DICTIONARY OF
Americain History

Third Edition

EDITORIAL BOARD

to one penny a gallon, applied alike to foreign and British imports, and the protests on the molasses duty ended. At this lower rate, molasses yielded an average of £12,194 annually from 1767 to 1775.

Other phases of the Sugar Act of 1764 were far more irritating to the colonists than was the lowered duty on molasses. One was a new duty on wine imported from Madeira, which had previously come in duty free and was the main source of profit for the fish and food ships returning from the Mediterranean. This part of the Sugar Act led to few direct protests, but it did produce some spectacular attempts at evasion, such as the wine-running episode in Boston involving a ship belonging to Capt. Daniel Malcolm, in February 1768. Even more provocative were measures imposing new bonding regulations that compelled ship masters to give bond, even when they loaded their vessels with nonenumerated goods. The most controversial of these features was a provision that shipmasters had to give bond before they put any article, enumerated or nonenumerated, on board. The universal American practice, however, was to load first and then clear and give bond, which made it difficult for shipmasters to give a new bond at a customhouse before he brought every new consignment on board. Under the Sugar Act, any ship caught with any article on board before a bond covering that article had been given was subject to seizure and confiscation. The customs commissioners profited greatly from this provision. The most notorious seizures for technical violations of the bonding provision included John Hancock's sloop *Liberty* (10 June 1768) and the *Ann* belonging to Henry Laurens of South Carolina.

BIBLIOGRAPHY

Andrews, K. R., et al. *The Westward Enterprise: English Activities in Ireland, the Atlantic, and America, 1480–1650.* Detroit, Mich.: Wayne State University Press, 1979.

McCusker, John J., and Russell R. Menard. *The Economy of British America, 1607–1789.* Chapel Hill: University of North Carolina Press, 1985.

O. M. Dickerson / s. b.

See also **Colonial Commerce; Colonial Policy, British; Enumerated Commodities; Navigation Acts; Rum Trade; Smuggling, Colonial; Triangular Trade; West Indies, British and French.**

SUGAR INDUSTRY dates back to the very founding of the New World, and has been intricately entangled with its history. Because of its role in the slave trade, sugar played an important role not only in the economy but also in how social relations developed in the New World. In the infamous "triangle trade," English colonies in the Caribbean shipped sugar to England for refining, and the products went to Africa where traders exchanged them for slaves, who were brought to the Caribbean plantations to raise more sugar. Sugar plantation work was among the most brutal and dangerous, as workers labored in oppressive heat and swampy conditions, and with dangerous tools.

Brought to the New World by Christopher Columbus, sugar cane was first cultivated successfully in Louisiana around the middle of the eighteenth century. Although efforts to make sugar from the cane juice succeeded in Louisiana as early as 1760 and in Florida a few years later, until the 1790s cane was cultivated in small quantities, mainly for the manufacture of syrup and rum. The spectacular success of a wealthy Louisiana planter, Jean Étienne Boré, in making sugar on a substantial scale in 1795 was followed in the next years by a rapid shift of planters from indigo to sugarcane. When the United States took possession of Louisiana in 1803, there was already a small but thriving sugar industry in south Louisiana. Likewise, when the United States acquired Puerto Rico and Hawaii in 1898, sugar culture was already well established in both areas. Though SLAVERY in the United States ended after the Civil War, sugar producers continued to keep sugar workers in slave-like conditions in parts of the South, supported by government programs.

The need for cane sugar laborers was a key reason that seventeenth-century plantation owners in the Caribbean began importing slaves, and the labor-intensive character of sugar growing later encouraged planters in the U.S. South to hold large numbers of slaves. Climatic conditions in the southern United States were not as favorable for cane culture as those of the West Indies, because of shorter growing seasons and the danger of freezes. Nevertheless, as a result of the availability of enslaved workers, a protective tariff, the introduction of cold-resistant cane varieties, the adoption of steam power for grinding cane, and advances in the processes of clarification and evaporation of cane juice, the cane sugar industry grew rapidly in the years prior to the Civil War. Major improvements were made in the manufacture of sugar, including the introduction in the 1820s of steam power for crushing cane and the invention in the 1840s by Norbert Rillieux, a Louisiana Creole, of a multiple-effect system for evaporating cane juice, which replaced the open kettle boilers and revolutionized sugar manufacture. Although cane was grown for syrup mainly on small farms in South Carolina, Georgia, Florida, Alabama, Mississippi, Louisiana, Arkansas, and Texas, only on the large plantations in south Louisiana and Texas was a successful sugar industry established. In 1850, on plantations worked by slaves, the southern states produced almost 114,000 tons of cane sugar, approximately one-half of the sugar consumed in the United States. Prior to 1861, most Louisiana cane sugar was shipped to cities throughout the Mississippi Valley and the East Coast, and much of it was consumed in the form of raw sugar. Refiners in eastern cities imported raw sugar from the West Indies and, by a refining process of melting the sugar, clarifying the juice in boneblack filters, and centrifugal drying, produced a dry, white sugar.

Beets, the other principle source for the sugar industry, have only in the twentieth century become a widespread source, though attempts at making beet sugar date centuries back. Sugar beets, which probably grew wild in Asia, were cultivated at an early time in Egypt and southern Europe. A German chemist, Andreas Marggraf, demonstrated in 1747 that sugar from beets was identical with cane sugar. Early in the nineteenth century, when France was cut off from overseas sugar supplies, Napoleon Bonaparte established the sugar beet industry. Although the industry declined with Napoleon's downfall, it gradually revived, spreading first to Germany and then to much of the rest of Europe.

One reason that the beet sugar industry was established so slowly in the United States is the large amount of hand labor required in growing beets; because of where beets grew, their growers could not rely on enslaved labor. In the late nineteenth and early twentieth centuries, the cultivation of sugar beets spread throughout the central and western states from the Great Lakes to California, and in both cane and beet processing, large expensive central mills came to dominate the manufacture of sugar. Four small beet sugar factories were constructed between 1838 and 1856, but all failed. The first successful one was established by E. H. Dyer at Alvarado, California (twenty-two miles east of San Francisco), in 1870 and operated through 1967. The next successful plants were established in Watsonville, California (1888); Grand Island, Nebraska (1890); and Lehi, Utah (1891). During the 1870s, Maine and Delaware offered a bonus for beet sugar manufactured within their limits, and factories destined to operate only a few years were built at Portland and Wilmington, respectively. The Portland factory inaugurated the practice of contracting with farmers for a specific acreage of sugar beets that would be raised from seed furnished by the company. This plan of operation, adapted from French practices, has persisted to the present. Despite the activity in Maine and Delaware, production in the United States has tended to concentrate in irrigated areas in the West.

By 1910 more beet than cane sugar was produced in the continental United States. In 1920 the output exceeded one million tons, and in 1972 it was about 3.5 million tons, which was more than one-fourth of the sugar consumed in the United States. In the 1970s, some sixty plants were producing beet sugar in eighteen states, with more than one-third of the total factory capacity located in California and Colorado. During the 1930s, studies began on the mechanization of growing and harvesting beets. Since World War II, mechanical devices have replaced much of the handcutting of cane, as machines for planting, cultivating, and harvesting beets—all requiring specialized technological changes—were developed by the beginning of World War II, and their adoption was hastened by shortages of hand labor during the war and by postwar prosperity.

By the 1960s, the refining branch of the sugar industry was dominated by large corporations and was concentrated in coastal cities, especially New York, New Orleans, Savannah, Baltimore, Philadelphia, Boston, and San Francisco. Refiners process raw sugar from Louisiana, Florida, Hawaii, Puerto Rico, and foreign countries. Refined sugar was marketed in more than one hundred varieties of grades and packaging to meet highly specialized demands. Per capita sugar consumption in the United States increased rapidly during the twentieth century and by the 1970s had been stabilized at about one hundred pounds per year. Although sugar production in Texas ended in the 1920s, a thriving modern sugar industry emerged in Florida south of Lake Okeechobee.

Since 1934 the U.S. government has assisted the sugar industry, which has a powerful lobby. Until the late twentieth century, sugar growers had access to extremely low-paid, non-unionized immigrant workers through a federal "guest worker" program for the industry. In the early twenty-first century, the sugar industry was receiving $1.6 billion from the U.S. government. Rather than making direct payments to growers, as the Agriculture Department does in other industries, the department gives sugar processors short-term loans, and maintains high domestic prices by strictly limiting imports. Critics of this policy note that sugar consumers pay two to three times the world market price. In fiscal year 2000, domestic growers grew more than the government-set limit, and the government had to spend $465 million to buy their excess sugar and cover the cost of processors' loan forfeitures. According to the Center for Responsive Politics, which tracks political campaign contributions, the sugar industry contributes more than one-third of the money that crop production and food processing interests spend on political campaigns. The industry has a growing U.S. market; sugar consumption has practically doubled in the past century, from 86 pounds per U.S. citizen to nearly 160. However, the fortunes of the U.S. sugar industry may change in the wake of the North American Free Trade Agreement, as Mexican imports are likely to flood the U.S. market beginning in fiscal 2004.

BIBLIOGRAPHY

Hall, Michael R. *Sugar and Power in the Dominican Republic: Eisenhower, Kennedy, and the Trujillos.* Westport, Conn.: Greenwood Press, 2000.

Melendy, H. Brett. *Hawaii, America's Sugar Territory, 1898–1959.* Lewiston, N.Y.: Edwin Mellen Press, 1999.

Mintz, Sidney Wilfred. *Sweetness and Power: The Place of Sugar in Modern History.* New York Penguin Books, 1986.

Roberts, Paul. "The Sweet Hereafter." *Harper's Magazine* 299, 1794 (November 1999): 54.

Rodrigue, John C. *Reconstruction in the Cane Fields: From Slavery to Free Labor in Louisiana's Sugar Parishes, 1862–1880.* Baton Rouge: Louisiana State University Press, 2001.

Sandiford, Keith Albert. *The Cultural Politics of Sugar: Caribbean Slavery and Narratives of Colonialism.* New York: Cambridge University Press, 2000.

Woloson, Wendy A. *Refined Tastes: Sugar, Confectionery, and Consumers in Nineteenth-Century America*. Baltimore: Johns Hopkins University Press, 2002.

Wayne D. Rasmussen
J. Carlyle Sitterson / D. B.

See also **Agricultural Machinery; Agricultural Price Support; Agriculture, Department of; Diets and Dieting; Plantation System of the South; Slave Trade; Subsidies.**

SUMMIT CONFERENCES, U.S. AND RUSSIAN,

the occasions for heads of state or government to meet directly in what is often termed "personal diplomacy." While summits are often depicted as the opportunity for top leaders to reach breakthroughs on difficult issues their subordinates have been unable to resolve through negotiation, more often agreements signed at summit meetings are the culmination of traditional diplomatic work. Summits offer participants a chance to evaluate their counterparts in person, and allow leaders to impress domestic and international audiences with their peacemaking ability or diplomatic prowess, although the expectations they raise for dramatic progress can easily be disappointed.

Every president since Franklin D. Roosevelt has met with the Soviet or Russian leadership. Although each summit meeting was marked by circumstances specific to the historical moment, one can speak roughly of four phases: wartime meetings of the Allied leaders to plan strategy during World War II; a continued multilateral approach to dealing with crucial international issues in the Dwight D. Eisenhower years; a shift to bilateral discussions of nuclear arms limitation in the 1960s through the 1980s; and the attempt to forge a new relationship in the post–Cold War era.

Allied Conferences in World War II

The first wartime summit took place from 28 November to 1 December 1943, when President Roosevelt met with Soviet Premier Joseph Stalin and British Prime Minister Winston Churchill at Tehran. Stalin pressed the Anglo-Americans to begin the promised cross-channel attack on German-held Europe, and promised to enter the war against Japan once Germany was defeated. Roosevelt proposed the creation of a postwar international organization to keep the peace, dominated by the "Four Policemen" (including China).

From 4 to 11 February 1945, the three met again at the Russian Black Sea resort of Yalta. Stalin consented to a four-power occupation of Germany (including a French force) and reaffirmed his promise to enter the war against Japan. But the central issue was the postwar fate of Eastern Europe, especially Poland. Stalin soon violated the Yalta agreement to assure representative government in Poland, made without provision for enforcement. This led Roosevelt's detractors to charge him with "betrayal" and to link the name of Yalta, like that of Munich, to appeasement, although the Yalta accords reflected the reality of the positions Allied armies had reached on the ground.

After Roosevelt's death and Germany's surrender, President Harry S. Truman traveled to Potsdam to meet Stalin and Churchill (replaced during the conference by Clement Attlee after his victory in British elections) from 17 July to 2 August 1945. They carved Germany into four occupation zones and settled on a policy of modest reparations and the rebuilding of Germany's basic infrastructure, rather than seeking the country's deindustrialization or dismemberment.

The sharpening of the Cold War after World War II brought a ten-year halt to U.S.-Soviet summit meetings. Summits were discredited in the minds of critics who believed that an ailing Roosevelt had been manipulated by a crafty Stalin at Yalta, and that there was nothing to be gained by personal diplomacy with untrustworthy rivals.

Summits on International Issues

The freeze began to thaw from 18 to 23 July 1955, when President Dwight D. Eisenhower met Premier Nikolai Bulganin and Communist Party chief Nikita Khrushchev, along with Prime Minister Anthony Eden of Britain and French Prime Minister Edgar Faure at Geneva in the first East-West summit of the Cold War. Neither Eisenhower's proposal for an "open skies" inspection plan permitting Americans and Soviets to conduct aerial reconnaissance over one another's territory, nor the Soviet proposal for mutual withdrawal of forces from Europe, made any headway. However, after a decade of no meetings, many welcomed the lessening of international tension associated with the "spirit of Geneva." This was followed by the "spirit of Camp David," when Khrushchev visited Eisenhower at the presidential retreat in Maryland from 25 to 27 September 1959 and retracted his ultimatum demanding a final settlement of the status of Berlin.

The thaw proved short-lived. Two weeks before a planned summit in Paris on 16 to 17 May 1960, an American U-2 spy plane was shot down deep inside Soviet airspace. Khrushchev used the opening of the summit to denounce American aggression and then walked out. When Khrushchev met the new President John F. Kennedy in Vienna on 3 and 4 June 1961, the two leaders eyed each other grimly. They agreed to avoid superpower confrontation over the civil war in Laos, but made no progress toward a proposed ban on nuclear weapons testing, and clashed over the fate of Berlin.

The outbreak of the Six-Day War in the Middle East prompted an emergency session of the United Nations General Assembly in New York, which Soviet Premier Alexei Kosygin planned to attend. Kosygin and President Lyndon B. Johnson met halfway between New York and Washington at Glassboro, New Jersey, from 23 to 25 June 1967. The Soviet premier called for American withdrawal from Vietnam and Israeli withdrawal from Egypt, and Johnson focused on nuclear issues. However, Kosygin had been given little power to negotiate by the Politburo, and no agreements were signed.

Détente and Nuclear Arms Talks

President Richard M. Nixon and his National Security Adviser Henry A. Kissinger sought to use negotiations with the Soviet Union to arrange an acceptable exit from the Vietnam War in exchange for improved relations. After Nixon's historic visit to China in 1972, Soviet leaders invited him to Moscow, where talks held from 22 to 30 May 1972, resulted in the signing of two agreements marking the beginning of "détente": a treaty limiting each country to the construction of two Anti-Ballistic Missile (ABM) systems, and an agreement limiting long-range land-based and submarine-based ballistic missiles, later known as the SALT I (Strategic Arms Limitation Talks) treaty.

Communist Party Secretary Leonid Brezhnev visited the U.S. from 18 to 25 June 1973, where he and Nixon signed a number of minor agreements regarding agriculture, transportation, and trade. A meeting in Moscow from 27 June to 3 July 1974, held in the shadow of the Watergate scandal and under pressure from conservative opponents of arms control, brought no further progress on strategic arms limitations, although the ABM treaty was amended to reduce the number of ABM systems permitted from two to one.

After Nixon's resignation, President Gerald R. Ford met Brezhnev at Vladivostok on 23 and 24 November 1974, where they agreed on the outlines for a SALT II agreement. From 30 July to 2 August 1975, the two leaders met again in Helsinki during a signing ceremony of the Conference on Security and Cooperation in Europe. Cooling relations brought about by the collapse of Saigon, superpower rivalry in Angola, and trade disputes lessened the possibility of progress toward a second SALT agreement, as did the upcoming American elections, in which Ford avoided all references to "détente" to resist challenges from the right.

The unpopularity of détente continued to grow during President Jimmy Carter's term. By the time he met Brezhnev in Vienna from 15 to 18 June 1979, relations with the Soviet Union had deteriorated over trade restrictions, Third World conflicts, U.S. rapprochement with China, and human rights. The two leaders were able to sign a SALT II agreement but Senate conservatives opposed the treaty and the Soviet invasion of Afghanistan in December ended any hope of ratification.

President Ronald Reagan's first term was marked by remilitarization and a heightening of Cold War tensions that sowed fears that the superpowers might be sliding toward nuclear war, creating a mass antiwar movement in the United States and Europe. In response, Reagan met the new, reformist Soviet leader, Mikhail Gorbachev, at a "get-acquainted summit" at Geneva from 19 to 21 November 1985, where despite a lack of agreement on nuclear arms reductions, the two leaders established warm personal relations. They met again in Reykjavik, Iceland, on 11 and 12 October 1986, and agreed to reduce intermediate-range nuclear missiles, but deadlocked over Reagan's devotion to space-based missile defense. At a third meeting in Washington from 7 to 10 December 1987, the two leaders signed the Intermediate-Range Nuclear Forces (INF) Treaty, requiring the elimination of all U.S. and Soviet INF missiles. A fourth meeting in Moscow from 20 May to 2 June 1988, was more notable for the media images of Reagan strolling through the heart of what he had formerly called "the Evil Empire" than for the minor arms control agreements signed, and a final meeting in New York on 7 December was largely ceremonial.

End of the Cold War

The rapid pace of political change in Eastern Europe in 1989 led President George H. W. Bush to hold a shipboard meeting with Gorbachev off Malta on 2 and 3 December 1989. Although no agreements were signed, statements of goodwill indicated, as Gorbachev put it, that the era of the Cold War was ending. This was reinforced at a Washington summit from 31 May to 3 June 1990, when agreements on a range of issues including trade and chemical weapons were signed in an atmosphere of cooperation not seen since the height of détente. Gorbachev was invited to a Group of Seven meeting in London on 17 and 18 July 1991, where he and Bush agreed to sign a START (Strategic Arms Reduction Talks) treaty at a full summit in Moscow on 30 and 31 July. The Moscow meeting proved to be the last superpower summit, as the Soviet Union collapsed at the end of the year.

Summits after the Cold War

Between 1992 and 2000, Presidents George Bush and Bill Clinton met more than twenty times with Russian Presidents Boris Yeltsin or Vladimir Putin at bilateral summits or individually at multilateral venues. Talks on further nuclear arms reductions and securing the former Soviet arsenal and nuclear materials were a feature of many of the summits. At a Moscow meeting on 2 and 3 January 1993, Bush and Yeltsin signed the START II Treaty, promising to reduce each country's nuclear arsenal to between 3,000–3,500 warheads within ten years. Yeltsin used various summit meetings to argue unsuccessfully against the eastward expansion of the North Atlantic Treaty Organization, and Clinton often pressed Yeltsin and Putin to seek a peaceful resolution to Russia's conflict with its secessionist province of Chechnya. Another regular feature of the discussions was the attempt by the Russian leaders to obtain better trade relations and economic aid from Western countries and institutions, and American pressure to link such concessions to structural reform of Russia's economy. The diminished drama and increased frequency of the meetings compared with the Cold War years confirmed the extent to which relations between the two countries had normalized by the end of the twentieth century.

ated by Congress to expedite cleanup of the nation's worst HAZARDOUS WASTE sites. National concern over the release of hazardous wastes buried beneath the residential community at LOVE CANAL in western New York State prompted its passage. The term also refers to the Superfund Amendment and Reauthorization Act (SARA) of 1986, which comprehensively revised the original act and added $9 billion to the fund. In response to a 1984 tragedy in Bhopal, India, in which three thousand people died and hundreds of thousands were reportedly affected by exposure to deadly methyl isocyanate gas that leaked from a Union Carbide plant, Congress included provisions in SARA requiring corporations to inform host communities of the presence of dangerous materials and to develop emergency plans for dealing with accidental releases of such materials. From the beginning Superfund met with harsh, and often justified, criticism. President Ronald Reagan's commitment to reduce government regulation of industry undermined the effectiveness of the legislation. At the end of five years the money was gone, and only six of the eighteen hundred hazardous waste sites identified at that time had been cleaned up. Another eighteen thousand suspected sites remained to be investigated. A new provision reauthorized the program to continue until 1994. Legal disputes had mired those willing to restore sites, and in 1994 the legislation was not reauthorized. Instead, the program has continued to function with special appropriated funding while Congress negotiates how to make the program more effective and efficient.

BIBLIOGRAPHY

Anderson, Terry, ed. *Political Environmentalism: Going Behind the Green Curtain.* Stanford, Calif.: Hoover Institution Press, 2000.

LaGrega, Michael D., Phillip L. Buckingham, and Jeffrey C. Evans. *Hazardous Waste Management.* Boston: McGraw Hill, 2001.

Vaughn, Jacqueline. *Environmental Politics: Domestic and Global Dimensions.* New York: St. Martin's Press, 2001.

John Morelli / F. H.

See also **Environmental Protection Agency; Times Beach.**

SUPERMARKETS AND SUPERSTORES. *See* Retailing Industry.

SUPERSONIC TRANSPORT.

In late 1962, the governments of France and Great Britain announced their intention to jointly develop a supersonic transport (SST) named the "Concorde." Anxious that the United States not trail the Europeans in the SST market as it had in the case of jet airliners, President John F. Kennedy, in a June 1963 speech at the Air Force Academy, called for a jointly funded government-industry program to design and build an American SST. The specifications, drawn from a government feasibility study, called for a passenger capacity of 300 and a cruising speed from 2.5 to 3 times that of sound—both better than Concorde's. Boeing and Lockheed, two of the three major commercial jet manufacturers, produced full-sized mockups for a 1967 design competition. Boeing's design was heavier and more complex but promised slightly better performance and a significantly more impressive, futuristic look. It won, but engineers later abandoned its most advanced features as they struggled to build a plane light enough to operate profitably. The final design, the 2707-300, mirrored Concorde in both appearance and performance.

Opposition to the SST project emerged on multiple fronts during the late 1960s. Environmentalists warned of catastrophic damage to the ozone layer. Homeowners along flight routes rebelled against the prospect of routine sonic booms. Members of Congress objected to the use of public funds for a commercial venture. Boeing officials worried, privately, that the SST might bankrupt the company if it failed. Dismayed by rising costs, mounting opposition, and unfulfilled promises, Congress cancelled the SST program in 1971.

BIBLIOGRAPHY

Ames, Mary E. "The Case of the U.S. SST: Disenchantment with Technology." In her *Outcome Uncertain: Science and the Political Process.* Washington, D.C.: Communications Press, 1978. Ties the cancellation to shifts in public opinion.

Horwitch, Mel. *Clipped Wings: The American SST Conflict.* Cambridge, Mass.: MIT Press, 1982. The definitive history.

A. Bowdoin Van Riper

See also **Aircraft Industry; Boeing Company.**

SUPPLY-SIDE ECONOMICS

is based on the premise that high tax rates hurt the national economy by discouraging work, production, and innovation. President Ronald Reagan's adoption of supply-side ECONOMICS as the underlying theory for his economic policy in the 1980s represented a major shift in U.S. economic thinking. Supply-side theory was far from new, however, its basic ideas dating back to the early-nineteenth-century works of Jean-Baptiste Say and David Ricardo. It had been ignored in the United States since the New Deal, because of the demand-side theories of the British economist John Maynard Keynes, who believed in raising income and reducing unemployment by expanding demand even if the government does so through deficit spending.

In the 1980s, supply siders found an audience looking for an alternative to deficit-oriented, demand-side policies. Arthur B. Laffer popularized the idea. He argued that cutting taxes, especially those of high income groups, would increase government revenues, because lower tax rates would produce more incentives for business and individuals to work and less reason for them to avoid taxes whether through non-productive investments in tax shelters or outright tax avoidance. Cutting taxes would result in more jobs, a more productive economy, and more government revenues. This theory fit nicely into the conservative political agenda, because it meant less interference with the economy and, when combined with spending cuts and deficit reduction, smaller government.

Supply-side economics dominated the administration of President Ronald Reagan, who instituted major tax cuts in 1981 and 1986, reducing the top U.S. rate from 70 percent to roughly 33 percent. However, Congress did not reduce federal spending to compensate for the reduced revenue, with the result that deficits soared to record levels. In the view of some advocates, the failure of Congress to adopt a balanced-budget amendment that would have controlled federal spending to match the tax cuts meant that supply-side theories were not really tried. Cutting taxes remained an important goal for subsequent Republican administrations, but by 2001, few argued that tax cuts would increase government revenue. Rather, tax cuts were a way to stimulate the economy, reign in government spending, and return the budget surplus to its rightful owners.

The legacy of supply-side economics has been more political than economic. In the mid-1990s, Republican House Speaker Newt Gingrich observed that supply-side economics has "relatively little to do with economics and a great deal to do with human nature and incentives." It contributed to the larger debate about the respective roles of government, individuals, and incentives in U.S. society as the nation faced a global economy.

BIBLIOGRAPHY

Canton, Victor A., Douglas H. Joines, and Arthur B. Laffer. *Foundations of Supply-Side Economics: Theory and Evidence.* New York: Academic Press, 1983.

Thompson, Grahame. *The Political Economy of the New Right.* London: Pinter, 1990.

Wilber, Charles K., and Kenneth P. Jameson. *Beyond Reaganomics: A Further Inquiry Into the Poverty of Economics.* Notre Dame, Ind.: University of Notre Dame Press, 1990.

Winant, Howard A. *Stalemate: Political Economic Origins of Supply-Side Policy.* New York: Praeger, 1988.

Brent Schondelmeyer / c. p.

See also **Debt, Public; Economics; Keynesianism; Radical Right; Taxation.**

SUPREME COURT. The Supreme Court is the final judicial authority in the U.S. system of government. Designated in Article III of the U.S. Constitution to have jurisdiction over all cases "arising under" the Constitution, the Court has the power to hear cases on appeal from the Federal appellate courts and the highest courts of each state. The Constitution also provides that the Court may act as a trial court in a limited number of cases: "Cases affecting Ambassadors, other public Ministers and Consuls, and those in which a State shall be Party." Though the Supreme Court is the final judicial authority in American government, it is not necessarily the final legal or political authority in the political system. While litigants may never appeal Supreme Court decisions to a superior court, disputes may proceed in other branches of government after a Supreme Court ruling. Congress and state legislatures may effectively alter or negate Supreme Court decisions involving statutory interpretation by amending or clarifying statutes, and may nullify constitutional decisions by amending the Constitution pursuant to Article V of the Constitution.

Several factors are important to understand the Court's role in American democracy, including: the continuing nature of the Court's relationship to Congress, the Executive Branch, and state governments; the influence of political and economic history on the Court; the intellectual underpinnings of Supreme Court decisions; and the internal dynamics of the Court as a distinct institution. Finally, the ambiguity of many key provisions of the Constitution is a source of both limits and power, for it creates the need for an authoritative voice on the Constitution's meaning and simultaneously makes such interpretations open to contestation. Created at the crossroads of law and politics, the Supreme Court's history is a history of controversy.

In addition to the possibility of legislative alteration of Supreme Court decisions, formal relationships the Constitution establishes between the Court and the other branches of the national government affects the Court's power. First, the President appoints each justice to the Court, subject to Senate confirmation. Second, Supreme Court justices, like all federal judges, serve for life, absent impeachment by the House of Representatives and removal by the Senate. Third, Congress controls the number of justices that serve on the Court at any given time. At various points in U.S. history, the Court has had as few as five justices and as many as ten. Since 1865, however, the number has held steady at nine, including one chief justice. Fourth, Congress controls the Court's operational budget, though actual compensation to the justices "shall not be diminished during [the Justices] Continuance in office." (Article III, Section 1). Fifth, the Constitution gives Congress power over much of the Court's appellate jurisdiction. These and other overlapping Constitutional functions of each branch of government have led scholars to proclaim that the three branches of government are "separate institutions, sharing powers."

Beyond constitutional overlap, the special institutional nature of the Supreme Court is important. For example, the Court lacks the power to decide cases unless the proper parties to a lawsuit bring the case to the Court. The Court also lacks the ability to implement its decisions of its own accord, having to rely upon the executive branch to carry out its will. As Alexander Hamilton wrote in Federalist 78, the Framers firmly expected that the Supreme Court, "no influence over either the sword or the

scope and power of the federal government, particularly over the depressed American economy. Two justices, Chief Justice Charles Evans Hughes and Justice Owen J. Roberts, were swing votes and tended to vote with those who opposed the New Deal legislation. The result was that the Court struck down eight out of ten major programs proposed by FDR, many by narrow majorities.

In February 1937, FDR announced his proposal to alter the composition of the judiciary, citing inefficiency and backlogged dockets as the reasons necessitating the change. The proposal would have impacted the American federal judicial system from top to bottom, but its primary goal was to pack the Supreme Court with justices he would appoint. His plan would have authorized the president to replace every judge or justice who had served more than ten years or had failed to retire within six months after reaching seventy years of age. At the time, the proposal would have authorized FDR to appoint as many as six new justices to the Supreme Court.

The proposal, the subject of tense debates, never made it out of committee, and Congress as a whole never voted on it. FDR and congressional New Deal supporters, however, still received their desired result. With the two 1937 cases of *West Coast Hotel v. Parrish* and *National Labor Relations Board v. Jones & McLaughlin Steel Corporation*, Justice Roberts changed his voting tendencies and began voting in favor of upholding sweeping New Deal legislation. Roberts denied that his "switch" was influenced by FDR's court packing proposal. There are many other viable explanations, but the saying "the switch in time that saved nine" emerged as the characterization of the Court packing events of 1937. The Court's new willingness to support President Roosevelt's favored legislation took the wind out of the sails of his court-packing plan.

Congress's attempts to pack the court have had more effect on the Supreme Court than presidential packing. Court packing bills have been designed to result in congressional control of the Supreme Court, which provides the largest check on congressional legislation and action. Congressional control of the Supreme Court disrupts the balance of powers and the system of checks and balances revered as fundamental to the system of government in the United States. The unsuccessful attempt by FDR and his Democratic allies in Congress to pack the Supreme Court was the last major concerted attempt by a president and Congress to alter the number of justices on the Supreme Court and thus change the direction of American law and life.

BIBLIOGRAPHY

Abraham, Henry J. *The Judiciary: The Supreme Court in the Governmental Process.* 10th ed. New York: New York University Press, 1996.

Leuchtenburg, William E. *The Supreme Court Reborn: The Constitutional Revolution in the Age of Roosevelt.* New York: Oxford University Press, 1995.

Rehnquist, William H. *The Supreme Court.* New York: Knopf, 2001.

Jacob E. Cooke, Akiba J. Covitz,
Esa Lianne Sferra, Meredith L. Stewart

SURFING. Riding a surfboard across the face of a breaking wave was once the preserve of ancient Polynesian islanders, but in the twentieth century it became something enjoyed by millions of people the world over. Modern surfing has spread well beyond its more recent Hawaiian, American, and Australian origins, becoming a global phenomenon of such magnitude that every minute of every day will find somebody, somewhere, trying to catch a wave. The talented and photogenic few are paid to surf by a multibillion dollar surfing industry. For the rest, it is an obsessive hobby, a statement of identity, and even a spiritual pursuit.

Surfing originated sometime between 1500 B.C. and A.D. 400 among the oceanic island cultures of Polynesia. From there, it spread to the Sandwich (Hawaiian) Islands,

Surfing Pioneer. Teenager Isabel Letham catches a wave, c. 1917. Duke Kahanamoku picked the locally known bodysurfer out of a crowd in 1915 to be the first person in Australia to ride a Hawaiian-style surfboard.

where it was witnessed by the British explorer Captain James Cook in 1778. The missionaries that followed in Cook's wake discouraged the practice to such an extent that it had practically vanished by the end of the nineteenth century. It was revived early in the 1900s by young Hawaiians and promoted by the local tourist industry and Alexander Hume Ford, who founded the Hawaiian Outrigger Canoe Club in 1908 in Honolulu. The Hawaiian surfers Duke Kahanamoku and George Freeth traveled to America and Australia to take part in exhibitions that helped spread surfing beyond Hawaii's shores.

The accessibility of the sport was limited by the athletic demands of the heavy redwood boards that were the Hawaiian norm. Only with the invention of lighter board materials in the 1940s and 1950s did surfing become more appealing to the general public. Surfing subcultures appeared in Hawaii, California, and Australia, developing a distinctive language, fashion, attitude, and lifestyle that gradually filtered into mainstream popular culture. The 1960s saw the emergence of glossy surfing magazines, surf music, and surf clothing and equipment companies, along with the release of numerous surf-related movies, all of which led to a huge increase in the surfing population. New inventions such as wetsuits, leashes, and more maneuverable short boards only added to surfing's worldwide popularity. Large national organizations were created to organize the sport and to hold competitions, leading eventually to a professional circuit that is funded, principally, by the surf industry and media sponsorship. The original extreme sport, surfing continues to push its boundaries. The development of tow-in surfing technology allows big-wave surfers to ride offshore waves that are more than sixty feet high.

BIBLIOGRAPHY

Finney, Ben, and James Houston. *Surfing: The History of the Ancient Hawaiian Sport.* San Francisco: Pomegranate Books, 1996.

Kampion, Drew. *Stoked: A History of Surf Culture.* Santa Monica, Calif.: General Publishing, 1997.

Young, Nat. *The History of Surfing.* Angourie, Australia: Palm Beach Press, 1998.

Rick Dodgson

See also **Honolulu; Sports.**

SURPLUS, FEDERAL. Federal budgets have varied considerably over our history. As indicated in the accompanying table, our first and second centuries were very different in terms of budget surpluses. Through our first 134 years, surpluses were the norm; in the last 75 years, they have been rare. A number of factors affect our budgetary history. The most pronounced are wars and economic recessions. However, philosophical and partisan values and beliefs also were critical.

TABLE 1

Years in Surplus or Deficit, 1792–2000

Years	Years in Surplus	Years in Deficit
1792–1800	5	4
1801–1825	17	8
1826–1850	16	9
1851–1875	17	8
1876–1900	19	6
1901–1925	14	11
1926–1950	8	17
1951–1975	5	20
1976–2000	3	22

SOURCE: U.S. Dept of Commerce, 1970, pp. 1104–1105.

For example, when the Jeffersonian Democrats defeated the Federalists in 1800, their philosophy of a limited national government replaced the Federalists' more activist role. As a result, the budget deficits that Treasury Secretary Alexander Hamilton was willing to run to provide federal services were replaced by Thomas Jefferson's desire to run surpluses to reduce the total public debt. His (and James Madison's) Secretary of the Treasury, Albert Gallatin, was able to produce surpluses in ten of fourteen years from 1801 to 1824, with the exceptions coming primarily during and after the War of 1812. Because Democrats were in power for most of the period prior to the Civil War, there were thirty-three years of budget surpluses from 1801 to 1850.

Since the total public debt was essentially eliminated by 1835, but both the Democrats, and especially the Whigs, believed in high protective tariffs, revenue consistently outpaced spending. The answer of what to do with the excess funds came in the form of the Deposit Act of 1836, which required the federal government to distribute any surplus over $5 million to the states in proportion to their electoral votes (hence their population). That act was short-lived because of major economic downturns commencing with the Panic of 1837. That recessionary period resulted in deficit spending during six of the next seven years.

Surpluses returned by 1844 and were common until the military buildup prior to and during the Civil War. The war resulted in eight years of deficits and an unimaginable increase in government spending and government debt. The latter rose from $64 million in 1860 to $2.8 billion in 1866. That debt was partly paid for by issuing war bonds, authorized by Lincoln's hard-driving Secretary of the Treasury, Samuel Chase. Tariff revenue declined substantially during the war. Thus, to help finance the war effort and to begin paying off the debt, Congress passed the first income tax in 1862, which remained in effect until its repeal in 1872.

Because of the income tax, the nation was able to return to surpluses in 1866. The fiscally conservative nature of the post–Civil War period, for both Republicans and Democrats, led to continuous surpluses from 1866 to 1894. As in the pre–Civil War period, surpluses eventually ended due to the nation's economic woes, which in the 1890s were much worse than anything the country had experienced before. Because of the enormity of the debt built up during the Civil War, the total debt had only been reduced to $1 billion by 1894 from the $2.8 billion that existed in 1866. Spending in the 1890s on the Spanish American War and veterans pension legislation contributed to five straight years of deficits at the end of the nineteenth century.

A mixed pattern of deficits and surpluses marked the period beginning in 1900 and ending in 1918 with U.S. entry into World War I. The war again produced a historic level of debt that was completely beyond anything previously imagined. It stood at $24 billion by 1921. However, the income tax had been reenacted in 1913 and was expanded dramatically during the war. By the end of the war it accounted for 56 percent of federal revenues. Using that tax engine, Secretary of the Treasury Andrew Mellon was able to produce surpluses in every year he was in power, which included three presidential administrations from 1921 to 1932. As the surpluses were acquired, Mellon would subsequently support reduction in taxes, with income tax rate reduction the primary target. Because of the strength of the economy during this period, even as tax rates were reduced, more taxes were collected and more surpluses created.

Those surpluses ended with the depression, and with the willingness of Franklin Roosevelt to use the federal government to help alleviate the nation's suffering—and to run deficits while doing so. Later during his thirteen years in office Roosevelt embraced the philosophy of John Maynard Keynes, which lent academic endorsement to the concept of deficit spending in times of recession.

The combination of growing expenditures for New Deal programs; the philosophical acceptance of Keynesian deficit spending; and wars in Europe, Korea, and Vietnam, along with a cold war with Russia, created a phenomenal period of growth in U.S. government, and with it an omnipresent budget deficit.

Beginning in the 1980s both the origin of deficits and the drive for budget surpluses took on a new dimension. For the first time in budget history, deficits were an unintended consequence of a major peacetime tax reduction occurring in 1981. The influence of Keynesian macroeconomic theory had waned in policy circles and for a short period was replaced by a supply-side theory in which tax reductions were viewed as the major engine of capital formation, and therefore economic growth. Some of the empirical evidence supporting the supply-side theory included the results of the surplus-generating actions of the Mellon era in the 1920s. Supply-siders argued that cutting tax rates would ultimately increase tax collections. The debate over supply-side theory continues, but the short-term effects are not subject to debate. Deficits exploded,

reaching $290 billion in 1992. The political result was a consistent effort to return the nation to surpluses. That legislative goal dominated legislative and presidential politics from 1982 to 1997. Spending restraints were imposed and peacetime tax increases were enacted for the first time since 1931.

With government having achieved the goal of returning to surpluses by the 1998 fiscal year, politics seemed to be returning to a prior period, as political pressures supporting tax reductions (accomplished in early 2001) and pent-up spending demands crowded the political agenda.

BIBLIOGRAPHY

Studenski, Paul, and Herman E. Krooss. *Financial History of the United States*. New York: McGraw-Hill, 1952.

U.S. Department of Commerce, Bureau of the Census. *Historical Statistics of the United States, Colonial Times to 1970*. New York: Basic Books, 1976.

Witte, John. *The Politics and Development of the Federal Income Tax*. Madison: University of Wisconsin Press, 1985.

John Witte

See also **Debt, Public; Deposit Act of 1836; Supply-Side Economics; Taxation.**

SURROGATE MOTHERHOOD is the process by which a woman bears a child for another couple, typically an infertile couple. There are two kinds of surrogate motherhood. In traditional surrogacy, the mother is artificially inseminated with sperm from the father or with sperm from a donor, if the father is infertile. In gestational surrogacy, sperm is taken from the father (or from a donor) and the egg is taken from the mother, fertilization happens in vitro, and the embryos are then implanted into the surrogate mother's uterus. Thus, the surrogate mother is not genetically related to the child.

For over one hundred years artificial insemination was used as a way of managing male infertility that kept the family intact and allowed children to be born to a married couple. Artificial insemination was generally kept secret. Couples did not tell friends, family, or the children themselves that donor sperm was used, thus maintaining the fiction of biological paternity.

Though stories of surrogate motherhood, often with familial surrogates, date back two thousand years, in 1976 the lawyer Noel Keane arranged the first formal agreement between a couple and a surrogate mother in the United States. The marketing of "surrogacy" developed as a solution to female infertility. Brokers entered the scene, hiring women to become pregnant via artificial insemination with the sperm of the husband of the infertile woman. In 1986 surrogacy came to national attention with the case of "Baby M." In this case, the woman hired as a surrogate, Mary Beth Whitehead, later refused to relinquish the child. After a protracted court battle, in which Whitehead's parental rights were stripped and then replaced, the hiring couple won custody of the baby, but Whitehead remained the legal mother with visitation rights.

Since the 1980s, advances in technology have increased the use of gestational surrogacy. As it has become more common, there has been an increase in the number of Latin American, Asian American, and African American surrogates.

The Center for Surrogate Parenting (CSP) estimates a cost of $56,525 for traditional surrogacy, in which artificial insemination is used, and a cost of $69,325 if another woman's egg is used. Approximately $15,000 of these fees are paid to the surrogate herself for the time and sacrifice of the pregnancy. When surrogacy agreements first surfaced in the mid-1970s, there was no payment for surrogate motherhood, and it tended to involve middle-class and blue-collar couples, with friends and sisters helping each other. Once payment became the norm, the demographic changed: "the majority of the couples remain largely upper-middle-class people, whereas the majority of the surrogates are working class women" (Ragoné, *Surrogate Motherhood*, p. 194).

In 2002, most states had no specific laws regarding surrogate motherhood. While many states do not uphold surrogacy contracts, all states recognize birth certificates and adoption certificates from other states, making surrogate services available to anyone with the money to hire them.

That surrogacy has become a business has not meant that contracting couples do not value the surrogate or that the surrogate does not care about the child or the couple. Very careful screening—approximately 95 percent of potential surrogates are rejected—ensures that situations similar to that of Mary Beth Whitehead do not happen. Surrogates are chosen for their commitment. In the only ethnographic study of surrogacy, Helena Ragoné found that couples adopted one of two strategies in dealing with their surrogate. "Egalitarians" wanted to maintain a relationship with the surrogate mother and did not see her as a means to an end. Since in all of Ragoné's cases the children were still quite young, it is difficult to know how this would play out. "Pragmatists" simply dropped the relationship with the surrogate, taking the child as theirs, and considering the payment sufficient acknowledgement of the role of the surrogate.

BIBLIOGRAPHY

Ragoné, Helena. *Surrogate Motherhood: Conception in the Heart.* Boulder, Colo.: Westview Press, 1994.

Rothman, Barbara Katz. *Recreating Motherhood: Ideology and Technology in a Patriarchal Society.* New York, Norton, 1989.

See also **Adoption; Childbirth and Reproduction; Children's Bureau; Family; Foster Care.**

SURROUNDED, THE a novel by the Native American author D'Arcy McNickle, was first published in 1936 by Dodd, Mead of New York City and republished in 1978 by the University of New Mexico Press. The economically stressed nation of the 1930s may not have been as ready to consider the tragic losses of American Indian peoples as they would be in the 1970s, despite the reforms of John Collier, President Franklin D. Roosevelt's commissioner of Indian affairs, who crafted the Indian Reorganization Act of 1934, and the rave review of Oliver LaFarge, Pulitzer Prize–winning novelist. *The Surrounded* depicts the many ways in which law constrained American Indians: laws that established the reservation system during the nineteenth century; the law of the Catholic Church missions that took as their task educating Salish and other traditional tribal people out of their "savagery," and laws that prohibited the practice of Native religions. In the novel, the limitations imposed on the Salish-Spanish protagonist, Archilde, and his people lead to his demise after he becomes a fugitive in an effort to protect his mother from being prosecuted for killing a game warden. In his many professional roles—Bureau of Indian Affairs official, scholar, anthropologist, writer, and founder of national organizations—McNickle devoted his life to drawing attention to the ways in which tribal peoples were "surrounded."

BIBLIOGRAPHY

McNickle, D'Arcy. *Native American Tribalism: Indian Survivals and Renewals.* New York: Oxford University Press, 1973.

Parker, Dorothy R. *Singing an Indian Song: A Biography of D'Arcy McNickle.* Lincoln: University of Nebraska Press, 1992.

Purdy, John Lloyd. *Word Ways: The Novels of D'Arcy McNickle.* Tucson: University of Arizona Press, 1990.

Kathryn W. Shanley

See also **Indian Policy, U.S.: 1830–1900, 1900–2000; Indian Reorganization Act; Tribes: Great Plains.**

SURVEY ACT of 1824, enacted by Congress twelve years after Treasury Secretary Albert Gallatin's "Report on Roads, Canals, Harbors, and Rivers" had generated interest in national internal improvements. The act authorized the president, with the aid of army engineers, to conduct surveys of such canal and turnpike routes as would serve an important national interest. Presidents Madison and Monroe had vetoed earlier efforts to appropriate money for such purposes, because each president thought an amendment to the Constitution was necessary to authorize federal expenditures for the construction of roads or canals. But the Supreme Court's decision in GIBBONS V. OGDEN (1824) regarding the scope of Congressional power over interstate commerce cleared the way for President Monroe to sign this bill. Congress repealed the act in 1838.

BIBLIOGRAPHY

Hill, Forest G. *Roads, Rails and Waterways: The Army Engineers and Early Transportation.* Westport, Conn.: Greenwood Press, 1977.

Larson, John L. "'Bind the Republic Together': The National Union and the Struggle for a System of Internal Improvements." *Journal of American History* 74 (September 1987): 363–387.

Malone, Laurence J. *Opening the West: Federal Internal Improvements before 1860.* Westport, Conn.: Greenwood Press, 1998.

L. W. Newton / C. P.

See also **Canals; Engineers, Corps of; River and Harbor Improvements; Roads.**

SURVEYING.   Using little more than a compass and a 66-foot chain, early American surveyors set out early to chart the United States of America. Surveys determine boundaries, chart coastlines and navigable streams and lakes, and provide for mapping of land surfaces. Much of this work done in the early days of the United States used rudimentary, although not necessarily inefficient, equipment.

For instance, surveyors set a 2,000-mile line for the transcontinental railroad in the 1860s without the benefit of maps, aerial views, or precise knowledge of topographical features. A century later, when surveyors set the line for Interstate 80 using everything their predecessors had not, the route followed the railroad's route almost exactly.

The primary tool used by surveyors in North America from the 1600s through the end of the 1800s was a "Gunter's chain," measuring 66 feet long, usually with 100 swiveled links. A retractable steel tape to replace the chain was patented in 1860 by W. H. Paine of Sheboygan, Wisconsin.

Surveyors relied on the compass to set the direction of their chain. Goldsmith Chandlee, a notable clock and instrument maker, built a brass foundry in Winchester, Virginia, in 1783 and made the most advanced surveying compasses of his day.

The biggest breakthrough in surveying technology came in England in 1773, when Jesse Ramsden invented the circular dividing engine, which allowed the manufacture of precise scientific and mathematical instruments. The first American to develop a capability for the mechanical graduation of instruments was William J. Young. Young built the first American transit in Philadelphia in 1831, replacing the heavier, more inconvenient theodolite, which measures horizontal and vertical angles. The transit has a telescope that can be reversed in direction on a horizontal axis. The transit built by Young differs little from the transit used in the early twenty-first century.

The increased demand for accuracy in railroad construction, civil engineering, and city surveys led to the rapid acceptance of the transit. An influx of tradesmen from the Germanic states in the 1830s and 1840s provided a means of manufacturing precision instruments in volume.

To help with mathematical calculations, surveyors began experimenting with a number of nonelectric calculators, including Thacher's Calculating Instrument, patented in 1881, which was the equivalent of a 360-inch-long slide rule precise to 1:10,000. Slide rules replaced

Makeshift Facilities. Photographers accompanying surveyors in the West had to process their film in a tent (as shown here) or wagon. LIBRARY OF CONGRESS

calculating instruments, calculators replaced slide rules, and computers have replaced calculators.

America's original thirteen colonies, as well as a few states such as Texas and Kentucky, were originally surveyed by metes and bounds, which is the process of describing boundaries by a measure of their length. On 7 May 1785, Congress adopted the Governmental Land Surveys, which provided for the "rectangular system," which measured distances and bearing from two lines at right angles and established the system of principal meridians, which run north and south, and base lines, running east and west.

Under the Northwest Ordinance of 1787, Ohio served as the experimental site for the new public lands surveying system. The lessons learned culminated in the Land Ordinance of 1796, which determined the surveying and numbering scheme used to survey all remaining U.S. public lands.

The first government-sanctioned survey was the Survey of the Coast, established in 1807 to mark the navigational hazards of the Atlantic Coast. Under Superintendent Ferdinand Hassler, the survey used crude techniques, including large theodolites, astronomical instruments, plane table topography, and lead line soundings to determine hydrography. Despite these techniques, the survey achieved remarkable accuracy.

By the time the Coast Survey was assigned to map Alaska's coast, after Alaska was acquired in 1867, technological advancements had provided new kinds of bottom samplers, deep-sea thermometers, and depth lines. A new zenith telescope determined latitude with greater accuracy, and the telegraph provided a means of determining longitudinal differences by flashing time signals between points.

Inland, surveys were more informal. Often under sponsorship from the Army, explorers such as Meriwether Lewis and William Clark, Zebulon Pike, and Stephen H. Long went out on reconnaissance missions, gathering geographic, geologic, and military information.

After the Civil War (1861–1865), westward migration created a need for detailed information about the trans-Mississippi West. Congress authorized four surveys named after their leaders: Clarence King, F. V. Hayden, John Wesley Powell, and George M. Wheeler. In addition to topography and geography, these surveys studied botany, paleontology, and ethnology.

The U.S. Geological Survey was formed in 1879 and began mapping in the 1880s, relying on the chain-and-compass method of surveying. By the early 1900s, surveyors were working with plane tables equipped with telescopic alidades with vertical-angle arcs, allowing lines of survey to be plotted directly from the field. Leveling in-

Surveying Camp. This 1912 photograph shows a noon camp of surveyors in the southwestern part of the Jornada Range Reserve, New Mexico. NATIONAL ARCHIVES AND RECORDS ADMINISTRATION

Swimsuit Scandal. Several women talk with a police officer after disobeying a prohibition on what many people regarded as skimpy bathing suits in Chicago, 1922. © UPI/CORBIS-BETTMANN

freestyle stroke, so the breaststroke was made a separate event.

The first American swimmer to achieve national fame was Duke Kahanamoku, a native Hawaiian who won three gold medals and two silvers in the 1912, 1920, and 1924 Olympics. Kahanamoku used six flutter kicks for each cycle of his arms, a technique that is now considered the classic freestyle form. In 1924, the twenty-year-old Johnny Weissmuller beat Kahanamoku, achieving international celebrity. In a decade of racing, Weissmuller set twenty-four world swimming records, won five Olympic gold medals, and never lost a race of between 50 yards and a half-mile. Weissmuller achieved even greater fame, however, when he went on to Hollywood to play Tarzan on the silver screen.

Women were excluded from Olympic swimming until 1912 because they were considered too frail to engage in competitive sports. In the 1910s, however, the newly formed Women's Swimming Association of New York gave women an opportunity to train for competition. Gertrude Ederle, the daughter of a delicatessen owner, began setting world records in distances of between 100 and 800 meters. Wanting to win fame for her swimming club, in 1926 she became the first woman to swim the English Channel. The nineteen-year-old's time of 14 hours and 31 minutes broke the existing men's record, and Ederle returned home to a ticker-tape parade. The first American woman to win an Olympic swimming title was Ethelda Bleibtrey, who captured three gold medals in 1920.

The early twentieth century also saw a boom in leisure swimming. Americans had been going to the beach for seaside recreation ever since railroads made public beaches more accessible in the late nineteenth century. The first municipal pool in the United States was built in Brookline, Massachusetts, in 1887, and by the 1920s many cities and some wealthy homeowners had installed pools. Leisure swimming had health as well as social benefits; President Franklin D. Roosevelt swam regularly to strengthen legs weakened by paralysis, while President John F. Kennedy swam to strengthen his back muscles.

Beginning in the 1930s, women's swimsuits became increasingly streamlined and revealing. (Fabric rationing during World War II [1939–1945] led to the introduction of the two-piece bathing suit, and the "bikini"—named for a U.S. nuclear testing site in the South Pacific—debuted in 1946.) Pin-up girls and starlets appeared in bathing attire, and in 1944 swimming champion Esther Williams made a splash in the film *Bathing Beauty*. Williams's appearance in a string of Hollywood swimming movies in the 1940s and 1950s helped popularize synchronized swimming.

Hollywood was not alone in turning a camera on swimmers. In 1934, Iowa University coach Dave Armbruster first filmed swimmers in order to study their strokes. To speed his breaststrokers, Armbruster developed a double overarm recovery known as the "butterfly." An Iowa swimmer, Jack Seig, paired this with a "dolphin kick," in which his body undulated from the hips to the toes. The butterfly was so exhausting that it was initially considered a novelty, but swimmers using the overhand stroke began dominating breaststroke races. In 1953, the butterfly was finally recognized as a separate competitive stroke.

The final years of the twentieth century were golden for American swimmers. Mark Spitz, a butterfly and freestyle racer, garnered seven gold medals and seven world records in the 1972 Munich Olympics, the most ever in a single Olympiad. In 1992, freestyler Matt Biondi matched Spitz's career record of 11 Olympic medals (The only other Olympian to win 11 medals was shooter Carl Osburn). In the 1980s, Tracy Caulkins became the only American swimmer ever to hold U.S. records in every stroke; she won three gold medals at the Olympics in 1984. Competing in the 1992, 1996, and 2000 Games, Jenny Thompson won ten butterfly and freestyle medals, including eight golds, the most ever captured by a woman.

BIBLIOGRAPHY

Gonsalves, Kamm, Herbert, ed. *The Junior Illustrated Encyclopedia of Sports.* Indianapolis, Ind.: Bobbs-Merrill, 1970.

USA Swimming Official Web site. Home page at http://www.usa-swimming.org.

Yee, Min S., ed. *The Sports Book: An Unabashed Assemblage of Heroes, Strategies, Records, and Events.* New York: Holt, Rinehart, and Winston, 1975.

Wendy Wall

SYMBIONESE LIBERATION ARMY,

SYMBIONESE LIBERATION ARMY, a violent revolutionary group that espoused vaguely Marxist doctrines and operated in California from 1973 to 1975, undertaking a highly publicized campaign of domestic terrorism. Their 1973 assassination of the Oakland superintendent of schools, Marcus Foster, brought them to national attention. They became even more notorious the following year when they kidnapped Patricia Hearst, a wealthy newspaper heiress. In a bizarre twist, Hearst joined her captors and became an active revolutionary. A shootout with the Los Angeles police in May 1974 left six of the radicals dead, but they continued to operate throughout 1975. Subsequently, the group dissolved, as its members ended up dead, captured, or in hiding. In 1999 the SLA was once again in the headlines with the arrest of Kathleen Soliah, one of its fugitive members. She ultimately pleaded guilty to charges of aiding and abetting a plot to plant bombs in police vehicles. As of 2002, she and three other former SLA members were facing murder charges stemming from a 1975 bank robbery.

BIBLIOGRAPHY

Bryan, John. *This Soldier Still at War.* New York: Harcourt Brace Jovanovich, 1975.

Hearst, Patricia. *Every Secret Thing.* Garden City, N.Y.: Doubleday, 1982.

Daniel J. Johnson

See also **Kidnapping; Terrorism.**

Patricia Hearst, Revolutionary. Before becoming the unlikely poster girl for the short-lived Symbionese Liberation Army, she was an heiress kidnapped by the group in 1974. AP/WIDE WORLD PHOTOS

SYMPHONY ORCHESTRAS.

SYMPHONY ORCHESTRAS. While Americans have enjoyed music making since their earliest days, colonial cities at first had insufficient size and disposable income to support orchestras. By the 1750s, however, Boston, Philadelphia, and Charleston had orchestras. In the early national period, music making assumed roles that involved more than mere entertainment. In Lexington, Kentucky, for example, an orchestra was developed as a means of competing with rival city Louisville in the hope that stronger levels of culture would attract entrepreneurs and trade. In Boston, the Handel and Haydn Society was founded in 1815. It maintained regular concerts and quickly became a center for the city's culture. This was the first music organization prominently to conceive and use its influence in explicitly conservative ways: to maintain established traditions and to discourage what were seen as corrupting "modern" trends.

German immigrants in the 1840s and 1850s sparked the formation of orchestras and festivals in many cities. In 1842, the New York Philharmonic Society was established. In 1878, a second orchestra, the New York Symphony, emerged. The two were rivals until they merged in 1928, although the New York music public had shown it could support two full orchestras. While there was a highbrow-lowbrow dichotomy in nineteenth-century America, the popularity of symphony orchestras, and opera as well, touched many beyond the wealthy classes, especially among immigrant groups, including German and Italian Americans. Grand orchestra concerts were a rage in mid-nineteenth-century America. While the proceeds were good and the mainstream public was satisfied, some critics and serious music lovers noted the often middling (or worse) quality of the music making.

In an age when corporations were eclipsing many older means of providing goods and services, the organization of the American symphony orchestra began to evolve from individual entrepreneurialism toward corporate forms. An example is the Boston Symphony, founded in 1881. The investment banker Henry L. Higginson, an ardent music lover, was impatient with the ragtag nature and substandard performances of American musical organizations. Higginson used his considerable financial power to hire the best conductors and musicians and bind them to contracts that restricted their outside activities and demanded regular rehearsals; he simply paid everyone enough to make the arrangement irresistible. While Higginson's corporate order restricted musicians' freedom, musically it worked wonders. Other cities followed suit, and the United States witnessed the establishment of many of its major orchestras in the generations after Higginson founded the Boston Symphony.

World War I interrupted not the quality but the character of American symphony orchestras. Before 1917, Austro-German traditions had utterly dominated the repertoire of orchestras. Also, conductors and personnel were largely German. The war changed this. Repertoire turned to French, Russian, and American composers, and while Austro-German music quickly reemerged in programming, it never again reached its position of prewar dominance. More starkly, personnel shifted markedly. Some German orchestra members returned home and never came back. War hysteria pressured several conductors. Frederick Stock of the Chicago Symphony had to resign his post for the war's duration. Two conductors—Ernst Kunewald of Cincinnati and Karl Muck of Boston—were investigated by the Justice Department and arrested under suspicion of subversion and spying. Both spent the war in an internment camp and were subsequently compelled to accept deportation.

Despite personnel shifts during the war, the quality of music making never flagged. Orchestras' popularity continued to grow, and in the 1920s many—especially the Boston Symphony of Serge Koussevitsky—began to champion works by American composers. This put the symphony orchestras more to the center of the major aesthetic issues among modern American artists, critics, and audiences. The heat of the debates here, combined with the increasing presence of music making among the general population with the proliferation of records and radio, made the symphony orchestras of the nation a central part of the country's cultural life in the 1920s and 1930s. Radio was especially important in maintaining this presence during the depression, when many smaller orchestras folded. The New Deal Works Progress Administration's music project helped too, as it sponsored many touring symphony orchestras and presented public concerts for minimal prices. Most famously, in 1937, the National Broadcasting Company (NBC) also began live radio concerts. Not content with the best orchestras in New York City or anywhere else, NBC president Robert Sarnoff hired conductor Arturo Toscanini to put together a hand-picked orchestra. The NBC orchestra concerts became a Sunday afternoon mainstay for millions of households. Many still think it was the greatest orchestra ever assembled. Walt Disney added further to the symphony's visibility in the cultural life of the nation when he hired Leopold Stokowski and the Philadelphia Orchestra for the animated movie *Fantasia* (1940).

After World War II, orchestras continued to flourish, especially with the breakdown of barriers that had prevented Jews, African Americans, and women from playing in significant numbers. The orchestra became a perfect neutral ground for the rise of anyone with musical talent. Indeed, to prevent bias, conductors often auditioned people from behind screens. Progress took some time, but talent won in the end.

Just as radio had boosted the musical presence of the symphony among virtually all levels of the American music public, television would do much the same in the 1950s and 1960s. Here the Columbia Broadcasting System's production of Leonard Bernstein's innovative Young People's Concerts with the New York Philharmonic were pivotal in introducing new generations to the symphony. Still, it was with the television generation and with the general economic prosperity of the era that Americans began gravitating steadily toward genres of music other than the symphonic.

Alternative musical forms and other entertainment in general had always been available, but a significant line seemed to be crossed in the 1970s, as in most cities the weekend symphony concert seemed less and less to be a central event as it had once been in various communities' cultural lives. In this regard, the life of the American symphony orchestra closed the last quarter of the twentieth century on less sure footing than it had been. The cities with the greatest symphonic traditions, like Boston, New York, Philadelphia, Cleveland, and Chicago, never felt significantly imperiled, although even they occasionally experienced labor strife and financial pinches. The orchestras of other cities became more seriously troubled, and in the early twenty-first century the fate of the symphony orchestra as a mainstay in the cultural life of most American cities has ceased to be the certainty it once was.

BIBLIOGRAPHY

Arian, Edward. *Bach, Beethoven, and Bureaucracy: The Case of the Philadelphia Orchestra.* University: University of Alabama Press, 1971.

Johnson, H. Earle. *Symphony Hall, Boston.* New York: DaCapo Press, 1979.

Kupferberg, Herbert. *Those Fabulous Philadelphians: The Life and Times of a Great Orchestra.* New York: Scribners, 1969.

Mueller, John Henry. *The American Symphony Orchestra: A Social History of Musical Taste.* Bloomington: Indiana University Press, 1951.

Mussulman, Joseph A. *Music in the Cultured Generation: A Social History of Music in America, 1870–1900.* Evanston, Ill.: Northwestern University Press, 1971.

Otis, Philo Adams. *The Chicago Symphony Orchestra: Its Organization, Growth, and Development, 1891–1924.* Freeport, N.Y.: Books for Libraries Press, 1972.

Swoboda, Henry, comp. *The American Symphony Orchestra.* New York: Basic Books, 1967.

Alan Levy

See also **Music Festivals; Music Industry; Music: Classical, Early American.**

SYNDICALISM, or revolutionary industrial unionism, originated in France but has been identified in the United States with the Industrial Workers of the World (IWW), founded in 1905. The IWW sought strong, centralized unions, while French syndicalists preferred smaller unions. Both opposed action through existing governments.

Syndicalists sought to establish a producers' cooperative commonwealth, with socially owned industries managed and operated by *syndicats*, or labor unions. Emphasizing class struggle, they advocated direct action through sabotage and general strikes. Opponents, criticizing the movement for militant actions, opposing political government, and condoning violence, secured antisyndicalist laws in several states. The syndicalist movement waned after World War I when many former adherents joined Communist, Trotskyite, or other Socialist groups.

BIBLIOGRAPHY

Kimeldorf, Howard. *Battling for American Labor: Wobblies, Craft Workers, and the Making of the Union Movement.* Berkeley: University of California Press, 1999.

Gordon S. Watkins / c. w.

See also **Communist Party, United States of America; Industrial Workers of the World; Labor.**

TABERNACLE, MORMON. This unique Salt Lake City auditorium, built by the Church of Jesus Christ of Latter-day Saints between 1864 and 1867 at a cost of about $300,000, was designated a National Historic Landmark in 1970 and a National Civil Engineering Landmark in 1971. Its interior is 150 feet wide, 250 feet long, and 80 feet high, and accommodates nearly 8,000 people. The Tabernacle's most distinctive feature is a nine-foot-thick tortoise-like roof, designed by a bridge-builder and constructed without nails. A network of lattice arches, resting on buttresses in the outside walls but with no interior support, forms this remarkable dome. Timbers were fastened together with wooden dowels. Split timbers were bound with rawhide that, as it dried, contracted and held them tight.

The tabernacle is notable also for its outstanding acoustics and its famous organ, which by the early twenty-first century contained over 11,600 pipes. In 1994 the Organ Historical Society cited it as "an instrument of exceptional merit, worthy of preservation."

The first meeting in the Tabernacle was a general conference of the church in 1867. These semiannual gatherings were held there until 1999, after which they were transferred to the new and more spacious conference center. In the early twenty-first century the building continued to be used for organ recitals, concerts, religious services, and various public functions. As the home of the renowned Mormon Tabernacle Choir, it also hosted regular Sunday broadcasts over the CBS radio and television networks.

BIBLIOGRAPHY

Anderson, Paul L. "Tabernacle, Salt Lake City." In *Encyclopedia of Mormonism*. Edited by Daniel H. Ludlow et al. New York: Macmillan, 1992.

Grow, Stewart L. *A Tabernacle in the Desert*. Salt Lake City, Utah: Deseret Book Company, 1958.

James B. Allen

See also **Latter-day Saints, Church of Jesus Christ of.**

TAFT COMMISSION. President William McKinley appointed the Taft Commission on 16 March 1900 to supervise the adjustment of the Philippine Islands' government from military command to civil rule. The five-member commission assumed legislative authority on 1 September 1900, less than two years after Spain ceded the Philippines to the United States following the SPANISH-AMERICAN WAR of 1898. On 4 July 1901, William Howard Taft, president of the commission, became the Philippines' first civilian governor.

The commission defined its mission as preparing the Filipinos for eventual independence, and focused on economic development, public education, and the establishment of representative institutions. The commission went on to establish a judicial system, organize administrative services, and create a legal code that included laws regarding health, education, agriculture, and taxation.

On 1 September 1901, three Filipinos were appointed to the Taft Commission, and each American member became an executive department head. However, unstable economic conditions became a catalyst for the creation of a Filipino resistance movement dedicated to achieving immediate independence. To quell growing opposition, the United States promulgated a Sedition Law on 4 November 1901, making the advocacy of independence punishable by death or long imprisonment.

In July 1902, a legislature was established that included a popularly elected Lower House and the Taft Commission, which was also known as the Second Philippine Commission. Five years later, the reorganization went into effect and elections for the assembly took place, but franchise was limited to owners of substantial property who were also literate in English or Spanish.

After considerable Filipino lobbying and the capture of resistance leader Emilio Aguinaldo, the Tydings-McDuffie Act was passed. It provided for a ten-year period of "Commonwealth" status, beginning in 1935. On 4 July 1946, the United States granted the Philippines complete independence.

James T. Scott

TAFT-HARTLEY ACT (1947). Passed by Congress over the veto of President Harry Truman, the Taft-Hartley Act enacted a number of significant amendments to the NATIONAL LABOR RELATIONS ACT of 1935. The 1935 law, known as the Wagner Act, may have been the most radical legislation of the twentieth century, recognizing and giving federal protection to workers' rights to organize, to form unions, to engage in strikes and other "concerted activities," including picketing, and to bargain collectively with their employers. The Wagner Act overturned a vast body of older, judge-made laws, which had enshrined, as a right of private property, employers' freedom to refuse to deal with unions or union workers. Now, the Wagner Act required them to bargain collectively with employees, and it forbade them to interfere with workers' new statutory rights. No longer could employers punish or fire pro-union employees or avoid independent unions by creating company-dominated unions; and no longer could they refuse to bargain in good faith with the unions that workers chose to represent them. What was more, the 1935 legislation created a new federal agency, the National Labor Relations Board (NLRB), to supervise union elections and bring "unfair labor practices" charges against employers who violated the Act.

The enforcement tools at the Board's disposal were never formidable; nonetheless, the spectacle of federal support behind vigorous industrial union drives both emboldened workers and enraged much of the business community and its supporters in Congress. During the dozen years since Congress passed the Wagner Act, the labor movement had quintupled in size, reaching roughly 15 million members, or 32 percent of the nonfarm labor force. A substantial majority of the workforce of such key industries as coal mining, railroads, and construction belonged to unions. Thus, by 1947 organized labor had become "Big Labor" and a mighty power in the public eye, and the complaints of business that the National Labor Relations Act was a one-sided piece of legislation began to resonate. The Act safeguarded workers' rights and enshrined collective bargaining but provided no protection for employers or individual employees against the abuses or wrongdoing of unions.

Changes after World War II

The end of World War II (1939–1945) saw a massive strike wave, which helped turn public opinion against "Big Labor." Thus, when the Republicans won both houses of Congress in the 1946 elections, new federal labor legislation was almost inevitable. Indeed, in the decade preceding 1946, well over 200 major bills setting out to amend the Wagner Act had been introduced in Congress. These bills had rehearsed the main themes of the complex and lengthy Taft-Hartley Act. The gist of Taft-Hartley, according to its proponents, was to right the balance of power between unions and employers. The Wagner Act, they claimed, was tilted toward unions; Taft-Hartley would protect employers and individual workers. For the latter, the new law contained provisions forbidding the closed shop and permitting states to outlaw any kind of union security clauses in collective agreements.

Already, several states, led by Florida and Arkansas, had adopted so-called right-to-work measures, outlawing any form of union security—not only the closed shop, but also contract provisions that required workers who declined to join the union to pay their share of expenses for bargaining and processing grievances. By sanctioning right-to-work statutes, Taft-Hartley did not injure "Big Labor" in the industrial heartland, so much as help thwart union advance in traditionally anti-union regions like the South and the prairie states.

The Taft-Hartley Act Brings Changes

For employers, the Act created a list of union "unfair labor practices," where previously the Wagner Act had condemned only employer practices. Taft-Hartley also greatly expanded the ability of both employers and the Board to seek injunctions against unions, thus undermining some of the protections against "government by injunction" that labor had won in the 1932 Norris-LaGuardia Act. It gave employers the express right to wage campaigns against unions during the period when workers were deciding and voting on whether to affiliate with a union. Previous Board policy generally had treated these processes as ones in which workers ought to be free to deliberate and decide free from employer interference. The new law also banned secondary boycotts and strikes stemming from jurisdictional disputes among unions. These provisions chiefly affected the older craft unions of the American Federation of Labor, whose power often rested on the capacity for secondary and sympathetic actions on the part of fellow union workers outside the immediate "unfair" workplace.

By contrast, Taft-Hartley's anticommunist affidavit requirement, like its sanction for right-to-work laws, fell most heavily on the Congress of Industrial Organizations (CIO). The statute required that all union officials seeking access to NLRB facilities and services sign an affidavit stating that they were not communists. The requirement rankled because it implied that unionists were uniquely suspect. The law did not require employers or their agents to swear loyalty, but it did demand that the representatives of American workers go through a demeaning ritual designed to impugn their patriotism or they would be unable to petition the Board for a representation election or to bring unfair labor practice cases before it.

Finally, the Act changed the administrative structure and procedures of the NLRB, reflecting congressional conservatives' hostility toward the nation's new administrative agencies, exercising state power in ways that departed from common-law norms and courtlike procedures. Thus, the Act required that the Board's decision making follow legal rules of evidence, and it took the Board's legal arm, its general counsel, out of the Board's jurisdiction and established it as a separate entity.

The CIO's general counsel, for his part, warned that by establishing a list of unfair union practices and by imposing on the NLRB courtlike fact-finding, the new law would plunge labor relations into a morass of legalistic proceedings. Already under the Wagner Act, employers had found that unfair labor practice cases stemming from discrimination against union activists, firings of union-minded workers, and the like could all be strung out for years in the nation's appellate courts, rendering the Act's forthright endorsement of unionization a hollow one.

Since the late 1930s the NLRB itself had been retreating from its initially enthusiastic promotion of industrial unionism. Now, with Taft-Hartley, the Board or the independent legal counsel, who might be at odds with the Board, would have even more reason to maintain a studied "neutrality" toward union drives and collective versus individual employment relations, in place of Wagner's clear mandate in behalf of unionism. The great irony, the CIO counsel went on to say, was that so-called conservatives, who had made careers out of criticizing the intrusion of government authority into private employment relations, had created a vast and rigid machinery that would "convert . . . [federal] courts into forums cluttered with matters only slightly above the level of the police court."

And so it was. Despite its restrictions on secondary actions and jurisdictional strikes, Taft-Hartley did little to hamper the established old craft unions, like the building trades and teamsters, whose abuses had prompted them; but it went a long way toward hampering organizing the unorganized or extending unions into hostile regions of the nation, and it helped make the nation's labor law a dubious blessing for labor.

BIBLIOGRAPHY

Millis, Harry A., and Emily C. Brown. *From the Wagner Act to Taft-Hartley: A Study of National Labor Policy and Labor Relations.* Chicago: University of Chicago Press, 1950.

Tomlins, Christopher. *The State and the Unions: Labor Relations, Law, and the Organized Labor Movement in America, 1880–1960.* New York: Cambridge University Press, 1985.

Zieger, Robert H. *The CIO: 1935–1955.* Chapel Hill: University of North Carolina Press, 1995

William E. Forbath

TAFT-KATSURA MEMORANDUM (29 July 1905), a so-called agreed memorandum exchanged between Secretary of War William Howard Taft, speaking for President Theodore Roosevelt, and Prime Minister Taro Katsura of Japan. The memorandum invoked Japanese-American cooperation "for the maintenance of peace in the Far East." Thus ornamented, it expressed an approval by the United States of Japanese suzerainty over Korea and a disavowal by Japan of "any aggressive designs whatever on the Philippines." Roosevelt assured Taft afterward that his "conversation with Count Katsura was absolutely correct in every respect," thus emphatically approving the agreement, which remained secret until 1925.

BIBLIOGRAPHY

Esthus, Raymond A. *Theodore Roosevelt and Japan.* Seattle: University of Washington Press, 1966.

Minger, Ralph E. "Taft's Missions to Japan: A Study in Personal Diplomacy." *Pacific Historical Review* 30 (1961).

Samuel Flagg Bemis / A. G.

See also **Diplomacy, Secret; Diplomatic Missions; Japan, Relations with.**

TAFT-ROOSEVELT SPLIT. When Republican President William Howard Taft took office in 1909 he did so with the support of his reform-minded predecessor Theodore Roosevelt. Within a year, however, Progressive reformers in Congress complained that the administration had allied itself with the conservative Congressional establishment. The reformers, known as Insurgents and led by Senator Robert M. La Follette of Wisconsin, took particular exception to Taft's controversial firing of Gifford Pinchot in January 1910. Pinchot, head of the Forest Service and a leading conservationist, had been a longtime friend of Roosevelt's and his firing became a rallying point for Progressives. On his return from a year-long trip to Africa, Roosevelt consulted with Pinchot and other Progressive leaders and plotted a political comeback. In a speech in Kansas in August 1910, Roosevelt attacked Taft's conservatism and proposed a sweeping program of reforms he called the "NEW NATIONALISM." At the 1912 Chicago convention, Roosevelt contested for the Republican nomination, but conservative party leaders defiantly renominated Taft. Outraged by the conservatives' heavy-handed tactics, Roosevelt organized the Bull Moose Progressive Party, and became its candidate for president. The split between Roosevelt and Taft allowed the Democratic candidate, Woodrow Wilson, to win the presidency with only about 42 percent of the vote.

BIBLIOGRAPHY

Broderick, Francis L. *Progressivism at Risk: Electing a President in 1912.* New York: Greenwood, 1989.

Harbaugh, William H. *The Life and Times of Theodore Roosevelt.* New York: Oxford University Press, 1975.

Mowry, George E. *Theodore Roosevelt and the Progressive Movement.* Madison: University of Wisconsin Press, 1946.

Edgar Eugene Robinson / A. G.

See also **Bull Moose Party; Conservation; Conventions, Party Nominating; Elections, Presidential: 1912; Progressive Movement; Progressive Party, Wisconsin; Republican Party.**

TAILHOOK INCIDENT. The Tailhook Association, named for the arresting gear on carrier-based aircraft, is a private group of navy and marine aviators. During the association's 1991 annual convention in Las Vegas, eighty-three women, many of them naval officers, alleged that they had been sexually assaulted passing through a hotel hallway filled with male officers. Secretary of the Navy H. Lawrence Garrett III and Chief of Naval Operations Adm. Frank B. Kelso II attended the convention, but both said they witnessed no improper behavior. A subsequent navy investigation was indecisive, and on 18 June 1992, Secretary Garrett asked the Defense Department's inspector general to take control of the inquiry. The next week several female victims, led by navy Lt. Paula A. Coughlin, a helicopter pilot and aide to Rear Adm. John W. Snyder, Jr., brought charges. On 26 June, Secretary Garrett resigned. Members of Congress criticized the pace of the investigation, the commitment of investigators, and the stonewalling of Tailhook members.

In April 1993, the Inspector General accused 140 officers of indecent exposure, assault, and lying under oath. About fifty were fined or disciplined. Accusations in more prominent cases did not lead to court-martial convictions or even demotions. In 8 February 1994, a navy judge ruled that Admiral Kelso had misrepresented his activities at the convention and had tried to manipulate the subsequent investigation. Denying these charges, Kelso decided to retire two months early with a full pension, in return for a tribute from Defense Secretary John J. Dalton that stated Kelso was a man of the "highest integrity and honor." During that same week Coughlin announced her resignation, saying her career in the navy had been ruined because she had chosen to bring charges. She later received monetary awards from lawsuits against the Tailhook Association, the Hilton Hotels Corporation, and the Las Vegas Hilton Corporation.

BIBLIOGRAPHY

McMichael, William H. *The Mother of All Hooks: The Story of the U.S. Navy's Tailhook Scandal.* New Brunswick, N.J.: Transaction, 1997.

O'Nelll, William L. "Sex Scandals in the Gender-Integrated Military." *Gender Issues* 16, 1/2 (Winter/Spring 1998): 64–86.

Zimmerman, Jean. *Tailspin: Women at War in the Wake of Tailhook.* New York: Doubleday, 1995.

Irwin N. Gertzog / c. r. p.

See also **Marine Corps, United States; Navy, United States; Sexual Harassment; Women in Military Service.**

TALK SHOWS, RADIO AND TELEVISION.

The talk show has been an important programming format for television and RADIO since its earliest origins. On television, the earliest such program was *Meet the Press*, which first aired in 1947. The original host, Martha Rountree, was also the only woman in the program's history to moderate discussion as politicians and other public leaders made appearances. As television's ability to impact society grew, so did the need for expansions of the talk show format. In 1952, the *Today* show made its first appearance on NBC with host Dave Garroway. Soon other networks followed with similar programs, such as the

The Dick Cavett Show. The talk show host *(center)* engages in conversation with heavyweight boxers Muhammad Ali *(left)* and Jurgen Blin, whom the once and future champion fought, and knocked out, at the end of 1971. AP/WIDE WORLD PHOTOS

Morning Show on CBS with host Walter Cronkite. As television reached more and more homes all over the country, the talk show changed to include more entertainment and human-interest features. The *Tonight Show*, first with Steve Allen in 1954 and eventually Johnny Carson, established the late-night genre that remains wildly popular today. A variety of daytime talk shows have covered a number of issues with very distinct methods of delivery. Serious, issue-oriented programs like *Donahue*, the *Oprah Winfrey Show*, and *Charlie Rose* have been important vehicles for the discussion of important social issues. Other television talk programs have featured hosts interjecting their personal opinions to guests while fielding questions from the audience. The growth of "trash TV" began in the early 1980s with the *Morton Downey, Jr. Show*. These programs featured incendiary guests who would often come to blows in discussions of race, sexual preference, and infidelity. Many times the hosts themselves would become involved, as when Geraldo Rivera suffered a broken nose during a fracas in one episode of his syndicated talk program. The *Jerry Springer Show* became a national force in the 1990s and found itself at the center of controversy about the violence and lack of moral content on television in America. These various forms of talk shows continued to dominate afternoon television programming at the turn of the twenty-first century.

Radio talk programs evolved over the years as the daily commute to and from work became a high-ratings time slot for that medium. Talk radio programs have become an important political force. Various liberal and conservative hosts voice their views in daily programs. Rush Limbaugh became one of the most well known and well paid of these political hosts, specializing in espousing conservative views and deriding then President Bill Clinton. National Public Radio, founded in 1970, serves over fifteen million listeners and provides two popular talk-news programs, *All Things Considered* and *Morning Edition*.

Cheers! The Schlitz Hotel Bar in Milwaukee, Wisc., shown here in the early twentieth century, displays a wide variety of alcoholic beverages. LIBRARY OF CONGRESS

TASK FORCE 58 was the long-range naval striking arm of the U.S. Pacific Fleet during the offensive against Japan in World War II. It became the major weapon system in the wartime and postwar U.S. Navy, replacing the battleship. During World War II the Navy created numbered fleets with subordinate numbered task organizations. In August 1943 the Navy divided the Pacific Fleet into the Third and Fifth Fleets, of which the fast carriers became Task Force 58 (TF 58). The Navy later subdivided TF 58 into task groups and they into smaller task units. This system, which allowed the Pacific Fleet to transfer ships between commands with a minimum of administrative detail, became the basis for postwar naval organization.

The tasks of TF 58, which the Navy renamed Task Force 38 in 1944, increased as the war progressed. In 1944, TF 58 sought out and destroyed the Japanese fleet and naval air forces at the Battles of the Philippine Sea and of Leyte Gulf. In 1943 and 1944 it provided defensive cover and air support for the amphibious forces that captured the Gilbert, Marshall, New Guinea, Mariana, Palau, and Philippine Islands and protected the forces that neutralized Truk. In 1945 it supported the amphibious landings at Iwo Jima and Okinawa, fought off Japanese kamikaze air attacks, and struck airfields and strategic targets in Formosa and Japan. The latter-type missions also dominated fast-carrier operations in the Korean and

Vietnam Wars, during which the carriers (in far fewer numbers) composed TF 77 as part of the Seventh Fleet.

BIBLIOGRAPHY

Belote, James H. *Titans of the Sea*. New York: Harper and Row, 1975.

Bradley, James. *Flags of Our Fathers*. New York: Bantam, 2000.

Cutler, Thomas J. *The Battle of Leyte Gulf, 23–26 October, 1944*. New York: HarperCollins, 1994.

Wildenberg, Thomas. *Destined for Glory*. Annapolis, Md.: Naval Institute Press, 1998.

Clark G. Reynolds/E. M.

See also **Aircraft Carriers and Naval Aircraft; Philippine Sea, Battle of the.**

TAVERNS AND SALOONS. Early New England taverns were actually private homes where the homeowner both served meals and opened rooms so travelers would have a place to stay. Taverns received travelers who came on canal boats, in stagecoaches, and by horseback. By the 1790s taverns were offering more services: if a horse needed stabling, stalls were to be had; clubs and boards of directors held meetings in their rooms; promoters of the arts used taverns for dances, stage productions, and art galleries; area residents met in taverns at the end of the day to discuss politics, transact business, or gossip. Many stagecoach stops were at taverns, which provided workers to load and unload freight. Early post offices were often in taverns.

Taverns, often the social and economic centers of communities, evolved and expanded along with the country. While always offering drink, both alcohol (licenses to serve alcohol had to be applied for and approved by the local government) and soft, they also made newspapers available to their patrons for reading, and were used as polling places during elections. Because the building was often large enough to accommodate a group, taverns were sometimes utilized as courtrooms. In times of war, taverns were used as military headquarters. In addition, many taverns served as a basic general store, selling staples such as molasses, cloth, kitchen utensils, and spices. (Some taverns, the nicer ones, had a parlor that was set apart for ladies or others who did not wish to be seated in the main room. The furnishings were usually more formal and included a fire in the colder months.)

Taverns had colorful names, the Eagle, the Star and Garter, the Bull's Eye, the Leather Bottle, the Globe, the Indian Queen, and the Mermaid Inn among them. The Mermaid opened shortly after James Simpson established Salem, Virginia, in 1802. At a time when many people were illiterate and before the practice of naming and numbering streets was common, signs were hung out to identify each tavern. Some were carved from wood and then painted; others were stone, tile, metal, and even stuffed animal heads.

Taverns were commonly absentee-owned, with the tavern keeper living in the building as a tenant, much like motel managers of the current day. The lodging was undoubtedly part of the tavern keeper's compensation.

By the end of the nineteenth century, taverns had died out as each area of their trade became specialized. Boardinghouses, restaurants, theaters, hotels, and saloons became stand-alone businesses. With the advent of the train, passengers and freight depots no longer had need of taverns for transfers.

Saloons

Saloons were the western version of a tavern but did not provide lodging; entertainment, however, took on a decidedly western flair. Instead of art displays, saloons offered prizefights or boxing matches. Saloons did not host formal dances; they had dance hall girls who danced with the men for a price.

Many saloon keepers built stages on which short plays and variety shows were held. The Apollo Hall in Denver opened in 1859 with the saloon on the ground floor and a theater on the second floor. Denver was only a year old, but ready for variety in entertainment. Saloon talent, however, was not especially sophisticated or refined; for example, the strong woman act of Mrs. De Granville; the entrepreneur who installed a stereoscope

with obscene pictures; and the man who was hired to walk to and fro on a platform above the bar in a Cheyenne saloon for 60 hours.

Saloons had liquor of the best, and the worst, qualities, depending on their location—a rich mining town or a hardscrabble settlement. Saloons had the most success in mining or cattle towns. In some of these settlements, saloons outnumbered stores and other establishments by two to one. Abilene, Kansas, with a year-round population of only 800, had eleven saloons. Abilene was on the trail of the cattle drives from Texas, thus the population would briefly increase by at least 5,000 cowboys. Regulations were few, so some saloons were open all day and night, seven days a week, especially in mining towns. Gunfights and other violence were common in both the cattle and mining towns.

Saloons located in farming communities were much quieter. Farmers were usually settled inhabitants, with a name to protect and consistent hard work facing them each morning. They discussed their successes and difficulties over snacks that the barkeeper supplied as they sipped their beers.

Many Americans thought that saloons and strong drink were the work of the devil (indeed, alcoholism was a major problem in the United States). Perhaps the most vociferous in that belief was Carry A. Nation, who traveled around the country preaching her temperance message, urging moderation in most things but complete abstinence of intoxicating liquor. She carried a hatchet in her underskirt, and more than once used it to destroy liquor bottles and bar equipment. Churches promoted the temperance movement, and it spread throughout the country during the last decades of the nineteenth century.

BIBLIOGRAPHY

Erdoes, Richard. *Saloons of the Old West.* New York: Knopf, 1979.

Grace, Fran. *Carry A. Nation: Retelling the Life.* Bloomington: Indiana University Press, 2001.

Schaumann, Merri Lou Schribner. *Taverns of Cumberland County 1750–1840.* Carlisle, Pa.: Cumberland County Historical Society, 1994.

Peggy Sanders

See also **Stagecoach Travel; Temperance Movement.**

TAX IN KIND, CONFEDERATE. *See* **Tithes, Southern Agricultural.**

TAXATION is the imposition by a government of a compulsory contribution on its citizens for meeting all or part of its expenditures. But taxation can be more than a revenue raiser. Taxes can redistribute income, favor one group of taxpayers at the expense of others, punish or reward, and shape the behavior of taxpayers through incentives and disincentives. The architects of American tax policy have always used taxes for a variety of social purposes: upholding social order, advancing social justice, promoting economic growth, and seeking their own political gain. The need for new revenues has always set the stage for pursuing social goals through taxation, and the need for new revenues has been most intense during America's five great national crises: the political and economic crisis of the 1780s, the Civil War, World War I, the Great Depression, and World War II. In the process of managing each of these crises, the federal government led the way in creating a distinctive tax regime—a tax system with its own characteristic tax base, rate structure, administrative apparatus, and social intention.

In the United States, progressive taxation—taxation that bears proportionately more heavily on individuals, families, and firms with higher incomes—has always enjoyed great popularity. Progressive taxation has offered a way of reconciling the republican or democratic ideals with the high concentrations of wealth characteristic of capitalist economic systems. During national crises, political leaders have been especially intent on rallying popular support. Consequently, the powerful tax regimes associated with great national crises have each had a significant progressive dimension.

The Colonial Era and the American Revolution, 1607–1783

Before the American Revolution, taxation was relatively light in the British colonies that would form the United States. Public services, such as education and roads, were limited in scale, and the British government heavily funded military operations. In 1763, after the expensive Seven Years' War, the British government initiated a program to increase taxes levied on Americans, especially through "internal" taxes such as the Stamp Act (1765) and the Townshend Acts (1767). But colonial resistance forced the British to repeal these taxes quickly, and the overall rate of taxation in America remained low until the outset of the Revolution, at least by contemporary British standards.

Tax rates and types of taxation varied substantially from colony to colony, and even from community to community within particular colonies, depending on modes of political organization and the distribution of economic power. British taxing traditions were diverse, and the various colonies and local communities had a rich array of institutions from which to choose: taxes on imports and exports; property taxes (taxes on the value of real and personal assets); poll taxes (taxes levied on citizens without any regard for their property, income, or any economic characteristic); excise (sales) taxes; and faculty taxes, which were taxes on the implicit incomes of people in trades or businesses. The mix varied, but each colony made use of virtually all of these different modes of taxation.

Fighting the Revolution forced a greater degree of fiscal effort on Americans. At the same time, the democratic forces that the American Revolution unleashed energized reformers throughout America to restructure state taxation. Reformers focused on abandoning deeply unpopular poll taxes and shifting taxes to wealth as measured by the value of property holdings. The reformers embraced "ability to pay"—the notion that the rich ought to contribute disproportionately to government—as a criterion to determine the distribution of taxes. The reformers were aware that the rich of their day spent more of their income on housing than did the poor and that a flat, ad valorem property levy was therefore progressive. Some conservative leaders also supported the reforms as necessary both to raise revenue and to quell social discord. The accomplishments of the reform movements varied widely across the new states; the greatest successes were in New England and the Middle Atlantic states.

During the Revolution, while state government increased taxes and relied more heavily on property taxes, the nascent federal government failed to develop effective taxing authority. The Continental Congress depended on funds requisitioned from the states, which usually ignored calls for funds or responded very slowly. There was little improvement under the Articles of Confederation. States resisted requisitions and vetoed efforts to establish national tariffs.

The Early Republic, 1783–1861

The modern structure of the American tax system emerged from the social crisis that extended from 1783 to the ratification in 1788 of the U.S. Constitution. At the same time that the architects of the federal government forged their constitutional ideas, they struggled with an array of severe fiscal problems. The most pressing were how to finance the revolutionary war debts and how to establish the credit of the nation in a way that won respect in international financial markets. To solve these problems, the Constitution gave the new government the general power, in the words of Article 1, section 8, "To lay and collect Taxes, Duties, Imposts, and Excises."

The Constitution, however, also imposed some restrictions on the taxing power. First, Article 1, section 8, required that "all Duties, Imposts and Excises shall be uniform throughout the United States." This clause prevented Congress from singling out a particular state or group of states for higher rates of taxation on trade, and reflected the hope of the framers that the new Constitution would foster the development of a national market. Second, Article 1, section 9, limited federal taxation of property by specifying that "No Capitation, or other direct, Tax shall be laid, unless in Proportion to the Census." The framers of the Constitution never clearly defined "direct" taxation, but they regarded property taxes and "capitation" or poll taxes as direct taxes. The framers' goals were to protect the dominance of state and local governments in property taxation, and to shield special categories of property, such as slaves, against discriminatory federal taxation.

As the framers of the Constitution intended, property taxation flourished at the state and local levels during the early years of the Republic. Most of the nation's fiscal effort was at these levels of government, rather than at the federal level, and the property tax provided most of the funding muscle.

Differences persisted among states regarding the extent and form of property taxation. Southern states remained leery of property taxation as a threat to the land and slaves owned by powerful planters. These states also had the most modest governments because of limited programs of education and internal improvements. One southern state, Georgia, abandoned taxation altogether and financed its state programs through land sales.

Northern states, in contrast, generally expanded their revenue systems, both at the state and local levels, and developed ambitious new property taxes. The reformers who created these new property taxes sought to tax not just real estate but all forms of wealth. They described the taxes that would do this as general property taxes. These were comprehensive taxes on wealth that would reach not only tangible property such as real estate, tools, equipment, and furnishings but also intangible personal property such as cash, credits, notes, stocks, bonds, and mortgages. Between the 1820s and the Civil War, as industrialization picked up steam and created new concentrations of wealth, tax reformers tried to compel the new wealth to contribute its fair share to promoting communal welfare. By the 1860s, the general property tax had, in fact, significantly increased the contributions of the wealthiest Americans to government.

At the federal level, a new tax regime developed under the financial leadership of the first secretary of the Treasury, Alexander Hamilton. His regime featured tariffs—customs duties on goods imported into the United States—as its flagship. Tariffs remained the dominant source of the government's revenue until the Civil War.

To establish precedents for future fiscal crises, Hamilton wanted to exercise all the taxing powers provided by Congress, including the power to levy "internal" taxes. So, from 1791 to 1802, Congress experimented with excise taxes on all distilled spirits (1791); on carriages, snuff manufacturing, and sugar refining (1794); and with stamp duties on legal transactions, including a duty on probates for wills (1797)—a first step in the development of the federal estate tax. In addition, in 1798 Congress imposed a temporary property tax, apportioned according to the Constitution, on all dwelling houses, lands, and large slave holdings.

Excise taxes proved especially unpopular, and the tax on spirits touched off the Whiskey Rebellion of 1794. President George Washington had to raise 15,000 troops to discourage the Pennsylvania farmers who had protested, waving banners denouncing tyranny and proclaiming "Liberty, Equality, and Fraternity."

In 1802, the administration of President Thomas Jefferson abolished the Federalist system of internal taxation, but during the War of 1812, Congress restored such taxation on an emergency basis. In 1813, 1815, and 1816, Congress enacted direct taxes on houses, lands, and slaves, and apportioned them to the states on the basis of the 1810 census. Congress also enacted duties on liquor licenses, carriages, refined sugar, and even distilled spirits. At the very end of the war, President James Madison's secretary of the Treasury, Alexander J. Dallas, proposed adopting an inheritance tax and a tax on incomes. But the war ended before Congress acted.

The Era of Civil War and Modern Industrialization, 1861–1913

The dependence of the federal government on tariff revenue might have lasted for at least another generation. But a great national emergency intervened. The Civil War created such enormous requirements for capital that the Union government had to return to the precedents set during the administrations of Washington and Madison and enact a program of emergency taxation. The program was unprecedented in scale, scope, and complexity.

During the Civil War, the Union government placed excise taxes on virtually all consumer goods, license taxes on a wide variety of activities (including every profession except the ministry), special taxes on corporations, stamp taxes on legal documents, and taxes on inheritances. Each wartime Congress also raised the tariffs on foreign goods, doubling the average tariff rate by the end of the war. And, for the first time, the government levied an income tax.

Republicans came to the income tax as they searched for a way to hold popular confidence in their party in the face of the adoption of the new regressive levies—taxes that taxed lower income people at higher rates than the wealthy. Republicans looked for a tax that bore a closer relationship to "ability to pay" than did the tariffs and excises. They considered a federal property tax but rejected it because the allocation formula that the Constitution imposed meant taxing property in wealthy, more urban states at lower rates than in poorer, more rural states. The Republican leadership then took note of how the British Liberals had used income taxation in financing the Crimean War as a substitute for heavier taxation of property. They settled on this approach, and the result was not only an income tax but a graduated, progressive tax—one that reached a maximum rate of 10 percent. This was the first time that the federal government discriminated among taxpayers by virtue of their income. The rates imposed significantly higher taxes on the wealthy—perhaps twice as much as the wealthy were used to paying under the general property tax. By the end of the war, more than 15 percent of all Union households in the northeastern states paid an income tax.

After the Civil War, Republican Congresses responded to the complaints of the affluent citizens who had accepted the tax only as an emergency measure. In 1872,

Congress allowed the income tax to expire. And, during the late 1860s and early 1870s, Republican Congresses phased out the excise taxes, except for the taxes on alcohol and tobacco.

Republicans, however, kept the high tariffs, and these constituted a new federal tax regime. Until the Underwood-Simmons Tariff Act of 1913 significantly reduced the Civil War rates, the ratio between duties and the value of dutiable goods rarely dropped below 40 percent and was frequently close to 50 percent. On many manufactured items the rate of taxation reached 100 percent. The system of high tariffs came to symbolize the commitment of the federal government to creating a powerful national market and to protecting capitalists and workers within that market. The nationalistic symbolism of the tariff in turn reinforced the political strength of the Republican Party.

After the Civil War, continuing industrialization and the associated rise of both modern corporations and financial capitalism increased Democratic pressure to reform the tariff. Many Americans, especially in the South and West, came to regard the tariff as a tax that was not only regressive but also protective of corporate monopolies. One result was the enactment, in 1894, of a progressive income tax. But in 1895 the Supreme Court, in *Pollock v. Farmers' Loan and Trust Company*, claimed, with little historical justification, that the architects of the Constitution regarded an income tax as a direct tax. Since Congress had not allocated the 1894 tax to the states on the basis of population, the tax was, in the Court's view, unconstitutional. Another result of reform pressure was the adoption in 1898, during the Spanish-American War, of the first federal taxation of estates. This tax was graduated according to both the size of the estate and the degree of relationship to the deceased. The Supreme Court upheld the tax in *Knowlton v. Moore* (1900), but in 1902 a Republican Congress repealed it.

State and local tax policy also began to change under the pressure of industrialization. The demand of urban governments for the funds required for new parks, schools, hospitals, transit systems, waterworks, and sewers crushed the general property tax. In particular, traditional self-assessment of property values proved inadequate to expose and determine the value of intangible property such as corporate stocks and bonds. Rather than adopt rigorous and intrusive new administrative systems to assess the value of such, most local governments focused property taxation on real estate, which they believed they could assess accurately at relatively low cost. Some states considered following the advice of the reformer Henry George and replacing the property tax with a "single tax" on the monopoly profits embedded in the price of land. Farm lobbies, however, invariably blocked such initiatives. Instead, after 1900, state governments began replacing property taxation with special taxes, such as income taxes, inheritance taxes, and special corporate taxes. Beginning in the 1920s, state governments would continue this trend by adding vehicle registration fees, gasoline taxes, and general sales taxes.

The Establishment of Progressive Income Taxation, 1913–1929

Popular support for progressive income taxation continued to grow, and in 1909 reform leaders in Congress from both parties finally united to send the Sixteenth Amendment, legalizing a federal income tax, to the states for ratification. It prevailed in 1913 and in that same year Congress passed a modest income tax. That tax, however, might well have remained a largely symbolic element in the federal tax system had World War I not intervened.

World War I accelerated the pace of reform. The revenue demands of the war effort were enormous, and the leadership of the Democratic Party, which had taken power in 1912, was more strongly committed to progressive income taxes and more opposed to general sales taxes than was the Republican Party. In order to persuade Americans to make the financial and human sacrifices for World War I, President Woodrow Wilson and the Democratic leadership of Congress introduced progressive income taxation on a grand scale.

The World War I income tax, which the Revenue Act of 1916 established as a preparedness measure, was an explicit "soak-the-rich" instrument. It imposed the first significant taxation of corporate profits and personal incomes and rejected moving toward a "mass-based" income tax—one falling most heavily on wages and salaries. The act also reintroduced the progressive taxation of estates. Further, it adopted the concept of taxing corporate excess profits. Among the World War I belligerents, only the United States and Canada placed excess-profits taxation—a graduated tax on all business profits above a "normal" rate of return—at the center of wartime finance. Excess-profits taxation turned out to generate most of the tax revenues raised by the federal government during the war. Thus, wartime public finance depended heavily on the taxation of income that leading Democrats, including President Wilson, regarded as monopoly profits and therefore ill-gotten and socially hurtful.

During the 1920s, three Republican administrations, under the financial leadership of Secretary of the Treasury Andrew Mellon, modified the wartime tax system. In 1921 they abolished the excess-profits tax, dashing Democratic hopes that the tax would become permanent. In addition, they made the rate structure of the income tax less progressive so that it would be less burdensome on the wealthy. Also in 1921, they began to install a wide range of special tax exemptions and deductions, which the highly progressive rates of the income tax had made extremely valuable to wealthy taxpayers and to their surrogates in Congress. The Revenue Acts during the 1920s introduced the preferential taxation of capital gains and a variety of deductions that favored particular industries, deductions such as oil- and gas-depletion allowances.

The tax system nonetheless retained its "soak-the-rich" character. Secretary Mellon led a struggle within the Republican Party to protect income and estate taxes from those who wanted to replace them with a national sales tax. Mellon helped persuade corporations and the wealthiest individuals to accept *some* progressive income taxation and the principle of "ability to pay." This approach would, Mellon told them, demonstrate their civic responsibility and help block radical attacks on capital.

The Great Depression and New Deal, 1929–1941

The Great Depression—the nation's worst economic collapse—produced a new tax regime. Until 1935, however, depression-driven changes in tax policy were ad hoc measures to promote economic recovery and budget balancing rather than efforts to seek comprehensive tax reform. In 1932, to reduce the federal deficit and reduce upward pressure on interest rates, the Republican administration of President Herbert Hoover engineered across-the-board increases in both income and estate taxes. These were the largest peacetime tax increases in the nation's history. They were so large that President Franklin D. Roosevelt did not have to recommend any significant tax hikes until 1935.

Beginning in 1935, however, Roosevelt led in the creation of major new taxes. In that year, Congress adopted taxes on wages and the payrolls of employers to fund the new social security system. The rates of these taxes were flat, and the tax on wages provided an exemption of wages over $3,000. Thus, social security taxation was regressive, taxing lower incomes more heavily than higher incomes. Partly to offset this regressive effect on federal taxation, Congress subsequently enacted an undistributed profits tax. This was a progressive tax on retained earnings—the profits that corporations did not distribute to their stockholders.

This measure, more than any other enactment of the New Deal, aroused fear and hostility on the part of large corporations. Quite correctly, they viewed Roosevelt's tax program as a threat to their control over capital and their latitude for financial planning. In 1938, a coalition of Republicans and conservative Democrats took advantage of the Roosevelt administration's embarrassment over the recession of 1937–1938 to gut and then repeal the tax on undistributed profits.

World War II, 1941–1945: From "Class" to "Mass" Taxation

President Roosevelt's most dramatic reform of taxation came during World War II. During the early phases of mobilization, he hoped to be able to follow the example of Wilson by financing the war with taxes that bore heavily on corporations and upper-income groups. "In time of this grave national danger, when all excess income should go to win the war," Roosevelt told a joint session of Congress in 1942, "no American citizen ought to have a net income, after he has paid his taxes, of more than $25,000." But doubts about radical war-tax proposals grew in the face of the revenue requirements of full mobilization. Roosevelt's military and economic planners, and Roosevelt himself, came to recognize the need to mobilize greater resources than during World War I. This need required a general sales tax or a mass-based income tax.

In October of 1942, Roosevelt and Congress agreed on a plan: dropping the general sales tax, as Roosevelt wished, and adopting a mass-based income tax that was highly progressive, although less progressive than Roosevelt desired. The act made major reductions in personal exemptions, thereby establishing the means for the federal government to acquire huge revenues from the taxation of middle-class wages and salaries. Just as important, the rates on individuals' incomes—rates that included a surtax graduated from 13 percent on the first $2,000 to 82 percent on taxable income over $200,000—made the personal income tax more progressive than at any other time in its history.

Under the new tax system, the number of individual taxpayers grew from 3.9 million in 1939 to 42.6 million in 1945, and federal income tax collections leaped from $2.2 billion to $35.1 billion. By the end of the war, nearly 90 percent of the members of the labor force submitted income tax returns, and about 60 percent of the labor force paid income taxes, usually in the form of withheld wages and salaries.

In making the new individual income tax work, the Roosevelt administration and Congress relied heavily on payroll withholding, the information collection procedures provided by the social security system, deductions that sweetened the new tax system for the middle class, the progressive rate structure, and the popularity of the war effort. Americans concluded that their nation's security was at stake and that victory required both personal sacrifice through taxation and indulgence of the corporate profits that helped fuel the war machine. The Roosevelt administration reinforced this spirit of patriotism and sacrifice by invoking the extensive propaganda machinery at their command. The Treasury, its Bureau of Internal Revenue, and the Office of War Information made elaborate calls for civic responsibility and patriotic sacrifice.

Cumulatively, the two world wars revolutionized public finance at the federal level. Policy architects had seized the opportunity to modernize the tax system, in the sense of adapting it to new economic and organizational conditions and thereby making it a more efficient producer of revenue. The income tax enabled the federal government to capitalize on the financial apparatus associated with the rise of the modern corporation to monitor income flows and collect taxes on those flows. In the process, progressive income taxation gathered greater popular support as an equitable means for financing government. Taxation, Americans increasingly believed, ought to redistribute income according to ideals of social justice and thus express the democratic ideals of the nation.

The Era of Easy Finance, 1945 to the Present

The tax regime established during World War II proved to have extraordinary vitality. Its elasticity—its ability to produce new revenues during periods of economic growth or inflation—enabled the federal government to enact new programs while only rarely enacting politically damaging tax increases. Consequently, the World War II tax regime was still in place at the beginning of the twenty-first century. During the 1970s and the early 1980s, however, the regime weakened. Stagnant economic productivity slowed the growth of tax revenues, and the administration of President Ronald Reagan sponsored the Emergency Tax Relief Act of 1981, which slashed income tax rates and indexed the new rates for inflation. But the World War II regime regained strength after the Tax Reform Act of 1986, which broadened the base of income taxation; the tax increases led by Presidents George H. W. Bush and William J. Clinton in 1991 and 1993; the prolonged economic expansion of the 1990s; and the increasing concentration of incomes received by the nation's wealthiest citizens during the buoyant stock market of 1995–2000. Renewed revenue growth first produced significant budgetary surpluses and then, in 2001, it enabled the administration of president George W. Bush to cut taxes dramatically. Meanwhile, talk of adopting a new tax regime, in the form of a "flat tax" or a national sales tax, nearly vanished. At the beginning of the twenty-first century, the overall rate of taxation, by all levels of government, was about the same in the United States as in the world's other modern economies. But the United States relied less heavily on consumption taxes, especially value-added taxes and gasoline taxes, and more heavily on social security payroll taxes and the progressive income tax.

BIBLIOGRAPHY

Becker, Robert A. *Revolution, Reform, and the Politics of American Taxation, 1763–1783.* Baton Rouge: Louisiana State University Press, 1980. Sees conflict within the colonies and states as an important part of the American Revolution.

Beito, David T. *Taxpayers in Revolt: Tax Resistance during the Great Depression.* Chapel Hill: University of North Carolina Press, 1989. A neoconservative approach to the history of taxation during the New Deal era.

Brownlee, W. Elliot. *Federal Taxation in America: A Short History.* Washington, D.C., and Cambridge, U.K.: Wilson Center Press and Cambridge University Press, 1996. Includes a historiographical essay.

Brownlee, W. Elliot, ed. *Funding the Modern American State, 1941–1995: The Rise and Fall of the Era of Easy Finance.* Washington, D.C., and Cambridge, U.K.: Cambridge University Press, 1996.

Fischer, Glenn W. *The Worst Tax? A History of the Property Tax in America.* Lawrence: University Press of Kansas, 1996. The best single volume on the history of property taxation.

Jones, Carolyn. "Class Tax to Mass Tax: The Role of Propaganda in the Expansion of the Income Tax during World War II." *Buffalo Law Review* 37 (1989): 685–737.

King, Ronald Frederick. *Money, Time, and Politics: Investment Tax Subsidies in American Democracy.* New Haven, Conn.: Yale University Press, 1993. Stresses a post–World War II victory for a "hegemonic tax logic" based on the needs of American capitalism.

Leff, Mark. *The Limits of Symbolic Reform: The New Deal and Taxation, 1933–1939.* Cambridge, U.K.: Cambridge University Press, 1984. Interprets President Franklin Roosevelt's interest in progressive taxation as symbolic rather than substantive.

Ratner, Sidney. *Taxation and Democracy in America.* New York: Wiley, 1967. The classic interpretation of the expansion of income taxation as a great victory for American democracy.

Stanley, Robert. *Dimensions of Law in the Service of Order: Origins of the Federal Income Tax, 1861–1913.* New York: Oxford University Press, 1993. Regards the income tax as an effort to preserve the capitalist status quo.

Stein, Herbert. *The Fiscal Revolution in America.* Rev. ed. Washington, D.C.: AEI Press, 1990. Explores the influence of "domesticated Keynesianism" on fiscal policy, including the Kennedy-Johnson tax cut of 1964.

Steinmo, Sven. *Taxation and Democracy: Swedish, British, and American Approaches to Financing the Modern State.* New Haven, Conn.: Yale University Press, 1993. A model study in comparative political economy applied to international tax policy.

Steuerle, C. Eugene. *The Tax Decade: How Taxes Came to Dominate the Public Agenda.* Washington: Urban Institute, 1992. The best history of the "Reagan Revolution" in tax policy.

Wallenstein, Peter. *From Slave South to New South: Public Policy in Nineteenth-Century Georgia.* Chapel Hill: University of North Carolina Press, 1987. The best fiscal history of a single state.

Witte, John F. *The Politics and Development of the Federal Income Tax.* Madison: University of Wisconsin Press, 1985. The leading history of the income tax from a pluralist point of view.

Zelizer, Julian E. *Taxing America: Wilbur D. Mills, Congress, and the State, 1945–1975.* Cambridge, U.K.: Cambridge University Press, 1998. Interprets the powerful chair of the House Ways and Means Committee as a reformer.

W. Elliot Brownlee

See also **Budget, Federal; Capitation Taxes; Debts, Revolutionary War; Excess Profits Tax; Hamilton's Economic Policies; Inheritance Tax Laws; Negative Income Tax; Poll Tax;** *Pollock v. Farmers' Loan and Trust Company;* **Revenue, Public; Revolution, American: Financial Aspects; Sales Taxes; Social Security; Stamp Act; Tariff.**

"TAXATION WITHOUT REPRESENTATION"

was at the center of the ideological underpinnings of the American Revolution. Resistance to the practice originated with the establishment of parliamentary supremacy in England, especially during the seventeenth century, when "no taxation without representation" was asserted as every Englishman's fundamental right. Colonial leaders also struggled during the seventeenth century to establish their provincial assemblies' sole power to tax within the colonies. When Parliament attempted to raise revenues

Taxes are not to be laid on the people but by their consent in person or by deputation . . . these are the first principles of law and justice and the great barriers of a free state, and of the British constitution in part. I ask, I want no more—Now let it be shown how 'tis reconcilable with these principles or to many other fundamental maxims of the British constitution, as well as the natural and civil rights which by the laws of their country all British subjects are entitled to, as their best inheritance and birthright, that all the northern colonies, who are without legal representation in the house of Commons should be taxed by the British parliament.

SOURCE: James Otis (Massachusetts lawyer and pamphleteer), "The Rights of the British Colonies Asserted and Proved," Boston, 1764.

in the colonies after 1763, colonial leaders vigorously protested, arguing that their rights as Englishmen guaranteed that, since colonists were not directly represented in Parliament, only their representatives in the colonial assemblies could levy taxes.

BIBLIOGRAPHY

Bailyn, Bernard. *The Ideological Origins of the American Revolution.* Enlarged ed. Cambridge, Mass.: Belknap Press, 1992.

Greene, Jack P. *The Quest for Power: The Lower Houses of Assembly in the Southern Royal Colonies, 1689–1776.* Chapel Hill: University of North Carolina Press, 1963.

Morgan, Edmund Sears. *The Birth of the Republic, 1763–89.* Chicago: University of Chicago Press, 1956.

Aaron J. Palmer

See also **Assemblies, Colonial; Colonial Policy, British; Stamp Act; Sugar Acts; Taxation;** *and vol. 9:* **Massachusetts Circular Letter; Patrick Henry's Resolves; Stamp Act.**

TAYLOR V. LOUISIANA, 419 U.S. 522 (1975). Billy Taylor, accused of rape, appealed to the Supreme Court claiming that a state law exempting women from jury duty infringed on his Sixth Amendment right to be tried by an impartial jury. The Court ruled in Taylor's favor, invalidating all state laws restricting jury duty on the basis of gender. In Louisiana women could be called for jury service only if they filed a written declaration of their willingness to serve. As a result, most Louisiana juries, including the one that convicted Taylor, were all-male. Louisiana's practice was similar to one that the Court had unanimously upheld in *Hoyt v. Florida* (1961), a decision that sustained the Florida law as a reasonable concession to women's family responsibilities. The Court had implied acceptance of states' exclusion of women from grand juries as recently as 1972. But *Taylor* ended special treatment for women. The Court quoted from an earlier case: "Who would claim that a jury was truly representative of the community if all men were intentionally and systematically excluded from the panel?" In *Duren v. Missouri* (1979) the Court extended its ruling in *Taylor* to a Missouri law allowing women to be exempted from jury service on the basis of their gender. Since *Taylor,* jury duty has been a responsibility shared equally by men and women.

BIBLIOGRAPHY

Baer, Judith A. *Women in American Law.* New York: Holmes and Meier, 1985–1991.

Judith A. Baer/A. R.

See also **Civil Rights and Liberties; Jury Trial; Women's Rights Movement: The 20th Century.**

TEA, DUTY ON. Tea coming to colonial America was subject to British import and excise or inland duties. The import duties were practically fixed at 11.67 percent, and the inland duties varied from four shillings to one shilling plus 25 percent ad valorem. The Revenue Act of 1767, which levied a duty of three pence per pound, stirred resentment against Britain and became the center of political resistance. Despite an attempted boycott against its importation, Americans would have their tea; between 1767 and 1774, more than 2 million pounds were imported and the American duty was paid.

In 1773 the East India Company was permitted to export tea directly to America and set up wholesale markets in Boston, New York, Philadelphia, and Charleston. This created a de facto monopoly, precipitating agitation across the colonies not unlike that over the sale of stamps. There had been no change in the tax since 1767, but the tea ships with their loads of taxed freight became a symbol of taxation tyranny. Tories claimed the tea was coming in without any tax being paid. Whigs exposed the subterfuge. In the ensuing newspaper and pamphlet warfare, Alexander Hamilton won his first reputation as a political writer. Every tea ship was turned back or had its tea destroyed, unless its cargo was landed under an agreement that it would not be sold (*see* BOSTON TEA PARTY). After 1774 the Association enforced a boycott on most English imports. Some tea filtered through, was entered at the customshouses, and had the regular duty paid on it.

BIBLIOGRAPHY

Brown, Richard D. *Revolutionary Politics in Massachusetts: The Boston Committee of Correspondence and the Towns, 1772–1774.* Cambridge, Mass.: Harvard University Press, 1970.

O. M. Dickerson/A. R.

See also **Smuggling, Colonial; Taxation; Tea Trade, Prerevolutionary.**

TEA TRADE, PREREVOLUTIONARY. The Dutch in mid-seventeenth-century New Amsterdam were the first people in North America to drink tea. The habit caught on more slowly among the British colonists who succeeded the Dutch. Although tea was available to seventeenth-century British colonists—William Penn quite likely carried tea with him when he arrived in Pennsylvania in 1682, and the first license to sell tea in Boston was issued in 1690—it was not until after 1720 that the consumption of tea blossomed in British North America. By the mid-century, nowhere in the Western world, other than Great Britain, was tea consumption more prevalent than along the eastern seaboard of North America. In 1774, approximately 90 percent of the affluent households in Massachusetts owned items associated with tea, such as teacups and teapots. Perhaps 50 percent of middling people and 42 percent of poor people also owned tea-making equipment on the eve of the American Revolution.

By 1760, tea ranked third, behind textiles and ironware, among the goods colonists imported from Britain. Like other goods imported into the colonies, tea was embedded in the British mercantile system of trade. The East India Company, which held a monopoly on the trade, shipped tea from China to London where wholesalers purchased it at auctions and then distributed it internally or exported it. The British government raised revenue through high import duties and heavy excise taxes on tea. Because of extensive smuggling, especially between 1723 and 1745 when taxes were at their highest, there is no way to measure accurately the amount of tea imported by the North American colonies. The illegal trade in tea, much of it from Holland, must have been sizeable, given that almost every ship the British seized or examined for smuggling included tea in its cargo.

The tea trade became a major point of contention between Britain and its American colonies in 1767, when tea was listed among the Townsend Duties. The nonimportation movement, which arose in response to the new duties, significantly reduced the quantity of tea entering the colonies. In New York and Philadelphia, the amount of tea imported from England fell from 494,096 pounds in 1768 to just 658 pounds in 1772. Exports to New England also declined from 291,899 pounds in 1768 to 151,184 pounds in 1772. When Parliament repealed the Townsend Duties in 1770, it retained the tax on tea as a symbol of the right and power of Parliament to tax the colonies.

The struggle over the tea trade climaxed in 1773 when parliament passed the Tea Act, lowering the tax on tea and enabling the financially troubled East India Company to export tea directly to North America. Parliament anticipated that the Tea Act would lower tea prices in America and increase profits for the East India Company. British colonists, however, interpreted the Tea Act as an attempt by the British government to force them to accept Parliament's right to tax them. In 1773, attempts to bring tea into the colonies resulted in a series of "tea parties" in Annapolis, Boston, New York, Philadelphia, and Charleston. The efforts of revolutionaries to halt the tea trade never fully succeeded, however. In 1775, the British exported 739,569 pounds of tea to the colonies.

BIBLIOGRAPHY

Scott, J. M. *The Great Tea Venture.* New York: Dutton, 1965.

Smith, Woodruff D. "Complications of the Commonplace: Tea, Sugar, and Imperialism." *Journal of Interdisciplinary History* 23, no. 2 (1992): 259–278.

Krista Camenzind

See also **Tea, Duty on.**

TEACHER CORPS, created by the Higher Education Act of 1965. Senators Gaylord A. Nelson of Wisconsin and Edward M. Kennedy of Massachusetts proposed the legislation, and President Lyndon B. Johnson gave the idea a name. This program grew out of the same Great Society optimism that fueled Head Start and Volunteers in Service to America. During its seventeen-year life, the corps conducted more than 650 projects in cities, small towns, and rural areas, focusing on educational innovation. The first broad concern of the Teacher Corps was to improve education for the disadvantaged. In the mid-1960s, policymakers likened it to the Peace Corps—idealistic young people would bring energy and commitment to schools in blighted urban areas and poor rural communities. The corps encouraged graduates of liberal arts colleges and members of minority groups to join. The perspectives of these nontraditional teachers led to curricular innovation in individual instruction and multicultural education.

A second innovation was in teacher training. After eight weeks of training, interns spent two years engaged simultaneously in university study, work-study in the schools, and work in communities, which included afterschool recreation activities, home visits, and health programs. During its last years, the Teacher Corps was more concerned with in-service training for teachers already in schools, focusing on professional development and innovations among veteran teachers. Cooperation among educators was important to the Teacher Corps. The Department of Health, Education and Welfare provided funds. At the state level, college and university teachers instructed interns and consulted with local schools. School districts and community groups then utilized the interns.

Controversy surrounded the Teacher Corps from the beginning. The corps threatened the traditional rights of the states in educational matters, and issues of trust and authority simmered beneath the surface of relations between teachers and interns, school districts and universities, and the national office and local educators. Community groups were concerned about being shuffled aside. By the late 1970s, the mission of the corps became difficult to define and its varied constituents hard to satisfy. In an effort to cut back federal involvement in education, President Ronald Reagan officially eliminated the corps as part of the 1981 Education Consolidation and Improvement Act. It ceased operations in 1983.

BIBLIOGRAPHY

Bernstein, Irving. *Guns or Butter: The Presidency of Lyndon Johnson.* New York: Oxford University Press, 1996.

Dallek, Robert. *Flawed Giant: Lyndon Johnson and His Times, 1961–1973.* New York: Oxford University Press, 1998.

Kaplan, Marshall, and Peggy L. Cuciti, eds. *The Great Society and Its Legacy: Twenty Years of U.S. Social Policy.* Durham, N.C.: Duke University Press, 1986.

Unger, Irwin. *The Best of Intentions: The Triumphs and Failures of the Great Society under Kennedy, Johnson, and Nixon.* New York: Doubleday, 1996.

Christine A. Ogren / A. E.

See also **Education; Great Society; Peace Corps.**

TEACHER TRAINING in the United States began in 1794 when the Society of Associated Teachers was formed in New York City to establish qualifications for teachers in that city. The Free School Society, established in 1805, also in New York City, began training teachers using public funds and organized a teacher-training course. In 1885, Brown University began to offer students courses in pedagogy, establishing one of the first university-level departments of EDUCATION. When the study of teaching methods began to receive recognition as a valid program in the twentieth century, the certification standards for teachers increased throughout the United States.

By the end of the twentieth century, almost all American teachers received preservice training in institutions of higher education with programs that complied with state guidelines for certification. These institutions usually have separate schools or departments of education, and prospective teachers are education majors. Nearly every teacher holds a bachelor's degree, and the vast majority have additional credits, with more than half holding one or more advanced degrees. Many states require graduate education for permanent liscensure. Education students must take courses in pedagogical techniques, and prospective secondary teachers need a specified number of credit hours in the specific subject they plan to teach. Training includes a student teaching requirement, a period of classroom teaching under the supervision of a certified teacher. States vary in their course content and credit requirements. Since the 1980s, the expanding role of computers in the classroom has made familiarity with high technology almost mandatory for teachers, and organizations such as the National Teacher Training Institute

offer them instruction on how best to integrate new technology into lesson plans.

Critics of teacher training programs cite an overemphasis on methods and psychological studies, the neglect of academic subjects, the need for accountability to ensure that training and certification are based less on academic credits and more on ability to function in the classroom, and the lack of uniform requirements among states. *A Nation at Risk*, the 1983 report of the National Committee on Excellence in Education, appointed by President Ronald Reagan, alerted the American public to the need to attract high-quality teaching candidates and to improve their training. By the mid-1990s, most states offered alternative routes to certification to mid-career people and liberal arts graduates via programs that provide on-the-job supervision. On the federal level, the Troops to Teachers program helps qualified retired servicemen and servicewomen begin second careers as teachers in public schools. The Teach for America program, supported by private, corporate, and government donations, trains recent college graduates at summer institutes. Program participants then teach for at least two years in rural and urban low-income areas.

BIBLIOGRAPHY

Britzman, Deborah P. *Practice Makes Practice: A Critical Study of Learning to Teach.* Albany: State University of New York Press, 1991.

Edwards, Elizabeth. *Women in Teacher Training Colleges, 1900–1960: A Culture of Femininity.* New York: Routledge, 2000.

Leavitt, Howard B., ed. *Issues and Problems in Teacher Education: An International Handbook.* New York: Greenwood Press, 1992.

Myrna W. Merron / A. E.

See also **Carnegie Foundation for the Advancement of Teaching; Education, Higher: Women's Colleges; Peabody Fund; Smith-Hughes Act; Teacher Corps.**

TEACHERS' LOYALTY OATH. Since 1863, nearly two-thirds of the states have adopted LOYALTY OATHS for teachers. Some oaths prohibit membership in subversive groups and the teaching of subversive doctrines, and others ask for sweeping disclaimers of past beliefs and associations. The early Cold War years following World War II produced a bumper crop of such oaths. In *Cramp v. Board of Public Instruction of Orange County, Florida* (1961), the Supreme Court struck down all-encompassing oaths infringing on FIRST AMENDMENT rights to freedom of thought and expression, but affirmed the constitutionality of generic teachers' oaths to uphold state and federal constitutions in *Knight v. Board of Regents of University of State of New York* (1967).

BIBLIOGRAPHY

Reutter, E. Edmund, Jr., and Robert R. Hamilton. *The Law of Public Education.* 2d ed. Mineola, N.Y.: Foundation Press, 1976.

Samuel H. Popper / c. w.

See also **Pierce v. Society of Sisters.**

TEAMSTERS. *See* **International Brotherhood of Teamsters.**

TEAPOT DOME OIL SCANDAL. In October 1929, Albert B. Fall, the former Secretary of the Interior under President Warren G. Harding, was convicted of accepting bribes in the leasing of U.S. Naval Oil Reserves in Elk Hills, California, and Teapot Dome, Wyoming. They were leased to private oil barons Edward L. Doheny and Harry F. Sinclair, respectively. Though the reserves had been set aside in 1912 for the Navy in case of war, responsibility for the reserves had been passed to the Department of the Interior at the outset of Harding's administration in 1921.

Responding to the concerns of conservationists and many in business, Montana Senator Thomas J. Walsh opened hearings in October 1923 to investigate the competitive bidding practices Fall used for the leases. Walsh's investigations eventually revealed that Doheny and Sinclair had together given Fall approximately $404,000 (about $4 million in 2000) either as loans or as investments in Fall's New Mexico cattle ranch while he was serving in the cabinet. All three men faced charges of bribery and conspiracy to defraud the U.S. government; the Supreme Court canceled the leases in 1927.

Sinclair was acquitted of conspiracy and bribery charges in 1928, and Doheny was acquitted in 1930. In a juridical paradox, the court ruled that regardless of Sinclair's and Doheny's intentions, Fall had, in fact, accepted the loans and investments as bribes and had been influenced by them. He was convicted in 1929 for accepting bribes and was imprisoned from 1931 to 1932. The political fallout of the scandal was enormous. Though Calvin Coolidge managed to hold on to the White House for the Republicans in 1924 by placing most of the blame on Fall and Harding (who died in office in 1923), the party faced charges of corruption through the 1950s. Moreover, Doheny's prominence and associations in the Democratic Party seemed to spread the corruption to all aspects of politics in the 1920s.

BIBLIOGRAPHY

Davis, Margaret L. *Dark Side of Fortune: Triumph and Scandal in the Life of Oil Tycoon Edward L. Doheny.* Berkeley: University of California Press, 1998.

Stratton, David H. *Tempest over Teapot Dome: The Story of Albert B. Fall.* Norman: University of Oklahoma Press, 1998.

Eric S. Yellin

See also **Scandals.**

TECHNOCRACY MOVEMENT of the 1930s advocated the radical reorganization of American society around the principles of advanced technology. William Henry Smyth, an inventor and social reformer from California, first coined the term "technocracy" in 1919. Engineer Howard Scott revived the idea of a technological society during the economic depression that swept the United States in the 1930s. Scott believed that "technocrats" familiar with modern machinery could automate production, distribute industrial wealth, increase consumption, and spark a national economic recovery. Scott also argued that technocrats could apply their skills to remake the nation's financial system and prevent future depressions. They could set a product's value by the amount of energy consumed in production and redesign a monetary system based on "energy certificates" good for a certain amount of consumption. In Scott's utopia, the government would also provide each citizen an annual income of $20,000 in exchange for a minimum amount of work. To lay the groundwork for his technological society, Scott and a group of coworkers conducted an energy survey of North America from office space provided by Columbia University. Although their efforts fueled public interest, they also attracted the scornful denunciation of professional economists, and the Technocracy Movement essentially ended in 1933. However impractical Scott's technocracy may have been, however, his theories highlighted the impact of machines on society and the pervasive economic inequality of the 1930s. Technocrats ultimately stimulated discussion of the nation's economic problems and probably helped create a climate favorable for increasing the federal involvement in the economy.

BIBLIOGRAPHY

Akin, William. *Technocracy and the American Dream.* Berkeley and Los Angeles: University of California Press, 1977.

Noble, David F. *Forces of Production: A Social History of Industrial Automation.* New York: Knopf, 1984.

Scott, Howard. *Introduction to Technocracy.* New York: J. Day Co., 1933.

Harris Gaylord Warren / e. m.

See also **Automation; Great Depression; Share-the-Wealth Movements; Townshend Plan.**

TECHNOLOGY. *See* **Industrial Research** *and individual industries.*

TECUMSEH'S CRUSADE.

At the end of the French and Indian War in 1763, France gave up its claims to its vast North American empire. Abandoning not only French settlements, France also withdrew from generations of economic, military, and political alliances with hundreds of thousands of American Indians. Forced to redefine their economies and polities, many Algonquian communities throughout the Ohio River valley and southern Great Lakes began negotiating with the British to assume many of the lost opportunities for trade, tribute, and protection. Slowly, the British assumed many of the former roles of the French and established trading outposts and forts throughout Algonquian territories.

It was within this mutually constructed Anglo-Algonquian world that the young Shawnee warrior, Tecumseh, was raised. Witnessing the erosion of British strength following the American Revolution, the Shawnee and other Great Lakes groups increasingly faced the advancing American nation by themselves. Bloody conflicts between American settlers and Shawnee, Delaware, Miami, and Wyandot communities, among others of the Algonquian group, became commonplace in the late-eighteenth and nineteenth centuries.

Despite the increased conflicts and pressures from American settlers, Algonquians and other Indian powers, including the Cherokee in Kentucky and Tennessee, continued to control the fertile lands to the Mississippi. Following the Louisiana Purchase of 1803, however, American settlers, surveyors, and politicians increasingly coveted the lands between the Ohio and Mississippi River. Many, including Thomas Jefferson, believed that Indians had either to adopt American farming economies or be removed permanently from American society, an idea of exclusion at odds with more than a century of Indian-white relations in the region. Conflicts continued to escalate in the early 1800s, and Algonquian communities had already begun taking up arms against American settlements when Britain again fought the United States in the War of 1812.

Organized around the military and political leadership of Tecumseh, Shawnee and other Indian communities had also recently begun a series of cultural reforms to spiritually revive and energize their communities. Under the influence of Tecumseh's brother, Tenskwatawa, also known as the Prophet, this religious movement facilitated Tecumseh's military and political efforts to organize Indian communities throughout the Great Lakes and into the South into a broad confederacy against the Americans.

Known for his impassioned oratory and strategic vision, Tecumseh, with the aid of the British in Canada, guided the confederacy through a series of battles with American forces under the leadership of the Indiana territorial governor William Henry Harrison. Facing overwhelming military odds, particularly the lack of supplies, and unable to get non-Algonquian groups, such as the Cherokee and Iroquois, to fully support the confederacy's efforts, Tecumseh's aspirations for an overarching Indian union capable of withstanding American aggression ended on 5 October 1813, when he perished at the Battle of the Thames. As the British sued for peace and the confederacy dissolved, Shawnee and other Great Lakes Indian communities became displaced from their homelands in Ohio, Michigan, Indiana, and Illinois to lands west of the Mississippi.

BIBLIOGRAPHY

Edmunds, R. David. *The Shawnee Prophet.* Lincoln: University of Nebraska Press, 1983.

Sudgen, John. *Tecumseh's Last Stand.* Norman: University of Oklahoma Press, 1985.

Ned Blackhawk

See also **Indian Policy, Colonial; Indian Policy, U.S.: 1775–1830; Indian Removal; Thames, Battle of the; Wars with Indian Nations: Colonial Era to 1783.**

TEEPEE. *See* Tipi.

TEHERAN CONFERENCE.

From 28 November to 1 December 1943, President Franklin D. Roosevelt, Prime Minister Winston Churchill, and Marshal Joseph Stalin met at Teheran, the capital of Iran, to coordinate Western military plans with those of the Soviet Union. Most important of all, the "big three" drew up the essential victory strategy in Europe, one based on a cross-channel invasion called Operation Overlord and scheduled for May 1944. The plan included a partition of Germany, but left all details to a three-power European Advisory Commission. It granted Stalin's request that Poland's new western border should be at the Oder River and that the eastern one follow the lines drafted by British diplomat Lord Curzon in 1919. The conference tacitly concurred in Stalin's conquests of 1939 and 1940, these being Estonia, Latvia, Lithuania, and a slice of Finland. Stalin reiterated his promise, made in October 1943 at Moscow, to enter the war against Japan upon the defeat of Germany, but he expected compensation in the form of tsarist territories taken by Japan in 1905. On 1 December 1943, the three powers issued a declaration that welcomed potential allies into "a world family of democratic nations" and signed a separate protocol recognizing the "independence, sovereignty, and territorial integrity" of Iran.

BIBLIOGRAPHY

Eubank, Keith. *Summit at Teheran.* New York: Morrow, 1985.

Mayle, Paul D. *Eureka Summit: Agreement in Principle and the Big Three at Teheran, 1943.* Newark: University of Delaware Press, 1987.

Sainsbury, Keith. *The Turning Point: Roosevelt, Stalin, Churchill, and Chiang-Kai-Shek, 1943: The Moscow, Cairo, and Teheran Conferences.* Oxford: Oxford University Press, 1985.

Justus D. Doenecke

See also **World War II.**

TELECOMMUNICATIONS.

The history of telecommunications is a story of networks. Alexander Graham Bell on his honeymoon wrote of a "grand system" that would provide "direct communication between any two places in [a] city" and, by connecting cities, provide a true network throughout the country and eventually the world (Winston, *Media Technology*, p. 244). From the telegraph to the telephone to e-mail, electronic communication has extended farther and reached more people with increasing speed. The advent of the Internet in combination with a satellite system that covers the entire surface of the earth has brought us closer to the "global village" envisioned by Marshall McLuhan in the 1960s.

The variety of media included under the umbrella of "telecommunications" has expanded since the early twentieth century. The term was adopted in 1932 by the *Convention Internationale des Telecommunications* held in Madrid (OED). At this point, the telegraph, the telephone, and the radio were the only widely used telecommunications media. The United States, the point of origin for only one of these three (Bell's telephone), soon came to dominate the telecommunications industries. The Radio Corporation of America (RCA) was created in 1919, three years before Britain's British Broadcasting Corporation (BBC). By 1950, the American Telephone and Telegraph Company (AT&T) provided the best telephone service in the world. American television led the way after World War II (1939–1945). Then, in the early 1980s, a new device was introduced: the personal computer. Although not intended as a tool for telecommunications, the personal computer became in the 1990s the most powerful means of two-way individual electronic communication, thanks to a network that goes far beyond any "grand system" dreamed of by Bell. The network we now call the Internet gives a person with a computer and an Internet connection the ability to send not only words, but graphs, charts, audio signals, and pictures, both still and moving, throughout the world.

Most telecommunications networks were created for specific purposes by groups with vested interests. The telegraph network was created to make scheduling trains possible. Telephones were first primarily for business use. The grandfather of the Internet, ARPANET, was commissioned by the Department of Defense in 1969 to develop a military communication network that could withstand a nuclear attack.

In general, the U.S. Congress has chosen to allow these networks to remain under private control with a modicum of regulation, in contrast to governments in Europe and Britain, which have turned these networks into public utilities. In the case of the Internet, we see the control moving from the military to the private sector, and Congress grappling with how to regulate "objectionable" communications such as pornography.

The Telegraph

The first practical means of electronic communication was the TELEGRAPH. The science on which it is based was over a century old when the sudden development of the railway system in the 1830s, first in England, then in America, made it necessary to communicate the movement of trains rapidly. The interconnection of the various technologies, one breeding the need for another, is well illustrated.

But while the telegraph was developed with this one purpose in mind, the potential uses of the new device were soon recognized, and information other than that dealing with train schedules began to flow across the wires. In 1844, the Democratic National Convention's nominee for vice president declined via telegraph, though the Convention, not trusting the new device, had to send a group from Baltimore to Washington, D.C., for face-to-face confirmation. Here we see an early example of the evolution of trust in these new networks.

While battles were waged over ownership, the technology continued to expand its influence as the stock market and the newspaper business, both in need of rapid transmission of information, began using the ever-expanding network. As with later technologies, there was debate in Congress over governmental control. Congress' decision was to let the private sector compete to exploit this new technology. That competition ended with the adoption of one specific "code," and Samuel Morse emerged as the Bill Gates of the telegraph.

The Telephone and the Fax

Telegraphy required training in Morse code on the part of both sender and receiver, so this form of telecommunication remained primarily a means of communication for business and for urgent personal messages sent from a public place to another public place. Bell's TELEPHONE, invented in 1876, brought telecommunication into the home, although the telephone remained primarily a business tool until after World War II, when telephones become common in American homes.

AT&T, formed in 1885, held a virtual monopoly on U.S. telephonic communication until 1982. The Justice Department forced the separation of Western Union from the company in 1913. At this point an AT&T vice president, Nathan Kingsbury, wrote a letter to the U.S. Attorney General, which came to be called the "Kingsbury Commitment." It formed the basis of AT&T's dominance of telephone service until 1982, when the Justice Department insisted that AT&T be severed into seven "Baby Bells" who each provided local service to a region.

Walkie-Talkies. Al Gross shows two early models of walkie-talkies that he invented, precursors of more sophisticated forms of modern telecommunications. AP/WIDE WORLD PHOTOS

The control that AT&T maintained probably contributed to the quality of phone service in the United States, but it also squelched some developments. For example, until 1968, only equipment leased from AT&T could be hooked to their network. Thus the facsimile machine (the fax), originally developed in the nineteenth century as an extension of telegraphy, did not come into use until after the 1968 FCC order forcing Bell to allow users to hook non-Bell equipment to the AT&T network. Factors other than technology often determine the evolution of telecommunications.

Radio and Television

RADIO and TELEVISION are quite different from the telegraph and telephone: they communicate in one direction and "broadcast" to many listeners simultaneously. The Italian Guglielmo Marconi, working in England in 1896, patented his wireless system and transmitted signals across the Atlantic in 1901. By 1919 RCA was formed, and in 1926, it created the National Broadcasting Company (NBC). The radio was a common household appliance by the time of President Franklin Delano Roosevelt's fireside

chats in 1933, and its effect on the public was demonstrated inadvertently by Orson Welles in his radio drama based on H. G. Wells's novel *The War of the Worlds.* Many people accepted the fictional tale of an invasion from Mars as fact and panicked.

In 1939, NBC began broadcasting television signals, but television broadcasting was halted until after World War II ended in 1945. Both radio and television altered many aspects of American society: home life, advertising, politics, leisure time, and sports. Debates raged over television's impact on society. Television was celebrated as an educational panacea and condemned as a sad replacement for human interaction.

The Internet

Like the Interstate Highway System, which carries a different kind of traffic, the INTERNET began as a Cold War postapocalypse military project in 1969. ARPANET was created to develop a means of effective communication in the case of a nuclear war. The Advanced Research Project Agency (ARPA), created in 1957 in response to the launch of *Sputnik*, advanced the case that such a network was necessary, illustrating again that necessity (or at least perceived necessity) is the mother of invention. Paul Baran, a RAND researcher studying military communications for the Air Force, wrote in 1964, "Is it time now to start thinking about a new and possibly non-existent public utility, a common user digital data communication plant designed specifically for the transmission of digital data among a large set of subscribers?"

As the ARPANET expanded, users developed software for sending electronic mail, soon dubbed e-mail, then just plain email. By 1973, about three-fourths of the traffic on this network connecting many research universities consisted of email. The network expanded to include other universities and then other local area networks (LANs). Once these local area networks became connected to one another, this new form of communication spread rapidly. In 1982, a protocol was developed that would allow all the smaller networks to link together using the Transmission Control Protocol (TCP) and the Internet Protocol (IP). Once these were adopted on various smaller "internets," which connected various LANs, "the Internet" came into being. Just as railroad companies had to adopt a common gauge of track to make it possible to run a train across the country, so the various networks had to adopt a common protocol so that messages could travel throughout the network. Once this happened, the Internet expanded even more rapidly. This electronic network, often dubbed "the information superhighway," continued to expand, and in the early 1990s, a new interface was developed that allowed even unsophisticated users of personal computers to "surf the Internet": the World Wide Web. With this more friendly access tool came the commercialization of this new medium.

The Access Issue

Access has been a key issue throughout the history of telecommunications. The term "universal service," coined in 1907 by Bell Chief Executive Officer Theodore Vail, came to mean, by midcentury, providing all Americans affordable access to the telephone network. There were still rural areas without electrical and telephone service in the mid-twentieth century (the two networks often sharing the same poles for stringing wires overhead), but by the end of the century, about 94 percent of all homes had phones (notable exceptions being homes in poverty zones such as tribal lands and inner-city neighborhoods). In the final decade of the twentieth century, cell phones became widely available, though they were not adopted as quickly in the United States as elsewhere. This new and alternative network for telephonic communication makes possible wireless access from remote sites, so that villages in central Africa, for example, can have telephone access to the world via satellite systems. In the United States, subscribers to cell phone services increased from about 5,000 in 1990 to over 100,000 in 2000, while average monthly bills were cut in half.

Despite the fact that access to the Internet expanded much faster than did access to earlier networks, there was heated political debate about the "digital divide" separating those who have such access from the have-nots. This points to the importance of this new form of telecommunication, which combines personal communication technology with information access. Thus, federal programs in the 1990s promoted Internet access to public schools and libraries. While 65 percent of public high schools had Internet access in 1995, the figure reached 100 percent by 2000. Once connected to this vast network, the computer becomes not only an educational tool but also a means of communication that can change the world. In 1989 news from Tiananmen Square protesters came out of China via email.

The Merging of the Media

By the mid-1990s, the impact of the Internet, the new digital technologies, the satellite systems, and fiber-optic cables was felt throughout the world of telecommunications. Radio stations began "web casting," sending their signals out over the Internet so listeners around the world could tune in. By the turn of the twenty-first century, not only pictures but also entire movies could be downloaded from the Internet. As use of computers increased, the digital format became increasingly important, and by the end of the century digital television was a reality, though not widely in use. A variety of mergers by telecommunications companies increased the need for government oversight. Congress grappled with regulation of this ever-expanding field that knows no borders or nationality. The Telecommunications Act of 1996 extended the quest for "universal service" to "advanced telecommunications services," but other attempts to regulate content on the Internet tended to be rejected by the courts as unconstitutional.

Effect of Medium on the Message

If television produced a generation that was more comfortable with the image than with the word, computers turned a later generation back to the word, and to new symbols as well. Marshal McLuhan in the 1960s said that "the medium is the message." The phenomenon of the medium affecting the communication process is well illustrated by the development of the "emoticon" in email chat room and instant messenger communications. Emoticons came about when email and Internet users discovered that the tone of their messages was often missed by receivers, who sometimes became offended when a joking tone was not inferred. Thus, the emoticon was proposed in 1979, first as a simple -) and then the more elaborate :-) to suggest tone, and soon this and other tone indicators came into widespread use.

Too often we limit ourselves to "just the facts" when considering technology, but its impact on the social sphere is important. Just as the automobile changed employment patterns (with rural residents commuting into the city) and architecture (creating the garage as a standard part of homes), so the telephone ended the drop-in visit and created telemarketing. It draws us closer electronically while distancing us physically. We are still debating the impact of the television, which seems to alter some family patterns extensively, and already we are discussing "Internet addiction." Telecommunications remains an expanding and changing field that alters us in ways we might fail to recognize.

BIBLIOGRAPHY

Baran, P. "On Distributed Communication Networks." *IEEE Transactions on Communications Systems* (1 March 1964).

"Digital Divide, The." *CQ Researcher* 10, no. 3 (Jan 28, 2000): 41–64.

Jensen, Peter. *From the Wireless to the Web: The Evolution of Telecommunications, 1901–2001.* Sydney: University of New South Wales Press, 2000.

Lebow, Irwin. *Information Highways and Byways: From the Telegraph to the 21st Century.* New York: IEEE Press, 1995.

Lubar, Steven D. *InfoCulture: The Smithsonian Book of Information Age Inventions.* Boston: Houghton Mifflin, 1993.

McCarroll, Thomas. "How AT&T Plans to Reach Out and Touch Everyone." *Time* 142 (July 5, 1993): 44–46.

Mitchell, William J. *City of Bits: Space, Place, and the Infobahn.* Cambridge, Mass.: MIT Press, 1995. Available at http://mitpress2.mit.edu/e-books/City_of_Bits/

Winston, Brian. *Media Technology and Society: A History: From the Telegraph to the Internet.* New York: Routledge, 1998.

William E. King

See also **AT&T**.

TELECOMMUNICATIONS ACT of 1996 represented a bipartisan effort to overhaul the nation's telecommunications laws. It encouraged deployment of new telecommunications technologies and promoted competition among providers of local telephone service, between local and long distance telephone companies, and among providers of cable and broadcast television programming. The act in large part replaced the Communications Act of 1934, which was enacted at a time when technology was less mature and telephone and broadcast telecommunications were largely compartmentalized.

The Telecommunications Act significantly restructured local and national telephone markets. Local phone service had long been considered a natural monopoly. States typically awarded an exclusive franchise in each local area to a specific carrier, which would own and operate the infrastructure of local telephone service. By the early 1990s, however, technological advances made competition among local carriers seem possible, and the act ended the regime of state-sanctioned monopolies. The act prohibited states from enforcing laws impeding competition and imposed on existing local carriers a number of obligations intended to encourage competition. The most prominent of these duties was the requirement that such carriers share their networks with potential competitors. In exchange for opening local markets to competition, the act removed restrictions that prevented local carriers from providing long distance telephone service. By removing limitations on competition in both the local and long distance markets, the act made it possible for telephone companies to offer integrated long distance and local telephone service to the public.

The act also made significant changes to the regulation of cable and broadcast television in order to encourage competition. One of the more important changes was the authorization of telephone companies to provide cable television services. The act also eliminated the regulation of cable television rates, except for basic broadcast service, and liberalized prior restrictions on "over-the-air" television broadcasters that limited the number of broadcast stations that any one entity could own.

In addition to its provisions encouraging competition, the act contained controversial rules regarding obscenity, indecency, and violence on cable and broadcast television and on the Internet. It pressured television networks to establish a rating system for their programs, and required manufacturers of television sets to install "V-chips," circuitry that would allow viewers to block violent or sexual programming. The act also required cable television operators that provide channels dedicated to sexually oriented programming either to completely scramble the channel or to limit the channel's programming to nighttime hours. In 2000, the Supreme Court struck down this latter provision in *United States v. Playboy Entertainment Group*, saying that the provision regulated speech protected by the First Amendment and that the provision was not the least restrictive means of protecting children from inadvertently viewing offensive programming.

The most contentious of the act's provisions sought to protect minors from "indecent" communications on the Internet through the use of criminal penalties for people sending such communications or for providers of Internet service that knowingly facilitated such communications. This part of the act was controversial in part because it regulated not only obscene communications, which do not receive constitutional protection under the First Amendment, but also those that were "patently offensive as measured by contemporary standards." The Supreme Court struck down this provision within a year after it was passed. In the 1996 case of *Reno v. American Civil Liberties Union*, the Court explained that the regulation of nonobscene communication was a content-based restriction of speech and that such a restriction merited careful scrutiny. The Court, troubled by the possible "chilling effect" the provisions would have on free speech, held that the provisions were too broad, vague, and undefined to survive constitutional challenge.

BIBLIOGRAPHY

Huber, Peter W., Michael K. Kellogg, and John Thorne. *The Telecommunications Act of 1996: Special Report.* Boston: Little, Brown, 1996.

Krattenmaker, Thomas G. "The Telecommunications Act of 1996." *Connecticut Law Review* 29 (1996): 123–174.

Wiley, Richard E., and R. Clark Wadlow, eds. *The Telecommunications Act of 1996.* New York: Practising Law Institute, 1996.

Kent Greenfield

See also **Censorship, Press and Artistic.**

TELEGRAPH. The word "telegraph" originally referred to any device that facilitated long-distance communication. Although various means of "telegraphing" began thousands of years ago, it was not until the early nineteenth century that the concept of using electrical devices took root. By that time, Alessandro Volta had developed the battery, Hans Christian Oersted had discovered the relationship between electrical current and magnetism, and Joseph Henry had discovered the electromagnet. Combining these new technologies into a reliable communication system was to be the work of Massachusetts-born artist Samuel F. B. Morse.

Morse worked with partners Alfred Vail and Leonard Gale to design his electromechanical device, which Morse described as the "Recording Telegraph." In 1837, Morse's newly patented telegraph featured a dot-and-dash code to represent numbers, a dictionary to turn the numbers into words, and a set of sawtooth type for sending signals. Morse demonstrated his telegraph at a New York exhibition a year later with a model that used a dot-dash code directly for letters instead of the number-word dictionary. "Morse code" was to become standard throughout the world. The dots or dashes, created from an interruption in the flow of electricity, were recorded on a printer or interpreted orally.

Samuel F. B. Morse. A painting of the artist with his invention, the telegraph, which transmitted messages using his "Morse code" of dots and dashes. LIBRARY OF CONGRESS

In 1844, Congress funded $30,000 for the construction of an experimental telegraph line that was to run the forty miles between Washington, D.C., and Baltimore. From the Capitol in Washington, Morse sent the first formal message on the line to Baltimore, "What hath God wrought?"

Rapid advances in telegraph use followed. Small telegraph companies began operations throughout the United States, including American Telegraph Company, Western Union Telegraph Company, New York Albany and Buffalo Electro-Magnetic Telegraph Company, Atlantic and Ohio Telegraph Company, Illinois and Mississippi Telegraph Company, and New Orleans and Ohio Telegraph Company. In 1861, Western Union built its first transcontinental telegraph line. The first permanently successful telegraphic cable crossing the Atlantic Ocean was laid five years later. The invention of "duplex" telegraphy by J. B. Stearns and "quadruplex" telegraphy by Thomas A. Edison in the 1870s enhanced the performance of the telegraph by allowing simultaneous messages to be sent over the same wire.

All rapid long-distance communication within private and public sectors depended on the telegraph throughout the remainder of the nineteenth century. Applications were many: Railroads used the Morse telegraph to aid in the efficiency and safety of railroad operations, the As-

sociated Press to dispatch news, industry for the transmission of information about stocks and commodities, and the general public to send messages. The telegraph's military value was demonstrated during the Civil War (1861–1865) as a way to control troop deployment and intelligence. However, the rival technologies of the telephone and radio would soon replace the telegraph as a primary source of communication.

Until the mid-1970s, Canada used Morse telegraphy, and Mexico continued with the system for its railroads up to 1990. However, the telegraph is no longer widely used, save by a small group of enthusiasts. Although radiotelegraphy (wireless transmission using radio waves) is still used commercially, it is limited in the United States to just a few shore stations that communicate with seafaring ships. Telephones, facsimile machines, and computer electronic mail have usurped the Morse model of long-distance communication.

BIBLIOGRAPHY

Bates, David Homer, and James A. Rawley. *Lincoln in the Telegraph Office: Recollections of the United States Military Telegraph Corps During the Civil War.* Lincoln: University of Nebraska Press, 1995.

Blondheim, Menahem. *News Over the Wires: The Telegraph and the Flow of Public Information in America, 1844–1897.* Cambridge, Mass.: Harvard University Press, 1994.

Gabler, Edwin. *The American Telegrapher: A Social History, 1860–1900.* New Brunswick, N.J.: Rutgers University Press, 1988.

Jolley, E. H. *Introduction to Telephony and Telegraphy.* London: Pitman, 1968.

Kym O'Connell-Todd

See also **Telecommunications; Western Union Telegraph Company.**

TELEPHONE. The telephone, a speech transmission device, dates from 1876, the year Alexander Graham Bell patented his "Improvements in Telegraphy." Many inventors had been experimenting with acoustics and electricity, among them Thomas Edison, Emil Berliner, and Elisha Gray. Each of these men, as well as Bell's assistant Thomas Watson, contributed modifications that resulted in the telephone we recognize today. Technology has advanced, but the fundamental principles remain the same.

When Bell Telephone Company formed to market its product in 1877, the telegraph was the reigning telecommunication service. Coast-to-coast communication had been possible since 1861, and 2,250 telegraph offices spanned the country. Earlier that year, Western Union had been offered the Bell patent but refused it, only to buy telephone technology from others. Although Bell held the patent for the device, 1,730 other companies were making telephones.

In 1882, the American Bell Telephone Company won a court judgment against Western Union and gained con-

Alexander Graham Bell. A photograph of the inventor *(seated)* demonstrating his telephone, patented in 1876. U.S. National Aeronautics and Space Administration

trolling interest in the company, an event that paved the way for modern telephone systems. In 1885, Bell formed a subsidiary, American Telephone & Telegraph (AT&T), which provided a network to which Bell-licensed companies could connect. For the first time, long-distance calling became possible.

As the twentieth century progressed, the importance of telephone service in the daily lives of Americans increased. The Bureau of the Census estimated that in 1920, 35 percent of households had telephones. Fifty years later the figure had risen to 90.5 percent. The Bell System manufactured and installed all telephone equipment and provided all the services. As a national monopoly, it had regulated rates. It was often written that Bell was the best telephone system in the world. The 1877 technology start-up had become the largest privately owned industry in United States history with more than 1 million employees and $152 billion in assets in 1983.

However, as the 1960s drew to a close, complaints of poor service and of "Ma Bell's" monopoly attracted government attention. In 1974, the Department of Justice filed an antitrust suit against AT&T that culminated in a 1984 court order that deregulated the industry. Bell Systems had lost its empire, but its pioneering engineers left an indelible mark on the world.

Bell Telephone announced the first transcontinental telephone service at the San Francisco World's Fair in 1915. Radiotelephone service to other countries and ships at sea was available after 1927. A transatlantic cable was laid in 1956. The transmission of calls by microwave began soon after World War II (1939–1945), and Bell Laboratories initiated satellite communications with the launch of *Telstar* in 1962.

The Bell Systems invention that had the most dramatic impact on the world was the transistor. Unveiled in 1948, it made small electronic devices possible. The transistor was vital to the development of hearing aids, portable radios, and the personal computer.

AT&T introduced modems for data transmission between computers over telephone lines in 1958. A Department of Defense computer network project from 1969 (ARPANET) developed into the Internet by 1992, and the popular World Wide Web appeared in 1994. By 2001, 143 million Americans, more than half the population, were communicating online, sending data and audio and video transmissions. Eighty percent of them relied on telephone dial-up connections.

BIBLIOGRAPHY

Grosvenor, Edwin, and Morgan Wesson. *Alexander Graham Bell: The Life and Times of the Man Who Invented the Telephone.* New York: Abrams, 1997.

Gwanthmey, Emily, and Ellen Stern. *Once Upon a Telephone: An Illustrated Social History.* New York: Harcourt Brace, 1994.

Katz, James Everett. *Connections: Social and Cultural Studies of the Telephone in American Life.* New Brunswick, N.J.: Transaction, 1999.

Noll, A. Michael. *Introduction to Telephones and Telephone Systems.* Norwood, Mass.: Artech House, 1999.

Christine M. Roane

See also **AT&T; Internet; Telecommunications.**

TELEPHONE CASES. Alexander Graham Bell's 1876 patent on the TELEPHONE had barely been filed before a legion of other inventors surfaced to claim rights to the invention. The WESTERN UNION TELEGRAPH COMPANY purchased the rights to Amos E. Dolbear's and Thomas A. Edison's telephone inventions and began manufacturing and installing telephones. The Bell Telephone Company brought suit and prevailed in court in 1879. Over the next two decades, the holders of the Bell patent battled more than six hundred lawsuits. Daniel Drawbaugh, an obscure Pennsylvania mechanic who claimed to have had a workable instrument as early as 1866, came nearest to defeating them, losing his Supreme Court appeal in 1887 by a vote of only four to three. The government sought from 1887 to 1897 to annul the patent, but failed.

BIBLIOGRAPHY

Harlow, Alvin F. *Old Wires and New Waves: The History of the Telegraph, Telephone, and Wireless.* New York: D. Appleton-Century, 1936.

Alvin F. Harlow / A. R.

See also **AT&T; Industrial Research; Patents and U.S. Patent Office; Telecommunications.**

TELEVANGELISM. As television became a staple of American culture in the second half of the twentieth century, a growing number of Protestant preachers embraced the new mass medium to deliver their messages. Catholics, too, took to the airwaves, most famously in the person of Bishop Fulton J. Sheen, who utilized the new medium of television to demonstrate the compatibility of American culture and Catholic faith. Televangelism emerged after World War II as an outgrowth of evangelicalism, a type of Protestant religion based on the idea that people needed to open their hearts and redirect their wills toward Christ, not only to secure an eternal place in heaven, but also to better their lives on earth. While evangelicals point to the New Testament story of Jesus commissioning disciples as the origin of their movement, modern evangelicalism emerged in eighteenth-century Britain and North America in the context of a burgeoning market economy. Preachers skilled at awakening religious feelings in their audiences used open-air stages to promote their beliefs and to enact the emotional process of repentance for sin and heartfelt commitment to God.

The foremost evangelical predecessor of televangelists was the Anglican preacher George Whitefield, an actor before his conversion, whose combination of religious fervor, theatrical flair, and marketing genius made him the most celebrated figure in America in the decades preceding the American Revolution. One of the first entrepreneurs to cultivate publicity for his performances through the fast-growing newspaper medium, Whitefield drew large audiences to his sermons, which included tearful reenactments of the lives of biblical characters. These gatherings, where rich and poor, slave and free, men and

Jim and Tammy Faye Bakker. Their "PTL (Praise the Lord) Club" was one of the most popular televangelist programs until the late 1980s, when Bakker confessed to adultery and then was convicted of defrauding his contributors. AP/WIDE WORLD PHOTOS

women rubbed shoulders, exerted a democratizing force, although Whitefield himself never condemned the institution of slavery and was a latecomer to the cause of American independence.

As evangelicalism developed in America, African Americans contributed elements of African religious tradition, such as spirit possession, call and response, and the five-tone musical scale, to the repertoire of evangelical performance. In nineteenth century America evangelicalism was often associated with social reform, especially antislavery, education, and temperance. In the early twentieth century, however, evangelicalism became increasingly tied to conservative politics, fundamentalist interpretations of the Bible, and hostility to liberal forms of Protestant theology and social reform. When Billy Graham began to make use of television in the 1950s, evangelicalism was almost as closely identified with anticommunism as it was with personal salvation.

The most famous televangelist of the twentieth century, Graham turned from radio to television to broadcast his message. Combining fervent preaching, heart-melting music, and personal testimonies from successful people, Graham's crusades traveled around the country and eventually around the world, carrying the evangelical mix of religious outreach, theatrical entertainment, and creative entrepreneurship to new levels of sophistication. Graham's evident personal integrity and continual prayers for the spiritual guidance of political leaders led to his visibility as a respected public figure and to his role as counselor to several American presidents.

Televangelism boomed in the 1970s and 1980s, when the Federal Communications Commission (FCC) changed its policy of mandating free time for religious broadcasts to allow stations to accept money for religious programs. This regulatory change inspired more than a few preachers to use television as a means of funding their ministries. Oral Roberts sought funds for the development of the City of Faith Medical and Research Center in Tulsa, Oklahoma, by introducing the concept of "seed faith," a means by which viewers might reap miracles from God in their own lives by donating to Roberts's ministry. In *The Hour of Power*, broadcast from the Crystal Cathedral in Garden Grove, California, Robert Schuller preached about the power of positive thinking, offering viewers the chance to purchase membership in his Possibility Thinkers Club along with a mustard seed cross as a sign of their faith. Pat Robertson's success in introducing a talk-show format to showcase interviews with people testifying to the power of faith led to the purchase of his own network, the Christian Broadcasting Network (CBN), which funded his bid for the Republican presidential nomination in 1988.

Televangelists' power to generate money contributed to the formation of conservative political constituencies, like Jerry Falwell's MORAL MAJORITY and the CHRISTIAN COALITION led by Robertson and Ralph Reed, which influenced public policy and political rhetoric in the United States. At the same time the money in televangelism stimulated various forms of corruption and scandal, leading to deepening distrust of televangelists on one hand and to more rigorous forms of accounting on the other.

In the 1990s and the early years of the twenty-first century televangelism grew along with communications technology and the increasing pluralism of American religious life. Satellite, cable, and Internet technologies offered new opportunities for evangelical outreach and made increasingly sophisticated forms of presentation readily available. This technological expansion fostered the development of niche programming—shows devoted to biblical prophecy, for example—as well as the extension of televangelism's mix of entertainment, self-promotion, and missionary outreach to other groups—for example, Catholics advocating devotion to Mary through dramatic reenactments of their own piety. As televangelism diversified, the distinctively Protestant character of its message blurred. Televangelism's success compromised Protestant evangelicalism's exclusive claim to salvation.

BIBLIOGRAPHY

Alexander, Bobby C. *Televangelism Reconsidered: Ritual in the Search for Human Community.* Atlanta, Ga.: Scholars Press, 1994.

Balmer, Randall. *Mine Eyes Have Seen the Glory: A Journey into the Evangelical Subculture in America.* Expanded ed. New York: Oxford University Press, 1993.

Schmidt, Rosemarie, and Joseph F. Kess. *Television Advertising and Televangelism: Discourse Analysis of Persuasive Language.* Philadelphia: J. Benjamins Publishing, 1986.

Schultze, Quentin J. *Televangelism and American Culture: The Business of Popular Religion.* Grand Rapids, Mich.: Baker Book House, 1991.

Stout, Harry S. *The Divine Dramatist: George Whitefield and the Rise of Modern Evangelicalism.* Grand Rapids, Mich.: Eerdmans, 1991.

Amanda Porterfield

See also **Evangelicalism and Revivalism; Protestantism; Religion and Religious Affiliation; Television: Programming and Influence.**

TELEVISION

This entry includes 2 subentries:
Programming and Influence
Technology

PROGRAMMING AND INFLUENCE

By 1947, the American Broadcasting Company (ABC), Columbia Broadcasting System (CBS), the Du Mont Network, and the National Broadcasting Company (NBC) had started regularly scheduling television programs on a small number of stations. Many more channels soon commenced operations, and a TV boom began. By 1960 just under 90 percent of all households had one or more sets. Because most channels had network affiliation agree-

ments—96 percent of all stations in 1960—the networks dominated the medium for over thirty years. (Du Mont ceased operations in 1955.) Especially in the evening, when most Americans watched TV, consumers very likely viewed a network program.

In the late 1940s, relatively few advertisers were prepared to follow the American radio model of producing and underwriting the cost of shows. Within a few years, however, and often by accident, the networks and a few advertisers developed individual programs that sparked interest in the medium. This, in turn, encouraged more companies to advertise on TV.

At first, television betrayed both a class and regional bias. The coaxial cable permitting simultaneous network telecasts did not reach Los Angeles, the center of the nation's motion picture industry and home to most popular entertainers, until September 1951. As a result, most network shows originated from New York. And programs tended to have a New York accent. At the same time, programmers often confused their own, more cosmopolitan, tastes with those of viewers. Network executives assumed audiences wanted culturally ambitious fare, at least some of the time. Some simply believed the TV audience was more educated and well-to-do, despite studies indicating little class bias to set ownership.

In the 1950s, television relied on a variety of program types or "genres." The first was the variety program, telecast live with a regular host. Milton Berle and Ed Sullivan starred in two of the most durable variety hours. Individual sponsors produced "dramatic anthologies," original dramas aired live. Although many TV plays were uneven or pretentious, some proved memorable, notably *Marty*, which was later remade as a feature film starring Ernest Borgnine. Other program types came from network radio: the dramatic series, situation comedy, and quiz (later game) show. They relied on one of radio's oldest objectives: create a consumer habit of tuning to a specific program every day or week. (Many closed with the admonition, "Same time, same station.") CBS, of the four networks, adhered most dutifully to this model of programming.

The success of CBS's situation comedy *I Love Lucy* (1951–1957) confirmed the network's strategy. More tellingly, repeats of episodes proved almost as popular. This greatly undermined another broadcast industry "rule": that audiences always wanted original programming, even in the summer when replacement series heretofore had been offered. By the late 1950s, most series were filmed. They had an additional advantage over the live telecast. They could not only be rerun in the summer but then rented or "syndicated" for re-airing by individual stations in the United States and overseas. *Lucy*, it should be noted, was the single most rerun series in the history of television.

TV's dependency on film accelerated in the late 1950s. ABC banked heavily on filmed action/adventure series—first westerns, then detective dramas—many of which gained large followings. CBS and NBC quickly seized on the trend. During the 1958–1959 season, seven of the ten most popular programs, according to the A. C. Nielsen ratings service, were westerns. Most were considerably more sophisticated than television's earliest westerns, such as *Hopalong Cassidy* and *The Lone Ranger,* which were plainly aimed at pre-adolescents. The new "adult" westerns and detective series also possessed higher production values. The large audiences especially for westerns also indicated a change in the television audience, as TV spread into smaller cities and towns in the South and West. Filmed programming satisfied small-town audiences, which, as movie exhibitors had long known, greatly preferred westerns over nightclub comedy or original drama.

By the end of the 1950s, the economics of television had become clear. Networks and stations derived most of their revenues from the sale of time to advertisers. Indeed, the stations that the networks owned were their most profitable properties. Producing successful programs was far more risky—too much for most stations to do extensively. Most new television series failed. Yet a popular program could be a moneymaker in syndication. With this prospect in mind, as well as a wish to wrest control from advertisers, the networks gradually began producing more of their own programming. Government regulations, however, severely restricted network participation in entertainment programming in the 1970s and 1980s.

News programming was the great laggard in early TV. The networks produced fifteen-minute early evening weekday newscasts and telecast special events, including the national party conventions and presidential inaugurations. Informational shows were considered "loss leaders," presented to satisfy TV critics and federal regulators. The Federal Communications Commission (FCC) assigned TV licenses, including the limited number that the agency permitted the networks to own. The FCC expected each license holder to devote a small proportion of its schedule to "public interest" programming, including news. Under no pressure to win audiences, news program producers had great latitude in story selection. That said, TV news personnel tended to be political centrists who took their cues from colleagues working at the prestigious newspapers.

For all its shortcomings, early television news had one great journalist, Edward R. Murrow of CBS. Revered for his radio coverage of World War II, Murrow co-produced and hosted the documentary series *See It Now,* beginning in 1951. Although widely praised and courageous in its treatment of domestic anti-Communism, *See It Now* never won a large audience. His less critically admired interview program *Person to Person,* was far more popular and, indeed, anticipated similar, more celebrity-centered efforts by Barbara Walters of ABC several decades later.

In the early 1960s, NBC and CBS began pouring more of their energies into their early evening newscasts, lengthening them from fifteen to thirty minutes in 1963. (ABC did not do so until 1967 and waited another decade before investing substantially in news.) The early evening newscast strategy reflected the "habit" rule of broadcasting, while proving very profitable. Although audiences did not equal those for entertainment shows later in the evening, the nightly newscasts drew enough viewers to interest advertisers. Similarly successful was NBC's *Today* show, which premiered in 1952. Aired in the early morning for two hours, *Today* offered a mix of news and features. ABC eventually developed a competitor, *Good Morning America.*

In the late 1950s and 1960s, all three networks occasionally produced documentaries, usually an hour long, that explored different public issues. Although they rarely had impressive ratings, documentaries mollified critics and regulators dismayed by the networks' less culturally ambitious programming. The opportunity costs (the value of goods or services that one must give up in order to produce something) of airing documentaries, however, grew with heightened advertiser demand for popular series in the late 1960s. The networks quietly reduced their documentary production. Although most TV critics were dismayed, the FCC, which had earlier encouraged such programming, said nothing. Partly relieving the networks of their former obligations was the Public Broadcasting Service (PBS), created by Congress in 1969. Although chronically underfinanced, PBS managed to produce some public affairs and informational programming, once the preserve of the commercial networks. The commercial network documentary had all but vanished by 1980.

In its place came a new type of news show. CBS's *60 Minutes,* which debuted in 1968, was the trendsetter. The documentary's great weaknesses, according to *60 Minutes* producer Don Hewitt, was its slow pacing. Largely because of its devotion of an hour or more to one "serious" issue like German unification, it bored the majority of viewers. Hewitt wanted to make news programming engaging. "Instead of dealing with issues we [will] tell stories," he remarked (Richard Campbell, *60 Minutes and the News,* p. 3). And he determined to mix it up. On *60 Minutes,* no single topic would absorb more than a quarter hour. The topics covered, in turn, would vary to attract as many in the audience as possible. It came to be known as the first TV "magazine" and eventually, *60 Minutes* nurtured a large following. Indeed, it became the first news program to compete successfully with entertainment series in evening prime time.

All three networks found airing newsmagazines irresistible. They were considerably cheaper than entertainment programming and the network could own and produce the program, and not pay fees to an independent company. (At the time, the FCC limited network ownership of entertainment programs.) This meant higher profits, even if a *60 Minutes* imitator accrued smaller ratings than a rival entertainment series.

The tone of network news changed over time. In the 1950s and early 1960s, TV news programs tended to be almost stenographic. A network newscast report on a cabinet secretary's speech was largely unfiltered. This approach had several explanations. Excessively critical coverage might upset federal regulators. Then, too, broadcast news people tended to share in many of the assumptions of newsmakers, especially in regards to the Cold War with the Soviet Union. Television's coverage of America's involvement in Vietnam, especially during the escalation of U.S. participation (1963–1967), was hardly hostile. Nor was TV's combat footage especially graphic. Still, the inability of the U.S. military to secure South Vietnam, despite repeated claims of progress, shattered the Cold War consensus while fostering a new skepticism toward those in power. So did the attempts by the Nixon administration to cover up scandals associated with the Watergate break-in of 1972. The networks did not cover the Watergate affair as searchingly as some newspapers, the *Washington Post* or *Los Angeles Times*, for example. Yet the scandals further damaged relations between government officials and network TV news correspondents. But correspondents had not become leftist ideologues, as many conservatives assumed; network reporters' politics remained strikingly centrist. Rather, TV correspondents tended to mediate government news more warily—regardless of which party controlled the executive branch. Network TV news also became more correspondent-centered. The reporter's interpretation of an announcement—not the announcement itself—dominated most network news accounts.

Still, in times of grave national crisis, network newscasters self-consciously assumed a special role. After the assassination of John F. Kennedy in 1963 and the resignation of Richard M. Nixon in 1974, television journalists sought to reassure and unite the nation. The sociologist Herbert J. Gans dubbed this the "order restoration" function of the national news media. The terrorist attacks of September 2001 prompted a similar response, as well as demonstrations of patriotism not seen on television news since the early Cold War.

Local news programming became especially important to individual stations. Stations initially aired news programs as a regulatory concession. Most followed the networks in expanding their newscasts from fifteen minutes in the 1960s. They were of growing interest to advertisers, and became the single most profitable form of local programming. Stations extended the length and frequency of their newscasts. Production values and immediacy increased as stations switched from film to videotape for their stories. As the competition among stations for ratings grew, the news agenda changed. Little time went to serious issues—which were often difficult to capture visually—as opposed to features, show-business news, and, in larger markets, spectacular fires and crimes.

Sporting events had long been a convenient means of filling the schedule. Because their audiences were disproportionately male, however, most sports telecasts could not command the same ratings as popular entertainment series, except for the championship series in baseball and the National Football League (NFL). Moreover, in airing sporting contests, television played favorites. Football proved to be the most "telegenic" sport, and began luring viewers on Sunday afternoons, which had long been considered a time when people would not watch television. Professional football broke another rule by achieving ratings success in prime time, with the debut of Monday night NFL telecasts on ABC in 1970. Cable television in the 1980s and 1990s created more outlets devoted to sports.

With a cable connection, subscribers could improve their TV's reception and greatly increase their programming choices. In the 1980s, the non-cable viewer could select from seven channels; the cable home had thirty-three. More and more consumers preferred to have more options, which multiplied in the 1990s. In the late 1980s, cable reached about half of all households. A decade later, just under 70 percent of all homes had cable.

Although cable offered an extraordinary range of choices, viewer preferences were strikingly narrow. Channels playing to certain, specialized tastes enjoyed the greatest success. Eight of the fifteen most watched cable telecasts the week of 17–23 December 2001, were on Nickelodeon, which programmed exclusively for young children. Professional wrestling and football programs placed five shows that week.

With cable's spread, the networks saw their share of the evening audience fall from 90 percent in the mid-1970s to just over 60 percent twenty years later. The network early evening newscasts suffered even larger declines. The creation of all-news cable channels, beginning with the Cable News Network (CNN) in 1980, ate away at the authority of the network news programs. Still, CNN's effects should not be overstated. Except during a national crisis, relatively few watched CNN. Entertainment cable channels actually posed the larger problem. The availability of such channels gave viewers alternatives to the newscasts they had not previously had.

All in all, cable had contradictory effects on the networks. News producers, anxious to retain audiences, made their newscasts' agenda less serious and more fixated on scandal (a trend also explained by the end of the Cold War). At the same time, entertainment programs, similarly losing viewers to cable, became more daring. This was not because cable programs, with a few exceptions on pay cable services, violated moral proprieties. Many cable channels aired little other than reruns of network programs and old feature films. For the networks, however, only a more relaxed standard could hold viewers, especially younger ones. While still voluntarily honoring some moral strictures, television series handled violence and sexual relations with a realism unimaginable a generation earlier. Old prohibitions against the use of profanity and nudity were partially relaxed.

No network hurried this trend along more enthusiastically than Fox. Formed in 1986, Fox carried a number of comedies, action dramas, and reality shows (*When Good Pets Go Bad*), some of which consciously crossed mainstream boundaries of good taste. Fox owner Rupert Murdoch, an Australian publisher of tabloid newspapers, lacked the self-conscious sensibility of his older rivals.

Fox's rise coincided with the relaxation of federal regulations. Between the 1920s and 1970s, the relative scarcity of on-air channels justified government oversight of broadcasting. The radio spectrum only permitted so many stations per community. With cable eliminating this rationale, the FCC in the 1980s systematically deregulated broadcasting. In the late twentieth century, television license holders aired news programs to make money, not to please federal officials. Congress approved this course, and the 1996 Telecommunications Act weakened remaining FCC rules limiting the number of stations that networks and others could own.

Institutional Impacts of Television

The nation's established mass media—radio, films, and newspapers—reacted differently to television's sudden presence in the American home. Radio felt the effects first, as audiences for radio programs, particularly in the evening, dropped sharply in the first half of the 1950s. Radio's relative portability allowed some recovery, especially with the development of the transistor. Then, too, in the 1950s, most Americans only owned one television. Those unhappy with what another family member insisted on watching could listen to a radio elsewhere in the house. Moreover, radio could be a diversion for those doing the dishes or cleaning a room. At the same time, radio listening while driving became much more common as more automobiles were equipped with radios, and the percentage of Americans who owned cars increased. In addition, some radio stations broke with an older industry tradition by targeting a demographic subgroup of listeners, specifically, adolescents. Stations hired disc jockeys who continuously played rock and roll music. Television stations and networks could only offer a few programs tailored to teens. Advertisers prized their parents more. Radio, in that regard, anticipated the direction of television's competitors after the 1960s. Radio stations continued to narrow their formats by age, race, and politics.

Television presented an enormous challenge to the film industry. Theater attendance dropped sharply in the late 1940s and early 1950s. however, box office receipts were declining even before television arrived in many communities. With marginal theaters closing, the studios responded by reducing the number of movies produced per year. To compete with TV, more films had elaborate special effects and were produced in color. (Not until 1972 did most homes have color televisions.) The collapse of film censorship in the mid-1960s gave Hollywood another edge: violence and sexual situations could be portrayed with an unprecedented explicitness that TV producers could only envy.

Although most large studios at first resisted cooperating with the television networks, by the mid-1950s virtually every movie company was involved in some TV production. With some exceptions, most of Hollywood's initial video work resembled the old "B" movie, the cheaper theatrical release of the 1930s and 1940s produced as the second feature for a twin billing or for the smaller theaters, most of which had ceased operations in the late 1950s. In the late 1960s, motion picture firms began producing TV movies, that is, two-hour films specifically for television. At first, they were fairly cheaply mounted and forgettable. But a few had enormous impact. ABC's *Roots*, telecast in 1977, chronicled the history of an African American family and prompted a new appreciation for family history. Although the TV films remained popular through the 1980s, higher costs caused the networks to lose their enthusiasm for the genre, which all but disappeared from the small screen in the 1990s.

No major mass medium responded more ineffectively to the challenge of television than newspapers. For more than two decades, newspaper publishers refused to regard TV as a threat to their industry. Indeed, the diffusion of television did not initially affect newspaper circulation. In the long run, however, TV undermined the daily newspaper's place in American life. As "baby boomers," those Americans born between 1946 and 1963, reluctantly entered adulthood, they proved less likely to pick up a paper. If they did, they spent less time reading it. Publishers belatedly responded by making their papers more appealing to a generation raised with television. They shortened stories, carried more pictures, and used color. Assuming, not always correctly, that readers already knew the headlines from television, editors insisted that newspaper stories be more analytical. Yet they were losing the war. The more interpretive journalism failed to woo younger readers, while many older readers deemed it too opinionated. Although Sunday sales were fairly stable, daily circulation per household continued to drop.

Like many newspaper publishers, America's political class only slowly recognized television's impact. John F. Kennedy's video effectiveness during the 1960 presidential campaign, however, changed many minds, as did some powerful television political spots by individual candidates later in the decade. TV advertising became an increasingly common electoral weapon, even though its actual impact was debated. Nevertheless, to candidates and their consultants, the perception that television appeals could turn an election mattered more than the reality. And, as the cost of television spots rose, so did the centrality of fundraising to politicians. TV, in that regard, indirectly contributed to the campaign finance problem besetting both political parties by making their leaders more dependent on the monies of large corporations and their political action committees.

Advertisers of goods and services, and not political candidates, were far and away commercial television's greatest patrons. (Political campaigns accounted for 7 percent of all advertising spending—print as well as video—in 1996.) During TV's first decade, sponsors had great power. They likely underwrote entire programs, and often involved themselves in aspects of the production. They sought product placement on the set, and sometimes integrated the middle commercial into the story. They also censored scripts. For example, a cigarette manufacturer sponsoring *The Virginian* forbade a cast member from smoking a cigar on camera.

In the early 1960s, sponsors lost their leverage. The involvement of some in the rigging of popular quiz shows had embarrassed the industry. Members of Congress and others insisted that the networks, and not sponsors, have the ultimate authority over program production (a power the networks themselves had long sought). Concomitantly, more advertisers wanted to enter television, creating a seller's market. Then, too, as the costs of prime time entertainment series rose, so did the expense of sole sponsorship. Advertisers began buying individual spots, as opposed to entire programs. The new economics of television, even more than the fallout over the quiz scandals, gave the networks sovereignty over their schedules. Yet the entry of so many more potential sponsors, demanding masses of viewers, placed added pressure on the networks to maximize their ratings whenever possible. Networks turned away companies willing to underwrite less popular cultural programming, such as *The Voice of Firestone*, because more revenue could be earned by telecasting series with a wider appeal.

The popularity of cable in the 1980s and 1990s marked a new phase in advertiser-network relations. The "niche marketing" of cable channels like MTV and Nickelodeon greatly eased the tasks of advertising agencies' media buyers seeking those audiences. The networks, on the other hand, confronted a crisis. Although willing to continue to patronize network programs, advertisers made new demands. These did not ordinarily involve specific production decisions, whether, for instance, a character on a sitcom had a child out of wedlock. Instead, media buyers had broader objectives. No longer did they focus exclusively on the size of a program's audience; they increasingly concerned themselves with its composition. A dramatic series like *Matlock* had a large audience, but a graying one. *Friends* and *Melrose Place*, on the other hand, were viewed by younger viewers. Advertisers assumed that younger consumers were far more likely to try new products and brands. Increasingly in the 1990s, the demographics of a series' audience determined its fate. This left viewers not in the desired demographic group in the wilderness of cable.

BIBLIOGRAPHY

Balio, Tino, ed. *Hollywood in the Age of Television*. Boston: Unwin Hyman, 1990.

Baughman, James L. *The Republic of Mass Culture: Journalism, Filmmaking, and Broadcasting in America since 1941*. 2d ed. Baltimore: Johns Hopkins University Press, 1997.

Bernhard, Nancy E. *U.S. Television News and Cold War Propaganda, 1947–1960*. Cambridge, U.K.: Cambridge University Press, 1999.

Bogart, Leo. *The Age of Television: A Study of Viewing Habits and the Impact of Television on American Life*. 3d ed. New York: Frederick Ungar, 1972.

Hallin, Daniel C. *We Keep America on Top of the World: Television Journalism and the Public Sphere*. London and New York: Routledge, 1994.

———. *The "Uncensored War": The Media and Vietnam*. New York: Oxford University Press, 1986.

Mayer, Martin. *About Television*. New York: Harper and Row, 1972. The best, most thoughtful journalistic account of the television industry before the cable revolution.

O'Connor, John E., ed. *American History/American Television: Interpreting the Video Past*. New York: Frederick Ungar, 1983.

Stark, Steven D. *Glued to the Set: The Sixty Television Shows and Events That Made Us Who We Are Today*. New York: Free Press, 1997.

James L. Baughman

See also **Celebrity Culture; Mass Media; Talk Shows, Radio and Television; Televangelism; Videocassette Recorder.**

TECHNOLOGY

Television is the process of capturing photographic images, converting them into electrical impulses, and then transmitting the signal to a decoding receiver. Conventional transmission is by means of electromagnetic radiation, using the methods of radio. Since the early part of the twentieth century, the development of television in the United States has been subject to rules set out by the federal government, specifically the FEDERAL COMMUNICATIONS COMMISSION (FCC), and by the marketplace and commercial feasibility.

Early Developments

Image conversion problems were solved in the latter part of the nineteenth century. In 1873 English engineer Willoughby Smith noted the photoconductivity of the element selenium, that its electrical resistance fluctuated when exposed to light. This started the search for a method to change optical images into electric current, and simultaneous developments in Europe eventually led to a variety of mechanical, as opposed to electronic, methods of image transmission.

In 1884 German engineer Paul Nipkow devised a mechanical scanning system using a set of revolving disks in a camera and a receiver. This converted the image by transmitting individual images sequentially as light passed through small holes in the disk. These were then "reassembled" by the receiving disk. The scanner, called a Nipkow disk, was used in experiments in the United States by Charles F. Jenkins and in England by John L. Baird to create a crude television image in the 1920s. Jenkins began operating in 1928 as the Jenkins Television Corporation near Washington, D.C., and by 1931 nearly two dozen stations were in service, using low-definition scanning based on the Nipkow system.

In the 1930s, American Philo T. Farnsworth, an independent inventor, and Vladimir K. Zworykin, an engineer with Westinghouse and, later, the Radio Corporation of America (RCA), were instrumental in devising the first workable electronic scanning system. Funding, interference from competitors, and patent issues slowed advances, but Farnsworth came out with an "image dissector," a camera that converted individual elements of an image into electrical impulses, and Zworykin developed a similar camera device called the iconoscope. Although Zworykin's device was more successful, in the end collaboration and cross-licensing were necessary for commercial development of television.

By 1938, electronic scanning systems had overtaken or, in some cases, incorporated elements of, mechanical ones. Advancements made since the early 1900s in the United States, Europe, and Russia by Lee De Forest, Karl Ferdinand Braun, J. J. Thomson, A. A. Campbell Swinton, and Boris Rosing contributed to the commercial feasibility of television transmission. Allen B. DuMont's improvements on the cathode-ray tube in the late 1930s set the standard for picture reproduction, and receivers (television sets) were marketed in New York by DuMont and RCA. The cathode-ray tube receiver, or picture tube, contains electron beams focused on a phosphorescent screen. The material on the screen emits light of varying intensity when struck by the beam, controlled by the signal from the camera, reproducing the image on the tube screen in horizontal and vertical lines—the more lines, the more detail. The "scene" changes at around the rate of 25 to 30 complete images per second, giving the viewer the perception of motion as effectively as in motion pictures.

Early Commercial Broadcasting

In 1939, the National Broadcasting Company in New York provided programming focused on the New York World's Fair. During the 1930s, RCA president David Sarnoff, a radio programming pioneer, developed research on programming for television, which was originally centered on public events and major news stories. In late 1939, the FCC adopted rules to permit the collection of fees for television services, in the form of sponsored programs. In the industry, the National Television Systems Committee (NTSC) was formed to adopt uniform technical standards. Full commercial program service was authorized by the FCC on 1 July 1941, with provisions that the technical standard be set at 525 picture lines and 30 frames per second. After more than forty years of experimentation, television was on the brink of full commercial programming by the beginning of World War II (1939–1945). After World War II, a television broadcasting boom began and the television industry grew rapidly, from programming and transmitting ("airing") to the manufacturing of standardized television sets.

Color Television

The development of color television was slower. Color television used the same technology as monochromatic (black and white), but was more complex. In 1940, Peter Goldmark demonstrated a color system in New York that was technically superior to its predecessors, going back to Baird's 1928 experiments with color and Nipkow disks. But Goldmark's system was incompatible with monochromatic sets. The delay in widespread use of color television had more to do with its compatibility with monochromatic systems than with theoretical or scientific obstacles. By 1954, those issues had been resolved, and in 1957 the federal government adopted uniform standards. For most Americans, however, color televisions were cost-prohibitive until the 1970s.

The Future of Television

The last three decades of the twentieth century were filled with as many exciting advancements in the industry as were the first three: Projection televisions (PTVs) were introduced, both front- and rear-projection and with screens as large as 7 feet; videotape, which had been used by broadcasters since the 1950s, was adapted for home use, either for use with home video cameras or for recording programmed broadcasting (by the 1980s videocassette recorders—VCRs—were nearly as common as TVs); cable television and satellite broadcasting began to make inroads into the consumer market; and in the early 2000s, digital videodiscs (DVDs) began to replace videotape cassettes as a consumer favorite. Also in the 1970s, advancements were made in liquid crystal display (LCD) technology that eventually led to flatter screens and, in the 1990s, plasma display panels (PDPs) that allowed for screens over a yard wide and just a few inches thick.

The 1990s brought about a revolution in digital television, which converts analog signals into a digital code (1s and 0s) and provides a clearer image that is less prone to distortion (though errors in transmission or retrieval may result in no image at all, as opposed to a less-than-perfect analog image). First developed for filmmakers in the early 1980s, high-definition television (HDTV) uses around 1,000 picture lines and a wide-screen format, providing a sharper image and a larger viewing area. Also, conventional televisions have an aspect ratio of 4:3 (screen width to screen height), whereas wide-screen HDTVs have an aspect ratio of 16:9, much closer to that of motion pictures.

Since the late 1980s, the FCC has been aggressively advocating the transition to digital television, largely because digital systems use less of the available bandwidth, thereby creating more bandwidth for cellular phones. Based on technical standards adopted in 1996, the FCC ruled that all public television stations must be digital by

May 2003, considered by many to be an overly optimistic deadline. As with the development of color television, the progress of HDTV has been hampered by compatibility issues. The FCC ruled in 1987 that HDTV standards must be compatible with existing NTSC standards. By 2000, however, the focus for the future of HDTV had shifted to its compatibility and integration with home computers. As of 2002, HDTV systems were in place across the United States, but home units were costly and programming was limited.

BIBLIOGRAPHY

Ciciora, Walter S. *Modern Cable Television Technology: Videos, Voice, and Data Communications.* San Francisco: Morgan Kaufmann, 1999.

Federal Communications Commission. Home page at http://www.fcc.gov

Fisher, David E. *Tube: The Invention of Television.* Washington, D.C.: Counterpoint, 1996.

Gano, Lila. *Television: Electronic Pictures.* San Diego, Calif.: Lucent Books, 1990.

Trundle, Eugene. *Guide to TV and Video Technology.* Boston: Newnes, 1996.

Paul Hehn

See also **Electricity and Electronics; Telecommunications.**

TELLER AMENDMENT, a disclaimer on the part of the United States in 1898 of any intention "to exercise sovereignty, jurisdiction or control" over the island of Cuba when it should have been freed from Spanish rule. It was proposed in the Senate by Henry M. Teller of Colorado and adopted, 19 April as an amendment to the joint resolution declaring Cuba independent and authorizing intervention. Spain declared war on the United States five days later. By August, the United States had expelled Spanish forces from the island. Despite Teller's amendment, the United States intervened in Cuban internal affairs deep into the twentieth century.

BIBLIOGRAPHY

LaFeber, Walter. *The New Empire: An Interpretation of American Expansion, 1860–1898.* Ithaca, N.Y.: Cornell University, 1963.

Perez, Louis A., Jr. *Cuba and the United States: Ties of Singular Intimacy.* Athens: University of Georgia Press, 1990.

Julius W. Pratt / A. G.

See also **Cuba, Relations with; Imperialism; Spain, Relations with; Spanish-American War.**

TEMPERANCE MOVEMENT. The movement to curb the use of alcohol was one of the central reform efforts of American history. From earliest settlement, consumption of alcohol was a widely accepted practice in America, and while drunkenness was denounced, both distilled and fermented beverages were considered nourishing stimulants. In 1673 the Puritan divine Increase Mather condemned drunkenness as a sin, yet said "Drink in itself is a good creature of God, and to be received with thankfulness." Alcohol was not prohibited but rather regulated through licensing.

Growth of the Temperance Movement

The half century after independence witnessed both a gradual change in attitudes toward alcoholic beverages and an increase in alcohol production and consumption. A pamphlet by the prominent Philadelphia physician Benjamin Rush entitled *An Inquiry into the Effects of Spirituous Liquors on the Human Mind and Body*, published in 1784, was an early voice denouncing the harmful effects of distilled liquors. The first temperance society of record was formed in Litchfield County, Connecticut, in 1789 by prominent citizens convinced that alcohol hindered the conduct of their businesses. In 1813 the Massachusetts Society for the Suppression of Intemperance was formed by society's elites—clergymen, town officials, and employers—"to suppress the too free use of ardent spirits, and its kindred vices, profaneness and gambling, and to encourage and promote temperance and general morality," as its constitution proclaimed. There was good reason for the concern of these early temperance advocates. The newly opened western lands in Pennsylvania, Tennessee, and Kentucky were producing grain more easily transported if converted to whiskey. Cheaper than rum, whiskey soon flooded the market. Estimates are that between 1800 and 1830 the annual per capita consumption of absolute alcohol among the drinking-age population (fifteen and older) ranged from 6.6 to 7.1 gallons.

By 1825 the forces of evangelical Protestantism mobilized for the temperance crusade. In that year, the Connecticut clergyman Lyman Beecher preached six sermons warning of the dangers of intemperance to a Christian republic. The next year sixteen clergy and laypersons in Boston signed the constitution of the American Society for the Promotion of Temperance. The reformers sensed divine compulsion to send out missionaries to preach the gospel of abstinence from the use of distilled spirits. Using an effective system of state, county, and local auxiliaries, the American Temperance Society (ATS) soon claimed national scope. Voluntary contributions enabled it to support agents who visited every part of the country, striving to affiliate all temperance groups with the national society. By 1831 the ATS reported over 2,200 known societies in states throughout the country, including 800 in New England, 917 in the Middle Atlantic states, 339 in the South, and 158 in the Northwest.

The efforts of the ATS were aimed at the moderate drinker to encourage total abstinence from distilled liquor. By the late 1830s, the national organization, now called the American Temperance Union, was attempting to distance itself from antislavery reformers to placate southern temperance societies, sponsor legislation against

Temperance Cartoon. This woodcut, c. 1820, blames rum for such evils as murder, fever, and cholera. © CORBIS

the liquor traffic, and adopt a pledge of total abstinence from all intoxicants, the teetotal pledge. However, each of these efforts sparked internal division and external opposition, which, along with the 1837 panic and ensuing depression, weakened the reform movement.

Interest in temperance revived with the appearance of the Washingtonian movement in 1840. Six tipplers in Baltimore took the abstinence pledge, formed a temperance organization named after the first president, and began to spread the temperance gospel. Aimed at inebriates rather than moderate drinkers, Washingtonian meetings featured dramatic personal testimonies of deliverance from demon rum akin to the revival meetings of the Second Great Awakening, as well as other social activities to replace the conviviality of the tavern. Orators such as John B. Gough and John H. W. Hawkins toured the country, including the South, lecturing on temperance. The Washingtonian impulse was strong but short-lived, owing to lack of organization and leadership.

The enthusiasm generated by the Washingtonians was captured and institutionalized by the Sons of Temperance, a fraternal organization formed in 1842 by some Washingtonians concerned about the frequency of backsliding. They proposed an organization "to shield us from the evils of Intemperance; afford mutual assistance in case of sickness; and elevate our character as men." A highly structured society requiring dues and a total abstinence pledge, the Sons introduced a new phase of the temper-

ance movement, the fraternal organization with secret handshakes, rituals, ceremonies, and regalia. The organization spread rapidly and all but a few states had Grand Divisions of the Sons by 1847. The peak year of membership was 1850, when the rolls listed over 238,000 members.

At the same time the Sons of Temperance was flourishing, Father Theobald Mathew, the well-known Irish Apostle of Temperance, undertook a speaking tour through the United States. Between July 1849 and November 1851, he traveled the country administering the temperance pledge to several hundred thousand people, many of them Irish Americans. His tour illustrated some of the dynamics affecting the temperance movement. Upon his arrival in America, Mathew was greeted by William Lloyd Garrison, who pressured him to reaffirm an abolition petition Mathew had signed some years earlier. Seeking to avoid controversy, and aware that he planned to tour the South, Mathew declined despite Garrison's public insistence. Word of the affair reached Joseph Henry Lumpkin, chairman of the Georgia State Temperance Society, who had invited Mathew to address the state temperance convention. Despite his insistence that temperance was his mission, Mathew's acknowledgement of his abolition sentiments led Lumpkin to withdraw his invitation to address the convention. Nonetheless, Mathew did successfully tour the South.

Carry Nation. The hatchet-wielding nemesis of saloons all over Kansas, and then across the country, in the first decade of the twentieth century. LIBRARY OF CONGRESS

During the antebellum era the temperance message was spread widely through the printed word. Weekly and monthly journals appeared devoted solely to temperance, while many religious periodicals carried news of the reform movement. Songs, poems, tracts, addresses, essays, sermons, and stories found their way into print, and temperance literature became a common part of the cultural landscape. Fiction like Timothy Shay Arthur's *Ten Nights in a Bar-Room, and What I saw There* (1854), portrayed the pain and shame experienced by drunkards and their families, as well as the joy of a life redeemed from demon rum. Temperance was trumpeted as the means to both social and domestic tranquility and individual economic advancement.

The ATS was among the first of voluntary benevolent reform organizations of the antebellum era to admit women, who participated in significant numbers. Women both joined men's societies and formed their own auxiliaries. According to the ideology of the day, woman's presumed superior moral influence, exercised mainly in the domestic sphere, added moral weight to the temperance cause. Also, women along with children were the main

victims of alcoholic excess in the form of domestic violence and economic deprivation.

From Moral to Legal Reform

By the late 1830s some temperance reformers were ready to abandon moral suasion (urging individuals to abstinence by personal choice) in favor of legal suasion (employing the coercion of law). In 1838 and 1839 temperance workers circulated petitions asking state legislatures to change license laws regulating liquor traffic. Some petitions sought to prohibit liquor sales in less-than-specified quantities ranging from one to twenty gallons. Others sought local option laws allowing communities to regulate liquor sales. While petition campaigns occurred in most states, they were usually unsuccessful.

After the revival of temperance interest in the 1840s, a second prohibition effort occurred in the next decade. The state of Maine, under the efforts of the merchant Neal Dow, passed a prohibitory statute in 1851 outlawing the manufacture and sale of intoxicants. The Maine Law became a model for state campaigns throughout the country. During the early years of the 1850s temperance was one of the issues along with nativism, slavery, and the demise of the Whig Party that colored state political campaigns. A number of states passed prohibitory laws, though most were declared unconstitutional or repealed by 1857. Despite the failure of these efforts, temperance had proven the most widespread reform of the antebellum era.

Following the Civil War, the PROHIBITION PARTY was formed in Chicago in 1869, and began nominating presidential candidates in 1872, though it languished in the shadow of the major parties. Perhaps more important was the emergence of greater involvement of women in the temperance cause with the appearance of the WOMAN'S CHRISTIAN TEMPERANCE UNION in 1874. Annual per capita consumption of absolute alcohol had dropped sharply during the 1830s and 1840s and remained relatively stable at one to two gallons through most of the second half of the century. As America shifted from a rural to urban culture, drinking patterns shifted as well, away from whiskey to beer, a more urban beverage, now readily available owing to technological developments like pasteurization and refrigeration. Saloons became familiar fixtures of the urban landscape, and for temperance workers, the symbol of alcohol's evil. The WCTU, largely a collection of Protestant women, adopted a confrontational strategy, marching in groups to the saloon and demanding that it close. Under the leadership of Frances Willard, who led the organization for two decades, the WCTU embraced a wide variety of reforms, including woman's suffrage, believing that only by empowering women in the public sphere could alcohol be eliminated and the home protected. The WCTU became the largest temperance and largest women's organization prior to 1900.

Building on the women's efforts to keep the alcohol issue before the public, the ANTI-SALOON LEAGUE was formed by evangelical Protestant men in 1895. Attacking the saloon was its method; its aim was a dry society. The Anti-Saloon League worked through evangelical denominations, winning statewide victories over the next two decades. Its crowning success was the passage of the Eighteenth Amendment in 1919, ushering in the Prohibition era that ran from 1920 to 1933.

BIBLIOGRAPHY

Blocker, Jack S., Jr. *American Temperance Movements: Cycles of Reform.* Boston: Twayne, 1989.

Bordin, Ruth. *Women and Temperance: The Quest for Power and Liberty, 1873–1900.* Philadelphia: Temple University Press, 1981.

Dannenbaum, Jed. *Drink and Disorder: Temperance Reform in Cincinnati from the Washingtonian Revival to the WCTU.* Urbana: University of Illinois Press, 1984.

Hampel, Robert L. *Temperance and Prohibition in Massachusetts, 1813–1852.* Ann Arbor, Mich.: UMI Research Press, 1982.

Krout, John Allen. *The Origins of Prohibition.* New York: Knopf, 1925.

Rorabaugh, W. J. *The Alcoholic Republic: An American Tradition.* New York: Oxford University Press, 1979.

Tyrrell, Ian R. *Sobering Up: From Temperance to Prohibition in Antebellum America, 1800–1860.* Westport, Conn.: Greenwood Press, 1979.

Douglas W. Carlson

See also **Prohibition.**

TEN-FORTIES, gold bonds issued during the CIVIL WAR that were redeemable after ten years and payable after forty years. Authorized by Congress on 3 March 1864 to allow greater freedom in financing the Civil War, their low 5 percent interest made them unpopular; less popular, at any rate, than the earlier "five-twenties," bonds with more flexible terms issued by the U.S. Treasury under the direction of financier Jay Cooke. Bond sales declined rapidly and forced the Treasury to rely more heavily on short-term loans, bank notes, greenback issues, and taxes.

BIBLIOGRAPHY

Rein, Bert W. *An Analysis and Critique of the Union Financing of the Civil War.* Amherst, Mass: Amherst College Press, 1962.

Reinfeld, Fred. *The Story of Civil War Money.* New York: Sterling Publishing, 1959.

Chester M. Destler / A. R.

See also **Cooke, Jay, and Company; Greenbacks; National Bank Notes; War Costs.**

TENEMENTS. The New York City Tenement House Act of 1867 defined a tenement as any rented or leased dwelling that housed more than three independent families. Tenements were first built to house the waves of immigrants that arrived in the United States during the 1840s and 1850s, and they represented the primary form of urban working-class housing until the New Deal.

A typical tenement building was from five to six stories high, with four apartments on each floor. To maximize the number of renters, builders wasted little space. Early tenements might occupy as much as 90 percent of their lots, leaving little room behind the building for privies and water pumps and little ventilation, light, or privacy inside the tenement. With a large extended family and regular boarders to help pay the rent, which could otherwise eat up over half of a family's income, a tenement apartment might house as many as from ten to twelve people at a time. These tenement residents often also worked in the building in such occupations as cigar rolling and garment making.

From the beginning, reformers attacked tenement conditions. In New York City, early attempts at reform included fire-prevention measures, the creation of a Department of Survey and Inspection of Buildings in 1862, and the founding of the Metropolitan Board of Health in 1866. Meanwhile, city tenements were getting increas-

Tenement. In this photograph by Jacob Riis, c. 1890, a woman does handiwork while smoking a pipe in her cramped tenement room in New York. © BETTMANN/CORBIS

ingly crowded: by 1864, approximately 480,400 of New York City's more than 700,000 residents lived in some 15,300 tenement buildings.

New York State passed a Tenement House Law on 14 May 1867, the nation's first comprehensive housing reform law. It established the first standards for minimum room size, ventilation, and sanitation. It required fire escapes and at least one toilet or privy (usually outside) for every twenty inhabitants. However, enforcement was lax.

An 1879 amendment to the 1867 legislation required more open space on a building lot and stipulated that all tenement rooms open onto a street, rear yard, or air shaft. The measure was designed to increase ventilation and fight diseases, such as tuberculosis, that ravaged tenement neighborhoods. To meet the standards of the 1879 law, builders designed the "dumbbell tenement" with narrow airshafts on each side to create a dumbbell-like shape from above. Despite slightly better fireproofing and ventilation, reformers attacked these buildings as only a limited improvement on existing conditions.

In 1890, Jacob Riis's *How the Other Half Lives* rallied middle-class reformers to the cause of improving tenement life. His photos and essays drew attention to the health and housing problems of tenement neighborhoods.

The most significant New York State law to improve deteriorating tenement conditions was the Tenement Act of 1901, promoted by a design competition and exhibition held by the Charity Organization Society in 1900. By that time, the city's Lower East Side was home to the most densely populated buildings on earth. The neighborhood's

Tenth Ward had a population of 69,944, approximately 665 people per acre.

The 1901 legislation, opposed by the real estate industry on the grounds that it would discourage new construction, improved tenement buildings. The law mandated better lighting and fireproofing. Most important, it required that privies be replaced with indoor toilet facilities connected to the city sewers, with one toilet for every two apartments.

Beginning in the New Deal era, reformers' strategies changed. Drawing on a tradition of "model tenements" and new government interest in housing construction, reformers designed public housing projects. Their plans emphasized open space, much as an earlier generation had passed laws to provide more light and fresh air for urban working-class families. The imposed standards, however, often created new problems. Building closures and slum clearance displaced many working-class families, while new high-rise public HOUSING often fell victim to segregation and neglect. Although reformers continued to attack working-class living conditions, social pressures sustained many of the problems of poverty and overcrowding.

Slums Breed Crime. A U.S. Housing Authority poster showing police making arrests outside a tenement building. NATIONAL ARCHIVES AND RECORDS ADMINISTRATION

BIBLIOGRAPHY

Bauman, John F., Roger Biles, and Kristin M. Szylvian. *From Tenements to the Taylor Homes: In Search of an Urban Housing Policy in Twentieth-Century America.* University Park: Pennsylvania State University Press, 2000.

Day, Jared N. *Urban Castles: Tenement Housing and Landlord Activism in New York City, 1890–1943.* New York: Columbia University Press, 1999.

Ford, James. *Slums and Housing, with Special Reference to New York City: History, Conditions, Policy.* Cambridge, Mass.: Harvard University Press, 1936.

Hall, Peter. *Cities of Tomorrow: An Intellectual History of Urban Planning and Design in the Twentieth Century.* New York: Blackwell, 1988.

Lower East Side Tenement Museum. Home page at http://www.tenement.org.

Plunz, Richard. *A History of Housing in New York City.* New York: Columbia University Press, 1990.

Riis, Jacob. *How the Other Half Lives: Studies among the Tenements of New York.* New York: Scribners, 1890.

Mark Ladov

See also **Poverty; Public Health; Urbanization;** *and vol. 9:* **In the Slums.**

TENNESSEE. Since its founding, Tennessee has traditionally been divided into three sections: East Tennessee, Middle Tennessee, and West Tennessee. East Tennessee includes part of the Appalachian Mountains, which stretch from Alabama and Georgia northward through East Tennessee to New England; the GREAT VALLEY, which is to the west of the Appalachians, slanting northeastward from Georgia through Tennessee into Virginia; and the Cumberland Plateau, which is to the west of the Great Valley, slanting from northeastern Alabama through Tennessee into southeastern Kentucky. The people of East Tennessee are often called "Overhills," because Tennessee was once part of North Carolina and was west over the mountains from the rest of North Carolina. Both the Cumberland Plateau and the Great Valley are fertile and ideal for growing many different crops; the Great Valley is well watered. The Tennessee Appalachian Mountains are rugged, with numerous small valleys occupied by small farms. The people of East Tennessee were from their first settlement an independent-minded group who valued hard work and self-reliance.

Middle Tennessee extends from the Cumberland Plateau westward to the Highland Rim. The people who live on the Highland Rim are often called "Highlanders." The lowlands include the Nashville Basin, are well watered, and are noted for their agriculture, especially for cotton and tobacco. The Highland Rim features many natural wonders, including many caves and underground streams.

Situated between East Tennessee and West Tennessee, Middle Tennessee has sometimes seemed to be a divided culture. Before the Civil War, it had more slaves than East Tennessee, but fewer than West Tennessee, and it tended to favor the small farm tradition of the east rather than the plantation system of the west. It was divided on its support for outlawing slavery, but after Reconstruction its politics were controlled by a political spoils system run by Democrats who controlled Tennessee until the 1970s.

West Tennessee lies in the Gulf Coastal Plain, a region that stretches northward from the Gulf of Mexico to Illinois along the Mississippi River. It was in this region that many local Native Americans made their last efforts to retain their remaining lands by petitioning the federal government for help. Land speculators of the early 1800s created towns and plantations throughout the area, and they brought with them the slave culture of North Carolina. Historians differ on the exact numbers, but between 40 percent and 60 percent of the people who lived in West Tennessee were slaves during the antebellum period. The plantations were notoriously cruel.

Tennessee is nicknamed the "Big Bend State" because of the unusual course of the TENNESSEE RIVER. It flows southwest from the Appalachian Mountains through the Great Valley into Alabama. There, it bends northwestward, reenters Tennessee at Pickwick Lake, and flows north along the western edge of the Highland Rim into Kentucky, eventually joining the OHIO RIVER. During the 1930s, the United States government established the Tennessee Valley Authority (TVA), a project to provide jobs for people who had lost their jobs during the Great Depression and intended to control flooding and to provide hydroelectricity to Tennessee and its neighbors. It was controversial, with many criticizing it as a waste of money, and others insisting that it was destroying Tennessee's environment. The TVA built dams on the Tennessee River and the Cumberland River, creating new lakes and reservoirs, as well as a system of over 650 miles of waterways that boats used to ship products around the state.

Tennessee is bordered on the north by Kentucky; along its northeastern border is Virginia. Its eastern boundary is along the western border of North Carolina. Its southern border extends along the northern borders of Georgia, Alabama, and Mississippi. Its western border is met by Arkansas in the south and Missouri in the north.

Prehistory

Tennessee has a complex ancient past; there is evidence throughout the state of numerous cultures that have come and passed in the regions now within its borders. Over 100,000 years ago, people crossed into North America from northeastern Asia. Traces of these earliest peoples are hard to find, partly because the glaciers of an ice age about 11,000 years ago would have destroyed their remains. Tennessee offers tantalizing hints as to what some of these migrants were like, because in some of Tennessee's caves are the remains of ancient cave dwellers. In West Tennessee there are caves that hold evidence of ancient fishermen. This evidence may represent several dif-

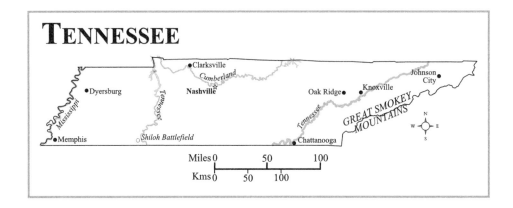

ferent cultures, but each seems to have practiced a religion. Their cave dwellings contain spearheads as well as fishhooks, and they may have hunted the big game of the Great Plains such as mammoths, camels, and giant bison.

About 9000 B.C., nomadic peoples known as Paleo-Indians began crossing North America. They were primarily hunters; in the Great Plains they hunted the large land mammals that roved in herds across grasslands. In Tennessee they would have hunted the same animals until the great forests covered much of Tennessee around 7000 B.C. They likely hunted bison and deer in these forests. Their spear points suggest that several different cultural groups of Paleo-Indians crossed the Mississippi into and through Tennessee.

Around 5000 B.C., another group of people, who archaeologists call Archaic Indians, may have begun migrating into Tennessee. The first Archaic Indians of the Midwest made a significant technological advance over the Paleo-Indians by developing the atlatl, a handheld device with a groove in which to hold a spear. It enabled a person to throw a spear with far greater force and accuracy than by throwing a spear with a bare hand. Archaeological remains from about 2000 B.C. show signs of people settling throughout Tennessee. They began making pottery that increased in sophistication over the next few thousand years.

Homes were made of log posts with walls of clay. Communities enlarged and engaged in public works projects to clear land, plant crops, and build places of worship. Pottery was commonplace and was used for cooking, carrying, and storage.

These ancient peoples began a practice that has puzzled and fascinated archaeologists: they built mounds, sometimes seven stories high. Few of the mounds that survive have been explored by scientists, but those that have reveal people to have been buried in them, sometimes just one, sometimes many. They have been mummified and have carved animals and people, as well as food, placed around them, indicating a belief in an afterlife in which game and food would be wanted, at least symbolically. That the different cultures who built these mounds had priests is clear, and clear also is that they had

a highly developed government that would have included many villages and towns.

By about A.D. 800, maize had become a crop, probably brought to Tennessee from central Mexico. By this time, the people in Tennessee were ancestors of modern Native Americans. They continued the mound-building tradition and were farmers. They lived in villages consisting of people related by blood, but they may have insisted that people marry outside their villages much as the Native Americans did when the first Europeans explored Tennessee. Their governments probably consisted of federations of villages, governed by a high chief.

When Hernando de Soto explored southern and western Tennessee in 1540, the peoples had undergone much turmoil for more than a century. The Mound Builders had been driven away, exterminated, or absorbed into invading tribes. Three language groups were represented in the area: Algonquian, Iroquoian, and Muskogean. Among the Iroquoian group were the Cherokees, who had probably migrated from the north into Tennessee. They had a settled society that claimed East and Middle Tennessee as their territory. The Iroquois Confederacy to the north claimed the Cherokees' territory, but the Cherokees resisted them. The Muskogean cultural tribes, Creeks and Chickasaws, claimed the rest of Tennessee, with the Creeks contesting the Cherokees for some of Middle Tennessee. The Chickasaws of western Tennessee were very well organized, with strong leadership and excellent military skills. The capital of the Cherokees was Echota (aka Chota), a city that was declared "bloodless," meaning no fighting was allowed. Weapons were not allowed either. It was a place created by the Native Americans to settle their disputes through diplomacy, and in the Cherokee and Creek tribes, in particular, skilled diplomats were awarded honors equal to those of skilled warriors.

Each village had a main house ("town house") where religious ceremonies took place. Villages consisted of clay houses, usually gathered around the main house. By the late 1600s, the Native Americans had horses, cattle, pigs, and chickens, imports from Europe. They farmed their lands and hunted wild game in their forests, but the Cherokees were fast developing livestock farming. Some of the Shawnees, of the Algonquian language group, had moved into the Cumberland Valley to escape the Iroquois Confederacy. The Cherokees and Creeks viewed them as interlopers, but the Shawnees had little choice; the Iroquois Confederacy sometimes settled its differences with its neighbors with genocide. In 1714, the Cherokee, Creek, and Iroquois Confederates drove the Shawnees out; the Shawnees sought sanctuary in the Ohio Valley. War with the Iroquois Confederacy often seemed imminent for the Cherokees, Creeks, and Chickasaws, but during the 1700s new threats came to preoccupy those Native Americans.

Land

By 1673, the French were trading to the north of Tennessee and had antagonized the Chickasaws to the point that the Chickasaws killed Frenchmen on sight. That year, a Virginian, Abraham Wood, commissioned explorer John Needham to visit the Cherokees west of the Appalachian Mountains in what is now Tennessee. John Needham visited the Cherokees twice, and he was murdered by them. His servant Gabriel Arthur faced being burned alive so bravely that his captors let him live.

In 1730, Alexander Cuming of North Carolina led an expedition across the Appalachians to make the acquaintance with the Cherokees of the Great Valley. He impressed the Native Americans with his boldness and eloquence, as well as his numerous weapons, and the chiefs agreed to affiliate themselves with England. Cuming took Cherokee representatives to England, where they were well treated. Among them was Attakullakulla (meaning "Little Carpenter"), who, upon returning home, became a great diplomat who several times prevented bloodshed.

In 1736, the French, having nearly wiped out the Natchez tribe, invaded West Tennessee with intention of eradicating the Chickasaws. The Chickasaws were forewarned by English traders and decisively defeated the French invaders. The French built Fort Assumption where Memphis now stands, as part of their effort to control the Chickasaws. They failed. In another war in 1752, the Chickasaws again beat the French. These victories of the Chickasaws were important for all the Native Americans in Tennessee, because a 1738 epidemic had killed about 50 percent of the Cherokees, leaving them too weak to guarantee the safety of their neighbors. From that time on, Cherokee politics were chaotic, with different chiefs gaining ascendancy with very different views at various times, making Cherokee policies wildly swing from one view to another.

During the Revolutionary War (1775–1783), some Cherokees allied themselves with Shawnees, Creeks, and white outlaws, and tried to retake East Tennessee. They were defeated by American forces under the command of Colonel Evan Shelby, who drove them into West Tennessee. In 1794, the Native Americans of Tennessee united in a war against the United States and were utterly de-

feated; they became subject to American rule. These battles had been over possession of land, and in 1794, the land belonged to the United States. On 1 July 1796, Tennessee became the sixteenth state of the United States, taking its name from Tenasie, the name of a Cherokee village.

Civil War

In the 1850s, the matter of slavery was a source of much conflict in Tennessee. The settlers in the east wanted it outlawed. Slave owners ignored laws regulating slavery and turned West Tennessee into a vast land of plantations worked by African American slaves. Literacy was forbidden to the slaves, and they were not even allowed to worship God, although they often did in secret. Newspapers and politicians campaigned against slavery in Tennessee, but others defended slavery with passion.

On 9 February 1861, Tennessee held a plebiscite on the matter of secession, with the results favoring remaining in the Union 69,387 to 57,798. The governor of Tennessee, Isham G. Harris, refused to accept the results and committed Tennessee to the Confederacy. He organized another plebiscite on whether Tennessee should become an independent state, with independence winning 104,913 to 47,238. He declared that the result meant Tennessee should join the Confederacy. The Confederacy made its intentions clear by executing people accused of sympathizing with the Union. Over 135,000 Tennesseans joined the Confederate army; over 70,000 joined the Union army, with 20,000 free blacks and escaped slaves. The surprise attack at Shiloh on 6–7 April 1862 seemed to give the Confederacy the upper hand in Tennessee, but the Union troops outfought their attackers. After the Stone's River Battle (near Murfreesboro) from 31 December 1862–2 January 1863, the Union dominated Tennessee. Over 400 battles were fought in Tennessee during the Civil War. The lands of Middle and West Tennessee were scourged. Fields became massive grounds of corpses, farms were destroyed, trees were denuded, and Tennessean refugees clogged roads by the thousands.

On 24 July 1866, Tennessee, which had been the last state to join the Confederacy, became the first former Confederate state to rejoin the United States. Prior to readmission, on 25 February 1865, Tennessee passed an amendment to its constitution outlawing slavery. Schools were soon accepting African Americans as well as whites and Native Americans, but in December 1866, the Ku Klux Klan was founded at Pulaski, Tennessee. Directed by "Grand Cyclops" Nathan Bedford Forrest, it murdered African Americans and white people who were sympathetic to them, raped white female schoolteachers for teaching African Americans, burned schools, and terrified voters, in resistance to Reconstruction.

Segregated Society

By 1900, Tennessee had a population of 2,020,616. It was racially segregated. In a decades-long effort to deny education to African Americans, the state managed to create an illiteracy rate among whites and blacks that was the third worst in the nation. Under the direction of Governor Malcolm R. Patterson (1907–1911), in 1909, the state enacted a general education bill.

When the United States entered World War I (1914–1918), thousands of Tennesseans volunteered, and Tennessee contributed the greatest American hero of the war, Sergeant Alvin York from Fentress County in northern Middle Tennessee. In 1918, the soft-spoken farmer and his small squad captured 223 Germans in the Argonne Forest; the sight of a few Americans leading hundreds of captured Germans to American lines was said to have been astonishing.

By 1920, the state population was 2,337,885. On 18 August of that year Tennessee ratified the Twenty-First Amendment of the Constitution of the United States, which gave women the vote. In 1923, Governor Austin Peay reorganized state government, eliminating hundreds of patronage positions, while consolidating government enterprises into eight departments. In 1925, the infamous Scopes "Monkey Trial" was held in Dayton, Tennessee. A new state law said that evolution could not be taught in Tennessee schools, but John Scopes taught it anyway and was charged with violating the law. Two outsiders came to try the case, atheist Clarence Darrow for the defense and three-time presidential candidate William Jennings Bryant for the prosecution. The trial was broadcast to the rest of the country by radio, and when Scopes was convicted and fined, the impression left was that Tennessee was home to ignorance and bigotry enforced by law, an image it had not completely escaped even at the turn of the twenty-first century. A man who did much to counter the image was statesman Cordell Hull, from Overton County, west of Fentress, in northern Middle Tennessee. He served in the U.S. House of Representatives and Senate and was Franklin Roosevelt's secretary of state. He helped create the "Good Neighbor Policy" that helped unify the nations of the New World, and he was important to the development of the United Nations. He received the 1945 Nobel Peace Prize for his work.

Civil Rights

By 1950, Tennessee's population was 55 percent urban. The cities controlled most of the state's politics, and they were becoming more cosmopolitan. Getting a bit of a head start in desegregating schools, the University of Tennessee admitted four African Americans to its graduate school in 1952. On the other hand, Frank Clement was elected governor on the "race platform," insisting that there would be no racial integration in Tennessee. Many other politicians would "play the race card" during the 1950s and 1960s, and many of these politicians would change their minds as Clement would as the civil rights movement changed the way politics were conducted. Memphis State University began desegregating in 1955, after the United States Supreme Court ruling in 1954 that

segregating the races was unconstitutional. In 1956, Clement called out the National Guard to enforce desegregation of schools in Clinton. Even so, schools elsewhere here bombed or forced to close by white supremacists.

By 1959, African Americans were staging well-organized nonviolent protests in NASHVILLE in an effort to have stores and restaurants desegregate. Meanwhile, the U.S. government, under a 1957 civil rights law, sued Democratic Party local organizations for their exclusion of African Americans from voting and holding office. Slowly, DESEGREGATION took hold in Tennessee; it took until 1965 for Jackson to begin desegregating its restaurants. In 1968, in Memphis, sanitation workers went on strike and Martin Luther King Jr., the preeminent figure in the CIVIL RIGHTS MOVEMENT, came to the city to help with negotiations. On 4 April 1968, King was shot to death by James Earl Ray.

Modern Era

In the 1970s, Tennessee made a remarkable turnaround in its image. With the election of Winfield Dunn as governor in 1971, the state for the first time since Reconstruction had a Republican governor and two Republican senators. This notable shift in political fortunes marked the coming of the two-party system to Tennessee, which had a positive effect on the politics and society of the state. If Democrats were to hold on to power, they needed African Americans as new allies. In 1974, the state's first African American congressman, Harold Ford of Memphis, was elected. The Democrats remained dominant in the state, but the competition with Republicans was lively and encouraged the participation of even those who had been disenfranchised, poor whites as well as African Americans, as recently as 1965.

Among the most notable politicians of the 1980s and 1990s was Albert Gore Jr., son of a powerful United States Senator, and widely expected to be a powerful politician himself. In 1988 and 1992, he ran for the presidential nomination of the Democratic Party, and he served from 1993–2001 as vice president of the United States under his longtime friend President Bill Clinton. His cosmopolitan views and his work for environmental causes helped to change how outsiders viewed Tennesseans.

By 2000, Tennessee's population was just under 5,500,000, an increase from 1990's 4,896,641. Although the urban population was larger than the rural one, there were 89,000 farms in Tennessee. The TVA had doubled the amount of open water in Tennessee from 1930 to 1960, and the several artificial lakes and streams became prime attractions for recreation in the 1990s; the state also had some of the most beautiful woodlands in the world. Memphis became a regional center for the arts, as well as a prime retail center for northern Mississippi, in addition to Tennessee; Nashville developed the potential for its music industry to be a magnet for tourists, and by the 1990s many a young musician or composer yearned to live there.

BIBLIOGRAPHY

Alderson, William T., and Robert H. White. *A Guide to the Study and Reading of Tennessee History*. Nashville: Tennessee Historical Commission, 1959.

Corlew, Robert E. Revised by Stanley J. Folmsbee and Enoch Mitchell. *Tennessee: A Short History*. 2d edition Knoxville: University of Tennessee Press, 1981.

Dykeman, Wilma. *Tennessee: A Bicentennial History*. New York: Norton, 1975.

Hull, Cordell, and Andrew H. T. Berding. *The Memoirs of Cordell Hull*. New York: Macmillan, 1948.

Kent, Deborah. *Tennessee*. New York: Grolier, 2001.

State of Tennessee home page. Available at http://www.state.tn.us.

Van West, Carroll. *Tennessee History: The Land, the People, and the Culture*. Knoxville: University of Tennessee Press, 1998. A wealth of information and opinion.

Vanderwood, Paul J. *Night Riders of Reelfoot Lake*. Memphis, Tenn.: Memphis State University Press, 1969.

Kirk H. Beetz

See also **Appalachia; Cherokee; Creek; Cumberland Gap; Iroquois; Shawnee.**

TENNESSEE, ARMY OF.

When General Braxton Bragg reorganized the Army of Mississippi on 20 November 1862 he named it the Army of Tennessee. After fighting at Stone's River, the army spent the summer campaigning in middle Tennessee. Aided by Virginia troops, the army won an outstanding victory at Chickamauga. After mounting an inconclusive siege at Chattanooga that led to defeat, the army retreated into northern Georgia. Leadership was in flux—William J. Hardee replaced Bragg; Joe Johnson replaced Hardee. Despite Johnson's rather successful efforts to slow Sherman's march toward Atlanta, Jefferson Davis replaced Johnson with John B. Hood. After several tough battles, the army left Atlanta and moved into Tennessee where it experienced defeats at Franklin and Nashville. Richard Taylor replaced Hood and retreated into Mississippi. After moving to the east to challenge Sherman, the army surrendered at the Battle of Bentonville.

BIBLIOGRAPHY

Daniel, Larry J. *Soldiering in the Army of Tennessee: A Portrait of Life in a Confederate Army*. Chapel Hill: University of North Carolina Press, 1991.

McPherson, James M. *What They Fought For, 1861–1865*. New York: Doubleday Anchor, 1994. A brilliant explanation of motivation, human nature, and military necessity.

———. *Ordeal by Fire: The Civil War and Reconstruction*. 3d ed. Boston: McGraw-Hill, 2001.

Donald K. Pickens

See also **Chickamauga, Battle of.**

TENNESSEE RIVER, formed by the confluence of the Holston River and the French Broad River, near Knoxville, Tennessee, follows a serpentine course into northern Alabama and from there northward to the Ohio River at Paducah, Kentucky. The length of the main stream is 652 miles, and the total drainage area is 40,569 square miles. Called for a time the Cherokee River, it was used extensively by Indians on war and hunting expeditions, especially by the Cherokees, some of whose towns were located along the branches of the river in southeast Tennessee. In the mid-eighteenth century, the Tennessee Valley played an important part in the Anglo-French rivalry for the control of the Old Southwest that culminated in the French and Indian War. The river was also an important route for migration of settlers into the Southwest after that war.

Use of the river for navigation was handicapped by the presence of serious obstructions, especially the Muscle and Colbert shoals at the "Great Bend" in northern Alabama. The problem of removing or obviating the obstructions to navigation has been a perennial one that has received spasmodic attention from the federal government as well as from the states of Tennessee and Alabama, including a grant of public lands to Alabama in 1828 for the construction of a canal, and several subsequent surveys and appropriations. In the twentieth century, discussion of the river shifted from navigation to power production and flood control. During World War I, construction of the Wilson Dam and nitrate plants at the Muscle Shoals initiated a nationwide controversy over the question of public or private ownership and operation of power facilities. Since the New Deal created the TENNESSEE VALLEY AUTHORITY (TVA) in 1933, the river has been the subject of an extensive program involving navigation and flood control, fertilizer experimentation, and the production and sale of electric power, all of which fueled the social and economic transformation of the Tennessee Valley. The river has been made into a chain of reservoirs, or lakes, held back by nine major dams. As a result of TVA improvements, freight traffic on the Tennessee, which had been one million tons in 1933, had reached twenty-seven million tons per year by the early 1970s. By 1985, the 234-mile Tenn-Tom waterway opened, connecting the river's Pickwick Lake to the Tombigbee River at Demopolis, Alabama.

BIBLIOGRAPHY

Colignon, Richard A. *Power Plays: Critical Events in the Institutionalization of the Tennessee Valley Authority*. Albany: State University of New York Press, 1997.

Davidson, Donald. *Tennessee: The Old River, Frontier to Secession*. Knoxville: University of Tennessee Press, 1978.

Droze, Wilmon Henry. *High Dams and Slack Waters: TVA Rebuilds a River*. Baton Rouge: Louisiana State University Press, 1965.

S. J. Folmsbee/H. S.

See also **River Navigation; Rivers;** *and vol. 9:* **Power.**

TENNESSEE VALLEY AUTHORITY.

The Tennessee Valley Authority (TVA), a federal corporation responsible for power generation in the Tennessee Valley, serves roughly 8.3 million people through 158 municipal and cooperative power distributors. TVA furnishes power to an 80,000-square-mile area, including the state of Tennessee and parts of Kentucky, Virginia, North Carolina, Georgia, Alabama, and Mississippi, thus making the corporation one of America's largest electrical power producers.

Born of President Franklin D. Roosevelt's innovative solution to help stimulate the area's economy during the Great Depression, the TVA development began after World War I (1914–1918). A government-owned dam and nitrate-producing facility at Muscle Shoals, on the Tennessee River in northwestern Alabama, became the seedling of the audacious experiment. Nebraska Senator George W. Norris hoped at the time to build more dams similar to the Wilson Dam at Muscle Shoals, bringing public control to the Tennessee River. Almost single-handedly, Norris held the dam in government ownership until President Roosevelt's vision expanded it into a broader concept of multipurpose development and regional planning. On 18 May 1933, Congress responded to Roosevelt's prodding and enacted the Tennessee Valley Act.

TVA was to be more than a flood control and power agency. It was seen as having a wide mandate for economic development, recreation, reforestation, and the production of fertilizer. But the agency was in sad shape at its start. The best timber had already been cut, the land had been farmed too long, and crop yields were declining.

Tennessee Valley Authority. Created by President Franklin Roosevelt to provide low-cost electricity and to stimulate economic development in the Tennessee Valley region during the Great Depression, the TVA also ran demonstration farms, such as the one shown here, to instruct farmers on the optimal use of fertilizers. In the photo, the healthy crops were treated with phosphate, while the barren crops were left untreated.
© FRANKLIN DELANO ROOSEVELT LIBRARY

Controversy also surrounded TVA. Private utilities fought the agency's power policies, and an internal feud between Chairman Arthur Morgan and directors David Lilienthal and Harcourt Morgan unsettled TVA's direction until 1938.

Nevertheless, the agency pushed forward. By 1941, it operated eleven dams with six more under construction, and it was selling low-cost electric power to 500,000 consumers throughout six states. TVA technicians developed fertilizers, and 25,000 demonstration farms taught local citizens the benefits of more scientific farming. Additionally, the agency helped replant forests, controlled forest fires, and improved habitat for wildlife. During World War II (1939–1945), 70 percent of TVA power went to defense industries, among them the Oak Ridge atomic project. At the war's end, TVA had completed a 652-mile navigation channel, becoming the largest electricity supplier in the United States.

Attacked for being too radical, TVA also found itself criticized for being too conciliatory to established interests and ideas. Director Lilienthal claimed that TVA practiced "grassroots democracy" by reaching out in a massive educational effort to involve the rural population of the valley. However, critics saw mostly manipulation in this approach.

The 1960s saw unprecedented growth in the Tennessee Valley. At the same time, TVA began building nuclear plants as a new source of power. The agency survived reproach from both conservatives and environmentalists and, by the early 1970s, claimed an impressive record. In 1972, an estimated $395 million in flood damages had been averted by TVA dams. Power revenues came to $642 million, of which TVA returned $75 million to the U.S. Treasury. Along with industrial customers, 2 million residential consumers used TVA power.

The TVA manages an integrated, technically advanced system of dams, locks, and reservoirs in the Tennessee River watershed. The balanced system facilitates navigation, controls flooding, and provides hydropower to benefit users. As of 2002, it included three nuclear generating plants, eleven coal-fired plants, twenty-nine hydraulic dams, five combustion turbine plants, a pumped-storage plant, and roughly 17,000 miles of transmission lines, making the TVA the largest public power system in the nation. TVA's generation mix consisted of 63 percent coal, 31 percent nuclear, and 6 percent hydroelectric.

The agency serves 158 local municipal and cooperative power distributors that deliver power to homes and businesses within the seven-state area. Also involving itself in technical assistance to communities and industries, TVA conducts economic research and analysis, industrial research, and conceptual site engineering and architectural services. It also provides technical and financial support to small and minority-owned businesses as well as working with regional industrial development associations to recruit new industry and develop strategies for creating jobs.

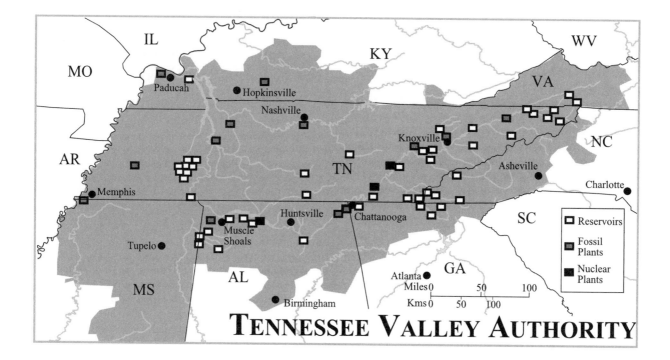

TENNESSEE VALLEY AUTHORITY

Legend:
□ Reservoirs
▧ Fossil Plants
■ Nuclear Plants

Preserving wildlife habitat, TVA oversees more than 122,000 acres of public land designated for natural-resource management. Forty percent of it is administered by other agencies, while the remainder falls under TVA management. The agency launched the Natural Heritage Project in 1976, with the help of the Nature Conservancy, to analyze and manage biodiversity on TVA lands and to improve compliance with federal environmental regulations. The project monitors threatened and endangered plant and animal species in the TVA service area. Since its beginnings, the Natural Heritage Project has supplied environmental data on TVA activities ranging from transmission-line construction to economic development.

TVA has also developed a land-use system of 10,700 acres classified as TVA Natural Areas. The specified sites are designated as Habitat Protection Areas, Small Wild Areas, Ecological Study Areas, or Wildlife Observation Areas and include limitations on activities that could endanger important natural features.

Throughout the Tennessee Valley, TVA operates roughly 100 public recreation facilities, including campgrounds, day-use areas, and boat-launching ramps.

BIBLIOGRAPHY

Callahan, North. *TVA: Bridge Over Troubled Waters.* South Brunswick, N.J.: A. S. Barnes, 1980.

Chandler, William U. *The Myth of TVA: Conservation and Development in the Tennessee Valley, 1933–1983.* Cambridge, Mass.: Ballinger, 1984.

Conkin, Paul K., and Erwin C. Hargrove. *TVA : Fifty Years of Grass-Roots Bureaucracy.* Chicago: University of Illinois Press, 1983.

Creese, Walter L. *TVA's Public Planning: The Vision, The Reality.* Knoxville: The University of Tennessee Press, 1990.

Tennessee Valley Authority Web Site. Home page at http://www.tva.com/.

Kym O'Connell-Todd

See also **New Deal;** *and vol. 9:* **Power.**

TENNIS, or more properly, lawn tennis, derives from the ancient game of court tennis. It was introduced in the United States shortly after Major Walter Clopton Wingfield demonstrated a game he called Sphairistike at a garden party in Nantclwyd, Wales, in December 1873. Formerly, some historians believed that Wingfield's game of Sphairistike, played on an hourglass-shaped court, was first brought to America by way of Bermuda. In 1875 Mary Ewing Outerbridge, an American, obtained a set of tennis equipment from British officers stationed there and her brother, A. Emilius Outerbridge, set up a court on the grounds of the Staten Island Cricket and Baseball Club in New York City, the home of the first national tournament in September 1880. However, Outerbridge was preceded by Dr. James Dwight (often called the father of American lawn tennis) and F. R. Sears Jr., who played the first tennis match in the United States at Nahant, Massachusetts, in August 1874. The present scoring system of 15, 30, 40, games, and sets became official at the first Wimbledon (England) Championship in 1877. In 1881, the newly formed U.S. National Lawn Tennis Association (USNLTA) (the "National" was dropped in 1920, the "Lawn" in 1975) hosted the first official tennis championship in the United States at the Newport Casino in Rhode Island. Richard D. Sears of Boston won the tournament, a feat he repeated annually through 1887.

From the Late Nineteenth to the Mid-Twentieth Century

Although tennis was initially confined mainly to the Northeast, by the 1880s and 1890s it was spreading throughout the United States, with tournaments and clubs organized in Cincinnati, Atlanta, New Orleans, Seattle, San Francisco, and Chicago, which was awarded the national doubles championships in 1893 as part of the World's Columbian Exposition there. The first Davis Cup matches, between the United States and Great Britain, were held at the Longwood Cricket Club in Brookline, Massachusetts, in 1900. The cup donor, Dwight F. Davis, was a native of St. Louis but was at Harvard when he put up the cup, as were Malcolm Whitman and Holcombe Ward, also members of the first Davis Cup team. At that time, there were 44 tennis clubs in the United States; by 1908, there were 115. Like golf, tennis was most popular among America's economic and cultural elite. African Americans, Jews, and recent immigrants were usually excluded from the private clubs where tennis thrived.

From its introduction in the United States, tennis greatly appealed to both sexes, yet women were initially forbidden from playing in public tournaments. American clubs, like those in Europe, often assigned female players different venues and imposed confining styles of dress that limited their range of motion. Nevertheless, the United States has consistently produced some of the strongest women players in tennis history. The English-born Californian May Sutton was national champion in 1904, and in 1905 became the first American to win at Wimbledon. Hazel Hotchkiss' volleying style of attack allowed her to win forty-three national titles. She was also the donor of the Wightman Cup, sought annually since 1923 by British and American women's teams. Fifty years later, Billie Jean King, winner of four U.S. titles, would defeat the aging Bobby Riggs in what was called the Battle of the Sexes, a landmark event in the histories of both tennis and feminism.

In 1916 the USNLTA funded a series of programs and clinics to develop the skills of budding tennis players and promote the sport on a wider scale. As a result, the following decades saw numerous American players receive worldwide acclaim. Over the course of his career, William T. Tilden II won seven U.S. titles and three Wimbledon championships. Beginning in 1923, Helen Wills won the first of seven U.S. women's championships and ultimately triumphed at Wimbledon for a record eight times. Her match at Cannes in 1926 with Suzanne Leglen, six-time Wimbledon champion, was the most celebrated women's contest in the history of the game. A decade later Don Budge, the first player to complete the coveted "grand slam" by winning at Wimbledon, the U.S. Open, the French Open, and the Australian Open, regained the Davis Cup for the United States in 1937 after

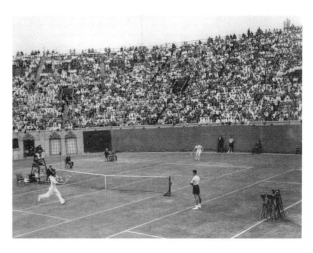

Grand Slam Winner. In 1938 Don Budge (in near court, opposite Fred Perry) became the first person to win a tennis Grand Slam, taking the titles of the Australian Open, French Open, Wimbledon, and the U.S. Open in the same year.
© CORBIS

a period of French and English domination. Following World War II, the development of young tennis players continued under the auspices of the Tennis Educational Association. School physical education instructors were trained to teach tennis, while inner-city programs attempted to spread tennis to underprivileged youths. At the same time, the American Tennis Association became an outlet for aspiring African American players, including Althea Gibson, who in 1950 became the first African American to participate in the U.S. Open.

Radical Innovations

The late 1960s saw revolutionary changes in tennis, both in the United States and worldwide. Until that time, the sport's most prestigious competitions were open exclusively to amateurs. However, in 1968 the International Lawn Tennis Federation sanctioned open tournaments, permitting amateurs to compete against professionals. This shift had a profound impact on both professional and amateur tennis. New promoters and commercial sponsors came into the game and the schedule of tournaments was radically revised and enlarged. The prize money available for professional players increased dramatically, with tennis superstars such as Rod Laver, Jimmy Connors, Arthur Ashe, Billie Jean King, and Chris Evert earning hundreds of thousands of dollars a year by the mid-1970s. Top players no longer struggled to earn a living under the rules governing amateur status; as a result, the mean age of competitive players rose sharply, as many found they could earn more playing tennis than in other careers. Matches were also increasingly televised, especially after 1970, when the introduction of the "sudden death" tiebreaker made it possible to control the length of matches.

Improvements in racket technology further revolutionized the sport of tennis during the 1960s and 1970s. Steel, aluminum, and graphite rackets soon replaced the traditional wooden designs. Over the next two decades, wood and metal rackets gave way to stronger and lighter synthetic materials, while conventional head sizes disappeared in favor of intermediate and oversized racket heads, first introduced by Prince Manufacturing in 1976. Competitive techniques and styles of play were greatly affected by the new racket technology. The two-handed backhand, popularized during the 1970s, proved ideally suited to the new, larger racket heads and became a staple of the competitive game. The new racket technology was clearly responsible for a greater reliance on power in both men's and women's competitive tennis throughout the 1990s.

U.S. Dominance

During the last three decades of the twentieth century, the United States remained the single most important source of world-class players. Between 1974 and 1999, Jimmy Connors, John McEnroe, Jim Courier, Pete Sampras, and Andre Agassi held the world's top men's ranking for a combined sixteen years. In the same period, Americans Billie Jean King, Chris Evert, Monica Seles, and Lindsay Davenport held the top women's ranking in a total of ten years, with Martina Navratilova, a naturalized American, adding another seven. Since the late 1970s, when an estimated thirty-two to thirty-four million Americans played tennis, the popularity of the sport has been in decline. Although interest in tennis experienced a resurgence during the early 1990s, by the decade's end only 17.5 million Americans were actually playing the sport. Particularly underrepresented have been Americans of color, despite the success and influence of such players as Michael Chang and Venus and Serena Williams. Nevertheless, tennis remains a multibillion-dollar industry worldwide, with top tournaments frequently hosting record crowds.

BIBLIOGRAPHY

Collins, Bud, and Zander Hollander, eds. *Bud Collins' Modern Encyclopedia of Tennis*. Farmington Hills, Mich.: Gale, 1994.

Gillmeister, Heiner. *Tennis: A Cultural History*. New York: New York University Press, 1998.

Parsons, John. *The Ultimate Encyclopedia of Tennis: The Definitive Illustrated Guide to World Tennis*. London: Carlton Books, 1998.

Phillips, Caryl. *The Right Set: A Tennis Anthology*. New York: Vintage, 1999.

Sports Illustrated 2002 Sports Almanac. New York: Bishop Books, 2001.

Allison Danzig
David W. Galenson
John M. Kinder

See also **Sports.**

TENURE OF OFFICE ACT, passed by Congress in 1867 over President Andrew Johnson's veto, was designed to restrict greatly Johnson's appointing and removing power. When Johnson attempted to remove Secretary of War Edwin M. Stanton, the Radical Republican Congress proceeded with its long-laid plans for the impeachment and trial of the president. As Stanton was not a Johnson appointee, the act could not be applied to him. Passed during, and as part of, the struggle between Johnson and Congress over Reconstruction, sections of the act were repealed early in Ulysses S. Grant's first administration; the rest of the act was repealed 5 March 1887.

BIBLIOGRAPHY

Benedict, Michael Les. *A Compromise of Principle: Congressional Republicans and Reconstruction, 1863–1869*. New York: Norton, 1974.

Kutler, Stanley I. *Judicial Power and Reconstruction*. Chicago: University of Chicago Press, 1968.

McKittrick, Eric L. *Andrew Johnson and Reconstruction*. Chicago: University of Chicago Press, 1960.

Thomas, Benjamin P., and Harold M. Hyman. *Stanton: The Life and Times of Lincoln's Secretary of War*. New York: Knopf, 1962.

Willard H. Smith / A. G.

See also **Impeachment Trial of Samuel Chase; Liberal Republican Party; Stalwarts; Wade-Davis Bill.**

TERMINATION POLICY. After World War II, pressure in Congress mounted to reduce Washington's authority in the West, end the reservation system, and liquidate the government's responsibilities to Indians. In 1953 the House of Representatives passed Resolution 108, proposing an end to federal services for thirteen tribes deemed ready to handle their own affairs. The same year, Public Law 280 transferred jurisdiction over tribal lands to state and local governments in five states. Within a decade Congress terminated federal services to more than sixty groups, including the Menominees of Wisconsin and the Klamaths of Oregon, despite intense opposition by Indians. The effects of the laws on the Menominees and the Klamaths were disastrous, forcing many members of the tribes onto public assistance rolls. President John F. Kennedy halted further termination in 1961, and Presidents Lyndon B. Johnson and Richard M. Nixon replaced termination with a policy of encouraging Indian self-determination with continuing government assistance and services. After years of struggle the Menominees and Klamaths succeeded in having their tribal status restored in 1973 and 1986, respectively.

BIBLIOGRAPHY

Fixico, Donald Lee. *Termination and Relocation: Federal Indian Policy, 1945–1960*. Albuquerque: University of New Mexico Press, 1986.

Peroff, Nicholas C. *Menominee Drums: Tribal Termination and Restoration, 1954–1974.* Norman: University of Oklahoma Press, 1982.

Frank Rzeczkowski

See also **Bureau of Indian Affairs.**

TERRITORIAL GOVERNMENTS.

The Constitution empowers Congress to govern the territory of the United States and to admit new states into the Union. However, territorial governments in the United States predate the Constitution. The Congress of the Confederation enacted the Northwest Ordinance of 1787 for the region north of the Ohio River and westward to the Mississippi. Under its terms the territories could look forward to eventual statehood on terms of equality with the original states. As modified by congressional enactments after the adoption of the Constitution in 1789, the Ordinance set forth the general framework of government for the territories that ultimately achieved statehood, beginning with Tennessee in 1796 and ending, most recently, with Alaska and Hawaii in 1959.

The Ordinance provided for three stages of government. Congress established each territorial government by way of an organic act, a federal law serving as a temporary constitution. In the initial or "district" stage, the president, with the consent of the Senate, appointed a governor, a secretary, and three judges. The governor served as head of the militia and superintendent of Indian affairs. He was authorized to establish townships and counties, appoint their officials, and, in conjunction with the judges, adopt laws for the territory.

The second stage began when the territory attained a population of at least 5,000 free adult males. The inhabitants could then establish a legislature consisting of a house of representatives elected for two years and a legislative council appointed by the president to serve for five years. The house and council would choose a nonvoting delegate to Congress. The governor enjoyed the authority to convene, adjourn, and dissolve the legislature, and could exercise a veto over legislative enactments. Congress retained the power to nullify the acts of territorial legislatures.

Finally, when the total population of a territory reached 60,000, it could petition Congress for admission into the Union. Admission was not automatic; indeed, the process often became entangled in struggles between partisan or sectional interests. For example, in the decades preceding the Civil War, Congress balanced the admission of each free state with the admission of a slave state. Once it decided to admit a territory, Congress would pass an enabling act authorizing the people of the territory to adopt a permanent state constitution and government.

Over the course of the nineteenth century Congress further modified the pattern set forth in the Ordinance. For instance, in later territories the governor, secretary, and judges were appointed for four years, and the electorate chose the members of the council and the nonvoting congressional delegate, who served for two-year terms. The governor shared appointive power with the council, and a two-thirds vote of the legislature could override his veto. The legislature apportioned itself, fixed the qualifications for suffrage, and organized judicial districts. Most local officials were elected. Legislative and gubernatorial acts were still subject to the approval of Congress. Judicial power was placed in supreme, superior, district, probate, and justice-of-the-peace courts.

The turn of the twentieth century ushered in a new period in territorial governance. In 1898, the United States won the Spanish-American War and took sovereignty over the Philippines, Puerto Rico, and Guam. It established governments in these territories that borrowed elements from the Ordinance, but varied widely according to local circumstances. For instance, under Puerto Rico's Organic Act, passed by Congress in 1900, the president appointed the governor and legislative council, while the electorate chose the members of a lower legislative chamber. Yet in Guam, Congress did not even pass an organic act until 1950; until then, the navy administered the territory.

The acquisition of these islands triggered a nationwide debate over whether Congress had an obligation to admit all U.S. territories into statehood eventually, or whether it could govern some territories as colonies indefinitely. Opposition to statehood for the former Spanish colonies was based in part on the view that their inhabitants were too different, racially and culturally, from the American mainstream. In the rhetoric of the time, the question was whether the Constitution "followed the flag" to the new territories. In the INSULAR CASES of 1901, the U.S. Supreme Court held that it did not. Distinguishing for the first time between incorporated and unincorporated territories, the Court explained that all territories acquired prior to 1898 (along with Hawaii, which became a U.S. territory in 1898) had been incorporated into the United States, while the new territories remained unincorporated. According to the Court, the decision whether to incorporate a territory was entirely up to Congress.

The incorporated/unincorporated distinction had two consequences. First, unincorporated territories were not considered to be on a path to statehood. Second, in legislating for incorporated territories, Congress was bound by all constitutional provisions not obviously inapplicable, but in the unincorporated territories, Congress was bound to observe only the "fundamental" guarantees of the Constitution. Neither the Court nor Congress attempted to specify precisely what these fundamental guarantees included. Later, the Supreme Court decided that such guarantees as the right to a trial by jury and an indictment by grand jury were not among these fundamental rights, but most provisions of the Bill of Rights were held applicable.

At the turn of the twenty-first century, the U.S. had five territories, none of which was incorporated: the Commonwealth of Puerto Rico, the Commonwealth of the

Northern Mariana Islands (CNMI), the U.S. Virgin Islands, Guam, and American Samoa. Although federal laws generally apply in the territories, and their inhabitants are U.S. citizens (or, in American Samoa, U.S. nationals), they cannot vote in presidential elections and do not have senators or representatives in the federal government. Instead, they elect nonvoting delegates to Congress, except for the CNMI, which simply sends a representative to Washington, D.C. The Departments of War, State, Interior, and the Navy have all played a role in the administration of territories. In 1873, Congress conferred upon the Department of the Interior statutory jurisdiction over territorial governments, but after 1898, Guam was assigned to the Navy Department, and the Philippines and Puerto Rico to the War Department. In 1934 President Franklin D. Roosevelt created by executive order the Division of Territories and Island Possessions within the Department of the Interior. In 1950 this division became the Office of Territories. In the early 2000s it was known as the Office of Insular Affairs.

BIBLIOGRAPHY

Eblen, Jack Ericson. *The First and Second United States Empires: Governors and Territorial Government, 1784–1912.* Pittsburgh, Pa.: University of Pittsburgh Press, 1968.

Farrand, Max. *The Legislation of Congress for the Government of the Organized Territories of the United States, 1789–1895.* Newark, N.J.: Baker, 1896.

Leibowitz, Arnold H. *Defining Status: A Comprehensive Analysis of United States Territorial Relations.* Dordrecht, Netherlands: Nijhoff, 1989.

Van Cleve, Ruth G. *The Office of Territorial Affairs.* New York: Praeger, 1974.

Christina Duffy Burnett

See also **Territories of the United States.**

TERRITORIAL SEA is a belt of coastal waters subject to the territorial jurisdiction of a coastal state. The territorial jurisdiction of the coastal state extends to the territorial sea, subject to certain obligations deriving from international law; the most significant of which is the right of innocent passage by foreign ships. The distinction between the territorial sea, in effect an extension of exclusive coastal state sovereignty over its land mass and the high seas, a global commons beyond the reach of any state's jurisdiction, dates at least to the early eighteenth century in Europe.

A limit to the territorial sea of three nautical miles from the coast was accepted by many countries until the latter part of the twentieth century, including by the United States, which claimed a three-mile territorial sea dating from the beginning of the republic. A United Nations–sponsored conference in 1958 adopted four major multilateral agreements on the law of the sea, but failed to secure an international agreement on a compromise limit to the territorial sea. The United States, along with other maritime powers such as the United Kingdom, Japan, and the Netherlands, argued for the traditional three-mile limit so as to preclude coastal-state encroachments into the navigational freedoms of the high seas. A second UN conference convened in 1960 was similarly unsuccessful. The Third United Conference on the Law of the Sea, initiated in 1973, adopted a major new multilateral convention in Montego Bay, Jamaica, in 1982. That agreement confirmed the emerging trend toward a twelve-mile limit. Although the United States is not a party to the 1982 convention, President Reagan in December 1988 claimed a twelve-mile territorial sea on behalf of the United States.

According to the Montego Bay convention, which has emerged as the international standard even for those states not party to it, measurement of the territorial sea from convoluted shorelines may be made from baselines connecting headlands. Baselines are also used for bays and estuaries with headlands not over twenty-four miles apart, between outer points of coastal inland chains that enclose internal waters, and for historic bays to which territorial claims have been established by long and uncontested use.

The territorial sea is now but one component of a larger international legal regime governing the interests of coastal states in their adjacent waters. The United States, like many states, claims limited jurisdiction in a "contiguous zone" of twelve additional miles beyond the territorial sea to enforce customs, fiscal, immigration, and sanitary laws, and to punish violations of its laws committed in its territory or territorial sea. U.S. courts have supported the arrest of smugglers hovering beyond territorial waters with the intent to violate customs laws. Legislation authorizing a four-league customs-enforcement zone was protested by other countries, but during Prohibition several countries agreed by treaty to arrests within a one-hour sailing distance from shore.

Many countries, following President Harry S. Truman's proclamation in 1945, have claimed jurisdiction over continental shelves extending off their coasts. This form of jurisdiction extends to the seabed and not the water column above it, primarily for the purpose of exploiting resources such as oil and gas. The extent of the continental shelf may vary, depending on the shape of the sea floor. "Exclusive economic zones," which govern the use of the water column primarily for the purposes of fishing, may extend up to 200 nautical miles from a coastal state's baseline. In 1983 President Reagan claimed an exclusive economic zone of 200 nautical miles on behalf of the United States.

BIBLIOGRAPHY

Jessup, Philip C. *The Law of Territorial Waters and Maritime Jurisdiction.* New York: Jennings, 1927.

McDougal, Myres S., and William T. Burke. *The Public Order of the Oceans: A Contemporary International Law of the Sea.* New Haven, Conn.: New Haven Press, 1987.

David A. Wirth

See also **International Law.**

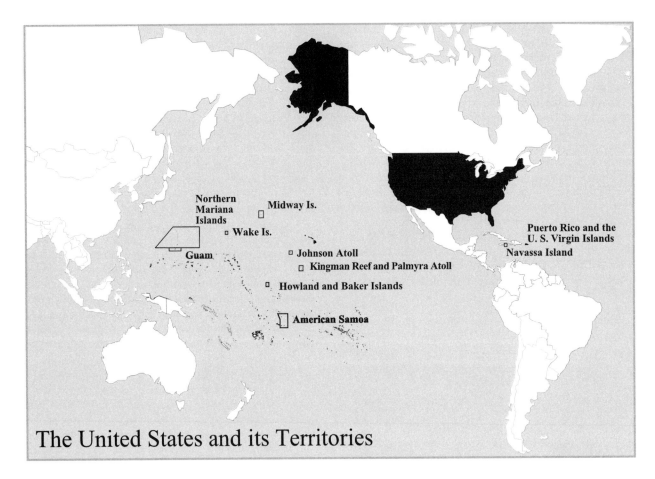

The United States and its Territories

TERRITORIES OF THE UNITED STATES are those dependencies and possessions over which the United States exercises jurisdiction. Until the turn of the nineteenth century, American experience was almost exclusively directed to the creation of territorial governments within the continental United States. The force of the Northwest Ordinance of 1787 set the precedent that territorial status was a step on the path to statehood, during which time residents of the territories maintained their citizenship and their protections under the Constitution. ALASKA and HAWAII, admitted in 1959, were the last of the territories to become states and the only exceptions to the pattern of contiguity with existing states and territories. Although new states were admitted, in the twentieth century the United States entered an era when the appropriate destiny of its territorial acquisitions was not necessarily statehood.

For the Spanish possessions ceded to the United States in 1898, the peace treaty did not include the promise of citizenship found in earlier treaties of annexation. Subject only to the limitations of the Constitution, Congress was free to determine the political status and civil rights of the inhabitants. In the INSULAR CASES, decided in 1901, the SUPREME COURT held that Congress could distinguish between incorporated and unincorporated territories and that the full guarantees and restraints of the Constitution need not be applied to the latter. Congress uniformly chose to treat its new acquisitions as unincorporated territories and so enjoyed a flexibility not present in the earlier pattern of territorial government.

In common with other dependencies PUERTO RICO was initially subject to military control, although this period was brief. Its inhabitants became U.S. citizens in 1917. Civil government with a gradual broadening of self-rule culminated in an act of Congress in 1950 that authorized Puerto Rico to formulate and adopt its own constitution, which came into effect in 1952. While commonwealth status is not the equivalent of statehood and did not terminate U.S. authority, the agreement that neither Congress nor the president should annul Puerto Rican legislation guaranteed the commonwealth the maximum degree of autonomy accorded to any of the territories.

The VIRGIN ISLANDS were purchased from Denmark in 1917 and citizenship was conferred in 1927. By the early 2000s, the islands had become a popular vacation destination.

GUAM did not attract significant attention until WORLD WAR II, after which it became the site of major military installations. Guamanians became citizens in 1950, framed and adopted a constitution in 1969, and since 1970 have elected their governor as well as members of the legislature.

American Samoa became a distinct entity in 1899 and remained under the administration of the U.S. Navy until 1951. In 1960 a constitution was formulated with Samoan participation and was then accepted and promulgated by the secretary of the Interior.

With the exception of Guam, islands of the Caroline, Marshall, and Mariana groups have been held by the United States as trust territories under the United Nations since 1947. The trust agreement charges the United States with the development of the islands toward "self-government or independence."

BIBLIOGRAPHY

Carr, Raymond. *Puerto Rico: A Colonial Experiment.* New York: New York University Press, 1984.

Stevens, Russell L. *Guam U.S.A.: Birth of a Territory.* Honolulu: Tongg Publishing, 1956.

Taylor, Bette A. *The Virgin Islands of the United States: A Descriptive and Historical Profile.* Washington, D.C.: Congressional Research Library, Library of Congress, 1988.

Robert L. Berg/A. G.

See also **Caroline Islands; Guantanamo Bay; Marshall Islands; Midway Islands; Paris, Treaty of (1898); Pribilof Islands; Samoa, American; Spain, Relations with; Spanish-American War; Teller Amendment.**

TERRORISM is a political tactic that uses threat or violence, usually against civilians, to frighten a target group into conceding to certain political demands.

The term "terrorism" was first used to describe the state terrorism practiced by the French revolutionaries of 1789–1795. Through kangaroo courts, executions by guillotine, and violent repression of political opponents, the revolutionaries tried to frighten the population into submission. Two great terrorist states of the twentieth century, Nazi Germany and Stalinist Russia, also practiced the threat and use of violence to keep their own citizens in line.

In the nineteenth century, terrorist tactics were adopted by individuals and groups that used assassinations, bombings, and kidnappings to undermine popular support for what the terrorists saw as unjust policies or tyrannical governments. Terrorist acts were first committed on a wide scale in the United States during the latter part of the nineteenth century. On 4 May 1886, an anarchist bomb killed eight policemen during a demonstration in Chicago's Haymarket Square, and on 16 September 1920, an anarchist bomb hidden in a wagon on Wall Street killed thirty people and seriously injured more than two hundred.

Although anarchist violence received the most newspaper coverage during this period, the white supremacist Ku Klux Klan (KKK) was the most important terrorist group in the United States from 1850 to the 1960s. The KKK used marches, beatings, and lynchings to intimidate

Terrorism in Alabama. Officials examine the destruction at the Sixteenth Street Baptist Church in Birmingham after a bomb killed four black girls attending Sunday school on 15 September 1963; the last conviction of the white supremacists responsible did not take place until nearly forty years later. AP/ WIDE WORLD PHOTOS

African Americans who wished to vote or otherwise participate in the political process.

Beginning in the late 1960s, extreme-left groups like the Weathermen engaged in kidnapping and bombings to protest the Vietnam War, while groups like the Symbionese Liberation Army engaged in armed actions against civilians or the police, hoping thereby to provoke a "people's revolution." These groups disappeared in the 1970s and 1980s only to be replaced by extreme-right terrorist organizations.

On 19 April 1995 a truck bomb exploded outside the Alfred P. Murrah federal building in Oklahoma City, destroying the building and killing 168 people. An act of domestic terrorism, the OKLAHOMA CITY BOMBING was the worst terrorist attack in U.S. history at the time. Testifying before the U.S. Senate in 1998, FBI Director Louis J. Freeh stated that, "The current domestic terrorist threat primarily comes from right-wing extremist groups, including radical paramilitary [militia] groups, Puerto Rican terrorist groups, and special interest groups."

The period after 1960 saw the rise of international terrorist attacks on Americans in the Middle East and in Latin America. The most dramatic instance of terrorism during this period was the 4 November 1979 attack by

Iranian students on the United States Embassy in Teheran, when sixty-six diplomats were held hostage until their release on 20 January 1981. According to the U.S. State Department, seventy-seven U.S. citizens were killed and 651 injured in international terrorist attacks between 1995 and 2000.

By the mid-1970s, international terrorists began to carry out operations on American soil. On 24 January 1975, the Puerto Rican Armed National Liberation Front killed four people when bombs exploded at the Fraunces Tavern in New York City. Eleven months later, on 29 December 1975, a bomb exploded in the TWA terminal at La Guardia Airport, killing eleven. No group ever claimed responsibility. The next major incident occurred on 26 February 1993, when a truck bomb exploded in the basement of New York's World Trade Center, killing six and wounding thousands. At his 1997 trial, bombing mastermind Ramzi Yousef stated, "I support terrorism so long as it was against the United States government and against Israel."

On 11 September 2001, in the most murderous terrorist attack American history had yet witnessed, almost three thousand people were killed. Nineteen Middle Eastern terrorists hijacked four airplanes; one crashed into the Pentagon, two destroyed the twin towers of New York City's World Trade Center, and one, possibly headed for the White House, crashed in a wooded area of Pennsylvania. Although the hijackers left no message, they were clearly motivated by hatred of the United States and by a desire to force a change in American policy in the Middle East.

The enormity of the attack pushed terrorism to the top of the American political agenda, with President George W. Bush declaring "war on terror" in his 20 September 2001 address to a joint session of Congress. President Bush predicted that this new war could last for years or even decades. The World Trade Center attack also led to a major change in the way the United States deals with terrorism. Before 11 September 2001, the United States followed a police-justice model whereby police and intelligence agencies identified and apprehended terrorists and then turned them over to the justice system. After those attacks, however, the Bush Administration adopted a preemptive-war model, whereby the United States intends to strike at individual terrorists or terrorist groups anywhere in the world and has threatened to use all means necessary, from special forces to massive military force, to attack what it identifies as "terrorist states" that support international terrorism.

The adoption of this model led President Bush in his 29 January 2002 State of the Union address to talk about Iran, Iraq, and North Korea together as an "axis of evil" and to threaten military action against Iraq. This statement led to much uneasiness among allies of the United States, who feared that the administration's war on terrorism signaled a move toward unilateralism in U.S. foreign policy and the destabilization of international relations.

BIBLIOGRAPHY

Harmon, Christopher. *Terrorism Today*. Portland, Ore.: Frank Cass, 2000.

Laqueur, Walter. *The New Terrorism: Fanaticism and the Arms of Mass Destruction*. New York: Oxford University Press, 2000.

Wilkinson, Paul, *Terrorism and the Liberal State*. New York: New York University Press, 1986.

Harvey G. Simmons

See also **9/11 Attack;** *and vol. 9:* **George W. Bush, Address to a Joint Session of Congress and the American People (As Delivered Before Congress), 20 September 2001.**

TEST LAWS.   Although the national government had used loyalty tests before the CIVIL WAR and RECONSTRUCTION, those eras witnessed an attempt to establish criteria of loyalty. Both Abraham Lincoln and Andrew Johnson considered loyalty oaths and disloyalty proceedings to be an integral part of war and reconstruction policy. Despite constant pressure from Congress, Lincoln maintained control of loyalty proceedings in the federal government. He did, however, have to compromise particularly in the case of the "IRONCLAD OATH." This oath required every federal officeholder to swear that he had "never voluntarily borne arms against the United States" or given any aid to those so doing or held any office "under any authority or pretended authority in hostility to the United States." Furthermore, each individual had to swear that he had "not yielded a voluntary support to any pretended government, authority, power, or constitution within the United States, hostile or inimical thereto. . . ." In 1864, Congress broadened the scope of the oath to include its own membership, which would effectively bar returning reconstructed state delegations. On 24 January 1865, Congress extended the oath to lawyers practicing in federal courts.

Under Johnson the issue of loyalty oaths became critical to Radical Republican policy. In Missouri and West Virginia, for example, adoption of the ironclad oath was fundamental to Radical Republican control. Both the federal and state oaths created serious constitutional difficulties, however. Opponents raised various constitutional challenges to the oaths, and in 1866, the Supreme Court heard *CUMMINGS V. MISSOURI* and *EX PARTE GARLAND*, the former a challenge to the state law and the latter a challenge to the federal test-oath act of 1865.

The decisions in these two cases had been preceded in December 1866 by *EX PARTE MILLIGAN*, which some Republicans had interpreted as dangerous to their ideas of reconstruction. The decisions rendered in the *Cummings* and *Garland* test-oath cases did not allay their suspicions. On 14 January 1867, the Supreme Court invalidated the test oath of 1865 because the oath provision was a bill of attainder and an ex post facto law.

Because of these decisions, Radical Republicans mounted various legislative proposals for curbing what they felt was abuse of judicial power. The Radical Republicans asserted the right of the legislative branch to decide "political" questions, which included the barring of "conspirators" and "traitors" from practicing in federal courts. Meanwhile, in 1867, the Court in *Mississippi v. Johnson* rejected an attempt to have it rule on the constitutionality of the congressional Reconstruction. It argued that an injunction in this case would interfere in the legitimate political functions of the legislative and executive branches. The Court's decision in 1868 to hear arguments in *Ex Parte McCardle* did lead to congressional action curtailing the Court's jurisdiction in all cases arising under the Habeas Corpus Act of 1867. The Court's acquiescence in this restriction of its power of judicial review and the acceptance of Congress's right in *Texas v. White* (1869) to guarantee republican governments in the states obviated any further threats to the Court at this time.

The test oath itself was modified in 1868 for national legislators, who now had only to swear to future loyalty. In 1871, Congress further modified the oath for all former Confederates to a promise of future loyalty. Finally, in 1884, Congress repealed the test-oath statutes.

BIBLIOGRAPHY

Foner, Eric. *A Short History of Reconstruction, 1863–1877.* New York: Harper and Row, 1990.

Kutler, Stanley I. *Judicial Power and Reconstruction.* Chicago: University of Chicago Press, 1968.

Sniderman, Paul M. *A Question of Loyalty.* Berkeley: University of California Press, 1981.

Joseph A. Dowling / A. E.

TET OFFENSIVE. In the spring of 1967, the communist Vietcong leadership began planning a nationwide offensive aimed at destroying the South Vietnamese government and forcing the Americans out of the Vietnam War. The communists were concerned about the growing U.S. military presence in Vietnam and their own mounting losses. The Vietcong believed that South Vietnam was ripe for revolution and saw the Saigon government as the weak link in the Allied war effort. The Politburo in Hanoi, in conjunction with leaders of the Vietcong, developed a plan for an all-out attack to take place during the Tet holiday at the end of January 1968. The communists expected that a general offensive, aimed primarily at South Vietnamese military and government installations, would encourage a majority of the citizens to turn against the Saigon government. The combination of military action and popular revolution would sweep away the Saigon regime, put in its place a procommunist slate of leaders, and thus force the United States to withdraw from the war. The communists christened their attack the Tong Cong Kich–Tong Khia Nghia, or TCK–TKN (General Offensive–General Uprising) plan.

The first phase of TCK–TKN began in the fall of 1967 with a series of attacks in western Vietnam near the borders with Laos and Cambodia. These attacks were designed to draw allied forces away from urban centers in the eastern part of the country, and gave the communists more opportunity to infiltrate troops and stockpile supplies near dozens of key cities and towns. The allied leaders detected signs of an imminent enemy offensive that would likely take place around the Tet holiday but concluded that the thrust would be limited to the three northern provinces of South Vietnam.

In the early morning hours of 30 January 1968, the communists in the mid-northern section of South Vietnam began their offensive one day early, apparently the result of a miscommunication with Hanoi. They attacked nine cities, including Da Nang, Nha Trang, Pleiku, and Kontum, which gave allied forces partial warning before the main offensive began in the early morning hours of the thirty-first. The communists, however, still managed to achieve a large measure of tactical surprise. Approximately 84,000 communist soldiers attacked Saigon and five of the largest urban centers, thirty-six of forty-four

Tet Offensive. The Cholon area of Saigon is hit by two 750-pound bombs during the shelling of the South Vietnamese capital in early 1968. © CORBIS

provincial capitals, and at least sixty-four of 242 district capitals. The communists wreaked havoc and caused confusion, but were soon overcome by the weight of American firepower and the surprisingly able resistance of the South Vietnamese army. With the exception of the city of Hué and the marine base at Khe Sanh, two battles that persisted until March, the offensive collapsed within the first week. As many as 45,000 Vietcong and North Vietnamese army soldiers perished in the offensive, and the popular uprising failed to materialize. However, the offensive caused significant political turmoil in the United States and strengthened the hand of those who wanted to limit or extinguish the American role in Vietnam.

BIBLIOGRAPHY

Davidson, Phillip B. *Vietnam at War: The History, 1946–1975.* Novato, Calif.: Presidio Press, 1988.

Karnow, Stanley. *Vietnam: A History.* New York: Viking, 1983.

Oberdorfer, Don. *Tet! The Turning Point in the Vietnam War.* Garden City, N.Y.: Doubleday, 1971.

Erik B. Villard

See also **Vietnam War.**

TEXAN EMIGRATION AND LAND COMPANY,

also known as the Peters' Colony Company, introduced 2,205 families into north central TEXAS between 1841 and 1848 as part of the basic settlement of seventeen present-day counties, which include the cities of DALLAS, Fort Worth, and Wichita Falls. Organized by W. S. Peters and associates of Louisville, Kentucky, and Cincinnati, Ohio, the company entered into contract with the Republic of Texas on 9 November 1841. The Republic of Texas distributed free land on its northern Indian frontier in parcels of 640 acres, while the company furnished the colonists with log cabins, rifles, and ammunition. Acrimonious disputes arose when other settlers, acting independently, moved into land unoccupied but promised to the company, and claimed homesteads by preemption. The only organized opposition in Texas to annexation in 1845 came from agents of the company, who feared abrogation of their colonization contract. Conflicts waxed after annexation, leading to two armed raids by settlers, in 1848 and 1852, on company headquarters at Stewartsville, Collin County. Land title claims were quieted only in 1853, when a law was passed granting settlers the right to land actually occupied as a homestead. The company was then compensated in part with a tract of unoccupied public land in west Texas.

BIBLIOGRAPHY

Connor, Seymour V. *Kentucky Colonization in Texas: A History of the Peters Colony.* Baltimore: Clearfield, 1994.

Sam H. Acheson / A. R.

See also **Annexation of Territory; Land Claims; Land Companies; Texas Public Lands.**

TEXAS.

The varied geography of Texas has helped to shape its history. The eastern third of the state's 266,807 square miles is mostly humid woodlands, much like Louisiana and Arkansas. A broad coastal plain borders the Gulf of Mexico. Much of southwest and far-west Texas is semiarid or arid desert, and west-central Texas northward through the Panhandle marks the southernmost part of the Great Plains. The central and north-central regions of the state are mostly gently rolling prairies with moderate rainfall. Moving from northeast to southwest, the major rivers are the Red, Sabine, Trinity, Brazos, Colorado, Guadalupe, Nueces, and Rio Grande; none has ever proven very suitable for navigation. The state is generally flat, with the exception of the Hill Country region west of the Austin–San Antonio area and the Davis Mountains of far west Texas.

The First Texans

Prior to the arrival of Europeans, Texas was home to a diverse collection of native peoples. Most numerous of these were the Hasinai branch of the CADDO Indians in east Texas, an agricultural society related to the mound-building cultures of the Mississippi Valley. Along the upper and central Gulf Coast ranged the nomadic Karankawas, and south Texas was home to various hunter-gatherers collectively known as Coahuiltecans. The APACHES were the dominant Plains nation, following the great herds of bison. Numerous small groups, including the Jumanos of southwest Texas and the Tonkawas of central Texas, lived in various parts of the state.

Spanish Texas

Europeans first viewed Texas in 1519, when an expedition led by the Spaniard Alonso Álvarez de Pineda mapped the

Gulf Coast from Florida to Mexico. In 1528 survivors of the Pánfilo de Narváez expedition, which had previously explored parts of Florida, washed ashore in the vicinity of Galveston Island during a storm. Only four men survived the first few months, including Álvar Núñez CABEZA DE VACA, whose memoir became the first published account of Texas. After more than seven years of harrowing adventure, the castaways finally made their way back to Mexico in 1536.

The tales of Cabeza de Vaca and his companions inspired the expedition of Francisco Vázquez DE CORONADO, who entered the Texas Panhandle from New Mexico in 1541. Although he failed in his search for gold, Coronado was the first European to see Palo Duro Canyon and to encounter the Apache Indians. In 1542, while Coronado was crossing the Panhandle, an expedition led by Luis de Moscoso Alvarado was entering east Texas from Louisiana. Moscoso perhaps reached as far as the Brazos River before returning to the Mississippi. When Coronado and Moscoso failed to find riches in Texas, Spain abandoned its efforts to explore or exploit Texas. For the next 140 years, Spain would claim the vast region, but only when the French suddenly appeared on the scene did Texas again become a priority.

In 1684 René Robert Cavelier, Sieur de LA SALLE, sailed from France with the intention of establishing a colony at the mouth of the Mississippi River. Overshooting his target by 400 miles, he landed instead at Matagorda Bay. At a well-concealed point at the head of the bay, he built a crude camp commonly known as Fort Saint Louis. Beset by disease, disunity, and hostile Indians, the settlement lasted only four years, with La Salle being killed by his own men in 1687. But the ill-fated French venture alerted the Spanish to the dangers of losing Texas, and La Salle unintentionally became the impetus for the creation of a permanent Spanish presence in Texas.

Between 1684 and 1689 Spain dispatched five sea and six land expeditions to locate and expel La Salle. Finally, in 1689 a party led by Alonso de León found the ruins of La Salle's settlement. The French were gone, but Spain was now determined to establish a presence in east Texas among the Hasinai. The following year the Spanish established Mission San Francisco de los Tejas in present-day Houston County. However, floods, disease, and poor relations with the Indians caused the Franciscan missionaries to abandon the effort in 1693.

Spain tried to move back into east Texas beginning in 1716, eventually founding six missions and a presidio there. In 1718 Martín de Alarcón, the governor of Coahuila and Texas, founded a mission and presidio on the San Antonio River in south central Texas to serve as a halfway station between the east Texas missions and the Rio Grande. In time, the San Antonio complex would become the capital and principal settlement of Spanish Texas.

Spain's second effort in east Texas proved little more successful than the first, and by 1731 most of the missions

in the east had been abandoned, leaving Spain with only a token presence in the area. Missions and presidios founded in other parts of Texas in the mid-1700s, such as the Mission San Sabá near present-day Menard, met with disease, Indian attack, or other problems and were all short-lived. In 1773, following an inspection tour by the Marqués de Rubí, the crown ordered the abandonment of the remaining east Texas settlements. Spain had acquired Louisiana from France in 1763 and no longer needed Texas as a buffer to French expansion. Some of the east Texas settlers resisted being resettled in San Antonio and eventually returned to east Texas, founding the town of Nacogdoches. By the late eighteenth century, then, Spanish Texas essentially consisted of San Antonio, Nacogdoches, and La Bahía (later renamed Goliad), which had been founded on the lower Texas coast in 1722. At its height around 1800, the non-Indian population of Spanish Texas numbered perhaps 4,000.

When the United States acquired the Louisiana Territory in 1803, Spain found itself with an aggressive new neighbor on its northern frontier. Over the next two decades Anglo-American adventurers known as "filibusters" launched repeated expeditions into Texas, with the intention of detaching it from New Spain. Two filibusters, Augustus Magee (1813) and James Long (1819, 1821), joined with Mexican revolutionary José Bernardo Gutiérrez de Lara to invade Texas from the United States. A Spanish royalist army crushed the rebels near San Antonio at the battle of Medina River and unleashed a reign of terror across Texas. By the time Mexico won its independence from Spain in 1821, the non-Indian population of Texas stood at no more than 3,000.

Mexican Texas

Hispanic Texans, or Tejanos, had supported the movement for Mexican independence, and they likewise endorsed the creation of a federal republic in the 1820s. Long neglected by Mexico City, many of these hardy settlers realized that trade with the United States held the best promise for prosperity. Therefore, when a bankrupt American businessman named Moses Austin proposed establishing a colony of 300 American families in 1821, his plan met with widespread support and gained the approval of Spanish authorities. Austin died before launching his colony, but his son, Stephen F. Austin, inherited the project and became Texas's first EMPRESARIO (colonization agent). Austin's colony encompassed parts of nearly forty present-day Texas counties along the lower watersheds of the Brazos and Colorado Rivers. By 1834 some 15,000 Anglos lived in Texas, along with 4,000 Tejanos and 2,000 African American slaves.

The Texas Revolution

Relations between the Texan settlers and the Mexican government began to sour in 1830, when the Mexican congress passed a law intended to weaken Anglo influence in the state. Among other provisions, the Law of 6 April, 1830 placed Mexican troops in East Texas and canceled all *empresario* contracts, although Austin and one other *empresario* were later exempted from the ban. Over the next five years, clashes between settlers and Mexican soldiers occurred repeatedly, often over customs regulations. Anglos demanded free trade, repeal of the 1830 law, and separate statehood for Texas apart from Coahuila, to which it had been joined for administrative purposes since 1824. Matters came to a head in 1835, when President Antonio López de Santa Anna abandoned federalism altogether, abolished the 1824 constitution, and centralized power in his own hands. Anglo Texans, joined by some Tejanos, resisted Santa Anna; hostilities commenced at Gonzales on 2 October 1835. One month later, the Texans declared a provisional state government loyal to the 1824 constitution.

In February 1836 a Mexican army of several thousand commanded by Santa Anna arrived in San Antonio, where they found the old Alamo mission held by approximately 200 defenders. After a thirteen-day siege, Santa Anna's soldiers stormed the mission on March 6, killing all the defenders, including James Bowie, William Barret Travis, and David Crockett. Shortly thereafter, James Fannin surrendered a force of about 400 volunteers at Goliad, who were subsequently executed at Santa Anna's order. On March 2 a convention at Washington-on-the-Brazos declared independence and authorized Sam Houston to take command of all remaining troops in Texas. On 21 April 1836, following a six-week retreat across Texas, Houston's army attacked one division of the Mexican army at SAN JACINTO and won a stunning victory. Some 800 Mexican troops were killed or wounded and that many more captured, while Texan deaths numbered fewer than ten. Santa Anna was captured the next day and ordered his remaining troops from Texas. Independence was won.

The Republic of Texas

In September 1836 Sam Houston was elected president of the Republic of Texas. He faced a daunting task in rebuilding the war-torn country, securing it against reinvasion from Mexico and hostile Indians, achieving diplomatic recognition from the world community, and developing the economy. Over the next decade the record on all of these matters was mixed at best. Twice in 1842 Mexican armies invaded and briefly occupied San Antonio. On the western frontier the COMANCHE Indians (immigrants to Texas in the mid-1700s) terrorized settlers with their brilliant horsemanship and fierce warrior code. In east Texas the Republic waged a brutal war of extermination against the CHEROKEES (also recent immigrants), driving the survivors into what is now Oklahoma. The Republic also undertook imprudent ventures such as the 1841 Santa Fe Expedition, intended to open a trade route between Texas and New Mexico, which resulted instead in the capture and imprisonment of nearly 300 Texans by Mexico. The wars against the Indians and the Santa Fe Expedition can largely be laid at the doorstep of Mirabeau B. Lamar, who replaced Houston as president in 1838 and

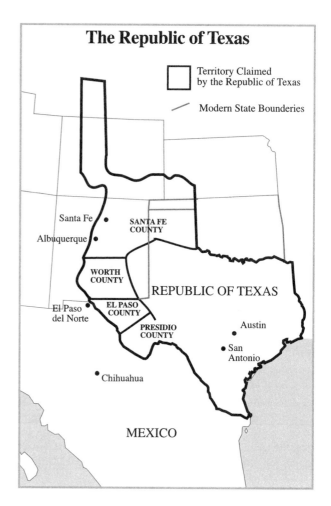

The Republic of Texas

☐ Territory Claimed by the Republic of Texas

╱ Modern State Boundaries

Santa Fe

Albuquerque

SANTA FE COUNTY

WORTH COUNTY

REPUBLIC OF TEXAS

El Paso del Norte

EL PASO COUNTY

PRESIDIO COUNTY

Austin

San Antonio

Chihuahua

MEXICO

believed in a sort of Texan version of MANIFEST DESTINY. Under Lamar, the national debt rose from $1 million to $7 million and the currency depreciated drastically. Typical of Lamar's grandiose thinking was his action in moving the capital to Austin, a new village on the far western frontier. Exposed to Indian and Mexican attacks and difficult to reach, the new capital was a luxury that the republic could scarcely afford, but Lamar envisioned its future as the centrally located seat of a vast Texan empire.

By the time Houston returned to office in 1841, the financial condition of the republic made annexation by the United States critically important. Texans almost unanimously desired annexation, but concerns about slavery effectively prevented American action. In 1844, though, pro-annexation candidate James K. Polk captured the Democratic presidential nomination. When Polk won the election, the outgoing president, John Tyler, viewed it as a mandate for annexation. Having previously failed to gain Senate approval for a treaty of annexation, Tyler resorted to the tactic of annexing Texas by means of a congressional joint resolution requiring only simple majorities in both houses of Congress. It succeeded, and Texas officially entered the Union on 29 December 1845. The new state retained ownership of its vast public domain; it also retained its massive public debt. The new constitution reflected the strong Jacksonian political leanings of most Texans, creating a government with limited powers.

The Republic had enjoyed considerable success on one front: In a decade the population had grown from about 40,000 to nearly 140,000. The Republic had made land available practically free to immigrants from the United States, and it also resurrected the *empresario* system to attract immigrants from the United States and Europe. In the last years of the Republic, some 10,000 colonists from Kentucky, Indiana, Illinois, and Ohio settled in the E. S. Peters colony in northeast Texas; about 7,000 Germans came to a grant in the Hill Country; and approximately 2,000 French Alsatians settled in Henri Castro's colony southwest of San Antonio. These immigrants gave Texas a more ethnically diverse population than most other southern states.

Statehood, Disunion, and Reconstruction

Immigration notwithstanding, after annexation Texas drew closer to the states of the Deep South, primarily due to the growth of SLAVERY and the COTTON economy. The enslaved population grew from 38,753 in 1847 to 182,566 in 1860. Cotton production increased from 58,000 bales in 1849 to 431,000 bales in 1859. As part of the Compromise of 1850, Texas surrendered its claims to parts of what are now New Mexico, Colorado, and Wyoming (thus assuming its modern boundaries) in return for federal assumption of its public debt. Texas thus enjoyed its most prosperous decade of the nineteenth century.

By 1860 Texas mirrored its fellow southern states economically and politically. Following Lincoln's election and the secession of the Deep South states, the state legislature called a secession convention and, over the strong opposition of Governor Sam Houston, voted to secede from the Union. Texas voters ratified the convention's decision by a three-to-one margin. About 60,000 Texans served the Confederacy, many of them in the eastern theatre of the war. Hood's Brigade and Terry's Rangers were among the better-known Texas units. On 19 June 1865, a date celebrated by black Texans as "Juneteenth," Union occupation troops under Gen. Gordon Granger landed at Galveston and declared the state's slaves free.

Texas' experiences in Reconstruction were typically southern. The state underwent Presidential Reconstruction in 1865 through 1866, resulting in the election of state and local governments dominated by former rebels, including Governor James Throckmorton, a former Confederate general. Black Codes returned African Americans to a condition of quasi-servitude.

When Congress took over the Reconstruction process in 1867, black males were enfranchised, many former Confederate officeholders were removed (including Governor Throckmorton), and the Reconstruction process began anew. With African Americans voting, the Republican Party rose to power. The Republican Constitution of 1869 gave the new governor, Edmund J. Davis, and the legislature sweeping new authority. Davis, a former judge who had lived in Texas since the 1840s, had served in the Union Army and championed the rights of blacks. His administration created a system of public education for children of both races; established a state police force to help protect the lives and property of all citizens; and worked to attract railroads to Texas using government subsidies. The measures galvanized the Democratic opposition, and in 1872 the Democrats recaptured the state legislature. In December 1873 the Democrat Richard Coke, a former Confederate officer, defeated Davis and "redeemed" Texas from Republican rule. The triumphant Democrats undid virtually all of the Republican programs, and in 1876 they ratified a new state constitution that returned the state to its Jacksonian, limited-government, white-supremacist roots.

Texas in the Gilded Age and the Progressive Era

The 1870s marked the beginning of the longest agricultural depression in the state's history. Cotton prices declined steadily through the 1880s and 1890s; land prices and interest rates rose. By century's end a majority of white farmers had joined African Americans in the ranks of tenants and sharecroppers, trapped in a vicious spiral of debt and dependence. In 1900 half of Texas farmers worked on rented farms.

RAILROADS finally came to Texas. The Missouri, Kansas, and Texas Railroad connected Texas to northern markets in 1872; by 1882 the Texas and Pacific and the Southern Pacific gave Texas east-west transcontinental connections. But the transportation revolution had come at a heavy price: The legislature had lured rail companies to Texas by granting them 32 million acres of the public domain.

One bright spot in the mostly bleak economic picture of the late nineteenth century was the growth of the CATTLE industry. The Spanish had first brought hardy longhorns to Texas in the 1700s. By the end of the Civil War millions of the animals roamed wild across the open grasslands south of San Antonio. Between 1866 and 1885, five million of these cattle were driven northward, first to Sedalia, Missouri, and later to a succession of railheads in Kansas. Thereafter the cattle industry declined precipitously. The arrival of railroads and the advance of the farming frontier ended the great overland cattle drives, confining cattle raising to ranches large and small. By this time, years of overgrazing had damaged the range and weakened herds. Then, in 1885 through 1886, two years of severe drought and an unprecedented blizzard killed thousands of cattle and drove many small operators out of business. Only the largest and most efficient ranches, such as the million-acre King Ranch in South Texas, survived.

As the farmers' depression deepened, complaints mounted against the established political parties, the railroads, and foreign capitalists. Many ordinary farmers

101

TEXAS

sought relief from self-help organizations such as the Patrons of Husbandry (popularly called the Grange) and the FARMERS' ALLIANCE. In 1891 Alliancemen founded the People's, or Populist, party. Between 1892 and 1896 the Populists competed vigorously with the Democrats, promising to rein in the monopolistic practices of railroads and large corporations, reform the nation's monetary system, and provide affordable credit for struggling farmers. The rise of POPULISM spurred the state Democrats to embrace limited reforms such as a railroad commission, which became a reality under Governor James S. Hogg (1891–1895). But Populism required far more government action than most Texans could stomach, and the party's willingness to appeal for African American votes further tainted it in the eyes of many whites. After 1896 Populism faded, but many of its ideas would resurface in progressivism and the New Deal.

In the aftermath of Populism, the Democratic Party sponsored electoral "reforms" that largely disfranchised blacks. Foremost among these, the 1902 poll tax also effectively eliminated large numbers of poor whites from politics. Middle-class white Texans embraced certain progressive reforms, such as woman's suffrage, prohibition, prison reform, and the commission plan of city government, but many elements of Texas progressivism were

aimed at limiting the influence of northern and foreign capital in the state's economy. Changes in banking and insurance laws, designed to give Texas-owned companies competitive advantages, constituted much of what passed for progressivism in the state.

The Emergence of Modern Texas

The twentieth century began with two history-altering events. The first, a massive hurricane, devastated Galveston in September 1900, costing 6,000 lives in one of the worst natural disasters in U.S. history. But the other event ultimately overshadowed even that tragedy. On 10 January 1901 the greatest oil gusher in history blew in at Spindletop, near Beaumont. Texas immediately became the center of the world's PETROLEUM INDUSTRY. Hundreds of new oil firms came into existence; some, like Texaco, became huge. Perhaps more important than the oil itself was the subsequent growth of the refining, pipeline, oil-tool, and petrochemical industries, which transformed the Gulf Coast into a manufacturing center, creating jobs and capital for investment. Growth of these industries, along with the discovery of massive new oil fields in east and west Texas, caused the Texas economy to modernize and begin diverging from the southern pattern of poverty and rurality.

As the economy modernized, however, Texas politics lagged behind. Governor James Ferguson, elected in 1914, three years later faced charges of corruption and suffered impeachment and a ban from future office holding. Undeterred, Ferguson ran his wife, Miriam, successfully twice, in 1924 and 1932, promising "two governors for the price of one." Most historians consider the Fergusons demagogues and an embarrassment to the state, characterizations that likewise applied to Governor W. Lee "Pappy" O'Daniel, a Fort Worth flour merchant who was elected governor in 1938 on a platform based on "the Ten Commandments and the Golden Rule." Progressive Democrats, such as the New Dealer James V. Allred (governor from 1935 to 1939), were rare in Texas.

World War II transformed Texas. In 1940 a majority of Texans still lived in rural areas, and sharecroppers plowing cotton fields behind mules were still everyday sights. But the war drew hundreds of thousands of rural Texans into the military or into good-paying manufacturing jobs. By 1950 a majority of Texans lived in urban areas. Farms had mechanized and modernized. Much of this prosperity was due to federal spending, and for the first time the U.S. government was spending more in Texas than the state's citizens paid in federal taxes. Texas cities, which had always been relatively small, began to grow rapidly. By 1960 Houston boasted a population of 938,219, followed by Dallas's 679,684 and San Antonio's 587,718.

The Texas economy boomed in the 1970s, when world oil prices skyrocketed. The boom ended in 1983 and bottomed out in 1986. The oil "bust" plunged the state into a near-depression, as thousands of oil companies and financial institutions failed. Unemployment soared, and state tax revenues declined by 16 percent. But in the long run the crisis may have benefited the state, for it forced the economy to diversify and become less oil-dependent. In the 1990s Texas became a center of the "high-tech" revolution, with dramatic growth in electronics, communications, and health care–related industries. Population growth resumed. The 2000 census revealed that Houston, Dallas, and San Antonio had grown respectively to about 2 million, 1.2 million, and 1.1 million people. Even more dramatic was suburban growth; the greater Dallas–Fort Worth metropolitan area grew faster than any other large metropolitan area in the nation in the 1990s, with 5.2 million people by 2000, larger than 31 states. Overall, Texas passed New York to become the country's second-largest state, with a population of nearly 21 million. Much of this growth was fueled by Hispanic immigrants, who made up 32 percent of the Texas population in 2000.

As the economy modernized, so did Texas politics. The Civil Rights Movement enfranchised African Americans and Hispanics, who heavily favored liberal Democrats, including Texan Lyndon B. Johnson. This drove many conservative white voters into the Republican Party. In 1978, William P. Clements, Jr., became the first Republican elected to the governorship since Reconstruction. Two other Texas Republicans, George H. W. Bush and his son, George W. Bush, claimed the nation's highest office in 1988 and 2000, respectively. Democrats continued to dominate politics in the large cities, but at the state level the Republican revolution was completed in 1998, when Republicans held every statewide elective office.

Texas, then, entered the twenty-first century very much in the mainstream of American life and culture. Texans continued to take pride in their state's colorful history, and many non-Texans persisted in thinking of Texas as the land of cowboys and oil tycoons. But as a modern, diverse, urban, industrial state, Texas had become more like the rest of the nation and less like the rough-and-tumble frontier of its legendary past.

BIBLIOGRAPHY

Barr, Alwyn. *Reconstruction to Reform: Texas Politics, 1876–1906.* Austin: University of Texas Press, 1971.

Buenger, Walter L. *Secession and the Union in Texas.* Austin: University of Texas Press, 1984.

Calvert, Robert A., Arnoldo De León, and Gregg Cantrell. *The History of Texas.* 3rd ed. Wheeling, Ill.: Harlan Davidson, 2002.

Campbell, Randolph B. *An Empire for Slavery: The Peculiar Institution in Texas, 1821–1865.* Baton Rouge: Louisiana State University Press, 1989.

Cantrell, Gregg. *Stephen F. Austin, Empresario of Texas.* New Haven, Conn.: Yale University Press, 1999.

Chipman, Donald E. *Spanish Texas, 1519–1821.* Austin: University of Texas Press, 1992.

Hogan, William R. *The Texas Republic: A Social and Economic History.* Norman: University of Oklahoma Press, 1946.

Lack, Paul D. *The Texas Revolutionary Experience: A Social and Political History, 1835–1836.* College Station: Texas A&M University Press, 1992.

Moneyhon, Carl H. *Republicanism in Reconstruction Texas.* Austin: University of Texas Press, 1980.

Montejano, David. *Anglos and Mexicans in the Making of Texas, 1836–1986.* Austin: University of Texas Press, 1987.

Smith, F. Todd. *The Caddo Indians: Tribes at the Convergence of Empires, 1542–1854.* College Station: Texas A&M University Press, 1995.

Spratt, John S. *The Road to Spindletop: Economic Change in Texas, 1875–1901.* Dallas, Tex.: Southern Methodist University Press, 1955.

Gregg Cantrell

See also **Alamo, Siege of the; Dallas; El Paso; Explorations and Expeditions, Spanish; Fort Worth; Galveston; Houston; Mexican-American War; "Remember the Alamo";** *and vol. 9:* **Memories of the North American Invasion; Mexican Minister of War's Reply to Manuel de la Peña y Peña; Message on the War with Mexico; The Story of Enrique Esparza.**

TEXAS NAVY. The southwestern borderlands were a serious barrier in 1836 to Mexico's attempts to crush the Texas revolution. Although Mexican President Antonio López de Santa Anna's advisers warned him to establish a Mexican Gulf fleet to protect the flow of seaborne military supplies along the coast before launching an overland campaign, Santa Anna refused to wait. In the meantime, the Texans, with only four small armed ships, seized control of the Gulf and disrupted Mexican supply routes throughout the war.

By the summer of 1837, however, Mexico had blockaded TEXAS and many residents feared a sea invasion. In 1838, France's navy fortuitously surrounded Mexico and destroyed its fleet. Alarmed by French withdrawal in 1839, President Mirabeau B. Lamar committed Texas to a naval program. By 1840, the new fleet consisted of an eleven-gun steamer, a twenty-two-gun flagship, and five smaller but effective men-of-war. The collapse of Texan James Treat's peace negotiations with Mexico caused Lamar to enter into a *de facto* alliance with the state of Yucatán, then fighting for independence from the Mexican union. As allies of Yucatán, the Texas navy captured Tabasco and, as late as the spring of 1843, fought engagements with new Mexican steam warships built and commanded by the British.

The Texas fleet kept Mexico busy and saved the young republic from re-invasion. By 1843, United States annexation was close at hand, and the president of Texas, Sam Houston, recalled the navy because he believed it was too expensive and was jeopardizing his diplomacy. After annexation, the remaining ships in the Texas navy became the property of the U.S. government.

BIBLIOGRAPHY

Francaviglia, Richard V. *From Sail to Steam: Four Centuries of Texas Maritime History, 1500–1900*. Austin: University of Texas Press, 1998.

Hill, Jim D. *The Texas Navy: In Forgotten Battles and Shirtsleeve Diplomacy*. Austin, Tex.: State House Press, 1987.

Montejano, David. *Anglos and Mexicans in the Making of Texas, 1836–1986*. Austin: University of Texas Press, 1987.

Jim Dan Hill/E. M.

See also **Annexation of Territory; Armored Ships; Mexican-American War; Mexico, Relations with.**

TEXAS PUBLIC LANDS. The 1845 treaty of annexation between the Republic of TEXAS and the United States made Texas the only state aside from the original thirteen colonies to enter the Union with control over its public lands. The state has since disposed of these lands in various ways. It sold land to settlers through various preemption acts and granted land as compensation for war service, bonuses for construction of railroads and other public works, payment for the construction of the state capitol, and support for education. By the COMPRO-MISE OF 1850, Texas also ceded claims to lands that now lie in other states. At the end of the nineteenth century, Texas had no unappropriated public lands left.

BIBLIOGRAPHY

Miller, Thomas L. *The Public Lands of Texas, 1519–1970*. Norman: University of Oklahoma Press, 1972.

Morgan, Andrea Gurasich. *Land: A History of the Texas General Land Office*. Austin: Texas General Land Office, 1992.

W. P. Ratchford/C. P.

See also **Land Grants: Overview.**

TEXAS RANGERS. In 1823 Stephen F. Austin hired ten men he called "rangers" to conduct a raid against the Indians. On 24 November 1835 the Texas legislature created a police force of three companies, fifty-six men each, known as Texas Rangers. Their numbers and reputation rose and fell, influenced by threats to the Texas Republic and governmental economy. Organized along military lines, the rangers had no uniforms in the nineteenth century. Later they began to wear suits with the ubiquitous cowboy hat.

Rangers served in the Texas Revolution as scouts, but their numbers remained small. In December 1838 Mirabeau B. Lamar, president of the Republic, added eight companies. Until the Mexican-American War the rangers were Indian fighters. During his second presidency of Texas, Sam Houston used 150 rangers under the command of Captain John Coffee Hays to protect the frontier from Indian raids, and the rangers gained a reputation for toughness and dedication to duty.

After Texas became a state, from 1848 to 1858, the rangers had no official duties since the United States controlled the border and the frontier. In January 1858 Senior Captain John S. "Rip" Ford led attacks on Indians from the Red River to Brownsville. During the Civil War and Reconstruction the rangers contributed little to law and order, but subsequently they pacified the border with Mexico and stopped various feuds in the state. Between 1890 and 1920 the state legislature dramatically reduced the number of rangers.

The Mexican Revolution changed the situation. Reacting to Pancho Villa's raid on Columbus, New Mexico, rangers killed approximately five thousand Hispanics from 1914 to 1919. Shocked, the state legislature set new standards of recruitment and professionalism. In the 1920s the rangers dealt with riots, labor strikes, the Ku Klux Klan, and oil strikes. The Great Depression marked a low point in the organization's history. Because the rangers supported her opponent in the Democratic primary, Miriam A. "Ma" Ferguson fired all forty-four rangers. The new force was only thirty-two men.

In 1935 legislators created the Texas Department of Public Safety and administratively combined the rangers, the highway patrol, and a state crime lab. The five companies of rangers were restored, and qualifying examinations and behavioral standards were instituted. Between 1938 and 1968 Colonel Homer Garrison Jr. shifted the rangers' focus to detective work. During that time, in response to World War II, fears of sabotage, the civil rights movement, and urbanization, the number of Rangers increased.

After 1968 the rangers worked closely with local police and improved their recruitment, training, and scientific methods. By 1993 the ninety-nine officers included two women, and by 1996 Texas had 105 rangers.

BIBLIOGRAPHY

Gillett, James B. *Six Years with the Texas Rangers, 1875–1881.* New Haven, Conn.: Yale University Press, 1925. A classic autobiography.

Procter, Ben. *Just One Riot: Episodes of the Texas Rangers in the Twentieth Century.* Austin, Tex.: Eakin Press, 1991. A brief scholarly evaluation.

Webb, Walter Prescott. *The Texas Rangers: A Century of Frontier Defense.* 2d ed. Austin: University of Texas Press, 1965. The major source for understanding the Rangers' behavior and their resulting reputation.

Donald K. Pickens

See also **Texas.**

TEXAS V. WHITE, 7 Wallace 700 (1869), was an attempt by the RECONSTRUCTION governor of TEXAS to prevent payment on federal bonds disposed of by the secessionist state government in payment of supplies for the Confederacy. The SUPREME COURT acknowledged the governor's competence to sue on the ground that Texas was now, and had never ceased to be, a member of "an indestructible Union"; hence the ordinance of SECESSION was void. But the Court denied the power of the secessionist government to dispose of state property for purposes of rebellion. The decision was overruled in 1885 in *Morgan v. United States.*

BIBLIOGRAPHY

Hyman, Harold M. *The Reconstruction Justice of Salmon P. Chase: In re Turner and Texas v. White.* Lawrence: University Press of Kansas, 1997.

Hyman, Harold M., and William M. Wiecek. *Equal Justice under Law: Constitutional Development, 1835–1875.* New York: Harper and Row, 1982.

Harvey Wish / A. R.

See also **Civil War; Confederate States of America.**

TEXTBOOKS constitute the de facto curriculum in many disciplines. Especially at the secondary level, where 85 percent of the nation's students take courses before graduation, American history is a controversial area because of disputes over content and interpretation. U.S.

history texts include the study of continental geography, political history, economic development, social history, and diverse cultures. Private corporations provide textbooks to state and local governments for a profit, an arrangement that differs from that prevailing in most industrialized countries, where the national government creates the curriculum and publishes textbooks. The total domestic market for instructional materials was an estimated $5 billion in 1992, of which more than $2 billion represented elementary and high school materials. Because the public-school systems of Texas and California buy so many textbooks, many corporations tailor the contents of their publications to meet the interests and needs of schools in those two states.

Since 1970 there have been considerable changes in textbooks, especially in U.S. history and social studies because of the influence of social history, revisionism, and multiculturalism on curriculum composition. Publishers expended considerable effort to make texts redress earlier omissions. Nevertheless, the state-level controversies of the late 1980s and early 1990s in California and New York showed that textbook publishers remained beset by the demands of special-interest groups, including ethnic activists, feminists, the disabled, environmentalists, homosexuals, and religious groups, all of whom desire favorable and prominent treatment. Such pressures make it difficult for publishers to balance academic integrity against market requirements. Several federal court cases in the 1980s reflect the perennial disputes over textbook censorship, content, and interpretation. Challenges have arisen over biology, health, literature, and history texts. Three significant federal cases originated in local complaints that textbooks promote secular humanism (*Smith v. Board of School Commissioners of Mobile County,* 1986), atheism (*Mozert v. Hawkins County Public Schools,* 1987), and the theory of evolution (*Aguillard v. Edwards,* 1987).

Textbooks remain useful and efficient devices for learning in all formal subjects, offering organized, convenient sequences of ideas and information for structured teaching and learning. In the 1990s schools at all levels began to experiment with CD-ROMs and other video technologies as curriculum supplements. The classroom use of CD-ROM reference works, electronic atlases, and on-line databases continues to grow, but it is far from certain that such media will supplant textbooks.

BIBLIOGRAPHY

Altbach, Philip G., Gail P. Kelly, Hugh G. Petrie, and Lois Weiss, eds. *Textbooks in American Society: Politics, Policy, and Pedagogy.* Albany: State University of New York Press, 1991.

Apple, Michael W., and Linda K. Christian-Smith, eds. *The Politics of the Textbook.* New York: Routledge, 1991.

DelFattore, Joan. *What Johnny Shouldn't Read: Book Censorship in America.* New Haven, Conn.: Yale University Press, 1992.

Jenkinson, Edward B. *Censors in the Classroom: The Mind Benders.* Carbondale: Southern Illinois University Press, 1979.

Gilbert T. Sewall/a. e.

See also **American Legion; Education; Educational Technology; McGuffey's Readers;** *New England Primer;* **Publishing Industry; School, District.**

TEXTBOOKS, EARLY.   Bibles, almanacs, embroidered samplers, and broadsheets were the most common textual materials in most colonial homes. Children used hornbooks to learn to read short phrases and proverbs. A hornbook consisted of a wooden paddle holding a piece of printed text that was covered with a layer of transparent cow's horn to protect the text.

As schools proliferated in New England, most used a version of *The New England Primer,* copied from English texts, and most schoolbooks were imported from England. After the Revolution, the schoolteacher Noah Webster lobbied for copyright legislation to protect his book, *A Grammatical Institute of the English Language,* later renamed *The American Spelling Book,* which he began marketing in 1783. He supplemented the speller with a grammar (1784) and a reader (1785), and by 1804, more than 1.5 million copies of his books had been sold. Webster's books met the new nation's need for a distinctly American product. He standardized American English spelling and grammar, and his books emphasized nationalism and patriotism. By the time Webster died in 1843, 24 million copies of his books had been sold.

Schoolbooks were a popular product as the nation expanded and public schools were established. In 1840 various publishers sold 2.6 million schoolbooks. In 1837, William McGuffey's *Eclectic Reader* was published, directed at the burgeoning western market. Truman and Smith Publishing Company in Cincinnati, Ohio, offered the job of compiling reading selections for four graded readers to Catharine Beecher, who had authored other texts, as well as coauthoring *Primary Geography for Children* with her sister Harriet Beecher Stowe. Beecher was too busy establishing the Western Female Institute in Cincinnati, and recommended McGuffey, an experienced educator. McGuffey gathered previously published pieces for the first edition and did little actual work on later editions. The McGuffey readers were revised numerous times, with all new material at three different points. Major editions were published in 1836 (7 million copies sold), 1857 (40 million sold), 1879 (60 million sold), and 1890–1920 (15 million sold).

As the century wore on, schoolbooks made fewer references to religion and more to honesty and self-reliance. Charity to others was extolled, as well as respect for authority. Illustrations grew more important as printing technology became more sophisticated, and by the 1880s the books were heavily illustrated, usually showing children and animals in idealized pastoral or natural settings.

McGuffey's First Reader. This woodcut illustrates the first lesson in the 1836 edition of the enormously popular and long-lived series. © Bettmann/corbis

Rural organizations such as the Farmer's Alliance and National Grange began challenging the reliance on textbooks. The Grange lobbied for more vocational training, practical knowledge, and science, and less rote memorization. Grange-sponsored schools were established in southern states, Michigan, and California. The Grange advocated free textbooks for children and urged states to buy books in bulk to save money. In 1890 the Farmer's Alliance charged textbook publishers with creating a "Textbook Trust," claiming the American Book Company (publisher of the McGuffey books) controlled the market and prices. Schoolbook publishers responded to local critics because they were subject to community approval; high school and college texts were not. By the end of the century, John Dewey, author of *School and Society* (1899), led progressive educational reforms, urging hands-on learning rather than complete reliance on texts.

BIBLIOGRAPHY

Apple, Michael W., and Linda K. Christian-Smith, eds. *The Politics of the Textbook*. New York: Routledge, 1991.

Tanner, Daniel, and Laurel Tanner. *History of the School Curriculum*. New York: Macmillan, 1990.

Laurie Winn Carlson

See also **Hornbook; McGuffey's Readers;** *New England Primer*; **Webster's Blue-Backed Speller.**

TEXTILES. Textile production played a crucial part in the American industrial revolution, the establishment of organized labor, and the technological development of this country. Once, textile production was simple enough that the entire process could and did take place in the home. Now, textiles represent a complex network of interrelated industries that produce fiber, spin yarns, fabricate cloth, and dye, finish, print, and manufacture goods.

Products and Services

About 35 percent of U.S. manufactured cloth is intended for apparel, 16 percent for home furnishings, and 24 percent for floor coverings. The remaining 25 percent is used in industrial textiles, which include sports equipment, conveyer belts, filtration materials, and agricultural and construction materials. So-called geotextiles are used for earth stabilization and drainage as well as reinforcement in roads and bridges. The aerospace industry uses industrial textiles in the nose cones of space shuttles, and medicine uses textiles as artificial arteries and dissolving stitches.

Fiber Producers

Until the early twentieth century, all textiles were derived from plants or animals. The invention of a process for regenerating cellulose from wood chips and cotton linters into a usable fiber marked the beginning of research, development, and innovation. Many of today's textile producers started as chemical companies.

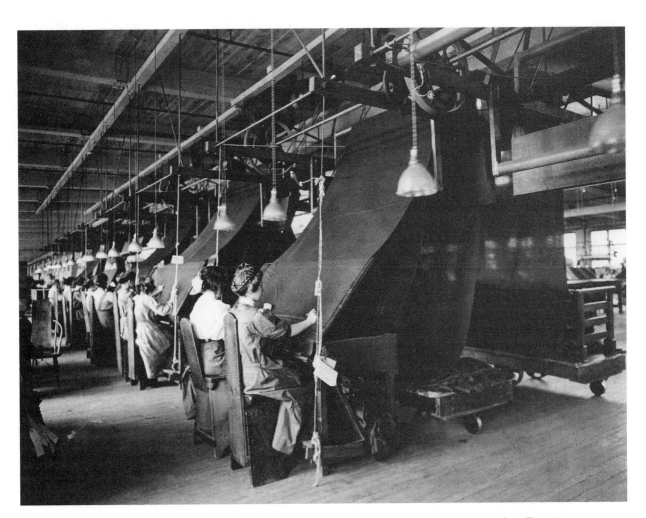

Woolen Mill. Female workers examine lengths of fabric and mark any imperfections at this Boston textile mill, 1912. © CORBIS

Producers of natural fibers are dependent on raw materials and often held hostage to nature. It is not easy for them to quickly increase or decrease output based on consumer demand. Most producers sell their fiber to mills or wholesalers for resale and seldom have any direct involvement after the fiber is sold. Trade organizations like Cotton Incorporated and the American Wool Council have been established to support producers by providing educational materials, helping with public relations, and assisting with advertising.

Manufactured fibers can be made from regenerated natural materials, or they can be synthesized from chemicals. Because many of these processes may be petroleum-based, such producers may be affected by events concerning the oil industry. The American Fiber Manufacturers Association is the primary association for the manufactured fiber industry. Manufactured fibers can be sold as unbranded fiber, where the fiber producer has no further involvement; trademarked fiber, where the fiber producer has some control over the quality of the fabric; or licensed trademarked fiber, where the fiber producer sets standards that must be met by the fabric manufacturer. An advantage of trademarked or licensed trademarked fiber is that the fabric manufacturers and, ultimately, the garment manufacturers, can capitalize on advertising and brand recognition.

Origins in America

The American colonies were viewed as rich deposits of natural resources for Europe, and the colonists were considered as a consumer pool. Because Holland and France were producing their own wool, England was forced to look west for a new market. England encouraged the culture of flax, hemp, and silk in the colonies, but only if it aided English industries. Though the colonists were capable of producing cloth through spinning and weaving, they found no real necessity to do so as long as cloth could be imported. Problems arose in the Massachusetts colony when the French captured supply ships. The lack of sufficient warm clothing in an inhospitable climate created great hardship in the northern settlements.

The Massachusetts colony recognized the need to be as self-sufficient as possible. It encouraged the development of raw materials and the manufacture of wool and linen cloth. A bounty was offered to weavers as inducement, and the coarse linen they produced was the first officially recorded American-produced textile.

In 1638, twenty families arrived in Massachusetts from Yorkshire, a wool-producing district in England. Five years later, they began the manufacture of cloth, establishing the textile industry in America. Although they worked primarily in wool, they also spun and wove flax and cotton. The mill they established continued in production into the nineteenth century. With increasing concern over the availability of goods, in 1645 the Massachusetts colony instructed the public to preserve and increase their flocks of sheep, make woolen cloth, and

advise friends and family still in England to emigrate and bring as many sheep with them as possible. By the beginning of the eighteenth century, there were a quarter of a million colonists. Textile production had become important enough to pose a threat to English merchants and manufacturers. The English enacted restrictions that detailed what goods could be exported to the colonies and by whom, and what items could be exported from the colonies and where. This only served to instill a greater sense of defiance among the colonists. George Washington was a great supporter of homespun American cloth and maintained a weaving house on his Mount Vernon estate, as did Thomas Jefferson at Monticello. Imported textiles became very unpopular, especially after the 1765 Stamp Act. England retaliated for colonial disobedience by disallowing the exportation of any textile goods, machinery, or equipment to the colonies. The American army suffered terribly during the Revolution because of lack of proper clothing. The freedom won by the former colonists allowed the textile industry to develop.

Industry Pioneers

George Cabot founded the first integrated American textile mill in Beverly, Massachusetts, in 1787. His mill hand-carded fiber, spun yarn, and wove cloth, all under one roof. The company produced a variety of cotton fabrics until the early 1800s.

Samuel Slater may be considered the father of the American industrial revolution. English by birth, he trained for seven years in a textile mill, and left England in 1789 at age twenty-one. Settling in Rhode Island, he built the first successful water-powered spinning mill in Pawtucket in 1793.

Francis Cabot Lowell, nephew of George Cabot, visited English textile mills and committed the workings of the power loom to memory. Upon his return, he worked with the inventor Paul Moody at Waltham, Massachusetts, to develop the first American power loom.

George Corliss contributed to steam engine design and succeeded in making Providence, Rhode Island, the center of steam engine manufacture in the 1850s. First used as a source of alternate power during the dry season, steam slowly replaced water as an energy source. It allowed a mill owner to build in a populous area without regard for waterpower.

How the Industry Developed

Cloth production is a two-part process: spinning fiber into yarn, and weaving yarn into cloth. A mechanized spinning frame was invented in England in 1764 that could spin eight spools of yarn at once. Within a few years, it was improved to spin 100 spools simultaneously. Richard Arkwright improved upon the original design so that all steps occurred in one machine. It was in the factory of his partner, Jedediah Strutt, that Samuel Slater was trained. Slater opened Slater Mill in 1793 with money from Providence investors. His organizational methods

Spinning Jenny. A 1765 engraving of James Hargreaves's revolutionary new invention, the mechanized spinning frame. © CORBIS

became the blueprint for successors in the Blackstone River Valley. Based on mills smaller than those used in Massachusetts, his plan was ideal for small rural mill villages. Seven more mills opened by 1800, and there were 213 by 1815. The mills flourished in areas where the rocky terrain made farming unsuitable.

The year after Slater opened his mill, Eli Whitney patented a machine that would lead to the revival of the declining practice of slavery and ultimately contribute to the causes of the Civil War. In 1790, there were 657,000 slaves in the southern states. In 1793, 187,000 pounds of cotton was harvested. Because one slave was able to clean only one pound of cotton fiber per day, the crop hardly was worth the trouble. Whitney's cotton gin, however, could process fifty pounds a day, enabling the harvest to grow to six million pounds in 1795. The business of slavery grew as well, so that in 1810 there were 1.3 million slaves and 93 million pounds of cotton harvested. Cotton became the largest U.S. export and textiles the most important industry before the Civil War.

Weavers could not keep up with the abundance of yarn being produced by the mechanized mills. This problem was solved when Francis Cabot Lowell and Paul Moody created their more efficient power loom and spinning apparatus in 1813 in Lowell's Waltham mill. With a dependable loom, weaving could now keep apace of spinning. Soon mills began to dot the rivers of New England. The fully integrated mill marked the shift from a rural, agrarian society to a manufacturing economy. Shortly after his death, Lowell's associates began to develop an area north of Boston where the Merrimack River and Paw-

tucket Falls had the waterpower to operate dozens of mills. Named for Lowell, the planned community was set up in 1823 and incorporated in 1826. By 1850 almost six miles of canals flowed through Lowell, drove the waterwheels of 40 mill buildings, and powered 320,000 spindles and almost 10,000 looms, operated by more than 10,000 workers.

The period from 1820 to 1860 saw the rapid development of many more factories. New England became the nation's textile center. In 1825, there were 16,000 mills in Maine, New Hampshire, Vermont, and New York. By 1850, there were 60,000 mills in the United States. New England alone had 896 power-driven mills, almost 500 of which were in northern Massachusetts, patterned after Lowell's Waltham mill. Virtually all mills were fully mechanized by the early part of the nineteenth century. Initially powered by water, the mills eventually switched to steam, then electricity. By 1910, the Lowell mills were using hydroelectricity.

The Civil War dramatically changed production. The cotton harvest shrunk to 200,000 bales in 1864, and after the war the western states began producing cotton. The South was faced with the need to reinvent itself and began to build spinning and weaving mills. Its lower wages, lower rate of unionization, and openness to new technology induced many northern mills to relocate southward in the years between the world wars.

Chemistry began to play an important part in the textile industry in the mid-nineteenth century when synthetic dyes were discovered. These were followed in 1891

LOWELL MILL GIRLS

Beginning in 1823, girls from farms and local villages were recruited to work in the Lowell mills for a few years before they left for marriage or other reasons. Most were between fifteen and thirty years old and worked an average of three years. They lived in dormitories and boarding houses with strict rules of curfew and moral conduct. In 1834, 800 young female mill workers went on strike to protest wage cuts, claiming the cuts threatened their economic independence. The Lowell Female Labor Reform Association was formed in 1844, the first organization of working women to try to bargain collectively for better conditions and higher pay. The economic downturn of the 1850s led to lower pay and longer hours, and as a result, immigrant Irish women replaced American farm girls. In the late nineteenth century, women held nearly two-thirds of all textile jobs in Lowell.

by the development of regenerated cellulose, the first manmade fiber. The first plant for manufacturing "artificial silk" in America opened in 1910. Later named rayon (1924), the fabric was followed by acetate and triacetate, also cellulose derivatives. Chemical companies set up research and development labs in the race to find new fibers.

DuPont established an experimental lab for the purpose of pure scientific research in 1928. Directed by Dr. Wallace Hume Carothers, the lab conducted work on polyesters but abandoned the project to pursue what would become known as nylon. After several years of development, the fiber was presented to consumers in the form of women's stockings. In 1940, when they became available to the general public, nylon stockings earned more than $3 million in profit in seven months, completely covering the cost of research and development. Nylon stockings ceased production during World War II when nylon was needed for parachutes, ropes, and tents.

British scientists picked up Carothers's work on giant molecules and further developed polyesters. DuPont bought the appropriate patent and opened the first U.S. plant to produce Dacron polyester in 1953. Subsequent developments include manufactured fibers for protection, high performance, durability, strength, and ease of care. Other important chemical contributions are finishes on traditional fabrics for wrinkle resistance, shrinkage control, and color fastness. Technological developments include computer-aided design (CAD) and computer-aided manufacture (CAM). CAD equipment is used in the design of yarns and fabrics and the development of coloration. Prints can easily be manipulated, and designs can be reconfigured in seconds. CAM is used for designing factory layouts and in textile production processes like the control of looms and robotics. Computers are invaluable in communications and for tracking inventory.

Concern for the impact of manufacturing on the environment led to the development of so-called environmentally improved textile products. One such product is lyocell, regenerated cellulose produced using a nontoxic solvent. Organic cotton and naturally colored cottons are being cultivated, and natural dyes have sparked interest. Attention is also being given to recycling materials such as old carpets as well as other used textile products into new materials. Plastic soda bottles are being processed into fiberfill, polar fleece, and geotextiles.

Statistics

By the end of the twentieth century, there were approximately 75,000 woolgrowers in the United States, active in almost every state, and 35,000 cotton growers, mainly in the South. Textiles were also being manufactured in almost all states, with the largest concentrations in Georgia, North Carolina, and South Carolina.

According to the U.S. Department of Commerce and the Bureau of Labor Statistics there were 5,117 companies, with 6,134 plants, in 1997. The companies employed 541,000 workers in 2000, but within a few years 177,000 jobs had been lost and more than 215 mills had closed. Though the industry income was $57.8 billion in 2000, shipments and exports soon dropped as the strength of the U.S. dollar against faltering Asian economies allowed for a surge of inexpensive imported textiles and clothing.

Changes in Business and Commerce

The textile industry has undergone significant changes in business practices in several key areas. Labor relations, trade practices, product labeling, product safety, and environmental and antipollution measures have been subjects of public scrutiny and federal legislation.

Employee and Labor Practices

Once farmers gave up rural self-sufficiency, they had to adapt to a mill whistle rather than the rhythm of nature. Life was difficult and unhealthy with long hours and poor conditions. Respiratory disease was common and there was always the danger of losing a limb in the machinery. The mills were cold and drafty in the winter and stifling in the summer, as well as dirty and noisy. Physical abuse occurred and it was not uncommon for mill owners to take advantage of workers. When labor was scarce, conditions improved, but conditions declined again when more workers became available.

Samuel Slater developed a management style that became known as the Rhode Island system. He hired entire families, who often lived in company housing, shopped in the company store, and attended company schools and churches. It was a clever means of control because bad behavior on one worker's part could get the entire family fired. Work was ten to twelve hours a day, six days a week. Sunday was for church and for children to learn basic reading, writing, and arithmetic. Though the mill complex did provide a measure of convenience for the workers, it was actually a way for the owner and investors to regulate every aspect of the workers' lives. Paid by the mill owner, teachers and ministers preached the party line.

By 1830, 55 percent of Rhode Island mill workers were children earning less than $1 a week. Children on farms worked equally long hours, and so for poor families, millwork was seen as an improvement. Textile machines lent themselves to child labor because they were simple enough for unskilled children to operate under adult supervision.

By 1900, 92 percent of southern textile workers lived in mill villages. By 1908, fewer than 7 percent had a living situation with anything more than a simple privy. Some villages had a rule that a family had to have one employee for each room in the house, further ensuring child entry into the workforce. School was discouraged so that children would have no option but to enter mill life. Schools were free to seventh grade, then charged tuition after that. Between 1880 and 1910 about one-fourth of southern cotton mill workers were under sixteen, having entered the mills full-time by age twelve. The Fair Labor Standards Act of 1938 finally regulated child labor.

In the 1890s, the National Union of Textile Workers held meetings throughout the Carolina Piedmont, organizing ninety-five locals by 1900. Unions continued to organize workers and in 1929 a wave of strikes began in Elizabethton, Tennessee. Thousands of mill workers walked out and stayed out three months even in the face of intimidation and the murder of Ella May Wiggins, organizer of the Gastonia, North Carolina, strike. Though hunger forced the workers back with only minor concessions from the owners, the stage was set for later protest.

In an effort to stimulate recovery from the 1929 stock market crash and the depression that followed, President Franklin D. Roosevelt signed the National Industrial Recovery Act (NIRA) into law in 1933. Under NIRA, a Cotton Textile Board was established to enforce a code of fair competition in the industry, limit destructive price competition, prevent overproduction, and guarantee mill hands a minimum wage. Unfortunately, the Board was controlled by mill owners, who used the minimum wage as the maximum and laid off even more workers.

The 1934 General Textile Strike led to the eventual abandonment of the mill village system. Twenty thousand Alabama workers walked out, demanding a minimum of $12 for a thirty-hour week and reinstatement of fired union members. The unrest spread, and when the United Textile Workers (UTW) called for a general strike an estimated 400,000 workers walked out, making it the largest labor conflict in American history. The governors of South Carolina, North Carolina, and Georgia called out the militias and the national guards to support the mill owners. Financial need forced workers back and the UTW called off the strike three weeks later. Many workers were fired and blacklisted.

In the early 1960s, African Americans made up fewer than 2 percent of textile industry employees. Although the industry was very competitive and most jobs were largely unskilled, it chose to overlook this source of labor. Integration occurred through the enforcement of the federal Civil Rights Act of 1964.

Prospects

In the 1980s, half a million jobs moved overseas in the search for cheap labor, and in the next decades jobs continued to be lost and mills shut down. Legislative efforts have been made to protect the American textile industry, which will also need continuing innovation and technological advances in order to survive.

BIBLIOGRAPHY

Collier, Billie J., and Phyllis G. Tortora. *Understanding Textiles*, 6th ed. Upper Saddle River, N.J.: Prentice Hall, 2001.

Hall, Jacquelyn Dowd, et al. *Like a Family: The Making of a Southern Cotton Mill World*. Chapel Hill: University of North Carolina Press, 1987.

Harris, J., ed. *Textiles, 5000 Years: An International History and Illustrated Survey*. New York: Abrams, 1993.

Kinnane, Adrian. *DuPont: From the Banks of the Brandywine to Miracles of Science*. Wilmington, Del.: DuPont, 2002.

Little, Frances. *Early American Textiles*. New York: Century Co., 1931.

Minchin, Timothy J. *Hiring the Black Worker: The Racial Integration of the Southern Textile Industry, 1960–1980*. Chapel Hill: University of North Carolina Press, 1999.

Tortora, Phyllis G., and Robert S. Merkel, eds. *Fairchild's Dictionary of Textiles*, 7th ed. New York: Fairchild, 1996.

Christina Lindholm

See also **Industrial Revolution; Labor; Labor Legislation and Administration; Mill Streams; Slavery; Strikes; United Textile Workers;** *and vol. 9:* **Mill Worker's Letter on Hardships in the Textile Mills.**

THAMES, BATTLE OF THE. The American effort to reclaim the upper Great Lakes, lost to the British in August 1812, was led by Gen. William Henry Harrison, who established Fort Meigs (above Toledo) as an advance base, and Capt. Oliver Hazard Perry, who built the fleet that, on 10 September, won the Battle of Lake Erie. Harrison's troops, convoyed by Perry's fleet, pursued British Gen. Henry A. Procter's forces into the interior of Ontario. The Americans engaged and defeated Proctor and his Indian allies, led by Tecumseh, a few miles east of Thamesville on 5 October 1813. Harrison's victory added to the future president's reputation as a military hero and restored American dominance in the Northwest.

BIBLIOGRAPHY

Morison, Samuel E. *"Old Bruin": Commodore Matthew C. Perry, 1794–1858.* Boston: Little, Brown, 1967.

Peterson, Norma Lois. *The Presidencies of William Henry Harrison and John Tyler.* Lawrence: University Press of Kansas, 1989.

Skaggs, David Curtis. *A Signal Victory: The Lake Erie Campaign, 1812–1813.* Annapolis, Md.: Naval Institute Press, 1997.

Sugden, John. *Tecumseh's Last Stand.* Norman: University of Oklahoma Press, 1985.

———. *Tecumseh: A Life.* New York: Holt, 1998.

M. M. Quaife/A. R.

See also **"Don't Give Up the Ship"; Ghent, Treaty of; Great Lakes Naval Campaigns of 1812; Lake Erie, Battle of; Tecumseh's Crusade; Tippecanoe, Battle of; War of 1812.**

THANKSGIVING DAY. Thanksgiving Day, a national holiday imitated only by Canadians, was first established as an annual event by Abraham Lincoln in a proclamation dated 3 October 1863. Expressing hope amidst the continuing Civil War, it was a response to the campaign of Sarah Josepha Hale, editor of *Godey's Lady's Book*, to nationalize an autumn festival already observed by most of the states. Sporadic days of thanksgiving had been previously appointed by national leaders, such as those honoring military victories during the American Revolution, the Whiskey Rebellion, and the War of 1812 and one by George Washington to celebrate the new Constitution on 26 November 1789. The origin of the holiday is rooted in New England practices of prayer and feasting, most symbolically enacted by the three-day harvest celebration in 1621 between the Pilgrim settlers of PLYMOUTH COLONY and ninety Wampanoag, an event briefly mentioned in the histories written by Plymouth governors William Bradford and Edward Winslow.

This First Thanksgiving has been widely promoted since the late nineteenth century as a source of national origins. The types of public events during Thanksgiving have changed over time and have included church services, shooting matches, and—in nineteenth-century cities—military parades, masquerades, child begging, and charity banquets. Persisting public activities include games between football rivals (beginning in 1876) and spectacular commercially sponsored parades, such as the Macy's parade in New York City starting in 1924. President Franklin Delano Roosevelt changed the traditional observance from the last to the penultimate Thursday in 1939 (a year when November had five Thursdays) to extend the holiday shopping season. The controversy surrounding the alteration, however, led to a congressional resolution in 1941 that fixed the official holiday as the fourth Thursday in November. The heavy volume of travel over the four-day weekend originated in the nineteenth-century tradition of homecoming, when urban residents returned to celebrate their rural roots and feast on native foods such as turkey (which is such a central symbol that the holiday is sometimes called Turkey Day).

BIBLIOGRAPHY

Appelbaum, Diana Karter. *Thanksgiving: An American Holiday, An American History.* New York: Facts On File, 1984.

Myers, Robert J. *Celebrations: The Complete Book of American Holidays.* Garden City, N.Y.: Doubleday, 1972.

Pleck, Elizabeth. "The Making of the Domestic Occasion: The History of Thanksgiving in the United States." *Journal of Social History* 32 (1999): 773–789.

Timothy Marr

See also **Holidays and Festivals.**

THEATER in America started as ritual performance by Native Americans and then, upon the arrival of the first white, Spanish settlers, became another sort of ritual, based on medieval European Christian morality plays. For many years, theater was outlawed in Colonial America, although the proscription hardly called a halt to performances. As everywhere, theater ranged between high and low: early "high" theater attempted to duplicate what was going on in Europe and included rewritten ("improved") Shakespeare and other, mostly British dramas, including *School for Scandal* by Richard Brinsley Sheridan. "Low" theater included riverboat shows, VAUDEVILLE, minstrel shows, and Wild West shows. It was not until the late eighteenth century that an authentic "American" voice began to emerge in the theater. This voice continued to develop throughout the nineteenth century and found itself being embraced on the world stage during the twentieth century.

Early American Theater

While there are no records of the earliest Native American performances, Indian rituals were noted by the early white settlers. Native Americans performed most of their theatrical pieces in honor of various gods or to celebrate changes in seasons, harvests, hunts, battles, and so on. Among the many performances were the summer and winter rituals of the Pueblo Indians. Pueblo dramas included the Deer Dance, Buffalo Dance, Corn Dance, Raingod Dance, and the Eagle Dance. Variations on Native American performance were later played out many times with white settlers in rituals and ceremonies focused around treaties and other meetings. These dramas included gift giving, dances, and speeches. Later, Indians—and cowboys—became stock characters in performances ranging from melodramas to vaudeville. In "Wild West" shows of the nineteenth century, Indian rituals were recreated for white audiences in the eastern United States and in Europe.

The first recorded white colonial performances were morality plays performed by missionaries for Spanish soldiers in Florida in 1567. These plays were intended to show the supremacy of the Spaniards' religion and its ultimate triumph in the New World. Although no record of the actual play exists, it can be assumed that it took the stylized and ritualistic form of medieval drama.

In Colonial days, theater was looked down upon by many of the Puritanical white settlers, so it was not until 1665 that the first play performed in English was recorded. *Ye Bare and Ye Cub* was performed by three men in Accomack County, Virginia. Apparently someone was offended by the offering, or simply by the idea of theater, because the players were sued. After the play was performed in court, the performers were found "not guilty of fault." Quakers were especially opposed to theatrical performances and had laws passed against them in most of the colonies, beginning with William Penn's in Pennsylvania. Proscriptions against theater were not passed in Virginia, and that is likely why it became the home of the first professional American theater, the Company of Comedians, led by entrepreneur Lewis Hallam.

Hallam's troupe of provincial players arrived from England in 1752. Like most of the companies to follow, the Company of Comedians was run by an actor/manager. After performing Shakespeare in Williamsburg, Virginia, Hallam built the first theater in New York City in 1753 and in Charleston in 1754. Hallam's fare also included such English staples as Restoration drama, farce, and operetta. His company played Philadelphia and toured the South and eventually moved to Jamaica, where Hallam died. While in Jamaica, Hallam's wife married another theater producer, David Douglass, who had founded theaters in Philadelphia and New York. Under Douglass, the company moved back to the States, calling itself the American Company. Hallam's son, Lewis Hallam the Younger, often performed opposite his mother and proved to be a talented comic. In 1767, Hallam played the lead in the first professional American drama, Thomas Godfrey's *Prince of Parthia*.

In 1775, theater was again banned, this time by the Continental Congress. While the ban was routinely ignored, it did put off professional theater producers—including David Douglass, who moved back to Jamaica—and fostered more amateur performances, especially those featuring patriotic themes.

Theater in the Early United States

After the Revolutionary War (1775–1783), the American Company returned to New York City and when David Douglass died, Hallam took over and produced what is widely believed to be the first important American play, one written by a Harvard-educated lawyer and army officer, Royall Tyler. Tyler's play, *The Contrast*, debuted in New York in March 1787. The characters in *The Contrast* include a Revolutionary War veteran and a man deemed a natural nobleman. The leading character, Jonathan, was the first in a long line of "Yankees" to grace the American stage. Tyler made comparisons between American and British attitudes that favored the American. In addition to its themes of patriotism and the belief that love con-

quers all, Tyler's play is filled with references to the fashions and topics of the time. *The Contrast* was an instant hit that was also performed in Baltimore, Philadelphia, and Boston and has seen revivals up to the twenty-first century.

During the early nineteenth century, touring groups continued to play a large role in American theater, and English actors were often imported to headline local productions. Among the more popular players were Edmund Kean and Junius Brutus Booth (father of actor Edwin Booth and actor/Lincoln assassin John Wilkes Booth). At this time, actors often specialized in one or two roles that they were known for.

The American-born actor credited with innovating a truly American style of acting was Edwin Forrest. After playing second leads to Edmund Kean, Forrest eventually became a leading man and played throughout the East, South, and Midwest. Forrest was an athletic actor who was a natural for heroic and rebellious roles. He found his greatest fame as star of *Metamora; or, The Last of the Wampanoags* (1829), a play that he found by sponsoring a contest for a tragedy, "of which the hero . . . shall be an aboriginal of this country." Forrest played the Indian Metamora throughout his career, and the success of the play caused many other dramas featuring the noble savage to be entered into the American repertory.

For the most part, when Black Americans were portrayed, it was not as noble persons but as buffoons. The 1840s saw the rise of minstrelsy, in which mostly white, but also black, performers sang and danced while made up in blackface, achieved by smearing coal on the face. Minstrel shows remained popular until the early twentieth century. Also wildly popular in midcentury were "Tom Shows," melodramatic productions based on Harriet Beecher Stowe's 1852 novel, *Uncle Tom's Cabin*. Other forms of diversion included vaudeville, which boasted such performers as Eddie Foy, W. C. Fields, and Sophie Tucker. P. T. Barnum sponsored singing tours by the "Swedish Nightingale," Jenny Lind, and opened the American Museum (1842) in New York City where he exhibited such freakish attractions as "Tom Thumb" and the Siamese twins Chang and Eng. Barnum, along with James A. Bailey, founded the Barnum and Bailey Circus in 1881.

Wild West shows were in vogue, especially Buffalo Bill's Wild West Show, organized by former Pony Express rider William Frederick Cody in 1883. Cody's Cowboy and Indian show toured throughout the United States and Europe. Showboats were also a popular venue for all manner of entertainment from vaudeville to Shakespeare.

Theater of the Gilded Age

The last thirty years of the 1800s, often referred to as the "Gilded Age," were dominated by melodrama. Many Civil War plays were produced; they often focused on romances between Northern and Southern lovers but skirted the political issues of the war. Nonetheless, American theater was edging ever closer to the realistic style of performance that would come to dominate it in the twentieth century.

A trend in late-nineteenth-century drama, attributed largely to California-born manager/playwright/producer David Belasco, was to greatly enhance the production values of a play. Belasco built enormous and spectacular three-dimensional sets that he deemed naturalistic. Belasco was among the forerunners of a small group of producers who were breaking away from the romantic style of acting that marked the nineteenth century as well. These producer/directors encouraged actors to perform in a naturalistic style that suited the actors' own personalities.

By 1888, it was estimated that there were more than 2,400 professional actors in the United States. A few earned as much as $100,000 a year—a tremendous amount at the time. Among the highly paid actors were many who came from theatrical families, including descendents of the Booths, the Davenports, the Jeffersons, and the Drew-Barrymores (Lionel, Ethel, and John Barrymore all worked on the New York stage in the early twentieth century). Lesser-known performers were often badly treated; sometimes no pay was given for weeks or even months of rehearsal. Thus, in 1894, the Actors' Society of America, later Actors' Equity, was formed to negotiate standard contracts for actors. Even before this, other stage employees organized unions.

The number of actors grew to around 15,000 at the turn of the twentieth century. Along with the increase in actors came an increase in acting schools. Among the first was the Lyceum Theatre School, founded in New York City in 1884 and renamed the American Academy of Dramatic Arts in 1892. The American Academy of Dramatic Arts remains perhaps the most prestigious acting school in the country.

In the mid-nineteenth century, stock companies rose in number and often traveled. The opening of the first transcontinental railroad in 1869 meant that productions could travel to the West Coast. Soon companies stopped developing a large number of new plays and instead produced long runs of a single, popular play that they often took on tour. By the early 1870s, there were about 50 resident stock companies in the country. In 1886, a group of booking agents and managers formed a partnership known as the Theatrical Trust (or Syndicate). For approximately thirty years, the Syndicate controlled virtually all bookings at professional theaters. Over 1,700 theaters were available to touring productions in 1905, according to Julius Cahn's *Official Theatrical Guide*, making the Syndicate's sphere of influence very great indeed. By the turn of the twentieth century, resident stock companies were nearly nonexistent.

A challenge to the Syndicate's authority came from independent producer David Belasco, who wanted to stage a play set in Japan at the 1904 World's Fair in St. Louis and was blocked by the syndicate. Belasco booked a theater anyway and, typically, the Syndicate mounted a rival play on the same topic as Belasco's. Even an antitrust suit, filed after the Sherman Antitrust Act of 1890 became law, failed to loosen the Syndicate's grip. What did finally stop the Syndicate was another group of theatrical monopolists, the New York–based Shubert brothers—Lee, Sam S., and Jacob J. The Shuberts, who initially worked with the Syndicate, eventually joined forces with David Belasco, actress Minnie Maddern Fiske, and others to overturn it.

The nineteenth century did see some accomplished American playwrights, including Edward Harrigan, William Dean Howells, and Steele MacKaye. However, the time and country that produced such memorable writers in other genres as Walt Whitman, Emily Dickinson, and Henry David Thoreau failed to nurture a truly great playwright until the twentieth century.

Theatre in the Early Twentieth Century

The early twentieth century mostly saw a continuation of commercialization and lack of originality in the theater. Melodrama, with subjects ranging from historical to romantic to Western to mystery, remained the form most often performed. Touring ceased to be the main way in which plays were presented and stock companies again formed. The continuing prosperity of America was reflected in the theater, and by 1912 there were some 8,000 theaters in America. By then, activities were focused in New York, especially off Times Square. Many of the theaters built during the boom of the 1920s were still used in 2002.

With the exception of some suffragist actresses, there were very few performers involved in political causes. However, in the Chicago slums, Jane Addams and Ellen Gates Starr recognized the possibilities of theater as a force for social good and opened Hull House in 1889 as an alternative entertainment for impoverished youth. Similar theaters followed, including the Henry Street Settlement in New York.

As more and more of the theatergoing public became exposed to the work of such groundbreaking European playwrights as Henrik Ibsen, Anton Chekhov, and George Bernard Shaw, a small but active theater intelligentsia was formed that looked for more sophisticated plays. In the teens, "Little Theaters" began to open around the country. Some of these were formed for the purpose of offering standard commercial fare at cut rates, but many were formed with a higher purpose in mind—to produce serious, realist drama. These little theaters, including Chicago's Little Theatre, New York's Neighborhood Playhouse and Washington Square Players, and the Cleveland Playhouse featured work by both contemporary European and American playwrights and were modeled after European art theaters such as the Moscow Art Theatre and Dublin's Abbey Theatre. American performances by these two theater companies and others greatly influenced the style of acting in America further toward naturalism.

In Massachusetts, the PROVINCETOWN PLAYERS were developing the early short sea plays (set on the sea) of the only American playwright ever to win a Nobel Prize (1936), Eugene O'Neill. O'Neill was the son of James O'Neill, a famous actor who felt he had squandered his talent playing mostly one role, in *The Count of Monte Cristo*, throughout his career. The plays were taken to New York and the Provincetown Players began a tradition of developing plays out of town before a New York opening. O'Neill was the first of many great American playwrights to work in the twentieth century. He is credited with first perfecting the realist voice of the American stage.

During the 1930s, the Great Depression brought a far greater interest in political theater. Such groups as the INTERNATIONAL LADIES GARMENT WORKERS UNION put on plays, and even the government got into the act through the federally sponsored and ill-fated Federal Theatre Project, which attempted to put 13,000 theater people on the government payroll. Meanwhile, the unions were represented by playwright Clifford Odets in his *Waiting for Lefty* on the legitimate stage. Lillian Hellman and Thornton Wilder were among the other prominent playwrights of the time.

The postwar 1940s were also a fascinating time for theater. It was then that the heartbreaking dramas of Mississippi playwright Tennessee Williams, *The Glass Menagerie* (1945) and *A Streetcar Named Desire* (1947), were staged. Marlon Brando, who studied the Stanislavski System of acting originated at the Moscow Art Theatre and taught at The Actors Studio (opened 1947), became an overnight sensation after starring in *A Streetcar Named Desire*. His intimate performance not only led to a long film career but also had a great influence on the way American actors performed.

Arthur Miller debuted works that deal with government corruption (*All My Sons*, 1947), the alienation of modern man (*Death of a Salesman*, 1949), and manipulation of public opinion through the House Un-American Activities Committee hearings of the early 1950s (*The Crucible*, 1953). In 1947, Julian Beck and Judith Malina formed the Living Theatre, an experimental theater devoted to producing avant-garde plays that promoted the ideals of pacifism and anarchy.

The 1940s also saw the development of the American musical, starting with *Oklahoma* (1943), written by Richard Rodgers and Oscar Hammerstein and choreographed by Agnes DeMille. Other musicals included *Brigadoon* (1947) and *My Fair Lady* (1956), by the team of Alan Jay Lerner and Frederick Loewe, and *West Side Story* (1957) by Leonard Bernstein and Arthur Laurents, and later, *Sweeney Todd* (1979), by Stephen Sondheim. The musical was to become the most American of theatrical genres; immense productions began to dominate the large theaters in New York by the 1950s and continue to do so.

Theatre in the Late Twentieth Century

The Civil Rights Movement, the war in Vietnam, and the other upheavals of the 1960s provided a rich time for theater. Playwrights including Amiri Baraka (then LeRoi Jones) championed the Black Arts Movement with such in-your-face plays as *Dutchman* (1964), in which a white woman stabs a black man on a subway. David Rabe wrote about Vietnam in *Stick and Bones* (1971). The 1960s also saw the first of many plays dealing openly with homosexuality. *The Boys in the Band* premiered in 1968. Later plays to deal with the subject included Larry Kramer's *The Normal Heart* (1985) and Tony Kushner's Pulitzer Prize–winning two-part epic, *Angels in America* (1991, 1993). The 1960s also ushered in the work of Neil Simon, probably the most popular writer of comedies in the late twentieth century.

Among other important playwrights of the last part of the century, California born and raised Sam Shepard writes plays about those who, like himself, rejected the mores of polite society; Christopher Durang lampoons the Catholic church that he was raised in; and Marsha Norman writes of a woman so disconnected she is planning suicide (*'night Mother*, 1982). Performance artists such as Karen Findley, whose work dealt with her own sexuality, Anna Deavere Smith, who explores social issues such as Black-Jewish relationships, and performer/musician Laurie Anderson rose to prominence in the 1980s.

Many of these performances were produced Off Broadway, including the New York Shakespeare Festival, founded in 1954 by Joseph Papp for the purpose of mounting Shakespeare productions in Central Park that were free and open to the public each summer. When Papp died in 1991, the innovative African American director George C. Wolfe became director of the festival. Papp also produced the surprise hit hippie musical of 1967, *Hair*, at his not-for-profit Public Theater. *Hair* was then moved to Broadway and the profits used for other, less commercial productions.

BROADWAY is still dominated by musicals and revivals of musicals, and it has seen a tremendous decline since the 1980s, largely because of escalating costs in mounting a production. In the 1950s, a grand musical such as *My Fair Lady* might have cost half a million dollars to produce, and tickets were less than ten dollars each. By the end of the twentieth century, costs soared so that a musical such as *The Lion King* (1997) could cost $15 million to produce and a ticket could cost up to $100.

Broadway budgets and ticket prices have long provided much of the momentum for Off Broadway and later for even smaller—less than 100-seat—houses called Off Off Broadway. Greenwich Village's Caffe Cino, founded in 1958 by Joe Cino, is generally thought to be the birthplace of Off Off Broadway, but Off Off Broadway's most enduring and important producer is Ellen Stewart of Café La Mama, which was founded in 1962, and renamed the La Mama Experimental Theater Club. Stewart is known for giving fresh voices a place in her theater, not because she likes the script—she often does not read them in advance—but rather because she has a good feeling about the person bringing an idea for a production to her. Off and Off Off Broadway venues, in addition to many regional theaters including Steppenwolf in Chicago, Magic Theater in San Francisco, and repertory companies including Yale Repertory Theater, American Conservatory Theater in San Francisco, Missouri Repertory Theater, and Chicago's Goodman Theater, are thought by many to be the most exciting places to view theater in the twenty-first century.

BIBLIOGRAPHY

Blum, Daniel. *Great Stars of the American Stage: A Pictorial Record.* New York: Greenberg, 1952.

Brustein, Robert. *Reimagining American Theatre.* New York: Hill and Wang, 1991.

Henderson, Mary C. *Theater in America: 250 Years of Plays, Players, and Productions.* New York: Abrams, 1996.

Hischak, Thomas S. *American Theatre: A Chronicle of Comedy and Drama, 1969–2000.* New York: Oxford University Press, 2001.

Londre, Felicia Hardison, and Daniel J. Watermeier. *The History of North American Theater: From Pre-Columbian Times to the Present.* New York: Continuum Publishing, 1998.

Lorca Peress contributed information on Off Off Broadway.

Rebekah Presson Mosby

See also **Dance, Indian; *Death of a Salesman, The*; Music: Theater and Film; Wild West Show.**

THEME PARKS. *See* **Amusement Parks.**

THEOCRACY IN NEW ENGLAND. This term was applied to the political regimes established in the Massachusetts Bay and New Haven colonies. These colonies were not theocracies in the traditional sense—that is, clergy did not establish or run their political systems. In both colonies, there was a clear separation of church and state. In Massachusetts, for instance, clergy were forbidden to hold public office, and both colonies maintained separate systems of political and religious leadership. But it was also the case that these political and religious systems were mutually reinforcing, and that early leaders hoped that every institution of their societies—the family, the church, and the magistracy—would function in concert to maintain a pious society based on Calvinist theology and religious practice. For this reason some have applied the term "theocracy" to seventeenth-century NEW ENGLAND.

Colonial leaders deliberately intended to create a BIBLE COMMONWEALTH, a society in which the fundamental law would be the revealed Word of God, and God would be regarded as the supreme legislator. Thus, John Winthrop announced the program before the settlement, "For the worke wee haue in hand, it is by a mutuall consent . . . to seeke out a place of Cohabitation and Consorteshipp under a due forme of Government both ciuill and ecclesiastical"; the "due forme" was that enacted in the Bible. John Cotton later argued that the New England colonies, having a clear field before them, were duty bound to erect a "Theocracy . . . as the best forme of government in the commonwealth, as well as in the Church." Consequently, the political theory assumed that the colonies were based on the Bible and that all specific laws would show biblical warrant.

The governments of the two colonies were founded on the theory that God had ordained all society as a check on depraved human impulses and, therefore, that all politics should ideally fulfill God's will. Hence, Winthrop explained in 1645, that after people entered a body politic, they gained the freedom to do only that "which is good, just and honest"—in other words, only that which God demands. The purpose of the state was to enforce God's will, and to ensure that every member of society would observe God's laws.

BIBLIOGRAPHY

Foster, Stephen. *The Long Argument: English Puritanism and the Shaping of New England Culture, 1570–1700.* Chapel Hill: University of North Carolina Press, 1991.

Gildrie, Richard P. *The Profane, the Civil, and the Godly: The Reformation of Manners in Orthodox New England, 1679–1749.* University Park: Pennsylvania State University Press, 1994.

Miller, Perry. *The New England Mind: The Seventeenth Century.* New York: Macmillan, 1939.

Noll, Mark A. *A History of Christianity in the United States and Canada.* Grand Rapids, Mich.: Eerdmans, 1992.

Perry Miller / S. B.

See also **Cambridge Agreement; Massachusetts Bay Colony; New England Way; New Haven Colony.**

THEOSOPHY is defined by its expounders as a religion-philosophy-science brought to America by "messengers of the guardians and preservers of the ancient Wisdom-Religion of the East." Its founder was an eccentric Russian noblewoman, Helena P. Blavatsky. In July 1848, at age sixteen, she was married to a forty-one-year-old government official. She ran away after three months to Constantinople and joined a circus. After extensive travels in the Far East where she claimed to have received instruction from "Sages of the Orient," she came to New York City on 7 July 1873 and, two years later, with William Q. Judge, Henry Steel Olcott, and fifteen others, formed the Theosophical Society. The purpose of the organization was to further a universal brotherhood of humanity without distinction of race, color, sex, caste, or creed; to further the study of the ancient scriptures and teachings such as Brahmanical, Buddhist, and Zoroastrian; and to investigate the "unexplained laws of Nature" and the psychic and spiritual powers latent in man.

At first, the theosophists displayed an interest in spiritualism but later repudiated it, stating that spiritistic phenomena "were but a meagre part of a larger whole." Later, Madame Blavatsky formed what she termed an "esoteric section," which was a select group of promising students gathered to study the more profound teachings of theosophy. Madame Blavatsky left the United States in 1878 and formed theosophical societies in England and India, which recognized her leadership until her death in 1891.

The teachings of theosophy stress universal brotherhood to be a fact in nature on which its philosophy and religion are based. Theosophy proclaims a "Deific Absolute Essence, infinite and unconditioned . . . from which all starts, and into which everything returns." Man has an immortal soul, but the soul is a tenant of many different bodies in many different lives. Every soul must become perfect before the next stage of existence can be entered upon, and those who go forward most rapidly must wait for all. For this, many reincarnations are necessary. Theosophy accepts the miracles of Jesus but denies their supernatural character, holding that they were accomplished through natural laws.

As of 2001, there were 130 theosophical study centers and theosophical societies—known as lodges—in the United States.

BIBLIOGRAPHY
Campbell, Bruce F. *Ancient Wisdom Revised: A History of the Theosophical Movement.* Berkeley: University of California Press, 1980.

Greenwalt, Emmet A. *The Point Loma Community in California, 1897–1942: A Theosophical Experiment.* Berkeley: University of California Press, 1955.

Washington, Peter. *Madame Blavatsky's Baboon: Theosophy and the Emergence of the Western Guru.* London: Secker and Warburg, 1993.

William W. Sweet / F. B.

See also **Asian Religions and Sects; Cults; New Age Movement; Utopian Communities.**

THINK TANKS are policy-oriented research organizations that provide expertise to government. By the year 2000 there were an estimated 1,200 nongovernment think tanks of various descriptions, various focuses on social and economic issues, and various sources of funding at work in the United States. Of the major think tanks, only the BROOKINGS INSTITUTION (1916) and the Carnegie Endowment for International Peace (1910) were founded before World War II. The American Enterprise Institute was founded in 1943.

Although think tanks are ostensibly nonpartisan, in many instances they function as extensions of state power, gaining and losing influence with changes in governments and shifts in the ideological climate of the country. In other cases, think tanks function more independently,

questioning and monitoring state strategies and structures. (For example, the Rand Corporation, founded in the aftermath of World War II, was created to monitor and evaluate Air Force programs, before it became an independent research organization in the 1950s.)

The course of the Brookings Institution reflects the kinds of changes that can occur in shifting ideological currents. Founded as the Institute for Government Research in 1916 and reorganized in 1927 by the St. Louis philanthropist Robert Brookings, the Brookings Institution sought to bring nonpartisan expertise to policy questions of the day. During the 1930s, however, the institution, under its first president, Harold Moulton, became a major critic of many New Deal programs, including the National Recovery Administration, the Agricultural Adjustment Administration, securities regulation, and Keynesian economic policy. Following World War II, Moulton warned repeatedly that the government had drifted into "uncharted seas, if not state socialism," and called for an end to "regimentation."

In response to the new postwar environment and the reluctance of foundations to fund an institution they perceived as ineffective and out of touch, Robert Calkins, former head of the General Education Fund at the ROCKEFELLER FOUNDATION, agreed to become president of Brookings. Calkins reorganized the institution and recruited social scientists with liberal credentials and government experience. This new group had close ties with government and, unlike the devotees of the earlier nonpartisan ideal, aligned themselves closely with presidential administrations. In 1965, when Calkins retired, the Brookings Institution was representative of mainstream Keynesian economic thinking, and its growing influence was reflected in renewed foundation support, especially from the Ford Foundation. Under Calkins's successor, Kermit Gordon, Brookings's reputation as a liberal Democratic think tank was well entrenched. Under Gordon, the Brookings Institution became a major center for policy innovation in welfare, health care, education, housing, and taxation policy.

In 1976, the board of trustees appointed Bruce MacLaury to head the institution. A former regional Federal Reserve banker and Treasury official, MacLaury successfully courted business support, increased corporate representation on the board of trustees, and moved the institution toward a more moderate ideological stance.

By the 1970s, the Brookings Institution confronted competition from other major policy research institutions, especially the American Enterprise Institute and the Heritage Foundation, both viewed as conservative research institutions close to the Republican party.

The American Enterprise Institute (AEI), founded in 1943 as the American Enterprise Association (AEA), illustrates the experience of a conservatively oriented research institution that expressed deep ambivalence about the post–World War II policy consensus. The key figure behind the establishment of the AEA was Lewis Brown, chairman of Johns-Manville Corporation. From the start, the AEA reflected a conservative bias.

In 1954, A. D. Marshall, head of General Electric, assumed the institution's presidency and immediately hired William Baroody and W. Glenn Campbell, both staff economists at the U.S. Chamber of Commerce, to head the research program. Under their guidance, AEA was gradually built into a modern research institute under its new name, the American Enterprise Institute. Principle support came from the Lilly Endowment, the Scaife Fund, and the Earhart and Kresge Foundations, as well as major corporate sponsors. The institution's reputation was enhanced when the Nixon administration called a number of AEI associates to government positions. The AEI also emerged as a successful proponent of economic deregulation.

In 1977, William Baroody retired and his son, William Baroody Jr., took over the presidency of the institution. To improve its standing in the academic community, the AEI assembled an impressive staff including Melvin Laird, William Simon, Robert Bork, Michael Novak, and Herbert Stein. The tenure of William Baroody Jr., however, ended abruptly in the summer of 1987, when an increasingly restive board of trustees forced his resignation because of cost overruns and declining revenues. Baroody's successor, Christopher DeMuth, bolstered the conservative orientation of the institute by bringing on board several former Reagan administration officials with strong rightist reputations.

The founding of the Heritage Foundation in 1973 revealed a new ideological climate in the analysis of public knowledge. Founded by Edwin Feulner and Paul Weyrich to provide rapid and succinct legislative analysis on issues pending before Congress, the Heritage Foundation sought to promote conservative values and demonstrate the need for a free market and a strong defense. The Heritage Foundation's articulation of conservative values in social policy, education, and government activities placed it at the forefront of New Right activity. The Heritage Foundation remained relatively small in its early years, but the election of Ronald Reagan to the presidency in 1980 enhanced the institution's prestige. By the mid-1980s the Heritage Foundation had established a solid place in the Washington world of think tanks as a well-organized, efficient, and well-financed research organization that called for the turning over of many government tasks to private enterprise, a strong defense, and a cautious approach to Russia and China.

During the 1960s, 1970s, and 1980s, a myriad of other think tanks emerged in Washington representing a range of ideological positions and specialized policy interests, including the left-oriented Institute for Policy Studies (1963) and the libertarian-oriented Cato Institute (1977). Think tanks concerned with national security included the Center for Strategic and International Studies (1962) and the Center for National Security Studies

(1962) affiliated with the AMERICAN CIVIL LIBERTIES UNION. The Urban Institute (1968) focused on domestic social, welfare, and family policy, while the National Women's Law Center (1972) worked on policies that affect women, especially reproductive rights, employment, and education. The Institute for International Economics (1981) became a major center for international economic and monetary policies, especially from a free-trade perspective. The traditionalist-oriented Ethics and Public Policy Center (1976) provided analysis of public policies related to religious issues.

BIBLIOGRAPHY

Critchlow, Donald T. *The Brookings Institution, 1916–1952.* DeKalb: Northern Illinois University Press, 1985.

Dixon, Paul. *Think Tanks.* New York: Atheneum, 1971.

Edwards, Lee. *The Power of Ideas: The Heritage Foundation at Twenty-Five Years.* Ottawa, Ill.: Jameson Books, 1997.

Friedman, John S., ed. *The First Harvest: An Institute for Policy Studies Reader, 1963–1983.* Washington, D.C.: Grove, 1983.

Lagemann, Ellen Condliffe. *The Politics of Knowledge: The Carnegie Corporation, Philanthropy, and Public Policy.* Middletown, Conn.: Wesleyan University Press, 1989.

Ricci, David. *The Transformation of American Politics: The New Washington and the Rise of Think Tanks.* New Haven, Conn.: Yale University Press, 1993.

Smith, James Allen. *The Idea Brokers: Think Tanks and the New Policy Elite.* New York: Free Press, 1991.

Donald T. Critchlow

THIRD PARTIES. The American political system has rarely been kind to third parties. No third party has won a presidential election in over a century. From the point of view of the two major parties, minor parties have functioned more as irritants or sideshows than as serious rivals. Parties such as the Libertarian Party, the American Vegetarian Party, the nativist Know-Nothing Party, and the agrarian Populist parties have been most valuable as safety valves for alienated voters, and as sources of new ideas, which, if they become popular, the major parties appropriate. In the historian Richard Hofstadter's classic formulation: "Third parties are like bees: once they have stung, they die."

Hofstadter explains this phenomenon by claiming that the major parties champion patronage not principle. A better explanation is more structural, and more benign. The "first to the post" nature of most American elections selects the candidate with the most number of votes even without a majority. Marginal parties that woo a consistent minority languish. On the presidential level, the "winner take all" rules for most states in the electoral college further penalize third parties by diffusing their impact. In 1992, Ross Perot received over 19 million votes, 18.8 percent of the popular vote, but no electoral votes, and, thus, no power. As a result, although there is nothing mandating it in the Constitution—and the Framers abhorred

George Wallace. The segregationist Alabama governor, who was a third-party candidate for president in 1968; his 1972 bid for the Democratic presidential nomination ended when an assassination attempt left him disabled. LIBRARY OF CONGRESS

parties—since the 1830s a two-party system has been the norm in American politics.

The classic American third party is identified with an issue, or a cluster of issues. The searing antebellum slavery debate spawned various third parties. James G. Birney ran with the antislavery Liberty Party in 1840 and 1844; former president Martin Van Buren won over 10 percent of the popular vote—but no electoral votes—with the Free Soil Party in 1848. By 1860, the antislavery Republican Party had captured the presidency, although with less than 40 percent of the popular vote in a rare four-way race. Some historians consider the Republican Party America's only successful third party. Others argue that the party debuted as a new major party assembled from old ones, not as a minor party that succeeded.

Third Parties after the Civil War
The century and a half following the Civil War witnessed an extraordinarily stable rivalry between the Republicans and the Democrats. Throughout, third parties erupted sporadically, commanded attention, made their mark politically, rarely gained much actual power, and then disappeared. In the late nineteenth century, the agrarian Populist protest movement produced a Greenback Party and the People's Party. The 1892 platform of the People's

Party heralded the reorientation in government power that shaped the twentieth century. "We believe that the power of the government—in other words of the people—should be expanded," the platform thundered. Some of the more radical Populist schemes proposing public ownership of the railroads, the telegraph, and the telephone failed. But many other proposals eventually became integrated into American political life, such as a national currency, a graduated income tax, the (secret) Australian ballot, and the direct election of United States senators. In 1892, James B. Weaver of the People's Party won more than a million popular votes and 22 electoral votes. That year Populists sent a dozen congressmen to Washington, while securing governor's chairs in Kansas, North Dakota, and Colorado.

In the early twentieth century, the Socialist, Socialist Workers, and Socialist Laborites helped radical Americans, particularly many immigrants, express frustration while staying within America's political boundaries. Typically, the perennial Socialist Party candidate, Eugene V. Debs, won hundreds of thousands of votes in 1904, 1908, 1912, and 1920, but not even one electoral vote. The only formidable third-party challenge from that era was a fluke. In 1912, the popular former president Theodore Roosevelt fought his handpicked protégé President William Howard Taft for the Republican nomination. When Taft won, Roosevelt ran as a Progressive. Thanks to Roosevelt, the Progressive Party won 88 electoral votes, and became the only modern third party to come in second for the presidency. Twelve years later, "Fighting Bob" Robert M. La Follette's Progressive campaign only won the electoral votes of his home state, Wisconsin. Still, as with the Populists, many Progressive ideas became law, such as woman's suffrage, prohibition of child labor, and a minimum wage for working women.

Third Parties in the Modern Era
In the latter half of the twentieth century, third parties were even more transitory and often had even fewer infrastructures. In 1948, Southerners rejecting the Democratic turn toward civil rights bolted the party to form the Dixiecrats or States' Rights Democratic Party. Their candidate Strom Thurmond won 1,169,063 popular votes and 39 electoral votes from various Southern states. That same year former Vice President Henry Wallace's breakaway party from the left side of the Democratic coalition, the Progressive Party, won 1,157,172 votes scattered in the North and Midwest, but no electoral votes. Twenty years later, civil rights issues again propelled a Southern breakaway party with George Wallace's American Independent Party winning almost 10 million votes and 46 electoral votes.

In the modern era, the most attention-getting third party revolts cast a heroic independent voice against mealy-mouthed and hypercautious major party nominees. In 1980, veteran Congressman John Anderson broke away from the Republican Party, after distinguishing himself in

119

the Republican primaries as a straight shooter. In 1992 and 1996 billionaire businessman Ross Perot bankrolled his own campaign and party, targeting the deficit. And in 2000, the long-time reformer Ralph Nader mounted a third-party effort that did not even win five percent of the popular vote, but whose more than 90,000 votes in Florida may have thrown the election to George W. Bush.

In an era of cynicism and political disengagement, public opinion polls show that Americans claim they would like to see a third party as an alternative. At the state and local level, some third parties have lasted, most notably New York City's Liberal and Conservative Parties and Minnesota's Farmer-Labor Party. In the 1980s, the Libertarian Party advanced in Alaska, and in the 1990s, Connecticut and Maine, among others, had independent governors, while Vermont had an independent-socialist congressman. Still, these are mere shooting stars in the American political universe. As their predecessors did, modern, consumer-oriented Americans approve of third parties in principle, but rarely in practice.

BIBLIOGRAPHY

Hofstadter, Richard. *The Age of Reform: From Bryan to F. D. R.* New York: Random House, 1955.

Polakoff, Keith I. *Political Parties in American History.* New York: Wiley, 1981.

Reichley, James. *The Life of the Parties: A History of American Political Parties.* New York: Free Press, 1992.

Rosenstone, Steven J. *Third Parties in America: Citizen Response to Major Party Failure.* Princeton, N.J.: Princeton University Press, 1984.

Gil Troy

See also **Machine, Political; Political Parties.**

THIRTY-EIGHTH PARALLEL. As World War II in the Pacific neared its end in August 1945, the United States began to dismantle the Japanese Empire and return conquered nations to indigenous rule. The United States had given little thought to the Korean peninsula before Japan's surrender. The region played a very minor role in America's strategic plan during the war, and many observers expected that the Soviet Union would assume the postwar occupation duties. However, Joseph Stalin's clear ambition to dominate Eastern Europe and parts of the Middle East convinced U.S. policymakers to limit Soviet influence in the Far East. The Soviet Union had 1.6 million battle-hardened troops on the Manchurian and Korean borders, but the United States wagered that Stalin would accept an American role in the postwar occupation of Korea if President Harry Truman's administration moved quickly.

When the Soviet Twenty-fifth Army entered Korea on 10 August and moved as far south as Pyongyang, the United States realized how little time it had to act. That same evening, the War Department instructed two U.S. Army officers, Colonel Dean Rusk and Colonel Charles H. Bonesteel III, to design an occupation plan for Korea. They proposed a demarcation line at the thirty-eighth parallel, with the Soviets handling the postwar occupation duties in the north and the Americans administering the southern half.

The choice was based on expediency—they were forced to make a quick decision and the thirty-eighth parallel was clearly marked on most maps of Korea. The decision was also made for bureaucratic convenience: the thirty-eighth parallel divided the country into two halves of roughly the same size (the northern part being slightly larger—48,000 square miles opposed to 37,000). However, it did not take into account the economic differences or such factors as demography and geography. As a result, the northern half included virtually all of the industrial facilities and mineral wealth, while the southern sphere incorporated most of the agricultural land and a majority of the population. The thirty-eighth parallel was designed to be a political border, but not a permanent one, and thus it did not take into account military defensibility. The United States immediately forwarded the occupation plan to Stalin and the Soviets accepted on 16 August. With the rapid ascent of the Cold War, however, the thirty-eighth parallel soon became a de facto international boundary between an emergent communist state led by Kim Il-sung in the north and a pro-Western autocratic state headed by Syngman Rhee in the south.

BIBLIOGRAPHY

Hickey, Michael. *The Korean War: The West Confronts Communism, 1950–1953.* Woodstock, N.Y.: Overlook Press, 1999.

Sandler, Stanley. *The Korean War: No Victors, No Vanquished.* Lexington: University of Kentucky Press, 1999.

Stueck, William Whitney. *The Korean War: An International History.* Princeton, N.J.: Princeton University Press, 1995.

Erik B. Villard

See also **Korean War.**

THIRTY-HOUR WEEK. In 1932, Senator Hugo Black (D-Alabama) introduced the Thirty-Hour Work Week Bill, 72nd Congress, to "prohibit, in interstate or foreign commerce, all goods produced by establishments where workers were employed more than five days a week or six hours a day." Black hoped that this bill, drafted by the American Federation of Labor, would create 6 million jobs. The Senate passed the bill on 6 April 1933, by a vote of 53–30.

President Franklin Delano Roosevelt privately expressed doubts, and the bill remained in House of Representatives committees for five years. When the FAIR LABOR STANDARDS ACT became law in 1938, the thirty-hour work week provision was not included.

BIBLIOGRAPHY

Hunnicutt, Benjamin Kline. *Work Without End: Abandoning Shorter Hours for the Right to Work.* Philadelphia: Temple University Press, 1988.

Kelly Boyer Sagert

See also **American Federation of Labor–Congress of Industrial Organizations; Great Depression.**

THOMAS CONFIRMATION HEARINGS.

On 28 June 1991, Thurgood Marshall, the first African American to serve on the Supreme Court, sent his resignation to President George H. W. Bush. Three days later, the president nominated Clarence Thomas, another African American, to fill the vacancy. But while Marshall had been a leading liberal on the Court and a champion of minorities and the poor, Thomas held much more conservative views. Born into a poor Georgia family, he graduated from Yale Law School in 1974 and rose in Missouri legal and political circles until moving to Washington, D.C., with Senator John Danforth. Thomas headed the Equal Employment Opportunity Commission from 1982 until

Anita Hill. The law professor testifies before the Senate Judiciary Committee that Clarence Thomas sexually harassed her while she worked for him at the Equal Employment Opportunity Commission. Thomas angrily denied the accusations and was narrowly confirmed to a seat on the U.S. Supreme Court. ASSOCIATED PRESS/WORLD WIDE PHOTOS

1990, when President Bush named him to the Court of Appeals for the District of Columbia.

The earliest phase of the nomination hearings centered on Thomas's political, social, and judicial views, his critics inquiring particularly into his lukewarm attitudes toward affirmative action and other social programs aimed at minority groups. The nominee maintained a discreetly noncommittal attitude when questioned on such controversial matters as abortion. The Senate Judiciary Committee was evenly divided and, in late September, sent the nomination forward with no recommendation. Before the full Senate could act, however, an explosive new element was injected into the debate.

Anita Hill, a young African American law professor at the University of Oklahoma, alleged that while working for Thomas she had been harassed by him. She charged that Thomas repeatedly addressed crude and sexually explicit remarks to her and made persistent and unwanted sexual advances. Hill made her allegations in televised testimony before the Senate Judiciary Committee, and much of the nation was transfixed by her dramatic charges and by Thomas's vehement and angry denial of every allegation (he called the proceedings "a high tech lynching"). Both principals were highly articulate and both seemed honest, but it was clear that one of them was not telling the truth. Proponents of Thomas felt that the Hill testimony was part of an orchestrated campaign to discredit a conservative. Opponents, on the other hand, believed that Hill's charges were convincing and damaging and that the Judiciary Committee (made up entirely of white males) was insensitive at best and harshly aggressive toward Hill at worst—Senators Arlen Spector, Orrin Hatch, and Alan Simpson came in for particular criticism because of their overtly hostile attitude toward Hill.

On 15 October 1991, the full Senate voted to confirm Thomas by a vote of 52–48, the narrowest confirmation vote of the twentieth century. Thomas took the oath of office on 23 October. One of the results of the hearings was a heightened consciousness of the problem of sexual harassment and a greater willingness on the part of many women to reveal their own experiences and, in some instances, to bring formal charges.

BIBLIOGRAPHY

Danforth, John. *Resurrection: The Confirmation of Clarence Thomas.* New York: Viking, 1994.

Hill, Anita. *Speaking Truth to Power.* New York: Doubleday, 1997.

Mayer, Jane, and Jill Abramson. *Strange Justice: The Selling of Clarence Thomas.* Boston: Houghton Mifflin, 1994.

United States Senate. *Nomination of Judge Clarence Thomas to be Associate Justice of the Supreme Court of the United States: Hearings before the Committee on the Judiciary.* 4 volumes. Washington, D.C.: Government Printing Office, 1991.

David W. Levy

See also **Confirmation by the Senate.**

Three Mile Island. An aerial view of the nuclear facility near Harrisburg, Pa. AP/WIDE WORLD PHOTOS

an eleven-year period, the cleanup of Three Mile Island's severely damaged reactor cost in excess of $1 billion.

BIBLIOGRAPHY

Cantelon, Philip L., and Robert C. Williams. *Crisis Contained: The Department of Energy at Three Mile Island.* Carbondale: Southern Illinois University Press, 1982.

President's Commission on the Accident at Three Mile Island. *Report of the President's Commission on the Accident at Three Mile Island: The Need for Change: The Legacy of TMI.* Washington, D.C.: Government Printing Office, 1979.

Stephens, Mark. *Three Mile Island.* New York: Random House, 1980.

Robert M. Guth
John Wills

See also **Electric Power and Light Industry; Nuclear Power; Nuclear Regulatory Commission.**

THREE MILE ISLAND, the site of the worst civilian nuclear power program accident in the United States, is located in the Susquehanna River near Harrisburg, Pennsylvania. In the early 1970s, Metropolitan Edison built two reactors on Three Mile Island for commercial energy production. On 28 March 1979, a faulty valve allowed water coolant to escape from Metropolitan Edison's second reactor, Unit 2, during an unplanned shutdown. A cascade of human errors and technological mishaps resulted in an overheated reactor core with temperatures as high as 4,300 degrees and the accidental release of radiation into the atmosphere. Plant operators struggled to resolve the situation. Press reporters highlighted the confusion surrounding the accident, while Governor Richard L. Thornburgh of Pennsylvania and President Jimmy Carter visited the stricken plant, urging the nation to remain calm. On 30 March, state officials evacuated pregnant women and preschool children from the immediate area as a safety measure. On 2 April, temperatures decreased inside the Unit 2 reactor, and government officials declared the crisis over on 9 April.

A commission authorized by President Carter investigated the calamity. Government analysts calculated that, at the height of the crisis, Unit 2 was within approximately one hour of a meltdown and a significant breach of containment. The lessons learned at Three Mile Island led to improved safety protocols and equipment overhauls at commercial reactors across the country. Three Mile Island also contributed to rising public anxiety over the safety of nuclear energy, anxieties fueled by the coincidental release of *The China Syndrome*, a fictional movie about the cover-up of a nuclear plant accident, just twelve days before the disaster at Three Mile Island. The Three Mile Island accident became a rallying cry for grassroots antinuclear activists. Wary of sizable cost overruns and public resistance, electrical utilities shied from constructing new nuclear plants in the years that followed. Over

THRESHER **DISASTER.** Launched in July 1960 and commissioned in August 1961, the USS *Thresher* was the lead boat for a revolutionary class of "hunter-killer attack" SUBMARINES designed to destroy Soviet ballistic missile submarines. A strong steel hull, although thinner than that of most submarines, permitted the *Thresher* to withstand greater damage and operate significantly deeper than its counterparts. Its advanced design incorporated a reduced-profile conning tower to increase maneuverability while providing maximum stealth and a highly sensitive, bow-mounted sonar array to detect the enemy at greater distances. The *Thresher*'s torpedo room was located aft of the conning tower, and the tubes angled upward to utilize SUBROC, or submarine rocket, torpedoes. More importantly, a nuclear reactor provided the submarine its power and extended its operational range. During an exhaustive two-year sea trial period, the *Thresher* suffered an unanticipated reactor shutdown and a collision with a tugboat in addition to the usual "shakedown" problems. After additional tests, the submarine began a nine-month overhaul in August 1962.

On 9 April 1963, the *Thresher* returned to sea and initiated a series of routine dives to "test depth," or maximum safe operating depth, estimated at approximately 1,000 feet. On 10 August the crew reported "minor difficulties" at 700 feet and attempted an emergency surface. The *Thresher* never reappeared, sinking in 8,500 feet of water, with all 129 men aboard killed. The submarine imploded from the extreme pressure at these depths, leaving only small fragments of wreckage to be located or recovered. Tests conducted at the time of the accident (and again in the 1980s) revealed that the nuclear reactor had remained intact and an environmental disaster averted. The ensuing inquiry into the navy's first loss of a nuclear-powered vessel suspected improperly welded brazed joints as leading to *Thresher*'s demise, but the official cause remained unknown. The disaster sobered proponents of a nuclear navy, who subsequently instituted the SUBSAFE program to review nuclear submarine construction and operations to ensure that safety would keep pace with technological innovation.

BIBLIOGRAPHY

Duncan, Francis. *Rickover and the Nuclear Navy: The Discipline of Technology.* Annapolis, Md.: Naval Institute Press, 1990.

Polmar, Norman. *Death of the* Thresher. Philadelphia: Chilton, 1964.

Rockwell, Theodore. *The Rickover Effect: How One Man Made a Difference.* Annapolis, Md.: Naval Institute Press, 1992.

Derek W. Frisby

See also **Navy, United States; Nuclear Power.**

THRIFT STAMPS. During World War I the American government turned to thrift stamps as one means of financing the war effort while instilling traditional values. War expenses totaled $33 billion, and the Treasury Department sold approximately $21 billion worth of Liberty bonds to meet the nation's new financial demands. However, to encourage thrift and support for the war effort among elements of the population who could not afford even the smallest bond, valued at fifty dollars, the Treasury Department was authorized to issue Thrift Stamps and War Savings Stamps. This revenue measure was often targeted at immigrants and school children. In many localities, public school teachers were authorized to implement the program and teach children the values of patriotism and saving.

Thrift Stamps cost twenty-five cents each, and when sixteen were collected they could be exchanged for War Savings Stamps or Certificates, which bore interest compounded quarterly at four percent and were tax free. War Savings Stamps could be registered at any post office, insuring the owner against loss, and sold back to the government through any post office with ten days written notice. The conditions placed on the program made it popular with small investors. The campaign began on 2 January 1918 and closed at the year's end. When the War Savings Stamps matured on 1 January 1923, the Treasury Department promised to pay the sum of five dollars for each certificate. In little more than a year over $1 billion was raised in this campaign, fulfilling its ideological and financial purposes.

BIBLIOGRAPHY

Kennedy, David. *Over Here: The First World War and American Society.* New York: Oxford University Press, 1980.

Wynn, Neil A. *From Progressivism to Prosperity: World War I and American Society.* New York: Holmes and Meier, 1986.

Ron Briley

See also **Savings Bonds.**

Defiance at Tiananmen Square. A lone protester stands up to the tanks during the government crackdown on the mostly peaceful, student-led demonstrations in Beijing. Years later, *Time* magazine named him one of the century's top twenty "leaders and revolutionaries" for his inspiring action. © CORBIS

TIANANMEN SQUARE PROTEST. On 15 April 1989, students held a vigil in Beijing's Tiananmen Square that commemorated the death of Hu Yaobang, a progressive leader who had sought reforms in China. They demanded freedom and empowerment for a young generation. The vigil became an ongoing protest in the square on 4 May and gave rise to a prodemocracy movement throughout China. Calling for a change in government through political liberalization and an end to official corruption, the demonstrators displayed Lady Liberty, meant to resemble the Statue of Liberty in New York Harbor and signaling a desire for an open way of life. Although the situation was far from a civil war, the scope of the largely nonviolent opposition to the government was very broad.

While the movement earned support for its agenda and sympathy abroad through wide international media coverage, the most potent challenge to the legitimacy and authority of the Communist Party since Mao Tse-tung's 1949 victory against the Nationalists was crushed at Tiananmen Square by military force on 3 and 4 June 1989, seven weeks after it had begun. Hundreds of protesters and bystanders were presumed dead, thousands wounded and imprisoned. From documents smuggled out of China and published in the United States, it appears that factional struggles among China's leaders and the fear of international shame delayed military action. President George H. W. Bush, acting upon public outrage, imposed minor diplomatic sanctions, but he subordinated human rights concerns to U.S. business interests, encouraging

Bill Clinton to denounce him as "coddling dictators" during the 1992 presidential campaign. In turn, however, Clinton's policies followed the pattern of engaging the Chinese commercially, claiming that trade and openness would facilitate political reforms. This policy was embodied in the ongoing grant of most-favored-nation trade status to China, the jailing of human rights activists notwithstanding.

BIBLIOGRAPHY

Nathan, Andrew, and E. Perry Link, eds. *The Tiananmen Papers.* 2001.

Wang, James C. F. *Contemporary Chinese Politics: An Introduction.* Englewood Cliffs, N.J.: Prentice-Hall, 2000.

Itai Sneh

See also **China, Relations with.**

TICONDEROGA, CAPTURE OF (1775).

The French fort built in October 1755 by Marquis de Lotbinière, commanding the route between lakes Champlain and George, fell into English hands during the FRENCH AND INDIAN WAR after Sir Jeffrey Amherst's successful siege in 1759. The English renamed it Fort Ticonderoga, New York.

In 1775, MASSACHUSETTS revolutionaries hatched a plan to capture Fort Ticonderoga to obtain cannon for the siege of Boston. Early in the morning of 10 May, Ethan Allen, Benedict Arnold, and eighty-three men crossed LAKE CHAMPLAIN in two boats. The expedition passed through the ruined walls and, without bloodshed, quickly subdued the sleepy garrison of two officers and forty-three men. On 5 December, Henry Knox arrived at Ticonderoga to supervise the moving of fourteen mortars and coehorns, two howitzers, and forty-three cannons. The guns were taken in groups by water to Fort George, at the southern end of Lake George; on sleds drawn by oxen and horses to Claverack, New York; and thence east through the mountains to Cambridge, Massachusetts. By 24 January 1776, Gen. George Washington was able to use these cannons to force the British from Boston.

In 1777, the British moved to recapture Fort Ticonderoga. British Gen. John Burgoyne's army of more than nine thousand was opposed by Gen. Arthur Saint Clair with about twenty-five hundred men. The British dragged cannon up Sugar Hill (Mount Defiance), which commanded the fort from the southwest. Shortly after midnight on 6 July, Saint Clair wisely retreated southward along the eastern shore of Lake Champlain, leaving the fort to the British.

BIBLIOGRAPHY

Billias, George Athan. *George Washington's Opponents: British Generals and Admirals in the American Revolution.* New York: Morrow, 1969.

Bird, Harrison. *March to Saratoga: General Burgoyne and the American Campaign, 1777.* New York: Oxford University Press, 1963.

French, Allen. *The Taking of Ticonderoga in 1775.* Cambridge, Mass.: Harvard University Press, 1928.

Gilchrist, Helen Ives. *Fort Ticonderoga in History.* [Fort Ticonderoga? N.Y.]: Printed for the Fort Ticonderoga Museum, [192-?].

Hargrove, Richard J. *General John Burgoyne.* Newark: University of Delaware Press, 1983.

Edward P. Alexander / A. R.

See also **Boston, Siege of; Bunker Hill, Battle of; Burgoyne's Invasion; Oriskany, Battle of.**

Fort Ticonderoga. This photograph shows a cannon facing Lake Champlain; the small British garrison was asleep when Americans crossed the lake and seized the fort, only three weeks after the Revolution began. © LEE SNIDER/CORBIS

TIDELANDS, lands lying under the sea beyond the low-water limit of the tide but considered within the territorial waters of a nation. The U.S. Constitution does not specify whether ownership of these lands rests with the federal government or with individual states. Perhaps because little commercial value was attached to tidelands, ownership was never firmly established but the states generally proceeded as if they were the owners.

The value of tidelands increased when it became known that vast oil and natural gas deposits lay within their limits and that modern technology made retrieval of these minerals commercially profitable. The first OFFSHORE OIL well began production in 1938 in shallow water in the Gulf of Mexico one mile off the Louisiana coast; in 1947, a second well began to operate off the coast of Terrebonne Parish, also in Louisiana. In that same year, the Supreme Court ruled, in *United States v. California,* that the federal government and not the states owned the tidelands. The decision meant the loss of untold millions of dollars in taxes and leasing fees by the states. The states whose tidelands were suspected of containing minerals objected strongly to the decision.

The issue became important in the 1952 presidential campaign. The Republican candidate, Dwight D. Eisenhower, pledged legislation that would restore the tidelands to the states. Eisenhower won the election, and, in 1953, Congress passed two acts that fulfilled his campaign promise. The Submerged Lands Act extended state ownership to three miles from their actual coastline—except for Florida and Texas, which received ownership of the tidelands to within 10.5 miles of their coastlines. The Outer Continental Shelf Lands Act gave the United States paramount rights from the point where state ownership leaves off to the point where international waters begin.

The 1953 acts did not end all controversy, however. The Submerged Lands Act, in particular, was so badly drawn up that state taxes and leasing fees had to be put in escrow pending final resolution of the numerous lawsuits that emerged. The Supreme Court finally decided the issue on 31 May 1960 when it ruled that Mississippi, Alabama, and Louisiana owned the rights to the offshore lands for a distance of 3.5 miles, and Texas and Florida owned rights to tidelands within three leagues, or approximately 10.5 miles, from their coastline boundaries (*United States v. States of Louisiana, Texas, Mississippi, Alabama, and Florida*). In the case of Texas, the claim to special boundary limits had been recognized by Congress in the Treaty of Guadalupe Hidalgo of 1848, which ended the Mexican-American War. The ruling for Florida was based on congressional approval of Florida's claims when the state reentered the Union after the Civil War.

Although the other Gulf states objected to what they considered preferential treatment for Florida and Texas, no new legislation resulted. In 1963, the U.S. Justice Department settled the last of the tidelands controversies by ruling that the 1953 act gave control to the states of islands near the shore that were created after the states had been admitted to the Union.

BIBLIOGRAPHY

Bartly, Ernest R. *The Tidelands Oil Controversy: A Legal and Historical Analysis*. Austin: University of Texas Press, 1953.

Galloway, Thomas D., ed. *The Newest Federalism: A New Framework for Coastal Issues*. Wakefield, R.I.: Times Press, 1982.

Marshall, Hubert R., and Betty Zisk. *The Federal-State Struggle for Offshore Oil*. Indianapolis, Ind.: Published for the Inter-university Case Program by Bobbs-Merrill, 1966.

Thomas Robson Hay / c. w.

See also **Constitution of the United States; Guadalupe Hidalgo, Treaty of; Natural Gas Industry; Territorial Sea.**

TIDEWATER is a term commonly used to designate that portion of the Atlantic coastal plain lying east of the points in rivers reached by oceanic tides. This region, the first to be occupied by settlers from the Old World, slowly became an area of comparative wealth. Merchants and shippers in the towns; and planters growing tobacco, rice, indigo, and COTTON, dominated the tidewater population. Since the tidewater coastal area is so narrow in New England, the terminology is more applicable elsewhere, particularly to the middle and southern Atlantic regions that were initially British colonies and the later states of the federal Union. First to settle and establish themselves economically, socially, and politically, tidewater region inhabitants secured control of the government. Almost inevitably, they used the machinery of government for their own benefit and in accordance with their own traditions and ideals, and they resisted any efforts to weaken their control. Nonetheless, the later population—composed largely of small farmers who moved out into the PIEDMONT REGION—found this governmental domination both unfair and injurious. A serious and long-standing sectional conflict resulted. Sometimes, as in the case of BACON'S REBELLION of 1676 in Virginia, the Paxton riots of 1764 in Pennsylvania, and the Regulator movement of 1768–1771 in North Carolina, the conflict resulted in open warfare. At times, manipulation and compromise kept violence down. Less violence accompanied the separation of West Virginia from the rest of Virginia in 1863 when the western counties, which had remained loyal to the Union, formed their own state. On all occasions, however, the serious conflict in ideals and interest had to be taken into consideration. The political history of the colonies, and later the states, can only be interpreted adequately in the light of this conflict.

The tidewater element of the population maintained control of the government largely by a device of disproportional representation that operated widely from Pennsylvania to Georgia. Another device was restricted suffrage, wherein a heavy property qualification benefited the wealthy of the tidewater region while it disadvantaged the poorer inhabitants of the interior. Using these devices to control the legislatures, the tidewater element pursued policies in regard to the Indians, debts, and taxes that were of most benefit to the tidewater population and therefore often injurious to the up-country population.

BIBLIOGRAPHY

Kars, Marjoleine. *Breaking Loose Together: The Regulator Rebellion in Pre-Revolutionary North Carolina*. Chapel Hill: University of North Carolina Press, 2002.

Kolp, John Gilman. *Gentlemen and Freeholders: Electoral Politics in Colonial Virginia*. Baltimore: Johns Hopkins University Press, 1998.

Lee, Wayne E. *Crowds and Soldiers in Revolutionary North Carolina: The Culture of Violence in Riot and War*. Gainesville: University Press of Florida, 2001.

Williams, John Alexander. *West Virginia: A History*. Morgantown: West Virginia University Press, 2001.

Alfred P. James / A. E.

See also **Fall Line; Indigo Culture; Insurrections, Domestic; Paxton Boys; Regulators; Rice Culture and Trade; Tobacco Industry; Sectionalism.**

TILL, EMMETT, LYNCHING OF.

Emmett Louis Till was murdered in the Mississippi Delta on 28 August 1955, making the fourteen-year-old Chicagoan the best-known young victim of racial violence in the nation's history.

Visiting relatives shortly before he would have started the eighth grade, Till entered a store in Money, in Leflore County, and as a prank behaved suggestively toward Carolyn Bryant, the twenty-one-year-old wife of the absent owner, Roy Bryant. This breach of racial etiquette soon provoked Bryant and his half brother, J. W. Milam, to abduct Till from his relatives' home, pistol-whip and then murder him, and finally to dump the corpse into the Tallahatchie River. Bryant and Milam were prosecuted in the early autumn. Despite forthright testimony by the victim's mother, Mamie Till, a jury of twelve white men quickly acquitted the defendants. The verdict was widely condemned even in the southern white press, and more sharply in the black press and the foreign press. The brutality inflicted upon a guileless teenager exposed the precarious condition that blacks faced—especially in the rural South—as did no other episode. Such violence in defense of racial supremacy and white womanhood helped to inspire the civil rights movement in the early 1960s.

Emmett Till. Murdered at fourteen in a small Mississippi town, because white men believed he had whistled at a white woman. © CORBIS

BIBLIOGRAPHY

Whitfield, Stephen J. *A Death in the Delta: The Story of Emmett Till.* New York: Free Press, 1988.

Stephen J. Whitfield

See also **Lynching.**

TILLMANISM.

Tillmanism, which was strongest during the years 1890 through 1918, was an agrarian movement in South Carolina led by "Pitchfork Ben" Tillman (1847–1918) and characterized by violent white supremacy, the lionization of farmers, and hostility toward northern business interests and the aristocratic southern leadership. The traditional interpretation claims that the movement embraced a legitimate populism that helped the rural poor (Tillman helped found Clemson University, for example), even if it was marred by racism. Recent scholarship, however, argues that Tillman's agrarian rhetoric was a crass tactic to gain control of Democratic Party machinery. In the current view farmers received little material benefit from Tillman's policies and suffered from the backward social system that white supremacy created.

BIBLIOGRAPHY

Kantrowitz, Stephen D. *Ben Tillman & the Reconstruction of White Supremacy.* Chapel Hill: University of North Carolina Press, 2000.

Jeremy Derfner

See also **White Supremacy.**

TIMBER CULTURE ACT.

An 1870s weather hypothesis suggested that growing timber increased humidity and perhaps rainfall. Plains country residents urged the Federal Government to encourage tree planting in that area, believing trees would improve the climate. Also, 1870 government land regulations dictated that home seekers in Kansas, Nebraska, and Dakota could acquire only 320 acres of land. To encourage tree planting and increase the acreage open to entry, Congress passed the Timber Culture Act in 1873, declaring that 160 acres of additional land could be entered by settlers who would devote forty acres to trees. Some 10 million acres were donated under this act, but fraud prevented substantive tree growth. The act was repealed in 1891.

BIBLIOGRAPHY

Gates, Paul W. *History of Public Land Law Development.* Washington, D.C.: Public Land Law Review Commission, 1968.

Paul W. Gates / F. B.

See also **Forestry; Great Plains; Land Speculation.**

TIME.

The first issue of *Time* magazine appeared on 3 March 1923. The magazine was founded by the twenty-four-year-old Yale graduates Briton Hadden and Henry Luce. They created a distinctive newsweekly that was "Curt, Clear, and Complete" to convey "the essence of the news" to the "busy man." Emphasizing national and international politics, *Time* contained brief articles that summarized the significant events of the week. Its authoritative and omniscient tone was created through the technique of "group journalism," in which the magazine was carefully edited to appear the product of a single mind.

Time peppered its articles with interesting details and clever observations. It sought to make the news entertaining by focusing on personality. In its first four decades, over 90 percent of *Time*'s covers featured a picture of an individual newsmaker. In 1927, the magazine began its well-known tradition of naming a "man of the year," making aviator Charles Lindbergh its first selection. *Time*'s formula proved successful, particularly in appealing to better-educated members of the white middle class. By the end of the 1930s, circulation neared one million and its journalistic innovations were much imitated—newspapers were adding week-in-review sections and former *Time* employees launched *Newsweek* in 1933.

Particularly after Hadden's death in 1929, *Time* reflected the empire-building vision of Henry Luce. Beginning in the 1930s, Luce expanded the operations of Time, Inc. In 1930, he created *Fortune*, a business magazine widely read by the nation's economic leaders. In 1936, he created *Life*, a vastly popular magazine that summarized the weekly news events through pictures and had a seminal influence on the development of photojournalism. Luce also launched "The March of Time," both a radio program and a newsreel.

Luce became a well-known advocate of the global expansion of American power and influence. In a famous 1941 *Life* editorial, Luce called for an "American Century" in which the United States would "accept wholeheartedly our duty and our opportunity as the most powerful and vital nation in the world and . . . exert upon the world the full impact of our influence, for such purposes as we see fit and by such means as we see fit." Luce's essay anticipated America's leadership of the capitalist world in the Cold War years, while his publications helped promote his patriotic, internationalist, and procapitalist views.

In the Cold War years, *Time*'s reporting of the news reflected Luce's anticommunism. Throughout the 1940s, *Time* contained flattering portraits of the Chinese dictator Chiang Kai-shek and urged greater U.S. effort to prevent the victory of Mao Zedong and communism in China. The magazine's support of Cold War principles is clearly represented in a 1965 *Time* essay declaring the escalating battle in Vietnam to be "the right war, in the right place, at the right time." The Cold War years were a time of great expansion for *Time*, as it became America's most widely read news magazine, reaching a circulation of over four million by the end of the 1960s.

After Luce's death in 1967, *Time* made a number of changes to its distinctive journalistic style. In response to the growing influence of television news, *Time* granted bylines to writers, expanded its article lengths, shifted its focus from personality to issues, and added opinion pieces. However, much of *Time*'s original journalistic vision of a news summary delivered in an authoritative and entertaining tone persisted, not just in *Time*, but also in the news media as a whole.

Meanwhile, Time, Inc., continued to expand. In the 1970s, Time acquired a large stake in the developing field of cable television. In 1989, it merged with Warner Brothers to become Time Warner. In 2001, it merged with America Online to become the gigantic media conglomerate AOL Time Warner, with large operations in television, publishing, music, film, and the Internet. Thus, even as the journalistic vision of the original *Time* had lost its distinctiveness, Luce's plan to make *Time* the cornerstone of a media empire was far more successful than his wildest expectations at the magazine's founding.

BIBLIOGRAPHY

Baughman, James L. *Henry R. Luce and the Rise of the American News Media.* Boston: Twayne, 1987.

Elson, Robert T. *Time, Inc.: The Intimate History of a Publishing Enterprise, 1923–1941.* New York: Atheneum, 1968.

——. *The World of Time, Inc.: The Intimate History of a Publishing Enterprise, 1941–1960.* New York: Atheneum, 1973.

Herzstein, Robert. *Henry R. Luce: A Political Portrait of the Man Who Created the American Century.* New York: Scribners, 1994.

Prendergast, Curtis, with Geoffrey Colvin. *The World of Time: The Intimate History of a Changing Enterprise, 1960–1980.* New York: Atheneum, 1986.

Daniel Geary

See also **Magazines.**

TIMES BEACH, a town in Missouri, came to national attention in December 1982, when Environmental Protection Agency (EPA) officials learned that soil samples taken from the town's dirt roads contained dioxin, a toxic chemical by-product, in concentrations hundreds of times higher than levels considered safe for human exposure. The EPA found that a contractor hired by Times Beach to control dust on its dirt roads had sprayed them with waste automotive oil mixed with industrial sludge from a defunct chemical company. The EPA purchased all the property in Times Beach and permanently evacuated its 2,000 residents. The buyout was the first under the Superfund program.

BIBLIOGRAPHY

Posner, Michael. "Anatomy of a Missouri Nightmare." *Maclean's* 96 (April 4, 1983): 10–12.

Times Square at Night. The Great White Way still shines despite the Great Depression, in this photograph by Irving Underhill from the early 1930s. LIBRARY OF CONGRESS

Switzer, Jacqueline Vaughn. *Environmental Politics: Domestic and Global Dimensions.* New York: St. Martin's Press, 1994.

John Morelli / c. w.

See also **Chemical Industry; Conservation; Environmental Protection Agency; Hazardous Waste; Superfund.**

TIMES SQUARE in New York City, formerly Longacre Square and often referred to as the "Great White Way" because of the Broadway theaters' lights that illuminate the district, is formed by the intersection of three streets—Broadway, Seventh Avenue, and Forty-second Street. It was renamed for the *New York Times* building erected at the opening of the twentieth century. By the 1920s the neighborhood became a concentrated entertainment district of theaters, vaudeville, cabarets, bars, and restaurants. The 1929 stock market crash took its toll on the area and many businesses that once attracted a well-heeled clientele turned to seamier forms of entertainment. In particular, pornographic movie houses, "peep shows," and the flesh trade gradually infested the district. By the 1960s the drug trade added an additional element of danger to the neighborhood. However, the area was never totally deserted by legitimate forms of entertainment and Broadway shows always guaranteed the retention of a certain flow of legitimate commercial traffic into the area. During the 1990s, New York City began a slow but steady push for its revitalization. In the early 2000s

that process, sometimes referred to as "Disneyfication," was nearly complete and the district was a mecca for family-oriented tourism and entertainment.

BIBLIOGRAPHY

Rogers, W. G. *Carnival Crossroads: The Story of Times Square.* Garden City, N.Y.: Doubleday, 1960.

Stone, Jill. *Times Square: A Pictorial History.* New York: Collier, 1982.

Taylor, William, ed. *Inventing Times Square: Commerce and Culture at the Crossroads of the World.* New York: Russell Sage Foundation, 1991.

Faren R. Siminoff

See also **Broadway.**

TIMUCUA. In the sixteenth century, prior to contact with the Spanish, around 200,000 Timucuans lived in what is today northern Florida and southern Georgia. Approximately thirty-five distinct chiefdoms divided the area politically. Their language, Timucua, is so strikingly different from other southeastern languages that some linguists have argued that the Timucuans may have originated in Central or South America, but archaeological evidence, some of it 5,000 years old, seems to undermine these claims.

Each of the chiefdoms consisted of two to ten villages, with lesser villages and leaders paying tribute to higher-status chiefs. Both men and women served as chiefs. Before contact with the Spanish, Timucuans lived in close proximity to wetlands, and supported themselves by hunting, fishing, and gathering. Because of their rapid demise after contact with the Spanish, little is known about Timucuan culture and lifeways. Archaeologists in recent decades have begun to fill in sorely needed details about diet, burial practices, and political structures.

Contact with the Spanish brought sweeping changes to Timucua country as each of the thirty-five chiefdoms received its own Franciscan mission between 1595 and 1630. The presence of Spanish missions brought about more than just religious change; the once locally oriented Timucuans were drawn into the broader struggle for empire on a global scale. In the missions, Timucuans built churches, forts, and barracks for the Spanish; they also raised pigs and sheep and grew corn. Indians grew the food and provided the labor that allowed the Spanish to dominate the Southeast throughout the seventeenth century. At the same time, disease imported from Europe wreaked havoc on Timucuan peoples. Epidemics caused severe depopulation: by the 1650s, only around 2,000 Timucuans remained.

Although their population declined drastically, mission life provided some measure of stability for Timucuans. This stability was short-lived, however. The founding of English colonies at Jamestown (1607) and Charles Town (1670) renewed conflict between Spain and Britain, and Carolina slavers and allied Native groups continually raided the Spanish missions for captives. When Spain evacuated Florida following the Seven Years' War, all of the remaining Timucuans were taken to Cuba. The last full-blooded Timucuan died in Cuba in 1767.

BIBLIOGRAPHY

Milanich, Jerald T. *The Timucua.* Cambridge, Mass.: Blackwell, 1996.

———. *Laboring in the Fields of the Lord: Spanish Missions and Southeastern Indians.* Washington, D.C.: Smithsonian Institution Press, 1999.

———. "The Timucua Indians of Northern Florida and Southern Georgia." In *Indians of the Greater Southeast: Historical Archaeology and Ethnohistory.* Edited by Bonnie G. McEwan. Gainesville: University Press of Florida, 2000.

Worth, John. *The Timucuan Chiefdoms of Spanish Florida.* 2 vols. Gainesville: University Press of Florida, 1998.

Matthew Holt Jennings

See also **Tribes: Southeastern.**

TIN PAN ALLEY, a phrase probably coined early in the 1900s, described the theatrical section of Broadway in NEW YORK CITY that housed most publishers of popular songs. As the music-publishing industry moved from the

Tin Pan Alley. A photograph by G. D. Hackett of several music-publishing companies in buildings on Twenty-eighth Street in Manhattan. GETTY IMAGES

area around Twenty-eighth Street and Sixth Avenue to Thirty-second Street and then to the area between Forty-second and Fiftieth streets, the name "Tin Pan Alley" moved with it. The term suggests the tinny quality of the cheap, overabused pianos in the song publishers' offices. As the songwriting and music-publishing industry moved to other parts of the city, and to other cities as well, Tin Pan Alley became a term applied to the industry as a whole.

BIBLIOGRAPHY

Furia, Philip. *The Poets of Tin Pan Alley: A History of America's Great Lyricists.* New York: Oxford University Press, 1990.

Jasen, David. *Tin Pan Alley: The Composers, the Songs, the Performers and their Times: The Golden Age of American Popular Music from 1886–1956.* New York: D. I. Fine, 1988.

Tawa, Nicholas. *The Way to Tin Pan Alley: American Popular Song, 1866–1910.* New York: Schirmer Books, 1990.

Stanley R. Pillsbury / H. R. S.

See also **Broadway; Music Industry.**

TINIAN (from 24 July to 1 August 1944). The invasion of Tinian by American forces was necessary to secure the occupation of its neighbor Saipan, captured the previous month. Landing beaches on northern Tinian were chosen to take advantage of field artillery based on Saipan. On the morning of 24 July, following several days of bombardment, the Fourth Marine Division came ashore and pushed rapidly inland, surprising the Japanese force of 8,000. Reinforcements from the Second and Fourth Marine Divisions landed on 25 July and swept to the southern tip by 1 August, killing most of the Japanese garrison. American casualties were 328 killed and 1,571 wounded. Tinian became a major U.S. Air Force base for the strategic bombardment of Japan.

BIBLIOGRAPHY

Crowl, Philip. *Campaign in the Marianas.* Washington, D.C.: Office of the Chief of Military History, Dept. of the Army, 1960.

Hoffman, Carl W. *The Seizure of Tinian.* Washington, D.C.: Historical Division, Headquarters, U.S. Marine Corps, 1951.

Hoyt, Edwin P. *To the Marianas: War in the Central Pacific, 1944.* New York: Van Nostrand Reinhold, 1980.

Philip A. Crowl/A. R.

See also **Air Power, Strategic; Marine Corps, United States; Philippine Sea, Battle of the; Saipan; Trust Territory of the Pacific; World War II; World War II, Air War against Japan.**

TIPI, a conical skin tent best known from the Plains Indians but with historical roots from the indigenous people of the Arctic. All tipis have a central fire hearth, an east-facing entrance, and a place of honor opposite the door. Plains tipis are actually tilted cones, with a smokehole down a side with controllable flaps, and an interior lining for ventilation and insulation. Tipi covers historically were bison hide, but modern tipis use canvas. Plains tipis use either a three- or a four-pole framework overlain with additional poles as needed. Covers are stretched over the poles, staked, or weighted down with stones. Tipis were an excellent adaptation for hunting and gathering peoples who needed a light, transportable, yet durable residence.

BIBLIOGRAPHY

Laubin, Reginald, and Gladys Laubin. *The Indian Tipi: Its History, Construction, and Use.* Norman: University of Oklahoma Press, 1977. Originally published in 1955, it is the most complete book on the tipi available and contains excellent illustrations throughout.

Davis, Leslie, ed. *From Microcosm to Macrocosm: Advances in Tipi Ring Investigation and Research.* Edited by Leslie Davis. *Plains Anthropologist* 28–102, pt. 2, Memoir 19 (1983). Twenty-three papers investigate tipi use on the Great Plains

Tipis. Young Man Afraid of His Horse, an Oglala chief of the Lakota tribe (part of the Sioux confederation), stands in front of several of these Plains Indian dwellings. NATIONAL ARCHIVES AND RECORDS ADMINISTRATION

from prehistory to the period after Euroamerican contact. Heavily illustrated.

Larry J. Zimmerman

See also **Tribes: Great Plains.**

TIPPECANOE, BATTLE OF   (7 November 1811).

In response to pressure from white settlers, the Shawnee leader Tecumseh organized a confederacy of Native American tribes in the Indiana and Michigan territories. The crisis came in the summer of 1811, when Tecumseh, after renewing his demands on Gen. William Henry Harrison, governor of the Indiana Territory, at Vincennes, departed to rally the tribes of the Southwest to the confederacy. Urged on by the frantic settlers, Harrison decided to strike first.

On 26 September Harrison advanced with 1,000 soldiers on the Indian settlement of Prophetstown, along Tippecanoe Creek, 150 miles north of Vincennes. He spent most of October constructing Fort Harrison at Terre Haute, resuming his march on 28 October. With the town in sight, Harrison yielded to belated appeals for a conference. Turning aside, he encamped on an elevated site a mile from the village. Meanwhile the Native American warriors, a mile away, were stirred to a frenzy by the appeals of Tecumseh's brother Tenskwatawa ("the Prophet"). Shortly before dawn (7 November), they drove in Harrison's pickets and furiously stormed the still-sleeping camp. Harrison's soldiers deflected the attack with a series of charges, attacked and razed the Indian town on 8 November, and began the retreat to distant Fort Harrison.

Although Tippecanoe was popularly regarded as a great victory and helped Harrison's political fortunes, the army had struck an indecisive blow. With almost one-fourth of his followers dead or wounded he retreated to Vincennes, where the army was disbanded or scattered. During the War of 1812, federal troops would again do battle with Tecumseh, who had formed an alliance with the British.

BIBLIOGRAPHY
Bird, Harrison. *War for the West, 1790–1813.* New York: Oxford University Press, 1971.
Edmunds, R. David. *The Shawnee Prophet.* Lincoln: University of Nebraska Press, 1983.
———. *Tecumseh and the Quest for Indian Leadership.* Boston: Little, Brown, 1984.
Peterson, Norma L. *The Presidencies of William Henry Harrison and John Tyler.* Lawrence: University Press of Kansas, 1989.

*M. M. Quaife/*A. R.

See also **Indian Policy, U.S., 1775–1830; Indiana; Shawnee; Tecumseh, Crusade of; Thames, Battle of the; "Tippecanoe and Tyler Too!"; War Hawks; War of 1812.**

"TIPPECANOE AND TYLER TOO!"   was the

campaign slogan of the Whigs in 1840, when William Henry Harrison, the hero of the Battle of Tippecanoe, and John Tyler were their candidates for the presidency and vice-presidency, respectively. The party cry typified the emotional appeal of the Whig canvass. Deliberately avoiding issues, its supporters wore coonskin caps, built campaign log cabins in almost every town of consequence, and freely dispensed hard cider to the voters, who were persuaded that Harrison had saved the country from untold Indian atrocities. Few American political slogans have been such unadulterated demagoguery.

BIBLIOGRAPHY
Gunderson, Robert G. *The Log-Cabin Campaign.* Lexington: University of Kentucky Press, 1957.
Varon, Elizabeth. "Tippecanoe and the Ladies, Too." *Journal of American History* 82 (September 1995).

*Irving Dilliard/*L. T.

See also **Elections; Elections, Presidential: 1840; Whig Party.**

TITANIC, SINKING OF THE.   On 12 April 1912

the White Star Line's royal mail steamer *Titanic*, a ship many considered unsinkable, set sail on its maiden voyage from Southampton, England, with stops at Cherbourg, France, and Queenstown, Ireland. On board were many of the most wealthy and influential people in early twentieth-century society and hundreds of emigrants. On 14 April, at 11:40 P.M., the *Titanic*, some four hundred miles from the coast of Newfoundland, hit an iceberg on its starboard side. Shortly after midnight the crew was instructed to prepare the lifeboats and to alert the passengers. The lifeboats had capacity for one-half of the passengers, and some of the boats left not fully loaded. At 2:20 A.M. the *Titanic* disappeared.

Although the *Titanic* sent out distress calls, few vessels carried wireless radios, and those that did staffed them only during daytime hours. The eastbound liner *Carpathia*, some fifty miles away, responded to the *Titanic*'s signals and began taking on survivors. The *Carpathia* rescued 705 people, but 1,523 died.

Five days after the sinking, the White Star Line chartered a commercial cable company vessel, the *Mackay-Bennett*, to search the crash area for bodies. Ultimately three other ships joined the search, and 328 bodies were recovered. To aid in identification, hair color, weight, age, birthmarks, jewelry, clothing, and pocket contents were recorded. Nevertheless 128 bodies remained unidentified.

Amid calls for an investigation of the tragedy, hearings began in the United States and in England. Neither inquiry blamed the White Star Line, but both issued a series of recommendations, including lifeboats for all passengers, lifeboat drills, a twenty-four-hour wireless, and an international ice patrol to track icebergs.

131

Titanic. Survivors in a lifeboat reach the *Carpathia* and safety.

BIBLIOGRAPHY

Ballard, Robert D., with Rick Archbold. *The Discovery of the "Titanic."* New York: Warner, 1987.

Biel, Steven. *Down with the Old Canoe: A Cultural History of the "Titanic" Disaster.* New York: Norton, 1996.

Eaton, John P., and Charles A. Hass. *"Titanic": Destination Disaster.* New York: Norton, 1987

———. *"Titanic": Triumph and Tragedy.* New York: Norton, 1995.

Lord, Walter. *A Night to Remember.* New York: Holt, 1955.

———. *The Night Lives On.* New York: Morrow, 1986.

Lynch, Don, and Ken Marschall. *"Titanic": An Illustrated History.* Toronto: Madison Press, 1992.

John Muldowny

See also **Disasters; Shipbuilding; Transportation and Travel.**

The *Titanic* story evolved into a major cultural phenomenon. The fascination began with the initial newspaper reports, which, while exaggerating stories of supposed heroism, led to the erection of countless memorial plaques, statues, fountains, and buildings in both England and the United States.

After this initial outpouring of grief, interest in the *Titanic* lagged, but following the publication in 1955 of Walter Lord's *A Night to Remember,* additional books and films about the tragedy appeared. Robert Ballard's discovery of the wrecked *Titanic* in 1985 and the subsequent publication in 1987 of his book, *The Discovery of the Titanic,* brought a deluge of Titanica. Included in this flood were video games, CD-ROMs, classical music scores, documentaries, and traveling exhibits of artifacts, mementos, and memorabilia from the ship. In 1997 a Broadway musical was staged, and in 1999 James Cameron directed an epic film. The discovery also revealed new information that it was not a long gash but a strategically placed hull puncture that sank the ship. This information in turn raised speculation about the strength and reliability of the steel and rivets used in its construction and renewed questions about the vessel's speed, iceberg warnings, the conduct of the crew and certain first-class passengers, treatment of third-class passengers, and the ship on the horizon.

The *Titanic* saga seems unending. It continually fascinates as a microcosm of the Edwardian world of the early twentieth century. The wealth and status of its passengers, like John Jacob Astor, Benjamin Guggenheim, Isadore and Ida Straus, and Charles Thayer, represent the equivalents of rock music, entertainment, and sports figures. The *Titanic* story has something for everyone—the ultimate shipwreck, strictures against overconfidence in technology, the results of greed and rampant capitalism, and what-ifs and might-have-beens. The *Titanic,* if sinkable in reality, remains unsinkable in cultural memory and imagination.

TITHES, SOUTHERN AGRICULTURAL, were an expedient of the Confederate congress for securing subsistence for its armies. Because taxes collected in the depreciated Confederate currency did not bring in enough revenue, the ten percent levy in kind was adopted on 24 April 1863, to tap the resources of the 7 or 8 million Confederate farms. Yeoman farmers were especially burdened under the system, and their grievances, which exacerbated preexisting class tensions, eroded Confederate morale in the final months of war. But the revenues produced by the tithes were indispensable in sustaining the southern war effort.

BIBLIOGRAPHY

Escott, Paul D. *After Secession: Jefferson Davis and the Failure of Confederate Nationalism.* Baton Rouge: Louisiana State University Press, 1978.

Francis B. Simkins / A. R.

See also **Civil War; Confederate States of America; Excess Profits Tax; Taxation; Union Sentiment in the South.**

TITLES OF NOBILITY. A title of nobility grants special privileges to an individual at the expense of the rest of the people. The U.S. Constitution prohibits both federal and state governments from granting titles of nobility, and prohibits federal officials from accepting them, but does not prohibit private citizens from accepting them.

No case regarding titles of nobility has reached the Supreme Court, but the issue has been raised at the trial level, where plaintiffs usually argue that the privileges of government officials or agents amount to constructive titles of nobility. This position is supported by an 1871 U.S. Attorney General ruling (13 Ops. Atty. Gen. 538) that a commission making someone a diplomatically accredited representative of a foreign government, with the special immunities diplomats enjoy, would constitute a title of nobility. The courts have, however, tended to avoid ruling on this argument, preferring to interpret "titles" narrowly, as the English titles, duke, marquis, earl, count, viscount, or baron, rather than consider the privileges that would create functional equivalents. In feudal tradition, those titles usually brought land or the income from land and special legal privileges; they also required special duties to the king.

It should be noted that both Constitutional prohibitions occur in the same sections with the prohibitions against ex post facto laws and bills of attainder, which are the obverse of titles of nobility, the legislative imposition of legal disabilities on persons without due process. The founders allowed for minor privileges and the kinds of disabilities that come with general regulations and taxes, but sought to exclude both extremes: great privileges and great deprivations of rights.

BIBLIOGRAPHY

Blackstone, William. *Commentaries on the Laws of England.* Book I Part I Section IV. Ed. St. George Tucker. 1803. Available from http://www.constitution.org/tb/tb-1104.htm.

Bouvier, John. *Bouvier's Law Dictionary.* 1856. Entry on "Nobility." Available from http://www.constitution.org/bouv/bouvier_n.htm.

The Federalist, Nos. 39, 44, 69, 84, 85. Available from http://www.constitution.org/fed/federa00.htm.

Segar, Simon. *Honores Anglicani: or, Titles of Honour. The temporal nobility of the English nation . . . have had, or do now enjoy, viz. dukes, marquis.* London, 1712.

Virginia Ratifying Convention, June 17, 1788, Speech by Edmund Randolph. Available from http://www.constitution.org/rc/rat_va_14.htm.

Jon Roland

See also **Constitution of the United States.**

TOBACCO AS MONEY. Because of the scarcity of specie, Virginia, Maryland, and North Carolina used tobacco as currency throughout most of the colonial period. In 1619 the Virginia legislature "rated" high-quality tobacco at three shillings and in 1642 made it legal tender. Nearly all business transactions in Maryland, including levies, were conducted in terms of tobacco. North Carolina used tobacco as money until the outbreak of the Revolution. Sharp fluctuations in tobacco prices led Virginia in 1727 to adopt a system of "tobacco notes," certificates issued by inspectors of government warehouses. The obvious weakness of tobacco as currency—notably, lack of portability and variability of value—became more apparent with time, and it was abandoned in the second half of the eighteenth century.

BIBLIOGRAPHY

Breen, T. H. *Tobacco Culture.* Princeton: New Jersey Press, 2001.

Hugh T. Lefler / A. R.

See also **Barter; Colonial Commerce; Cotton Money; Maryland; Tobacco Industry.**

TOBACCO INDUSTRY. Tobacco in the form of leaf, snuff, chew, smoking tobacco, cigars, and factory-made cigarettes has often been called the United States' oldest industry. Since its introduction to Europeans by American Indians, no other agricultural crop has been more thoroughly entwined with the history of the United States than the growing, processing, and manufacturing of tobacco. In addition, no one product has enjoyed deeper ties to the colonization of the New World and to the expansion of international trade between the New World and Europe, Asia, and the Middle East over the last four centuries. The prospect of farming tobacco and selling it to England brought the earliest British colonists to Virginia and Maryland, and at the end of the twentieth century U.S. companies such as Philip Morris and RJR Nabisco continued to dominate the international cigarette market and stood among the most profitable transnational corporations. U.S. tobacco growing, manufacturing, distribution, marketing, and sales contributed $15 billion in wages to some 660,000 American workers. For many centuries tobacco has been identified with the New World, especially the United States. In the form of the mass-produced cigarette, U.S. tobacco became the virtual international symbol of American modernity. Indeed, students of the industry have argued that the advent of machine-made cigarettes in the 1880s helped inaugurate in the United States the modern era of mass consumer products, mass advertising and promotion, and the professionally managed modern corporation.

However, the last half of the twentieth century saw the U.S. tobacco industry come under pressure from the demonstrated health hazards of smoking and the subsequent steady decline in smoking in the United States and other highly industrialized nations. In response, the industry aggressively pursued expanding into markets in Asia, Eastern Europe, and Africa, prompting the World Health Organization to accuse tobacco manufacturers of fomenting a tobacco epidemic. Equally worrisome for the industry, at century's end the growth of class-action lawsuits, the publication of documents revealing corporate manipulation of the political and legal process and the willful distortion and suppression of scientific findings, and the rise of government antitobacco measures further clouded the future of the domestic tobacco market. Cigarette makers faced the prospect of being demoted to the status of a rogue industry in the eyes of U.S. citizenry.

Early History: Production and Consumption

Most modern tobacco consumption derives from *Nicotiana tabacum,* which is a species of nightshade plant. The general consensus is that the tobacco plant originated in South America and was spread by American Indians to North America and the South Pacific and Australia. The arrival of Europeans in the New World introduced them

Sorting Tobacco. African American workers, mostly women, sort tobacco at the T. B. Williams Tobacco Company in Richmond, Va., c. 1899 . LIBRARY OF CONGRESS

to tobacco, and by the early seventeenth century commercial tobacco became a driving force of colonization in North America and the Caribbean. The Jamestown colony in Virginia owed its very survival to tobacco. A cash crop requiring very intensive labor from planting to harvesting to curing, its cultivation created a demand for conscripted labor, first in the form of indentured European servants on family farms and soon afterward in the form of African slave labor on large landholdings. Two types of tobacco leaf were grown, principally for pipe smoking and, later on, snuff. They were both dark varieties: the more expensive leaf grown in Virginia and the stronger, cheaper orinoco leaf grown in Maryland. In England, demand for tobacco rapidly grew and by 1628 the Chesapeake colonies exported 370,000 pounds annually to England, procuring substantial tax revenues for the state, which overcame early Crown hostility to tobacco cultivation and consumption. Tobacco farming spread quickly to North Carolina, South Carolina, Kentucky, Tennessee, and Georgia. It also extended to two other regions in which cigar (Cuban) leaf cultivation would come to dominate in the nineteenth century: the Northeast (Pennsylvania, New York, Connecticut, and Massachusetts) and, later, the Midwest (Ohio, Illinois, Wisconsin, Minnesota, and Missouri). In 1700 exports of raw leaf from the British Chesapeake colonies reached 37 million pounds and by the outbreak of the American Revolution in 1776 upward of 100 million pounds. At the end of the eighteenth century, the main producers of tobacco were the United States, Brazil, and Cuba. After a decline following the American Revolution, U.S. production rebounded, but only slowly due to the Napoleonic Wars (1799 through 1815) and the War of 1812. Production then rose sharply to 434 million pounds in 1860 and, after a drop due to the Civil War, resumed its growth, averaging 660 million pounds in 1900 through 1905, of which one-

half was consumed domestically. From 1945 to the 1980s, U.S. annual production averaged two billion pounds.

Throughout most of their history, Americans overall and men in particular remained the heaviest consumers of tobacco worldwide, principally in the form of chewing and smoking tobacco. Europeans consumed tobacco by smoking it in clay pipes until the eighteenth century, when manufactured snuff became dominant starting in Spain. While chewing tobacco was rare in Europe, it was quite popular in the United States among men and remained so up to the early twentieth century. Pipe smoking was also popular among men and some women in the nineteenth century Women also used snuff. It was taken by New York society women and by women of all classes in the South. In Europe, pipe smoking made a comeback in the nineteenth century at the expense of snuff, but was soon forced to accommodate the new vogues for cigar and cigarette smoking popular both there and in North America. These shifts in consumption patterns stemmed in part from the development in the nineteenth century of new, lighter leaves of the bright and the burley varieties, which were more suitable for chewing and cigarette smoking and competed with the dark leaf grown in Virginia and Maryland. By the end of the nineteenth century, the bulk of U.S. tobacco production had shifted away from low-lying areas of Maryland and Virginia to the Virginia–North Carolina Piedmont region and to Kentucky, where the bright and the burley varieties flourished. By 1919 bright accounted for 35% of the U.S. tobacco crop, burley for 45%.

Industrializing Tobacco and the Rise of the Cigarette
Until 1800 tobacco manufacturing proper was largely carried out in Europe. Initially, U.S. factories were dispersed in the tobacco-growing regions of Virginia, North Carolina, Tennessee, Kentucky, and Missouri, which used slave labor. New York, a center of snuff production, was the exception. Manufacturing of tobacco also thrived among planters who prepared tobacco for chew. After the Civil War, the introduction of steam-powered shredding and cigarette machines and pressures stemming from the rise of national markets led to the concentration of tobacco manufacturing in that sector. Cigar manufacturing underwent a similar evolution somewhat later. Cigars first became popular in the United States after the Mexican-American War, and their manufacture was fairly dispersed in cigar leaf-growing regions. However, by 1905 the greatest centers of cigar manufacturing were Philadelphia, New York, Boston, Cincinnati, Chicago, Baltimore, Richmond, Tampa, and Key West.

In the United States, the convenience and simplicity of smoking cigarettes made from the bright variety of tobacco was discovered by Union and Confederate troops alike during the Civil War. Ready-made cigarettes using mixtures of bright and burley tobacco allowed U.S. manufacturers to develop cheaper brands. U.S. cigarette production boomed between 1870 and 1880, rising from 16 million cigarettes (compared to 1.2 billion cigars) annually to over 533 million, reaching 26 billion by 1916. The growth of the U.S. population between 1880 and 1910 and the decline of chewing tobacco due to antispitting ordinances further expanded the market for cigarettes. With this growth arose new aggressive methods of packaging (striking colors, designs, logos, brand names), promoting (gifts, picture cards, free samples, discounts and rebates to jobbers, retailers, etc.), and advertising (newspapers, billboards, posters, handbills, endorsements) cigarettes to an emerging national market.

In 1881 James Bonsack patented a new cigarette-making machine that turned out over 120,000 cigarettes per day. Until then, factory workers rolled up to 3,000 cigarettes a day. The Bonsack machines made the fortune of James B. Duke, who adopted them in 1884. By securing exclusive rights over Bonsack machines and devoting 20% of his sales revenues to advertising, Duke helped create a mass national market, which he soon dominated. By 1889 W. Duke and Sons had become the world's leading manufacturer of cigarettes, with 40% of the U.S. market. That same year Duke pressured his rivals into forming the American Tobacco Company with Duke as president. The trust did not own any tobacco farms, and employed its considerable leverage to depress the price of tobacco leaf. This unequal relationship to the detriment of growers reached a crisis point forty years later during the Great Depression, necessitating the tobacco price support program of 1933—still in place at the end of the twentieth century—which rescued tobacco growers, many of them tenant farmers, from certain ruin. The trust also proceeded to absorb important rivals as well as manufacturers of chew, snuff, smoking tobacco, and cigars including R.J. Reynolds, P. Lorillard, Liggett and Myers, the American Snuff Company, and the American Cigar Company.

The geometric increase in cigarette production spurred the trust to make a major innovation in modern corporate practices: to seek outlets in foreign markets (not controlled by state monopolies), often by buying local companies outright (United Kingdom, Japan) and later by setting up factories abroad (China). American Tobacco Company's incursion into Britain provoked British companies to form a cartel, Imperial Tobacco. In turn, in 1902 Imperial Tobacco formed a joint company, but with minority interest, with American Tobacco called the British-American Tobacco Company (BAT). Together the U.S. and U.K. cartels exploited overseas markets while withdrawing from each other's domestic market. At the turn of the century, upward of one-third of the U.S. trust's cigarettes were exported and 54% or 1.2 billion were exported to China alone. By 1910, the year before its demise, the trust accounted for 75 percent of U.S. tobacco production of all kinds. In 1911, the Supreme Court found the American Tobacco Company in violation of the Sherman Antitrust Act and ordered its breakup into four major companies: the American Tobacco Company, Liggett and Myers, R.J. Reynolds, and P. Lorillard.

In 1900 machine-made cigarettes still accounted for only 3 to 4 percent of U.S. tobacco leaf production. Their greatest growth lay ahead: by 1940 the figure had risen to 50 percent (or 189 billion cigarettes) and by 1970 to 80 percent (or 562 billion cigarettes). In 1913 the newly independent R.J. Reynolds launched Camels, the "first modern cigarette." An innovative blend of burley and Turkish tobacco backed by a massive publicity campaign, Camels were quickly imitated by American's Lucky Strike and Liggett and Myers' revamped Chesterfield cigarettes (in 1926 Lorillard jumped in with its Old Gold brand). All three brands stressed their mildness and catered their appeal to men and women alike. Between them the three brands enjoyed 65 to 80 percent market share through the 1940s. The 1920s saw the "conversion" of many tobacco consumers to the cigarette in the Unites States, United Kingdom, Europe, China, and Japan. Between 1920 and 1930, U.S. cigarette consumption doubled to 1,370 cigarettes per capita.

Smoking and Health

As in the previous century, war was to prove a boon to U.S. tobacco, especially cigarettes. The rations of American soldiers and sailors included tobacco. With each world war, U.S. consumption of tobacco jumped and that of cigarettes soared, leaping 57 percent between 1916 and 1918 and 75 percent between 1940 and 1945. Per capita consumption in the United States reached almost 3,500 per year by 1945, a rate matched only by the United Kingdom and Canada. It would be twenty years before nations in continental Europe and East Asia would achieve similar rates. By 1955 in the United States, 57 percent of men and 28 percent of women smoked. A veritable culture of cigarette smoking had arisen. It was a culture of glamour, style, and modern individualism featured and promoted in fashion magazines and Hollywood films It would appear that the widespread movement by women to adopt cigarettes began prior to advertising campaigns actively directed at them and coincided with the culmination of the suffragette movement's drive to obtain the right to vote. Commentators openly associated cigarettes with women's emancipation. Estimates vary, but by 1929 around 16 percent of women smoked cigarettes, a figure that rose to 25 to 35 percent in the late 1940s and peaked at around 30 to 35 percent in the early 1960s.

Ever since King James I's denunciation of tobacco in the seventeenth century as detrimental to one's health and character, tobacco had been the object of recriminations by politicians, religious leaders, heads of industry, and social commentators. At the very moment cigarettes took off as a popular consumer product in the 1880s and 1890s, antismoking crusaders were waging successful campaigns banning the sale or consumption of tobacco in seventeen states, but their success was short-lived: World War I undid most of the legislation. Prior to World War II, cases of lung cancer were relatively rare in the United States, the United Kingdom, and Canada, the heaviest-smoking countries, but rates in men were rising fast, prompting

Processing Tobacco. African American men process tobacco at the T. B. Williams Tobacco Company in Richmond, Va., c. 1899. LIBRARY OF CONGRESS

medical researchers to initiate the first statistical studies of the disease. Results of early studies in the United States and the United Kingdom appeared in 1950 just as the Federal Trade Commission was castigating the tobacco industry for making false health claims for their products. Reports of other studies followed over the next two years resulting in a health scare that precipitated a temporary 10 percent drop in consumption. The industry responded in two ways: by promoting filtered-tipped cigarettes (42 percent of all cigarettes by 1956 through 1960) and mentholated brands, which they claimed to be less harsh and harmful; and by questioning the validity of the studies, a tactic it would pursue with each unfavorable new scientific finding up through the 1990s, especially through its Council for Tobacco Research and the industry's lobbying arm, the Tobacco Institute. Meanwhile, tobacco in the United States, as in many countries, because of its economic importance, the substantial tax revenues it contributed to federal and state coffers ($3 billion in 1964 and $13.4 billion in 1998), and its campaign contributions, benefited from its special status as neither a food nor a drug and thus escaped formal government regulation as to its effects.

Under pressure from health organizations, the government published in 1964 a landmark report of the Surgeon General warning the American public of the dangers of smoking. It was the first in a long series of Surgeon General reports that reviewed existing studies on tobacco-related diseases and, beginning in the 1980s, on women and smoking, nicotine addiction, modified cigarettes, cessation, secondhand smoke, youth initiation, and smoking among racial and ethnic minority groups. The political and economic picture of the domestic market for the tobacco industry had changed. In 1965, the industry had to work vigorously to keep the new cigarette warning labels watered down, and in 1970 the industry withdrew all radio and television ads voluntarily in order to eliminate free broadcast time awarded by the Federal Trade Commission starting in 1967 for antismoking public service announcements. Segregation of smokers in airplanes and other forms of public transportation began in 1972 and was extended to public buildings in Arizona (1974) and Minnesota (1975). New studies on the dangers of secondhand smoke in the 1980s and 1990s galvanized the antismoking movement to pressure federal, state, and local governments to ban smoking completely in public buildings, public transportation, stores, theaters, and schools, establish smoking sections in workplaces and restaurants, and, in the case of California, ban smoking in all indoor public areas including workplaces, restaurants, and bars. U.S. cigarette consumption began to decline. Men's and women's rates had already dropped from 52 and 34 percent, respectively, in 1965 to 44 and 32 percent in 1970 and to 38 and 29 percent by 1980, respectively. By 1990, the rates had dropped precipitously to 28 and 23, respectively, and by 1999 to 26 and 22 percent. Per capita cigarette consumption peaked in the early 1970s at around 4,000 and steadily dropped from 1980 (3,850) to 1999 (2,000). Meanwhile, tobacco-related diseases (lung cancer, emphysema, coronary heart disease, stroke) became the leading preventable causes of death—over 400,000 deaths in 1990. For women, the number of deaths due to lung cancer surpassed those due to breast cancer in 1987.

Industry adjusted by offering low-tar and nicotine cigarettes (a 40 percent drop in yields between 1967 and 1981), cheaper brands, and promotion gimmicks such as coupons and giveaways and by opposing systematically growing legal challenges. In a changing market, one company that rose to preeminence was Philip Morris, thanks to its innovative marketing. Its market share surpassed that of previous leader R.J. Reynolds in 1983, and it also took the lead in industry sponsorship of cultural institutions, concerts, and national sporting events. To cover declining U.S. sales, it exploited a traditional outlet for U.S. cigarettes somewhat neglected since World War II: overseas markets. With the help of the U.S. Trade Representative and North Carolina Senator Jesse Helms in 1986, Philip Morris, along with R.J. Reynolds, forced open East Asian markets previously dominated by state monopolies, and in the 1990s snapped up privatized state-run companies in former communist countries in Eastern Europe. By the end of the century, Philip Morris held 50 percent of the U.S. cigarette market followed by R.J. Reynolds (23 percent), Brown & Williamson (12 percent), and Lorillard (10 percent).

Although faced with a changing market, leading U.S. cigarette manufacturers remained among the nation's most profitable companies. In the 1980s and 1990s they repositioned themselves by diversifying into the beverage and food industry (Nabisco, Kraft Foods), blurring their corporate identities. In 2002 Philip Morris executives proposed renaming the parent company from Philip Morris Companies, Inc., to Altria Group, Inc. The threat of successful lawsuits resulted in the Master Settlement Agreement signed on 23 November 1998 with forty-six states attorneys general. This agreement stipulated payment of $206 billion to states over twenty-five years, reigned in industry promotion practices, especially those targeting youth, and provided $5.5 billion over ten years in aid to vulnerable tobacco growers. To cover the settlement's costs the industry increased prices forty-five cents per pack and Philip Morris announced a 16 percent cut in its U.S. workforce. Down from a high of 75,000 in 1955, in 1990 cigarette manufacturing in the United States directly employed 41,000 people; the number dropped to 26,000 by 1999. In 1999 through 2000, debt-ridden RJR Nabisco sold off its overseas tobacco operations to Japan Tobacco and its food products company to Philip Morris, and spun off its domestic tobacco operations as R.J. Reynolds Tobacco. Finally, at decade's end India had moved ahead of the United States in total leaf and cigarette production (behind China), and the United States fell behind Brazil and Zimbabwe in the export of tobacco leaf while remaining ahead of the United Kingdom and the Netherlands in cigarette exports. U.S. tobacco leaf production, exports, and employment are expected to continue to fall as domestic consumption declines and as productivity, competition from cheaper foreign leaf, and the growth in off-shore manufacturing by U.S. companies increase.

BIBLIOGRAPHY

Brandt, Allan M. "The Cigarette, Risk, and American Culture." *Daedalus* 119 (1990): 155–177.

Centers for Disease Control and Prevention. Tobacco Information and Prevention Source. Available at http://www.cdc.gov/tobacco. On-line access to U.S. data including Surgeon General reports.

Cox, Howard. *The Global Cigarette. Origins and Evolution of British American Tobacco 1880–1945*. New York: Oxford University Press, 2000.

Glantz, Stanton A., John Slade, Lisa A. Bero, Peter Hanauer, and Deborah E. Barnes. *The Cigarette Papers*. Berkeley: University of California Press, 1996.

Goodman, Jordan. *Tobacco in History: The Cultures of Dependence*. New York: Routledge, 1993. Most complete international history.

Jacobstein, Meyer. *The Tobacco Industry in the United States*. New York: Columbia University Press, 1907. Reprint, New York, AMS, 1968. Important early statistics.

Klein, Richard. *Cigarettes Are Sublime*. Durham, N.C.: Duke University Press, 1993. The significance of cigarettes in modern culture.

Kluger, Richard. *Ashes to Ashes: America's Hundred-Year Cigarette War, the Public Health, and the Unabashed Triumph of Philip Morris*. New York: Knopf, 1996. Prize-winning history of U.S. industry's marketing and political strategies.

Parker-Pope, Tara. *Cigarettes: Anatomy of an Industry from Seed to Smoke*. New York: New Press, 2001. Lively short account.

Rabin, Robert L., and Stephen D. Sugarman, eds. *Regulating Tobacco*. New York: Oxford University Press, 2001. Recent U.S. developments including the 1998 Master Settlement Agreement.

Robert, Joseph C. *The Story of Tobacco in America*. Chapel Hill: University of North Carolina Press, 1967.

Schudson, Michael. "Symbols and Smokers: Advertising, Health Messages, and Public Policy." In *Smoking Policy: Law, Politics, and Culture*. Edited by Robert L. Rabin and Stephen D. Sugarman. New York: Oxford University Press, 1993.

Tobacco Control Archives. Available at http://www.library.ucsf.edu/tobacco. Important review of secret industry documents.

Roddey Reid

See also **American Tobacco Case; Tobacco and American Indians; Tobacco as Money.**

TOCQUEVILLE. *See Democracy in America.*

The *Today* Show. Before 1952, network television programming did not start until 10:00 A.M. That changed when NBC president Sylvester Weaver created a two-hour show called the *Today* show that ran from 7:00 until 9:00 A.M. each day. Fifty years later, in 2002, the show was still successful and had spawned copycat shows on each of the other major networks. Bryant Gumbel, here interviewing former President Richard Nixon in 1990, was one of the show's most popular hosts; he ended a fifteen-year stint as host of *Today* in 1997. © AP/WIDE WORLD PHOTOS

TODAY. In 1952, no network television programming was scheduled earlier than 10:00 A.M. (EST). NBC president Sylvester "Pat" Weaver created *Today* with the idea that people might watch TV early in the morning before going to work and sending their children off to school. The two-hour show, running from 7:00 A.M. to 9:00 A.M. (EST), was designed to unfold in small modular segments, with the expectation that few viewers would watch from beginning to end. News, interviews, feature stories, and weather were combined in an informal style by friendly hosts. *Today* went on the air on 14 January 1952 and has remained there with relatively minor changes ever since. It was not until 1954 that another network, CBS, scheduled a program, *The Morning Show*, in the same time slot, and it was not until the 1970s, when *Good Morning, America* was introduced on ABC, that any program challenged the ratings dominance of *Today*. Fifty years after the beginning of *Today*, all early morning network shows were essentially copies of it. *Today* replaced the daily newspaper as a first source of information for millions of Americans at the start of each day, providing news and weather reports as well as discussions of books, trends, and other cultural and domestic topics.

From 1952 to 1961, the *Today* team included Dave Garroway, Betsy Palmer, Jack Lescoulie, Frank Blair, and

for a few years of comic relief, a chimpanzee named J. Fred Muggs. In 1961, the news department at NBC took over production of the show, and the lead host position went successively to John Chancellor (1961–1962), Hugh Downs (1962–1971), and Frank McGee (1971–1974). Barbara Walters became the first woman to co-host the show, which she did from 1974 to 1976. Walters was paired with a series of co-hosts until Jim Hartz got the permanent job. In 1976, Walters and Hartz were replaced by Tom Brokaw (1976–1981) and Jane Pauley (1976–1989). Subsequent hosts included Bryant Gumbel (1982–1997), Deborah Norville (1989–1991), Katie Couric (1991–), and Matt Lauer (1997–).

BIBLIOGRAPHY

Kessler, Judy. *Inside* Today: *The Battle for the Morning.* New York: Villard, 1992.

Metz, Robert. *The* Today *Show: An Inside Look at Twenty-five Tumultuous Years.* Chicago: Playboy Press, 1977.

Robert Thompson

See also **Television: Programming and Influence.**

TOHONO O'ODHAM. *See* **Akimel O'odham and Tohono O'odham.**

TOLEDO, the fourth largest city in Ohio in the early twenty-first century, began in 1680 as a French trading post. Ceded to the British in 1763, it became part of the U.S. Northwest Territory in 1787. Canals and railroads helped establish Toledo as a major inland port and center of industry. During the Progressive Era, Toledo won national recognition for urban reform. Historically, Toledo has been a major producer of glass and automotive products, but these industries declined, and from 1970 to 2000 employment in the Toledo metropolitan area decreased markedly. During this same period, population declined from 383,062 to 313,619, although city leaders question the accuracy of the 2000 federal census. Toledo has experienced other problems. A 1967 race riot caused extensive property damage, injuries, and arrests. Public schools were closed for several weeks in 1976 and 1978 because of teacher strikes. In July 1979 a bitter dispute between the city government and police and firemen led to a two-day general strike and costly arson fires. In the 1980s and 1990s, Toledo sought to emphasize its strong medical, cultural, and higher educational institutions. New downtown buildings and the Portside festival marketplace along the Maumee River were indicative of business leaders' commitment to the city.

BIBLIOGRAPHY

Jones, Marnie. *Holy Toledo: Religion and Politics in the Life of "Golden Rule" Jones.* Lexington: University Press of Kentucky, 1998.

Korth, Philip A., and Margaret R. Beegle. *I Remember Like Today: The Auto-Lite Strike of 1934.* East Lansing: Michigan State University Press, 1988.

McGucken, William. *Lake Erie Rehabilitated: Controlling Cultural Eutrophication, 1960s–1990s.* Akron, Ohio: University of Akron Press, 2000.

John B. Weaver/A. E.

See also **Boundary Disputes Between States; Canals; Great Lakes; Labor; Michigan, Upper Peninsula of; Northwest Territory; Ohio; Railroads.**

TOLERATION ACTS provided for varying degrees of religious liberty in the American colonies. In New England, where the Congregational Church enjoyed legal establishment, the law required taxpayers to support the Puritan churches. Strong dissent in Massachusetts and Connecticut during the early eighteenth century resulted in legal exemptions for Quakers, Baptists, and Episcopalians. Rhode Island was the exception in New England, granting full freedom of worship.

The middle colonies offered broad religious liberty. William Penn's Charter of 1682 provided for freedom of conscience to all Pennsylvanians who believed in God. Later, however, royal pressure forced the legislature to restrict liberties for Jews and Catholics. The New Jersey proprietors offered religious liberty in order to attract settlers. In New York, although the Anglican Church enjoyed official establishment, the realities of religious diversity and local control resulted in *de facto* religious liberty for most denominations.

The Anglican Church was stronger in the southern colonies and often encroached on dissenters' religious practice, particularly in Virginia and Maryland. Virginian evangelicals met with resistance, as did Maryland Catholics, although the latter enjoyed protection under the Toleration Act of 1649. Georgia's royal charter (1732) confirmed religious liberty for all except Catholics. In North Carolina, Anglicans maintained tenuous power.

The American Revolution reinforced the doctrine of individual liberty, including religious freedom. Most state constitutions framed in this era sanctioned freedom of conscience to some extent. Local religious establishment continued in many states (until Massachusetts separated church and state in 1833). The NORTHWEST ORDINANCE (1787) extended religious liberty to the Northwest Territory. The First Amendment of the federal Constitution forbade Congress to abridge the free exercise of religion.

BIBLIOGRAPHY

Bonomi, Patricia U. *Under the Cope of Heaven: Religion, Society, and Politics in Colonial America.* New York: Oxford University Press, 1986.

Curry, Thomas J. *The First Freedoms: Church and State in America to the Passage of the First Amendment.* New York: Oxford University Press, 1986.

Hall, Timothy L. *Separating Church and State: Roger Williams and Religious Liberty.* Urbana: University of Illinois Press, 1998.

Isaac, Rhys. *The Transformation of Virginia, 1740–1790.* Chapel Hill: University of North Carolina Press, 1982.

Shelby Balik
Winfred T. Root

See also **Dissenters; First Amendment; Maryland; Massachusetts Bay Colony; Religion and Religious Affiliation; Religious Liberty; Virginia.**

TOLL BRIDGES AND ROADS, a system that developed as a means of transportation improvement in the face of limited public funding. Local, colonial, and state governments, burdened by debt, chartered private turnpike and bridge companies with the authority to build, improve, and charge tolls. While toll bridges appeared in New England by 1704, the first toll roads of the turnpike era were in Virginia, which authorized tolls on an existing public road in 1785, and Pennsylvania, which chartered the sixty-two-mile Philadelphia and Lancaster Turnpike in 1792.

Toll Rates. Photographed in 1941 by Jack Delano, this sign on the New Hampshire side of a bridge across the Connecticut River near Springfield, Vt., lists rates ranging from "foot passengers" and bicyclists to automobiles and motorcycles, as well as vehicles drawn by various numbers of "horses or beasts." LIBRARY OF CONGRESS

From 1790 to 1850, private toll roads were the nation's primary land-based venue of transportation. More than four hundred turnpikes, many paved to the French engineer Pierre-Marie Tresaguet's specifications, facilitated trade and communication with and movement to western areas. By the 1830s, toll canals, toll bridges over such major rivers as the Connecticut, and between 10,000 and 20,000 miles of private toll roads composed the heart of the national transportation network. However, lack of profitability and competition from railroads, which hauled heavy freight at relatively low costs and high speeds, led most turnpike and bridge authorities to dissolve by 1850, leaving their roads and bridges to public ownership.

A second wave of toll bridges and roads began in the 1920s and 1930s. In 1927, Congress ruled that federal highway aid could be used for toll bridges built, owned, and operated by the states. Bridge authorities in New York, California, and elsewhere thereafter sold revenue bonds amortized by tolls to finance new bridges, including the George Washington, Triborough, and San Francisco–Oakland Bay. But restrictions on using federal aid for toll road construction, coupled with heavy traffic on existing roads and cash-strapped treasuries, led states to create special authorities that designed and built new toll roads, which like the bridges were financed through revenue bonds. These limited-access, high-speed roads included New York City–area parkways (beginning in 1926), Connecticut's Merritt Parkway (1937), the Pennsylvania Turnpike (1940, first to accommodate trucks), and the Maine Turnpike (1947, the first postwar toll road).

The 1956 Federal-Aid Highway Act, authorizing the interstate highway system, allowed toll bridges, roads, and tunnels to join the system if they met interstate standards and contributed to an integrated network. However, tolls were prohibited on all interstates beyond the 2,447 miles of toll expressways operating or under construction in 1956; additionally, federal highway aid could not be used for new toll facilities except for high-cost bridges and tunnels and extensions to existing toll roads.

These policies discouraged new toll road construction, until 1987 and 1991 legislation made federal highway aid available for noninterstate public and private toll roads, and allowed the imposition of tolls on federally funded noninterstate highways. Toll roads constructed thereafter included the private Dulles Greenway in Virginia and the public E-470 beltway near Denver. In the 1990s, Houston, San Diego, and Orange County, California, introduced high-occupancy toll, or HOT, lanes on otherwise free highways, permitting solo drivers to access carpool lanes by paying a toll; critics charged that this traffic management strategy created a road system stratified by class. In 2000, the Federal Highway Administration listed 4,927 miles of toll roads and 302 miles of toll bridges and tunnels nationwide.

BIBLIOGRAPHY

American Public Works Association. *History of Public Works in the United States, 1776–1976*. Chicago: American Public Works Association, 1976.

Gómez-Ibáñez, José A., and John R. Meyer. *Going Private: The International Experience with Transport Privatization*. Washington, D.C.: Brookings Institution, 1993.

Klein, Daniel B. "The Voluntary Provision of Public Goods? The Turnpike Companies of Early America." *Economic Inquiry* 28 (October 1990): 788–812.

Jeremy L. Korr

See also **Interstate Highway System; Transportation and Travel.**

TOLLS EXEMPTION ACT, an act of Congress, 24 August 1912, exempting American vessels in coast-wise traffic from the payment of tolls on the Panama Canal. The Hay-Pauncefote Treaty of 1901 had provided that the canal should be free and open to the ships of all nations without discrimination, so the act raised a serious moral and legal question. President Woodrow Wilson, on 5 March 1914, eloquently requested repeal as a matter of sound diplomacy and international good faith. Prominent Republicans seconded his efforts, and the act was repealed a few weeks later. Congress, however, expressly denied any relinquishment of the right to grant exemptions to coastwise shipping.

BIBLIOGRAPHY

Collin, Richard H. *Theodore Roosevelt's Caribbean: The Panama Canal, the Monroe Doctrine, and the Latin American Context*. Baton Rouge: Louisiana State University Press, 1990.

W. A. Robinson / c. w.

See also **Hay-Pauncefote Treaties; Panama Canal; Panama Canal Treaty.**

TOMAHAWK appears to derive from the Algonquian *tamahawk*, or cutting utensil. The earliest English reference to the word came from John Smith, who indicated that it could mean "axe" or "war club." Over time the term came to denote metal trade hatchets rather than other forms. Tomahawks were among the most popular items Europeans brought to the fur trade. Innumerable varieties developed, from simple hand-forged tomahawks to those elaborately inlaid with precious metals; some featured a spike or hammer head opposite the blade. Spontoon tomahawks had a spearlike blade, suitable for war, not woodcutting. One of the most popular types was the pipe tomahawk, featuring a pipe bowl opposite the blade and a handle drilled through to allow for smoking.

Metal trade tomahawks became much prized throughout North America, and were widespread in eastern North America by 1700. Their spread coincided with growth in the fur and hide trade. Tomahawks coexisted with older forms of clubs and hybrid weapons well into the nineteenth century. While very popular with both Indians and white settlers, tomahawks and other hand weapons were increasingly reduced to a ceremonial role in Native Amer-

O.K. Corral, Tombstone. The site of the most famous shootout in the history of the West: Wyatt Earp, his brothers Virgil and Morgan, and John "Doc" Holliday against Ike and Billy Clanton, Frank and Tom McLaury, and Billy Clairborne, 26 October 1881. © CORBIS

ican life by the advent of repeating firearms in the midnineteenth century. Symbolically, tomahawks remain synonymous with North American Indian warriors and warfare.

BIBLIOGRAPHY

Hartzler, Daniel D., and James A. Knowles. *Indian Tomahawks and Frontiersman Belt Axes.* Baltimore: Windcrest, 1995.

Peterson, Harold L. *American Indian Tomahawks.* Rev. ed. New York: Heye Foundation, 1971.

Robert M. Owens

See also **Indian Trade and Traders.**

TOMBSTONE. A former silver boomtown located east of the San Pedro River valley in southeastern Arizona, Tombstone is some twenty-five miles north of the Mexican border. Prospector Ed Schieffelin, who discovered silver nearby in 1877, named the site as he did because of remarks by soldiers at Camp Huachuca that the only thing he would find was his tombstone. Large-scale silver production began in 1880. The district yielded about $30 million over the next thirty years and about $8 million thereafter. Politics, feuds, greed, and conflicting town lot claims produced violence that culminated in the 26 October 1881 shootout near the O.K. Corral between the Earp brothers and Doc Holliday on one side and the

Clantons and McLaurys on the other. Labor strife and flooding curtailed mining operations in the mid-1880s. Despite extensive efforts to pump water out of the underground shafts, nearly all the mines were abandoned by 1911. Tombstone's population declined from 5,300 in 1882 to 849 in 1930. In 1929 the Cochise County seat was moved from Tombstone to Bisbee. With the publication of Walter Noble Burns's *Tombstone, an Iliad of the Southwest* (1927) and Stuart Lake's *Wyatt Earp, Frontier Marshal* (1931), along with the institution of the town's first Helldorado Days celebration in 1929, Tombstone capitalized on its notoriety as The Town Too Tough to Die. Subsequent books, motion pictures, and television shows have enhanced its reputation as a place where legends of the Old West were played out. The town became a national historic landmark in 1962, and is a major tourist attraction. Its population was 1,504 in 2000.

BIBLIOGRAPHY

Marks, Paula Mitchell. *And Die in the West: The Story of the O.K. Corral Gunfight.* New York: Morrow, 1989.

Shillingberg, William B. *Tombstone, A.T.: A History of Early Mining, Milling, and Mayhem.* Spokane, Wash.: Arthur H. Clark, 1999.

Bruce J. Dinges
Rufus Kay Wyllys

See also **Mining Towns; Silver Prospecting and Mining.**

Heeeree's Johnny! Beginning in 1954, NBC tried to create a latenight talk show that would keep viewers up after the local news. For ten years a number of hosts tried to make the show work, with only Jack Paar (1957–1962) achieving any real success. All this changed in October 1962 when Johnny Carson became the host of *The Tonight Show with Johnny Carson.* For thirty years Carson ruled late-night television with his comfortable comedic style that featured a nightly monologue, topical humor and sketches, and guests from the entertainment industry. Carson is shown here behind his familiar desk interviewing Frank Sinatra in 1976. © AP/WIDE WORLD PHOTOS

TONIGHT. "The Tonight Show," the generic title used to describe the many iterations of NBC TV's late-night comedy-talk show, was originally developed by Sylvester "Pat" Weaver, the president of NBC in the early 1950s. *Tonight!* was the initial title. It ran from 1954 through 1956, hosted by Steve Allen. In its final year, Allen shared hosting duties with the comedian Ernie Kovacs. In 1957, the title was changed to *Tonight! America After Dark*, with Jack Lescoulie as host. Unlike Allen's show, which emphasized comic sketches and music, *Tonight! America After Dark* concentrated on news, interviews, and live remote broadcasts, much like the *Today* program. After six months, Al Collins replaced Lescoulie and a month later the format was overhauled once again. *The Jack Paar Show* debuted in July 1957 in a format that emphasized interviews and "desk comedy." Paar also conducted political crusades on the air, supporting Fidel Castro's revolution in Cuba, broadcasting from the Berlin Wall, and including presidential candidates John F. Kennedy and Richard M. Nixon among his guests in 1960. When Paar left the show in March 1962, guest hosts filled in on the re-titled *The Tonight Show* until October of that year.

From October 1962 through May 1992, Johnny Carson established and sustained *The Tonight Show Starring Johnny Carson* as an American institution. The format of his show, an opening comic monologue—often about news events—followed by interviews, occasional comic pieces, musical performances, and chats with the audi-ence, would be copied by nearly all of the late-night talk shows that followed. Carson retired in 1992 and NBC awarded the vacated position to Jay Leno, who had been a frequent guest host since 1987, and re-titled it *The Tonight Show with Jay Leno.* David Letterman, angry that he had been passed up for the job, left his NBC program and moved to CBS to compete with Leno.

Since the Jack Paar era, the program has enjoyed an important place in American culture.

BIBLIOGRAPHY

Carter, Bill. *The Late Shift: Letterman, Leno, and the National Battle for the Night.* New York: Hyperion, 1994.

Metz, Robert. *The Tonight Show.* Chicago: Playboy Press, 1980.

Robert Thompson

See also **Television: Programming and Influence.**

TONKIN GULF RESOLUTION. On 2 August 1964, the USS *Maddox*, engaged in an electronic spying operation in the Tonkin Gulf, was involved in a firefight with North Vietnamese PT boats. On 4 August, the *Maddox* was apparently attacked again in international waters. Although that second attack was never confirmed, President Lyndon B. Johnson informed the American people that he was retaliating against North Vietnam's aggression by ordering air attacks on its military installations and that he was also asking Congress for its support in the form of a congressional resolution.

Drafted weeks earlier by the executive, this resolution was designed to grant the president the authority he desired to protect and defend American interests in Southeast Asia. Managing the Senate floor debate on behalf of the administration was Senator J. William Fulbright of Arkansas, a respected member of that body who also was a good friend of the president. He sought to quell existing doubts about the seemingly open-ended nature of the resolution by informing several skeptical colleagues that the president sought no wider war in Southeast Asia. According to Fulbright, that was the president's intent and the nature of his policy. Thus, given the strong public support for the president's action and congressional unwillingness to challenge his authority, Congress passed the resolution on 7 August 1964 with only two dissenting votes in the Senate.

The resolution charged that North Vietnam had attacked American ships lawfully present in international waters, which was part of a systematic campaign of aggression it has been waging against its neighbors. Congress approved and supported "the determination of the President, as Commander in Chief, to take all necessary measures to repel any armed attack against the forces of the United States and to prevent further aggression." In addition, it also authorized the president "to take all necessary steps, including the use of armed force, to assist any [SEATO] member or protocol state . . . requesting assistance in defense of its freedom."

President Johnson believed passage of the resolution had given him the necessary legal authority to take whatever action he deemed appropriate in Vietnam. But as disillusionment with the war widened and deepened, and as more information surfaced about provocative American actions in the gulf prior to the alleged incident involving the *Maddox*, Congress grew increasingly unhappy with how it had been deceived by the president in August 1964. Consequently, it repealed the resolution, which became invalid in 1971. President Richard M. Nixon, disregarding Congress's action, continued to wage war in Vietnam while acting in his capacity as commander in chief.

BIBLIOGRAPHY

Hess, Gary. *Presidential Decisions for War: Korea, Vietnam, and the Persian Gulf.* Baltimore: Johns Hopkins University Press, 2001.

Mirsky, Jonathan. "The Never Ending War." *New York Review of Books* (25 May 2000).

William C. Berman

TOPEKA CONSTITUTION.

The movement for statehood launched by free-state Kansans in opposition to the proslavery territorial government was inaugurated in the late summer of 1855, when a "people's" assembly at Topeka called an election for members of a constitutional convention. Thirteen of the delegates were natives of southern states, ten of New York and Pennsylvania, eight of the Old Northwest, four of New England, and two of foreign countries. They chose James H. Lane, a popular sovereignty Democrat as president.

The constitution contained standard provisions for the forms and functions of government. The bill of rights prohibited slavery and declared invalid indentures of blacks executed in other states. The service of free blacks in the militia was prohibited, but the fundamental question of admitting them to Kansas was referred to the voters along with the constitution and a general banking law. After the Constitution was ratified, Lane went to Washington, D.C., to petition Congress for Kansas statehood. On 4 March 1856, the legislature assembled at Topeka and elected U.S. senators. The House of Representatives passed a bill 3 July 1856, to admit Kansas under the Topeka Constitution, although five days later the Senate substituted its own measure authorizing a constitutional convention. The Senate's actions terminated the ambitions laid out in the Topeka Constitution.

BIBLIOGRAPHY

Fehrenbacher, Don E. *Sectional Crisis and Southern Constitutionalism.* Baton Rouge: Louisiana State University Press, 1995.

Rawley, James A. *Race and Politics: "Bleeding Kansas" and the Coming of the Civil War.* Philadelphia: Lippincott, 1969.

Wendell H. Stephenson / H. S.

See also **Border Ruffians; Kansas; Kansas-Nebraska Act; Sectionalism.**

TORIES. *See* **Loyalists.**

TORNADOES.

A product of an unusually powerful thunderstorm, a tornado is a naturally occurring atmospheric vortex of air spiraling at a very high speed, usually about 250 miles per hour or more, forming a funnel, and extending from the ground to the base of a convective cloud. The shape of the funnel depends on air pressure, temperature, moisture, dust, rate of airflow in the vortex, and whether the air in the tornado's core is moving upward or downward. A tornado can also have multiple vortices. Double vortices are often produced when the upper vortex turns in the direction opposite to the circular motion of the lower vortex. Because of all these factors, very few tornadoes look like true funnels. Tornadoes cause one-fifth of natural-disaster losses each year in the United States. The most intense tornadoes can toss a car a half-mile or shatter a house. However, about 80 percent of tornadoes are weak and cause no more damage than severe winds. A tornado can last fewer than 10 seconds or more than two hours. Tornadoes can occur singly or in swarms. There is no agreement among experts on any single theory of tornado formation.

The typical tornado has ground contact for about six miles, marking a path up to 500 feet wide. Tornadoes travel as fast as 35 to 60 miles per hour. The average number of tornadoes in the United States ranges between 700 and 800 per year, exceeding 1,000 in some years, most notably 1973, 1982, 1990, and 1992. Tornadoes occur most frequently in Texas, followed by Oklahoma and Kansas. Most tornado fatalities happen in the deep South and generally total fewer than 100 per year, although 350 people died in the 1974 tornado that swept through Alabama, Georgia, Tennessee, Kentucky, and Oklahoma on 3 and 4 April.

Although tornadoes have been reported in every state, most occur in the Gulf States and in the Midwest. The west-to-east airflow across the United States is interrupted by the Rocky Mountains, which push the air currents upward; they fall suddenly as they reach the Great Plains. If moisture-laden air is pulled in from the Gulf of Mexico and meets the high dry air over the plains, that confluence creates the conditions for a tornado. Tornado season begins in early spring in the deep South and progresses northward, with two-thirds of tornadoes occurring from March to June. Tornadoes are most likely to form in late afternoon, but they can occur at any time of day on any day of the year.

The National Severe Storms Forecast Center in Kansas City, Missouri, is responsible for issuing warnings of approaching tornadoes. Tornado predictions are based on meteorological conditions in combination with unusual patterns on the weather radar. Although the approach of a tornado can be forecast only 50 percent of the time, warnings have become important in reducing the death toll.

BIBLIOGRAPHY

Eagleman, Joe R. *Severe and Unusual Weather.* New York: Van Nostrand Reinhold, 1983.

Grazulis, Thomas P. *The Tornado: Nature's Ultimate Windstorm.* Norman: University of Oklahoma Press, 2001.

Mary Anne Hansen

See also **Disasters; Great Plains; Meteorology; Midwest.**

TORPEDO WARFARE. Robert Whitehead's self-propelled torpedo—a cigar-shaped weapon with an explosive charge and powered by a small engine—became standard in all major navies by the 1870s. Torpedoes increased rapidly in speed, range, and explosive power. By the eve of World War I, torpedoes effectively ranged near 7,000 yards with top speeds over 40 knots. The largest torpedoes had bursting charges of 700 pounds of explosive.

Until about 1900 torpedo boats—small, very fast vessels designed for torpedo attacks—were the principle torpedo carriers. As protection against such vessels large warships acquired batteries of quick-firing guns, and in the 1890s began to rely on a new type of warship, the torpedo boat destroyer, for protection. By the outbreak of World War I, the destroyer, grown to about 1,000 tons, had largely usurped the torpedo boat.

Submarines, however, have made the greatest use of torpedoes. During World War I, German submarines sank more than 11 million tons of British shipping, forced the British fleet to operate with extraordinary precaution, and nearly won the war for the Central Powers.

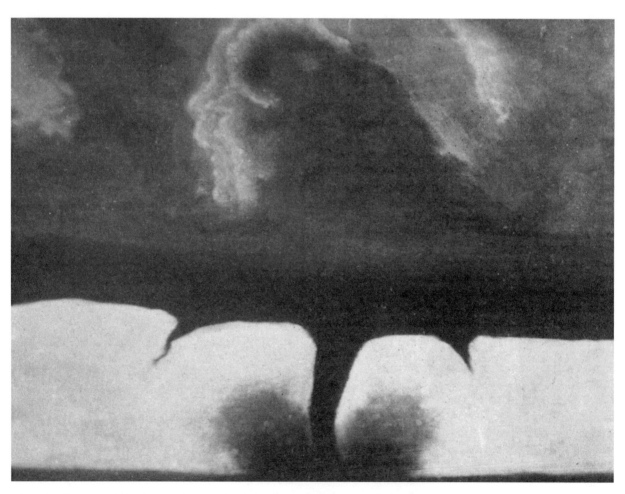

Tornado. This is the oldest known photograph of a tornado, taken 28 August 1884, twenty-two miles southwest of Howard, S.D.
NATIONAL OCEANIC AND ATMOSPHERIC ADMINISTRATION/DEPARTMENT OF COMMERCE

Between the wars, airplanes added a new dimension to torpedo warfare. In World War II a small force of British "swordfish" torpedo planes put half the Italian battle fleet out of action at Taranto harbor in 1940, and in 1941 Japanese torpedo planes helped cripple the American fleet at Pearl Harbor.

In World War II, German U-boats sank millions of tons of Allied shipping before the Allies finally won the long Battle of the Atlantic. In the Pacific, American submarines devastated the Japanese merchant marine, accounting for 28 percent of all Japanese naval shipping sunk during the war.

BIBLIOGRAPHY

Gannon, Robert. *Hellions of the Deep: The Development of American Torpedoes in World War II.* University Park: Pennsylvania State University Press, 1996.

Gray, Edwyn. *The Devil's Device: Robert Whitehead and the History of the Torpedo.* Annapolis, Md.: Naval Institute Press, 1991.

Ronald Spector / c. w.

See also **Munitions; Ordnance; Submarines.**

TOURISM. From sunbathers at Myrtle Beach to Civil War buffs at Gettysburg, Americans travel to many different destinations for a variety of reasons. Today, tourism plays an integral role in American economy, society, and culture. The Travel Industry Association of America reported that in 2001 tourism generated 7.8 million American jobs and revenues in excess of $545 billion. Yet tourism is relatively new. In less than two hundred years, touring has changed from the activity of a small elite to a mass phenomenon spurred by a thriving economy, improved transportation, national pride, and an increased desire to escape the pressures of modern life.

Before the 1820s, Americans rarely traveled for pleasure. In the next two decades, however, the fruits of industrialization created the necessary environment for tourism, as more Americans possessed the time, money, and opportunity for recreational travel. With the invention of the steamboat and increased use of railroads after 1830, Americans could travel faster, more inexpensively, and in relative comfort.

For most of the nineteenth century, Americans traveled in pursuit of improved health, sublime scenery, and social opportunities. Large spas sprang up in upstate New York and the Valley of Virginia, where the elite could "take" the waters. Americans also traveled the country searching for picturesque wonders. Popularized by the British, the "picturesque" tourist sought sublime scenes that astonished by their grandeur, beautiful vistas that soothed through pastoral serenity, and landscapes that intrigued by their quaintness. Favorite destinations included the White Mountains of New Hampshire, the villages along the Hudson River, and most of all, Niagara Falls. The historian John Sears has shown that such journeys

Yosemite National Park. In this 1922 photograph, naturalist A. F. Hall shows visitors a giant sequoia knocked down by a storm in 1919, when it was 996 years old; the labels on tree rings indicate when historic events took place during the life of the California tree. © BETTMANN/CORBIS

became sacred pilgrimages as tourists found spiritual renewal gazing on the power and beauty of the divine in nature. A popular itinerary, the "fashionable tour," combined health and the picturesque as visitors steamed up the Hudson River to Albany, traveled west along the Erie Canal stopping at the Ballston or Saratoga Springs, and ended up at Niagara Falls. Popular guidebooks such as Theodore Dwight's *The Northern Traveller* (1825) showed tourists where to visit, how to get there, and what to experience. In turn, trips became a sign of status for the individuals and of cultural identity for their new nation.

After the Civil War, attention focused on Florida and the West. Northerners gathered to winter in Jacksonville, a semitropical Eden according to a multitude of guidebooks from the 1870s and 1880s. Popular excursions included a cruise down the St. John's River and a visit to America's oldest city, St. Augustine. Even more people flocked to the state after the oil tycoon Henry M. Flagler constructed a railroad along Florida's eastern coast and built a string of luxury hotels including the lavish 1,150-room Royal Poinciana Hotel in Palm Beach, completed in 1894 and at the time the largest wooden structure in the world. Henry B. Plant used similar methods to lure tourists to the state's Gulf Coast.

The West, however, attracted visitors more out of curiosity than climate. The completion of the transcontinental railroad in 1869 and luxurious Pullman Palace cars enticed visitors to California. Visitors to the West marveled at the wonders of Yosemite and Pike's Peak and stayed in luxury resorts such as the Hotel Del Monte in Monterey. Americans increasingly viewed the West as a mythic, golden land. Railroads busily promoted this image in guidebooks and pamphlets while travel agents, such as the Raymond and Whitcomb Company, helped smooth the journey westward.

During the late nineteenth and early twentieth centuries, preservation groups worked on several popular sites. In 1860, the Mount Vernon Ladies Association purchased and restored George Washington's Virginia home

Nantucket. A poster created by Ben Nason, c. 1938, for the New Haven Railroad (one of a series of seven he made, which the railroad distributed into the 1950s), advertising the popular island vacation spot south of Cape Cod, Mass.; passengers changed from the train to the ferry at Woods Hole. © SWIM INK/CORBIS

and in the process spurred similar efforts that rescued such sites as the Hermitage and Jamestown Island. Cities and states created chambers of commerce and tourism boards that urged patriotic citizens to "see America first." The federal government responded to pressures for preservation and conservation by establishing Yellowstone as a national park in 1872. Later, the National Parks Act of 1916 established the National Park Service (NPS), whose mission was to conserve the scenery, natural and historic objects, and wildlife of America for future generations.

In the decades after World War I, the automobile spurred a great expansion of tourism. By 1930, 23 million Americans owned cars, and middle-class Americans traveled the country staying at hotels, motels, and campgrounds. Federal legislation earmarked large sums for roads, highways, and turnpikes, including the scenic Blue Ridge Parkway. During the Great Depression close to $4 billion was spent by the Works Progress Administration (WPA) to build, repair, or improve 651,087 miles of highway and 124,031 bridges. The WPA also issued guidebooks for several states and key cities through the Federal Writers Program.

After 1945, America tourism experienced phenomenal growth. Most Americans enjoyed a two-week vacation that had been denied them during the years of depression and war. As Americans' disposable income rose, so did the promotion of tourism. Major destinations included cities, ski resorts, and national parks. Several cities revitalized their downtown areas to attract tourists. San Antonio's Riverwalk and Baltimore's Inner Harbor are but two examples. And beginning with the 1955 opening of Disneyland in Anaheim, California, there has been phenomenal growth in theme parks with attendance totaling more than 163 million in 1998.

After the attacks of 11 September 2001, air travel plummeted and domestic tourism suffered, though by spring 2002 the World Trade Organization had announced that recovery was well underway.

BIBLIOGRAPHY

Aron, Cindy S. *Working at Play: A History of Vacations in the United States.* New York: Oxford University Press, 1999.

Brown, Dona. *Inventing New England: Regional Tourism in the Nineteenth Century.* Washington, D.C.: Smithsonian Institution, 1995.

Cocks, Catherine. *Doing the Town: The Rise of Urban Tourism in the United States, 1850–1915.* Berkeley: University of California Press, 2001.

Sears, John F. *Sacred Places: American Tourist Attractions in the Nineteenth Century.* New York: Oxford University Press, 1989.

Shaffer, Marguerite. *See America First: Tourism and National Identity, 1880–1940.* Washington, D.C.: Smithsonian Institution, 2001.

Rebecca C. McIntyre

Barge. African American refugees transport their household belongings along a canal in Richmond, Va., at the end of the Civil War. LIBRARY OF CONGRESS

See also **Amusement Parks; National Park System; Recreation; Transportation and Travel.**

TOWBOATS AND BARGES.

The deficiencies of railroad transportation during World War I led to the TRANSPORTATION ACT OF 1920, which created the Inland Waterways Corporation (1924) and its Federal Barge Line. The completion of the nine-foot channel of the OHIO RIVER in 1929 was followed by similar improvements on the Mississippi and its tributaries and the Gulf Intra-Coastal Canals. Each improvement marked a giant step by the U.S. Army Engineers (Corps of Engineers) in promoting inland waterways development. Private capital followed these improvements with heavy investments in towboats and barges.

In the years before World War II, towboat power soared steadily from 600 to 1,200 to 2,400. The shift from steam to diesel engines cut crews from twenty or more on steam towboats to an average of eleven to thirteen on diesels. By 1945 fully 50 percent of the towboats were diesel; by 1955, the figure was 97 percent. Meanwhile the paddlewheel had given way to the propeller, the single propeller to the still-popular twin propeller; the triple propeller became fairly common during the 1960s. In 1974 the Valley Line added the 10,500-horsepower triple-screw *W. J. Barta* to its fleet of twenty-one towboats and 750 barges. Capable of handling forty barges with a capacity of 50,000 tons, the *W. J. Barta* transported twenty-two times the record-breaking 9,266 cotton bales carried by the *Henry Frank* in 1881. By the end of the twentieth century, 10,500-horsepower towboats were common on the Mississippi.

The pilothouse is the key to modern towboat expansion. Electronics are everywhere: main control panels, radar, computers, communication systems, and circuit television scanners that monitor the entire boat for the pilot, who can communicate with pilots of approaching boats. The pilot is in telephone communication with the numerous marine services that have sprung up to cut out barges from a tow while it is under way, thus saving time and money. Some towboats have thrusters (like the bowboats of rafting days) that aid the pilots in passing other large tows, negotiating sharp bends, passing bridges, or entering locks.

Traffic on the Mississippi system climbed from 211 million short tons to more than 330 million between 1963 and 1974. The growth in river shipping did not abate in the final quarter of the century. Traffic along the Upper Mississippi rose from 54 million tons in 1970 to 112 million tons in 2000. The change from riveted to welded barges, the creation of integrated barges, and the innovation of double-skinned barges have led to improved economy, speed, and safety. Shipping on Mississippi barges became substantially less expensive than railroad transport, but at a cost to taxpayers. Barge traffic is the most heavily subsidized form of transport in the United States. A report in 1999 revealed that fuel taxes cover only 10 percent of the annual $674 million that the U.S. Army

Corps of Engineers spends building and operating the locks and dams of the Mississippi River.

BIBLIOGRAPHY

Clay, Floyd M. *History of Navigation on the Lower Mississippi.* Washington, D.C., 1983.

Petersen, William J. *Towboating on the Mississippi.* Washington, D.C.: National Waterways Study, U.S. Water Engineer Water Resource Support Center, Insitute for Water Resources, 1983.

Willliam J. Petersen / A. R.

See also **Bargemen; Engineers, Corps of; Inland Lock Navigation; Inland Waterways Commission; Lakes-to-Gulf Deep Waterway; Mississippi River; River Navigation; Waterways, Inland.**

TOWER COMMISSION. Appointed by President Ronald Regan in November 1986, the Tower Commission investigated allegations that the administration sold arms to Iran in exchange for U.S. hostages in Lebanon and then diverted money from the arms sales to the Nicaraguan contras, which violated congressional legislation. Headed by former Senator John Tower, the commission also was charged with proposing changes in the National Security Council (NSC) to prevent any such action in the future. Its 1987 report concluded that members of the NSC staff were responsible for the secret diversion of funds and that President Reagan was out of touch with the actions of his own government in the White House.

BIBLIOGRAPHY

Koh, Harold Hongju. *The National Security Constitution: Sharing Power After the Iran-Contra Affair.* New Haven, Conn.: Yale University Press, 1990.

United States. President's Special Review Board. *The Tower Commission Report: The Full Text of the President's Special Review Board.* New York: Times Books, 1987.

Katy J. Harriger / A. G.

See also **Iran-Contra Affair; Political Scandals; Special Prosecutors.**

TOWN GOVERNMENT or township government is the lowest level of general-purpose local government in the northeastern and midwestern states. Generally the jurisdiction of towns or townships extends only to areas outside of incorporated cities. Towns were the principal units of local government in colonial New England, providing schools, poor relief, roads, and other necessary services. The town meeting, an assembly of all enfranchised townspeople, was the primary decision-making body, but over the course of the colonial period the elected selectmen seemed to grow increasingly important in determining town policy. Towns or townships also existed in New York, New Jersey, and Pennsylvania, though in these middle colonies counties played a greater role in local government than in New England. The southern colonies did not develop townships. This basic geographic pattern persisted throughout the following centuries. In the northernmost states towns were most significant. In the middle swath of states they existed but were less important, and they were foreign to the southern half of the nation.

During the nineteenth century the trans-Appalachian states stretching from Ohio to the Dakotas adopted township government. In each of these states township officials were responsible for roads, cemeteries, and poor relief. Moreover they ensured that farmers maintained their fences and impounded stray livestock. States could assign other tasks to townships as well. In Ohio township clerks were authorized to record livestock brands, and Kansas lawmakers empowered townships to eliminate prairie dogs. In New York, New Jersey, Michigan, Illinois, Wisconsin, and Nebraska the chief township officer was the supervisor, and the country governing boards were composed of the supervisors from each township. The township supervisor was therefore both a township and a county official.

By the first half of the twentieth century many observers believed the town or township was obsolete. In New England the town meeting seemed ill suited to the larger towns with thousands of voters. Many indifferent townspeople failed to exercise their right to participate, abdicating decision making to the random few hundred people who attended the meetings. In 1915, in response to this situation, Brookline, Massachusetts, adopted the representative town meeting. All town voters could attend these meetings and express their views, but only elected representatives could vote on the issues. By the last decade of the twentieth century forty-two Massachusetts towns, seven Connecticut towns, and one Vermont community had adopted the representative town meeting. To preserve a semblance of broad-based democracy, these assemblies usually included over two hundred voting representatives.

Another alternative to the town meeting was the town council. This was a small legislative body comparable to a city council, and it often hired a town manager with duties corresponding to those of a city manager. In other words, under the town council plan a town was governed like a city but retained the title of town. In 1945 Bloomfield became the first Connecticut community to opt for this plan, and in 1971 Agawam was the first Massachusetts town to embrace council rule. By the 1990s twenty-nine Massachusetts towns operated under the council plan. In a majority of New England towns the traditional town meeting survived, though only a minority of voters attended. Lauded as bastions of direct democracy, town meetings actually appeared to be prime examples of democratic apathy.

Meanwhile, most students of local government were growing increasingly critical of township rule outside of New England. They condemned the townships as obso-

they could get tossed in jail—just as they wished would happen to many of the "captains of industry" whom many Americans blamed for the depression.

Two other phenomena once again revolutionized the toy industry after World War II (1939–1945). They were the introduction of a suitable plastic for toys, and the baby boom. The plastic known as polystyrene actually first appeared in 1927. But World War II perfected the use of plastics in industry. That, coupled with a postwar prosperity and the largest new generation in American history, set the stage for a toy boom.

The classics of the age were born. In 1952, the Hassenfeld Brothers—Hasbro—of Providence, Rhode Island, introduced an unlikely toy: plastic eyes, noses, ears, and lips that kids could stick into potatoes and other vegetables or fruits. Hasbro called the odd toy Mr. Potato Head, and it quickly caught on. In the 1960s, Hasbro marketed Mr. Potato Head with plastic potatoes, and even plastic carrots, green peppers, and french fries. A Mrs. Potato Head appeared, but the spuds lost their appeal by the 1970s. In 1995, however, Pixar's movie *Toy Story* repopularized Mr. Potato Head.

Television and movie tie-ins created new toy markets in the 1950s. Disney's *Mickey Mouse Club* spurred a demand for mouse-ear hats, as did Disney's *Davy Crockett* series a demand for coonskin caps. Disney's *Zorro* encouraged little boys to ask for black plastic swords tipped with chalk so they could slash a "Z" on sidewalks, trees, and buildings.

In 1959, Mattel introduced Barbie, the most popular plastic doll of all time. Mattel engineered a marketing coup with Barbie, by offering not only the doll but a range of accessories as well. Changes of clothes, purses, gloves, shoes—no Barbie was complete without a decent wardrobe, and a Barbie box to carry it in. Soon Barbie had a boyfriend, Ken, and a sister, Skipper. Barbie was born into the suburban housewife era and has lived through the hippie age of the 1960s, the do-your-own-thing era of the 1970s, and the flamboyant 1980s. While feminists have decried that Barbie, with her exaggerated hourglass figure, is sexist, foisting upon young girls an image of womanhood that is hard to achieve, she has nevertheless endured.

In 1965, Hasbro took the social risk of introducing a doll for boys—G.I. Joe. At almost a foot tall, Joe was loosely based on a new television series called *The Lieutenant*. In reality, Joe arrived in a year when the United States was celebrating the twentieth anniversary of its victory in World War II. Joe represented a time before the Cold War when Americans were victorious on the battlefield. Not that six-year-old boys cared, but Joe won the favor of their parents, and that was half the battle. Joe also followed Barbie's marketing scheme, by offering accessories like M-1 Rifles, hand-grenades, dress blues, and jungle camouflage. Boys could even outfit Joe in enemy uniforms; but they were enemies from the "good ol'

days"—Germans and Japanese—not the North Vietnamese or Vietcong of the 1960s. Indeed, Joe would suffer, as would all Americans, from United States involvement in Vietnam. As victory eluded the United States there and things military faded from fashion in the wake of war protests, Joe changed from a soldier to an adventurer. In 1970, Hasbro began marketing Joes as the "Adventure Team." Bewhiskered Joes drove All-Terrain Vehicles instead of Jeeps, and hunted for stolen mummies and white tigers. Joe became anemic as the United States began to doubt itself on the battlefield. By the mid-1970s, Joe had faded away. He returned, however, as a smaller action figure in the early 1980s to battle an elite group of terrorists known as Cobra. In the late 1990s, Hasbro returned the original G.I. Joe to the markets. The target audience was grown-up baby boomers who once played with the original.

Toy cars had long been around. Jack Odell introduced finely crafted miniatures he called Matchbox Cars in 1952, and in 1957 Tonka trucks and cars hit the market. Larger-scale, metal vehicles with free-rolling wheels, Tonkas were virtually indestructible. Mattel revolutionized the market once again in 1966 with the introduction of Hot Wheels. The cars had low-friction wheels and used gravity to speed them down strips of yellow track that boys could attach to tabletops then run down to the floor. The cars depicted stock autos, like Mustangs and Camaros, and fanciful show and concept cars.

The release of George Lucas's *Star Wars* in 1977 brought new interest in miniature play figures, popularly called "action figures." In the early twenty-first century, toy buyers can expect tie-in toys to hit the shelves a month or more before their associate movie, but *Star Wars* arrived in the summer of 1977 with no affiliated toys. Not until the next year did figures of Luke Skywalker, Darth Vader, and the rest appear. Compared with later action figures, the original Kenner *Star Wars* figures are simple, yet toy collectors highly prize them. In the 1980s, virtually every kid-oriented movie from *E.T.* to *Beetlejuice* had action figure/toy tie-ins.

The 1980s also saw reverse tie-ins, when toy manufacturers contracted animation studios to produce cheap half-hour cartoons to support toys. He-Man, She-Ra, G.I. Joe, and Teenage-Mutant Ninja Turtles capitalized on such marketing strategy.

Electronics have also made their mark on toys. In 1972, Magnavox introduced Odyssey, the first video game that could be hooked into a television. Atari followed in 1976 with Pong. While home video games boomed briefly, they faded quickly in the early 1980s as large, coin-fed games in arcades attracted players. In 1983, Nintendo pried the home video game market back open with games like Super Mario Brothers. Now video games are a staple for both televisions and computers.

153

BIBLIOGRAPHY

The History of Toys and Games. Available at http://www .historychannel.com/exhibits.toys.

Ketchum, William C., Jr. *Toys and Games.* Washington, D.C.: Cooper-Hewitt Museum of the Smithsonian Institution, 1981.

Miller, G. Wayne. *Toy Wars: The Epic Struggle between G.I. Joe, Barbie, and the Companies that Make Them.* New York: Times Books, 1998.

Spilhaus, Athelstan, and Kathleen Spilhaus. *Mechanical Toys: How Old Toys Work.* New York: Crown Publishers, 1989.

R. Steven Jones

See also **G.I. Joe; Barbie Doll; Middlebrow Culture; "Monopoly"; "Scrabble"; Vacation and Leisure.**

TRACK AND FIELD athletics in the United States had multiple origins in the early- to mid-nineteenth century. British models were most influential. Scottish immigrants formed Caledonian Clubs in many American cities, and through these the tradition of Highland Games (also called Caledonian Games) brought track and field competition to the East Coast through the mid-1870s. Boston, for example, held its first Highland Games in 1842. In 1849 English long-distance runners demonstrated their sport to large American crowds.

Another important thread, older and harder to trace, is the Native American running and games traditions. One of the first American runners to compel English athletes' notice was Louis "Deerfoot" Bennett, a Seneca Indian who ran in England in 1862, dressed for effect in wolfskin and a feathered headband.

Yet another venue for organized competition was county and state fairs.

As in England, social class distinguished the structures that contained and sponsored track and running events. Caledonian Club events tended to invite all comers, no matter what race or ethnicity. Other British imports, such as the races called "pedestrians," were often largely working-class events. One of the first American pedestrians was held in 1835 at the Union racetrack in New York. Runners competed to cover ten miles in less than an hour. (One out of nine entrants achieved this goal.) Another type of pedestrian was the "six day go as you please" staged in several cities in the mid-nineteenth century. These were endurance events characterized by betting and by the rough informality of that era's urban spectacles. One race in Boston in the mid-1880s was run indoors by contestants from a wide variety of social backgrounds who had coaches and stood to win some money. A final category was the women's walking contest, quite popular in the 1870s. Often lucrative for the winners, these marathon contests, involving thousands of quarter-mile track circuits per meet, disappeared in the 1880s and are barely remembered today. By the late-nineteenth century the other pedestrians had also shriveled because of widespread corruption and the increasing attraction of more elitist and "legitimate" competitions.

Collegiate and club track and running competitions eventually overwhelmed more populist events. For these athletes, amateur status was a badge of honor. In the 1880s and 1890s, the athletic club model caught on among American elites. These clubs varied from social clubs with fine athletic facilities to clubs primarily for amateur athletes, but in America's gilded age, most clubs developed membership policies defined by income and social prestige. The New York Athletic Club (NYAC) was founded in 1868, and the Boston Athletic Association in 1887. By the late nineteenth century, most American cities had amateur athletic clubs, and the international aspirations of the American clubs were captured in the first American-British meet held at Travers Island, New York, in June 1895, in which the NYAC hosted its London counterpart.

On the collegiate scene, perhaps due to their relative age and their links to elite preparatory schools with track programs and to the city athletic clubs, northeastern universities nurtured many outstanding amateur track and field athletes at the turn of the century. The growth of organized collegiate sports partly reflected middle-class concerns about the fate of rugged manliness in an urban, electrified world. The Intercollegiate Association of Amateur Athletics was founded in 1876. By the 1880s, track and field events encompassed the 100- and 220-yard sprints, the quarter-, half-, and mile runs, hurdles, the broad jump, long jump, pole vault, shot put, 56-pound throw, and hammer throw, and sometimes the half-mile walk. (The marathon would be an Olympic addition.)

In 1896 a fourteen-man team sponsored by the Boston Athletic Association traveled to Athens for the first modern Olympic Games. The young Americans won nine of the twelve track and field events. By the 1912 games, United States track athletes had put the Olympics on their calendars and continued their impressive record of victories. The remarkable Carlisle Indian School graduate, Jim Thorpe, won both the pentathlon and decathlon.

The 1912 team also included several African American members, as had the 1908 team. The development of American track and field has reflected the evolution of various groups' access to social competition in general. Into the early twentieth century, American white men dominated the track and field events sponsored and fostered by the white athletic clubs and the white-dominated colleges. Yet African Americans competed in track and field from its American beginnings, largely through venues that paralleled those of white male athletes. Most black track athletes, as in baseball and other sports, functioned in segregated settings. The "colored" YMCAs nurtured athletic skills and organizational knowledge. American blacks also founded urban athletic clubs to foster recreation and competition; in fact, like whites of various ethnic and class groupings, African Americans fully participated in the club movement of the late nineteenth century. Limited community resources hampered these clubs, and members usually had to use public facilities for their activities. Black colleges, founded after the Civil War, offered a crucial staging ground for black athletes. After initial hesitation to commit their scarce resources to athletics, by the 1890s college administrators were backing a varsity movement. More public resources might have come their way through the Second Morrill Act of 1890, except that southern white state legislators diverted funds intended for black land-grant colleges to white uses.

Even in those years, the outstanding competitive skills of individual black men occasionally emerged. A few black athletes were able to participate in white-controlled events like the Highland Games. A few black students attended white colleges and universities, sometimes only after being required to graduate from a black college. These included outstanding athletes like Amherst's W. T. S. Jackson, the University of Pennsylvania's J. B. Taylor, Howard Smith, and Dewey Rogers, and Harvard's N. B. Marshall and Ted Cable (a graduate of Andover Academy). Other venues for blacks to compete against whites included the military, where black units could field competitors against white units' teams. American meets and teams contained increasing numbers of black American world-class athletes, including of course Jesse Owens, whose winning performance offered an ironic commentary on the Third Reich's racial philosophy in the 1936 Berlin Olympic Games.

In the mid-1890s college women began testing their skill in track and field events. Vassar College held the first of forty-two consecutive women's field days in 1895. For thirty years, women track athletes strove against the physical educators' received wisdom, which echoed cultural repression of women's physical exertion on the grounds that women were incapable of extended exercise. In the early 1920s, track and field boomed as a sport for college women, then fell victim by the 1930s to social fears of the "mannish" and unnatural (read: "lesbian") female types who might thrive in sports so dependent on "masculine" strength and speed (rather than the grace and agility one could read into gymnastics, skating, and even tennis and golf, which had their own social cachet).

Colleges were not the only breeding ground for women (or men) track athletes. Though access to good tracks, coaches, and practice time made a difference in results, one could compete for relatively little money in events sponsored by the Amateur Athletic Union and thus qualify for distinction. While the blight on female track athletics hit colleges first, non-collegiate athletes continued to compete and draw audiences into the 1930s. There was room in public regard for Mildred "Babe" Didrikson, who gained celebrity in the 1931 nationals by breaking the world's record for the 80-meter hurdles and achieved Olympic distinction in 1932. (In the longer run, her blunt speech and avoidance of dresses seemed to confirm stereotypes of women athletes.) Didrikson and many other non-collegiate women athletes were sponsored by indus-

Jesse Owens. The track and field phenomenon, in midair during a broad jump in 1936, the year he won four gold medals and broke world records at the Olympic Games in Berlin. AP/WIDE WORLD PHOTOS

trial leagues, part of the "welfare capitalism" movement of the 1920s.

As female participation in track and field became culturally complicated, black women emerged as the individuals able to withstand the stigma of speed, endurance, and strength to compete in national and international meets. Alice Coachman was the first black woman to win an Olympic gold medal in the high jump, in London in 1948. Wilma Rudolph won Americans' hearts with her Olympic performance in 1960, when she won three gold medals; and she was only one member of an Olympic women's squad dominated by black collegiate athletes. (The entire relay team was from Tennessee State University.) Since the 1960s a host of black American women athletes have starred on the world stage of Olympic competition, including Evelyn Ashford, Valerie Brisco-Hooks, Gail Devers, Florence Griffith Joyner, Jackie Joyner-Kersee, Marion Jones, and Wyomia Tyus.

Black men have matched black women's track and field brilliance in the last fifty years. Again, a partial list includes Bob Beamon, Leroy Burrell, Milt Campbell, Lee Evans, Carl Lewis, Michael Johnson, Edwin Moses, and

155

Mike Powell. The bitter side of African American success is the continuing social and "scientific" conversation about whether there are physiological causes of black athletic domination. Besides linking to a long Euro-American history of slandering black Africans and their descendants as more animalistic and primitive than whites, this debate implies that blacks may have to work less hard and thus deserve less credit for their athletic achievements.

As with other sports, track and field's twentieth century has been characterized by both technical and technological developments contributing to progressively faster, longer, higher results. Technological improvements encompass the materials used in equipment, including shoes and clothing, as well as timing, starting, and measurement methods. There have also been illegitimate technological developments, notably the use of drugs, particularly anabolic steroids, to enhance physical development and performance.

Technical improvements include training regimes, nutritional knowledge, and research toward systematizing and enhancing the psychosocial aspects of training and competition.

The final major development has been the erosion of distinctions between amateur and professional athletic status. Endorsements and sponsorships from corporations and other organizations allow outstanding track athletes to enhance and extend their careers. Many other professional athletes may earn far more, but professionalization has contributed to the visibility and democratization of track and field.

BIBLIOGRAPHY

Ashe, Arthur R., Jr. *A Hard Road to Glory: A History of the African-American Athlete 1619–1918*. Volume I. New York: Amistad, 1993.

Cahn, Susan K. *Coming On Strong: Gender and Sexuality in Twentieth-Century Women's Sport*. New York: Free Press, 1994.

Chalk, Ocania. *Black College Sport*. New York: Dodd, Mead, 1976.

Guttmann, Allen. *Women's Sports: A History*. New York: Columbia University Press, 1991.

McNab, Tom. *The Complete Book of Track and Field*. New York: Exeter Books, 1980.

Rader, Benjamin G. *American Sports: From the Age of Folk Games to the Age of Televised Sports*. 3rd ed. Englewood Cliffs, N.J.: Prentice Hall, 1996.

Riess, Steven A. *City Games: The Evolution of American Urban Society and the Rise of Sports*. Urbana: University of Illinois Press, 1989.

Tricard, Louise Mead. *American Women's Track and Field: A History, 1895 through 1980*. Jefferson, N.C.: McFarland, 1996.

Mina Carson

See also **Olympic Games, American Participation in; Sports.**

TRADE AGREEMENTS. When two or more nations wish to establish or modify economic relations and set tariffs on international commerce they enter into a trade agreement. Any authorized government official may negotiate such an agreement, but all participating governments must formally ratify the proposed treaty before it becomes effective. As a result, domestic political forces and interest groups exert considerable influence over the provisions of any trade agreement. The United States negotiated few trade agreements in the eighteenth and nineteenth centuries. Domestic political pressures determined how high or low import taxes (tariffs) would be. From the earliest debates in the First Congress, some political leaders favored low tariffs designed to raise revenue while others favored much higher rates to protect domestic producers from foreign competition. Lower rates generally prevailed through the 1850s, but protectionist tariffs were sponsored by the dominant Republican party during and after the Civil War. To encourage particular types of trade within the forbiddingly high post–Civil War tariff structure some leaders favored bilateral trade agreements in which each nation agreed to reduce rates in return for reciprocal reductions.

In the 1870s the United States signed a reciprocal trade agreement with the then-independent Hawaiian government that gave Hawaiian sugar exporters tariff-free access to the U.S. market. In the early 1890s Secretary of State James G. Blaine negotiated reciprocal trade agreements that softened the effect of the highly protectionist McKinley Tariff Act of 1890, but the 1894 Wilson-Gorman Tariff Act made such agreements impossible. With the exception of the Underwood Act, which passed in 1913 but never went into effect because of World War I, protectionist rates remained until the Great Depression, when it appeared that the nation's high import duties were not only detrimental to world trade but also might be harmful to the domestic economy.

In the election of 1932 the Democrats came to power on a program involving "a competitive tariff" for revenue and "reciprocal trade agreements with other nations." Cordell Hull, President Franklin D. Roosevelt's secretary of state, was the driving force behind congressional action in getting the Trade Agreements Act made law on 12 June 1934. The Reciprocal Trade Agreements Act of 1934 permitted reduction of trade barriers by as much as half in return for reductions by another nation. Moreover, the new act, in form an amendment to the 1930 Tariff Act, delegated to the president the power to make foreign-trade agreements with other nations on the basis of a mutual reduction of duties, without any specific congressional approval of such reductions. The act limited reduction to 50 percent of the rates of duty existing then and stipulated that commodities could not be transferred between the dutiable and free lists. The power to negotiate was to run for three years, but this power was renewed for either two or three years periodically until replaced by the Trade Expansion Act of 1962. In the late

1930s and 1940s U.S. negotiators arranged a great number of bilateral trade agreements. In fact, between 1934 and 1947 the United States made separate trade agreements with twenty-nine foreign countries. The Tariff Commission found that when it used dutiable imports in 1939 as its basis for comparison, U.S. tariffs were reduced from an average of 48 percent to an average of 25 percent during the thirteen-year period, the imports on which the duties were reduced having been valued at over $700 million in 1939.

Although Congress gave the State Department the primary responsibility for negotiating with other nations, it instructed the Tariff Commission and other government agencies to participate in developing a list of concessions that could be made to foreign countries or demanded from them in return. Each trade agreement was to incorporate the principle of "unconditional most-favored-nation treatment." This requirement was necessary to avoid a great multiplicity of rates.

During World War II the State Department and other government agencies worked on plans for the reconstruction of world trade and payments. They discovered important defects in the trade agreements program, and they concluded that they could make better headway through simultaneous multilateral negotiations. American authorities in 1945 made some far-reaching proposals for the expansion of world trade and employment. Twenty-three separate countries then conducted tariff negotiations bilaterally on a product-by-product basis, with each country negotiating its concessions on each import commodity with the principal supplier of that commodity. The various bilateral understandings were combined to form the General Agreement on Tariffs and Trade (GATT), referred to as the Geneva Agreement, which was signed in Geneva on 30 October 1947. This agreement did not have to be submitted to the U.S. Senate for approval because the president was already specifically empowered to reduce tariffs under the authority conferred by the Trade Agreements Extension Act of 1945.

After 1945 Congress increased the power of the president by authorizing him to reduce tariffs by 50 percent of the rate in effect on 1 January 1945, instead of 1934, as the original act provided. Thus, duties that had been reduced by 50 percent prior to 1945 could be reduced by another 50 percent, or 75 percent below the rates that were in effect in 1934. But in 1955 further duty reductions were limited to 15 percent, at the rate of 5 percent a year over a three-year period, and in 1958 to 20 percent, effective over a four-year period, with a maximum of 10 percent in any one year.

In negotiating agreements under the Trade Agreements Act, the United States usually proceeded by making direct concessions only to so-called chief suppliers—namely, countries that were, or probably would become, the main source, or a major source, of supply of the commodity under discussion. This approach seemed favorable to the United States, since no concessions were extended to minor supplying countries that would benefit the chief supplying countries (through unconditional most-favored-nation treatment) without the latter countries first having granted a concession. The United States used its bargaining power by granting concessions in return for openings to foreign markets for American exports.

Concessions to one nation through bilateral negotiations were often extended to all others through the most-favored-nation principle. Many international agreements included a clause stating that the parties would treat each other in the same way they did the nation their trade policies favored the most. If in bilateral negotiations the United States agreed to reduce its import duties on a particular commodity, that same reduction was automatically granted to imports from any nation with which the United States had a most-favored-nation arrangement. The high tariff walls surrounding the United States were gradually chipped away through bilateral agreements that established much lower rates for all its major trading partners.

From the original membership of twenty-three countries, GATT had expanded by the mid-1970s to include more than seventy countries, a membership responsible for about four-fifths of all the world trade. During the numerous tariff negotiations carried on under the auspices of GATT, concessions covering over 60,000 items had been agreed on. These constituted more than two-thirds of the total import trade of the participating countries and more than one-half the total number of commodities involved in world trade.

With the expiration on 30 July 1962, of the eleventh renewal of the Reciprocal Trade Agreements Act, the United States was faced with a major decision on its future foreign trade policy: to choose between continuing the program as it had evolved over the previous twenty-eight years or to replace it with a new and expanded program. The second alternative was chosen by President John F. Kennedy when, on 25 January 1962, he asked Congress for unprecedented authority to negotiate with the European Common Market for reciprocal trade agreements. The European Common Market had been established in 1957 to eliminate all trade barriers in six key countries of Western Europe: France, West Germany, Italy, Belgium, the Netherlands, and Luxembourg. Their economic strength, the increasing pressure on American balance of payments, and the threat of a Communist aid and trade offensive led Congress to pass the Trade Expansion Act of 1962. This act granted the president far greater authority to lower or eliminate American import duties than had ever been granted before, and it replaced the negative policy of preventing dislocation by the positive one of promoting and facilitating adjustment to the domestic dislocation caused by foreign competition. The president was authorized, through trade agreements with foreign countries, to reduce any duty by 50 percent of the rate in effect on 1 July 1962. Whereas the United States had negotiated in the past on an item-by-item, rate-by-rate basis, in the future the president could decide to cut tariffs on an industry, or across-the-board, basis for all products, in exchange for similar reductions by the other countries. In order to deal with the tariff problems created by the European Common Market, the president was empowered to reduce tariffs on industrial products by more than 50 percent, or to eliminate them completely when the United States and the Common Market together accounted for 80 percent or more of the world export value. The president could also reduce the duty by more than 50 percent or eliminate it on an agricultural commodity, if he decided such action would help to maintain or expand American agricultural exports.

After Kennedy's death, President Lyndon B. Johnson pushed through a new round of tariff bargaining that culminated in a multilateral trade negotiation known as the Kennedy Round. The agreement, reached on 30 June 1967, reduced tariff duties an average of about 35 percent on some 60,000 items representing an estimated $40 billion in world trade, based on 1964 figures, the base year for the negotiations. As a result of the tariff-reduction installments of the Kennedy Round, by 1973 the average height of tariffs in the major industrial countries, it is estimated, had come down to about 8 or 9 percent.

Although both Johnson and President Richard M. Nixon exerted pressure on Congress to carry some of the trade expansion movements of the Kennedy Round further, Congress resisted all proposals. Since 1934 U.S. trade negotiations have been an executive responsibility, but Congress has maintained a strong interest in both procedures and outcomes. In the 1960s and 1970s it called upon the U.S. Tariff Commission to identify "peril points," where reduction of specific duties might cause serious damage to U.S. producers or suppliers. Other federal legislation provided for relief measures if increased imports cause injury to a domestic industrial sector. The crisis in foreign trade that developed in 1971–1972 was the result of stagnation as well as of an unprecedented deficit in the U.S. balance of payments. Some pressure groups from both industry and labor tried to revive the protectionism that had flourished before 1934, but they had had small success except on petroleum imports by the mid-1970s.

The world's acceptance of more liberal trade agreements has had different effects on U.S. producers. Most likely to benefit are those engaged in the nation's traditionally export-oriented agricultural sector. Production costs are relatively low in the U.S. heartland, so a freer market tends to benefit domestic agricultural exporters. At the same time, labor-intensive industries, such as textiles, electronics, and automobiles, have suffered from the gradual reduction of import restrictions. U.S. wage rates range far higher than comparable rates in certain countries that have built very efficient textile mills and fabrication plants for electronic devices and appliances. The recovery of the U.S. auto industry in the 1990s, however, demonstrated that increasing the use of industrial robotics and automated assembly lines can help undermine the cost advantage of foreign manufacturers. As more liberal trade agreements promote competition among producers, each nation is likely to develop stronger and weaker economic sectors that complement those of its global trading partners. The ultimate trade agreement is one in which all national barriers disappear. The European Union (formerly the European Economic Community) represents an approximation of that goal, as does the 1993 North American Free Trade Agreement (NAFTA) among the United States, Canada, and Mexico. NAFTA cancels all major barriers to exchange of goods and services among the participants, leaving the GATT structure in control of imports and exports outside the free-trade area.

BIBLIOGRAPHY

Grinspun, Ricardo, and Maxwell A. Cameron, eds. *The Political Economy of North American Free Trade.* New York: St. Martin's Press, 1993.

McCormick, Thomas J. *America's Half Century: United States Foreign Policy in the Cold War and After.* Baltimore: Johns Hopkins University Press, 1995.

McKinney, Joseph A., and M. Rebecca Sharpless, eds. *Implications of a North American Free Trade Region: Multi-Disciplinary Perspectives.* Waco, Texas: Baylor University, 1992.

John M. Dobson
Sidney Ratner / A. G.

See also **European Union; General Agreement on Tariffs and Trade; North American Free Trade Agreement; Reciprocal Trade Agreements; Trade, Foreign.**

TRADE DOLLAR. The currency law of 1873 created a special silver dollar, weighing 420 grains instead of the standard 412.5 grains, ostensibly to encourage trade with China, but more probably to provide a market for domestic silver producers (see CRIME OF 1873). The bulk of the 36 million pieces coined went to China, but at least 6 million were forced into circulation in the United States, despite the fact that after 1887 they were no longer legal tender. Many were bought at a discount and paid out at par to immigrant laborers who were forced to take the loss. Hoping to force the government to buy new silver, the silver interests delayed government redemption of the coins until 1887.

BIBLIOGRAPHY

Carothers, Neil. *Fractional Money: A History of the Small Coins and Fractional Paper Currency of the United States.* New York: Wiley, 1930.

Schwarz, Ted. *A History of United States Coinage.* San Diego, Calif.: Barnes, 1980.

Neil Carothers / A. R.

See also **China Trade; Currency and Coinage; Free Silver; Money; Silver Prospecting and Mining.**

HIGHLIGHTS OF THE DEVELOPMENT OF DOMESTIC TRADE, 1492–2002

1492–1607, The New World Evolves

The Old World (Europe) and the New World begin to blend together as the pioneers bring livestock andother necessities for survival. Fishing starts a dominant industry in the North.

1607–1783, The Colonial Era

Native Americans taught the colonists to raise new crops, including corn, squash, potatoes, and tobacco. Ships were sent from Europe full of luxuries to trade. The first permanent trading post was established.

1784–1860, A New Nation

The Constitution was adopted. A national currency and a banking system were developed.

1861–1865, The Civil War

The North was thriving economically as a result of war expenditures. The South was just barely surviving. Its agricultural lands had been turned into battlefields, and what little was produced was not being marketed because the North blockaded the Southern ports.

1865–1889, Reconstruction

The development of the railroads connecting the Middle West and the South to the West made trading much faster and more profitable. Also, the Great Lakes became a hub of commerce between the East and the Middle West.

1890–1913, The Progressive Era

The creation of the Federal Trade Commission brought control and regulation to interstate trade. For the first time, more people were employed by industry than working on farms.

1914–1928, World War I and the Jazz Age

The Eighteenth Amendment was ratified, prohibiting the manufacture of alcoholic beverages for sale. Illegal industries evolved in active trade in wines and liquor. America enjoyed prosperity, along with demanding more goods and services.

1929–1939, The Great Depression

The stock market crashed in October 1929. A domino effect occurred in the nation's economy, and consumer spending collapsed. Trade was nearly at a standstill.

1941–1945, World War II

Demand for goods and services was once again placed on need only, although government spending on the war effort helped bring the country out of the Great Depression. Production for consumer goods declined, and production for war necessities increased.

1945–Present, The Modern Era

Since World War II, goods increasingly have been mass-produced to meet the needs and wants of consumers. Companies seek lower production costs and less time in the production process. America has seen a shift from domestic production to foreign production. Some American companies have bought land in foreign countries, built factories there, and used their labor because it is cheaper. America is helping the underdeveloped countries to develop as a result of trade.

The technological revolution beginning in the mid-1980s has brought even faster production methods and a new set of industries. Consumer spending is at an all-time high. Trade is evolving on a worldwide basis.

TRADE, DOMESTIC. Trade can be defined as engaging in an exchange for goods and services. For trade to take place, there must be at least two parties with different wants and needs. These people may not be able to produce the goods or services alone and seek others who can do so.

People need the basics to survive such as food, clothing, and shelter. They may want large houses, fashion clothing, and exotic food. Specialization is extremely important to trade. Each worker or company focuses on producing a type of service or product, creating interdependency. Whether they are consumers, workers, producers, or the government itself, everyone benefits from trade in various ways.

Workers benefit from securing jobs with companies that are expanding and desire labor. A producer or company can grow as a result of the demand for its product or service. Consumers are able to make better choices because they create the demand for products and services and indirectly create competition among producers. The government benefits because of the taxes on producers, workers, and consumers. Since colonial times, trade has contributed greatly to the standard of living of the United States, which is among the highest in the world.

Early Trade, 1492–1783

The people who came to America did so to seek freedom of religion, freedom of political views, and economic opportunity. Great Britain still had control over the colonies. As the American colonies were being settled, trade became a means of survival. The Native Americans assisted the colonists in growing food. They introduced them to potatoes, corn, and tobacco, which the colonists in turn traded for goods from Europe.

Indigenous people had their settlements either near waterways or near trails they had created. The colonists used both the waterways and the trails as transportation routes to conduct trade. As America was being explored, trade was evolving.

To make trade easier, trading posts were set up in towns. A popular one, called the Aptucxet Trading Post, was founded by the Pilgrims in 1627. It has often been referred to as "the cradle of American commerce." Fur, lumber, luxury goods, and food were just a few things that were traded. The Native Americans as well as the Pilgrims used the trading post, exchanging beaver skins for blankets, guns, hatchets, and rum. As the colonial trade grew, hostilities developed with Britain and also among the colonists themselves over trade issues. As the colonists were prospering, Britain was losing money as a result of its war with France over territories in North America. Britain's unsuccessful efforts to tax the colonists helped spark the Revolution. During the war, little trade took place outside the colonies. People became more self-sufficient and interdependent, or they just did without things that they were used to having.

By 1762 merchants had been complaining that there was no central bank in the colonies. A central bank was starting to evolve by the end of the Revolution. The signing of the Constitution in 1787 created a strong government that supported Americans who were trying very hard to maintain an economy based on domestic trade, with an emphasis on agriculture.

A New Nation, 1783–1860

In the late 1700s, the newly discovered Ohio Valley waterways made inland trade easier for New England and the middle and southern colonies. The steamboat made a successful appearance in the Ohio Valley in 1811. It was mainly used to get crops to market areas. The "river cities," including Cincinnati, Louisville, Saint Louis, and New Orleans, became trading hubs as manufacturing developed along the waterways. By the 1820s there was a central bank and a national currency. In almost every large town and new cities, banks were being built.

The opening of the Erie Canal in 1825, connecting Lake Erie to the Hudson River, also furnished a new outlet for the Northwest traffic. New York City wasn't just a market anymore but also a commercial center for trade.

Waterways continue to be important, but the landlocked towns began to prosper from trade as a result of the railroads. They spread quickly from Baltimore to Wisconsin. Most of the northern Atlantic Coast turned to manufacturing as the railroad continued to grow.

Civil War, 1861–1865

At the time of the Civil War, the South was producing mostly agricultural products, with an emphasis on cotton and tobacco as major commodities for trade. The North cut off the South's markets when the war started, and its trade was almost at a standstill. Also, with so many men in the army, it was impossible for the women left behind to operate the transportation systems to get the products to markets. The South was mostly self-sufficient and poor once again.

By 1863, the North was seeking profits on goods related to the war, such as the high demand for army uniforms. The North was thriving economically and making quick money.

Reconstruction, 1865–1889

The two decades from 1870 to 1890 marked the development of railroads connecting the Middle West and the South to the West. People migrated to the West in search of a profitable economic future. New settlements sprang up quickly along with the manufacturing and agricultural trade. With the development of a more sophisticated transportation system came a demand for material possessions. The Great Lakes were transformed to provide the needs and wants of commerce between the East and the Middle West.

The Progressive Era, 1890–1914

The Progressive Movement started in about 1890 as a protest against the excesses of the preceding century and the corruption in government at the time.

One result of this movement was more effective regulation on business and trade. Journalists (some of whom became known as muckrakers) exposed the sins of corporate giants like Standard Oil Corporation to the socially conscious public.

The turn of the century saw the establishment of large corporations and trusts, which attempted to control both supply and demand of their product category and to exercise authority over newly organized labor unions. These new corporations controlled vast amounts of money and resources, which they used for expansion, competition with foreign business, political influence, control of large blocks of stock, and the pooling of patents. The creation of the Federal Trade Commission under President Woodrow Wilson brought control and regulation to interstate trade.

Cities were growing explosively because of their role as centers for great industrial corporations. Cities had the money and the employment, and to them came the vast armies of workers, the expanding railway systems, and the crowded and often unhealthy factories. Department stores flourished and became centers of shopping, enabled by improvements in transportation, such as tramways and motorcars. For the first time in United States history, there were more people employed by industry than working on farms.

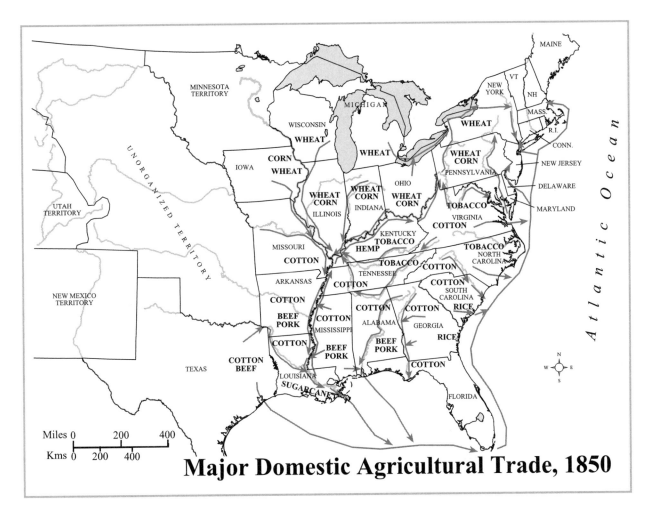

Major Domestic Agricultural Trade, 1850

In spite of the move to the cities, agricultural trade also grew. The shift on the farm from manual labor to machines allowed for the expansion in commercial farming. The expanding population in the cities provided a large market for the farmers' products, but there was still enough left to sell to foreign countries. The number of farms in the United States tripled between 1860 and 1910, from 2 million to 6 million.

At the turn of the century, America was a land of abundance. Supplies of many natural resources surpassed those of the rest of the world. By this time, there was a well-established trade both domestically and internationally in iron, steel, coal, cotton, corn, and wheat.

World War I and The Jazz Age, 1914–1928

In 1917 the United States entered World War I, and from that experience first became a major world power. During the brief period that the country was involved in the war, the shortage of men at home meant that there were plenty of jobs available and full employment. Lucrative government contracts meant a full workload.

Immediately following the war, there was a glut of returning veterans seeking work. The end of wartime contracts meant fewer jobs, business owners attempted to drive down wages and to break unions in an effort to maintain profits, and the unions began to revolt. Scarcity of available money stalled the shift to a consumer goods economy.

In 1919 the Eighteenth Amendment was ratified, prohibiting the manufacture of alcoholic beverages for sale. It spawned an illegal cottage industry that resulted in an active trade in wines and liquors. In addition, the period gave rise to a new industry: the underworld. Trading in alcohol and the demand for union busters gave illegal activity new strongholds.

During the 1920s, America enjoyed an era of prosperity, and big business regained control. New wealth brought more leisure time and the growth of the entertainment business: organized sports, silent films, radio, mass-oriented magazines, and recorded music. Corporations issued stock publicly on a wide scale, and millions of Americans were able to buy stock in these giant companies.

The Great Depression, 1929–1939

All of this affluence came to a crashing end when the stock market collapsed in October 1929. Just prior to the crash in 1929, the Gross National Product was $87 billion; four

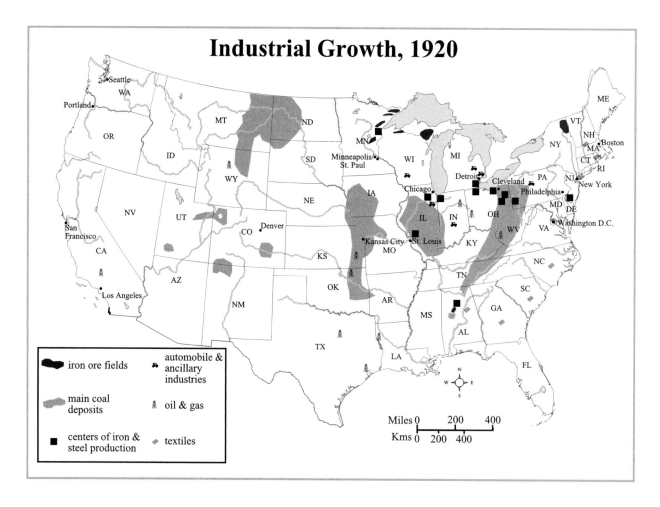

Industrial Growth, 1920

years later, it had shrunk to $41 billion. Every day, factories closed and banks and businesses failed. In 1930 the jobless numbered 7 million; by 1932 the number had risen to 15 million out of a total workforce of 45 million.

Farmers were also hurt, as thousands lost their land and homes through foreclosure. In the South, the collapse of the export market for cotton and tobacco and problems with overproduction led to looting and riots in 1931. American businessmen found that the overseas markets for their goods were drying up because the depression was becoming global.

In 1933 President Franklin Delano Roosevelt led Congress to enact a wide variety of emergency economic and social legislation called the New Deal, which brought some relief to the ailing country. The Securities and Exchange Commission was created in 1934. Its purpose was to police corporations that were issuing new securities. The National Recovery Administration was created in 1933 to establish codes for fair competition and to guarantee workers the right to form unions. Minimum wages and maximum work hours were established, and the Social Security system was created to provide relief to the elderly and infirm.

During this decade, Hollywood became the movie capital of the world. With the sensational boom in "talk-ing" movies, an industry was born that would supply entertainment to the country and abroad.

Isolationism was the U.S. foreign policy in Roosevelt's first term in office, a policy in opposition to America's efforts to regulate international currency and trade.

World War II, 1941–1945

All of this changed on 7 December 1941 when Japan bombed American ships in Pearl Harbor and America entered World War II. Some say that this marked the end of the depression. World War II saw the beginning of what came to be called the military industrial complex. This alliance between government and big business led to unprecedented production records; manufacturing production in 1943 doubled over the year before, as thousands of previously civilian businesses shifted into manufacturing items for war. With so many men in the armed forces, there were new job opportunities for women.

Farmers were also affected, as the increasing mechanization of equipment led to a 35 percent rise in output in those years—enough food for civilians, American armed forces, and allies like England and the Soviet Union. At home, Americans moved to cities to find work and to consolidate families whose men had gone to war. Manufacturing plants in the north brought African Americans from the south to work. Job opportunities existed for this group of workers but the results were crowded working conditions, inadequate housing and transportation, and urban blight. Volatile racial tensions occurred with the result in Detroit, Michigan, being one of the bloodiest riots in history.

The Modern Era, 1945 to the Present

At the close of World War II, the United States was the most powerful nation in the world, both politically and economically. The GI bill provided $15 billion for veterans' college educations and low-cost mortgages for new homes in the suburbs. Factories and businesses sprang up in record numbers, and women in the workforce added to the new affluence of families. America entered the consumer culture in the 1950s, and this trend continued throughout the rest of the century.

The 1960s were a period of revolt and change in America. The 1970s continued this radical movement, as the baby boom generation (born just after World War II) came of age and provided new areas of consumer demand for punk rock music, drugs, hippie fashion, and vegetarian cuisine.

The late 1970s saw massive inflation, and the Arab oil embargo had a profound effect on the cost of living as oil prices soared for business, home, and auto. The American automobile business lost its domestic position dominance, as more fuel-efficient cars from Japan became popular. This business suffered badly until the end of the 1980s, when cooperative deals between American and Japanese automobile manufacturers resulted in Japanese auto plants being built in the United States.

Shortly after the end of World War II, the General Agreement on Tariffs and Trade (GATT) was established, reducing world tariffs and allowing for increased imports. Revisions to GATT in December 1993 provided for the elimination of all quotas on clothing and textiles on 1 January 2005. Also in 1993, the North American Free Trade Agreement (NAFTA) was signed. This agreement set new guidelines for cooperative trade between the United States, Mexico, and Canada.

Since the 1970s a sharp rise in low-cost imports has led to the decline of industry in America, and the United States has lost its place as a world leader in manufacturing.

Between 1980 and 1991, the number of workers in the manufacturing sector fell by 2 million. At the same time, United States workers were increasingly finding employment in the service sector in areas like health care, computer programming, insurance, food service, banking and finance, and entertainment. Multinational companies became the vogue, and mergers and acquisitions and joint ventures defined the business landscape.

Domestic trade in the last decades of the twentieth century was strong in the areas of automobiles, housing, computers, and environmental and health-related products. The computer business was the fastest-growing in-

dustry in the United States between 1973 and the late 1990s, and the cellular telephone business boomed.

As manufacturing in the United States declined and large corporations suffered, there was a sharp increase in small businesses (those with 500 or fewer employees). At the turn of the twenty-first century, 95 percent of all businesses in the United States were classified as small businesses.

BIBLIOGRAPHY

Badger, Anthony J. *The New Deal: The Depression Years 1933–40.* New York: Hill and Wang, 1989.

Batra, Ravi. *The Myth of Free Trade: A Plan for America's Economic Revival.* New York: Scribners, 1993.

Boyer, Paul S., ed. *The Oxford Companion to United States History.* New York: Scribners, 1993.

"Doubtless as Good": Growing Pains. Available at www .americanhistory.si.edu/doubtless

Nash, Gerald D. *The Great Depression and World War II: Organizing America, 1933–1945.* New York: St. Martin's Press, 1979.

An Outline of American History. Available at www.usinfo .state.gov/usa/infousa/facts/history

Samhaber, Ernst. *Merchants Make History: How Trade Has Influenced the Course of History Throughout the World.* Transl. E. Osers. New York: John Day, 1964.

Sitkoff, Harvard. *Postwar America: A Student Companion.* New York: Oxford University Press, 2000.

Streissguth, Tom. *An Eyewitness History: The Roaring Twenties.* New York: Facts on File, 2001.

Uschan, Michael V. *A Cultural History of the United States Through the Decades: The 1940s.* San Diego, Calif.: Lucent Books, 1999.

Donna W. Reamy
Rosalie Jackson Regni

TRADE, FOREIGN. The United States throughout its history has been relatively self-sufficient; yet foreign trade has, since the colonial period, been a dominant factor in the growth of the nation. The colonies were founded basically for the purpose of commerce: the shipment of products, particularly raw materials, to the mother country and the sale of finished goods from the shops of England in the colonies. Even had colonial plans not been centered around the welfare of Englishmen at home, the results could scarcely have been different. The Atlantic coast is particularly suited to commerce on the high seas. Deep harbors in the North and bays, indentations, and rivers and smaller streams from New York southward provided excellent ports for loading and unloading the ships of the day. Moreover, the settlements, clustered around the places where the ships came in or scattered along the rivers and creeks, were almost completely isolated from each other. As late as 1794 it took a week (under the most favorable conditions) to make the trip by coach from Boston to New York. Although the seas were infested with privateers and pirates (and the distinction was sometimes a thin one) and the ships were small and the journey long, the hazards of overland trading were still greater and the returns more uncertain.

Foreign trade was primarily in outgoing raw materials and incoming manufactured goods during the colonial period. Simple economic necessity had turned the colonists to agriculture. When surplus food production became possible, economic specialization appeared. Dictated by climatic and soil conditions, as well as by a host of other factors, production in each section determined the course of its commerce. The trade of the colonies south of Pennsylvania was chiefly with England. Ships from British ports called at the wharves of plantations along the rivers of Maryland and Virginia for tobacco and the next year returned with goods ordered from the shops of London and other cities. Furs, skins, naval stores, and small quantities of tobacco made up the early cargoes that went out from the Carolinas, but after 1700 rice quickly gained the lead as the most important export. Before the middle of the century indigo had become a profitable crop not only because it offered employment for the slaves when they were not busy in the rice fields but also because the demand for the dye in England had induced Parliament to vote a bounty. On the eve of the Revolution indigo made up by value about 35 percent of the exports of South Carolina.

The commerce of New England and the middle colonies ran counter to economic plans of empire. Grain, flour, meat, and fish were the major products of Pennsylvania and New Jersey and the colonies to the north. Yet shipment of these materials to England endangered long-established interests of Englishmen at home. Although small amounts of naval stores, iron, ship timbers, furs, whale oil and whalebone, oak and pine plank, and staves, barrels, and hoops went off to London, other markets had to be sought in order to obtain means of paying for the large amounts of goods bought in England. The search for sales brought what is often referred to as the triangular trade. Southern Europe, Africa, and the West Indies bought 75 percent of the exports of New England and more than 50 percent of those of New York and Pennsylvania.

On the eve of the Revolution the middle colonies were shipping annually to southern Europe more than 500,000 bushels of wheat and more than 18,000 tons of bread. Fish, meat, grain, ship timbers, lumber, and materials for barrels, kegs, and casks also went out in large quantities from Pennsylvania, New York, and New England. Rum was exchanged in Africa for slaves, and the slaves in turn sold in the West Indies for specie or for more molasses for New England rum distilleries. These islands, in fact, provided an inexhaustible market for fish, meat, foodstuffs, and live animals, as well as pearl ash, potash, cut-out houses, lumber, and finished parts for making containers for sugar, rum, and molasses. Corn,

wheat, flour, bread, and vegetables found their greatest outlet in the islands.

Unfortunately the sellers of raw materials—the colonists—were almost always in debt to the manufacturers of finished goods—the British. Carrying charges by English shipowners ate up the favorable balance of the southerners, and the debts of the planters became virtually hereditary. Northern commercial men, selling more than they bought everywhere except in England, gained enough specie to settle their accounts in London with reasonable promptness. The persistent drainage of money to the mother country, however, was a significant factor in the discontent that developed in America.

Although the Revolution did not destroy American trade, even with the British, the former colonies obviously lost their preferred position in the world of commerce and also the protection of the powerful empire fleet. British trade regulations of 1783 (emphasized by further regulations in 1786–1787) closed the ports of the West Indies to the ships of the new nation and protected others by heavy tonnage duties. Only Sweden and Prussia agreed to reciprocity treaties. Yet this critical postwar period was far less discouraging than it is sometimes pictured to be. Varying tariffs in the ports and hostile action and counteraction among the states did keep commerce in perpetual uncertainty and prevented retaliation against European discriminations, but trade went on either in traditional channels or in new markets. Shipping interests in the new Congress secured legislation favoring American-owned ships. The tonnage registered for foreign trade increased in the years 1789–1810 from 123,893 to 981,000, and imports and exports in American bottoms jumped roughly from about 20 percent to about 90 percent.

The Napoleonic Wars turned production forces to military goods, drove merchant ships from the seas, and pushed prices upward rapidly. Although many ships were seized, American merchant captains and the nation prospered until President Thomas Jefferson, seeking to maintain peace, induced Congress in 1807 to pass the Embargo Act. Exports dropped from $108.3 million to $22.4 million within a year; imports fell from $138.5 million to $56.9 million. Repeal of the embargo brought some revival, but other restrictions and the war against England drove exports to $6.9 million in 1814 and imports to $12.9 million.

Foreign trade in the years between 1815 and 1860, though fluctuating often, moved generally upward. Agricultural products made up the major part of the exports. Cotton led all the rest—production mounted from about 200,000 bales in 1821 to more than 5 million in 1860, 80 percent of which was sold abroad. Great Britain and France were the two greatest purchasers, but Germany, Austria, Belgium, Holland, and Russia bought appreciable quantities. The West Indies and South America took large amounts of grain and flour, and English demands increased steadily after the repeal of the corn laws in 1846. Tobacco, rice, meat, and meat products, as well as lumber,

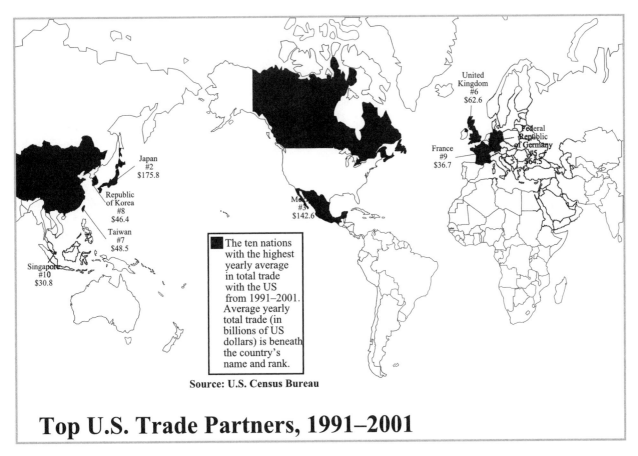

The ten nations with the highest yearly average in total trade with the US from 1991–2001. Average yearly total trade (in billions of US dollars) is beneath the country's name and rank.

Source: U.S. Census Bureau

Top U.S. Trade Partners, 1991–2001

naval stores, barrels and kegs, staves, and hoops moved out in large quantities. Cottons, woolens, silks, iron, cutlery, china, and a miscellany of other items made up the bulk of the incoming cargoes. But the glory of the clipper ship was being obscured by the iron-hulled steamers that came from the British shipyards; the day of the whalers was ending even before oil began to flow out of the first well at Titusville, Pa., in 1859.

As the nation became increasingly industrialized between the Civil War and World War II, domestic production and domestic trade were its basic concerns. Railroads knit marketing centers together and economic specialization reached maturity. Agriculture, spreading into the West, increased each year its outpouring of foodstuffs; and industry, entrenched behind a high protective tariff, grew with astounding rapidity. The American merchant marine declined rapidly as investors turned their dollars into railroads and other industrial ventures at home. The percentage of foreign trade carried in American bottoms decreased from 66.5 percent in 1860 to 7.1 percent in 1900. That did not mean, however, any lessening in total ocean commerce. The value of exports and imports combined rose from $686,192,000 in 1860 to $4,257,000,000 in 1914. Cotton, wheat, flour, and other farm products continued to move out in ever-larger amounts, but it was obvious that agriculture was losing out to manufactured goods. The changing nature of exports and imports clearly revealed the fact that Europe was becoming each year relatively less important in American foreign trade. Shipments to and from Asia, Oceania, Africa, Canada, and Latin America were growing rapidly.

World War I restored temporarily the supremacy of Europe as a consumer of American agricultural products. But new goods also made up large portions of the cargoes—chemicals, explosives, firearms, special woods for airplane propellers, barbed wire, and a host of other needs of fighting forces. The value of exports and imports more than doubled during the war. The huge purchases of the Allies were based on government credits in the United States, and the slow growth for the next decade was financed largely by American loans. The economic structure fell apart in 1929. Prices declined sharply everywhere; world credit and world finance broke down; foreign exchange transactions were curtailed or taken over completely by government in many places; and the principal powers sought to maintain themselves by hiding behind high tariffs, trade licenses, and fixed quotas. The United States had for a decade been shutting itself off from the world. The climax was reached in the Smoot-Hawley Tariff of 1930, which brought retaliatory restrictions from other nations. Foreign trade of the nation dropped to $2.9 billion in 1932. The slow climb upward to $6.6 billion in 1940 was in part the result of the insistence of Secretary of State Cordell Hull that reciprocity agreements rather than trade restrictions were essentials in commercial revival. By authority of the Reciprocal

Trade Agreements Act of 1934 he made a series of executive agreements with foreign nations by which he encouraged American trade, and, by applying the most-favored-nation clause, spread the gains widely over the world.

In the war years 1941–1945 more than $50 billion in goods went out of American ports, and $17 billion came in. But about $32.9 billion of the exports were lend-lease war materials to fighting allies and no payment was expected. That was a startling change in the customary creditor-debtor relationship following World War I, but the experiences of that war dictated the decision. The whole international economic structure was, in fact, undergoing a basic revolution.

By the end of the war production facilities had roughly doubled; the nature of the outpouring products had changed astoundingly; and the people of the nation in general and the agricultural and industrial working force in particular had not only found new homes but also new wants and new hopes.

Tired of rationing and eager for a new world, Americans were at the end of the war impatient with the delays in transforming the industrial plants from war goods to peace goods and intolerant of any threats of wage cuts. But reconstruction in the nation was slow. Shelves were long empty and shortages of many essentials developed. Europe was paralyzed, and multilateral trade had all but ended.

Fearful of communism and convinced that hunger must be eliminated if traditional nations were to be re-established and if new ones were to be created on the principle of freedom of choice, the United States initiated (1947) the MARSHALL PLAN, which, as proposed by U.S. Secretary of State George C. Marshall, provided $12 billion in aid for the economic recovery of Europe. Already American loans, credits, grants, and relief—private and public—had exceeded that amount by several billion dollars. The plan was not envisioned as a relief program but as a cooperative venture that would restore, or create, economic well-being for all. On 3 April 1948, President Harry S. Truman signed the European Recovery Act, which, through the Economic Cooperation Administration, headed by Paul G. Hoffman and a European coordinating body, the Organization for European Economic Cooperation, gave out through sixteen national offices in Europe and a mission in China at least $17 billion over a four-year period.

Machinery for regulating international monetary and trade relations had already been established by the end of the 1940s. The International Monetary Fund (IMF) and the International Bank for Reconstruction and Development (the World Bank) had been created at a meeting in Bretton Woods, N.H., in 1944. The General Agreement on Tariffs and Trade (GATT), with authority to agree on tariff rates in the free world, floundered for a while but became firmly established by late 1947.

If the 1940s were years of destruction and reconstruction, the 1950s were, throughout the free world, years of growth and of adjustments in a transition from a basically nationalistic thinking concerning tariffs and trade to a basically international philosophy of freedom of world commerce from deadening restrictions. The experiences of the Great Depression and World War II turned thoughts earnestly toward free trade. Led by the social philosophers and economists the movement gained remarkable headway, even among political leaders.

Conscious of the disadvantages of small and sometimes jealous countries in building an industrial structure and in bargaining with great nations, such as the United States and the Soviet Union, Europe turned to unity. Assuming an independent stance, although still drawing appreciable amounts of U.S. aid, France, Belgium, West Germany, Luxembourg, Italy, and the Netherlands in 1957 formed the European Economic Community (EEC), most often referred to as the Common Market. Since the primary purpose of the organization was to improve the economy of all the members by throwing a common barrier around the whole and harmonizing restrictions within, various interests in the United States, especially farmers, were deeply concerned.

Within three years after the formation of the Common Market, Great Britain, Sweden, Norway, Denmark, Austria, Switzerland, and Portugal formed the European Free Trade Association (EFTA). (Finland became an associate member in 1961.) With the United States and Canada, the groupings came to be called the Atlantic Community.

But not all was harmony in the new economic community. The mercantilists quarreled with the tariff reformers everywhere, and in the United States there was opposition to shifting control of tariff rates from Congress to an international body. The decade of the 1960s was at times a period of bitter controversy. President John F. Kennedy early in 1962 requested Congress to delegate some of its authority over tariffs to the executive department so that he might make revisions at home and might, in the meetings of GATT, bargain for ends that would further the trade of all of the countries involved. The Trade Expansion Act of 1962 granted much authority to the president, notably the power to reduce tariffs on a linear basis by as much as 50 percent on a most-favored-nation basis.

American delegates and officials of the Common Market, who were determined to assert themselves politically and economically, gathered in Geneva in 1964, in what is called the Kennedy Round of the GATT discussions. The ministers of the various countries had met the year before in a somewhat vain effort to work out ground rules for the proceedings. Agreements concerning rates on even the simplest industrial groups were troublesome to reach, and reductions in agricultural tariffs were arrived at—if at all—only with great difficulty. After nearly four years of controversy, the meeting adjourned with average tariff rates lowered to somewhere between 35 and 40 percent. Many industrialists and laborers in the United States, wholly dissatisfied, returned to protectionism. Members of the Common Market were unhappy in many ways also, but obviously pleased that they possessed the power to challenge the United States.

The foreign trade of the United States had undergone profound changes. The great surpluses that had marked U.S. world commerce from the 1870s began in the 1950s a decline that reached significant proportions in the 1960s. The great steel empire that Andrew Carnegie and Henry Clay Frick had done much to make the wonder of the industrial world was crumbling because of new mills and less costly labor in other countries. Freighters put into ports on the Atlantic, the Pacific, and the Gulf and even traveled down the Saint Lawrence Seaway to Cleveland, Detroit, and Chicago to unload finished industrial goods in the heart of America. As Europe and other countries of the free world made a remarkable recovery from the war years, products from their new plants poured into the stream of international commerce. Between 1960 and 1967 finished goods in U.S. imports increased 150 percent. Steel, automobiles, textiles, and electronic goods led the new imports. Incoming steel, until 1957, was insignificant in amount and had grown only to some 3 million tons in 1960. But by 1967 shipments had reached 11.5 million tons, and the next year reached 18 million. In 1971 steel imports amounted to 18.3 million tons—nearly 18 percent of all steel sold in the nation that year, when total employment in American mills also fell to its lowest point since 1939.

Competing steelmaking plants, although new, were not appreciably more efficient than those of the United States. Basically the steel problem was too much steel. Production facilities over the world were far in excess of need; yet Japan, for instance, although having to both bring in raw materials and send its finished product to faraway markets, ever increased its output. Even production in Mexico, South Korea, Spain, and the Philippines, for example, grew steadily as capacity outside the United States doubled in the 1960s.

American steelmakers were both unwilling and unable to bargain in the marketplace. They blamed cheap labor (the European advantage, they asserted, was about $20 a ton; the Japanese roughly twice that amount) and liberal governmental assistance in the form of border taxes, license requirements, special levies, quotas, export rebates, hidden subsidies, value added tax, and other monetary and legislative provisions for hindering exports from the United States and encouraging exports to the United States. They turned to Congress for help. Both European and Japanese producers agreed to limit further shipments of steel for the next three years to an annual growth of 2.5 percent.

The automobile industry was turned topsy-turvy also. Large British and French cars—once popular as prestige vehicles—steadily declined among American imports as small European cars, encountering little American competition, began to appear in ever-larger numbers in the United States. Only in the export of trucks, buses, and automotive parts and equipment did the United States keep the unfavorable trade to a reasonable limit in the automotive field.

Textile and footwear manufacturers, too, protested the loss of markets because of competing goods from other countries, especially Japan. Some agreements were reached concerning shipments of cotton cloth into the United States, but the whole field of synthetic fibers remained open. Between 1965 and 1969 American imports of man-made fiber textile increased from 79 million pounds to 257 million pounds. During the same period imports of wearing apparel of man-made fibers grew from 31 million pounds to 144 million pounds. The number of imported sweaters rose from 501,000 dozen in 1965 to about 6.9 million dozen in 1969. Imports of footwear were increasing also: 96 million pairs in 1965; 202 million pairs in 1969. In the first four months of 1970, one-third of the demand for footwear was being met by foreign shops.

Electronic goods in foreign trade added appreciably to the deficit in the United States. Between 1963 and 1970 such imports, by value, mostly from Japan, increased at the annual rate of 32 percent. By 1970 they accounted for 37 percent of the television sets, 63 percent of the phonographs, 92 percent of the radios, and 96 percent of the tape recorders sold in the United States—though some of the parts were made in American plants or in American-owned foreign plants. Even the developing countries exported local products, including tropical fruits and novelties, and such substantial products as special steels.

The basic problem in American foreign trade in the early 1970s was that imports had increased more rapidly than exports. Building on the foundation of American aid after World War II, and to an appreciable extent on borrowed American technology, Europe and parts of Asia performed an industrial miracle and captured markets over the world, especially in the United States, with their well-made goods. Moreover, the United States, suffering from persistent inflation and its consequent high prices, could not effectively compete in world markets. Imports were cheap in comparison with domestic prices, and foreign goods flowed freely into the ports.

Many industrialists and wage earners in the United States resented the economic penalties they thought the changing foreign trade situation had brought. During the 1960s ever-increasing numbers of U.S. corporations and individuals set up factories throughout the world. Some said they were fleeing behind the protective walls that prevented Americans from selling in many world markets; others said they were escaping the high wages at home that choked them out of world competition; a few said they were getting away from the irresponsible American workmen. Discontent in the nation continued to grow, and American industrialists and laborers and a great number of other citizens, convinced that the whole international experiment had been a failure, turned to protection. Arguments by theoretical scholars and realistic statisticians that free trade had created more jobs than it had destroyed and that a return to the old order would bring economic tragedy were unconvincing to factory owners with limited markets or to men without jobs.

American foreign trade was involved not only in the complex industrial world but also in the even more complex monetary world. The annual unfavorable balance of payments, sometimes of several billion dollars, made it difficult for the nation to pay its bills. The merchandise exchange was with few exceptions favorable to the United States; it was the balance of payments that embarrassed the nation. Military commitments in Europe and elsewhere, the Vietnam War, heavy expenditures of American tourists abroad, shipping charges, and a host of other payments left the nation each year through the 1960s and at the beginning of the 1970s heavily indebted. This debt steadily increased the claims on the gold reserves of the United States and brought an ever-growing doubt concerning the dollar.

The essential monetary difficulty was not so much the problem of gold as it was the problem of adjusting the existing monetary system to the needs of the new international situation and the overvalued dollar—the only currency in the free world with a fixed value based on a specific amount of gold. (The designers of the IMF at Bretton Woods had set up that standard with all other currencies having a parity relation to it. There was a modest permissible variation in the rate of exchange.) If, however, the unit value of any currency became too cheap or too expensive in terms of other currencies, it could be devalued or revalued upward to be realistically realigned with the dollar. In the 1960s most of the currencies of the major countries had become greatly undervalued in terms of the dollar, notably the West German mark and the Japanese yen. Thus imports were temptingly cheap in American ports, and exports discouragingly costly in foreign markets.

Through the 1960s U.S. imports grew twice as fast as exports, and the small trade surplus fell each year far short of meeting the persistent foreign debt. Dollar claims piled up in Europe. In 1968 additional reserves (often referred to as paper gold) were provided by the creation of Special Drawing Rights issued by the IMF. But the imbalance continued. There was no lack of suggested remedies: devalue the dollar; increase the price of gold; widen the parity margin; float all currencies; desert gold altogether. Each proposal stirred some doubts, and each one presented a plethora of known and unknown difficulties. As the 1970s began, there was no question that the dollar was under tremendous pressure.

The impending crunch came in August 1971, when higher interest rates in the United States, rumors of revaluations, and a growing American deficit, swelled by strikes and threatened strikes, poured a flood of unwanted dollars into Europe. Speculators, corporations, commercial banks, and other holders, protecting themselves from changes in currency values, began to scurry out from under their surplus dollars. They returned to the United States $4 billion in the second week of August. The nation at the time held only $13 billion in its gold reserve against some $60 billion in short-term obligations. On 15 August President Richard M. Nixon closed the door on gold redemptions and levied a 10 percent surtax on dutiable imports. The drastic action, it was hoped, would force Japan and the major European countries to revalue their currencies upward, remove some of their manifold barriers to United States trade, and share the costs of American military forces stationed abroad. Despite many fears that the action might disrupt the monetary world, the situation cleared appreciably, although the bitternesses that had long existed did not disappear.

By February 1972 the monetary situation had begun to deteriorate rapidly. Fearful that Congress, dissatisfied with promised trade concessions from the Common Market, Canada, and Japan, would severely amend the devaluation proposal, Europe began to enact currency controls. American foreign trade throughout the year remained the largest in the world, but exports made no appreciable gains on imports. The surtax, soon removed, had not lessened appreciably the amount of goods coming into American ports. Tariff walls had come down, but other barriers had gone up.

The dollar, devalued again in February 1973 and further deteriorated through the succeeding currency float, continued to decline relative to the currencies of the Common Market and Japan. A gasoline shortage developed with the oil embargo of October 1973, and by the early months of 1974 the economic situation was recognized by even the most optimistic as a full-blown depression, with further unemployment but no end to inflation. Quarrels in the free world intensified as the United States established détente with the Soviet Union and offered a friendly hand to China. Sales of grain to the Soviets, reductions in military and other world expenditures, augmented returns from foreign investments, and other favorable factors pushed the balance of trade substantially in favor of the United States by the beginning of 1976.

Between the 1970s and the mid-1990s the U.S. post–World War II dominance of world trade came to an end. Major changes in transportation, finance, corporate structures, and manufacturing restructured the global economy, erasing the significance of international economic boundaries. Whole industries in the United States were largely eliminated, unable to compete effectively against cheaper and often better imports. In labor-intensive industries, such as textiles, shoes, and assembly work, the competition came from low-wage developing countries; in the automobile, steel, and electronics industries it came from technological innovators abroad who developed new products and efficient manufacturing.

Texas Press, 1985. The original edition was published San Antonio, Texas: Jackson Printing, 1920–1923.

J. Frank Dobie / c. w.

"TRAIL OF BROKEN TREATIES."

A central protest event of the Red Power activist period of the 1970s, the "Trail of Broken Treaties" was organized by members of the AMERICAN INDIAN MOVEMENT (AIM) to bring national attention to Native grievances. The "trail" began on the West Coast in the late summer of 1972 as an automobile caravan composed of Indians from across the country who intended to demonstrate their concerns in Washington, D.C. As it proceeded east, the caravan stopped by reservations and urban Indian communities to drum up support, recruit participants, conduct workshops, and draft an agenda for Indian policy reform. The caravan arrived in Washington, D.C., in the early days of November, just before the 1972 presidential election, a time considered ideal for anyone seeking media coverage.

As it traveled across the country, the caravan grew, numbering several hundred when it arrived in the capital. Initially the group was orderly, but when housing for the protesters disintegrated, the original goals of the organizers shifted from meetings and demonstrations to a weeklong occupation of the Bureau of Indian Affairs building. The occupation was reported on the front pages of the *New York Times* and many other newspapers. The publicity drew attention to Indian rights and provided a platform for the protesters to present their "20-Point Program" to increase the role of tribes in the formation of Indian programs. The "self-determination" federal legislation of the mid-1970s that shifted more local control to recognized tribes should be understood against the backdrop of the Red Power protest era, especially the Trail of Broken Treaties and the protests it inspired.

Another important outcome of the Trail of Broken Treaties and the other protests of the era was a surge of Native pride and consciousness. For example, the Lakota author Mary Crow Dog describes the response to militant Indians such as those in the American Indian Movement:

> The American Indian Movement hit our reservation like a tornado, like a new wind blowing out of nowhere, a drumbeat from far off getting louder and louder. . . . I could feel this new thing, almost hear it, smell it, touch it. Meeting up with AIM for the first time loosened a sort of earthquake inside me. (pp. 74–75)

BIBLIOGRAPHY

Crow Dog, Mary, and Richard Erdoes. *Lakota Woman.* New York: Grove Weidenfeld, 1990.

Josephy, Alvin M., Jr., Joane Nagel, and Troy Johnson, eds. *Red Power.* 2d ed. Lincoln: University of Nebraska Press, 1999.

Joane Nagel

See also **Wounded Knee (1973).**

TRAIL OF TEARS,

most closely associated with the Cherokees, is perhaps the most well known injustice done to Native Americans during the removal period of the 1830s. Historically, the Cherokees occupied lands in several southeastern states including North Carolina and Georgia. Acting under the Removal Act of 1830, federal authorities sought to win the tribe's agreement to exchange tribal lands for a reservation in the West. In 1835, approximately 500 Cherokees, none of them elected officials of the Cherokee nation, gathered in New Echota, Georgia, and signed a treaty ceding all Cherokee territory east of the Mississippi to the United States in exchange for $5 million and new homelands in Indian Territory (modern Oklahoma). Though a majority of the tribe protested this illegal treaty, it was ratified—by a single vote—by the U.S. Senate on 23 May 1836.

In May 1838, federal troops and state militia units supervised by General Winfield Scott rounded up the Cherokees who refused to accept the New Echota agreement and held them in concentration camps until they were sent west in groups of approximately 1,000 each. Three groups left that summer, traveling 800 miles from Chattanooga by rail, boat, and wagon, primarily on the water route. In November, with river levels too low for navigation and with inadequate clothing and supplies, twelve more groups traveled overland, under close military supervision and primarily on foot, in spite of roads rendered impassable by autumn rains and the subsequent onset of winter. By March 1839, all survivors had arrived in their new home. Of the 15,000 Cherokees who began the journey, about 4,000—a fifth of the total Cherokee population—perished along the route.

Though local and state governments along with private organizations and individuals made some efforts to recognize this tragic event in American history, it was not until 1987 that Congress designated the Trail of Tears as a National Historic Trail under the supervision of the National Park Service.

BIBLIOGRAPHY

Anderson, William L., ed. *Cherokee Removal: Before and After.* Athens: University of Georgia Press, 1991.

Hoig, Stan. *Night of the Cruel Moon: Cherokee Removal and the Trail of Tears.* New York: Facts on File, 1996.

National Park Service. *Certification Guide: Trail of Tears National Historic Trail.* Santa Fe, N. Mex.: National Park Service, 1994.

Perdue, Theda, and Michael D. Green, eds. *The Cherokee Removal: A Brief History with Documents.* Boston: Bedford Books, 1995.

Michael Sherfy

See also **Cherokee; Cherokee Nation Cases; Indian Land Cessions; Indian Removal; Indian Territory; Removal Act of 1830.**

Trailer Park Community. A mobile home park in Gillette, Wyo. © CORBIS

TRAILER PARKS began to appear in the 1920s as roads improved and Americans enjoyed a fascination with motoring and highway travel as leisure pursuits. Trailers were originally designed for recreational uses such as family camping or adventure. Industry pioneers began designing vehicles for their own families, and soon found themselves manufacturing and selling house trailers. Informal sites where motorists towing house trailers could park and live in a community of other travelers were formed independently, and as the number of trailer campers increased, the need for specially designated campgrounds arose. These were originally established as free municipal facilities but they soon became fee facilities in order to discourage the poor and limit users to a tourist population.

Tourists were not the only people using house trailers, however, and by 1936 an estimated one million people were living in them for part or all of the year.

Eventually the industry split; house trailers produced for travel became recreational vehicles (RVs) while mobile homes were produced specifically as dwellings.

During World War II a boom occurred in trailer living among military and construction workers who followed jobs and assignments. The postwar housing crisis perpetuated the popularity of trailers as dwellings. In the 1950s, trailer parks evolved into communities intended for permanent dwelling rather than as tourist parks, while RV campgrounds replaced the original trailer parks.

Trailer parks are frequently associated with tornadoes. That is because mobile homes are destroyed more easily and, therefore, in greater numbers than more structurally substantial houses.

BIBLIOGRAPHY

Santiago, Chiori. "House Trailers Have Come a Long Way, Baby." *Smithsonian* 29, no. 3 (June 1998): 76–85.

Thornburg, David A. *Galloping Bungalows: The Rise and Demise of the American House Trailer.* Hamden, Conn.: Archon Books, 1991.

Wallis, Allan D. *Wheel Estate: The Rise and Decline of Mobile Homes.* New York: Oxford University Press, 1991.

Deirdre Sheets

See also **Housing; Transportation and Travel.**

TRAIN ROBBERIES were more frequent in the United States than anywhere else in the world in the latter half of the nineteenth century. Vast stretches of sparsely inhabited country permitted robbers to escape undetected; carelessness and lack of adequate security on trains also made robberies easier. The robbery of $700,000 from an Adams Express car on the New York, New Haven, and Hartford Railroad, the first train robbery on record, occurred in 1866. That same year, the four Reno brothers stole $13,000 in their first train holdup. They went on to stage a number of bold bank and train robberies in southern Indiana and Illinois before the Pinkerton Detective Agency, just coming into prominence, tracked them down

Jesse James. One of Quantrill's Raiders, a Confederate guerrilla band in the Civil War (this photograph is from 1864, when he was seventeen), he was subsequently the legendary leader of a gang of robbers (first of banks, then of trains) in the Midwest, until "that dirty little coward" Robert Ford—as a sympathetic "ballad" of the day put it—killed him for a bounty in 1882.

in 1868. Vigilantes executed three of the four brothers before their cases came to trial. The Farringtons operated in 1870 in Kentucky and Tennessee. Jack Davis of Nevada, after an apprenticeship robbing stagecoaches in California, started operations at Truckee, California, by robbing an express car of $41,000.

Train robberies peaked in 1870. The colorful and daring Jesse James gang began to operate in 1873 near Council Bluffs, Iowa. No other robbers are so well known; legends and songs were written about their deeds. For nine years they terrorized the MIDWEST, and trainmen did not breathe freely until an accomplice shot Jesse, after which his brother Frank retired to run a WILD WEST SHOW. Sam Bass in Texas, the Dalton boys in Oklahoma, and Sontag and Evans in California were other robbers with well-known records. After 1900 the number of holdups declined conspicuously.

BIBLIOGRAPHY

DeNevi, Don. *Western Train Robberies*. Millbrae, Calif.: Celestial Arts, 1976.

Pinkerton, William Allan. *Train Robberies, Train Robbers, and the "Holdup" Men*. New York: Arno Press, 1974. The original edition was published in 1907.

Carl L. Cannon / c. w.

TRANS-APPALACHIAN WEST. The Trans-Appalachian West is the region west of the Appalachian Mountains and east of the Mississippi River. It stretches from the U.S. border with Canada down to Mexico. Originally blanketed with coniferous and deciduous forests, it was home to numerous Native American groups. The United States gained control of the region after the Treaty of Paris (1783), which ended the American Revolution. Treaties with the local Indian populations resulted in a flood of settlement over the next seventy years. The region's economy has been based on both agriculture and manufacturing. Nine states were formed out of the region and it is home to over 65 million people.

Polly Fry

See also **Paris, Treaty of (1783).**

TRANSCENDENTALISM was a movement for religious renewal, literary innovation, and social transformation. Its ideas were grounded in the claim that divine truth could be known intuitively. Based in New England and existing in various forms from the 1830s to the 1880s, transcendentalism is usually considered the principal expression of romanticism in America. Many prominent ministers, reformers, and writers of the era were associated with it, including Ralph Waldo Emerson (1803–1882), Henry David Thoreau (1817–1862), Margaret Fuller (1810–1850), Theodore Parker (1810–1860), Bron-

son Alcott (1799–1888), and Orestes Brownson (1803–1876).

Various organizations and periodicals gave the movement shape. The earliest was the so-called "Transcendental Club" (1836–1840), an informal group that met to discuss intellectual and religious topics; also important was the "Saturday Club," organized much later (1854). Many transcendentalists participated in the utopian communities of Brook Farm (1841–1848; located in West Roxbury, Massachusetts), founded by George Ripley (1802–1880) and his wife, Sophia Dana Ripley (1803–1861), and the short-lived Fruitlands (1843–1844; located in Harvard, Massachusetts), founded by Alcott. A number of transcendentalist ministers established experimental churches to give their religious ideas institutional form. The most important of these churches were three in Boston: Orestes Brownson's Society for Christian Union and Progress (1836–1841); the Church of the Disciples (founded 1841), pastored by James Freeman Clarke (1810–1888); and Theodore Parker's Twenty-Eighth Congregational Society (founded 1845–1846). The most famous transcendentalist magazine was the *Dial* (1840–1844), edited by Fuller and then by Emerson; other major periodicals associated with the movement included the *Boston Quarterly Review* (1838–1842), edited by Brownson, and the *Massachusetts Quarterly Review* (1847–1850), edited by Parker.

Transcendentalism emerged from Unitarianism, or "liberal Christianity"—an anti-Calvinist, anti-Trinitarian, anticreedal offshoot of Puritanism that had taken hold among the middle and upper classes of eastern Massachusetts. The founders of transcendentalism were Unitarian intellectuals who came of age, or became Unitarians, in the 1820s and 1830s. From Unitarianism the transcendentalists took a concern for self-culture, a sense of moral seriousness, a neo-Platonic concept of piety, a tendency toward individualism, a belief in the importance of literature, and an interest in moral reform. They looked to certain Unitarians as mentors, especially the great Boston preacher William Ellery Channing. Yet transcendentalists came to reject key aspects of the Unitarian worldview, starting with their rational, historical Christian apologetic.

The Unitarian apologetic took as its starting point the thesis of the British philosopher John Locke that all knowledge, including religious knowledge, was based on sense data. The Unitarians were not strict Lockeans; under the influence of the Scottish "Common Sense" philosophers, notably Thomas Reid and Dugald Stewart, they held that some fundamental knowledge could be known intuitively—for example, that certain things were morally right and wrong, and that the world that human senses perceive in fact exists. Nonetheless, Unitarians held that only "objective" evidence could prove Jesus had delivered an authoritative revelation from God. They believed they had found such evidence in the testimony, provided in the Gospels, of Jesus' miracles. The Unitarians valued the historical study of Gospel accounts, in order to prove them "genuine" and therefore credible.

Transcendentalists rejected as "sensual" and "materialistic" Unitarianism's Lockean assumptions about the mind, and were inspired instead by German philosophical idealism. Its seminal figure, Immanuel Kant, argued that sense data were structured by the mind according to certain "transcendental" categories (such as space, time, and cause and effect), which did not inhere in the data, but in the mind itself. The transcendentalists liked the Kantian approach, which gave the mind, not matter, ultimate control over the shape of human experience. The name of their movement was derived from Kant's philosophical term. Yet the transcendentalists, unlike Kant but like other Romantics (and, to an extent, the Common Sense philosophers), held that religious knowledge itself could be intuitively known. According to this view, people could tell "subjectively" that Jesus had given a revelation from God, because his doctrine was self-evidently true and his life self-evidently good.

The transcendentalist apologetic turned out to have radical implications. Because transcendentalists believed religious truth could be known naturally, like any other truth, they tended to reject the idea of miraculous inspiration as unnecessary and to dismiss as false the claim made for the Bible that it had unique miraculous authority. Transcendentalists still respected Jesus, but the more radical of them, like Emerson in his Divinity School Address (1838), and Parker in *Discourse on the Transient and Permanent in Christianity* (1841), attacked the miracle stories in the Gospels as pious myths. Such attacks were highly controversial; theologically conservative Unitarians accused the transcendentalists of being infidels and atheists. Meanwhile, the transcendentalists began to see religious value in sacred writings beyond the Bible, including those of Buddhists, Hindus, and Muslims. The transcendentalists became pioneers in the American study of comparative religion.

Another implication of intuitionism had to do with the role of the artist. The transcendentalists believed all human inspiration, whether biblical or not, drew from the same divine source. They did not hold religious inspiration to be mundane, like artistic and intellectual inspiration; rather, they held that artistic and intellectual inspiration, like religious inspiration, were divine. The artist, in particular the poet, gained new importance to the transcendentalists as a potential prophet figure, and poetry as a potential source of divine revelation. Emerson was being characteristically transcendentalist when in his first book, *Nature* (1836), he sought to achieve wholly honest, beautiful, and original forms of expression. In his address "American Scholar" (1837), meanwhile, he called on American writers to stop imitating foreign models; actually, the transcendentalists promoted American interest in foreign Romantic writers, especially Samuel Taylor Coleridge (1772–1834), Thomas Carlyle (1795–1881), and Johann Wolfgang von Goethe (1749–1832).

Intuitionism also affected the transcendentalist approach to social and political problems. Transcendental-

Ralph Waldo Emerson. The profoundly influential nineteenth-century essayist, poet, lecturer, abolitionist, and leading light of transcendentalism. © BETTMANN/CORBIS

ists believed laws should be disobeyed if moral intuition held them to be unjust. Thoreau famously argued this point in his essay "Civil Disobedience" (1848; also called "Resistance to Civil Government"). He here advised individuals to disobey unjust laws so as to prevent their personal involvement in evil.

More broadly, the transcendentalists held that inspiration was blunted by social conformity, which therefore must be resisted. This is a theme of Emerson's essay "Self-Reliance" (1841) and Thoreau's book *Walden* (1854). When approaching the education of children, the transcendentalists advocated innovative methods that supposedly developed a child's innate knowledge; Alcott tried out transcendentalist methods at his famous experimental Boston school in the mid-1830s. Elizabeth Palmer Peabody (1804–1894), who later played a major role in bringing the European kindergarten to America, described Alcott's approach in her *Record of a School* (1835), as did Alcott himself in his *Conversations with Children on the Gospels* (1836).

Transcendentalists also came to criticize existing social arrangements, which they thought prevented individual spiritual development. There were calls and attempts to change what were seen as oppressive economic structures. Orestes Brownson, in his *Boston Quarterly Review* articles on the "Laboring Classes" (1840), advocated abolition of inherited private property. George and Sophia Ripley, with others, tried to make Brook Farm a place with no gap between thinkers and workers. Eventually, the Farmers adopted a system inspired by the French socialist Charles Fourier, who believed that in a properly organized society (one he planned in minute detail), people could accomplish all necessary social work by doing only what they were naturally inclined to do. Margaret Fuller, meanwhile, criticized the lack of educational, political, and economic opportunities for women of the era. In the famous series of "conversations" she led for women (1839–1844), Fuller set out to encourage their intellectual development, and in her *Woman in the Nineteenth Century* (1846), issued a famous manifesto in favor of women's rights. She came to embody many of the principles she advocated, and became a significant literary critic and journalist, as well as a participant in the Roman Revolution of 1848.

The transcendentalists saw slavery as inherently wrong because it crushed the spiritual development of slaves. They protested against slavery in various ways and a few of them, most notably Parker, became leaders of the abolitionist movement. Finally, the transcendentalists laid great value on the spiritual value of nature; Thoreau, particularly, is regarded as a principal forerunner of the modern environmental movement.

Transcendentalism has always had its critics. It has been accused of subverting Christianity; of assessing human nature too optimistically and underestimating human weakness and potential for evil; of placing too much emphasis on the self-reliant individual at the expense of society and social reform. Yet even those hostile to transcendentalism must concede that American literature, religion, philosophy, and politics have been shaped by the movement in profound ways.

BIBLIOGRAPHY

Capper, Charles, and Conrad E. Wright, eds. *Transient and Permanent: The Transcendentalist Movement and Its Contexts.* Boston: Massachusetts Historical Society, 1999.

Miller, Perry, ed. *The Transcendentalists: An Anthology.* Cambridge, Mass.: Harvard University Press, 1950.

Packer, Barbara, "The Transcendentalists." In *The Cambridge History of American Literature.* Edited by Sacvan Bercovitch. Vol. 2: *Prose Writing 1820–1865.* New York: Cambridge University Press, 1995.

Dean Grodzins

See also **Individualism; Philosophy; Romanticism; Utopian Communities;** *Walden.*

TRANSCONTINENTAL RAILROAD, BUILDING OF.

The Transcontinental Railroad was the result of the U.S. commitment to Manifest Destiny and its burgeoning industrial might. Long distances and slow transportation hampered contact between eastern and western commercial centers. Both the United States government and entrepreneurs sought faster transportation to link the two sections. For a decade after 1850, Congress studied possible transcontinental routes, but arguments over sectionalism and slavery blocked all plans. Not until after the South seceded and the Civil War had begun could Congress pass an effective transcontinental plan, the Pacific Railroad Act of 1862. It called for two railroad companies to complete the transcontinental line. The railroad would be a "land-grant railroad," meaning that the government would give each company 6,400 acres of land and up to $48,000 for every mile of track it built. The money capitalized the project, and the railroads could use the land to entice settlers to the West, who in turn would need the railroads to haul freight. But Congress, afraid to fund a project that would never be completed, wrote a caveat into the act: the railroads had to complete the project by July 1, 1876, or they would forfeit the land, money, and all of the constructed track.

The Union Pacific Railroad, a corporation formed for the venture, would build the eastern half of the line starting in Nebraska. The Central Pacific Railroad, owned by a group of California entrepreneurs including Collis Huntington and Leland Stanford, would build the western half.

Preliminary work began, even as the nation still fought the Civil War. Surveyors and engineers had to scout and map workable routes. After the war, several army generals served as engineers on the project. They included Grenville Dodge, a favorite general of Ulysses S. Grant and William T. Sherman, who became the Union Pacific's chief engineer.

Work progressed rapidly after the Civil War. The project attracted many former soldiers, both Union and Confederate, as well as Irish and Chinese immigrants. The Central Pacific quickly had to tackle the rugged Sierras in California. Rather than go over or around them, engineers chose to go through them. But such a plan required tons of dynamite and someone to set the charges. The Chinese were often willing to do the hazardous work for less pay than other Americans, and they became a backbone of the Central Pacific work crew. Men working on both lines braved the extremes of heat and cold, hostile Native Americans, and disease as they advanced.

The two railroads reached northern Utah at about the same time, and the work crews passed by each other, for no one had decided where the rails were to join. Government engineers stepped in and selected Promontory Point, Utah, for the connection. In a ceremony that included the driving of a symbolic golden railroad spike, the two lines linked on May 10, 1869, seven years ahead of schedule.

BIBLIOGRAPHY

Billington, Ray Allen, and Martin Ridge. *Westward Expansion: A History of the American Frontier.* Albuquerque: University of New Mexico Press, 2001.

R. Steven Jones

See also **Central Pacific–Union Pacific Race; Land Grants for Railways.**

TRANSPLANTS AND ORGAN DONATION.

Transplantation (grafting) is the replacement of a failing organ or tissue by a functioning one. Transplantation was a dream in antiquity. The Hindu deity Ganesha had his head replaced by an elephant's head soon after birth (Rig-Veda, 1500 B.C.). In the Christian tradition Saints Cosmas and Damian (fl. 3rd century A.D.) are famous for replacing the diseased leg of a true believer with the leg of a dark-skinned Moor, thereby becoming the patron saints of physicians and surgeons.

Transplantation may be from the same person (autologous), from the same species (homologous—the allograft can come from a genetically identical twin, genetically close parent or sibling, living unrelated person, or cadaver) or from a different species (xenotransplant).

Human tissues carry highly specific antigens, which cause the immune system to react to "foreign" materials. An antigen is a substance that when introduced into an organism evokes the production of substances—antibodies—that destroy or neutralize the antigen. Grafts of a person's own tissue (such as skin grafts) are therefore well tolerated. Homologous grafts are plagued by attempted rejection by the recipient human. The biological acceptability of the graft is measured by tissue typing of the donor and recipient using the human leucocyte antigen, or HLA, panels. The closer the match between the donor and the recipient, the greater the chance of graft acceptance and function. Xenotransplantation is as yet entirely experimental because of tissue rejection and the possibility of transmitting animal diseases to the human recipient.

Organ transplantation has two sets of problems. The first relate to the recipient: the magnitude of the procedure and the intricacies of the surgical technique, the avoidance of rejection (acute or chronic) of the grafted tissue because of antigens in the tissue, and temporary and long-term suppression of the recipient's immune processes, with resulting infections and cancers. The second set of problems relates to the graft itself: the source of the graft and its collection, preservation, and transport to the recipient. Associated problems are ethical and economic, including the expense of the procedure and the cost of long-term monitoring and support of the patient.

Transcontinental Railroad. The Union Pacific and the Central Pacific ceremonially link up at Promontory Summit, Utah, just north of the Great Salt Lake, on 10 May 1869; the spot is now the Golden Spike National Historic Site. NATIONAL ARCHIVES AND RECORDS ADMINISTRATION

Many of the technical problems associated with transplantation are gradually being overcome, and solutions are being constantly improved. Obtaining donor organs and distributing them equitably remain critical problems.

Transplantation is well established for skin, teeth, bone, blood, bone marrow, cornea, heart, kidney, liver, and to a lesser extent for the lung, pancreas, and intestines. On occasion two transplants are combined, such as heart and lung or pancreas and kidney.

Grafting an individual's own skin was well known to the ancient Hindus and has been widely used in the Western world since the middle of the nineteenth century. Skin grafting is a major resource in treating large wounds and burns. Artificially grown skin analogues and frozen pigskin can temporarily meet massive immediate needs.

Blood transfusion was attempted in the seventeenth century in France and England but was abandoned because of adverse reactions, including death. The identification of blood types in the early twentieth century and the discovery of methods of separating and preserving blood and its components have made transfusion a common and effective therapy. An important side effect of World War II and later conflicts has been improvement in all aspects of blood transfusion—collection, preservation, and delivery. The recognition of HLA types was based largely on the practices of blood transfusion and skin grafting. Transplantation of bone marrow and stem cells (precursors from which blood cells develop) is used to treat patients with malignancies of the blood and lymphatic system, such as the leukemia and lymphoma. Donor cells may be from the patient or from antigenmatched donor(s). Usually the patient's bone marrow (with the stem cells) is totally destroyed by chemotherapy, sometimes with whole body irradiation afterward. Donor cells are then introduced into the body, with the expectation that they will take over the production of new blood cells.

The commonest organ transplanted is the kidney. The first successful kidney transplant was done in 1954 in the United States between identical twins; before immunosuppressive procedures were developed, twins were the most successful donors. Transplantation between twins evokes the least immune reactions as the HLA types of twins are identical or nearly so. In 2001, about 14,000 kidney transplants were performed in the United States, 63 percent using kidneys obtained from cadavers. Patient survival using cadaveric donor kidneys is more than 90 percent at 1 year after surgery, and 60 to 90 percent at 5 years. For living donor kidneys, survival is above 98 percent at 1 year and 71 to 98 percent at 5 years. Corneal transplants have a high rate of success because the cornea does not have blood vessels and hence is not highly antigenic. Cadaver corneas can be successfully preserved and stored in eye banks for delivery as needed. More than 30,000 corneas are grafted each year in the United States.

More than 5,000 liver transplantations were done in the United States in 2001. Some of these transplants were portions of livers from living donors. In living adult liver donors, significant surgical complications and even a few deaths have raised some questions about the procedure. Though this is a controversial procedure, the great demand for donor livers will certainly keep this practice going. The heart is the fourth most common organ replaced. The first heart transplantation was done in South Africa in 1967; the high risk made it very controversial at the time. In 2000, almost 2,200 heart transplants were performed in the United States. Graft rejection remains a problem, and immunosuppresion (with its attendant dangers) has to be continued lifelong. If patients do not have other significant diseases, they return to near-normal functioning. More than 80 percent of patients function satisfactorily 1 year after surgery, and 60 to 70 percent at 5 years. At any given time, thousands of patients are waiting for donated organs. With progressive technical improvement in keeping seriously ill patients alive and making transplantation less risky, the need for organs continues to rise. Bioengineering is the application of engineering principles to biology—this includes the artificial production of cells and organs, or that of equipment that can perform functions of organs such as the kidneys or the heart. Bioengineered cells and tissues are a promising field in transplantation. Bioengineered skin is widely used for short-term coverage. Bioengineered corneas appear to be promising. Primitive heart-muscle cells (myoblasts) are being transplanted into diseased hearts, chondrocytes or cartilage cells are being cultured for use in degenerated joints, and there is considerable interest in xenografts.

Since 1968 a Uniform Anatomical Gift Act allows adults to donate their organs for transplantation after death. In every state, some form of donor card is associated with driver's licenses, and health care providers in most states are required to ask permission for postmortem organ procurement. (In some European countries consent for organ donation is presumed.) The United Network for Organ Sharing (UNOS) was established in 1977 to coordinate the distribution of kidneys and later other organs nationally and to maintain a registry of persons awaiting transplant. The UNOS generally prefers that donated organ(s) be used in the local community. All transplant centers are required to join the network and abide by its rules. By May 2002, UNOS membership included 255 Transplant Centers, 156 Histocompatibility Laboratories, and 59 Operating Organ Procurement Organizations. With all these efforts, the shortage of organs persists.

BIBLIOGRAPHY

Cooper, David K. C., and Robert P. Lanza. *Xeno: The Promise of Transplanting Animal Organs into Humans.* Oxford and New York: Oxford University Press, 2000.

Fox, Renée C., and Judith P. Swazey, with the assistance of Judith C. Watkins. *Spare Parts: Organ Replacement in American Society.* New York: Oxford University Press, 1992.

183

Lock, Margaret M. *Twice Dead: Organ Transplants and the Reinvention of Death*. Berkeley: University of California Press, 2002.

Munson, Ronald. *Raising the Dead: Organ Transplants, Ethics, and Society*. Oxford and New York: Oxford University Press, 2002.

Murray, Joseph E. *Surgery of the Soul: Reflections on a Curious Career*. Canton, Mass.: Science History Publications, 2001.

Parr, Elizabeth, and Janet Mize. *Coping With an Organ Transplant: A Practical Guide to Understanding, Preparing For, and Living With an Organ Transplant*. New York: Avery, 2001.

United States Congress, House Committee on Commerce. *Organ and Bone Marrow Transplant Program Reauthorization Act of 1995: Report (to Accompany S. 1324)*. Washington, D.C.: U.S. General Printing Office, 1996.

United States Congress, House Committee on Commerce, Subcommittee on Health and the Environment. *Organ Procurement and Transplantation Network Amendments of 1999: Report Together with Dissenting Views (to Accompany H.R. 2418)*. Washington, D.C.: U.S. General Printing Office, 1999.

United States Congress, House Committee on Government Reform and Oversight, Subcommittee on Human Resources. *Oversight of the National Organ Procurement and Transplantation Network: Hearing Before the Subcommittee on Human Resources of the Committee on Government Reform and Oversight*. 105th Cong., 2nd sess., 8 April 1998. Washington, D.C.: General Printing Office, 1998.

Youngner, Stuart J., Renée C. Fox, and Laurence J. O'Connell, eds. *Organ Transplantation: Meanings and Realities*. Madison: University of Wisconsin Press, 1996.

Internet Sources

For current national statistical data, see the Web sites of the Scientific Registry of Transplant Recipients, http://ustransplant.org/annual.html, and the United Network for Organ Sharing, http://www.unos.org/frame_default.asp.

For general information for patients, updated regularly, see http://www.nlm.nih.gov/medlineplus.

Ranes C. Chakravorty

See also **Medicine and Surgery.**

TRANSPORTATION, DEPARTMENT OF

(DOT) was established by an act of Congress (P.L. 89-670) on 15 October 1966, and formally opened for business on 1 April 1967. It consists of the Office of the Secretary and fourteen Operating Administrations, each of which has statutory responsibility for the implementation of a wide range of regulations, both at its headquarters in Washington, D.C., and at the appropriate regional offices.

Mission

The Department's mission is to develop and coordinate policies that provide an efficient and economical national transportation system, with due regard for its impact on safety, the environment, and national defense. For example, DOT regulates safety in the skies, on the seas, and on the roads and rails. The department regulates consumer and economic issues regarding aviation and provides financial assistance for programs involving highways, airports, mass transit, the maritime industry, railroads, and motor vehicle safety. It writes regulations carrying out such disparate statutes as the Americans with Disabilities Act and the Uniform Time Act. It promotes intermodal transportation (utilizing different modes of transportation for one trip) and implements international trade and transportation agreements.

The Structure

The Office of the Secretary (OST) oversees the formulation of America's national transportation policy, including the promotion of intermodalism and safety. The office includes the secretary, the deputy secretary, one under secretary, five assistant secretaries, and the office of the general counsel. Four of the assistant secretaries are appointed by the president and confirmed by the Senate. The fifth, the assistant secretary for administration, has a career civil service appointee at its helm. In addition to the general counsel, these four offices include Aviation and International Affairs, Budget and Financial Management, Governmental Affairs, and Transportation Policy.

The Operating Administrations, which are responsible for implementing the department's mission, include: (1) the United States Coast Guard (USCG); (2) the Federal Aviation Administration (FAA); (3) the Federal Highway Administration (FHWA); (4) the Federal Motor Carrier Safety Administration (FMCSA); (5) the Federal Railroad Administration (FRA); (6) the National Highway Traffic Safety Administration (NHTSA); (7) the Federal Transit Administration (FTA); (8) the Maritime Administration (MARAD); (9) the Saint Lawrence Seaway Development Corporation (SLSDC); (10) the Research and Special Programs Administration (RSPA); and (11) the Transportation Security Administration (TSA). Each is headed by a presidential appointee who is subject to Senate confirmation. The Bureau of Transportation Statistics (BTS), the Transportation Administrative Service Center (TASC), and the Surface Transportation Board (STB) provide specialized functions.

DOT's Immediate Pre-History

From the outset, the drive behind the establishment of a Department of Transportation was to develop a viable national transportation policy. When DOT was formed, the federal government had no less than thirty-four agencies and functions to handle the nation's transportation programs. The need to nationalize these programs under a single roof gained steady adherence in the years following the Civil War; and since that time, members of Congress attempted to pass legislation resolving this issue on ninety-two occasions. The first Hoover Commission (1947–1949), as part of its mandate to reorganize the executive branch, proposed to put all the transportation functions under the Department of Commerce, which President Harry S. Truman did—to almost no one's satisfaction.

President Dwight Eisenhower's Advisory Committee on Governmental Organization proposed a cabinet-level Department of Transportation and Communications; however, this proposal faced several political obstacles. Consequently, when the retiring administrator of the still-independent Federal Aviation Agency proposed to President Lyndon Baines Johnson the establishment of a Department of Transportation, the staff of the Bureau of the Budget, who had been working on proposals to reorganize the executive branch, seized upon his proposal. Noting that "America today lacks a coordinated [intermodal] transportation system," Johnson agreed, and within two years, in October 1966, the Department of Transportation became a reality.

From Many to One

As such, DOT proved valuable in the development of a national transportation policy, particularly during the administrations of Presidents Gerald Ford and George H. W. Bush. During President Ronald Reagan's administration, not only had the maritime administration successfully been brought into the Department, but DOT had managed to withstand serious efforts to pry away the Coast Guard and the FAA as well. It even saw commercial space transportation and residual functions of the Civilian Aeronautics Board (CAB) and the Interstate Commerce Commission (ICC) become significant parts of the mix.

Guided by President William Clinton's National Performance Review (the Reinventing Government Initiative) and Congress's passage of the Chief Financial Officers Act of 1990 and the Government and Performance Results Act of 1993, the Department pursued a "One DOT" management strategy, replete with customer service proposals, strategic planning, and performance appraisals. As an example, NHTSA adopted as its slogan, "People Saving People."

Following the 11 September 2001 attacks on the World Trade Center and the Pentagon, on 19 November 2001, Congress passed the Aviation and Transportation Security Act, which established the Transportation Security Administration (TSA), responsible for securing all modes of transportation in the United States.

BIBLIOGRAPHY

Burby, John F. *The Great American Motion Sickness; or, Why You Can't Get From There to Here.* Boston: Little, Brown, 1971.

Davis, Grant Miller. *The Department of Transportation.* Lexington, Mass.: D.C. Heath Lexington, 1970.

Hazard, John L. *Managing National Transportation Policy.* Westport, Conn.: Eno Foundation for Transportation Policy, 1988.

Whitnah, Donald Robert. *U.S. Department of Transportation: A Reference History.* Westport, Conn.: Greenwood Press, 1998.

R. Dale Grinder

See also **Transportation and Travel.**

TRANSPORTATION ACT OF 1920, also known as the Esch-Cummins Act. The U.S. government took over and ran the railroads from 26 December 1917 to 1 March 1920. During the period of government operation, the tracks were obliged to carry a heavy volume of traffic with little attention to replacements or ordinary maintenance. This was more a result of circumstances than the fault of the government; nevertheless, the railroads were in a deplorable condition when, after a little more than two years, they were returned to private operation.

As a result, some remedial legislation was imperative. The Transportation Act of 28 February 1920 was the result. The Senate bill, introduced by Sen. Albert B. Cummins, and the House bill, proposed by Rep. John Jacob Esch, required a conference committee to produce a compromise measure, which became effective on 1 March, a little more than three months after President Woodrow Wilson returned the railroads to private operation.

To help the railroads financially, the bill authorized consolidations, established a six-month guarantee period, and authorized extensive loans for a variety of purposes. Congress provided for arbitration without power of enforcement and established voluntary adjustment boards to settle labor disputes. These provisions were to be enforced by the Railroad Labor Board, consisting of nine members and having national jurisdiction. Hotly contested in Congress, the Transportation Act of 1920 engendered controversy for years thereafter. Advocates contended that favorable terms were necessary to avoid paralysis of the national transportation system; detractors claimed that railroads and financial interests had dictated terms to their own advantage.

BIBLIOGRAPHY

Berk, Gerald. *Alternative Tracks: The Constitution of American Industrial Order, 1865–1917.* Baltimore: Johns Hopkins University Press, 1994.

Himmelberg, Robert F., ed. *Business-Government Cooperation, 1917–1932: The Rise of Corporatist Policies.* Vol. 5 of *Business and Government in America since 1870.* New York: Garland, 1994.

W. Brooke Graves/c. w.

See also **Railroad Administration, U.S.; Railroads; Transportation and Travel.**

TRANSPORTATION AND TRAVEL. Travel in the United States for most of its history was arduous. Nineteenth-century transportation systems, notably the railroad, improved travel between and within cities, but most Americans could go only as far as their horses could carry them. The vast country remained largely inaccessible to all but the most intrepid pioneer or explorer.

The United States was transformed in the twentieth century into the most mobile society in human history. Americans traveled far more often and covered many

Pullman Car. The interior of a sleeping car on the Chicago, Milwaukee, St. Paul and Pacific Railroad. GETTY IMAGES

more miles during the twentieth century compared not only to their ancestors but also to their contemporaries in other countries. The principal agent of the unprecedented ability to travel was a transportation system based on near universal ownership of private motor vehicles.

Colonial Era

Most settlers lived near a body of water, so water transportation was the usual means of travel. A short journey down a river could be undertaken by canoe, while a longer-distance trip across a protected bay or sound could be made by shallop, sloop, schooner, or other small sailboat.

For those who could afford a horse, land-based travel could be accomplished by riding on a trail traced initially by deer, buffalo, and other animals. Otherwise, a traveler had to set off on foot. Colonists moved goods between east coast cities by mule and packhorse. In the west, fur traders, farmers, and settlers widened footpaths by riding horses or attaching horses to wagons.

Colonial road building officially started in 1639, when the Massachusetts General Court directed that each town lay out roads connecting it with adjacent villages. Roads were built by other colonial governments, but the condition of these dirt roads was generally poor and money

was not available to maintain and improve them. Operating horse-drawn passenger vehicles was difficult during much of the colonial era because of the poor roads.

The first regular stagecoach route was inaugurated on 8 March 1759, between New York City and Philadelphia, and by the end of the colonial period a network of services connected the larger towns. A covered wagon service known as the "flying machine," operated by John Mercereau during the 1770s, was advertised as a miracle of speed because it covered the 100-mile distance between New York City and Philadelphia in only a day and a half, and it had a reputation for sticking precisely to a published timetable.

Nineteenth-Century Transportation

Through the nineteenth century, the top transportation objective in the United States was to open routes between eastern population centers and sparsely inhabited territories to the west. In the first quarter century after independence, construction of roads across the Appalachian Mountains received priority. As American settlement pushed further westward during the nineteenth century, first water and then rail transport emerged as leading forms of transport.

Turnpikes. To stimulate road construction during the last decade of the eighteenth century and the first decade of the nineteenth, states chartered private companies to build, operate, and maintain turnpikes, so named because poles armed with pikes were turned to allow travelers to pass through after paying. The first turnpike, between Philadelphia and Lancaster, Pennsylvania, was chartered in 1790, begun in 1792, and completed in 1794. The sixty-two-mile road was thirty-seven feet wide, paved with stone, and covered with gravel. Its high quality and financial success generated interest from hundreds of companies in turnpikes. By 1811 New York had chartered 137 companies, which constructed 1,400 miles of roads, and Pennsylvania had 2,380 miles of road built by 102 companies. High tolls discouraged using the turnpikes to transport bulky products at a profit.

Some turnpikes were built with state and federal government aid. Most prominent was the Cumberland Road or National Pike, authorized by Congress in 1806. Financing was arranged through an agreement in which states exempted from taxation for five years federal land sold to settlers in return for the federal government agreeing to appropriate 5 percent of the proceeds from the land sales for building the road. The first 130-mile stretch of the National Pike from Cumberland, Maryland, west to Wheeling, West Virginia, was completed in 1818.

The National Pike was an engineering marvel, eighty feet wide, with bridges across streams. Its most distinctive feature was a thirty- to forty-foot-wide center track made not of dirt but of the new macadam technology, a ten-inch layer of compacted small stones. The route reached what proved to be its westward terminus at Vandalia, Illinois, in 1852 and was not extended further west to Jefferson City, Missouri, as planned, because water and rail had by then emerged as better choices for long-distance travel.

Canals. Movement of people and especially goods by barge was much cheaper than by road because a horse could drag a load that was fifty times heavier on water than across land. But water travel to the west from east coast population centers was impractical because navigable rivers, especially in the Northeast, such as the Delaware and Hudson, flowed generally north-south.

Water routes to the west were opened through canals, a technique already widely used in Great Britain. New York State under the leadership of Governor DeWitt Clinton authorized construction of the Erie Canal in 1817 to connect the Hudson River with Lake Erie. Forty feet wide and four feet deep, the Erie Canal rose over 500 feet through 83 locks. The first 15 miles between Utica and Rome were opened in 1819, the entire 363-mile canal between Troy (Albany) and Buffalo on 26 October 1825. With the opening of the Erie Canal, transporting a ton of freight between New York City and Buffalo took eight days instead of twenty and cost about $10 instead of $100. Cities in Upstate New York along the route, such as Syracuse, Rochester, and Buffalo, thrived, and New York City surpassed Philadelphia as the country's most populous city and most important seaport.

In the Midwest, the state of Ohio in 1825 authorized two canals to connect Lake Erie with the Ohio River, including the Ohio and Erie, completed in 1832 between Portsmouth and Cleveland, and the Miami and Erie between Cincinnati and Toledo, substantially finished in 1835, though not completely until 1845. In Indiana, the Wabash and Erie Canal, begun in 1832 and completed in 1843, connected Evansville on the Ohio River with Toledo and the Miami and Erie Canal near the Ohio-Indiana state line. The United States had 3,326 miles of canals in 1840, and 3,698 in 1850.

Canals were built and financed mostly by states because private individuals lacked sufficient capital. But states overreached, constructing canals that could never generate enough revenue to pay off the loans. Inability to repay canal construction loans was a major contributor to the panic of 1837, the worst economic depression of the nineteenth century. Subsequent nineteenth-century transportation improvements would be financed by private speculators.

Robert Fulton first demonstrated the practicability of steam power in 1807 when he sailed his boat the *Clermont* 150 miles up the Hudson River from New York City to Albany in thirty-two hours. On the western rivers such as the Ohio and Mississippi, flat-bottomed two-deck steamboats quickly became the cheapest means for long-distance hauling of large quantities of goods. The 1,200-mile journey up the Mississippi from New Orleans to St. Louis could be completed in four days. More than 1,000

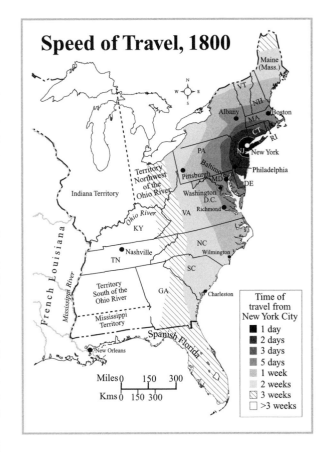

steamboats plied the Mississippi and its tributaries during the 1850s.

Railroads. It was the railroad that first succeeded in knitting together a unified coast-to-coast transportation network for the United States. The first railroad in the United States was the Baltimore and Ohio. Given the honor of placing the first rail, on 4 July 1828, was the Maryland native Charles Carroll, who as the country's only surviving signer of the Declaration of Independence symbolically linked the political revolution of the eighteenth century with the industrial revolution of the nineteenth. The first 13 miles, between Baltimore and Ellicott City, Maryland, opened in 1830, and by 1835 the B&O had 135 miles of track. Other early-1830s U.S. rail lines included New York's Mohawk and Hudson and South Carolina's Charleston and Hamburg, a 136-mile route, then the world's longest.

U.S. railroad mileage grew rapidly through the nineteenth century: 23 miles of track in 1830, 2,818 miles in 1840, 9,021 miles in 1850, 30,626 miles in 1860, 52,914 miles in 1870, 93,296 miles in 1880, 163,597 miles in 1890, and 193,346 miles in 1900. Rail companies succeeded in digging through the Appalachians and bridging the Mississippi during the 1850s. Barely a decade later, the first transcontinental railroad was completed.

187

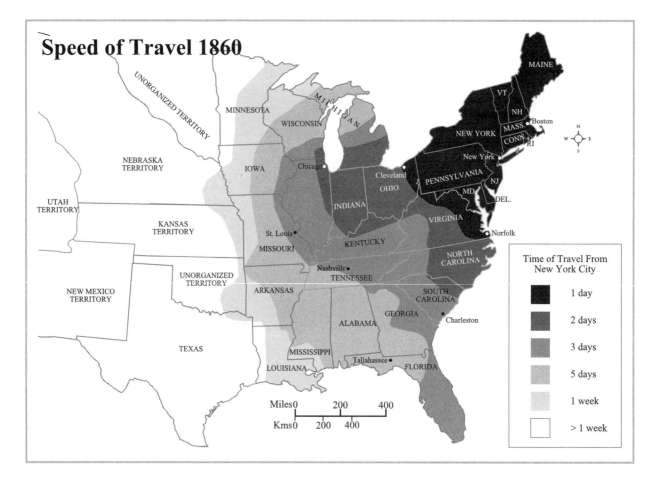

Congress created the Union Pacific Railroad Company in 1862 for the purpose of building a road from Nebraska west to California. Meanwhile, Sacramento, California, merchants organized the Central Pacific Railroad to build eastward. To encourage rapid construction, the two railroads were granted ownership of ten square miles of federal land for every mile of track laid, raised in 1864 to twenty square miles. They also received subsidies of $16,000 for every mile of track laid in the plains, $32,000 in the foothills, and $48,000 in the mountains. The two lines met at Promontory Point, Utah, on 10 May 1869, where Leland Stanford, a California grocer and Central Pacific investor, drove in the last spike, made of California gold. Several other transcontinental railroads were quickly constructed, also backed by generous grants of public land.

Rail-based transportation systems were also built within cities during the nineteenth century to help ease congestion resulting from rapid growth. Horse-drawn streetcars were widely used beginning in the 1850s until replaced by electric streetcars during the 1880s and 1890s. In larger cities, elevated railroads were constructed beginning in the 1870s, and the first underground railroad (subway) opened in Boston in 1897.

After a half-century of rapid construction, the United States had 40 percent of the world's total rail mileage in

1900. For every 10,000 inhabitants, the United States had 27 miles of tracks, compared to 4.8 miles in Europe and 1.3 miles in the rest of the world. For every 100 square miles of territory, the United States had 9.6 miles of tracks, compared to only 5.1 miles in Europe and 0.3 miles in the rest of the world.

Train service made possible rapid movement between major cities in the late nineteenth century, but for the majority of Americans who still lived in rural areas railroads offered little service because they stopped infrequently between major cities. The routes of the main rail lines controlled the fate of rural communities. The rural and small-town stations where the trains did stop were like pearls strung along the railroad line. Around the stations economic and social activity bustled. Beyond a ten-to-twelve-mile radius of the stations, most farmers lived in isolation, able to reach the outside world only by riding horses over dirt trails. In 1900, the United States still had 30 million horses, an average of more than one per household.

Seven groups—Vanderbilt, Pennsylvania, Morgan, Gould, Moore, Harriman, and Hill—controlled two-thirds of U.S. rail service in 1900. To most Americans, the railroad owners were hated and feared robber barons insensitive to the public interest. As monopolies, U.S. railroads paid more attention to wealthy riders willing to pay high

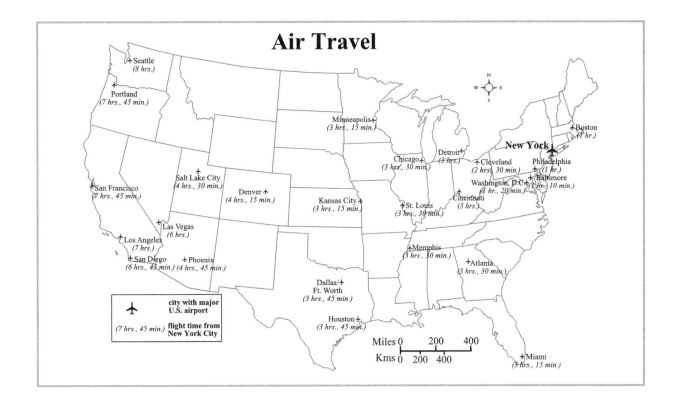

Air Travel

Seattle
(8 hrs.)

Portland
(7 hrs., 45 min.)

Minneapolis
(3 hrs., 15 min.)

Boston
(1 hr.)

Detroit
(3 hrs.)

New York

Chicago
(3 hrs., 30 min.)

Cleveland
(2 hrs., 30 min.)

Philadelphia
(1 hr.)

Salt Lake City
(4 hrs., 30 min.)

Denver
(4 hrs., 15 min.)

Washington, D.C.
(1 hr., 20 min.)

Baltimore
(1 hr., 10 min.)

San Francisco
(7 hrs., 45 min.)

Kansas City
(3 hrs., 15 min.)

St. Louis
(3 hrs., 30 min.)

Cincinnati
(3 hrs.)

Las Vegas
(6 hrs.)

Los Angeles
(7 hrs.)

San Diego
(6 hrs., 45 min.)

Phoenix
(4 hrs., 45 min.)

Memphis
(3 hrs., 30 min.)

Atlanta
(3 hrs., 30 min.)

Dallas/
Ft. Worth
(3 hrs., 45 min.)

city with major
U.S. airport

(7 hrs., 45 min.) flight time from
New York City

Houston
(3 hrs., 45 min.)

Miles 0   200   400
Kms 0   200   400

Miami
(3 hrs., 15 min.)

prices for a luxurious ride than to average Americans eager to travel but unable to afford a ticket. The railroad was ripe for a challenge from a viable alternative for intercity travel. In the twentieth century, that viable alternative turned out to be the private motor vehicle.

Twentieth Century

Nineteenth-century transportation improvements made it possible for groups of Americans to travel long distances together with relative speed and comfort. The twentieth century brought personal and affordable travel to each individual American. Itinerary and departure time were determined by the stagecoach, steamboat, or railroad operator during the nineteenth century. During the twentieth century, the motor vehicle enabled individuals to decide for themselves where and when to travel.

Motor vehicles. The Duryea Motor Wagon Company, organized by brothers J. Frank and Charles E. Duryea in Chicopee Falls, Massachusetts, was the first company in the United States to manufacture automobiles in volume, thirteen in 1896. Duryea had gained fame by winning a race through the streets of Chicago on 28 November 1895, the first important event involving motor vehicles in U.S. history.

Because motor vehicles quickly captured the public imagination for their speed and performance, early producers assumed that the market was primarily for high-end recreation and leisure purposes. Early vehicles were purchased as novelty items, akin to motorized bicycles, and with an average cost of about $2,000 only wealthy

people could afford them. Motor vehicles in fact were known as pleasure cars until World War I, when the motor vehicle industry launched a successful campaign to call them passenger cars instead, because "pleasure" sounded unpatriotic in the midst of a world war.

The Ford Motor Company, organized in 1903 by Henry Ford, led the transformation of the motor vehicle from a toy into an indispensable tool of daily life. Ford believed that desire to own motor vehicles was universal, limited only by their high cost, and that once in possession of them Americans would find them extremely useful and practical. To build cars cheaply, Ford pioneered such production methods as offering only one model, designing an easy-to-build car, standardizing parts, placing machines in a logical sequence in the factory, assigning a very specialized job to each worker, and above all bringing the tasks to the workers along a continuously moving assembly line.

Sales of the Ford car, known as the Model T, increased from 13,840 in 1909, its first year of production, to a peak of 1.4 million in 1924. When production ended in 1927, the Model T cost only $290, and Ford had sold more than 15 million of them over eighteen years. During the 1910s and 1920s, half of the world's motor vehicles were Ford Model Ts.

General Motors overtook Ford as the leading motor vehicle producer in the 1920s by offering a wide variety of vehicles with styling changed every year. GM stimulated sales through readily available low-interest loans and

189

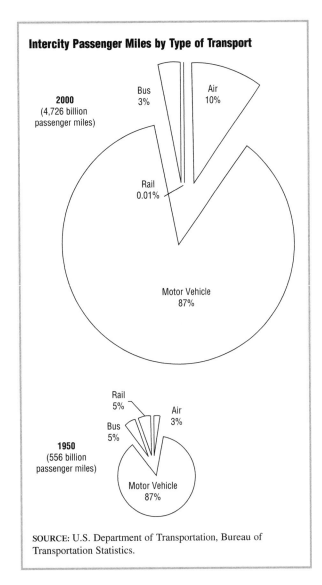

Intercity Passenger Miles by Type of Transport

2000
(4,726 billion passenger miles)

Bus 3%
Air 10%
Rail 0.01%
Motor Vehicle 87%

1950
(556 billion passenger miles)

Rail 5%
Bus 5%
Air 3%
Motor Vehicle 87%

SOURCE: U.S. Department of Transportation, Bureau of Transportation Statistics.

increased profits through innovative financial management practices.

At the onset of the Great Depression in 1929, the number of motor vehicles in the United States was nearly as great as the number of families, at a time when possession of a motor vehicle was extremely rare in the rest of the world. Through the first half of the twentieth century, the United States accounted for more than three-fourths of the world's production and sales of motor vehicles. As a result of a high car ownership rate, the United States had a very different transportation system for much of the twentieth century than anywhere else in the world. As early as 1930, the U.S. Census Bureau reported that one-fourth of U.S. cities with more than 10,000 inhabitants had no public transit and so depended entirely on cars for transportation. Even in the country's largest cities, most trips were being made by car in 1930.

Use of motor vehicles had been limited during the first two decades of the twentieth century by poor road conditions. The first inventory of U.S. roads by the Office of Public Roads Inquiry in 1904 found only 153,662 miles of roads with any kind of surfacing. The 1916 Federal Aid Road Act appropriated $75 million over five years to pay half of the cost of building rural post roads, with states paying the remaining half. In 1921 the amount was increased to 75 million per year. The amount of surfaced roads in the United States increased from 257,291 miles in 1914 to 521,915 miles in 1926. The Federal Highway Act of 1921 called for designation of a national highway system of interconnected roads. The complete national system of 96,626 miles was approved in 1926 and identified by the U.S. highway numbers still in use.

The first limited-access highway—the Pennsylvania Turnpike—opened in 1940. The Interstate Highway Act of 1956 called for construction of 44,000 miles of limited-access highways across the United States. The federal government paid for 90 percent of the cost to construct the highways. Most of the miles of interstate highways were constructed to connect cities, but most of the dollars were spent to cross inside cities.

Construction of new highways could not keep pace with increased motor vehicle usage during the second half of the twentieth century. Between 1950 and 2000, the number of Americans nearly doubled and the number of roads doubled, but the number of vehicles more than quadrupled and the number of miles driven more than quintupled. As a result, the United States had more motor vehicles than licensed drivers in 2000.

The federal government played an increasing role in the design of safer, cleaner, more efficient motor vehicles, especially during the 1960s and 1970s. The National Traffic and Motor Vehicle Safety and Highway Safety Acts of 1966 mandated safety features, such as seat belts. A cabinet-level Department of Transportation was established in 1967 to coordinate and administer overall transportation policy. The 1970 Clean Air Act specified reductions in polluting emissions. The 1975 Energy Policy and Conservation Act specified minimum fuel efficiency. However, improvements in passenger car safety and fuel efficiency during the late twentieth century were offset by Americans' preference for purchasing trucks instead.

Aviation. The federal government was crucial in shaping the role of aviation in the U.S. transportation system during the 1920s and 1930s. After the Wright Brothers' first successful manned flight in 1903, airplanes were flown primarily for entertainment and military purposes until 15 May 1918, when Army pilots started daily airmail service between New York and Washington. The Post Office—then a cabinet-level federal department—was authorized under the 1925 Kelly Act to award private aviation companies with contracts to carry mail on the basis of competitive bidding. Because carrying airmail accounted for 90 percent of airline revenues during the 1920s, carriers with contracts were the ones to survive the industry's initial shakeout and then evolve into the dominant passenger-carrying services during the 1930s.

The first privately contracted airmail routes started on 15 February 1926, from Detroit to Chicago and Cleveland, and the federal government stopped flying its own airmail planes on 31 August 1927. Regularly scheduled passenger service started in 1926, when airmail contractors first provided a limited number of seats in their planes. Aviation companies started carrying cargo that year as well.

The Civil Aeronautics Board (CAB, originally called the Civil Aeronautics Authority), created under the 1938 Civil Aeronautics Act, certified airlines as fit to fly, specified pairs of cities between which they could fly passengers, and regulated their fares. The Federal Aviation Administration (FAA), established in 1958, regulated safety and other standards for aircraft, airports, and pilots.

Passenger service grew rapidly during the 1950s and 1960s, especially after the introduction of large jet-engine planes capable of flying more people longer distances at higher speeds. Between 1938 and 1978, the number of passengers increased from 1 million to 267 million and revenue passenger miles increased from 533 million to 219 billion. Routes supported by the Post Office back in the 1920s formed the backbone of the passenger services certified during the next half-century of government regulation.

The federal government dramatically restructured the industry in 1978 through passage of the Airline Deregulation Act. Airlines could now fly wherever they wished inside the United States and charge passengers whatever they wished. The CAB—its regulatory role rendered obsolete—was disbanded in 1984, and its safety oversight functions transferred to the FAA.

Deregulation set off a wave of airline acquisitions, mergers, and bankruptcies during the 1980s and 1990s. A handful of surviving airlines dominated the U.S. air system by terminating most point-to-point flights between pairs of cities and instead concentrating most flights in and out of a few hub airports. Regional airlines fed more passengers from smaller cities into the hubs. As a result, most airports offered nonstop flights to fewer cities but one-stop flights (via transfer at a hub) to many more cities. Low-cost airlines filled in gaps in the hub-and-spokes system by offering inexpensive flights between pairs of underserved airports.

In the first two decades of deregulation, U.S. air travel increased even more rapidly than in the past—from 275 million passengers in 1978 to 466 million in 1990 and 666 million in 2000, and from 219 billion passenger miles in 1978 to 458 billion in 1990 and 693 billion in 2000. Free to charge passengers whatever they wished, airlines employed sophisticated yield management models to constantly change fares for particular flights depending on demand.

Surviving nineteenth-century transportation systems. Squeezed between motor vehicles for shorter distances and airplanes for longer distances, the railroads lost nearly

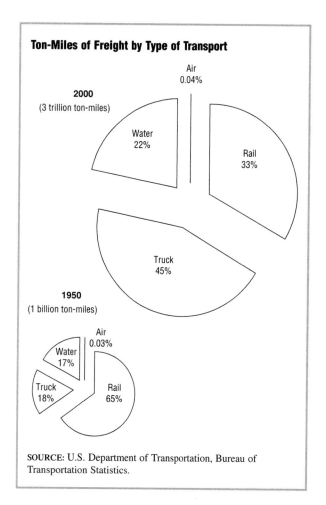

Ton-Miles of Freight by Type of Transport

2000
(3 trillion ton-miles)

Air 0.04%
Water 22%
Rail 33%
Truck 45%

1950
(1 billion ton-miles)

Air 0.03%
Water 17%
Truck 18%
Rail 65%

SOURCE: U.S. Department of Transportation, Bureau of Transportation Statistics.

all of their intercity passengers during the second half of the twentieth century. The handful of remaining intercity passenger routes were taken over in 1971 by Amtrak, with federal financial support. Most of Amtrak's 22 million passengers in 2000 were traveling between the large cities in the Northeast. Amtrak operated some suburban commuter rail lines, although most were transferred to local or regional public authorities.

Railroads and truck companies shared about evenly in the growth of freight handling during the first half of the twentieth century, but after completion of the interstate highway system trucks captured virtually all of the growth while railroads stagnated. Conrail was created by the federal government in 1976 to take over a number of bankrupt freight-hauling lines, including the Penn Central, the nation's largest when it was created in 1968 through the merger of the Pennsylvania and New York Central railroads.

Within urban areas, rail-based transit enjoyed a modest revival in the late twentieth century, especially in construction of new subway and streetcar (now called light rail) lines. The 1991 Intermodal Surface Transportation Efficiency Act and 1998 Transportation Equity Act enabled state and local governments to fund a mix of highway and transit improvements.

On major inland waterways, such as the Mississippi and Ohio Rivers, the federal government widened and straightened river channels and constructed locks and dams to make shipping by barge faster and safer. Dredging operations permitted oceangoing vessels to reach inland cities such as Tulsa, Oklahoma. In 2000, the United States had about 25,000 miles of navigable inland channels, not including the Great Lakes. Movement of freight became much easier in the late twentieth century by packing goods in containers that could be moved easily from ship to rail to truck.

Into the Twenty-first Century

The United States entered the twenty-first century with the prospect that travel would be slower and more difficult than during the twentieth century. After the 11 September 2001 terrorist attack on the World Trade Center and Pentagon employed four airplanes as weapons, strict security checks instituted at U.S. airports increased total travel time and made more Americans afraid to fly. On the ground, roads and bridges deteriorated at a faster rate than they could be repaired, while motor vehicle usage continued to increase. As a result, driving time between and within cities increased.

BIBLIOGRAPHY

Air Transport Association of America. *Annual Report*. Washington, D.C.: Air Transport Association of America, published annually.

Davies, R. E. G. *Fallacies and Fantasies of Air Transport History*. McLean, Va.: Paladwr, 1994.

Dunbar, Seymour. *A History of Travel in America*. 4 vols. Indianapolis: Bobbs-Merrill, 1915.

Flink, James J. *The Automobile Age*. Cambridge, Mass.: MIT Press, 1988.

Hilton, George W., and John F. Due. *The Electric Interurban Railways in America*. Stanford, Calif.: Stanford University Press, 1960.

Jarrett, Philip, ed. *Modern Air Transport: Worldwide Air Transport from 1945 to the Present*. London: Putnam Aeronautical Books, 2000.

Rubenstein, James M. *Making and Selling Cars: Innovation and Change in the U.S. Automotive Industry*. Baltimore: Johns Hopkins University Press, 2001.

Taylor, George Rogers. *The Transportation Revolution, 1815–1860*. New York: Rinehart, 1951.

Vance, James E., Jr. *The North American Railroad: Its Origin, Evolution, and Geography*. Baltimore: Johns Hopkins University Press, 1995.

Vranich, Joseph. *Derailed: What Went Wrong and What to Do about America's Passenger Trains*. New York: St Martin's Press, 1997.

Womack, James P., Daniel T. Jones, and Daniel Roos. *The Machine That Changed the World*. New York: Rawson, 1990.

James M. Rubenstein

See also **Air Transportation and Travel; Airline Deregulation Act; Amtrak; Cumberland Road; Erie Canal; Federal-Aid Highway Program; Federal Aviation Administration; Interstate Highway System; Railroads; Railways, Interurban; Railways, Urban, and Rapid Transit; Transportation, Department of.**

TRAVELING SALESMEN are representatives of business firms who travel through assigned territories to solicit orders for future deliveries of their employers' goods and services. Unlike peddlers or canvassers, they seek orders from other business firms and public institutions rather than from individual consumers or households. Also, unlike peddlers and other itinerant merchants, they usually sell from samples or descriptions of their products rather than carry goods for immediate delivery.

Although itinerant dealers, such as seagoing and overland traders, emerged early in American economic life, traveling salesmen were virtually nonexistent before the mid-nineteenth century. Thin, sparsely developed market areas, small-scale manufacturing, and the lack of branded merchandise lines provided little incentive for the use of salesmen. Wholesale merchants, who maintained their own contacts with suppliers, dominated trade. Retailers either made periodic buying trips to major wholesale centers to replenish their inventories or patronized local wholesale jobbers. After 1840 manufacturers began to take the initiative and send salesmen in search of customers. This change resulted from (1) the growth of market opportunities as America became more urban; (2) transportation improvements that reduced travel time and expense; and (3) growth in manufacturing capacity and the consequent need to sell greater quantities of goods.

The pioneer traveling salesmen cannot be precisely identified, in part because of definitional problems. For example, should a company owner or partner who made an occasional visit to distant customers or agents be classified as a traveling salesman? A Wilmington, Del., railway equipment manufacturing company, Bonney and Bush (subsequently Bush and Lobdell and then Lobdell Car Wheel Company), employed a traveling agent starting in the 1830s and added additional salesmen in the 1850s. Scovill Manufacturing Company of Waterbury, Conn., which made brassware, experimented with a traveling salesman from 1832 to 1835 but did not finally adopt that selling method until 1852. The Rogers Brothers Silverware Company and other metalworking firms also began using traveling salesmen in the early 1850s.

Many states and municipalities, acting at the behest of their local wholesalers, imposed costly licensing requirements on traveling salesmen entering their jurisdictions. These barriers proved ineffective and eventually were declared unconstitutional in *Robbins v. Taxing District* (1887). The U.S. Census reported 7,262 traveling salesmen in 1870 and 223,732 in 1930, but these figures may represent only one-half to one-third of the true numbers. The number of salesmen undoubtedly increased after 1930.

Salesmanship in the twentieth century became increasingly professionalized and scientific. The early sales management textbooks of the 1910s and 1920s were followed by a steadily expanding stream of books, periodicals, and college courses; more careful planning of salesmen's itineraries; attention to new methods of testing, selecting, and training salesmen; and experimentation with various commission and salary methods of compensation.

Traveling salesmen continued to ply their trade well into the twenty-first century. But while salesmen selling to businesses thrived—selling drugs to doctors or cosmetics to salons, for example—the door to door salesman became extremely rare. The rise of the two-income family after the 1970s deprived door to door salesmen of daytime access to customers. In addition, the rise of the Internet as a marketing device and the trend toward gated and policed suburban subdivisions created steep barriers for door to door work. In many parts of the United States by the end of the twentieth century, the door to door salesman was a thing of the past.

BIBLIOGRAPHY

Hollander, S. C. "Nineteenth Century Anti-Drummer Legislation." *Business History Review* 38 (1964).

Moore, Truman E. *The Traveling Man: The Story of the American Traveling Salesman.* Garden City, N.Y.: Doubleday, 1972.

Porter, Glenn, and Harold C. Livesay. *Merchants and Manufacturers: Studies in the Changing Structure of Nineteenth-Century Marketing.* Baltimore: Johns Hopkins Press, 1971.

Spears, Timothy B. *100 Years on the Road: The Traveling Salesman in American Culture.* New Haven: Yale University Press, 1995.

Stanley C. Hollander / L. T.; A. R.

See also **Advertising; Consumerism; Marketing.**

TREASON. Traditionally, treason was betrayal of the state, which, in most countries meant the monarch. A person who commits treason is a traitor. However, the framers of the U.S. Constitution chose to adopt a restricted definition of treason, making it the only term defined in the body of the Constitution. James Wilson was the principal author of the provision:

> Art. III Sec. 3: Treason against the United States, shall consist only in levying War against them, or in adhering to their Enemies, giving them Aid and Comfort. No person shall be convicted of Treason unless on the Testimony of two witnesses to the same overt Act, or on confession in open Court.
>
> The Congress shall have Power to declare the Punishment of Treason, but no Attainder of Treason shall work Corruption of Blood, or Forfeiture except during the Life of the Person attainted.

Their reason for defining treason was the common English practice of charging political opponents with a capital offense, often on weak evidence, under the doctrine of "constructive treason." A classic case was the trial of Algernon Sidney, beheaded in 1683 for plotting against the king. The case against him was based largely on passages from his treatise, *Discourses Concerning Government*, which was not even published until after his death, in 1698. The term treason was familiar in the common law before it was used in the Statute of 25 Edward III (1350), from which the Constitution derives its language concerning the levying of war and adhering to enemies, giving them aid and comfort. However, the Constitution's treason clause contains no provision analogous to that by which the Statute of Edward III penalized the compassing (intending) of the king's death, since in a republic there is no monarch and the people are sovereign. Charges of treason for compassing the king's death had been the main instrument used in England for the most drastic, "lawful" suppression of political opposition or the expression of ideas or beliefs distasteful to those in power.

The Statute of 7 William III (1694) introduced the requirement of two witnesses to the same or different overt acts of the same treason or misprision (concealment) of treason, made several exceptions to what could be considered treason, and protected the right of the accused to have copies of the indictment and proceedings against him, to have counsel, and to compel witnesses—privileges not previously enjoyed by those accused of common law crimes. This statute served as a model for colonial treason statutes.

The first major cases under the U.S. Constitution arose from an 1807 conspiracy led by Aaron Burr, who had served as vice president under Thomas Jefferson in 1801–1805. The conspirators planned to seize parts of Mexico or the newly acquired Louisiana Territory. Burr and two confederates, Bollman and Swartwout, were charged with treason.

Chief Justice John Marshall opened the door for making actions other than treason a crime in *EX PARTE BOLLMAN* when he held that the clause does not prevent Congress from specifying other crimes of a subversive nature and prescribing punishment, so long as Congress is not merely attempting to evade the restrictions of the treason clause. But he also stated, "However flagitious [villainous] may be the crime of conspiring to subvert by force the government of our country, such conspiracy is not treason. To conspire to levy war, and actually to levy war, are distinct offences. The first must be brought into open action by the assemblage of men for a purpose treasonable in itself, or the fact of levying war cannot have been committed. So far has this principle been carried, that . . . it has been determined that the actual enlistment of men to serve against the government does not amount to levying of war." On the basis of these considerations and because no part of the crime charged had been committed in the District of Columbia, the Court held that

TREASON TRIALS

Ex parte Bollman, 4 Cr. (8 U.S.) 75 (1807).
United States v. Burr, 4 Cr. (8 U.S.) 469 (1807).
Annals of Congress, Tenth Congress, First Session, Senate, Debate on Treason and Other Crimes, 1808.
Wharton's State Trials of the United States (Philadelphia, 1849), and *Lawson's American State Trials* (17 volumes, St. Louis, 1914–1926), trials of Thomas Wilson Dorr (1844) and of John Brown (1859).
Cramer v. United States, 325 U.S. 1 (1945).
Haupt v. United States, 330 U.S. 631 (1947).
Kawakita v. United States, 343 U.S. 717 (1952).
United States v. Rosenberg, 195 F.2d 583 (2d. Cir.), cert den., 344 U.S. 889 (1952).

Bollman and Swartwout could not be tried in the District and ordered their discharge. Marshall continued by saying, "the crime of treason should not be extended by construction to doubtful cases."

Burr was acquitted 1 September 1807, after an opinion rendered by Chief Justice Marshall in *U.S. v. Burr* that further defined the requirements for proving treason. The Court held that Burr, who had not been present at the assemblage of men on Blennerhassett Island, could be convicted of advising or procuring a levying of war only upon the testimony of two witnesses to his having procured the assemblage, but the operation was covert and such testimony was unobtainable. Marshall's opinion made it extremely difficult to convict someone of levying war against the United States unless the person participated in actual hostilities.

The Burr and Bollman cases prompted the introduction in 1808 of a Senate bill to further define the crime of treason. The debate on that bill, which was rejected, provides insight into the original understanding of the treason clause: its purpose was to guarantee nonviolent political controversy against suppression under the charge of treason or any other criminal charge based on its supposed subversive character, and there was no constitutional authority to evade the restriction by creating new crimes under other names.

Before 1947, most cases that were successfully prosecuted were not federal trials but rather state trials for treason, notably the trials of Thomas Wilson Dorr (1844) and John Brown (1859) on charges of levying war against the states of Rhode Island and Virginia, respectively.

After the Civil War, some wanted to try Southern secessionists for treason, and former the Confederate

president Jefferson Davis was charged with treason in *U.S. v. Jefferson Davis.* The constitutional requirement in Art. III Sec. 2 Cl. 3 that an offender be tried in the state and district where the offense was committed would have meant trying Davis in Virginia, where a conviction was unlikely, so the case was dismissed. Although the United States government regarded the activities of the Confederate States as a levying of war, the president's Amnesty Proclamation of 25 December 1868 pardoned all those who had participated on the Southern side.

Since the Bollman case, the few treason cases that have reached the Supreme Court have been outgrowths of World War II and charged adherence to enemies of the United States and the giving of aid and comfort. In the first of these, *Cramer v. United States,* the issue was whether the "overt act" had to be "openly manifest treason" or whether it was enough, when supported by the proper evidence, that it showed the required treasonable intention. The Court in a five to four opinion by Justice Jackson took the former view, holding that "the two witness principle" barred "imputation of incriminating acts to the accused by circumstantial evidence or by the testimony of a single witness," even though the single witness in question was the accused himself. "Every act, movement, deed, and word of the defendant charged to constitute treason must be supported by the testimony of two witnesses."

The Supreme Court first sustained a conviction of treason in 1947 in *Haupt v. United States.* Here it was held that although the overt acts relied upon to support the charge of treason (defendant's harboring and sheltering in his home his son who was an enemy spy and saboteur, assisting him in purchasing an automobile and in obtaining employment in a defense plant) were all acts that a father would naturally perform for a son, this fact did not necessarily relieve them of the treasonable purpose of giving aid and comfort to the enemy.

In *Kawakita v. United States,* the petitioner was a native-born citizen of the United States and also a national of Japan by reason of Japanese parentage and law. While a minor, he took the oath of allegiance to the United States, went to Japan for a visit on an American passport, and was prevented from returning to this country by the outbreak of war. During World War II he reached his majority in Japan, changed his registration from American to Japanese, showed sympathy with Japan and hostility to the United States, served as a civilian employee of a private corporation producing war materials for Japan, and brutally abused American prisoners of war who were forced to work there. After Japan's surrender, he registered as an American citizen, swore that he was an American citizen and had not done various acts amounting to expatriation, and returned to this country on an American passport. The question whether, on this record, Kawakita had intended to renounce American citizenship was peculiarly one for the jury, said the Court in sustaining conviction, and the jury's verdict that he had not so intended was based on sufficient evidence. An American citizen, it continued, owes allegiance to the United States wherever he may reside, and dual nationality does not alter the situation. This case is notable for extending U.S. criminal jurisdiction to the actions of U.S. civilian citizens abroad, which would have originally been considered unconstitutional.

World War II was followed by the Cold War, which resulted in political prosecutions of several persons for treason and other charges on dubious evidence. The trials of the Axis broadcasters—Douglas Chandler, Robert H. Best, Mildred Gellars as "Axis Sally," Iva Ikuko Toguri d'Aquino as "Tokyo Rose" (later pardoned by President Ford when it was revealed she had been a double agent for the allies)—and the indictment and mental commitment of Ezra Pound, muddied the jurisprudence of the treason clause. Their actions provided no significant aid or comfort to an enemy and were not committed within the territorial jurisdiction of the United States. In *United States v. Rosenberg*, the Court held that in a prosecution under the ESPIONAGE ACT for giving aid to a country (not an enemy), an offense distinct from treason, neither the two-witness rule nor the requirement as to the overt act was applicable. However, no constitutional authority for the Espionage Act itself was proven.

BIBLIOGRAPHY

Chapin, Bradley. *The American Law of Treason: Revolutionary and Early National Origins.* Seattle: University of Washington Press, 1964.

Elliot, Jonathan. *Debates in the Several State Conventions on Adoption of the Federal Constitution.* Philadelphia, 1836, p. 469 (James Wilson).

Hurst, James Willard. *The Law of Treason in the United States: Collected Essays.* Westport, Conn.: Greenwood Publishing, 1971.

Kutler, Stanley I. *The American Inquisition: Justice and Injustice in the Cold War.* New York: Hill and Wang, 1982.

Jon Roland

See also **Arnold's Treason; Civil Rights and Liberties; Davis, Imprisonment and Trial of; Rosenberg Case.**

TREASURY, DEPARTMENT OF THE.

At its inception in 1789 the U.S. Treasury Department quickly came to dominate the executive branch. Alexander Hamilton, the first secretary of the treasury, became a virtual prime minister in the Washington administration. Although the department's role diminished somewhat under future secretaries, it remained the cabinet branch most central to the operation of the federal government.

The administrative reach of the Treasury Department is enormous. Early Congresses mandated that the department create and oversee the U.S. Customs Service, the Internal Revenue Service, the U.S. Mint, the Coast Guard, and the First Bank of the United States, along with other responsibilities. This oversight meant that Secretary Hamilton and his successors guided fiscal policy and influenced foreign trade; collected and disbursed the revenue of government; maintained the stability of the national currency; were responsible for funding the national debt; made the lion's share of federal appointments in the new nation; influenced the development of American manufacturing; and policed America's territorial waters.

The Treasury Department's reach and authority changed over the next two centuries, depending on both the forcefulness and personality of the incumbent secretary and the addition or subtraction of a particular responsibility. But within the cabinet framework of constitutional executive power, the department always remained at the center of domestic policy, foreign and domestic commerce, and national fiscal oversight.

Hamilton's goals were twofold: shift the equilibrium between states' rights and federal authority created by the Constitution to the advantage of national power, and diversify the American economy, making it more balanced by augmenting dependence on agriculture with strong encouragement of elite commercial and manufacturing interests. He achieved both goals and in doing so he set the terms for a national debate that endured into the twentieth century. He funded the national debt, a product of the Revolution, in a way that immediately shifted power away from the states; he created the First Bank of the United States in 1791, both consolidating federal control over fiscal policy and stimulating foreign trade. His 1791 Report on Manufactures established a standard that engaged the federal government on behalf of elite-led industrialization over the next quarter-century and beyond. Using the Treasury Department as the instrument of his will in implementing his vision of a strong diversified economy in a nation led by a landed and moneyed gentry, he also renewed the ideological debate over the very shape of the republic established by the American Revolution.

Nineteenth Century

Even when Hamilton's enemy Thomas Jefferson became president in 1801, and despite his agrarian and democratic rhetoric—echoed faithfully by his secretary of the treasury, Albert Gallatin—Hamiltonian economic reforms, and the ideology behind them, endured. Gallatin served two presidents (Jefferson and James Madison) for fourteen years with great ability. But his department legacy, sometimes in conflict with his own and his administrations' principles, was to implement and solidify Hamilton's vision of America. Gallatin's 1810 Report on Manufactures to Congress, building on earlier submissions, encouraged American industrial development. President James Madison completed his own version of Hamiltonian treasury policies in 1816, when he signed bills chartering the Second Bank of the United States and introducing America's first protective tariff. These measures had the cumulative effect of strengthening the Treasury Department's hand in shaping government policy.

Under Andrew Jackson's strong executive leadership, the Treasury Department was at the forefront in 1830s attempts to reverse Hamiltonian policy. Treasury secretaries Louis McLane and especially Roger Taney carried the banner in assaulting what Jacksonian Democrats saw as entrepreneurial excess and economic elitism. The Second Bank of the United States in particular was seen to drain federal control of fiscal policy, foreign and domestic commerce, and even westward expansion of America's farmers. It was Roger Taney who drafted Jackson's famous and ideologically crucial 1832 message vetoing the recharter of the Second Bank of the United States. And it was the Treasury Department that ultimately inherited the residue of bank power over American fiscal and economic policy when the Independent Treasury was legislated in 1840. It was the Treasury Department that issued the Specie Circular of 1836, granting enormous financial leverage to Jackson's state-oriented "Pet Banks," meant to oversee the financing of a more rapid and democratic agrarian expansion into the west. So the department during the 1830s became the chief executive means of implementing populist, agrarian Jacksonian Democracy.

Civil War. The practical result of Jacksonian policies, however, was to unwittingly open the door to unrestrained free enterprise and industrial expansion. Jacksonian ideology finally undermined the Treasury Department's role in controlling economic development. Until the Civil War restored its centrality, the department shared the fate of the executive branch as a whole as its power to exercise leadership dwindled under the weak presidents who presided through the 1850s. Abraham Lincoln's secretary of the treasury, Salmon P. Chase, was an able administrator and politically a powerful and well-placed Republican Party leader. Facing the crisis of the Civil War, he quickly moved to restore the fiscal health of the department and find the revenue and credit needed to prosecute the war. He used the power of the department to collect the new taxes mandated by Congress; and he restored the authority of a Customs Service fractured by secession. Chase also used Treasury Department guarantees to borrow large amounts of money from private capital sources to finance the war until his tax policies could kick in; and via the National Bank Acts of 1863 and 1864, drafted by him and passed at his urging, he reformed the nation's truncated banking system by, among other things, eliminating competition for borrowed funds by taxing the state banks to the breaking point. The national banks already chartered were forced by the new laws to invest one-third of their capital in government bonds to help finance the war, a provision made possible by the weakening of the state banks and thus the elimination of competition from that source.

But Chase's restoration of the Treasury Department to something near its former eminence was short-lived and did not survive much beyond the Civil War. In the post-war nineteenth century the department shared the fate of a weakened presidency in general, and it mostly failed to exercise much fiscal or economic restraint on the Gilded Age.

Twentieth Century

Progressive Era. Efforts to correct the economic, political, and social excesses of the late nineteenth century also began the process of restoring the Treasury Department to its earlier eminence in directing domestic executive policies. It remained at the center of government for much of the twentieth century. The Federal Reserve Act of 1913, part of the Progressive reform package delivered by Woodrow Wilson, was the most important piece in the puzzle. William McAdoo was secretary of the treasury from 1913 to 1918, and he oversaw both its complicated passage through Congress and its implementation. The fact that he was Wilson's son-in-law did not hurt his leverage. The Federal Reserve Act created a new and original banking system.

While after the 1960s the Federal Reserve Board created by the act achieved a greater degree of autonomy, the board started life under the Progressives as very much the creature of the Treasury Department. Both the secretary and the comptroller of the treasury were voting members of the board, as were six regional directors appointed by the president of the United States. For at least a half-century the secretary of the treasury wielded immense de facto authority over economic policy, interest rates, currency (via federal reserve notes), and commercial paper through his ability to move the Federal Reserve Board. Even later, more conservative administrations fell in line as bankers admitted that the Federal Reserve introduced a financial stability to the nation that it had not seen since the tenure of Alexander Hamilton.

Progressive impetus also achieved final ratification of the Sixteenth Amendment, making constitutional the passage of a graduated federal personal income tax. This opened the door to a resurgence of Treasury Department authority. First introduced in the waning days of Teddy Roosevelt's administration, the amendment was ratified in 1913, in time for the Wilson administration to implement a graduated income tax. While it did not dramatically result in a "soak the rich" policy, it did increase the amount of federal funds overseen by the Treasury Department, and it significantly increased the bureaucracy within the department through the revitalization of the Internal Revenue Service, which dated back to 1791. In general, as federal oversight of economic and social conditions increased in the twentieth century, the Treasury Department's role in that oversight increased as well.

This became evident immediately following the Progressive Era. Both the politically conservative 1920s and the dramatically liberal 1930s made clear the strong resurgence of the Treasury Department at the center of domestic policy. Two powerful secretaries oversaw this comeback: Andrew Mellon and Henry Morgenthau. The ideological divide between the two men was immense.

Secretary from 1921 to 1932, Mellon successfully lobbied Congress to reduce taxes for the wealthy, whether they be individuals or corporations viewed in law as individual entities. In an era of fiscal speculation, Mellon's department gave corporate America free rein in generating stock market–oriented wealth. Mellon espoused the theory of "trickle down economics," which held that wealth at the top would filter down to the lower classes. So the secretary was instrumental in gutting even the modest graduation of the new income tax, and he almost entirely removed the tax burdens the Progressives had imposed on the well-to-do. Mellon's popularity soared until 1929. He was seen as the architect of the theory, best enunciated by President Calvin Coolidge, that "the business of government is business." The secretary of the treasury was the spokesman for the "New Prosperity" of paper profits generated by Wall Street, gains that fueled the Roaring Twenties mentality of easy wealth for the upper-middle classes and new rich. And Mellon was, with President Herbert Hoover, the fall guy on whom the Great Depression of the 1930s was blamed after the stock market collapse of 1929.

The Great Depression and the New Deal. The depression discredited the conservative economic leadership of the 1920s. Under the New Deal, which began with Franklin Delano Roosevelt's election in 1932, Secretary of the Treasury Henry Morgenthau oversaw the strongly liberal policy of government intervention on the side of labor and the small farmer. He was no less an icon of what a modern secretary of the treasury should be for the rural and urban working classes than Mellon was for capitalists and entrepreneurs. Secretary from 1934 to 1945, Morgenthau was one of a cadre of important liberals responsible for the legislation that transformed Mellon's policy of government hands off free enterprise to a dramatically new policy of welfare capitalism, invoking vast government control over the private sector of the economy. Some argue that the New Deal destroyed real capitalism in America; others claim that FDR and his administration saved capitalism from failing completely. However one reads the record, the Treasury Department was at the center of New Deal domestic policy.

In drafting most depression-era legislation, Morgenthau was secondary to New Dealers like FDR guru Harry Hopkins, Labor Secretary Frances Perkins, and Brain Truster Raymond Moley, but the Treasury Department was central to its revolutionary implementation. And in a few areas, the treasury did find legislative solutions as well. In 1935, for example, Morgenthau came up with the plan to find the vast funding needed to secure passage of the Social Security Act. He convinced the president to levy a payroll tax to build up the trust fund that made Social Security a self-financed old-age benefit independent of congressional budgeting. Initially, he argued in the midst of vast unemployment, financing would come

from taxes only on those working, a de facto elite in the 1930s. The secretary was a key player too in shaping legislation for a graduated corporate income tax that included those holding companies far removed legally from their profitable corporate subsidiaries.

When recovery foundered in 1937, Morgenthau was instrumental in convincing FDR to move more conservatively in the economic sector, advice that FDR heeded in launching what historians now call "the second New Deal." There followed a renewed increase in deficit spending as the administration once again pumped money into public spending designed to increase employment. The Treasury Department was at the center of this "second New Deal," as it had been at the center of the first. The radical reforms of the first New Deal were consolidated, insuring that "welfare capitalism" (conservatives were already calling it the welfare state) would remain a permanent part of twentieth- century economic and social policy.

For twelve critical years the treasury remained front and center in guiding domestic policy. Even post–World War II Republican secretaries were unwilling (or unable) to undo New Deal economic and social reform. In the years between the New Deal and Lyndon Johnson's Great Society newly created cabinet-level departments, especially Health, Education, and Welfare and Housing and Urban Development, siphoned off some of the near monopoly the treasury had exercised over domestic affairs. In the 1980s Ronald Reagan's conservative policies cut taxes and returned to the massive deficit spending that marked the New Deal. This effort thrust the treasury once more into the center of executive branch oversight; the arrival of Robert Rubin, secretary of the treasury beginning in 1993 during Bill Clinton's administration, cemented the treasury's central role in domestic policy yet again.

Balanced budgets and free trade. Rubin first pushed successfully to balance the budget, largely by means of more disciplined spending, trimming back federal bureaucracy, and tax reform that increased revenue by imposing more taxes on the well-to-do and corporate America. These were openly acknowledged to implement Rubin's vision. The Treasury Department then moved to restore American and global economic health by moving America rapidly toward free trade through NAFTA (North American Free Trade Agreement); expansion of most-favored-nation status for China; and closer cooperation with the European Union as it moved toward full economic integration. The Treasury Department, working with the Federal Reserve (still nominally under its jurisdiction), oversaw a long period of prosperity lasting into the new millennium. It did this while both keeping inflation in check and balancing the budget. Like a few earlier secretaries, Rubin, who served through nearly two terms under Bill Clinton, won enormous public confidence in personal terms. Thus his support and that of his department translated into bipartisan popular and congressional support for any policies they espoused. Rapidly rising

197

stock markets, dynamic expansion of stock investments by the public at large, growing employment opportunities, massive gains in the new high-tech economy and low inflation all contributed to sustaining perhaps the longest period of uninterrupted prosperity in the nation's history.

One major result of America's domination of a new global economy was to elevate the Treasury Department to virtually the same supreme driving force in government in the 1990s that it had enjoyed two centuries earlier under the aegis of Alexander Hamilton.

BIBLIOGRAPHY

Elkins, Stanley M., and Eric McKitrick. *The Age of Federalism.* New York: Oxford University Press, 1993.

Kennedy, David M. *Freedom from Fear: The American People in Depression and War, 1929–1945.* New York: Oxford University Press, 1999.

Link, Arthur. *Woodrow Wilson and the Progressive Era, 1910–1917.* New York: Harper, 1954.

Sellers, Charles G. *The Market Revolution: Jacksonian America, 1815–1846.* New York: Oxford University Press, 1991.

Walston, Mark. *The Department of the Treasury.* New York: Chelsea House, 1989.

Carl E. Prince

See also **Bank of the United States; Coast Guard, U.S. ; Crédit Mobilier of America; Customs Service, U.S.; Debts, Revolutionary War; Gilded Age; Granger Movement; Great Society; Railroads; Tariff.**

TREATIES, COMMERCIAL. From its earliest years, the United States' foreign policy has focused as much on commercial interests as on all other concerns (including military) combined. This focus comes from what Americans and their government have perceived as their needs and from the way America views its role in international affairs. The Revolution itself was motivated in part by English restrictions on foreign trade by the American colonies. One of the United States' very first treaties was the Treaty of Amity and Commerce of 1778, which opened American ports and markets to French traders and opened French ports and markets to Americans. France's colonial markets had great value to American merchants as sources of raw materials to manufacture into goods for sale, not only in America but overseas. This treaty led to navigation treaties with several European powers, eventually opening markets in the Far East that proved very profitable in the late 1700s and early 1800s.

There was already a global economy, and commercial treaties were becoming highly complicated agreements among several nations at once, often with each new treaty requiring adjustments to old ones. Sometimes the State Department or the president concluded treaties known as executive agreements. The Senate occasionally challenged these executive agreements, arguing that the Constitution required formal Senate confirmation of commercial trea-

ties; these were called formal accords. This vagueness between executive agreements and formal accords often made commercial treaty negotiations difficult because foreign countries could not tell whether years of hard negotiations with the president or State Department would be accepted by the Senate. In 1936, *United States v. Curtis-Wright Export Corporation,* the Supreme Court tried to clarify the distinctions between executive agreements and formal accords and affirmed that the president had the authority to make commercial treaties without always needing the Senate's approval. This decision was controversial, especially when the United States gave "most-favored-nation" status to communist Hungary in 1978 and to communist China annually from the late 1980s through the early 2000s.

During the 1800s, the creation of commercial treaties was haphazard because of America's conflicting impulses to isolate itself from foreign affairs and to create new markets for its goods. Americans also believed that free trade was a liberating force that would bring political freedom and would raise the standard of living for America's trading partners. For example, when Admiral Matthew Perry sailed warships to Japan to pressure Japan into making a commercial treaty with the United States, America regarded it as doing the Japanese people a good turn by opening their country to benefits of a modern economy.

By the 1920s it was clear that having a trading agreement with the United States was good for a country; nations as disparate as Japan and Argentina were creating wealth for themselves by selling consumer goods to Americans. By 1923 the principle of most-favored-nation status became a permanent part of American foreign policy: It clarified the trading rights of American commercial partners, making it easier to negotiate economic ventures with American companies. In the second half of the twentieth century, the United States participated in four sweeping commercial agreements: the World Bank, the World Monetary Fund (WMF), the General Agreement on Tariffs and Trade (GATT), and the North American Free Trade Agreement (NAFTA). Americans believed that it was in everybody's best interest to improve the economies of impoverished nations. The World Bank, to which the United States was by far the major contributor, was intended to make long-term loans to build private industries, and the World Monetary Fund, with the United States again the major contributor, was created to loan governments money to stabilize their economies and to help them promote economic growth. The WMF became very controversial in the 1990s, because some people saw it as creating a global economy (they were about three hundred years too late) that would lead to international corporations oppressing the peoples of the world.

GATT was intended to eliminate the trade barriers presented by tariffs. It recognized that economies can change, and it provided a mechanism for changing the treaty to meet changing times called the "round" of negotiations. The first round took place in Geneva in 1947 and focused on coordinating tariffs to help nations devastated by World War II. A single round could last for years, and no wonder: the first round alone covered more than 45,000 trade agreements. GATT is probably the supreme achievement of twentieth-century commercial treaties, generating more wealth for its member nations through free trade than any other treaty America was party to.

NAFTA was a response to creation of the European Union and efforts among Southeast Asian countries to form a trading block. By eliminating trade barriers among its members, the European Union created a powerful economic machine in which member nations could coordinate and finance large industrial enterprises and challenge America for world dominance in foreign trade. The United States and Canada already had a free trade agreement that allowed shipping across their borders almost without impediment. Negotiated mainly during the administration of George Bush the elder (1989–1993), NAFTA sought to include all of North America in a single economic engine that would be unmatched in its resources. Mexico readily participated in negotiations with Canada and the United States, but the nations of Central America, most of which were in social upheaval, did not, although President Bush envisioned that both Central America and South America would be included in the future. NAFTA required adjustments to GATT, because it affected almost every trading partner's treaties with the United States. It was to be a formal accord, requiring the Senate's consent, and passage was a tricky business in 1993–1994; the new president, Bill Clinton, had said he opposed NAFTA during his campaign. This brought into play an interesting characteristic of American treaty negotiations: the promise to treaty partners that subsequent presidential administrations will honor agreements made by previous ones. This consistency has been upheld by presidents since Thomas Jefferson, and President Clinton persuaded the Senate to approve NAFTA.

Kirk H. Beetz

BIBLIOGRAPHY

Appleton, Barry. *Navigating NAFTA: A Concise User's Guide to the North American Free Trade Agreement.* Rochester, N.Y.: Lawyer's Cooperative Publishing, 1994.

MacArthur, John R. *The Selling of "Free Trade": NAFTA, Washington, and the Subversion of American Democracy.* New York: Hill and Wang, 2000.

Morrison, Ann V. "GATT's Seven Rounds of Trade Talks Span More than Thirty Years." *Business America* 9 (7 July 1986): 8–10.

Wilson, Robert R. *United States Commercial Treaties and International Law.* New Orleans, La.: Hauser Press, 1960.

TREATIES WITH FOREIGN NATIONS. In international usage the term "treaty" has the generic sense of "international agreement." Rights and obligations, or status, arise under international law irrespective of the form or designation of an agreement. In constitutional usage, however, treaties are sometimes distinguished from less formal agreements by special requirements for negotiation or ratification, limitations of subject matter, or distinctive effects in domestic law.

The U.S. Constitution distinguishes treaties from other agreements and compacts in three principal ways. First, only the federal government can conclude a "Treaty, Alliance, or Confederation." States can make an "Agreement or Compact" with other states or with foreign powers but only with consent of the Congress (Article I, section 10).

Second, treaties are negotiated and ratified by the president, but he or she must obtain the advice and consent of the Senate, two-thirds of the senators present concurring (Article II, section 2, clause 2). President George Washington understood this provision to include Senate advice during both treaty negotiation and ratification. He attempted to consult with the Senate at an executive council concerning a proposed Indian treaty, but after a frustrating experience he declared that he "would be damned" if he ever did that again. Washington's successors sought the advice and consent of the Senate only after treaty negotiations, during the period of ratification.

Third, the Constitution distinguishes international treaties from "agreements and compacts" by making treaties part of the supreme law of the land that judges in every state are bound to enforce (Article VI, clause 2). The U.S. Supreme Court has on occasion asserted that it may nullify unconstitutional treaties, but it has never done so. International treaties are generally obligatory after signature and before formal ratification. In the United States, however, this is only true when a treaty is designated as "self-executing." Otherwise, under U.S. law, treaties are sent to Congress for legislative ratification and implementation.

Early American Treaties

After declaring independence from Great Britain in 1776, the United States concluded fifteen treaties before the ratification of the U.S. Constitution in 1789. These early treaties reflected the problems of political decentralization at the time. Commissioners appointed largely ad hoc by the Continental Congress negotiated the treaties and the agreements were subject to a very uncertain ratification process. Between 1776 and 1781 the assent of all states voting was required for treaty approval, with nine states constituting a quorum. After the creation of the Articles of Confederation in 1781, nine of the thirteen states had to approve each treaty.

These provisions posed many difficulties for America's nascent diplomats, operating without an established foreign service or a reliable framework of legislative support. At critical moments, the Continental Congress often skirted its stated rules to obtain desired treaty ratification. The Treaty of Alliance with France in 1778—a vitally important part of America's revolutionary struggle against Great Britain—obtained congressional ratification with a vote recorded as unanimous. Yet the representatives of two states were certainly absent from the vote. Two more states may also have failed to ratify the treaty. Proponents of the alliance with France disguised the absence of required consent for the treaty by depicting a vote of eight states, rather than the necessary nine, as a unanimous congressional voice.

Often employing similar procedures, the Continental Congress ratified the Treaty of Paris in 1783, which ended the war with Great Britain on very favorable terms for Americans. London acknowledged American independence and conceded the new nation free navigation of the Mississippi River, the key inland estuary for north-south commerce and communication. Americans also concluded a series of commercial treaties around this same time with the Netherlands (1782), Sweden (1783), Prussia (1785), and Morocco (1786). In 1788 the United States concluded a formal consular convention with France, assuring high diplomatic standing for American representatives in Paris.

After 1789, treaty making under the U.S. Constitution focused upon assuring American economic independence, freedom from entanglement in the Napoleonic Wars that convulsed the European continent, and territorial expansion in North America. In 1794 John Jay negotiated a treaty with Great Britain—Jay's Treaty—that sought to reduce growing tensions between the Americans and their former colonial masters. U.S. citizens objected to British restrictions on American trade with London's adversaries, especially France, and they found the British impressment of captured American sailors into British military service deeply offensive. Jay's Treaty did not prohibit London's continued attacks on American shipping, but it did secure the final withdrawal of British troops from a string of occupied western forts around the Great Lakes. The treaty also opened U.S. trade with British-controlled India and the West Indies. Many Americans, including then–Secretary of State Thomas Jefferson, opposed the Jay Treaty as too deferential to Britain. They demanded a stronger assertion of American neutral shipping rights. Recognizing that Jay had done the best he could from a position of U.S. weakness, President Washington personally pushed the treaty through the Senate, barely gaining ratification. The debate about the Jay Treaty began a long history of domestic controversy over the necessary and acceptable compromises required by the vagaries of international politics. Jay's "realism" was pragmatic, but it contradicted many of America's stated ideals.

Thomas Pinckney followed Jay's work by negotiating a treaty with Spain in 1795 known as Pinckney's Treaty. Under this agreement Spain granted the United States access to the Mississippi River—especially the port of New Orleans, under Spanish control—and the territories around the estuary. The Spanish also promised to help curb Indian attacks on American settlements. In return, the United States promised to respect Spanish holdings in North America. The Pinckney Treaty offered the United States unprecedented access to western and southern territories and it consequently avoided the controversies surrounding the Jay Treaty. The Senate ratified the Pinckney Treaty with minimal debate.

The Jay and Pinckney Treaties set precedents for American diplomatic efforts in the early republic. In each case a group of elite American representatives negotiated with their foreign counterparts in search of an agreement that would assure stability in European-American relations and U.S. domination on the North American continent. President Thomas Jefferson's treaty with Napoleon Bonaparte in 1803 accomplished both ends. Despite his revulsion at the despotism of the French emperor, Jefferson purchased the vast Louisiana Territory from Napoleon at the cost of $15 million. The new lands—828,000 square miles—provided room for America to grow and expand westward relatively free from the warfare that convulsed Europe at the time. Jefferson's distrust of a strong central government did not stop him from concluding a treaty that doubled the size of the United States and asserted a presidential right to transform the shape of the country.

The Treaty of Ghent, signed in 1814 at the conclusion of America's ill-considered War of 1812 with Great Britain, acknowledged U.S. predominance in North America. It also marked the end of Anglo-American hostilities. The so-called "special relationship" between leaders in Washington and London—based on general amity, trust, and cooperation—began in very nascent form with the signing of this treaty. Great Britain continued to assert a right of impressment over American shipping, but after 1814 London rarely exercised this prerogative. The United States, in return, pledged not to attack British-controlled Canada, as it had during its struggle for independence and during the War of 1812.

Treaties negotiated by the U.S. government between 1814 and 1848, including the Webster-Ashburton Treaty of 1842 and the Oregon Boundary Treaty of 1846, secured further expansion of American territorial holdings without jeopardizing British claims in Canada. The Treaty of Guadalupe-Hidalgo, signed at the conclusion of the Mexican-American War in 1848, provided the United States with possession of present-day California, Arizona, Nevada, and Utah, as well as parts of New Mexico, Colorado, and South Dakota. In return the administration of President James K. Polk paid Mexico a paltry $15 million and promised not to annex any further Mexican territory, despite contrary pressures from many American citizens.

By the middle of the nineteenth century America had, through warfare and treaty making, established itself as a colossal land power stretching from the Atlantic to the Pacific Ocean. The nation's asserted Manifest Destiny to dominate the continent reflected racial, religious, and cultural assumptions of American superiority that found their way into the treaties of the period. Time and again, American leaders asserted their right to expand. Time and again, they laid claim to territories they had never before controlled. The non-Americans—Indians, Mexicans, and others—who resided on many of the new U.S. territories received little voice in the treaties negotiated during this period.

Treaties and American Overseas Expansion

After the conclusion of the Civil War in 1865, U.S. treaties focused on expanding American economic, political, and cultural interests outside of North America. In 1867 Secretary of State William Henry Seward secured a treaty with Russia, which agreed to sell the territory of Alaska to the United States for $7.2 million. Seward foresaw that this northern "icebox" would provide important natural resources and help extend American economic interests across the Pacific Ocean. The U.S. Senate almost rejected this treaty, as it rejected many of Seward's other expansionist schemes. Nonetheless, the Alaska treaty created a precedent for American overseas expansion that would slowly reach its fruition around the end of the nineteenth century.

Following a few short months of warfare with the overextended and declining Spanish Empire, at the end of 1898 the United States secured the Treaty of Paris with Madrid's representatives. By the terms of this treaty, Spain vacated its colony in Cuba, acknowledging America's sphere of influence in the area. The Spanish also ceded Puerto Rico, Guam, and the Philippine archipelago to the United States. With Senate approval in early 1899, these islands became America's first extended foreign colonies. The provisions for American occupation of the Philippines allowed President William McKinley to wage forty-one months of brutal ground warfare against a native Filipino resistance. By 1902, when the American counter-insurgency forces asserted nearly complete control over the archipelago, as many as twenty-thousand Filipino rebels had died opposing American colonialism. Some 4,200 Americans also perished in this battle to enforce U.S. occupation under the terms of the Treaty of Paris. Many Americans, the so-called anti-imperialists, opposed U.S. military activities in the Philippines, but President McKinley acted with the legitimacy provided by the treaty with Spain.

Following the Panamanian Revolution of 1903, the administration of President Theodore Roosevelt used a similar tact. Secretary of State John Hay negotiated the Hay-Bunau–Varilla Treaty with the newly created state of Panama in the same year. The treaty granted the United States the right to construct and operate an isthmian canal linking the Caribbean Sea with the Pacific Ocean. When completed in 1914, the fifty-one-mile canal allowed ships to travel between the Atlantic and Pacific Oceans, saving the thousands of miles required to circumnavigate South America before the existence of this passage. The new transport route greatly facilitated trade between the productive eastern seaboard of the United States and the large markets of Asia. The Hay-Bunau–Varilla Treaty allowed for American construction of and control over the Panama Canal. After many subsequent treaty revisions—the most significant in 1977—the Panamanian government attained sovereignty over the canal zone in 2000.

The treaties negotiated by the United States with Russia, Spain, and Panama after the Civil War indicated that American interests had extended far beyond the North American continent and its established trading routes with Europe. An industrializing nation that had reached the end of its western frontier looked overseas for new markets and strategic possessions. American foreign expansion occurred primarily through treaties negotiated with declining empires (Spain), established states seeking new allies (Russia), and new regimes subject to foreign pressure (Panama). U.S. imperialism in the late nineteenth and early twentieth centuries was relatively costless for Americans because their leaders attained so much at the negotiating table.

Multilateral Treaties and a Liberal International Order

In the aftermath of World War I, many Americans sought new mechanisms for building international cooperation and averting future military conflicts. President Woodrow Wilson called for a new kind of diplomacy that rejected the competing alliances, autocracies, and arms races of old. Instead, he argued that only what he called a League of Nations could promise free trade, collective security, and long-term international stability. America had entered World War I to "make the world safe for democracy," according to Wilson, and he sought a peace treaty at the close of hostilities that carried this vision to fruition.

At the Paris Peace Conference in 1919 Wilson pressured his allied counterparts—particularly Georges Clemenceau of France, Vittorio Orlando of Italy, and David Lloyd George of Great Britain—to formulate a treaty that emphasized European reconstruction and cooperation rather than war revenge. The American president succeeded only in part, but he did manage to include a covenant creating a League of Nations in the final treaty authored largely by France, Italy, Great Britain, and the United States. On 28 June 1919 the defeated leaders of Germany signed the treaty at the Chateau de Versailles outside Paris, the site of more than five months of heated negotiations on the text of what became known as the Versailles Treaty.

In the next year, rancorous Senate debate resulted in the rejection of the Versailles Treaty by the United States. Despite President Wilson's tireless public speeches on behalf of the treaty, isolationists, led by Republican senator Henry Cabot Lodge, managed to depict Wilson's League of Nations as a harmful encumbrance that would embroil Americans in additional overseas difficulties. Lodge and his colleagues added numerous reservations to the treaty that would restrict American participation in the League.

201

On 19 March 1920 these reservations and the Versailles Treaty itself failed to receive the necessary two-thirds majority in the Senate. An odd collection of Republican isolationists and Democratic supporters of Wilson's original proposal had prohibited American participation in a nascent liberal international order.

Through the 1920s and 1930s this isolationist sentiment spurned official U.S. alliance with foreign powers. Washington did, however, enter into a series of multilateral treaties aimed at naval disarmament (the Washington Treaty of 1921 and the London Treaty of 1930) and outlawing war (the Kellogg-Briand Pact of 1928). These treaties had few enforcement mechanisms, but they sought to guarantee a peaceful and open climate for American businesses that were then expanding their activities overseas.

World War II illustrated the shortcomings in these platitudinous treaties. When Germany, Italy, and Japan began to pursue militaristic policies in the early 1930s, the international community lacked the legal mechanisms and political will to react with necessary force. Without American participation, the League of Nations was a very weak reed. Without forceful penalties for treaty violations, the fascist powers were not deterred from attacking neighboring states.

During the course of World War II, many Americans vowed to correct the mistakes of the past. President Franklin Roosevelt made it clear that the war would only end with the unconditional surrender of the fascist powers and the creation of a new series of international treaties that guaranteed, with force, the kind of liberal international order envisioned by Wilson. In particular, Roosevelt called for a United Nations that would include a Security Council of the great powers, capable of employing force for collective security.

The United Nations Charter, signed in San Francisco on 26 June 1945, made this vision into a reality. In contrast to its rejection of the League of Nations in 1920, on 28 July 1945 the U.S. Senate approved the United Nations Charter by a vote of 89 to 2. A series of arrangements for multilateral economic cooperation came to fruition around this same time. The Bretton Woods agreements of 1944 stand out because they created the International Bank for Reconstruction and Development (the World Bank) and the International Monetary Fund (IMF), both designed to regulate and support capitalist wealth creation across the globe. At the center of these new international institutions, the United States took on an unprecedented role as the primary financier for global economic exchanges. Unlike the UN Charter, the groundbreaking Bretton Woods agreements were not handled as treaties, but rather as economic legislation, in the U.S. House of Representatives and Senate. At the time, international economics did not attract the same high political attention as issues of military security.

Cold War hostilities between the United States and the Soviet Union distorted American multilateralism. After 1945 U.S. treaties focused on building collective security alliances with states imperiled by communist infiltration and possible invasion. The North Atlantic Treaty Organization (NATO), created in 1949, provided for mutual security and close military cooperation among Western Europe, Canada, and the United States. Each government pledged that it would regard an attack on one member as an attack on all. By approving NATO the Senate affirmed a new bipartisan anticommunist consensus in the United States. In place of prior isolationist urgings, American politicians firmly committed themselves to the containment of communism abroad through extensive and long-term U.S. military and economic intervention. The creation of NATO marked the end of American isolationism by treaty.

In the 1950s the United States extended the NATO precedent to other areas of the world. In 1954 it joined Great Britain, France, Australia, New Zealand, the Philippines, Thailand, and Pakistan in the creation of the Southeast Asia Treaty Organization (SEATO). America also concluded a mutual defense treaty with the Guomindang government of Taiwan in late 1954. SEATO and the Taiwan treaty pledged their signatories to cooperate for mutual defense against communist threats. The treaties also obligated the governments to promote free markets and democracy.

SEATO commitments contributed to increasing American intervention in Southeast Asia after 1954. This was particularly true in Indochina, where the United States became the chief sponsor of an anticommunist South Vietnamese government. Belligerent autocrats in South Vietnam—as well as in Taiwan and Pakistan—used their nations' treaties with the United States to call upon American military support for anticommunist warfare rather than domestic development and democratization. The failure of U.S. military activities in Vietnam between 1965 and 1975 proved that SEATO and other treaties had misdirected American policies.

In the aftermath of the Vietnam War, the United States shied away from new treaties of defensive alliance. Instead, American officials focused on arms control in their attempts to reduce tensions with the Soviet Union. In 1972 the two superpowers signed the Strategic Arms Limitation Treaty (SALT I), which for the first time limited the future construction of nuclear weapons delivery systems. It also included an Anti-Ballistic Missile (ABM) Treaty that prohibited the two governments from building more than two missile defense sites. In 1974 they reduced this limit to one missile defense site for each nation.

SALT II, signed in 1979, pledged the two superpowers to additional limits on nuclear weapons delivery systems. President James Earl Carter withdrew the treaty from Senate consideration after the Soviet invasion of Afghanistan in December 1979, but his successor, Ronald Reagan, voluntarily followed through on the SALT II limitations. Despite Reagan's assertion that the Soviet Union was an "evil empire," he pressed forward with arms control negotiations. The world was too dangerous to do otherwise and the treaties of the 1970s had attracted strong support among citizens, intellectuals, and policymakers.

Reagan negotiated the most far-reaching arms control treaties of any American president. The Intermediate Nuclear Forces Treaty (INF) of 1988 eliminated an entire group of weapons for the first time: the intermediate and short-range nuclear missiles stationed by both superpowers in Europe. In 1991 Reagan's successor, George H. W. Bush, concluded negotiations for the Strategic Arms Reduction Treaty (START I) that reduced both American and Russian nuclear arsenals by 30 percent. These treaties contributed to the peaceful end of the Cold War.

In the post–Cold War world, where America's vision of a liberal international order appears triumphant, U.S. leaders have proven unsure about future treaty negotiations. Presidents William Jefferson Clinton and George W. Bush have pursued policies embracing both American unilateralism and international cooperation. President Bush, for example, withdrew from the ABM Treaty in 2001 while he was managing an international coalition of states fighting terrorist influences in Afghanistan and other areas. American presidents often prefer to act without the restrictions and senatorial oversight of treaty negotiations. This is likely to remain true in the twenty-first century, but future leaders will surely rely on treaties to affirm serious and long-standing political, military, and economic commitments abroad.

BIBLIOGRAPHY

Bundy, McGeorge. *Danger and Survival: Choices about the Bomb in the First Fifty Years.* New York: Random House, 1988.

Cooper, John Milton, Jr. *Breaking the Heart of the World: Woodrow Wilson and the Fight for the League of Nations.* New York: Cambridge University Press, 2001.

Dallek, Robert. *Franklin D. Roosevelt and American Foreign Policy, 1932–1945.* New York: Oxford University Press, 1979.

Gaddis, John Lewis. *Strategies of Containment: A Critical Appraisal of Postwar American National Security Policy.* New York: Oxford University Press, 1982.

Garthoff, Raymond L. *Détente and Confrontation: American-Soviet Relations from Nixon to Reagan.* Rev. ed. Washington, D.C.: Brookings Institution, 1994.

———. *The Great Transition: American-Soviet Relations and the End of the Cold War.* Washington D.C.: Brookings Institution, 1994.

LaFeber, Walter. *The American Search for Opportunity, 1865–1913.* New York: Cambridge University Press, 1993.

McMahon, Robert J. *The Limits of Empire: The United States and Southeast Asia since World War II.* New York: Columbia University Press, 1999.

Perkins, Bradford. *The Creation of a Republican Empire, 1776–1865.* New York: Cambridge University Press, 1993.

C. H. McLaughlin
Jeremi Suri

See also **Bretton Woods Conference; Cold War; Ghent, Treaty of; Guadalupe Hidalgo, Treaty of; Internationalism; Jay's Treaty; Louisiana Purchase; Manifest Destiny; North Atlantic Treaty Organization; Paris, Treaty of (1783); Paris, Treaty of (1898); Pinckney's Treaty; Southeast Asia Treaty Organization; Strategic Arms Limitation Talks; United Nations; Versailles, Treaty of.**

TREATIES WITH INDIANS. *See* **Indian Treaties.**

TREATIES, NEGOTIATION AND RATIFICATION OF. A treaty is a formal agreement signed by one or more countries. Article II, Section 2, of the Constitution gives the president the "Power, by and with the Advice and consent of the Senate, to make Treaties, provided two thirds of the Senators present concur." Although the drafters of the Constitution intended for the president and the Senate to collaborate in negotiating and ratifying treaties, throughout U.S. history, the responsibility for treaty making has rested with the chief executive.

In the United States, only the federal government can make treaties with other nations. Article I, Section 10, of the Constitution provides that "No State shall enter into any Treaty, alliance, or Confederation" nor "without the Consent of Congress . . . enter into any Agreement or Compact with another state, or with a foreign power."

There are five stages in arriving at a treaty. In the first stage, the president prepares instructions about the terms of the treaty. The president assigns a representative to negotiate the agreement with counterparts from the other nation or nations and president then signs the draft of the treaty. In the second stage, the president submits the treaty to the Senate for its consideration. The Senate can consent to the treaty; reject it, block it by tabling it; or consent with reservations. If the Senate consents, the president proceeds to the third stage, known as ratification. In the fourth stage, the president exchanges ratifications with the co-signing country. The U.S. Department of State and American diplomats abroad typically handle this step. In the fifth and final stage, the president proclaims the treaty the law of the land.

If the Senate refuses to consent to the treaty, the process is halted and the president cannot ratify the agreement. Or, if the Senate attaches reservations or amendments to the treaty, the president may accept or reject them. Congress did not change seventy-two percent of treaties until 1945. Since World War II, however, presidents have evaded Senate oversight of treaty making by entering into what are called "executive agreements" with foreign nations. These agreements do not have the force of law but are generally binding on the courts while they are in effect, which is the term in office of the president who made them.

Executive agreements have varied widely in importance. Some have concerned inconsequential matters, such as adjusting the claim of an individual citizen. Or they have involved routine diplomacy, such as recognizing a government.

However, many of America's most significant international accords have been in the form of executive agreements. Examples are the Open Door Notes (1899) concerning American trade in China, the exchange of American destroyers for access to British military bases (1940), and the Yalta and Potsdam agreements after World War II.

Since World War II, the number of executive agreements has far exceeded the number of treaties. From time to time, Congress has tried to limit the President's ability to enter into such agreements. Sen. John W. Bricker of Ohio launched the most ambitious attempt to curtail what he perceived as a usurpation of power by the executive branch. In 1953, Bricker proposed a constitutional amendment that would give Congress the power to "regulate all Executive and other agreements with any foreign power or international organization." The amendment failed in the Senate by one vote in February 1954 and was never passed.

Trade and Territory

For much of American history, U.S. treaty making has primarily involved two areas of interest: the promotion of overseas business and the acquisition of land across North America.

During the early decades of the Republic, American leaders sought trade and territory while dealing with the unfinished business of the revolutionary war. The most important treaties signed by the United States in the eighteenth century were Jay's Treaty (1794) and the Pinckney Treaty (1795), which established peaceful relations with Britain and Spain.

Despite the formal end to warfare between the United States and England (Treaty of Paris, 1783), relations between the revolutionary upstart and the Mother Country remained poor. In 1794, President Washington appointed John Jay to negotiate a settlement of American and British grievances to avert another war. Under the terms of the Jay Treaty, signed on 19 November 1794, the central source of friction was removed when Britain agreed to cede control of military forts on the northwestern frontier to the United States. The United States agreed to grant England most-favored-nation trading status.

Under the Pinckney Treaty with Spain, the border separating the United States and Spanish Florida was established at the thirty-first parallel. The United States also gained vital trading rights along the Mississippi River in addition to the right of deposit at the port of New Orleans.

By virtue of these two treaties, the United States could reasonably expect to extend its grasp as far west as the Mississippi and south to include Florida. During the next half century, those territorial aims were exceeded as

a result of the Louisiana Purchase (1803) and later annexation treaties.

In what is considered one of history's greatest land deals, the Louisiana Purchase, President Thomas Jefferson spent $15 million to buy 828,000 square miles of North American land from Napoleon Bonaparte, the French emperor. With the purchase, the United States doubled in size and extended its domain west to the Rocky Mountains, north to Canada, and south to the Gulf of Mexico. The deal was signed on 30 April 1803. President James Monroe's secretary of state, John Quincy Adams, subsequently obtained Florida from Spain in the Adams-Onis Treaty signed on 22 February 1819.

In 1844, President John Tyler signed a treaty with the leaders of the breakaway Republic of Texas to bring that former Mexican territory into the Union. As a result of anti-slavery opposition in the Senate, the treaty was rejected. However, Tyler was able to obtain Texas the following year when Congress approved the annexation through a joint resolution. Because Mexico did not accept the loss of Texas, war broke out between the neighboring countries. These hostilities were ended with the treaty of Guadalupe Hidalgo (2 February 1848), which not only secured the American claim to Texas but added California and New Mexico to the United States.

With the ratification of the Gadsden Purchase Treaty with Mexico in 1854, America gained the southernmost areas of Arizona and New Mexico. Secretary of State William Seward's Alaska Purchase Treaty with Russia in 1867 was the United States' last major land deal.

In the years preceding the Civil War, the United States expanded its overseas trade via treaties with England, Russia, Siam, China, Hawaii, and Japan. To increase business in Latin America, U.S. leaders signed a series of accords establishing the right to trade across the strategic Isthmus of Panama and eventually build a canal in one of the Central American countries.

Overseas Expansion and International Agreements

At the end of the nineteenth century, the United States became one of the world's great powers by virtue of its growing overseas commerce. Having become a great power, the United States began acting more like one. The naval fleet was vastly enlarged, and efforts were taken to obtain territory abroad. Many of the treaties signed by the U.S. during this period resulted from this new imperialism. Some of these treaties were hotly debated in the Senate, reflecting the limits to popular support for the notion of American colonial expansion.

In the peace treaty signed by the United States and Spain after the 1898 war, the U.S. acquired the Philippines and Puerto Rico. The treaty was highly controversial. Although it received Senate approval, it barely earned the necessary two-thirds majority.

Prior to World War I, the United States was most assertive in its traditional sphere of influence in Central and South America. President Theodore Roosevelt sought to oust British influence from the region, and he boldly proclaimed the American right to intervene with military force to bring order to Latin America.

Under the Hay-Pauncefote Treaty (5 February 1900), the U.S. obtained from Britain exclusive rights to operate a future canal in Panama, then under the control of Colombia. After instigating a rebellion in Panama, leading to its independence from Colombia, the U.S. was able to sign the Hay-Bunau-Varilla Treaty (18 November 1903), establishing complete American sovereignty over the Canal Zone and opening the door to construction of the canal.

Also, at the end of the eighteenth century, the U.S. began involvement in international conferences producing multilateral treaties. For example, in 1890, the U.S. signed an international agreement calling for suppression of the slave trade in Africa, which the Senate ratified in 1892. After the First and Second International Peace Conferences at The Hague, the U.S signed an accord to participate in the Permanent Court of Arbitration. Still wary of involvement in Old World politics, the Senate approved The Hague treaty with the reservation that the U.S. would not officially depart from its non-interventionist policy toward Europe.

Versailles Treaty and the Return to Isolationism

The most fiercely debated treaty of the twentieth century was the Versailles Treaty, which settled the outstanding issues of World War I. President Wilson had raised the stakes for passage incredibly high. He desperately wanted to see creation of the world's first collective security organization, the League of Nations, which was the centerpiece of the treaty.

Wilson led the American team that traveled to France in January 1919 to negotiate the treaty. The president personally commanded the intense lobbying effort he hoped would ensure Senate passage of the accord. However, too many Republican Senators opposed the League on grounds that it posed a threat to American autonomy over foreign affairs. Wilson refused to compromise and the Senate rejected the treaty.

The demise of the League ushered in a return to isolationism in the United States. The treaties the U.S. entered into in the 1920s and 1930s reflected the nation's desire to retreat from Europe's troubles. Most notable was American participation in the Pact of Paris, also known as the Kellogg-Briand Pact (27 August 1928), which called on the United States and sixty-two other co-signing countries to renounce war as an "instrument of national policy."

Postwar Internationalism and Collective Security

After World War II, the United States spearheaded the drive to create a new collective security organization. In 1945, the U.S. became the first nation to sign the U.N. charter. Unlike consideration of the League of Nations, the Senate eagerly approved American participation. There were no longer any questions raised about the United States' ability to safeguard its own interests while participating in the world body. The U.S., as a permanent member of the U.N. Security Council, would have veto power over any decisions rendered by the organization.

Europe and vast parts of Asia were utterly devastated after the war, and the United States and the Soviet Union emerged as the two most powerful nations in the world. The rivalry between the superpowers prompted the United States to break with its 150-year-old tradition of avoiding "entangling" alliances. Due to fears about the spread of communism, for the first time in American history, the United States joined a series of peacetime military alliances. These alliances were arranged through multilateral treaties.

The 1949 ratification of the Atlantic Pact establishing the twelve-member North Atlantic Treaty Organization was considered a major turning point in American foreign policy. The treaty committed the United States to the permanent defense of Western Europe. During the next decade, the U.S. entered into numerous other security treaties around the globe. The U.S. signed the Pacific Security Pact with Australia, and New Zealand (1951); a Japanese security treaty (1951); the Southeast Asia Treaty Organization (1954) with the United Kingdom, France, Australia, New Zealand, the Philippines, Thailand, and Pakistan; and defense treaties with South Korea, Pakistan, and Taiwan.

The deep mistrust underlying the Soviet-American relationship made it difficult to establish peace treaties with the defeated Axis powers. The United States, for example, completed no peace treaty with Germany, even as it claimed a major role in rebuilding the devastated country. In 1954, however, the U.S. signed the Treaty of Paris, formally ending the allied occupation of West Germany. In addition, it took a decade of talks following the war to settle the status of Austria, strategically located on the border of the Iron Curtain. The delay worked to America's favor. By 1955, when the U.S. and Soviet Union signed the Austrian State Treaty establishing its neutrality, Austria had firmly committed itself to democratic government.

It should be noted that, after America's two major Asian wars in the latter half of the twentieth century, no treaties terminated the hostilities. After lengthy negotiations, the Korean War ended with a ceasefire and the signing of an armistice (1953) that reestablished the prior division of the country. Following the North Vietnamese-Vietcong Tet Offensive in 1968, the U.S. and Hanoi began peace talks that dragged on for five years. These talks resulted in a 1973 accord in the form of an executive agreement. The agreement permitted the U.S. to continue its support for South Vietnam, but by 1975, communist forces had ousted the remaining American presence and had taken Saigon, which they renamed Ho Chi Minh City.

Nuclear Arms Treaties

The most important treaties of the late twentieth century were designed to slow the pace of the nuclear arms race between the Americans and the Soviets. The terrifying Cuban Missile Crisis (1962) inspired the superpowers to sign the Nuclear Test Ban Treaty (1963), outlawing nuclear missile tests in the atmosphere, space, and underwater. A 1968 treaty signed by the United States sought to limit the proliferation of nuclear arms.

President Richard Nixon initiated the Strategic Arms Limitation Talks (SALT) with the Soviet Union, resulting in two treaties signed on 26 May 1972. The Anti-Ballistic Missile Treaty (ABM Treaty) prohibited the Superpowers from deploying nationwide ABM defenses. The SALT I Treaty banned the development, testing and deployment of space-based, sea-based, air-based, mobile, and land-based ballistic missiles.

SALT II (18 June 1979) initiated restraints on existing and future strategic nuclear arms systems. The 8 December 1987 Intermediate Nuclear Forces Treaty, signed by U.S. president Ronald Reagan and Soviet leader Mikhail Gorbachev, was considered the most stringent nuclear-control treaty until the collapse of the Soviet Union in 1989. The break-up of the Soviet empire led Russia and the United States to sign several groundbreaking accords calling for the destruction of thousands of nuclear bombers and warheads.

BIBLIOGRAPHY

Beisner, Robert L. *From the Old Diplomacy to the New, 1865–1900.* Arlington Heights, Ill.: Harlan Davidson, 1986.

Gaddis, John Lewis. *Strategies of Containment: A Critical Appraisal of Postwar American National Security Policy.* New York: Oxford University Press, 1982.

Kissinger, Henry. *Diplomacy.* New York: Simon and Schuster, 1994.

Tucker, Robert W., and David C. Hendrickson. *Empire of Liberty: The Statecraft of Thomas Jefferson.* New York: Oxford University Press, 1990.

Ellen G. Rafshoon

See also **Foreign Policy; Reciprocal Agreements; Trade Agreements;** *and individual treaties.*

TREATY COUNCILS (INDIAN TREATY-MAKING).

Prior to the American Revolution, formal relations between European colonial societies and the numerous Native Americans in North America were governed by various means, including enslavement, war, and carefully regulated trade. The United States entered its first treaty with a Native American nation, the Delawares, in 1778, during the Revolutionary War. Several wartime agreements were reached with other groups, but the first formal treaties negotiated under the U.S. Constitution were approved in 1789. In the years after the Revolution, U.S. treaties with the Native American nations on the Atlantic seaboard acknowledged Native American sovereignty, determined the boundaries between the Native American nations and the United States, restricted American settlers from occupying or seizing Indians' land, prohibited Native Americans from forging alliances with any nation other than the United States, and governed trade relations.

Treatymaking between the United States and Native American nations changed significantly in May 1830, when Congress passed the Indian Removal Act, which established the policy that the United States should secure the exchange of Native Americans' land in the East for land west of the Mississippi River. This law triggered a series of "removal treaties" that extinguished the landholdings of many eastern tribes and established reservations for them in the West. Removal treaties were signed with Native American nations in the Southeast, such as the Cherokee, and also with nations in the Ohio Valley. When Native Americans resisted removal, the federal government relied on military force to obtain their compliance. Most removals involved military pressure. Some, such as the relocation of the Seminoles, required repeated invasion and warfare.

Following the removal era, Congress initiated a number of treaties that reduced the size of tribal landholding in and restricted Native Americans to reservations. These agreements involved relatively small tribes in the Midwest, California, the Northwest, and the Great Lakes region as well as large hunting societies on the Plains and in the Southwest.

The next major shift in treatymaking occurred on 3 March 1871, when Congress determined that the federal government would no longer enter into formal treaties with Native American nations. Despite the end of formal treatymaking, Congress continued to approve agreements negotiated with tribes. In the late nineteenth century most of these agreements were related to the implementation of the 1887 General Allotment Act, a statute that divided reservations into parcels of land that were allocated to individual Native Americans as private property. The act also mandated the sale of the remaining "surplus" land to the federal government.

In 1934 Congress passed the Indian Reorganization Act, which prohibited future land allotment, and restored to the Native American nations limited independent authority over their internal affairs. Since then, Native Americans and Congress have relied on federal and state laws to address contemporary issues such as water rights and land use. The United Nations oversaw international agreements that affected indigenous peoples including Native Americans.

BIBLIOGRAPHY

Deloria, Vine, Jr., and David E. Wilkins. *Tribes, Treaties, and Constitutional Tribulations.* Austin: University of Texas Press, 1999.

Petersburg. Union soldiers in December 1864 occupy a trench, part of the elaborate complex that each side constructed during the ten-month siege of this crucial Virginia city south of the Confederate capital of Richmond. LIBRARY OF CONGRESS

Prucha, Francis Paul. *Great Father: The United States Government and the American Indians.* Lincoln: University of Nebraska Press, 1984.

———. *American Indian Treaties: The History of a Political Anomaly.* Berkeley: University of California Press, 1994.

Barbara Krauthamer

See also **Indian Removal; Indian Reorganization Act; Indian Reservations; Indian Treaties; Indian Treaties, Colonial.**

TREATY OF PEACE, 1783. *See* **Paris, Treaty of (1783).**

TRENCHES IN AMERICAN WARFARE. Field trenches seldom played a role in the American colonial wars, but they became more prominent in the American Revolution: opposing forces began to use hasty field entrenchments at the Battle of Bunker Hill, and General George Washington used trenches continually and freely throughout the war as a means of keeping his army in the field; he constantly warned, however, against allowing trenches to become a trap.

Trenches were little used in the War of 1812 and the Mexican-American War, and, at the beginning of the Civil War, soldiers on both sides resented work on trenches—even though they quickly realized their error. The Battle of Chancellorsville, Virginia, was a trench battle, and thereafter both sides acquired great skill and ingenuity in digging.

The ultimate development in trenches was at Petersburg, Virginia, in 1864–1865, with trenches dug there that foreshadowed those of World War I in France. The two sides created parallel lines of trenches that required a minimum force to hold yet kept a maximum force free for maneuver. When the line became so long that General Robert E. Lee's weakened army could not hold it, he had to abandon Richmond and tried in vain to escape to the Carolinas. Similar events in France after the Battle of the Marne in 1914—often called the Race to the Sea—produced a different result because shorter distances and larger forces meant that maneuvering flanks reached the English Channel before trench-holding elements lost control.

The foxhole, a more temporary shelter, largely replaced the trench in World War II and the Korean War. In the Vietnam War the bunker afforded some protection against artillery.

BIBLIOGRAPHY

Bull, Stephen. *Trench Warfare: Battle Tactics.* London: Brassey's, 2002.

Coffman, Edward M. *The War to End All Wars: The American Military Experience in World War I.* New York: Oxford University Press, 1968.

Johnson, J. H. *Stalemate! Great Trench Warfare Battles.* London: Cassell Academic, 1999.

Tuchman, Barbara W. *The Guns of August.* New York: Macmillan, 1962.

Oliver Lyman Spaulding / C. W.

See also **Chancellorsville, Battle of; Fortifications; Petersburg, Seige of.**

TRENT **AFFAIR.** When Captain Charles Wilkes, commanding the sloop *San Jacinto*, arrested two Confederate delegates onboard the British ship *Trent* on the high seas, he created an incident that endangered Union relations with neutral Great Britain during the Civil War. James M. Mason and John Slidell had been selected by the Confederate president Jefferson Davis to ask Great Britain and France for material aid and diplomatic recognition. After running the Union blockade, Mason and Slidell took passage on the *Trent* in Havana, Cuba, on 7 November 1861. The next day the ship was stopped, the arrests were made, and the *Trent* was allowed to continue on its voyage.

Rejoicing in the Northern states soon gave way to more sober contemplation. Although Secretary of the Navy Gideon Welles had given orders to apprehend Mason and Slidell, Wilkes had violated accepted maritime behavior. International law would have prescribed seizing the *Trent*, placing a crew aboard, and sailing it into a harbor for adjudication by a prize court that would determine if the *Trent* had violated neutrality. Arresting Mason and Slidell without taking the *Trent* as a prize was considered equivalent to the impressment the Americans had so vehemently opposed fifty years earlier.

Immediately the British protested and demanded the release of the prisoners. When the Union realized that Great Britain was preparing for war with the Union and was sending troops to Canada, Mason and Slidell were released on 26 December 1861.

BIBLIOGRAPHY

Ferris, Norman B. *The "Trent" Affair: A Diplomatic Crisis*. Knoxville: University of Tennessee Press, 1977.

Warren, Gordon H. *Fountain of Discontent: The "Trent" Affair and Freedom of the Seas*. Boston: Northeastern University Press, 1981.

Michael Wala

See also **Civil War; Confederate States of America; Great Britain, Relations with.**

TRENTON, BATTLE OF. During the American Revolution, following General George Washington's evacuation of New Jersey, the British general William Howe established two unsupported cantonments of 1,500 Hessians each, at Bordentown and Trenton. Washington, sure the enemy only awaited the freezing of the Delaware River to seize Philadelphia, planned a simultaneous surprise movement against both cantonments, with the main blow falling at Trenton.

On Christmas night, with 2,500 troops, he crossed the Delaware at McKonkey's Ferry, eight miles above Trenton. Delayed by floating ice and a storm of sleet and snow, his two columns, under his command and that of General John Sullivan, reached the village at 8:00 A.M., in broad daylight. The Hessians, who had spent Christmas night celebrating, were completely surprised. Their commandant, Colonel Johann Rall, who had ignored warn-

ings of the attack, seemed nonplussed. The Americans fired from houses and cellars and from behind trees and fences, while their artillery raked the two main streets of the town. In the battle, lasting scarcely forty minutes, thirty Hessians were killed (including Rall), and one thousand were taken prisoner, while the Americans had only two officers and two privates wounded. Two supporting divisions failed to cross the river until the following day; meanwhile, the Hessians at Bordentown safely withdrew.

Coming so swiftly after a succession of bitter defeats, this victory infused new life into the revolutionary cause, restored confidence in Washington both at home and abroad, strengthened the resolution of Congress, and, coupled with the victory at Princeton a few days later, practically freed New Jersey of British control.

BIBLIOGRAPHY

Bill, Alfred H. *The Campaign of Princeton, 1776–1777*. Princeton, N.J.: Princeton University Press, 1948.

Dwyer, William M. *The Day Is Ours!: November 1776–January 1777: An Inside View of the Battles of Trenton and Princeton*. New York: Viking, 1983.

Stryker, William S. *The Battles of Trenton and Princeton*. Boston: Houghton Mifflin, 1898. Reprint, Spartanburg, S.C.: Reprint Co., 1967.

C. A. Titus/A. R.

See also **Delaware, Washington Crossing the; German Mercenaries; New Jersey; Princeton, Battle of; Revolution, American: Military History.**

TREVETT V. WEEDEN, a decision rendered by Judge David Howell of Rhode Island in September 1786, is frequently cited as a precedent for the doctrine of judicial review laid down by Chief Justice John Marshall in *Marbury v. Madison* (1803). Acts of the legislature provided heavy fines for those refusing to accept the state's depreciated paper currency at par. The defendant, John Weeden, a butcher, was acquitted on the ground that the acts were unconstitutional and void.

BIBLIOGRAPHY

Clinton, Robert L. *Marbury v. Madison and Judicial Review*. Lawrence: University Press of Kansas, 1989.

W. A. Robinson/A. R.

See also **Judicial Review;** *Marbury v. Madison.*

TRIANGLE SHIRTWAIST FIRE. Late on the afternoon of Saturday, 25 March 1911, a fire broke out at the Triangle Shirtwaist Company on New York City's Lower East Side, where some 500 garment employees worked overtime to fill back orders. The floors were littered with inflammable chemical fluids and piles of fabrics, ensuring that the fire spread quickly through the congested building. When workers rushed to the doors,

Triangle Shirtwaist Factory. A view of the ruins after the fire on 25 March 1911, in which 146 trapped sweatshop workers, mostly women and young girls, were killed. AP/WIDE WORLD PHOTOS

BIBLIOGRAPHY

Dubofsky, Melvyn. *When Workers Organize.* Amherst: University of Massachusetts Press, 1968.

Foner, Philip S. *Women and the American Labor Movement.* New York: Free Press, 1979.

Park, David W. "Compensation or Confiscation," Ph.D. diss., University of Wisconsin, Madison, 2000.

David Park

See also **National Labor Relations Act; New York City; Progressive Movement; Workers' Compensation.**

they found some locked, just one of several safety regulations habitually violated. The only fire escape, a flimsy and narrow ladder, immediately collapsed. In a matter of some 15 minutes, the fire snuffed out the lives of 146 workers, most of them Jewish girls and young women. On 5 April, while many of the victims were being buried in another part of the city, half a million spectators watched some 75,000 to 100,000 workingmen and workingwomen march in protest up Fifth Avenue in lower Manhattan.

The Triangle fire occurred soon after a fatal accident in a lamp factory in Newark, New Jersey, on 26 November 1910 and major industrial disasters at the Monongah Mine in West Virginia on 6 December 1907 and at the Cherry Mine in Illinois on 13 November 1909. Consequently, the Triangle fire prompted some Americans to condemn corporate greed. The state of New York immediately formed the Factory Investigating Commission and overhauled or enacted three dozen laws dealing with factory safety between 1912 and 1914. A large number of states, including Colorado, Minnesota, New Hampshire, Ohio, and Wisconsin, soon followed New York's lead. The incident also provided a decisive impetus for further protective labor legislation with stringent provisions in the remaining years of the Progressive Era, including employers' liability, worker's compensation, workday and workweek laws, occupational disease and comfort laws, and industry-specific health and safety laws for mining, railroading, and construction. New York Senator Robert F. Wagner, who served as chair of the Factory Investigating Commission, became the principal author of the National Labor Relations Act, called the Wagner Act, in 1935. Much of the protective labor legislation and enforcement of the Progressive Era formed an ideological and constitutional-legal foundation for New Deal labor legislation.

TRIANGULAR TRADE. At least two overlapping patterns of trans-Atlantic trade developed in the colonial era whereby profits from rum and other American and British manufactured goods sold on the west coast of Africa financed the purchase of enslaved Africans. Those slaves were then taken to the Americas, where their sale in turn funded the shipment of sugar, molasses, and other New World raw materials to the point of origin for the manufactured products. There the whole three-cornered process began anew. In one version of this triangular trade, the manufactured goods originated in British ports, notably Liverpool. In the similar American triangular trade route, the manufactured goods, especially rum, went from New England ports to the Gold Coast of Africa. In both patterns, the second leg of the triangle became known as the infamous "middle passage" in which enslaved Africans were carried to destinations in the Americas, usually islands in the West Indies, but in some instances locations on the North American mainland, especially Charleston, South Carolina.

After they sold their slave cargoes at great profit to colonial purchasers, ship captains took on molasses, sugar, or other local crops, mostly to avoid sailing back to their home ports in ballast. Especially for New England merchants, the middle passage was by far the most lucrative of the three legs of the triangular trade. The English triangular trade commenced almost as soon as European colonies in the New World began to import African slaves. The American variant had roots in the seventeenth century but was mostly an eighteenth-century phenomenon. Although greatly reduced by the end to the legal slave trade in 1808, the triangular pattern continued to exist in an illicit form until the Civil War ended slavery in the United States.

The large slave-carrying ships out of Liverpool required deep-water anchorage, limiting them to a few European-controlled ports on the African coast. They were too specialized to accommodate nonhuman cargoes efficiently, yet often suffered from long periods of unprofitable idle time in America as captains scrambled for local products to ship back to England. Ultimately, many returned laden only with ballast, leaving it to other sorts of British ships to carry goods along the leg of the triangle

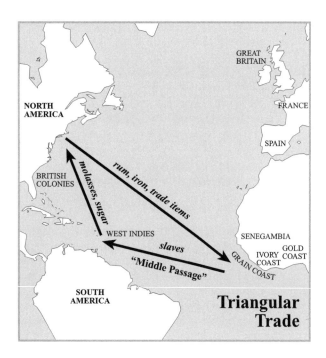

Triangular Trade

trade model perfectly, they conformed in a general sense. Lopez's vessels all left Newport with large quantities of rum, to which he added smaller amounts of foodstuffs, manufactured items, and forest products. His captains sold those goods in African ports, where they purchased slaves for the American market. Typically, they sold the slaves in several West Indian ports and sometimes at Charleston, South Carolina, taking on board whatever local produce might be available, but with a special interest in West Indian rum and the molasses that New England distilleries would convert into their own brand of the drink, thereby providing the raw materials for yet another "Guinea Voyage."

The economic dislocations occasioned by the American Revolution disrupted participation in the Atlantic slave trade. In an 1807 statute, Great Britain outlawed the slave trade altogether, and the United States followed suit in 1808. The British navy began to suppress the trade on the high seas. Some slave ships continued to make their way to American ports, but the heyday of the Atlantic slave trade, triangular or otherwise, was over.

BIBLIOGRAPHY

Coughtry, Jay. *The Notorious Triangle: Rhode Island and the African Slave Trade, 1700–1807.* Philadelphia: Temple University Press, 1981.

Klein, Herbert S. *The Middle Passage: Comparative Studies in the Atlantic Slave Trade.* Princeton, N.J.: Princeton University Press, 1978.

Minchinton, Walter E. "The Triangular Trade Revisited." In *The Uncommon Market: Essays in the Economic History of the Atlantic Slave Trade.* Edited by Henry A. Gemery and Jan S. Hogendorn. New York: Academic Press, 1979.

Platt, Virginia Bever. "'And Don't Forget the Guinea Voyage': The Slave Trade of Aaron Lopez of Newport." *William and Mary Quarterly,* 3rd. Ser. 32 (1975): 601–618.

James P. Whittenburg

See also **Middle Passage; Slave Trade; Slavery;** *and vol. 9:* **Spanish Colonial Official's Account of Triangular Trade with England.**

between England and the New World. Instead of being a simple three-legged route for any one vessel, then, the triangular path from England to Africa to America was in reality a general arrangement for the movement of goods, credits, and slaves around the Atlantic world, often with different ships running different legs of the route.

In America, Rhode Island was the principal mainland American point on the triangle. Vessels out of Bristol and Newport were generally much smaller and far less specialized than the ships employed by Liverpool slave traders. They could negotiate shallow water, giving them access to locations the Liverpool slavers could not reach. They were also easily converted from carrying slaves to carrying nonhuman cargoes. This versatility minimized down time in port and maximized the chances for profits from the classic triangular trade pattern. While the triangular slave trade was never the prime feature of Rhode Island's commercial activity, it was important there. Indeed, contemporaries claimed that New England distilleries dominated the enormous rum trade into Africa.

The activities of the Newport merchant Aaron Lopez are perhaps the best-known evidence for the existence of the triangular trade. In his first brush with the slave trade in 1761–1762, Lopez and his partner and cousin, Jacob Rodriguez Rivera, sent more than 15,000 gallons of rum, American foodstuffs, and a small quantity of tobacco to Africa on the *Greyhound,* a brig under the command of an experienced Newport slaving captain named William Pinnegar. Apparently, Lopez enjoyed a substantial profit from this venture, for thirteen similar voyages by a variety of Newport ships and commanders in his employ followed through 1774. Although not all of them fit the triangular

TRIBAL COLLEGES. The Tribal College and University (TCU) movement was founded in the late 1960s to counterbalance the near eradication of all things American Indian within the educational system of the United States. TCUs have developed a philosophy that protects and enhances tribal cultures while embracing much of modern education. They understood that, to enhance American Indian communities, students must be knowledgeable about their own cultures and prepared to survive in the non-Indian world. Navajo Community College (Diné College), founded in 1968, was the first institution to develop the tribal college philosophy. Other communities have followed this blueprint when founding their own institutions.

Each TCU has been chartered by its respective tribal government and is governed by a local board of regents. TCUs adhere closely to their mission statements as they develop curriculum and work closely with regional accreditation agencies. TCUs within the United States serve approximately 25,000 students; individual school enrollments range from 50 to 4,500 students. Although TCU students represent many racial and social backgrounds, the majority at each college comes from the local tribe or tribes. The TCU students' average age is twenty-seven, and a majority of students are female and live below the poverty line; most are first-generation college students.

TCUs interact with the federal government in much the same way as state institutions interact with state governments. The passage of Public Law 95-471, the Tribally Controlled Community College Assistance Act, in 1978 provided the financial foundation for TCUs. TCUs gained land grant status in 1994 with the passage of the Equity in Education Land Grant Status Act, which in turn strengthened the linkages between TCUs and other land grant institutions. In 1996, an executive order was issued making federal systems more accessible to TCUs and encouraging partnerships with the private sector. Private philanthropic foundations have been a source of support to the TCUs since their beginnings, contributing importantly to the growth of the TCUs and their national institutions, the American Indian Higher Education Consortium (AIHEC) and the American Indian College Fund (AICF). The AIHEC was founded by the presidents of the first six tribal colleges in 1972. By 2002, the AIHEC had grown to represent more than thirty tribal colleges in the United States and Canada. Its mission is to support the work of the tribal colleges and the national movement of American Indian self-determination. The AICF was created by the tribal colleges in 1989. Its mission is to raise funds from individuals, foundations, and corporations to build an endowment for the support of the colleges and student scholarships.

The treaty relationship between the United States and Indian tribes assures the future of the TCUs, which have a major role in preparing students to be the next leaders for American Indian nations. TCUs have also become role models for the indigenous peoples of the world who would emulate what has been accomplished by the TCU movement in the United States.

BIBLIOGRAPHY

Stein, Wayne J. *Tribally Controlled Colleges: Making Good Medicine.* New York: Peter Lang, 1992.

St. Pierre, Nate, and Wayne J. Stein. *Tribally Controlled Colleges: Facts in Brief.* Bozeman: Montana State University 1997.

Wayne J. Stein

See also **Education, Indian.**

DINÉ COLLEGE MISSION

To strengthen personal foundation for responsible learning and living consistent with Sa'ah Naaghháí Bik'en Hózhóón.

To prepare students for careers and further studies.

To promote and perpetuate Navajo language and culture.

To provide community services and research.

TRIBES

This entry includes 9 subentries:
Alaskan
California
Great Basin
Great Plains
Northeastern
Northwestern
Prairie
Southeastern
Southwestern

ALASKAN

Alaska is the traditional home of three major groups of aboriginal people, commonly known as Eskimos, Aleuts, and Indians (Eskimos and Aleuts are non-Indians). Aleuts live along the cold, rocky, treeless Aleutian Island archipelago and the west end of the Alaska Peninsula. Northern Eskimos, properly Inupiat people, who speak a language called Inupiaq, live along the Arctic Coast of Alaska, Canada, and Greenland. Yuit people, speaking Yup'ik, live along the southwest Alaska coast and the lower Kuskokwim and Yukon Rivers. Athapascan Indians live along the interior rivers and around upper Cook Inlet. Tlingit and Haida Indians, who are Pacific Northwest Coast people, live in more than a dozen villages in the Alexander Archipelago in Alaska's southeast panhandle. While the Indian populations are descended from Paleolithic people who entered America via Beringia, the "ice-age" land connection, the Eskimo and Aleut people arrived later than most other groups.

Aleuts

Divided into three language subgroups—western, central, and eastern—the Aleuts lived in villages of about fifty people and ate fish, seal, and other sea mammals, which they hunted using detachable harpoons and one-hatch kayaks made of walrus intestine stretched over a driftwood frame. Aleut hunters were legendary in kayaking and hunting skills. Kinship was matrilineal, and the basic

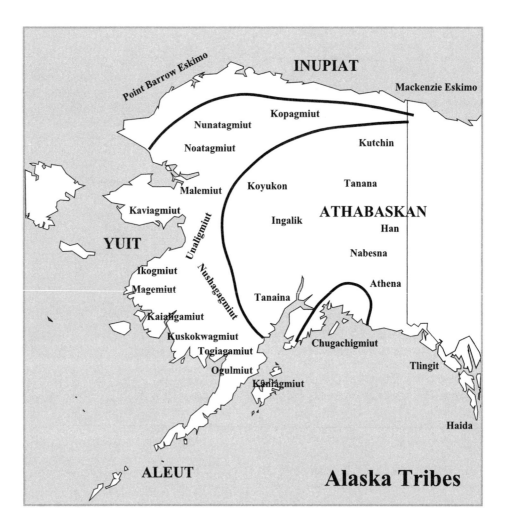

Alaska Tribes

social unit was the house-group. Women owned the houses, which were partially subterranean, but the eldest male usually made decisions for the group.

The Aleuts were the first Alaska Natives to encounter Europeans, Russian sea otter hunters who came following Vitus Bering's 1741 voyage. These fur trappers subjugated the Aleut people, and through disease and brutality reduced their population from 20,000 to 2,000. Years later, during World War II, the remaining islanders were evacuated for three years to dilapidated, substandard camps in southeast Alaska, where 80 of 881 died.

Inupiats

Traditionally, the Inupiats lived in semisubterranean houses in communities of from twenty-five to fifty. They relied on mixed fishing and hunting, especially for caribou, and organized whale hunts using an open skin boat called an umiak. The umialik, or boat captain, was a position of leadership and prestige. The Inupiats traced kinship bilaterally. They developed several methods of establishing quasi-kinship relationships, including trading partnerships between men from different groups, short-term spouse exchange, and adoption. Food brought to the community was shared by everyone.

Before contact the Inupiats numbered about 10,000. Widespread European contact did not occur until the middle of the nineteenth century, when Yankee whaling ships began to hunt in the northern Bering Sea and Arctic Ocean. Influenza between 1918 and 1922 and tuberculosis in the 1940s and 1950s took a high toll among the Inupiat. Due partly to local governmental authority and the corporations established by the Alaska Native Claims Settlement Act (ANCSA), the remaining Inupiat villages enjoy modestly comfortable material circumstances.

Pacific Yuits

The Pacific Yuits (southern Eskimos), who include the people of Kodiak Island (Alutiiq), lived mostly in partial dugout and framed houses, though the Alutiiqs used Aleut-type underground dwellings. Kinship was matrilineal, except on St. Lawrence Island, where it was patrilineal. All Yuit communities except those on St. Lawrence Island also had a larger dwelling, called a kashim, where a group of matrilineally related men lived in winter and where the women brought them their food. The Yuits relied heavily on salmon, which are prolific along Alaska's southwest coast, though some groups also took caribou and marine mammals. Numbering 30,000 before contact,

an era of rapid change for Great Basin Indians. Whereas Spanish authorities had deliberately tried to curb the influence of French, British, and American traders in their empire, Mexican national officials encouraged foreign traders and even settlers. At the same time, the western expansion of the United States following the Louisiana Purchase attracted new waves of white settlement. As a consequence, Native groups throughout the intermountain West faced dramatic increases in foreign traffic, trade, and settlement. In the 1820s, American and British trappers quickly descended into the northern Great Basin along the Snake and Humboldt Rivers and virtually exterminated beaver and other fur-bearing animals. Such escalated foreign trade and traffic altered Great Basin Indian subsistence, as precious game, water, and grasses became consumed by outsiders and their large animal herds.

Such ecological and economic disruptions were exponentially compounded following the American conquest of northern Mexico in 1848. As the United States acquired control of the West, hundreds of thousands of Euro-American migrants moved through the Great Basin, drawn by the prospect of gold during the California gold rush and by lands in western states, such as the Oregon Territory. Western migration came through Indian homelands and initiated conflict, warfare, and impoverishment for Great Basin Indians. As white migrants eventually settled in the region, particularly along fertile rivers, settlers increasingly competed with Indian groups for land, resources, and power. In Utah and southern Idaho, Mormons and other settlers fought a series of wars with Utes and Shoshones, in which hundreds of Indians were often killed in single encounters. More commonly, white migrants and militia deployed indiscriminate violence and terror to consolidate American power throughout the region. From Owens Valley, California, to the Colorado Plateau, Great Basin Indians found their communities and homelands increasingly targeted by institutions of the American state, particularly the federal army and Indian agents.

Beginning in the 1850s and 1860s, the U.S. government negotiated a series of treaties with most Great Basin Indians to isolate Indian groups away from white settlements. In the 1880s and 1890s, the federal government initiated a series of assimilative efforts to divide Indian communal reservation lands under the auspices of the Dawes General Allotment Act while also attempting to "reform" Indian education, religion, and culture. The effects of these government policies were disastrous for many Great Basin groups. In Colorado and Utah the once sizable reservations established for Ute groups were opened to non-Indians, and millions of acres of the Mountain Ute, the Southern Ute, and the Uintah-Ouray reservations passed into non-Indian hands. Meanwhile, the intertwined attacks of assimilation sent Indian children away to boarding schools, outlawed traditional religious practices, and curbed many forms of economic subsistence.

To survive American conquest required that Great Basin Indians make tremendous adjustments. Many Shoshone groups in Nevada and California did not receive federally protected reservation lands as stipulated by government treaties and were forced to work in white communities for survival. Paiute and Shoshone women worked as domestics and cooks, while Indian men labored as ranch hands, miners, and day laborers. The renowned Paiute author and activist Sarah Winnemucca Hopkins noted in her autobiography, *Life Among the Piutes* (1883), that Indian women throughout the region were often targeted by white men for sexual pleasure. Enduring such challenges taxed many community and individual resources, and many groups suffered bitter poverty throughout the first decades of the twentieth century.

With the Indian policy reforms of the 1930s, many Great Basin Indian communities received federal recognition, and a few scattered reservations, and "colonies," federally recognized urban Indian communities, were established for mainly Shoshone groups in Nevada. The creation of the Indian Claims Commission (ICC) in 1946 offered many groups a new avenue for legal redress. The Western Shoshone, for example, initiated ICC cases that have yet to be fully resolved.

During World War II, many Ute, Shoshone, and Paiute soldiers served their communities and country, often venturing away from their homelands for the first time. Their increasing familiarity with the larger national culture and the continued poverty within their communities brought many Great Basin Indians to larger regional and urban centers, such as Reno, Nevada, Salt Lake City, Utah, and Denver, Colorado. Indian urbanization coincided with the postwar relocation policies of the Bureau of Indian Affairs, which encouraged Indian youth to move to urban centers for job-training and placement programs. Additionally, during the postwar termination era, the federal government extinguished federal trust status for Indian reservations, including the Southern Paiute reservations in southwestern Utah, and turned matters of Indian affairs over to state and local governments. Only in the 1970s did these assimilation efforts give way to an era of self-determination, in which Indian peoples and tribal governments began formulating more actively the laws and policies under which their communities lived.

BIBLIOGRAPHY

Crum, Steven J. *The Road on Which We Came: A History of the Western Shoshone.* Salt Lake City: University of Utah Press, 1994.

Inter-Tribal Council of Nevada. *Newe: A Western Shoshone History.* Reno: Inter-Tribal Council of Nevada, 1976.

Madsen, Brigham D. *The Shoshoni Frontier and the Bear River Massacre.* Salt Lake City: University of Utah Press, 1985.

Stewart, Omer C. *Indians of the Great Basin: A Critical Bibliography.* Newberry Library Center for the History of the American Indian Bibliography Series. Bloomington: University of Indiana Press, 1982.

Sturtevant, William C., ed. *Handbook of North American Indians.* Volume 11: *Great Basin*, edited by Warren L. D'Azevedo. Washington, D.C.: Smithsonian Institution, 1986.

Trenholm, Virginia Cole, and Maurine Carley. *The Shoshonis: Sentinels of the Rockies.* Norman: University of Oklahoma Press, 1964.

Ned Blackhawk

See also **Indian Land Cessions; Indian Reservations; Indian Trade and Traders; Indian Treaties.**

GREAT PLAINS

The image of buffalo-hunting, horseback-mounted, teepee-dwelling Plains warriors is the dominant stereotype of American Indians. But this static, one-dimensional picture is not an accurate representation of Native Americans as a whole, nor does it reflect the diversity among Plains tribes. Six different linguistic groups are represented among Plains peoples. Their dwellings varied from the earth lodges built by horticulturalists such as the Mandans, Hidatsas, Arikaras, and Pawnees of the central river valleys, to the woven-grass lodges of the Witchitas and other southeastern Plains groups, to the "classic" buffalo-skin lodges of the Blackfeet, Lakotas, Crows, Comanches, and other nomadic peoples. The lives of all, moreover, were dramatically altered by European animals, goods, diseases, and settlers.

The oldest dwellers of the Plains were nomadic Paleo-Indian big-game hunters. Occupation of the Plains has been dated as far back as the Clovis Phase (15,000–11,000 before common era) and the Folsom Phase (11,000–8,000 B.C.E.). The disappearance of species such as mammoths and mastodons at the end of the last ice age, combined with a climactic shift from a moist and cool environment to a drier, warmer ecosystem, may have spurred some groups to leave the area. At the time of European contact, two major cultural traditions existed on the Plains. One comprised small bands of nomadic hunters living in buffalo-hide teepees; the other comprised horticulturalists who lived in semipermanent villages in the major river valleys and who raised maize, beans, squash, and other crops. By 1750 horticultural groups included (besides those already mentioned) the Iowas, Kansas (Kaws), Missouris, Omahas, Osages, Otos, Poncas, Quapaws, and Witchitas. Hunters included the Assiniboines, Gros Ventres, Cheyennes Arapahos, Kiowas, Yankton and Yanktonai Sioux, Kiowa-Apaches, and Plains Crees and Ojibwas. Both groups engaged in large communal buffalo hunts and maintained extensive trade networks. Both horticulturalists and hunters developed elaborate ceremonial and religious systems based on the idea of an interconnected universe.

European contact with Plains tribes probably began in 1540, when Francisco Vasquez de Coronados reached the Witchitas in what is now Kansas, but European influences arguably arrived even sooner. Recurring epidemic diseases such as smallpox, cholera, measles, and scarlet

Great Plains Tribes

fever both preceded and followed Europeans, and decimated Native communities. Sometime in the seventeenth century, the arrival of horses and European-manufactured trade goods altered the balance of power on the Plains. Initially introduced in the sixteenth century by the Spanish in the Southwest, horses conferred unprecedented power and mobility on their owners. Horses enabled nomadic bands to follow and exploit the buffalo more effectively, and allowed the accumulation and transportation of greater quantities of goods and supplies. Guns obtained from French and British fur traders, meanwhile, enabled groups who had formerly lived on the fringes of the region, including the Lakotas and Yankton Sioux and the Blackfeet and Crees, to push onto the Plains and displace established groups. These new technologies may have also aided the Crow Indians in separating from their Hidatsa relatives and becoming equestrian buffalo hunters. The Cheyennes likewise made a similar shift from horticulture on the prairies of Minnesota and the eastern Dakotas to a nomadic hunting lifestyle. Other groups, such as the Comanches and Kiowas, migrated south from the area of present-day Wyoming to the southern Plains.

In the early nineteenth century other Indian groups entered the Plains following their removal from their homelands in the eastern and southeastern United States. More than two dozen eastern tribes—either in whole or in part—suffered removal to Indian Territory. Portions of other tribes, including Apaches from the southwest and Modocs from northern California, were also relocated to the territory by federal officials before the end of the century.

Prior to the 1840s, belief that the Plains constituted a "Great American Desert" enabled U.S. policymakers to envision a permanent Indian frontier, beyond which Native Americans could live undisturbed. However, the acquision of western lands, followed by the discovery of gold in California and the Rocky Mountains, placed Plains tribes under increasing pressure. Although disease killed far more emigrants than did Indians, the destruction of game and other resources, as well as the diseases emigrants brought, heightened tensions. Although agreements such as the 1851 Treaty of Fort Laramie attempted to reduce the level of conflict, the decentralized nature of Plains societies and the speed of American expansion made such agreements difficult to enforce. Continued confrontations soon led to warfare. After the Civil War, pressure increased as settlers pushed onto the Plains. Although Native peoples won some victories, notably in the Bozeman Trail conflict of 1866–1867 and at the Little Bighorn in 1876, continued American military pressure and the destruction of the buffalo eventually forced tribes onto reservations.

Cultural warfare followed military conflict, as government officials, missionaries, and other reformers attempted to impose assimilation upon tribes. Traditional social and religious practices were banned, and children were forbidden from speaking their Native language in schools. Many cultural practices were either lost outright or forced underground. Reservations themselves came under assault in the Dawes General Allotment Act of 1887, which sought to break up reservations and force Indians to accept individual parcels of land. Indians responded to these conditions with a combination of adaptation, resistance, and innovation, including new religious forms such as the Ghost Dance and peyotism. Plains tribes also fought continuing legal battles, commencing early in the twentieth and continuing into the twenty-first century, to protect water and mineral rights and to obtain either compensation for or the return of land taken by the U.S. government. In 1980 the Supreme Court upheld a 1979 Court of Claims decision that awarded the Lakotas $102 million for the illegal taking of the Black Hills, but the Lakotas refused to accept the money, insisting that the land be returned.

In the early 2000s many Plains tribes continued to struggle with issues of poverty, economic underdevelopment, and the legacy of decades of cultural genocide. Plains communities also continued to meet these challenges in innovative ways, ranging from the development of tribal colleges and curriculum programs to sustain tribal cultures and provide vocational training, to casino gaming and the restoration of the buffalo. Unlike the static image of the mounted warrior, the strength of Plains tribes has been in their ability to adapt and survive through centuries of change.

BIBLIOGRAPHY

Carlson, Paul H. *The Plains Indians*. College Station: Texas A&M University Press, 1998.

Hoxie, Frederick E. *Parading through History: The Making of the Crow Nation in America, 1805–1935*. New York: Cambridge University Press, 1995.

Iverson, Peter, ed. *The Plains Indians of the Twentieth Century*. Norman: University of Oklahoma Press, 1985.

West, Elliot. *The Contested Plains: Indians, Goldseekers, and the Rush to Colorado*. Lawrence: University Press of Kansas, 1998.

Frank Rzeczkowski

See also **Indian Policy, U.S.**

NORTHEASTERN

All the indigenous tribes of New England were speakers of languages belonging to the widespread Algonquian family. The adaptive expansion of the Algonquians into the region was made possible by their possession of the bow and arrow, pottery, and fishing technology that earlier inhabitants of the region seemingly lacked.

Although the Micmac language of New Brunswick and Nova Scotia appears to have diverged earlier, most of the Northeastern Algonquians started to diverge from the main body around A.D. 600. This process was later accelerated by the northward expansion of Iroquoian speakers to the west in the interior of the Northeast, which cut the Eastern Algonquians off from those in the Great Lakes region. The Eastern Algonquians subsequently spread southward along the coast, and were established as far south as North Carolina upon European contact.

The Eastern Algonquians were largely patrilineal in their social organization. They lived in tribal societies dominated by big men (sagamores); only rarely did fragile and short-lived chiefdom organizations emerge over time. Their first well-documented contacts with Europeans resulted from the expedition of Giovanni da Verrazano in 1524. The explorer stopped in both southern and northern New England before sailing home. He noticed, as did later explorers, that New England tribes practiced agriculture in the south but were hunters and gatherers in the north. The division between the two adaptations fell in the vicinity of modern coastal New Hampshire.

Later explorations of the Maine coast by George Weymouth and Samuel Champlain, both in 1605, and John Smith in 1614, left records that provide an unusual wealth of detail about local Indian communities. From these and later sources we know that the tribes of northern New England included the Western Abenaki of New Hampshire and Vermont, the Eastern Abenaki of Maine, the Maliseet of northern Maine and New Brunswick, and the coastal Passamaquoddy, closely related to the Maliseet but resident in eastern Maine. The Penobscot tribe, which survives on a reservation at Old Town, Maine, descends from more general Eastern Abenaki origins.

The people of northern New England lived part of the year in villages of up to four hundred houses. Local leadership tended to be in the hands of one or two big men. While leaders appear to have been chosen for life, leadership was not necessarily hereditary. Homes contained senior men and small extended families. These family units were also the economic units that lived to-

219

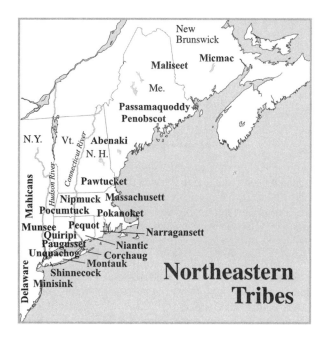

Northeastern Tribes

gether at special-purpose camps located away from the main villages. Travel in northern New England was typically by canoe along the coast and inland streams. Dense forests restricted foot travel to portages and the immediate vicinities of villages and camps. A short growing season made horticulture too risky in northern New England, so the people depended mostly upon wild food resources. Coastal camps were used when migratory birds and shellfish could be exploited. Fish runs in the spring and fall took them to key places along major rivers, where their villages were also located. They dispersed to interior hunting camps in the winter. The last became increasingly important in the seventeenth century, when demand for furs by European traders reached a peak. Depletion of furs and competition from intruding English colonists led many Abenakis to move to refugee villages in Canada. Those that remained played out a political balancing act between the colonial English and French until the latter were expelled from Canada in 1763. The Indians subsequently lost land to English colonists at an accelerating rate. Following the American Revolution, the state of Massachusetts (of which Maine was a part until 1820) and later the state of Maine acquired more land by means that were in violation of federal law. Compensation was finally realized in the 1970s and the Penobscots, Maliseets, and Passamaquoddys of Maine have survived into the present century with prosperity and identities intact.

The Eastern Algonquian tribes of southern New England enjoyed a longer growing season, and the native American crops of maize, beans, and squash spread to the region after A.D. 1000. Verrazano noted many fields, often with small summer houses that were occupied by people tending the crops. Travel was by overland trails and dugouts on larger streams. Population densities here were ten or twenty times higher than those of northern New En-

gland. There were probably only about 34,000 people in northern New England compared to 108,000 in the smaller southern portion. The lack of suitable fibers from plants or animals meant that the Indians had to rely on hides for clothing here as elsewhere in the Northeast. Deer were the primary source of both hides and protein from meat. However, beans combined with maize provided a partial protein substitute, somewhat relaxing what would have been a severe constraint on population growth.

Little is known about the political and social organization of southern New England tribes. Their social organizations were patrilineal or bilateral and local communities were led informally by big men. The emergence of chiefdoms or other, more complex or more permanent political entities was rare. A severe epidemic involving hepatic failure that began in southeastern New England in 1615 drastically reduced and scattered local populations. Many survivors became dependents in English colonial settlements and others regrouped in new refugee communities, erasing many of the previous social and political patterns. Despite the confusion, ethnohistorians have settled on a set of generally accepted tribal names for the seventeenth century. The Massachusett lived in what became eastern Massachusetts and Rhode Island. Their subdivisions included the Pawtucket, from northeastern Massachusetts to southern Maine, the Massachusett proper around Boston, the Pokanokets (Wampanoags) of southeastern Massachusetts, and the Narragansetts of Rhode Island. The Nipmucks lived in central Massachusetts and the Pocumtucks resided west of the Connecticut River in western Massachusetts. The Western and Eastern Niantics occupied small coastal enclaves in eastern Connecticut. The Pequot-Mohegans occupied the Thames River drainage north of the Niantics and the coastline between them. Small tribes closely related to the Pequot-Mohegans, namely the Corchaugs, Shinnecocks, and Montauks, lived on eastern Long Island. Western Connecticut and central Long Island were occupied by several related local groups such as the Quiripis, Paugussets, and Unquachogs, which are not covered by a single term. Munsee people, speakers of a Delaware language and related to the Minisinks of New Jersey, occupied western Long Island and the southern Hudson River. The Mahicans, not to be confused with either the Mohegans or the fictional "Mohicans," lived in the middle Hudson Valley.

Political divisions, such as the split between the closely related Pequots and Mohegans, were common and often short-lived in the disruptive context of European colonization. King Philip's War in 1675 and 1676 led to the death, deportation, or dislocation of most communities. Fourteen "praying towns" were established to accommodate missionized Indians. Many others fled to live with the Iroquois nations or to form refugee communities like Schaghticoke and Stockbridge in western Connecticut and Massachusetts. Subsequent intermarriage with people of European or African descent changed the composition of many surviving communities. Notable among them are the Gay Head, Mashpee, Hassanamisco, Schaghticoke, and Mashantucket Pequot communities of southern New England, and the Poospatuck and Shinnecock communities on Long Island.

BIBLIOGRAPHY

Feidel, Stuart J. "Correlating Archaeology and Linguistics: The Algonquian Case." *Man in the Northeast* 41 (1991): 9–32.

———. "Some Inferences Concerning Proto-Algonquian Economy and Society." *Northeast Anthropology* 48 (1994): 1–11.

Snow, Dean R. *The Archaeology of New England.* New York: Academic Press, 1980. The archaeology is dated but the historical sections remain useful.

Sturtevant, William C., gen. ed. *The Handbook of North American Indians.* Vol. 15, *Northeast.* Edited by Bruce G. Trigger. Washington, D.C.: Smithsonian Institution, 1978.

Dean Snow

See also **Agriculture, American Indian; French and Indian War; Indian Economic Life; Indian Intermarriage; Indian Land Cessions; Indian Languages; Indian Policy, Colonial: English, French; Indian Policy, U.S., 1775–1830; Indian Policy, U.S., 1900–2000; Indian Political Life; Indian Reservations; Stockbridge Indian Settlement; Wars with Indian Nations: Colonial Era to 1783.**

NORTHWESTERN

The northwestern region is bordered on the north by Yakutat Bay and on the south by Cape Mendocino, on the east by the crest of the Rocky Mountains and on the west by the Pacific Ocean. Four language families dominate the region. Two, Salish and Penutian, incorporate the majority of the inland population, although two Na-Dene groups, the Carriers and Chilcotins, live in the region, as do the Kutenais, whose language is of unknown affiliation. Salish groups—including the Lillooets, Sanpoils, Flatheads, and many others—dominate the northern interior. South of them, Penutian speakers—including the Nez Perces, Cayuses, and Wascoes—are most common. On the coast, the Na-Dene speaking Tlingits and Hupas are respectively the northernmost and southernmost of the Northwestern coastal tribes. Interspersed in between are Salish groups—the Tillamooks, for example—and Penutians such as the Chinooks. Wakashans—including the Nootkas, Makahs, Kwakiutls, and several others—are also interspersed along the coast.

Although useful, these linguistic labels do not indicate hard ethnic distinctions: broad cultural behaviors and values were shared across linguistic lines. Groups throughout the region joined into constantly shifting networks based on economic and ceremonial co-participation. Only

The Makah Tribe. The Makahs, who were part of the Wakashan group, lived along the coastline at Nee-oh Bay; shown here is the Makah tribe c. 1890 on the beach at Port Townsend, Washington. NATIONAL ARCHIVES AND RECORDS ADMINISTRATION

Northwestern Tribes

Salish language group
Penutian language group
Na-Dene language group
Washakan language group

Tlingit

Lillooet

QUEEN CHARLOTTE ISLAND

Carrier

VANCOUVER ISLAND

Kwakiutl   Kutenai

Chilcotin

Nootka

Puget Sound

Sanpoil

Juan de Fuca Strait

Makah   Flathead

Chinook   *Nez Percé*

Columbia River

Pacific Ocean

Tillamook   Yakima

Wascoe   Cayuse

Hupa

since the mid-nineteenth century, when the Canadian and United States governments denominated a number of discrete tribes in the region, did today's clearly identifiable polities come into existence.

Fishing, hunting, and gathering constituted the primary economic activities throughout the region. Intergroup trade allowed individual groups to engage in maximal exploitation of local resources with assurance that surpluses could be bartered for outside goods. Although disparities in economic power between groups occurred, environmental variability generally corrected inequalities. Still, both coastal and plateau groups adopted ceremonies involving the redistribution of accumulated goods, which was the foundation for the well-known potlatch, through which prestige was earned by giving away material wealth.

The Fur Trade and Accompanying Disruptions
During the late eighteenth and early nineteenth centuries, a series of European intrusions disrupted traditional Northwestern culture. The first of these, the fur trade, arrived in the 1740s with the Russian fur hunters, followed over the next century by Canadian, British, and United States companies. This new trading presence did not immediately disrupt traditional societies as Indian groups consistently marshaled the trade to their own ends. It led, however, to increasing intergroup disparities and a much more elaborate potlatch to address resulting tensions.

Four cultural introductions that accompanied the fur trade—epidemic disease, horses, guns, and Christianity—were more disruptive than the trade itself. Disease was most immediately devastating: estimates suggest a mortality rate of between 80 and 90 percent in areas of sus-

tained contact. Horses and guns had their greatest impact on Plateau groups such as the Nez Perces and Flatheads, whose acquisition of horses from neighboring Shoshones during the mid-eighteenth century embroiled them in the Plains raiding and trading economy, generating a demand for guns among the Plateau groups. This demand for guns and potential allies against aggressive Plains tribes facilitated deeper penetration by fur traders. Coincidentally it also facilitated penetration by missionaries when, in 1825, the Hudson's Bay Company initiated a Christianization policy as a way of cementing trading relations. Perhaps in an effort to thwart a British monopoly, a party of Flatheads and Nez Perces ventured to St. Louis in 1831 to request that American missionaries come to the region.

This 1831 delegation's journey had far-reaching consequences. Steeped in expansionism and a national religious revival, people in the United States responded to the Nez Perce invitation with enthusiasm. Several missionary parties embarked for the Northwest during the 1830s, where their activities were instrumental in creating a fertile environment for American settlement. In fact, missionary Marcus Whitman led the first major overland party along the Oregon Trail in 1843. Thereafter, migrants from the United States would annually flood into the region by the thousands.

U.S. Settlement: Reservation and Allotment Policies
The presence of increasing numbers of settlers and the demand for a transcontinental railroad route through the region pressured government officials to remove Indians from large expanses of land. In a series of treaties drafted between 1843 and 1855, federal authorities synthesized tribal units out of contiguous village groups and relegated them to reservations. This policy often led to reservation communities that had no ethnic coherence. As disease and poverty took their toll, community institutions often disintegrated. Still, large numbers of Indians in western Oregon refused to accede, forcing state authorities to award them small individual enclaves. When Congress failed to ratify these de facto arrangements, it effectively dispossessed those groups. Reaction in the interior was more violent: the Yakimas went to war against the United States following an 1855 treaty cession and in 1877 a band of Nez Perces under Chief Joseph (Heinmot Tooyalakekt) sought to escape to Canada rather than relocate onto a "tribal" reservation to which they felt no kinship.

Federal authorities reversed this process of consolidation in 1887 when the General Allotment Act (Dawes Act) broke up reservations into homesteads assigned to individual Indian heads of household. The government declared all remaining lands, almost 90 percent of reservation territory in the area, "surplus," folding it into the public domain. Some Northwestern Indians lived up to the Dawes Act's expectation by becoming farmers, but most were pushed into casual labor in the logging and fishing industries or into seasonal farm work.

Revival: Reassembling Reservations, Establishing Businesses, and Reclaiming Culture

A period of severe economic, psychological, and cultural depression followed the allotment era. However, a new dawn of hope arose in 1934 when Congress passed the Indian Reorganization Act (Wheeler–Howard Act), which effectively repealed the Dawes Act and provided support for tribal communities to reassemble lost reservation holdings and develop communal businesses. For example, Walla Wallas, Wascoes, and Paiutes used the new federal law in 1937 to incorporate as the Confederated Tribes of the Warm Springs Reservation. Five years later they formed the Warm Springs Lumber Company, using much of the proceeds to support legal action to recover lost properties. A $4 million legal settlement in 1957 capitalized their building of Kah-Nee-Ta, a vacation resort. With this as an economic foundation, the tribal corporation branched out to start several businesses and continue expanding existing ones. Then, after the U.S. Supreme Court in *California v. Cabazon Band of Mission Indians* (1987) legitimized Indian-owned gambling establishments, they opened the Indian Head Casino in 1996, expanding their economic horizons significantly. Since that time they have increasingly devoted corporate earnings to repurchasing lost lands while expanding their economic self-sufficiency.

Other Northwestern tribes have followed suit, with varying degrees of success. A number of Indian-owned casinos dot the landscape throughout the Northwest and Native corporations have launched lumber businesses, fisheries, and various tourist industries. Much of the money being earned through these operations is being invested in rebuilding tribal land bases and reassembling population lost to dispossession and off-reservation jobs. Much is also being invested in building educational institutions and funding cultural reclamation by reassembling dying languages and recording tribal lore. While such activities suggest a hopeful future for the Northwestern tribes, it should be noted that alcoholism, endemic health problems, and poverty still beset many descendents of the region's aboriginal population and that the vagaries of federal law and whims of Congress still determine the limits of Indian self-sufficiency in the area, lending an air of uncertainty to the future.

BIBLIOGRAPHY

Harmon, Alexandra. *Indians in the Making: Ethnic Relations and Indian Identities around Puget Sound.* Berkeley and Los Angeles: University of California Press, 1998.

Miller, Christopher L. *Prophetic Worlds: Indians and Whites on the Columbia Plateau.* New Brunswick, N.J.: Rutgers University Press, 1985.

Ruby, Robert H., and John A. Brown. *Indians of the Pacific Northwest: A History.* Norman: University of Oklahoma Press, 1981.

Sturtevant, William C., gen. ed. *Handbook of North American Indians.* Vol. 7, *Northwest Coast,* edited by Wayne Suttles. Washington, D.C.: Smithsonian Institution, 1990.

——, gen. ed. *Handbook of North American Indians.* Vol. 12, *Plateau,* edited by Deward E. Walker Jr. Washington, D.C.: Smithsonian Institution, 1998.

Christopher L. Miller

See also **Dawes General Allotment Act; Fur Trade and Trapping; Indian Land Cessions; Indian Languages; Indian Reorganization Act; Indian Reservations; Nez Perce; Oregon Trail; Yakima Indian Wars.**

PRAIRIE

Tall-grass prairies interspersed with deciduous forests once stretched from central Indiana to eastern Nebraska. Vast meadows supported big game animals common on the western Plains. In contrast, rivers and streams flowing into the Missouri and Mississippi Rivers attached the land and its people to woodland environments and the white-tailed deer and small game animals that thrived there.

The Siouan- and Algonquian-speaking peoples who lived there developed distinctive cultures on these specific prairie environments. Western tribes, such as the Omaha, Ponca, Kansa, and Otoe-Missouria, constructed earth lodges common among the village-dwellers of the Plains. They also used buffalo-hide tepees during buffalo hunts. Rituals, such as the Sun Dance, celebrated both the buffalo hunt and the growth of corn. Eastern prairie tribes, including the Ioways, SAUKS, Quapaws, and OSAGES, built houses reflective of the woodlands. They preferred rectangular and circular lodges made of wooden poles covered with grass, bark, and woven mats. Southeastern prairie tribes, such as the CADDOS and Quapaws, incorporated the Green Corn Ceremony, common among their heavily agricultural neighbors to the southeast.

Yet in this conversation across cultures, the prairie tribes developed shared traits that defined them as a people. First, they adhered to a diverse subsistence cycle, based on hunting, horticulture, and gathering. Second, prairie tribes had strong patrilineal descent systems based on clans. Third, tribal clans regulated individual rights and one's rank in society. Finally, most of the prairie tribes became allies with the French and Spanish between the sixteenth and eighteenth centuries, and were relative strangers to the Americans at the dawn of the nineteenth century.

Several different language families made up the prairie tribes. The Dhegiha SIOUX (Osages, Quapaws, Kansas, Poncas, and Omahas) were the farthest west and, as such, became closely associated with the Plains tribes. Through oral tradition, the Dhegihas maintain that they were once a single tribe, united in what is now the lower Ohio valley. Between the late seventeenth and early eighteenth centuries they migrated beyond the Mississippi, where they separated and formed independent tribes between eastern South Dakota and Nebraska (Omahas, Poncas), eastern Kansas and western Missouri (Kansas, Osages), and eastern Arkansas (Quapaws).

The Chiwere Sioux (Ioways, Otoes, Missourias, and Winnebagos) migrated from modern Wisconsin during this time period. The Otoes and Missourias settled in southeastern Nebraska and northwestern Missouri, respectively. The Ioways ranged from eastern Iowa to southern Minnesota, where they developed close ties with the Sioux. The Winnebagos remained in their original homeland of Wisconsin until their removal from the state in 1837.

Central Algonquian tribes, including the Illinis, Sauks, MESQUAKIES (Foxes), MIAMIS, Prairie POTAWATOMIS, and KICKAPOOS, occupied the prairies of Indiana and Illinois. The Sauks and Mesquakies lived near the Ioways in northern Illinois and southern Wisconsin. Two closely related tribes, the Kickapoos and Prairie Potawatomis, dominated the Grand Prairie of north-central Illinois, while the Illini confederacy controlled the region below modern St. Louis. The Miamis lived between the attenuated prairies and dense forests of north-central Indiana.

Prairie peoples worked hard to integrate the economic, religious, and political functions of their tribes to insure their survival as a people. Many tribes appointed respected men and subordinates whose responsibilities included organizing the hunt and conducting rituals that affirmed the power of men to take life. In contrast, the more heavily agricultural central Algonquian tribes appointed female elders who organized the planting of corn and spring rituals associated with the feminine powers of renewal and fertility. Since approximately A.D. 900, prairie tribes planted the "three sisters": corn, beans, and squash. Western tribes, such as the Ioways, Omahas, and Poncas, also raised corn, but buffalo hunting sustained them.

The introduction of horses by the Spanish between 1680 and 1750, along with virulent Old World diseases such as smallpox, devastated the prairie tribes. Horses provided the mobility necessary for village dwellers to leave on semi-annual buffalo hunts on the short-grass Plains. Soon thereafter, a genocidal competition for hunting territory and access to European traders with the western Sioux led to the subjugation of the prairie peoples. Farther south, tribes such as the Osages and Caddos became rich for a time through the sale of horses and Indian slaves to the French. Others, such as the Ioways and Mesquakies, were less fortunate. They became embroiled in a series of intertribal wars directed in part by the French that decimated their populations. More importantly, village dwellers living along rivers were particularly hard hit by epidemics, which reduced their populations by between 50 and 95 percent. Some of the heaviest recorded epidemics struck the prairie tribes between 1778 and 1782, 1801 and 1802, and 1837. To cite one example, Omaha populations declined from 2,800 people in 1780 to 800 in 1855.

Prairie tribes then lost the majority of their land to the United States during a narrow band of time between the Louisiana Purchase in 1803 and the creation of the Indian Territory in 1825. More than 60,000 American Indians from the eastern United States were relocated to their former homelands between the Indian Removal Act of 1830 and the 1840s. Most of the prairie tribes were similarly relocated to Indian Territory in modern Kansas and Oklahoma between 1825 (Osages) and 1878 (Poncas).

The Poncas, led by Chief Standing Bear, resisted removal to Oklahoma after one-third of their people, including Standing Bear's son and daughter, died on the trail southward. Standing Bear fought for the right to return to Nebraska to bury his son. The case ultimately reached the federal district court, which ruled in *United States ex rel. Standing Bear v. Crook* (1879), that "an Indian is a person within the meaning of the laws of the United States." The court affirmed Standing Bear's rights under the U.S. Constitution and enabled him to remain in Nebraska with a handful of his people. The Poncas are divided into two separate tribes, the "Warm Ponca" of Oklahoma and the "Cold Ponca" of Nebraska. The Sauks, Mesquakies (Foxes), Potawatomis, and Ioways are similarly divided into separate federally recognized tribes.

Since removal, the prairie tribes have adjusted to sweeping changes brought by the Dawes Act (1887), the Indian Reorganization Act (1934), and the Termination and Relocation programs of the 1950s. Pan-Indian religious movements, such as the Native American Church and the GHOST DANCE, have also proliferated. New religions and new surroundings have challenged, and sometimes eliminated, more traditional religious practices. Despite these changes, tribal populations continue to recover and many tribal members remain committed to the preservation of their cultures.

BIBLIOGRAPHY

DeMallie, Raymond J., ed. *Handbook of North American Indians.* Volume 13: *Plains.* Washington, D.C.: Smithsonian Institution, 2001.

Fowler, Loretta. "The Great Plains from the Arrival of the Horse to 1885." In *The Cambridge History of the Native Peoples of the Americas.* Volume 1: *North America, Part 2*, edited by Bruce G. Trigger and Wilcomb E. Washburn. New York: Cambridge University Press, 1996.

Tanner, Helen Hornbeck, ed. *Atlas of Great Lakes Indian History.* Norman: University of Oklahoma, 1987.

White, Richard. *The Middle Ground: Indians, Empires, and Republics in the Great Lakes Region, 1650–1815.* New York: Cambridge University Press, 1991.

Stephen Warren

See also **Buffalo (Bison); Grand Prairie; Illinois (Indians); Indian Language; Indian Reservations; Prairie; Sauk Prairie; Winnebago/Ho-Chunk.**

SOUTHEASTERN

When Europeans and Africans arrived in North America in the 1500s, Southeastern Indians were in the midst of a significant social transformation. Only some two hundred years earlier, they had been living in Mississippian societies, chiefdoms characterized by cities and ceremonial centers. Cahokia, the largest Mississippian city (in present-day East St. Louis), once covered five square miles and contained over one hundred earthen mounds, including one of enormous proportions that spread over sixteen acres and rose one hundred feet high. Cahokia and settlements like it began to decline in the 1300s and 1400s, however, perhaps because of environmental pressures, such as drought, deforestation, and overpopulation. By 1500, some Indians, including the Natchez of present-day Louisiana, lived in the remnants of mound-building centers. Others lived in smaller, scattered settlements. The total population numbered between 600,000 and 1,200,000.

Southeastern Tribes

Early Colonization

The arrival of Europeans and Africans completed the destruction of Mississippian societies, for though the colonial presence in the Southeast was small in the 1500s, its impact was great. By introducing smallpox and other European diseases into the region, Spanish explorers—most prominently Pánfilo de Narváez (1527), Hernando de Soto (1539–1543), and Pedro Menéndez (1565)—destabilized native communities. Eventually, Old World epidemics reduced the native population by as much as 90 percent.

Coastal Indians bore the brunt of early European settlement. In Florida, after disease lowered their numbers, the Apalachees, Timucuas, and Guales survived by attaching themselves to the Spanish missions that were constructed in their homelands in the late sixteenth and seventeenth centuries. Further north, the Powhatan chiefdom remained strong enough to contest the settlement of Virginia in 1607. After a series of wars culminated in their defeat in 1644, however, they were confined to a few local reservations.

By the eighteenth century, the survivors of these devastating epidemics and wars had coalesced into new and powerful nations: the Choctaws, Chickasaws, Creeks, Cherokees, and Catawbas. (The Seminoles did not emerge as a separate people until the mid-1700s.) In all, they numbered about 130,000, still nearly twice the black and white population in the South.

The Eighteenth Century

In the early and mid-1700s, these new tribes dominated the Southeast by using the French, Spanish, and English presence to their advantage. The English had their base along the eastern seaboard, while the French centered their power in New Orleans and the Spanish in Florida. Native peoples held the balance of power in the region, and they skillfully played one colonial empire off another. The deerskin trade proved particularly profitable to both Indians and Europeans. So, too, did the trade in Indian slaves. Larger tribes, such as the Creeks, Chickasaws, and Cherokees, regularly sold captives to Carolina plantations. Indian slavery declined significantly after the Yamasee War of 1715, an intertribal uprising against Carolina's practice of enslaving Indians, but the deerskin trade continued to flourish.

In the late eighteenth century, two events converged to reshape the political landscape in the Southeast. First, the Seven Years' War, or French and Indian War (1754–1763), pushed both Spain and France out of the region, leaving indigenous southerners at the mercy of a single colonial power. Second, the American Revolution (1775–1781) produced the ambitious new American Republic. Freed from the moderating influence of their London superiors, victorious Americans moved aggressively onto Indian lands.

At the same time, a new generation of leaders arose among the Choctaws, Chickasaws, Cherokees, and Creeks.

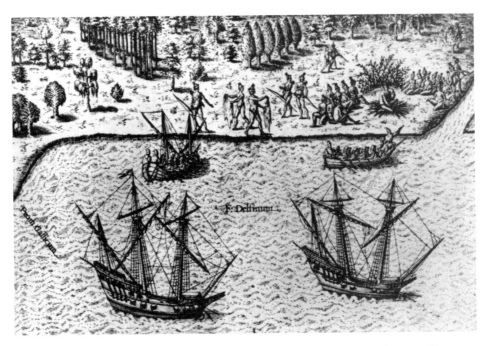

Calusa. The illustration, first published in the 1560s, shows an early encounter between this southern Florida tribe and Europeans. LIBRARY OF CONGRESS

Able diplomats and politicians who were well-versed in the English language, they used their skills to protect their nations' independence. They introduced constitutions and written laws into their tribes, and they also embraced plantation slavery. These adaptations would eventually lead white Americans to refer to the Choctaws, Chickasaws, Cherokees, Creeks, and Seminoles as the Five Civilized Tribes.

Indian Removal

Official U.S. policy in the postwar years called for the "civilization" of Native Americans. Named after its foremost proponent in the White House, Jeffersonian Indian policy schooled Native Americans in the English language, taught them to farm like white Americans, and instructed them in Christianity. As cotton cultivation grew in the South, however, so did white hunger for Indian lands. By 1830, many whites were calling for the removal of all Native peoples from the Southeast, and in that year President Andrew Jackson signed the Indian Removal Act into law. Under this statute, removal was voluntary, but many Native southerners left for Indian Territory (present-day Oklahoma) only after U.S. troops forced them at gunpoint.

In Indian Territory, the nations thrived until the onset of the allotment policy in the 1880s. Many Indians lost their allotments to fraud; others sold them for cash in order to purchase food. In 1934, the Indian Reorganization Act reversed the Dawes General Allotment Act and permitted Indians to reestablish their nations. Today, the Chickasaws, Choctaws, Creeks, Cherokees, and Seminoles each have national governments located in Oklahoma.

Survival and Adaptation in the South

Despite the efforts of U.S. troops, not all native peoples left the Southeast during removal. One thousand Cherokees hid out in the mountains of North Carolina. In 1866, they received state and federal recognition, and are now known as the Eastern Band of Cherokee Indians. In Mississippi, hundreds of Choctaws remained behind as well, working as sharecroppers and wage laborers. In 1939, the United States authorized the secretary of the interior to establish a reservation for them in that state. In Florida, thousands of Seminoles fought U.S. soldiers in three separate conflicts: the Seminole Wars of 1817–1818, 1835–1842, and 1855–1858. The Second Seminole War became nineteenth-century America's Vietnam. Defeated by unfamiliar terrain, hostile public opinion, and the tenacity of Seminole warriors, the United States finally conceded permanent Florida reservations to the Seminoles in the 1850s.

Many other Indians, pursuing a different survival strategy, remained in the Southeast by disappearing into the wider population. They worked for white planters, labored in southern cities, or sold their crafts on the streets. Living with other marginalized southerners, they helped build multiracial black, Indian, and white communities that still exist. Some of these peoples proudly embrace their Indian heritage. The Lumbees of North Carolina, for example, numbering 40,000, successfully fought for state recognition as an Indian tribe and were seeking federal recognition as well.

BIBLIOGRAPHY

Galloway, Patricia. *Choctaw Genesis, 1500–1700.* Lincoln: University of Nebraska Press, 1995.

McLoughlin, William G. *After the Trail of Tears: The Cherokees' Struggle for Sovereignty, 1839–1880.* Chapel Hill: University of North Carolina, 1993.

Merrell, James H. *The Indians' New World: Catawbas and Their Neighbors from European Contact through the Era of Removal.* Chapel Hill: University of North Carolina Press, 1989.

Rountree, Helen C. *Pocahontas's People: The Powhatan Indians of Virginia through Four Centuries.* Norman: University of Oklahoma Press, 1990.

Saunt, Claudio. *A New Order of Things: Property, Power, and the Transformation of the Creek Indians, 1733–1816.* New York: Cambridge University Press, 1999.

Usner, Daniel H., Jr. *American Indians in the Lower Mississippi Valley: Social and Economic Histories.* Lincoln: University of Nebraska, 1998.

Claudio Saunt

See also **Cahokia Mounds; Catawba; Cherokee; Chickasaw-Creek War; Choctaw; Civilized Tribes, Five; Creek; Lumbee; Natchez; Seminole; Seminole Wars.**

SOUTHWESTERN

The original inhabitants of the American Southwest occupied a vast area characterized by striking variations in topography and a sweeping aridity. From the northern plateau country of southern Utah, Nevada, and Colorado, to the rugged mountains of eastern Arizona, western New Mexico and northwestern Mexico, to the deserts of southern California, Arizona, New Mexico, and Texas, the indigenous peoples of the Southwest adapted to a land of little rain and extreme temperatures.

In the period just prior to European contact, two distinct subsistence patterns evolved among the tribes of the Southwest. Some tribes, like the Pueblo people of northeast Arizona and the Rio Grande Valley of New Mexico, developed an agrarian system. Living in permanent villages constructed of adobe or stone, the Pueblos cultivated corn, beans, cotton, squash, and other foodstuffs.

Other tribes, such as the late-arriving Apaches and Navajos, developed seminomadic lifestyles. Living in small communities of brush-covered wicki-ups or earth-covered hogans, these Athapaskan speakers relied on summer rains to nourish small crops while they roamed traditional hunting territories or raided neighboring agrarian tribes.

In the sixteenth and seventeenth centuries, Spanish conquistadors and Jesuit priests were the first Europeans to intrude on the people of the Southwest. In southern Arizona and northern Mexico, Padre Eusebio Kino converted the peaceful, agrarian Tohono O'Odham (formerly known as the Papagos) of the Sonoran desert. Kino

Southwestern Tribes

eventually urged the O'Odham into missions scattered throughout southern Arizona. Kino introduced foods such as citrus fruits, grapes, figs, and olives into the O'Odham diet, and taught his neophytes to raise horses, cattle, sheep, and goats. Using native labor, Kino built missions like San Xavier del Bac, known today as the "White Dove of the Desert," southwest of Tucson. Their close cousins to the north, the Piman-speaking Akimel O'Odham, settled along the Gila River; their great fields of crops would one day feed American pioneers on their way to California.

Today, many O'Odham still worship in the old mission and participate in the annual saguaro fruit harvest; wine made from this stately cactus is used in ceremonies to ensure abundant summer rain in an otherwise dry desert. In addition to relying on tourist dollars generated by their world-famous mission, the modern O'Odham economy is augmented by cattle ranching, mineral leases, and a lucrative casino. The Akimel O'Odham farmers are almost completely self-sufficient, accepting little aid from the federal government.

On the high mesas of northeastern Arizona and the fertile valley of the Rio Grande, the descendants of the Anasazi, known today as the Pueblos—residents of western settlements such as Hopi and Zuni, and Rio Grande towns such as Taos and San Juan—first encountered Franciscan priests in 1598. Suffering under repressive Spanish rule, these Pueblos eventually staged a revolt in 1680, driving the foreigners from their lands.

When the Spanish reimposed their rule in 1692, their approach had changed. The Pueblos managed to retain many of their traditional beliefs and they tolerated the presence of the Spanish and their priests. After American acquisition of the Pueblo region in the 1840s, the United

States recognized the Pueblo people's historic right to the their traditional lands. In the early twentieth century, traditional Pueblo pottery makers found a market in American tourists, and today, Hopi kachinas, Pueblo pottery, and Zuni jewelry provide income for talented Pueblo artisans.

The Yuman-speaking Pais, another indigenous group occupying the northern reaches of the Southwest, lived relatively undisturbed on the south rim of the Grand Canyon in thatched huts, eking a living from the sage, juniper, piñon, and small game of the high Mojave Desert. They watched as Apaches and Navajos prevented the Spaniards from migrating north of the Gila River or west of the Hopi villages. Originating on the lower Colorado River, the migrating Havasupais eventually occupied a side canyon of the Grand Canyon, where they live today; their cousins, the Hualapais, settled to their west.

The Yavapais migrated south, in time settling in central Arizona, where they warred with the Apaches. Living in mineral-rich lands, by the 1870s they had been invaded by American miners and subdued by the United States military. The Hualapais and Havasupais lived unmolested until the 1850s, when surveying parties for American railroads traversed through their country.

The Uto-Aztecan–speaking Southern Paiutes, who believe they originated near present-day Las Vegas, Nevada, eventually settled north of the Grand Canyon, where they farmed along tributary creeks and developed a spiritual worldview closely tied to the majestic Canyon. When Mormons settled their territory in the mid-nineteenth century, the Paiutes worked as laborers for their new neighbors. Today, the various Pai reservations sustain themselves through a combination of timber harvesting, grazing leases, tourism in the Grand Canyon, and casino gaming.

Back on the Colorado River, the Mojaves remained in the shadow of Spirit Mountain, from which they believe they originally emerged. Below them on the river lived the Quechans, and further south lived the Cocopahs. Along the Colorado, the people lived well, harvesting fish and farming on the rich flood plain of the river. There, in a land of abundance, they lived in rancherías and learned to acquire power through dreams. At death, the Mojaves ceremonially cremated their dead. Today, the Mojaves live on their riverside reservation or on the Colorado River Indian Tribes reservation, where the land is shared with Chemehuevis, as well as Navajos and Hopis who migrated to the reservation in the twentieth century. On these fertile lands, the Colorado River tribes still farm, and in recent years have added gaming to their economic development. In addition, the Cocopahs, straddling the United States–Mexico border, work as laborers on large corporate-owned farms on the lower Colorado River.

The Apaches, who call themselves the Inde, and the Navajos, the Diné, migrated from western Canada sometime after 1000 A.D. While the Navajos settled in the Four Corners region of Arizona, New Mexico, Colorado, and Utah, the Apaches eventually occupied the rugged, piney forests of eastern Arizona and western New Mexico. Additionally, the Mescalero and Jicarilla Apaches occupied land from west Texas to central New Mexico. Fierce warriors and raiders, the Navajos and Apaches harried their agrarian neighbors, battled the Yavapais, and raided Spanish settlements in Mexico, until the arrival of Americans in the region in the 1850s. Soon, wagon trains, stage lines, and the Pony Express crossed their lands. Even so, the Apaches largely refrained from fighting with Americans until the 1860s, when a misunderstanding caused the powerful Chiricahua Apache chief Cochise to declare war on Americans.

By the 1870s, the Western Apaches of central Arizona had joined forces with the American military against the Chiricahuas. Although they fought bitterly under their war chief and shaman Geronimo, the Chiricahuas were defeated in 1886 and exiled to Alabama and Florida. By the end of the nineteenth century, the Chiricahuas had been moved to Fort Sill, Oklahoma, on land given to them by the Comanches. In 1894, many Chiricahuas returned to the Southwest to live with the Mescalero Apaches, but others chose to remain in Oklahoma, where they live today. The Apaches still practice their G'an, or Mountain Spirits dance, and girls' puberty rites. Today, tribal economic development revolves around recreation industries such as hunting, fishing, skiing, and gaming.

The Navajos, settling in the Four Corners region, absorbed many of the agrarian practices of their neighbors, the Pueblos. They fought American incursion until 1864, when American troops forced them to march to Bosque Redondo, New Mexico. Hundreds of Navajos died during the ordeal. Some Navajos filtered back to northeastern Arizona, while others remained in New Mexico and in 1868 signed a treaty with the United States guaranteeing them a reservation on their homeland.

Today, the Navajo reservation includes land in four states, constituting the largest Indian reservation in the United States. Like their ancestors, modern Navajos raise sheep and goats, and maintain spiritual beliefs based on their close relationship to the land. The Navajos matrilineal clan system has absorbed people of many origins—Indian, Mexican, and American—while maintaining cohesiveness as a people. Though Navajos have resisted the gaming industry as a means of economic development, they are well known for their fine silverwork and blanket weaving. In addition to handcrafts, the Navajo economy depends on mineral leases and tourism.

The Pascua Yaqui Indians, or Yoeme, are the most recent arrivals to the Southwest. Originating in Mexico, their homeland encompassed some of the richest land in Sonora. Firmly resisting Spanish conquerors, the Yaquis were eventually missionized by Jesuits. In the early twentieth century, the Mexican government persecuted the Yaquis, killing many and exiling others to Yucatan. Many Yaquis fled north to Arizona, where they settled in Tucson and Phoenix. They received a reservation in the 1970s.

Today, the Yaquis practice a mix of Catholicism and traditional beliefs. Their Easter season ceremonies have been practiced uninterrupted for over four hundred years. At their main reservation near Tucson, the Yaqui Nation has prospered in the late twentieth century from casino gaming.

BIBLIOGRAPHY

Dobyns, Henry F., and Robert C. Euler. *The Walapai People*. Phoenix, Ariz.: Indian Tribal Series, 1976.

———. *The Havasupai People*. Phoenix, Ariz.: Indian Tribal Series, 1976.

Fontana, Bernard L. *Of Earth and Little Rain: The Papago Indians*. Flagstaff, Ariz.: Northland Press, 1981.

Gifford, Edward W. "The Southeastern Yavapai." *University of California Publications in American Archaeology and Ethnology* 29, no. 3 (1932).

———. "Northeastern and Western Yavapai." *University of California Publications in American Archaeology and Ethnology* 34, no. 4 (1936).

Iverson, Peter. *The Navajo Nation*. Albuquerque: University of New Mexico Press, 1983.

Jefferson, James, Robert Delaney, and George C. Thompson. *The Southern Utes: A Tribal History*. Ignacio, Colo.: Southern Ute Tribe, 1972.

Mails, Thomas E. *The People Called Apache*. Englewood Cliffs, N.J.: Prentice-Hall, 1974.

Ortiz, Alfonso, ed. *Handbook of North American Indians*. Volume 9, *Southwest*. Washington, D.C.: Smithsonian Institution Press, 1979.

———. *Handbook of North American Indians*. Volume 10, *Southwest*. Washington, D.C.: Smithsonian Institution Press, 1983.

Sando, Joe S. *The Pueblo Indians*. San Francisco: Indian Historian Press, 1976.

Spicer, Edward S. *Cycles of Conquest: The Impact of Spain, Mexico and the United States on the Indians of the Southwest, 1533–1960*. Tucson: University of Arizona Press, 1962.

———. *The Yaquis: A Cultural History*. Tucson: University of Arizona Press, 1980.

Spier, Leslie. *Yuman Tribes of the Gila River*. Chicago: University of Chicago Press, 1933.

Trimble, Stephen. *The People: Indians of the American Southwest*. Santa Fe, N.M.: School of American Research Press, 1993.

Victoria A. O. Smith

See also **Apache; Hopi; Indian Policy, Colonial; Navajo; Pueblo; Pueblo Revolt; Zuni.**

TRIBUTE. Thomas Jefferson's new administration faced a crisis regarding the Barbary pirate-nations of North Africa. For years, European nations and the United States had paid tribute, or ransom, to these rogue nations to ensure protection of commercial vessels and keep sailors from being captured and sold into slavery. But the practice was expensive. From 1795 to 1802, the United States had paid more than $2 million in tributes. Nevertheless, this sum did not prevent the North African nation of Tripoli from declaring war against the United States; Tripoli wanted a larger share of the money. From 1801 to 1805, American naval operations against the pirates proved inconclusive. On February 16, 1804, U.S. naval officer Stephen Decatur's ship destroyed a captured American ship, denying the enemy the benefits of the capture. Military operations on land were successful enough to force Tripoli's government to sue for peace. It was a temporary solution. During the Napoleonic Wars, the pirates resumed their attacks. Finally, in 1815, Decatur's navy forced Tripoli to renounce the practice of paying tribute. The extended campaign against the Barbary states was over and no tribute was paid after 1815. In an indirect fashion, the United States had also helped Europe, since paying a tribute became a relic of the past for both.

BIBLIOGRAPHY

Allen, Gardner Weld. *Our Navy and the Barbary Corsairs*. Boston: Houghton Mifflin, 1905. An old and factual account.

Irwin, Ray Watkins. *The Diplomatic Relations of the United States with the Barbary Powers, 1776–1816*. Chapel Hill: University of North Carolina Press, 1931. A close, informative narrative.

Donald K. Pickens

TRICKLE-DOWN ECONOMICS. A derogatory term applied to Reaganomics, or supply-side economics, trickle-down economics is the theory that tax cuts for the wealthy merely "trickled down" to the bottom groups and that the rich benefited at the expense of the economy. Similar criticisms were raised about the supply-side tax cuts enacted by Treasury Secretary Andrew Mellon in 1921 but not for those made by John Kennedy in the 1960s. Supply-side cuts involve cutting taxes across the board but most dramatically for those in the top tax brackets. The rationale was that those who paid the most taxes would then be able to reinvest their tax "savings." Thus, supporters have countered the phrase "trickle-down" with the one coined by John Kennedy: "a rising tide lifts all boats."

BIBLIOGRAPHY

Brookes, Warren. *The Economy in Mind*. New York: Universe Books, 1982.

Brownlee, W. Elliot. *Federal Taxation in America: A Short History*. Washington, D.C.: Woodrow Wilson Center Press, 1996.

Canto, Victor A., Douglas H. Joines, and Arthur B. Laffer, eds. *Foundations of Supply Side Economics: Theory and Evidence*. New York: Academic Press, 1983.

Schweikart, Larry. *The Entrepreneurial Adventure: A History of Business in the United States*. Ft. Worth, Tex.: Harcourt, 2000.

Larry Schweikart

See also **Laissez-Faire; Reaganomics; Supply-Side Economics; Taxation.**

TRIPARTITE AGREEMENT. The Tripartite Agreement was an international monetary agreement entered into by France, England, and the United States in September 1936 to stabilize their currencies both at home and in the exchange. Following suspension of the gold standard by England in 1931 and the United States in 1933, a serious imbalance developed between their currencies and those of the gold bloc countries, particularly France. At the same time, in both England and America there was a sharpening of the controversy between "sound money" advocates, who urged stabilization, and those who favored complete demonetization of gold and a managed currency. The gold bloc countries were also urging stabilization of sterling and the dollar, because their fluctuating values were having an adverse influence on the exchange value of gold bloc currencies. Because devaluation had raised import prices and lowered export prices in England and America, the gold bloc countries would eventually have to devaluate unless international stabilization was agreed on by leading monetary powers. Parallel to the announcement of the Tripartite Agreement, France devalued its currency.

By this informal and provisional agreement the three powers pledged to refrain from competitive depreciation and to maintain currencies at existing levels as long as that attempt did not interfere seriously with internal prosperity.

BIBLIOGRAPHY

Gardner, Lloyd C. *Economic Aspects of New Deal Diplomacy.* Madison: University of Wisconsin Press, 1964.

Leuchtenburg, William E. *Franklin D. Roosevelt and the New Deal, 1932–1940.* New York: Harper and Row, 1963.

Kenneth Potter / A. G.

See also **France, Relations with; Gold Exchange; Gold Standard; Great Britain, Relations with; Great Depression.**

TROLLEYS. *See* **Railways, Urban, and Rapid Transit.**

TRUAX V. CORRIGAN, 257 U.S. 312 (1921), a case in which the Supreme Court held unconstitutional a pro-union law of Arizona (1913) that forbade state courts from granting injunctions against picketing. Considering a dispute between a restaurant owner and his striking employees, the Court ruled that the action of the strikers was a violation of the plaintiff's right of property and a denial of free access of employees, owners, and customers to the place of business. The five-to-four opinion further held that the Arizona law deprived the owner of property without due process of law and hence violated the Fourteenth Amendment.

BIBLIOGRAPHY

Forbath, William E. *Law and the Shaping of the American Labor Movement.* Cambridge, Mass.: Harvard University Press, 1991.

Gordon S. Watkins / A. R.

See also **Boycotting; Due Process of Law; Injunctions, Labor; Labor Legislation and Administration; Picketing; Yellow-Dog Contract.**

TRUCKING INDUSTRY had its inception in France about 1769 with Nicolas J. Cugnot's experimental artillery tractor. It was introduced in America in the nineteenth century, but neither the times, nor the technology, nor the roads were prepared for such an innovation, and the occasional builders of experimental vehicles received little encouragement for their efforts, particularly given the stellar successes of the rail industry in transporting heavy goods.

In the 1890s numerous experimental motor vehicles began to appear throughout the country, and among them were a few motor wagons. A few commercial motor vehicles reached the market during the last three years of the century. Like the passenger vehicles that were widely known as "horseless carriages," these earliest motor wagons resembled their horse-drawn predecessors, with their motors and other machinery suspended under their bodies. This design prevailed through the first decade of the twentieth century. Because the heavy machines were limited to short hauls on paved urban roads, the nascent trucking industry favored the more reliable electric wagons over those powered by as-yet-crude gasoline or steam engines. No early trucks were very efficient or reliable, however, and most carried only small loads. Consequently, people found them most valuable as advertisements, because of their novelty. Inexperienced drivers, who abused and neglected the vehicles, the general conservatism of the business world, and inadequate design all retarded the use of motor trucks during these years.

By 1910, improvements in truck design had begun to break down the conservative bias against the new vehicles, and increased profits for the manufacturers enabled more rapid development. Following innovations first worked out in the passenger-car market, vertical four-cylinder engines, located under a hood in front of the driver, began to replace the single-cylinder and double-opposed engines. Sliding gear transmissions superseded planetary transmissions and the less efficient friction transmissions. During the period 1913–1915, there was a noticeable trend away from chain drive in favor of several forms of gear drive.

Important developments of 1912 were the tractor and semitrailer, the former having been introduced for use with the many serviceable wagons designed to be drawn by horses, the tractor and its rear wheels replacing the horses and front wheels of the wagons. Truck use increased rapidly during that decade. The production of

25,000 trucks in 1914 tripled in 1915, and total registrations of 99,015 in 1914 rose to 1,107,639 by 1920. Poor rural roads and the 15 mile per hour maximum speed of these solid-tired trucks kept most of these vehicles confined to city streets.

World War I and its aftermath had an immense effect on truck use and development. The immediate need for trucks by the military and the army's truck-standardization program focused the attention of truck engineers on component design and furthered the cause of the assembled truck as against the manufactured truck. As the railroads became woefully congested and inefficient because of the tremendous increase in traffic when the United States entered the war in 1917, Roy Chapin's Highway Transport Committee of the Council for National Defense experimented with the first long-distance truck shipments, sending trucks bound for overseas military use under their own power from midwestern manufacturing centers to eastern seaports, primarily Baltimore. At that time, too, pneumatic tires capable of withstanding heavy truck loads were being developed; previously pneumatic tires had rarely been used on anything heavier than a three-quarter-ton truck. When the improved tires became available, they enabled trucks to double their former speed, an enormous advantage and a practical necessity for intercity trucking. Immediately after the war the good-roads movement began to achieve major results as the federal-aid system began to develop, resulting in the dramatic expansion of the nation's hard-surfaced highway system over the next two decades.

Interstate trucking increased steadily during the 1920s along with the new road system. As the decade closed such developments as power-assisted brakes, six-cylinder engines, and three-axle trucks began to contribute to the safety and efficiency of highway operation. The lean years of the early 1930s had some adverse effects on trucking, but there was also some progress, as the use of the semitrailer, better adapted to heavier loads, increased 500 percent from 1929 to 1936. Likewise, in the early 1930s cooperative trailer-switching arrangements between carriers permitted through service by eliminating the extra freight handling that shifting loads from truck to truck had previously required and, at the same time, led to standardization in size, fifth wheels, brakes, and other new components. The diesel truck, introduced in the early 1930s, was not found in significant numbers until the 1950s.

The shortages of steel, rubber, and gasoline during the war years of the 1940s curtailed the growth of motor freighting, but trucks served as a mobile assembly line on the home front and were often the decisive factor in the theaters of war, causing Gen. George S. Patton to remark, "The truck is our most valuable weapon." After the war the trucking industry resumed a steady and rapid growth. An important development of the late 1950s and 1960s was "piggybacking" or "intermodal" shipping—the long-distance movement of loaded semitrailers on railway flatcars; 1,264,501 semitrailers were loaded on flatcars in 1970. Intermodal trucking activity increased even more dramatically in the 1980s, following the 1980 Staggers Act, which weakened the Interstate Commerce Commission's regulatory control over railroads, and the 1980 Motor Carrier Act, which partially deregulated trucking. As a result, the number of piggybacking semitrailers jumped by 70 percent between 1981 and 1986. The 1991 Intermodal Surface Transportation Efficiency Act (ISTEA) further boosted intermodal shipping.

The last three decades of the twentieth century saw a large increase in highway trucking as well, in large part due to the rapid construction of the 42,500-mile system of interstates begun in 1956, which facilitated the use of larger trucks carrying heavier loads at lower per-mile cost. By 1970 the national truck total of 18,747,781 more than tripled the 1941 figure. Following the deregulation of the truck industry in 1980, the number of licensed carriers grew from 17,000 to over 40,000 by 1990. In addition, the number of carriers with permission from the ICC to operate on a nationwide basis grew from under 100 in 1980, when operating rights sold for hundreds of thousands of dollars, to an unprecedented 5,000 carriers in 1990.

BIBLIOGRAPHY

Automobile Manufacturers Association. *Motor Truck Facts.* New York: Annually, 1935–1975.

Denham, A. F. *Twenty Years Progress in Commercial Motor Vehicles (1921–1942).* Washington, D.C.: Automotive Council for War Production, 1943.

Karolevitz, Robert F. *This Was Trucking: A Pictorial History of the First Quarter Century of Commercial Motor Vehicles.* Seattle, Wash.: Superior, 1966.

Motor Vehicle Manufacturers Association. *Motor Vehicle Facts and Figures.* Detroit, Mich.: Annually 1975–current.

U.S. Department of Transportation. *America's Highways, 1776–1976: A History of the Federal-Aid Program.* Washington, D.C.: U.S. Government Printing Office, 1977.

Don H. Berkebile
Christopher Wells

See also **Automobile; Deregulation; Interstate Commerce Commission; Interstate Highway System; Motor Carrier Act; Roads; Staggers Rail Act.**

TRUMAN DOCTRINE. The 12 March 1947 announcement of the Truman Doctrine marked the beginning of a new, aggressive American posture toward the Soviet Union. The administration of President Harry S. Truman abandoned efforts to accommodate the Soviet Union, which had emerged as America's principal rival after World War II. Now the two superpowers engaged in the Cold War. The doctrine called on Congress to approve $400 million in military assistance for Greece, which was fighting communist insurgents, and neighboring Turkey, also believed to be threatened by Soviet subversion. The doctrine was formulated after Britain indicated it no longer had the wherewithal to support the royalist Greek government. But during the previous year, the Truman administration had grown increasingly suspicious of Soviet intentions as the nations of Eastern Europe disappeared behind what the former British prime minister Winston Churchill had termed the "iron curtain."

Although it was specifically targeted to Greece, the Truman Doctrine was envisioned to have a much broader reach. Truman made this clear when he framed his request as part of a general policy to "support free peoples who are resisting attempted subjugation by armed minorities or by outside pressures." The doctrine was to be the first step in a strategy of containment of the Soviet Union, designed to prevent communist influence throughout Western Europe. The United States subsequently agreed to launch the massive recovery plan for Europe known as the Marshall Plan and entered its first peacetime military alliance, the North Atlantic Treaty Organization. The eruption of the Korean War in 1950 prompted a further expansion of the Truman Doctrine and the containment policy. The United States was committed to fighting communism in Asia and around the world.

BIBLIOGRAPHY

Gaddis, John Lewis. *The United States and the Origins of the Cold War, 1941–1947.* New York: Columbia University Press, 1972.

Harbutt, Fraser J. *The Iron Curtain: Churchill, America, and the Origins of the Cold War.* New York: Oxford University Press, 1986.

Ellen G. Rafshoon

See also **Cold War; Greece, Relations with; Iron Curtain; Marshall Plan.**

TRUST TERRITORY OF THE PACIFIC.

The Trust Territory of the Pacific was a United Nations Trust Territory administered by the United States from 1947 to 1996. It consisted of the Marshall Islands, Caroline Islands, Palau Islands, and the northern Marianas Islands— all of Micronesia except for Guam. Scattered across roughly three million square miles of the western Pacific, these island groups were geographically and culturally heterogeneous; their population included at least six distinct ethnic groups and nine mutually unintelligible languages.

All of Micronesia was claimed by Spain from the sixteenth century until 1898. However, after the Spanish-American War, Guam became a possession of the United States while the rest of Micronesia was purchased by Germany. The islands remained in German hands only until World War I, when they were captured by Japan. Until World War II they were League of Nations Class C mandates, effectively Japanese colonies. The region was the site of several major land and sea battles during the latter conflict, including those of Tarawa, Saipan, Peleliu, and the Philippine Sea.

After Japan's surrender, the islands were placed under the administration of the U.S. Navy, and then incorporated into a new trust territory. The Trust Territory of the Pacific was unique among all trust territories in that it was a "strategic" trust, one whose administrator answered to the UN Security Council, where the United States had a veto, rather than the UN General Assembly.

From 1948 until about 1996, the Trust Territory was administered as a de facto American colony. There was very little economic development on the islands; literacy levels were raised and basic health care was provided, but otherwise there were no major changes in the standard of living.

During this period, the islands were used for a variety of purposes by the U.S. military. Sixty-seven nuclear weapons tests were conducted in the Marshall Islands between 1946 and 1958, while Saipan was used as a training center for Nationalist Chinese forces. The islands were kept under military security: foreigners were excluded and travel by the islanders themselves was strictly regulated.

Beginning around 1962, however, the United States began to take a more liberal approach toward governing the Trust Territory. The Kennedy administration ended most travel restrictions, permitted limited foreign investment, and sharply increased the territory's budget. In 1965 the territory was granted limited self-government in the form of a bicameral Congress of Micronesia.

During this period a debate over the territory's future emerged and quickly became acute. Most islanders wanted independence, but a large minority wanted some form of association with the United States, while a local majority in the Northern Marianas Islands wanted to become an American commonwealth or territory. Furthermore, there was sharp disagreement over whether the territory should evolve into a single independent state or a group of smaller entities. This debate was resolved in 1975, when negotiators for the Northern Marianas and the United States agreed that the former should become an American commonwealth.

Over the next twenty years, four separate entities emerged from the Trust Territory. The Northern Marianas Islands broke away first, becoming an American commonwealth in 1978 with a status roughly equivalent to Puerto Rico. Then, in 1979, the Marshall Islands became an independent state, while Chuuk, Yap, Pohnpei, and Kosrae combined to form the Federated States of Micronesia. The last entity to emerge from the Trust Territory was the Republic of Palau. Its independence was delayed for nearly a decade by a protracted dispute over making Palau a nuclear-free zone. Full independence was finally granted on 1 October 1994 and the world's last trust territory came to an end.

The historical legacy of the Trust Territory is mixed. The Trust Territory government spread American concepts of democracy, human rights, and the rule of law across the Micronesian islands and the successor states are, by the standards of the region, stable and free. However, while the Northern Marianas have seen considerable economic development since the breakup of the Trust Territory, the Marshall Islands and the Federated States of Micronesia remain among the poorest states in the Pacific, and remain heavily dependent upon American aid.

The Republic of Palau, the Republic of the Marshall Islands, and the Federated States of Micronesia are all internationally recognized sovereign states with seats in the United Nations. However, all three have signed treaties that bind them quite closely to the United States politically, diplomatically, and economically. Although the Trust Territory of the Pacific is no more, the United States remains the dominant military and diplomatic influence in Micronesia.

BIBLIOGRAPHY

Kluge, P. F. *The Edge of Paradise: America in Micronesia.* Honolulu: University of Hawaii Press, 1993.

Willens, Howard, and Deanne Siemer. *National Security and Self-Determination: United States Policy in Micronesia.* Westport, Conn.: Praeger, 2000. There is no single-volume history of the Trust Territory of the Pacific, but Willens and Siemer provide a straightforward chronicle of the period from 1962 to 1975.

Douglas M. Muir

"TRUST-BUSTING," a term that referred to President Theodore Roosevelt's policy of prosecuting monopolies, or "trusts," that violated federal antitrust law. Roosevelt's "trust-busting" policy marked a major departure from previous administrations' policies, which had generally failed to enforce the SHERMAN ANTITRUST ACT of 1890, and added momentum to the progressive reform movements of the early 1900s.

BIBLIOGRAPHY

Brands, H. W. *T. R.: The Last Romantic.* New York: Basic Books, 1997.

Gould, Lewis L. *The Presidency of Theodore Roosevelt.* Lawrence: University Press of Kansas, 1991.

Myron W. Watkins/A. G.

See also **Codes of Fair Competition; Implied Powers; Laissez-Faire; Pujo Committee; Taft-Roosevelt Split.**

TRUSTS. The term "trust" derives from English common law. Not until the 1880s, however, with the rise of big business in the United States, did the modern definition of trust come into use.

In 1879, John D. Rockefeller, a rich industrialist and owner of Standard Oil, was facing a crisis. A self-made man who began his career as a bookkeeper at the age of sixteen, Rockefeller had built up Standard Oil through a system of mergers and acquisitions. A persistent entrepreneur, Rockefeller was involved in various industries, including the rapidly expanding railroads. By 1879 the New York State Legislature was looking into Rockefeller's dealings, specifically his railroad mergers, and when the investigation's findings were published in the *Atlantic Monthly* in 1881, public outcry made further mergers impossible.

Anxious to expand Standard Oil beyond Ohio, Rockefeller had been limited by antimonopoly laws and sentiment. Rockefeller, realizing that he was stymied after the legislative investigation and that he needed a change of direction, was intent on finding a backdoor to monopoly. His attorney, Samuel Dodd, provided the answer.

Dodd proposed the formation of a trust company, controlled by a board of nine trustees. This board would select directors and officers of component companies and would determine the dividends of the companies within the trust. Rather than acquiring companies directly, Rockefeller would instead control such companies indirectly via the trust. Such a form of corporate organization insured against a direct hierarchy with Rockefeller at the top; this legal technicality allowed Rockefeller to expand and continue to control his business. On 2 January 1882, the Standard Oil Trust became a reality, changing the face of big business.

As the U.S. economy expanded, so did the number of trusts, attracting such men as steel maker Andrew Carnegie, railroad tycoon Jay Gould, and financier J. P. Morgan. All would use the trust form to crush their competition and achieve monopolies in their industries.

Such concentration meant almost certain death for small businessmen and companies just getting started—they could not be competitive. The cry of "unfair" was quickly heard. Thomas Nast, the famous cartoonist who had exposed the corruption at TAMMANY HALL during the early 1870s, inflamed the public with caricatures of rich, powerful industrialists controlling everything from corn to Congress, while MUCKRAKERS such as Ida M. Tarbell exposed the greed and power behind the ROBBER BARONS. By 1888, popular antipathy toward the trusts made them a key issue in the presidential election. Both the Democratic candidate, Grover Cleveland, and the Republican, Benjamin Harrison, were forced to make a campaign promise to fight trusts. In a closely contested election, Harrison would receive fewer popular votes, but would win the electoral college and become president.

Sherman Antitrust Act

Eager to gain public support, Harrison was prepared to sign into law antitrust legislation. Congress responded with the SHERMAN ANTITRUST ACT, named after Ohio senator John Sherman. The Senate passed the bill by 51 to 1 on 8 April 1890. The bill then went on to the House, where it was passed unanimously.

Section 1 of the bill stated that "every contract combination in the form of trust or otherwise, or conspiracy, in RESTRAINT OF TRADE or commerce among the several States, or with foreign nations, is declared to be illegal." Section 2 extended the law to anyone who attempted to "monopolize any part of the trade or commerce among the several States, or with foreign nations." Violation was ordained a felony, with each violation punishable by a fine of $350,000 and up to three years in jail.

Unfortunately, the bill was poorly worded. The legislators had failed to define the terms "restraint of trade," "combination," and "monopolize." What was to be considered restraint of trade, and how to determine "good" trusts from "bad?" were some immediate questions. This Act was used throughout the 1890s to block strikes. Companies such as Pullman Palace Railcar maintained that unions were prohibited under the "conspiracy to restrict trade" clause. Accepting this argument, the federal government sent troops to put down the Pullman strike of 1892.

A further setback came in 1895, when the Supreme Court, in the case of UNITED STATES V. E. C. KNIGHT CO. ruled that not all combinations constituted trusts that restrained interstate commerce, and such combinations could therefore not be prosecuted under the new law. The Court noted a distinct difference between commerce and manufacture, declaring that not all that is produced can be considered commerce. "Commerce succeeds to manufacture," the majority decision stated, "and is not a part of it . . . The fact that an article is manufactured for export to another state does not of itself make it an article of interstate commerce, and the intent of the manufacturer does not determine the time when the article or product passes from the control of the state and belongs to commerce." This decision implied that Congress did not have a right to control all products manufactured, since the simple manufacturing of a product did not make it "interstate commerce" and weakened the already ineffectual INTERSTATE COMMERCE COMMISSION.

The 1896 presidential campaign again brought the need for reform to the forefront. William Jennings Bryan, the popular orator and Democratic candidate for president, compared the rich industrialists to hogs. "As I was riding along," he declared, "I noticed these hogs rooting in a field, and they were tearing up the ground, and the first thought that came to me was that they were destroying a good deal of property. And that carried me back to the time when as a boy I lived upon a farm, and I remembered that when we had hogs we used to put rings in the noses of the hogs, and the thought came to me, 'Why did we do it?' Not to keep the hogs from getting fat. We were more interested in their getting fat than they were. The sooner they got fat the sooner we killed them; the longer they were in getting fat the longer they lived. But why were the rings put in the noses of those hogs? So that, while they were getting fat, they would not destroy more property than they were worth."

Bryan was not a socialist, but he did not want the Rockefellers, the Goulds, and the Morgans taking more than their share by way of muddy legal maneuvers. His opponent, William McKinley, meanwhile, received large donations from industrialist supporters, enabling his campaign to spend at least $4 million, a tremendous sum at the time. Some called this bribery, but Rockefeller and other industrialists insisted that they had a right to contribute money to candidates who supported their ideas. McKinley won the election by a comfortable margin, and the issue of trusts and monopolies seemed to be put on the backburner, especially with the advent of the Spanish-American War in 1898. McKinley was reelected in 1900; serious trust reform, it seemed, would have to wait. But McKinley's assassination in September 1901 brought Theodore Roosevelt into the White House.

Trust-Busters
Roosevelt, the "Hero of San Juan Hill" and former governor of New York, where he was outspoken in his criticisms of government policy toward business, quickly took big business to task, attacking the trusts and the newer "holding companies." Five months into Roosevelt's term, Morgan gave him the perfect opportunity to show his mettle when the financier formed the Northern Securities Company. The Northern Securities Company was a $4 million combination of all major groups competing for rail traffic in the northwest, including Rockefeller. Morgan thought that he would be able to negotiate with Roosevelt, even going so far as to suggest that "his man" meet with Roosevelt's "man" (Attorney General Philander C. Knox) to settle the matter.

Roosevelt was not interested in Morgan's negotiations. Instead, in 1902 he ordered Knox to bring suit against Northern Securities for violation of the Sherman Antitrust Act. The case went to the Supreme Court, and in a split five-to-four decision in *Northern Securities Co. v. United States* (1904), the Court sided with Roosevelt, proclaiming, "Congress has authority to declare, and by the language of its act, as interpreted in prior cases, has, in effect, declared, that the freedom of interstate and international commerce shall not be obstructed or disturbed by any combination, conspiracy, or MONOPOLY that will restrain such commerce, by preventing the free operation of competition among interstate carriers engaged in the transportation of passengers of freight."

Roosevelt's challenge of Northern Securities quickly gained him popularity as a "trustbuster." The wave of support for Roosevelt forced Congress to create a Bureau of Corporations in the Department of Commerce and Labor to investigate the activities of corporations. Congress also passed the ELKINS ACT of 1903, which outlawed rebates to large shippers and increased the powers of the Interstate Commerce Commission. Although he preferred to regulate corporations rather than "bust" them, Roosevelt went on to file forty-three more antitrust suits. His successor, William Howard Taft, filed sixty-five suits against trusts; Taft is rarely given credit for his vigorous enforcement activities.

The robber barons were losing ground. In *Standard Oil Co. v. United States* (1911), a case pushed strongly by the Taft administration, the Supreme Court ruled that Rockefeller's Standard Oil combination had to be dissolved; the Court, however, left a small loophole that would later prove crucial in allowing some combinations, including U.S. Steel, to survive. The Court invoked a "Rule of Reason," declaring that the restraint upon trade must be "undue" or "unreasonable." As long as their tactics were not "unreasonable," the alleged robber barons could proceed.

In 1914, during the presidency of Woodrow Wilson, Congress passed the Clayton Antitrust Act; this Act prohibited mergers and acquisitions that tended to "substantially . . . lessen competition, or . . . to create a monopoly." The Act also outlawed the "interlocking" of corporate executives on boards of companies issuing more than $1 million in stocks and bonds, and forbade stock purchases and price discriminations in which the intent was to limit competition. Labor unions were exempted from these restrictions, and Congress included provisions for labor's right to strike.

That same year, the FEDERAL TRADE COMMISSION (FTC) was created to replace the Bureau of Corporations. The FTC was granted the authority to investigate corporate activities and to make rulings on unfair monopolistic business practices; it was further empowered to regulate advertising and to keep Congress and the public informed of the efficiency of antitrust legislation.

The Depression and the NEW DEAL brought more antitrust legislation. In 1934 Congress created the Securities and Exchange Commission to protect investors from "rags to riches" schemes and maintain the integrity of the securities market.

In 1936, the ROBINSON-PATMAN ACT was passed. Its purpose was to protect small businessmen who were trying to get back into the market. While many small businesses had been wiped out by the Depression, most of the larger ones had managed to stay afloat. It was widely feared that these companies might expand in such bad times and use methods such as price discrimination to stifle competition. Robinson-Patman forbade firms involved in interstate commerce to engage in price discrimination when the effect would be to lessen competition or to create a monopoly. (This law is frequently referred to as the "Anti-Chain Store Act," as it has often been applied to them.) Through the 1940s and 1950s, the government would continue trust-busting activities. In 1969, the government filed suit against IBM, the corporate giant; the suit dragged on for thirteen years before the case was dismissed. By then IBM's business was threatened by personal computers and networked office systems. Many critics of antitrust legislation declared government intervention pointless, noting that technology is often its own safeguard against monopoly. In 1973, however, the government would succeed in forcing giant AT&T to dissolve.

During the late twentieth and early twenty-first centuries, the government engaged in a massive antitrust lawsuit against Microsoft, the computer-programming giant. The FTC began its attempt to dismantle Microsoft in 1989, accusing the company and its officers of engaging in price discrimination and claiming that the company deliberately placed programming codes in its operating systems that would hinder competition. Microsoft responded by changing its royalty policy. In 1997 Microsoft would come to trial once again, with the Department of Justice claiming that the company violated Sections 1 and 2 of the Sherman Antitrust Act. The case stemmed from the fact that Microsoft's Windows® program required consumers to load Microsoft's Internet browser, giving Microsoft a monopolistic advantage over other browser manufacturers. Microsoft claimed that this was a matter of quality service, not of monopoly. Microsoft claimed that it had produced a superior, more compatible product and that its intent was not to restrict commerce. In late 1999, the judge hearing the case ruled that Microsoft was, in fact, a monopoly and should be broken up. Two years later, in July 2001, an Appeals Court found that Microsoft had acted illegally but reversed the lower court ruling ordering a breakup.

BIBLIOGRAPHY

Abels, Jules. *The Rockefeller Billions: The Story of the World's Most Stupendous Fortune.* New York: MacMillan, 1965.

Brands, H. W. *TR: The Last Romantic.* New York: Basic Books, 1997.

Chernow, Ron. *The Death of the Banker: The Decline and Fall of the Great Financial Dynasties and the Triumph of the Small Investor.* New York: Vintage Books, 1997.

Garraty, John A. *Theodore Roosevelt: The Strenuous Life.* New York: American Heritage Publishing, 1967.

Geisst, Charles R. *Monopolies in America: Empire Builders and their Enemies, from Jay Gould to Bill Gates.* New York: Oxford University Press, 2000.

Laughlin, Rosemary. *John D. Rockefeller: Oil Baron and Philanthropist.* Greensboro, N.C.: Morgan Reynolds, 2001.

Tompkins, Vincent, ed. "Headline Makers." In *American Eras: Development of the Industrial United States, 1878–1899.* Detroit, Mich.: Gale Research, 1997.

Wheeler, George. *Pierpont Morgan and Friends: The Anatomy of a Myth.* Englewood Cliffs, N.J.: Prentice-Hall, 1973.

David Burner
Ross Rosenfeld

TUBERCULOSIS was the leading cause of death in the United States during the nineteenth century, responsible at times for as many as one of every four deaths. Although the death rate from tuberculosis steadily declined beginning in the mid-nineteenth century, it persisted as a major public health problem well into the twentieth century, when programs of public health education, disease surveillance and diagnosis, and the availability of antibiotics and vaccination helped to curb its incidence. After World War II, the death rate was only a small fraction of what it was a century earlier, but by the 1990s, the emergence of tuberculosis strains resistant to antibiotics and the connections between tuberculosis and AIDS again made it a significant health concern.

Before the late nineteenth century, various names—including consumption and phthisis—were used to describe the dry, persistent cough, throat irritations, chest and shoulder pains, and difficult breathing accompanied by emaciation that characterized pulmonary tuberculosis. The incidence of tuberculosis grew dramatically in Europe beginning in the eighteenth century, and although its incidence in the United States was less severe, it had grown into the leading cause of death in the United States by the mid-nineteenth century. Other than being slightly more prevalent in women than men, the disease respected no boundaries, afflicting Americans of all ages, races, ethnicities, and social and economic stations.

Tuberculosis in Nineteenth-Century Life

While sudden and dramatic epidemics of cholera, diphtheria, smallpox, and yellow fever commanded public attention, tuberculosis quietly became a regular feature of nineteenth-century American life. Healers diagnosed tuberculosis on the basis of its physical symptoms, but they were at a loss to offer a definitive cause or cure for the disease. For much of the nineteenth century, it was thought that tuberculosis was hereditary, and therefore, that it was noncontagious and could not be transmitted from person to person. It was presumed that there was some familial disposition that made a person susceptible to the disease and that the interaction of the inherited constitution with environmental or behavioral "irritations," such as rich diets, sedentary occupations, and cold, wet climates, brought on the disease. The remedies emphasized changing the irritants, whether to a mild or bland diet, to an active lifestyle with exercise, or to a residence that was mild and dry. Between 1840 and 1890, thousands of Americans with tuberculosis, particularly from New England, became "health seekers," moving to where they believed the wholesome, restorative climates would give them relief. These "lungers," as tuberculosis patients were colloquially called, moved first to Florida, and later to the West and Southwest, settling in the deserts and mountains of Arizona, California, Colorado, and New Mexico. One in four migrants to California and one in three migrants to Arizona during the second half of the nineteenth century went looking to improve their health.

During the 1830s, tuberculosis was responsible for one in every four deaths, but by the 1880s, the mortality rate had declined to one in every eight deaths. In major American cities, the death rate from tuberculosis at the end of the nineteenth century (200 deaths per 100,000 population) was essentially half of what it was a century earlier. Improvements in diets and in living conditions, along with natural selection and genetic resistance in the

population, contributed to the declining rates. Even as the mortality rates from tuberculosis declined in the general population, it persisted as a significant health problem among America's growing immigrant population, most of whom lived in the crowded, dank, and dirty tenements of America's urban centers—living conditions that were ripe for the rapid spread of the disease. The incidence of tuberculosis became increasingly associated with immigrants and the impoverished and the overcrowded living conditions they experienced.

Tuberculosis in the Age of Bacteriology

In March 1882, the German bacteriologist Robert Koch announced the discovery of *Mycobacterium tuberculosis*, the bacillus or bacterium that causes tuberculosis. But medical explanations attributing the cause of tuberculosis to heredity, climate, diet, lifestyle, poor ventilation, and other factors endured through the century and decades would pass before physicians were fully convinced that tuberculosis was contagious and could be transmitted between persons. The medical landmark of Koch's discovery accompanied the growing number of tuberculosis sanatoria being built in Europe and the United States after the 1850s and 1880s, respectively. The sanatorium movement emphasized a therapy regimen based on fresh air, proper diet, and rest, but they also served to remove and to isolate patients with tuberculosis from areas where they might infect others. Among the sanatoria were two founded by America's most prominent physicians of tuberculosis: Edward Livingston Trudeau established a sanatorium at Saranac Lake in the Adirondack Mountains of northeastern New York, and Lawrence Flick established a sanatorium at White Haven, in the Pocono Mountains of eastern Pennsylvania. Trudeau and Flick themselves suffered from tuberculosis, and learned of the benefits of an outdoor life in seeking a cure for their own afflictions. Trudeau's Saranac Lake sanatorium, founded in 1884, became a model for other sanatoria. Flick, believing that tuberculosis was contagious, advocated for a scientific approach to its diagnosis and treatment, as well as the registration of patients and the education of the public about the disease. In 1892, Flick founded the Pennsylvania Society for the Prevention of Tuberculosis, the first state organization in the nation devoted to the control and the elimination of tuberculosis. As other state societies against tuberculosis developed, Flick joined Trudeau, Hermann Biggs, William Welch, William Osler, and others to found in 1904 the National Association for the Study and Prevention of Tuberculosis (NASPT), the forerunner to the American Lung Association, which unified efforts, led public health education campaigns, and raised funds for research.

By the turn of the twentieth century, as the presence of the tubercle bacillus rather than the physical symptoms became the basis for diagnosis, the new understanding of what caused tuberculosis and how it was spread brought important changes in public health and the medical care of patients. The goal of Progressive Era public health work against tuberculosis was to improve social condi-

War on Tuberculosis. A poster created for the City of Chicago Municipal Tuberculosis Sanitarium and dated 1939 promotes testing. LIBRARY OF CONGRESS

tions and to control the behaviors that fostered the disease. Health departments instituted education campaigns that used films, posters, and lectures to dissuade individuals from practices that spread germs, such as spitting and coughing. In addition to maintaining clean, well-ventilated homes, the use of nonporous building materials such as metals, linoleum, and porcelain was encouraged over wood and cloth, which could harbor disease-causing germs. Public health officials inspected and fumigated dwellings that posed health risks, required physicians to report cases of tuberculosis, and forcibly isolated individuals who did not seek treatment. New diagnostic tests such as the tuberculin skin test and radiological examinations were used in mass screenings for tuberculosis, and new surgical therapies involving the collapse or partial section of the lungs were introduced. Infected individuals were required to seek treatment through a sanatorium or through a dispensary that engaged in disease surveillance and patient education.

Tuberculosis after World War II

The result of the far-reaching and aggressive public health campaign was that the incidence of tuberculosis, which had been steadily declining since the 1870s (when the mortality rate exceeded 300 deaths per 100,000 population), fell to unprecedented low levels by the 1930s (when the mortality rate fell below 50 deaths per 100,000 population). Disease mortality fell even lower (to 10 deaths per 100,000 population in 1954) after the development of an antibiotic, streptomycin, by the microbiologist Selman Waksman in 1943. Although other countries in the 1950s instituted vaccination campaigns using the Bacillus-Calmette-Guérin (BCG) vaccine, it was not adopted for wide use in the United States as public health programs emphasized the identification of patients exposed to the bacillus rather than universal vaccination against the disease.

Between 1954 and 1985, the incidence of tuberculosis in the United States declined 75 percent, and by 1989, public health officials confidently predicted its eradication in the United States by 2010 and worldwide by 2025, believing it would no longer pose a public health threat. These expectations were dashed as a worldwide pandemic of tuberculosis began in 1987 and the World Health Organization declared that tuberculosis posed a global emergency in 1993. The displacement of populations through immigration and political conflicts; the emergence of drug-resistant strains; the high rates of incarceration, homelessness, and intravenous drug use; the prevalence of mass air travel; the collapse of medical services in eastern Europe; the persistence of widespread poverty; and the progress of the AIDS pandemic, in which tuberculosis emerged as an opportunistic infection, all contributed to a worldwide public health crisis. By 2002, the World Health Organization reported that tuberculosis was the leading infectious killer of youth and adults and a leading killer of women, and that a third of the world's population was infected with the tuberculosis bacillus. In response, nearly 150 countries, including the United States, agreed to adopt the Directly Observed Treatment Short-Course (DOTS) system in which countries would promote public health programs of case detection, standardized treatment regimens using multiple drugs, patient surveillance to monitor compliance, and the forcible detention of noncompliant patients. Once thought to be on the verge of eradication, in 2002 it was not known if and when the worldwide incidence of tuberculosis would return to levels experienced only a half century before.

BIBLIOGRAPHY

Bates, Barbara. *Bargaining for Life: A Social History of Tuberculosis, 1876–1938.* Philadelphia: University of Pennsylvania Press, 1992.

Ellison, David L. *Healing Tuberculosis in the Woods: Medicine and Science at the End of the Nineteenth Century.* Westport, Conn.: Greenwood Press, 1994.

Tucson. Dancers in traditional Mexican costume perform in this southern Arizona city, part of Mexico until 1853.

Feldberg, Georgina. *Disease and Class: Tuberculosis and the Shaping of Modern North American Society.* New Brunswick, N.J.: Rutgers University Press, 1995.

Lerner, Barron H. *Contagion and Confinement: Controlling Tuberculosis Along the Skid Road.* Baltimore: Johns Hopkins University Press, 1998.

Ott, Katherine. *Fevered Lives: Tuberculosis in American Culture since 1870.* Cambridge, Mass.: Harvard University Press, 1996.

Rothman, Sheila. *Living in the Shadow of Death: Tuberculosis and the Social Experience of Illness in America.* New York: Basic Books, 1994.

Ryan, Frank. *The Forgotten Plague: How the Battle against Tuberculosis Was Won—And Lost.* Boston: Little, Brown, 1993.

Teller, Michael. *The Tuberculosis Movement: A Public Health Campaign in the Progressive Era.* New York: Greenwood Press, 1988.

D. George Joseph

See also **Epidemics and Public Health.**

TUCSON, the second-largest city in Arizona, takes its name from a Tohono O'Odham (Papago) Indian village that stood at the base of Stjukshon Mountain, later known as Sentinel Peak. Situated in the lower Sonoran Desert basin, Tucson is flanked by the Santa Catalina and Santa Rita Mountains. In 1700 Jesuit missionary Eusebio Francisco Kino founded San Xavier del Bac Indian mission, and the Spanish established the Presidio de San Augustín de Tuguisón in 1775. Tucson became U.S. territory with the Gadsden Purchase in 1853, and served as the capital of Arizona Territory from 1867 to 1877. The Southern Pacific Railroad reached Tucson in 1880 and the city was incorporated in 1883.

From World War II to the year 2000, the city grew by more than four times, to a population of 486,699, with the metropolitan area including 843,746 residents. Tucson's economy in the 1990s included everything from agriculture and mining to state-of-the-art electronics. The rapid population growth threatened a dwindling water supply, but in 1992 the Central Arizona Project began supplying Colorado River water to Tucson. One of the most environmentally conscious cities in Arizona, Tucson is home to the Biosphere experiment and several national environmental groups.

The city offers activities for every taste. Wilderness enthusiasts enjoy mountain climbing and desert trekking, wealthy tourists visit expensive resorts and art galleries, while modest spenders patronize the Arizona-Sonora Desert Museum and Old Tucson, a movie site for more than two hundred films. All visitors can enjoy cultural and athletic events at the University of Arizona plus a variety of theater, symphony, ballet, and opera productions.

BIBLIOGRAPHY

Logan, Michael F. *Fighting Sprawl and City Hall: Resistance to Urban Growth in the Southwest.* Tucson: University of Arizona Press, 1995.

Sonnichsen, C. L. *Tucson: The Life and Times of an American City.* Norman: University of Oklahoma Press, 1982.

Walker, Henry P., and Don Bufkin. *Historical Atlas of Arizona.* Norman: University of Oklahoma Press, 1979.

Roger L. Nichols

See also **Arizona; Gadsden Purchase; Southwest.**

TULSA, city in northeastern OKLAHOMA located on the Arkansas River. Sitting in the middle of some of the richest OIL FIELDS in the United States, Tulsa grew in conjunction with the rise of the railroad and oil industries in the late nineteenth and early twentieth centuries. Settled by the Creek tribe after the TRAIL OF TEARS in 1836, it was originally named Tulsee Town from the word Tullahassee or "old town." As more whites began to settle, the town changed its name to Tulsa in 1879 and incorporated as a city in 1898. The discovery of oil in the early 1900s expanded the city's economy. In 1921 racial tensions led to one of the most violent riots of the twentieth century, resulting in the deaths of an official number of thirty-six people, primarily African Americans, though unofficial estimates run as high as 250 to 400 people. The city's economy further benefited as electronics and aircraft manufacturing jobs arrived in the region during World War II. Though no longer the "oil capital of the world," Tulsa continues to have a very close relationship with the energy industry. The city has a total land area of 182.7 square miles and a 2000 Census population of 393,049 persons, up from 367,302 in 1990.

BIBLIOGRAPHY

Ellsworth, Scott. *Death in a Promised Land: The Tulsa Race Riot of 1921.* Baton Rouge: Louisiana State University Press, 1982.

Halliburton, R., Jr. *The Tulsa Race War of 1921.* San Francisco: R and E Research Associates, 1975.

Matthew L. Daley

See also **Creeks.**

TULSA RACE RIOT (1921), one of the worst American civil disturbances of the twentieth century. Perhaps as many as one hundred people lost their lives, and more than thirty-five blocks were destroyed in the African American section of Tulsa, Oklahoma, known as Greenwood.

The riots began on the evening of 31 May, when World War I veterans heard that a young black man being held in the Tulsa County Courthouse on charges of assaulting a young white woman might be lynched. The veterans followed the advice of a local black newspaper, the *Tulsa Star,* which encouraged them to take action to protect against a lynching. They put on their uniforms, got guns, and went to the courthouse. When some white men tried to disarm them, shots were fired, and the riot

Tulsa Race Riot. Smoke billows over the African American section of this Oklahoma city in 1921. LIBRARY OF CONGRESS

started. The police department hastily deputized several hundred men to help put down the "Negro uprising."

Around dawn on 1 June the deputies and Tulsa-based units of the National Guard began to sweep through Greenwood, disarming and arresting the residents, then taking them to "concentration" camps around the city, ostensibly for their protection. Some who refused to give up their guns were shot. Mobs of looters, some wearing deputy badges or police uniforms, followed soon after. The looters took what they could and then burned the buildings. In later years, the Oklahoma legislature contemplated paying reparations to survivors in recognition of the wrong done them.

BIBLIOGRAPHY

Brophy, Alfred L. *Reconstructing the Dreamland: The Tulsa [Race] Riot of 1921—Race, Reparations, Reconciliation.* New York: Oxford University Press, 2002.

Ellsworth, Scott. *Death in a Promised Land: The Tulsa Race Riot of 1921.* Baton Rouge: Louisiana State University Press, 1982 .

Alfred L. Brophy

See also **Lynching; Race Relations; Riots.**

TUNNELS. The digging of permanent tunnels is the most difficult, expensive, and hazardous of civil engineering works. Although extensive tunneling has characterized deep-level mining and the construction of water supply systems since ancient times, transportation tunnels have been largely the products of nineteenth-century technology. The earliest such tunnels in the United States were built for canals. The pioneer work was constructed in 1818–1821 to carry the Schuylkill Canal through a hill at Pottsville, Pa., and it was shortly followed by the tunnel of the Union Canal at Lebanon, Pa. (1825–1827). Possibly the first tunnel to exceed a length of 1,000 feet was excavated in 1843 for the passage of the Whitewater Canal through the ridge at Cleves, Ohio, near Cincinnati.

The first U.S. railway tunnel was probably that of the New York and Harlem Railroad at Ninety-first Street in New York City (1837). Until 1866 all tunnels had to be laboriously carved out by hand techniques, with drills, picks, and shovels as the primary tools.

The beginning of modern rock tunneling in the United States came with the digging of the railroad tunnel through Hoosac Mountain, Mass., which required twenty-two years for completion (1854–1876). The enterprise was initially carried out by hammer drilling, hand shoveling, and hand setting of black-powder charges. This method was suddenly changed in 1866, when Charles Burleigh introduced the first successful pneumatic drill, and the chief engineer of the project, Thomas Doane, first used the newly invented nitroglycerin to shatter the rock. With a length of 4.73 miles, the Hoosac was the longest tunnel in the United States for half a century following its completion.

For tunneling through soft ground an entirely different technique is necessary, since the problem is more one of removing the muck and holding the earth in place than digging through it. An adequate solution to the problem involved the use of the tunnel-driving shield, originally patented in 1818 by the British engineer Marc Isambard Brunel for a tunnel under the Thames River. It was introduced in the United States by Alfred Ely Beach for the abortive Broadway subway in New York City (1869–1870), a successful work that was abandoned in the face of political opposition.

Various forms of pneumatic and shield tunneling were most extensively employed in the great subaqueous tunnel system of New York City. The first Hudson River tunnel, the trouble-plagued enterprise of the promoter De Witt C. Haskin, dragged on from 1873 to 1904. Haskin began operations by pneumatic excavation, the technique employed in the pressure caissons developed for building bridge piers, but a blowout in 1880 cost twenty lives and led to its abandonment. Work was resumed in 1889 by means of the shield invented by the English engineer James H. Greathead for working in near-fluid alluvial sediments, but lack of capital held up completion for another fifteen years. The tunnel eventually became part of the Hudson and Manhattan Railroad system. The longest of all the tunnels underlying metropolitan New York is the second Croton Aqueduct (1885–1890), blasted largely through igneous rock for a total length of thirty-one miles. Still another variation on the Greathead shield was introduced by James Hobson for mining the Grand Trunk Railroad's Saint Clair Tunnel (1886–1891) between Port Huron, Mich., and Sarnia, Ontario, the first to unite Canada with the United States.

The extensive tunnel system of the Pennsylvania Railroad's New York extension (1903–1910) required for its completion all the existing techniques of tunneling. The soft sediments of the Hudson River bed allowed the use of the shield; the igneous rock of Manhattan called for power drills and blasting or cut-and-cover methods, while the gravel underlying the East River necessitated mining in front of the shield under a vast blanket of clay laid down on the bed to prevent the blowouts that would have occurred in the porous material.

The safest and most economical method of tunneling—the trench method—was first used at the beginning of the twentieth century. The Detroit River Tunnel of the Michigan Central Railroad (1906–1910) was the first to be built by the trench method: cylindrical concrete sections with sealed ends were poured on land, towed to position, sunk into a trench previously dredged in the riverbed, and covered with gravel. The longest tunnel built by this method is the subaqueous portion of the Chesapeake Bay Bridge and Tunnel (1960–1964).

With all the techniques of excavation and lining well established, tunnel engineers were able to build the big rail and vehicular bores necessary to keep pace with the expanding traffic that followed World War I. The pioneer automotive tube was the Clifford M. Holland Tunnel under the Hudson River at New York City (1920–1927), which was followed by three others under the East and Hudson Rivers. The Moffat Tunnel (1923–1928) of the Denver and Salt Lake Railroad through James Peak in Colorado held the short-lived record for transportation tunnel length, 6.1 miles, and was the first long rail tunnel designed with a forced-draft ventilating system for the operation of steam locomotives. The Cascade Tunnel (1925–1929) of the Great Northern Railway in Washington, 7.79 miles long, is the longest tunnel in the United States. The complete mechanization of rock tunneling was finally achieved in 1952 by means of the mechanical mole, a cylindrical drilling machine as large as the tunnel interior equipped with rotating hardened-steel cutters that can grind through the densest rock.

American engineers led advances in tunnel technology in the nineteenth and early twentieth century. But the completion of the national highway grid and a tendency to rely on automobiles and aviation, rather than railways, resulted in fewer new tunnel projects. Probably the most extensive of the late twentieth century was the Central Artery/Tunnel Project in Boston, Mass. (dubbed by locals as the Big Dig). Begun in 1991 and scheduled to be finished in 2004, this massive project extended the Massachusetts Turnpike through a tunnel to Logan Airport while putting the elevated Central Artery underground, freeing hundreds of acres in downtown Boston for redevelopment.

The Big Dig notwithstanding, the most ambitious and technologically advanced tunnels in the early twenty-first century were being built in nations with growing public transportation systems in Europe and Asia. The Seikan railway tunnel under the Tsugaru Strait in Japan, built in 1988, is 33.5 miles in length, two miles longer than the Chunnel, the railway link under the English Channel linking England with Normandy, France, completed in 1994. Various other European countries planned Alpine tunnels that would span even longer distances.

BIBLIOGRAPHY

Beaver, Patrick. *A History of Tunnels*. London: P. Davies, 1972.

Bickel, John O., and T. R. Kuesel, eds. *Tunnel Engineering Handbook*. New York: Van Nostrand Reinhold, 1982.

Sandström, Gösta E. *Tunnels*. New York: Holt, Rinehart and Winston, 1963.

West, Graham. *Innovation and the Rise of the Tunnelling Industry*. New York: Cambridge University Press, 1988.

Carl W. Condit / A. R.

See also **Hoosac Tunnel; Interstate Highway System; Railways, Urban, and Rapid Transit.**

TUSKEGEE UNIVERSITY. In 1880 Lewis Adams, a mechanic and former slave, and George W. Campbell, a banker and former slaveowner, both of Tuskegee, Alabama, saw the need for the education of black youth in Macon County and secured a charter, which appropriated $2,000 annually for teachers' salaries, from the state legislature. Booker T. Washington was chosen to head the school, and the coeducational Normal School for Colored Teachers was established by an act of the Alabama general assembly on 12 February 1881. Washington became the first principal and opened the school on 4 July. Spectacular growth and development took place under Washington, who was President from 1881 to 1915, and continued under his successors: Robert Russa Moton (1915–1935), Frederick D. Patterson (1935–1953), Luther H. Foster (1953–1981), and Benjamin F. Payton (1981–). In 1881 the school was renamed Tuskegee State Normal School; subsequent names include Tuskegee Normal School (1887–1891), Tuskegee Normal and Industrial Institute (1891–1937), and Tuskegee Institute (1937–1985). In 1985 the institution became known as Tuskegee University.

Tuskegee University is a small university, offering undergraduate degrees in six major areas—arts and sciences, applied sciences, education, engineering, nursing, and veterinary medicine—and degrees at the master's level in each area except nursing. The program is fully accredited by the Southern Association of Colleges and Schools, and many of the professional areas are approved by national agencies. The school's enrollment, predominantly undergraduate, was 3,000 in 2001, with students representing most U.S. states and many foreign countries. Twenty-five degree-granting courses make up the curricula of six areas. The campus has over 150 buildings on more than 5,000 acres of land.

Tuskegee University has achieved or maintains numerous distinctions. Distinguished doctoral programs are offered in material science, engineering, and veterinary medicine. More than 75 percent of the world's African American veterinarians graduate from Tuskegee. The university is the number-one producer of African American aerospace science engineers and is also an important producer of such engineers in chemical, electrical, and mechanical specializations. The first nursing baccalaureate program in Alabama and one of the earliest in the United States was developed at Tuskegee University. The university is also the only college or university campus in the nation to ever be designated a National Historic Site by the U.S. Congress. Famous alumni or faculty include Daniel "Chappie" James, the first African American four-star General; and Ralph Ellison, the first African American writer to win the National Book Award.

BIBLIOGRAPHY

Dozier, Richard K. "From Humble Beginnings to National Shrine: Tuskegee Institute." *Historic Preservation* 33, no. 1 (1981): 40–45.

Jackson, McArthur. *A Historical Study of the Founding and Development of Tuskegee Institute (Alabama)*. Ed.D. diss., University of North Carolina Greensboro, 1983.

Washington, Booker T. *Up From Slavery*. New York: Oxford University Press, 2000.

Daniel T. Williams
A. J. Wright

See also **African Americans; Education, African American; Education, Higher: African American Colleges.**

TWA FLIGHT 800. On 17 July 1996 Trans World Airlines flight 800, headed for Paris from John F. Kennedy airport in New York City, exploded off Long Island, killing all 212 passengers and 18 crew members, more than 150 of them American, on board the Boeing 747 jumbo jet. During the weeks following the tragedy, divers recovered 95 percent of the plane and 220 bodies from the ocean. After rebuilding the entire plane, investigators discovered that the center tank had exploded in flight.

TWA Flight 800. On 17 July 1996, tragedy struck when TWA Flight 800, carrying 230 crew and passengers from New York City to Paris, exploded in flight off the coast of Long Island; there were no survivors. Divers recovered 95 percent of the plane's body, and experts reassembled it in a nearby airplane hanger, shown here. © AP/WIDE WORLD PHOTOS

Three primary possible explanations for the explosion emerged: a bomb, a mechanical failure, or a missile hit. The last theory, even though rejected by government investigators, attracted much media attention after the former ABC newsperson Pierre Salinger, using numerous eyewitness accounts, claimed that an Aegis guided missile from a U.S. Navy ship had mistakenly hit the plane. (One amateur photograph showed an object resembling a missile near the airplane seconds before the explosion, but U.S. military authorities claimed that no such object appeared on radar screens. Further declassification will be required before the official theory of an accidental explosion can be dismissed.) Others also advanced the theory that the plane could have been lost to a terrorist attack with one of the Stinger missiles the United States had sent to anti-Soviet guerrillas during the Afghanistan War (1980–1988). Should the terrorist theory be accurate, TWA flight 800 would join the World Trade Center bombing (26 February 1993), the OKLAHOMA CITY BOMBING (19 April 1995), and the suicide-hijacking attacks on the Pentagon and the World Trade Center (11 September 2001) as one of the worst acts of domestic terrorism in U.S. history.

Mechanical failure was the explanation eventually favored by governmental investigators. In its final report of 22–23 August 2000, the National Transportation Safety Board (NTSB) concluded that the probable cause of the accident was an explosion of the center wing fuel tank due to the ignition of the flammable fuel-air mixture in the tank. The NTSB recommended that the flammability of the mix be reduced, the tank be isolated from heat and ignition sources, and aging aircrafts be better monitored.

BIBLIOGRAPHY

Milton, Pat. *In the Blink of an Eye: The FBI Investigation of TWA Flight 800.* New York: Random House, 1999.

Sanders, James D. *The Downing of Flight 800.* New York: Zebra Books–Kensington Publishing, 1997.

Philippe R. Girard

See also **Air Transportation and Travel; Disasters; Terrorism.**

TWEED RING. In the late 1860s and early 1870s, William Marcy Tweed, New York State senator and Democratic Party boss, along with his political associates, robbed the New York City treasury of at least $30 million, and perhaps far more. Matthew J. O'Rourke, a journalist who—while county bookkeeper—exposed the frauds, reckoned $200 million as the total stealings of the ring and its subrings. The Tweed Ring infiltrated nearly every segment of public life in New York City. The ring included the governor, the mayor, the city comptroller, and countless other prominent citizens in both the public and private sectors. It operated by granting municipal contracts to its political cronies and by embezzling funds intended for hospitals and charitable institutions. The ring's recklessness and the magnitude of its thefts quickly

William Marcy Tweed. The boss of New York City's powerful Democratic machine, Tammany Hall, and the epitome of urban corruption. © CORBIS

pushed the city to the verge of bankruptcy. This, coupled with a struggle between Tweed and reformer Samuel J. Tilden for Democratic Party control, led to the ring's undoing. The corruption racket involved so many notable figures in New York City that a complete list of the ring's beneficiaries was never released. Although Tweed himself made a partial confession and spent the remainder of his life in jail, the vast majority of the ring's participants were never brought to justice. Long after Tweed's death, his name remained synonymous with shameless political graft.

BIBLIOGRAPHY

Mandelbaum, Seymour J. *Boss Tweed's New York.* New York: Wiley, 1965.

Summers, Mark Wahlgren. *The Era of Good Stealings.* New York: Oxford University Press, 1993.

Anthony Gaughan
Denis Tilden Lynch

See also **Corruption, Political; Political Scandals; Rings, Political.**

TWENTY-ONE GUN SALUTE. Originally, British naval tradition recognized seven guns as the British national salute. British regulations provided that ships could fire seven guns only, but forts could fire three shots for every shot afloat. At that time, powder made from sodium nitrate was easier to keep ashore than shipboard. When the use of potassium nitrate in place of sodium nitrate improved gunpowder, the sea salute came to equal the shore salute of twenty-one guns. The British proposed that the United States return their salutes "gun for gun." Accordingly, on 18 August 1875 the United States adopted the twenty-one gun salute and the gun-for-gun return.

BIBLIOGRAPHY

Jessup, John E. et al., eds. *Encyclopedia of the American Military: Studies of the History, Traditions, Policies, Institutions, and Roles of the Armed Forces in War and Peace.* New York: Scribner, 1994.

Louis H. Bolander / A. E.

TWO PENNY ACT, enacted in 1755 by the Virginia assembly in anticipation of a low-yielding tobacco crop, permitted payment of obligations due in tobacco over a ten-month period at a commutation rate of two pence per pound. In 1758 the assembly passed a similar act of one year's duration. The Anglican clergy, whose salaries were fixed in terms of tobacco, objected to the measure. They secured a royal disallowance of the act and sought to collect the difference between two pence and the market price. The suits to recover back salaries, known as the "parson's cause," proved unsuccessful.

BIBLIOGRAPHY

Isaac, Rhys. *The Transformation of Virginia, 1740–1790.* Chapel Hill: University of North Carolina Press, 1982; New York: Norton, 1988.

Wesley Frank Craven / S. B.

See also **Parson's Cause; Royal Disallowance.**

TWO-PARTY SYSTEM. Although there have been minor political parties, or third parties, throughout most of American history, two major, competitive parties have dominated the American party system. Beginning with the Federalists and the Antifederalists in the 1790s, only two political parties usually have had any substantial chance of victory in national elections. Indeed, since the Civil War, the same two parties, the Democratic and Republican, have constituted the American two-party system.

Because of the two-party system, all American presidents and almost all members of Congress elected since the Civil War have been either Democrats or Republicans. Furthermore, the competition of the two parties has been consistently close. From 1860 through 2000, only four presidents won more than 60 percent of the total popular vote: Warren G. Harding in 1920; Franklin D. Roosevelt in 1936; Lyndon B. Johnson in 1964; and Richard M. Nixon in 1972.

While the two-party system has long characterized national politics, it has not invariably marked the politics of the states. In some measure, the national two-party system of the late nineteenth century was an aggregate of one-party states. The incidence of that statewide one-partyism declined in the twentieth century, but the Democrats maintained a one-party supremacy in the states of the Deep South from the Reconstruction period into the 1960s and in some cases into the 1970s (the Republicans dominated the South from the late 1980s into the early twenty-first century). Occasionally, too, states have had three-party systems for short periods of time. Wisconsin, North Dakota, and Minnesota all included a party from the Progressive movement in their party systems in the 1930s and 1940s. In the 1990s and early 2000s, a number of third-party presidential candidates, including Pat Buchanan and Ross Perot, both of the Reform Party, and Ralph Nader, of the Green Party, challenged Democratic and Republican candidates but with little success.

The American two-party system results in part from the relative absence of irreconcilable differences within the American electorate about basic social, economic, and political institutions and in part from the absence of electoral rewards for minor parties. The traditions of plurality elections from single-member constituencies and of a single elected executive give few chances of victory or reward to parties that cannot muster the plurality.

BIBLIOGRAPHY

Jelen, Ted G., ed. *Ross for Boss: The Perot Phenomenon and Beyond.* Albany: State University of New York Press, 2001.

Lowi, Theodore J., and Joseph Romance. *A Republic of Parties? Debating the Two-Party System.* Lanham, Md.: Rowman and Littlefield, 1998.

Rosenstone, Steven J., Roy L. Behr, and Edward H. Lazarus. *Third Parties in America: Citizen Response to Major Party Failure.* Princeton, N.J.: Princeton University Press, 1996.

Sifry, Micah L. *Spoiling for a Fight: Third-Party Politics in America.* New York: Routledge, 2002.

Frank J. Sorauf / A. E.

See also **Antifederalists; Democratic Party; Elections, Presidential; Federalist Party; Political Parties; Republican Party; Republicans, Jeffersonian; Third Parties; Whig Party.**

TWO-THIRDS RULE. The two-thirds rule is used at all levels of government and in many social and political organizations to prevent the dominance of a small majority over a large minority. The U.S. Constitution, for example, gives the Senate sole authority to ratify treaties proposed by the President of the United States and to try impeachments but makes this contingent upon a two-thirds majority, thus ensuring broad support for such important measures. In 1832, the Democratic Party adopted a two-thirds rule for nominating a presidential candidate. Frequent attempts to change the rule were resisted by those who believed it to be a convenient tool to prevent a candidacy they opposed. It was finally repealed in 1936.

BIBLIOGRAPHY

Bass, Harold F. "Presidential Party Leadership and Party Reform: Franklin D. Roosevelt and the Abrogation of the Two-Thirds Rule." *Presidential Studies Quarterly* 18 (1988): 303–317.

Michael Wala

TYDINGS-McDUFFIE ACT. In January 1933 Congress passed the Hawes-Cutting Act over President Herbert Hoover's veto, providing for the independence of the Philippine Islands after twelve years and for trade relations with the United States after ten years of authorized commonwealth government. The Philippine legislature rejected this act because of its tariff and immigration provisions. The Tydings-McDuffie Act of 24 March 1934 eliminated objectionable provisions of the Hawes-Cutting Act, and the Philippine legislature passed and ratified it on 1 May 1934, shortly thereafter inaugurating its new government. To cushion the economic effects of this act, Congress passed the Philippine Economic Adjustment Act in 1939.

BIBLIOGRAPHY

Ninkovich, Frank. *The United States and Imperialism.* Malden, Mass.: Blackwell, 2001.

Thomas Robson Hay
Christopher Wells

See also **Immigration Restriction; Philippines; Tariff.**

TYPEWRITER. The idea of the typewriter emerged long before the technology existed for its practical or economical production. A patent was issued in England in 1714 to Henry Mill, "engineer to the New River Water Company," for "an Artificial Machine or Method for the Impressing or Transcribing of Letters Singly or Progressively one after another, as in Writing, whereby all Writings whatsoever may be Engrossed in Paper or Parchment so Neat and Exact as not to be distinguished from Print." No drawing or other description has survived, and it is not known if a machine was actually made.

Subsequently, inventors in many countries planned and produced writing machines. The most notable were Friedrich von Knauss in Germany and Pierre Jacquet-Droz of Switzerland in the late eighteenth century and Pietro Conti in early-nineteenth-century Italy.

Christopher Latham Sholes. The inventor with one of his early models of a typewriter. © CORBIS

William A. Burt of Detroit, Michigan, received the first U.S. patent for a writing machine in 1829 for his typographer. This was an indicator type machine using printer's type arranged on a swinging sector. It was slow but surprisingly effective. The tempo of such inventions increased as the century advanced, many of them made to aid blind persons, some to record telegraph messages. Giuseppe Ravazza in Italy in 1855, William Francis in the United States in 1857, and Peter Mitterofer in Austria in 1866 used individual keys for each character, and typebars pivoted around an arc so that all printed at the common center.

The first really successful machine used the same general arrangement of bars pivoted around an arc. The inventor was Christopher Latham Sholes of Milwaukee, Wisconsin, who had already pioneered new methods for addressing newspapers and numbering pages. Sholes acquired two patents in 1868, and James Densmore, a long-time friend of Sholes's, had fifteen machines made in Chicago. These machines were failures, but under Densmore's dominating personality Sholes was induced to continue tests and improvements. By 1872 what essentially became the modern key arrangement had been developed to permit speed without the interference of one letter with another. Production began again in that year at Milwaukee but was not profitable. In 1873 Densmore convinced E. Remington and Sons, arms manufacturers of Ilion, New York, to build and sell the machine. Their first act was to redesign the component parts, adapting them to more economical manufacture. The first examples, completed in 1874 and priced at $125, typed only capital letters. Not until 1878, with the introduction of a smaller machine with a shift key, could both uppercase and lowercase characters be typed. The American inventor Luciean S. Crandall perfected the means for shifting the cylinder, or platen; another American, Byron A. Brooks, developed multicharacter typebars. These features added so much to the versatility of typing that all subsequent machines had to offer similar writing ability.

In order to avoid the specifics of preexisting patents, inventors had to be clever in finding other means to a similar end. Out of this effort came the large class of typewheel machines, of which the Hammond and the Blickensderfer were the most widely accepted. Both this class of machine and the typebar machines often used a double-shift design, in which there were separate shift keys—one for capitals and another for characters and numbers. This double shift reduced the number of parts and thus the cost, and in the case of type-wheel machines reduced the mass of moving parts, thus increasing speed and lessening wear. Another approach, popular for a time, used a double keyboard with a separate key for each character, typified by such once-popular machines as the Caligraph and the Smith-Premier. During the formative years there were many other varieties of keyboard as well, some with the keys disposed on circular arcs instead of in straight rows, and others with such accessories as the space bar in different locations. Through all of this period the basic arrangement, used since 1874 on Remington machines, remained popular and eventually became standard with the Underwood typewriter, which appeared about 1895. It was not until 1908 that Remington adopted a fast visible-writing machine, in which the carriage did not have to be lifted up in order to read the written line.

Meanwhile, typewriting had become so extensively accepted by the public that a host of slow, primitive machines, such as the Odell, found a wide market. These machines required the use of one hand to select the letter or character to be printed and the other hand to make the impression. Their only justification was a very low selling price; they appealed to those whose need for typewritten copy was only occasional and who did not require speed. Although often mistaken for pioneer machines, these primitive typewriters did not appear until practical machines had created a market for them.

The early years of the twentieth century saw the universal acceptance of visible writing, a uniform keyboard, and the scaling down of size to create portable machines. Several electric machines were introduced; the most successful was made by Blickensderfer in Stamford, Connectinut, prior to 1909. Beginning in 1930, with the introduction of a motor-driven variety by Electromatic Typewriters, Inc., of Rochester, New York, electric type-

Early Typewriter. A woman sits next to a model in this 1912 photograph. Library of Congress

writers gradually replaced manual typewriters. The electric typewriter introduced in 1961 by International Business Machines Corporation (IBM) eliminated the heavy sliding carriage and the basket of typebars. Instead, the type was on a swiveling ball-shaped shuttle on a light carriage that traveled inside the framework of the machine. Printing was by means of a wide carbon ribbon in a readily changeable cartridge. Errors were corrected by striking over with a correction ribbon.

IBM's "memory" typewriter, introduced in 1974, reflected the company's role in the development of the personal computer. Seven years later IBM introduced its IBM PC, using integrated chips from its memory typewriters. Thereafter, personal computers with powerful word-processing programs, hooked up to fast dot matrix—and, later, laser—printers, replaced the electric typewriter for the favored spot on the desks of clerical workers. The role of typewriters quickly waned.

BIBLIOGRAPHY

Bliven, Bruce. *The Wonderful Writing Machine.* New York: Random House, 1954.

Current, Richard N. *The Typewriter and the Men Who Made It.* 2d ed. Arcadia, Calif.: Post-Era Books, 1988.

Weller, Charles E. *The Early History of the Typewriter.* La Porte, Ind.: Chase and Shepard, 1918.

Edwin A. Battison / A. R.

See also **Business Machines; Computers and Computer Industry; Newspapers; Office Technology.**

U

U-2 INCIDENT. On 1 May 1960 a U-2 reconnaissance and research aircraft piloted by Francis Gary Powers, on a surveillance mission for the CIA, was shot down over the Soviet Union (over Sverdlovsk, now Yekaterinburg) by a SAM-2 missile. The mission had originated in Peshawar, Pakistan, and aimed at capturing aerial pictures of military installations to monitor the progress of the Soviet missile programs. Upon entering Soviet air space Powers activated his antiradar scrambler, but the plane was spotted by Soviet military authorities. The Soviets shot the plane down; Powers surprisingly enough survived the crash unharmed but unconscious due to lack of oxygen. (Spy plane pilots were not expected to be captured alive if their mission could not be completed.) He was arrested by the KGB and admitted being a spy who had flown across the USSR to reach a military airfield in Norway while collecting intelligence information. On 5 May Premier Nikita Khrushchev denounced this act of U.S. aggression. The U.S. government and the CIA responded by denying that they had authorized the flight, but the Kremlin remained unconvinced. Powers was tried publicly (from 17 to 19 August) and sentenced to three years in prison and seven years in a labor camp. Finally, the United States admitted that the U-2 flights were supposed to prevent surprise attacks against American interests.

This incident disrupted the peace process between Washington and Moscow and ruined the Paris summit: the conference was adjourned on 17 May despite President Eisenhower's promise to stop the flights. On 19 February 1962 Powers was finally exchanged for Colonel Rudolph Ivanovich Abel, a Soviet spy.

BIBLIOGRAPHY

Gaddis, John L. *We Now Know: Rethinking Cold War History.* Oxford University Press, 1998.

Powers, Francis G., and Curt Gentry. *Operation Overflight: A Memoir of the U-2 Incident.* Brasseys, Inc., 2002.

Frédéric Robert

See also **Cold War.**

UFOS. *See* **Unidentified Flying Objects.**

UNABOMBER. From 1978 until April 1996, Theodore John Kaczynski, the Unabomber, conducted a campaign of letter-bomb terror against people symbolizing technology. Kaczynski, a Harvard-trained mathematician, left academia for the seclusion of a shack near Helena, Montana. Between 1978 and 1995, Kaczynski's bombs killed three and wounded twenty-three. In 1995 he threatened a reign of terror if his 35,000-word manifesto against science and technology was not published in the national media. *The New York Times* and *Washington Post* complied to save lives. David Kaczynski, his brother, recognized similarities between the language of the manifesto and his brother's letters. His tip led to an arrest and a search of his brother's cabin. The search yielded substantial evidence, and in April 1996 Kaczynski was indicted on ten counts of illegal transportation, mailing, and use of bombs, as well as murder. Because of conflicts between Kaczynski and his lawyers, the trial in Sacramento, California, which began in November 1997, was a confused proceeding. Ultimately Kaczynski entered a plea of guilty to thirteen federal charges in exchange for the government dropping its demand for the death penalty. In February and August

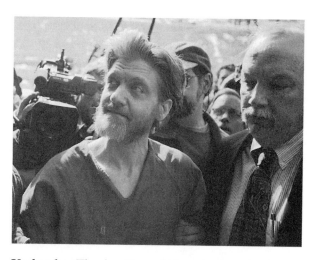

Unabomber. Theodore Kaczynski (*center*), a letter-bomb terrorist for eighteen years, is escorted by U.S. marshals after his arrest in 1996. AP/WIDE WORLD PHOTOS

2001 Kaczynski lost federal appeals for a new trial, and as of 2002 he remains incarcerated.

BIBLIOGRAPHY

Gelernter, David Hillel. *Drawing Life: Surviving the Unabomber.* New York: Free Press, 1997.

Mello, Michael. *The United States of American versus Theodore John Kaczynski: Ethics, Power and the Invention of the Unabomber.* New York: Context Books, 1999.

Gordon Morris Bakken

See also **Terrorism.**

UNCLE SAM, a nickname of the U.S. government, first used during the War of 1812. Critics of the war applied the term somewhat derisively to customhouse officers and to soldiers while the "war hawks" generally avoided it. As contemporary newspapers show, the term was doubtless a jocular expansion of the letters "U.S." on uniforms and government property.

The name is also identified with Samuel Wilson of Troy, N.Y. (1766–1854), known as "Uncle Sam" Wilson, who supplied barrels of beef to the government. In 1961 Congress recognized Wilson as a namesake for America's symbol, which over the years has lost its negative connotations.

BIBLIOGRAPHY

Ketchum, Alton. *Uncle Sam: The Man and the Legend.* New York: Hill and Wang, 1959.

Albert Matthews/c. w.

See also **War Hawks; War of 1812.**

Uncle Sam. In this 1917 poster, Uncle Sam appeals to the patriotism of viewers to bolster sales of government bonds. LIBRARY OF CONGRESS

UNCLE TOM'S CABIN, an antislavery novel written by Harriet Beecher Stowe and published in book form in 1852. In 1862, Abraham Lincoln apocryphally referred to Harriet Beecher Stowe as "the little woman who started this big war," underscoring the enormous influence of *Uncle Tom's Cabin; Or, Life Among the Lowly* to antebellum audiences. Stowe claimed to have been inspired by grief over her baby's death in 1849 and resistance to the Fugitive Slave Law of 1850. Published serially in the *National Era* from 5 June 1851 to 1 April 1852 and in book form in March 1852, the novel sold 300,000 copies in the first year and more than a million by 1860. By 1900 it had spawned a theatrical tradition, inspired a market tie-in, and been translated into forty-two languages. Abolitionists thrilled to what Jane Tompkins has called the novel's "sentimental power," its emotional appeal, especially to middle-class women readers, to identify with black families separated by slavery (*Sensational Designs*, pp. 122–146). But the novel was viciously attacked by proslavery readers, even after Stowe defended the research on which she based the novel in *A Key to Uncle Tom's Cabin* (1853).

A later generation also attacked the novel, arguing that Stowe's stereotyped characters revealed her own historically conditioned racism. Indeed, for the African American author James Baldwin and others the term "Uncle Tom" came to imply a black person who pandered to a racist white power structure. More recently, Stowe's novel sparked an interest in uncovering other nineteenth-century women writers. Readers also noted the novel's geographical sweep from New Orleans to Canada, Paris, and Liberia; its Christian radicalism; and its relationship to slave narratives. The novel's popularity and its controversy have endured. For example, the 1956 film *The King and I* contains a Siamese version of the "Uncle Tom" plays that flooded American stages, and in the 1991 San Francisco Mime Troupe's acclaimed *I Ain't Yo' Uncle*, Stowe's characters confront their creator. *Uncle Tom's Cabin* continued to catalyze discussions about race in the United States in the twenty-first century.

BIBLIOGRAPHY

Hedrick, Joan. *Harriet Beecher Stowe: A Life*. New York: Oxford University Press, 1994.

Lowance, Mason I., Jr., Ellen E. Westbrook, and R. C. De Prospo, eds. *The Stowe Debate: Rhetorical Strategies in "Uncle Tom's Cabin."* Amherst: University of Massachusetts Press, 1994.

Tompkins, Jane. *Sensational Designs: The Cultural Work of American Fiction, 1790–1860*. New York: Oxford University Press, 1985.

Lisa MacFarlane

See also **Antislavery; Literature: Popular Literature.**

UNCONDITIONAL SURRENDER

UNCONDITIONAL SURRENDER came into the American political lexicon during the Civil War, when the Union General Ulysses Simpson Grant rejected a request for negotiations and demanded the "unconditional surrender" of the Confederate-held Fort Donelson, Tennessee, in 1862. U. S. Grant's strict terms became his nickname.

Since then, every major international war to which the United States was a party was ended by a negotiated settlement, except for World War II. In that conflict, the Allies' demand that the Axis powers surrender unconditionally, first announced by President Franklin D. Roosevelt at a Casablanca summit meeting with British Prime Minister Winston Churchill on 24 January 1943, has been praised for holding together the alliance and criticized for prolonging the war.

Legend holds that Roosevelt surprised Churchill by the sudden announcement, but an agreement to demand unconditional surrender had actually been reached after discussions within the State Department, the Joint Chiefs of Staff, and the British Cabinet. With their statement, the Anglo-Americans hoped to reassure Soviet Premier Joseph Stalin that the Western Allies would not seek a separate peace with Germany. The Allies also hoped to prevent any public debate over appropriate surrender terms and, above all, wished to prevent Germans from later claiming that they had not been militarily defeated, as Adolf Hitler did after the 1919 Versailles settlement of World War I.

Critics have claimed that the demand for unconditional surrender bolstered the Axis nations' will to fight and eliminated the possibility of an earlier, negotiated end to the war. In the case of Germany, this argument is largely speculative. Evidence suggests that a faction in the Japanese government sought peace even before the atomic bombs were used, provided that Japan be permitted to retain its emperor—a condition rejected by the Allies before the atomic bombings, but ultimately accepted in the peace settlement of 2 September 1945. Whether an earlier concession on the emperor's status could have ended the war without the use of the atomic bomb is intensely debated among historians.

BIBLIOGRAPHY

Hikins, James W. "The Rhetoric of 'Unconditional Surrender' and the Decision to Drop the Atomic Bomb." *Quarterly Journal of Speech* 69, no. 4 (1983): 379–400.

O'Connor, Raymond G. *Diplomacy for Victory: FDR and Unconditional Surrender*. New York: Norton, 1971.

Max Paul Friedman

See also **World War II;** *and vol. 9:* **Total Victory.**

UNDERGROUND RAILROAD

UNDERGROUND RAILROAD, a term that was coined during the 1840s to designate a system of secret networks of escape routes and hiding places used by runaway blacks seeking safety as they made their way from the southern slave states to freedom in the North. To aid these runaways, sympathetic Americans served as "conductors" along these land and sea routes stretching out of the South through the North and into Canada.

The concept of a system of escape routes out of slavery predates the antebellum era, when the development of train travel inspired the clever appellation "Underground Railroad." During the colonial period, a viable system of escape routes existed as both a protest and political movement. The "railroad" of these years engaged enslaved and free blacks, whites, and significantly, Native Americans. Its changing character over time allows for a generalized thesis about the railroad's three phases of development.

During the initial phase, Native American nations like the Tuscaroras aided fugitive slaves as part of their war against the colony of North Carolina at the beginning of the eighteenth century. Tuscaroras and blacks formed a community, first in eastern North Carolina, and then as maroons in the great Dismal Swamp. When the Tuscaroras were invited to join the Five Nations of the Iroquois Confederacy, the center for the Native American freedom networks shifted to Iroquois country in colonial New York. After American independence, fugitives could fabricate free identities through the Iroquois binational system of encampments. Native Americans in the Deep South often accommodated slavery, but on the frontier of planter society they endangered the slaveholders' enterprise. The outlying Seminole nation, an Afro-Indian people in Florida, took abetting fugitive slaves to its logical limit. Blacks among the Seminoles became not only free but also constituent citizens and soldiers.

The early freedom networks organized by European settlers in British North America originally stemmed from religious conscience. German Quakers in Pennsylvania were the first to renounce slavery on religious authority in 1688. Quakers and other pietists slowly moved from benevolence toward blacks to a faith-driven collaboration to aid fugitives. Like the "righteous gentiles" of a later period, these conscientious believers took personal responsibility for the earthly fate of the oppressed. Quakers,

"A Bold Stroke for Freedom." In this illustration from *The Underground Railroad* by William Still (1821–1902), African American slaves flee as slave catchers shoot at them. © CORBIS

Dunkers, Mennonites, and Shakers, later joined by those from the theologically radical wings of Baptism and Methodism, almost certainly constituted the first institutional skeleton of the later, secular, and more elaborate Underground Railroad.

In its third phase, the sophistication of the Underground Railroad of the antebellum period was propelled by a number of important developments. The rise of a republican "conscience"—a secular antislavery sensibility parallel to the Christian one—swelled the numbers of Americans willing to risk aiding fugitives. The ideology of the Revolution and consequent state emancipations in New England raised serious doubts about the compatibility of republicanism and slavery. Moreover, the rapidly growing class of free blacks became the new engine for the railroad. Harriet Tubman's amazing career is emblematic of this important shift. Free blacks identified with the slaves, provided places of refuge in their settlements, and were most often the engineers to freedom in both the South and the North.

The Underground Railroad as a social movement matured during the first half of the nineteenth century, when its various constituencies began to merge ideologically as abolitionists and intellectually as a spiritually influenced grassroots republican faction. The spokesmen for slavery were right to fear this movement. The railroad was, in an important sense, simply a functional arm of radical abolitionism. It engaged abolitionists committed to immediate and concrete action against slavery. In addition, in helping individual women and men escape to freedom, the railroad facilitated creation of the most potent weapon of abolitionism: first-hand testimony on the evils of slavery. Frederick Douglass was the most famous of these witnesses. Douglass, in turn, assisted hundreds of runaways to freedom from his home base in Rochester, New York.

The political, moral, and financial effectiveness of the railroad was underscored in the congressional debates of 1850, out of which grew the Fugitive Slave Act of 1850. This extreme extension of federal power in the interest of slavery incited fierce protest in the North and set the fugitive slave clause of the Constitution against and over the Fourth, Fifth, and Sixth amendments. The railroad almost certainly provoked this political blunder.

In its final fifteen years, the influence of the Underground Railroad increased due to continued resistance to the Fugitive Slave Act in the North, while simultaneously providing clandestine aid to fugitives and free blacks there, especially those subject to the racial violence that swept the region. The railroad disbanded when emancipation was assured by the Thirteenth Amendment to the Constitution.

BIBLIOGRAPHY

Bland, Sterling Lecatur, Jr. *Voices of the Fugitives: Runaway Slave Stories and Their Fictions of Self-Creation*. Westport, Conn.: Greenwood Press, 2000.

Buckmaster, Henrietta. *Let My People Go: The Story of the Underground Railroad and the Growth of the Abolitionist Movement*. New York: Harper, 1941.

Franklin, John Hope, and Schweninger, Loren. *Runaway Slaves: Rebels on the Plantation, 1790–1860*. New York: Oxford University Press, 1999.

Hunter, Carol M. *To Set the Captives Free: Reverend Jermain Wesley Loguen and the Struggle for Freedom in Central New York, 1835–1872*. New York: Garland, 1993.

Mitchell, William M. *The Under-ground Railroad*. Westport, Conn.: Negro Universities Press, 1970.

Harold S. Forsythe

See also **Antislavery; Fugitive Slave Acts; Slave Insurrections; Slave Rescue Cases; Slavery.**

UNDERWATER DEMOLITION TEAMS

(UDTs) are special units of the United States Navy. During World War II, Germany and Japan devised extensive underwater defenses in anticipation of Allied amphibious landings. The U.S. Marines assault at Tarawa Island in the western Pacific in November 1943 demonstrated the need to detect and destroy underwater obstructions and mines close to shore, where minesweepers could not go. The U.S. Navy organized intensively trained men into teams of expert swimming scouts whose duties were the reconnaissance of the seaward approaches to landing beaches; the location, improvement, and marking of usable channels for landing craft; and the demolition of natural and artificial obstacles. Often swimming two miles in shallow waters over coral reefs, under fire by the enemy in broad daylight, these men, nicknamed "frogmen," were unarmed except for a sheath knife. Working underwater, they scouted shores, demolished reef barriers, and neutralized enemy mines. UDTs were "first in" at Kwajalein, Saipan, Tinian, Guam, Peleliu, Anguar, Leyte, Lingayen, Luzon, Borneo, Iwo Jima, and Okinawa in the Pacific. In Europe, UDTs combined with U.S. Army beach clearance personnel at Normandy and in southern France in 1944 and suffered heavy casualties during the Normandy landings. During the Korean War, UDTs prepared the way for the amphibious Inchon landing and cooperated with special U.S. Marine Corps raider units striking far inland to blow up bridges, tunnels, dams, power plants, and highways. In the Vietnam War special volunteer units recruited from UDTs called SEALs (Sea-Air-Land approaches) made intelligence forays and commando raids into Vietcong-held territory in South Vietnam.

BIBLIOGRAPHY

Fane, Francis D., and Don Moore. *The Naked Warriors*. New York: Appleton-Century-Crofts, 1956.

Fawcett, Bill, ed. *Hunters and Shooters: An Oral History of the U.S. Navy Seals in Vietnam*. New York: Morrow, 1995.

Hutchins, Joel. *Swimmers among the Trees: SEAL Operations in the Vietnam War*. Novato, Calif.: Presidio, 1996.

Welham, Michael. *Combat Frogmen: Military Diving from the Nineteenth Century to the Present Day*. Wellingborough, U.K.: Stephens, 1989.

James J. Stokesberry/E. M.

See also **Korean War; Navy, United States; Vietnam War; World War II.**

UNEMPLOYMENT.

Few economic indicators are as important as the unemployment rate. A high unemployment rate, such as during the Great Depression, can precipitate tremendous political and legal change. Low unemployment is one of the surest signs of a healthy economy.

To be classified as unemployed by the U.S. Bureau of Labor Statistics (BLS), a person must be jobless, but must also be willing and able to take a job if one were offered, and must have actively looked for work in the preceding four weeks. The unemployment rate is calculated by dividing the number unemployed by the number in the labor force, where the labor force is the sum of the unemployed and the employed. The BLS calculates the unemployment rate monthly by surveying a random sample of about 50,000 households. The unemployment rate is criticized by some because it excludes "discouraged workers," that is, people who do not have jobs and are not actively seeking them because they believe that a job search would be fruitless.

Table 1 contains estimates of the average unemployment rate by decade beginning with the 1890s. The earliest figures come from Stanley Lebergott, who argues that unemployment in the early 1800s was very low—for example 1 to 3 percent in the 1810s—largely because the economy was dominated by agriculture, self-employment, and slavery. With the industrialization of the economy, the growth of wage labor, and the frequent occurrence of eco-

TABLE 1

Decadal Estimates of the Average Unemployment Rate

	Lebergott/BLS (percent)	Adjusted Figures (percent)
1890–1899	10.4	8.9
1900–1909	3.7	4.6
1910–1919	5.3	5.3
1920–1929	5.0	5.5
1930–1939	18.2	14.0
1940–1949	5.2	4.1
1950–1959	4.5	
1960–1969	4.8	
1970–1979	6.2	
1980–1989	7.3	
1990–1999	5.8	

nomic recessions and panics, unemployment became a serious problem after the Civil War. Lebergott guesses that unemployment averaged about 10 percent in the 1870s and 4 percent in the 1880s. Beginning in 1890, the decennial census asked questions about unemployment and Lebergott links these to other economic indicators to provide annual estimates of unemployment. Christina Romer argues that Lebergott's method overstates swings in the unemployment rate, because it incorrectly assumes that changes in employment mirror changes in annual output. This assumption contradicts a persistent relationship, known as Okun's Law, whereby changes in output are typically 2.5 to 3 times larger than changes in unemployment. Romer's estimates of unemployment (1890–1929) are given in the right-hand column. Her assumptions seem more realistic than Lebergott's but her estimates are still imprecise in comparison to estimates for later years. Figures after 1930 come from the BLS, but they have been criticized too. Michael Darby maintains that official figures vastly overstate unemployment between 1931 and 1942 because they improperly count millions of workers supported by federal work relief programs as unemployed. He argues that these jobs were substantially full-time and paid competitive wages, so these workers should be counted as government employees. (On the other hand, there was substantial part-time work and work-sharing during the Great Depression, which is not reflected in unemployment figures.) Darby's estimates of unemployment for the 1930s and 1940s are given in the right-hand column.

The estimates in Table 1 show that the Great Depression was truly exceptional and that the second half of the twentieth century saw an upward drift in the unemployment rate, with a reversal at the end. Unemployment peaks were reached between 1894 and 1898 when the rate exceeded 10 percent for five years running. A strong spike occurred in 1921—11.7 percent by Lebergott's series, 8.7 percent according to Romer. In 1933 the official unemployment rate was 25 percent and exceeded 37 percent of non-farm employees. The highest postwar rate was 9.7 percent in 1982. The lowest rates have occurred during wartime, with a record low of 1.2 percent during World War II. Overall, the unemployment rate averaged about three percentage points lower than normal during wartime.

Economists distinguish among frictional, seasonal, structural, and cyclical unemployment. Frictional unemployment refers to the normal turnover of workers (and firms) in any dynamic market economy. Seasonal unemployment occurs because production in some sectors varies over the year. Structural unemployment refers to the mismatch between workers and jobs. The mismatch can be spatial—for example entry-level jobs in the suburbs may go begging because unemployed youths in central cities cannot easily get to them, or workers in the rust belt can be unable to find jobs while there are vacancies they could fill in sunbelt states. Structural unemployment can also be caused by skill-based mismatches—such as when blue-collar workers losing jobs in declining sectors cannot fill high tech white-collar job vacancies. Many commentators have worried, especially during the Great Depression era, that technological advances would cause continually increasing structural unemployment rates, as machines took away the jobs of people. The trends in Table 1 show that these fears were ill founded, especially in the long run, as rising productivity brought rising incomes and demands for new services. Together, frictional and structural unemployment define a natural rate of unemployment, one to which the economy tends in the long run. The natural rate is notoriously difficult to estimate, but seems to have risen and then fallen in the last four decades of the twentieth century. Part of this change was probably due to demographic forces. Because younger workers generally have higher unemployment rates, as the baby boom generation entered the labor force, the unemployment rate first climbed, and then dropped as boomers aged. Another probable part of this change was the restructuring of the economy with the move away from heavy industry and increased international competition. Cyclical unemployment arises during recessions.

There is no universally accepted theory of the causes of unemployment. Some economists argue that all unemployment is voluntary, because there are always job openings, even in a recession. Instead of taking such jobs, the unemployed rationally choose to wait for better offers. Other economists hold that unemployment arises because wages are too high in terms of supply and demand. Why don't wages fall to the point where the supply and demand for labor are equal and unemployment disappears? Wage "stickiness"—the failure of wages to fall when demand for labor falls—increased significantly in the late 1800s and has been attributed to rising bargaining power among workers and employers' fears that cutting wages during a recession would undermine worker morale, harm productivity, and spawn strikes. Furthermore, after World War I, firms shifted toward longer-term relationships with their employees and found that wage cutting could increase turnover and clashed with internal pay structures. Many firms, then, were unwilling to cut wages during a downturn in product demand and responded instead by laying off workers, protecting the majority of employees from the problem. In addition, some laws, such as the Fair Labor Standards Act, which established a minimum wage beginning in 1938, or the wage codes established temporarily under the National Recovery Administration in 1933, can keep wages above the equilibrium level and cause unemployment.

The duration and incidence of unemployment spells changed to a great extent between the late nineteenth century and the late twentieth century. Unemployment spells were much briefer in the earlier period, but the odds of any individual becoming unemployed were noticeably higher. Compared with workers in the late 1970s, those in 1910 faced a 37 percent higher monthly rate of entry into the ranks of the unemployed. On the other hand,

"Parade of Unemployed." Men demonstrate on a New York street for jobs and social justice, 31 May 1909. Library of Congress

they also had a 32 percent higher rate of exiting unemployment, so the average spell of unemployment lasted less than four months. Data from the late 1800s suggest an even more rapid pace of workers entering and leaving unemployment, with an average unemployment spell lasting about seventy days, much less than the late 1970s rate of almost half a year. Evidence suggests that nearly 80 percent of employees laid off in the late 1800s were eventually recalled and rehired by their initial employers, a rate that was about the same in the late twentieth century. In the late 1800s and early 1900s, unemployment was influenced by personal characteristics, but to a much smaller degree than in the post–World War II period when educated, married, middle-aged, and experienced workers had significantly lower unemployment rates than others. Although unemployment was fairly indiscriminate in the earlier period, workers in industries with a high risk of layoff commanded higher wages—usually high enough to fully compensate them for the greater income risks they faced.

In the late twentieth century, the incidence of unemployment differed little by gender, but greatly by race. The nonwhite unemployment rate was 1.8 times higher than the white rate in 1950 and 1970 and 2.2 times higher in 1990. This gap opened up only after World War II— the nonwhite unemployment rate was slightly lower than the white rate in 1890 and 1930 and only 1.15 times higher in 1940. Another significant change has been the gradual decline in seasonal unemployment. In the late 1800s, employment in agriculture was very seasonal, as was manufacturing employment. In 1900 most industries saw considerable employment drops—often 10 to 15 percent— in the winter and again, to a smaller degree, in the summer. Seasonality faded slowly as America industrialized and as technology circumvented the vagaries of climate.

Until the Great Depression, federal and state governments did very little to explicitly combat or ameliorate the effects of unemployment. During the deep recession of the 1890s, for example, almost all the help to the unemployed came from the traditional sources, private charities and local governments. However, in 1935, as part of the Social Security Act, the federal government established a system of unemployment insurance, administered at the state level. The American system of unemployment insurance differs in important respects from that in other developed countries. The economists who framed this legislation, led by John Commons, believed that employers had enough leeway to substantially reduce seasonal and other layoffs, and constructed a system that included incentives to avoid layoffs. Unemployment insurance taxes were "experience rated," so that firms with higher layoff rates were taxed at higher rates. Evidence suggests that subsequently within the United States, seasonal differences in employment fell the most in states where experience rating was highest. Likewise, seasonality in the construction industry fell by two-thirds between 1929 and 1947 to 1963, a much faster rate than in Canada where firms were not penalized for laying off workers.

Unemployment insurance in the United States was designed to reduce unemployment and also to provide workers with extra income so that they could continue spending during a job loss and mount effective job searches, rather than accepting substandard jobs. By the standards of other countries, American unemployment insurance has covered a smaller portion of the workforce and has provided benefits that are lower in comparison to average wages. Unemployed workers are normally eligible for benefits for twenty-six weeks, although this can be extended to thirty-nine weeks if unemployment in a state is unusually severe or if Congress votes an extension. In comparison, during the postwar period most countries in Western Europe established maximum benefit durations of a year or more. Many economists argue that the generosity of European unemployment insurance helps explain why unemployment rates there surged past the American rate in the 1980s and became about twice as high in the 1990s.

Another way in which government has combated unemployment is by taking an active role in managing the economy. The Employment Act, adopted in 1946, declared the "responsibility of the Federal Government to use all practicable means . . . to coordinate and utilize all its plans, functions, and resources for the purpose of creating and maintaining . . . conditions under which there will be afforded useful employment opportunities . . . and to promote maximum employment." Congress essentially committed itself to "do something" to prevent depression, recessions, and other macroeconomic malfunctions. During the Great Depression the intellectual underpinnings for such an activist policy were laid out in the writings of British economist John Maynard Keynes, who called for governments to cut taxes or boost spending at the appropriate time to reduce the negative effects of recessions. By the late 1950s some leading economists argued that there was a consistent, stable relationship between inflation and unemployment—the Phillips Curve—which allowed policymakers to keep unemployment perpetually at a low rate: a 3 percent unemployment rate was attainable if we accepted an inflation rate of 7 percent, according to one set of calculations by two future Nobel laureates. Beginning in the late 1960s, however, it was learned that the additional government spending on the Vietnam War and new social programs could not push down the unemployment rate much below its long-term trend and that additional spending fueled accelerating inflation. The U.S. Full Employment and Balanced Growth Act of 1978 (also known as the Humphrey-Hawkins Act) "required" the federal government to pursue the goal of an overall unemployment rate equal to 4 percent. The goal was achieved only briefly during 2000. By the 1980s the federal government had largely given up on using taxation and expenditures to steer the economy and the role of macroeconomic stabilization was left primarily to the Federal Reserve. The Federal Reserve's principal goal, however, appeared to be controlling inflation, rather than reducing unemployment.

BIBLIOGRAPHY

Baicker, Katherine, Claudia Goldin, and Lawrence F. Katz. "A Distinctive System: Origins and Impact of U.S. Unemployment Compensation." In *The Defining Moment: The Great Depression and the American Economy in the Twentieth Century*. Edited by Michael D. Bordo, Claudia Goldin, and Eugene N. White. Chicago: University of Chicago Press, 1998.

Bewley, Truman. *Why Wages Don't Fall during a Recession*. Cambridge, Mass.: Harvard University Press, 1999.

Bureau of Labor Statistics. Latest statistics and explanations of measurements available at stats.bls.gov.

Darby, Michael. "Three-and-a-Half Million U.S. Employees Have Been Mislaid: Or, an Explanation for Unemployment, 1934–1941." *Journal of Political Economy* 84, no. 1 (1976): 1–16.

Ehrenberg, Ronald G., and Robert S. Smith. *Modern Labor Economics: Theory and Public Policy*. Rev. and updated 7th ed. Reading, Mass.: Addison-Wesley-Longman, 2000.

Goldin, Claudia. "Labor Markets in the Twentieth Century." In *The Cambridge Economic History of the United States*. Volume 3: *The Twentieth Century*, edited by Stanley L. Engerman and Robert E. Gallman. New York: Cambridge University Press, 2000.

Keyssar, Alexander. *Out of Work: The First Century of Unemployment in Massachusetts*. New York: Cambridge University Press, 1986.

Lebergott, Stanley. *Manpower in Economic Growth: The American Record since 1800*. New York: McGraw-Hill, 1964.

Nelson, Daniel. *Unemployment Insurance: The American Experience, 1915–1935*. Madison: University of Wisconsin Press, 1969.

Romer, Christina. "Spurious Volatility in Historical Unemployment Data." *Journal of Political Economy* 94, no. 1 (February 1986): 1–37.

Vedder, Richard, and Lowell Gallaway. *Out of Work: Unemployment and Government in Twentieth Century America*. New York: Holmes and Meier, 1993.

Robert Whaples

See also **Employment Act of 1946; Great Depression; Social Security;** *and vol. 9:* **Advice to the Unemployed in the Great Depression.**

UNIDENTIFIED FLYING OBJECTS. The UFO phenomenon consists of reports of unusual flying objects that remain unidentified after scientific inquiry. It first came to public attention in the United States in 1947, when a pilot reported seeing nine unusual objects flying in formation in the state of Washington. Since 1947, the U.S. federal government, private research institutions, and individual scientists have collected data about the phenomenon. Although UFOs are not a phenomenon unique to the United States, American organizations and private individuals have taken the lead in collecting, analyzing, and publishing sighting reports.

The most publicized collection agency was the U.S. Air Force through its Projects Sign (1948), Grudge (1948–1951), and Blue Book (1951–1969). The Air Force also sponsored research by the Battelle Memorial Institute in 1955 and the University of Colorado in the late 1960s. The Federal Bureau of Investigation, the Central Intelligence Agency, and other U.S. government agencies also looked into the phenomenon. Congressional hearings were held on the subject in 1966 and 1968. The goal of the U.S. government was to determine whether the UFO phenomenon was a threat to national security. Unable to find the threat, the government stopped collecting reports from the public in 1969.

Private research institutions, including the Aerial Phenomenon Research Organization (APRO), the National Investigations Committee on Aerial Phenomena (NICAP), the Mutual UFO Network, the J. Allen Hynek Center for UFO Studies, and the Fund for UFO Research, have collected and analyzed reports since 1952. Even the American Institute of Aeronautics and Astronautics (AIAA) conducted a study in 1971.

Nearly all research efforts have determined that a small but significant number of sightings remain "unidentified" after scientific investigation. This is especially true with reports made by the most articulate witnesses and containing the most data. Although the primary objective of private UFO researchers was to collect and analyze reports, they also sought to convince the public and the scientific community of the legitimacy of the subject. Their task was made all the more difficult by ridicule, caused in part by the perceived unlikelihood of the phenomenon's extraterrestrial origin, and in part by publicity-hungry charlatans and self-promoters ("contactees") who, beginning in the 1950s, made fictitious claims about meeting "space brothers" and traveling to distant planets, or hinted darkly about secret government conspiracies with aliens.

In addition to the problem of ridicule, serious researchers found it difficult, although not impossible, to gather "hard" evidence of the unconventional nature of the phenomenon. They amassed photos, films, videotapes, radar tracings, and great numbers of multiple witness reports of objects on or near the ground. They reported studies of UFO effects on electrical and mechanical devices, animals, and humans. They studied soil samples

Unidentified Flying Object? A hat, along with a cigar, is among the most common shapes of purported flying saucers that have been spotted in the skies since 1947. AP/WIDE WORLD PHOTOS

purportedly altered by landed UFOs. In spite of all this, they were unable to present artifacts of a UFO—the hard evidence that most scientists demanded.

Since the late 1940s, the UFO phenomenon has entered U.S. popular culture, and it has become a staple of motion pictures, television shows, advertising copy, and media images. As early as 1950 it proved to be one of the most recognized phenomena in Gallup Poll history, and it has continued to play an important role in popular culture.

In the early 1960s, people began to claim that they were abducted into UFOs. Although UFO researchers at first considered these reports to be an "exotic"—and probably psychological—sidelight of the main sighting phenomenon, abduction accounts grew steadily in number. Evidence for abductions was mainly derived from human memory, usually retrieved through hypnosis. But the people who reported being abducted were not "contactees" or self-promoters and appeared to be genuinely concerned about what had happened to them. In the 1980s, the numbers of people who came forward with abduction accounts had begun to rise dramatically, and a 1998 Roper Poll of 5,995 adults suggested that as many as a million Americans believed they had been abducted. By the end of the twentieth century, the abduction phenomenon had come to dominate UFO research.

In spite of extensive efforts in the second half of the twentieth century, attitudes toward the legitimacy of the UFO phenomenon and the research into it changed little. At the beginning of the twenty-first century, researchers had failed to convince the scientific community of the phenomenon's legitimacy, they had not developed a standardized methodology to retrieve alleged abduction accounts, and no UFO organization had gained the academic backing to professionalize both UFO and abduction research. Yet after half a century of study, UFO proponents had advanced knowledge of the subject greatly, and some even claimed that a solution to the mystery of UFO origins and motivations seemed possible.

In the twenty-first century, the UFO phenomenon persisted, apparently unaffected by societal events. It continued to maintain a ubiquitous presence in popular culture, researchers continued to study it, and, although scientists and academics still scorned it, ordinary people continued to report both sightings and abduction accounts.

BIBLIOGRAPHY

Clark, Jerome. *The UFO Encyclopedia*. 2d ed. Detroit, Mich.: Visible Ink, 1998.

Dean, Jodi. *Aliens in America*. Ithaca, N.Y.: Cornell University Press, 1997.

Hopkins, Budd. *Intruders*. New York: Random House, 1981.

Jacobs, David M. *The UFO Controversy in America*. Bloomington: Indiana University Press, 1975.

———. *Secret Life*. New York: Simon and Schuster, 1992.

David Jacobs

UNIFORM CODE OF MILITARY JUSTICE

(UCMJ) replaced the traditional system known as the Articles of War, which governed the conduct of military personnel from 1775 to the UCMJ's passage in 1950. The Articles of War contained eighteenth-century language inappropriate to the post–World War II military and contained separate legal systems for the army and navy. The UCMJ was a product of the newly created Office of the Secretary of Defense, which centralized and regularized many facets of military life.

The UCMJ was written entirely by civilians, with Secretary of Defense James Forrestal making many of the key decisions himself. The UCMJ more closely aligned military justice procedure with civilian federal procedure, though it delegated to the president the authority to modify rules of evidence and other procedures. In 1951, President Harry Truman issued his *Manual for Courts-Martial*, which directs military courts on the implementation of the UCMJ.

In many of its aspects, the UCMJ is significantly more restrictive than civilian law. For example, the UCMJ restricts the First Amendment right of free speech and more closely regulates the sexual behavior of military members, specifically forbidding homosexuality and adultery. These features of the UCMJ have drawn the most criticism in recent years.

BIBLIOGRAPHY

Byrne, Edward. *Military Law: A Handbook for the Navy and Marine Corps*. Annapolis, Md.: Naval Institute Press, 1981.

Michael S. Neiberg

See also **"Don't Ask, Don't Tell"; Military Law.**

UNIFORMS, MILITARY.

The American model for uniform military dress is derived from concepts in tactics

Confederate Zouave. This style of uniform, adapted from French colonial uniforms, was worn by soldiers on both sides in the Civil War. © CORBIS

and weaponry introduced into European armies in the mid-seventeenth century. Uniforms became a vital element in these new European national standing armies with large numbers of soldiers. Brightly colored, distinctive uniforms made soldiers recognizable on crowded and smoke-filled battlefields. Equally important, uniforms shaped actions and habits, imposing a discipline that transformed individual strength into collective power in these modern, permanently mobilized armies. Uniforms embodied a hierarchy of organization within the military and overt political references outside of it.

Styles of uniforms did not change as often as civilian fashion until late in the twentieth century. The military wardrobe expanded to accommodate a larger, modern, and less-isolated armed force with styles often indistinguishable from civilian casual dress. Distinctive military features have been sustained over long periods, however, or have reappeared in tribute to the heritage of the population from which the armies are drawn. Epaulettes, for example, were first used on army and navy uniforms to attach a shoulder belt for a sword or a bugle and to protect the shoulder while carrying a musket. Later they were decorated with rank or service insignia. Now epaulettes are used primarily for ceremonial dress. Shoulder boards with rank insignia are a derivation of epaulettes and are a feature of most contemporary uniforms. Likewise, horizontal rows of braid on the chests of the uniform coats of West Point cadets, band uniforms, and other "full dress" uniforms descend from the Hungarian national costume via Hungarian Hussars serving with the Austrian army in the late-seventeenth century.

In America, when pre-revolutionary militia units and the independent volunteer companies wore uniforms, they wore British uniforms. British and French officers garrisoned in colonial America often followed the example of Native Americans and colonial irregulars like ROGERS' RANGERS, wearing indigenous clothing such as fringed shirts, moccasins, leggings, cocked hats (with brims later swept up to become bicorns and tricorns), and deerskin trousers. American Indian feather headdresses may have inspired the striking Scots Highlanders' feather bonnet that appeared when the Highlanders were serving in colonial America. The frontier style, worn by some American forces through the War of 1812, introduced features that would later emerge in post–Civil War martial wear: the buckskin coats of George Armstrong Custer and his officers; the Indian Scout uniform that in the late nineteenth century combined traditional Indian leggings and moccasins with regulation army uniform items; and at the turn of the twentieth century leggings and puttees, precursors of World War II paratrooper boots.

Red Cross Nurses. These World War II nurses stroll a London street neatly garbed in the dark colors originally prescribed by Dorothea Dix during the Civil War. © HULTON-DEUTSCH COLLECTION/CORBIS

From 1776 until late in the nineteenth century, standard uniforms for American armed forces followed the styles of European uniforms. Blue uniforms, British in appearance, were officially designated for the American army during the Revolutionary War, and blue remained the national American uniform color for more than a century. The American navy and marine services, like virtually all maritime services, followed a tradition set early by the British navy, issuing dark blue winter apparel and white summer apparel. Unlike the army, which authorized special summer wear only intermittently before the twentieth century, from the start the navy had separate winter and summer clothing. Naval uniforms were formally regulated in the late nineteenth century.

The colorful close-fitting jackets, tight trousers, and outsized headwear of the Napoleonic style of military uniform swept Europe in the first decades of the nineteenth century. Although subdued in American uniforms, the Napoleonic influence is evident in the design, if not the color, of the first West Point uniform in 1816 and of American uniforms during the half century that followed.

Another colorful French contribution to military apparel, the Zouave uniform, reached America in the mid-nineteenth century. First adopted by French colonial soldiers in North Africa in the 1830s, the popular costume with balloon trousers and cropped jacket quickly spread worldwide. In the Civil War, dozens of Zouave units fought for and against the Union. Most Union soldiers wore an unstructured sack coat modeled after fashionable informal civilian jackets, foreshadowing modern American uniforms. Worn with the celebrated French-styled forage cap or kepi, sack coats were the comfortable and

West Point Cadets. Cadets stand at attention in this 1933 photograph. © BETTMANN-CORBIS

Desert Uniform. A special forces soldier poses with his weapon at Fort Bragg, N.C., in 1991. © LEIF SKOOGFORS/CORBIS

the *pickelhaube*, that projected the aura of military repression in America it had already gained in Europe.

The U.S. Army first wore khaki military uniforms in the Spanish-American War. Olive drab service uniforms followed in 1902, standardizing colors and styles that would change only superficially during the twentieth century. While blue remained the general color of navy uniforms and the primary color of army dress uniforms, the new drab-colored field uniforms represented a concession to the increased range of modern small arms and the greater battlefield visibility afforded by weapons using smokeless powder.

By the mid-twentieth century, patterned camouflage field uniforms obscured soldiers from the air as well as on land. More recently, camouflage uniforms have been worn by military men and women for fatigue dress and by civilians for hunting and casual wear. U.S. Army Captain Anson Mills developed woven webbing that was used during the early twentieth century for wear with khaki uniforms as waist and cartridge belts. It shortly became integral to military field wear, transforming the way a wide range of military and civilian equipment was safely attached—parachute straps, belts and straps for sports equipment, automobile seat belts, infant car seats, and others.

Patriotism, progressivism, and a widespread concern for military preparedness at the beginning of the twentieth century triggered a proliferation of civilian organizations in which members, women and men, wore uniforms with overt military features. The wearing of uniforms reached its apogee during World War I. Women volunteers officially served in the armed forces for the first time in World War I; the uniforms authorized for them by the War Department closely resembled those worn by women volunteers in the American Red Cross, Salvation Army, YMCA, YWCA, and the many other secular and religious groups that participated in war service.

New technologies spurred innovation in the development of fabrics and more practical uniforms used during World War II. A variety of special-function and field uniforms were introduced for ground troops, the army air corps, paratroopers, and mountain units. These included layered uniforms suitable for widely varied climates, special jungle boots, and cotton olive drab fatigues and coveralls. This trend continued through the late twentieth century with highly specialized apparel for special forces, high-altitude pilots, and astronauts, along with more new materials—kevlar helmets, lightweight moisture-wicking fabrics, high-tech footwear, and more.

At the start of the twenty-first century, standard military uniforms have become more casual. Military apparel retains drab colors even as it expands into the realm of civilian casual wear. Undress uniforms serve for duty and off-duty, while dress and service uniforms are less frequently worn.

popular predecessors of the fatigue and multiple-function uniforms of the expanding armed forces in America.

Women's uniforms also appeared during the Civil War. Dorothea Dix's appointment to superintendent of women nurses, charged with organizing and overseeing nurses in military hospitals, extended official sanction to women's age-old support role in the military. Dix immediately issued directives for nurses to dress uniformly in brown or black frocks with no adornment or hoops, following a standard set by Florence Nightingale little more than a decade earlier. Civil War veterans proudly wore their wartime uniforms at regular reunions until the uniforms of organized veterans' associations became popular. By the late nineteenth century, versions of military uniforms were worn in many veteran, quasi-military, and fraternal organizations, as well as in some women's associations and drill corps.

Still strongly influenced by the smart, tight uniforms of European armies, the army uniform of the 1870s and 1880s was Prussian in appearance. It was topped by a version of the famous 1840s Russian-Prussian spiked helmet,

BIBLIOGRAPHY

Abler, Thomas S. *Hinterland Warriors and Military Dress: European Empires and Exotic Uniforms.* New York: Berg, 1999.

Mollo, John. *Military Fashion.* New York: Putnam, 1972.

Roche, Daniel. *The Culture of Clothing: Dress and Fashion in the "Ancien Régime."* Cambridge: Cambridge University Press, 1994.

Margaret Vining

UNION COLONY. In December 1869 Nathan C. Meeker, the agricultural editor of the *New York Tribune*, sought fellow temperance advocates to establish a cooperative community in COLORADO that would adhere to their conception of high moral standards. The Union Colony, with 450 residents, settled in the Cache la Poudre Valley, north of Denver, and, in 1870, established the town of Greeley, named for Horace Greeley, the editor of the *Tribune*. In return for fees that varied from $50 to $200, members received farming land, access to the system of IRRIGATION, and the right to buy lots in the colony town. The success of this semicooperative venture stimulated similar undertakings. Greeley was incorporated as a city in 1885.

BIBLIOGRAPHY

Willard, James F., ed. *The Union Colony at Greeley, Colorado, 1869–1871.* Boulder, Colo., 1918.

Colin B. Goodykoontz / A. R.

See also **Agrarianism; "Go West, Young Man, Go West"; Temperance Movement; Utopian Communities.**

UNION, FORT (North Dakota). In 1827 the American Fur Company purchased its rival, the Columbia Fur Company. The following year Kenneth McKenzie, director of the newly created Upper Missouri Outfit, began construction of Fort Union, located on the north bank of the Missouri River near its junction with the Yellowstone. The fort, occupied in 1832, was the hub of a prosperous trade with Assiniboines, Crees, Crows, Lakotas, and Blackfeet for almost forty years. Although a decline in beaver pelts prompted a sale to Pratt, Chouteau and Company in 1834, the outpost remained profitable, thanks to a steady supply of buffalo robes and elk skins. Sadly, however, smallpox epidemics frequently ravaged the region's American Indians.

Fort Union welcomed several distinguished visitors, including the artists Karl Bodmer and George Catlin. Other prominent guests included the naturalist John J. Audubon and Pierre Jean De Smet, a Jesuit missionary. In 1853, Fort Union served as a rendezvous site for the Northern Pacific Railroad survey. The Plains Wars of the 1860s, coupled with a decline of fur-bearing animals and the denial of an application for a license renewal, hastened the post's demise. In November 1867 the military de-molished Fort Union, so its materials could be used at nearby Fort Buford. Restoration of the historic post was completed by the National Park Service in 1991. The Fort Union Trading Post National Historic Site is located near Williston, North Dakota.

BIBLIOGRAPHY

Barbour, Barton H. *Fort Union and the Upper Missouri Fur Trade.* Norman: University of Oklahoma Press, 2001.

Ewers, John C. *Plains Indian History and Culture: Essays on Continuity and Change.* Norman: University of Oklahoma Press, 1997.

Jon Brudvig

See also **Fur Companies; Fur Trade and Trapping.**

UNION LABOR PARTY was organized in Cincinnati, Ohio, in 1887 in an attempt to unite the remnants of the Greenback Labor Party with wage earners who had been politicized by industrial conflicts. The Haymarket Riot of 1886 led to a major backlash against organized labor and created a political climate hostile to labor parties. Consequently, during the 1888 presidential campaign neither major party made overtures to organized labor, and the Union Labor Party remained on the political fringe. Alson J. Streeter of Illinois, presidential nominee in 1888, received only 147,000 votes, the bulk of which came from the agricultural South and West.

BIBLIOGRAPHY

Brody, David. *The American Labor Movement.* New York: Harper and Row, 1971.

Montgomery, David. *The Fall of the House of Labor: The Workplace, the State, and American Labor Activism, 1865–1925.* New York: Cambridge University Press, 1987.

Chester M. Destler / A. G.

See also **Greenback Movement; Haymarket Riot; Labor Parties.**

UNION PARTY, a fusion party conceived by Republicans in 1861 to combine people of all political affiliations into a single movement committed to the preservation of the Union and to war. Republicans wanted to project an image of wartime nonpartisanship, and they also expected to capitalize on wartime patriotism to siphon off Democratic support. Most Democrats, including a significant number willing to tone down their partisan rhetoric, refused to bolt their party altogether to join the Union coalition (the War Democrats were the notable exception). After 1862 and for the duration of the war, Republicans and occasionally War Democrats ran against regular Democrats under the Union Party banner.

BIBLIOGRAPHY

Silbey, Joel H. *A Respectable Minority: The Democratic Party in the Civil War Era, 1860–1868.* New York: W.W. Norton, 1977.

Jeremy Derfner

See also **War Democrats.**

UNION SENTIMENT IN BORDER STATES.

After the outbreak of the Civil War in the spring of 1861, a large majority of the people of Maryland, western Virginia, and Missouri rallied to the Union cause, and by September, Kentucky also openly sided with the North in its struggle against the secessionist South. Unionist sentiment ran strongest in the cities and in communities accessible to railroads and navigable rivers. Confederate sympathizers emerged as a significant minority faction in some areas of the border states, particularly among slaveholders. Although much harassed by Confederate raids and guerrilla bands, the border states contributed heavily in men to the Union armies and played a major role in the Confederacy's defeat.

BIBLIOGRAPHY

Donald, David Herbert. *Why the North Won the Civil War.* Baton Rouge: Louisiana State University Press, 1960.

McPherson, James M. *Battle Cry of Freedom: The Civil War Era.* New York: Oxford University Press, 1988.

E. C. Smith / A. G.

See also **Army, Union; Cumberland, Army of the; Impressment, Confederate; Jayhawkers; Mosby's Rangers; Tennessee, Army of.**

UNION SENTIMENT IN THE SOUTH,

widespread throughout the Civil War but strongest in the mountainous parts of Virginia, North Carolina, Tennessee, Georgia, and Alabama. Many residents in these states loved the Union and viewed secession with dismay. Many previously loyal Confederates, disaffected by Confederate conscription, impressment, and tax-in-kind laws, came to prefer the Union to the heavy-handed Richmond administration.

Unionists organized themselves into secret peace societies to provide mutual protection, render aid to Union troops, and weaken Confederate forces. By burning bridges, encouraging desertion, and transmitting military information to the enemy, these societies greatly embarrassed the Confederate government and compelled it to use a part of its strength in controlling its own disaffected citizens.

BIBLIOGRAPHY

Thomas, Emory M. *Confederacy as a Revolutionary Experience.* Columbia: University of South Carolina Press, 1991.

Richard E. Yates / C. W.

See also **Impressment, Confederate; States' Rights in the Confederacy.**

UNIONS. *See* **Labor; Trade Unions.**

UNIT RULE.

The unit rule, a practice formerly observed by the Democratic Party at its national conventions, required that the entire vote of a state delegation be cast as a unit for the candidate preferred by a majority of that delegation. The 1968 Democratic convention voted to release all delegates from the unit-rule constraint, and reforms adopted before the 1972 convention outlawed the unit rule at all stages of delegation selection. The survival of the unit rule until 1968 was largely a concession to the often dissident southern delegations in the party.

BIBLIOGRAPHY

David, Paul T., Ralph M. Goldman, and Richard C. Bain. *The Politics of National Party Conventions.* Lanham, Md.: University Press of America, 1984.

Parris, Judith H. *The Convention Problem: Issues in Reform of Presidential Nominating Procedures.* Washington, D.C.: Brookings Institution, 1972.

Robert Eyestone / A. G.

See also **Conventions, Party Nominating; Democratic Party.**

UNITED AMERICANS, ORDER OF.

The Order of United Americans, formed in New York in 1844, was a nativistic benevolent association that quickly attained nationwide membership, which was limited to American laborers. Although members gained retirement benefits, the society was principally an agency for the dissemination of anti-Catholic and antiforeign propaganda. Members' xenophobia stemmed from the conviction that most immigrants, especially Catholics, were not worthy of American freedoms and would corrupt the American way of life. Although not expressly opposed to violence against immigrants, the Order of United Americans concentrated more on the mutual-aid aspect of its organization. A decade later the Know-Nothing Party copied its secret methods and elaborate rituals.

BIBLIOGRAPHY

Bennett, David H. *The Party of Fear: From Nativist Movements to the New Right in American History.* Chapel Hill: University of North Carolina Press, 1988.

Knobel, Dale T. *America for the Americans: The Nativist Movement in the United States.* New York: Twayne, 1996.

Ray Allen Billington / A. E.

See also **Know-Nothing Party; Nativism; Secret Societies.**

UNITED AUTOMOBILE WORKERS OF AMERICA

(UAW) was the largest and most politically im-

UAW. With police keeping them apart from a large crowd, workers outside Chevrolet Parts Plant no. 9 in Flint, Mich., maintain their strike against General Motors in 1937—a defining moment in the history of that union. © CORBIS

portant trade union during the heyday of the twentieth-century labor movement. Although the UAW held its first convention in 1935, its real founding took place the next year, when it became one of the key unions within the new Committee for Industrial Organization. After a dramatic, six-week sit-down strike at General Motors during the winter of 1937, the UAW won union recognition from that company, then the nation's largest corporation. Chrysler and numerous supplier plants followed within a few months, after which it took four difficult years to organize workers at the Ford Motor Company, an intransigent union foe. By 1943, the UAW had organized more than a million workers in the auto, aircraft, and agricultural equipment industries.

The UAW was a uniquely democratic and militant union for three reasons. First, under conditions of mass production, supervisors and unionists fought bitterly and continuously over the pace of production, the distribution of work, and the extent to which seniority would govern job security. Second, the UAW enrolled hundreds of thousands of Poles, Hungarians, Slavs, Italians, African Americans, and white Appalachian migrants for whom unionism represented a doorway to an engaged sense of American citizenship. Finally, the founders and officers of the UAW were a notably factional and ideological cohort,

among which socialists, communists, Catholic corporatists, and Roosevelt liberals fought for power and office.

Homer Martin, who served as union president from 1936 until 1939, was a former Protestant minister whose maladroit leadership nearly wrecked the union during the sharp recession of 1938. He was followed by R. J. Thomas, who tried to straddle the rivalry that made the former socialist Walter Reuther and his "right wing" faction the bitter enemies of Secretary Treasurer George Addes and Vice President Richard Frankensteen and their communist supporters. Reuther won the union presidency in 1946, and his anticommunist caucus, which nevertheless embodied the radicalism of many shop militants and progressive unionists, took full control of the UAW the next year. Reuther served as president until 1970, when he died in an airplane crash.

During its first quarter century, the UAW established the template that defined much of modern U.S. unionism. In bargaining with the big three auto corporations, the union raised and equalized wages between plants, regions, and occupations. It established a grievance arbitration system that limited the foreman's right to hire, fire, and discipline, and it won for its members a wide array of health and pension "fringe benefits" when it became clear that the unions and their liberal allies could not expand the U.S. welfare state. The real income of automobile workers more than doubled between 1947 and 1973.

But the UAW was thwarted in many of its larger ambitions. During World War II, the union sought a role in administering the production effort and sharing power with corporate management. Immediately after the war, Reuther led a 113-day strike against General Motors not only to raise wages but also to pressure both that corporation and the administration of President Harry Truman to limit any subsequent rise in the price of cars, thus enhancing the purchasing power of all workers.

The defeat of the UAW on both of these issues paved the way for a midcentury accord with most of the big auto firms. The union abandoned most efforts to challenge management pricing or production prerogatives, in return for which the corporations guaranteed autoworkers a slow but steady increase in their real pay. But this industry–UAW accord was not peaceful. Individual UAW locals struck repeatedly to humanize working conditions and to defend unionists victimized by management. At the companywide level, both sides probed for advantage. Thus, long strikes occurred at Chrysler in 1950 and 1957, at Ford in 1955 and 1967, and at General Motors in 1964 and 1970.

Politically, the UAW was a liberal presence in national Democratic politics and in those states, such as Michigan, Missouri, Ohio, Illinois, New York, Iowa, California, and Indiana, where it had a large membership. Until 1948, many in the UAW leadership supported forming a labor-based third party, but after Truman's unexpected victory, the UAW sought a liberal "realignment" of the Democrats. The union pushed for aggressive Keynesian fiscal policies to lower unemployment, fought for an expanded welfare state, and favored détente with the Soviets. The UAW funded numerous civil rights activities in the 1960s, despite or perhaps because its role in Detroit municipal politics and in numerous auto and aircraft factories was an equivocal one on racial issues. The UAW did not break with President Lyndon Johnson over Vietnam. But it withdrew from the AFL-CIO from 1968 to 1981, because of what Reuther considered the conservative posture and stolid anticommunism of that union federation and of George Meany, its longtime president. In 1972 the UAW vigorously supported the presidential candidacy of George McGovern.

Until the late 1970s, UAW membership fluctuated between 1.2 and 1.5 million, but the back-to-back recessions of the late 1970s and the early 1980s combined with automation, the deunionization of the auto parts sector, and the closing of many older factories slashed UAW size to about 750,000. When Chrysler verged on bankruptcy in 1980 and 1981, the union agreed to a series of contract concessions that for the first time in forty years broke wage parity among the major auto firms. The UAW eventually reestablished the industry wage pattern and won employment guarantees for many of its remaining mem-bers, but the concession bargaining of the early 1980s spread rapidly across industrial America with devastating results for millions of workers.

After the mid-1980s, the UAW no longer played the "vanguard" role within the labor movement once hailed by Reuther. Until 1983 it was led by Leonard Woodcock and Douglas Fraser, both union pioneers and labor spokesmen of national stature. The UAW voice was more muted during the subsequent presidencies of Owen Bieber and Steven Yokich. The union cooperated with the auto industry to dilute government-mandated fuel efficiency standards and to stanch Japanese imports. But when foreign firms built assembly and parts plants in the United States, the union could not organize the workers. For more than a decade the UAW accommodated management efforts to deploy team production and employee involvement schemes, which often eroded work standards and eviscerated union consciousness. By the early twenty-first century the UAW was the nation's fifth largest union.

BIBLIOGRAPHY

Boyle, Kevin. *The UAW and the Heyday of American Liberalism, 1945–1968*. Ithaca, N.Y.: Cornell University Press, 1995.

Halpern, Martin. *UAW Politics in the Cold War Era*. Albany: State University of New York Press, 1988.

Jefferys, Steve. *Management and Managed: Fifty Years of Crisis at Chrysler*. New York: Cambridge University Press, 1986.

Lichtenstein, Nelson. *The Most Dangerous Man in Detroit: Walter Reuther and the Fate of American Labor*. New York: Basic Books, 1995.

Moody, Kim. *Workers in a Lean World: Unions in the International Economy*. London: Verso, 1997.

Nelson Lichtenstein

See also **American Federation of Labor–Congress of Industrial Organizations; Automobile Industry; Labor; Sitdown Strikes; Strikes;** *and vol. 9:* **Ford Men Beat and Rout Lewis.**

UNITED BROTHERHOOD OF CARPENTERS AND JOINERS.

In 1881, thirty-six carpenters from eleven cities, representing 2,000 members met in Chicago and over a four-day period established the United Brotherhood of Carpenters and Joiners. Members elected Peter J. McGuire as the executive secretary. A factory carpenter, McGuire gained national fame for his participation in the St. Louis carpenter's strike in the spring of 1881. Like other carpenters, McGuire saw the mechanization of his trade and the mass production of such items as wooden doors, stairs, and floors as a threat. He also feared the carpenters' loss of control over prices and wages since the end of the Civil War. The Brotherhood, then, was a response to the changes brought on by the modern industrial economy. Shortly after the formation of the union, McGuire moved its headquarters to New York. There he worked with Samuel Gompers to establish what became the American Federation of Labor. With the exception of four years, the Brotherhood had a key officer on the executive council of the Federation for its first seventy-five years.

The slogan that appeared in the union's newspaper, the *Carpenter*, reflected the union's philosophy: Organize, Agitate, Educate. Although the Brotherhood agitated for an eight-hour working day and better wages, McGuire also campaigned for a day to honor the workers of America. Because of his efforts, he is given credit for establishing LABOR DAY. By the mid 1890s membership surpassed 100,000 and included African American carpenters, making the organization one of the few multiracial unions in the country. McGuire remained the authoritative figure of the union until his death in 1906, when membership reached nearly 200,000.

In 1915, William L. Hutcheson ascended to the office of the presidency. The son of a migrant worker, Hutcheson held the executive office until 1952 when membership reached a historic high of 850,000. During that time Hutcheson worked to establish the union as a mainstream patriotic organization, untouched by the more radical elements within the industry. In 1918, he dropped German editions of the *Carpenter* and spoke out against such groups as the Wobblies (see INDUSTRIAL WORKERS OF THE WORLD). He continued the battle against what he perceived as a threat from radical workers by challenging the recruitment efforts of the Congress of Industrial Organizations in the 1930s. But he also defeated challenges to the Brotherhood from the establishment. In 1938 Hutcheson defended the union against antitrust charges brought by Assistant Attorney General Thurman W. Arnold. Following World War II, Hutcheson, a life-long Republican, organized the Stop Taft movement at the 1952 Republican convention. In 1964 the union abandoned its policy of not endorsing presidential candidates and cast its support for Lyndon Johnson. The Brotherhood faced questions of jurisdiction with two competing unions in the 1970s and the challenges of the economic recession of the 1980s. As it had in previous years, the union publicly supported the country's military engagement in the Vietnam and Persian Gulf Wars. In 2000, an estimated 700,000 members belonged to the Brotherhood.

BIBLIOGRAPHY
Galenson, Walter. *United Brotherhood of Carpenters: The First Hundred Years.* Cambridge, Mass.: Harvard University Press. 1983.

David O'Donald Cullen

See also **American Federation of Labor–Congress of Industrial Organizations, Labor; Trade Unions.**

UNITED CHURCH OF CHRIST. Although the United Church of Christ (UCC) is a relatively young Protestant denomination, formed in 1957, the historical roots of its four constituent bodies go much deeper. The UCC brought together the Congregational Christian Church—itself the product of a 1931 union of Congregationalist and Christian churches—with the Evangelical and Reformed church—the product of a 1934 merger between the German Reformed and Evangelical Synod churches. This diverse historical background encompasses Calvinism, American revivalism, and German pietism, but to a considerable degree the four traditions have shared a common commitment to social witness and ecumenical efforts toward Christian unity.

Congregationalism arrived in New England in the 1620s and 1630s as a movement of Calvinist dissenters from the Anglican Church, emphasizing the autonomy of local congregations from state and episcopal control. Although these seventeenth-century Puritans did not champion religious tolerance—theological mavericks might be banished or summarily executed—they did affirm the necessity of informed individual assent to church teaching. The Congregational tradition thus placed great emphasis on an educated clergy and laity—a commitment realized in the formation of Harvard in 1636 and in the myriad of smaller colleges established in the nineteenth century, including several schools (Howard and Fisk) for African Americans. Although by the end of the nineteenth century two-thirds of all Congregationalists still resided in New England, the denomination's early leadership in foreign missions, abolitionism, and women's rights testified to its powerful and generally progressive role as cultural arbiter. In the late-nineteenth century, Congregationalists like Washington Gladden and Josiah Strong led the Social Gospel movement's call for social action among Protestant churches. Similarly, churchmen like George A. Gordon, Henry Ward Beecher, and Lyman Abbott popularized the tenets of the New Theology—emphasizing the immanence of God in creation, the humanity of Christ, and the importance of scientific learning for religious thought—in pulpits and seminaries.

The 1931 merger of the Congregationalist and Christian churches was in some ways an unlikely one. The Christian church was a product of early-nineteenth-century revivalism, a movement whose emotional excesses inspired distrust among many more rationally inclined Congregationalists. But the two traditions shared a dislike of ecclesiastical hierarchy, creedal tests, and sectarian competition; the early Christian churches modeled themselves on the first-century church and refused any denominational title. The Bible was to be their only arbiter of practice and teaching, and the unity of all believers their final goal. The movement was indebted to three main founders: James O'Kelly of Virginia, who left the Methodist Episcopal Church and founded the Republican Methodists (later Christians) in 1794; Abner Jones, a former Baptist who established the First Free Christian Church in Lyndon, Vermont, in 1801; and Barton W. Stone, who led a dissenting group of Kentucky Presbyterians out of the denomination in 1803. In 1820, these groups formed the Christian Connection, a relatively loose affiliation that enabled them to sustain two colleges (Defiance and

Elon) and a vigorous publishing effort, dating back to Elias Smith's *Herald of Gospel Liberty* in 1808. But the group remained relatively small: at the time of the 1931 merger, the General Convention of the Christian Church numbered only 100,000 members, mostly in the Upper South and Ohio Valley, compared with about one million Congregationalists.

The Evangelical and Reformed merger brought together two German immigrant groups. The German Reformed church originated in 1747, when Michael Schlatter organized a German-speaking synod (coetus) in Philadelphia. In 1793 this body, then numbering around 15,000 members, declared itself the Synod of the German Reformed Church in the United States of America. As the denomination grew, it established a foreign mission board (1838), and various colleges and seminaries, including Mercersburg (later Lancaster) Theological Seminary in Pennsylvania, Heidelberg College in Tiffin, Ohio, and Franklin and Marshall College, also in Lancaster, Pennsylvania. Two professors at Mercersburg, Philip Schaff and John W. Nevin, were influential critics of American Protestantism, particularly its incipient anti-Catholicism and its sectarian divisions. The Mercersburg Theology emphasized the importance of historic creeds, catechism, and liturgy as means of unifying a divided Christendom.

The Evangelical Synod of North America, which joined with the Reformed church in 1934, originated in 1817, when Prussia's King Frederick William III united his country's Lutheran and Reformed churches into one state-controlled body, the Evangelical Church of the Prussian Union. In 1833, under the sponsorship of the Basel Missionary Society, the denomination began sending pastors to German immigrants in the United States. In 1840, ministers in the St. Louis area formed the German Evangelical Church Society of the West, which in 1866 became not a formal denomination but a more loosely organized "synod." In 1872, this German Evangelical Synod of the West joined with two other regional synods in the upper Midwest and Northeast; five years later the denomination was renamed the German Evangelical Synod of North America. The word "German" was dropped in 1927. Itself the product of missionary endeavor and heavily influenced by pietist zeal, the Evangelical Synod soon developed a wide array of evangelistic and humanitarian projects, including deaconess hospitals in Cleveland, Detroit, Chicago, and Evansville, Indiana. The denomination's two schools, Eden Theological Seminary and Elmhurst College, produced two leading American theologians, Reinhold Niebuhr, a central figure in the neo-orthodox movement, and H. Richard Niebuhr, an ethicist and church historian. At the 1934 merger, the Evangelical Synod numbered about 280,000 members and the German Reformed some 350,000.

The merger of these four traditions became final in June 1957, at the Uniting General Synod in Cleveland, Ohio. Not all congregations participated: the National Association of Congregational Christian Churches and the Conservative Congregational Christian Conference did not join because of disagreements on polity and theology. Since the 1960s, the UCC, like most other mainline American denominations, has endured membership losses and theological turmoil. Between 1960 and 1970, the UCC lost 12.5 percent of its members; in 2001, membership stood at about 1.4 million. The UCC has found much of its identity in social witness, particularly the civil rights movement, antiwar protest, and support for the ordination of women and homosexuals. It has pursued ecumenism as a member of the World and National Councils of Churches, the World Alliance of Reformed Churches, and in ecumenical partnership with the Disciples of Christ.

BIBLIOGRAPHY

Dunn, David, et. al. *A History of the Evangelical and Reformed Church.* Philadelphia: Christian Education Press, 1961. Reprint. New York: Pilgrim Press, 1990.

Gunneman, Louis. *The Shaping of the United Church of Christ: An Essay in the History of American Christianity.* New York: United Church Press, 1977.

Von Rohr, John. *The Shaping of American Congregationalism, 1620–1957.* Cleveland, Ohio: Pilgrim Press, 1992.

Zikmund, Barbara Brown, ed. *Hidden Histories in the United Church of Christ.* 2 vols. New York: United Church Press, 1984.

Margaret Bendroth

See also **Calvinism; Congregationalism; Evangelicalism and Revivalism; Reformed Churches; Social Gospel.**

UNITED COLONIES OF NEW ENGLAND.
See **New England Confederation.**

UNITED CONFEDERATE VETERANS.

The United Confederate Veterans (UCV) was organized at New Orleans, Louisiana on 10 June 1889. Fifty-two delegates representing nine Confederate veterans' organizations elected General John B. Gordon of Georgia as their first commander in chief, a position that he held until his death in 1904. The military type of command was elaborated at Chattanooga, Tennessee in 1890, with authority over the Trans-Mississippi and East of Mississippi departments. In 1894 the latter was reorganized as the departments of the Army of Northern Virginia and the Army of Tennessee; the Division of the Northwest was added at a later date. The basic constitution and by-laws were adopted at Houston, Texas in 1895.

In January 1893 Sumner A. Cunningham began monthly publication at Nashville, Tennessee of the *Confederate Veteran*, which became the unofficial organ of the UCV and other Confederate societies until its demise in December 1932. By 1899 it enjoyed a circulation of more than twenty thousand, a modest number in view of the 1903 estimate of 246,000 living Confederate veterans—of whom 47,000 were active and 35,000 inactive members of 1,523 UCV camps.

United Farm Workers. César Chávez (*center*) and others march during the 1966 grape strike and boycott. MAGNUM PHOTOS, INC.

Matthiessen, Peter. *Sal Si Puedes: Cesar Chavez and the New American Revolution.* New York: Random House, 1969.

Benjamin H. Johnson

See also **California; Strikes.**

UNITED KINGDOM. *See* **Great Britain, Relations with.**

UNITED MINE WORKERS OF AMERICA (UMWA), a labor union founded in 1890 by bituminous coal miners from the United States and Canada who met to consolidate the union efforts of the Knights of Labor Trade Assembly No. 35 and the National Progressive Union of Miners and Mine Laborers. The UMWA was organized industrially (meaning that it represented miners as well as other workers who labored in and around the mines) and was one of the first interethnic and interracial affiliates of the American Federation of Labor (AFL). Throughout the 1890s, organizers worked to build the union and gain recognition, finally achieving these goals for the majority of its members after the victorious 1897 strike. In January 1898, operators and UMWA representatives met in a joint conference and signed the first agreement; it included union recognition, wage increases, the checkoff system (operators' guarantee that union dues would be deducted from wages), uniform standards for weighing coal (which determined wage rates), and the eight-hour day for coal mine workers in the Central Competitive Field (Pennsylvania, Illinois, Ohio, and Indiana).

The 1898 agreement was a tremendous achievement for miners and organized labor. It allowed the industry to overcome much of the economic chaos, price fluctuations, and imbalanced supply and demand of coal, which wreaked havoc on mineworkers and operators alike. In addition, the checkoff system ensured funding for continued organizing efforts, expansion of representation in the mines, and knowledgeable organizers who lent their expertise to union drives in other industries. But the UMWA's success was tempered by the union's limited reach. While it had members in regions beyond the Central Competitive Field—Kansas, Alabama, Iowa, West Virginia, and Wyoming, for example—operators in these states refused to engage in collective bargaining.

The UMWA's efforts to strengthen and build its organization continued through the first decades of the twentieth century. The success was a product of the organizational structure, rank-and-file militancy, and strategic leadership, starting with John Mitchell. Mitchell expanded organizing efforts into Maryland, Kansas, Missouri, Michigan, and Arkansas and consolidated the UMWA's control in Kentucky, Alabama, and Indiana. One of Mitchell's most controversial decisions concerned the fight for union recognition in Pennsylvania's anthracite field. Railroad companies controlled most of the mining interests in that state and refused to bargain collectively. In 1902, miners attempted to change this. Though

267

they failed in their effort for recognition, Mitchell claimed the strike a victory because the UMWA was able to win public support and governmental backing for the cause. The strike had worn on for months when President Theodore Roosevelt hosted a meeting between operators and union officials in hopes of settling the conflict. In the end, the miners won wage increases and publicity through the establishment of an investigating commission; in addition, a board was established to hear grievances. Many union members believed that Mitchell had acquiesced at a moment when the strike, and therefore recognition, could have been won. Mitchell's decision did reveal a more conservative trade unionism, something his critics condemned. Indeed, the tension between conservatives and radicals in the movement threatened to undermine the miners' union from the Progressive Era through the Great Depression.

Miners' militancy shaped the UMWA and union culture throughout the United States. At the onset of the Great Depression, United Mine Workers' members reinvigorated the campaign to change the craft structure of the AFL. At the forefront of this movement was John L. Lewis, leader of the miners' union since 1919. Lewis was ambitious, heavy-handed, sharp-witted, and controversial. His post–World War I strategy to maintain wages rather than jobs made him both hated and beloved, and his autocratic rule is blamed for a revolt within the union which was not overcome until the early 1930s. These experiences seem to have had a profound impact on Lewis. In 1935, he led an insurgency of industrial unionists in the AFL who formed the Committee for Industrial Organization (later the Congress of Industrial Organizations, CIO). Within three years, the UMWA, along with four million other organized workers and thirty-eight unions, affiliated with the CIO. The connection between the two organizations was tenuous, and in 1947, the miners broke with the CIO, affiliating again with the AFL-CIO in 1989.

During the first part of the century, the UMWA concerned itself with recognition, uniform wage scales, and building the organization. After World War II, its main concern became advocating coal as a viable energy source and winning health and safety reforms. Membership in the 1950s and 1960s began to decline because mechanization and the country's move to cleaner fuel meant fewer jobs. But miners were also disenchanted with a corrupt leadership. Tony Boyle, president from 1963 to 1972, was convicted of the murder of his rival, Joseph Yablonski and his family. As a part of the Miners for Democracy (MFD) movement, Yablonski had challenged Boyle's leadership and questioned his honesty. The MFD won control of the union in 1972 and began a legacy of reform in the last quarter of the twentieth century. By the end of the twentieth century, the UMWA was once again at the forefront of changes within the AFL-CIO.

As of 2002, the United Mine Workers of America was about half the size it had been at midcentury, but it continues its legacy of fighting for economic and social justice.

BIBLIOGRAPHY

Baratz, Morton S. *The Union and the Coal Industry.* New Haven, Conn.: Yale University Press, 1955.

Coleman, McAlister. *Men and Coal.* New York: Farrar and Rinehart, 1969.

Fox, Maier B. *United We Stand: The United Mine Workers of America, 1890–1990.* Washington, D.C.: United Mine Workers of America, 1990.

Long, Priscilla. *Where the Sun Never Shines: A History of America's Bloody Coal Industry.* New York: Paragon, 1989.

Caroline Waldron Merithew

See also **American Federation of Labor–Congress of Industrial Organizations.**

UNITED NATIONS. The United States was a key force behind the establishment of the United Nations (UN) at the end of World War II. The term, the "United Nations," was first used on 1 January 1942 in an agreement that pledged that none of the Allied governments would make a separate peace with the Axis Powers. The actual Charter of the United Nations that was finalized in 1945 was very much a U.S. document, in contrast to the Covenant of the LEAGUE OF NATIONS that had been based primarily on both U.S. and British drafts. The UN Charter flowed from discussions at Dumbarton Oaks (outside Washington, D.C.) in 1944 between the United States, Britain, the Soviet Union, and later China. Fifty governments signed the Charter in June 1945. UN membership exceeded 120 by the early 1970s, was over 150 by 1980, and reached 185 nation-states by the 1990s. Despite the central role of the United States in the establishment of the UN, and in many of its subsequent operations, Washington's relationship with the organization has not been without friction over the years.

The Origins and Establishment of the United Nations

There is considerable debate about the United States' motives for the establishment of the UN. From the point of view of some commentators, the administration of President Franklin Delano Roosevelt (1933–1945) viewed the UN as a potential pillar of a wider effort to construct an international order in which U.S. manufacturers and investors would be able to continue to benefit economically following the end of World War II. Other observers emphasize the role of liberal (or Wilsonian) idealism in the foundation of the UN and its importance as an effort to move beyond the Great Power rivalry of the pre-1945 era. Related to this perception is the view that Roosevelt envisioned the UN as a vehicle by which the Soviet Union could be brought into a more cooperative and less confrontational international order. From this perspective, the UN was a way of maintaining and broadening the alliance after 1945 between the victorious powers in World War II.

At the same time, even if the establishment of the UN represented an immediate response to World War II, it built on rather than displaced the ideas about, and the practices of, international relations that had emerged prior to the 1940s. For example, the UN was clearly a successor organization to the League of Nations. But, given the discredited reputation of the League, the UN could not be established directly on its foundations. Many observers regard the UN as an improvement on the overall structure of the League of Nations. From the perspective of the United States and its wartime allies, one of the most significant improvements was to be the way in which the UN was even more explicitly grounded in the principle of the concert (or concerted action) of the Great Powers. The notion that the Great Powers had unique rights and obligations in international relations was already a major element behind the establishment of the League of Nations, particularly its main decision-making body, the Council. In the UN, however, the major allied powers were given permanent seats on the Security Council, which came with the right of veto on any UN security initiative. The main framers of the UN also sought to enlarge the organization's role in social and economic affairs (in contrast to the League). This flowed from the knowledge that a broad international effort would be required to deal with a range of problems related to reconstruction following the end of World War II. There was also a sense that mechanisms for countering the kind of wholesale violation of human rights that had characterized the Nazi regime needed to be set up. Furthermore, in light of both the Great Depression and World War II there was a growing concern that economic inequality and poverty facilitated crisis and war.

The Operation and Growth of the United Nations

The Security Council, as already suggested, is the most important body of the UN. It is in permanent session and is responsible for the maintenance of international peace and security. It has the power to call on the armed forces of member governments to provide peacekeeping forces and to intervene in conflicts and disputes around the world. The Security Council was established with five permanent members and ten rotating members. The permanent members are the major allied powers that won World War II: the United States, the Soviet Union (now Russia), Great Britain, France, and China (Taiwan held the Chinese seat until 1971). The five permanent members all have an absolute veto on any resolution of the Security Council. After 1945 international power politics, as played out at the UN, were directly linked to the (sometimes dubious) proposition that these five states were the most politically and militarily significant in world affairs. The veto also meant that although these five powers were prevented, in theory, from using force in a fashion that went against the UN Charter, their veto in the Security Council protected them from sanction or censure if they

UN Security Council. Delegates meet on the Bronx, N.Y., campus of Hunter College in 1946, before moving to interim quarters on Long Island while awaiting completion of the UN complex in Manhattan, in 1952. © CORBIS

did engage in unilateral action. The Security Council thus represented a major arena for COLD WAR politics at the same time as the Cold War, which pitted its members against each other, ensured that the ability of the Security Council to act was often profoundly constrained.

While the Security Council's focus was on issues of peace and war, the General Assembly was given particular responsibility for social and economic issues. Over the years, as this brief has grown, a range of specialized, often semiautonomous, agencies have emerged. For example, the INTERNATIONAL LABOR ORGANIZATION, which had been set up by the League of Nations, was revitalized. The UN also established the World Health Organization, the United Nations Educational, Scientific, and Cultural Organization, and the Food and Agriculture Organization, not to mention the United Nations Conference on Trade and Development and the United Nations Development Programme. By the 1990s there were nineteen separate UN agencies. Some of the most significant UN organizations that emerged after 1945 now operate almost entirely independently. This is particularly true of the INTERNATIONAL MONETARY FUND (IMF) and the International Bank for Reconstruction and Development (the World Bank).

The Cold War, Decolonization, and the United Nations in the 1940s, 1950s and 1960s

The UN, as already emphasized, was profoundly shaped by the emerging Cold War. In this context the United States increasingly perceived it as an important element in its policy toward Moscow. For example, a U.S. Department of State memorandum in April 1946 observed, "[t]he Charter of the United Nations affords the best and most unassailable means through which the U.S. can implement its opposition to Soviet physical expansion." Meanwhile, Moscow's early resistance to Washington's preferred candidates for the presidency of the General Assembly and the post of the UN's first Secretary-General ensured that the UN would be an important forum for the wider Cold War. The UN was also directly involved in and shaped by the rising nationalist sentiment against colonialism and the move toward decolonization, as well as the question of racial discrimination that was directly or indirectly connected to the colonial question. For example, the UN passed a resolution on 29 November 1947 that called for the end of the British mandate in Palestine and the creation of a Jewish state and an Arab state, with Jerusalem being put under international administration. The Arab delegates at the UN were unhappy with these proposed arrangements and responded by walking out of the General Assembly. On 14 May 1948 the state of Israel was officially proclaimed, followed by the start of open warfare between the new state of Israel and neighboring Arab states. A cease-fire was eventually agreed to under the mediation of Ralph Bunche (a U.S. citizen and senior UN official), who subsequently received the Nobel Peace Prize. Israel was formally admitted to the UN in May 1949. The conflict between the Dutch colonial government in the Netherlands East Indies and the de facto government of the Republic of Indonesia was also brought before the UN in the late 1940s. The United States exerted its influence inside and outside the UN, and in March 1949 the Dutch government agreed to move quickly to decolonize and recognize Indonesian independence. The Cold War backdrop was important in this trend. The United States was concerned that Moscow's support for national liberation movements, such as that in Indonesia, might enhance the influence of the Soviet Union, and it realized at the same time that U.S. support for decolonization would advance U.S. influence.

The KOREAN WAR (1950–1953) was a turning point for the UN, and for U.S. Cold War policy. In September 1947 the United States placed the Korean question before the General Assembly. This was done in an effort to wind back the United States' commitment to the Korean peninsula. Subsequently the General Assembly formally called for the unification of what was at that point a Korea divided between a northern government allied to the Soviet Union (and later the Peoples' Republic of China, or PRC) and a southern government allied to the United States. Following the outbreak of war between the north and the south on 25 June 1950, the Security Council quickly began organizing a UN military force, under U.S. leadership, to intervene in Korea. This was made possible by the fact that Moscow had been boycotting the Security Council since the start of 1950. The Soviet Union was protesting the fact that China's permanent seat on the Security Council continued to be held by the Kuomintang (KMT) government that had been confined to Taiwan since the Chinese Communist Party's triumph on the mainland at the end of 1949. In Korea it quickly became clear that the United States (and its UN allies) were en-

tering a major war. The resolutions of the General Assembly on Korean unification were soon being used to justify a full-scale military effort against the North Korean regime. The initial aim of U.S.-UN intervention to achieve the limited goal of ending northern aggression was quickly transformed into a wider set of aims, centered on the reunification of the peninsula under a pro-U.S.–UN government. The ensuing conflict eventually brought the PRC directly into the war.

It was initially thought that U.S.-UN intervention in Korea indicated that the UN had overcome the paralysis that had afflicted the League of Nations in any conflict where the rival interests of Great Powers were involved. But, once the Soviet Union resumed its seat on the Security Council in August 1950, Moscow challenged the validity of the resolutions of the Security Council that underpinned UN operations in Korea. Meanwhile, the Soviet Union was also highly critical of Secretary-General Trygve Lie's keen prosecution of UN actions in Korea. Moscow opposed his reelection in 1951, but the United States managed to ensure that he remained in the post until the end of 1952. At the same time, Moscow's delegation at the UN avoided having anything to do with the Secretary-General, dramatically weakening his position. In the wake of the signing of an armistice agreement in Korea on 27 July 1953, U.S. influence at the UN went into relative decline. Another result of the Korean War was two decades of Sino-U.S. hostility. Until 1971 Washington successfully prevented all attempts at the UN to have the PRC replace the KMT in China's permanent seat in the Security Council.

The decline of U.S. influence in the 1950s was primarily a result of the way in which the process of decolonization increasingly altered the balance of power in the General Assembly. A key event in the history of decolonization and the growth of the UN was the SUEZ CRISIS that followed the seizure of the Suez Canal on 26 July 1956 by the Egyptian government of Gamal Abdel Nasser (1954–1970). The canal was of considerable commercial and strategic importance to Great Britain and France. Despite the objections of the Security Council, London and Paris, with the support of the Israeli government, attacked Egypt. The UN responded, with U.S. and Soviet support, by setting up and dispatching a 6,000-strong United Nations Emergency Force (UNEF) to manage a cease-fire and the withdrawal of Anglo-French troops from the Canal Zone. The UNEF, which continued to operate as a buffer between Egypt and Israel from 1956 to 1967, was important for the history of future peacekeeping efforts. It flowed from a resolution of the General Assembly and clearly set the precedent (not always followed) that UN peacekeeping forces should work to prevent conflict between opposing sides rather than engage in the conflict.

The growing significance of decolonization for the UN became clear when, following Congo's independence from Belgium in 1960, a UN force (Opération des Nations Unies au Congo, or ONUC) was asked to intervene. The UN operation in the Congo, from July 1960 to June 1964, was the biggest UN action since the war in Korea in the early 1950s. The Congo crisis started with a mutiny in the former Belgian colonial military establishment (Force Publique) that had become the Armée Nationale Congolaise following independence. When troops attacked and killed a number of European officers, the Belgian administrators, and other Europeans who had remained behind after independence, fled the country, opening the way for Congolese to replace the European military and administrative elite. Shortly after this, Moise Tshombe led a successful secessionist effort to take the wealthy Katanga province out of the new nation. At the end of 1960 President Kasa Vubu dismissed the new prime minister, Patrice Lumumba, and a week later Colonel Joseph Mobutu seized power, holding it until February 1961, by which time Lumumba had been killed. Meanwhile, Belgian troops intervened to protect Belgian nationals as civil war spread in the former Belgian colony. The assassination of Lumumba precipitated a Security Council resolution on 21 February 1961 that conferred on ONUC the ability to use force to stop the descent into civil war. Prior to this point ONUC had only been allowed to use force in self-defense. During operations in the Congo, Secretary-General Dag Hammarskjöld was killed in a plane crash and was awarded the Nobel Peace Prize posthumously. Even with upwards of 20,000 UN-sponsored troops in the Congo, however, a cease-fire was not agreed to and Katanga was not brought back into the Congo until 1963. All ONUC troops were withdrawn by the end of June 1964, in part because the UN itself was on the brink of bankruptcy (a result of the French and Soviet government's refusal to contribute to the costs of ONUC). It was not until the UN operation in Somalia in 1992, almost thirty years later, that the UN again intervened militarily on the scale of its operation in the Congo in the early 1960s.

The UN and the Third World in the 1970s and 1980s

By the 1970s the emergence of a growing number of new nation-states in Africa and Asia over the preceding decades had clearly altered the balance in the UN in favor of the so-called "Third World." This shift was readily apparent when the Sixth Special Session of the General Assembly of the United Nations in April 1974 passed the Declaration and Programme of Action for the Establishment of a New Economic Order. This represented a formal call for a New International Economic Order in an effort to improve the terms on which the countries of the Third World participated in the global economy. In the late 1970s the UN also established the Independent Commission on International Development (the Brandt Commission), presided over by former West German Chancellor Willy Brandt. However, by the start of the 1980s, calls at the UN and elsewhere to address the North-South question were increasingly rebuffed, particularly with the

Debt Crisis and the subsequent spread of neoliberal economic policies and practices. With the support of Margaret Thatcher's government in Britain (1979–1990) and the administration of Ronald Reagan (1981–1989) in the United States, the IMF and the World Bank increasingly encouraged the governments of the Third World to liberalize trade, privatize their public sectors, and deregulate their economies. This trend was strengthened by the end of the Cold War, by which time virtually all branches of the UN had become sites for the promotion of economic liberalism and what has come to be known as globalization.

The United Nations after the Cold War

The Cold War had undermined the expectation, prevalent in the late 1940s and early 1950s, that the UN would provide the overall framework for international security after 1945. With the end of the Cold War, however, the UN was presented with an opportunity to revive the major peacekeeping and security activities that many of its early proponents had anticipated. For example, while the UN dispatched a total of 10,000 peacekeepers to five operations (with an annual budget of about $233 million) in 1987, the total number of troops acting as peacekeepers under UN auspices by 1995 was 72,000. They were operating in eighteen different countries and the total cost of these operations was over $3 billion. Early post–Cold War initiatives were thought to augur well for the UN's new role. The major civil war in El Salvador, which had been fueled by the Cold War, came to a negotiated end in 1992 under the auspices of the UN. Apart from El Salvador, the countries in which the UN has provided peacekeepers and election monitors include Angola, Bosnia-Herzegovina, Cambodia, Croatia, East Timor, Macedonia, Mozambique, Rwanda, Somalia, and the Western Sahara. While Cambodia and East Timor, for example, are seen as UN success stories, the failure of the UN in Angola and Somalia highlights the constraints on the UN's role in the post–Cold War era.

The UN's new post–Cold War initiative in relation to peacekeeping was linked to the appointment of Boutros Boutros-Ghali as Secretary-General at the beginning of 1992. Shortly after taking up the new post, Boutros-Ghali presented the Security Council with his "Agenda for Peace." This document laid out a range of major reforms to facilitate a greatly expanded peacekeeping role. Boutros-Ghali wanted member states to provide permanently designated military units that could be deployed quickly and overcome the UN's well-known inability to act quickly in a time of crisis. A number of states expressed an interest in such an arrangement at the same time as changes were made at UN headquarters in New York. The UN military advisory staff was expanded with a focus on intelligence activities and long-range planning, and efforts were made to enhance communications between officers on the ground and UN headquarters. There was even some talk of forming a multinational military establishment, made up of volunteers that would be under the direct control of the UN. These initiatives made little progress, however, in the context of an organization comprised of nation-states that were very wary of providing soldiers and equipment in ways that might diminish their sovereignty. Furthermore, there was little or no possibility of a more effective and united intervention by the UN in situations where the national interests of the major powers were thought to be at stake. At the same time, the fact that a number of countries, including the United States and Russia, fell behind in their payment of dues to the UN suggested the prospects for a more activist and revamped UN were still limited. As a result of concerted U.S. opposition, Boutros-Ghali was not reappointed as Secretary-General for a second term, further dampening the momentum toward a more assertive UN. His replacement, Kofi Annan, who was awarded the Nobel Peace Prize in 2001, has emerged as a much more cautious and conciliatory Secretary-General.

BIBLIOGRAPHY

Armstrong, David. *The Rise of the International Organisation: A Short History.* London: Macmillan, 1982.

Hilderbrand, Robert C. *Dumbarton Oaks: The Origins of the United Nations and the Search for Postwar Security.* Chapel Hill: University of North Carolina Press, 1990.

Meisler, Stanley. *United Nations: The First Fifty Years.* New York: Atlantic Monthly Press, 1995.

Wesley, Michael. *Casualties of the New World Order: The Causes of Failure of UN Missions to Civil Wars.* Basingstoke, U.K.: Macmillan, 1997.

Mark T. Berger

See also **Dumbarton Oaks Conference; United Nations Conference; United Nations Declaration.**

UNITED NATIONS CONFERENCE on International Organization was held in San Francisco from 25 April to 26 June 1945. Fifty nations attended, forty-six of them signatories of the United Nations Declaration of 1 January 1942, to finalize the proposals for an international organization designed at the Dumbarton Oaks Conference held from August to October 1944 and the Yalta Conference of February 1945. The United States delegation included the Democratic senator Tom Connally from Texas and Republican senator Arthur Vandenberg from Michigan, ranking members of the Senate Foreign Relations Committee; the Democratic representative Sol Bloom of New York and Republican Charles Eaton of New Jersey; Harold Stassen, former Republican governor of Minnesota and then a naval officer; and Virginia Gildersleeve, dean of Barnard College.

The conference drafted an eloquent preamble to the UN charter. It established an International Court of Justice based upon a statute drafted by a committee of jurists who had met in Washington, D.C., from 9 to 20 April 1945. The conference designed a form of trusteeship for nations considered "dependent," although leaving the exact lands to be placed under trusteeship to later

decisions. The new Trusteeship Council could receive reports on economic, social, and educational conditions, but could only make inspection visits if the trustee nation approved. The new UN General Assembly was given authority to make recommendations on any subject to the new Security Council. On 2 June, the Soviet diplomat Andrei A. Gromyko almost broke up the conference by insisting that the Security Council not even be able to discuss a dispute unless each of the five permanent members voted to place it on the council's agenda. On 6 June, however, Stalin concurred with the American objection, remarking it was "an insignificant matter." Yet to meet Soviet concerns, the conference drafted Article 27, which in most imprecise language gave permanent members of the Security Council the right to prevent a substantive issue, as opposed to "procedural matters," to come before it. In the conference's technical committee, Australia, Belgium, the Netherlands, and the Latin American nations all sought to end the permanent members' veto on issues of peaceful settlement, but even the United States would not budge.

Thanks to the United States, the conference adopted Article 51, which declared that "nothing in the present Charter shall impair the inherent right of individual or collective self-defense if an armed attack occurs against a Member of the United Nations, until the Security Council has taken the measures necessary to maintain international peace and security." This article severely modified the Dumbarton Oaks draft, which had forbidden members to enforce the peace "under regional arrangements or by regional agencies without the authorization of the Security Council." It thereby gave legitimacy to the Act of Chapultepec of 4 April 1945, a regional security agreement binding for the duration of the war. The United States was able to block the seating of the Polish government, already a Soviet satellite, whereas the Soviets were unable to block the seating of Argentina, which had only declared war against the Axis on 27 March 1945. (Poland was later admitted.) The delegates finished the charter by 18 June and unanimously approved it on 26 June 1945.

BIBLIOGRAPHY

Benedicks, William. "The San Francisco Conference on International Organization, April–June 1945." Ph.D. diss., Florida State University, 1989.

Campbell, Thomas M. *Masquerade Peace: America's UN Policy, 1944–1945.* Tallahassee: Florida State University Press, 1973.

Campbell, Thomas M., and George C. Herring. *The Diaries of Edward R. Stettinius, Jr., 1943–1946.* New York: New Viewpoints, 1975.

Russell, Ruth. *A History of the United Nations Charter: The Role of the United States, 1940–1945.* Washington, D.C.: Brookings Institution, 1958.

Justus D. Doenecke

See also **Dumbarton Oaks Conference; International Court of Justice; United Nations; United Nations Declaration.**

UNITED NATIONS DECLARATION. Soon after Japan's attack on Pearl Harbor (7 December 1941), British Prime Minister Winston Churchill hastened to Washington, D.C., and with President Franklin D. Roosevelt announced a "Declaration by United Nations," open to all nations, the signatories to which constituted a military alliance against "Hitlerism." In the declaration, the signatories affirmed the principles of the Atlantic Charter (1941) and pledged to employ their full economic and military resources against the Axis powers. They also vowed not to make separate armistice or peace agreements with enemy. The Declaration marks the first official use of the term "United Nations." It was signed 1 January 1942, by the United States (making its first military alliance since the alliance with France in 1778), the United Kingdom, and twenty-four other nations.

BIBLIOGRAPHY

Dallek, Robert. *Franklin D. Roosevelt and American Foreign Policy, 1932–1945.* New York: Oxford University Press, 1979.

Charles S. Campbell

UNITED PRESS INTERNATIONAL. *See* **Press Associations.**

UNITED STATES V. BUTLER, 297 U.S. 1 (1936), also known as the Hoosac Mills case, eviscerated the Agricultural Adjustment Act of 1933 (AAA), dealing a blow to New Deal agricultural policy. AAA provided payments to farmers who agreed to reduce production acreage; these benefits were paid from the proceeds of a tax on commodities processors. In a 6 to 3 decision, the Supreme Court found that while the tax itself was justified under the "general welfare" clause of the Constitution, its intended use was "coercive" and thus unconstitutional. AAA violated the Tenth Amendment by attempting to use the taxing power to regulate agricultural production—a matter that the Court determined was the sole jurisdiction of the states.

BIBLIOGRAPHY

Brinkley, Alan. *The End of Reform: New Deal Liberalism in Recession and War.* New York: Knopf, 1995.

Harvey Pinney
R. Volney Riser

See also **New Deal.**

UNITED STATES V. CRUIKSHANK, 92 U.S. 542 (1876). The Enforcement Acts of 1870 forbade interference with a citizen's constitutional rights on the basis of race and were designed to protect African American voters from Ku Klux Klan violence. However, in 1876 the U.S. Supreme Court overruled the conviction of a num-

UNITED NATIONS DECLARATION

The Governments signatory hereto,

Having subscribed to a common program of purposes and principles embodied in the Joint Declaration of the President of the United States of America and the Prime Minister of the United Kingdom of Great Britain and Northern Ireland dated August 14, 1941, known as the Atlantic Charter.

Being convinced that complete victory over their enemies is essential to defend life, liberty, independence and religious freedom, and to preserve human rights and justice in their own lands as well as in other lands, and that they are now engaged in a common struggle against savage and brutal forces seeking to subjugate the world *Declare*:

1. Each government pledges itself to employ its full resources, military or economic, against those members of the Tripartite Pact and its adherents with which such government is at war.

2. Each Government pledges itself to co-operate with the Governments signatory hereto and not to make a separate armistice or peace with the enemies.

The foregoing declaration may be adhered to by other nations as which are, or which may be, rendering material assistance and contributions in the struggle for victory over Hitlerism.

ber of whites who had rioted to prevent AFRICAN AMERICANS from voting. The Court ruled that the Constitution did not grant the rights of assembling peaceably and bearing arms; it merely prohibited Congress from infringing upon those rights. The Fourteenth Amendment's due process and equal protection clauses guaranteed citizens protection against encroachment by the states, but not against encroachment by other citizens, the Court ruled.

BIBLIOGRAPHY

Gillette, William. *The Right to Vote: Politics and the Passage of the Fifteenth Amendment.* Baltimore: Johns Hopkins University Press, 1965.

Rogers, Donald W., and Christine Scriabine, eds. *Voting and the Spirit of American Democracy.* Urbana: University of Illinois Press, 1992.

Ransom E. Noble Jr. / A. R.

See also **Civil Rights and Liberties; Disfranchisement; Equal Protection of the Law; Force Acts; Jim Crow Laws; Mississippi Plan; Reconstruction; Supreme Court.**

UNITED STATES V. E. C. KNIGHT COMPANY,
156 U.S. 1 (1895), the case in which the U.S. Supreme
Court first applied the Sherman Antitrust Act (1890) and
severely limited its reach. Through mergers, American
Sugar Refining had acquired 98 percent of the national
sugar market, and it was fixing sugar prices. The U.S.
government sought an injunction. The Court held business acquisitions, refining, and manufacturing did not
amount to interstate commerce, and so were not in violation of the act, protecting manufacturing trusts and monopolies from regulation. The distinction between manufacture and commerce, and this immunity from federal
regulation, was overturned in NATIONAL LABOR RELA-
TIONS BOARD V. JONES AND LAUGHLIN STEEL CORPORATION
(1937).

BIBLIOGRAPHY

Taft, William H. *The Anti-Trust Act and The Supreme Court.*
    1914. Reprint, Littleton, Colo: Rothman, 1993.

Steve Sheppard

UNITED STATES V. HARRIS, 106 U.S. 629 (1883),
a case in which the U.S. Supreme Court held unconstitutional the 1871 Ku Klux Klan Act provision that
penalized all conspiracies to deprive any person equal
protection of the laws. The act was broader than the
Fourteenth Amendment warranted, explained Justice William B. Woods, and neither the Fourteenth Amendment
nor the Fifteenth Amendment authorized Congress to
legislate directly upon the acts of private persons, irrespective of state civil rights efforts.

BIBLIOGRAPHY

Avins, Alfred. "The Ku Klux Act of 1871." *St. Louis University
    Law Journal* 11 (1967): 331–374.
Hyman, Harold M. *A More Perfect Union: The Impact of the Civil
    War and Reconstruction on the Constitution.* New York: Knopf,
    1973.

Ransom E. Noble Jr./A. R.

See also **African Americans; Civil Rights and Liberties; Equal
    Protection of the Law; Force Acts; Ku Klux Klan;
    Reconstruction.**

UNITED STATES V. LEE, 106 U.S. 196 (1882). In
1857, upon the death of George Washington Parke Custis, his Arlington House estate passed to his daughter,
Mary Lee, wife of Robert E. Lee, for the term of her
lifetime. The property was then to pass to Custis's eldest
grandson, Mary's son George Washington Custis Lee.

During the CIVIL WAR the estate was seized by agents
of the U.S. government for delinquent taxes, offered for
sale, and, despite bids from friends of the Lee family, purchased by an army officer, who converted it into a national
cemetery and military post. After Mrs. Lee's death, her

son brought a court action to eject the superintendent of
Arlington Cemetery on the grounds that he was trespassing. The United States pleaded the immunity of a sovereign, but in the 1882 case, the SUPREME COURT held
that the doctrine of immunity did not extend to the misuse of authority by agents of the government. Eventually
the matter was settled when the government paid for
ownership of the property.

BIBLIOGRAPHY

Beth, Loren P. *The Development of the American Constitution,
    1877–1917.* New York: Harper and Row, 1971.

Leonard C. Helderman/A. R.

See also **Arlington National Cemetery; Cemeteries, National;
    Government Ownership; Public Domain; Sovereignty,
    Doctrine of.**

UNITED STATES V. LOPEZ, 514 U.S. 549 (1995),
curtailed congressional regulatory authority under the
COMMERCE CLAUSE (U.S. Constitution, Article 1, section
8) and called into question the post-1937 understanding
of judicial review and the separation of powers. From
1880 through 1937, the Supreme Court had often restrained congressional commerce power, relying on an
artificial distinction between "manufacturing" and "commerce," as well as a supposed state sovereignty acknowledged by the Tenth Amendment. After 1937, however, the
Court seemingly authorized unrestricted congressional
power to regulate economic matters under its commerce
power.

Chief Justice William H. Rehnquist's opinion for a
5-4 majority in *Lopez* therefore came as a surprise, holding
unconstitutional the federal Gun-Free School Zones Act
on the grounds that school violence did not "substantially
affect" interstate commerce. The majority relied on a distinction between "commercial" and "noncommercial" activity to delineate federal power. Justice Clarence
Thomas, concurring, tried to disinter the manufacturing-
commerce distinction. The dissenting justices would have
upheld the statute, finding an adequate connection between interstate commerce and the effects of school
violence.

United States v. Morrison (2000) confirmed the assumption that *Lopez* signaled a significant departure from
previous commerce clause precedent. In striking down
the federal Violence Against Women Act, Chief Justice
Rehnquist for the same 5-4 majority extended the doctrine of *Lopez* to distinguish "truly national" from "truly
local" activities. He ignored a former criterion that relied
on the aggregate effects of the regulated activity and
thereby seemed to be returning to a pre-1937 understanding of the commerce clause.

BIBLIOGRAPHY

Lessig, Lawrence. "Translating Federalism: *United States v. Lo-
    pez.*" *Supreme Court Review* 5 (1996): 125–215.

Tribe, Laurence H. *American Constitutional Law*. 3d ed. Mineola, N.Y.: Foundation Press, 2000.

William M. Wiecek

UNITED STATES V. REESE, 92 U.S. 214 (1876), was the first significant voting rights case decided by the U.S. Supreme Court under the Fifteenth Amendment. The Court struck down the Enforcement Act of 1870 because one of its sections permitted federal prosecution for refusal to accept votes without limiting the offense to denials based on race or prior condition of slavery. "The Fifteenth Amendment does not confer the right of suffrage upon any one," Chief Justice Morrison R. Waite stated. *Reese* enabled the southern states to deny the vote to blacks on seemingly nonracial grounds, such as literacy, and thus was the foundation for later black disfranchisement.

BIBLIOGRAPHY

Gillette, William. *Retreat from Reconstruction, 1869–1879*. Baton Rouge: Louisiana State University Press, 1979.

Stephenson, D. Grier. "The Supreme Court, the Franchise, and the Fifteenth Amendment: The First Sixty Years." *University of Missouri Kansas City Law Review* 57 (1988): 47–65.

William M. Wiecek

See also **Force Acts; Voter Registration.**

UNITED STATES V. SIOUX NATION, 448 U.S. 371 (1980). The Lakota, or Sioux, controlled the northern Plains throughout most of the nineteenth century. Allied Lakota bands negotiated a series of treaties with the U.S. government at Fort Laramie, Wyoming, in 1851 and 1868 and were granted the Great Sioux Reservation by the 1868 Fort Laramie Treaty. Encompassing all of South Dakota west of the Missouri River and additional territory in adjoining states, the Great Sioux Reservation, including the sacred Black Hills, was to be "set apart for the absolute and undisturbed use and occupation" of the Lakota. Following the discovery of gold in the Black Hills in the early 1870s, white prospectors and U.S. Army troops invaded the reservation, and the Lakota responded militarily, defeating the U.S. Seventh Cavalry at the Little Big Horn in 1876. Outraged, Congress passed legislation that opened the Black Hills to white occupation and abrogated the articles of the Fort Laramie Treaty.

Throughout the twentieth century, Lakota leaders demanded redress for the illegal seizure of Lakota treaty lands. Filing a series of cases against the U.S. government, including a failed Court of Claims attempt in 1942, Lakota leaders finally received a full hearing through the Indian Claims Commission, created in 1946 by Congress to adjudicate outstanding Indian land disputes. In 1975 the ICC ruled that Congress's 1877 law was unconstitutional and amounted to an illegal seizure, or "taking," of Lakota lands. The Lakota, the commission ruled, were entitled

to the 1877 estimated value of the seized lands, roughly 17.1 million dollars, plus interest. The U.S. government appealed, and in *United States v. Sioux Nation*, the Supreme Court upheld the ICC ruling. This landmark ruling established the legal basis for the compensation for illegally seized Indian lands. Maintaining that the Black Hills are sacred sites and that no monetary amount could compensate their communities, Lakota leaders refused the settlement and demanded return of the Black Hills, most of which remained under the control of the federal government in 2002.

BIBLIOGRAPHY

Lazarus, Edward. *Black Hills, White Justice: The Sioux Nation Versus the United States: 1775 to the Present*. New York: Harper Collins, 1991.

Ned Blackhawk

See also **Black Hills; Black Hills War; Indian Claims Commission; Laramie, Fort, Treaty of (1851); Laramie, Fort, Treaty of (1868); Sioux; Sioux Wars.**

UNITED STATES V. TRANS-MISSOURI FREIGHT ASSOCIATION, 166 U.S. 290 (1897), involved the attempt of eighteen western railroads to fix freight rates by mutual agreement. The government brought suit to dissolve the association under the SHERMAN ANTITRUST ACT. By a 5 to 4 decision the SUPREME COURT held that the Sherman Act did apply to railroads and that it prohibited all contracts in restraint of interstate or foreign commerce, not merely those in which the restraint was unreasonable. Justice Edward Douglass White's dissenting opinion, that "reasonable" contracts do not contravene the act, became substantially the majority view fourteen years later in the Standard Oil and American Tobacco cases.

BIBLIOGRAPHY

Kolko, Gabriel. *Railroads and Regulation, 1877–1916*. Princeton, N.J.: Princeton University Press, 1965.

Letwin, William. *Law and Economic Policy in America: The Evolution of the Sherman Antitrust Act*. New York: Random House, 1965.

Ransom E. Noble Jr./A. R.

See also **Addyston Pipe Company Case; Antitrust Laws; Commerce Clause; Monopoly; Pools, Railroad; Standard Oil Company; *United States v. E. C. Knight Company*.**

UNITED STATES V. VIRGINIA et al., 518 U.S. 515 (1996) redefined the standard for how state or federal governments determine constitutional and unconstitutional sex discrimination under the Fourteenth Amendment. Previous to this case, the Supreme Court of the United States used an "intermediate" standard of scrutiny to determine that all discrimination based on sex by state and federal government violates the Fourteenth Amendment's Equal Protection Clause, unless the government wishing to discriminate can show "important governmental objectives" for the discrimination, and that the discrimination is "substantially related" to achieving those objectives. The Supreme Court had already set a stricter standard for determining constitutional and unconstitutional discrimination based on race or national origin in 1976. The Court, however, had refused to institute the same strict standard for discrimination based on sex.

This case potentially raised the intermediate standard for sex discrimination closer to the strict standard for race and nationality discrimination by stating that, if the government of Virginia wished to discriminate based on sex, it must show an "exceedingly persuasive justification" rather than a "substantially related" justification. The Supreme Court found that the Virginia Military Institute, a state-funded, all male, military style, collegiate institution, could no longer deny women admission. The Court found that Virginia violated the Fourteenth Amendment under the Court's newly articulated sex discrimination standard, because Virginia's governmental objectives of single-sex educational benefits and diversity of education were not "exceedingly persuasive justification" for excluding women. They also found that the creation of a military-influenced program at a private women's college was an insufficient remedy.

The seven to one majority opinion by Justice Ruth Bader Ginsburg was written narrowly, and did not explicitly adopt the strict scrutiny standard for sex discrimination cases. At the beginning of the twenty-first century, it was uncertain whether the Court would use the newly articulated higher standard for determining unconstitutional and constitutional sex discrimination in other cases.

BIBLIOGRAPHY

Ayres, Ian. *Pervasive Prejudice? Unconventional Evidence of Race and Gender Discrimination.* Chicago: University of Chicago Press, 2001.

Baer, Judith A. *Women in American Law.* New York: Holmes and Meier, 1991.

Falk, Gerhard. *Sex, Gender, and Social Change: The Great Revolution.* Lanham, Md.: University Press of America, 1998.

Sunstein, Cass R. *One Case at a Time: Judicial Minimalism on the Supreme Court.* Cambridge, Mass.: Harvard University Press, 1999.

Akiba J. Covitz
Esa Lianne Sferra
Meredith L. Stewart

See also **Discrimination: Sex; Equal Protection under the Law.**

UNITED STATES V. WONG KIM ARK,

169 U.S. 649 (1898), was an important interpretation of the clause in the Fourteenth Amendment to the Constitution declaring that "all persons born or naturalized in the United States and subject to the jurisdiction thereof, are citizens of the United States and of the State wherein they reside." Wong Kim Ark was an American-born Chinese laborer whose parents were ineligible for citizenship under the naturalization laws. On his return to the United States after a visit to China, an attempt was made to debar him from entry under the CHINESE EXCLUSION ACT. Claiming that his birth in San Francisco, California, conferred citizenship, Wong Kim Ark secured a writ of habeas corpus. His case eventually reached the SUPREME COURT, which upheld his contention, with two justices dissenting. The principle laid down in this decision also served to protect Asians born in the United States against discriminatory state legislation.

BIBLIOGRAPHY

Schuck, Peter H., and Rogers M. Smith. *Citizenship Without Consent: Illegal Aliens in the American Polity.* New Haven, Conn.: Yale University Press, 1985.

Shklar, Judith N. *American Citizenship: The Quest for Inclusion.* Cambridge, Mass.: Harvard University Press, 1991.

W. A. Robinson / A. R.

See also **Chinese Americans; Citizenship; Constitution of the United States; Naturalization.**

UNITED STATES – CANADA FREE TRADE AGREEMENT

(1988). President Ronald Reagan and Prime Minister Brian Mulroney signed the United States-Canada Free Trade Agreement (FTA) on 2 January 1988. The agreement went into effect on 1 January 1989, after implementing legislation was passed in each country. The FTA was an attempt to expand the markets of each country by reducing the barriers to trade in goods, services, and investment. The main goal of the agreement was to eliminate all tariffs on trade between the United States and Canada by January 1998. In addition it provided a code of principles on service trade and improved access to government procurement. The agreement addressed foreign investments, telecommunications, tourism, financial services, bilateral energy trade, and provided procedures for dispute settlement. It was viewed by many as a North American response to the increase in competition due to free trade in Europe, as a result of the European Economic Community, and in the Asian Pacific Rim countries. The agreement was suspended on 1 January 1994 when the NORTH AMERICAN FREE TRADE AGREEMENT (NAFTA) went into effect. In addition to including Mexico, NAFTA also mandated free trade in areas that had only been principles of agreement in FTA. Until the passage of NAFTA, the FTA was the most comprehensive bilateral free trade agreement.

BIBLIOGRAPHY

Ritchie, Gordon. *Wrestling with the Elephant: The Inside Story of the Canada-US Trade Wars* Toronto: Macfarlane Walter and Ross, 1997.

Schott, Jeffery. *United States-Canada Free Trade: An Evaluation of the Agreement*. Washington, D.C.: Institute for International Economics, 1988.

Steger, Debra. *A Concise Guide to the Canada-United States Free Trade Agreement*. Toronto: Carswell, 1988.

Shira M. Diner

See also **Free Trade.**

UNITED STEELWORKERS OF AMERICA.

The United Steelworkers of America began life on 17 June 1936 as the Steelworkers Organizing Committee (SWOC) of the Congress of Industrial Organizations (CIO). John L. Lewis of the United Mine Workers of America (UMWA) formed the CIO in order to encourage the American Federation of Labor, the umbrella organization for nearly all labor unions in the country, to organize the largely unorganized manufacturing industries. Steelmaking in America had been mostly nonunion since the Homestead Lockout of 1892. Of all the organizing campaigns the CIO undertook, Lewis was particularly concerned about the steel industry because some steel firms controlled nonunion mines that the UMWA wanted to organize. The UMWA vice president Philip Murray served as the first head of the new committee.

The SWOC concentrated its early efforts on the United States Steel Corporation, by far the largest firm in the industry at that time. Like many other companies worried about organized labor's growing strength during the Great Depression, U.S. Steel had set up "company unions" in their plants, employee organizations that management created and controlled. By satisfying the collective bargaining requirements of the National Labor Relations Act, company unions were supposed to keep independent unions like the SWOC out of the mills. However, the SWOC convinced many of U.S. Steel's workers who served on these company unions to support independent union representation. As a result of this campaign, the U.S. Steel chairman Myron Taylor agreed to conduct secret talks with Lewis. These negotiations culminated on 17 March 1937 with a signed contract between the SWOC and U.S. Steel. This marked the first major victory for steel unionism in decades and was all the more surprising because the SWOC won the contract without a strike.

Other large firms in the industry known as "Little Steel" (because they were smaller than U.S. Steel) chose to fight the SWOC on the picket line rather than sign a contract. The Little Steel Strike of 1937 was marked by violence and ill will on both sides. The most famous incident of this dispute was the MEMORIAL DAY MASSACRE. Police killed ten strikers during a march on a Republic Steel plant in Chicago. Although the Little Steel firms managed to delay organization, the union filed multiple grievances under the National Labor Relations Act as a result of the strike. Thanks to legal victories in these cases and pressure for production due to war mobilization, the vast majority of steel firms in the United States recognized the USWA by the end of World War II.

The SWOC changed its name to the United Steelworkers of America (USWA) on 22 May 1942 and elected Philip Murray its first president. The union made strong membership gains during World War II thanks to a decision not to strike in exchange for government mandates to employers that spurred organizing. Dues collected from new members under government auspices solved the organization's chronic financial problems. The USWA entered the postwar era determined to improve upon progress made in wages and working conditions won during the conflict.

Employers had other ideas. The industry fought the USWA over wages, benefits, and working conditions throughout the immediate postwar era. The USWA led five nationwide strikes between 1946 and 1959, and it at least threatened to strike during most years of this period.

These strikes resulted in great gains for the union. In 1947, the USWA completed a massive effort to evaluate and classify every job in the steelmaking industry. This allowed it to bargain for the first industrywide wage rate structure in U.S. history. The earlier system had been widely recognized as grossly unfair. During the 1949 strike, the USWA won the right to negotiate pensions for its members. By 1960, steelworkers were among the best-paid manufacturing workers in America.

The cost to employers of these wage and benefit victories contributed to the collapse of the American steel industry in the face of foreign competition. In order to forestall strikes that might have further damaged the industry, the USWA agreed to an unprecedented arrangement that required that all bargaining issues be submitted to arbitration, the Experimental Negotiating Agreement of 1973 (ENA). The plan failed to save the industry. By the time the parties abandoned the ENA in 1983, plant closings and the layoff of union workers had devastated the USWA's membership rolls.

The USWA has to some extent counteracted the decline in membership brought on by the collapse of the American steel industry by adding other industries to its jurisdiction. In 1967, it merged with the 40,000-member International Union of Mine, Mill, and Smelter Workers. In 1970, it added 20,000 members of the United Stone and Allied Product Workers of America. In 1995 the USWA merged with the United Rubber, Cork, Linoleum, and Plastic Workers of America, which had 98,000 workers at that time. In 1997, the USWA merged with the Aluminum, Brick, and Glass Workers International Union. As of 1996, the USWA had approximately 700,000 members. Only 150,00 of them were employed in the American steel industry.

The USWA has frequently championed the notion of cooperation with both management and government in order to gain wage and benefit increases. During World War II it proposed creating joint works councils in order to oversee production. It has offered strong support to the Democratic Party since the late 1930s. In 1974, the union agreed to a precedent-setting consent decree with the industry and the Equal Employment Opportunity Commission to compensate African American and Hispanic steelworkers for past racial discrimination and prevent it from happening in the future. By the end of the twentieth century, the leadership and rank and file of the union had become considerably more militant and more racially diverse.

BIBLIOGRAPHY

Brody, David. *Steelworkers in America: The Nonunion Era.* Cambridge, Mass.: Harvard University Press, 1960.

Clark, Paul F., Peter Gottlieb, and Donald Kennedy, eds. *Forging a Union of Steel: Philip Murray, SWOC, and the United Steelworkers.* Ithaca, N.Y.: ILR Press, 1987.

Hoerr, John P. *And the Wolf Finally Came.* Pittsburgh, Pa.: University of Pittsburgh Press, 1988.

Tiffany, Paul A. *The Decline of American Steel.* New York: Oxford University Press, 1988.

Jonathan Rees

See also **American Federation of Labor–Congress of Industrial Organizations; Homestead Strike.**

UNITED TEXTILE WORKERS. Created in 1901 when several independent textile unions met in Washington, D.C., the United Textile Workers of America (UTW) was affiliated with the American Federation of Labor (AFL). However, the demographics of the textile industry hampered the first two decades of the UTW. The majority of textile workers were foreign-born, but foreign-born membership in the UTW never exceeded 10 percent. The executive council of the UTW reflected the suspicion, held by the governing board of the AFL, that foreign workers brought "foreign" ideologies with them. Indeed, a sizeable number of textile workers openly expressed their political allegiance to socialism, syndicalism, and communism. Some workers in New England, for example, opened their meetings with the singing of the "International." For thirty years the UTW focused its organizing efforts on New England, ignoring the growing number of textile workers in the South.

Southern textile mills proved, however, to be the most important chapter in the history of the UTW. In 1934 the National Industrial Recovery Act established the right of non-farm workers to organize and bargain collectively. This federal protection acted as a catalyst for the UTW to renew its organizing efforts and concentrate its energies in the South. Within a few months membership increased from 40,000 to just over 270,000. Much of this number resided in the Southern Piedmont area. By 1934 the depression exacerbated the problems for mill workers. In particular, the use of the stretch-out (requiring workers to do more work with no increase in pay) by mill owners alienated the already overworked, underpaid worker. The UTW called for a nationwide strike against the mill owners. Beginning on Labor Day 1934, Francis Gorman of the UTW led the strike effort. Among the demands of the UTW was an end to the stretch-out, a thirty-hour workweek, and recognition of the union. The strike closed mills from Maine to Alabama as 400,000 workers walked out. However, mill owners used strikebreakers, state police, evictions from company housing, and violence to end the walkout. Within a month the strike was over, and many workers found themselves blacklisted. But the strike did lead to the passage of the Farm Labors Standard Act of 1938. However, the blacklist and evictions dramatically reduced UTW membership, which dropped to 37,000 in 1936. That year the Congress of Industrial Organizations (CIO) made overtures to the humbled UTW. Union president Thomas McMahon, a member since the group's beginnings in 1901, supported the creation of the Textile Workers Organizing Committee. That group supervised the union's shift in 1939 from the AFL to the CIO under a new name, the Textile Workers Union of America (TWU). However, beginning in 1948 the CIO became the target of the federal government's anticommunism campaign. As a result, in 1953 the leaders of the TWU successfully campaigned to return to the AFL. The last major organizing effort of the TWU began in the early 1960s when the union targeted the mills of J. P. Stevens in the Southeast. The difficulty of this project resulted in the merging of the TWU with the Amalgamated Clothing Workers in 1976, taking the name Amalgamated Clothing and Textile Workers Union. Although the merged union failed to achieve its ambitious goals, its work did result in the intervention of the National Labor Relations Board and federal action against J. P. Stevens.

BIBLIOGRAPHY

Daniel, Cletus E. *The Culture of Misfortune: An Interpretive History of Textile Unionism in the United States.* Ithaca, N.Y.: ILR Press, 2001.

Hodges, James A. "J. P. Stevens and the Union Struggle for the South." In *Race, Class, and Community in Southern Labor History.* Edited by Gary M. Fink and Merl E. Reed. Tuscaloosa: University of Alabama Press, 1994.

Marshall, F. Ray. *Labor in the South.* Cambridge, Mass.: Harvard University Press, 1967.

David O'Donald Cullen

See also **Amalgamated Clothing Workers of America, American Federation of Labor-Congress of Industrial Organizations, Labor; Trade Unions.**

"UNITED WE STAND, DIVIDED WE FALL," a favorite toast, in varying forms, of political orators from Benjamin Franklin to Abraham Lincoln. It gained currency after John Dickinson's "Liberty Song" was published on 18 July 1768, in the *Boston Gazette.* The work contained the lines:

> Then join in hand, brave Americans all—
> By uniting we stand, by dividing we fall!

The slogan regained widespread usage three-quarters of a century later when the popular writer George Pope Morris's "The Flag of the Union" appeared. The poem quoted the sentiment as given above, from the motto of Kentucky, which had been adopted in 1792. Gaining new currency during times of national crisis, the phrase was most recently a popular slogan after the attacks upon the World Trade Center and the Pentagon on 11 September 2001.

BIBLIOGRAPHY

Furtwangler, Albert. *American Silhouettes: Rhetorical Identities of the Founders.* New Haven, Conn.: Yale University Press, 1987.

Irving Dilliard / L. T.

See also **Liberty, Concept of; Nationalism; 9/11 Attack.**

UNIVERSITIES, STATE. State universities have long been an important element in the complex structure of American higher education, but in the early Republic, only the private, church-related colleges established deep roots. Those private colleges educated an elite in a narrow, classical liberal arts curriculum and confirmed the dominant Protestant religious groups. The westward movement planted denominational liberal arts colleges of this type across the land, and they remained a feature of American higher education into the twentieth century.

With the birth of the nation in the late eighteenth century came the conviction that the public had a responsibility to support higher education, giving rise to the earliest state universities. State institutions first appeared in the Southeast, where private colleges had not gained a foothold during the colonial period. Georgia pioneered in chartering a state university in 1785, North Carolina followed in 1789, and South Carolina in 1801. Thomas Jefferson's vision of a public university culminated in the 1819 charter of the University of Virginia. Often, the initiation of instruction occurred several years after the charter.

As the nation expanded, settlers carried the idea of state universities to new frontiers. Vermont provided for a state university in 1791, and Tennessee did so in 1794. The Northwest Ordinance of 1787 encouraged schools and the means of education, and Ohio University (1804) in Athens, Ohio, and Miami University (1809) in Oxford, Ohio, were the first state universities established in the Northwest Territory. By 1861, twenty of the existing thirty-four states had founded publicly supported universities, including new institutions in Indiana (1816), Michigan (1817), Missouri (1821), Iowa (1846), and Wisconsin (1848). In seven of the other fourteen states, private colleges had been established at an early date; for example, Harvard, Yale, Princeton, King's College (now Columbia), and Brown. The remaining seven new states, Illinois, Maine, Arkansas, Florida, Texas, Oregon, and Kansas, failed to act on a university between the time of their admission to the Union and the outbreak of the Civil War.

A massive reconstruction of higher education created the modern American university. The leaders of an educational reform movement that began in the 1820s and gathered momentum in the 1840s criticized the entrenched liberal arts colleges as lacking relevance for a democratic and expanding nation. They demanded that the federal government help create an educational system open to all social and economic classes and to women as well as men, and they demanded a curriculum designed to prepare students for the world of work and practical pursuits.

The reform movement culminated in the Morrill Land Grant Act (1862), which entitled each state to select 30,000 acres of public land for each legislator it sent to Washington, D.C. in 1860. The states were to invest the proceeds from the disposition of this bounty at 5 percent and use the returns to endow within two years at least one college where

> the leading object shall be, without excluding other scientific and classical studies, and including military tactics, to teach such branches of learning as are related to agriculture and the mechanic arts, in such manner as the legislatures of the states may respectively prescribe, in order to promote the liberal and practical education of the industrial classes in the several pursuits and professions of life.

The enormous federal endowment stimulated the rise of state universities and initiated a new era in American higher education.

The MORRILL ACT threw the burden of responsibility on the states. By 1863, fourteen states had acted, and by 1870, the two-year deadline having been extended, a total of thirty-six states had accepted the legislation. The federal subsidy was too large to refuse but too small by itself to support a college. Some states were slow to meet the challenge. To further the cause of public colleges and universities, the Hatch Act (1887) provided $15,000 a year to establish an agricultural experiment station affiliated with a land-grant college or university in each state. The second Morrill Act (1890) provided a permanent annual endowment starting at $15,000 and rising to $25,000 for each land-grant college established under the provisions of the 1862 act, and it allowed states to use a portion of the federal appropriation to endow and maintain land-grant colleges for black youths in states that maintained separate educational facilities. Many of the resulting institutions became agricultural and mechanical colleges.

Starting around the middle of the twentieth century, most state-supported teacher's colleges in the United States were transformed into state universities. In 1994, the Carnegie Foundation for the Advancement of Teaching classified 3,595 American colleges and universities according to the highest level of degrees conferred. At that time, 765 institutions granted degrees beyond a baccalaureate, including 529 in which the highest degree awarded was a master's and 236 that granted doctorates. Well over

279

half of the latter (151, or 64 percent) were public institutions. Of this group, sixty-six were classified as doctoral universities and eighty-five as research universities. The doctoral universities offered baccalaureate programs and graduate studies through doctorates, and they were subdivided into two categories according to the number of doctoral degrees awarded annually. The research universities offered baccalaureate programs and graduate studies through doctorates and gave high priority to research. They were subdivided into Categories I and II. The former received annually $40 million or more in federal support; the latter received between $15.5 and $40 million annually in federal support. Of the public research universities, fifty-nine were classified in Category I and twenty-six were classified in Category II.

American state universities educate a large proportion of the young people engaged in postsecondary studies. In 1994, public universities that granted doctorates enrolled 12.072 million students, 79.1 percent of the total number of students pursuing such studies, compared to 3.191 million students in private institutions of the same type. Public colleges and universities offering a master's as the highest degree enrolled 2.292 million or 73 percent of the total number of students involved in such studies, compared to 848,000 in private institutions of the same type.

Most of the state universities classified as Category I research universities are clustered in three geographical areas in the United States: along the Atlantic seaboard in Massachusetts, Connecticut, New York, New Jersey, Pennsylvania, Maryland, Virginia, North Carolina, Georgia, and Florida; in the middle of the land, in Ohio, Indiana, Illinois, Michigan, Wisconsin, Minnesota, Iowa, Nebraska, Missouri, and Kansas; and along the Pacific Coast in Washington, Oregon, and California.

Rapid changes following World War II erased many of the qualitative distinctions that formerly had distinguished the best private universities from the best state universities. Some critics suggested that the leading private universities, with their historical commitment to the liberal arts, emphasize quality in the humanities more so than the best state universities. But the United States in 2002 supported a number of world-class state universities whose educational and research programs are essential to the advancement of knowledge and to human welfare. The state universities have contributed significantly to the shaping of American democracy and to elevating the intellectual and cultural life of the nation.

BIBLIOGRAPHY

Brody, Alexander. *The American State and Higher Education: The Legal, Political, and Constitutional Relationships.* Washington, D.C.: American Council on Education, 1935.

Heller, Donald E., ed. *The States and Public Higher Education Policy: Affordability, Access, and Accountability.* Baltimore: Johns Hopkins University Press, 2001.

National Center for Education Statistics. *Digest of Education Statistics 2000.* Washington, D.C.: U.S. Department of Education, 2001.

Nevins, Allan. *The State Universities and Democracy.* Urbana: University of Illinois Press, 1962.

Ross, Earle D. *Democracy's College: The Land-Grant Movement in the Formative Stage.* Ames: Iowa State College Press, 1942.

Serving the World: The People and Ideas of America's State and Land-Grant Universities. Washington, D.C.: National Association of State Universities and Land-Grant Colleges, 1987.

Solberg, Winton U. *The University of Illinois, 1867–1894: An Intellectual and Cultural History.* Urbana: University of Illinois Press, 1968.

———. *The University of Illinois, 1894–1904: The Shaping of the University.* Urbana: University of Illinois Press, 2000.

Thackrey, Russell I. *The Future of the State University.* Urbana: University of Illinois Press, 1971.

Winton U. Solberg

See also **Education; Education, Higher; Land Grants: Land Grants for Education.**

UNIVERSITY OF CALIFORNIA. *See* **California Higher Educational System.**

UNIVERSITY OF CHICAGO, which opened in 1892, was one of a number of cultural institutions established in the period of Chicago's growth, all of which were financed by a small group of entrepreneurs and visionaries in the merchandising, meatpacking, and shipping industries. Key leaders in the university's planning stages included Thomas W. Goodspeed, an alumnus of the original Baptist College (also called the University of Chicago, 1857–1886); Frederick T. Gates, secretary of the American Baptist Society; and William Rainey Harper, the university's first president. Gates persuaded John D. Rockefeller to finance the university on the condition that additional funds would be raised. Chicago's wealthy businessmen and philanthropists contributed money and land, and brought the initial funding to $1 million. Harper, young, gifted, and energetic, had been Professor of Semitic Languages at Yale's Divinity School, when the trustees appointed him in 1891. He and Gates envisioned a large research institution with a small college and a number of affiliations, where the first commitment of faculty and students would be to scholarship. Harper's ideas had been shaped in the 1870s and 1880s, with the establishment of the first graduate school at Johns Hopkins (1876) and of new research institutions, including Stanford (1891) and Clark (1889). The university opened with an academy, a college, two graduate schools, and a divinity school. In an unprecedented move, Harper hired nine women to the faculty in the 1890s. Undergraduate and graduate enrollments were coeducational; women exceeded 50 percent of the undergraduate student body by 1901. Fear of feminization prompted Harper to attempt an unsuccessful and short-lived program of separate classes for men and women. At the urging of deans Alice Freeman Palmer and Marion Talbot, Chicago also instituted a small number of graduate fellowships for women. Faculty and students became involved in Chicago's social, cultural, and political institutions, such as Jane Addams's Hull House, the Chicago public schools, the Field Museum, the Chicago Civic Federation, and the juvenile courts. The university established its own press and developed a variety of scholarly journals. Such expansion kept the university in debt for its first fifteen years, but Rockefeller continued his support. Harper's successor Harry Pratt Judson (1906–1923) placed the university on secure financial ground and expanded its faculty and graduate programs. By 1910, Rockefeller had contributed $35 million, augmented by donations from prominent Chicago families. In the 1920s, various Rockefeller Foundation units supported biomedical, social science, and other research in the university. Ernest DeWitt Burton (1923–1925) expanded student activities to enrich college life and instituted better advising and other services for undergraduates, before his untimely death. Max Mason (1925–1928) continued to build the science faculty and saw to completion a large-scale examination of undergraduate education. By the late 1920s, the university was considered one of the preeminent research universities in the United States. In 1928 the trustees appointed Robert M. Hutchins to the presidency (1929–1951). A young man known for his high intelligence and quick wit, Hutchins reorganized the university's college and graduate school into four divisions: social sciences, humanities, and natural and physical sciences; and pushed the faculty to form interdisciplinary committees and to initiate and maintain a new general education curriculum in the college, which included extensive exposure to the great books. This latter innovation occurred in the 1930s, when many colleges and universities were experimenting with curricular reforms. Chicago's program, emulated by a number of institutions, had the most lasting influence on the curricular reorganization of St. Johns' College in the late 1930s with an entirely great books curriculum. Hutchins faced much faculty opposition, but every proposal increased media coverage of the university and its reforms. Permitting the university to serve as the site of the first self-sustained nuclear reaction to release atomic energy contributed to Allied strength in World War II and enhanced the physics faculty. His staunch defense of academic freedom in the mid-1930s and again during the McCarthy era elicited faculty loyalty, but opening the college to students out of the sophomore year of high school and enabling them to finish college early stirred faculty opposition into the 1940s. During Hutchins's tenure, undergraduate enrollment declined. The curriculum was perceived as unrelated to students' future plans, and other graduate schools were not accepting the early Chicago bachelor's degree. Succeeding presidents, though quite competent, did not have the charisma or impact of Harper or Hutchins. Lawrence Kimpton (1951–1960) pulled the university out of debt,

stabilized the neighborhood with rehabilitation projects, and increased undergraduate enrollment by abandoning Hutchins's early college plan.

Edward Levi (1968–1975) urged the faculty to experiment with undergraduate curriculum, connecting the reforms with the Hutchins era, which was viewed more favorably by the 1970s. Hanna H. Gray (1978–1993) encouraged reorganization of graduate programs. Hugo F. Sonnenschein (1993–2000) stabilized the university's finances and enriched undergraduate student life. Each president faced responsibility for maintaining and enhancing the university's international distinction as a first-class research institution, protecting the university's assets in the Hyde Park neighborhood, and offering undergraduate programs designed to attract some of the nation's brightest students.

BIBLIOGRAPHY

Diner, Steven J. *A City and Its Universities: Public Policy in Chicago, 1892.* Chapel Hill: University of North Carolina Press, 1980.

Dzuback, Mary Ann. *Robert M. Hutchins: Portrait of an Educator.* Chicago: University of Chicago Press, 1991.

Goodspeed, Thomas W. *The Story of the University of Chicago, 1890–1925.* Chicago: University of Chicago Press, 1925.

Manuscripts and Special Collections, Joseph Regenstein Library, University of Chicago.

McNeill, William H. *Hutchins' University: A Memoir of the University of Chicago, 1929–1950.* Chicago: University of Chicago Press, 1991.

Storr, Richard J. *Harper's University: The Beginnings; A History of the University of Chicago.* Chicago: University of Chicago Press, 1966.

University of Chicago. *One in Spirit: A Retrospective View of the University of Chicago on the Occasion of Its Centennial.* Chicago: University of Chicago Press, 1991.

Mary Ann Dzuback

See also **Education, Higher: Colleges and Universities.**

UNIVERSITY OF MICHIGAN was established by an act of the Michigan Territory legislature on 26 August 1817, funded with several private grants, including lands ceded by area Native Americans. The act provided for a complete structure of state-supported education that would include a "Catholepistemiad or University of Michigania." The vision, based on Napoleonic concepts of state-based public instruction, never fully materialized and little is known of the first two decades of the university. When Michigan became a state in 1837, its first constitution provided for a complete system of public instruction overseen by a superintendent. The first to hold that office, John D. Pierce, proposed that the state establish a university with three departments: literature, science, and the arts; medicine; and law. The legislature adopted the proposal and the university was located in Ann Arbor, where construction began on a new campus, partially funded through the sale of lands from the university's earlier presence in Detroit. During the first years, the presidency of the university rotated among its small faculty.

In 1851, Michigan revised its constitution and provided for the university to be separated from the office of the superintendent and charged an elected board of regents to "have the general supervision . . . and control of all expenditures." This constitutional independence has been a critical factor in the development of the university. Funds for the university were designated through a land tax, which grew as the state quickly developed in the latter part of the century. In 1852, the regents named Henry Philip Tappan the first appointed president of the university. Tappan had high ambitions fueled by his interest in emerging German models of instruction and scholarship. This combination of constitutional independence, strong finances, and energetic leadership largely accounts for the prominence achieved by the university so early in its history.

Over the years, the university expanded to engage as wide a range of intellectual and professional concerns as any university in the country. The College of Literature, Science, and the Arts was established in 1841, followed by medicine (1850); law (1859); dentistry (1875); pharmacy (1876); engineering (1895); a graduate school (1912), named for Horace H. Rackham in 1935; architecture and urban planning (1913), named in 1999 for A. Alfred Taubmann; education (1921); business administration (1924); natural resources and the environment (1927); music (1940); nursing (1941); public health (1941); social work (1951); information (1969), formerly library science; art and design (1974); kinesiology (1984); and public policy (1995), named in 2000 for President Gerald R. Ford, who graduated from the university in 1935. Through a gift from the Mott Foundation a branch campus was established in Flint in 1958, and through a gift from Ford Motor Company, a branch was established in Dearborn on the grounds of the Henry Ford Estate in 1959.

In 1870 the regents passed a resolution allowing women to attend the university. Other notable events in the history of the university include the announcement on 12 April 1955 of the successful field test of the Salk vaccine under the direction of Professor Thomas Francis; John F. Kennedy's speech on 14 October 1960 on the steps of the Michigan Union, where he defined the idea of a "peace corps"; and President Lyndon B. Johnson's commencement speech on 22 May 1964, in which he outlined a vision of America that he called the "Great Society."

The university is among the most prominent public research universities in the country. Total enrollment on all campuses in fall 1999 was 52,602, of which 37,828 were on the Ann Arbor Campus. University libraries in 2000 held more than 7.2 million volumes. Sponsored research in the academic year 1998–1999 amounted to just under $500 million. The University Health System included three hospitals and more than 150 health centers and clinics. The total operating budget for the university was $2.9 billion in 1998–1999.

BIBLIOGRAPHY

Peckham, Howard H. *The Making of the University of Michigan.* Edited and updated by Nicholas H. Steneck and Margaret L. Steneck. Ann Arbor, Mich.: Bentley Historical Library, 1994.

Shaw, Wilfred Byron, ed. *University of Michigan: An Encyclopedic Survey.* 8 vols. Ann Arbor: University of Michigan, 1941–1958.

Francis X. Blouin

See also **Education, Higher: Colleges and Universities; Universities, State.**

UNIVERSITY OF PENNSYLVANIA, located in Philadelphia, emerged from a sequence of experimental trusts. Starting from a 1740 plan for a charity school, in 1749 it became a public academy, as Benjamin Franklin had suggested in his *Proposals* and the *Constitutions.* The resulting institution was significant because never before in the history of higher education had anyone founded an educational institution on purely secular and civil objectives, without patronage from a religious group, a private sponsor, or a government. Instruction began at the academy in 1751 and included some classes for poor children. In 1755 a rechartering that denominated the school a "College and Academy" epitomized Franklin's commitment to higher education.

During the eight years between 1749 and 1757 that Franklin shepherded the infant institution, he exemplified the spirit of compromise needed to moderate the conflict and bitterness that can strangle academic progress. Instead of insisting on the primarily utilitarian curriculum he preferred, he agreed to a major classical emphasis in order to attract important trustees, and thus, there emerged a balance between classical and scientific education unique in the colonies. Through the succeeding two centuries, the example of resilience set by Franklin more than once moderated academic fright over prospective change and permitted some venturesome innovations, such as the first medical school in the colonies in 1765 and the first department of botany in 1768.

Despite Franklin's example, little progress occured between 1790 and 1850. The medical school was faltering, and the pioneer law professorship of 1790–1791, which was the first in the United States, failed to inspire the establishment of a law school until 1850. Fortunately, vigor was on the point of resuming, as proved by the addition of the Towne Scientific School in 1875, the School of Dentistry in 1878, the Wharton School of Business in 1881, the Graduate School of Arts and Sciences in 1882, and the Veterinary School in 1884. Affiliation with the Free Museum of Science and Arts, which later became the University Museum in 1938, began in 1887.

The twentieth century brought medicine forward at the university. The Graduate School of Medicine was founded in 1919, the School of Nursing in 1935, and the School of Allied Medical Professions in 1950. The university became affiliated with several hospitals and diverse medical facilities. The spectrum of academic inquiry broadened further with the founding of the Moore School of Electrical Engineering in 1923, the College of Liberal Arts for Women in 1933, the Fels Institute of State and Local Government in 1937, and the Annenberg School of Communications in 1959. In 1974 the College of Liberal Arts for Women merged with its male counterpart.

Such rapid and varied growth called for taking stock, and in 1954 the university commissioned a critical five-year survey by outside specialists. Adoption of many of the suggested alterations resulted in the expenditure of $100 million for new buildings and a proliferation of experiments in curricula, student lifestyles, and community relations. Currently, the university stresses the value of interdisciplinary learning, a dedication that the establishment of the Institute for Medicine and Engineering, the Joseph H. Lauder Institute for Management and International Studies, and the Management and Technology of Program exemplifies. The university also is committed to improving the overall quality of life in West Philadelphia. The total yearly operating expenditures of the university were $3.05 billion in 2000. Franklin's little academy, which opened its doors in 1751 to 145 pupils, had become a multiform university of approximately 22,000 students in 2000.

BIBLIOGRAPHY

Brands, H. W. *The First American: The Life and Times of Benjamin Franklin.* New York: Doubleday, 2000.

Lucas, Christopher J. *American Higher Education: A History.* New York: St. Martin's Press, 1994.

Meyerson, Martin, and Dilys Pegler Winegrad et al. *Gladly Learn and Gladly Teach: Franklin and His Heirs at the University of Pennsylvania, 1740–1976.* Philadelphia: University of Pennsylvania Press, 1978.

Wechsler, Louis K. *Benjamin Franklin: American and World Educator.* Boston: Twayne Publishers, 1976.

Jeannette P. Nichols / A. E.

See also **Chemistry; Education; Education, Higher: Colleges and Universities; Engineering Education; Medical Education; Universities, State; Veterinary Medicine.**

UNIVERSITY OF VIRGINIA, founded by Thomas Jefferson at Charlottesville, gained statutory existence in 1819. Developed from an academy charter of 1803, construction began on its buildings in 1817, and eight schools opened in 1825. Its foundation was one of the landmarks in the development of higher public education in America. Jefferson, who was also the architect, spoke of himself as its "father," and in writing the inscription for his tombstone, mentioned his connection with its foundation as one of the three achievements of his life by which he wished to be remembered.

A chairman of the faculty administered the university until 1904, when Edward A. Alderman became the first president. The university has made three specific contributions to American education. First, the University of Virginia secularized scientific thought. The university's devotion to secularism is clear even in the first architectural plans that Jefferson drew up for the institution in which a library rather than a chapel stood at the center of the campus. Second, in 1842 Henry St. George Tucker and his colleagues installed a system of student self-government along lines suggested by Jefferson in 1818. Third, it established, as part of larger tenets of freedom in teaching and learning, an elective system of study. In 1944 Mary Washington College for women, established in 1908 at Fredericksburg, combined with the University of Virginia. Two community colleges, Clinch Valley College and George Mason College, are also associated with the university. In the early 1950s, the previously racially segregated University of Virginia enrolled its first black students. In 1970 the school became coeducational at the undergraduate level.

Outstanding features are its beautiful grounds and neoclassical buildings, its honor system, and its association with Jefferson, James Madison, and James Monroe. Famous students have included Edgar Allan Poe, Woodrow Wilson, and Walter Reed. As of 2002, the university enrolled just under 19,000 students with an operating budget of $816.3 million for the academic division and $575.6 million for the medical center. It consistently ranks as one of the top public universities in the United States. Because the quality of its instruction compares favorably with that of the finest private schools in the country, it has earned the unofficial label of a "public ivy" school. Currently, ten schools make up the University of Virginia: the School of Architecture, the College and Graduate School of Arts and Sciences, the McIntire School of Commerce, the School of Engineering and Applied Science, the School of Nursing, the Darden Graduate School of Business Administration, the School of Law, the School of Medicine, the Curry School of Education, and the School of Continuing and Professional Studies.

BIBLIOGRAPHY

Brawne, Michael. *University of Virginia, the Lawn: Thomas Jefferson.* London: Phaidon, 1994.

Dabney, Virginius. *Mr. Jefferson's University: A History.* Charlottesville: University Press of Virginia, 1981.

Hellenbrand, Harold. *The Unfinished Revolution: Education and Politics in the Thought of Thomas Jefferson.* Newark: University of Delaware Press, 1990.

Lucas, Christopher J. *American Higher Education: A History.* New York: St. Martin's Press, 1994.

John Cook Wyllie / A. E.

See also **Architecture; Education, Higher: Colleges and Universities; Ivy League; Universities, State; Virginia.**

UNIVERSITY OF WISCONSIN. The origins of higher education in Wisconsin came in the provision of the new state's 1848 constitution mandating the founding of a public, nonsectarian institution of higher learning, financed by the sale of the state's designated public lands. Its first legislature elected a governing board of twelve regents, charged with choosing a chancellor, purchasing a site, erecting buildings, buying books and scientific apparatus, and administering the university fund, derived primarily from land sale revenues. The new university was established at Madison in 1849.

Over the years, the state legislature gradually assumed the lion's share of the university's funding, supplemented by student tuition and fees and by federal subsidies. The legislature also mandated the organization of four university departments: science, literature, and the arts; law; medicine; and elementary education. The allocation of another 240,000 acres of public lands by the Morrill Land Grant Act led to the Legislative Organic Act of 1866, which provided for appointment of the regents by the governor and mandated instruction in agricultural and technical subjects, as well as military tactics. While several other midwestern states established a second institution for those purposes, Wisconsin subsumed all of its higher education activities under a single aegis; it also consistently resisted subsequent efforts to establish a separate agricultural college.

That situation persisted until the founding of the University of Wisconsin–Milwaukee in 1956 and of additional campuses in Green Bay and Kenosha-Racine (Parkside) in the late 1960s. In 1971, the legislature merged the four university campuses with those of the several Wisconsin state universities and two-year "centers," as well as the complex Extension Division, into a single University of Wisconsin System. By the end of the century, that system consisted of thirteen four-year and thirteen two-year campuses, a faculty of 6,559, a staff of 26,080, a student body of 155,298, and a budget of $2,922,311,886. Despite this expansion, the Madison campus remained the system's "flagship" and continued to be regarded by many, both within and without the state, as *the* University of Wisconsin.

Since 1851, the University of Wisconsin has become one of the country's preeminent universities; the majority of its academic disciplines and professional and graduate programs consistently rank among the top twenty-five in the nation. In addition, it has gained lasting distinction for a number of innovations in public higher education, beginning with the 1894 adoption by the regents of a specific guarantee of academic freedom: "Whatever may be the limitations which trammel inquiry elsewhere, we believe that the great state university of Wisconsin should ever encourage that continual and fearless sifting and winnowing by which alone the truth can be found." Just a few years earlier, the campus embarked on what soon became the country's most extensive and celebrated system of educational outreach—the Extension Division, with its myriad courses and programs that reach an estimated audience of more than one million per year and provide abundant evidence for the claim that the boundaries of the campus are coextensive with those of the state. At least equally renowned has been its role in what came to be known as the "Wisconsin Idea." Led by some of its most famous graduates—Robert M. La Follette Sr., Charles R. Van Hise, and Charles McCarthy—and several of its most distinguished faculty—John R. Commons, Richard T. Ely, Edward A. Ross, and Fredrick Jackson Turner—university personnel established an enduring tradition of public service, drafting legislation, testifying before legislative committees, and serving on investigative and regulatory commissions.

BIBLIOGRAPHY

Bogue, Allan G., and Robert Taylor, eds. *The University of Wisconsin: One Hundred and Twenty-Five Years.* Madison: University of Wisconsin Press, 1975.

Curti, Merle, Vernon Carstensen, E. David Cronon, and John W. Jenkins. *The University Of Wisconsin: A History.* 4 vols. Madison: University of Wisconsin Press, 1949–.

John D. Buenker

See also **Universities, State; Wisconsin; Wisconsin Idea.**

UNKNOWN SOLDIER, TOMB OF THE, in Arlington National Cemetery near Washington, D.C., was dedicated in 1921 by President Warren G. Harding as a memorial to all American soldiers and sailors who lost their lives in World War I. An unknown serviceman was chosen and buried with a two-inch layer of earth brought

Tomb of the Unknown Soldier. Photographed on 22 March 1996, Sergeant Heather Lynn Johnsen of Roseville, Calif., was the first woman selected to guard the famous tomb at Arlington National Cemetery, outside Washington, D.C. AP

from France so that he could rest on the earth on which he died. The tomb itself was not completed until 1932. In 1958, President Dwight D. Eisenhower participated in ceremonies at which two other nameless soldiers, one to represent members of the armed forces lost in World War II and one to represent those who died in the Korean War, were also buried in the tomb. At that time, the monument was renamed the Tomb of the Unknowns. In 1973, Congress authorized plans to add a burial place for an unidentified casualty of the Vietnam War. The Vietnam unknown was interred in 1984, although his remains were disinterred in May 1998 after his body was identified using methods previously unavailable. His body was returned to his family, and the crypt remains empty. The bodies within the tomb have been selected with great care to avoid future identification. The present tomb was designed by Thomas Hudson Jones and Lorimer Rich and dedicated in 1932 on the site of a former uncompleted monument. A perpetual military guard is maintained at the tomb.

Frederick P. Todd
Honor Sachs

See also **Cemeteries, National; Memorial Day; Prisoners of War;** *and vol. 9:* **Dedicating the Tomb of the Unknown Soldier.**

UNSAFE AT ANY SPEED. Published in 1965 by the then-unknown lawyer Ralph Nader, this exposé of the American automobile industry's disregard for consumer safety became a best-seller that electrified the consumer advocacy movement. *Unsafe at Any Speed* showed how the automobile industry consistently ignored and even covered up the dangers their products posed for the public. The public outrage provoked by the book helped assure the passage of the National Traffic and Motor Vehicle Safety Act in 1966, which created a regulatory agency empowered to set design standards for automobiles, such as mandatory seatbelts. Along with Rachel Carson's environmentalist classic *Silent Spring* (1962), *Unsafe at Any Speed* reinvigorated a progressive regulatory impulse in American politics that had been in abeyance since at least World War II. But Nader's aim was not just to savage the design defects of one vehicle—General Motors' best-selling Corvair—or even to criticize the automobile industry generally. Rather, Nader's true target was elite control of the state and of business–government linkages—what he called "the power of economic interests." Like Upton Sinclair's muckraking socialist classic *The Jungle* (1906), however, Nader's book failed to convince the public that capitalism itself contained flaws, but did result in greater consumer protection in one specific industry.

Nils Gilman

See also **Automobile Safety; Consumer Protection; National Traffic and Motor Vehicle Safety Act.**

URBAN LEAGUE. *See* **National Urban League.**

URBAN REDEVELOPMENT. Nineteenth-century slum housing in the United States consisted of buildings with warrens of tiny, poorly ventilated rooms that resulted in a high incidence of infant mortality and infectious diseases among the European immigrant population. Reform movements began in 1901, with the New York State Tenement House Law and continued in the 1930s with zoning ordinances (intended to separate residential areas from the health-endangering waste products of industrial activities) and federal loans to build housing for workers who had fallen on hard times during the GREAT DEPRESSION.

During the 1940s and 1950s, as immigrants prospered and moved out of the TENEMENTS, much increasingly decrepit housing stock was still in place in Northeastern and Midwestern cities, which had become destinations for southern blacks seeking better-paid factory employment. Rampant housing discrimination created racially segregated neighborhoods. Lacking an adequate tax base and political clout, these areas and populations lagged in the quality of schools, roads, police protection, and other city services. Nevertheless, even segregated neighborhoods of this period generally included solidly middle-class residents and thriving businesses.

After World War II, urban planners (then largely concerned with accommodating the increasing presence of automobiles) and social reformers (focused on providing adequate affordable housing) joined forces in what proved to be an awkward alliance. The major period of urban renovation in the United States began with Title I of the 1949 Housing Act: the Urban Renewal Program, which provided for wholesale demolition of slums and the construction of some eight-hundred thousand housing units throughout the nation. The program's goals included eliminating substandard housing, constructing adequate housing, reducing de facto segregation, and revitalizing city economies. Participating local governments received federal subsidies totaling about $13 billion and were required to supply matching funds.

Bad News for the Inner City

Sites were acquired through eminent domain, the right of the government to take over privately owned real estate for public purposes, in exchange for "just compensation." After the land was cleared, local governments sold it to private real estate developers at below-market prices. Developers, however, had no incentives to supply housing for the poor. In return for the subsidy and certain tax abatements, they built commercial projects and housing for the upper-middle class. Title III of the Housing Act of 1954 promoted the building of civic centers, office buildings, and hotels on the cleared land. Land that remained vacant because it was too close for comfort to remaining slum areas often became municipal parking lots.

CASE STUDY: THE HILL DISTRICT

A well-to-do neighborhood in the nineteenth century, the Hill District bordering downtown Pittsburgh, Pennsylvania, gained a different population after 1870, as the new trolley service allowed the gentry to move away from downtown. The new residents were European immigrants and African Americans from the South seeking factory jobs in an area said to be a haven from segregation laws. During the 1930s and 1940s the Hill District was home to nightclubs featuring top jazz performers. Even in the 1950s, it was a vibrant community with shops, theaters, churches, and social organizations.

As early as 1943, however, a member of the Pittsburgh City Council noted that "approximately 90 percent of the buildings" in the Hill District were "substandard." He urged that these aging stores and residences be destroyed. In 1955, the U.S. government provided the Lower Hill Redevelopment plan with $17.4 million in loans and grants. More than eight thousand residents, overwhelmingly African American, were displaced when thirteen hundred buildings were demolished to make way for what was to be a twenty-nine-acre cultural district anchored by the eighteen-thousand-seat Civic Arena (now Mellon Arena, a hockey rink). After the arena was built, however, the cultural district plan was abandoned.

Former residents received little compensation and minimal benefits from the federal government. Many moved across the Allegheny River to the city's North Side, where, in turn, more than five hundred buildings were razed to make room for a shopping mall, office tower, and private housing complex. Elsewhere in the city, new highways and the Three Rivers Stadium displaced even more low-income residents.

Efforts to build new housing in the Hill District lagged until the early 1990s, when community groups worked with a commercial developer to initiate a $40-million, five hundred-unit residential project on a nearby site, with some government-subsidized units for low-income residents. But the land cleared in the 1950s remained largely unused. By 2002, it had become one of the city's most valuable parcels of undeveloped real estate, prompting the local hockey team—which wants to build a new arena—to propose a $500-million office, retail, and housing development.

The district's city council representative, Sala Udin, was a ten-year-old when his family was uprooted in the 1950s. He supports the plan, but only if the arena (viewed by some as worthy of preservation) is razed, allowing the city grid to be adjusted to reconnect the district's streets to downtown Pittsburgh and to create what he calls "a healthy, organic neighborhood."

Interstate highways funded by the Highway Act of 1956 not only hastened "white flight" (the departure of middle-class white residents to new suburban housing developments) but also physically divided cities. Little thought was given to the results of leveling inner-city neighborhoods to build the new interstates: the destruction of neighborhoods and displacement of low-income residents.

More than two thousand construction projects on one thousand square miles of urban land were undertaken between 1949 and 1973, when the urban renewal program officially ended. Roughly six hundred thousand housing units were demolished, compelling some two million inhabitants to move. Thousands of small businesses were forced to close. In New York City, more than one hundred thousand African Americans were uprooted, destroying the social and economic fabric of many neighborhoods.

The original legislation had stipulated that for each new unit of housing built, at least one old unit of housing was to be torn down. Yet only 0.5 percent of all federal expenditures for urban renewal between 1949 and 1964 was spent on family relocation. A 1961 study of renewal projects in forty-one cities found that 60 percent of the tenants (even more in large cities) were merely relocated to other slums, exacerbating the problem of overcrowding. Slum evacuees who found better housing often had to pay higher rents.

After 1960, federally subsidized loans increasingly underwrote the rehabilitation, rather than wholesale demolition, of blighted neighborhoods. In 1964 Congress passed legislation to assist relocated persons who could not afford their new rents. Still, despite the good intentions that prompted urban renewal, most observers now agree that the process was deeply flawed.

The Public Housing Debacle

The public housing built in the 1950s—ironically, based on the utopian architecture of European modernist Charles-Édouard Jeanneret Le Corbusier—was designed to squeeze as many families as possible onto expensive urban real estate. Slab-like high-rise complexes, poorly planned and constructed, housed as many as twelve thousand people (in the notorious Pruitt-Igoe project in St. Louis, Missouri). Known by residents as "the projects," these buildings were increasingly plagued by vandalism, drug use, rape, assault, robbery, and murder.

A 1969 law that abolished minimum rents and stipulated that no family would have to pay more than 25 percent of its income to rent an apartment in public housing lacked federal subsidies to make up for the lost revenue. While public housing authorities went bankrupt, the projects increasingly filled with people who had no income at all. The 1981 Omnibus Budget Reconciliation Act created priority categories for public housing that insured only the "truly needy" were served while ignoring poor working families who had spent years on waiting lists.

"Cross Out Slums." An undated poster put out by the U.S. Housing Authority vehemently rejects the slums depicted at the bottom in favor of the more appealing housing at the top.

Literally and figuratively walled off from the rest of the city, the projects became islands of despair and dereliction.

Allied to the failures of urban development as a means of alleviating housing shortages was and is owner abandonment of rental apartment housing; they stop making repairs and paying taxes, and accumulate so many building violations that legal occupation is no longer permitted. Destroyed by vandalism or arson, these buildings become city property, to be torn down or rehabilitated at public expense. Other apartment buildings are "warehoused," awaiting gentrification of the neighborhood, when they may be rehabilitated and sold at a profit.

Urban Redevelopment after 1973

New thinking about the nature and function of American cities has led to public-private partnerships that frequently succeed in modest, yet measurable, ways where large-scale methods have failed. The Housing and Community Development Act of 1974 emphasized rehabilitation, preservation, and gradual change rather than demolition and displacement. Under the Community Development Block Grant program, local agencies bear most of the responsibility for revitalizing decayed neighborhoods. Successful

programs include urban homesteading, whereby properties seized by the city for unpaid taxes are given to new owners who promise to bring them "up to code" within a given period—either by "sweat equity" (doing the work themselves) or by employing contractors—in return for free title to the property. Under the Community Reinvestment Act, lenders make low-interest loans to help the neighborhood revitalization process.

The federal Empowerment Zone program, initiated in 1994 in Atlanta, Baltimore, Chicago, Detroit, New York, and Philadelphia-Camden, with two "supplementary" awards to Los Angeles and Cleveland, gave each city $100 million plus a package of tax benefits to encourage economic development in blighted areas. Provisions include tax-exempt bond financing for business expansion and tax credits for investments in distressed areas. More cities were added to the program in 1998 and 2001.

Two basic design directions have prevailed in urban redevelopment: creating new pedestrian zones and reclaiming underused or deteriorating areas of a city by blending them into a city's historic fabric. Widening sidewalks, permitting mixed-use zoning (mingling residential and business uses), planting trees, adding lighting, and establishing a pleasing variety of building facades promote economic vitality by encouraging people to spend time downtown.

Several theories about the overall failure of city planning are currently in vogue. An argument for greater involvement of local residents—as a counterweight to the dictates of distant professional planners—is often coupled with the need to empower poor and minority groups to lobby for changes that will benefit them. Another view emphasizes the significance of global forces, including foreign investment in U.S. cities and overseas labor costs, as well as other factors (such as interest rate fluctuations and energy prices), over which city planners, investors, and local politicians have no control.

Today, major league stadiums, hotel-convention centers, and entertainment districts, which cater largely to middle-class nonresidents, are believed to be prime components of a successful urban center. Yet studies have shown that these increasingly larger and more costly projects—often built despite lack of voter approval and costing more in job-creation funds than other economic development programs—rarely pay for themselves. These sleek edifices contrast with the all-too-common scenario, particularly in poorer urban centers, of severe cutbacks in essential city services. Ultimately, it is hard to disagree with urban historian Witold Rybczynski that "neighborhoods are the lifeblood of any city." By preserving neighborhoods, a city proclaims that it is a place where people want to be.

BIBLIOGRAPHY

Anderson, Martin. *The Federal Bulldozer: A Critical Analysis of Urban Renewal: 1949–1962.* Cambridge, Mass.: MIT Press, 1964.

CASE STUDY:
THE LOWER GARDEN DISTRICT

Built in the early nineteenth century around a spacious park, the once-affluent Lower Garden District in New Orleans, Louisiana, began its long decline after the Civil War. In the 1970s, the crumbling old homes found new buyers, activists who fought to stop a proposed bridge over the Mississippi River that would have split the district in half and cut off access to the park. A decade later, however, many homes were abandoned and storefronts on the main commercial thoroughfare, Magazine Street, were nearly all vacant.

In 1988, the Preservation Resource Center, a local advocacy organization, launched Operation Comeback, a nonprofit program to help potential homebuyers purchase and rehabilitate vacated buildings in seven New Orleans neighborhoods. Owners pay the monthly interest on the loan, carried by Operation Comeback, and contribute their own labor. Architects donate their expertise, and contractors are paid in stages by Operation Comeback through a bank line of credit. When the renovations are finished, the owners buy their homes for the fair market value purchase price plus taxes, fees, and the cost of repairs.

In 1992, working with a $220,000 budget and two-person staff, Operation Comeback had rescued, or helped others to rescue, one hundred houses. Magazine Street bloomed again with restaurants, shops, and small businesses. Another Preservation Resource Center program, Christmas in October, organizes teams of volunteers to repair rundown homes occupied by poor, elderly, and disabled residents as well as blighted community buildings.

As an outgrowth of these middle-class renovation efforts, a combination of private money and government matching grants—under a Department of Housing and Urban Development (HUD) program to rid the United States of the one hundred thousand worst public housing units—revived the blighted fifteen-hundred-unit St. Thomas Public Housing complex, built in New Orleans in 1939 for the working poor. Begun in 1999, the multimillion-dollar project consists of tearing down older sections of the complex and replacing them with public housing designed to blend in with traditional neighborhood residences. Both symbolically and practically, these efforts help to create more cohesive neighborhoods, the building blocks of livable cities.

Friedan, Bernard J., and Lynne B. Sagalyn. *Downtown, Inc.: How America Rebuilds Cities.* Cambridge, Mass.: MIT Press, 1989.

Hall, Peter. *Cities of Tomorrow: An Intellectual History of Urban Planning and Design in the Twentieth Century.* Oxford: Basil Blackwell, 1988.

Jacobs, Jane. *The Death and Life of Great American Cities.* New York: Random House, 1961.

Judd, Dennis R., and Paul Kantor, eds. *The Politics of Urban America: A Reader.* New York: Longman, 2001.

Kemp, Roger L., ed. *The Inner City: A Handbook for Renewal.* Jefferson, N.C.: McFarland, 2001.

Mumford, Lewis. *The City in History: Its Origins and Transformations and Its Prospects.* New York: Harcourt, Brace and World, 1961.

O'Connor, Thomas. *Building a New Boston: Politics and Urban Renewal 1950–1970,* Boston: Northeastern University Press, 1993.

Teaford, Jon C. *The Rough Road to Renaissance: Urban Revitalization in America 1940–1985.* Baltimore: Johns Hopkins University Press, 1990.

Whyte, William H. *City: Rediscovering the Center.* New York: Doubleday, 1988.

Wilson, James Q., ed. *Urban Renewal: The Record and the Controversy.* Cambridge, Mass.: MIT Press, 1966.

Wright, Gwendolyn. *Building the Dream: A Social History of Housing in America.* New York: Pantheon, 1981.

Cathy Curtis

See also **Housing; Housing and Urban Development.**

URBANIZATION. Cities have been the pioneers of American growth. From the beginnings of European exploration and conquest, towns and cities were the staging points for the settlement of successive resource frontiers. Boston and Santa Fe in the seventeenth century, Philadelphia and San Antonio in the eighteenth century, Cincinnati and Denver in the nineteenth century, and Anchorage and Miami in the twentieth century all played similar roles in organizing and supporting the production of raw materials for national and world markets. It has been city-based bankers, merchants, and journalists who have linked individual resource hinterlands into a single national economy.

The reality of the "urban frontier" clashes with the ingrained American frontier myth. In his famous essay, "The Significance of the Frontier in American History" (1893), Frederick Jackson Turner asked his readers to take an imaginative stance over the Cumberland Gap to watch the "procession of civilization . . . the Indian, the fur-trader and hunter, the cattle raiser, the pioneer farmer." City makers, by implication, trailed far to the rear. From James Fenimore Cooper's novels and Theodore Roosevelt's *Winning of the West* (4 vols., 1889–1896) to Paul Bunyan stories and John Wayne movies, there is little place for the bustling levees of New Orleans, the surging crowds of Broadway, or the smoky cacophony of Pittsburgh steel mills.

A comparison of urbanization in the United States to the rest of the world contradicts the national self-image.

Americans have prided themselves on their youth as a nation, which consequently was late to urbanize. In sober fact, however, the United States was a pioneer among urbanizing nations. Along with Britain, France, Belgium, and the Netherlands, it was among the very first to feel the effects of the urban-industrial revolution. The history of American cities is substantially a story of the invention of new institutions and technologies to cope with two centuries of massive urbanization.

Stages of Urbanization

American urbanization has followed the same demographic pattern found in every urbanizing society for the last two centuries. The word "urbanization" itself refers to an increase in the proportion of national or regional population living in cities. For the first six thousand years of urban life, no society was long able to maintain an urban percentage greater than from 5 to 10 percent. Starting in late eighteenth-century England, however, one nation after another experienced an accelerating shift from rural to urban population. After several generations of rapid urbanization, the process leveled off toward a new equilibrium in which about three-quarters of the population lived in cities and many of the rest pursued city-related activities in smaller towns. The result, when the urban proportion of a population is graphed against time is an s-shaped curve that turns up sharply for perhaps a century and then tapers off.

Urban growth in the United States has clearly followed these three stages of gradual growth, explosive takeoff, and maturity. First, the era of colonial or premodern cities stretched from the seventeenth century to the 1810s. Second, the rise of the industrial city dominated a century of rapid urbanization from 1820 to 1920. Finally, the third era of the modern city has run from 1920 onward. At each stage, the available technologies of communication and transportation shaped the internal patterns of cities and their distribution across the continent.

The first century of British and Dutch colonization along the Atlantic seaboard depended directly on the founding of new cities, from New Amsterdam (1625) and Boston (1630) to Providence (1638), Charleston (1672), Norfolk (1680), Philadelphia (1682), and Savannah (1733). These colonial towns resembled the provincial market centers in the British Isles. Compact in size and small in population, they linked the farms, fisheries, and forests of the Atlantic colonies to markets in Europe and the Caribbean. With populations that ranged from 15,000 to 30,000 at the time of the American Revolution, the four largest cities dominated the commerce of regional hinterlands. Portsmouth, Salem, Springfield, and Providence looked to Boston; Albany traded via New York; Philadelphia took its profits from the rich farms of the Delaware and Susquehanna Valleys; Charleston centralized the trade of Savannah, Wilmington, and New Bern.

Colonial capitals looked to the sea. William Penn's Philadelphia was designed to march inland from the Delaware River, but the economic life of the port drew settlement north and south along the river. Charleston faced the Cooper River and the Atlantic beyond its barrier islands. New York City similarly faced its harbor on the East River. Taverns and warehouses lined the wharves. Merchants crowded the coffeehouses to share the latest shipping news and arrange for their next cargoes. The elite built near the governor's residence on lower Broadway to enjoy the fresh air off the Hudson River and a relaxing view of the green New Jersey shore.

Taken together, the twenty-four recognized cities with 2,500 people or more at the first census of 1790 accounted for only 5 percent of the national population. A generation later, after the disruptions of the War of 1812, with its British attacks on Washington, Baltimore, and New Orleans, and the panic of 1819, the 1820 census still counted only 700,000 urban Americans—a scant 7 percent of the national total. A century later, the 1920 census found a nation that was 51 percent urban, giving 1920 as much symbolic meaning for American history as the supposed closing of the frontier in 1890.

Nineteenth-century urbanization meant more cities and bigger cities. From 1820 to 1920, the New York metropolitan area expanded from 124,000 people on the lower end of Manhattan Island to 7,910,000 spread across fourteen counties. Philadelphia's metropolitan region grew from 64,000 to 2,407,000. Over the same period, the number of cities from the Mississippi River to the Pacific Ocean increased from a handful of settlements to 864 cities, topped by San Francisco and Los Angeles.

New city people came from farms and small towns on both sides of the Atlantic. Whether it involved a transatlantic voyage from Liverpool or Hamburg or a fifty-mile train ride into Indianapolis, migration from farm to city was the other great population movement in nineteenth-century America. It simultaneously balanced and was part of the westward movement across the continent. The physical construction of cities—houses, bridges, sewers, streets, offices, factories—was a complementary process of capital formation that, likewise, balanced the development of farms and their supporting railroads.

By the end of the nineteenth century, American cities fell into two categories. The nation's industrial core stretched from Boston and Baltimore westward to St. Louis and St. Paul, accounting for the overwhelming majority of manufacturing production and wealth. Many of these cities were specialized as textile towns, steel towns, shoemaking towns, pottery towns, and the like. Their industrial labor force drew from the millions of European immigrants and their children who made up more than two-thirds of the population of cities like Detroit, Chicago, Milwaukee, Pittsburgh, and New York City. Cities in the South, the Great Plains, and the Far West were the suppliers and customers. They funneled raw materials to the industrial belt: cotton from Mobile, lumber from Norfolk, metals from Denver, cattle from Kansas City. In

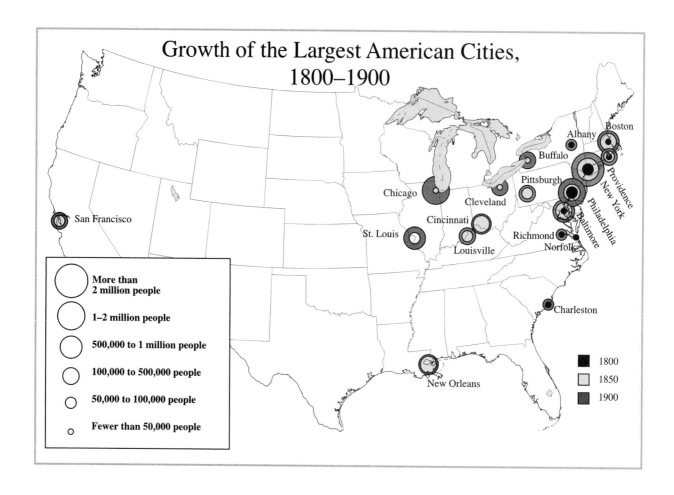

Growth of the Largest American Cities, 1800–1900

San Francisco

Chicago
Buffalo
Albany
Boston
Pittsburgh
Providence
New York
Cleveland
Philadelphia
Cincinnati
Baltimore
St. Louis
Richmond
Louisville
Norfolk

Charleston

New Orleans

More than
2 million people

1–2 million people

500,000 to 1 million people

100,000 to 500,000 people

50,000 to 100,000 people

Fewer than 50,000 people

1800
1850
1900

return, they distributed the manufactured goods of the Northeast.

Chicago was the great exemplar of the growing industrial city. Between 1880 and 1920, 605,000 immigrants and 790,000 Americans moved into the city. Chicagoans lifted their entire city ten feet to improve its drainage. They built the world's first skyscrapers and some of its first grain elevators. They remade American taste with the World's Columbian Exposition of 1893. They competed with Odessa as a grain port, Pittsburgh as a steel city, Cincinnati as a meatpacker, and London and Paris as a national railroad center. Looking at Chicago and other mid-continent cities, Charles Francis Adams commented that "the young city of the West has instinctively . . . flung herself, heart, soul, and body, into the movement of her time. She has realized the great fact that steam has revolutionized the world, and she has bound her whole existence up in the great power of modern times" (*North American Review*, pp. 6–14).

Urban growth after 1900 revolved around the adaptation of American cities to twentieth-century technologies of personalized transportation and rapid communication. The 1910s and 1920s brought full electric wiring and self-starting automobiles to middle-class homes. George F. Babbitt, the eponymous hero of Sinclair Lewis's

1922 novel, lived in a thoroughly modern Dutch colonial house in the bright new subdivision of Floral Heights in the up-to-date city of Zenith. He awakened each morning to "the best of nationally advertised and quantitatively produced alarm-clocks, with all modern attachments." His bathroom was glazed tile and silvered metal. His business was real estate and his god was Modern Appliances.

The metropolis that Babbitt and millions of real automobile owners began to shape in the 1920s broke the physical bounds of the nineteenth century industrial city. In 1910 the Census Bureau devised the "metropolitan district" to capture information about the suburban communities that had begun to ring the central city. The definition has been repeatedly modified to match the realities of urban-regional geography. In 2000, the federal government recognized 280 metropolitan regions with a total population of 276 million. The metro areas of middle-sized cities like Atlanta, Phoenix, Minneapolis–St. Paul, and Houston stretched for from seventy-five to one hundred miles from one suburban margin to the other.

The cities of post–World War II America have had the greatest ethnic variety in national history. They have been destinations for a massive northward movement. Rural southerners, both black and white, moved north (and west) to cities and jobs. Starting with the Great Migration of 1917 and 1918, the African American experience became an urban experience, creating centers of black culture like Harlem in the 1920s and feeling the bitter effects of ghettoization by the 1930s and 1940s. During the Great Depression and World War II, Appalachian whites joined black workers in middle western cities like Cincinnati and Detroit. Okies and Arkies left their depressed cotton farms in Oklahoma and Arkansas for new lives in Bakersfield and Los Angeles.

The northward movement also crossed oceans and borders. Puerto Rican immigrants after World War II remade the social fabric of New York City and adjacent cities. Half a million Cubans made an obvious impact on Miami after the Cuban Revolution of 1959. The Puerto Ricans and Cubans were followed to eastern cities by Haitians, Jamaicans, Colombians, Hondurans, and others from the countries surrounding the Caribbean. Mexicans constitute the largest immigrant group in cities in Texas, Arizona, Colorado, and California. Temporary workers, shoppers, visitors, legal migrants, and illegal migrants fill neighborhood after neighborhood in El Paso, San Antonio, San Diego, and Los Angeles, creating bilingual labor markets and downtowns.

From the 1970s, Asia matched Latin America, with each accounting for 40 percent of documented immigrants. Asians have concentrated in the cities of the Pacific Coast and in New York City. Los Angeles counts new ethnic neighborhoods for Vietnamese, Chinese, Japanese, Koreans, and Samoans. Honolulu looks to Asia as well as the continental United States for business and tourism. A new generation of migrants has revitalized fading Chinatowns in New York City, Chicago, Seattle, and Los Angeles.

The rise of Latin American and Asian immigration is part of a rebalancing of the American urban system. What journalists in the 1970s identified as the rise of the Sun Belt is part of a long-term shift of urban growth from the industrial Northeast toward the regional centers of the South and West—from Detroit, Buffalo, and Chicago to Los Angeles, Dallas, and Atlanta. The causes include the concentration of defense spending and the aerospace industry between 1940 and 1990, the growth of a leisure economy, the expansion of domestic energy production, and the dominance of information technology industries. The result has been booming cities along the South Atlantic coast from Washington to Miami, through the greater Southwest from Houston to Denver, and along the Pacific Coast from San Diego to Seattle.

At the start of the twenty-first century, nine metropolitan areas had populations of five million or more: New York City, Los Angeles, Chicago, Washington-Baltimore, San Francisco–Oakland–San Jose, Philadelphia, Boston, Detroit, and Dallas–Fort Worth. Their eighty-four-million residents accounted for 30 percent of all Americans. The fastest-growing metropolitan areas from 1990 to 2000 were all found in the South or West.

In total, metropolitan areas contained 80 percent of the American population.

Cities and American Values

Urbanization has been a cultural as well as demographic process. The United States lagged behind Great Britain and a handful of nations in northwestern Europe in urbanization, but led the rest of the world. One result has been ambivalent Americans who have praised cities with one voice and shunned them with another. Public opinion polls repeatedly show that most Americans would prefer to live in a small town. A few extra questions have revealed that they also want easy access to the medical specialists, cultural facilities, and business opportunities that are found only in cities. Indeed, there was scarcely any place in late-twentieth-century America not thoroughly penetrated by urban values and tied into urban networks.

Thomas Jefferson set the tone for American anti-urbanism with the strident warning that cities were dangerous to democracy. At the time of Philadelphia's deadly yellow fever epidemic of 1800, Jefferson wrote to Benjamin Rush that "when great evils happen, I am in the habit of looking out for what good may arise from them as consolations. . . . The yellow fever will discourage the growth of great cities in our nation, and I view great cities as pestilential to the morals, the health, and the liberties of man." Jefferson feared that American cities would become facsimiles of eighteenth-century London and Paris as areas of poverty and breeders of riotous mobs. He also feared that because city dwellers were dependent on others for their livelihoods, their votes were at the disposal of the rich. Should Americans become "piled upon one another in large cities, as in Europe," he wrote to James Madison, they would become "corrupt as in Europe."

If Jefferson feared foremost for the health of the republic, many of the antiurban writers who followed feared instead for the morals of the individual. George Foster drew stark contrasts between rich and poor in *New York in Slices, by an Experienced Carver* (1849) and *New York by Gaslight* (1850). Others indicted city life as a corrupter of both rich and poor. For example, in *The Dangerous Classes of New York* (1872), Charles Loring Brace warned of the threat posed by the abjectly poor and the homeless. With no stake in society, they were a riot waiting to happen and a responsibility for more comfortable citizens. Jacob Riis used words and photographs to tell the middle class about the poor of New York City in *How the Other Half Lives* (1890). A few years later, W. T. Stead wrote *If Christ Came to Chicago!* (1894) to show the big city as un-Christian because it destroyed the lives of its inhabitants.

The first generation of urban sociologists wrote in the same vein during the 1910s, 1920s, and 1930s. Robert E. Park worked out a theory of urban life that blamed cities for substituting impersonal connections for close personal ties. As summarized by Louis Wirth in "Urbanism as a Way of Life" (1938), the indictment dressed up Thomas Jefferson in the language of social science. Wirth's

291

city is the scene of transitory and superficial relationships, frantic status seeking, impersonal laws, and cultural institutions pandering to the lowest common denominator of a heterogeneous society.

The attack on city living was counterbalanced by sheer excitement about the pace of growth. By the 1830s large numbers of Americans had come to look on cities as tokens of American progress. The pages of booster pamphlets and histories of instant cities were drenched in statistics of growth. *Pittsburgh as It Is* (1857) offered statistics on coal mining, railroads, real estate values, population, employment, boat building, banks and a "progressional ratio" comparing the growth of Pittsburgh to the rest of the nation. Boosters counted churches, schools, newspapers, charities, and fraternal organizations as further evidence of economic and social progress. Before the Civil War, one Chicago editor wrote that "facts and figures . . . if carefully pondered, become more interesting and astonishing than the wildest vision of the most vagrant imagination." His words echoed seventy years later as George Babbitt sang the praises of "the famous Zenith spirit . . . that has made the little old Zip City celebrated in every land and clime, wherever condensed milk and pasteboard cartons are known." Urban advocates in the twentieth century extended the economic argument to point out the value of concentrating a variety of businesses in one location. The key is external economies: the ability of individual firms to buy and sell to each other and to share the services of bankers, insurance specialists, accountants, advertising agencies, mass media, and other specialists.

American writers and critics as disparate as Walt Whitman and Ralph Waldo Emerson have also acknowledged cities as sources of creativity. "We can ill spare the commanding social benefits of cities," Emerson wrote in his essay "The Young American" in 1844. Nathaniel Hawthorne allowed his protagonist in *The Blithedale Romance* (1852) to take time off from the rigors of a country commune for the intellectual refreshment of Boston. George Tucker, professor of moral philosophy and political economy at Jefferson's University of Virginia, analyzed urban trends in 1843. He stated: "The growth of cities commonly marks the progress of intelligence and the arts, measures the sum of social enjoyment, and always implies increased mental activity. . . . Whatever may be the good or evil tendencies of populous cities, they are the result to which all countries, that are at once fertile, free, and intelligent tend" (*Progress of the United States in Population and Wealth*, p. 127).

Livable Cities

Americans had to learn not only to plan their cities but also to live comfortably in the fast-growing communities that they erected. They needed to adapt their lives to the urban pace and to develop institutions to bring order out of the seeming chaos. In a city like Philadelphia, rates of accidental deaths and homicides began to drop after 1870 as city dwellers learned to control reckless behavior and

pay attention on the streets. The end of the century also brought a decline of spontaneous mobs and endemic drunkenness at the same time that the saloon developed as a stable social institution in immigrant neighborhoods.

Cities developed community institutions that linked people in new ways. Apartment buildings offered a new environment for the middle class. Novelist William Dean Howells reflected contemporary concerns by devoting the first hundred pages of *A Hazard of New Fortunes* (1890) to Basil March's search for an apartment appropriate for a newly appointed New York City magazine editor. Department stores, penny newspapers, vaudeville theaters, and baseball provided common meeting grounds and interests for heterogeneous populations. Department stores such as A. T. Stewart's, John Wanamaker's, Marshall Field's, and others of the 1860s, 1870s, and 1880s made emerging central business districts acceptable places for women as consumers and helped to introduce women into the clerical labor force. Ballparks and theaters were shared spaces where allegiances and jokes crossed ethnic lines. Ethnic banks, newspapers, and mutual insurance societies offered training in American ways at the same time that they preserved group identity.

The openness of the American city to continued growth brought the need for professionalism in public services. At the start of the nineteenth century, private companies or amateurs provided everything from drinking water to police protection. In the flammable wooden cities of colonial times, householders were expected to keep buckets and respond to calls for help. By the 1820s and 1830s, more cities had added groups of citizens who drilled together as volunteer fire companies, answered alarms, and fought fires as teams. Problems of timely response and the development of expensive steam-powered pumpers, however, required a switch to paid fire companies in the 1850s and 1860s. Firemen who were city employees could justify expensive training and be held accountable for effective performance. By 1900 most observers agreed that fire protection in the United States matched that anywhere in Europe.

Effective fire protection required a pressurized water supply. Residents of colonial cities had taken their water directly from streams and wells or bought it from entrepreneurs who carted barrels through the streets. Philadelphia installed the first large-scale water system in 1801. Boston reached twenty miles into the countryside with an aqueduct in the1840s. From 1837 to 1842, New York City built the Croton Reservoir and an aqueduct that brought fresh water forty miles from Westchester County to a receiving reservoir in what is now Central Park. Changing theories of disease and the availability of abundant water for municipal cleaning helped to cut New York City's death toll in the 1866 cholera epidemic by 90 percent from the 1849 epidemic.

The public responsibilities of nineteenth-century cities generally fell into the three categories of public health and safety (police, sewers, parks), economic development

Growth of the Largest American Cities, 1900–1990

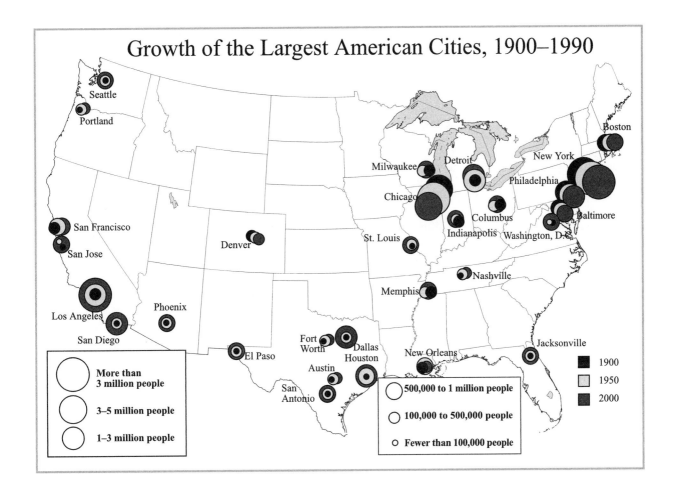

Seattle
Portland

Milwaukee
Detroit
New York
Boston

Chicago
Philadelphia

San Francisco
Columbus
Baltimore

San Jose
Indianapolis
Washington, D.C.

Denver
St. Louis

Los Angeles
Phoenix
Nashville

San Diego
Memphis

El Paso
Fort Worth
Dallas
Jacksonville

Austin
Houston
New Orleans

San Antonio

More than
3 million people

3–5 million people

1–3 million people

500,000 to 1 million people

100,000 to 500,000 people

Fewer than 100,000 people

1900
1950
2000

(street drainage and pavement), and public education. Such expanding responsibilities fueled the municipal progressivism of the early twentieth century. Led by local business interests, cities implemented civil service employment systems that based hiring and promotion on supposedly objective measures. The city manager system placed the daily operations of government under a professional administrator. As the system spread after the 1910s, city government became more and more the realm of engineers, planners, budget analysts, and other trained professionals.

Public intervention came later in other areas like low-income housing. Cities long preferred to regulate the private market rather than to intervene directly. New York City pioneered efforts to legislate minimum housing standards with tenement house codes in 1867, 1882, and 1901. However, providing the housing remained a private responsibility until the federal government began to finance public housing during the 1930s. Even the massive investments in public housing spurred by federal legislation in 1937 and 1949, however, failed to meet the need for affordable living places.

A full social agenda for local government awaited the 1960s. Assistance to the poor was the realm of private philanthropy in the nineteenth century, often coordinated through private charity organization societies. The crisis of the 1930s legitimized federal assistance for economically distressed individuals, but city government remained oriented to public safety and economic development. By the start of the 1960s, however, criticisms that the urban renewal programs of the 1950s had benefited real estate developers at the expense of citizens added to an increasing sense that America's multiracial cities were in a state of crisis. In 1964 President Lyndon Johnson declared a nationwide "war on poverty." On the front lines was the Office of Economic Opportunity with its Neighborhood Youth Corps for unemployed teenagers, its Head Start and Upward Bound programs to bolster public schools, and its Community Action Agencies to mobilize the poor to work for their own interests. Two years later the Model Cities program sought to demonstrate that problems of education, child care, health care, housing, and employment could be attacked most effectively by coordinated efforts.

The last quarter of the century left American cities with comprehensive social commitments but limited resources. Presidents Richard Nixon and Ronald Reagan redirected federal resources to meet the development needs of politically powerful suburbs. Cities and city people absorbed roughly two-thirds of the budget cuts in the first Reagan budget, leaving them without the resources to fund many needed social programs.

Cities and American Society

"I am an American, Chicago born—Chicago, that somber city—and go as I have taught myself, free-style, and will make the record in my own way: first to knock, first admitted; sometimes an innocent knock, sometimes a not so innocent." These opening lines from *The Adventures of Augie March* (1953) capture one of the essential features of the American city. The hero of Saul Bellow's novel about growing up during the 1920s and 1930s knew that cities are the place where things happen. They are centers of opportunity that bring people together to exchange goods, services, ideas, and human company.

At their best, American cities are among the most livable environments in the world. Americans have solved—or know how to solve—many of the physical problems of traffic, pollution, and deteriorated housing. Failures have come from lack of commitment and political will, not from the inherent nature of cities. The poor are often expected to tax themselves for public services that they cannot afford as private citizens. As in the nineteenth century, the centers of our cities display the polarization of society between the very rich and the very poor.

What cities will continue to do best is to protect diversity. The key to urban vitality is variety in economic activities, people, and neighborhoods. This understanding implies that the multicentered metropolitan area built around automobiles and freeways is a logical expression of American urbanism. In the words of historian Sam Bass Warner Jr., the contemporary city offers "the potential of a range of personal choices and social freedoms for city dwellers if we would only extend the paths of freedom that our urban system has been creating" (*The Urban Wilderness*, p. 113).

The political expression of the urban mosaic is metropolitan pluralism, facilitated by the civil rights movement, the Voting Rights Act, and the war on poverty. Diverse groups defined by ethnicity, social class, or residential location have developed the capacity to pursue their goals through neighborhood organizations, suburban governments, and interest groups. Pluralistic politics has given previously ignored groups and communities entry to public and private decisions about metropolitan growth and services, particularly Hispanics and African Americans. However, cities still need strong area-wide institutions to facilitate the equitable sharing of problems and resources as well as opportunities. Most promising are regional agencies like the Twin Cities Metropolitan Council in Minnesota and Metro in Portland, Oregon, that have assumed responsibility for planning and delivering specific regional services such as parks or public transportation.

Toward the close of the New Deal, a number of the nation's leading specialists on urban growth summed up the promise of urban America in a report called *Our Cities:* *Their Role in the National Economy* (1937). "The city has seemed at times the despair of America," it said, "but at others to be the Nation's hope, the battleground of democracy. . . . The faults of our cities are not those of decadence and impending decline, but of exuberant vitality crowding its way forward under tremendous pressure—the flood rather than the drought."

BIBLIOGRAPHY

Abbott, Carl. *The Metropolitan Frontier: Cities in the Modern American West.* Tucson: University of Arizona Press, 1993.

Adams, Charles Francis. "Boston." *North American Review* (Jan. 1868): 6–14.

Bender, Thomas. *New York Intellect: A History of Intellectual Life in New York City, from 1750 to the Beginnings of Our Own Time.* New York: Knopf, 1987.

Borchert, John R. "American Metropolitan Evolution." *Geographical Review* 57 (1967): 301–332.

Cronon, William. *Nature's Metropolis: Chicago and the Great West.* New York: Norton, 1991.

Gillette, Howard, Jr., and Zane L. Miller. *American Urbanization: A Historiographic Review.* New York: Greenwood, 1987.

Goldfield, David R. *Cotton Fields and Skyscrapers: Southern City and Region, 1607–1980.* Baton Rouge: Louisiana State University Press, 1982.

Jackson, Kenneth T. *Crabgrass Frontier: The Suburbanization of the United States.* New York: Oxford University Press, 1985.

Lemon, James T. *Liberal Dreams and Nature's Limits: Great Cities of North America since 1600.* New York: Oxford University Press, 1996.

Monkkonen, Eric H. *America Becomes Urban: The Development of U.S. Cities and Towns, 1780–1980.* Berkeley: University of California Press, 1988.

Monti, Daniel J., Jr. *The American City: A Social and Cultural History.* Malden, Mass.: Blackwell, 1999.

Nash, Gary. *The Urban Crucible: Social Change, Political Consciousness, and the Origins of the American Revolution.* Cambridge, Mass.: Harvard University Press, 1979.

Tucker, George. *Progress of the United States in Population and Wealth in Fifty Years, As Exhibited by the Decennial Census.* New York: Press of Hunt's Merchants' Magazine, 1843.

Wade, Richard C. *The Urban Frontier: The Rise of Western Cities, 1790–1830.* Cambridge, Mass.: Harvard University Press, 1959.

Warner, Sam Bass, Jr. *The Urban Wilderness: A History of the American City.* New York: Harper and Row, 1972.

Weber, Adna F. *The Growth of Cities in the Nineteenth Century: A Study in Statistics.* New York: Macmillan, 1899.

White, Morton, and Lucia White. *The Intellectual versus the City: From Thomas Jefferson to Frank Lloyd Wright.* Cambridge, Mass.: Harvard University Press, 1962.

Carl Abbott

See also **City Planning; Housing; Immigration; Migration, Internal; Poverty; Suburbanization; Tenements; Urban Redevelopment.**

URSULINE CONVENT, BURNING OF (11 August 1834). In the early 1830s, a self-proclaimed "escaped nun," Rebecca Theresa Reed, began spreading tales of immoral acts committed in the Ursuline convent school of Charlestown, Massachusetts. Tensions peaked in 1834 when another nun, Elizabeth Harrison, fled to the home of her brother. She later returned voluntarily, but rumors that she was being forcibly detained brought forth a mob; the sisters and pupils were expelled, and the convent was burned. The prompt acquittal of the mob leaders, the state's refusal to reimburse the Ursuline order, and the thinly veiled satisfaction voiced by the press led to a nationwide campaign against Roman Catholicism in the following decades.

BIBLIOGRAPHY

Billington, Ray Allen. "The Burning of the Charlestown Convent." *New England Quarterly* 10 (1929).

———. *The Protestant Crusade, 1800–1860: A Study of the Origins of American Nativism.* New York: Rinehart, 1952. The original edition was published in 1938.

Grimsted, David. *American Mobbing, 1828–1861: Toward Civil War.* New York: Oxford University Press, 1998.

Ray Allen Billington / A. R.

See also **Anti-Catholicism; Catholicism; Know-Nothing Party; Nativism; United Americans, Order of.**

Andrew Carnegie. The industrialist, philanthropist, and founder of Carnegie Steel, whose merger with the Federal Steel Company in 1901 resulted in the first billion-dollar company in the United States.

U.S. STEEL was incorporated in New Jersey in 1901. At the time, it was the first billion-dollar company in America, having authorized capitalization of $1.4 billion. U.S. Steel was formed by combining the assets of the Federal Steel Company, controlled by J.P. Morgan and Elbert H. Gary, with Carnegie Steel, purchased from its owner, Andrew Carnegie. After its first year of operation, U.S. Steel was producing over 65 percent of the steel in the United States. For the next eighty years, U.S. Steel created many subsidiaries and joint ventures connected with steel production, such as ore mining and taconite pellet production.

However, the 1980s brought a number of economic changes to the steel industry, most notably, the importing of foreign steel into the American marketplace. In response, U.S. Steel began a series of restructuring ventures, both domestic and foreign. It reduced its domestic raw steel production and became involved in the energy industry by its acquisition of Marathon Oil Company in 1982. Further diversification included the selling or combining into joint ventures the chemical and agri-chemical business and worldwide raw materials properties.

In late 1986, U.S. Steel changed its name to USX Corporation. It is headquartered in Pittsburgh, Pennsylvania. Although it is now involved with energy and other diversified businesses, it remains the largest integrated steel producer in the United States.

Robert M. Bratton

See also **Iron and Steel Industry.**

USURY. *See* Interest Laws.

UTAH. In a nation without an established church, Utah represents the closest thing to a theocracy that the United States has ever seen. With a land area of 82,168 square miles and despite a swelling urban population in the late twentieth century, Utah remains one of the least densely populated states in the United States with 27.2 persons per square mile. Physically, the Wasatch Mountains divide the state of Utah into the Central Rocky Mountain Province, the Colorado Plateau Province, and the Great Basin, where the greatest concentration of hot springs in the United States is to be found. Elevation varies from a high of 13,258 feet to a low of 2,350 feet and there is considerable climatic variation, with the highest rainfall in the mountains. The 2000 Census reported 2,233,169 residents, 89.2 percent of whom were white and only 0.8 percent black, with 9.0 percent of Hispanic ori-

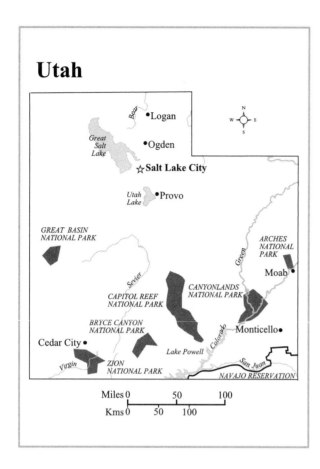

Utah

Logan
Ogden
Great Salt Lake
☆ **Salt Lake City**
Utah Lake • Provo
Bear
GREAT BASIN NATIONAL PARK
ARCHES NATIONAL PARK
Green
Moab •
CANYONLANDS NATIONAL PARK
CAPITOL REEF NATIONAL PARK
Sevier
BRYCE CANYON NATIONAL PARK
Monticello •
Colorado
Cedar City •
Lake Powell
San Juan
Virgin
ZION NATIONAL PARK
NAVAJO RESERVATION

Miles 0   50   100
Kms 0   50   100

gin. More than two-thirds of Utah's residents belong to the Church of Jesus Christ of Latter-day Saints (LDS).

From Native Americans to Latter-day Saints

Utah's earliest inhabitants, the Anasazi, occupied southern Utah, living in permanent villages and using floodplain agriculture. Around A.D. 1100, the Numic Indians settled the Great Basin with more efficient harvesting technology, an organization that was familial, and with weak tribal structures. Although Utah lay on the borders of the Spanish Empire, trade developed with Spanish communities in present-day New Mexico and further south. It was not until the 1820s, however, that American and British fur trappers entered the region, erecting a number of forts that were later to provide assistance to migrants crossing to California. Increasing acquaintance with the Utah region drew the attention of the Church of Jesus Christ of Latter-day Saints, seeking land in the remote West after the murder in 1844 of its leader, Joseph Smith. In February 1846 the Mormons left Illinois, led by their president, Brigham Young. The members of an advance party reached the Salt Lake Valley on 22 July 1847, where they found fertile soils and an adequate growing season at the crossroads of the overland route to California. By 1860, forty thousand Euro-Americans resided

in Utah. The church used a lottery to assign town lots and distributed land and water rights systematically, with water held on the principle of cooperative ownership. Although more sympathetic to the Numic Indians than other Euro-Americans, the Mormons still sought to acquire their lands and interfered in the Ute trade in slaves, leading to the Walker War of 1853.

The First Years of Settlement

Negotiations in 1849 to create a state proved abortive and instead Utah Territory was established. Conflict arose in 1857, after the territory had accorded local probate courts original jurisdiction in civil and criminal cases to avoid federally administered justice. That year President James Buchanan sent out the army to remove Brigham Young as governor of the territory. After a standoff in which the Mormons destroyed Forts Bridger and Supply, fortified Echo Canyon, and sought to deny the invaders access to grass and livestock that they would need, a compromise was reached whereby the federal government offered an amnesty in return for submission, although federal troops remained until 1861. The Mormon state continued to grow, with twenty thousand new immigrants arriving between 1859 and 1868. They spread out into the higher valleys and created settlements to mine minerals and grow cotton and flax. During the Civil War they remained loyal to the Union, despite passage of the Morrill Anti-bigamy Act (1862), which targeted the practice of polygamy in the territory. In 1868, the church established Zion's Cooperative Mercantile Institution to serve as wholesaler and distributor for a network of cooperative enterprises in Mormon communities. At Brigham Young's behest, an attempt was also made to foster a more comprehensive cooperative system—the United Order—but it ultimately failed.

Economic Development

During the 1860s, the first commercial mining of silver took place at Bingham Canyon. The full potential of mining was only realized, however, with the completion of a trans-state rail link in 1869. The new mines that resulted benefited from new technologies, outside investment, and the cooperation of the Mormon communities, many of which were involved in selling agricultural produce to the mining districts. Although not initially working as miners, Mormons were increasingly encouraged by the church to do so, provided they continued to work their farms. Despite the fact that mine work was dangerous, most Mormon miners refused to join unions and were regarded unfavorably by their non-Mormon neighbors. By 1880, Utah Territory had become dependent on coal mining, while wheat, sugar beets, and growing numbers of sheep and cattle gave a boost to commercial agriculture. The LDS Church created Zion's Central Board of Trade to plan home industry and provide a market for goods; the board also worked with non-Mormon businesses. By 1890, 36 percent of Utah Territory's residents lived in cities, a greater proportion than in the rest of the nation, although water supply and sewerage systems remained of low quality. Culturally, too, Utah attracted attention, with the formation of the Salt Lake Art Association in 1881 (later to become the Utah Art Association) and the new prominence accorded the Mormon Tabernacle Choir after its appearance at the 1893 World's Columbian Exposition in Chicago.

The War Against Polygamy

Such progress, however, was hampered by the federal prosecution of the practice of polygamy by members of the LDS Church. The territory's chief justice, James Mc-Kean, worked to exclude Mormons from jury service and brought charges of immorality against Mormon leaders. Although around three-quarters of Mormon families were monogamous, polygamy was often regarded as the basis for holding high office in the church. In 1882, the Edmunds Act provided sanctions for unlawful cohabitation and allowed exclusion of jurors who supported polygamy. Over one thousand Mormons were imprisoned during the 1880s for violating the act, but the Mormon-dominated People's Party retained control of the legislature. The Edmunds-Tucker Act of 1887 targeted the LDS Church by providing for the confiscation of all church property above fifty thousand dollars. During the 1880s, moreover, the gentile population of Utah Territory rose considerably and the anti-Mormon Liberal Party gained control of the cities of Ogden and Salt Lake City. The threatened confiscation of church property led LDS president Wilford Woodruff to issue the Manifesto of 1890, which revoked the practice of polygamy. The church also had some of its prominent figures join the Republican Party in order to avoid a political schism on religious lines since, prior to statehood, most Mormons had belonged to the national Democratic Party, which was more sympathetic to their call for states' rights. In preparation for statehood in 1896, Utah drafted a constitution that enshrined religious freedom and prohibited polygamy. At the same time, church property and civil rights were restored to the Latter-day Saints.

Commercial Agriculture and Mining

Before 1896 the farm frontier was concentrated on the irrigated and urbanized Wasatch Front and Sanpete Valley. Afterward, it shifted to more rural areas, aided by dry farming, made possible by hoarding moisture from winter rain; this helped increase farm size. Dairy farming came to northern Utah around 1900 and horticulture to the central Utah Valley in the early twentieth century. Attitudes toward water rights became less communitarian, allowing owners to buy and sell them, but in 1898 the state supreme court ruled that water could not be appropriated except for a beneficial purpose. Damage to grazing land led to the setting aside of forest reserves in 1897 and 1902 to protect watersheds and timberlands, a move supported by the LDS Church and Senator Reed Smoot. Mining production also expanded dramatically, rising from a return of $10.4 million in 1896 to $99.3 million in 1917.

The exploitation of low-grade copper was a key factor here, and the world's largest copper smelter was installed at Garfield in 1906. The mines attracted Italian and Greek immigrants who were not Mormons and had their own network of ethnic associations and churches. They formed the basis for new industrial unions like the Western Federation of Miners, which established its headquarters in Salt Lake City for a time during the late 1890s. In strikes by the United Mine Workers against the Utah Fuel Company in 1903–1904 and by the Western Federation of Miners against the Utah Copper Company in 1912 the unions were decisively beaten.

The Progressive Era

Republicans exploited the rising tide of national prosperity at the turn of the century to achieve political dominance. In 1903, LDS apostle Reed Smoot gained a U.S. Senate seat and built a political machine in Utah known as the Federal Bunch. Only in 1916 did Progressives succeed in electing its first Democratic governor, Simon Bamberger, and a new legislature that enacted statewide prohibition, established public utility and industrial commissions, and allowed peaceful picketing. The Progressive impulse extended to Salt Lake City, where the Utah Federation of Women's Clubs was active in social reform. A Civic Improvement League was created in 1906, bringing together a variety of interest groups of different religious and political backgrounds that called for better paving and more parks. A comprehensive planning system for the city was conceived in 1917 and carried through in the 1920s. One aspect of this effort at urban improvement was the fight against air pollution, led by businessman and state legislator George Dern, who sponsored a bill in 1915 to set up a cooperative research program to investigate the smelter smoke problem from the burning of soft coal.

During World War I, the LDS Church and its affiliates were active in Liberty Bond work and offered Americanization classes for new immigrants, while Utah provided 20,872 recruits for the armed services of whom 447 were killed. With the coming of the 1920s, the state turned back to the Republican Party, but in 1924 Democrat George Dern was elected governor thanks to Republican intraparty strife. Although the legislature remained under Republican control, it signed on to the federal Sheppard-Towner Maternity and Infancy Act of 1923 that provided matching health-care grants for infants and their mothers. The state also participated in negotiations that led to the Colorado River Compact, designed to ensure reasonable use of the river's water by states through which it flowed.

The Great Depression

Mining and agricultural activity remained at a comparatively low level during the 1920s. After 1920, Utah's mining and agricultural sectors failed to sustain the levels enjoyed during the first two decades of the twentieth century. When the Great Depression struck the Utah economy it completely collapsed. Per capita income stood at only $300 in 1933, farm income fell from $69 million in 1929 to $30 million in 1932, and unemployment reached 36 percent in 1932–1933. Governor Dern called for an increase in the money supply and short-term federal aid for the unemployed. Relief was initially handled by county governments and private charity, of which the LDS Church was an important source, and in 1931 Dern appointed Sylvester Cannon of the LDS Church to chair the State Advisory Council on Unemployment. Victorious in 1932, the new Democratic governor, Henry Blood, called for a reasonable minimum wage, old age insurance, unemployment relief, and a state anti-injunction law to protect the rights of organized labor. Blood quickly turned to the federal government for assistance, seeking $57 million in building, sewage, and reclamation work from the Federal Emergency Relief Administration, the Civilian Conservation Corps, and the Works Progress Administration. A new burst of unionization took place in Carbon County, where the United Mine Workers achieved recognition in most mines. The Democratic Party was dominant in Utah throughout the 1930s, with state senator Herbert Maw as the party's radical champion. In 1936, Utahns voted 63.9 percent for President Franklin Roosevelt and the New Deal, despite an LDS Church decision to publish a front-page editorial in the Church-operated *Deseret News* that some interpreted as a tacit endorsement of Republican presidential nominee Alfred Landon. Unhappy with the extensive federal intervention of the Roosevelt administration, the church in 1936 adopted its own welfare plan in an effort to divorce the Saints from secular government by providing them with church-sponsored work.

World War II and the Transformation of Utah

A great transformation of Utah came with World War II. In the mid-1930s, it was decided to upgrade Ogden Arsenal and build Hill Air Force Base to provide storage and training facilities for the military. This vastly expanded federal presence fueled dramatic in-migration as civilian defense jobs increased from 800 in 1940 to 28,800 in 1945. The government also built the Geneva Steel Plant near Provo for $214 million, although it was operated under private contract. Governor Herbert Maw proved particularly effective in lobbying the president for locating military sites in Utah. An activist for his state, he created the Department of Publicity and Industrial Development in 1941 to plan for the postwar economic world. The new demand for labor also led to an increased hiring of women workers, who constituted 37 percent of the labor force by 1944. Some 71,000 Utahns served in the armed forces and 3,600 were killed. By 1943, 52,000 people were working in defense installations and pressure for new housing was high, while food and clothing costs grew dramatically.

The Postwar Economy

Defense employment declined in the late 1940s but revived during the Korean War, when Hill Air Force Base was assigned responsibility for storing and repairing jets.

Nuclear weapons were stored and tested in Utah and Nevada; atomic tests from 1951 to 1958 at the Nevada Test Site released radiation that affected residents of southwestern Utah. The new demand for uranium fueled Utah's economy and Moab, located near uranium ore deposits, became a boomtown in the mid-1950s. The new prosperity led to a conservative shift in politics, with Republicans making striking gains in 1946 and 1948. The Republican Party in Utah was racked by dissension, however, after Senator Arthur Watkins, one of its own, chaired the committee investigating censure of Joseph McCarthy. The resulting split between moderates and conservatives in Utah helped Democrat Frank Moss to defeat Watkins in 1958. In the same period, the appointment of Hugh Brown to the First Presidency in 1961 placed a liberal Democrat in an influential advisory position to the president of the LDS Church, while in secular politics democrat Calvin Rampton served as governor from 1965 to 1977.

The Minority Question

Minorities in Utah faced challenges in the 1950s and 1960s. The redistribution of tribal lands to the Paiute Indians by the federal government did not begin to compensate for their loss of access to federal health insurance, education, and employment programs, and many were forced to sell their new land because it generated so little income. The position of African Americans improved in the late 1940s, when many businesses and swimming pools were integrated, and again in the mid-1960s when Utah, along with the federal government, began to pass civil rights legislation. The LDS Church found itself obliged to reflect on its own ban, dating from the nineteenth century, against black males holding priestly office, and in 1978 President Spencer Kimball received a revelation that permitted African Americans to enter the priesthood.

Modern Utah

Since 1970 Utah has become a Republican stronghold, voting 54 percent to 33 percent for Bob Dole over Bill Clinton in 1996 and 67 percent to 26 percent for George W. Bush over Al Gore in 2000. Democrats have not won a majority in the legislature since the 1974 election and have not held the governorship since 1985. A part of the reason for this shift has been the negative reaction to federal ownership of public lands. President Clinton's creation of the 1.7-million-acre Grand Staircase-Escalante National Monument helped defeat conservative Democratic U.S. representative Bill Orton that year. Even former Democratic governor Scott Matheson argued that the federal government had encroached too far on the rights of the states.

A new post-industrial economy in Utah has arisen, in which sixteen of the twenty-four largest employers are neither military nor absentee. The electronics industry includes WordPerfect, Novell, and Unisys, while manufacturing has shifted to electronic and aerospace components. Delta Airlines has made Salt Lake City a national hub, opening the Wasatch Front to business and tourism.

During the 1990s, the state's population grew by 29.6 percent. Utah had a high school graduation rate of 82.1 percent in 1989 and was fifth in the nation in SAT scores in 1994. The state boasted good public health indicators and low rates of cancer. Cultural institutions include the Utah Symphony, the Mormon Tabernacle Choir, Ballet West, the Brigham Young University Folk Dance Ensemble, and the Utah Shakespearean Festival.

BIBLIOGRAPHY

Alexander, Thomas G. *Utah, the Right Place: The Official Centennial History.* Salt Lake City, Utah: Gibbs Smith, 1995.

Arrington, Leonard J. *Great Basin Kingdom: An Economic History of the Latter-day Saints, 1830–1900.* Cambridge, Mass.: Harvard University Press, 1958.

———, Feramorz Y. Fox, and Dean L. May. *Building the City of God: Community and Cooperation Among the Mormons.* Salt Lake City, Utah: Deseret Book Company, 1976.

Hundley, Norris, Jr. *Water and the West: The Colorado River Compact and the Politics of Water in the American West.* Berkeley: University of California Press, 1975.

Logue, Larry M. *A Sermon in the Desert: Belief and Behavior in Early St. George, Utah.* Urbana: University of Illinois Press, 1988.

May, Dean L. *Utah: A People's History.* Salt Lake City: University of Utah Press, 1987.

———. *Three Frontiers: Family, Land, and Society in the American West, 1850–1900.* New York: Cambridge University Press, 1994.

Papanikolas, Helen Z., ed. *The Peoples of Utah.* Salt Lake City: Utah State Historical Society, 1976.

Powell, Allan Kent. *The Next Time We Strike: Labor in Utah's Coal Fields, 1900–1933.* Logan: Utah State University Press, 1985.

Stegner, Wallace. *Mormon Country.* Lincoln: University of Nebraska Press, 1981. Originally published in 1942.

Jeremy Bonner

See also **Copper Industry; Latter-day Saints, Church of Jesus Christ of; Mormon Expedition; Mormon Trail; Mormon War; Polygamy; Salt Lake City; Tabernacle, Mormon; Tribes: Southwestern.**

UTE. Ute Indians are Southern Numic speakers of the Uto-Aztecan language family. Utes (from the Spanish "Yutas") call themselves Nuciu or Nuche, the People. When they first came in contact with Europeans, the Utes inhabited over 130,000 square miles of eastern Utah and western Colorado—environments ranging from the arid valleys and mountains of the Great Basin, to the eroded Colorado Plateau, to the alpine Rocky Mountains, to the high Plains of eastern Colorado. Eleven Ute bands included the Tumpanuwacs, Uinta-ats, San Pitches, Pahvants, and Sheberetches in Utah, and the Yamparkas, Parianucs, Taviwacs, Weeminuches, Moaches, and Kapotas in Colorado. These bands shared a common language and customs, traded and intermarried, but maintained no

Captured Utes. Utes are transported to Fort Meade, S. Dak., by way of Belle Fourche, S. Dak., c. 1906. © Louis G. Billings.

larger tribal organization. Members traveled in local residence groups of from 50 to 100 people, with seasonal band gatherings for annual rituals like the spring Bear Dance, a world renewal ceremony (performed to ensure the continuation or rebirth of the world as they knew it). Leadership was chosen by proven ability and group consensus, with distinctions between civil, war, and hunt leaders emerging in the nineteenth century. Women maintained an informal but notable voice in local group decision making as a consequence of their subsistence contributions.

Ute subsistence systems were remarkably flexible and adapted to their varied environments. Families and bands moved through known territories taking advantage of the seasonal abundance of food and material resources. Men hunted deer, elk, buffalo, mountain sheep, rabbits, small mammals, and migratory waterfowl with bows and arrows, spears, snares, and nets. Women gathered seed grasses, piñon nuts, berries, yampa roots, and greens, and prepared foods for consumption or storage in parfleche bags or woven baskets. Colorado Utes focused more on large mammals, while Utah bands took advantage of spawning fish in Utah Lake and of grasshoppers and crickets, drying and storing both for trade and winter use. Ute families lived in brush shelters and hide tepees, wore both leather and woven fiber clothing, and used implements of bone, horn, stone, and wood.

Ute contact with Spanish colonists in New Mexico began in the 1610s and the Utes acquired horses by 1680. Especially among the Colorado Utes, horses increased their mobility, enabling them to focus on hunting buffalo and using their meat and hides. This reliance on buffalo led to incorporation of traits and material culture of the Plains Indians, whose society had traditionally relied on buffalo. By the nineteenth century, the Utes were respected raiders and middlemen in the southwestern horse and slave trade. Few Spaniards ventured into their territory so the Utes were able to remain free from colonial rule. Between 1810 and 1840, a growing number of fur trappers passed through Ute lands, but the full impact of Euro-American contact came with the arrival of Mormon settlers in 1847 and the Colorado gold rush of 1859.

As Mormon settlers took up residence in Utah, they disrupted Ute subsistence rounds and interfered with their slave trade. Two Ute uprisings—the Walker War (1853–1854) and the Black Hawk War (1863–1868)—were responses to this subsistence displacement, violence, and plans to remove Utah Utes to the two million acre Uintah Valley Reservation, established in eastern Utah in 1861. Between 1868 and 1877, battered Utah Utes moved to the reservation. During the same period, Colorado Ute bands confronted encroaching miners. Treaties in 1863 and 1868, and an 1873 agreement reduced their homelands to 11.5 million acres and established reservation agencies at Los Pinos (later Uncompahgre) and White River. In 1882, following a Ute uprising at White River Agency, the government forcibly removed White River Utes to the Uintah Reservation and Uncompahgre Utes to the adjoining two million-acre Ouray Reservation. In 1883, the government combined administration of the Uintah-Ouray Reservation. The Weeminuche Utes managed to avoid removal and retain the small Ute Mountain Ute Reservation, while the Moache and Kapota bands kept the Southern Ute Reservation in Colorado.

Between 1887 and 1934, Utes on the three reservations lost another 80 percent of their reservation lands through allotment and the sale of allotments, leaving them with 873,600 acres. Attempts to create a viable agricultural economy were largely unsuccessful. At the same time, Ute populations tumbled from approximately 11,300 in 1868, to 3,975 in 1880, to 1,771 Utes in 1930. Utes adopted the sun dance and peyotism to bolster their tribal identities, but internal tensions and conflicts with neighboring whites continued. Southern Ute factionalism led to settlement of the Allen Canyon and later White Mesa Ute communities in southern Utah, while Northern Utes at Uintah-Ouray terminated mixed-blood Utes in 1954 in an attempt to consolidate their cultural identity.

Since 1940, the Northern Ute, Southern Ute, and Ute Mountain Ute tribes have organized tribal governments and programs to protect their land and people. They have used settlements from successful court cases to repurchase alienated lands and establish tribal enterprises. Oil and gas exploration, mining, timber, livestock, and tourism have become their chief sources of income, but poverty, unemployment, and alcoholism are persistent problems. Enrolled Utes numbered 5,788 in 1995. Each tribe remains active in promoting Ute language, culture, and sovereignty.

BIBLIOGRAPHY

Callaway, Donald, Joel Janetski, and Omer C. Stewart. "Ute." In *Handbook of North American Indians*, edited by William C. Sturtevant et al. Vol. 11: *Great Basin*, edited by Warren L. D'Azevedo. Washington, D.C.: Smithsonian Institution, 1986.

Conetah, Fred A. *A History of the Northern Ute People*, edited by Kathryn L. MacKay and Floyd A. O'Neil. Salt Lake City: University of Utah Printing Services for the Uintah-Ouray Ute Tribe, 1982.

Delaney, Robert W. *The Ute Mountain Utes*. Albuquerque: University of New Mexico Press, 1989.

Jefferson, James, Robert W. Delaney, and Gregory C. Thompson. *The Southern Utes: A Tribal History*. Ignacio, Colo.: Southern Ute Tribe, 1972.

Simmons, Virginia McConnell. *The Ute Indians of Utah, Colorado, and New Mexico*. Niwot: University Press of Colorado, 2000.

David Rich Lewis

UTOPIAN COMMUNITIES. Although they date to the earliest days of U.S. history, Utopian communities, intentional communities created to perfect American society, had become institutionalized in American thought by the 1840s. Various groups, struggling under the pressures of urbanization and industrialization, challenged the traditional norms and social conservatism of American society. Their desire to create a perfect world often lay in sharp contradiction to the world in which they lived, one in which capitalism, the INDUSTRIAL REVOLUTION, immigration, and the tension between the individual and the community challenged older forms of living.

The first American Utopias grew out of Robert Owen's attempt to create a model company town in New Lanark, Scotland. In the United States, Owen organized the New Harmony Community along the Wabash River in western Indiana in 1825. There the residents established a socialist community in which everyone was to share equally in labor and profit. Just months after the creation of a constitution in January 1826, the thousand residents at New Harmony divided into sub-communities that then disintegrated into chaos. In 1825 Francis Wright established another Owenite community at Nashoba in Tennessee. Wright had hoped to demonstrate that free labor was more economical than slavery, but Nashoba attracted few settlers, and the community closed its doors within a year.

Transcendentalist Influence

Transcendentalists of the 1840s believed that the true path lay in the perfection of the individual, instead of reform of the larger society. The individualistic quality of TRANSCENDENTALISM gave it a more spiritual than social quality, one that also influenced later Utopian movements. Many of the figures of transcendentalism embraced the liberating qualities of INDIVIDUALISM, making man free of the social, religious, and family restrictions of the past. Ralph Waldo Emerson, for example, rejected the decaying Puritan lifestyle of New England's past in favor of the Romantic world of William Wordsworth and Samuel Taylor Coleridge. For transcendentalists, a higher reality lay behind that afforded by the senses; a reality in which people could understand truth and eternity. To reach that world, humankind had to transcend the concrete world of the senses in favor of a more mystical definition of nature. To escape the modern world, transcendentalists fled into model Utopian communities.

The most important of these communities was BROOK FARM, established in West Roxbury, Massachusetts, in 1841. Residents hoped to free themselves from the competition of the capitalist world so as to work as little as possible, all the while enjoying the fruits of high culture. Unlike their European counterparts, American transcendentalists embraced the quest for a higher moral law. Far from a simple rejection of American society, the creators of Brook Farm, chief among them George Ripley, a Unitarian minister from Boston, wanted to create an alternative to the capitalist state, to found a new "city on a hill." The life of the mind that the transcendentalists so valued was one of the most important components of life at Brook Farm. Emerson, Nathaniel Hawthorne, Henry David Thoreau, and *Dial* editor Margaret Fuller all made regular visits. While the cultural life of Brook Farm blossomed, management of its practical matters languished. Ripley's decision to recruit more farmers over thinkers eventually alienated even Emerson. After a serious fire in 1846, the farm was sold in 1847 and the society dissolved.

Not long after the failure of Brook Farm, another transcendentalist community was established at Fruitlands, Massachusetts. The residents of Fruitlands, originally organized in 1843 by Bronson Alcott and Charles Lane, rejected the market economy and chose a life of subsistence agriculture. But Fruitlands attracted the eccentric more than the genuinely alienated, including a number of "body purists"—one of whom advocated nude moonbathing. As a group, they rejected clothing made of cotton (as it was manufactured by slave labor) and that made of wool (as it was taken from sheep without their consent), as well as root vegetables and all animal food products in favor of fruit and corn meal. As in later Utopian experiments, women failed to enjoy the full benefits of the cooperative society. Instead, as Abigail Alcott noted, women did most of the work while the men passed the day in deep conversation. The colony lasted only through the end of 1844 and was eventually sold at auction, with Lane jailed for nonpayment of taxes.

As Brook Farm and Fruitlands dissolved, converts to the ideas of Charles Fourier in the United States grew to take the place of the transcendentalists. Fourierists believed that small, highly organized communities (or phalanxes) would allow residents to perfectly develop their talents and inclinations, free from the influence of traditional capitalist society. The standard phalanx consisted of 1,620 people living in common dwellings and working in their natural trades. In America, Arthur Brisbane became the chief advocate of phalanxes, hoping that they would complete what, to him, was the unfinished Revolution of 1776 by ending wage slavery. By the 1840s, Brisbane and his disciples had founded more than one hundred phalanxes across the country, from New York to Texas. Although most of these communities failed in short order, their existence underscored the general dissatisfaction some workers felt with industrialization and the triumph of the capitalist order.

Other mid-nineteenth century Utopian experiments found some success by organizing themselves around a religious principle or charismatic leader. The SHAKERS, whose origins dated to the visions of Ann Lee Stanley during the American Revolution, believed that mankind suffered due to the lust of Adam and Eve. Mother Ann favored celibacy as the path to perfection. She and a small group of followers founded a church outside of Albany, New York, in 1774, where they became known as "Shaking Quakers," or Shakers. They withdrew into isolated communities where they could escape from the larger society's wicked nature. They abolished not only property but marriage, demanding a strict commitment to celibacy. By the 1840s, more than twenty Shaker communities had been established in greater New England. Due to their strict rejection of marriage and a reduced number of available converts, the Shaker movement slipped into decline by midcentury and never recovered.

Oneida

The ONEIDA COLONY, established in New York in 1848 by John Humphrey Noyes, combined the cooperativist movement of the Fourierists and the marriage taboo of the Shakers to produce a new form of Utopian community. At Oneida, the community practiced the doctrine of complex marriage, where all members of the community were married to each other. The community rejected monogamy and marriage as sources of gender inequality and strictly regulated childbirth and childcare. Unlike previous attempts at self-sufficiency, Oneida's silverware production remained profitable well after Noyes himself had been forced to flee to Canada to avoid persecution for adultery.

By the late nineteenth-century, a number of separatist communities were established in the United States. These communities were often constructed on the frontier, where participants could practice their religion free from outside influence. One such group was the Hutterites, an association of German-speaking separatists that established hundreds of communities in the United States and Canada. Unlike the AMISH, who rejected the use of machinery, the Hutterites were willing to use modern tools and dress in contemporary clothing, within certain limitations. Hutterite society was strictly ordered and work schedules centrally planned. Founded by Jakob Hutter in the sixteenth century, the Hutterites embraced pacifism and a communal lifestyle. Each community in the Hutterite Brethren played an important role in the creation of new Hutterite colonies. Once a colony reached between one hundred and one hundred fifty members, the community split and established a new settlement. Hutterites migrated to the United States in the 1860s and 1870s, settling heavily in the Dakotas. Their numbers

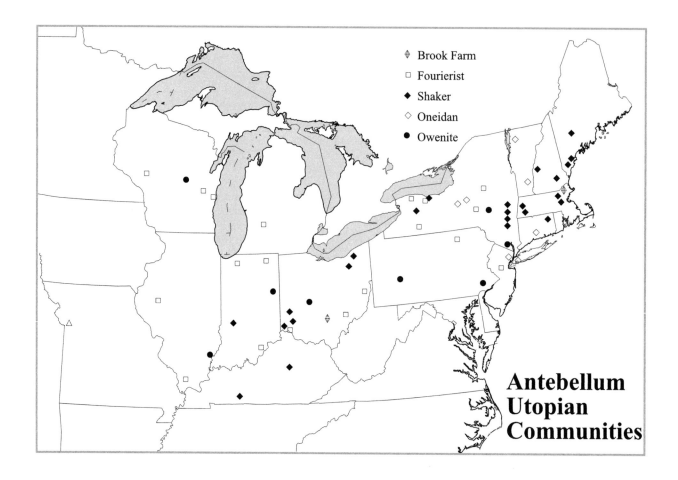

Antebellum Utopian Communities

grew until World War I, when compulsory military service and anti-German sentiment led many to migrate to Canada. The Hutterite Brethren's separatist model, shared by many other religious and secular communities, became common in the following century. Other separatist communes could be found among the Jewish migrants of the Am Olam movement in Louisiana, South Dakota, and Oregon.

Religious Utopian Communities

The industrial problems and the power of Darwinism in the late nineteenth century encouraged the formation of a number of religious Utopian communities. Christian Socialists led by Ralph Albertson established the Christian Commonwealth Colony in Georgia in 1896. There they advocated applied Christianity and published *The Social Gospel* before disbanding four years later due to financial problems. A group of disaffected Methodists, growing out of the Holiness Movement, created the Society of the Burning Bush. Burning Bush established the Metropolitan Institute of Texas in eastern Texas where profits and property were held in common. The community thrived until the agricultural troubles of the 1920s led to a forced sale. Another in the series of the short-lived communes of the 1890s, the Koreshan Unity communes of Cyrus

Teed attacked the Copernican system and taught that the earth was hollow. Teed mixed more standard Utopian ideals of community and cooperation with newer Asian religious traditions. They created communities in Chicago and San Francisco. Eventually, the Chicago group established a third community in Estero, Florida—"New Jerusalem," where most of the Chicago group migrated before eventually dispersing in the 1920s and 1930s. In 1900, another Chicago group, led by the charismatic John Alexander Dowie, established Zion City, which eventually had a population of eight thousand. Dowie raged against the intrusion of the secular world into the religious world. Yet Dowie found little wrong in capitalism. He believed business principles were divinely ordained, attacking even the leaders of the Pullman strike of 1894. Dowie kept a tight grip on community life in Zion City before being overthrown in 1906. Still, Zion City served as jumping off point for numerous post-war healing evangelists, many of whom were Pentecostal, including F. F. Bosworth and Mary Woodworth-Etter. Zion was one of more than twenty-five of these religious Utopian communities established between 1865 and 1920.

Secular Utopias

Secular Utopian communities were also common at the end of the nineteenth century. Many of these were socialist in nature, and many were inspired by Edward Bellamy's *Looking Backward: 2000–1887*. Published in 1888, Bellamy's novel describes how the capitalism of the late nineteenth century matured to a state-sponsored and centrally planned economy that ensured equal wages and equality. It sold over one million copies and influenced a number of communes. One such colony was Equity Colony in Washington. Founded by Wallace Lermond, the colony served as a model for socialist government, one residents hoped would later convert the United States to socialism. Named after Bellamy's 1894 novel, it too ran short of money and was later placed under the management of the New York anarchist Alexander Horr. Another socialist colony was created outside of Nashville, Tennessee, by Julius A. Wayland in 1895. Publisher of the socialist newspaper *The Coming Nation*, Wayland purchased eight hundred acres where middle-class urbanites could mix with socialist intellectuals and poor Tennessee farmers. As it grew larger, the divisions within the community surfaced and ultimately doomed the experiment. In the 1880s, the Kaweah Co-Operative Commonwealth in Tulare County, California, revived the earlier traditions of Brook Farm. Residents included many artists, musicians, and spiritualists. The group fell into infighting, however. Accused of various criminal activities, they were eventually evicted, and Kaweah became part of Sequoia National Park. Still other communities returned to the Shaker and Oneida positions on sexuality and family. The Dawn Valcour Community, a spiritualist–free love commune in Vermont and New York, rejected the rigid Victorian family structure and challenged traditional Protestant definitions of love and marriage.

Anarchist and Other Utopias

In competition with the socialist Utopias were anarchist versions. Josiah Warren founded one such community in Tuscarawas County, Ohio. It was the first American anarchist community, and members invested in the local sawmill. The community eventually collapsed because of epidemic disease and poor finances. Still other societies embraced Henry George's plan to levy a single tax on land values to counteract the wealth accumulated by rental income. Some socialists attempted to establish Single Tax colonies between the 1890s and the 1930s. Fiske Warren of Massachusetts created several such intentional communities, including Tahanto in Massachusetts and Halidon in Maine. While anarchist communities revolved around local control and grassroots democracy, some businesses in the United States found interest in planned communities. One of the most famous of the period was Pullman, Illinois, founded and funded in the 1880s by George Pullman, who manufactured railway cars. Pullman refused to allow its residents, all of whom worked for him, to buy their homes. Residents were paid in Pullman dollars and had to buy from his company store, often at inflated prices. In 1894, Pullman workers protested a planned wage reduction with a strike that eventually led to a national boycott by the American Railway Union, one that made Pullman a symbol of corporate control.

Government Communities

Utopian communities waned in the 1920s. The depression of the 1930s, however, led the U.S. government to create a number of similar settlements, though the theory behind those experiments was not quite "utopian." The RESETTLEMENT ADMINISTRATION, in particular, created a number of agricultural communities, hoping to address the growing refugee problem among sharecroppers in the South. Dyess Colony and St. Francis River Farms in Arkansas were two such, though both of them reverted to planter control almost immediately. In the 1930s a few private communities held on, but they remained small and less influential. Two exceptions were the Sunrise Community (Stelton, New Jersey) and the Catholic Worker Movement, both of which ultimately failed as Utopian communal movements.

In the aftermath of World War II, Utopian communities flourished in the United States, especially during the 1960s and 1970s. The youth counterculture of the 1960s spawned not only the Free Speech Movement and antiwar protests, but a longing for rural communes in California, New Mexico, and as far east as Vermont. These communes, like the Utopians of the 1840s, organized in ways that challenged the economic and sexual standards of the day. They rejected materialism in favor of self-sufficiency and were especially important in their early advocacy of stricter environmental policies. Some were clearly escapist, like The Farm Eco-Village, created in 1971 by hippies from the Haight-Ashbury section of San Francisco. Based in Summertown, Tennessee, the Farm produced its own food and power and embraced the simplicity and self-reliance common to Utopian communities of the nineteenth century.

Still others migrated to new religious communities. The Jesus People Movement grew out of the charismatic revivals of the 1960s. They combined the hippie lifestyle with a deep devotion to Christianity. The "Jesus Freaks" represented the power of the new charismatic Christianity among American youth. New Age movements, ranging from yoga and transcendental meditation to the disciples of Sun Myung Moon and his Unification Church, also attracted a large following in the United States. Still others migrated to more cultic communities. The mass suicide and murder of nine hundred members of the People's Temple at Jonestown, Guyana, in 1977 underscored the danger of ideologically homogenous communities led astray by a charismatic leader. Many of the new cults of the 1970s and 1980s encouraged their members to wall themselves off from larger society, often painting apocalyptic visions of a future filled with totalitarianism, race riots, and communist control. Especially disturbing was the emergence of many neo-fascist and racial-religious communities like Identity Christians, who embraced anti-Semitism and the inevitability of a racial revolution, leading in turn to a popular backlash against such extremism.

Internet as Utopia

While religious fanaticism had given Utopian communities a bad name by the end of the twentieth century, other forces worked to revive them. The numbers of and faith in technology-based Utopian experiments grew throughout the last half of the century. Some Utopian communities consisted of groups of people spread across the United States fighting for a better and safer world, like the SIERRA CLUB and Greenpeace. Others continued to employ the older Utopian model of visionary settlements isolated from the larger world. One such technological community was Celebration, a corporate-sponsored Utopian dream of the Disney Company to create the ideal twenty-first century community. Modern Utopian communities increasingly cross into the digital world. By the 1990s, some believed the early Internet could become the long-promised Utopian paradise, where class, gender, and racial stereotypes might be stripped away in favor of complete equality. At first the Internet seemed the triumph of the anarchist ideal. In many places small groups came together on bulletin board systems (BBS), among other media, to create online communities modeled closely on the Utopian ideals of the nineteenth century. One of the best of the early BBSes of the mid-1990s was Heinous.net, where mostly young midwestern university students came together to discuss art, politics, and culture in a professionally moderated and intellectually intense environment. Yet, by the end of the decade, most of these boards were in decline. The Internet grew more corporate and mirrored the larger society from which the early Internet pioneers hoped to flee.

Many of these communities shared a similar set of assumptions and concerns. The Industrial Revolution had challenged American social institutions, forcing working-class Americans to turn first to labor unions and then to POPULISM. At the same time, industrial society also challenged the assumptions of the Victorian middle class. Many in the transcendentalist era longed for a free-market Utopia, where government nearly ceased to exist and workers profited from a fair balance between capital and labor. Other technocratic Utopians, like Edward Bellamy, Fiske Warren, and George Pullman, believed that the most capable, in contrast to the most political, should be placed in positions of power. Many others, like John Noyes and the Hutterites, found solace in religion, believing that new religious movements would better protect and structure human society. Still others based their Utopias in nature or technology. Many of these philosophies were certainly at odds with one another. Yet the search for an ideal society remained a constant theme throughout the course of American history, dating from the Puritans to the "Jesus Freaks" of the 1970s. All but the most dystopian of the religious movements believed that American society fell short of the ideal and needed great change to ensure the prosperity of all.

BIBLIOGRAPHY

Fogarty, Robert S. *All Things New: American Communes and Utopian Movements, 1860–1914*. Chicago: University of Chicago Press, 1990.

Halloway, Mark. *Heavens on Earth: Utopian Communities in America, 1680–1880*. New York: Dover, 1961.

Kern, Louis. *An Ordered Love: Sex Roles and Sexuality in Victorian Utopias*. Chapel Hill: University of North Carolina Press, 1981.

Shi, David E. *The Simple Life: Plain Living and High Thinking in American Culture*. Athens: University of Georgia Press, 2001.

J. Wayne Jones

See also **Fourierism; New Age Movement.**

VACATION AND LEISURE.

VACATION AND LEISURE. Vacationing began as a privilege of the colonial elite in the eighteenth century, when southern planters and wealthy northerners started to make periodic retreats to mineral springs and seashores. Early destinations included Saratoga Springs in New York, Stafford Springs in Connecticut, Berkeley Springs in Virginia, and Newport in Rhode Island. The Antebellum period saw the number of vacationers and vacation retreats increase. Added to the list of destinations during this time were the resorts around the mineral springs in the Virginias like Red Sulfur Springs and White Sulfur Springs; seaside resorts like Cape May in New Jersey and Cape Cod in Massachusetts; and the Catskill, Adirondack, White, and Green Mountains. Meanwhile, Niagara Falls became the preeminent tourist destination of the nineteenth century. But the vacation remained largely confined to the upper classes and was intended primarily for health reasons. In fact, the word "vacation" to describe these types of journeys did not enter into the American lexicon until the middle of the nineteenth century, and it was at about this time that a considerable debate emerged. Taking time away from work for leisure ran counter to the Puritan ethic, which had pervaded for two centuries; idle time away could be justified for health reasons, but not simply for amusement. The eventual change in public opinion, the emergence of the middle class, and changes in transportation technology following the Civil War gave rise to a vast array of resorts and types of vacations for leisure, recreation, education, and, indeed, health.

The railroads changed the vacation landscape dramatically. With the introduction of the luxurious Pullman Palace Cars after the Civil War, the railroads developed a wider tourist trade. In addition, the completion of the transcontinental railroad in 1869 made the West a viable tourist destination. Mineral springs remained popular and proliferated throughout the country, including Waukesha, Wisconsin, in the Midwest, Hot Springs, Arkansas, in the South, and Congress Springs, California, in the West, to name a few. Seaside resorts began to spring up on the West Coast, for example, in San Diego, where the famous Hotel Del Coronado first opened its doors in 1886, and in Monterey Bay, where the equally famous Hotel Del Monte opened a year later. The railroads were also the main proponents of America's first national parks; The Northern Pacific promoted Yellowstone; the Santa Fe marketed the Grand Canyon; and the Great Northern was instrumental in the development of Glacier National Park in northern Montana.

Hunting, fishing, and outdoor recreation in general became widely popular in the decades bracketing the end of the nineteenth century, especially among America's growing, urban population. Backwoods resort regions emerged across the country wherever there was a concentration of lakes, forests, or mountains. The typical resort was operated on what was called the American plan, which meant that literally everything was provided for guests, including food, shelter, transportation, entertainment, and guides.

The twentieth century witnessed dramatic changes in vacation and leisure activities. The automobile and the development of a nationwide highway system liberated the vacationer from the railroad; they were free to travel virtually anywhere. Camping and inexpensive motels brought the vacation experience within the grasp of almost the entire American population. Attendance swelled at national and state parks in the decades following World War II. Theme parks like Disneyland and Disney World paved the way for new types of family-based vacations, while the thrill of gambling and nightlife put Las Vegas on the map. Once exclusively for the wealthy, inexpensive air travel in the latter decades of the twentieth century allowed middle class Americans to travel to vacation destinations in Europe, Mexico, the Caribbean, and Hawaii.

BIBLIOGRAPHY

Aron, Cindy. *Working at Play: A History of Vacations in the United States.* New York: Oxford University Press, 1999.

Belasco, Warren. *Americans on the Road: From Autocamp to Motel, 1910–1945.* Cambridge, Mass.: MIT Press, 1979.

Jakle, John. *The Tourist: Travel in Twentieth-Century North America.* Lincoln: University of Nebraska Press, 1985.

Timothy Bawden

See also **Hotels and Hotel Industry; Recreation; Resorts and Spas.**

VALLANDIGHAM INCIDENT. Clement L. Vallandigham of Dayton, Ohio, a Copperhead leader and former congressman, was arrested on 5 May 1863 for violating General Ambrose E. Burnside's General Order No. 38, prohibiting expressions of sympathy for the enemy during the American CIVIL WAR. He was convicted by court-martial and sentenced to prison, but President Abraham Lincoln commuted Vallandigham's sentence to banishment to the Confederacy. Vallandigham later left the South for Canada. From exile, he was nominated as the Democratic candidate for governor of Ohio but lost the race.

In early 1864, Vallandigham lost his appeal to the U.S. Supreme Court, which said it lacked authority to overrule a military commission. Vallandigham returned to the United States in June 1864 and was not reimprisoned, even though the terms of his banishment required his detention if he returned.

BIBLIOGRAPHY

Porter, George H. *Ohio Politics during the Civil War Period.* New York: AMS Press, 1968. The original edition was published New York: Columbia University, 1911.

Charles H. Coleman / c. w.

VALLEY FORGE, Continental army encampment during the winter and spring of 1777–1778, is situated on the west bank of the Schuylkill River, in Chester County, Pa., about twenty-five miles northwest of Philadelphia.

After the American defeats at BRANDYWINE, Paoli, and GERMANTOWN and after the British had occupied Philadelphia (then the national capital), Gen. George Washington led 11,000 regular troops to Valley Forge to take up winter quarters. The site provided convenient access to key roads, nearby military supplies, local farmlands, and a nearby health resort that could serve as a hospital for troops. Some officers also thought that the sloping hills, flanked by the Schuylkill and supported in the rear by the high, winding, wooded gorge of Valley Creek, could be made impregnable against attack. As a further safeguard, picket parties were detached to watch the movement of the British.

The encampment at Valley Forge was plagued by bad weather and poor conditions. An unexpectedly early winter, with heavy snows and abnormally freezing weather during Christmas week, prevented the delivery of regular supplies. A January thaw brought mud so deep on the roads that hundreds of army wagons had to be abandoned. Even when transport was available, the Continental Congress's neglect of the army and the commisary officers' failure to forward food, clothing, and supplies by the most available routes added to the troops' sufferings. At one point Washington reported that he had almost 3,000 men who were unfit for duty because they were barefoot "and otherwise naked." On several occasions, he expressed his fears that only extraordinary efforts could prevent the army from disbanding. Many soldiers deserted; the civilian governor of Philadelphia, Joseph Galloway, stated that more than 2,000 deserters had asked for his help. Camp

fever—probably typhus—and smallpox were epidemic during the army's stay at Valley Forge, and medical supplies were lacking. About 2,500 men died and were buried in unmarked graves.

Despite the difficulties, however, the encampment at Valley Forge proved an important turning point for the Continental Army. Marquis de Lafayette, a French aristocrat who embraced the American cause, suggested new practices in training and command that helped boost the troops' morale. At the same time, Baron Friedrich von Steuben introduced efficient drilling techniques that improved military discipline. The formal Franco-American alliance, news of which reached Valley Forge in May 1778, resulted in improved equipment and supplies for the soldiers. All told, efforts like these helped reduce desertions and solidify a core military force in the Continental Army.

BIBLIOGRAPHY

Bill, Alfred Hoyt. *Valley Forge: The Making of an Army.* New York: Harper, 1952.

Boyle, Joseph Lee. *Writings from the Valley Forge Encampment of the Continental Army.* Bowie, Md.: Heritage Books, 2000.

Middlekauff, Robert. *The Glorious Cause: the American Revolution, 1763–1789.* New York: Oxford University Press, 1982.

Harry Emerson Wildes / s. b.

See also **Army, United States; France, Relations with; Revolution, American;** *and vol. 9:* **Life at Valley Forge, 1777–1778.**

VANCOUVER EXPLORATIONS. In 1791, the British dispatched Captain George Vancouver on a multifaceted naval mission to the Pacific Northwest. He was to resolve a fur-trading dispute centering on the island that would become the British Columbia city that bears his name. He was also ordered to explore the river systems of Puget Sound, particularly the Columbia River, to determine how far into the continent they were navigable. Finally, he was to map the entire Pacific Northwest, an area that encompasses Oregon, Washington, and British Columbia. A naval captain with training as a scientist, he was eminently suited to the task. Evidence of this mission is made clear in his 1798 three-volume publication, *A Voyage of Discovery to the North Pacific Ocean and Round the World.*

Unfortunately for Britain's deepening interest in the area, the London publication made common knowledge of the economic and strategic potential of the Pacific Northwest in general, and the Columbia River area in particular. It was the first authoritative study of the area; during the ensuing generation, key Americans were made aware of the volumes and absorbed its contents for various reasons.

Among them, President Thomas Jefferson was made familiar with Vancouver's work. It was a motivating force

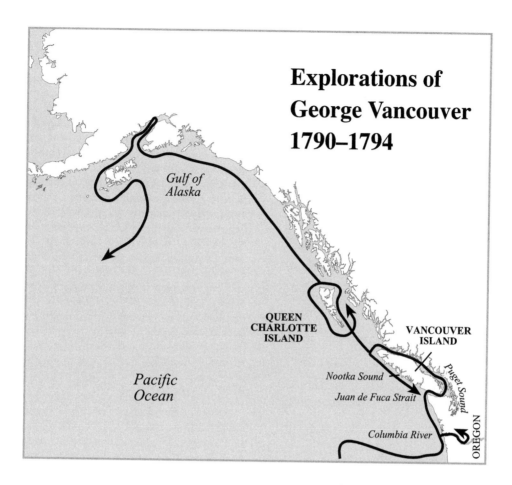

Explorations of George Vancouver 1790–1794

Gulf of
Alaska

QUEEN
CHARLOTTE
ISLAND

VANCOUVER
ISLAND

Pacific
Ocean

Nootka Sound

Juan de Fuca Strait

Puget Sound

Columbia River

OREGON

in Jefferson's decision to authorize the Lewis and Clark Expedition in 1803 to explore an overland route to the Pacific Northwest. The book defined American interest in the area at the highest level. Lewis and Clark's mapping and exploration, reported in 1807, in turn moved John Jacob Astor to secure an economic as well as territorial foothold by establishing his fur-trading outpost in Astoria, in what later became Oregon. The War Hawks in Congress in 1812 stirred the expansionist dreams that would become the notion of Manifest Destiny a generation later.

But in the interim, John Quincy Adams—first as a student in London, later as a diplomat in Europe, and finally as a Secretary of State (1817–1825) and President (1825–1829)—understood clearly the inexorability of the westward movement. He knew intimately from its first publication the detailed and significant work George Vancouver had undertaken for the British government. As Secretary of State, Adams picked up on Jefferson's interest in establishing a territory west of the Cascade Mountains and touching the Pacific Ocean. Secretary Adams, in 1818, fixed the Canadian-U.S. border at the forty-ninth parallel in the West beyond the Rockies, leaving open the door to America's successful 1846 claim to the territory that would become the states of Oregon and Washington.

Behind all of this complex American interest lay the hard-won knowledge that George Vancouver's exploration uncovered. That his discovery was so facilely transmitted early on to the rest of the world is strange. Why was he allowed to publish his findings in such detail? Although he was a scientist in his own right, he was also a naval captain whose expedition was wholly publicly financed. One can only conclude that, for whatever reason, Whitehall was "asleep at the switch."

BIBLIOGRAPHY

Bemis, Samuel Flagg. *John Quincy Adams and the Foundations of American Foreign Policy.* Westport, Conn.: Greenwood Press, 1981.

Malone, Dumas. *Jefferson and His Time.* 6 vols. Boston: Little, Brown, 1981.

Carl E. Prince

See also **Astoria; Lewis and Clark Expedition; Manifest Destiny; War Hawks.**

VANDALIA COLONY was an aborted settlement on the OHIO RIVER, sponsored in the early 1770s by the Grand Ohio Company, often referred to as the Walpole

Company. Although the colony never materialized, the movement behind it was typical of the great land speculation schemes that were so numerous in England and America in the eighteenth century. This project counted among its backers many prominent persons—Benjamin Franklin, for example—on both sides of the Atlantic.

The plan originated in the Indiana land grant, offered by the Six Nations to a group of PENNSYLVANIA traders in 1768 to reimburse them for losses sustained in Pontiac's War. Samuel Wharton and William Trent, agents of the Indiana Company, proceeded to England early in 1769 to seek royal confirmation of the grant. This group was reorganized on 27 December 1769 as the Grand Ohio Company. It then petitioned to purchase an additional tract of some 20 million acres south of the Ohio River.

The new colony, to be called Vandalia, would have a separate government of the royal type. Although many of the proprietors were Englishmen holding high official positions, the project encountered strong opposition from influential British quarters and from rival speculative interests in VIRGINIA that claimed almost the same territory. In 1773 the grant appeared imminent, but the outbreak of hostilities in 1775 ended all hope of success. In 1781 Wharton and others tried to persuade Congress to recognize the abortive Vandalia grant, but strong opposition finally killed it.

BIBLIOGRAPHY

James, Alfred P. *The Ohio Company: Its Inner History.* Pittsburgh, Pa.: University of Pittsburgh Press, 1959.

Wayne E. Stevens / A. R.

See also **Baynton, Wharton, and Morgan; Land Companies; Migrations, Internal; Ohio; Ohio Company of Virginia; Westward Migration.**

VANHORNE'S LESSEE V. DORRANCE, 2 U.S. (2 Dallas) 304 (1795), was one of the earliest cases in which a federal court asserted the right to disregard a state law that was held to be in conflict with the state constitution. A Pennsylvania law divesting one person of property and vesting it in another without compensation, according to Justice William Paterson, was inconsistent with the "inherent and unalienable rights of man." Paterson also viewed the Pennsylvania law as a violation of the sanctity of contracts as guaranteed by the state constitution and the Constitution of the United States, and therefore declared it unconstitutional and void.

BIBLIOGRAPHY

Hall, Kermit L. *The Supreme Court and Judicial Review in American History.* Washington, D.C.: American Historical Association, 1985.

P. Orman Ray / A. R.

See also **Appeals from Colonial Courts; Contract Clause; *Holmes v. Walton;* Judicial Review; Judiciary; *Marbury v. Madison; Trevett v. Weeden.***

VATICAN II. Numerous commentators agree that the Second Vatican Council (1962–1965) was the single most important event in twentieth-century religious history, although seldom is it cited for its significance in U.S. history. Yet Vatican II was a watershed in American cultural life, comparable in significance to often-cited events like the Armory Show of 1913 or the 1969 Woodstock music festival. Like these events, Vatican II illuminated and ratified a series of influential cultural trends. Not only did it influence tens of millions of U.S. Catholics, but thanks to the broad knowledge of it among the American public, Vatican II also promoted sustained conversation among multiple belief systems—Catholicism, Protestantism, Judaism, and a variety of other religions and spiritual movements. As such, it helped foment the historically unparalleled blending of religious traditions and practices characteristic of the late-twentieth-century United States, and consequently, it served as a critical event in cultural history, announcing the arrival of what some have called religion's postmodern age. Vatican II gave evidence of a new deference on the part of church authorities to the idea that both the secular and religious world provided multiple sources of truth and of the common good, and it represented a notable democratizing influence within the Catholic Church.

Vatican II was an extended meeting in Rome of over 2,600 Catholic bishops from around the world with 240 U.S bishops attending, and it had five especially defining goals: aiming to elaborate a positive relationship between Catholicism and the modern world; abandoning the format of harsh denunciations (anathemas) used at previous church councils; affirming the fundamental human right to religious liberty; affirming that fundamental truths were taught by religions other than Roman Catholicism; and reforming Catholic spirituality and church governance. By the mid-twentieth century, church leaders had long pronounced their opposition to modern Enlightenment principles that eroded belief in the supernatural, divine revelation, and hierarchical authority; however, Vatican II sought to reconcile church teachings with modern principles, praising the advances of science and technology, democratic government, and religious toleration. At the request of its instigator, Pope John XXIII, the Vatican Council adopted a conciliatory rhetoric in each of its official pronouncements, avoiding the customary confrontational language and critical statements directed toward other religious bodies or governments. Its civility, in turn, elicited praise for the Council from numerous non-Catholic sources. Marking a major transformation in official teaching, the Vatican II document *On Religious Freedom* (drafted by the U.S. Jesuit priest and theologian John Courtney Murray) stated that each individual possessed the right to choose his or her religion and practice it free from political persecution; previously, official church teaching was that "error possesses no rights," and that since other religions, unlike Catholicism, advocated religious errors, they did not command the protection of law. Further, pronouncements on ecumenism and non-

Christian religions acknowledged that numerous world religions also taught fundamental truths, rescinding past denunciations, yet stopping short of rescinding the excommunication of key figures like Protestant reformer Martin Luther.

While Vatican II's other distinguishing marks involved external affairs, the reform of spirituality and church governance prompted internal renovation. Thanks to modern modes of communication that permitted rapid transmission of information, Vatican II was the most uniform and comprehensive reform initiative in church history. Where the reform program of the sixteenth-century Council of Trent took many decades to disseminate and implement throughout the Catholic world, Vatican II reforms spread swiftly. Consequently, the period after 1965 brought rapid transformation and turmoil, often inducing bitter division and disagreement among Catholics. The two most significant changes in spiritual life were, first, the reform of the Mass (celebration of Eucharist), especially the use of the vernacular language rather than Latin and the increased participation of lay people in its sacred rituals, and, second, the "universal call to holiness," which asserted that each individual possessed a fundamental responsibility for cultivating the spiritual life and bringing spiritual principles to bear in society, culture, and politics. Additionally, the reform of church governance provoked the establishment of deliberative bodies at the local and national levels, and lay Catholics were encouraged to assist in governance and leadership through democratically elected parish councils and numerous ministerial activities. Lay leadership grew, in part, due to the declining number of priests in the decades after 1960. Increased emphasis on individual responsibility and an increase in democratic governance frequently led to clashing viewpoints, encouraging the formation of opposing ideological camps among many lay Catholics, often referred to as the "liberal" and "conservative" wings within the church. Additionally, the emphasis on individual responsibility helped normalize public dissent from the teachings of the church hierarchy and led to the notably heightened value of individual conscience in the moral and religious imagination.

BIBLIOGRAPHY

Appleby, R. Scott, and Mary Jo Weaver, eds. *Being Right: Conservative Catholics in America.* Bloomington: Indiana University Press, 1995.

Flannery, Austin, ed. *Vatican II: Constitutions, Decrees, and Declarations.* Collegeville, Minn.: Liturgical Press, 1992. Source for official Vatican II pronouncements.

Komonchak, Joseph A., and Guiseppe Alberrigo, eds. *History of Vatican II.* 5 vols. Maryknoll, N.Y.: Orbis Press, 1995–2002. A comprehensive survey of the deliberations in Rome.

Morris, Charles R. *American Catholic: The Saints and Sinners Who Built America's Most Powerful Church.* New York: Time Books, 1997.

Weaver, Mary Jo, ed. *What's Left? Liberal American Catholics.* Bloomington: Indiana University Press, 1999.

Wuthnow, Robert. *After Heaven: Spirituality in the United States since the 1950s.* Berkeley: University of California Press, 1998.

James P. McCartin

See also **Catholicism; Religion and Religious Affiliation.**

VAUDEVILLE. Vaudeville flourished as a form of variety theater from the 1880s to the late 1930s, when it succumbed to competing forms of popular entertainment, particularly "talking" pictures. Recent historians have portrayed vaudeville as a place of struggle over class, race, and gender relations and identities in industrial America. Vaudeville also saw the application of consolidation and franchise techniques to the organization of popular entertainment. Benjamin Franklin Keith may have been the first American entrepreneur to use the term vaudeville, adapted from the French *vaux-de-vire*, referring to popular songs from the French province of Normandy (the valleys of Vire), or from *voix de ville* (voices of the town).

Keith is also credited with refining the vaudeville format. He and a partner opened a "dime museum" in Boston in 1883, and then expanded their operations to include singers and animal acts. By the mid-1890s, Keith and his subsequent partner, Edward Albee, owned vaudeville theaters in Boston, Philadelphia, New York, and Providence. According to Keith, vaudeville differed from variety shows, burlesque, minstrel shows, and sideshows in its intentional appeal to "higher" cultural tastes and audiences that included women and children. The Keith vision of genteel popular entertainment resonated with Progressive Era acculturation anxieties, racialist ideologies, and campaigns to sanitize and organize American cities.

Although performers and audiences may have been disciplined to a bourgeois cultural standard on the "bigtime" Keith and later Orpheum circuits (the western circuit that merged with the Keith enterprise in 1927), the "small-time" vaudeville theaters nourished their own local audiences, often working class, immigrant, or African American, and their own kinds of humor. While there was an all-black circuit, managed by the Theatre Owners Booking Association (TOBA), from the beginning African American performers also appeared in white-owned vaudeville (which blacks called "white time"). The Whitman Sisters maintained a popular African American vaudeville company that included Bill "Bojangles" Robinson. In a brutally racist society, African American performers and audiences found ways to resist segregation on stage and in the theaters.

When vaudeville's popularity began to fade in the 1920s, some of its stars carried vaudeville forms into the new media of radio, nightclub entertainment, films, and later, television. These included George Burns and Gracie Allen, Jack Benny, Milton Berle, Sarah Bernhardt, Eubie Blake, Sammy Davis Jr., W. C. Fields, Cary Grant, the Marx Brothers, Phil Silvers, and Ethel Waters.

Crystal Hall. A theater on East Fourteenth Street in New York City, c. 1900, where the performances included "A Russian Spy" and "Love in the Ghetto."

BIBLIOGRAPHY

George-Graves, Nadine. *The Royalty of Vaudeville: The Whitman Sisters and the Negotiation of Race, Gender, and Class in African American Theater, 1900–1940.* New York: St. Martin's Press, 2000.

Kibler, M. Alison. *Rank Ladies: Gender and Cultural Hierarchy in American Vaudeville.* Chapel Hill: University of North Carolina Press, 1999.

Slide, Anthony. *The Encyclopedia of Vaudeville.* Westport, Conn.: Greenwood Press, 1994.

Mina Carson

See also **Burlesque.**

VCR. *See* **Videocassette Recorder.**

VEAZIE BANK V. FENNO, 75 U.S. (8 Wallace) 533 (1869). In 1866 Congress imposed a 10 percent tax on the notes issued by state banks in order to drive the notes out of circulation. In 1869 the Supreme Court, in *Veazie Bank v. Fenno,* upheld the constitutionality of the enactment on the ground that this destructive use of the taxing power was for an object clearly within the constitutional powers of Congress—the power to regulate the currency of the nation.

BIBLIOGRAPHY

Bensel, Richard Franklin. *Yankee Leviathan: The Origins of Central State Authority in America, 1859–1877.* New York: Cambridge University Press, 1990.

W. A. Robinson / A. R.

See also **Banking: State Banks; Legal Tender; Money; Reconstruction; Taxation.**

VEGETARIANISM, the practice of eating a diet composed primarily or wholly of vegetables, grains, fruits, nuts, and seeds, with or without eggs and dairy products, was endorsed in the United States in 1838 by the American Health Convention. Various proponents such as William Alcott (1798–1859) advanced the vegetarian cause for ethical and health reasons throughout the late nineteenth and early twentieth centuries. Vegetarianism enjoyed new attention and became a political stance with the counterculture of the 1960s as abuses and inefficiencies of mass-market meat production were brought to light. Still, in 1971 only 1 percent of U.S. citizens described themselves as vegetarians. But vegetarianism became an increasingly attractive and accepted dietary option by the century's end. A 2000 Zogby Poll sponsored by the Vegetarian Resource Group found that 2.5 percent of respondents reported not eating meat, poultry, or fish while 4.5 percent reported not eating meat. Additionally, the National Restaurant Association reported that in 2001 approximately eight out of ten restaurants offered vegetarian entrees.

BIBLIOGRAPHY

Root, Waverly Lewis, and Richard de Rochemont. *Eating in America: A History.* New York, 1976.

Spencer, Colin. *The Heretic's Feast: A History of Vegetarianism.* Hanover, N.H.: University Press of New England, 1995.

Loren Butler Feffer

See also **Diets and Dieting; Health Food Industry; Nutrition and Vitamins.**

VENEREAL DISEASE. *See* **Sexually Transmitted Diseases.**

VERACRUZ INCIDENT. When Victoriano Huerta seized the Mexican presidency in 1913, the United States refused to recognize him. Early in 1914, when Tampico was under martial law, some U.S. Marines were arrested there, but they were quickly released, with apologies. Admiral Henry T. Mayo insisted that Mexico fire a twenty-one gun salute to the American flag, and President Woodrow Wilson supported this demand. When Mexico refused to comply, Wilson ordered a fleet to Veracruz. Troops landed on 21 April 1914 and, aided by bombardment, took the city, with an American loss of seventeen killed and sixty-three wounded. American political pressure forced Huerta out in July; he fled to Jamaica.

BIBLIOGRAPHY

Quirk, Robert E. *An Affair of Honor: Woodrow Wilson and the Occupation of Veracruz.* New York: Norton, 1967. The original edition was published in 1962.

Alvin F. Harlow / c. w.

See also **Defense, National; Mexico, Relations with.**

VERMONT. What we now know as Vermont is believed to have had an ABENAKI Indian presence since 9000 B.C., peaking in population during the sixteenth century. Even before direct contact with Europeans, however, Vermont's inhabitants, western Abenakis, were depleted through wars with the Iroquois and by pathogens introduced by Europeans and transmitted through eastern Abenakis from Canada. In 1609, the French explorer Samuel de Champlain became the first European to reconnoiter Vermont, sailing up the lake that bears his name and initiating an alliance between the French and the Abenakis against the English and the Iroquois Confederacy that persisted until the French were driven from North America in 1763.

During that time the struggle for North America kept the region in turmoil, and Vermont attracted few European settlers. The Abenakis, augmented by a southern New England diaspora after KING PHILIP'S WAR (1675–1677), joined with the French to raid southern New England settlements in the Connecticut River valley during the colonial wars. In 1724, to protect settlers from these attacks, Massachusetts erected Fort Dummer, the first British settlement in Vermont, situated near present-day Brattleboro and west of the Connecticut River. The French were simultaneously occupying the Lake Champlain valley, building forts from Isle La Motte (1666) south to Ticonderoga (1755), but, focusing on the fur trade, they made relatively little effort at colonization. By 1754, New France numbered 75,000 European settlers contrasted with 1.5 million in British America.

Land Disputes and the Revolutionary Era

The FRENCH AND INDIAN WAR (1754–1763), the North American counterpart to the Seven Years' War in Europe, ended with a British victory, and what was to become Vermont fell totally under British sovereignty. The region, inaccurately mapped and sparsely settled, was plagued with conflicting charters and overlapping land claims. Royal decrees at times compounded the confusion. Shortly after a boundary dispute between Massachusetts and New Hampshire was resolved in New Hampshire's favor, New Hampshire was ordered to maintain Fort Dummer or have it restored to Massachusetts jurisdiction. Seizing upon this as having established New Hampshire's border west of the Connecticut River, New Hampshire governor Benning Wentworth claimed his province's boundary extended to Lake Champlain and in 1750 issued a grant for the town of Bennington at the westernmost edge of his claim. At the outbreak of the French and Indian War he had chartered fifteen additional towns, and in 1759, after the French were driven from the Champlain valley, he resumed issuing New Hampshire patents until by 1763 they totaled 138. Meanwhile New York Province, brandishing a 1664 grant by King Charles II to his brother the Duke of York (later James II), maintained that its eastern border extended to the Connecticut River and began issuing patents more remunerative to the crown and occasionally overlapping New Hampshire's.

In 1764 a king's order in council ruled the New York border to be the west bank of the Connecticut River, placing all of modern-day Vermont under New York jurisdiction. New Hampshire titleholders interpreted "to be" to mean from the date of the order in council, thus validating land titles issued before 1764. New York contended the ruling was retroactive and attempted to eject settlers on New Hampshire grants. In 1770 the issue was argued before an Albany County court at which Ethan Allen served as agent for the Wentworth titleholders. The court dismissed New Hampshire claims, and the Wentworth titleholders responded with the GREEN MOUNTAIN BOYS, unofficial military units led by Ethan Allen, Seth Warner, and others from western Vermont that used force and intimidation to frustrate New York's efforts at ejection. Many of the Green Mountain Boys held heavy investments in New Hampshire titles. East of the Green Mountains, where smaller landholders dominated, title disputes were resolved through payment to New York of reconfirmation fees, but other issues, particularly high court costs and debt proceedings, precipitated a March 1775 courthouse riot in Westminster that left two dead and collapsed New York authority in the Connecticut Valley.

In April, with Concord and Lexington sparking the American Revolution, New York lost any chance of reclaiming Vermont, especially when Ethan Allen and the Green Mountain Boys, along with Benedict Arnold, stormed the British Fort Ticonderoga in New York that May, capturing cannon for the Continental army in Boston and closing the Champlain-Hudson corridor to in-

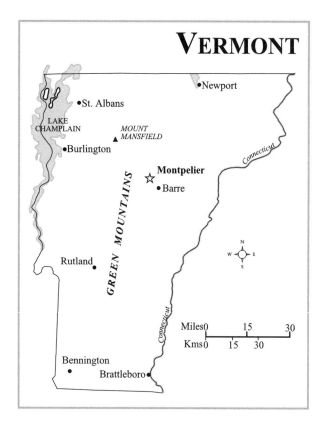

VERMONT

Newport

St. Albans

LAKE CHAMPLAIN

MOUNT MANSFIELD

Burlington

GREEN MOUNTAINS

Montpelier

Barre

Connecticut

Rutland

N
W · E
S

Connecticut

Miles 0 — 15 — 30
Kms 0 — 15 — 30

Bennington

Brattleboro

vasion from Canada until it was recaptured by the British. Shortly afterward the Continental Congress authorized an army regiment of Green Mountain Rangers that fought under the command of Seth Warner. In January 1777 representatives from New Hampshire Grant towns declared their independence from New York and Great Britain and in July drafted a constitution, scheduled elections, and established a government for the state of New Connecticut (estimated population 10,000), later renamed Vermont.

Despite its assertions of independence, Vermont's existence was in immediate jeopardy. That July, British general John Burgoyne, leading an army from Canada to the Hudson River, recaptured Fort Ticonderoga and sent Vermont settlers scurrying south. A rear guard detachment commanded by Seth Warner to cover the retreat from Ticonderoga was defeated at Hubbardton (the only Revolutionary War battle fought in Vermont), but in August the tide turned. New Hampshire and Vermont troops under General John Stark defeated a British force near Bennington. In September, Burgoyne surrendered his army at the Battle of Saratoga (see SARATOGA CAMPAIGN).

New York's opposition to Vermont's independence and the failure of Congress to admit it as a state until 1791 induced Vermont to assume initiatives associated with a sovereign nation, most notably coining its own currency

and maintaining a foreign policy. The Haldimand Negotiations (1781) were dealings with the governor-general of Canada that involved Vermont's return to the British empire in return for British promises not to invade Vermont or New York. The negotiations collapsed after General Cornwallis' defeat at Yorktown. They are still debated as either sincere negotiations or ploys by Vermont to obtain military security. Another Vermont initiative was to annex amenable border towns in western New Hampshire and eastern New York, so-called east and west unions, which aroused considerable New Hampshire, New York, and congressional displeasure. Vermont relinquished control of the towns, anticipating this would promote admission into the United States, but it was not until 4 March 1791, after Vermont "bought itself free" by paying New York $30,000 to settle disputed land titles, that it was admitted as the fourteenth state.

Statehood and Nineteenth-Century Vermont
Statehood marked the eclipse of Vermont's first generation of leaders. Thomas Chittenden, who, save for one year had served as governor from 1778, continued to serve until 1797, but his political allies were succeeded by younger men, legally trained Revolutionary War veterans and more recent settlers who poured into the state from southern New England. The census of 1791 recorded a population of 85,341 and the 1810 census 217,895. The War of 1812 put an end to Vermont's prosperity and population growth. It was the first state without an ocean port, and western Vermont was dependent upon trade with Canada down Lake Champlain. The suspension of this trade in 1808 and then by the war stimulated popular support for smuggling and political opposition to the party of Jefferson as well as the war itself. East of the Green Mountains, the Connecticut River was the principal commercial artery, linking Vermont with southern New England, but the war was no more popular in that area.

A modest prosperity was restored by the mid 1820s after the American consul in Lisbon returned to Vermont with 200 head of merino sheep. By 1840 the state boasted almost 1,690,000 merinos and preeminence among wool-producing states. Sheep grazing, which was possible on rocky uplands and less labor intensive than most other forms of agriculture, stimulated land clearing and emigration. It declined after 1840, the victim of western competition and the lowering of the protective tariff, and dairying began a steady growth. Before 1840 daughters of farm families frequently left the homesteads to work in textile mills, some as far away as New Hampshire or Massachusetts, never to return. After 1840 immigrants increasingly staffed textile mills in Vermont and elsewhere.

The Vermont economy had also been transformed by the Champlain-Hudson cutoff to the Erie Canal that opened in 1823. Promoted for its potential to provide access to a wider market for Vermont produce, it instead opened Vermont to western wheat and helped redirect the state's economy toward sheep farming, textile mills, and dairying. The Champlain-Hudson cutoff also loosened western Vermont's ties to Canada and, by reducing the cost and difficulty of immigration, opened the West for settlers from Vermont.

Railroads reached Vermont in 1848, and by 1855 there were over 500 miles of track. Designed to carry freight between Atlantic ports and the Great Lakes rather than to serve Vermont, the railroads nonetheless had a tremendous impact on the state and were the largest Vermont enterprises until the twentieth century. Thousands of Irish entered the state as construction workers, and, along with French-Canadians who worked in textile mills and on farms, constituted almost the entire immigrant population. These new immigrants, mostly Catholic, were often viewed by the almost exclusively Protestant natives as threatening American values. Their apprehensions were heightened in 1853 when the Burlington Catholic Diocese was established.

Economic and demographic disruptions spawned ferment. Vermont became virulently anti-Masonic, electing an Anti-Masonic Party governor and in 1832 becoming the only state to vote for the Anti-Mason presidential candidate (see ANTI-MASONIC MOVEMENTS). By 1836 the Anti-Masons gave way to the newly formed Whig Party, and workingmen's associations thrived alongside religious revivals that included Millerites, whose founder was sometime Poultney resident William Miller, and John Humphrey Noyes's Perfectionist Society, founded in Putney. Mormon founders Joseph Smith and Brigham Young were Vermont natives. Temperance and antislavery, both church-rooted movements, had widespread appeal. Temperance societies dated from the 1820s, and in 1853 the state banned the manufacture and sale of liquor by a narrow vote. Not always rigidly enforced, it remained law until 1902. Antislavery enjoyed even broader support. Vermonters, evincing pride that their 1777 constitution was the first to prohibit slavery and provide universal male suffrage, championed congressional antislavery resolutions, state acts to annul fugitive slave laws, and gave rise to the LIBERTY PARTY and then the FREE SOIL PARTY, which along with the feeble Democratic Party were able to deny the Whigs popular majorities and left the election of governor to the legislature.

In 1854 state government was paralyzed by party fractionalization after passage of the nationally divisive KANSAS-NEBRASKA ACT, occurring as it did on the heels of the temperance contest and the 1853 election of a Democratic governor by a legislative coalition of Free Soilers and Democrats. In July 1854, Whigs and Free Soilers convened, agreed upon a common platform and slate of candidates, referred to themselves as Republicans, won a large popular majority, and in 1856 and 1860 led the nation in support of Republican presidential candidates. Vermont's overwhelming support for Lincoln and the Union cause accommodated a wide range of attitudes toward slavery along with an anti-southern bias. In addition to resenting such pro-southern measures as the Kansas-

Nebraska Act, Vermonters blamed southern opposition for their failure to obtain a higher tariff and national banking legislation. What most united Vermonters, however, was their support for the Union.

Almost 35,000, one of four adult males, served in the army during the Civil War, and casualty rates were among the highest of any state. The war brought economic prosperity while shifting much of the burden of farm work and financial management to women. In some instances war casualties cost towns almost their entire male populations. The northernmost action of the war occurred in October 1864 when Confederate soldiers crossed the Canadian border to rob St. Albans banks. Although the St. Albans raid provoked heated diplomatic negotiation between Britain, Canada, and the United States, it had no impact on the war.

After the war, the Republican Party dominated Vermont politics. Having saved the Union and enacted a protective tariff and national banking act with critical support from Congressman Justin Morrill, Republicanism became a civic religion, escaping meaningful challenge until the second half of the twentieth century. The state frequently returned over 200 Republicans to a Vermont house (with 246 members) and all 30 of its state senators. Agriculture remained the state's major economic pursuit, with dairy farming shaping its landscape. With the advent of the refrigerated railway car, shipping cream, butter, and cheese gave way to the more lucrative marketing of fresh milk. Sustained by a treaty with Canada, the lumber industry built Burlington into one of the busiest inland ports in the nation. The machine-tool industry in the Connecticut River valley, the platform-scale works in St. Johnsbury, independent marble companies in the Rutland area (consolidated into the Vermont Marble Company by Redfield Proctor), and independent Barre granite operations along with the railroads constituted the bulk of Vermont industry.

Vermont governors, who invariably served a single two-year term, were almost always business-oriented industrialists, some of whom presided over reform administrations. Vermont's political agenda, however, was usually dominated by the legislature. With one representative from each town irrespective of population, farmers were often a legislative majority and always the largest occupational category despite declining numbers. Vermont farms could seldom support large families, and emigration was so common that by 1860 over 40 percent of native-born Vermonters lived in other states. European immigration barely kept the population constant, and while the larger communities gained population, the smaller communities declined to where it became increasingly difficult to amass the personnel and other resources to meet municipal obligations. Soon after the Civil War the legislature began voting to shift expenditures from towns to the state on a need basis. From 1890 until 1931, when a state income tax was enacted, state levies on town grand lists were applied to bolster educational, welfare, and highway resources among the poorer communities.

The Twentieth Century

Efforts to stimulate the state economy through tourism, initially undertaken by the railroads, became a government operation. As the railroad gave way to the automobile, Vermont's transportation network proved inadequate for either tourism or its internal needs. In the fall of 1927 the state suffered a disastrous flood that cost lives, wiped out homes and industrial sites, and destroyed much of the state's transportation network. Within weeks a recovery effort, planned and financed with federal support, ushered Vermont into the era of hard-surfaced roads and state debt to support improvements. Even the Great Depression, however, could not seduce Vermont from its Republican Party allegiance, although the state was an enthusiastic participant in many New Deal programs. Until 1958, Democratic challenges were usually ceremonial. The real contests were Republican primaries.

The first signs of recovery from the Great Depression appeared in 1939 in the machine-tool industry that created a boom in the Springfield area never achieved in the rest of the state, although World War II brought prosperity to most sectors of the economy along with an increased presence of organized labor among both blue- and white-collar workers. There were 1,200 killed or missing in action among the 30,000 men and women who served in the military, and returning veterans contributed mightily to Colonel Ernest Gibson's upset of the more conservative candidate in the 1946 Republican gubernatorial primary. Although more traditional Republican governors succeeded Gibson in office, the state retained his policy of implementing state and federal welfare, education, and construction programs. This policy was accelerated with the election of a Democratic governor, Philip Hoff, in 1962, and the implementation of Great Society initiatives.

In 1965 the Vermont legislature convened under court reapportionment orders. The house was reapportioned down from 246 to 150 delegates with districts determined by population. (Previously, the twenty-two largest cities and towns had housed over half the state's population and paid 64 percent of the state's income tax and 50 percent of the property tax, but elected only 9 percent of the house members.) The senate was kept at 30 members, but county lines were no longer inviolate. Without reapportionment it is unlikely Republicans would ever have lost control of the legislature. Since Hoff, the governor's office has alternated between parties, and in 1984, Democrats elected Madeleine Kunin, the state's first female governor. In 1964 it cast its electoral votes for a Democratic presidential candidate for the first time, and since 1992 it has been regularly in the Democratic column. Yet the state has also demonstrated a tolerance for mavericks. In 2000, Vermont's congressional delegation was made up of one Democrat senator, one Republican senator, and one Independent House member. In 2001, Senator James Jef-

fords left the Republican Party to become an independent, throwing the control of the Senate to the Democrats while attaining favorable poll ratings. Elections during this period have been dogged by controversy over Vermont Supreme Court decisions leading to legislation equalizing educational resources statewide and providing same-sex couples rights similar to those possessed by married couples.

The latter, labeled the Civil Union Act (2000), was the first of its kind in the nation, and observers attributed its passage to the state's evolving demography and economy. Native-owned industries have been absorbed into conglomerates, and IBM, which moved into the state in 1957, has become Vermont's largest private employer. Economic development attracted additional growth. In 2000, Vermont's population stood at 608,827, with two-thirds of the growth since 1830 occurring after 1960. The interstate highway system brought Vermont to within a few hours of over 40 million urban dwellers. Tourism grew rapidly. Skiing spread from its 1930s roots to mountains and hillsides irrespective of environmental degradation or the ability of the local government to provide essential services. In 1970, Republican Governor Deane Davis gained approval of Act 250 to mandate permits requiring developers to prove the project's ecological soundness. Despite flaws and opposition, Act 250 and subsequent modifications have proven salutary.

A related effort has been made to retain Vermont's pastoral landscape of rapidly disappearing dairy farms. From 1993 to 2000 the number of dairy farms decreased from 2,500 to 1,700, with most of the decrease among farms of fewer than 100 cows. Yet because average production rose to 17,000 pounds of milk per cow per year, production increased. Some farmers participated in a 1986 federal program to curb overproduction by selling their herds to the federal government and subsequently selling their land to developers. In 1993 the National Trust for Historic Preservation designated the entire state an "endangered place." Nonetheless, farmland preservation projects that utilize differential tax rates and conservation trusts have been operating with some success.

With a population less than 609,000, Vermont is the second-smallest state in the nation, boasting the least-populated state capital and the smallest biggest city of any state. With a larger percentage of its population living in communities of fewer than 2,500 than any other state, it lays claim to being the most rural.

BIBLIOGRAPHY

Albers, Jan. *Hands on the Land: A History of the Vermont Landscape.* Cambridge, Mass.: MIT Press, 2000.

Anderson, Elin L. *We Americans: A Study of Cleavage in an American City.* Cambridge, Mass.: Harvard University Press, 1937. Reprint, New York: Russell and Russell, 1967. Burlington in the 1930s.

Bassett, T. D. Seymour. *The Growing Edge: Vermont Villages, 1840–1880.* Montpelier: Vermont Historical Society, 1992.

Bellesiles, Michael A. *Revolutionary Outlaws: Ethan Allen and the Struggle for Independence on the Early American Frontier.* Charlottesville: University Press of Virginia, 1993.

Bryan, Frank M. *Yankee Politics in Rural Vermont.* Hanover, N.H.: University Press of New England, 1974.

Gillies, Paul S., and D. Gregory Sanford, eds. *Records of the Council of Censors of the State of Vermont.* Montpelier: Secretary of State, 1991.

Graffagnino, J. Kevin, Samuel B. Hand, and Gene Sessions, eds. *Vermont Voices, 1609 Through the 1990s: A Documentary History of the Green Mountain State.* Montpelier: Vermont Historical Society, 1999.

Kunin, Madeleine. *Living a Political Life.* New York: Knopf, 1994.

Ludlum, David M. *Social Ferment in Vermont, 1790–1850.* New York: Columbia University Press, 1939. Reprint, New York: AMS Press, 1966.

Roth, Randolph A. *The Democratic Dilemma: Religion, Reform, and the Social Order in the Connecticut River Valley of Vermont, 1791–1850.* New York: Cambridge University Press, 1987.

Shalhope, Robert E. *Bennington and the Green Mountain Boys: The Emergence of Liberal Democracy in Vermont, 1760–1850.* Baltimore and London: Johns Hopkins University Press, 1996.

Sherman, Michael, ed. *Vermont State Government Since 1965.* Burlington: Center for Research on Vermont and Snelling Center for Government, 1999.

Samuel B. Hand

VERRAZANO-NARROWS BRIDGE. This suspension bridge connects Brooklyn and Staten Island in NEW YORK CITY. Though the idea had been discussed for more than eighty years, the bridge became part of Robert Moses's plan to modernize the city and open avenues of automotive transportation. Moses's influence overcame objections to the bridge, and construction began in September 1959, according to a design by Swiss engineer Othmar Ammann. The bridge, named for Giovanni da Verrazano—the first European to enter New York harbor, opened to the public on 21 November 1964. Moses called it a "triumph of simplicity and restraint."

BIBLIOGRAPHY

Rastorfer, Darl. *Six Bridges: The Legacy of Othmar H. Ammann.* New Haven, Conn.: Yale University Press, 2000.

Reier, Sharon. *The Bridges of New York.* New York: Quadrant Press, 1977.

Talese, Gay. *The Bridge.* New York: Harper and Row, 1964.

Ruth Kaplan

See also **Bridges.**

VERSAILLES, TREATY OF. The Treaty of Versailles, which formed the core of the peace settlement after World War I, was signed on 28 June 1919. Outside the German delegation, it was signed by two countries of the initial Triple Entente that had gone to war against Germany in August 1914, France and the United Kingdom (the third one, Russia, having already signed a separate treaty at Brest-Litovsk on 3 March 1918), and by a number of nations that had joined them at later stages in the war, the major ones being Italy, Japan, and the United States (1917). This widely different experience of the war explains why unity of purpose was so difficult to achieve among the Allies during the peace conference that opened in Paris on 18 January 1919.

The League of Nations

Whereas British and French official policy followed traditional lines of territorial and colonial ambitions, combined with guarantees of military security and reparations from the defeated, American peace aims were expressed in President Woodrow Wilson's ideal of self-determination and his FOURTEEN POINTS, first put forward before Congress in January 1918 as the foundation of a just, durable peace. These included the novel concept of "A general association of nations . . . for the purpose of affording mutual guarantees of political independence and territorial integrity to great and small states alike." The Fourteen Points had been seen by Germany as an honorable way out of the war, and they were therefore central to the Allied negotiations in Paris, which finally led to the treaty as presented to the Germans, who had been excluded from the conference. The American president, who headed the U.S. delegation in person, played a leading role in getting his allies to agree on a common text. He often acted as an arbiter between their rival claims and as a moderator of their territorial and financial demands from Germany and its allies, though the British prime minister, David Lloyd George, maintained that it was he who acted as the conciliator between Wilson, the naive idealist, and French premier Georges Clemenceau, the wily realist.

Wilson's greatest personal achievement in this respect was the early acceptance of his association of nations by Britain and France, which had been reluctant to relinquish any parcel of their sovereignty to an international organization, and its elaboration into the Covenant of the LEAGUE OF NATIONS, which formed Part I of the treaty. An article in it effectively ruled out the possibility of a long war between the signatories, let alone a world war, if the European great powers, Japan, and the United States adhered to it: "Should any Member of the League resort to war in disregard of its covenants . . . it shall ipso facto be deemed to have committed an act of war against all Members of the League. . . . It shall be the duty of the Council in such case to recommend to the several Governments concerned what effective military, naval, or air force the Members of the League shall severally contribute to the armed forces to be used to protect the covenants of the League." The French were still unconvinced that this protected them forever against renewed attack by a demographically and economically stronger Germany, and they insisted on further guarantees of military security from Britain and the United States, which they verbally obtained in April. Since the vexed question of "making Germany pay" was to be decided later by a Reparations Commission, the way was now clear for a settlement ostensibly based on Wilson's conceptions of a "peace between equals." Indeed, contrary to general belief, derived from very effective German propaganda, there was no mention of war guilt as such in the wording (by Americans Norman Davis and John Foster Dulles) of Article 231, which was couched in purely legal terms so as to give a justification to the reparations already provided for in the clauses of the armistice.

Territorial and Financial Provisions

The territorial losses in Europe were defined in Part II: Alsace-Lorraine went to France, the Eupen-Malmédy area to Belgium, and western Prussia and the province of Posen (now Poznań) to Poland, with the creation of a "Polish corridor" to the sea around Danzig (now Gdańsk). Memel (now Klaipėda) went to Lithuania, and plebiscites were to be held in North Schleswig, Upper Silesia, and the Saar (whose mines were given to the French as compensation for the flooding of their mines by German troops). The loss of territory amounted to 25,000 square miles with a population of 6 million, but most of the loss had already been envisaged in the Fourteen Points and accepted in the armistice.

Overseas possessions (mostly carved up between the British and French empires) were examined in Part IV. Other parts defined German obligations in Europe, including the prohibition of an *Anschluss* with Austria; the demilitarization of the Rhineland and a band extending fifty kilometers deep on the right bank of the Rhine; a ban on conscription, all air forces, and combat gasses; the severe limitation of the navy, army, and munitions industry; the right of aerial navigation over Germany for the Allies; and international control of German ports, waterways, and railways to guarantee Central European countries unobstructed access to the sea. The financial provisions were defined in Parts VII to X (with the guarantees stipulated in Part XIV): Germany had to pay an immediate sum of $5 billion in cash or in kind before the Reparations Commission published the final amount in 1921. "Voluntary default" by Germany was covered by clauses that gave the Allies power to take measures in Germany and to seize German private property abroad.

U.S. Rejection of the Treaty

The central question remains whether the treaty was "too gentle for the harshness it contained"—in other words, whether it was enforceable as it stood, and if yes, why it was never really enforced. The decisive blow probably came from the U.S. Senate's refusal, on 19 March 1920, to ratify the treaty, a refusal that included rejection of U.S. membership in the League of Nations. The League was bitterly opposed by Republican senator Henry Cabot Lodge, chairman of the Committee on Foreign Relations, on the same grounds of sacred national sovereignty as invoked in 1918–1919 by the British and French pre-

miers. The United States signed a separate peace treaty at Berlin on 2 July 1921. Then President Wilson did not push the Treaty of Guarantee to France promised in April 1919 (wherein the United States would declare war on any country that challenged the existing French frontiers), and Britain indicated that its own commitment fell. Collective security guaranteed by the major powers, the outstanding innovation of the treaty, thus remained a pious hope.

It was clear that by 1920 Great Britain, France, and the United States had no common German policy left—if they had ever had one—and their increasing disagreements over the amount of reparations and how to get Germany to pay them drew a constant wedge between them, gradually eroding whatever credibility the peace terms might have had in the first place. The exclusion of Soviet Russia from the settlement and the specter of Bolshevik revolution also explain why many moderates believed that nothing should be done to destabilize the German Republic, and with it central and eastern Europe, which was slowly adapting to the postwar order. There is no consensus on the relative weight to be given to these considerations, but the most recent historiography at least agrees on one thing: the popular image of Versailles as a punitive "diktat" leading to the ruin of Germany and the inevitable advent of Hitler rests on manipulation rather than fact.

BIBLIOGRAPHY

Allied and Associated Powers. *Treaty of Peace with Germany, June 28, 1919.* Washington, D.C.: Government Printing Office, 1919. The text of the Treaty of Versailles, with U.S. Senate reservations.

Boemeke, Manfred M., et al., eds. *The Treaty of Versailles: A Reassessment After Seventy-five Years.* Cambridge, U.K., and New York: Cambridge University Press, 1998.

Dockrill, Michael, and John Fisher, eds. *The Paris Peace Conference, 1919: Peace Without Victory?* New York: Palgrave, 2001.

Keylor, William R., ed. *The Legacy of the Great War: The Peace Settlement of 1919 and Its Consequences.* Boston: Houghton Mifflin, 1997.

Temperley, H. W. V., ed. *History of the Peace Conference of Paris.* 6 vols. London: H. Frowde and Hodder & Stoughton, 1920–1924. Reprint, London and New York: Oxford University Press, 1969.

United States Department of State. *The Paris Peace Conference, 1919.* In *Papers Relating to the Foreign Relations of the United States.* 13 vols. Washington, D.C.: Government Printing Office, 1942–1947. The final volume was also published separately in 1947 as *The Treaty of Versailles and After: Annotations of the Text of the Treaty.*

Antoine Capet

See also **World War I;** *and vol. 9:* **The Fourteen Points.**

VESEY REBELLION was an attempted uprising by slaves and freedmen in and around Charleston, South

Carolina, in the spring of 1822. Some estimates put the number of participants at as many as 3,000 men.

The revolt was planned, over the course of 1821 and 1822, by a former slave and local carpenter named Denmark Vesey. Few details survive about Vesey's origin, but he was most likely born on the sugar plantation island of Saint Thomas in 1767 with the name Telemaque. He was bought by a sea captain named Joseph Vesey in 1781. Telemaque worked for Captain Vesey at sea and after he settled in Charleston. In 1799 Denmark Vesey won $1500 in the East Bay Lottery. He was able to purchase his own freedom, but not that of his wife or children. This would be his principal reason for plotting the revolt.

A devout Christian, Vesey recruited groups of followers from the AFRICAN METHODIST EPISCOPAL CHURCH as well as from among artisans and rural slaves. The final date set for the revolt was 16 June 1822. Vesey proposed that the insurgents take the city ammunitions depository, plunder the local banks, slaughter every white person in the city, and sail to Saint Dominique. A week prior to the attack, insiders began to alert the authorities. The revolt was foiled, and Vesey and thirty-five others were hanged.

BIBLIOGRAPHY

Egerton, Douglas R. *He Shall Go Out Free*. Madison, Wisc.: Madison House Press, 1999.

Robertson, David. *Denmark Vesey*. New York: Knopf, 1999.

Michael K. Law

See also **Slave Insurrections.**

VETERANS AFFAIRS, DEPARTMENT OF.

On 3 July 1930, Congress established the Veterans Administration and charged it with handling all matters of disability compensation, pensions, home and educational loan benefits, medical care, and housing for American war veterans. Offices for veterans' affairs prior to 1930 originated in the common colonial practice of supporting those disabled in the defense of the colony. A federal veterans' pension provision was administered by the secretary of war under the supervision of Congress from 1776 to 1819, when the program passed entirely to the War Department. In 1849 it moved to the Interior Department, where it remained until 1930 as the Bureau of Pensions.

In 1866 the National Home for Disabled Volunteer Soldiers was founded, with branches around the country for invalid servicemen. After World War I other offices for veterans' compensation, vocational reeducation, and insurance were brought into existence, and were consolidated as the Veterans Bureau in 1921.

After its establishment in 1930, the Veterans Administration expanded rapidly in scope and complexity. It originally served 4.6 million veterans, 3.7 percent of the U.S. population. By 1971 veterans numbered 28.3 million, a sizable 13.7 percent of the citizenry. It was esti-

mated that they had approximately 97.6 million relatives, making 47 percent of the U.S. population actual or potential beneficiaries of the VA.

In 1987 President Ronald Reagan threw his support behind a movement to raise the Veterans Administration, an independent government agency since its creation in 1930, to a cabinet-level department, and in 1988 he signed a bill creating the Department of Veterans Affairs (VA). In 1989 the secretary of veterans affairs became the fourteenth member of the president's cabinet. The VA is the second-largest cabinet-level department of the government; only the Department of Defense is larger.

The VA is responsible for administering a wide variety of benefits for military veterans and their dependents, including medical care, insurance, education and training, loans, and guardianship of minors and incompetents. Some 60 percent of the budget goes to compensation and pensions, the former to recompense veterans for the loss of earning power because of injury or disease arising from military service. Pensions recognize an obligation to give aid when necessary for non-service-connected disease or death. Some 20 percent of the VA budget goes for medical programs. In 1972 the VA maintained 166 hospitals and 298 other facilities, such as nursing homes and clinics, serving 912,342 inpatients. Health benefits administered by the VA include hospitals, nursing homes, and outpatient medical and dental care. More than half the practicing physicians in the United States received part of their training within the health care system administered by the VA. There is a Prosthetics Assessment and Information Center, and programs include vocational as well as physical rehabilitation.

Within the VA are the Veterans Health Services and Research Administration, the Veterans Benefits Administration, and the National Cemetery System. Their heads and the general counsel for the VA are appointed by the president and confirmed by the Senate. The VA oversees military pensions, compensation for disabilities and death, and insurance and loans for veterans. The GI BILL of 1944 provided housing and educational benefits for World War II veterans, and benefits have been continued for veterans of the Korean, Vietnam, and Persian Gulf Wars, all administered by the VA. More than 20 million veterans have received GI Bill benefits for education and job training since the program's inception. Cumulative GI Bill outlays surpass $73 billion.

The Department of Veterans Affairs currently represents the interests of more than 25 million veterans and their dependents in the United States. The VA managed a budget of $49 billion in fiscal year 2001, with $21 billion for health care and $28 billion for benefits.

BIBLIOGRAPHY

Daniels, Roger. *The Bonus March: An Episode of the Great Depression*. Westport, Conn.: Greenwood Pub. Co., 1971.

Greenberg, Milton. *The GI Bill: The Law that Changed America*. New York: Lickle Publishing, 1997.

Whitnah, Donald R., ed. *Government Agencies: The Greenwood Encyclopedia of American Institutions.* Westport, Conn.: Greenwood Press, 1983.

Richard W. Moodey / A. G.

See also **Army, United States; Bonus Army; Bonuses, Military; Defense, Department of; Demobilization; Pensions, Military and Naval; Pension Plans; Soldiers' Home.**

VETERANS' ORGANIZATIONS.

In their purest form, veterans' organizations, which are voluntary associations, restrict their membership to former members of the military. Mostly social, fraternal, and service-oriented in their activities, veterans' organizations have also lobbied Congress, and later the Department of Veterans Affairs, for members benefits. Some also actively participate in electoral politics.

Most veterans' organizations emerged after specific wars; that is, their members served mainly in particular conflicts. General Henry Knox and other Revolutionary War officers formed the Society of the Cincinnati at Newburgh, New York, in 1783 to ensure their political clout in the new republic. The Cincinnati members soon turned to lobbying Congress for back pay and pensions. With the death of its last actual veteran in 1854, the society became exclusively hereditary. The Aztec Club, for officers of the Mexican-American War, successfully lobbied Congress to appropriate funds for the creation and maintenance of the current American soldiers' cemetery in Mexico City.

Individual Civil War units formed local veterans' organizations: in the North, posts; in the South, encampments. Benjamin F. Stephenson, of Decatur, Illinois, merged northern posts into the GRAND ARMY OF THE REPUBLIC in 1866. In 1890 the GAR counted over 400,000 members. S. Cunningham and J. F. Shipp federated the southern state and local encampments into the UNITED CONFEDERATE VETERANS at New Orleans in 1889. At the time of their 1911 gathering at Hot Springs, Arkansas, the UCV numbered over 12,000. The United Spanish War Veterans (1899) also took in veterans of later conflicts in the Philippines, Haiti, and Central America, giving the USWV a total membership of 19,000 as late as 1964.

Amvets (1944) copied this ploy. Originally a strictly World War II veterans' organization, it added veterans from Korea, Vietnam, and peacetime service for a membership of 176,000 in 2000. The Vietnam War produced several veterans' organizations: the National Vietnam and Gulf War Veterans Coalition (1983), representing 325,000 veterans in 2000; the Vietnam Veterans of America (1978), with 45,000 members in 2002; and Veterans of the Vietnam War, with 15,000 members in 2002.

After World War I and the acceptance of universal conscription, many veterans began to see themselves as an emerging social class with political power. The Veterans of Foreign Wars of the United States originally sought to rival the United Spanish War Veterans by accepting only those involved in overseas conflicts, but soon focused on the two World Wars, reaching two million members in 2000. The AMERICAN LEGION began as a professional association for volunteer soldiers, but in 1919 the AMERICAN EXPEDITIONARY FORCE officers in Paris, France, turned it into a veterans' organization; it had three million members in 2000. These two organizations actively advocated an extreme form of patriotism that they both labeled "Americanism." The American Veterans Committee (1944) began as a liberal alternative, but its ties with U.S. communists kept it small in size, with 15,000 members in 2000. All three organizations tirelessly promulgated outreach programs to school children, flag rituals, and anniversary observances. Like service clubs, they flourished in small-town America.

After World War II, specialized veterans' organizations for branch of service, military unit, naval vessel, and military specialization emerged. They existed primarily for their reunions and history-related activities, accepting all family members of both veterans and nonveterans. In 1964, sixty-one national veterans' organizations had 7.8 million members. In 2002, the U.S. Department of Veterans Affairs recognized sixty-eight national organizations with 8.5 million members.

BIBLIOGRAPHY

Minott, Rodney. *Peerless Patriots: Organized Veterans and the Spirit of Americanism.* Washington, D.C.: Public Affairs Press, 1962.

U.S. Department of Veterans Affairs. *Directory of Veterans Organizations.* Washington, D.C.: GPO, 1981.

Encyclopedia of Associations. Detroit, Mich.: Gale Group, 1961– . Thirty-six editions as of 2000.

Bill Olbrich

See also **Cincinnati, Society of the.**

VETERINARY MEDICINE.

The Indians of North America had no domestic animals until they captured progeny of horses and cattle that had escaped from Spanish explorers during the early sixteenth century, and their animals received only the most primitive veterinary care. Animals brought to the Virginia and New England colonies with the first settlers arrived in a nearly disease-free environment and, despite generally poor care, disease did not become widespread until the late seventeenth century.

Europe had no veterinary schools before 1760, but self-tutored cow doctors and farriers plied their trade and wrote books, some of which found their way to America, and a few early colonists gained local recognition for prowess in animal doctoring. A Virginia lawsuit of 1625, when a William Carter was brought to court over a cow he had guaranteed to cure, provides what is likely the first reference to such a practitioner.

The first American work to discuss animal disease, the anonymous *Husband-man's Guide* (1710), devoted a dozen pages to "The Experienced Farrier." An early work of some consequence, because it and others of its genre retarded the development of scientific veterinary medicine for nearly a century, was *The Citizen and Countryman's Experienced Farrier* (1764) by J. Markham, G. Jeffries, and Discreet Indians, which essentially rehashed a wretched British work, *Markham's Maister-peece* (1610).

Few serious animal diseases broke out in America before 1750; one of the first was "horse catarrh" (equine influenza, still a periodic problem) in 1699 and again in 1732 in New England. Canine distemper is said to have originated in South America in 1735 and by 1760 caused many deaths among dogs along the North Atlantic seaboard. In 1796–1797 a "very fatal" form of feline distemper (a different disease) appeared in New York and Philadelphia, where an estimated nine thousand cats died before it spread over most of the northern states. Rabies, or hydrophobia, was recorded as early as 1753 and reached alarming proportions in many areas by 1770. About 1745 a "mysterious malady" attacked cattle from the Carolinas to Texas and decimated local herds along the way to northern markets. This likely was piroplasmosis (Texas fever), a blood disease transmitted by the cattle tick, which later threatened the entire cattle industry of the United States.

America's first veterinary surgeon was John Haslam, a graduate of the Veterinary College of London (established 1791) who came to New York in 1803. His few writings in the agricultural press mark him as one whose rational practice was ahead of its time. As in Britain, few considered veterinary medicine a fit pursuit for educated persons, and by 1850 only a dozen or so graduate veterinarians practiced in America. Until about 1870 the numerous agricultural journals, several of which advertised "a free horse doctor with every subscription," supplied most contemporary information on animal disease.

In 1807 the eminent physician Benjamin Rush advocated the establishment of a school of veterinary medicine at the UNIVERSITY OF PENNSYLVANIA, but this did not materialize until 1884. George H. Dadd, a British medical man who had emigrated to America and turned to veterinary practice about 1845, opened a proprietary school, the Boston Veterinary Institute, in 1855. The school had only six graduates when it closed in 1858, and Dadd became better known for two of his several books, *The American Cattle Doctor* (1850) and *The Modern Horse Doctor* (1854). Dadd was an early advocate of rational medical treatment and humane surgery, including the use of general anesthesia. Dadd also founded and edited the *American Veterinary Journal* (1851–1852; 1855–1859). The first veterinary journal to have real impact was the *American Veterinary Review*, established in 1875 by Alexandre Liautard. The American Veterinary Medical Association purchased the *Review* in 1915 and since has published it as the *Journal of the American Veterinary Medical Association*.

Organized veterinary medicine had its shaky beginning in Philadelphia in 1854, when Robert Jennings, a nongraduate practitioner, helped found the American Veterinary Association. This group was superseded in 1863, when a separate group founded the U.S. Veterinary Medical Association (USVMA) in New York with a London graduate, Josiah H. Stickney of Boston, as its first president. In 1898 the USVMA, which had only belatedly attracted proper support by the still-fledgling veterinary profession, changed its name to the American Veterinary Medical Association. In the years since it has had a major influence on veterinary education and practice.

The veterinary educational system in the United States began with a series of some two dozen proprietary schools, which until 1927 had about eleven thousand graduates, who, for many years, made up the majority of the profession. Following the ill-fated attempt in Boston and another in Philadelphia (1852, no graduates), the New York College of Veterinary Surgeons (1857–1899) became the first viable school, although the American Veterinary College (New York, 1875–1898) soon overshadowed it. Most successful were the schools in Chicago (1883–1920) and Kansas City (1891–1918), with about 4,400 graduates. These schools depended entirely on student fees, offered a two-year curriculum, and emphasized the study of the horse. At the turn of the century, increasing demands for an extension of the period of instruction to three and then four years (now six), together with a broadening of scope to include the study of other species, spelled the doom of schools lacking university support.

Iowa State University founded the first of the university schools (1879), followed by the University of Pennsylvania (1884). By 1918 nine more schools had opened at land grant universities in Ohio, New York, Washington, Kansas, Alabama, Colorado, Michigan, Texas, and Georgia. Increasing demand for veterinary services after World War II resulted, by 1975, in the establishment of a school at Tuskegee Institute and eight at land-grant institutions, mostly in the Midwest, with more schools in the planning stage.

After 1750, records indicate numerous local outbreaks of animal disease, serious enough in some areas to cause considerable hardship, but the isolation of settlements and continuing availability of new land kept animal disease at tolerable levels nationally. The rise of large-scale animal disease in the United States in about 1860 in part explains the formation of the U.S. Department of Agriculture in 1862 and its Bureau of Animal Industry (BAI) in 1884. The Morrill Land Grant Act of 1862 accelerated the establishment of agricultural colleges, and most of the twenty-two in existence by 1867 offered instruction in veterinary science. Unusually competent educators and researchers staffed many of these departments, such as James Law of Cornell, and many of their early students became prominent veterinary scientists.

With Daniel E. Salmon as its first chief, the BAI formed when efforts by the states to stem the rising tide

319

of animal plagues proved inadequate, threatening the livestock industry of the entire nation with extinction. Contagious pleuropneumonia of cattle originated with a single cow imported from England to New York in 1843, and a major outbreak in Massachusetts in 1859 stemmed from four imported Dutch cows. By 1880 the disease had spread to most of the states east of the Mississippi, and the BAI's first task was to eradicate it by slaughtering infected and exposed cattle, which it accomplished in 1892.

After Theobold Smith discovered the protozoan cause of Texas fever in 1889, Fred L. Kilborne proved, in about 1893, that the cattle tick was the necessary vector in the disease's transmission. Delineation of the tick's life cycle by Cooper Curtice then paved the way for control of the disease by dipping cattle to kill the ticks.

Hog cholera originated in Ohio in 1833, infecting herds throughout the United States by 1870, when losses in the Midwest exceeded $10 million annually. BAI scientists began searching for its cause in 1884, eight years before any viral cause of disease had been demonstrated; discovery of the hog cholera agent in 1904 led to its control by vaccination. However, the use of virulent virus in vaccine maintained a reservoir of the disease, and in 1960 the country began a program of total eradication. In 1974, with the program completed, experts declared the country completely free of hog cholera.

In less than two decades, BAI veterinarians found the means for combating three distinct types of animal plagues by three vastly different means: a bacterial disease by slaughter, a viral disease by vaccination, and, for the first time in the history of medicine, a protozoan infection by elimination of the vector. In the ensuing years veterinarians also eradicated by slaughter several outbreaks of so-called exotic diseases, such as foot-and-mouth disease in cattle. These efforts have been successful—the outbreak of foot-and-mouth disease in England in 2000 did not affect livestock in the United States.

Veterinary practice, which began with self-denominated farriers and cow doctors (who often called themselves veterinary surgeons), shifted to the hands of graduates who, from 1870 to about 1920, were concerned primarily with the horse. Practitioners dealt mainly with individual animals, and veterinary medicine remained more of an art than a science. Attention increasingly turned to cattle and pet animal practice. After World War II employment opportunities for veterinarians broadened greatly, and many graduates entered such areas as public health, laboratory animal medicine, zoo animal practice, medical research, and various specialties including radiology, ophthalmology, and equine practice.

Few women became veterinarians during the early 1900s. By 1950 they constituted only about 4 percent of the workforce, but by 1970 they made up more than 20 percent of student enrollees and increased thereafter. Between 1900 and 1996, 60 percent of veterinary school graduating classes were women. By 1999 about 30 percent of the 59,000 veterinarians in the United States were women, and the numbers were still rising.

BIBLIOGRAPHY

Bierer, Bert W. *A Short History of Veterinary Medicine in America.* East Lansing: Michigan State University Press. 1955.

Dunlop, Robert H. *A Short History of Veterinary Medicine in America.* St. Louis: Mosby, 1996.

Smithcors, J. F. *The American Veterinary Profession: Its Background and Development.* Ames: Iowa State University Press, 1963.

J. F. Smithcors/c. w.

See also **Cattle; Epidemics and Public Health; Horse; Medical Research; Medicine and Surgery.**

VETO, LINE-ITEM. In 1996 President Bill Clinton received what presidents had wanted for many years, the "line-item veto." This gave the president the power to select out undesirable items in appropriations bills, in bills granting certain tax breaks, and in bills creating or augmenting entitlements to prevent those items from becoming law while approving the portions of the bill to his or her liking. The constitutions of the majority of the states give their governors some form of line-item veto, but the U.S. Constitution has no comparable provision.

Lawmakers agreed that a statute that purported to allow the president to literally strike some items from a bill would be unconstitutional since the Constitution clearly requires that the president either sign a whole bill or veto it, not pick and choose among its parts. Congress sought to circumvent this prohibition by allowing the president to sign the whole bill and within ten days choose not to spend the money allocated for disfavored projects or programs. Congress then had thirty days to reject the president's decisions. But to prevail Congress needed two-thirds of both houses, since the president could veto any bill and a two-thirds vote is required to override a veto.

Congress was aware that the bill had serious constitutional problems, so it included a special provision allowing an immediate and expedited challenge by members of Congress. Members recognized that giving the president line-item veto authority undermined their powers as legislators. A lawsuit was filed, and the district judge agreed that the law was unconstitutional. The case, *Raines v. Byrd* (1997), went directly to the Supreme Court, which dismissed it without reaching the merits. The Court found that the members of Congress lacked standing, effectively holding the special standing provision unconstitutional. According to the opinion, written by Chief Justice William Rehnquist with only Justices John Paul Stevens and Stephen Breyer dissenting, the plaintiffs suffered no personal injury, and any harm to them in their legislative capacities was not the kind of injury that is a proper basis for a constitutional challenge in the federal courts. Although only a procedural ruling, it was an important victory for the executive branch because it had the effect of sharply limiting if not completely eliminating cases in

December 1874. Other such incidents also occurred in the latter part of the Reconstruction period, after President Ulysses S. Grant's reluctance to use the military in the South became apparent. White citizens of Vicksburg and Warren County had organized to oppose the policies and actions of the Reconstruction state government. When federal authorities refused requests by state officials for U.S. troops, disturbances began. Two whites and twenty-nine blacks were killed in the riots.

BIBLIOGRAPHY

Harris, William C. *The Day of the Carpetbagger: Republican Reconstruction in Mississippi.* Baton Rouge: Louisiana State University Press, 1979.

Mack Swearingen / A. R.

See also **Mississippi; Reconstruction; Riots.**

VICTORIANISM.

Queen Victoria reigned as monarch of Great Britain from 1837 until her death at the age of eighty-two in 1901. Although the people who lived during her reign had no special name for themselves, historians have termed them "Victorians," and the period itself the Victorian age. Nineteenth-century Great Britain and the United States shared a common language, some political institutions, and a similar culture, and thus the Victorian period is taken to encompass America as well. Victorian America is generally seen to denominate the period stretching from the outbreak of the Civil War to the beginning of World War I.

The later nineteenth century saw the United States become a world power. This political development was accompanied, and in part caused, by the emergence of a newly self-confident society, itself propelled by the twin engines of wealth and progress. Marked by a newly ascendant Anglo-Saxon middle class, increased bureaucratization, a consumer revolution aided by new communication technologies, and a growing consensus that power should be achieved through education and expertise rather than solely through wealth, Victorian America emerged from the crucible of the Civil War and Reconstruction a self-conscious and vibrant society. Alongside this confidence existed anxieties that America represented perhaps the "last best hope for mankind." Victorian America endured a fratricidal struggle, as well as periodic concerns that the great rush to modernization brought with it the onset of moral decay. Victorian culture, with its attendant worldview, was a central component of this new society, and indeed served to mark the GILDED AGE in America.

The Importance of Being Earnest

The term "Victorianism" denotes no specific movement or ideology, but rather encompasses the varied and sometimes conflicting moral, cultural, social, and material components of American society during this period. If Victorianism has any central or defining characteristic, it would be the primacy of virtues, what in modern usage

we term "values." Above all, Victorian Americans viewed life as a serious proposition, imbued with moral purpose. This view was derived in the main from religion, of which Evangelical PROTESTANTISM and METHODISM were the most influential. Since earthly existence was a preparation for the afterlife, one should adhere to moral laws, with the Bible the guiding force. Every task served this moral purpose, and thus reading, work, and even leisure bore significance above and beyond their daily utility. Consequently, self-control was a highly prized trait. More broadly, Victorianism embodied attention to proper "character" and the maintenance of "respectability," the public display of one's inner morality. Practices such as covering furniture legs with pantaloons were largely myth, the stock-in-trade of the Victorian satirist, and the prudery of Thomas Bowdler (whose sanitized *Family Shakespeare*, appearing in ten volumes between 1804 and 1818, has given us the word "bowdlerized" to denote partial censorship) was less predominant as the century wore on. But Victorians paid great heed to propriety and appearances. Victorianism connoted absolute notions of right and wrong, and individuals were judged accordingly. This view was also applied to the world more generally. Victorians measured the success of their civilization according to its adherence to moral law, and judged other cultures accordingly. Here, Victorian values intertwined with nineteenth-century ideas of race, a social Darwinian outlook that conceived of a racial hierarchy, atop which were the Anglo-Saxon peoples.

Victorianism was not entirely as harsh as this sketch implies. Indeed, the Victorians employed a lighter view of life as well. If a strict adherence to moral law was the ideal, it was nonetheless recognized that men and women were very human creatures. Thus, lapses in moral judgment—a man's recourse to soliciting a prostitute, or a woman's purchase of an expensive dress—are not seen by historians as signs of hypocrisy, but rather examples of the ideological dissonance at the heart of daily life. Victorians also valued humor and leisure. Works of literature such as Mark Twain's *The Adventures of Tom Sawyer* (1876) and *The Adventures of HUCKLEBERRY FINN* (1884), which highlighted the sense of adventure and play central to life in Victorian America, proved vastly more popular than the work of more serious writers, such as Herman Melville, who sought to deconstruct such realist celebrations of American life.

The valuation of moral law and respectability also had a positive influence. Victorians' devotion to self-control and the development of proper "character" led them to pursue laudable humanitarian and charitable goals. While self-reliance may have been the ultimate goal—see, for example, the incredible popularity of the novelist Horatio Alger's *Ragged Dick* (1867) and *From Canal Boy to President* (1881), which championed the theme of poor-boy-makes-good—many Victorians devoted themselves to working with the downtrodden of society and supporting charities. Often such work was religious in organization, such as the YOUNG MEN'S CHRISTIAN ASSOCIATION. Still, the motive behind Victorian charitable work was to offer a "hand up," not a "handout." Other Victorian social causes included the abolition of slavery, though here of course were marked regional divides. Indeed, Victorianism was stronger in the northern states, where economic opportunities were more plentiful, and a stronger cultural Anglophilia was present. While Victorianism was closely linked with middle-class values, it was not intrinsically tied to social class. The wealthy man who hoarded his profits was no more respectable than the poor man who refused to improve himself.

The aspect of Victorianism that is perhaps most familiar is the divide between the private and public spheres. The Victorians cherished the home and the family as cornerstones of respectability, physical and social environments where the individual found solace from the vicissitudes of daily life. Women had a special role in maintaining home and family, and thus assumed a position as moral guardian. In this sense, Victorian women enjoyed a degree of influence. Women also assumed influence in the wider role through their work for various humanitarian and reform causes. That said, Victorianism dictated strict gender roles. Individuals, and especially women, were generally ignorant of their sexuality, and women furthermore were divorced from power because they had few legally recognized ownership rights. The "cult of domesticity" was as much a hindrance as a source of self-pride.

Victorianism was also embodied in the various manifestations of the visual arts. Victorian culture was intensely visual and demonstrative, from architecture and furniture to the 1893 WORLD'S FAIR in Chicago. Aesthetics and function were given equal weight. Although not as prevalent as in England, Pre-Raphaelitism and the arts and crafts movement were influential in America during the Victorian era. Special attention must also be paid to the importance of the decorative arts in the Victorian world. As the place where the private and the public coincided, the material culture of the Victorian parlor displayed the tenets and concerns of Victorianism.

Victorianism After the Victorians

Victorianism has generated widely variant interpretations in the century since the death of its eponymous patron. Originally used simply as a broad designation for the previous century, early-twentieth-century commentators quickly called the term into rebuke, charging the Victorians with emotional aridity, a crass and ugly visual culture, and an arrogant self-confidence that encouraged racial and patriarchal hierarchies. Critics such as H. L. Mencken asserted that Victorian culture was the epitome of philistinism, valuing popularity over merit, and watering down great works of art so as to make them palatable to an uncultured mass. The Bible was praised not because of its message, but because it was a "best-seller." The rise of modernism in the arts in the wake of World War I further delegitimized Victorianism by calling into question the Victorian notion of representational, or mimetic,

art and the belief that the arts were imbued with moral teachings. Victorian individualism, and the importance of self-reliance, fell into disrepute with the development of Franklin D. Roosevelt's New Deal and the rise of the welfare state.

By the second half of the twentieth century, however, Victorianism enjoyed something of a revival. Critics such as Walter Houghton and the socialist Raymond Williams pointed to the critical trends present in Victorian culture, with Williams in particular revealing an organic and consensual strain in Victorian thought that served as the impetus for positive reform. Victorian visual culture has also received a more sympathetic examination by American historians of architecture, including Henry Russell Hitchcock, who see in it the precursor to contemporary design movements. On a separate front, commentators such as the conservative historian Gertrude Himmelfarb point with favor to the Victorians' moral code, which in her view was a force for good in that it encouraged personal responsibility and rejected state patronage, a more effective recipe for dealing with social problems such as poverty.

Whether it is viewed as a mental and cultural world that championed progress, morality, and self-worth, or as a social code that promoted stultifying hierarchies and a base philistinism, Victorianism has proved of central significance in explaining the formative decades of the emergence of the United States as a dynamic cultural and political power.

BIBLIOGRAPHY

Himmelfarb, Gertrude. *The De-Moralization of Society: From Victorian Virtues to Modern Values.* New York: Knopf, 1995.

Houghton, Walter Edwards. *The Victorian Frame of Mind.* New Haven, Conn.: Yale University Press, 1957.

Howe, Daniel Walker. "Victorian Culture in America." In *Victorian America.* Philadelphia: University of Pennsylvania Press, 1976.

Ickingrill, Steve, and Stephan Mills, eds. *Victorianism in the United States: Its Era and Its Legacy.* Amsterdam: VU University Press, 1992.

Schlereth, Thomas J. *Victorian America: Transformations in Everyday Life, 1876–1915.* New York: HarperCollins, 1991.

Stevenson, Louise L. *The Victorian Homefront: American Thought and Culture, 1860–1880.* New York: Twayne, 1991.

Williams, Raymond. *Culture and Society.* New York: Columbia University Press, 1958.

Daniel Gorman

See also **Art: Decorative Arts; Arts and Crafts Movement; Class; Family Values; Gender and Gender Roles; Racial Science; Social Darwinism.**

VICTORY LOAN OF 1919.

The Victory Loan of 1919 was a bond issue intended to help pay World War I costs. The act authorizing this loan provided for the issue of two series of three-to-four-year 4.75 percent and 3.75

percent convertible gold notes; the issue, dated 29 May 1919, totaled $4.5 billion. Bearer notes were issued in denominations ranging from $50 to $10,000, registered notes from $50 to $100,000. The maturity date was 20 May 1923, but both series were callable for redemption in whole or in part on 15 June or 15 December 1922, on four months' notice. Some notes were called at these earlier dates.

BIBLIOGRAPHY

Gilbert, Charles. *American Financing of World War I.* Westport, Conn.: Greenwood, 1970.

W. Brooke Graves/c. w.

See also **Liberty Loans; War Finance Corporation; World War I, Economic Mobilization for.**

VIDEO GAMES

VIDEO GAMES encompass a range of electronic games, including coin-operated arcade games, console and cartridge games, various handheld electronics, and games on diskette and CD-ROM ranging in sophistication from simple geometric shapes to virtual reality programs with movielike qualities.

Massachusetts Institute of Technology student Steve Russell developed the first computer game, Spacewar, in 1962. Ralph Baer, an engineer at defense contractors Sanders and Associates, developed the first home video game console, the Magnavox Odyssey. The Odyssey connected to a regular television antenna terminal and was hardwired with twelve games, all variations of Ping-Pong. There was no sound or color, and each of the games required a different plastic overlay for the television screen, but 100,000 were sold by 1972. At the same time, another young entrepreneur, Nolan Bushnell, developed Pong and formed Atari. By 1974, 150,000 versions of home Pong had sold, and two years later there were over seventy companies making clones. The development of the game cartridge made hardwired consoles and tabletop games obsolete. Instead of buying a piece of hardware with a permanent set of games, consumer could buy one piece of hardware, the console, and as many games, or software, as companies could manufacture. By 1980 third-party companies such as Activision began producing games for other companies' consoles.

As PC technology advanced, so did gaming technology. In the early 1980s the market was dominated by Atari, Intellivision, and ColecoVision, then in 1985 Nintendo released the Nintendo Entertainment System (NES), using an eight-bit processor. By the 1990s, Nintendo released the sixteen-bit Super Nintendo and was joined by Sega. With the proliferation of video games in the 1980s, arcades became standard in American malls. Teenagers dropped 20 billion quarters into games by 1981. The video game industry also benefited from the increasing power and decreasing cost of home computers and the Internet. The Internet provides a virtual arcade where players can challenge opponents from all over the world

Video Game Center. The emergence of the electronic gaming industry in the 1970s and 1980s stimulated business opportunity and social concern. © Michael S. Yamashita/ CORBIS

using the vast array of data transmission methods. A 2000 survey found that 61 percent of players are over age eighteen, with an average age of twenty-eight. The home console market, dominated by Nintendo, Sony, and Sega, has taken advantage of advances in computer technology to increase processor speed to sixty-four-bit and enable consoles to connect to the Internet.

As the popularity of video games grew, controversy developed over the addictiveness of the games and related health problems stemming from hours of stationary play. The violent nature of many games has also become an issue, as graphics technology allowed for increasingly realistic images. In 1993 a rating system, much like the system for rating movies, was put in place.

BIBLIOGRAPHY

Herz, J. C. *Joystick Nation.* Boston: Little, Brown, 1997.

Kent, Steven L. *The Ultimate History of Video Games.* Roseville, Calif.: Prima, 2001.

Lisa A. Ennis

See also **Computers and Computer Industry; Internet; Software Industry; Toys and Games.**

VIDEOCASSETTE RECORDER

VIDEOCASSETTE RECORDER (VCR) is a device that records, stores, and plays back television programs on magnetic tape; VCRs are also used to play prerecorded commercial cassettes. Videocassette recorders for consumers evolved from models used by broadcast professionals. By the early 1970s, two competing types of VCRs were available: the Betamax format, produced by the Sony Corporation, and the VHS format, produced by the Matsushita Corporation. Although Betamax was widely acknowledged to be technologically superior, the consumer market ultimately abandoned this format because it lacked several desirable features, such as recording times that could accommodate movies and longer programs on a single tape.

The introduction of the VCR not only transformed the television-viewing habits of Americans by allowing them to tape programs and time-shift their viewing; it also shook the roots of the powerful movie industry. Initially, industry leaders feared that the availability of recorded movies to be watched at home would cause Americans to leave theaters in droves. But their fears proved to be unfounded, and over the next decades the revenue from videocassette sales and rentals became a significant portion of the profits from Hollywood films. The introduction of inexpensive camcorders—movie cameras that use videotape recording—gave another boost to the popularity of VCRs as families used them to make home movies that they could later view on their television sets and share with relatives and friends.

Videocassette recorders gave Americans new flexibility, privacy, and control in viewing television programs and movies. They were perhaps the first technology that enabled consumers to personalize their viewing experiences, a trend that continues to grow in importance.

BIBLIOGRAPHY
Dobrow, Julia R., ed. Social and Cultural Aspects of VCR Use. Hillsdale, N.J: L. Erlbaum Associates, 1990.
Gaggioni, H. P. "The Evolution of Video Technologies." IEEE Communications Magazine 25 (Nov. 1987): 20–36.
Graham, Ian. Television and Video. New York: Gloucester Press, 1991.
Wolpin, Stewart. "The Race to Video." American Heritage of Invention and Technology 10 (Fall 1994): 52–63.

Loren Butler Feffer

See also Electricity and Electronics; Film.

VIETNAM, RELATIONS WITH.

On 25 April 1976 the Democratic Republic of Vietnam was renamed the Socialist Republic of Vietnam; its government controlled both northern and southern parts of the country. After a period of cool diplomatic relations in the aftermath of the VIETNAM WAR, the United States and Vietnam established diplomatic relations on 12 July 1995 and exchanged ambassadors in May 1997. President Bill Clinton visited Vietnam in 2000.

By 2002, the United States was fully committed to normalization of diplomatic, political, and economic relations with Vietnam, including accounting for POW/MIAs, resettlement abroad for Vietnamese refugees, protection of intellectual property rights, economic and commercial cooperation, democratic reforms, and repayment of sovereign debt.

On 10 December 2001 the U.S.-Vietnam Bilateral Trade Agreement took effect; it established normal trade relations—allowing Vietnam to export products to the United States at standard tariff rates. Vietnam pledged to

continue economic reforms that would allow and encourage U.S. companies to invest in the country. Vietnamese exports to the United States totaled more than $1 billion in 2001 and were expected to increase in 2002; concurrently, the two nations were engaging in an unprecedented cultural exchange. As young Vietnamese-Americans returned to rural villages to meet their grandparents for the first time, former American servicemen visited earlier enemies in an attempt to understand the legacy of the war.

BIBLIOGRAPHY
Berman, Larry. No Peace, No Honor: Nixon, Kissinger, and Betrayal in Vietnam. New York: Touchstone, 2002.
Sheehan, Neil. After The War Was Over. New York: Vintage Books, 1992.

Larry Berman
Jason Newman

See also Southeast Asia Treaty Organization; Southeast Asian Americans.

VIETNAM SYNDROME

refers to both a collective and an individual ailment stemming from America's involvement in the VIETNAM WAR. On the collective level, Vietnam syndrome describes America's general reluctance to use military force abroad because of the psychological trauma caused by different aspects of the Vietnam War. Causes cited are America's military "loss" in Vietnam despite U.S. wealth and military superiority, unprecedented media access to the most horrific images of combat, guilt over the mistreatment of Vietnam veterans, and a public perception that U.S. involvement was fundamentally, and even morally, wrong.

The Vietnam syndrome resulted in a political, military, and civilian body unwilling to risk military engagement for fear of "another Vietnam." The syndrome meshed into American foreign and military policy from Richard M. Nixon's presidency to Bill Clinton's. After the fall of Saigon, U.S. policy was one of extreme caution. One of the most vocal advocates of cautiousness was Casper Weinberger, Ronald Reagan's secretary of defense. Requirements for U.S. military involvement abroad included that the conflict be short and have minimal American losses, overwhelming public support, and no civilian restriction on military authority.

During the Persian Gulf crisis of 1990–1991, President George H. W. Bush deliberately attempted to heal the effects of the Vietnam syndrome. As war with Iraq loomed, Bush repeatedly assured the American public that the conflict would not be "another Vietnam." Further, the American public welcomed the chance to support American servicemen and women. Only three days after the fighting stopped, Bush declared the effects of Vietnam were buried in "the desert sands of the Arabian Peninsula."

On an individual level Vietnam syndrome refers to a form of POST-TRAUMATIC STRESS DISORDER (PTSD) found in 20 to 60 percent of Vietnam veterans. The symptoms include not only all the classic PTSD symptoms such as anxiety, rage, depression, and addiction but also intrusive combat-related thoughts, nightmares, and flashbacks. Guilt is also a significant part of Vietnam syndrome. Soldiers not only experienced guilt for surviving when their friends did not but also guilt over the Vietnamese killed, especially women and children. The strategies veterans developed to cope with life in a combat zone did not translate back into civilian life and manifested as dysfunctional behaviors. Treatment for veterans with Vietnam syndrome symptoms includes drug therapy, individual as well as group therapy, and behavior management techniques.

BIBLIOGRAPHY

Friedman, Matthew J. "Post-Vietnam Syndrome: Recognition and Management." *Psychosomatics* 22 (1981): 931–935, 940–943.

Isaacs, Arnold R. *Vietnam Shadows: The War, Its Ghosts, and Its Legacy.* Baltimore: Johns Hopkins University Press, 1997.

Lisa A. Ennis

VIETNAM WAR, fought from 1957 until spring 1975, began as a struggle between the Republic of Vietnam (South Vietnam) supported by the United States and a Communist-led insurgency assisted by the Democratic Republic of Vietnam (North Vietnam). Eventually, both the United States and North Vietnam committed their regular military forces to the struggle. North Vietnam received economic and military assistance from the Soviet Union and the People's Republic of China. The Republic of Korea, Australia, New Zealand, Thailand, and the Philippines furnished troops to the U.S.–South Vietnamese side. With 45,943 U.S. battle deaths, Vietnam was the fourth costliest war the country fought in terms of loss of life.

The Vietnam War was a continuation of the Indochina War of 1946–1954, in which the Communist-dominated Vietnamese nationalists (Viet Minh) defeated France's attempt to reestablish colonial rule. American involvement began in 1950 when President Harry S. Truman invoked the Mutual Defense Assistance Act of 1949 to provide aid to French forces in Vietnam, Laos, and Cambodia. Early U.S. aims were to halt the spread of Communism and to encourage French participation in the international defense of Europe.

Even with U.S. aid in the form of materiel and a Military Assistance Advisory Group (MAAG), the French could not defeat the Viet Minh use of both guerrilla warfare and conventional attacks. Ending the Indochina War, the GENEVA ACCORDS OF 1954 divided Vietnam at the seventeenth parallel with a three-mile Demilitarized Zone (DMZ). The partition in effect created two nations: the Democratic Republic of Vietnam in the north with its capital at Hanoi, and the Republic of Vietnam in the south with its capital at Saigon. Vietnam's neighbors, Laos and

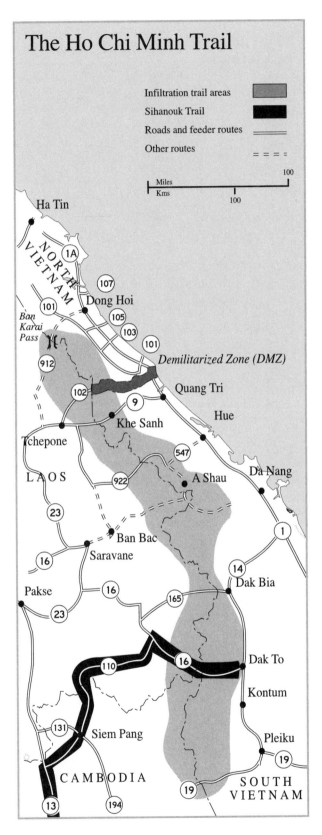

The Ho Chi Minh Trail

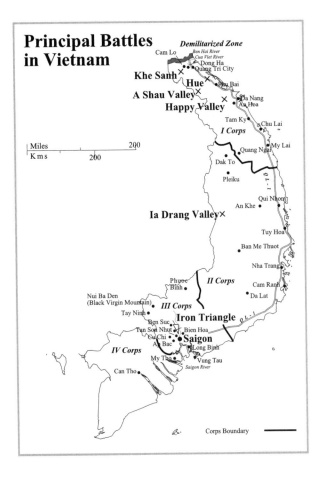

Principal Battles in Vietnam

Cambodia, became independent nations under nominally neutralist governments.

The administration of President Dwight D. Eisenhower provided aid and support to the government of Ngo Dinh Diem. The MAAG, which grew in strength from 342 personnel to nearly 700, helped Diem to build up his armed forces. In 1956, with Eisenhower's concurrence, Diem refused to participate in the national elections called for in the Geneva Accords, asserting that South Vietnam had not acceded to the agreement and that free elections were impossible in the north, and declared himself president of the Republic of Vietnam.

During the first years of his rule, Diem, assisted by the MAAG, American civilian advisers, and by $190 million a year in U.S. financial aid, established effective armed forces and a seemingly stable government. He defeated or co-opted South Vietnamese rivals, resettled some 800,000 Catholic refugees from North Vietnam, initiated land reform, and conducted a campaign to wipe out the Viet Minh organization that remained in the south. Although strong on the surface, however, Diem's regime was inefficient and riddled with corruption. Its land reform brought little benefit to the rural poor. Commanded by generals selected for loyalty to Diem rather than ability, the armed forces were poorly trained and low in mo-

rale. The anti–Viet Minh campaign alienated many peasants, and Diem's increasingly autocratic rule turned much of the urban anticommunist elite against him.

Anticipating control of South Vietnam through elections and preoccupied with internal problems, North Vietnam's charismatic leader, Ho Chi Minh, at first did little to exploit the vulnerabilities of the southern regime. Nevertheless, Ho and his colleagues were committed to the liberation of all of Vietnam and had accepted the Geneva Accords only with reluctance, under pressure from the Russians and Chinese, who hoped to avoid another Korea-type confrontation with the United States. In deference to his allies' caution and to American power, Ho moved slowly at the outset against South Vietnam.

Beginning in 1957, the southern Viet Minh, with authorization from Hanoi, launched a campaign of political subversion and terrorism, and gradually escalated a guerrilla war against Diem's government. Diem quickly gave the insurgents the label Viet Cong (VC), which they retained throughout the ensuing struggle. North Vietnam created a political organization in the south, the National Front for the Liberation of South Vietnam (NLF), ostensibly a broad coalition of elements opposed to Diem but controlled from the north by a Communist inner core. To reinforce the revived insurgency, Hanoi began sending southward soldiers and political cadres who had regrouped to North Vietnam after the armistice in 1954. These men, and growing quantities of weapons and equipment, traveled to South Vietnam via a network of routes through eastern Laos called the Ho Chi Minh Trail and by sea in junks and trawlers. At this stage, however, the vast majority of Viet Cong were native southerners, and they secured most of their weapons and supplies by capture from government forces.

Building on the organizational base left from the French war and exploiting popular grievances against Diem, the Viet Cong rapidly extended their political control of the countryside. Besides conducting small guerrilla operations, they gradually began to mount larger assaults with battalion and then regimental size light infantry units. As the fighting intensified, the first American deaths occurred in July 1959, when two soldiers of the MAAG were killed during a Viet Cong attack on Bien Hoa, north of Saigon. By the time President John F. Kennedy took office in 1961, it was clear that America's ally needed additional help.

Kennedy viewed the conflict in South Vietnam as a test case of Communist expansion by means of local "wars of national liberation." For that reason, as well as a continuing commitment to the general policy of "containment," Kennedy enlarged the U.S. effort in South Vietnam. He sent in more advisers to strengthen Diem's armed forces, provided additional funds and equipment, and deployed American helicopter companies and other specialized units. To carry out the enlarged program, Kennedy created a new joint (army, navy, air force) headquarters in Saigon, the Military Assistance Command,

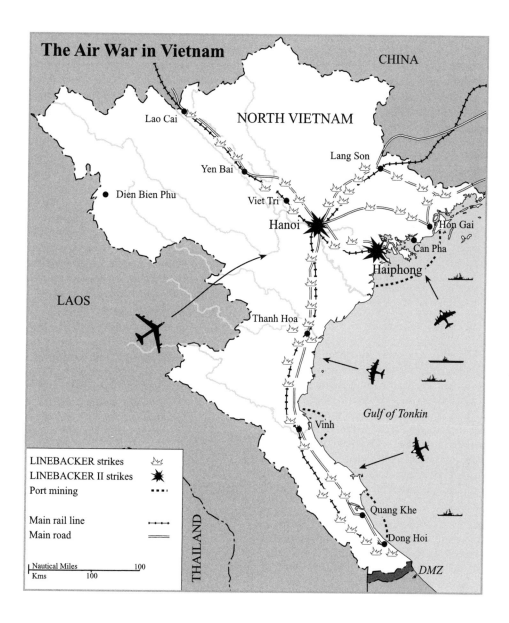

The Air War in Vietnam

CHINA

NORTH VIETNAM

Lao Cai

Lang Son

Yen Bai

Dien Bien Phu

Viet Tri

Hon Gai

Hanoi

Can Pha

Haiphong

LAOS

Thanh Hoa

Gulf of Tonkin

Vinh

LINEBACKER strikes
LINEBACKER II strikes
Port mining

Main rail line
Main road

Nautical Miles   100
Kms   100

THAILAND

Quang Khe

Dong Hoi

DMZ

Vietnam (MACV). The number of Americans in South Vietnam increased to more than 16,000 and they began engaging in combat with the Viet Cong.

After a promising start, the Kennedy program faltered. Diem's dictatorial rule undermined South Vietnamese military effectiveness and fed popular discontent, especially among the country's numerous Buddhists. An effort to relocate the rural population in supposedly secure "strategic hamlets" collapsed due to poor planning and ineffective execution. With support from the Kennedy administration, Diem's generals overthrew and assassinated him in a coup d'etat on 1 November 1963.

Diem's death, followed by the assassination of President Kennedy on 22 November 1963, did nothing to improve allied fortunes. As a succession of unstable Saigon governments floundered, the Viet Cong began advancing from guerrilla warfare to larger attacks aimed at destroying the South Vietnamese Army (ARVN). To reinforce the campaign, Hanoi infiltrated quantities of modern Communist-bloc infantry weapons, and in late 1964, began sending units of its regular army into South Vietnam. Kennedy's successor, Lyndon B. Johnson, during 1964 increased American military manpower in South Vietnam to 23,300 and tried to revive the counterinsurgency campaign. However, political chaos in Saigon and growing Viet Cong strength in the countryside frustrated his efforts and those of the MACV commander, General William C. Westmoreland.

Johnson and his advisers turned to direct pressure on North Vietnam. Early in 1964, they initiated a program of small-scale covert raids on the north and began planning for air strikes. In August 1964, American planes

President Johnson Visits the Troops. Rallying the national will was essential to the U.S. strategy. © CORBIS

raided North Vietnam in retaliation for two torpedo boat attacks (the second of which probably did not occur) on U.S. destroyers in the Gulf of Tonkin. Johnson used this incident to secure authorization from Congress (the TONKIN GULF RESOLUTION) to use armed force to "repel any armed attack against the forces of the United States and to repel further aggression." That resolution served as a legal basis for subsequent increases in the U.S. commitment, but in 1970 after questions arose as to whether the administration had misrepresented the incidents, Congress repealed it.

Committed like his predecessors to containment and to countering Communist "wars of national liberation," Johnson also wanted to maintain U.S. credibility as an ally and feared the domestic political repercussions of losing South Vietnam. Accordingly, he and his advisers moved toward further escalation.

During 1964, Johnson authorized limited U.S. bombing of the Ho Chi Minh Trail. In February 1965, after the Viet Cong killed thirty-one Americans at Pleiku and Qui Nhon, the President sanctioned retaliatory strikes against North Vietnam. In March, retaliation gave way to a steadily intensified but carefully controlled aerial offensive against the north (Operation Rolling Thunder), aimed at reducing Hanoi's ability to support the Viet Cong and compelling its leaders to negotiate an end to the conflict on U.S. terms.

At the same time, Johnson committed American combat forces to the fight. Seven U.S. Marine battalions and an Army airborne brigade entered South Vietnam between March and May 1965. Their initial mission was to defend air bases used in Operation Rolling Thunder, but in April, Johnson expanded their role to active operations against the Viet Cong. During the same period, Johnson authorized General Westmoreland to employ U.S. jets in combat in the south, and in June, B-52 strategic bombers

began raiding Viet Cong bases. As enemy pressure on the ARVN continued and evidence accumulated that North Vietnamese regular divisions were entering the battle, Westmoreland called for a major expansion of the ground troop commitment. On 28 July, Johnson announced deployments that would bring U.S. strength to 180,000 by the end of 1965. Westmoreland threw these troops into action against the Viet Cong and North Vietnamese's large military units. Taking advantage of their helicopter-borne mobility, U.S. forces won early tactical victories, but the cost in American dead and wounded also began to mount and the enemy showed no signs of backing off.

Additional deployments increased American troop strength to a peak of 543,400 by 1969. To support them, MACV, using troops and civilian engineering firms, constructed or expanded ports, erected fortified camps, built vast depots, paved thousands of miles of roads, and created a network of airfields.

Desiring to keep the war limited to Vietnam, President Johnson authorized only small-scale raids into the enemy bases in Laos and Cambodia. As a result, in South Vietnam, General Westmoreland perforce fought a war of attrition. He used his American troops to battle the North Vietnamese and Viet Cong regular units while the ARVN and South Vietnam's territorial forces carried on the pacification campaign against the Viet Cong guerrillas and political infrastructure. As the fighting went on, a

Aftermath of a Misdirected Napalm Attack. Vietnamese civilians were frequently caught between the warring parties.

stable government emerged in Saigon under Nguyen Van Thieu. These efforts, however, brought only stalemate. Aided by Russia and China, the North Vietnamese countered Operation Rolling Thunder with an air defense system of increasing sophistication and effectiveness. In South Vietnam, they fed in troops to match the American buildup and engaged in their own campaign of attrition. While suffering heavier losses than the U.S. in most engagements, they inflicted a steady and rising toll of American dead. Pacification in South Vietnam made little progress. The fighting produced South Vietnamese civilian casualties, the result of enemy terrorism, American bombing and shelling, and in a few instances—notably the MY LAI MASSACRE of March 1968—of atrocities by U.S. troops.

In the U.S., opposition to the war grew to encompass a broad spectrum of the public even as doubts about America's course emerged within the administration. By the end of 1967, President Johnson had decided to level off the bombing in the north and American troop strength in the south and to seek a way out of the war, possibly by turning more of the fighting over to the South Vietnamese.

Late in 1967, North Vietnam's leaders decided to break what they also saw as a stalemate by conducting a "General Offensive/General Uprising," a combination of heavy military attacks with urban revolts. After preliminary battles, the North Vietnamese early in 1968 besieged a Marine base at Khe Sanh in far northwestern South Vietnam. On the night of 31 January, during the Tet (Lunar New Year) holidays, 84,000 enemy troops attacked seventy-four towns and cities including Saigon. Although U.S. intelligence had gleaned something of the plan, the extent of the attacks on the cities came as a surprise.

Viet Cong units initially captured portions of many towns, but they failed to spark a popular uprising. Controlling Hué for almost a month, they executed 3,000 civilians as "enemies of the people." ARVN and U.S. troops quickly cleared most localities, and the besiegers of Khe Sanh withdrew after merciless pounding by American air power and artillery. At the cost of 32,000 dead (by MACV estimate), the TET OFFENSIVE produced no lasting enemy military advantage.

In the United States, however, the Tet Offensive confirmed President Johnson's determination to wind down the war. Confronting bitter antiwar dissent within the Democratic Party and a challenge to his renomination from Senator Eugene McCarthy, Johnson rejected a military request for additional U.S. troops and halted most bombing of the north. He also withdrew from the presidential race to devote the rest of his term to the search for peace in Vietnam. In return for the partial bombing halt, North Vietnam agreed to open negotiations. Starting in Paris in May 1968, the talks were unproductive for a long time.

Taking office in 1969, President Richard M. Nixon continued the Paris talks. He also began withdrawing U.S. troops from South Vietnam while simultaneously building up Saigon's forces so that they could fight on

Black GI in Vietnam. Major African American participation in the war was marked by racial tensions on account of domestic social inequities. GETTY IMAGES

with only American advice and materiel assistance. This program was labeled "Vietnamization."

Because the Viet Cong had been much weakened by its heavy losses in the Tet Offensive and in two subsequent general offensives in May and August 1968, the years 1969–1971 witnessed apparent allied progress in South Vietnam. The ARVN gradually took on the main burden of the ground fighting, which declined in intensity. American troop strength diminished from its 1969 peak of 543,400 to 156,800 at the end of 1971. The allies also made progress in pacification. American and South Vietnamese offensives against the enemy sanctuaries in Cambodia in April and May 1970 and an ARVN raid against the Ho Chi Minh Trail in February 1971 helped to buy time for Vietnamization. On the negative side, as a result of trends in American society, of disillusionment with the war among short-term draftee soldiers, and of organizational turbulence caused by the troop withdrawals, U.S. forces suffered from growing indiscipline, drug abuse, and racial conflict.

In spring 1972, North Vietnam, in order to revive its fortunes in the south, launched the so-called Easter Offensive with twelve divisions, employing tanks and artillery on a scale not previously seen in the war. In response, President Nixon, while he continued to withdraw America's remaining ground troops, increased U.S. air support to the ARVN. The North Vietnamese made initial territorial gains, but the ARVN rallied, assisted materially by U.S. Air Force and Navy planes and American advisers on the ground. Meanwhile, Nixon resumed full-scale bombing of North Vietnam and mined its harbors. Beyond defeating the Easter Offensive, Nixon intended these attacks, which employed B-52s and technologically advanced guided bombs, to batter Hanoi toward a negotiated settlement of the war. By late 1972, the North Vietnamese, had lost an estimated 100,000 dead and large amounts of equipment and had failed to capture any major towns or populated areas. Nevertheless, their military position in the south was better than it had been in 1971, and the offensive had facilitated a limited revival of the Viet Cong.

Both sides were ready for a negotiated settlement. During the autumn of 1972, Nixon's special adviser, Henry A. Kissinger, and North Vietnamese representative Le Duc Tho, who had been negotiating in secret since 1969, reached the outlines of an agreement. Each side made a key concession. The U.S. dropped its demand for complete withdrawal of North Vietnamese troops from South Vietnam. Hanoi abandoned its insistence that the Thieu government be replaced by a presumably Communist-dominated coalition. After additional diplomatic maneuvering between Washington and Hanoi and Washington and Saigon, which balked at the terms, and after a final U.S. air campaign against Hanoi in December, the ceasefire agreement went into effect on 28 January 1973.

Under it, military prisoners were returned, all American troops withdrew, and a four-nation commission supervised the truce. In fact, the fighting in South Vietnam continued, and the elections called for in the agreement never took place. During 1973 and 1974, the North Vietnamese, in violation of the ceasefire, massed additional men and supplies inside South Vietnam. Meanwhile, the Nixon administration, distracted by the WATERGATE scandal, had to accept a congressional cutoff of all funds for American combat operations in Southeast Asia after 15 August 1973.

Early in 1975, the North Vietnamese, again employing regular divisions with armor and artillery, launched their final offensive against South Vietnam. That nation, exhausted by years of fighting, demoralized by a steady reduction in the flow of American aid, and lacking capable leadership at the top, rapidly collapsed. A misguided effort by President Thieu to regroup his forces in northern South Vietnam set off a rout that continued almost unbroken until the North Vietnamese closed in on Saigon late in April. On 21 April, President Thieu resigned. His successor, General Duong Van Minh, surrendered the country on 30 April. North Vietnamese and Viet Cong troops entered Saigon only hours after the U.S. completed an emergency airlift of embassy personnel and thousands of South Vietnamese who feared for their lives under the Communists. Hanoi gained control of South Vietnam, and its allies won in Cambodia, where the government surrendered to insurgent forces on 17 April 1975, and Laos, where the Communists gradually assumed control.

The costs of the war were high for every participant. Besides combat deaths, the U.S. lost 1,333 men missing and 10,298 dead of non-battle causes. In terms of money ($138.9 billion), only World War II was more expensive. Costs less tangible but equally real were the loss of trust by American citizens in their government and the demoralization of the U.S. armed forces, which would take years to recover their discipline and self-confidence. South Vietnam suffered more than 166,000 military dead and possibly as many as 415,000 civilians. North Vietnamese and Viet Cong deaths amounted to at least 937,000. To show for the effort, the U.S. could claim only that it had delayed South Vietnam's fall long enough for other Southeast Asian countries to stabilize their noncommunist governments.

BIBLIOGRAPHY

Andrade, Dale. *America's Last Vietnam Battle: Halting Hanoi's 1972 Easter Offensive.* Lawrence: University Press of Kansas, 2001.

Berman, Larry. *Planning a Tragedy: The Americanization of the War in Vietnam.* New York: Norton, 1982.

Duiker, William J. *The Communist Road to Power in Vietnam.* Boulder, Colo.: Westview, 1996.

Halberstam, David. *The Best and the Brightest.* New York: Random House, 1972.

Herring, George C. *America's Longest War: The United States and Vietnam, 1950–1975.* Boston: McGraw-Hill, 2002.

McMaster, H. R. *Dereliction of Duty: Lyndon Johnson, Robert McNamara, the Joint Chiefs of Staff, and the Lies that Led to Vietnam.* New York: Harper Collins, 1997.

McNamara, Robert S. *In Retrospect: The Tragedy and Lessons of Vietnam.* New York: Vintage, 1996.

Oberdorfer, Don. *Tet!* Baltimore: Johns Hopkins University Press, 2001.

Palmer, Bruce. *The 25-Year War: America's Military Role in Vietnam.* Lexington: University Press of Kentucky, 1984.

Thompson, Wayne. *To Hanoi and Back: The U.S. Air Force and North Vietnam, 1966–1973.* Washington: Smithsonian Institution Press, 2000.

Turley, William S. *The Second Indochina War: A Short Political and Military History, 1954–1975.* Boulder, Colo.: Westview, 1987.

Westmoreland, William C. *A Soldier Reports.* New York: Da Capo, 1989.

Graham A. Cosmas

See also **Agent Orange; Cambodia, Bombing of; Domino Theory; Pentagon Papers;** *and vol. 9:* **The Christmas**

Bombing of Hanoi Was Justified; The Pentagon Papers; Dear America: Letters Home from Vietnam; Letter to Nguyen Van Thieu; Pardon for Vietnam Draft Evaders; President Lyndon B. Johnson's Speech Declining to Seek Re-election; Vietnamization and the Silent Majority; Statement by Committee Seeking Peace with Freedom in Vietnam; The Fall of Saigon.

VIETNAM WAR MEMORIAL.

The Vietnam Veterans Memorial was dedicated on the Washington Mall in November 1982. Maya Ying Lin, a Yale University architecture student who won the national design competition, erected two elongated, tapered walls of black granite that joined at the higher ends at a 125-degree angle to form an open "V." The back sides of the walls were landscaped to be even to the ground. Open front sides sloped downward into the earth to a depth of ten feet where the wings met. The names of the 57,939 American men and women dead or missing in action in the war were etched, chronologically, in white on the polished granite. At the dedication, veterans and family members read the names of the dead in alphabetical order, a tribute that required more than three days.

The organizers of the Vietnam Memorial intended their project as a symbol of reconciliation. Their nonpolitical memorial would not comment on the rightness or wrongness of the Vietnam War. By focusing simply on those who served and died, the organizers hoped to conciliate the war's supporters and opponents. Their choice of a site across from the Lincoln Memorial meant, as one

veteran put it, that "no one could ignore it." The wall's stark design offended some conservatives and veterans groups, who agitated for a more heroic memorial. As a compromise, sculptor Frederick Hart prepared a statue of three U.S. soldiers—one black, one white, and one Eurasian—as a counterpoint to the abstract simplicity of the wall. Since its unveiling, the Vietnam Memorial has been the third most visited site in Washington, D.C.

BIBLIOGRAPHY

Hass, Kristin Ann. *Carried to the Wall: American Memory and the Vietnam Veterans Memorial.* Berkeley: University of California Press, 1998.

Scott, Wilbur J. *The Politics of Readjustment: Vietnam Veterans since the War.* New York: Aldine De Gruyter, 1993.

Senie, Harriet F., and Sally Webster, eds. *Critical Issues in Public Art: Content, Context, and Controversy.* New York: Icon Editions, 1992.

J. Garry Clifford / F. B.

See also **Art: Sculpture; War Memorials; Washington, D.C.**

Vietnam War Memorial. Roni DeJoseph grieves for a fallen friend while seeing the Vietnam Wall Experience—the three-quarter-scale traveling replica of the permanent memorial in Washington, D.C.—in Brooklyn, N.Y., during the Memorial Day parade in 1996. AP/WIDE WORLD PHOTOS

VIETNAMIZATION,

an American term first used in the spring of 1969 by Secretary of Defense Melvin Laird to describe the policy, strategy, and programs adopted by the administration of Richard M. Nixon for the Vietnam War. Vietnamization entailed the progressive withdrawal of U.S. forces from South Vietnam combined with efforts to enhance the training and modernization of all South Vietnamese military forces to enable the government of South Vietnam to assume greater responsibility for the conduct of the war. The policy also encompassed U.S. support for Saigon to more vigorously pursue rural pacification and development to win the loyalty of the peasants and to strengthen its political base through village and hamlet elections, social and economic reforms, and expanded social services.

Under General Creighton W. Abrams, who succeeded General William C. Westmoreland as the overall U.S. military commander in South Vietnam in June 1968, allied military strategy under Vietnamization emphasized operations to weaken the enemy's capabilities by attacking its logistical bases in South Vietnam and neighboring Cambodia and Laos. Operations such as the May 1970 American ground incursion into Cambodia and the January 1971 South Vietnamese incursion into Laos, Lam Son 719, were justified as means to gain additional time for Vietnamization to progress. These operations only temporarily disrupted the enemy's plans. The poor showing of Saigon's forces in Lam Son 719 cast doubt on the efficacy of Vietnamization, as did the heavy reliance of Saigon's forces on U.S. airpower to repulse North Vietnam's 1972 Easter offensive.

Vietnamization was a useful facade for the withdrawal of American forces from Vietnam between 1969 and 1973. However, despite the extensive equipment the departing U.S. forces turned over to Saigon's armed forces, the latter were ill prepared after 1973 to face North Vietnamese forces in the absence of sustained, direct American military support.

BIBLIOGRAPHY

Clarke, Jeffrey J. *Advice and Support: The Final Years, 1965–1973.* Washington, D.C.: Center of Military History, 1988.

Kimball, Jeffrey. *Nixon's Vietnam War.* Modern War Studies. Lawrence: University Press of Kansas, 1998.

Nguyên, Duy Hinh. *Vietnamization and the Cease-Fire.* Washington, D.C.: Department of the Army, 1980.

Vincent H. Demma

See also **Vietnam War;** *and vol. 9:* **Speech on Vietnamization and Silent Majority.**

VIEUX CARRÉ ("Old Square"), the name commonly applied to the old French and Spanish section of New Orleans. It is bounded by the Mississippi River on the southeast, Rampart Street on the northwest, Canal Street on the southwest, and Esplanade Avenue on the northeast. Retaining much of its antique character, the section is a popular tourist attraction. Today it is commonly known as "The French Quarter."

BIBLIOGRAPHY

Arthur, Stanely Clisby. *Old New Orleans: A History of the Vieux Carré, Its Ancient and Historical Buildings.* New Orleans, La.: Harmanson, 1950.

Remini, Robert Vincent. *The Battle of New Orleans.* New York: Viking, 1999.

Walter Pritchard/A. G.

See also **Louisiana; New Orleans; River Navigation; Urbanization.**

VIGILANTES were members of citizens' committees set up in frontier towns and rural communities in the nineteenth century to keep order and put down illegal activity. Vigilante committees organized when citizens found law enforcement absent or inadequate. Occasionally, communities really were threatened with destruction by criminals. In those cases, citizens typically mimicked the duties and procedures of the legal authorities they supplanted, holding formal trials before administering punishment (usually hanging). For example, in the early 1860s a vigilante committee broke up a large Montana outlaw gang, headed by Sheriff Henry Plummer, which terrorized the citizens in the mining communities. John Beidler from Pennsylvania is said to have presided at many of the trials.

In many cases, however, although vigilantes cited a breakdown in law and order, other factors seemed to motivate their actions. Some vigilantes seemed to be frustrated by the inefficiency and expense of law enforcement, storming jails to hang persons already in custody. Some-

times vigilantes sought to enforce prevailing moral standards or attack their political opponents. The San Francisco Vigilance Committee of 1856, which had several thousand mostly Protestant and native-born members, wrested political control of the city by exiling the Irish Catholic leaders of the Democratic Party.

Today "vigilante" describes actions by groups or individuals who punish real or perceived wrongdoings outside the legal system. Dissatisfaction with law enforcement or the legal process remains the principal motive. Typically that dissatisfaction is shared by other individuals who see vigilante actions as heroic. Among the many cases receiving media coverage in the late twentieth century was that of Bernard Goetz. His 1984 shooting of four black youths, who he believed were attempting to rob him in a New York City subway car, gained Goetz national celebrity status.

BIBLIOGRAPHY

Gilje, Paul A. *Rioting in America.* Bloomington: Indiana University Press, 1996.

Slotkin, Richard. *The Fatal Environment: The Myth of the Frontier in the Age of Industrialization, 1800–1890.* Middletown, Conn.: Wesleyan University Press, 1985.

Stock, Catherine McNicol. *Rural Radicals: Righteous Rage in the American Grain.* Ithaca, N.Y.: Cornell University Press, 1996.

White, Richard. *"It's Your Misfortune and None of My Own": A New History of the American West.* Norman: University of Oklahoma Press, 1991.

Robert M. Guth
Cynthia R. Poe

See also **Regulators; Revolutionary Committees; White League;** *and vol. 9:* **Constitution of the Committee of Vigilantes of San Francisco.**

VILLA RAID AT COLUMBUS (9 March 1916). Mexican outlaw raids against U.S. nationals and their property on both sides of the border culminated on the night of 8–9 March 1916, in Pancho Villa's raid on Columbus, N.M. Units of the U.S. Thirteenth Cavalry stationed at Columbus, totaling 12 officers and 341 enlisted men, drove the Mexicans, variously estimated to number from 500 to 1,000 men, back across the border. American losses were seven soldiers killed, five soldiers wounded, eight civilians killed, and two civilians wounded; Mexican losses were approximately 190 killed or wounded. The raid was directly responsible for U.S. Gen. John J. Pershing's punitive expedition into Mexico.

BIBLIOGRAPHY

Eisenhower, John S. D. *Intervention!: The United States and the Mexican Revolution, 1913–1917.* New York: Norton, 1995.

Link, Arthur S. *Woodrow Wilson and the Progressive Era, 1910–1917.* New York: Harper and Row, 1954.

Mason, Herbert M., Jr. *The Great Pursuit.* New York: Random House, 1970.

Stout, Joseph A. *Border Conflict: Villistas, Carrancistas, and the Punitive Expedition, 1915–1920.* Fort Worth: Texas Christian University Press, 1999.

C. A. Willoughby / A. R.

See also **Army, United States; Cavalry, Horse; Foreign Policy; Mexican-American War; Mexico, Punitive Expedition into; Mexico, Relations with; New Mexico; Southwest.**

VINLAND refers to the southernmost region on the Atlantic coast of North America visited and named by Norse voyagers about A.D. 1000. Sagas and archaeological findings suggest this European contact with North America was part of the Norse westward movement across the Atlantic from the islands of Orkney, Shetland, and Faroe (A.D. 780–800) to Iceland (A.D. 870) and Greenland (A.D. 985–986). The first sighting is attributed to the Icelander Bjarni Herjulfsson about 986 and the first landing a few years later to Leif Eriksson (called Leif the Lucky), son of Erik the Red. The first attempt at colonization was made by an Islandic trader, Thorfinn Karlsefni. The settlement lasted approximately three years and was abandoned; it is hypothesized that this was prompted by native opposition. Other written evidence for Vinland settlement can be attributed to a German cleric, Adam of Bremen (c. 1076) as well as to the "Islandic Annals," which mention voyages to or from America in 1121 and 1347. The pre-Columbian Norse discovery and seaborne connection over a period of 400 years, remarkable achievements though they were, had little influence on subsequent American and Canadian history.

Nordic sagas, stories passed down orally through several generations, were often altered and enriched before they were written down. Two sagas, "The Greenlanders' Saga" and "Erik the Red's Saga," both dating from the 1200s, describe the Viking voyages, sailing directions, latitude, topography, flora, fauna, and the indigenous population. Additionally, these sagas tell of three lands west or southwest of Greenland named Holluland (Flatstoneland), Markland (Woodland), and Vinland (Wineland). The most northerly, Helluland, an area of glaciers, mountains, and rock, is commonly identified as the area from the Torngat Mountains to Baffin Island. There has been increasing acceptance of Markland as the large area around Hamilton Inlet in central Labrador. Vinland, so named for the grapes found growing abundantly in the area, is thought to be the region beginning in northern Newfoundland and extending to the south an indeterminate distance.

Archaeological evidence supporting the stories of Norse arrival in North America was found by a Norwegian archaeologist, Helge Ingstad, and his wife, Anne Stine, in the 1960s. The discovery of a Viking settlement, L'Anse aux Meadows (Meadow Cove) at Epaves Bay in Newfoundland contributed artifacts in the form of eight sod-walled structures, iron nail pieces, a soapstone spindle whorl, and a bronze-ringed pin.

The "Vinland Map" (perhaps dating to 1440) housed at the Beinecke Library at Yale University depicts Europe, the Atlantic Ocean, a large, relatively accurate Greenland, and a larger island to the southwest labeled "Island of Vinland." Since its discovery in 1957, the map has prompted debate over its authenticity. By 2002 chemical and historical analyses had not yet verified the map's integrity. Although many experts today question the validity of the "Vinland Map" and whether the Norse settlement at L'Anse aux Meadows was actually Vinland, it is widely accepted that the Norse were the first Europeans to reach North America around A.D. 1000.

BIBLIOGRAPHY

Jones, Gwyn. *A History of the Vikings.* New York: Oxford University Press, 2001.

Gwyn Jones
Janet S. Smith

See also **New England; Norsemen in America.**

VIOLENCE. Human history has been marked and marred by violence; the United States has proved to be no exception. Violent conflict between Native Americans and settlers and immigrants flared soon after the English colonization of Virginia in 1607 and lasted nearly three centuries until the defeat of the Lakotas at WOUNDED KNEE, South Dakota in 1890. In the numerous wars fought, both sides engaged in massacres. Six massacres stand out for the numbers slaughtered: 400 Pequot Indians in Rhode Island (1637); 300 Sioux at Wounded Knee; some 200 at Wyot in Humboldt Bay, California (1860); 200 Cheyennes at Sand Creek, Colorado (1864); 173 Blackfeet on the Marias River in Montana (1870); and 103 Cheyennes on the Washita River in Oklahoma (1868).

Similar to white-Indian racial violence were the black uprisings; the first was in Virginia in 1691 followed by significant revolts in New York City in 1712 and 1741. By far, the greatest number of these rebellions was in the South—the most notable of which was led by NAT TURNER in Virginia in 1831.

Blacks as Targets

Following the Civil War, former slaves were killed in great numbers in riots by whites in New Orleans and Memphis (1866), and in Colfax, Louisiana (1873). Most devastating of all were LYNCHINGS—the hanging of persons (usually black men) by mobs. Primarily a southern phenomenon, lynchings occurred from the 1880s well into the twentieth century. At its peak from 1889 to 1918, lynching was responsible for the execution of 2,460 African Americans in the South.

As more blacks fled the South for great cities in the North and West, urban violence became the rule. Riots in East St. Louis (1917), Chicago (1919), and Detroit (1943), primarily targeted black neighborhoods. During the 1960s, residents of black ghettos rioted in the WATTS

"Madman Murders, Commits Suicide." Seemingly random violence, increasingly sensationalized by the news media, has troubled Americans increasingly. This news photograph, from Mineola, N.Y., dates from 1935.

area of Los Angeles (1965); Newark and Detroit (1967); and Washington, Chicago, Baltimore, and Kansas City in 1968. The 1968 riots were in reaction to the assassination of black leader Martin Luther King Jr. (see KING, MARTIN LUTHER, ASSASSINATION). The 1992 riot in Los Angeles saw members of other minority groups joining African Americans in the greatest urban riot (54 deaths) of the twentieth century (see LOS ANGELES RIOTS). Over a century before, the New York City antidraft riot of 1863, one of the biggest urban riots in American history, was motivated to a significant degree by racial prejudice against blacks (see DRAFT RIOTS). This riot found lower-class whites violently protesting the newly imposed draft of men into the Union army. Rioting New Yorkers killed more than 110 people, most of them black.

Farmer and Frontier Violence

Racial minorities were not the only aggrieved Americans to resort to violence. Among the most chronically discontented were the white farmers, who over 260 years engaged in uprisings such as BACON'S REBELLION (Virginia, 1676), the Anti-Rent movement (New York, 1700s and 1800s), SHAYS'S REBELLION (Massachusetts, 1784–

1786), the WHISKEY REBELLION (Pennsylvania, 1794), the MUSSEL SLOUGH INCIDENT (California, 1878–1882), the Kentucky Night Riders (early twentieth century), and the Farm Holiday movement in the Midwest (1930s).

Frontier whites were at the center of a distinctive type of American violence: vigilantism—taking the law into their own hands. Beginning with the South Carolina "REGULATORS" (1767–1769), vigilantism gradually spread westward, reaching the Pacific Coast where, in 1856, the powerful San Francisco Committee of Vigilance, with between 6,000 and 8,000 members, became the largest such movement in American history. Although Indiana, Illinois, and Iowa had strong VIGILANTE groups, the strongest groups were to be found in the West, especially in California, Texas, and Montana. Between 1767 and 1904, more than 300 vigilante movements sprung up in the United States, taking at least 729 lives. Their targets and victims were overwhelmingly lawless white members of turbulent pioneer communities.

Labor Violence

Oppressive labor conditions during the nineteenth and early twentieth centuries frequently precipitated violence.

In 1877, railroad employees spontaneously and violently rebelled from coast to coast. Strikes by workers and lockouts by management often led to tragedy as in the HOMESTEAD STRIKE of 1892, in which clashes between workers and PINKERTON guards hired by the Carnegie Steel Company led to the deaths of sixteen, and in the unsuccessful strike of miners against a Rockefeller-controlled coal company near Ludlow, Colorado, in 1913–1914. The Ludlow strike and management's response led to the death by suffocation of thirteen women and children in April 1914. Members of union families had taken underground refuge from antilabor militia in a deep dugout that came to be known as the "Black Hole of Ludlow" (see LUDLOW MASSACRE).

Industrial violence between capitalists and their employees declined greatly after the labor reforms initiated by President Franklin D. Roosevelt's "New Deal" in the 1930s. New Deal reforms in the interest of hard-pressed farmers also brought to an end some agrarian violence.

Assassinations, Mass Murder, and Riots

Assassination of those who hold public office is the apex of political violence. U.S. presidents have been unusually vulnerable to assassination: Abraham Lincoln (1865), James A. Garfield (1881), William McKinley (1901), and John F. Kennedy (1963). Ronald Reagan was badly wounded in a 1981 assassination attempt. Also felled by an assassin's bullet was the great nonviolent civil rights leader, Martin Luther King Jr., shot in Memphis in 1968.

The greatest episode of mass killing in the nineteenth and twentieth centuries actually took place outside the United States. The combination of mass suicide and murder ordered by the California cult leader, Jim Jones, in 1978 took his own life as well as the lives of 912 (including many children) of his followers at the cult's compound in Guyana, South America (see JONESTOWN MASSACRE).

The portrayal of violence changed enormously in the second half of the twentieth century with television news coverage and entertainment. TV coverage of the 1965 Watts riot in Los Angeles showed the anarchy and destruction of that massive riot. In 1991, repeated replays on television of the video recording of the police beating a black motorist, Rodney King, were followed a year later by live TV coverage of the multiracial looting and burning of far-flung areas of Los Angeles in anger over a suburban jury's acquittal of the police who beat King.

Television's most riveting broadcast of violence was the assassination of President John F. Kennedy on 22 November 1963. Two days later, live TV caught Jack Ruby shooting Lee Harvey Oswald, the accused Kennedy assassin. The Kennedy assassination was the tragic introduction to one of the most violent decades in U.S. history—a decade graphically portrayed on TV.

Terror

Beginning in 1993, horrific acts of terrorism were perpetrated, starting with a great explosion at the WORLD TRADE CENTER, New York City. In 1995 antigovernment terrorist Timothy McVeigh bombed the Alfred P. Murrah federal building in OKLAHOMA CITY, killing 168. Few thought that the Oklahoma City horror could be exceeded, but on 11 September 2001 terrorist attacks in New York City, Pennsylvania, and the Pentagon in Virginia took at least 3,063 lives (see 9/11 ATTACK). The television images of two of the hijacked airliners being deliberately flown into the twin towers of New York City's World Trade Center, which collapsed in less than two hours, traumatized the nation. Americans were reminded of the surprise attack on Pearl Harbor on 7 December 1941. While the emotional impact of Pearl Harbor on the public was huge, the stunning visual impact of the televised destruction of the World Trade Center had an immeasurably greater and more immediate effect.

BIBLIOGRAPHY

Ayers, Edward L. *Vengeance and Justice: Crime and Punishment in the Nineteenth-Century South.* New York: Oxford University Press, 1984.

Brown, Richard Maxwell. *No Duty to Retreat: Violence and Values in American History and Society.* New York: Oxford University Press, 1991.

Clarke, James W. *American Assassins: The Darker Side of American Politics.* Princeton, N.J.: Princeton University Press, 1982.

Dray, Philip. *At the Hands of Persons Unknown: The Lynching of Black America.* New York, Random House, 2002.

Gilje, Paul A. *Rioting in America.* Bloomington: Indiana University Press, 1996.

Gottesman, Ronald, and Richard M. Brown, eds. *Violence in America: An Encyclopedia.* 3 vols. New York, Scribners, 1999.

Hofstadter, Richard, and Michael Wallace, eds. *American Violence: A Documentary History.* New York: Knopf, 1970.

Richard M. Brown

See also **Assassinations and Political Violence, Other; Assassinations, Presidential; Crime; Indian Removal; Indian Warfare; Insurrections, Domestic; Riots; Serial Killings; Slave Insurrections;** *and articles on individual massacres, riots, and other violent incidents.*

VIOLENCE AGAINST WOMEN ACT was introduced in Congress in January 1991 by Senator Joseph Biden of Delaware. In 1991 an estimated 4 million women were victims of DOMESTIC VIOLENCE, with 20 percent of all assaults that were reported to the police occurring in the home. The bill was made part of the Violent Crime Control and Law Enforcement Act and was signed into law on 13 September 1994, by President Bill Clinton.

The act authorized $1.6 billion to be spent over six years on the creation of rape crisis centers and battered women's shelters and authorized additional local police, prosecutors, victim advocates, and a domestic violence hotline. Funds were also made available to provide special training for judges who hear domestic violence cases. Provisions of the act expanded rape shield laws, created offenses for interstate spousal abuse, and allowed victims of gender-based crimes to sue those responsible in federal court. The act requires victims to prove the crime was not random and was motivated by animus based on gender. Portions of the act not originally part of the Violence Against Women Bill include restrictions on gun purchases for persons guilty of domestic abuse, safeguards to protect the confidentiality of information kept by state motor vehicle bureaus, and increased penalties for hate crimes in which the victim is targeted on the basis of race, gender, religion, or sexual orientation. Although Republicans attempted to remove domestic violence provisions from the act, on the grounds that funding them constituted government waste, they were narrowly defeated in the House of Representatives and by a cloture vote ending a filibuster in the Senate.

BIBLIOGRAPHY

Brooks, Rachelle. "Feminists Negotiate the Legislative Branch: The Violence Against Women Act." In *Feminists Negotiate the State: The Politics of Domestic Violence.* Edited by Cynthia R. Daniels. Lanham, Md.: University Press of America, 1997.

Justice Research and Statistics Association. *Domestic and Sexual Violence Data Collection: A Report to Congress under the Violence Against Women Act.* Washington, D.C.: U.S. Department of Justice, 1996.

Schneider, Elizabeth M. *Battered Women and Feminist Lawmaking.* New Haven, Conn.: Yale University Press, 2000.

U.S. Senate Committee on the Judiciary. *Turning Act into Action: The Violence Against Women Law.* Washington, D.C.: G.P.O., 1994.

*Irwin N. Gertzog/*H. S.

See also **Rape; Women in Public Life, Business, and Professions.**

VIOLENCE COMMISSION.

After the assassinations of Martin Luther King Jr. and Senator Robert F. Kennedy, President Lyndon Johnson signed an executive order creating the National Commission on the Causes and Prevention of Violence. Its mandate was to explain the forces that were creating a more violent society and make recommendations for reducing the level of violence. Johns Hopkins president emeritus Milton S. Eisenhower chaired the commission, and federal judge A. Leon Higginbotham served as vice-chair. Other members included the longshoreman and libertarian philosopher Eric Hoffer, Terrence Cardinal Cooke, then archbishop of the New York archdiocese, and U.S. House majority whip Hale Boggs. The commission heard testimony from two hundred experts and collected and analyzed data. The final report was transmitted to President Richard Nixon on 10 December 1969. Titled *To Establish Justice, To Insure Domestic Tranquillity*, it argued that the growing violence was a symptom of enduring social and economic inequality, and that the only long-term answer to controlling violence in a democratic society was to rebuild the cities and provide jobs and educational opportunity for the poor. The commission recommended a $20 billion increase in spending for work and social service programs, as well as a recommitment to a full-employment economy. It also recommended handgun control legislation and highlighted the connection between television and real-life violence. The commission's liberal recommendations were ignored by the administration of Richard Nixon. The commission's work, however, influenced a generation of liberal criminologists.

BIBLIOGRAPHY

United States. National Commission on the Causes and Prevention of Violence. *To Establish Justice, To Insure Domestic Tranquillity: Final Report.* Washington, D.C.: U.S. Government Printing Office, 1969.

Richard M. Flanagan

See also **Assassinations and Political Violence, Other; Crime; Riots.**

VIRGIN ISLANDS.

The Virgin Islands of the United States, formerly known as the Danish West Indies, are located fifty miles east of the island of PUERTO RICO in the Caribbean Sea. Their 108,612 inhabitants (2000 census) live primarily on St. Croix, St. Thomas, and St. John, the largest of the sixty-eight islands composing the archipelago.

Before their acquisition by the United States, the islands belonged to the kingdom of Denmark, the ruling power since 1754. American interest in the islands can be dated much earlier than their acquisition in 1917. During the Civil War, Secretary of State William H. Seward, who wanted to secure naval bases for the defense of the American coastline and U.S. interests in the Caribbean, and prepare for the control of major maritime routes to Central and Latin America, made the first official openings to Denmark over a possible purchase.

Because of internal difficulties in Denmark and the declining economy of the islands, Danish authorities—represented by their minister to the United States, General von Raasloff—opened negotiations leading to a treaty of purchase (for $7.5 million), which was signed on 24 October 1867. In spite of a favorable plebiscite and a speedy ratification by the Danish Parliament, Secretary Seward failed to secure the support of Congress and public opinion.

A chain of circumstances led to the treaty's defeat: a natural disaster in St. John; the 1868 impeachment of President Andrew Johnson; and debate on the treaty to purchase Alaska. Furthermore, public opinion was against foreign expansion in the context of Reconstruction and westward expansion. The treaty languished in the Senate and was eventually rejected in 1869.

Subsequent efforts to purchase the islands were led by Secretary of State John Hay in 1902, who was suspicious of German schemes to obtain naval bases in the Caribbean. However, the Danish were no longer willing to cede the islands, hoping to benefit from the forthcoming isthmian canal.

During World War I, growing concern over German expansionism in Central America prompted Secretary of State Robert Lansing to reopen negotiations. A treaty was signed on 4 August 1916 and ratifications were exchanged on 17 January 1917. After a favorable plebiscite in the islands and the payment of $25 million, the transfer became effective on 31 March 1917. Virgin Islanders were made American citizens in 1927. During World War II, St. Thomas was developed as a defense base, along with Water Island.

After a period of administration by the Department of the Navy, the islands were turned over to the Office of Insular Affairs in the Interior Department in 1931, where it remained until 1971. As an organized, unincorporated territory of the United States, the islands were given a limited form of self-government by the Organic Act of 1936. Their degree of self-rule was enhanced by the Revised Organic Act of 1954, which gave legislative power to a unicameral legislature of fifteen popularly elected senators, and by the Elective Governor Act of 1968, which provided for the election of the governor.

The economy of the islands is largely founded on tourism, with two million visitors a year. While the agricultural sector is small, the manufacturing sector is flourishing. However, the islands are subject to substantial damage from storms and other natural hazards. Their trading partners are almost exclusively the mainland United States and Puerto Rico.

The purchase of the Virgin Islands can be considered as an important step in the consolidation of American hegemony over Cuba, Puerto Rico, and Panama. It thereby helped to assure U.S. geopolitical security and economic prosperity.

BIBLIOGRAPHY

Dookhan, Isaac. *A History of the Virgin Islands of the United States.* Kingston, Jamaica: Canoe Press, 1994.

Pedersen, Erik Overgaard. *The Attempted Sale of the Danish West Indies to the United States of America, 1865–1870.* Frankfurt, Germany: Haag und Herchen, 1997.

Tansill, Charles Callan. *The Purchase of the Danish West Indies.* Baltimore: Johns Hopkins Press, 1932. The most complete study to date.

Aissatou Sy-Wonyu

See also **Caribbean Policy; Imperialism; Navy, United States.**

VIRGINIA. Before the arrival of Europeans in the New World, several groups of Indians related to the IROQUOIS, Algonquins, and CHEROKEES occupied the present state of Virginia. The Powhatans were the most powerful and numerous. They inhabited the eastern shore and tide-water regions and lived in settled villages. The Powhatans and other Virginia Indians maintained themselves through hunting, fishing, and growing garden crops. The Indian population of Virginia was never great, numbering perhaps 17,000 at the time of English settlement, and fell sharply after the coming of the colonists. English settlers adopted many Indian place names, such as Appomattox, Nansemond, Rappahannock, and Shenandoah.

On 24 May 1607, English colonists established their first permanent settlement on a peninsula of the James River. Operating under a charter granted by James I, the London Company organized an expedition to colonize Virginia. The company, seeking to gain profit, instructed the colonists to search for the ill-fated colony established by Sir Walter Raleigh in 1587, to seek a northwest passage, and to prospect for gold and other treasure. They realized none of these goals, and for several years, the settlement suffered through great adversity. The stockade village, called Jamestown in honor of the king, unfortunately stood in a malarial swamp. Little fresh water or tillable soil was available in the immediate area. Disease, "starving times," low morale, poor leadership, bickering, and Indian attacks combined to threaten the struggling settlement with extinction on several occasions. Having gained no profit from the venture, the London Company was bankrupt by 1624. Tired of the mismanagement and scandal attending the failure of the enterprise, James I revoked the company's charter, and thereafter the colony came under the direct administration of the crown.

After the establishment of royal administration, the colony enjoyed greater stability and growth. However, the real catalyst in the eventual prosperity of Virginia was the discovery that tobacco could be grown for a profit and that black slaves could be exploited to the advantage of the spreading tobacco agriculture. These three factors of British royal government, tobacco, and slavery produced in Virginia a distinctive culture that spread from there through much of the North American south. British institutions transformed into a system of deferential democracy, while tobacco and slavery produced an economic, social, and political organism dominated by a native oligarchy of superior farmers called the planter aristocracy.

The early settlement of Virginia generally proceeded up the main waterways that empty into Chesapeake Bay. The James, the York, and the Rappahannock rivers served first as avenues into the wilderness and then as convenient outlets for trade. Eventually, the estates of the slaveholding elite were located adjacent to the important watercourses of the tidewater region. During the early eighteenth century, the pattern of settlement shifted as German and Scotch-Irish emigrants began to enter Virginia down the Allegheny ridges from Pennsylvania. These self-sufficient people established small farms in the upper piedmont and Shenandoah Valley regions and generally manifested little interest in acquiring slaves or participating in the culture of the east. Thus the planters of

**Virginia During
the Early Republic**

the tidewater and the farmers of the west had little in common. A dichotomy of interests developed early, which periodically disturbed the social and political stability of Virginia until after the Civil War.

Civil government in provincial Virginia evolved from a modification of the British system. Under the London Company, an appointed governor and council, with, after 1619, an elected assembly called the House of Burgesses, administered the colony. After royal authority replaced the London Company, the king appointed the governor and council while the qualified citizenry elected the burgesses. During the second half of the seventeenth century, the council and the burgesses gradually developed into a two-house legislature known as the General Assembly. The General Assembly eventually enjoyed considerable power over the affairs of the province and jealously guarded its power against encroachments from the governor or the crown. Experience in the assembly raised the political leadership of the province to a high degree of maturity. A property qualification for voting and office-holding somewhat restricted the electorate, but the House of Burgesses was fairly representative of the sentiments and interests of the farmers and planters of the tidewater region.

Toward the end of the seventeenth century, considerable political and social instability plagued the colony as planters and newcomers competed for land, position, and influence. Nathaniel Bacon, a recent arrival from England, led an unsuccessful uprising of those dissatisfied with the prevailing order in 1676 (see BACON'S REBELLION). Once a home-grown elite firmly entrenched themselves in power in the tidewater, political and social affairs became stable during the first half of the eighteenth century. This elite dominated the council and burgesses, and the citizenry deferred in judgment to those considered superior in status and experience. Although all recognized a distinct social hierarchy, the gentlemen moved with ease and grace among the people, and in turn the masses respected them.

Black SLAVERY was intimately associated with the growth of provincial Virginia. The first blacks arrived in 1619 and, like many whites entering the colony at that time, became indentured to the London Company. The spreading tobacco culture encouraged the cultivation of large landholdings, and eventually the emerging aristocracy found indentured servitude unsatisfactory. Masters freed indentured servants after a short period of time. Thus, they became potential competitors for land and position. Chattel slavery, limited to blacks, became institutionalized during the second half of the seventeenth century, an occurrence that coincided with the growing unrest among poorer whites during the era of Bacon's Rebellion. After a series of preliminary measures defining the status of slaves in the 1670s and 1680s, the General Assembly issued a comprehensive slave code in 1705, which stated that all blacks should "be held, taken, and adjudged real estate." As late as 1670, blacks constituted only 4 percent of the population of the province, but by 1730, the proportion had risen to 40 percent. During the 1660s and 1670s, there were reports and rumors of unrest and conspiracy among slaves. Fear of insurrection thus contributed to the urge of the planters to fix slavery.

While Virginia remained a predominantly rural area for three centuries, villages and towns played an important role in its culture. Jamestown never became important, owing largely to its unfavorable location. In 1699 WILLIAMSBURG became the capital of the province; RICHMOND was laid out on land owned by William Byrd II in 1737 and became the seat of government in 1779. Williamsburg reigned as capital during the colony's golden age. Nurtured by the College of William and Mary, the General Assembly, and the town's several law offices and taverns, the Williamsburg environment spawned a generation of political leaders of unusual ability and intellect. The chief port of the province was Norfolk, which had achieved a population of 6,000 by the eve of the American Revolution. During the eighteenth century, the population of Virginia grew from an estimated 72,000 to over 807,000, with about 42 percent of that population enslaved.

Virginians played a major role in the American independence movement and the founding of the new nation. Thomas Jefferson, George Mason, and James Madison were foremost revolutionary theoreticians, while George Washington pulled the dispirited continental forces into an army capable of forcing the British out of the thirteen colonies. Virginia was a major scene of battle during the latter stages of the war for independence; the final surrender of British forces took place at Yorktown on 19 October 1781. Jefferson's Declaration of Independence and Statute of Virginia for Religious Freedom, and Mason's Declaration of Rights for Virginia serve as notable examples of American revolutionary ideology and theory. Madison, widely schooled in classical and modern political philosophy, was a major author of the U.S. Constitution of 1787 and *The Federalist.* Virginians dominated the presidency from the beginning of the new nation until 1824. Four of the first five chief executives, Washington, Jefferson, Madison, and James Monroe, were natives of Virginia, giving rise to the term "Virginia Dynasty." As a consequence of the independence movement, these men gained a national reputation and experience that allowed them successfully to transcend provincial and sectional interests and to make a lasting contribution to the establishment of a truly national edifice of government in the United States.

Agriculture remained the chief occupation of a majority of Virginians after the founding of the nation. Soil exhaustion and erosion caused by decades of overplanting tobacco resulted in the abandonment of many acres of land in the tidewater and southside areas. Many planters moved to Alabama and Mississippi in order to recoup declining fortunes in the ongoing cotton boom of the Deep South. Advocates of scientific farming gradually convinced farmers of the advantages to be gained from deep plowing, the use of fertilizers, and crop diversification. Tobacco remained an important staple in the southside, but increasingly farmers planted wheat, other grains, and garden crops in the tidewater and lower piedmont. Richmond became one of the nation's important flour-milling centers. Cattle raising and orchard cultivation were important in the Shenandoah Valley and the Blue Ridge foothills. A slight decline in slavery attended the changing pattern of agriculture. Slaves composed 40 percent of the population of Virginia in 1810, but only 33 percent by 1850. Many impoverished planters sold unwanted slaves to the flourishing cotton planters of the Deep South.

By the early national period, the free white population of the tramontane region outnumbered that of eastern Virginia, but the General Assembly remained under the control of traditional tidewater and piedmont interests. As early as 1816, a convention of westerners met in Staunton to call for reapportionment, suffrage expansion, and constitutional reform. The increasing numbers of workers in the iron foundries and textile mills of Wheeling found difficulty in meeting the property qualification for voting and resented that the slaveholders in the east refused to recognize the peculiarity of western interests. In addition, western appeals for internal improvements frequently fell on deaf ears.

In 1829 a convention took place in Richmond to revise the state constitution. The western part of the state received slightly increased representation in the General Assembly, but the convention refused to allow full white manhood suffrage. Concern that uncertain democratic forces in the west would take over the state led the convention to vote to continue the control of Virginia by the slaveholding elite.

In the wake of the 1829 convention, a broad discussion of slavery occupied the attention of the General Assembly session of 1831–1832. Thomas Jefferson Randolph presented a plan for the gradual emancipation of slaves in Virginia, but a vote of seventy-three to fifty-eight in the House of Delegates defeated the proposition. The recent memory of a slave uprising on 21–22 August 1831, led by NAT TURNER, no doubt influenced the decision. In addition to defeating gradual emancipation, the 1831–1832 assembly imposed a more rigid slave code as a response to the Turner insurrection. Democratic ferment in the western part of the state and black upheaval thus conspired to create an atmosphere of fear in which the entrenched elements in Virginia were able to reinforce traditional institutions. The choice associated Virginia with the South in the developing sectional controversy, and it ultimately led the western counties to form the separate state of West Virginia during the Civil War.

After Virginia cast its lot with the South and joined the Confederacy, the state became the scene of almost continuous warfare between 1861 and 1865. About 170,000 Virginians served in the Confederate Army. A native son, Robert E. Lee, led the ARMY OF NORTHERN VIRGINIA against the Union and became the major Confederate hero. The contest largely destroyed extensive areas of the state, including Petersburg and Richmond. The war came to a practical end when Lee surrendered his forces to Ulysses S. Grant at APPOMATTOX Courthouse on 9 April 1865. Earlier, on 20 June 1863, the fifty western counties of the Old Dominion joined the Union as the state of West Virginia. The state thus lost nearly 35 percent of its land area and about 25 percent of its population.

As a result of the Civil War, nearly 500,000 Virginia slaves gained their freedom, and the state had to accept the provisions of the Reconstruction Acts of 1867 in order to regain statehood in the Union. In October 1867, a convention met in Richmond. The resulting constitution contained all the required measures, and on 6 July 1869, the new electorate approved it. In January 1870, Virginia returned to the Union. Not surprisingly, the Constitution of 1869, frequently referred to as the Underwood Constitution, was never popular among the large numbers of Virginians who cherished antebellum institutions.

The post-Reconstruction period witnessed many changes in Virginia. The present-day city of Roanoke had a population of 669 in 1880; it had grown to the size of 16,159 by 1890. In the 1880s, a political insurgency called the READJUSTER MOVEMENT disturbed the state. At issue was the state's burdensome debt, which maintained taxes at a high level and almost destroyed the new public school system. Movement leader Gen. William Mahone raised the specter of class antagonism by appealing to poor whites and blacks to unite in a movement of self-interest and reform. He spent a term in the U.S. Senate as a Republican, but a rejuvenated Democratic party defeated his party and principles in 1883. The Democrats successfully exploited the baiting and intimidation of blacks in their effort to drive the Readjuster-Republicans out of office.

Conservatism and white supremacy became the talisman of Virginia's Democratic party. The first political objective of the organization was the replacement of the 1869 Underwood Constitution and the establishment of white control over the electorate. In 1902 Democrats accomplished this with the promulgation of a new frame of government, which set forth a literacy test and a poll tax as requisites for voting, which halved the electorate and denied nearly all blacks the right to vote. Two early-twentieth-century governors, Andrew J. Montague and Claude A. Swanson, led the state in the adoption of many progressive reforms, such as a revitalized public school system, penal reform, the passage of a pure food and drug statute, and the establishment of a state corporation commission that other states widely copied. The organization was able to survive over the years by adopting and exploiting potentially popular issues, such as prohibition, and opposing unpopular federal programs that appeared to encroach on state sovereignty. After the adoption of the constitution of 1902, the Republican party ceased to be an important force in state politics until revived in the 1960s.

The issue of school integration brought profound changes to the political and social system of Virginia. In 1956 the Democratic party under Virginia Senator Harry F. Byrd announced a firm intention to preserve segregation. A campaign of massive resistance opposed implementation of the 1954 Supreme Court ruling in BROWN v. BOARD OF EDUCATION OF TOPEKA. Rather than comply with court-ordered integration, Gov. J. Linsey Almond Jr. closed public schools in Norfolk, Charlottesville, and Warren County. In 1959 the Virginia Supreme Court of Appeals condemned such action, but the controversy continued when in the same year, the supervisors of Prince Edward County decided to abandon public schools altogether. White students attended hastily prepared private academies while black children were without schools for five years. At length the impetus behind massive resistance died down, as adverse publicity drove prospective investors from the state and parents tired of the uncertainty in the schools. The Democratic party became divided over massive resistance and related issues, eventually splitting into warring conservative and liberal camps. Many organization supporters defected to the Republican party in the 1960 national elections. The Democratic party began to disintegrate rapidly after the death of Byrd in 1966.

Political changes dating from the 1960s continued over the ensuing decades. In 1964 the Twenty-fourth Amendment ended the poll tax as a condition of voting in federal elections, and in a 1966 case that arose in Virginia, the U.S. Supreme Court struck down the tax in state elections as well. The Supreme Court rendered decisions that forced reapportionment in elections to Congress and to the Virginia state legislature. These changes led to the defeat of long-term incumbents, such as U.S. Senator A. Willis Robertson and U.S. Representative Howard W. Smith. The newly reapportioned legislature enacted a sales tax in 1966, and in 1969 a Republican, A. Linwood Holton, won the governorship, which broke the stranglehold of rural white Democrats on Virginia politics and delivered the final blow to the Virginia Democratic party. The Republican party controlled the governorship during the 1970s, but the Democrats took over in the 1980s and early 1990s. In the later 1990s, Virginia again had Republican governors, but in the most recent election, Mark R. Warner, a conservative Democrat, won the office. In legislative races, Republicans and Democrats faced each other as equals in the 1990s. As late as 1975, the hundred-member Virginia House of Delegates included only seventeen Republicans, but by 1994 the num-

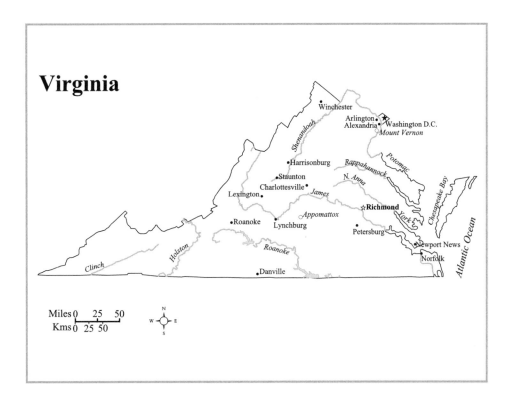

Virginia

Winchester
Arlington
Alexandria
Washington D.C.
Mount Vernon
Shenandoah
Harrisonburg
Staunton
Charlottesville
Lexington
Rappahannock
N. Anna
Potomac
James
Appomattox
Richmond
Roanoke
Lynchburg
Petersburg
York
Chesapeake Bay
Roanoke
Holston
Clinch
Danville
Newport News
Norfolk
Atlantic Ocean

Miles 0 25 50
Kms 0 25 50

ber was forty-seven. By 2000, the Republicans enjoyed a sixty-four to thirty-six majority in the House of Delegates. Meanwhile, Virginia became a Republican state in presidential elections. As early as 1948, although President Harry S. Truman took the state that year, Virginia Democrats had begun to abandon their party in presidential elections. Black Virginians abandoned the Republican party and embraced the Democrats but were swamped by the stream of white voters heading in the other direction, who together with many new residents voted Republican. From 1952 through 2000, the Democratic presidential candidates won Virginia's electoral votes only in 1964.

In terms of race and gender, Virginia politics in the late twentieth and early twenty-first centuries differed greatly from the l960s. In the late 1960s, for the first time since the 1880s, black candidates won election to the state legislature, and the number of women, most of them white, increased slowly as well. By the 2001 session, fifteen of the legislature's 140 members were black and twenty-two were women. Meanwhile, after the 1985 elections, Mary Sue Terry began the first of two four-year terms as state attorney general. L. Douglas Wilder, after sixteen years in the state senate, became lieutenant governor in 1985 and in 1989 became the first African American elected governor of any state. The declining significance of race in Virginia politics is obvious in that while a majority of white voters pulled the Republican lever, Wilder's victory depended on the support of far more whites than blacks. After the 1992 elections, Virginia's congressional delegation, like the state legislature, was no longer all white and all male. Robert C. Scott became only the second African American to win a seat from the Old Dominion, 104 years after John Mercer Langston's election in 1888, and Leslie L. Byrne became the first woman ever elected to Congress from Virginia, although Byrne lost her bid for reelection in 1994. In 2002, while neither of Virginia's senators was female or black, one woman and one African American did serve in the House of Representatives as part of the state's eleven-person delegation.

Major changes also occurred in higher education in Virginia in the last decades of the twentieth century. Such changes involved finance, numbers of students, the racial desegregation that came to Virginia in the 1950s and 1960s, and expansion of opportunities for women. The 1966 legislature inaugurated a statewide system of community colleges. By the 1990s, Virginia Polytechnic Institute and State University, Virginia Commonwealth University, George Mason University, and Northern Virginia Community College each enrolled more than 20,000 students. The UNIVERSITY OF VIRGINIA was not far behind. Before the 1950s, only one public institution of higher education in Virginia, now known as Virginia State University, admitted black students. By the 1990s, blacks attended every school although the numbers were still well below the African American percentage of Virginia residents. The University of Virginia only first admitted women as undergraduates in 1970, but by the 1990s, men and women were attending in almost equal numbers. Although women had begun attending law school there in 1920, they comprised 10 percent of the total number of law students only after congressional enactment of Title IX in 1972. By the 1990s, women comprised one-third of each graduating class. In the 1990s, the state reversed a quarter-century-long trend and trimmed its spending on higher education. Those budget cuts drove up tuition costs.

Virginia's economic prosperity in the twentieth century depended more on industry and government than on traditional agriculture. Until the 1990s, government was the second largest source of employment in Virginia, but the reduction of the United States military in that decade has meant the loss of thousands of military-related jobs. Tourism had developed into a billion-dollar-a-year enterprise by 1970 and remains an important industry. In the sphere of Virginia agriculture, which continues to decline in relative importance, the most significant changes came in the development of increasing numbers of dairy farms in the northern part of the state and of truck farms on the eastern shore. Peanut growing and processing centered around Suffolk, and the production of Smithfield hams replaced tobacco as the standard staple among a large number of southside farms. The significance of manufacturing also has fallen recently in Virginia's economy, with jobs in trade and service increasing to replace it. Nonetheless, the per capita income of Virginians remains almost 10 percent above the national average.

The population of Virginia more than tripled between 1900 and 2000, growing from 1,854,000 to nearly 7,079,000. Net immigration accounted for fully half the growth during the last forty years, which illustrates significant changes in Virginia's recent history, as the state had been a large exporter of people throughout the nineteenth century and well into the twentieth. During the same period, the population of the state also became highly urbanized, with nearly a 70 percent urban concentration in 1990 compared to only 18 percent in 1900. Thus northern and southeastern Virginia have become part of the "urban corridor" that stretches from Boston down the Atlantic seaboard, and the formerly rural counties of Henrico and Loudoun have found themselves absorbed into metropolitan Washington, D.C. From 1900 to 1970, the proportion of black people residing in the state steadily declined from over 35 percent to 18 percent, as many thousands of black Virginians decided to join the general tide of migration out of the south. Between 1970 and 2000, however, the black population began to stabi-

lize at around 19 percent. Meanwhile, residents of Asian ancestry increased from a negligible number at the time of the 1965 Immigration Act to a figure approaching 4 percent in 2000. Hispanics make up about 3 percent of Virginia's population.

BIBLIOGRAPHY

Blair, William A. *Virginia's Private War: Feeding Body and Soul in the Confederacy, 1861–1865.* New York: Oxford University Press, 1998.

Brundage, W. Fitzhugh. *Lynching in the New South: Georgia and Virginia, 1880–1930.* Urbana: University of Illinois Press, 1993.

Dailey, Jane Elizabeth. *Before Jim Crow: The Politics of Race in Postemancipation Virginia.* Chapel Hill: University of North Carolina Press, 2000.

Faggins, Barbara A. *Africans and Indians: An Afrocentric Analysis of Relations between Africans and Indians in Colonial Virginia.* New York: Routledge, 2001.

Hadden, Sally E. *Slave Patrols: Law and Violence in Virginia and the Carolinas.* Cambridge, Mass.: Harvard University Press, 2001.

Lassiter, Matthew D., and Andrew B. Lewis, eds. *The Moderates' Dilemma: Massive Resistance to School Desegregation in Virginia.* Charlottesville: University Press of Virginia, 1998.

Lewis, Charlene M. Boyer. *Ladies and Gentlemen on Display: Planter Society at the Virginia Springs, 1790–1860.* Charlottesville: University Press of Virginia, 2001.

Morgan, Edmund S. *American Slavery, American Freedom: The Ordeal of Colonial Virginia.* New York: Norton, 1975.

Sobel, Mechal. *The World They Made Together: Black and White Values in Eighteenth-Century Virginia.* Princeton, N.J.: Princeton University Press, 1987.

Raymond H. Pulley
Peter Wallenstein / A. E.

See also **Civil War; Colonial Assemblies; Confederate States of America; Desegregation; Plymouth; Reconstruction; Revolution, American: Political History; Slavery; South, the; Suffrage: African American Suffrage; Tidewater; Tobacco Industry;** and vol. 9: **The History and Present State of Virginia.**

VIRGINIA BEACH, located on Cape Henry at the entrance to Chesapeake Bay in Virginia, the site of the first landing of the Jamestown colonists in 1607. Later in the 1620s, a community known as Lynnhaven grew up in what became Princess Anne County by 1691. After piracy in the area was eradicated in the early eighteenth century, trade emerged as a mainstay of the local economy. To diminish dangers to merchant shipping, the Cape Henry lighthouse was erected in 1792.

In the 1880s Virginia Beach became a popular seaside resort with several luxury hotels. The most famous of these, the Cavalier Hotel, opened in 1927 and became known as the "Queen of the Beach." Although the tourist industry remained a crucial part of the local economy through the twentieth century, the U.S. military—particularly Oceana Naval Air Station—proved an essential catalyst for the city's rapid post–World War II growth.

Another factor in that growth was "white flight," as nearby Norfolk desegregated in the late 1950s and 1960s. In 1963 city and county merged, creating Virginia's largest city. Public hostility kept African Americans from moving in significant numbers to "the Beach," making the city somewhat of an anomaly among southern cities; the 2000 population of 425,257 was overwhelmingly white relative to other urban areas in Virginia and the region.

BIBLIOGRAPHY

The Beach: A History of Virginia Beach, Virginia. Virginia Beach: Virginia Beach Public Library, 1996.

J. Fred Saddler

See also **Sun Belt.**

VIRGINIA CITY, the largest and most famous of Nevada's early mining towns, came into existence in 1859. By 1861, when Congress organized Nevada Territory, it was a town of importance with a population of more than 3,000. It was incorporated as a city in 1864, and by the 1870s, its population had grown to about 30,000. The city declined in the 1880s when the ores of the great Comstock mining region failed. Disincorporated, Virginia City was eventually abandoned and became a ghost town. A number of buildings were preserved or restored, however, which makes Virginia City a popular tourist attraction.

BIBLIOGRAPHY

James, Ronald M., and C. Elizabeth Raymond, eds. *Comstock Women: The Making of a Mining Community*. Reno: University of Nevada Press, 1998.

James, Ronald M. *The Roar and the Silence: A History of Virginia City and the Comstock Lode*. Reno: University of Nevada Press, 1998.

Rupert N. Richardson/A. E.

See also **Bonanza Kings; Boomtowns; Comstock Lode; Gold Mines and Mining; Mining Towns; Nevada.**

VIRGINIA COMPANY OF LONDON was a commercial enterprise established on 10 April 1606 that governed the colony of Virginia from 1609 to 1624. The Society of Adventurers, or investors, was patented to Sir Thomas Gates, Sir George Somers, and their associates. The company, headquartered in London, was a body of stockholders who acquired interest in the company by paying money, rendering service, or settling on land in Virginia. Investors had to raise funds, furnish supplies, and send out expeditions. The company was presided over by a treasurer and conducted all of its business through its regularly elected officers or through special committees. The governing council in England was subordinate to the king regarding affairs in Virginia. Each colony was to be governed by a council in London and in day-to-day matters by a local council. The Virginia Company of London and the Virginia Company of Plymouth were patented to settle between 34 and 45 degrees north latitude. The London Company was allowed to settle between 34 and 41 degrees north latitude and the Plymouth Company, between 38 and 45 degrees north latitude. Settlements could not be within 100 miles of each other in the overlapping area of 38 to 41 degrees.

From 1606 to 1609, the private investors had little influence on affairs or commercial matters in Virginia. Business management was left to a joint-stock company, and the storehouse was controlled by a treasurer and two clerks elected by the president and council in the colony. In 1609, a second charter was granted to the company, converting it to a corporation and permitting public sale of stock. The entrepreneurs, with Sir Thomas Smith as treasurer, retained commercial responsibilities, assumed governmental functions, and reduced royal supervision. This new charter allowed the company to appoint a governor for the colony and the council in Virginia became an advisory body. The council of the company in London was chosen by the investors to act as a standing committee.

Another charter in 1612 strengthened the authority of the company, making it overlord of a proprietary province. Major decisions of the company were to be prepared at the quarter courts, which were stockholder meetings held four times per year. Extending over a period of seven years, a system for the joint management of land and exemption from English customs duties promised dividends to the investors and support for the planters. There was also enacted a running lottery that collected auxiliary money for the settlement and jurisdiction over newly discovered Bermuda. By 1617, many indentured servants fulfilled their obligations to the Virginia Company. Those settlers who had arrived before 1616 got one hundred acres fee simple.

In 1619 the Virginia Company adopted its Orders and Constitutions that were intended to ensure the legality of action and were read at one quarter court each year. The company allowed private landholding in order to encourage settlement. An investor might also obtain stock within three years by paying the passage for settlers and peopling his land. Emigration to Virginia by laborers, artisans, and apprentices was encouraged to attain production of grain, silk, and industries other than tobacco. A representative assembly was also enacted to offer settlers a voice in policy.

Between 1619 and 1622, factions developed within the company as a result of the administration of Samuel Argall, deputy governor of the colony. He exploited the lands and the trade of the company for private benefit. This led to the formation of an administration under Lord Cavendish, John Ferrar, Nicholas Ferrar, Sir Edwin Sandys, and the earl of Southampton with unconstructive changes. The Sandys-Southampton party supported the parliamentary opposition in England, and thus the king and Sandys became bitter political rivals. An Indian massacre in 1622 added to the colony's problems.

On 17 April 1623, a committee headed by Lord Cavendish was summoned before the Privy Council to defend the company against grievances. On 9 May 1623, the Privy Council announced that a commission would be appointed to inquire into the state of Virginia and Somers Island plantation. The commission found the colony had been in a state of disorder since the massacre by the Indians; there was quarreling among the factions of the company and masses of unprepared and unprovisioned settlers that Sir Edwin Sandys had sent to the new land. The king also wanted to maximize his revenues from customs duties on tobacco, even though he despised the commodity. On 24 May 1624, the company was dissolved, terminating in bankruptcy, and on 15 July, a commission was appointed to replace the Virginia Company of London and establish the first royal colony in America. The king sought the advice of the company on questions affecting the government of the colony, but Sandys was unsuccessful in his attempt to secure a new patent. Its function as a trading organization ceased.

BIBLIOGRAPHY

Andrews, Kenneth R. *Trade, Plunder, and Settlement: Maritime Enterprise and the Genesis of the British Empire, 1480–1630.* Cambridge: Cambridge University Press, 1984.

Billings, Warren M., Thad W. Tate, and John E. Selby. *Colonial Virginia: A History.* White Plains, N.Y.: KTO Press, 1986.

Craven, Wesley Frank. *Dissolution of the Virginia Company: The Failure of a Colonial Experiment.* Gloucester, Mass.: P. Smith, 1964.

———. *The Virginia Company of London, 1606–1624.* Williamsburg: Virginia 350th Anniversary Celebration Corporation, 1957.

Morton, Richard Lee. *Colonial Virginia.* Chapel Hill: University of North Carolina Press, 1960.

Neill, Edward D. *History of the Virginia Company of London, with Letters to and from the First Colony Never Before Printed.* New York: B. Franklin, 1968.

Rabb, Theodore K. *Enterprise & Empire: Merchant and Gentry Investment in the Expansion of England, 1575–1630.* Cambridge, Mass.: Harvard University Press, 1967.

Michelle M. Mormul

See also **Colonial Charters; Plymouth, Virginia Company of; Proprietary Colonies; Royal Colonies; Trading Companies.**

VIRGINIA DECLARATION OF RIGHTS

was formulated by George Mason. A convention of members of the Virginia House of Burgesses adopted this listing of first principles of government and of civil liberties on 12 June 1776, seventeen days before it adopted the constitution that made Virginia an independent state. Virginia's Declaration of Rights furnished a model for similar declarations in other state constitutions and also for the first ten amendments to the U.S. Constitution (the Bill of Rights).

BIBLIOGRAPHY

Adams, Willi Paul. *The First American Constitutions: Republican Ideology and the Making of the State Constitutions in the Revolutionary Era.* Rita Kimber and Robert Kimber, trans. Chapel Hill: University of North Carolina Press for Institute of Early American History and Culture, 1980.

Conley, Patrick T., and John P. Kaminski, eds. *The Bill of Rights and the States: The Colonial and Revolutionary Origins of American Liberties.* Madison, Wisc.: Madison House, 1992.

Rutland, Robert A. *The Birth of the Bill of Rights, 1776–1791.* Chapel Hill: University of North Carolina Press for Institute of Early American History and Culture, 1955.

Rutland, Robert A., ed. *The Papers of George Mason: 1725–1792.* Chapel Hill: University of North Carolina Press, 1970.

Veit, Helen E., Kenneth R. Bowling, and Charlene Bangs Bickford, eds. *Creating the Bill of Rights: The Documentary Record from the First Federal Congress.* Baltimore: Johns Hopkins University Press, 1991.

Matthew Page Andrews/c. p.

See also **Bill of Rights in U.S. Constitution; Constitution of the United States; Coutume de Paris;** *and vol. 9:* **Virginia Declaration of Rights.**

VIRGINIA DYNASTY,

a term applied to the succession of Virginia presidents in the late eighteenth and early nineteenth century. Between 1789 and 1825, four Virginians held the presidency for thirty-two of thirty-six years: George Washington, who served from 1789 to 1797; Thomas Jefferson, who served from 1801 to 1809; James Madison, who served from 1809 to 1817; and James Monroe, who served from 1817 to 1825. The only interruption in the Virginia Dynasty's control of the presidency came from 1797 to 1801, when John Adams, a native of Massachusetts, served a single term as president. Although Washington, like Adams, was a member of the Federalist Party, Jefferson, Madison, and Monroe all belonged to the Democratic-Republican Party. Jefferson's defeat of Adams in the 1800 presidential election ended the Federalists' control of the presidency and inaugurated an era of growing sectional conflict. Jefferson and his two Virginian successors shared a commitment to limited government, STATES' RIGHTS, and SLAVERY, views that generated sharp political opposition from northeastern Federalists. Resentful of the South's political influence in the federal government, the Federalists accused the Virginia Dynasty of pursuing policies biased toward southern interests. The dynasty finally ended in 1825 with the inauguration of John Quincy Adams, a resident of Massachusetts and son of John Adams, as the sixth president of the United States. A native Virginian would not hold the White House again until William Henry Harrison became president in 1841. The last Virginia native to become president was Woodrow Wilson, who served from 1913 to 1921.

BIBLIOGRAPHY

Ellis, Joseph J. *American Sphinx: The Character of Thomas Jefferson*. New York: Knopf University Press, 1998.

McCoy, Drew R. *The Elusive Republic: Political Economy in Jeffersonian America*. New York: Norton, 1982.

———. *The Last of the Fathers: James Madison and the Republican Legacy*. New York: Cambridge University Press, 1989.

Styron, Arthur. *The Last of the Cocked Hats: James Monroe and the Virginia Dynasty*. Norman: University of Oklahoma, 1945.

James Elliott Walmsley / A. G.

See also **Federalist Party; Jeffersonian Democracy; President, U.S.; Republicans, Jeffersonian; Virginia.**

VIRGINIA INDIAN COMPANY

VIRGINIA INDIAN COMPANY was created in 1714 to improve relations with the Indians. The Tuscarora War in North Carolina in 1711–1715 threatened Virginia's stability and its access to the lucrative trade in deerskins and Indian slaves to the south. Throughout the 1690s, Governor Francis Nicholson unsuccessfully advocated the creation of a strong trading concern to reduce trader abuses and limit French activities in the west, but fears that unscrupulous traders would cause another war finally prodded the colonial assembly to act. Authorized by provincial statute in 1714, the Virginia Indian Company was a private company of shareholders given exclusive control over traffic with the Indians in exchange for running the fort and Indian school at company headquarters at Fort Christanna. The organization supplied tribes, reopened trade with the Catawbas and Cherokees, and sponsored the discovery—made in the spring of 1716—of a passage through the Blue Ridge Mountains at or near Swift Run Gap. The act creating the corporation was disallowed by the English Privy Council in 1717 on the grounds that the enterprise constituted a monopoly. The history of Virginia affords no other example of a private stock company being given complete control of Indian trade.

BIBLIOGRAPHY

Robinson, Walter S. *The Southern Colonial Frontier, 1607–1763*. Albuquerque: University of New Mexico Press, 1979.

W. Neil Franklin / J. H.

See also **Fur Trade and Trapping; Indian Policy, Colonial: Dutch, French, Spanish, and English.**

VIRGINIA RESOLVES

VIRGINIA RESOLVES is a name applied to several sets of resolutions. The most important were the Virginia Resolves on the STAMP ACT. Patrick Henry introduced six resolutions, which were adopted by the Virginia House of Burgesses on 30 May 1765 except for the last two, which were considered too radical. Seven, slightly reworded, were published widely in newspapers, and similar sets were adopted by the legislatures of eight colonies by the end of 1765.

Earlier in 1765 the British Parliament had passed the Stamp Act, which placed a tax on newspapers, almanacs, pamphlets, and broadsides, all kinds of legal documents, insurance policies, ship's papers, licenses, dice, and playing cards. This led to widespread protest in the American colonies and to the slogan, "NO TAXATION WITHOUT REPRESENTATION!"

The key resolution of the official version of the Virginia Resolves was

> That the general assembly of the colony, together with his majesty or his substitute have in their representative capacity the only exclusive right and power to levy taxes and impositions on the inhabitants of this colony and that every attempt to vest such a power in any person or persons whatsoever other than the general assembly aforesaid is illegal, unconstitutional, and unjust, and has a manifest tendency to destroy British, as well as American freedom.

The Virginia Resolves concerning the TOWNSHEND ACTS were prepared by George Mason and introduced 16 May 1769 by George Washington in the House of Burgesses. They were adopted unanimously that day as a protest against the 1767 Townshend Acts, which had been adopted by the British Parliament after the repeal of the Stamp Act in 1766. The Townshend Acts created a tax on imported goods, such as paper, glass, paints, and tea shipped from England.

In February 1768, Samuel Adams drew up and issued the Circular Letter, which reported that the Massachusetts General Court had denounced the Townshend Acts in violation of the principle of no taxation without representation, reasserted that the colonies were not represented adequately in the British Parliament, and attacked the Crown's attempt to make colonial governors and judges independent of people by providing them a source of revenue independent of taxation and appropriations by colonial legislatures.

Resolutions passed by the Virginia House of Burgesses in 1769 asserted that only the Virginia governor and legislature had the power to tax Virginians. They also condemned the British government for censuring Adams's Circular Letters, multiple copies of which had been sent by various colonies, and attacked proposals in Parliament that dissidents be taken to England for trial. Within a few months, similar sets of resolutions were adopted by other colonial assemblies.

Written by James Madison and introduced by John Taylor of Caroline County, the Virginia Resolutions of 1798 was adopted by the Virginia Senate on 24 December 1798. Together with the Kentucky Resolutions of 1798 authored by Thomas Jefferson, it protested the ALIEN AND SEDITION ACTS of 1798, calling for state actions to obstruct their enforcement. That approach came to be called state nullification of U.S. laws. These protests established the Doctrine of '98 for interpretation of the Constitution, which drove the Democratic-Republican Party that elected Jefferson to the presidency and took control of Congress in 1800. That event came to be called the Revolution of 1800, which ushered in the Jeffersonian era that lasted through 1824.

BIBLIOGRAPHY

Loring, Caleb William. *Nullification, Secession, Webster's Argument, and the Kentucky and Virginia Resolutions Considered in Reference to the Constitution.* New York, 1893.

Jon Roland

See also **Massachusetts Circular Letter.**

VIRGINIA V. WEST VIRGINIA. When Congress admitted West Virginia to the Union in 1863, the West Virginia constitution contained provision for assumption of an "equitable" portion of the undivided state's debt. After decades of futile collection efforts, Virginia brought suit in the U.S. Supreme Court in 1906. In 1915 the Court decreed that West Virginia should pay $12,393,929, which was to go to certificate holders in final settlement. In 1918 the Court asserted its power to enforce its decision but postponed further action in the belief that West Virginia would now discharge its plain duty. Thereupon West Virginia paid.

BIBLIOGRAPHY

McGregor, James Clyde. *The Disruption of Virginia.* New York: Macmillan, 1922.

C. C. Pearson / A. R.

See also **State Constitutions.**

VIROLOGY. *See* **Microbiology.**

VIRTUAL REALITY refers to computer-generated, three-dimensional simulations that allow a participant to experience and interact with a setting or situation. In the most intense forms of virtual reality, a participant wears a headset that incorporates high-resolution video displays and audio speakers, immersing the participant in a computer-generated experience. The participant also wears a special glove or body suit studded with sensors that monitor all movement. Data from the participant's movements are then fed into a computer, which modifies the simulation accordingly. Virtual reality systems allow a participant to experience, navigate through, and manipulate a hypothetical area filled with imaginary structures and objects. This area is often referred to as "cyberspace," a term first used by author William Gibson in his 1984 novel, *Neuromancer.* By the end of the twentieth century, virtual reality not only encapsulated a specific technology, but also signaled a broader set of cultural questions about the place of technology in modern life.

The growth of the INTERNET, along with the advent of inexpensive and increasingly powerful computers and the development of sophisticated computer graphics techniques, has led to faster and more detailed virtual reality systems, adding to the realism of the experiences they deliver. The use of virtual reality technology in the entertainment industry holds the potential to provide consumers with a choice of exotic, surreal, or breathtaking experiences without any physical risk. Virtual reality has also been employed for more serious ends. Astronauts at the National Aeronautics and Space Administration used virtual reality devices as part of their training for the 1993 space shuttle flight, during which they repaired the HUBBLE SPACE TELESCOPE. Department of Energy experts employ a virtual reality version of a nuclear weapon in a shipping container to train emergency workers to handle trucking accidents involving such devices. Another application of virtual reality technology is telepresence, or giving the participant a sensation of being in a distant location. Telepresence systems, for example, can allow a physician in a hospital to perform emergency surgery on a soldier by remote control while the soldier is still on the battlefield, rather than wait until the soldier is transported to the hospital. Telepresence also holds the potential to be used for operating robotic rovers on the moon or on Mars for scientific purposes, or for profit-generating entertainment ventures.

While virtual reality provides the possibility of creating new communities in cyberspace, critics of virtual reality—and of technology in general—warn that it might overwhelm and erode established networks of human existence. Some educators, for instance, debate the effectiveness of virtual reality to provide a "distance learning" experience that could substitute for the traditional, four-year undergraduate education. At the most extreme, however, criticism of technology has taken the form of terrorism, as in the case of the UNABOMBER, Theodore Kaczynski.

BIBLIOGRAPHY

Heim, Michael. *The Metaphysics of Virtual Reality.* New York: Oxford University Press, 1993.

———. *Virtual Realism.* New York: Oxford University Press, 1998.

Rheingold, Howard. *Virtual Reality.* New York: Summit, 1991.

Vincent Kiernan
Jason Scott Smith

See also **Educational Technology; Medicine.**

VOICE OF AMERICA (VOA) is a multilingual radio broadcasting service begun in 1942 and administered since 1953 by the United States Information Agency (USIA). The first VOA broadcast originated from New York City on 24 February 1942, just seventy-nine days after the United States entered World War II. Speaking in German, announcer William Harlan Hale told his listeners, "Here speaks a voice from America. Every day at this time we will bring you the news of the war. The news may be good. The news may be bad. We shall tell you the truth."

The agency is responsible for the dissemination of U.S. policy and other types of information to foreign countries and for combating enemy propaganda. In essence, it creates a face for the nation for foreign listeners. In administering the VOA, the director of the USIA reports to the secretary of state and the president of the United States. Under its congressionally mandated charter, the VOA seeks to broadcast reliable news stories, present a balanced view of U.S. culture, and report on U.S. policy. Programming is intended for non-U.S. audiences, and under provisions of the Smith-Mundt Act (1948) and a clarifying amendment in 1972, programs may not be broadcast within the United States without congressional approval.

VOA broadcasts have been blocked by communications services in some countries, which have criticized its programming as anticommunist propaganda, but the agency has continued to receive support from Congress and U.S. presidents into the post–Cold War years. In 1983, VOA established the International Broadcast Training Center in Washington to train broadcasters from developing countries and to demonstrate the value of a free press. In 1985, VOA founded Radio Marti for broadcasting to Cuba and in 1990 expanded its efforts to deliver uncensored news to that nation with the establishment of TV Marti. Voice of America continued its work in the 1990s with programs ranging from the promotion of democracy to the war on drugs.

In 2002 VOA broadcast over 900 hours of news, informational, educational, and cultural programs every week to an audience of some 94 million worldwide. VOA programs are produced and broadcast in English and fifty-two other languages through radio, satellite television, and the Internet.

BIBLIOGRAPHY

Krugler, David F. *The Voice of America and Domestic Propaganda Battles, 1945–1953*. Columbia: University of Missouri Press, 2000.

Rawnsley, Gary D. *Radio Diplomacy and Propaganda: The BBC and VOA in International Politics, 1956–1964*. New York: St. Martin's Press, 1996.

Laura A. Bergheim

See also **America as Interpreted by Foreign Observers; Propaganda; Radio.**

VOLCANOES are mountains with a vent from which molten material from deep within the earth can spew under the appropriate conditions. Volcanoes have existed for geologic eons, but many are no longer active. The number of volcanoes worldwide that earth scientists consider active—those that can erupt—was about five hundred in

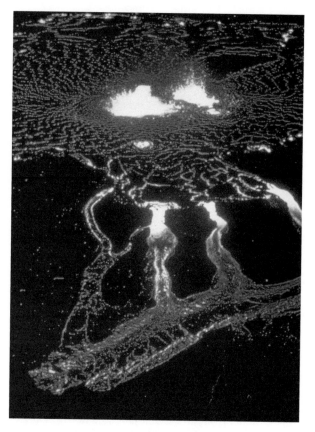

Kilauea. Eruptions at the volcano, on the island of Hawaii, create a spectacular lava flow. JLM VISUALS

the mid-1990s. Volcanoes are usually located at the junction of the earth's lithospheric plates. In the United States most active volcanoes are located in Alaska or in Hawaii, which consists of a group of islands formed by earlier volcanic eruptions. The West Coast of the continental United States also has a relatively inactive volcanic zone.

The two principal volcanoes in the United States are Mauna Loa and Kilauea, both in the Hawaiian island chain. Mauna Loa, the world's largest volcano, erupted most recently in 1975 and 1984. Kilauea is in almost continual eruption. Alaskan eruptions occurred in 1989, when Mount Redoubt, along Cook Inlet, southwest of Anchorage, erupted; in 1992, when Mount Spurr erupted; and in 1996, when an unnamed volcano on Augustine Island (also in Cook Inlet) erupted. Although not in the United States, Mount Pinatubo in the Philippines projected enough ash into the stratosphere during its eruption in 1991 to have a significant cooling effect on the U.S. climate for several years. Eruptions in the lower forty-eight states are rare but certainly not unknown: for example, the widely publicized eruption of MOUNT ST. HELENS in Washington State in 1980. Despite dire predictions and a minor eruption in 1990, the area surrounding Mount St. Helens had largely recovered from the effects of the 1980 eruption by 2000.

There are two volcanic observatories in the United States. One, established on Kilauea in 1912, is the second oldest in the world, ranking behind only one in Italy, on Mount Vesuvius. Following the eruption of Mount St. Helens in 1980, an observatory was established there.

BIBLIOGRAPHY

Decker, Robert W., and Barbara B. Decker. *Mountains of Fire: The Nature of Volcanoes.* New York: Cambridge University Press, 1991.

Scarth, Alwyn. *Volcanoes: An Introduction.* College Station: Texas A&M University Press, 1994.

Nancy M. Gordon / c. w.

See also **Alaska; Geology; Hawaii; Paleontology.**

VOLSTEAD ACT. The Eighteenth Amendment (ratified 29 January 1919) needed enforcement, and in October 1919 Congress passed the National Prohibition Act, introduced by Representative Andrew J. Volstead of Minnesota. President Woodrow Wilson vetoed the measure on 27 October, but Congress overrode the veto the next day. The act fixed penalties for liquor sales; provided for injunctions against establishments found selling liquor; contained a search and seizure clause; and, oddly, continued the taxation of alcoholic beverages. It permitted the retention of private stocks of liquor bought before the act went into effect, and allowed beer manufacturing, on condition that brewers reduce the alcoholic content to 0.5 percent before sale.

BIBLIOGRAPHY

Hamm, Richard F. *Shaping the Eighteenth Amendment.* Chapel Hill: University of North Carolina Press, 1995.

Alvin F. Harlow / c. w.

See also **Alcohol, Regulation of; Brewing; Constitution of the United States; Prohibition; Temperance Movement.**

VOLUNTEER ARMY. Use of volunteers for military service was popular throughout the first hundred years of U.S. history. Volunteers fought in the American Revolution, the Indian wars of the late 1700s, the War of 1812, the Mexican-American War, on both sides of the Civil War, and in the Spanish-American War. Permanent state militia units tended to put military training on a volunteer basis, and until World War I, individuals volunteered for national military service through the state quota system in state units.

With the passage of the Selective Service Act of 1917, volunteer forces began to diminish. Passage of the National Defense Act of 1920 rendered all state volunteers, who served in the National Guard, subject to federal military call whenever necessary. The state militias and National Guard kept up the supply of volunteers, but in the national military service, the numbers severely lessened.

The advent of mechanized warfare and strict planning of maneuvers made a great amount of training necessary, which virtually eliminated the untrained war volunteer. Tactics and equipment operation took time to learn, and in the case of the old-fashioned war volunteer, there was not enough time.

The furor during the Vietnam War over the draft reawakened interest in building an all-volunteer army, but there was much dissension over the practicality of such a move. Nevertheless, in 1973 the federal government abolished the Selective Service System. Prospective volunteers in the all-volunteer army receive incentives. Volunteers choose their branch of service and the course of study to follow while fulfilling their military obligations.

Throughout the 1970s, efforts to attract recruits in the quantity and quality required achieved only mixed success, and these difficulties prompted critics to question the feasibility of relying exclusively on volunteers. In the 1980s, however, recruiting methods and the quality of recruits improved. By the late 1980s and early 1990s, a string of U.S. military successes seemed to vindicate the decision to revert to the volunteer tradition.

BIBLIOGRAPHY

Bachman, Jerald G. *The All-Volunteer Force: A Study of Ideology in the Military.* Ann Arbor: University of Michigan Press, 1977.

Fredland, J. Eric, et al., eds. *Professionals on the Front Line: Two Decades of the All-Volunteer Force.* Washington, D.C.: Brassey's, 1996.

Keeley, John B., ed. *The All-Volunteer Force and American Society.* Charlottesville: University Press of Virginia, 1978.

Andrew J. Bacevich
Angela Ellis

See also **Conscription and Recruitment; Enlistment.**

VOLUNTEERISM may be defined as contributing one's time or talents for charitable, educational, social, political, or other worthwhile purposes, usually in one's community, freely and without regard for compensation. Since the seventeenth century, Americans have shaped their nation by their voluntary efforts: providing services, organizing political action, caring for the poor, reaching out to the disadvantaged, providing education, ensuring equality and civil rights for all citizens, and working for change.

Too numerous to count, American voluntary efforts have served many purposes. For example, thousands of Americans have contributed their resources to achieve political ends, providing invaluable service in times of war. During the Revolution men formed committees of correspondence to keep the colonies in constant contact; joined MILITIAS, like the MINUTEMEN of Concord, to fight the British army; and organized the BOSTON TEA PARTY, a raid on ships in Boston Harbor, during which crates of

Americorps Volunteer. Americorps, a federally sponsored program enacted early in the first Clinton administration, provided stipends for community-oriented volunteer work. AP/ Wide World Photos

expensive tea were thrown overboard to protest taxes imposed by the crown. At the same time, women used their economic power to boycott luxury items and cloth imported from Britain, producing their own goods for their family's needs. During the Revolution and later wars, women visited hospitals and prisons, rolled bandages, organized food drives, nursed soldiers, and sometimes worked as spies. In the nineteenth century, African Americans and white Americans undertook the dangerous task of moving escaped slaves to freedom along the UNDERGROUND RAILROAD. Children volunteered also, contributing their pennies and participating in drives to conserve food, clothing, and other resources. Americans continue to volunteer for political purposes by joining the military, working for political parties at elections, participating in voting drives, organizing block associations, protesting, marching, lobbying, and raising funds.

Volunteers have also provided relief to people in need. At first, citizens willingly organized to provide a service for their town or county. In the nineteenth century, public need began to overwhelm local resources. Women then seized the opportunity to become actively engaged in public life and policy. They organized, built, and maintained shelters for the homeless, soup lines, or-

phanages, homes for single mothers and abandoned children, and hospitals for the needy. Often established by religious and ethnic groups, these institutions assisted individuals and families, filling in the gaps that government did not have the authority or ability to cover. Similarly, from slavery through the beginning of the twenty-first century, African Americans have organized to provide relief, churches, burial, and religious instruction for their communities. Children have helped raise funds in their neighborhoods for schools, missions, and foreign aid organizations like UNICEF (United Nations Children's Fund). Volunteers continue to visit and nurse the sick, offer food to the hungry, clean up after disasters, build homes, give blood, raise money, and publicize the needs of others.

The volunteer force in the early 2000s was as large as it was diverse. Americans of every age, race, religion, and ethnic group contributed their time and abilities to local communities as well as to the nation. People worked independently and through organizations that coordinated volunteers to help provide healthcare, accessible public transportation, and decent schools and to support urban revitalization, public information, recycling, environmental protection, religious missions, and charities, among many other efforts.

BIBLIOGRAPHY

Ellis, Susan J., and Katherine H. Noyes. *By the People: A History of Americans as Volunteers.* Revised ed. San Francisco: Jossey-Bass, 1990.

Trattner, Walter I. *From Poor Law to Welfare State: A History of Social Welfare in America.* 6th ed. New York: Free Press, 1999.

Wuthnow, Robert, Virginia A. Hodgkinson, and Associates. *Faith and Philanthropy in America: Exploring the Role of Religion in America's Voluntary Sector.* San Francisco: Jossey-Bass, 1990.

Regina M. Faden

See also **Americorps; Peace Corps; Philanthropy; Welfare System.**

VOLUNTEERS. *See* **Conscription and Recruitment; Enlistment.**

VOTER REGISTRATION is a government responsibility in most European countries; in the United States, it is a task each voter must accomplish individually. From 1968 through 2000, 87.5 percent of registered voters cast ballots in American presidential elections. But in 2000, only 69.5 percent of citizens of voting age were registered. White and black registration rates were comparable (70 percent and 68 percent), but rates for Asian American and Hispanic citizens were substantially lower, at 52 and 57 percent, respectively. It is the double barrier of achieving registration and turning out to vote that accounts for the

Registering to Vote. A group of African Americans gathers outside the Voter Registration Headquarters of the A. Philip Randolph Institute in Cincinnati. A. PHILIP RANDOLPH INSTITUTE

notoriously low American participation rates: only 55 percent of voting-age citizens voted in 2000.

Personal registration is the largest remaining barrier to political participation in America. It was designed that way. Before the Civil War, only a few New England states forced voters to register. After 1865, state legislatures required men who lived in large cities, and later in smaller cities and rural areas, to register periodically, often before each major election. Adopted by 31 of the 37 northern states by 1920, the laws were touted as efforts to combat ballot fraud, but many proponents also wished to eliminate lower-class, often immigrant, voters, especially those who favored parties opposed to the reformers. They succeeded. The best estimate is that registration laws were responsible for 30 to 40 percent of the 29 percentage point decline in turnout in the northern states between 1896 and 1924.

In the post-Reconstruction South, registration laws were even more openly used for racial and partisan disfranchisement. Registrars, almost always white Democrats, often had absolute discretion to add anyone they pleased to the voting lists and to reject as insufficient the information provided by others. Such power was dramatically employed before voting on constitutional changes in suffrage regulations. In Louisiana before an 1898 referendum on whether to hold a constitutional convention to disfranchise most African Americans, authorities wiped the registration books clean and allowed re-registration by fewer than 10 percent of blacks and 40 percent of whites who had previously been registered.

Gradually during the 1950s and 1960s, the laws were liberalized and registration offices were professionalized. By 1970 nearly all states made registration permanent, if registrants voted at least every two or four years, and in 1970 Congress amended the VOTING RIGHTS ACT so that people could register until thirty days before a federal election. Many states began accepting applications by mail, opening convenient temporary offices in the weeks before the deadline, and allowing volunteers to distribute and return registration forms.

Still, registration rates were low, especially among young, poor, and minority voters. So Michigan and other states began to offer voting registration to people obtaining or renewing their driver's licenses, and after a twenty-year struggle Congress passed the National Voter Registration Act (NVRA) of 1993, popularly known as "Motor Voter." By 1999–2000, 38 percent of the 45.6 million people who registered initially or changed addresses did so at motor vehicle offices, and another 31 percent used the mails. The NVRA also regulated purges of inactive voters or felons and required the Federal Election Commission to gather and disseminate information about the election process in each state. Nonetheless, discriminatory purging of registration rolls and failures to send registration information from motor vehicle and other offices to registrars and officials at the polls disfranchised thousands of voters throughout the country in 2000 and probably determined the result of the presidential election in Florida and therefore the nation.

BIBLIOGRAPHY

Federal Election Commission. *The Impact of the National Voter Registration Act of 1993 on the Administration of Elections for Federal Office, 1999–2000.* Washington, D.C.: Federal Election Commission, 2001.

Jamieson, Amie, Hyon B. Shin, and Jennifer Day. *Voting and Registration in the Election of November 2000.* Washington, D.C.: U.S. Census Bureau, 2002.

Kleppner, Paul. *Who Voted? The Dynamics of Electoral Turnout, 1870–1980.* New York: Praeger, 1982.

Kousser, J. Morgan. *The Shaping of Southern Politics: Suffrage Restriction and the Establishment of the One-Party South, 1880–1910.* New Haven, Conn.: Yale University Press, 1974.

J. Morgan Kousser

See also **Suffrage;** *and vol. 9:* **An Interview with Fannie Lou Hamer.**

VOTER RESIDENCY REQUIREMENTS

VOTER RESIDENCY REQUIREMENTS prohibit otherwise qualified people from voting unless they have lived in a particular state, county, or election district for a specified period of time. Virtually unknown before the Civil War, they were imposed by permanent residents to keep recent migrants from influencing elections, to discourage fraud, and to give voting officials the ability to disfranchise political opponents, especially African Americans in the South. When fully enforced, they had substantial effects on voting participation because Americans have always been highly geographically mobile and because proving residency at a particular time in the past is often difficult and leaves much to the discretion of voting registrars.

In the nineteenth and early-twentieth centuries, some states required residency of up to two years. As late as the mid-1960s, requirements that typically amounted to a year in the state and two to six months in the particular district were estimated to disfranchise nearly a tenth as many Americans as were registered to vote. To encourage higher voter turnout and to minimize discrimination, Congress in its 1970 amendments to the VOTING RIGHTS ACT limited residency requirements in federal elections to thirty days, and the Supreme Court in *Dunn v. Blumstein* (1972) applied the same standard to state and local elections.

Although residency requirements have now essentially been eliminated, Americans' mobility still inhibits voting. In 1997–1998, 16 percent of Americans changed residences, and 10 percent of whites, 13 percent of African Americans, and 16 percent of Latinos moved to another county. Nearly twice as high a proportion of single and divorced people as married persons living with their spouses moved during that typical year, and renters were four times as likely to move as homeowners. Perhaps because they were insufficiently familiar with public services in their new communities, or perhaps because they were just too busy, only 38 percent of people who lived in a community for less than one year reported voting in the 2000 general election, compared to 72 percent of those who had lived there for five or more years. Thus, while geographic mobility promotes economic opportunity for individuals, it makes the political system as a whole more conservative—more dominated by married, white, geographically stable homeowners than is the population as a whole.

BIBLIOGRAPHY

Jamieson, Amie, Hyon B. Shin, and Jennifer Day. *Voting and Registration in the Election of November 2000.* Washington, D.C.: U.S. Census Bureau, 2002.

J. Morgan Kousser

See also **Suffrage.**

VOTING

VOTING. The defining act of American democracy, voting is as complicated as its history. Colonial American governments imported property tests for SUFFRAGE from England, but the requirement that one own land or personal property worth forty or fifty pounds or land that would rent for forty or more shillings a year was much less restrictive in sparsely populated America than in Britain. Almost any white male who lived in the colonies long enough could accumulate that much property, and historians estimate that between 50 and 97 percent of the white male colonists could vote. Apparently, even these property tests were rarely enforced, especially in close elections. By 1800, property qualifications had been weakened or a taxpaying qualification substituted in all but three states. Noisy battles over universal white male suffrage in New York in 1821 and Rhode Island in the 1830s and 1840s were not typical struggles, but last, doomed efforts by opponents of white male equality. In 1860, only four states retained taxpaying or other minor requirements, while the rest had adopted virtually universal white native male suffrage. In addition, several states allowed free African American men to vote, and from 1777 to 1807, New Jersey enfranchised propertied women.

Then as now, not all those who were eligible voted. Although few early election returns survive, from 1730 on turnouts in various colonies ranged from 10 to 45 percent of the free adult males, with close contests stimulating more campaigning and voting than races dominated by one candidate or party. Turnout slumped during the turmoil of the Revolution, when pro-English Tories were often disfranchised; rebounded during the 1780s and 1790s, especially in states where Federalists and ANTIFEDERALISTS or Jeffersonian Republicans were both well organized; and fell off again as the FEDERALIST PARTY collapsed after 1812. Presidential election turnout rose to 55 percent of those eligible to vote with the election of Andrew Jackson in 1828, reached 78 percent in the election of 1840, and continued above 60 percent until 1912, peaking at 83 percent in 1876.

Votes do not always count equally. At first, state legislators, not voters, usually chose members of the ELECTORAL COLLEGE, who then chose the president. Elite control soon eroded, and by 1828 political parties ensured that the winner of a plurality of the vote in a state would get all or nearly all of the state's electoral votes. Ironically, democracy reduced the value of the votes for losing presidential candidates in a state to nothing. Likewise, before 1842, some states elected members of Congress on the "general ticket" system, instead of by districts, allowing voters from one party to elect every congressman in a state. Other states drew noncontiguous districts or tidier districts with wide population disparities. Not until 1872 were congressional districts required to be contiguous and nearly equal in population; these mandates were never strictly enforced and were completely abandoned after 1911. Before the Civil War, under the Constitution slaves counted for three-fifths as much as free people in congressional and electoral college apportionment, enhancing the power of the slaveholding South. Since 1788, every state, no matter how large or small, has been entitled to two members in the U.S. Senate, giving a resident of Wyoming in 2000, for instance, 69 times as much representation in the Senate as a resident of California.

After the Civil War, more African Americans sought the vote, and abolitionist Republicans granted it. Congress first secured voting rights to blacks in the federally controlled District of Columbia, then, in 1867, in ten states of the former Confederacy, and finally, through the Fifteenth Amendment in 1870, in the nation as a whole. Since black suffrage had lost in twelve of fifteen referenda in northern states from 1846 through 1869, the Republicans' actions might have seemed foolhardy. But the passage of the Fifteenth Amendment robbed northern Democrats of an issue—the imaginary horrors of black suffrage, and it gave southern blacks a weapon with which to defend themselves—by voting Republican. As a further shield, Congress in 1870–1871 passed enforcement and supervisory acts to guard black voters against violence, intimidation, and corrupt or unequal balloting practices. Unfortunately, the Supreme Court emasculated these laws in 1876 in UNITED STATES v. REESE and UNITED STATES v. CRUIKSHANK.

The "white terror" that ended RECONSTRUCTION in the South in the mid-1870s did not immediately terminate African American voting. A majority of black males continued to vote in the South in the 1880s and in some states until 1900. African Americans were elected to Congress until 1901 and to southern state legislatures until 1907. It was legal, not extra-legal methods, that first constrained black political power, and then largely eliminated it. Gerrymandering, the substitution of at-large for district elections, and the establishment of partisan election boards facilitated fraud and elected racist Democratic state legislators. The new legislators then passed registration, POLL TAX, and secret ballot laws, which diminished voting by the poor and illiterate, white as well as black, Republicans, and Populists. These restrictions on the electorate, as well as continued ballot-box stuffing, allowed Democrats after 1890 to pass literacy and property tests for suf-

Voting in Alabama, 1966. The Voting Rights Act of 1965 outlawed the tactics that had disenfranchised most African Americans in the South for decades. After its enactment, voter registration increased dramatically among African Americans in the region. © FLIP SCHULKE/CORBIS

frage in constitutional conventions or referenda. Biased administration of these and other regulations of voting, such as the all-white Democratic primary, disfranchised nearly all southern blacks and many poor whites until the 1940s and 1950s.

Because women were less predictably Republican than were former slaves, who owed their legal status to the party of Lincoln, and because adding another radical reform might have nullified the opportunity for any change whatsoever, Republicans rejected the bid by the fledgling women's rights movement to add a ban on gender discrimination to that on race in the Fifteenth Amendment. It took women fifty years, innumerable local and state campaigns, and ideological shifts by the suffragists away from racial and antiliquor crusades before they secured the vote nationally with the ratification of the Nineteenth Amendment in 1920. Continued discrimination against women by male political leaders, as well as such barriers as the poll tax in the South, which disproportionately diminished women's votes, curtailed electoral opportunities for women until a third wave of feminism in the 1970s. By the 1990s, women turned out to vote at higher rates than men, and female elected officials had become commonplace.

While the fact is seldom emphasized, European (though not Asian) immigrants to America obtained the right to vote with some controversy, but little real difficulty, despite the fact that many from the mid-nineteenth century on differed in language and religion from the dominant English-speaking Protestants. Politics in nineteenth-century America was a white male melting pot—a limited achievement, to be sure, but one that other countries' histories might make us appreciate.

Although the NEW DEAL revived voter enthusiasm, along with active government, political power remained unequally distributed. One response was the Supreme Court's decisions in such malapportionment cases as BAKER V. CARR (1962) and *Reynolds v. Sims* (1964), which ended the practice of having one election district with up to 422 times as many people as another in the same state. In 1965, Congress passed the Voting Rights Act, which reenfranchised blacks in the Deep South and gave courts and the U.S. Department of Justice the tools necessary to ensure that electoral rules were not biased against ethnic minorities. A third reform, the National Voter Registration Act of 1993, sought to increase levels of participation, especially among the young and the poor, by allowing people to register to vote by mail and in government offices, including departments of motor vehicles, and regulating purges of voter rolls. Still, in the 2000 presidential election, only 55 percent of adult American citizens voted, one of the lowest percentages in a national election of any developed country. As the aftermath of that election reminded us, with its tales of incorrect registration records, confusing ballots, defective voting machines, inconsistent vote counts, biased officials, unprecedented judicial intervention, and defeat of the winner of the popular vote, voting involves much more than simply showing up at the polls.

BIBLIOGRAPHY

Keyssar, Alexander. *The Right to Vote: The Contested History of Democracy in the United States.* New York: Basic Books, 2000.

Kornbluh, Mark Lawrence. *Why America Stopped Voting: The Decline of Participatory Democracy and the Emergence of Modern American Politics.* New York: New York University Press, 2000.

Kousser, J. Morgan. *Colorblind Injustice: Minority Voting Rights and the Undoing of the Second Reconstruction.* Chapel Hill: University of North Carolina Press, 1999.

J. Morgan Kousser

See also **Ballot; Election Laws; Elections; Gerrymander; League of Women Voters; Suffrage.**

VOTING RIGHTS ACT OF 1965 (VRA) abolished a set of tactics that had prevented most African Americans in the South from voting since the beginning of the twentieth century. The VRA also established a variety of oversight mechanisms that gave the law the teeth absent from the CIVIL RIGHTS ACTS passed in 1957, 1960, and 1964. The provisions included the preclearance of any changes in state and local election laws with the federal government (section 5), authorization of federal "registrars" who would make sure that blacks were being allowed to register (sections 6 and 7), and provision for federal observers who would oversee elections (section 8).

By 1964, 43.3 percent of voting-age blacks in the South were registered to vote, up from only 3 percent in 1940. However, in Alabama, Georgia, Mississippi, North Carolina, and South Carolina, black registration was only 22.5 percent. Continued resistance in these states, along with the violence against peaceful voting rights demonstrators in Selma, Alabama, early in 1965, galvanized national public opinion in favor of the VRA.

President Lyndon Johnson signed the VRA into law on 6 August 1965. The positive effects were immediate and substantial; within two years, black registration in Mississippi increased from 6.7 percent to 59.8 percent, and in Alabama it went from 19.3 percent to 51.6 percent. The impact on black officeholders was even more dramatic. Only seventy-two blacks served in elective office in the South in 1965. By 1985 there were 143 blacks in state houses (10.8 percent of the total), 33 in state senates (7.8 percent), 425 on county councils (5.9 percent), and 1,330 on city councils (5.6 percent).

Many states actively resisted the growing influence of black voters. Initial legal challenges to the constitutionality of the VRA were rejected by the Supreme Court in *South Carolina v. Katzenbach* (1966). Other tactics were more invidious. Racial gerrymanders, at-large elections, prohibition of "single-shot" voting in multimember districts, majority runoff provisions, and impediments to voter registration were used widely throughout the South. In a landmark ruling in *Allen v. Board of Election* (1969), the Supreme Court gave the Justice Department the ability to challenge these practices under the section 5 preclearance provision of the VRA. Ruling that the right to vote encompassed the entire electoral process, not simply the acts of registering or casting a ballot, the Court significantly expanded the reach of the VRA. In 1975, section 4 was expanded to include language minorities in Texas, Alaska, Arizona, and parts of several other states.

The most important of the VRA amendments, passed in 1982, extended key provisions of the law for twenty-five years and overturned *City of Mobile v. Bolden* (1980). The *Bolden* case had required that plaintiffs demonstrate the intent to discriminate rather than discriminatory effects, which made it almost impossible to prove a vote dilution claim. The 1982 VRA amendments restored the pre-*Bolden* standard of proof by amending section 2 to prohibit any voting procedure that results in protected classes having "less opportunity than other members of the electorate to participate in the political process and to elect representatives of their choice." This amendment was the impetus behind the racial redistricting of the early 1990s, which was subsequently challenged in a series of court cases, starting with *Shaw v. Reno* (1993). While this area of the law is in flux, the VRA has remained the single most important contribution to minority voting rights in U.S. history. The VRA is up for renewal in 2007. The outcome of that legislative process will determine the direction of voting rights for the next generation.

BIBLIOGRAPHY

Davidson, Chandler, and Bernard Grofman, eds. *The Quiet Revolution in the South: The Impact of the Voting Rights Act, 1965–1990.* Princeton, N.J.: Princeton University Press, 1994.

Grofman, Bernard, Lisa Handley, and Richard G. Niemi. *Minority Representation and the Quest for Voting Equality.* New York: Cambridge University Press, 1992.

Kousser, J. Morgan. *Colorblind Injustice: Minority Voting Rights and the Undoing of the Second Reconstruction.* Chapel Hill: University of North Carolina Press, 1999.

David Canon

See also **Civil Rights Movement; Discrimination: Race; Disfranchisement.**

VOYAGEURS, or *engagés*, were a class of men employed by fur traders—especially by the North West, the American, and the Hudson's Bay Companies—to paddle their canoes and perform other menial tasks connected with the securing of furs and the maintenance of posts in the interior. The term was first used by French writers around the middle of the seventeenth century, when it became necessary to travel (*voyager*) long distances into the interior in order to get furs. From that time until the third quarter of the nineteenth century, these men formed a rather distinct class that was recognized as such by their contemporaries. There were on average 5,000 voyageurs in Canada and the United States in any one year of the late eighteenth and early nineteenth centuries.

Voyageurs had distinct dress, customs, and vocabulary, and a whole repertoire of songs. Their unique culture sustained them during long and arduous trips to collect furs from the indigenous people who had trapped and cleaned them. Collectively, voyageurs bore the responsibilities of ensuring safe delivery of valuable furs, and negotiating prices and quantity with Indian suppliers. They also formed crucial alliances with indigenous peoples, helping fur companies obtain furs and European governments to negotiate relations more effectively with Indian leaders. Voyageurs were generally divided by two criteria: (1) according to experience, the pork eaters (MANGEURS DE LARD) and the winterers; and (2) according to skill, the guides, middlemen, and end men (*bouts*). The pork eaters were the novices; the winterers had spent at least one winter in the interior. The guides were capable of directing the course of a brigade of canoes. The middlemen (*milieux*) sat in the middle of the canoe and merely propelled it in unison without attempting to guide its course, which was governed by the *bouts*. The *bouts* themselves were divided into the *avant*, standing in the prow, and the steersman (*gouvernail*) standing in the stern. In the interior the voyageurs helped construct the posts, cut shingles, made canoes, fished and hunted, went out among the natives, and were generally versatile men. They even served their countries during the American Revolution and the War of 1812 as soldiers. Certain companies, especially in the Canadian armies, were composed of and named by them.

BIBLIOGRAPHY

Lavender, David. *The Fist in the Wilderness.* Lincoln: University of Nebraska Press, 1998.

Nute, Grace Lee. *The Voyageur.* New York: D. Appleton, 1931.

Ray, Arthur J. *Indians in the Fur Trade: Their Role as Trappers, Hunters, and Middlemen in the Lands Southwest of Hudson Bay, 1660–1870.* Toronto: University of Toronto Press, 1974.

Grace Lee Nute/ T. D.

See also **French Frontier Forts; Fur Companies; Fur Trade and Trapping; Grand Portage; Hudson's Bay Company; Indian Trade and Traders.**

W

WACO SIEGE, a fifty-one-day siege by federal agents of the Branch Davidian religious group's commune headquarters outside Waco, Texas, in early 1993. The siege, which began after a botched and bloody attempt on 28 February 1993 to arrest the group's leader, David Koresh, on a weapons charge, ended in the deaths of four federal agents and seventy-eight Branch Davidians. The stalemate ended when U.S. Attorney General Janet Reno ordered the use of force on April 19. Soon after federal agents moved, fire engulfed the compound, killing seventy-two, provoking controversy over the use of force in dealing with dissident sects. Although some surviving members of the sect were acquitted of manslaughter, they received harsh sentences when convicted on lesser charges. In August 1999, new documents surfaced indicating that the FBI had fired three flammable tear gas canisters during the raid on the compound. Following a ten-month investigation, Senator John C. Danforth released a report concluding that although federal agents had mishandled evidence, they had neither started the fire nor improperly employed force.

BIBLIOGRAPHY

Reavis, Dick J. *The Ashes of Waco: An Investigation.* New York: Simon and Schuster, 1996.

End of the Waco Siege. The Branch Davidians' compound goes up in flames on 19 April 1993, killing seventy-two members of the religious group. AP/WIDE WORLD PHOTOS

Tabor, James D., and Eugene V. Gallagher. *Why Waco? Cults and the Battle for Religious Freedom in America.* Berkeley: University California Press, 1995.

Wright, Stuart A. *Armageddon in Waco: Critical Perspectives on the Branch Davidian Conflict.* Chicago: University of Chicago Press, 1995.

Bruce J. Evenson
Christopher Wells

See also **Cults; Millennialism.**

WADE-DAVIS BILL, passed by Congress 2 July 1864, was a modification of Abraham Lincoln's plan of Reconstruction. It provided that the government of a seceded state could be reorganized only after a majority of the white male citizens had sworn allegiance to the United States and approved a new state constitution that contained specified provisions. Rep. Henry W. Davis of Maryland and Sen. Benjamin F. Wade of Ohio, sponsors of the bill, believed, along with other Radical Republicans, that Lincoln's policy was inadequate because it allowed white southern Unionists to determine the status, rights, and conditions for freedpersons in their states. Abraham Lincoln's pocket veto of this bill on 4 July angered the radicals and presaged the contest over Reconstruction between President Andrew Johnson and Congress.

BIBLIOGRAPHY

Hyman, Harold H. *A More Perfect Union: The Impact of the Civil War and Reconstruction on the Constitution.* Boston: Houghton Mifflin Company, 1975.

Willard H. Smith / C. P.

See also **Radical Republicans; Reconstruction.**

WAGES AND HOURS OF LABOR, REGULATION OF. The historical pattern of hourly wages in the United States—rapidly rising money wages, more slowly rising real wages, and persisting differences in occupational, industrial, and sectional wages—can largely be explained in terms of broad productivity trends and competitive market forces. The long-term, sometimes pronounced, decline in the workweek resulted as much from pressures exerted by organized labor, government, and society in general, as from the traditional influences of supply and demand.

The Fair Labor Standards Act of 1938 comprised the principal NEW DEAL-era legislation aimed at regulating wages and hours after the U.S. Supreme Court invalidated the wage and hour codes under the National Industrial Recovery Act in 1935 (SCHECHTER POULTRY CORPORATION V. UNITED STATES). With respect to wages, the 1938 law limited itself to fixing a minimum rate only, which rarely established more than an absolute floor for the least-skilled jobs. (As late as 1975, the minimum wage stood at only $2.10 per hour for nonfarm workers and $1.80 for farm workers, lower than the rates actually being paid in most fields.) In setting a maximum standard of forty hours per week and eight hours per day, beyond which it required employers to pay time-and-a-half wages, the 1938 law established a standard that remained close to the prevailing practice for the next half century. Only for employees in big-city offices and in a few fields, such as construction and the needle trades, did standard work-hour schedules fall below these levels.

At the beginning of the nineteenth century, the number of work hours ranged upward from twelve hours a day, six days a week. Public agitation in the 1820s eventually led to a new norm of ten hours a day and sixty hours a week in most industries. After the Civil War, the eight-hour day became the focus of a national movement, but this level was not widely adopted until the 1920s, and the working world did not generally accept the five-day workweek until the 1930s.

Before the founding of the American Federation of Labor in 1886, recurring efforts were made to pass federal and state laws limiting hours of work for all classes of labor. Resorting to legislation tended to be especially frequent when unemployment rates rose and direct bargaining prospects looked unfavorable. Employers vigorously resisted these efforts, and during the nineteenth century the courts struck down many of these laws on the grounds that they abridged freedom-to-contract rights.

State legislatures became increasingly active in limiting hours of work for women and children, and Massachusetts enacted the first enforceable law in 1879. The courts, too, gradually began to reverse their position on such laws, and in 1908 the SUPREME COURT upheld Oregon's ten-hour law for women in mechanical establishments, laundries, and factories (MULLER V. OREGON).

The legal regulation of hours of labor for men followed a different course because businesses mounted a much stronger resistance in the courts. One approach was for the federal, state, and local governments to establish shorter work hours for public employees; President Martin Van Buren, for example, issued an executive order in 1840 limiting work in navy yards to ten hours a day. In another more widely used approach, legislators enacted state and federal statutes limiting men's hours in specified

industries, such as mining and railroads. A noteworthy event occurred in 1916 when Congress passed the ADAMSON ACT, which provided for the eight-hour day for operating railroad employees, with time-and-a-half for overtime. Finally, the continuing effort to win court approval for general hours legislation succeeded in 1917 when the Supreme Court upheld an Oregon law establishing ten-hour days for most men in mills, factories, or manufacturing establishments (Bunting v. Oregon).

Government efforts to establish minimum wage standards traditionally centered on protecting women and children. The Supreme Court brought these efforts to a halt in 1923, when it ruled that such legislation deprived individuals of their freedom to contract (ADKINS V. CHILDREN'S HOSPITAL). The demoralization of labor market standards with the onset of the GREAT DEPRESSION prompted further minimum wage action along more inclusive lines; in 1937 the Supreme Court upheld the authority of the states to enact such legislation (WEST COAST HOTEL COMPANY V. PARRISH), and in 1941 it upheld the national minimum wage law as a valid exercise of the federal power to regulate interstate commerce (United States v. F. W. Darby Lumber Company). The federal government also established minimum wages for special categories of employment, such as airline pilots and construction workers under federal contracts.

Although Congress took a series of steps to increase the initial minimum rate set by the Fair Labor Standards Act in 1938 (25 cents per hour), the 1976 rate of $2.30 was actually no higher in relation to prevailing wages. The law's main economic impact resulted from its extended coverage rather than its level: by 1975 it applied to nearly 80 percent of all nonsupervisory employees in private industry; in 1960 it covered only about 55 percent. The newly covered workers, moreover, were in such low-wage industries as farming, where the law's effect was clearly greatest. Whatever broad social benefits may be achieved by the legislation, on the other hand, it is clear that it tends to reduce employment opportunities in low-paying fields by reducing the number of available jobs.

Government regulation of wages has largely been aimed at setting minimum rates only. Any effort to set maximum rates as a means of checking inflation has traditionally been limited to war periods. On 15 August 1971, however, the federal government adopted a policy of limiting most wage increases to 5.5 percent per annum, along with maximum ceilings on price increases, in hopes of checking inflationary pressures. These pressures soon reasserted themselves, and controls, which had begun to be phased out in late 1973, expired on 30 April 1974.

From 1976 to 1981, the federal minimum wage continued to rise each year, from $2.30 to $3.35. The federal minimum wage remained steady throughout the rest of the 1980s during the Reagan administration and did not increase again until the early 1990s, when it became $3.80 in 1990 and $4.25 in 1991. In 1996 it increased to $4.75, but a year later, the federal minimum wage rose yet again to $5.15, where it has remained ever since. Despite these recent increases, however, the federal minimum wage has not kept up with the rate of inflation. Although in the 1960s and 1970s, a full-time, year-round minimum-wage worker could make enough to support a family of three above the poverty level, that is no longer the case. By 1999 that same worker only made about $10,700 annually, which was more than $2,500 below the poverty line for a family of three. Eleven states, however, require higher minimum wages than the federal government does, and in those states, the greater state wage prevails.

BIBLIOGRAPHY

Dankert, Clyde E., Floyd C. Mann, and Herbert R. Northrup, eds. *Hours of Work*. New York: Harper and Row, 1965.

Montgomery, David. *The Fall of the House of Labor: The Workplace, the State, and American Labor Activism, 1865–1925*. Cambridge, U.K., and New York: Cambridge University Press, 1987.

Northrup, H. R., and G. F. Bloom. *Government and Labor: The Role of Government in Union-Management Relations*. Homewood, Ill.: R. D. Irwin, 1963.

Frank C. Pierson / c. w.; A.E.

See also **American Federation of Labor-Congress of Industrial Organizations; Fair Labor Standards Act; National Recovery Administration; Price and Wage Controls; Walsh-Healey Act;** *and vol. 9:* **Women in Industry (Brandeis Brief).**

WAGES AND SALARIES. The vast majority of American adults gain their livelihoods by working for a corporation or partnership that they do not own. This is true of people who work in factories, stores, or offices. It is also true of many highly educated workers, such as doctors, and non-tenured college professors (who have no property rights in their jobs). Most unskilled and semi-skilled workers are paid by the hour, most professionals or semiprofessionals are paid by the month or the year. Although hourly employees are called wage workers and others are generally considered salaried, all depend for their livelihoods on payment by the owners of productive property (capital) who make a profit on their labor. In that sense they are all wage workers.

The average major league ballplayer in 2000 earned $1,895,630, worked for only seven months, and was not likely to think of himself as a wage earner. But like assembly line workers, wages are ballplayers' primary source of income, and they are employed by corporations that make a profit from their work. If an owner's team consistently loses money, players will be paid less—or traded. The vast discrepancy in compensation among wage earners is one factor that makes today's workforce so different from that of the nation's period of industrialization in the late nineteenth century. In the last decades of the nineteenth century, although the proportion of workers on railroads or in factories rose steadily, most of the working population, rural or urban, were independent producers. In the north and west, they worked on family-owned farms, while in the south about two-thirds of blacks (and many poor whites) were sharecroppers who rented their farms from large landowners, to whom they usually paid half their crops.

Whole families worked on these farms and received no wages or salaries. Skill and providence mattered, but elements over which they had little or no control—the weather, the market, their relationship with banks and railroads, on whom they depended for credit and access to markets—were just as important. Tenants were also at the mercy of landlords who owned the local stores where the sharecroppers were required to buy seed, tools, and staples, often at exorbitant prices. Still, tenants, too, were independent producers.

As the internal market grew in the years before 1900, farm productivity increased rapidly, and fewer and fewer farmers were needed to feed and clothe the nation. In these decades a steady stream of people left farms and went to work for wages in urban factories. By 1900, the balance of the American population had shifted from rural to urban in a process that still continues. At the turn of the twenty-first century, less than 3 percent of the workforce were farmers.

In manufacturing, productivity also grew rapidly. By the early 1900s capital-intensive technology and large-scale corporate organization also raised the value of manufactured goods more rapidly than the number of workers needed to produce them. As increasing productivity in manufacturing reduced the relative amount of labor required to produce all the goods that the market could absorb, capital sought new areas of investment. Large amounts of surplus capital, the emergence of overproduction (or underconsumption), and growing chronic unemployment spurred the drive to increase consumer spending. This initiated the shift from competitive industrialization to today's corporation-dominated consumer society.

The social and political turmoil of the Progressive Era (1900–1920) reflected these changes in the national economy. Beginning in these years, whole new areas of enterprise—and employment—began to change the way people lived. From the expansion of production of newly manufactured things, such as automobiles and radios, to the creation of new consumer goods and services such as popular fashion and entertainment, new industries invaded areas that had previously been the domain of small independent producers. By the 1920s the great increases in labor productivity showed in the accelerated growth of chronic unemployment and dislocations, and increasing underconsumption led to stagnation in major sections of the economy—even as corporate profitability increased. In retrospect, these changes foreshadowed the need to create a consumer society and a welfare state. Yet their significance was overlooked as the nation struggled with the stock market crash of 1929, the GREAT DEPRESSION, and World War II.

After the war, however, as large amounts of capital shifted to service industries, government and corporate leaders consciously promoted suburbanization and popular consumption. As a result, small businesses of all kinds disappeared as giant chains of supermarkets, pharmacies, and fast food restaurants covered the land. This process created some well-paid employment, especially in electronics and then computers—and in military production—but it created many more full- and part-time jobs paying minimum wage or just above it.

The expansion of corporate capital has also affected college-educated professionals. In 1900 a professional degree was the equivalent of capital for those who had private practices. But with the growth of large-scale manufacturing such degrees lost value. Engineers for example, were transformed from independent consultants to employees, and with the growth of for-profit hospital chains and HMOs, many doctors began to work for wages.

The expanded corporate economy has created new jobs mostly at the income extremes. As factories have reduced their labor forces—or simply moved overseas—many well-paid semiskilled and unskilled union members have found work only at near-minimum-wage jobs; many now work two or even three jobs. Many highly educated people, however, are very well paid, especially if they are licensed to practice medicine, law, or other professions. For such people, skill or educational level is a determinant of income and working conditions. Yet many other highly educated people, even those with doctorates, find themselves working for wages not much above poverty level.

In the industrializing years of the nineteenth century, few workers made more than the barest subsistence wage, and most worked ten or more hours a day, six days a week. Some skilled workers responded by organizing unions. On the railroads, for example, the brotherhoods of locomotive engineers, firemen, and brakemen had guild-like unions, while in factories small numbers of machinists and others formed craft unions that won concessions from management, including a shortening of the work day.

Even today, with unionized manufacturing on the decline, a clear gap exists between the wages of union and nonunion workers. In 2002 full-time unionized workers median wage was $718 a week, while nonunion workers earned $575. Unions also affect wages because many nonunion employers raise their workers' wages in order to keep unions out of their shops.

BIBLIOGRAPHY

Marx, Karl. *Capital: A Critique of Political Economy*. Chicago: Charles H. Kerr, 1909.

Ray, Marshall F. *Back to Shared Prosperity: The Growing Inequality of Wealth and Income in America*. Armonk, N.Y.: M.E. Sharpe, 2000.

Seidel, Michael. *Ted Williams: A Baseball Life*. Lincoln: University of Nebraska Press, 2000.

Sklar, Martin J. *The United States As a Developing Country: Studies in U.S. History in the Progressive Era and the 1920s*. Cambridge, U.K.: Cambridge University Press, 1992.

James Weinstein

See also **Labor; Railroad Brotherhoods; Trade Unions.**

WAGON MANUFACTURE.

Even as the United States changed from a largely agricultural society to an industrial one in the nineteenth century, the wagon maker remained indispensable. Farmers depended on all-purpose wagons no less than did teamsters on freight wagons. Railroads decreased the need for cross-country wagons, but the intown need greatly increased along with the growth of commerce and industry.

Local craftsmen in small shops only a few miles from their customers dominated wagon manufacture in the eighteenth and early nineteenth century. During the American Industrial Revolution, simple machinery came into use for carriage- and wagon-building in the 1820s, although substantial progress was not made in this area until the 1870s. This machinery permitted interchangeable parts, thus lowering costs by eliminating hand fitting. It also gave rise to a separate parts industry, enabling still further cost reduction.

Early specialists focused on producing machine-made wheels, for laboriously handmade wheels were a major factor preventing low-cost wagons. Improved wheelmaking and wood-bending machinery—the latter for bending rims—cut wagon costs shortly after the Civil War. Increasing use of malleable iron castings eliminated many hours of smithwork needed for each wagon.

These twin features of mechanization and specialization led to more precisely constructed wagons. Wagon manufacturers thus became assemblers, purchasing all necessary components at discount prices from parts manufacturers. By the early 1900s these methods had reduced prices of lightweight farm and delivery wagons to as little as $30, while heavier wagons cost as little as $60. Equally important, these features of wagon and carriage manufacture were carried over into the infant automobile industry and helped to introduce the techniques of automotive mass production.

BIBLIOGRAPHY

Goldman, Joanne Abel, Merri McIntyre Ferrell, et al. *Nineteenth Century American Carriages: Their Manufacture, Decoration, and Use*. Stony Brook, N.Y.: Museums at Stony Brook, 1987.

Snyder, Charles McCool. *Buggy Town: An Era in American Transportation*. Lewisburg: Pennsylvania State University Press, 1984.

Don H. Berkebile / c. w.

See also **Agricultural Machinery; Industrial Revolution; Railroads.**

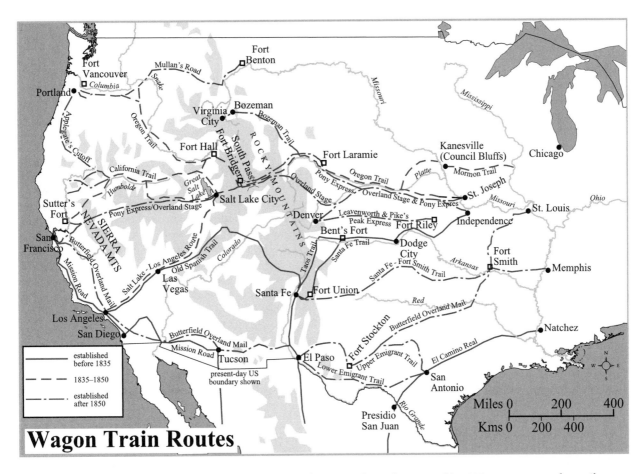

Wagon Train Routes

established before 1835

1835–1850

established after 1850

Miles 0   200   400

Kms 0   200   400

present-day US boundary shown

WAGON TRAINS. For purposes of protection and efficiency, traders and emigrants of the trans-Mississippi West before 1880 customarily gathered their wagons into more or less organized caravans or trains. William L. Sublette, a partner in the reorganized Rocky Mountain Fur Company, conducted a ten-wagon, mule-drawn train over the Oregon Trail from St. Louis, Missouri, as far as the company's Wind River rendezvous (in present-day Wyoming) between 10 April and 16 July 1830, returning to St. Louis on 10 October. Captain Benjamin L. E. Bonneville is usually credited with the distinction of having taken the first wagons through South Pass; in July 1832 his twenty-wagon train reached the Green River by that route.

At Elm Grove, Missouri, beginning in 1842, settlers came in covered wagons each spring, elected their captains, guides, and other officers, and began the long trek westward via the Oregon Trail. The caravan of 1842, organized by Dr. Elijah White, traveled as far as Fort Hall (in present-day Idaho) before the wagons were abandoned. From there the people traveled on foot, horseback, or by raft down the Snake and Columbia Rivers. The following year more than one thousand immigrants moved over the same route in many wagons, some of which reached the banks of the Columbia River.

It was not until 1843 that the celebrated "cow column" Oregon emigrant party of about one thousand persons brought most of its 120 wagons over the trail to arrive near the Columbia River on 10 October, the first wagon train to reach Oregon Country. By some accounts the so-called Stevens-Murphy-Townsend party of some fifty persons was the first group to bring wagons all the way from Missouri and through the Sierra Nevada by the California Trail, Donner Lake, and Truckee Pass, from October to December of 1844. William Becknell, a Missouri merchant, took the first wagon train, of three wagons, to Santa Fe (in present-day New Mexico), from May to July 1822; and the first wagon trail from Santa Fe to southern California seems to have been marked during the Mexican-American War by Lt. Col. Philip St. George Cooke with his Mormon Battalion (19 October 1846–29 January 1847), by way of Guadalupe Pass, the Gila River, and the Colorado Desert to San Diego.

The eastern section of the Old Spanish Trail, from the Wasatch Mountains through present-day Utah, Colorado, and New Mexico to Santa Fe, was seldom traversed by wagons, although Mexican pack trains had used it at least as early as 1830. During the gold rush the western section of this trail, through southwestern Utah and across Nevada and California to the vicinity of Los Angeles, bore waves of wagon trains of emigrants as they turned southward from Salt Lake City, in Utah Territory. A number of well-marked wagon routes ran across Texas from its coastal towns and from Louisiana, Arkansas, and

Indian Territory (present-day Oklahoma) to El Paso, Texas, or other points on the Rio Grande, from which connections could easily be made with the Gila Trail. Caravans of twenty-five wagons or more were used largely to transport trade goods over the Santa Fe Trail valued at $35,000 in 1824, $90,000 in 1826, and $150,000 in 1828.

The number of wagons making the overland journey annually from 1843 to 1848 is difficult to determine with accuracy. One report, dated 23 June 1849, estimated that 5,516 wagons had passed Fort Kearney on the Platte River (in present-day Nebraska), bound for California or the Columbia Valley.

During the 1850s, caravans, large and small, were thronging all roads across the Great Plains. Randolph B. Marcy conducted a caravan of one hundred wagons from Fort Smith, Arkansas, to the New Mexico Territory via the Canadian River in 1849, on the first leg of its journey to California; the Indian agent William Bent estimated that sixty thousand emigrants crossed the plains along the Arkansas route in 1859. Heavy freight caravans plied the routes between San Antonio, Texas, and Chihuahua, Mexico, between Santa Fe and Chihuahua, and from points in present-day Nebraska, Kansas, and Colorado to the far West by 1860. A well-known road from Council Bluffs, Iowa, to the Great Salt Lake in Utah Territory via Fort Bridger (in present-day Wyoming), was traveled by thousands of Mormon pilgrims from 1847 to 1860. By 1865, trains five miles long were occasionally reported. An average caravan was composed of scores of giant prairie schooners, each capable of transporting between four thousand and seven thousand pounds and drawn usually by five or six yoke of oxen.

The organization and daily routine of a wagon train depended on the danger expected from the Native American tribes into whose territory it had traveled, the terrain, and the size of the caravan. Mormon trains, in particular, had a semimilitary formation. It was customary to elect a captain as central authority, and several lieutenants were put in charge of keeping order in assigned sections of the train. One function of the captain was usually to select each night's camping site, on the advice of a guide or the reports of horsemen sent out in advance during the day. At night the wagons were commonly drawn up in a circle or a square, end to end, so as to form a corral for at least the more valuable horses, mules, and cattle, as well as a fortress for the passengers. Indian thefts, buffalo herds, storms, and animal stampedes made life in the wagon camps treacherous. Horse- or mule-drawn wagons could make from ten to fifteen miles a day.

Wagon Train. This 1887 photograph by J. C. H. Grabill shows oxen pulling wagons filled with freight through the Black Hills of South Dakota. © CORBIS

Even after the completion of the Union Pacific-Central Pacific tramontane railway line in May 1869, caravan trade and travel persisted for a decade. However, the wagon trains and caravans decreased in size, except in the case of freighting lines. The establishment of stagecoach lines, the military defeat and relocation of the Rocky Mountain and Great Plains Indians, the decimation of the buffalo herds, and the building of other far western railways in the 1880s all combined to transform the wagon train into a means of freighting heavy goods rather than of carrying passengers. It became increasingly safe for poorer emigrant families to make their way westward in a single covered wagon.

BIBLIOGRAPHY

Butruille, Susan G. *Women's Voices from the Oregon Trail.* Boise, Idaho: Tamarack Books, 1993.

Connor, Seymour V., and Jimmy M. Skaggs. *Broadcloth and Britches: The Santa Fe Trade.* College Station: Texas A&M University Press, 1977.

Faragher, John Mack. *Women and Men on the Overland Trail.* New Haven, Conn.: Yale University Press, 1979.

Gardner, Mark L. *Wagons for the Santa Fe Trade.* Albuquerque: University of New Mexico Press, 2000.

Hafen, Le Roy R., and Ann W. Hafen. *Old Spanish Trail: Santa Fé to Los Angeles.* Lincoln: University of Nebraska Press, 1993.

MacGregor, Greg. *Overland: The California Emigrant Trail of 1841–1870.* Albuquerque: University of New Mexico Press, 1996.

Walker, Henry P. *The Wagonmasters: High Plains Freighting from the Earliest Days of the Santa Fe Trail to 1880.* Norman: University of Oklahoma Press, 1966.

Rufus Kay Wyllys / A. R.

See also **Carriage Making; Conestoga Wagon; Gold Rush, California; Mormon Trail; Oregon Trail; Prairie Schooner; Santa Fe Trail; Stagecoach Travel; Westward Migration;** *and vol. 9:* **Across the Plains to California in 1852.**

WAGONERS OF THE ALLEGHENIES

transported merchandise from the ports of the East to the trade centers of the West and returned with agricultural products; they rose to prominence during 1810 to 1820, but finally succumbed to the competition of the railroads. Their chief routes were the Pennsylvania Road from Philadelphia to Pittsburgh and the CUMBERLAND ROAD from Baltimore to Wheeling. Their wagons, referred to as Conestoga or Pittsburgh wagons, were about twenty feet long, six to eight feet wide; powered by teams of six or eight horses, they could carry loads of over 6,000 pounds.

There were two classes of wagoners—regulars and sharpshooters. Regulars engaged in hauling the year round; sharpshooters were farmers who, when freight rates were high, undertook hauling for short periods. Sharpshooters paid higher tolls because their ordinary farm wagons had narrow-rimmed wheels that cut up the road. The regulars' wagons had broad-rimmed wheels. Wagoners traveled about fifteen miles a day, more for sharpshooters, and stayed overnight at taverns along the road.

Wagoners ran a brisk and profitable traffic through the Alleghenies; in 1822 a congressman estimated that 5,000 wagons had passed over the southern road that year, and in 1836, during a period of five weeks, thirty wagons passed daily over the northern road. Rivalry with canals caused the wagoners to form associations or to join transportation lines; and competition from the railroads forced the wagoners out of a large share of the business shortly before the Civil War.

BIBLIOGRAPHY

Raitz, Karl, ed. *The National Road.* Baltimore: Johns Hopkins University Press, 1996.

Shumway, George. *Conestoga Wagon, 1750–1850.* York, Pa.: G. Shumway and Early American Industries Association, 1966.

John W. Harpster / A. R.

See also **Allegheny Mountains, Routes Across; Baltimore Bell Teams; Connestoga Wagon; Pack Trains.**

WAKE, DEFENSE OF

(8–23 December 1941). The resolute defense of Wake Atoll by a small force of U.S. Marines against an overwhelming Japanese assault provided the only encouragement America could claim during the dark days after PEARL HARBOR. Wake, a mid-Pacific atoll flanked by the Japanese-held Marshall and Mariana islands, was garrisoned by 449 marines, under navy Commander Winfield Scott Cunningham and marine Major James P. S. Devereux, armed with artillery, antiaircraft guns, small arms, and a marine fighting squadron (VMF-211) with twelve Grumman F4F-3 fighters.

Lacking radar, Wake was surprised by the initial Japanese air onslaught and lost seven Grummans on the ground. By heroic feats of maintenance, VMF-211 kept two to four fighters airborne daily through 22 December, when the last defending planes were shot down. Twenty-one Japanese aircraft were destroyed over Wake.

The first Japanese ground attack on 11 December was repulsed: two enemy destroyers were sunk, seven other warships and transports were damaged, and some 700 Japanese killed. This was the only time in the Pacific war that an amphibious assault by either side was ever defeated. As Japanese bombers pounded Wake in preparation for another, stronger landing, a U.S. carrier task force bringing ground and aviation reinforcements attempted to reach Wake, but failed because of the commander's decision to refuel rather than press ahead of the Japanese.

Wake fell on 23 December, eleven hours after landings commanded by Rear Admiral Sadamichi Kajioka that cost the attackers two more destroyers and approximately

300 casualties. Eighty-one U.S. marines were killed or wounded throughout the defense.

BIBLIOGRAPHY

Cressman, Robert. *A Magnificent Fight: The Battle for Wake Island*. Annapolis, Md.: Naval Institute Press, 1995.

Devereux, James P. S. *The Story of Wake Island*. Philadelphia: Lippincott, 1947.

Urwin, Gregory J. W. *Facing Fearful Odds: The Siege of Wake Island*. Lincoln: University of Nebraska Press, 1997.

Robert Debs Heinl Jr. / A. R.

See also **Aircraft, Fighter; Marine Corps, United States; Marshall Islands; Midway, Battle of; World War II; World War II, Navy in.**

WALDEN. Henry David Thoreau (1817–1862) published *Walden* in 1854. It is based on the two years (1845–1847) he spent living in a cabin beside Walden Pond, near Concord, Massachusetts, and describes his simple way of life, along with meditations on nature and society. It has become a classic for environmentalists, nature mystics, and advocates of the simple life, while embodying one aspect of the transcendentalist creed.

Thoreau was convinced that most of his countrymen worked too hard and gave themselves too little time for relaxation and meditation, that they let themselves be imprisoned by their property and their acquisitive desires. Accordingly, he aimed to live as simply as possible, doing only the work sufficient to feed and shelter himself, which he claimed amounted to just six weeks out of each year. He bought the planks for his cabin from a migratory Irish railroad worker, built it beside the pond for $28 (as he tells the reader in a chapter titled "Economy"), made a table and a few simple chairs, planted and hoed beans, and spent his days fishing, searching for berries and chestnuts, or studying the plants and forest creatures. In winter he went out on the ice and, lying face-down, stared through it to the mysterious waters below. In summer he lay on his back and watched the sky.

Thoreau in *Walden* relishes paradox. He argues the superiority of shabby clothes, cold, hunger, and loneliness in a light-hearted and teasing tone (perfected after seven years of careful editing of his original journals). Conversely, he denigrates what many of his contemporaries regarded as the great achievements of their age: the railroad, the division of labor, capitalist efficiency, and philanthropy. By living at one remove from society (Walden was close to town, within easy reach of neighbors, and not in a "wilderness" setting), he said he was able to "live deliberately, to front only the essential facts of life."

BIBLIOGRAPHY

Harding, Walter Roy. *The Days of Henry Thoreau*. New York: Knopf, 1965.

McGregor, Robert Kuhn. *A Wider View of the Universe: Henry Thoreau's Study of Nature*. Urbana: University of Illinois Press, 1997.

Worster, Donald. *Nature's Economy: A History of Ecological Ideas*. New York: Cambridge University Press, 1994. See chapter 3.

Patrick N. Allitt

See also **Transcendentalism.**

WALKING DELEGATE, an important factor in the development of American trade unionism, was either a union organizer or business agent. As an organizer, his function was to persuade nonunion employees to join the union and demand union standards of wages, hours, and conditions of employment. As a business agent, his responsibility was to safeguard the terms of the trade agreement and adjust grievances that arose in its interpretation and application.

BIBLIOGRAPHY

Litwack, Leon. *The American Labor Movement*. Englewood Cliffs, N.J.: Prentice-Hall, 1962.

Montgomery, David. *The Fall of the House of Labor: The Workplace, the State, and American Labor Activism, 1865–1925*. New York: Cambridge University Press, 1987.

Gordon S. Watkins / T. D.

See also **Collective Bargaining; Labor; Trade Unions.**

WALL STREET EXPLOSION. The Wall Street Explosion occurred in New York City on 16 September 1920, across from the headquarters of the J. P. Morgan Company on Wall Street, near the corner of Broad Street. Forty persons in the street were killed, although no one inside J. P. Morgan headquarters was harmed. Authorities believed the bombing to have been caused by a bomb carried in the back of a ramshackle, one-horse wagon, which witnesses later remembered having seen near the spot. Both the horse and wagon were entirely destroyed in the blast, however, and the perpetrator was never discovered.

BIBLIOGRAPHY

Carosso, Vincent P. *The Morgans: Private International Bankers 1854–1913*. Cambridge, Mass.: Harvard University Press, 1987.

Alvin F. Harlow / C. W.

See also **Terrorism.**

WALL STREET JOURNAL. Charles Dow and Edward Jones, owners of Dow, Jones and Company, began publishing the daily *Wall Street Journal* on 8 July 1889. Both Dow and Jones were New Englanders with mutual

Charles Henry Dow. The founder, with Edward Jones, of the *Wall Street Journal* and Dow, Jones and Company, including the creation of early versions of the influential Dow Jones industrial average and other stock indicators. © CORBIS

Barron. Kilgore redesigned the paper, expanding its coverage to include all aspects of business, economics, and consumer affairs, including general news that had an impact on business. Other business news ventures of the parent Dow Jones Company included the Dow Jones News Service, Barron's, and the new international editions of the journal. Together they provided mutual support in reporting business and financial news. Starting in the late 1940s the journal published regional editions. The company purchased the *Chicago Journal of Commerce* in 1951 and effectively became a national newspaper.

With the growth of post–World War II prosperity and investments in the United States, the journal's circulation grew rapidly, reaching over a million copies in 1960 and almost 2 million by the 1990s. As the readership and breadth of coverage of the journal grew, so did the importance of the journal's editorial opinions. Avoidance of government policies seen as promoting price inflation or excessive levels of debt were the editorial preferences of the journal. Consistently sympathetic to conservative business principles, the journal emerged as the voice of political conservatism in American journalism. Such an editorial perspective, when combined with broad national distribution, provided strong circulation and advertising revenue growth, reaching $2.3 billion in the year 2000 and profits before special items of $294.6 million.

The breadth of the journal's circulation expanded further with the launch of the *Asian Wall Street Journal* in 1976 and the *Wall Street Journal Europe* in 1983. The special editions in thirty-eight local languages worldwide, the *Wall Street Journal Sunday*, and WallStreetJournal.com were added in the last decade of the twentieth century. Leading this growth, the flagship *Wall Street Journal* had become the largest circulation newspaper in the United States.

BIBLIOGRAPHY

Dealy, Francis X., Jr. *The Power and the Money: Inside the Wall Street Journal.* Secaucus, N.Y.: Carol Publishing Group, 1993.

Rosenberg, Jerry M. *Inside the Wall Street Journal: The History and the Power of Dow Jones and Company and America's Most Influential Newspaper.* New York: Macmillan, 1982.

Wendt, Lloyd. *The Wall Street Journal: The Story of Dow Jones and the Nation's Business Newspaper.* Chicago: Rand McNally, 1982.

Michael Carew

See also **Dow Jones; Stock Market.**

roots in journalism in Providence, Rhode Island. Their company had been founded seven years earlier as a financial news agency serving the burgeoning New York City financial community. Following their initial success, the founders sold their company to their Boston correspondent Clarence Barron in 1902.

NEWSPAPERS in the United States have been primarily concerned with general news and the perspectives of their local communities. The *Wall Street Journal* was designed for the business community: "Its object is to give fully and fairly the daily news attending the fluctuation in prices of stocks, bonds and some classes of commodities" (Wendt, p. 28). The journal initiated several indexes of price movements of stocks, including the Dow Jones Indexes. The top left-hand column covered general market and financial movements. The second from left covered the details of the day's market movements. The rest of the four-page paper was thoroughly business oriented, reporting general news in the context of its effect on the markets. Daily circulation reached 7,000 copies by 1900, 18,750 copies in 1920, and 29,780 copies in 1939. By comparison, the daily circulation of the *New York Times* in 1939 was 482,000 copies.

Bernard Kilgore became managing editor of the journal in 1945, seventeen years after the death of Clarence

WALLA WALLA SETTLEMENTS began in July 1818 when the North West Fur Company established an Indian trading post, Fort Nez Perce, later Fort Walla Walla, on the east bank of the Columbia River at its junction with the Walla Walla River. Waiilatpu, the mission of Marcus Whitman, built in October 1843, twenty miles up the river from the post, was the next white settlement. Although Whitman, his family, and twelve other missionary residents were massacred in a Cayuse raid in 1847, a new settlement of French-Canadians and Indians sprang up nearby, known as Whitman, or French Town.

A few white families had settled in the Walla Walla Valley by 1855, at the time of the Indian uprising in eastern Washington, but these families were ordered out by the U.S. Indian agent and Fort Nez Perce was closed. A new Fort Walla Walla, a U.S. military post, was erected in November 1856, about twenty-eight miles up the river (on the site of the present city of Walla Walla).

The Washington territorial legislature created Walla Walla County in 1854. By 1859, with the end of the YAKIMA INDIAN WARS, 2,000 white settlers lived in the valley. In 1862 the city of Walla Walla was incorporated, and in the early 1870s a railroad was completed connecting it to the town of Wallula at the mouth of Walla Walla River. These towns prospered during the gold rushes in eastern Oregon and western Idaho, beginning in 1860.

BIBLIOGRAPHY

Daugherty, James H. *Marcus and Narcissa Whitman: Pioneers of Oregon.* New York: Viking Press, 1953.

Jeffrey, Julie Roy. *Converting the West: A Biography of Narcissa Whitman.* Norman: University of Oklahoma Press, 1991.

Miller, Christopher L. *Prophetic Worlds: Indians and Whites on the Columbia Plateau.* New Brunswick, N.J.: Rutgers University Press, 1985.

R. C. Clark/A. R.

See also **Columbia River Exploration and Settlement; Indian Missions; Indian Trade and Traders; Indian Treaties; Oregon Trail; Washington, State of.**

WALLOONS, French-speaking people of Celtic stock in northeastern France (present-day Belgium) who became Protestant in large numbers during the Reformation. Many, exiled to Holland, England, and Germany, emigrated to America beginning in the early 1620s. They were the first colonizing settlers in New Netherland (first called Nova Belgica): at Manhattan (called New Avesnes), at Fort Orange (Albany), at Wallabout (Brooklyn), and at Boompjes Hoek on the Delaware River (Gloucester, New Jersey). They later settled on Staten Island and in the Walkill Valley. They brought seed, fruits, and cattle. Immigration continued, and they often intermarried with Dutch and Huguenot settlers.

BIBLIOGRAPHY

Griffis, W. E. *The Story of the Walloons.* Boston: Houghton Mifflin, 1923.

Augustus H. Shearer/F. B.

See also **Huguenots; New Netherland.**

WAL-MART was founded by Samuel Moore Walton in Rogers, Arkansas, in July 1962. He built a chain of huge discount stores mostly situated in small rural towns. Wal-Mart's success was based on everyday low prices, item merchandizing, volume movement of goods, and customer-orientated, non-unionized employees known as "associates." By Walton's death in 1992, Wal-Mart had displaced thousands of small town "Main Street" stores and become America's biggest retailer. During the 1990s Wal-Mart successfully expanded into Canada, Latin America, Europe, and the Far East. At the beginning of the twenty-first century, Wal-Mart was the largest employer in the United States and the world's biggest retailer.

BIBLIOGRAPHY

Ortega, Bob. *In Sam We Trust: The Untold Story of Sam Walton, and How Wal-Mart is Devouring America.* New York: Times Business, 1998.

Vance, Sandra S., and Roy V. Scott. *Wal-Mart: A History of Sam Walton's Retail Phenomenon.* New York: Twayne, 1994.

Richard A. Hawkins

See also **Retailing Industry.**

WALSH-HEALEY ACT (30 June 1936), established minimum standards for work on federal contracts. The act required federal purchases of supplies exceeding $10,000 to contain an agreement on the part of the contractor to conform to the standards prescribed by the act. These standards required contractors to pay prevailing wages as determined by the secretary of labor; establish an eight-hour day and forty-hour week; employ no male under sixteen or female under eighteen; and use no convict labor. Contractors were required to be manufacturers of, or regular dealers in, the materials and supplies purchased by the government.

BIBLIOGRAPHY

U. S. Employment Standards Administration. *A Guide to the Walsh-Healey Public Contracts Act.* Washington, D.C.: U.S. Department. of Labor, Employment Standards Administration, 1976.

Herbert Maynard Diamond/C. W.

See also **Government Regulation of Business; Price and Wage Controls; Wages and Hours of Labor, Regulation of; Wages and Salaries.**

WAMPANOAG. In the seventeenth century the Gay Head (or Aquinnah) Indians of Martha's Vineyard were members of a confederacy of Wampanoag communities in southeastern Massachusetts. After epidemic diseases struck Martha's Vineyard in the 1640s, dropping its Indian population from 3,000 to 1,500, the terrorized survivors embraced Christianity and allied with the English. These shifts led Vineyard Natives to fight alongside col-

Wampanoag Indians. On Martha's Vineyard off the coast of Massachusetts, the Gay Head Indians of the Wampanoag tribe swore allegiance to the British colonists after the tribe suffered catastrophic disease outbreaks in the 1640s. As a result, they found themselves fighting against the mainland tribes of the Wampanoags when the British went to war with the Indians in King Philip's War (1675–1676). This illustration shows two Gay Head women mourning their dead during the height of the epidemic. © NORTH WIND PICTURE ARCHIVES

onists when they successfully battled mainland Wampanoags in King Philip's War of 1675–1676.

In 1685 the Gay Head Indians deposed their sachem (chief) for selling land. However, a mixed blessing occurred when a missionary organization, the New England Company, acquired the title to Gay Head. The company supervised Gay Head until the Revolution, and although Indians resented its oversight, it kept the colonists from seizing Wampanoag territory. Secure land and Indian church leadership stabilized Gay Head throughout the eighteenth century as its people struggled with indebtedness, indentured servitude, male whaling deaths, exogamous marriages, and the loss of the Wampanoag language.

In 1871 Massachusetts made Gay Head a town and divided its common lands. Nevertheless it remained a Wampanoag place because the Natives discouraged treating land as capital, passed on the people's stories, and rallied around their church. In 1983 the Wampanoags of Gay Head-Aquinnah successfully petitioned the United States to become a federal tribe and established a reservation.

BIBLIOGRAPHY

McBride, Kevin, and Suzanne G. Cherau. "Gay Head (Aquinnah) Wampanoag Community Structure and Land Use Patterns." *Northeast Anthropology* 51 (1996): 13–39.

Mandell, Daniel R. *Behind the Frontier: Indians in Eighteenth-Century Eastern Massachusetts.* Lincoln: University of Nebraska Press, 1996.

Silverman, David J. "Conditions for Coexistence, Climates for Collapse: The Challenges of Indian Life on Martha's Vineyard, 1524–1871." Ph.D. diss., Princeton University, 2000.

Simmons, William S. *Spirit of the New England Tribes: Indian History and Folklore, 1620–1984.* Hanover, N.H.: University Press of New England, 1986.

Starna, William A. " 'We'll All Be Together Again': The Federal Acknowledgement of the Wampanoag Tribe of Gay Head." *Northeast Anthropology* 51 (1996): 3–12.

David J. Silverman

See also **Massachusetts; New England Company.**

WAMPUM. The beads known as wampum were of great value to the American Indians of the eastern GREAT LAKES and NEW ENGLAND regions. The word itself is from the Algonquian language, and the concept of wampum first appeared among the Algonquian-speakers of the eastern woodlands. The strings of wampum, smoothly polished tubular and disc beads of white, purple, and blue shells, placed on carefully woven threads, were manufactured by coastal New England Indians who traded them with Iroquois and other peoples of the interior. Wampum was valued by them as a sacred marker of prestige. Arrangements of beads served as mnemonic devices for the recounting of events, messages, treaties, or for the correct rendition of a ritual. Although Native Americans did not consider wampum a form of money, New England colonists introduced a material value by using it to pay for furs or to replace coinage that was scarce through the middle of the seventeenth century.

BIBLIOGRAPHY

Martien, Jerry. *Shell Game: A True Account of Beads and Money in North America.* San Francisco: Mercury House, 1995.

Robert F. Spencer / J. H.

See also **Currency and Coinage; Indian Economic Life; Iroquois; Money.**

WAR, LAWS OF. The laws of war are the rules of international law that govern the conduct of war between nation-states, and are especially concerned with whether a use of force is allowed, when a state of war exists, the weapons and conduct of war, and the treatment of opponents, prisoners, neutrals, and noncombatants. They apply to the United States through enactments by Congress, the president, the Department of Defense, and specific commanders—as well as through the ratification of treaties including the Charter of the United Nations, and through those obligations of international custom binding according to the U.S. Constitution.

Early Limits on War

There have been limits on the conduct of war throughout military history. These limits persist even though they are frequently violated, often without punishment. The degree to which a nation complies with them is the degree to which that nation is perceived as civilized, just as compliance on the part of a nation's military is what distinguishes it as professional. Furthermore, in the twentieth century, principles of state and personal responsibility have led to the possibility of effective criminal enforcement.

Ancient laws of war dealt mostly with immunity from combat and with the commencement of hostilities. By custom and treaties, the city-states of ancient Greece respected truces, armistices, peace treaties, alliances, flags of truce and the immunity of heralds, truces to bury the dead, surrender conditions, and the inviolability of victory monuments. The neutrality of religious temples, the Olympic games and, sometimes, third-party states were ordinarily respected. Conformity to these rules was thought necessary to be civilized, to obey the gods, and to justify similar treatment from opponents.

The Roman *iustum bellum* required that attacks could not be made unless there had been a prior declaration of war or unless prior demands had not been satisfied. Roman law did not, of course, limit conquest, although the treatment of conquered lands and people was closely regulated.

Religion and manners were the sole limits on medieval warfare. Both Christianity and Islam placed limits on treatment of their faithful in war that did not apply to heretics or infidels. Both cultures evolved forms of chivalry that constrained the forms of battle and the treatment of prisoners, although such rules were often beneficial only to those with high rank. Neither could enslave a captured enemy of the same religion. The Christian church evolved a doctrine of just war and doctrines protecting noncombatants from death in war. These doctrines were reflected in canon law but not in national legal systems, which tended to follow the view associated with Niccolò Machiavelli and Carl von Clausewitz, that war is justified as a rational instrument of national policy, even for the purpose of conquest. Various attempts were made by popes and kings to improve the treatment of civilians in surrendered towns and to limit the horrors of war by banning devious or inhumane weapons, such as the crossbow or, later, the bayonet. While these attempts yielded no means of enforcement, still, armies often followed some humanitarian customs of war for the ancient reason of ease to the army, particularly by limiting looting.

The Seventeenth through Early Twentieth Centuries

The modern law of war was invented during the age of the English colonies in North America. During the Thirty Years' War (1618–1648), Dutch jurist and ambassador Hugo Grotius published *On the Law of War and Peace,* an extended and systematic argument that nations are bound by natural law to respect other nations, that they should only engage in wars justified by grounds that would be satisfactory as claims for legally cognizable harms, and that they must respect the rights of noncombatants. This argument gained much attention but slow acceptance.

During the American Revolution, the guiding principle was not a law of war but the customs of the armies and navies of Europe; however, these customs were often violated, as with the American habit of sharpshooting enemy officers. One custom that was honored was the execution of spies. The U.S. Army's Articles of War (1775) did, however, codify many customs, such as the requirements of uniforms and organization.

By the mid-nineteenth century, there was both more formal organization of the U.S. military and greater agreement about the rules. In the Mexican War, General Winfield Scott created military commissions to prosecute U.S. soldiers and Mexican civilians for violations of the rules of war.

The first codification of the law of war by the United States was General Order 100, issued at the direction of President Lincoln by General-in-Chief Henry Halleck, enacting the rules set forth in a report by Francis Lieber, a German-American law professor at Columbia College in New York. Entitled *Instructions for the Government of Armies of the United States in the Field*, it augmented the 1775 articles but went much further, setting humane standards for the handling and exchange of prisoners, the freeing of slaves, the treatment of people and property in occupied territory, and the treatment of opposing combatants. With the notable exception of Sherman's surprise bombardment of Atlanta, the union Army appears to have complied with Lieber's Code, and the Southern armies seem to have emulated it. The U.S. Supreme Court acknowledged it as federal law in *Ex parte Vallandigham*, 68 US 243 (1863).

Lieber's Code immediately influenced international law. Translated into German by Johann Bluntschli, it formed the basis of his *Das Moderne Kriegsrecht* (1866) and was reprinted whole in most international law texts for the next fifty years. Its terms and ideas influenced the European powers at the first Geneva Convention (1864) to agree to standards of treatment for wounded prisoners of war. International conferences at The Hague in 1899 and 1907 codified much of the Code regarding the definition of combatants and treatment of neutrals into the international laws of war.

The Crimean War, the U.S. Civil War, and the Franco-Prussian War all provoked codification of the laws of war. The Declaration of Paris of 1856 outlawed privateering, made naval warfare a matter for state professionals, and established clearer rules regarding blockades and the rights of neutral shippers. The Geneva Convention of 1864 drafted the first code for the treatment of the enemy's wounded. The 1868 Declaration of Saint Petersburg announced that the only legitimate use of war is to weaken an enemy's military, and it restricted the use of small explosive or incendiary projectiles. A convention at The Hague in 1899 rejected the use of expanding bullets and asphyxiating gasses.

While the great states of Europe negotiated and signed conventions, the United States was slow to do so, although it abided by these norms separately. Only during World War I did the U.S. agree to abide by the Declaration of Paris of 1856. The U.S. did not sign the convention of 1864, the declaration of St. Petersburg, the 1899 Hague Convention, or the first Geneva Convention. Even so, the Hague Conventions of 1899 and 1907 were both derived from Lieber's *Instructions*, which the United States reissued in 1898, and in 1914 the U.S. Army first compiled *The Rules of Land Warfare*, a handbook for soldiers in battle.

American interest in international regulation of law increased dramatically with the presidency of Theodore Roosevelt. In 1904 Roosevelt called a meeting under terms of the 1899 convention, seeking to codify and extend the earlier conventions. The resulting Second Hague Peace Conference ended in 1907 with fourteen treaties, setting forth standards for the commencement of hostilities, cus-toms and duties of warfare on land and sea, and the standards of neutrality. The U.S. signed and ratified these conventions, making them the first significant international laws of war to be law in the U.S. through treaty. This was not the only method by which the laws of war became U.S. law, however, and in *The Paquete Habana*, 175 US 677 (1900), the U.S. Supreme Court had recognized that the customary international law of war was enacted into U.S. law by the Constitution.

World Wars I and II and Their Consequences

The horrors of World War I, including the widespread violation of earlier pacts, led interwar peace conferences toward attempts at the prevention of war and the limiting of inhumane tactics and weapons, but these efforts met with only moderate success. The 1923 Hague Convention, on the rules of aerial warfare, failed to achieve sufficient ratification to come into force. The Geneva Gas Protocol (1925) prohibited the use in war of asphyxiating, poisonous, or other gases and of bacteriological methods of warfare. The Geneva Conventions of 1929 detailed the treatment of prisoners of war and of the enemy sick and wounded. The Washington Disarmament Conference (1921–1922) and the Treaty of London of 1930 limited submarine warfare against noncombatant ships. Despite occasional breaches, it is notable that there was widespread compliance with these treaties in the subsequent world war.

The great exceptions to this tendency toward compliance were the peace treaties, commencing with the Bryan Treaties of 1913 and 1914, and the controversial Versailles Treaty of 1919, all of which promoted limits on the grounds for commencing war, including requirements for investigation, arbitration, and peaceful settlement of disputes. This process culminated in the Kellogg-Briand Pact of 1928.

Named for French foreign minister Aristide Briand and U.S. secretary of state Frank B. Kellogg, this initially bilateral treaty was eventually signed by nearly all of the nations then on earth, each renouncing war as an instrument of national policy and agreeing to settle all disputes by peaceful means. A surfeit of qualifications allowed wars in defense of the Covenant of the League of Nations, other military treaties, the Monroe Doctrine, and for self-defense. More damning, there was no mechanism for enforcement, and the treaty was ineffective as a prior restraint to aggression. It was, however, one of the key bases for trials after World War II on charges of waging aggressive war in violation of international law.

Even so, none of these instruments prevented the horrors of World War II. At the war's end, the allies established tribunals at Nuremberg and Tokyo to try defeated leaders, soldiers, and sailors accused of war crimes, mainly crimes against peace, which included the planning, initiating, and waging of wars of aggression in violation of international law; crimes against humanity, including exterminations, deportations, and genocide; war crimes on the battlefield; and conspiring to commit the criminal acts of the first three counts. Of twenty-four major German defendants, three were acquitted, four imprisoned from ten to twenty years, three imprisoned for life, and twelve sentenced to hang. (Two were not tried, one owing to suicide and one to physical incapacity.) Of twenty-five major defendants in Japan, two received prison terms, sixteen life imprisonment, and seven were sentenced to hang. Both tribunals adopted the "Nuremberg principle," which held the individual and not just the state liable for violations of the laws of war. This principle was soon a maxim of military training in most developed nations.

With the adoption of the United Nations Charter in 1945, almost all the nations of the world committed to the peaceful settlement of disputes and agreed to renounce war except in self-defense. Under the sponsorship of the United Nations, additional conventions have been adopted outlawing genocide and crimes against humanity; further limiting the use of weapons of mass destruction, such as nuclear and biological weapons, and of particular inhumanity, such as exploding bullets; and further refining standards for the treatment of prisoners and the wounded. The Geneva Conventions of 1949 refined duties to the wounded and sick on land, to the wounded, sick, and shipwrecked at sea, to prisoners of war, and to civilians. Conventions in 1954 and 1977 sought to protect property of great cultural significance and to end deliberate acts of war that harm the environment.

The Cold War and After

The Cold War between the U.S. and the Soviet Union, the Korean War, and the American war in Vietnam raised new questions about the nature and application of the laws of war. The laws of war traditionally applied only to conflicts between de jure states, and controversies arose over the legality of U.S. actions when war was not declared, as with U.S. involvement in Vietnam and Cambodia in the 1960s. The Vietnam War also led to debates over the legal definition of war as a civil war, guerrilla war, or national war; the applicability of the laws of war in the absence of a uniformed enemy; the adherence of the parties to the laws and conventions of war; and the tactics used by the belligerents, particularly the American use of carpet bombing and defoliants, which damaged noncombatant areas.

Blame in these disputes was not one-sided. The North Vietnamese and Vietcong used terrorism and refused to adhere to the 1949 Geneva Convention—they did not, for example, permit the International Red Cross to inspect prisoner-of-war camps.

Greater agreement on matters of international law and the law of war followed the end of the Cold War in the 1990s. With American support, the U.N. Security Council created the International Criminal Tribunal for the Former Yugoslavia in 1993 and the International Criminal Tribunal for Rwanda in 1994. Both tribunals applied the Nuremberg principle and actively investigated and convicted individuals, including former Yugoslav president Slobodan Milosevic, for violations of the Geneva Convention of 1949. They were charged to investigate and prosecute genocide, violations of the laws and customs of war, and crimes against humanity. The violation of the laws and customs of war included using poisonous weapons or other weapons calculated to cause unnecessary suffering; wanton destruction of civilian areas not justified by military necessity; attack or bombardment of undefended towns; seizing or harming buildings dedicated to religion, charity, or education, or to the arts and sciences, or historic monuments and works of art and science; and plundering public or private property.

At Rome in 1998 a U.N. conference opened for signature a treaty establishing an International Criminal Court, with global jurisdiction to try individuals whose governments are unwilling to try them when they have been accused of any of various "crimes against humanity"—the definitions of which are similar to those established by the Yugoslavia and Rwanda tribunals. To become effective the treaty needed the ratification of sixty states, a goal that was achieved in April 2002. The United States had signed in 2000, but withdrew its signature in 2002.

On 11 September 2001 an attack by a terrorist organization undirected by any state, but apparently sheltered by a theocratic de facto government in Afghanistan, destroyed the towers of the World Trade Center in New York, one of the largest office buildings in history and a center of the commercial world. The attack killed nearly three thousand people, mainly Americans but including people from many nations. The response of the United States and its allies was to demand surrender of the leaders of the attack, and, in the absence of satisfaction, to attack the armies of the Afghan government while seeking to arrest the terrorists. As much criminal enforcement as military action, this response further signaled a comprehensive change in the structure of the laws of war, which now include an element of the enforcement of international criminal law.

BIBLIOGRAPHY

Best, Geoffrey. *War and Law Since 1945*. Oxford and New York: Clarendon, 1994.

Brownlie, Ian. *International Law and the Use of Force by States*. Oxford: Clarendon, 1963.

Holland, Thomas Erskine. *The Laws of War on Land (Written and Unwritten)*. Oxford: Clarendon, 1908.

Jennings, R. Y., and A. Watts. *Oppenheim's International Law*. 9th ed. London: Longmans, 1992

Roberts, Adam, and Richard Guelff. *Documents on the Laws of War*. Oxford: Clarendon, 1989.

Taylor, Telford. *The Anatomy of the Nuremberg Trials: A Personal Memoir*. New York: Knopf, 1992.

United States. War Department. General Staff. *Rules of Land Warfare*. Washington, D.C.: Government Printing Office, 1914. U.S. Army field manual.

Steve Sheppard

See also **Geneva Conventions; Hague Peace Conferences; Kellogg-Briand Pact; Versailles, Treaty of.**

WAR AND ORDNANCE, BOARD OF. On 12 June 1776, the Continental Congress authorized the Board of War and Ordnance to assume administrative control of the army, previously exercised by congressional resolutions. Included among its duties were control of all military supplies and munitions; supervision of the raising, equipping, and dispatching of troops; keeping a register of officers; and recording accounts of the condition and disposition of troops. General Horatio Gates served briefly as president, during which time the board became involved in the CONWAY CABAL. On 7 February 1781, Congress authorized a department of war, and the Board of War theoretically ceased to exist.

BIBLIOGRAPHY

Mintz, Max M. *The Generals of Saratoga: John Burgoyne and Horatio Gates*. New Haven, Conn.: Yale University Press, 1990.

Angela Ellis

See also **Army, United States; Revolution, American: Military History.**

WAR AND THE CONSTITUTION. Although concerned about national security, the framers of the U.S. Constitution produced a document that failed to make an unequivocal assignment of responsibility for the initiation of hostilities or to provide the national government with wartime emergency powers. Presidents and Congresses supplemented the constitutional text and the U.S. Supreme Court has validated their creations. In wartime, however, the Court has proved far more willing to sanction novel exercises of governmental authority than to enforce constitutional guarantees of individual rights.

The Power to Initiate Hostilities

Although inadequate, the national security provisions of the Constitution represent a vast improvement over those of the Articles of Confederation. The latter gave Congress neither effective control of foreign affairs nor an independent source of revenue with which to pay for a navy capable of protecting American commerce or an army big enough to defend the frontier and expel British troops from U.S. territory. The new Constitution written at Philadelphia in 1787, its proponents claimed, corrected these deficiencies. It would improve national defense and empower the federal government to deal effectively with other nations.

One reason was that the Constitution created the presidency, an office with the energy, efficiency, and capacity for secrecy that effective conduct of military and foreign affairs required. To ensure civilian control of the armed forces, the framers provided in Article II, section 2 that the president should be the "Commander in Chief of the Army and Navy" and of the militia when it was in federal service.

Article I, section 8 gave Congress the power "to declare war." What the framers meant by that is unclear. The declaration of war was a medieval custom, associated with chivalry, which required one belligerent to notify another formally before commencing hostilities. By 1787 it had fallen into disuse, and the Constitutional Convention probably was trying to do something more than merely designate Congress as the body that would give such notification in the small minority of conflicts where it was employed. The Committee on Detail originally proposed authorizing Congress to "make war." The full Convention changed that to "declare war" after a brief and unenlightening discussion. It was apparently trying to ensure that the president could respond immediately if the nation were attacked. However, by choosing an abstruse term while giving the president the ability to start a war simply by deploying the armed forces of which he was commander in chief, it precipitated continuing conflict over which branch has the authority to initiate hostilities.

Generally, presidents have done so. Congress declared war on Great Britain in 1812, Mexico in 1846, Germany in 1917, and the Axis powers in 1941. In addition, in 1898 it authorized President William McKinley to take military action against Spain if the Spanish did not relinquish their authority over and withdraw their armed forces from Cuba. For most of the hundreds of conflicts in which the American military participated between 1787 and 1973, however, ranging from small skirmishes with Indian tribes to the Korean and Vietnam Wars, there was no congressional declaration.

The Supreme Court has never ruled on whether such undeclared wars are constitutional. During the Vietnam conflict several litigants asked it to do so, but the Court refused to decide their cases. The closest thing to a relevant ruling is the *Prize Cases* (1863), in which the issue was actually whether Abraham Lincoln had violated international law by blockading the South in the absence of a declaration of war. In the process of holding that he had not, the Court proclaimed that a president was bound "to resist force by force" and might do so "without waiting for any special legislative authority" or "for Congress to baptize it with a name."

While the Supreme Court has imposed no limitations on presidential war making, Congress has attempted to do so with quasi-constitutional legislation. The War Powers Resolution of 1973 permits the president to take military action under certain circumstances without a declaration of war, but requires him to notify Congress promptly and to desist if it does not subsequently grant him affirmative authorization. Beginning with Richard Nixon, who tried unsuccessfully to veto this law, presidents from both parties have disputed its constitutionality while failing to comply with its provisions.

Before George H. W. Bush launched Operation Desert Storm in 1991, however, he obtained from Congress an Authorization for the Use of Military Force against Iraq, which stated that it was intended to constitute the statutory authorization contemplated by the War Powers Resolution. His son secured a similarly worded resolution before commencing the war on terrorism in 2001. The chairman of the Senate Foreign Relations Committee pronounced it the functional equivalent of a declaration of war.

Domestic War Power
Although Congress seldom makes the decision to initiate hostilities, war inevitably enhances congressional authority. No single constitutional provision grants it the "war power," but Article I, section 8 authorizes Congress not only "to declare war," but also to "raise and support Armies," "provide and maintain a Navy," "make Rules for the Government and Regulation of the land and naval Forces," and "provide for organizing, arming, and disciplining the Militia" and for governing it when it is in federal service. The Supreme Court has held that these grants of authority, in conjunction with the Necessary and Proper Clause, empower Congress to do things in wartime that would be unconstitutional in peacetime. Thus, in *Hamilton v. Kentucky Distillers* (1919) it upheld a national prohibition statute as a war emergency measure, although banning alcoholic beverages in peacetime required a constitutional amendment. In *Hamilton* and later cases, the Court explained that this congressional war power remained operative during an ill-defined period of reconversion after fighting ended.

War also expands the president's power. One reason is that Congress generally delegates substantial authority to the executive in wartime. During the Civil War it even ratified actions already taken by Abraham Lincoln that encroached upon legislative prerogatives. Lincoln claimed that powers inherent in the presidency were sufficient to justify his actions. Out of the clause making the president commander in chief and the provision in Article II, section 3 directing the president to "take Care that the Laws be faithfully executed," he forged an essentially unlimited presidential "war power." Although Lincoln made his expansive claims concerning the domestic prerogatives of the presidency in the context of a unique internal conflict, by the end of the nineteenth century, commentators were pointing to his actions as examples of what any president could do during any war. World War II saw Franklin Roosevelt claim his authority was so extensive that he could ignore congressional legislation he thought interfered with the war effort.

In *Youngstown Sheet and Tube Company v. Sawyer* (1952), the Supreme Court dealt a blow to such expansive claims of presidential prerogative, holding that Harry Truman might not seize the nation's steel mills in order to prevent a strike that threatened to disrupt defense production during the Korean War. It did so, however, mainly because Truman had refused to employ the means for dealing with such a labor crisis that Congress had provided in a statute. A majority of the justices indicated that in the absence of legislation, the president could do even something as drastic as take over an entire industry.

During the Vietnam conflict, neither Lyndon Johnson nor Richard Nixon made use of the inherent presidential war power. They did not have to, for by then Congress had enacted well over four hundred statutes giving the president extraordinary powers during national emergencies. Johnson and Nixon could exercise those because a proclamation of national emergency, issued by Truman in 1950, had never been withdrawn. Congress took away the authority it conferred in 1976, but in 2001 George W. Bush proclaimed a new national emergency.

Civil Liberties
While expanding presidential and congressional power, war tends to restrict civil liberties. The judiciary is reluctant to enforce constitutional guarantees of individual rights if doing so would require it to challenge military authority. When Chief Justice Roger Taney held in *Ex Parte Merryman* (1861) that Lincoln had no authority to suspend the writ of habeas corpus, the president and the army ignored him. Since then, the Supreme Court has generally deferred to military power during wars and rendered rulings enforcing the Bill of Rights only after the fighting ends. Thus, a year after Appomattox in *Ex Parte Milligan* (1866), it held unconstitutional the trial of civilians before military commissions when the civil courts are open and functioning.

Although *Milligan* proclaimed that constitutional guarantees are not suspended during the great exigencies of government, in fact they often are when those exigencies are military. Thus, the Court affirmed numerous convictions of political dissidents under the World War I Espionage Act (1917) and Sedition Act (1918), despite the apparent conflict between those laws and the First Amendment's guarantees of freedom of expression. In *Schenck v. United States* (1919) Justice Oliver Wendell Holmes Jr. declared that there were many things which might be said in time of peace that no court would regard as protected by any constitutional right "so long as men fight." In *Korematsu v. United States* (1944) the Court upheld the removal of Japanese Americans from the West Coast because the military deemed that action necessary. Although acknowledging that in peacetime singling out a group for disfavored treatment because of its race would constitute unconstitutional discrimination, the Court insisted this was permissible in wartime because "hardships are part of war."

Thus, the Constitution is different in wartime than in peacetime. In the interests of national security, it invests government with greater power while affording less protection to individual rights.

BIBLIOGRAPHY

Belknap, Michal R. "Vietnam and the Constitution: The War Power under Lyndon Johnson and Richard Nixon." *This Constitution*, no. 10 (spring 1986): 12–19.

Ely, John Hart. *War and Responsibility: Constitutional Lessons of Vietnam and Its Aftermath*. Princeton, N.J.: Princeton University Press, 1993.

Koh, Harold Hongju. *The National Security Constitution: Sharing Power after the Iran-Contra Affair*. New Haven, Conn.: Yale University Press, 1990.

Marks, Frederick, III. *Independence on Trial: Foreign Relations and the Making of the Constitution*. Wilmington, Del.: Scholarly Resources, 1986.

Rehnquist, William H. *All the Laws but One: Civil Liberties in Wartime*. New York: Knopf, 1998.

Reveley, W. Taylor. *War Powers of the President and Congress: Who Holds the Arrows and Olive Branch?* Charlottesville: University of Virginia Press, 1981.

Michal R. Belknap

See also **Constitution of the United States;** *Ex Parte Merryman; Ex Parte Milligan;* **Japanese American Incarceration; Prize Cases, Civil War;** *Schenck v. United States;* **War Powers; War Powers Act.**

WAR CASUALTIES.

The term "war casualty" applies to any person who is lost to a military unit by having died of wounds or disease, having received wounds, or having been injured but not mortally. War casualties are classified into two categories: hostile and nonhostile (disease and nonbattle injuries). A hostile casualty is any person who is killed in action or wounded by any civilian, paramilitary, terrorist, or military force that may or may not represent a nation or state. Also included in this classification are persons killed or wounded accidentally either by friendly fire or by fratricide, which occurs when troops are mistakenly thought to be an enemy force. Nonhostile casualties are not attributable to enemy action. These occur due to an injury or death from environmental elements, disease, self-inflicted wounds, or combat fatigue.

The table shows the number of persons who served in the U.S. military in each of its ten major wars, the total deaths from wounds, disease and nonbattle injuries, and wounds received but not fatal. This data shows that more soldiers, sailors, airmen, and marines died from diseases and other nonbattle injuries than from battle wounds.

It was not until the Civil War that the techniques of battlefield treatment began. The surgeon Jonathan Letterman devised a system of collecting casualties and transporting them from the battlefield to field hospitals, where doctors would perform surgery.

With the discovery of antisepsis, disease and nonbattle deaths began to decline. Disease was no longer the principal threat to military forces. Prior to World War I, however, advances in technology increased weapon lethality. During the war, the number of casualties from combat wounds began to approach the number of disease and nonbattle injuries. In World War II, for the first time, battle casualties exceeded disease casualties. The medic or corpsman was first used during World War I. These individuals would accompany the infantry in combat and administer first aid to the injured, before they were evac-

United States Casualties by Conflict

Conflict	Total Who Served	Battle Deaths	Disease/Nonbattle Deaths	Wounds Not Mortal
American Revolution 1775–1783	Estimated 184,000 to 250,000	4,435	N/A	6,188
War of 1812 1812–1815	286,730	2,260	N/A	4,505
Mexican-American War 1846–1848	78,718	1,733	11,550	4,152
Civil War (Union Only) 1861–1865	2,213,363	140,414	224,097	281,881
Spanish-American War 1898–1899	306,760	1,000	5,400	1,662
World War I 1917–1918	4,734,991	53,402	63,114	204,002
World War II 1941–1945	16,112,566	291,557	113,842	671,846
Korean War 1950–1953	5,720,000	33,686	2,830	103,284
Vietnam War 1964–1973	8,744,000	47,410	10,788	153,303
Gulf War 1990–1991	467,159	148	151	467

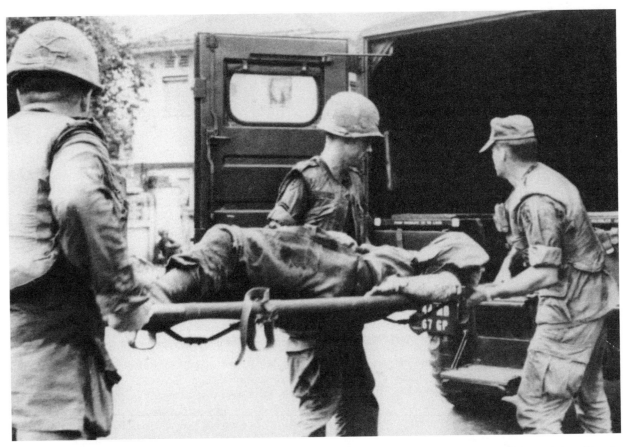

Vietnam War Casualty. American soldiers move the body of a fellow soldier, killed in the bombing of the U.S. bachelor officers' quarters in Saigon, South Vietnam, during the Tet offensive in early 1968. NATIONAL ARCHIVES AND RECORDS ADMINISTRATION

uated to field hospitals. Significant advances in military medicine helped to minimize casualties in World War II. Discoveries in antibiotic drug treatments, such as penicillin and sulfa (sulfanilamide), decreased wound infections, and the use of blood plasma helped prevent shock and replace blood volume. During the Korean War, the helicopter was routinely used to evacuate casualties from the battlefield to nearby mobile army surgical hospitals (MASH), where new lifesaving surgical techniques, such as arterial repair, saved many lives. These advances continued in military medicine during the Vietnam War with more sophisticated surgery and additional antibiotics and equipment. These developments contributed to just 2.5 percent of casualties dying from wounds received, the lowest number ever. During the Gulf War of 1990–1991, disease and nonbattle injury rates were markedly lower than expected. In addition, the number of combat casualties was never so high as to test the capabilities of the medical force.

BIBLIOGRAPHY

Depuy, Trevor N. *Attrition: Forecasting Battle Casualties and Equipment Losses in Modern War.* Fairfax, Va.: Hero Books, 1990.

Reister, Frank A. *Battle Casualties and Medical Statistics: U.S. Army Experience in the Korean War.* Washington, D.C.: Office of the Surgeon General, Department of the Army, 1973.

U.S. Department of Defense. "Service and Casualties in Major Wars and Conflicts (as of Sept. 30, 1993)." *Defense Almanac* 94, no. 5 (September–October 1994).

Robert S. Driscoll

See also **Medicine, Military.**

WAR COSTS. Any estimate of war costs must be based on arbitrary assumptions as to the nature of those expenses that are properly chargeable to war. Granting that wartime military expenditures by the government are a basic element, it has been questioned whether or not the normal peacetime operating costs of the military establishment should also be included. It is also arguable that both the prewar buildup of military expenditures in anticipation of hostilities and the postwar tapering off of such expenditures should be included. The question has also been raised concerning the deduction of the costs of feeding, clothing, and housing military personnel from military appropriations, considering, on the one hand, that the personnel would have had to be provided for anyway and, on the other, that they would have been productively occupied. Property damage, the lost economic value of people killed or disabled in war, the costs of wartime economic disruption, and, conversely, the "negative" costs—that is, economic gain—of a wartime boom are also factors to consider in determining war costs. Part of the costs is transferred to future generations in the form of interest charges on war debts, and these charges usually continue long after the debts themselves have lost their identity in the total national debt. In a similar category are the costs of veterans' pensions and bonuses and medical and hospital care.

For the revolutionary war the estimates include the specie value of Treasury expenditures and certificates of indebtedness for the years 1775–1783, foreign loans, and state war debts assumed by the federal government. The estimate of war costs of the Confederacy is based solely on military appropriations by the Confederate congress; since no effort has been made to estimate other categories of loss to the Confederacy, no valid figure for total Civil War costs can be arrived at. Allied war debts in World War I ($7.4 billion) and lend-lease transfers in World War II ($50.2 billion), both reduced by postwar repayments, have been included in the net military costs. Costs for both world wars have been reduced by the value of surplus assets of the armed services; they also include expenditures by certain nonmilitary agencies. Allowance has also been made for recoveries of excess profits under the World War II renegotiation process.

The Korean War poses a special problem. It is virtually impossible to separate the costs growing out of operations in Korea from those of the mobilization and expansion of military forces during the same period resulting from the expectation of new Communist aggressions in Europe and elsewhere. Defense expenditures following the war, moreover, continued at a high level, clearly as a consequence of that expectation. In the interests of consistency with other war cost figures, net military expenditures for the Korean War have been limited to the war period, reduced by estimated normal peacetime costs as for the other wars.

For the war in Southeast Asia, net military costs are official Defense Department data defined as "the net difference between wartime and peacetime needs"—that is, substantially the same kinds of costs as shown for the other wars. They include expenditures for operations and maintenance of all U.S. forces in Southeast Asia and offsore in support of South Vietnam from fiscal year 1965 through fiscal year 1975. Military and economic assistance in Southeast Asia and Korea is not shown in the table; in the war in Southeast Asia military and economic assistance went to the three countries of Indochina (Vietnam, Laos, Cambodia), as well as to Thailand and South Korea, for those countries' contributions in forces, bases, and facilities. The bulk of military assistance expenditures

TABLE 1

Costs of U.S. Wars

	Military Costs[1] (in millions of dollars)
Revolutionary War	101
War of 1812	90
Mexican-American War	71
Civil War	
Union	3,183
Confederacy	1,520
Spanish-American War	283
World War I	31,627
World War II	316,227
Korean War	54,000
Southeast Asia War	111,400
Persian Gulf War	61,000[2]

1. Not including debt interest or veteran's benefits.
2. Allied paid the United States approximately 88% of this amount.

is included in net military costs; for the Southeast Asia conflict such service-funded military assistance to Indochina, Thailand, and South Korea came to more than $17 billion. Aggregate economic and military aid to Indochina and Thailand since 1950 totals more than $30 billion; to South Korea more than $12 billion.

The Persian Gulf War of 1991 was one of the least expensive of America's twentieth-century wars. Its allies paid most of its $61 billion price tag, leaving only $8 billion to be paid by American taxpayers. During the 1990s, the U.S. became entangled in several war-like operations in response to a United Nations resolution (like its humanitarian intervention in Somalia in 1993) or as part of a NATO coalition (as with the air campaign against Yugoslavia in 1999). It is difficult to quantify the cost of these increasingly frequent peacekeeping missions. At the beginning of the new millenium, however, it was clear that the terrorist attacks of 2001 and the subsequent "war on terrorism" threatened to reverse the post–Cold War decline in American military spending relative to overall government expenditures.

BIBLIOGRAPHY

Gilbert, Charles. *American Financing of World War I.* Westport, Conn.: Greenwood Press, 1970.

Murphy, Henry C. *The National Debt in War and Transition.* New York: McGraw-Hill, 1950.

Weidenbaum, Murray L. *Small Wars, Big Defense: Paying for the Military after the Cold War.* New York: Oxford University Press, 1992.

Richard M. Leighton / A. R.

See also **Civil War; Korean War; Mexican-American War; Persian Gulf War of 1991; Revolution, American: Military History; Spanish-American War; Vietnam War; War of 1812; World War I; World War II.**

WAR CRIMES TRIALS. From November 1945 to October 1946, at Nuremberg, Germany, the surviving leaders of the Nazi regime were tried before an international tribunal (the United States, Great Britain, Russia, and France) as war criminals. They were charged with violations of international law, with having waged aggressive warfare, and in general with "crimes against humanity." Of twenty-two high officials brought to trial, nineteen were found guilty. Twelve, including Hermann Göring, Joachim von Ribbentrop, and Artur von Seyss-Inquart, were sentenced to death. Eight were eventually hanged. In addition a number of lesser officials were tried, most of whom were convicted.

Comparable trials of Japanese leaders were held at Tokyo, from May 1946 to November 1948, with similar results, although on a much larger scale. The Allies executed not only Hideki Tojo, the military dictator of Japan, and many of his top lieutenants, but also several hundred lower-ranking Japanese officers who were convicted of torturing and murdering Allied prisoners-of-war.

The trial of war criminals rested on the assumption that aggressive warfare was a crime, and on the still broader assumption that the principles of jurisprudence as developed in England and the United States applied to international relations as well. Yet many people objected that these principles were themselves disregarded in the trials. Thus it was charged that to try men for committing acts that were only later designated as crimes was to pass judgment *ex post facto*. The only answer to this was that the crimes of the Nazi leaders—the full magnitude of which became apparent only as the trials unfolded—were so horrible as to deserve, if not to demand, such punishment.

During the Cold War stand-off between the United States and Soviet Union, war crimes trials receded from the international scene. After the demise of the Cold War, however, an international consensus built in favor of resurrecting war crimes tribunals, particularly for perpetrators of genocide. In the first years of the twenty-first century, under the auspices of the United Nations, war crimes trials were held to prosecute those accused of committing "crimes against humanity" during the Balkans' Wars of the 1990s, including Slobodan Milosevic, former dictator of Yugoslavia. The United Nations expected to hold similar tribunals to prosecute the perpetrators of the 1994 genocide in Rwanda. During a 1998 United Nations conference in Rome, representatives of over 50 countries agreed to establish a permanent International Criminal Court for the prosecution of war crimes.

BIBLIOGRAPHY

Bloxham, Donald. *Genocide on Trial: The War Crimes Trials and the Formation of Holocaust History and Memory.* New York: Oxford University Press, 2001.

Persico, Joseph. *Nuremberg: Infamy on Trial.* New York: Viking, 1994.

Christopher Lasch / A. G.

See also **Cold War; Extradition; Genocide; Germany, Relations with; Helsinki Accords; International Law; Yugoslavia, Relations with.**

WAR DEMOCRATS were those who ceased normal party activity in 1861 and 1862 on the grounds that any partisan criticism of the Republican government during the Civil War amounted to disloyalty. Most regular Democrats supported the war effort but continued to oppose the Lincoln administration, arguing that the policies of individuals in office were easily separable from the cause of the Union. The War Democrats ran some candidates of their own, but they tended to cooperate with the Republicans. Though they embarrassed their party, they did not win enough votes to significantly change the political demographics of the period. Vice President Andrew Johnson was the best known of the War Democrats.

BIBLIOGRAPHY

Dell, Christopher. *Lincoln and the War Democrats: The Grand Erosion of Conservative Tradition.* Rutherford, N.J.: Fairleigh Dickinson University Press, 1975.

Silbey, Joel H. *A Respectable Minority: The Democratic Party in the Civil War Era, 1860–1868.* New York: Norton, 1977.

Jeremy Derfner

WAR DEPARTMENT. In 1789 Congress created the War Department to administer the field army commanded by the president and secretary of war. After the War of 1812, Secretary of War John C. Calhoun reorganized the department and introduced a system of bureau chiefs with a commanding general in the field. The bureau chiefs advised the secretary of war and commanded their own troops and field installations. The secretary typically supported the bureaus in disputes with the commanding general. Congress regulated the bureaus in minute detail, and their bureau chiefs often relied on federal lawmakers for support. The Spanish-American War demonstrated a need for more effective control over the department and its bureaus, and the debate over how to do so reshaped the War Department during the twentieth century. In 1903 Secretary Elihu Root asserted department control by appointing a chief of staff and a general staff for planning. Yet, his successor, William Howard Taft, reversed this position, subordinated the chief of staff to the adjutant general, and reinvigorated the traditional secretary–bureau chief alliance. In 1911 Secretary Henry L. Stimson revived Root's reforms and tried to rein in the bureaus. Congress undermined his efforts with the National Defense Act of 1916, which reduced the size and functions of the general staff. During World War I, Secretary Newton D. Baker and President Woodrow Wilson opposed efforts to control the bureaus and war industry, until competition for limited supplies almost paralyzed the American economy. Baker soon yielded to pressure from Congress and big business. He placed Benedict Crowell in charge of munitions, named George W. Goethals acting quartermaster general, and made Peyton C. March chief of staff. Assisted by industrial advisers, they reorganized the army's supply system and nearly eliminated the bureaus as independent agencies. March also reorganized the general staff along similar lines and gave it direct authority over departmental operations. Nevertheless, after the war, the bureaus regained their former independence from Congress. General John J. Pershing realigned the general staff on the pattern of his American Expeditionary Forces field headquarters. Although the general staff had little effective control over the bureaus, the chiefs of staff had gained substantial authority over them when General George C. Marshall assumed that office in 1939. Marshall believed that the department was a "poor command post" and, supported by Henry L. Stimson, who once again held the post of secretary of war, took advantage of the War Powers Act to reorganize the department following Pearl Harbor. He created three new commands to run the department's operations: the Army Ground Forces, the Army Air Forces, and the Army Service Forces. The Operations Division served as Marshall's general planning staff. After World War II, the federal government abandoned Marshall's organizational scheme and returned to the fragmented prewar structure, while the independent military services parried efforts to reestablish firm executive control over their operations. Under the National Security Act of 1947, as amended in 1949, the War Department became the Department of the Army within the Department of Defense, and the secretary of the army became an operating manager for the new secretary of defense.

BIBLIOGRAPHY

Cline, Ray S. *Washington Command Post: The Operations Division.* Washington, D.C.: Office of the Chief of Military History, Department of the Army, 1951.

Hewes, James.E. *From Root to McNamara: Army Organization and Administration, 1900–1963.* Washington, D.C.: Government Printing Office, 1975.

Skelton, William B. *An American Profession of Arms: The Army Officer Corps, 1784–1861.* Lawrence: University Press of Kansas, 1992.

James E. Hewes Jr. / E. M.

See also **Army, United States; Defense, Department of; Defense, National; Federal Agencies; Military Policy; Mobilization.**

WAR FINANCE CORPORATION.

The War Finance Corporation was created by Congress on 5 April 1918 to facilitate the extension of credit to vital war industries during World War I, primarily by making loans to financial institutions. During its six months of wartime existence, the corporation advanced $71,387,222. In 1919 it greatly assisted the director general of railroads and railroad companies, and until 1920 it served as the chief agency through which the Treasury purchased government obligations. With the return of peace, amendments to the corporation's charter greatly expanded its activities. After 1919 it actively financed the American agricultural and livestock industries until the Agricultural Credits Act terminated the corporation in 1924, after it had lent $700 million.

BIBLIOGRAPHY

Gilbert, Charles. *American Financing of World War I.* Westport, Conn.: Greenwood Press, 1970.

Leuchtenburg, William E. *The Perils of Prosperity, 1914–1932.* Chicago: University of Chicago Press, 1993.

Charles C. Abbott / C. W.

See also **Credit; Livestock Industry; World War I, Economic Mobilization for.**

WAR HAWKS.

John Randolph of Roanoke, opposed to the foreign policies of Jefferson and Madison after 1806, called the young leaders of the war party in the Twelfth Congress (1811–1813) "war hawks," and the epithet stuck. He continued the bird-simile, declaring they had a single cry: "Canada! Canada!" He might have detected another, "Florida!", for American expansionism pointed southward as well as westward and northward. Kentucky's young U.S. Senator Henry Clay switched to the House, leading the hawks as speaker. Clay appointed others as chairs of committees, and steered legislation for military preparations. Powerfully effective hawks were four South Carolinians: John C. Calhoun, William Lowndes, Langdon Cheves, and David R. Williams. John A. Harper of New Hampshire, Peter Porter of western New York, Richard Mentor Johnson of Kentucky, Felix Grundy of Tennessee, and George M. Troup of Georgia further proved that the war hawks represented frontier areas of the young republic. Born in the era of the American Revolution, these men expressed a burning desire to defend independence, which they supposed Britain threatened. They resented Britain's Orders-in-Council and impressments just as strongly as they denounced British encouragement of Indian resistance to U. S. expansion—most notably Tecumseh's confederation. Their national leaders, the Virginia Presidents Jefferson and Madison, also vigorously promoted territorial expansion, Indian removal, and the freedom of the seas throughout their public service. Most of the war hawks had distinguished careers during and after the war.

BIBLIOGRAPHY

Hickey, Donald R. *The War of 1812: A Forgotten Conflict.* Urbana: University of Illinois Press, 1989. Follows the hawks through the war in political, military, and diplomatic roles.

Perkins, Bradford. *Prologue to War: England and the United States, 1805–1812.* Berkeley: University of California Press, 1961. Demonstrates Jefferson's and Madison's determined pursuit of the freedom of the seas.

Pratt, Julius W. *Expansionists of 1812.* New York: Macmillan, 1925. Argues that the war hawks and the expansionist urge they embodied caused the War of 1812.

Robert McColley

See also **War of 1812.**

WAR INDUSTRIES BOARD. The War Industries Board was a wartime agency of 1917–1918 designed to coordinate the war role of American industry. Its parent body, the Council of National Defense, enjoyed only advisory powers and could not compel anyone to accept its advice. There were five procurement agencies in the War Department, and they frequently competed for the same materials and manufacturing facilities, leading to shortages of transportation, labor, and material that seriously slowed the war program in the winter of 1917–1918.

The War Industries Board, formed in July 1917, was as powerless as the other agencies had been. When Congress discussed the extremely limited production of military equipment early in 1918, many leaders aimed to establish a munitions ministry on the English model. In order to forestall this thinly veiled censure, President Woodrow Wilson, on 4 March 1918, appointed Bernard M. Baruch as chairman of the War Industries Board and greatly augmented its powers. This enabled the War Industries Board to use all the agencies of the Council of National Defense, to mobilize industry, and to force adoption of its orders. This board controlled all available resources and manufacturing facilities, fixed prices, raised the volume of munitions produced, and brought order out of industrial chaos. It was terminated by executive order on 1 January 1919.

BIBLIOGRAPHY

Baruch, Bernard M. *American Industry in the War: A Report of the War Industries Board.* New York: Prentice-Hall, 1941.

Leuchtenburg, William E. *The Perils of Prosperity, 1914–32.* Chicago: University of Chicago Press, 1993.

H. A. DeWeerd / c. w.

See also **Council of National Defense; Munitions; War Department; World War I, Economic Mobilization for.**

WAR LABOR BOARD. *See* **National War Labor Board.**

WAR MEMORIALS. The American national identity remains inexorably intertwined with the commemoration and memory of past wars. Most earlier war memorials sparked as much controversy over their purpose

War Memorial. The Women's Airforce Service Pilots Monument in Sweetwater, Texas, honors thirty-eight WASPs killed on training flights at Avenger Field there during World War II. SUSAN E. EDGAR

and cost as later ones such as the Vietnam Veterans (1982) and World War II (construction began in 2002). Monument styles changed dramatically over two hundred years. Before the Civil War, simple stone shafts predominated, including the Bunker Hill Monument (1842) and the mass gravestone at the Mexican War cemetery in Mexico City (1851). After the Civil War, European-trained sculptors created beaux-arts edifices and statues at battlefield parks like the ones at Gettysburg, Pennsylvania, and Vicksburg, Mississippi. The late-nineteenth-century City Beautiful movement convinced city governments to purchase elaborate war monuments, such as the Soldiers and Sailors Monument in Indianapolis, Indiana (1902). Most of the twentieth century saw "useful" memorials such as the stadium at Soldier Field in Chicago (1925), where Gold Star Mothers talked City Hall into changing the name from Grant Park Municipal Stadium. A B-17 Flying Fortress bomber airplane named *The Memphis Belle*, residing in Memphis, Tennessee, since 1946, helped to popularize preserved military equipment. The American Battle Monuments Commission, established in 1923, oversees twenty-seven monuments worldwide commemorating twentieth-century American wars.

BIBLIOGRAPHY

Mayo, James M. *War Memorials As Political Landscape: The American Experience and Beyond.* New York: Praeger, 1988.

Piehler, G. Kurt. *Remembering War the American Way.* Washington, D.C.: Smithsonian Institution Press, 1995.

Bill Olbrich

See also **Vietnam War Memorial.**

WAR OF 1812, fought under the motto "free trade and sailor's rights," was the result of British maritime policies during the wars between Great Britain and France, the desire of President James Madison to strengthen republicanism, and the American belief that it could secure possession of Canada as a bargaining chip against Great Britain.

Neither Britain nor France cared much about the rights of neutrals in their struggle, which lasted with only short interruptions from 1793 to 1815. Britain's major asset was its navy, which contained France by closing off large stretches of the European coastline. The British blockade from Brest to the mouth of the Elbe River; Napoleon's Berlin Decree of 21 November 1806, declaring a blockade of the British Isles and prohibiting ships from entering French harbors if they previously had been in British waters; the British Orders in Council of 1807 that all neutral ships coming from France would be seized if they had not previously visited British harbors; and Napoleon's Milan Decree of 17 December 1807 that all neutral ships that concurred with the British demands would be seized had little impact on the war in Europe but affected the United States and its profitable maritime trade. Americans were in no position to do anything about this sort of war. Great Britain, straining for sailors on their warships, insisted on the right of its naval officers to "impress" from American ships deserters from the Royal Navy or other British subjects liable to naval service. British sailors had deserted by the thousands to the American merchant marine. Many who had taken out naturalization papers were nonetheless the victims of the British policy.

Anger over the British practices reached a climax on 22 June 1807, when the USS *Chesapeake* was stopped by the British frigate *Leopard*. When the American captain denied the British request to search his ship for deserters, the *Leopard* shelled the American vessel. Not prepared for a military engagement, the *Chesapeake* suffered casualties quickly. After firing one shot, the American captain allowed the British to board his ship. They took four sailors prisoner and put out to sea again. This arrogant provocation injured American national pride. Although President Thomas Jefferson seemed ready to go to war, he resorted to economic warfare. At his request, Congress

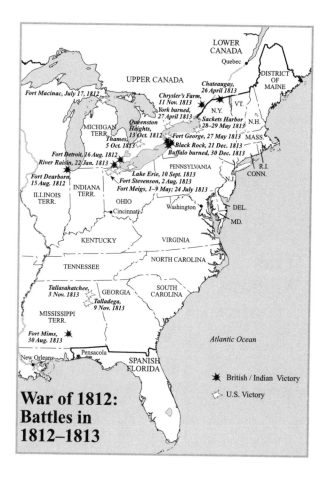

War of 1812: Battles in 1812–1813

passed the Embargo Act of 1807, which was intended to prevent additional entanglement in European affairs by prohibiting the export of American goods on both American and foreign vessels. While the British and French embargoes had led to seizures of American merchantmen, they had provided an opportunity for traders to reap huge profits by counting on the fast and sleek American ships to run the blockades. Prohibiting the ships from leaving harbor prevented seizure and impressment, but it also put an end to a lucrative situation. Although smuggling became routine, the Embargo Act severely hurt communities in New England and cotton planters and farmers in the West and South who depended on the European markets, particularly the British markets.

The embargo had little impact on Great Britain and France. Amidst growing protests against the embargo, under the impression of election victories by the rival Federalists, and with New Englanders airing secessionist ideas, President Jefferson asked for a modification of the Embargo Act shortly before he left office. Congress repealed the act and on 1 March 1809 passed the Nonintercourse Act. The new law prohibited trade with Great Britain and France and banned British and French ships from U.S. waters, but it permitted trade with the rest of the world. Great Britain had found ready suppliers in Central and Latin America, and like the embargo, nonintercourse did not change British naval conduct. Having

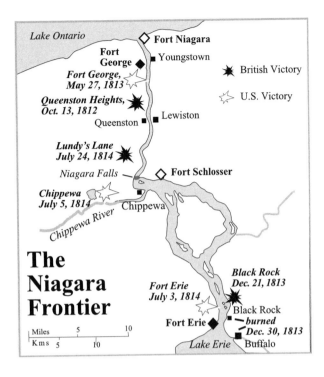

The Niagara Frontier

(Map labels: Lake Ontario; Fort Niagara; Fort George; Youngstown; Fort George, May 27, 1813; British Victory; U.S. Victory; Queenston Heights, Oct. 13, 1812; Queenston; Lewiston; Lundy's Lane July 24, 1814; Niagara Falls; Chippewa July 5, 1814; Chippewa River; Chippewa; Fort Schlosser; Fort Erie July 3, 1814; Black Rock Dec. 21, 1813; Black Rock burned Dec. 30, 1813; Fort Erie; Lake Erie; Buffalo)

Miles 5 10
Kms 5 10

The War Hawks argued that British crimes were not confined to the high seas. On the northwestern frontier, in Ohio and the territories of Indiana, Illinois, and Michigan, Native Americans, led by the Shawnee prophet Tenskwatawa and his brother Tecumseh and supported by the British in Canada, resisted the relentless white encroachment on their lands. Tenskwatawa preached a return to the customary way of living, Native American brotherhood, and abstinence. Strongly opposed to the extensive land cessions secured by the Americans and using anti-white rhetoric, he attracted many young warriors. After the Treaty of Fort Wayne, in which chiefs opposed to Tenskwatawa ceded 3 million acres of land to the United States, Tenskwatawa threatened to prevent settlement of the land by force. Tecumseh would supply the necessary military and political leadership. Americans suspected that Tenskwatawa and Tecumseh were agents of British interests, and while Tecumseh traveled into the South to enlist other Native American nations, the Indiana governor William Henry Harrison moved against what he perceived to be a threatening Native American coalition. He destroyed their town at the Tippecanoe River, providing an additional incentive for the Native Americans to seek support from the British in Canada. The attacks against white settlers did not end, and the War Hawks, holding Great Britain responsible for those attacks, advocated ousting the British from North America by conquering Canada. Oth-

accomplished nothing, the United States backed down and replaced the Nonintercourse Act with Macon's Bill No. 2, a bill introduced by Representative Nathaniel Macon that barred armed vessels of the belligerents from entering American ports but reopened trade with France and Great Britain. Macon's Bill promised that, if either England or France revoked the blockade, nonintercourse would be imposed against the other.

Napoleon reacted swiftly. He instructed his foreign minister, Jean-Baptiste Nompère de Champagny, duc de Cadore, to notify the Americans that the Milan and Berlin Decrees were revoked. Although the note the Americans received from Cadore was vague and stated that repeal of the decrees was contingent on resumption of American nonintercourse with Great Britain, President James Madison proclaimed the French in compliance with Macon's Bill. This gave the British until February 1811 to revoke the Orders in Council.

Great Britain remained intractable, and by the time Congress assembled in November, Madison was ready to put the nation on a war footing. Many members of Congress, however, were reluctant to go to war with the mightiest naval power on the globe. The most vocal group calling for war or at least some action was called the War Hawks. They were for the most part a group of young Jeffersonian Republicans from the West and the South who had recently been voted into office. Among them was Henry Clay of Kentucky, who had never served in the House of Representatives before and was only thirty-four years old but was nonetheless elected to the influential position of speaker of the House. Clay made sure that a number of his colleagues willing to go to war were appointed to important committees.

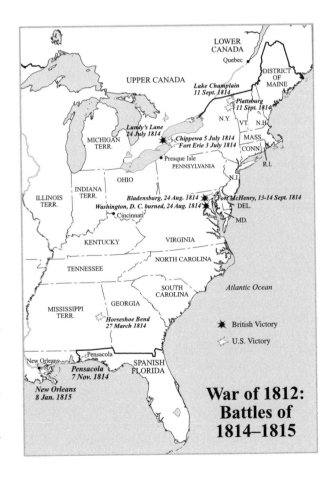

War of 1812: Battles of 1814–1815

(Map labels: LOWER CANADA; Quebec; DISTRICT OF MAINE; UPPER CANADA; Lake Champlain 11 Sept. 1814; Plattsburg 11 Sept. 1814; N.Y.; VT.; N.H.; Lundy's Lane 24 July 1814; MICHIGAN TERR.; Chippewa 5 July 1814; Fort Erie 3 July 1814; MASS.; CONN.; R.I.; Presque Isle; PENNSYLVANIA; N.J.; INDIANA TERR.; OHIO; ILLINOIS TERR.; Bladensburg, 24 Aug. 1814; Fort McHenry, 13–14 Sept. 1814; DEL.; Washington, D.C. burned, 24 Aug. 1814; MD.; Cincinnati; KENTUCKY; VIRGINIA; TENNESSEE; NORTH CAROLINA; SOUTH CAROLINA; Atlantic Ocean; MISSISSIPPI TERR.; GEORGIA; Horseshoe Bend 27 March 1814; British Victory; U.S. Victory; Pensacola; New Orleans; Pensacola 7 Nov. 1814; SPANISH FLORIDA; New Orleans 8 Jan. 1815)

Women and War. As in all wars, some women—like this one, shown passing cannonballs to artillerymen—played an unofficial and usually unacknowledged part in the War of 1812, even in battle. DOUBLE DELTA INDUSTRIES, INC.

ers from the Southwest and the South saw an opportunity to conquer East and West Florida. The United States had long claimed that West Florida was part of the Louisiana Purchase and had begun absorbing it piecemeal.

Frontier grievances and ambitions were debated in Congress, but they were hardly sufficient by themselves to bring about war with Great Britain. Some may have hoped to incorporate Canada into the United States, but most members of Congress simply perceived Canada as an easy target because Britain was too occupied with France to divert men and arms to defend its dominion in North America. Canada was to serve as a bargaining chip to force Great Britain to change its conduct on the high seas.

After more than half a year of deliberations and persuasion, Congress declared war on 18 June 1812. The House voted 79 to 49 on 4 June 1812, with 17 Republicans voting against war and 10 abstaining. Not one Federalist voted for war. The Senate approved the declaration by a narrow margin of 19 to 13 on 17 June. Madison signed it the following day. Two days before and unknown to the members of Congress, the British Parliament had repealed the Orders in Council. When the news reached the United States, it was already too late.

Invasion of Canada

Despite the long period of debates in Congress, the nation was hardly prepared to actually wage the war it declared on a formidable enemy. Inadequate military, naval, and financial preparation resulted in insufficient and ill-trained troops. Military incompetence and defective strategy led to a series of military disasters, particularly during the first year of the war, when American troops tried to invade Canada. The army was additionally hampered by a militia that generally defined itself as a defensive force and was unwilling to partake in a war of conquest and by obstruction of the war effort in the Federalist-controlled New England states. General William Hull had to surrender Detroit on 16 August 1812, Generals Stephen van Rensselaer and Alexander Smyth failed dismally on the Niagara River in October, and General Henry Dearborn broke off a feeble attempt to march on Montreal in November. On Lake Erie, U.S. forces achieved their greatest success under the command of Oliver H. Perry in September 1813. Detroit was recovered the following year, and Harrison defeated the British at the Thames River on 5 October 1813, a battle in which Tecumseh was killed, breaking Native American resistance. The year closed, however, with the complete failure of a renewed campaign against Montreal by General James Wilkinson on 11 No-

Death of a General. This engraving depicts the mortally wounded Sir Edward Pakenham, the British commander at the Battle of New Orleans, on 8 January 1815. HULTON/GETTY IMAGES

vember 1813, the British capture of Fort Niagara on 18 December 1813, and the destruction of a number of towns, including Buffalo, New York, by the British during December 1813.

By the summer of 1814 many incompetent officers had been replaced, and under the command of Generals Jacob Brown and Winfield Scott, the northern army, although failing to conquer any substantial territory, stood its ground at Chippewa River on 5 July 1814, Lundy's Lane on 25 July 1814, and the siege of Fort Erie in August 1814. In September, despite an overwhelming majority, the British broke off an attack against upper New York when their naval support was defeated on Lake Champlain.

British Landing Operations

After Napoleon's abdication in April 1814, Britain was free to transfer battle-hardened troops from Europe to North America, which made landing operations in Maine and the Chesapeake Bay possible. The British were successful in Maine, and their attack against Washington, D.C., brought about the infamous routing of the American militia and troops at Bladensburg, Maryland, and the burning of official buildings in the nation's capital, including the White House and the Capitol on 24 and 25 August 1814. In early September, the British moved against Baltimore, but there they were driven off. That battle inspired Francis Scott Key to write "The Star-Spangled Banner."

Blockade of the American Seaboard

During the first six months after the declaration of war, the Royal Navy was slow to use its superiority, but by the end of 1813, the American East Coast was under blockade. Only the New England states were exempted by Admiral John B. Warren until May 1814, because they opposed the war and supplied the British in Canada and the West Indies. American exports dropped sharply, and even coastal trade became increasingly dangerous. Harbor towns were affected severely, but farmers and planters in the West and the South also suffered heavily. Most American ships, navy and merchant marine, were bottled up in port, and single-ship actions on the high seas failed to affect the overwhelming superiority of the British fleet. Even privateers, who had been quite successful in previous years, found few prizes because most British ships now sailed in convoys.

Peace

Both the Americans and the British were eager to enter into negotiations. Russia offered to mediate the conflict, and American and British peace commissioners met in Ghent, Belgium, in August 1814. The American delegation had hoped to put impressment on the negotiation table but soon found that the British would not be moved on this issue. Anxious to protect Canada and their Native American allies, the British first demanded territory, a Native American buffer state, and demilitarization of the Great Lakes. In view of little encouraging news from

have deployed U.S. forces range from a show of force to minor hostilities to large-scale warfare. Although such actions have not been uniformly popular, the persistence of a consensus regarding U.S. foreign policy has usually muted any discord about presidents exceeding their constitutional prerogatives.

That consensus collapsed with the Vietnam War. Presidents Lyndon B. Johnson and Richard M. Nixon cited the Tonkin Gulf Resolution of August 1964 as congressional authorization for U.S. involvement in and escalation of the Vietnam War. The conflict proceeded without any formal declaration of war and became increasingly unpopular as it dragged on. Critics attributed the costly U.S. involvement to a failure to prevent successive presidents from usurping authority that rightly belonged to the legislative branch. This perception provoked calls for Congress to reassert its prerogatives. Such thinking culminated in passage of the War Powers Resolution of November 1973 over President Nixon's veto. The resolution directed the president to consult Congress prior to introducing U.S. forces into hostilities; it required the president to report to Congress all nonroutine deployments of military forces within forty-eight hours of their occurrence; and it mandated that forces committed to actual or imminent hostilities by presidential order be withdrawn within sixty days unless Congress declared war, passed legislation authorizing the use of U.S. forces, or extended the deadline. The sixty-day time limit could be extended to ninety days if the president certified the need for additional time to complete the withdrawal of U.S. forces.

Heralded as a congressional triumph, the War Powers Resolution proved limited in practice. Presidents continued to insist that the resolution infringed on constitutional executive authority. Time and again, they circumvented or disregarded its provisions. Among the notable presidential flouters were Gerald Ford in 1975, at the time of the *Mayaguez* operation; Jimmy Carter in 1980 with the Desert One hostage rescue attempt; Ronald Reagan in 1983 with the intervention in Grenada and in 1986 with the air attack on Libya; and George Bush with the 1989 invasion of Panama. Even the U.S. military response to the Iraqi invasion of Kuwait in August 1990 lacked a congressional mandate. President Bush relied on executive authority in ordering the U.S. buildup of 500,000 troops in the Persian Gulf, showing more interest in the endorsement of the United Nations Security Council than of the U.S. Congress. Only when U.S. forces were in place and the decision to use force had been made did Bush consult Congress, less for constitutional than for political reasons. On 12 January 1991 Congress narrowly passed a resolution authorizing Bush to do what he clearly intended to do anyway—forcibly eject Iraqi troops from Kuwait. When Operation Desert Storm began four days later, the usefulness of the War Powers Resolution seemed more problematic than ever, and the goal of restoring a division of war-making powers ever more elusive.

BIBLIOGRAPHY

Caraley, Demetrios, ed. *The President's War Powers: From the Federalists to Reagan.* New York: Academy of Political Science, 1984.

Kohn, Richard H., ed. *Military Laws of the United States from the Civil War Through the War Powers Act of 1973.* New York: Arno Press, 1979.

May, Christopher N. *In the Name of War: Judicial Review and the War Powers since 1918.* Cambridge, Mass.: Harvard University Press, 1989.

Andrew J. Bacevich / c. w.

See also **Grenada Invasion; Hostage Crises; Mayaguez Incident; Panama Invasion; Persian Gulf War of 1991; Tonkin Gulf Resolution; War and the Constitution; War Powers.**

WAR TRADE BOARD.

The War Trade Board was created by President Woodrow Wilson through an executive order dated 12 October 1917, issued under the authority of the Trading with the Enemy Act (6 October). The order vested the agency with control over both imports and exports. The board members were representatives of the secretaries of state, treasury, agriculture, and commerce, and of the food administrator and the chairman of the U.S. Shipping Board, with Vance C. McCormick as the chairman. An executive order transferred the duties and functions of the board to the Department of State on 1 July 1919.

BIBLIOGRAPHY

Leuchtenburg, William E. *The Perils of Prosperity, 1914–1932.* Chicago: University of Chicago Press, 1993.

Erik McKinley Eriksson / c. w.

See also **Shipping Board, U.S.; State, Department of; Trade with the Enemy Acts; World War I.**

WARD'S COVE PACKING CO., INC., V. ATONIO,

490 U.S. 642 (1989), briefly redefined the standards used to judge employment discrimination. Since 1971 courts had been following the "disparate impact" theory of the *Griggs v. Duke Power Company* case. If a plaintiff could show that an employer action harmed a protected group, then the employer had the burden of proving that its actions were a business necessity. The *Ward's Cove* case shifted the burden of proof to employees, making it harder to prove discrimination. The plaintiffs (nonwhite employees) sued the Alaskan salmon canning company on the basis of a disparate impact theory, providing statistical evidence on the disparity in the racial composition of jobholders in skilled and unskilled cannery work. The Supreme Court held that the plaintiffs had to do more than show disparate impact: they had to prove the specific relationship between employer practices and a discriminatory outcome. In addition, the Court replaced the

business-necessity defense with a less stringent "business-justification" standard. Civil rights groups, decrying this and other Supreme Court decisions of the 1980s, fought for substantive legislative amendments, an effort culminating with the passage of the Civil Rights Act of 1991. That legislation overturned the decision, restoring the *Griggs* standards for disparate-impact suits.

BIBLIOGRAPHY

Apruzzese, Vincent J. "Selected Recent Developments in EEO Law: The Civil Rights Act of 1991, Sexual Harassment, and the Emerging Role of ADR." *Labor Law Journal* 43 (1992): 325–337.

Halpern, Stephen C. *On the Limits of the Law: The Ironic Legacy of Title VI of the 1964 Civil Rights Act.* Baltimore: Johns Hopkins University Press, 1995.

Gilbert J. Gall / A. R.

See also **Affirmative Action; Civil Rights Act of 1964; Civil Rights Act of 1991; Civil Rights and Liberties;** *Griggs v. Duke Power Company.*

WARE V. HYLTON, 3 Dall. (3 U.S.) 199 (1796), 4 to 0. In this case the Supreme Court decided that federal laws have precedence over state laws. The Treaty of Paris (1783) provided that British creditors could recover debts without interference from state law. A Virginia statute absolved its citizens of responsibility if they paid such debts into the state treasury, thus confiscating the amounts due. The Court's decision in *Ware v. Hylton* nullified this statute. There were four opinions, but the most important was that of Justice Samuel Chase, who held that all state laws in conflict with federal treaties were "prostrate" before them. John Marshall, in his only appearance as an advocate before the Supreme Court, unsuccessfully argued the case for Virginia.

BIBLIOGRAPHY

Casto, William R. *The Supreme Court in the Early Republic: The Chief Justiceships of John Jay and Oliver Ellsworth.* Columbia: University of South Carolina Press, 1995.

Goebel, Julius, Jr. *Antecedents and Beginnings to 1801.* Vol. 1 of *History of the Supreme Court of the United States,* edited by the United States Permanent Committee for the Oliver Wendell Holmes Devise. New York: Macmillan, 1971.

Stephen B. Presser

WARFARE, INDIAN.

Warfare represents a vital aspect of Native American history for many reasons, not least of which is the tremendous impact of armed conflict on Native communities after the arrival of European intruders. Additionally, many enduring negative stereotypes of Native Americans stem from their supposedly "warlike" and "savage" nature. Native American peoples do indeed possess a strong military tradition, yet they used military force consciously to control the consequences of warfare within their communities. That struggle became much more difficult after the arrival of European intruders.

Pre-Contact Warfare

Modern authorities do not agree about the nature of warfare among Native Americans prior to the arrival of Europeans. Those who rely on literary sources and indigenous oral tradition contend that pre-contact warfare was comparatively limited. They believe that Indians went to war for only a few reasons: to avenge the deaths of relatives; to obtain plunder, prestige, or acceptance as an adult member of the community; and to take captives. According to these scholars, pre-contact conflicts tended to be small-scale, limited in range, and seasonal in duration. Archaeologists and others who rely on physical evidence, however, object to the characterization of pre-contact warfare as game-like and ineffective, and point to discoveries of palisaded enclosures, mass graves, and skeletal remains with imbedded projectile points and gruesome, intentional damage. This latter group of scholars maintains that the weak logistical capacities of pre-state societies in the Americas affected their ability to sustain continuous combat, but did not lessen their capacity to conduct brutal warfare.

Pre-contact warfare in North America included formal battles, small ambush raids, and large-scale assaults. Each variety played a role in Native societies, and each was deeply imbued with ritual. Considerable attention has been given to the elaborate, pre-arranged "set-piece" battles, which involved ornate dress and accoutrements, roughly equivalent armament, mutual taunting by the opposing sides, and relatively low rates of casualties resulting from hand-to-hand combat. However, small-scale ambushes and raids were by far the most common forms of inter-group conflict before the arrival of Europeans. These raids brought food, material goods, livestock, and human trophies (scalps and captives) to the aggressor nations, and they provided a means for individual warriors or their families to achieve social prestige within their communities. The social gains resulting from warfare, which in many groups included advancement to adult status for young men, outweighed concern over the potential for loss of life.

Ambush tactics seldom permitted the aggressor nation to acquire new territory or to assimilate a rival group. Instead, they killed a few people at a time, often individuals or small groups isolated from their home population, including a higher proportion of women. Archaeological evidence suggests that a significant percentage of ambush victims, surprised and often outnumbered, received fatal wounds as they attempted to flee. These wounds included scalping, an indigenous practice that was later encouraged by Europeans through the offering of scalp bounties.

In addition to economic and political motivations, many Indian groups found in war a means to redirect the self-destructive emotions associated with grief arising from the deaths of community members. These "mourning wars" were intended to fill the void in the community's spiritual power caused by the loss of an individual (whether by natural causes or in battle) by capturing an equal number of enemy personnel. The captives were adopted into the community, publicly tortured to death, or, in some cases, ritually cannibalized to appropriate the victim's spiritual power. This renewed sense of balance served to enhance group cohesion and identity.

Warfare might have occurred as a private conflict initiated by aggrieved families against an enemy or as a national conflict that involved a significant portion of a group's fighting men. Whatever the case, because most Native American peoples kept military activities segregated from their normal peacetime routine, specific ceremonies were necessary to prepare warriors, and even entire communities, for war and a return to peace. Fasting, sexual abstinence, and group rituals of singing and dancing were the most common ways in which warriors prepared themselves. Warriors departed after receiving provisions and some form of protection from community spiritual authorities. Because war parties were voluntary in nature and members were often linked by kinship, their leaders were especially unwilling to sustain losses. A war party's activities usually ended with a single successful battle or the death of a member of the group, even if accidental. Upon their return, purification rituals helped warriors reintegrate into community life.

Many scholars have noted the role of animal hunting in training future warriors; they believe that warfare functioned in large part to provide young men with another positive outlet for their aggressive tendencies by establishing clear guidelines for advancing their status through military exploits. Men between the ages of twelve and forty filled the ranks of warriors in most Native nations, and war honors tended to place a greater premium on courage, individual initiative, and stealth than on mere body or scalp counts. Traditional enemies were also valued, insofar as they provided permanent and comparatively predictable targets. Some conflicts went on for centuries as a result of seemingly endless cycles of ambush, murder, and retaliation. Given the various benefits of warfare for Native communities prior to the arrival of Europeans, however, it seems clear that it was not in one nation's best interests to totally obliterate or assimilate an enemy people, even when it was within their capacities to do so.

The Early Contact Period, 1600–1815

However frequent and brutal pre-contact indigenous warfare was, it differed markedly from the style of warfare practiced by European colonists. Native warriors soon learned that these new, uninvited neighbors tended to pursue sustained campaigns that persisted until their enemies were completely defeated or, at least, widely dispersed. European colonists were equally surprised by what they considered a cowardly approach to warfare among Native peoples, but after some initial scoffing at the In-

dians' "skulking way of war," many learned to respect the threat posed by Native war parties that could "approach like foxes, fight like lions, and disappear like birds."

After the arrival of Europeans, who brought epidemic diseases and subsequent catastrophic demographic losses among Native Americans, new motives for warfare developed among Native nations. These included defense of territorial boundaries from colonial encroachment; competition with other nations for good hunting territory to supply pelts and skins to European traders; aggression by groups possessing new technological advantages over neighboring peoples; aiding a colonial ally during imperial conflicts; and raids for new sources of material wealth (including cash bounties for scalps and revenue from the ransom of captives). As a consequence, warfare grew more frequent and deadly at a time when most Native nations could ill afford decreased populations. Scholars estimate that over one thousand battles and wars between Native groups and peoples of European descent took place between 1500 and 1890.

Historical portrayals of warfare between North American colonists and the Native population have emphasized the excessively brutal nature of these conflicts, comparing them unfavorably to the supposedly less sanguine battles in contemporary Europe. The stereotype of the inherently "savage" Native American has persisted, bolstered by a few ghastly examples of Indian hostility toward noncombatants. Yet considerable evidence suggests that Native Americans were equally appalled by the European practices of "total war," such as the burning of the Pequot village on Connecticut's Mystic River and the indiscriminate massacre of its residents by a colonial army in 1637. In the end, neither European colonists nor Native Americans held a monopoly on cruelty; typical assaults on settlements, whether by Natives or by colonists, involved killing noncombatants, destroying crops and livestock, burning dwellings, and taking captives.

By 1700, Indian warriors had largely converted from bows and arrows to the Europeans' flintlock muskets. While slower, noisier, less reliable, and less accurate than archery, firearms sent bullets to their targets more quickly than bows, and bullets caused greater damage on impact. The early adoption of firearms gave certain groups temporary advantages, the classic examples being the "Beaver Wars," involving the Dutch-armed Iroquois against neighboring Native peoples in the Northeast and Midwest (1643–1680), and the expansion of the western Sioux in the northeastern plains following their adoption of horses and firearms after 1700. In addition, the Indians' use of flintlocks for both warfare and hunting produced higher levels of marksmanship among Native warriors than among their colonial counterparts. As lighter, more accurate guns appeared over the course of the eighteenth century, Native riflemen became even more formidable in conflicts with the less capable settler militias and European regular troops.

The widespread adoption of firearms by virtually all Native American groups brought about dependence on European arms and ammunition. This dependence was greatly mitigated first by the rivalries among the different colonial powers, who were always seeking to secure Native allies with offers of guns, and second by the development of metalworking skills among many Native groups. One element, however, eventually proved critical in determining the ultimate military fate of Native Americans: gunpowder. This highly refined and fragile commodity remained a European monopoly, and occasional shortages or embargoes greatly diminished the threat posed by Native armies to the settler population.

Firearms dominated, but Native Americans retained bows and arrows as stealth weapons and continued to carry hand-to-hand combat weapons such as hatchets, knives, clubs, and spears. A common stratagem among Native war parties during the seventeenth and eighteenth centuries was a modified version of their earlier form of ambush; the enemy would be surprised with an initial volley of gunfire or arrows, and then these weapons would be discarded as the aggressors rushed out of their concealed positions to engage in hand-to-hand fighting. A preference for surprise attacks, however, did not preclude occasional assaults by Native groups on the fortified locations of both Native and non-Native enemies. Indian warriors also adapted flanking formations employed in communal hunting to sustained engagements with enemies, controlling movements with field signals consisting of hand movements and imitations of animal noises. They took advantage of the landscape to maintain steady fire on their targets and utilized a "half-moon" formation to outflank their enemies, adding a degree of terror to their actions with what witnesses described as blood-curdling yelling. Evidence also indicates that Native warriors adapted their advances and retreats to the logistics of their firearms by having warriors with loaded weapons cover the movements of those who needed to reload their guns.

The military talents of Native warriors did not go unnoticed by European colonists. As early as the mid-seventeenth century, colonial authorities attempted to recruit "friendly" Indians for service as scouts to guide colonial armies through unfamiliar territory, and often, to locate the enemy and prevent ambushes. Native allies received supplies, pay, and plunder for these services; as such, they often exploited opportunities provided by auxiliary service to pursue their own, parallel conflict with an enemy. European and colonial officers generally regarded their allied Indian warriors as troublesome, undisciplined, and untrustworthy, yet very few were willing to dispense with Indian auxiliaries entirely.

The capacity of Native warriors to adapt new technology to their own objectives is clearly illustrated in PONTIAC'S WAR (1763–1766), when the Algonquian nations of the Great Lakes initiated a committed effort to expel British military and Anglo American settlers from their territory. Native warriors attacked British forts and settlements for more than fifteen months after the outbreak of hostilities in May 1763, killing over two thousand settlers and four hundred British soldiers. The Algonquians also captured, destroyed, or forced the abandonment of nine interior forts, employing a melding of traditional Algonquian and European means of warfare. These included surprise assaults on military personnel, flaming arrows, carts and barges loaded with combustibles, and undermining the walls of at least one fort by tunneling. The tactical resourcefulness demonstrated by the Algonquians of Pontiac's War enabled them to achieve a military stalemate and favorable terms of peace in 1766. Success of this degree for Native peoples in warfare would, however, become increasingly rare after the United States achieved independence from Great Britain in 1783. Native Americans faced an aggressively expansionist American population, one convinced of its right to appropriate, occupy, and improve land that they believed "savages" merely roamed.

Under charismatic spiritual leadership and assuming an increasingly "pan-Native" character, new confederacies of allied Native American nations continued armed resistance for three decades after the Peace of Paris (1783). Aided by British and Spanish officials in Canada and Florida, throughout the 1780s, groups of dedicated Native militants waged effective guerrilla attacks on settlers streaming across a frontier from eastern Ohio to Tennessee. Initial efforts by the small American regular army to put down Native resistance proved futile, as the confederate Indian forces inflicted extremely heavy casualties in two successive campaigns (1790–1791).

Under General "Mad" Anthony Wayne, a reorganized American force succeeded in defeating the Northern Confederacy at Fallen Timbers (1794). The subsequent Treaty of GREENVILLE (1795) secured to the United States extensive cessions of Native territory in the Old Northwest. Yet, ongoing pressure by American settlers motivated Shawnee war leader Tecumseh, and his brother Tenskwatawa, to undertake what proved to be the final organized pan-Native resistance to United States expansion east of the Mississippi River. Guided by Tenskwatawa's spiritual message opposing accommodation to white civilization after 1805, the Shawnee militants reconstituted a pan-tribal military force at Prophet's Town (near modern Lafayette, Indiana). After a moderately successful preemptive American attack on Tecumseh's warriors at the November 1811 Battle of Tippecanoe, Native American resistance leaders moved to exploit the new conditions arising from the War of 1812 between the United States and Great Britain. Despite several battlefield victories early in the conflict, eastern Native American efforts to roll back the American settlement frontier were undermined by the loss of Tecumseh at the October 1813 Battle of the Thames and by the decline of the War of 1812.

The Demise of Independent Warring, 1815–1890

The acquisition of huge tracts of land by the United States in the LOUISIANA PURCHASE (1803) and the Treaty of GUADALUPE HIDALGO (1848) brought Native nations west of the Mississippi River into conflict with American settlers and armies. Many of these western Indian groups had only recently taken advantage of imported horses and firearms to move onto the Plains and create a new cultural complex founded on equestrian buffalo hunting. Nevertheless, many of the most powerful western nations possessed highly skilled cavalries, sustained by an intense warrior ethos. The policies of the United States federal government during the tenure of President Thomas Jefferson (1801–1809), however, aimed to transform the Native Americans of the Plains from mobile hunters to sedentary agriculturists. Prior to 1849, the War Department was responsible for the administration of Indian affairs, and fighting Natives who resisted became the principal occupation of the United States Army during the first half of the nineteenth century. The high stakes of these conflicts are reflected in the large number of American political leaders who rose to prominence following careers as "Indian fighters."

Native American warfare after 1800 revolved around the defense of large tracts of buffalo-hunting territory, protection of arms- and horse-trading routes, and revenge for atrocities by enemies. Inter-group conflicts continued, but after the INDIAN TRADE AND INTERCOURSE ACT of 1834, the United States military had authorization to intervene. Native warriors usually prevailed in initial engagements with trespassing frontier settlers and poorly organized local militias, but they were then subjected to harsh punitive attacks from increasingly skilled and heavily armed American regular troops and penalized with appropriations of their territory. After 1832, the United States Army reintroduced cavalry for fighting mounted Indian warriors.

By 1845, over 80 percent of the Native population living east of the Mississippi River had been relocated, under military supervision, to "Indian Territory" in the area that became Oklahoma and Kansas. The massive territorial expansion of the American nation during the 1840s and 1850s, motivated in part by the discovery of gold in California in 1848, meant that a frontier no longer existed between Native and settler populations in the west. After 1865, General William T. Sherman assumed control of the "Indian Wars," launching year-round attacks on hostile Native communities and advocating destruction of both tribal horse herds and the buffalo, the basis of Native American subsistence on the Plains.

The final phase of Indian warfare in the United States produced many renowned Native leaders whose names became part of the American vernacular: Red Cloud and Crazy Horse (Oglala Lakota); Chief Joseph (Nez Perce); and Cochise and Geronimo (Apache). Despite their heroic efforts, ultimately they could not contend with the waves of settlers entering their territory by wagon and by train, who killed vast numbers of life-giving buffalo and who were supported by a determined and experienced military that relied heavily on native scouts.

Mató-Tópe (Four Bears). This portrait of the Mandan chief is by George Catlin, c. 1832—just a few years before smallpox and cholera nearly wiped out the remaining members of this dwindling tribe in present-day North Dakota. © ACADEMY OF NATURAL SCIENCES OF PHILADELPHIA/CORBIS

The final conflict of the "Indian Wars" occurred on 29 December 1890 at Wounded Knee, a remote corner of the Pine Ridge Sioux reservation in South Dakota. Here, the Seventh Cavalry used artillery and barrages from soldiers carrying repeating rifles to destroy Big Foot's band and killed at least 150 Sioux men, women, and children.

Conclusion

By any measure, warfare exacted a heavy toll on Native communities after the arrival of Europeans in North America. By 1890, virtually all Native American nations lived in confinement on reservations, often at great distances from their traditional homelands. Militarily defeated, their communities struggled to cope with the collapse of traditional values and institutions that attended their loss of independence and self-government. The experience of the "Indian wars" has promoted enduring stereotypes of Native peoples as wild, bloodthirsty savages and has influenced administrative policies aimed at complete subordination of Native Americans. The schizophrenic attitude of the dominant American culture toward Native Americans in the late nineteenth century is illustrated by the appearance of nostalgic "Wild West" shows reenacting famous battles, government officials strenuously tried to dismantle traditional Native American life. Despite attempts to eliminate the threat of Native warriors, it is important to note that Native American men and women have entered all branches of the United States' armed forces during the twentieth century in numbers far exceeding their proportion of the population. As soldiers, sailors, and pilots, Native Americans have consistently earned distinction for their talents and courage.

BIBLIOGRAPHY

Axtell, James, and William C. Sturtevant. "The Unkindest Cut, or Who Invented Scalping?" *William and Mary Quarterly* 3d ser., 37 (1980): 451–72.

Given, Brian J. *A Most Pernicious Thing: Gun-Trading and Native Warfare in the Early Contact Period.* Ottawa, Ont.: Carleton University Press, 1994.

Holm, Tom. "The Militarization of Native America: Historical Process and Cultural Perception." *Social Science Journal* 34 (1997): 461–74.

Keeley, Lawrence H. *War before Civilization: The Myth of the Peaceful Savage.* Reprint, New York: Oxford University Press, 1997.

Malone, Patrick M. *The Skulking Way of War: Technology and Tactics among the New England Indians.* Baltimore: Johns Hopkins University Press, 1993.

Otterbein, Keith F. *The Evolution of War: A Cross-Cultural Study.* New Haven, Conn.: Human Relations Area Files Press, 1970.

Prucha, Francis Paul. *The Sword of the Republic: The United States Army on the Frontier, 1783–1846.* Bloomington: Indiana University Press, 1977.

Richter, Daniel K. "War and Culture: The Iroquois Experience." *William and Mary Quarterly* 3d ser., 40 (1983): 528–59.

Secoy, Frank Raymond. *Changing Military Patterns of the Great Plains Indians (17th Century through Early 19th Century).* Lincoln: University of Nebraska Press, 1992.

Starkey, Armstrong. *European and Native American Warfare, 1675–1815.* Norman: University of Oklahoma Press, 1998.

Steele, Ian Kenneth. *Warpaths: Invasions of North America.* New York: Oxford University Press, 1994.

Utley, Robert Marshall. *The Indian Frontier of the American West, 1846–1890.* Albuquerque: University of New Mexico Press, 1984.

Jon Parmenter

See also **Wars with Indian Nations; Wounded Knee Massacre;** *and vol. 9:* **Captivity Narrative of a Colonial Woman; General Custer's Last Fight; Logan's Speech; Sleep Not Longer, O Choctaws and Chickasaws; Speech of Little Crow.**

WARREN COMMISSION. On 29 November 1963, one week after the murder of John F. Kennedy, President Lyndon Johnson signed Executive Order No. 11130, creating the President's Commission on the Assassination of President John F. Kennedy. The executive order instructed the seven-man panel to "evaluate all the facts and circumstances surrounding [the] assassination, including the subsequent violent death of the man charged with the assassination," Lee Harvey Oswald. Johnson directed all federal agencies to cooperate with the special panel, which soon became known as the Warren Commission, after its chairman, U.S. Supreme Court Chief Justice Earl Warren.

The panel represented a careful political balancing act by Johnson. Warren was a towering figure among liberals because of the Supreme Court decisions reached under his stewardship. To offset him, Johnson picked Georgia Democratic senator Richard B. Russell, whose reputation (among conservatives) was the equal of Warren's. Other members from Congress were Senator John Sherman Cooper, a Kentucky Republican; Representative Hale Boggs, a Democrat from Louisiana; and then-Representative Gerald R. Ford, a Michigan Republican. Because of the international repercussions and intelligence issues involved, Johnson also appointed two lawyers with broad government experience: Allen W. Dulles, former director of the Central Intelligence Agency, and John J. McCloy, a former assistant secretary in the War Department.

Over the next ten months, the commission reviewed and expanded upon FBI, Secret Service, and CIA investigations; weighed the testimony of 552 witnesses; visited the site of the assassination; and oversaw the writing of the 888-page final report, which was presented to President Johnson on 24 September 1964 and made public three days later. Subsequently, twenty-six additional volumes of testimony and exhibits were printed, making the full Warren Report one of the most voluminous documents about a single episode ever published by the U.S. government.

The commission unanimously concluded that Oswald, acting alone, assassinated President Kennedy, and that Jack Ruby was a self-appointed vigilante when he killed Oswald two days later. Contrary to popular belief, the commission did not conclude definitively that there was no conspiracy. Rather, the panel stated that despite its best efforts, it had been unable to find any evidence of a conspiracy. This finding reflected the commission's recognition that pertinent records in communist bloc countries were beyond its reach.

President Johnson formed the commission to provide a forum for fact-finding (in the absence of a purgative trial) and to prevent competing, televised investigations in Congress. Initially, these goals were achieved. Congress declined to investigate, and upon publication, the Warren Report persuaded most Americans that the truth was known, insofar as it was knowable. Over time, confidence in the commission's probity and the report's validity eroded. The commission, operating as it did in the midst of the Cold War, had to keep some facts secret, and some information was kept from it. None of the revelations that trickled out in the years following the assassination, however, altered the accuracy of the commission's findings. But critics, only some of whom were well-meaning, repeatedly exploited the contradiction between the need for answers and the need for secrecy to suggest that the commission was either incompetent or intentionally avoided the truth. The Warren Commission's reputation also suffered collaterally from later cynicism engendered by the Vietnam War and Watergate scandal.

BIBLIOGRAPHY

Holland, Max. "After Thirty Years: Making Sense of the Assassination." *Reviews in American History* 22, no. 2 (June 1994): 191–209.

Manchester, William. *The Death of a President: November 20–November 25 1963.* New York: Harper and Row, 1967.

Report of the President's Commission on the Assassination of President John F. Kennedy. Washington, D.C.: Government Printing Office, 1964.

Max Holland

See also **Assassinations, Presidential.**

WARS WITH INDIAN NATIONS

This entry includes 3 subentries:
Colonial Era to 1783
Early Nineteenth Century (1783–1840)
Later Nineteenth Century (1840–1900)

COLONIAL ERA TO 1783

Warfare between colonists and the Native population in North America before 1783 played a vital role in shaping the attitudes and identities that emerged among both Native Americans and citizens of the United States. For Native people, these conflicts occurred in a context of catastrophic losses during the sixteenth and seventeenth centuries, caused by their exposure to European diseases. Between 1513 and 1783, contact between Europeans and Indians changed the nature of warfare for both parties: Native peoples experienced new levels of lethality as a result of imported weapons and tactics of mass destruction, while European colonists learned to exploit divisions among the Native population and incorporated such Indian tactics as ambush and firing from cover into their own strategies.

Clash on Contact: Invasions and Self-Defense, 1513–1609

In early April 1513, the Spanish explorer Juan Ponce de León landed on Florida's Atlantic coast, south of modern St. Augustine. Hoping to find new sources of gold or slaves, his expedition instead discovered an extraordinar-

ily hostile Native population. Entering a Timucua village, the Spanish were attacked and put to flight. Further scouting up the coast led to a fierce conflict with eighty canoes full of Calusa archers. The Natives of Florida eventually drove off the Spaniards with bows and arrows.

Such immediate hostility was not the universal Native response to contact with Europeans. Native people reacted to Europeans with a mixture of fear and curiosity, but more frequent interactions over the course of the sixteenth century often proved disastrous. European aggressiveness and contempt for Native lifeways—particularly their proclivity for kidnapping Indians to gain intelligence and linguistic expertise—undermined amicable relations between the groups.

Sailing for the French in 1524, the Italian navigator Giovanni de Verrazzano was welcomed by Narragansetts and other Native peoples on the southern coast of New England, while those peoples he encountered farther north (who had dealt with European fishermen for decades) expressed hostility. Barging into the Pueblo settlement at Zuni in June 1540, the Spanish conquistador Francisco Vázquez de Coronado inadvertently profaned sacred rituals associated with the summer solstice and narrowly escaped with his life. That same year, a powerful Choctaw leader named Tuscaluza, who had grown tired of the brutalities inflicted by the Spaniard Hernando de Soto's gold-seeking expedition (1539–1543) throughout the American Southeast, assembled 5,000 warriors and engaged the intruders in pitched battle. The Battle of Mabila on 18 October 1540 lasted seven hours, and while the Choctaws and their allies suffered casualties in excess of 50 percent, their effort inspired other groups to resist De Soto's invasion with force. In 1541, the French explorer Jacques Cartier enraged the St. Lawrence Iroquoian town of Stadacona on his third voyage to Canada by failing to return any of the people he had kidnapped on his voyage in 1536, and by building a fortified settlement west of the town without permission. The Stadaconans secured assistance from all the Indians in the vicinity of modern Quebec City and besieged Cartier's post over the winter of 1541–1542, killing thirty-five colonists and eventually forcing the abandonment of the colony. Despite the difficulty competitive Native polities experienced in formulating common policies, and despite the Europeans' advantage in military technology, Native Americans achieved a degree of success in expelling a range of European invaders from North America during the sixteenth century.

Seventeenth-Century Conflicts: Campaigns and Massacres, 1609–1689

On 30 July 1609, Samuel de Champlain, military governor of the new French settlement at Quebec, accompanied sixty Montagnais and Huron warriors to an arranged battle with the latter's Mohawk enemies on the shores of modern Lake Champlain. The French soldiers introduced the Mohawks to European firearms, killing dozens with volleys of musket balls fired from matchlock arquebuses, and rendering the Mohawks' massed, open-field battle tactics and their wooden armor immediately obsolete.

The establishment of permanent English, French, Spanish, and Dutch settlements in North America led the European powers to attempt to impose their legal authority on the Native population. This caused increased friction in the everyday contacts between colonists and Native peoples. Once colonists became capable of withstanding Native resistance, however, Indians had to adopt a mixed strategy of accommodation and resistance. Some groups sought alliances with Europeans to secure protection from hostile neighbors, while others employed alliances to extend their control over weaker peoples. The absence of solidarity among Native Americans in opposition to European invaders meant that, in conflicts after 1600, Native people were increasingly found on opposing sides of the battlefield.

Since 1607, English settlers at Jamestown, Virginia, had experienced uneasy relations with neighboring Algonquian peoples, owing to their growing appetite for Native lands. On 22 March 1622, the Pamunkey leader Opechancanough inflicted a surprise attack on the scattered plantations that resulted in the loss of 25 percent of the colony's population; he also led a second uprising in 1644 that killed 500 settlers. Brutal retaliatory attacks on the villages and crops of Virginia's Natives lasted for the

next two years, as the colonists sought to eliminate the prospect of future threats. Similar belief in the need for the total defeat of enemy Indians arose in 1637 among Connecticut settlers, who procured Mohegan and Narragansett assistance to surround, burn, and slaughter an entire village of Pequots that had refused to submit to colonial legal jurisdiction. Dutch settlers in New York and their Mahican allies launched an extremely violent cycle of murders and massacres against the Raritans, Wecquaesgeeks, and Wappingers during Governor Willem Kieft's war (1641–1645). French efforts to bypass the Iroquois Confederacy as "middlemen" in the fur trade with Native peoples in the Great Lakes, and Iroquoian efforts to replace their people lost to disease through a captive-seeking "mourning war" combined to produce a protracted series of wars from 1635 through 1701. Indiscriminate attacks on neighboring Native peoples provided a rallying point for Virginia frontier settlers under Nathaniel Bacon in their rebellion against royal governor William Berkeley in 1676. In 1680, Popé, a Tewa spiritual leader of San Juan Pueblo, organized a joint uprising of the Pueblos in New Mexico against the Spanish imperial presence, targeting the Franciscan missionaries who had endeavored to effect dramatic changes in the Pueblos' daily lives. In the deadliest conflict of the century, King Philip's War (1675–1676), the Wampanoag leader Philip responded to the

Battle of Lake Champlain. This engraving, first published in Samuel de Champlain's account of his explorations of New France (now Canada), depicts his one-sided victory over Mohawks on 30 July 1609, at the lake between New York and Vermont that bears his name. © BETTMANN/CORBIS

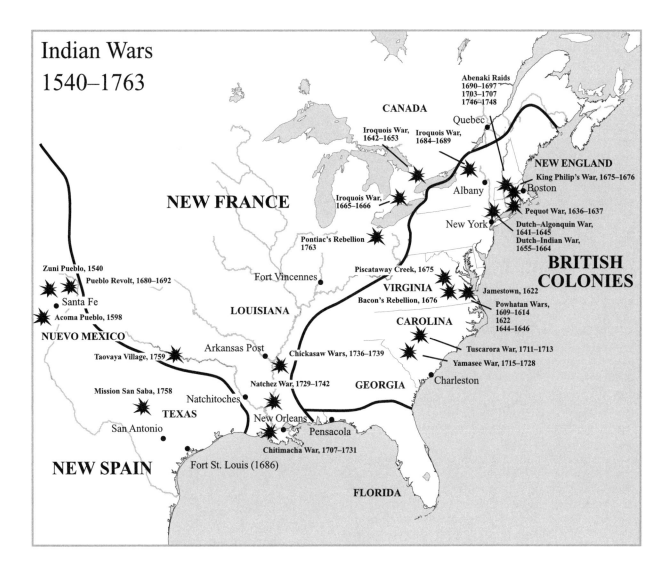

Indian Wars 1540–1763

Abenaki Raids
1690–1697
1703–1707
1746–1748

CANADA

Quebec

Iroquois War, 1642–1653

Iroquois War, 1684–1689

NEW ENGLAND

King Philip's War, 1675–1676

NEW FRANCE

Albany

Boston

Iroquois War, 1665–1666

New York

Pequot War, 1636–1637

Dutch–Algonquin War, 1641–1645

Dutch–Indian War, 1655–1664

Pontiac's Rebellion 1763

BRITISH COLONIES

Zuni Pueblo, 1540

Pueblo Revolt, 1680–1692

Piscataway Creek, 1675

Fort Vincennes

VIRGINIA

Bacon's Rebellion, 1676

Jamestown, 1622

Santa Fe

LOUISIANA

Powhatan Wars, 1609–1614 1622 1644–1646

Acoma Pueblo, 1598

NUEVO MEXICO

CAROLINA

Taovaya Village, 1759

Arkansas Post

Chickasaw Wars, 1736–1739

Tuscarora War, 1711–1713

Yamasee War, 1715–1728

Mission San Saba, 1758

Natchez War, 1729–1742

GEORGIA

Charleston

Natchitoches

TEXAS

New Orleans

San Antonio

Pensacola

Chitimacha War, 1707–1731

NEW SPAIN

Fort St. Louis (1686)

FLORIDA

execution of three of his warriors charged with murder by Massachusetts authorities by organizing an effective campaign of frontier attacks on New England settlements. Plunging the Puritans into an intense spiritual crisis with terrifying guerrilla-style warfare that killed more than a thousand colonists, Philip elicited the combined wrath of the New England colonies, whose troops, with the assistance of Christian Indian allies, finally hunted him down in August 1676 and subjected his people to ruthless vengeance.

The Age of Imperial Wars: Alliances and Transformations, 1689–1760

On the night of 29 February 1704, a force of 48 Canadian militiamen and 200 allied Abenakis, Kahnawakes, and Hurons concluded a journey of nearly 300 miles overland to launch a surprise attack on the town of Deerfield, Massachusetts. The raiders killed between 40 and 50 residents, secured 109 prisoners, and burned the town. The prisoners were marched back to Montreal, and those who survived the arduous winter trek experienced varied fates

of incarceration, redemption, or adoption into French-Canadian or Native American families.

Beginning in 1689, the imperial conflicts of Europe were exported to North America, and Native Americans became entangled in the wars between the English, French, and Spanish. As these conflicts grew increasingly professionalized, with the involvement of European regular troops and advanced techniques of fortification and siegecraft, Native Americans pursued their own objectives while fighting with their European allies as scouts and auxiliaries. They dominated warfare on the frontiers, attacking settlements at will, and defeating both settler militias and European regulars on many occasions.

The first two imperial conflicts, King William's War (1689–1697) and Queen Anne's War (1702–1713), quickly became stalemates in their North American theaters and thus had comparatively minimal impact on Native communities. Yet this period witnessed the rise of a new series of conflicts. Colonial encroachment on Native lands and Native resentment of the behavior of colonial traders, who supplied a range of goods (including firearms) many Native nations had come to depend on for their survival, led to the Tuscarora War in North Carolina (1711–1713), the Yamasee War in South Carolina (1715–1728), and the conflict known as Dummer's, or Grey Lock's, War in modern Maine and Vermont (1722–1727). The French experienced a series of wasting conflicts with interior nations who resisted the expansion of their military posts into the Upper and Lower Mississippi valleys, including the Fox of modern Wisconsin (1712–1730), the Natchez of Louisiana (1729–1742), and the Chickasaws of modern Alabama (1736–1739). King George's War (1744–1748) once again brought European rivalries to North America, but the neutral stance of the Iroquois Confederacy contributed to its indecisive conclusion. The most critical of the imperial conflicts was the last: the so-called Seven Years' War (1754–1763) began with Anglo-French rivalry for the Ohio Valley and ended with a peace that transformed the North American political landscape. English politicians poured unprecedented military resources into the final war for American empire and ultimately broke the pattern of colonial military stalemate, which left Native Americans to face an aggressively expansive Anglo-American settler population without a committed European ally.

The Revolutionary Era: The Rise of Pan-Indian Cooperation, 1760–1783

In November 1776, the Cherokee war leader Dragging Canoe made a difficult decision. Unable to convince the senior civil leaders of his nation to continue hostilities against the newly declared United States after a summer of harsh defeats, he led a migration of 500 Cherokees out of their traditional homeland in the Carolinas to the vicinity of modern Chattanooga, Tennessee. Known thereafter as Chickamaugas, Dragging Canoe's community hosted warriors from numerous eastern Native nations, and waged a relentless campaign of attacks on frontier settlers who encroached on Cherokee hunting territory through the era of the American Revolution (1775–1783) and beyond.

The years immediately following the Seven Years' War witnessed the first pan-Indian movements of resistance against the European colonial presence. The final phase of North American conflicts prior to 1783 was spurred on by the combined influence of nativistic leaders who preached of the need to reject the assimilative force of settler material culture and to return to traditional Native lifestyles, and by widespread Native resentment of the increasing arrogance of the victorious Anglo-American regime.

In 1759, the Cherokees were the first to strike out against the frontier settlements of the Carolinas, but their inability to secure any Native allies led to their crushing defeat in 1761 at the hands of British regulars. The Algonquian nations of the Great Lakes region united to fight Pontiac's War (1763–1766). Joined by Delawares,

Shawnees, and Senecas, the Indians destroyed nine British forts, and killed an estimated 400 British troops and 2,000 colonial settlers before negotiating terms of peace. Virginian settlers who chose to ignore the treaty boundaries established to protect Native settlement and hunting territories in the Ohio Valley caused renewed hostilities with the Shawnees in Lord Dunmore's War (1774). No Native nation east of the Mississippi completely escaped the consequences of the American Revolution. Both British and American officials abandoned initial promises of permitting Native Americans to remain neutral in the conflict. After 1776, both combatants sought allies and pursued "enemy" Indians with equal aggression. More Native Americans sided with the British, considering them the lesser of two evils, but in the end they could not withstand the more numerous Americans' relentless and incredibly destructive assaults on their villages, crops, and population, best exemplified by General John Sullivan's devastating 1779 expedition in Iroquois country. Unable to protect their Native allies' settlements from the Americans during the war, the British abandoned the Indians entirely in the 1783 Treaty of Paris, surrendering all land east of the Mississippi to the United States without reference to extant Native claims of ownership. This action guaranteed that the early years of the new American republic would be marred by ongoing conflicts with the Native American population.

Conclusion

Warfare with colonists further disrupted Native subsistence patterns already rendered precarious by the demographic losses of the contact period, exacerbated intergroup rivalry and competition, and produced dramatic shifts in the political structures of Native communities as younger war leaders gradually gained ascendancy over elder civil headmen. The experience of the Indian wars of the colonial era also left deep imprints on the people who came to inhabit the United States after 1783. The frequency and brutality of conflict with Native Americans between 1513 and 1783 hardened feelings toward Native people and led to a persistent belief in their inherently "savage," treacherous, and warlike nature. Although subsequent military and administrative policies toward Native peoples frequently held assimilative intentions, they were based on assumptions of the Indians' status as beaten but still potentially dangerous obstacles to settler expansion.

BIBLIOGRAPHY

Calloway, Colin G. *The American Revolution in Indian Country: Crisis and Diversity in Native American Communities.* New York: Cambridge University Press, 1995.

Dowd, Gregory E. *A Spirited Resistance: The North American Indian Struggle for Unity, 1745–1815.* Baltimore: Johns Hopkins University Press, 1992.

Ferling, John E. *A Wilderness of Miseries: War and Warriors in Early America.* Westport, Conn.: Greenwood Press, 1980.

Leach, Douglas E. *Arms for Empire: A Military History of the British Colonies in North America, 1607–1763.* New York: Macmillan, 1973.

Lepore, Jill. *The Name of War: King Philip's War and the Origins of American Identity.* New York: Knopf, 1998.

Selesky, Harold E. "Colonial America." In *The Laws of War: Constraints on Warfare in the Western World.* Edited by Michael Howard, George J. Andreopoulos, and Mark R. Shulman. New Haven, Conn.: Yale University Press, 1994.

Starkey, Armstrong. *European and Native American Warfare, 1675–1815.* Norman: University of Oklahoma Press, 1998.

Steele, Ian K. *Warpaths: Invasions of North America.* New York: Oxford University Press, 1994.

Jon Parmenter

See also **Explorations and Expeditions: French, Spanish; Indian Treaties, Colonial; Indian Policy, Colonial: Dutch, French, Spanish, and English; Warfare, Indian;** *and individual conflicts, e.g.,* **King Philip's War, Pueblo Revolt;** *and vol. 9:* **Logan's Speech.**

EARLY NINETEENTH CENTURY (1783–1840)

Warfare between the United States and the Indian Nations in the twelve years following the American Revolution involved the American attempt to occupy the region north of the Ohio River, a region Native Americans still claimed as their own. Since the British occupied Detroit throughout this period, British agents encouraged the Indians to resist and provided them with arms and ammunition.

Between 1785 and 1789, the federal government tried to purchase part of the Ohio Country in three treaties (Ft. McIntosh, 1785; Ft. Finney, 1786; and Ft. Harmar, 1789), but the tribes denounced these agreements as fraudulent. After Indian attacks forced settlers in the region to abandon their farms, the government ordered General Josiah Harmar to attack the Miamis and Wyandots, whom they accused of promoting the resistance. In October 1790, Harmar and 1,450 men marched from modern Cincinnati to the headwaters of the Maumee in northeastern Indiana. On 19 October 1790 part of Harmar's army was ambushed and defeated by a large war party led by Miami chief Little Turtle; two days later the Indians surprised the Americans again, killing forty regulars, including Major John Wyllis. Harmar retreated back to Cincinnati. He had lost 75 regulars, 108 militia, one-third of his packhorses, and much of his equipment. Meanwhile, a diversionary raid launched by Kentucky militia against Indian towns on the lower Wabash suffered no casualties and burned a few empty Indian villages, but failed to intimidate the tribesmen.

One year later Governor Arthur St. Clair and another army of over 2,000 men, including over half the standing army of the United States, retraced Harmar's route north toward the Maumee, but the results were even more disastrous. About one-third of the army (Kentucky militia and "volunteers") deserted enroute, but on the morning of 4 November 1791, near the headwaters of the Wabash, St. Clair's army was surprised by an immense war party of over 1,000 warriors. After a three-hour battle, the Americans broke through the Indian lines and fled, abandoning their wounded and most of their equipment. St. Clair's Defeat is the greatest Native American victory over an American military force in history. St. Clair survived, but he lost at least 647 men killed, and hundreds were wounded. Indian losses totaled about 150 warriors.

In response, the government ordered General Anthony Wayne, a strict disciplinarian, to rebuild the American army in the West. By 1794, Wayne was ready. He marched north from Cincinnati with 2,000 regulars and 1,500 volunteers, constructing a series of forts as supply posts for his forces. On 20 August 1794, he attacked a large force of warriors ensconced behind a natural barricade of storm-felled trees on the north bank of the Maumee River. The warriors fought back, but then retreated, intending to make another stand at Fort Miamis, a recently constructed British post just downstream from the fallen trees. Surprisingly, however, the British refused to allow the Indians entrance and the tribes dispersed into the forests. The Battle of Fallen Timbers was a major American victory. One year later, with the British still unwilling to support the Ohio tribes, the Indians signed the Treaty of Greenville (1795) in which they relinquished control of much of Ohio, and allowed the American military to construct posts at Ft. Wayne, Ft. Dearborn (Chicago), and other strategic locations.

By 1800, white settlement again spilled over onto Native American lands, and a renewed Indian resistance emerged, led by the Shawnee war chief Tecumseh, and his brother the Shawnee Prophet. The Shawnee brothers attempted to unite the tribes and prevent any further land loss, but in November 1811, Governor William Henry Harrison of Indiana Territory marched against their village at Prophetstown, near modern Lafayette, Indiana, and following the Battle of Tippecanoe, Harrison dispersed Tecumseh's followers and destroyed their village.

In the Northwest, the Battle of Tippecanoe was the opening engagement of the War of 1812, and much of the warfare in this theatre was fought between Indian and American forces. In early July 1812, an American army from Detroit attempted to invade Canada, but was forced back by British and Indian forces. After other British and Indians captured Fort Michilimackinac, on the straight between Lakes Huron and Michigan, Tecumseh and his British allies besieged the Americans at Detroit. In August they turned back two American attempts (the battles of Monguagon and Brownstown) to reestablish contact between Detroit and American forces in Ohio, and on 16 August 1812, the Americans surrendered Detroit to Tecumseh and the British.

The warfare spread from Ohio to Chicago. In mid-August Potowatomi warriors attacked the garrison of Ft. Dearborn after the army evacuated the post and was retreating toward Indiana. And in September the Kickapoos

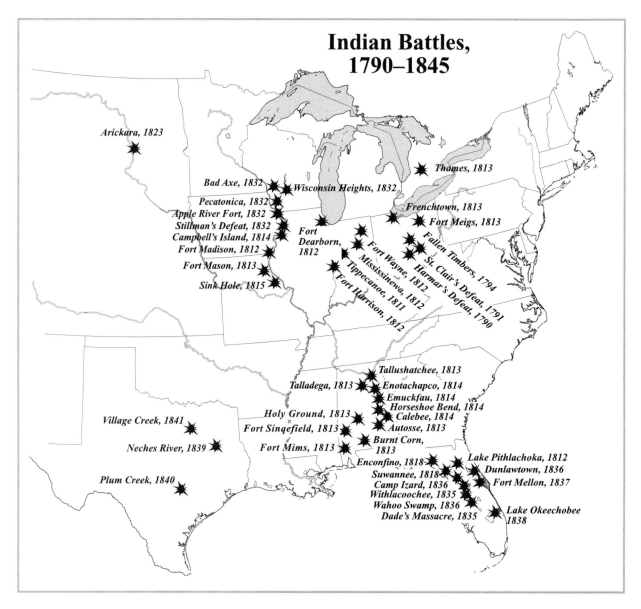

Indian Battles, 1790–1845

Arickara, 1823

Bad Axe, 1832

Wisconsin Heights, 1832

Thames, 1813

Pecatonica, 1832

Frenchtown, 1813

Apple River Fort, 1832

Fort Meigs, 1813

Stillman's Defeat, 1832

Campbell's Island, 1814

Fort Dearborn, 1812

Fallen Timbers, 1794

Fort Madison, 1812

Fort Wayne, 1812

St. Clair's Defeat, 1791

Fort Mason, 1813

Mississinewa, 1812

Harmar's Defeat, 1790

Tippecanoe, 1811

Sink Hole, 1815

Fort Harrison, 1812

Tallushatchee, 1813

Talladega, 1813

Enotachapco, 1814

Emuckfau, 1814

Horseshoe Bend, 1814

Holy Ground, 1813

Calebee, 1814

Village Creek, 1841

Fort Sinqefield, 1813

Autosse, 1813

Neches River, 1839

Fort Mims, 1813

Burnt Corn, 1813

Lake Pithlachoka, 1812

Plum Creek, 1840

Enconfino, 1818

Dunlawtown, 1836

Suwannee, 1818

Fort Mellon, 1837

Camp Izard, 1836

Withlacoochee, 1835

Wahoo Swamp, 1836

Lake Okeechobee 1838

Dade's Massacre, 1835

surrounded Ft. Harrison, an American post on the central Wabash. Other Potawatomis besieged the American garrison at Fort Wayne, but in September the post was relieved by an army of militia and volunteers led by William Henry Harrison. In January 1813, the two sides clashed again when a force of Kentuckians were defeated by the Indians at Frenchtown, in southeastern Michigan.

During the spring of 1813, the Indians and British mounted another offensive. In May almost 2,400 Indians and British troops surrounded Ft. Meigs, an American post near modern Toledo, Ohio. The Americans withstood the siege, but on 4 May, the Indians surprised and killed or captured almost 600 Kentuckians led by William Dudley who had arrived to reinforce the American garrison. Two months later the Indians and British again surrounded Ft. Meigs, then abandoned the siege and launched an unsuccessful attack on Ft. Stephenson, a small post on the Sandusky River.

Following Commodore Oliver Perry's victory on Lake Erie, the Americans regained the initiative in the war and in September, they invaded Canada. Although Major Henry Proctor, the British commander, attempted to retreat to Toronto, Tecumseh demanded that the British stand and fight, and on 5 October 1813, at the Battle of the Thames, the Shawnee war chief was killed after British troops abandoned their positions and the Americans concentrated all their firepower on the Indians. After Tecumseh's death, effective Indian resistance in the Northwest during the War of 1812 crumpled.

Indians and Americans also clashed in the South during the War of 1812. Many Creeks had been receptive to Tecumseh's pleas for Indian unity, and in the spring of 1813, anti-American Creeks, or "Red Sticks," led by mixed-blood William Weatherford attacked and overran Fort Mims, a poorly constructed stockade on the Alabama River, killing over 500 unfortunate settlers. In response, Andrew Jackson assembled an army of militia and pro-American Creeks and destroyed Creek villages at Tallushatchee, on the Coosa River, and at Talledega, just east of modern Birmingham. Many Red Sticks then retreated to Tohopeka, a fortified town on a horseshoe-shaped bend on the Tallapoosa River. In March 1814 Jackson, pro-American Creeks, and 2,000 volunteers attacked Tohopeka, eventually killing over 500 of the 900 warriors, in addition to many Native American women and children.

In the 1830s, violence flared again. In 1830 federal officials forced the majority of the Sacs and Fox tribes to remove from Illinois to Iowa, but one band, led by the old war chief Black Hawk, occupied its ancestral village at Rock Island, Illinois, until the summer of 1831, when the Illinois militia also forced them across the Mississippi.

Short of food and shelter, Black Hawk and his followers spent a miserable winter (1831–1832) in Iowa, and in April 1832, the old chief and about 1,000 followers, including at least 600 women and children, recrossed the Mississippi, intent upon reoccupying their former village and harvesting corn they had left standing the previous summer. Settlers fled their farms in panic and regular troops commanded by General Henry Atkinson were dispatched from St. Louis to force the Sacs and Foxes back into Iowa. Meanwhile, units of the Illinois militia rushed toward the Rock River Valley, also intent on intercepting the Indians. On 14 May 1832, Black Hawk attempted to surrender to a force of Illinois troops led by Major Isaiah Stillman, but 300 mounted militiamen fired upon the Sacs' white flag and attacked Black Hawk's surrender party. Black Hawk and about forty other Sac warriors returned the fire and the Americans fled in panic.

For Black Hawk, the Battle of Stillman's Run was a costly victory. Additional militia units joined the volunteer army and Andrew Jackson dispatched 800 regulars to Chicago to assist in the campaign against the Indians. The Sacs and Foxes retreated up the Rock River into Wisconsin, then turned westward still attempting to reach the Mississippi and return to Iowa. Black Hawk held off his pursuers at the Battle of Wisconsin Heights, on the Wisconsin River, but the Sacs and Foxes lost almost seventy warriors while the Americans suffered only one casualty. The Sacs and Foxes reached the Mississippi at the mouth of the Bad Axe River on 2 August. Again, their attempts to surrender were rejected, and as they crossed over onto several low sandy islands in the Mississippi, they were caught between the fire from American troops on the bank, and cannons fired from an American gunboat in the river. The Battle of the Bad Axe lasted almost eight hours, but when the firing stopped, over 200 Indians lay dead on the islands or in the river. The Americans lost eleven killed and had sixteen wounded. Black Hawk escaped but was later captured and imprisoned at St. Louis. He eventually was released and died in Iowa in 1838.

American military campaigns against the Seminoles were more costly. Prior to 1819 Florida was controlled by Spain and the region was a haven for African Americans fleeing slavery in Alabama and Georgia. Since the Seminoles allowed the refugees to settle within tribal territory, plantation owners accused the Indians of harboring runaways, and in 1817, bloodshed occurred when an American military expedition attacked a Seminole village in southwestern Georgia, and the Seminoles retaliated by ambushing against American supply boats on the Apalachicola River. In response, during March 1818, Andrew Jackson led an army of 1,200 men into Florida where he found few Seminoles, but burned several villages; captured St. Marks (a Spanish fort); and executed two British traders. Jackson's success in the First Seminole War demonstrated that the region was vulnerable to American military power, and in 1819, Spain ceded Florida to the United States.

With Florida ostensibly under American control, demands for Seminole lands in the state increased. In 1823 Seminole leaders signed the Treaty of Moultrie Creek, which opened both Florida coastlines to white settlement, but retained the peninsula's interior for the Indians. But the Seminoles refused to surrender runaway slaves and plantation owners clamored for their removal. In 1832 at the Treaty of Payne's Landing, the Seminoles signed what they believed was a treaty allowing them to send an "exploring party" to Oklahoma to examine lands in the west. If the Seminoles approved of the lands, they would agree to remove; if not they could remain in Florida. Evidence suggests that government agents bribed interpreters to misrepresent the terms of the agreement to the Indians, and when the Seminoles rejected the western lands, federal officials informed them that removal was not an option: they must leave Florida. The Seminoles refused and federal attempts to force their removal resulted in the Second Seminole War.

In 1835 Florida erupted in warfare. After stockpiling arms and ammunition, the Seminoles began to steal horses and other livestock. On 28 December 1835 a large war party of Seminoles led by Micanopy, Alligator, and Jumper ambushed a force of 107 officers and men led by Major Francis Dade just north of modern Tampa. The Seminoles killed 103 of the Americans while losing only three Indians. On the same day, Osceola and another smaller war party overran the Indian Agency near Fort King, killing seven other Americans.

Seeking retribution, General Duncan Clinch and an army of 700 regulars and volunteers pursued the Seminoles into the Wahoo Swamp on the Withlacoochee River, but were attacked and turned back before reaching any Seminole villages. Two months later, another party of Seminoles and ex-slaves attacked General Edmund Gaines near modern Citrus Springs. Although the Americans outnumbered their enemy, they remained on the defensive and after a series of skirmishes that extended over five days, the Seminoles withdrew and the Americans refused to follow them.

In January 1836, General Winfield Scott took over command of American forces in Florida, but he proved

401

ineffectual in either finding the Seminoles or defeating them. In May he was succeeded by Governor Richard Call of Florida, who in turn was relieved by General Thomas Sidney Jesup in December. By early 1837, Jesup had 8,000 troops in the field, including friendly Creek and northern Indians, and although he could not catch the Seminoles, he destroyed many of their villages and gardens. The Seminoles faced growing shortages of ammunition. In March 1837 Seminole leaders agreed to a truce at Fort Dade where those tribe members who wished to go to Oklahoma would board ships for removal, but when white slaveholders arrived and attempted to seize both African Americans and Indians, the Seminoles again fled. The federal government committed 1,700 more troops to the campaign, and the army pursued the Seminoles relentlessly.

The pursuit took its toll, but Jesup augmented his campaign with treachery. On 25 October 1837, he invited Osceola and other Seminole leaders to meet under a flag of truce, but when they again refused removal he surrounded them with troops and imprisoned them in St. Augustine. In November Wildcat and eighteen other warriors escaped, but Osceola suffered from malaria and could not accompany them. Jesup then transferred Osceola to Fort Moultrie in South Carolina, where he died on 31 January 1838.

Following Osceola's death the Seminole resistance continued, but its intensity diminished. Yet the war also took it's toll on American military commanders. Five officers commanded American troops between 1838 and 1842. When Colonel William J. Worth took command in May 1841, fewer than 800 Seminoles remained in Florida. In March Wildcat was captured and he then used his influence to persuade other Seminoles to surrender. Small bands led by Billy Bowlegs and Halleck Tustenugge remained free of government control until August 1842, when the government established a small reservation, just west of Lake Okeechobee. Although no formal peace treaty was signed, the Second Seminole War had ended. About 600 Seminoles remained in Florida.

The costs of the war were staggering. The army had committed over 9,000 men against no more than 1,300 Seminole warriors and their African American allies. Eventually the government removed 4,400 Seminoles from Florida, but the cost totaled at least $20,000 per Indian, a colossal figure in the 1840s. Moreover, Jesup's violation of a flag of truce was disgraceful. It was neither the government's nor the army's finest hour.

BIBLIOGRAPHY

Covington, James W. *The Seminoles of Florida*. Gainesville: University Press of Florida, 1993.

Gilpin, Alec R. *The War of 1812 in the Old Northwest*. East Lansing: Michigan State University Press, 1958.

Hagan, William T. *The Sac and Fox Indians*. Norman: University of Oklahoma Press, 1958.

Mahon, John K. *History of the Second Seminole War, 1835–1842*. Gainesville: University of Florida Press, 1967.

Prucha, Francis Paul. *Sword of the Republic: The United States Army on the Frontier, 1783–1846*. Toronto: Macmillan, 1969.

Sword, Wiley. *President Washington's Indian War: The Struggle for the Old Northwest, 1790–1795*. Norman: University of Oklahoma Press, 1985.

R. David Edmunds

See also **Fallen Timbers, Battle of; Greenville Treaty; Indian Policy, U.S.: 1775–1830; Ohio Wars; Seminole Wars; Tecumseh's Crusade; Tippecanoe, Battle of; War of 1812; Warfare, Indian;** *and vol. 9:* **Sleep Not Longer, O Choctaws and Chickasaws.**

LATER NINETEENTH CENTURY (1840–1900)

These wars were a constant and recurring feature of American westward expansion. Until the Civil War, the federal government regarded the various tribes as independent nations. Prior to 1860, federal policy was to establish a permanent frontier between whites and Indians in an Indian country that would keep them apart. But the acquisition of California and the Southwest as a result of the Mexican-American War provided more opportunities for westward settlement and conflict with the native population there. The policy of creating one "Indian Territory" clearly would not work. The indigenous population of the Great Plains, Southwest, and West Coast represented a problem to many Americans since they occupied lands that the whites wanted. Federal policies and acceptance of tribal sovereignty was insufficient in the face of mounting white pressure for admittance to these lands. These demands would not be deterred by federal efforts in the early 1850s to place the various tribes on defined reserves in order to give whites access to the most desirable Indian lands. Eventually, Indians would begin to resist white encroachment.

In 1851, with the Treaty of Fort Laramie the federal government tried to curtail growing friction between Indians and the wagon trains crossing their lands. This agreement brought several Plains Indian tribes off the main routes of white advances by defining large tribal territories and pledging the tribes to peace. The federal government promised to provide food supplies in return. However, not all tribal members, some of whom were suspicious that the government would break its promises, accepted these treaties. Corrupt and unreliable Indian agents and the inability of the U.S. Army to keep white settlers from intruding on reservation lands led to warfare in the last half of the 1850s.

In southern Oregon near the California border, tribes known collectively as the Rogue River Indians turned to war to resist the invasion of gold-seeking prospectors in 1855, after efforts to negotiate treaties that would set aside lands for them failed. A similar discovery of gold in the new Washington Territory led to warfare between prospectors and the Yakima Indians at about the same

Seattle, 1856
Connell's Prairie 1856
Haller's Defeat, 1855
Cascades, 1856
Umatilla, 1848
Grande Ronde, 1858
Galice Creek, 1855
Grave Creek, 1855
Evans Creek, 1853
Rogue River, 1851
The Meadows, 1856
Lava Beds, 1873
Pit River, 1867
Lake Abert, 1868
Owyhee Forks, 1868
Four Lakes, 1858
Steptoe Butte, 1858
Touchet, 1848
Clearwater, 1877
Walla Walla, 1855
White Bird Canyon, 1877
Baker's Battle, 1872
Big Hole, 1877
Camas Meadows, 1877
Bear River, 1863
Pyramid Lake, 1860
Truckee, 1860
Bear Paw Mountains, 1877
Cedar Creek, 1876
Yellowstone, 1873
Little Big Horn, 1876
Sturgis' Battle, 1877
Muddy Creek, 1877
Rosebud, 1876
Wolf Mountain, 1877
Piney Island, 1867
Fetterman's Defeat, 1866
Hole-in-the-Wall, 1876
Point of Rocks, 1874
Grattan's Defeat, 1854
Mud Springs, 1865
Fort Sedgwick, 1865
Milk Creek, 1879
Beecher's Island, 1868
Killdeer Mountain, 1864
Big Mound, 1863
Dead Buffalo Lake, 1863
Stony Lake, 1863
Little Missouri, 1864
Fort Abercrombie, 1862
White Stone Hills, 1863
Slim Buttes, 1876
Wood Lake, 1862
Redwood Ferry, 1862
Acton, 1862
Birch Coolie, 1862
Fort Ridgely, 1862
New Ulm, 1862
Wounded Knee, 1890
Rush Creek, 1865
Ash Hollow, 1855
Fort Kearney, 1867
Beaver Creek, 1867
Sand Creek, 1864
Crooked Creek, 1859
Chustenahlah, 1861
Bird Creek, 1861
Round Mountain, 1861
Antelope Hills, 1858
Adobe Walls, 1864, 1874
Washita, 1868
Palo Duro Canyon, 1875
Wichita Village, 1858
Yellow House Canyon, 1878
Pino Altos, 1862
Apache Pass, 1862
Salt Creek Massacre, 1872
Dove Creek, 1863

Indian Battles, 1846–1890

time. The Rogue River War was ended with a decisive defeat of the Indians and their removal to reserves in the Coast Range. The Yakima War ended inconclusively in September 1856, but in 1858 the tribes of the Columbia River area joined together to resist further white encroachment. Colonel George E. Wright defeated the Indians at the Battles of Four Lakes and Spokane Plains in September 1858. Wright then marched through the Indian country, hanging chiefs and others suspected of fomenting war. All resistance to white settlement ended in the Northwest by 1860.

Confined to an inadequate reservation and exploited by Indian agents, the eastern Sioux turned to war in this period, striking out under the leadership of Little Crow in 1862. Seven hundred whites were killed before federal troops and militia subdued them. In eastern Colorado, the Arapaho and Cheyenne came into conflict with miners

who were settling in their territory. Seeking to recover the lands they were losing, these Indians attacked stage lines and settlements.

From 1862 to 1867, with federal troops largely diverted east because of the U.S. Civil War, Indian raids on isolated settlements and homesteads were conducted with devastating effect; whites struck back, often carrying the conflict to the "civilian" element of the indigenous population. Sioux raids in Minnesota in August 1862 led to the deaths of more than four hundred whites. After the military had defeated the Indians, capturing 2,000, a military commission tried the captives and ordered the execution of 303 of them. President Lincoln reduced the number to be hanged to thirty-eight, and the executions were carried out in December. The remaining Sioux in Minnesota were resettled in the Dakota Territory. Little Crow was fatally shot by a white farmer in the summer of 1863. In

403

1864 at the Sand Creek reserve in Colorado, retaliating for raids that might have involved some of the Arapaho warriors on the reservation, militia forces slaughtered almost all of the Indians there. In late January 1870, a cavalry troop led by Major Edward M. Baker charged into a Piegan Blackfeet village in Montana, slaughtering 173 Indians, primarily women and children, many of whom were suffering from smallpox.

In the New Mexico Territory, war with the Navajo began in 1862, as that tribe resisted efforts to relocate them to the Bosque Redondo along the Pecos River. American forces led by Colonel Kit Carson under the direction of Brigadier General James H. Carleton, who commanded the Department of New Mexico, broke their resistance in January 1864. By the end of that year 8,000 Navajos had been transported to Bosque Redondo. After enduring harsh conditions for four years, the federal government allowed the Navajos to return to their homes in 1868, and the tribe remained peaceful afterwards.

After the Civil War, war broke out on a broad front. The longest running clash was in Montana, where the army was building the Bozeman Trail into the new mining areas being opened in the Black Hills. Angered by the intrusion into their hunting lands, the western Sioux, led by Red Cloud, were able to keep the army from completing the roadway. The Red Cloud War ended when Red Cloud signed a peace treaty late in 1868; the advance of the Union Pacific railroad to the south, which offered better routes into Montana, nullified his victory.

The SAND CREEK MASSACRE led to a federal investigation and the creation of a new policy that resulted in peace treaties that placed the major tribes on a pair of large reservations, one in the Dakotas and the other in Oklahoma Indian Territory. Further, the government decided to work toward the assimilation of Native Americans into white culture, and Congress ended the practice of treating Indian nations as sovereign in 1871.

Indian resistance had not ended, however. The Modoc War began after the Modoc leader Kintpuash left the reservation in 1872, along with sixty or seventy other families, for their old lands in northern California. Efforts of Indian agents to persuade him to return to the reservation failed and force was applied. After an attack on their village in November 1872, Kintpuash and his followers took refuge in a lava formation that served as a natural fortress and held out for several months. Peace talks between the two sides ended in April 1873 when the Modocs murdered General Edmund R. S. Canby, who led the peace commission. Eventually, dissension among the tribal leaders led to their defeat. Kintpuash and three others were hanged, and the Modocs were moved to the Indian Territory 1,500 miles to the east.

The confining nature of reservation life, continued white encroachment, and slaughter of the buffalo herds led to the Red River War of 1874–1875. Although they lived on the reservation, Kiowa, Cheyenne, and Comanche warriors often raided into Texas, Mexico, and occasionally Kansas. After the military lifted restrictions about carrying out operations on reservations, about 5,000 Kiowa, Cheyenne, and Comanche moved west beyond the boundaries of the reserves. Five columns of soldiers pursued them through the last half of 1874 and into early 1875. By autumn, some of the Indians were already returning to the reservation; all of them had come back by the spring of 1875.

In 1875 large numbers of Sioux, angered by crooked Indian agents and uneasy about white miners entering the Black Hills, began to organize. Under the leadership of Sitting Bull and Crazy Horse, they gathered in Montana. Three army columns were sent to round them up in the early summer of 1876, including the 7th Cavalry, commanded by George Armstrong Custer. In the battle at Little Big Horn, General Custer and his men were trapped by an overwhelming Indian force and wiped out. Lacking any real organization, however, the Indians soon began to disperse in small groups. These bands were eventually rounded up and returned to the reservation, and they ceased to pose a threat to white settlement.

In 1877 the Nez Perce refused to be restricted to an undersized reservation in Oregon and were compelled to resist efforts to keep them there. Following their leader, Chief Joseph, the Nez Perce tried to flee to Canada after defeating the military at White Bird Canyon. Following a pursuit that covered nearly 1,300 miles in twenty-five days, Joseph and his people were caught near the Canadian border and relocated to Indian Territory in Oklahoma.

A group of Cheyenne, led by Dull Knife and Little Wolf, fled the Indian Territory in 1878 in a futile effort to return to their lands in Montana. Caught and detained at Fort Robinson, Nebraska, in midwinter, the Indians made a desperate effort to escape. Soldiers gunned down many fleeing and unarmed Indians. The last organized resistance came from the Apache, who fought the whites from the 1860s into the late 1880s. Early leaders included Mangas Coloradas, who was killed during the Civil War, and Cochise, who accepted a peace treaty and agreed to move his people to a reservation in 1872. Other Apache leaders, notably Geronimo and Victorio, continued to fight, however. Victorio was killed in 1880; Geronimo surrendered in 1886. Geronimo's capture brought an end to the formal resistance between Indians and whites.

In 1890 panicked responses to a religious revival led to one final, tragic occurrence. The white assault on Indian life and culture contributed to the emergence of an emotional religion that originated in Nevada and spread swiftly among the Plains Indians. This new faith emphasized the coming of a messiah and featured the "Ghost Dance," which was believed to inspire visions in its ceremonies. Fearing an outbreak of violence, agents on the Sioux reserve sent for federal troops. The murder of Sitting Bull by an Indian policeman at Standing Rock prompted some of the Indians to flee the reservation. They were caught at Wounded Knee, South Dakota, and

George, James L. *History of Warships: From Ancient Times to the Twenty-First Century.* Annapolis, Md.: Naval Institute Press, 1998.

Landstrom, Bjorn. *The Ship.* London: Allen and Unwin, 1961.

Sprout, Harold, and Margaret Sprout. *The Rise of American Naval Power, 1776–1918.* Princeton, N.J.: Princeton University Press, 1966.

R. W. Daly
Paul B. Ryan
Ronald Spector / A. R.

See also **Armored Ships; Battle Fleet Cruise Around the World;** *Bonhomme Richard–Serapis* **Encounter;** *Constitution;* **Dreadnought; Gunboats; Ironclad Warships;** *Nautilus;* **Navy, United States; Privateers and Privateering; "White Squadron"; World War II, Navy in.**

WASHINGTON, D.C. Most Americans think of Washington, D.C., their national capital, as either a marble-columned theme park for visiting high-school civics classes or a cluster of government palaces housing activities so corrupt that aspirants to federal office regularly seek advantage over their incumbent rivals by accusing them of having spent too much time in Washington. To a degree, Washington is both of these things, yet it is also a real city, home to more Americans than is Wyoming, and (with Baltimore) a nucleus of the nation's fourth-largest metropolitan area. For Washingtonians, the presence of the federal government is both a blessing and a curse, for the city's status as capital provides steady employment and unparalleled cultural institutions but strips its people of basic rights of citizenship taken for granted by the residents of the fifty states.

Founding and Early History

For most of the War of Independence, Congress met in Philadelphia, the largest city in the thirteen colonies. Fearing urban mobs and not trusting the Pennsylvania government to control them, in 1783 Congress decided to create a new capital apart from any state, and in 1787 the framers of the Constitution provided for a capital district of up to 100 square miles in which Congress would "exercise exclusive legislation." For the next three years, Congress considered promising river ports up and down the Atlantic Coast, with northerners favoring a site on the Delaware or Susquehanna while southerners held out for the Potomac. Finally, Thomas Jefferson, Alexander Hamilton, and James Madison brokered a deal by which the South would agree to federal assumption of state war debts in return for a southern capital. President George Washington, himself a Potomac man, chose the exact spot for the square, straddling the river and embracing the towns of Georgetown, Maryland, and Alexandria, Virginia.

Rather than seating the federal government in either town, Washington called for a brand-new city to be built on the low land between the Potomac and Anacostia Rivers. To plan it, he turned to the thirty-six-year-old Pierre-Charles L'Enfant, a French artist and veteran of the Continental Army. L'Enfant, deeply influenced by the baroque plan of Versailles, began by emphasizing the site's topography. He reserved the most prominent hills for the Capitol and President's House (later nicknamed the White House), then gave each building a spectacular vista over an open, green Mall. To connect these and lesser nodes he drew a grand design of wide, diagonal avenues, superimposed on a practical American grid. Though L'Enfant was fired after a tiff with a local landowner, his plan provided the basic layout for Washington City (its name chosen by three presidentially appointed commissioners) within the larger territory of Columbia. In December 1800, the government arrived.

Washington and L'Enfant had hoped that the capital would grow into a major commercial city, a point of transshipment between the inland, Potomac trade, and seagoing vessels moored in an Anacostia harbor. But congressional neglect, rivalry among Georgetown, Alexandria, and Washington City, and the difficulty of opening the Potomac to navigation stifled the city's growth. When, in 1814, British troops raided the city, they found little worth torching except the White House and the Capitol. Congress did subscribe funds for the Chesapeake and Ohio Canal, designed to make Washington the Atlantic

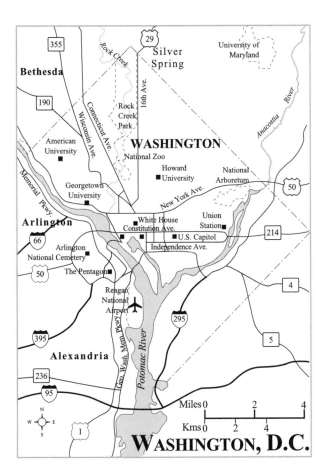

WASHINGTON, D.C.

port for the Ohio River valley, but the city had bet on the wrong technology. Baltimore put its money into Baltimore and Ohio Railroad, outpacing the canal and making that city the dominant port of the Chesapeake. L'Enfant's enormous avenues remained unpaved and undeveloped.

Politically, the capital did not fare much better. Congress did grant elected municipal governments to Washington, Georgetown, and Alexandria, but to a large degree the District remained a congressional pawn to be pushed back and forth across the board. This was particularly true in the matter of the slave trade. In the 1830s, northern abolitionists flooded Congress with petitions to abolish slavery in the District, and southern congressmen responded by ruling that such petitions would be automatically tabled. Finally, in 1846, Congress returned the portion of the District on the right bank of the Potomac to Virginia. Since this included the city of Alexandria, the District's major slave market, retrocession helped make possible the Compromise of 1850, which banned the slave trade in the remaining portion of the District, now only sixty-seven square miles.

Ten years later, as the Compromise collapsed into secession, Washington turned into an armed camp, surrounded by slave states. Northern troops rushed into the city, both to secure it for the Union and to use it as a base of operations against the Confederate capital of Richmond, only 100 miles away. The Capitol, Patent Office, and other government buildings were pressed into service, first as emergency barracks, then as emergency hospitals as wounded soldiers staggered back from Bull Run and points south. The Army of Northern Virginia threatened the city during its 1862 and 1863 invasions of the North, and in 1864 General Jubal Early actually entered the District before being repulsed at Fort Stevens.

Following the war, triumphant Midwesterners spoke of relocating the capital to the interior of the country, perhaps to St. Louis. Instead, in 1871, Congress decided to remain in Washington and modernize the city, merging the jurisdictions of Washington City, Washington County, and Georgetown, and giving the newly unified District a territorial government—the same form used by aspiring states. In just three years as vice president of the Board of Public Works and later as territorial governor, "Boss" Alexander Shepherd rebuilt the city's public spaces, paving streets, installing sewers, and planting tens of thousands of trees. But he also massively overdrew the city's Treasury account. In 1874 an appalled Congress abolished territorial government, and in 1878 it passed the Organic Act, which provided for government by three presidentially appointed commissioners, one of them an officer in the Army Corps of Engineers. To compensate District residents for their lost franchise, Congress promised to pay half of the District's budget, a promise that gradually eroded in subsequent decades.

Reinventing Washington

With the approach of the capital's centennial in 1900, a group of architects, eager to promote their profession, saw a chance to revive L'Enfant's baroque vision for the Mall, which had been cluttered with winding carriage roads and a dangerously sited train station. At the request of Senator James McMillan, the architects Daniel Burnham and Charles McKim, the landscape architect Frederick Law Olmsted Jr., and the sculptor Augustus Saint-Gaudens proposed a City Beautiful plan of green, open spaces and white neoclassical buildings. The railroad station on the Mall was demolished and its trains rerouted to Burnham's monumental Union Station north of the Capitol. The plan was capped in 1922, with the dedication of the Lincoln Memorial on land reclaimed from the Potomac.

Ironically, Lincoln's temple overlooked a racially segregated city. Woodrow Wilson, the first southern-born president since Andrew Johnson, encouraged racial discrimination within the civil service. Though libraries and public transit were integrated, the city's schools, restaurants, theaters, and hotels remained rigidly segregated. Despite these restrictions, Washington was home to a thriving black community. Howard University, founded during Reconstruction, and some of the nation's top black high schools attracted African American intellectuals from across the country. Blacks built their own theaters, clubs, and hotels along U Street, north of downtown. The author Jean Toomer and the musician Duke Ellington were born and raised in the neighborhood, and the many other artists, scholars, and activists who spent time in the area made Washington second only to Harlem as a center for black culture.

The expansion of the federal government during the New Deal and World War II made Washington a boomtown. In 1942 alone, more than 70,000 newcomers arrived to work in temporary buildings on the Mall, in the newly built Pentagon, or wherever they could find space for a typewriter. Thanks to the cold war, the federal government did not contract after victory, but it did disperse. Concerned about atomic attack and traffic congestion, federal planners scattered the new agencies—the Atomic Energy Commission, the Central Intelligence Agency, the National Security Agency, and the like—to suburban campuses miles from downtown. Private employers, particularly high-tech defense contractors, followed them, as did many families. These were good jobs, and by 1949 the region had the highest mean salary per family of any major metropolitan area.

Though the cold war boom turned metropolitan Washington into the nation's fastest-growing metropolitan area, the District's population, which had peaked in the 1950 census at over 800,000, fell to 764,000 by 1960. For the first time the District housed less than half of the metropolitan region's residents. The bulk of Washingtonians moving to the suburbs were white, while most newcomers were black, so in 1957 Washington became the nation's first major city to be majority African American.

National Rallying Point. A view from the Lincoln Memorial past the Reflecting Pool to the Washington Monument—the site of numerous mass demonstrations for a variety of causes.

Home Rule

With an almost all-white Congress and a southern-dominated House District of Columbia Committee ruling over a mostly black city, the civil rights element of home rule for the District became more pressing than ever. Presidents Kennedy, Johnson, and Nixon each took up the cause. Kennedy appointed the first African American district commissioner, as well as the first White House advisor on national capital affairs, while Congress approved the Twenty-third Amendment, allowing District residents to vote for presidential electors. Johnson, unable to get a home rule bill through Congress, nevertheless replaced the three commissioners with an appointed mayor, deputy mayor, and city council, a training ground for District leaders. Meanwhile, the District gained the right to send a nonvoting delegate to the House of Representatives. Finally, with Nixon's support, in 1973 Congress passed a home rule act. In 1974, the city—by now three-fourths black—held its first elections for top municipal office in a century.

The 1970s were rough on the city. Crime rates rose, downtown streets were torn up for subway construction, and the city lost its major-league baseball team. Escaping congressionally imposed height limits in Washington it-self, developers took their skyscrapers, and jobs, to Virginia. In contrast, the 1980s were boom years. Metro, the flashy new regional rapid transit system, brought commuters and investors back to the center, and Mayor Marion Barry gained a reputation as a business-friendly leader. There was even talk of granting the city full representation in Congress, either through statehood or a constitutional amendment. But Republicans had no desire to let the majority-black, and overwhelmingly liberal, city send two new Democrats to the Senate. Moreover, the city's image—and its claim to political maturity—suffered when federal agents videotaped Mayor Barry smoking crack cocaine in a hotel room, amplifying criticism that he had bloated the city's bureaucracy with patronage jobs. Combined with unfinished business from home rule, Barry's misadministration left the District essentially bankrupt. In 1995, Congress established an appointed Control Board to oversee the government until the city could balance its own budget.

At the start of the twenty-first century, the city had climbed out of insolvency. Though the year 2000 census count of 572,059 was lower than the 1990 figure, it was significantly higher than projected, suggesting that the population had bottomed out in the early 1990s and was climbing again. With a respectable mayor, a healthier economy, and encouraging demographics, local activists were ready to try again to gain voting representation in Congress and an end to congressional meddling with the city's laws and budget. They even persuaded the city council to replace tourist-friendly slogans on the District license plates with the defiant motto: "Taxation without Representation." But as the newly elected president George W. Bush shrugged off their demands, it seemed unlikely that Washingtonians would become full American citizens anytime soon.

BIBLIOGRAPHY

Abbott, Carl. *Political Terrain: Washington, D.C., from Tidewater Town to Global Metropolis.* Chapel Hill: University of North Carolina Press, 1999.

Bowling, Kenneth R. *The Creation of Washington, D.C.: The Idea and Location of the American Capital.* Fairfax, Va.: George Mason University Press, 1991.

Cary, Francine, ed. *Urban Odyssey: A Multicultural History of Washington, D.C.* Washington, D.C.: Smithsonian Institution Press, 1996.

Gillette, Howard, Jr. *Between Justice and Beauty: Race, Planning, and the Failure of Urban Policy in Washington, D.C.* Baltimore: Johns Hopkins University Press, 1995.

Green, Constance McLaughlin. *Washington.* Princeton, N.J.: Princeton University Press, 1962–1963.

Lessoff, Alan. *The Nation and its City: Politics, "Corruption," and Progress in Washington, D.C., 1861–1902.* Baltimore: Johns Hopkins University Press, 1994.

Reps, John William. *Washington on View: The Nation's Capital Since 1790.* Chapel Hill: University of North Carolina Press, 1991.

United States National Capital Planning Commission. *Worthy of the Nation: The History of Planning for the National Capital.* Washington, D.C.: Smithsonian Institution Press, 1977.

Zachary M. Schrag

See also **Capitol at Washington.**

WASHINGTON, STATE OF, has a wide variety of environments, from the lush San Juan Islands in the northwest to prickly pear cactus scattered in the high desert along the Snake River in the southeast. The rugged coastal Cascade Mountain range separates the urbanized Puget Sound region from the less-populated eastern portion of the state. Early settlements were constrained by the difficulty of passing over the mountains, resulting in a coastal region that relied on oceangoing international trade and an interior that relied on river transport and later railroad links to markets for agricultural, timber, and mining products.

White Exploration and Settlement

The Spanish captain Juan Pérez explored the seacoast by ship in 1774, but he made no settlements on land due to scurvy and bad weather. Other Spanish explorers attempted a presence, but scurvy and weather continued to restrict them. The Spanish established a fur trade post at Nootka on Vancouver Island, which led to conflict between Spain and Britain, resulting in the Nootka Convention of 1790 and Spain's eventual withdrawal from the Pacific Northwest. After the British captain James Cook's voyage to the Pacific Northwest in 1778, Americans entered the lucrative Pacific fur trade, selling Alaskan sea otter furs to China. The American Robert Gray was the first to identify and sail up the Columbia River, naming it after his ship, in 1792. That same year, George Vancouver explored the body of water he called Puget's Sound for Britain.

The Columbia River, which enters the state at the Canadian border and runs south to form the state's southern border, was a river route for early fur traders who entered the region immediately after the Lewis and Clark Expedition discovered the river and used it to reach the Washington coast on 14 November 1805. British fur traders made the earliest attempts at settlement, establishing outposts at the mouth of the Columbia River. After the War of 1812, Britain and the United States agreed to share the region, which was called the Oregon Country. By 1824, the British Hudson's Bay Company controlled the area, building Fort Vancouver on the north side of the Columbia and shipping furs to London. The company established forts and corporate farms but prohibited settlers. By the 1840s the fur era was over, and the Hudson's Bay Company moved operations north to British Columbia.

In 1836 the first Americans to settle in Washington came overland to establish Protestant missions to the Indians. Marcus and Narcissa Whitman, Henry and Eliza Spalding, and William Gray established mission stations at Waiilatpu, near Walla Walla in the southeast corner of the state, and near Lapwai, Idaho. Two years later, reinforcements arrived overland, establishing another mission station near the Hudson's Bay Company's Fort Colville. In 1838, Catholic priests from Canada began a series of missions in the region, assisted by the Jesuit Pierre Jean De Smet. American immigrants soon followed, and in 1843 a thousand came by wagon train to the region. Most settled in Oregon's Willamette Valley. In 1847, five thousand passed through the Whitman's mission at Walla Walla, bringing measles, which were caught by both whites and the local Indians. When the whites recovered and the Cayuse did not, the Cayuse thought they were being poisoned and attacked, killing the missionaries and several other Americans. As a result the missions were closed and Americans evacuated from the region. A period of white-Indian wars ensued.

Territory and Early Statehood

Most Americans settled south of the Columbia River during this time, thinking it would be the U.S.–Canadian boundary. In 1846 one party, led by a black cattleman from Missouri, George Washington Bush, located near

WASHINGTON, OREGON, AND IDAHO

today's Olympia, because Oregon citizens prohibited any blacks, free or slave, from settling in Oregon. Bush and thirty others established the first private settlement in the state. In 1853, Washington became a territory, with four thousand American residents who wanted it named Columbia. Congress thought that would be too easily confused with the District of Columbia and instead named it after the first president. Olympia was designated the capital, and Isaac Stevens was appointed governor. Stevens immediately set out to sign treaties with Indian tribes in 1854 and 1855, to gain legal title to their lands in exchange for goods and promises.

The Donation Land Claim Act of 1850, by allowing 320 acres of homestead land free to white males and an additional 320 to their wives, encouraged white settlers and resulted in few minorities coming to the area to settle. Gold discoveries in the 1850s and 1860s, particularly in Idaho and British Columbia, brought rushes of immigrants to the region and created markets for supplies. The California gold rush created a demand for lumber, fueling the sawmill industry around Puget Sound. The surge in settlement led to increased conflict with the area's Native inhabitants and a series of Indian wars from 1856 to 1859.

On 8 September 1883, the Northern Pacific rail line connecting Puget Sound at Tacoma with the Great Lakes was completed. The Northern Pacific was financed by government grants of public lands in forty-mile-wide sections on either side of the rail line. The government deeded every other section to the railroad upon completion of each twenty-five miles of track, keeping the alternating sections of land public. This checkerboard of ownership extended across the region. The Northern Pacific opened up its lands to settlers, and a rush of immigrants

recruited from Germany, Britain, and Scandinavia between 1880 and 1910 gave a distinct ethnic makeup to the region. At the same time, thousands of railroad laborers were recruited from China, which created animosities after railroad construction ended and competition for available jobs ensued. In 1882, Congress passed the Chinese Exclusion Act, which limited importing Chinese labor; Japanese and Filipino laborers were then recruited to fill jobs in the fish canneries and logging camps of Puget Sound. In 1885–1886, anti-Chinese riots broke out in Seattle and Tacoma, and many Chinese were expelled.

In 1889, Washington was admitted as a state along with North Dakota, South Dakota, and Montana under the Omnibus Bill. During the Progressive Era, an alliance of labor, farmer groups, and middle-class urban reformers pushed Washington to the forefront of national reform, enacting changes between 1907 and 1914 that included the right to voter initiative (which allows citizens to pass laws through a petition process), referendum (which allows voters to reject laws passed by legislators), and recall, as well as woman's suffrage, a direct primary, child labor laws, worker's compensation, the eight-hour workday for women, and prohibition.

By 1910, wheat was the most profitable crop across eastern and central Washington. Whitman County in the Palouse region of eastern Washington was identified as the wealthiest county per capita in the United States. Wheat in burlap sacks was carried by steamboat to Portland or shipped by rail to ports at Tacoma and Seattle. By 1900 apple orchards were significant in the Yakima, Wenatchee, and Okanogan Valleys. Apple growers also relied on rail to reach distant markets.

Competition between Portland and Seattle for sea-going markets, as well as between Seattle and neighboring Tacoma, influenced regional development. Seattle boosters exploited the Klondike gold rush in 1897, promoting the city as the jumping-off point for gold seekers stampeding to the Yukon and Alaskan goldfields. Seattle passed Tacoma in the census of 1900 and Portland in 1910, to become the premier city in the region.

Union Radicalism and World War I

In the early twentieth century, most wage earners were single men, employed in logging, agriculture, or mining. Jobs were seasonal and low-paying. Many workers joined the International Workers of the World (IWW), pressing for labor reforms. The "Wobblies" sought to overturn capitalism by consolidating all trades into "one big union," a worldwide effort to organize industrial workers.

Resistance to U.S. entry into World War I was widespread in Washington. Farmers, labor, and German Americans resisted. The Wobblies led protests against the war, to the chagrin of lumber companies and the federal government. The Sedition Act of 1918, which made criticizing the war a crime, silenced the IWW by imprisoning many of its spokespeople. War hysteria fostered by propaganda resulted in losses of First Amendment rights, so the Wobblies led "free speech fights," reading aloud the Constitution, the Bill of Rights, and the Declaration of Independence. Authorities and business owners reacted violently, inciting mobs that beat up demonstrators. The violence culminated in two tragic incidents, the Everett Massacre in 1916 and Centralia Massacre in 1919. In the latter, an American Legion parade to commemorate the war's end disintegrated into an attack on the IWW labor hall by an estimated thousand residents. The IWW member Wesley Everest was kidnapped from jail and lynched. Mob action against Wobblies followed in several towns, and support for the IWW faded.

The Seattle General Strike in February 1919 created intense anticommunist hysteria, which spread across the nation. It came at the end of the war, when workers demanded wage increases that had been suspended during the war. It was the first general strike to hit an American city, and alarmed citizens thought that the Bolshevik Revolution might spread to the United States. The strike faded after a week, from opposition and ineffective leadership, but it left an indelible mark on the nation, and in Washington State it led to the Centralia Massacre later that year.

World War I brought economic vitality to the state: the demand for wood to build airplanes and ships caused lumber prices to soar; wheat exports to Europe were profitable; and a fledgling aircraft industry began. William Boeing received federal contracts to build military aircraft, but after war's end those disappeared. The company hung on, however, and came to prominence in the next war. The end of World War I brought about the general collapse of an economy suddenly deprived of foreign or government orders. Sawmills closed and wheat farmers were in debt and facing drought. Union demands faded along with job opportunities. The Depression of the 1930s hit rural Washington in the 1920s.

The Depression and World War II

By the Great Depression of the 1930s, unemployment in Seattle was 40 to 60 percent; in some lumber mill towns along the coast it reached 80 percent. The national average was 25 percent. A severe drought hit the western states in 1928, lasting twelve years. Like the dust bowl of the Midwest, Washington endured dust storms in the Columbia Basin for years. Devastating forest fires erupted at the same time. Transients moved to the area seeking opportunity, resulting in thousands of migrant farm workers in squatters' camps.

In 1933, President Franklin Roosevelt instituted federal projects to construct hydroelectric dams at Bonneville and Grand Coulee on the Columbia River. In 1937, the Bonneville Power Administration (BPA) was created to market the electricity generated by those dams at minimal wholesale rates. Cheap, abundant electric power would stimulate the stagnant regional economy and raise the standard of living. A federal program to promote electric power ensued, utilizing Woody Guthrie singing "Roll On, Columbia," among other songs promoting the project. That song became the state's official folk song in 1987.

Legislation allowing labor organizing resulted in heavy involvement in labor unions, with resulting strikes and battles between opposing factions, both from outside and within unions. The state became one of the most heavily unionized in the nation. World War II revived the declining fortunes of the region, with a surge in manufacturing and production due to Washington's unique Pacific Coast ports and Columbia River drainage. Cheap hydropower was instrumental in building aluminum plants in the state, which supplied the Boeing Airplane Company, revived with federal aircraft orders. Henry J. Kaiser built massive shipyards, employing thousands in the war effort. When the war broke out in the Pacific, Washington's ports became vital to national defense, supplying operations in the Pacific. Overnight, farms, fish, and lumber were replaced by vigorous aluminum, airplane, and ship industries.

In 1939, President Roosevelt began the secret Manhattan Project to build the first atomic bomb. One component was constructed at Hanford, Washington, an isolated semidesert farm town. The Hanford Nuclear Facility was built to produce plutonium, necessary to bomb construction, by processing uranium in reactors cooled with vast amounts of fresh water, using huge amounts of electric power. Hanford was isolated—near Grand Coulee Dam for cheap electricity, and along the Columbia, a source of fresh water. Thousands of men and women arrived to live and work at Hanford, but newspapers censored the goings-on to maintain secrecy. Even workers had no idea what they were working on. Speculation was considerable, but few knew their purpose until the atomic bomb was dropped in Japan, ending the war.

The war transformed the state. Seattle became a bustling industrial center, with a large influx of African Americans who arrived to work in wartime factories, pushing the number of African Americans in Seattle to 30,000. Mexican men had been brought to the state as farm laborers under the Bracero program, which ended with the war. Nearly 40,000, Braceros were working in the Northwest between 1943 and 1947. An influx of Chicanos from southern states occurred during the war, boosting the state's Hispanic population in rural towns.

During the war, Japanese Americans who lived along the coast were ordered to relocate to the nation's heartland, out of fears they would assist the Japanese war effort against the United States. Federal authorities moved those who refused to relocate to the Minidoka Relocation Center, near Twin Falls, Idaho. Ten thousand Japanese Americans lived there during the war. They were allowed to return home in 1944. In 1988, Congress passed a reparations bill that gave $20,000 and an apology to each of the individuals relocated during the war. The bill was inspired by a court decision that evolved from the efforts of the University of Washington law student Gordon Hirabayashi, who refused to move, was convicted, and persisted with appeals through the court system.

Since World War II
When the war ended, Washington residents feared a repeat of World War I's drastic effect on the economy. There had been eighty-eight shipyards and boatyards, employing 150,000 people; Boeing had employed almost 50,000 people in Seattle during the war. Those jobs were gone, but a building boom ensued across the nation, fueled by pent-up demand and the GI Bill, which provided home loans to returning veterans, creating demand for Washington lumber. Thousands of jobs were created in sawmills and logging.

The Cold War boosted Washington's economy with federal defense contracts for aircraft and Minuteman missile construction going to Boeing. Aircraft manufacturing was boosted by the Korean War and later by the Vietnam War. In Hanford, research on atomic weapons continued, expanding until the greatest number of nuclear weapons were built at Hanford between 1956 and 1963. The interstate highway system, begun in 1956, improved Washington's transportation links with other states through Interstate 90, which runs from Seattle to Boston, and Interstate 5, which runs from Canada to Mexico. Federal dam-building projects accelerated, and a dozen new dams were built on the Columbia and Snake Rivers after 1950. For two decades, well-paid dam construction jobs were created with over $100 million in federal funds. The ensuing "slackwater" turned Clarkston into an inland port, where barges carrying wheat, paper pulp, and logs load to move down the Snake to the Columbia, for export at

Portland. The dams included the Columbia Basin Project, intended to provide irrigation for family farms; by the completion of the project, however, most irrigated farms were large-scale, corporate entities. The irrigation project eventually watered 550,000 acres of land and resulted in major food-processing plants locating in the region.

Washington pioneered health care delivery with the first health maintenance organization (HMO) in the nation, formed at the end of World War II in Seattle. Labor union members and farmers joined together, forming a cooperative of four hundred members, to purchase a clinic and hospital. The Group Health Cooperative of Puget Sound (now known as Group Health) was widely copied across the nation. Members pay a monthly fee for health services from physicians hired by the organization. Another national trend started in Washington when the Northgate Shopping Center opened north of Seattle in 1950. It was the first regional shopping center in the world, with more than a hundred shops, a hospital, and movie theater. Similar centers spread across the country.

By the 1970s, the state was facing major environmental issues. Judge George Boldt of the federal district court in Tacoma ruled in 1974, in *United States v. Washington*, that the state's Indian population was entitled to fish at their "usual and accustomed place," as stated in the treaties Governor Isaac Stevens had worked out in 1855. Ignored for over a century, the treaty language was important because environmental issues had become paramount. Judge Boldt determined that the Indians should receive half the annual catch from Washington waters. A landmark decision, it has shaped Indian-white relations as well as driven environmental protection practices for the logging, mining, and construction industries. In 1974, Spokane was the site for a World's Fair dedicated to the environment. In 1962, Seattle's World's Fair had been a response to the Russian launch of Sputnik and the beginning of the Cold War space race; a bit over a decade later, the environment was becoming the issue. As if to punctuate nature's continuing importance, one of the state's volcanoes, Mount Saint Helens, erupted in 1980, covering several states with volcanic ash and killing fifty-seven people. In February 2001, a 6.8 magnitude earthquake rocked Seattle and Tacoma, damaging buildings, streets, and bridges.

By the end of the twentieth century, effects from many of the major projects were being felt. Irrigation water had increased production, but at the cost of profit. Prices for many products, such as apples, were at historic lows. When drought hit, irrigation water and hydroelectric power were both in limited supply, putting a crunch on the region's economy. Aluminum plants halted production, selling their contracted electricity instead. The dams nearly devastated the annual runs of migrating salmon, interfering with movement both upstream to spawn and downstream to mature in the ocean. Hanford, a major entity in the central part of the state, became suspect after years of radiation releases into both the air and the Columbia River. Wheat growers no longer found a profitable export market as countries like India, former customers, now began exporting, too. Wheat prices were at historic lows, supported with extensive federal subsidy payments to growers.

In the 1990s, Seattle became a center for the computer software industry and the headquarters of the Microsoft Corporation, founded by the Seattle native Bill Gates. Many computer- and Internet-related firms located in the Puget Sound region.

Washington voters elected mostly Republicans between 1900 and 1930. Between about 1940 and 2000, they chose mostly Democrats for Congress, with the governorship roughly balanced between Democrats and Republicans. The 2000 census figures ranked the state fifteenth in population, with 5,894,121 residents, a 21 percent increase from 1990. The state had 441,509 Hispanic residents, 322,335 Asians, 190,267 African-Americans, and 93,301 Native Americans.

BIBLIOGRAPHY

Green, Michael, and Laurie Winn Carlson. *Washington: A Journey of Discovery.* Layton, Utah: Gibbs Smith, 2001.

Hirt, Paul W., ed. *Terra Pacifica: People and Place in the Northwest States and Western Canada.* Pullman: Washington State University Press, 1998.

Schwantes, Carlos Arnaldo. *The Pacific Northwest: An Interpretive History.* Rev. ed. Lincoln: University of Nebraska Press, 1996.

Stratton, David H., ed. *Washington Comes of Age: The State in the National Experience.* Pullman: Washington State University Press, 1992.

Laurie Winn Carlson

See also **Boeing Company; Columbia River Exploration and Settlement; Hudson's Bay Company; Industrial Workers of the World; Microsoft; Mount St. Helens; Puget Sound; Seattle; Tribes: Northwestern.**

WASHINGTON, TREATY OF.

The Treaty of Washington was concluded 8 May 1871 between the United States and Great Britain for the amicable settlement of the so-called *Alabama* Claims. During the Civil War, Confederate ships sailing from British ports raided U.S. shipping across the North Atlantic. After defeating the Confederacy in 1865, the U.S. government demanded financial compensation from Great Britain for its role in aiding and abetting the Southern rebellion. After five years, British reluctance to negotiate was removed by the following factors: the Franco-Prussian War and the ensuing denunciation of the Black Sea agreement by Russia, which threatened European complications; pressure from financial interests; and the appointment of the conciliatory Lord Granville as foreign secretary. The reluctance of some American elements to negotiate was modified by difficulties with Spain, pressure from American bankers,

and general realization that the hope of peaceable annexation of Canada was in vain.

John Rose, a former Canadian statesman who had become a London financier, came to Washington, D.C., in January 1871. He and U.S. Secretary of State Hamilton Fish readily made arrangements with the British minister, Sir Edward Thornton, for submission of the various disputes to a joint high commission. This had been Fish's desire since taking office. The British commissioners were soon at work in Washington with the American commissioners. The principal questions at issue were the *Alabama* claims, the rights of American fishermen in Canadian waters, and the water boundary between British Columbia and the state of Washington. The fisheries question was settled by agreement that a mixed commission should sit at Halifax, Nova Scotia, and determine the relative value of certain reciprocal privileges granted by the two nations. The northwestern, or San Juan Island, boundary dispute was submitted to the German emperor. Most important, the first eleven of the forty-three articles of the treaty provided that the *Alabama* claims should be adjudicated at Geneva, Switzerland, by five arbitrators, appointed, respectively, by the presidents of the United States and Switzerland and by the rulers of Great Britain, Italy, and Brazil.

The treaty was distinguished by two unprecedented features. One was the British confession of wrongdoing incorporated in the preamble, where the imperial commissioners expressed regret for the escape of the *Alabama* and other cruisers. The other was agreement on three rules of international law for the guidance of the Geneva tribunal in interpreting certain terms used in the treaty. The most important of these rules asserted that "due diligence" to maintain absolute neutrality "ought to be exercised by neutral governments" in exact proportion to the risks to which belligerents were exposed by breaches. The other two made explicit the impropriety of letting a vessel be constructed, equipped, and armed under such circumstances as attended the building of the *Alabama* and dealt with the use of neutral territory by belligerent vessels. The treaty preserved peaceful relations between Great Britain and the United States and partially alleviated American resentment at Britain's role in aiding the Confederacy during the Civil War.

BIBLIOGRAPHY

Bernath, Stuart L. *Squall Across the Atlantic: American Civil War Prize Cases and Diplomacy.* Berkeley: University of California Press, 1970.

Bourne, Kenneth. *Britain and the Balance of Power in North America, 1815–1908.* Berkeley: University of California Press, 1967.

Crook, David P. *The North, the South, and the Powers, 1861–1865.* New York: Wiley, 1974.

Allan Nevins/A. G.

See also ***Alabama*** **Claims; Bayard-Chamberlain Treaty; Civil War; Confederate States of America; Great Britain, Relations with; Treaties with Foreign Nations.**

WASHINGTON BURNED. During the War of 1812, the capture and burning of Washington, D.C., authorized by Admiral Alexander Cochrane and executed by British forces under the command of Major General Robert Ross and Rear Admiral George Cockburn, was meant to demoralize the government and to punish Americans for their depredations in Canada.

On 24 August, seasoned British regulars quickly routed the raw, poorly organized, and badly led militia opposing them at Bladensburg, Maryland, near Washington. That evening, without encountering further opposition, the invaders took possession of Washington. News of the British approach had thrown the city into chaos, and many of the city's inhabitants had fled.

That night a detachment of British troops, headed by Ross and Cockburn, began their work of destruction by burning the Capitol, the White House, and the Treasury. Temporarily interrupted by a great thunderstorm, they renewed their incendiary activities the following morning and by noon had reduced to ruins the buildings housing the departments of state and war; some private dwellings; two ropewalks; a tavern; several printing establishments, including the office of the *National Intelligencer*; and such naval structures and supplies as the Americans had not themselves destroyed.

BIBLIOGRAPHY

Coles, Henry L. *The War of 1812.* Chicago: University of Chicago Press, 1965.

Pitch, Anthony. *The Burning of Washington: The British Invasion of 1814.* Annapolis, Md.: Naval Institute Press, 1998.

Ray W. Irwin/A. R.

See also **Architecture; Capitals; Capitol at Washington; Ghent, Treaty of; Niagara Campaigns; Thames, Battle of the; Treasury, Department of the; War of 1812; Washington, D.C.; White House.**

WASHINGTON MONUMENT. Pierre L'Enfant's plan for the federal city called for an equestrian monument honoring George Washington at the key location where the axes of the Capitol and president's house intersected. The Washington National Monument Society, formed in 1833, raised funds for a design competition, but no plans realized their expectations. In 1845 Robert Mills suggested an obelisk with a colonnaded base. After many sites had been considered, the cornerstone was laid 4 July 1848, near the spot designated on L'Enfant's plan. In 1854 members of the Know-Nothing Party, angered by the donation of an interior stone by the Vatican, stole the stone and took over the society. The project came to a halt, remained unfinished through the Civil War, and

Washington Monument. A dramatic photograph by Theodor Horydczak of the famous obelisk, c. 1933. LIBRARY OF CONGRESS

resumed only in 1876, when Congress took control of funding and construction. The monument was finally dedicated 21 February 1885. At 555 feet, 5⅛ inches it was, and still is, the tallest masonry structure in the world. The obelisk has had its admirers and detractors, but many commentators have noted a congruence between the form of the monument and the man it commemorates: "simple in its grandeur, coldly bare of draperies theatric" (James Russell Lowell), "a perfect simulacrum of our first president . . . powerful . . . eternal . . . elemental" (Richard Hudnut).

BIBLIOGRAPHY

Allen, Thomas B. *The Washington Monument: It Stands for All.* New York: Discovery Books, 2000.

Harvey, Frederick L. *History of the Washington National Monument and of the Washington National Monument Society.* Washington, D.C.: U.S. Government Printing Office, 1902.

Jeffrey F. Meyer

WASHINGTON NAVAL CONFERENCE, officially the International Conference on Naval Limitation, was called by Secretary of State Charles Evans Hughes to end a burgeoning naval race and stabilize power relationships in the Pacific. It took place from 12 November 1921 to 6 February 1922. Other U.S. delegates included Senators Henry Cabot Lodge and Oscar W. Underwood and former secretary of state Elihu Root. At the opening session, Hughes stunned his audience by calling for a ten-year freeze on capital ship construction (which included battleships), and scrapping 1.8 million tons of ships, naming actual ships in his address. Subsequently, nine treaties were drafted and signed by the participants. The Four-Power Treaty of 13 December 1921, involving the United States, Great Britain, France, and Japan (the Big Four), committed the signatories to respect each other's rights over island possessions in the Pacific and in essence superseded the Anglo-Japanese alliance of 1902. Another Big Four treaty pledged each country to consult the others in the event of "aggressive action" by another power. The Five-Power Naval Treaty of 6 February 1922 declared a ten-year holiday on capital ship construction and fixed the ratio of capital ship tonnage between the United States, Great Britain, Japan, France, and Italy at 5:5:3: 1.67:1.67. It made no mention of cruisers, destroyers, and submarines, for the conference could reach no agreement concerning such items. The Nine-Power Treaty, also signed on 6 February, pledged all conference participants (the Big Four, Italy, Portugal, China, Belgium, and the Netherlands) to affirm the Open Door principle ("equal opportunity for the commerce and industry of all nations throughout the territory of China"); they also agreed to respect "the sovereignty, the independence, and the territorial and administrative integrity of China," a clause that abrogated the Lansing-Ishii Agreement of 1917. A fifth treaty outlawed poison gases and pledged protection for civilians and noncombatants during submarine bombardment. The four remaining treaties dealt with increased Chinese sovereignty, including the withdrawal of Japan from Shantung, and involved Japanese recognition of American cable rights on Yap.

The conference's accomplishments, although less than some contemporary leaders claimed, were substantial. The post–World War I capital ships arms race was halted by the first naval disarmament agreement among the major powers. Because of the extensive scrapping of naval tonnage by the United States, Great Britain, and Japan and the agreements between the Big Four on the Pacific, general security in the area was much enhanced.

BIBLIOGRAPHY

Buckley, Thomas H. *The United States and the Washington Conference, 1921–1922.* Knoxville: University of Tennessee Press, 1970.

Goldstein, Erik, and John H. Maurer, eds. *The Washington Conference, 1921–22: Naval Rivalry, East Asian Stability and the Road to Pearl Harbor.* Portland, Ore.: Frank Cass, 1994.

Murfett, Malcolm H. "Look Back in Anger: The Western Powers and the Washington Conference of 1921–22." In *Arms Limitation and Disarmament: Restraints on War, 1899–1939.*

Edited by Brian J. C. McKercher. Westport, Conn.: Praeger, 1992.

Justus D. Doenecke
John R. Probert

WASHINGTON V. GLUCKSBERG.

This case (521 U.S. 702 [1997]) addressed the question of whether or not Washington State could constitutionally prohibit doctors and others from assisting people in committing suicide. The Court of Appeals for the Ninth Circuit held that the state's ban violated the due process rights of the plaintiffs, who were in the terminal phases of painful illnesses and who desired the aid of their doctors in ending their ordeals. The Supreme Court unanimously overturned the Ninth Circuit.

Writing for the Court, Chief Justice William Rehnquist declared an examination of the "nation's history, legal traditions, and practices" revealed that an individual does not have a fundamental constitutional right to terminate his or her life. Because individuals did not have a fundamental right to commit suicide, the state could legitimately prohibit people from aiding another's suicide. The Court rejected analogies to the constitutional right to refuse unwanted medical treatment, recognized in the 1990 case of *Cruzan v. Director, Missouri Department of Health*, and the right to obtain medical intervention to cause an abortion, recognized in 1973 in *Roe v. Wade* and preserved in the 1992 case of *Planned Parenthood of Southeastern Pennsylvania v. Casey.*

Though all nine justices agreed that the Ninth Circuit should be overturned, four justices (John P. Stevens, David Souter, Ruth Bader Ginsburg, and Stephen Breyer) declined to join the chief justice's opinion for the Court. Each wrote separately to declare individual rationales and to clarify that the Court's opinion did not bar a future reconsideration of the issue.

BIBLIOGRAPHY

Rotunda, Ronald D., and John E. Nowak. *Treatise on Constitutional Law: Substance and Procedure.* 3d ed. Volume 3. St. Paul, Minn.: West, 1999.

Urofsky, Melvin I. *Lethal Judgments: Assisted Suicide and American Law.* Lawrence: University Press of Kansas, 2000.

Kent Greenfield

See also **Assisted Suicide; "Right to Die" Cases.**

WASHINGTON'S FAREWELL ADDRESS.

Having decided against serving a third term as president, George Washington faced the task of bequeathing to the nation his understanding of America. In his farewell address, which initially appeared on 19 September 1796 in but one newspaper, the retiring statesman did just this. He warned Americans against political factionalism, something he had avoided through his two terms in office. In conjunction with a call for unity at home, Washington stressed his desire to preserve a nation distinct from Europe. A little over half of the address warned Americans that political division at home might lead to entanglements abroad. Evenhandedness marked this statement, as the revered general urged citizens not to express too much hatred or fondness for any one nation. Commercial enterprise, not political ties, should govern the nation's conduct with the outside world. With the address, Washington brought his presidency to a close. Power transferred peacefully to the incoming administration, and republicanism survived its first and possibly greatest test.

BIBLIOGRAPHY
Spalding, Matthew, and Patrick J. Garrity. *A Sacred Union of Citizens: George Washington's Farewell Address and the American Character.* New York: Rowman & Littlefield, 1996.

Matthew J. Flynn

See also **Free Trade; Intervention; Isolationism; Jay's Treaty;** *and vol. 9:* **Washington's Farewell Address.**

WASTE DISPOSAL. Societies have always had to deal with waste disposal, but what those societies have defined as waste, as well as where would be that waste's ultimate destination, has varied greatly over time. Large-scale waste disposal is primarily an urban issue because of the waste disposal needs of population concentrations and the material processing and production-type activities that go on in cities. Waste is often defined as "matter out of place" and can be understood as part of a city's metabolic processes. Cities require materials to sustain their life processes and need to remove wastes resulting from consumption and processing to prevent "nuisance and hazard." Well into the nineteenth century, many American cities lacked garbage and rubbish collection services. Cities often depended on animals such as pigs, goats, and cows, or even buzzards in southern cities, to consume slops and garbage tossed into the streets by residents. In the middle of the century, health concerns stimulated such larger cities as New York to experiment with collection, often by contracting out. Contractors and municipalities often discarded wastes into nearby waterways or placed them on vacant lots on the city fringe.

Rapid urbanization in the late nineteenth century increased the volume of wastes and aroused concern over nuisances and hazards. People had always viewed garbage as a nuisance, but the public-health movement, accompanied by widespread acceptance of anticontagionist theory, emphasized the rapid disposal of organic wastes to prevent epidemics. Concern about potential disease drove municipalities to consider collection, usually by setting up their own services, granting contracts, or allowing householders to make private arrangements. By the late nineteenth century, cities were relying on contractors, although there were shifts between approaches. Cities apparently preferred contracting to municipal operation because of cost as well as the absence of a rationale for government involvement in a domain with many private operators.

During the first half of the twentieth century, municipal control over collection gradually increased to between 60 and 70 percent, largely for health and efficiency reasons. Just as they had moved from private to public provision of water because of concerns over inability of the private sector to protect against fire and illness, cities began to question leaving waste removal to contractors. Contractor collection was often disorganized, with frequent vendor changes, short-term contracts, and contractor reluctance to invest in equipment. Municipal reformers concluded that sanitation was too important to be left to profit-motivated contractors. Initially, responsibility went to departments of public health, but as the germ theory of disease replaced anticontagionism, control over the function shifted to public works departments. Increasingly, cities viewed garbage collection as an engineering rather than a public health problem, and municipal concern shifted from health to fire hazards and the prevention of nuisances such as odors and flies.

Changes in both composition of wastes (or solid wastes, as they were now called) and collection and disposal methods occurred after World War II. A major fraction of municipal solid wastes before the war had been ashes, but as heating oil and natural gas displaced coal, ashes became less important. The solid wastes generated by individuals did not decrease, however, because there were sharp rises in the amount of nonfood materials, such as packaging and glass. Another change occurred in regard to disposal sites. Before the war, cities had disposed of wastes in dumps, on pig farms (a form of recycling), by ocean dumping, or by incineration. A few cities used garbage reduction or composting. For nuisance and health reasons, cities found these methods unacceptable, and in the decades after 1945, they adopted the so-called sanitary landfill method of waste disposal, which involved the systematic placing of wastes in the ground using a technology such as a bulldozer or a bull clam shovel. The sanitary landfill, or tipping, had been widely used in Great Britain before the war. In the late 1930s, Jean Vincenz, director of public works in Fresno, California, had developed it. Vincenz used the sanitary landfill to deal with solid wastes at army camps during the war. Public works and public health professionals and municipal engineers viewed the technique as a final solution to the waste disposal problem. Between 1945 and 1960, the number of fills increased from 100 to 1,400.

A further development, starting in the late 1950s, involved a rise in private contracting. Firms that provided economies of scale, sophisticated management, and efficient collection absorbed smaller companies and replaced municipal operations. Sharp rises in the costs of disposal as well as a desire to shift labor and operating costs to the private sector also played a role. In the 1980s, private contracting grew rapidly because it was the most cost-effective method available.

In the 1960s, the environmental movement raised questions about solid-waste disposal and the safety of sanitary landfills, both in terms of the environment and health. In the 1950s, states had strengthened environmental regulations, while the federal government followed with the Solid Waste Act in 1965 and the Resource Conservation and Recovery Act in 1976. Higher standards for landfills raised costs. Increasingly, society sought disposal methods such as recycling that appeared protective of health and environmentally benign. By the last decade of the twentieth century, as new techniques for utilizing recycled materials and controlling waste generation developed, society seemed on its way to a more sustainable balance.

The tendency of Americans to consume ever-increasing amounts of goods, however, has dampened the rate of improvement. For instance, Americans are discarding an increasing number of computers every year. Monitors especially consistitute an environmental danger because they contain lead, mercury, and cadmium. If disposed of in landfills, they may leach these dangerous metals into the soil and groundwater. Therefore, concerned consumers are pushing manufacturers to create collection and recycling programs for outdated equipment.

Nevertheless, recycling programs have not proven the anticipated panacea for problems in solid-waste disposal. Quite simply, the supply of recyclable materials generally outstrips demand. A strong market exists for aluminum cans, but newspaper, plastic, and glass remain less attractive to buyers. For example, removing the ink from newspapers is expensive, and the wood fibers in paper do not stand up well to repeated processing. Thus, just because it is theoretically possible to recycle a material, it does not mean that recycling actually will happen. This difficulty suggests that consumers hoping to limit the amount of material in landfills would do well to buy products with less initial packaging and of materials that recycle easily.

BIBLIOGRAPHY

Luton, Larry S. *The Politics of Garbage: A Community Perspective on Solid Waste Policy Making.* Pittsburgh, Pa.: University of Pittsburgh Press, 1996.

Melosi, Martin V. *The Sanitary City: Urban Infrastructure in America from Colonial Times to the Present.* Baltimore: Johns Hopkins University Press, 2000.

———. *Effluent America: Cities, Industry, Energy, and the Environment.* Pittsburgh, Pa.: University of Pittsburgh Press, 2001.

Whitaker, Jennifer Seymour. *Salvaging the Land of Plenty: Garbage and the American Dream.* New York: W. Morrow, 1994.

Joel A. Tarr / A. E.

See also **Environmental Business; Environmental Movement; Environmental Protection Agency; Food, Fast; Haz-** ardous Waste; Plastics; Printing Industry; Recycling; Water Pollution.

WATER LAW. Central issues in the history of U.S. water law are: (1) the development and evolution of state systems—both legal doctrines and institutions—for determining ownership and for allocating use of water and (2) the impact of those systems upon industrial, agricultural, and urban development. Colonists who settled along the Atlantic coast encountered in the "new world" a landscape crisscrossed with rivers. To create order upon this landscape, they applied the English common-law riparian doctrine, which recognized the right of riverbank owners to use the water in a river in ways that would not diminish or alter the river for downstream users—a right to the "natural flow" of the stream. A riparian owner could, for example, use the river for fishing, watering stock, cleaning, or travel, but could not alter the course of the river, reduce its volume, or pollute it so that downstream owners could not reuse the water. This riparian right could not be sold independently of the land adjoining the waterway, and all riparian owners along a river had an equal right to use the water.

The common law natural-flow regime was suited for places where demand for water was low, as was the situation in the East during much of the colonial period. In the eighteenth century, colonies, and then states, began to chip away at the common law by passing mill acts that allowed mill owners to build dams by making them pay damages when the dams overflowed on the lands of upstream neighbors. By the beginning of the nineteenth century, the natural-flow doctrine had become an impediment to industrial development, which required the use and diversion of large amounts of water to power manufacturing plants and mills. To accommodate changing economic circumstances, courts modified riparian law further by fashioning a reasonable use doctrine that allowed riparian owners to use up, alter, or divert a portion of the stream for reasonable purposes, typically defined as the usual practices or best interests of a community. These legal changes were both the product and cause of conflicts over water use in a rapidly changing world.

While courts in the eastern states were modifying the common law in light of changing economic circumstances, miners in the western states were developing an informal water-rights regime based not on riparianism, but on first use. The doctrine of prior appropriation recognizes that the person who diverts the water first and puts it to a recognized beneficial use has the best, most senior right to the water. Subsequent users can claim rights to any water still remaining in the stream. This right is not limited to riparian landowners, and it is a vested property interest that one can sell, trade, or give away. Reservation of federal land for a particular purpose (for instance, a national park) includes an implicit reservation of the amount of yet unappropriated, appurtenant water necessary to meet the purposes of the reservation.

Courts, and then state legislatures, ratified the miners' system. Today, almost all western states, the major exception being California, have adopted prior appropriation by statute. Some states also recognize, through case law, riparian rights. Many historians explain the widespread use of prior appropriation in western states by pointing to the relative scarcity of water in the West and the need to divert water to places where it did not exist. Others point to different local economic conditions or to the difference in the nature of nineteenth-century water use in the West (consumptive) and in the East (for power generation).

The legal rules for groundwater diversion evolved independent of these surface water doctrines because little was known about the relationship between groundwater and surface water in the nineteenth century. Courts developed several distinct approaches to groundwater law including variations of the riparian reasonable use rules and prior appropriation. Today, several states, particularly in the west, use sophisticated state or local management systems that authorize and supervise the pumping levels of groundwater users.

Because bodies of water do not recognize the political boundaries humans have created, states have developed administrative structures—such as levee, irrigation, and swamp drainage districts—that allow people within a region to jointly make decisions affecting shared water resources. States have also entered into agreements with each other to determine the allocation and use of water that moves across state boundaries. The Colorado River Compact is an example of one such interstate agreement. States, however, do not have absolute power to determine water rights or use. The Federal Government has rights to water through reservation and has the responsibility under the U.S. Constitution to protect and regulate navigable and coastal waters. To fulfill these responsibilities, Congress has passed far-reaching legislation such as the Clean Water Act and the Coastal Zone Management Act. Finally, Indian tribes have rights to water under their treaties with the federal government.

BIBLIOGRAPHY

Baxter, John O. *Dividing New Mexico's Waters, 1700–1912*. Albuquerque: University of New Mexico Press, 1997.

Goldfarb, William. *Water Law*. 2d ed. Chelsea, Mich.: Lewis Publishers, 1988.

Miller, Char, ed. *Fluid Arguments: Five Centuries of Western Water Conflict*. Tucson: University of Arizona Press, 2001.

Pisani, Donald J. *To Reclaim A Divided West: Water, Law, and Public Policy, 1848–1902*. Albuquerque: University of New Mexico Press, 1992.

Rose, Carol. "Energy and Efficiency in the Realignment of Common-Law Water Rights." *Journal of Legal Studies* 19 (June 1990): 261–296.

Shurts, John. *Indian Reserved Water Rights: The Winters Doctrine in Its Social and Legal Context, 1880s–1930s*. Norman: University of Oklahoma Press, 2000.

Steinberg, Theodore. *Nature Incorporated: Industrialization and the Waters of New England*. New York: Cambridge University Press, 1991.

Cynthia R. Poe

See also **Boundary Disputes Between States; Clean Water Act; Common Law; National Waterways Commission; River and Harbor Improvements; Rivers; Water Supply and Conservation.**

WATER POLLUTION. Extensive water pollution in the United States began in the nineteenth century as a result of urbanization, industrial development, and modern agricultural practices. Although lumbering and mining despoiled individual lakes and rivers, the nation's cities were the sites of the most severe pollution. Early industrial by-products joined human sewage and animal waste to foul drinking water supplies. By the early 1800s, even horses declined New York City's public water, and one-quarter of Boston's wells produced undrinkable water. Severe epidemics of the waterborne diseases cholera and typhoid fever swept through major cities, most notably New York in 1832.

The early response to such pollution was not so much to clean the water but rather to build reservoirs and aqueducts to import fresh water for direct delivery to neighborhoods and even some individual homes. Cities built large sewer systems to flush these waters away, usually either out to sea or down a nearby river. Sewers thus spread the previously more localized pollution, often fouling the water sources of other cities.

In the 1890s, scientists decisively linked many diseases, including typhoid and cholera, to the presence of human waste in water supplies. Cities began to filter their drinking water with remarkable results. The national urban death rate from typhoid, 36 per 100,000 in 1900, dropped to only 3 per 100,000 by 1935 and was virtually nonexistent by the twentieth century's end. The urban water projects that combined filtration, delivery, and disposal ranked among the largest public works projects in the nation's history. Chicago, for example, reversed the direction of the Chicago and Calumet Rivers, so by 1900 they no longer carried the city's waste into Lake Michigan, its primary source of fresh water. By the end of the twentieth century, New York City moved about 1.5 billion gallons of fresh water through more than 300 miles of aqueducts and 27 artificial lakes.

The industrial pollution of bodies of water not used for drinking proved more difficult to control. In 1912, Congress charged the Public Health Service (PHS) with investigating water pollution. Two years later, the PHS established the first water quality standards. In the 1920s, the service investigated industrial pollution but with little effect. State governments retained the primary responsibility for water regulation. Following the lead of Pennsylvania, many states sought to balance environmental quality with the needs of industry by giving relatively high protection to waters used for drinking supplies while allowing others to be freely used for waste disposal. New Deal programs provided significant federal funds to water pollution control, and over the course of the 1930s the population served by sewage treatment nearly doubled. But those programs left pollution control in the hands of state governments.

After World War II, continued urban pollution and runoff from artificial fertilizers increasingly used in agriculture degraded the water quality of many lakes. Eutrophication occurs when plants and bacteria grow at abnormally high rates due to elevated quantities of nitrogen or phosphorus. The decomposition of this elevated biomass consumes much of the water's oxygen, often leading to a cascade of changes in aquatic ecosystems. Many species of fish grow scarce or die off altogether, and algae "blooms" can make water unsafe to swim in or to drink. Although small urban lakes suffered from eutrophication as early as the 1840s, after World War II, population growth, increasing nitrogen-rich agricultural runoff, and the addition of phosphates to detergents polluted even bodies of water as large as Lake Erie. By 1958, the bottom portion of a 2,600-square-mile portion of the lake was completely without oxygen, and algae grew in mats two feet thick over hundreds of square miles more. The nation's economic prosperity intensified problems, as pollution from heavy industry made some rivers and streams lifeless. In the 1960s, Cleveland authorities pronounced the Cuyahoga River a fire hazard, and at the end of the decade the river actually caught on fire. The more mobile and long-lasting industrial products polluted even waters remote from cities and industry. DDT, other pesticides and synthetic chemicals, mercury, and acid rain threatened numerous species and previously unaffected lakes and streams.

Such manifestations of a deepening pollution crisis prompted environmentalists and lawmakers to redouble pollution-control efforts. The major response, the 1972 Clean Water Act, shifted responsibility for the nation's waterways and water supply to the federal government. In the following decades, federal funds and regulations issued under the act's authority significantly raised standards for water purity. Repeatedly amended, the act halted the rate of water pollution, even in the face of decades of population and economic growth. Most industries and municipalities greatly reduced their pollution discharges, with the consequent reversal of the eutrophication of many bodies of water, including Lake Erie. Nevertheless, "nonpoint" pollution sources, such as agricultural runoff and vehicle exhaust, continued to degrade water quality. The act made virtually no progress in improving groundwater contamination. At the end of the twentieth century, regulating groundwater quality and grappling with nonpoint pollution remained the most formidable obstacles to those seeking to reverse water pollution.

BIBLIOGRAPHY

Elkind, Sarah S. *Bay Cities and Water Politics: The Battle for Resources in Boston and Oakland.* Lawrence: University Press of Kansas, 1998.

Melosi, Martin V. *The Sanitary City: Urban Infrastructure in America from Colonial Times to the Present.* Baltimore: Johns Hopkins University Press, 2000.

Outwater, Alice. *Water: A Natural History.* New York: Basic Books, 1996.

Benjamin H. Johnson

See also **Clean Water Act; Conservation; Sanitation, Environmental; Waste Disposal; Water Law; Waterways, Inland.**

WATER SUPPLY AND CONSERVATION.

Water covers about three-quarters of the earth and makes up more than two-thirds of the human body. Without water (which supports animal habitats, the food chain, and human life) life as we understand it would be impossible. An abundant and invaluable resource, water can be poisoned and poorly used.

Each of us lives in a watershed, a landmass that drains into a body of water. Natural forces, such as gravity and condensation, distribute rainwater throughout the watershed, giving life to the plants and animals within.

When Europeans first began settling the New World, natural resources were considered basically inexhaustible. Over the centuries, however, trees were clear cut, animals over-hunted, and water used without concern for CONSERVATION or for maintaining it in an unpolluted state. As settlers pushed westward, they continued earlier practices—using (sometimes abusing) natural resources without thought for the future.

The largest damage human beings caused to the environment came with the INDUSTRIAL REVOLUTION. Factories dumped toxic materials freely into waterways and filled the air with particulate pollutants. Expansionists cut down trees to build railroads and settle new lands without regard to watersheds or the disruption of ecosystems. Forests, which are important to watersheds because of their ability to absorb water and prevent flooding, were completely cut down for timber throughout the country. The business of men was deemed more important than the business of nature, and those few voices that spoke out against expansion were labeled antiprogress.

Although Yellowstone, Sequoia, and Yosemite National Parks were created in the late nineteenth century, it was not until Theodore Roosevelt assumed the presidency in 1901 that a widespread program of conservation began. The word "conservation" probably originates with Gifford Pinchot, head of the United States Forest Service during the administration of Theodore Roosevelt. Roosevelt, greatly influenced by environmentalists such as John Muir, took advantage of the Forest Reserve Act of 1891 that permitted the president to set aside lands as national forests. Presidents William Henry Harrison,

Grover Cleveland, and William McKinley had transferred some 50 million acres of timberland into the federal reserve system prior to Roosevelt; the conservation movement fully supported Roosevelt as he expanded these efforts, eventually adding another 150 million acres. Congress would complement Roosevelt's measures in 1911 with the WEEKS ACT, which allowed for multiple uses of public lands. Conservation in this era was not done for the benefit of nature itself, but for the benefit of people. A broad-based deep respect for nature, or even a firmly preservationist ethic, was in the future.

The Dust Bowl

The DUST BOWL of the 1930s would show Americans how nature could inflict more harm to man than man could to nature. Already in the midst of the Great Depression, the West and Southwest experienced lengthy droughts. Drought is actually the most deadly natural phenomenon in the world; agriculture eventually collapses as crops will not grow without water, the parched topsoil blows away, and animals and humans starve. The years of drought in the 1930s hurt not just the farmer, but all those who depended on him. Crop yields reached all-time lows, and migrant workers, without crops to help harvest, quickly became vagrants.

Franklin Delano Roosevelt, elected president in 1932, did not hesitate to apply his New Deal to nature. With the help of Congress, he created the TENNESSEE VALLEY AUTHORITY (TVA) and the CIVILIAN CONSERVATION CORPS (CCC). The TVA built dams, at once helping to preserve the natural resources of the Tennessee Valley, but also inadvertently destroying some of them. The CCC enlisted able-bodied young men to dig ditches, plant trees, and beautify parks.

Silent Spring

World War II and the Cold War put the issue of conservation on the backburner for some time, but a new movement would emerge in the 1960s, initiated by the writings and efforts of one woman. By far the most influential piece of literature written on the subject, Rachel Carson's Silent Spring (1962) forecast the terrible consequences of the damage being done to the environment by field chemicals such as DDT (dichloro-diphenyl-trichloro-ethane). Carson, a marine biologist, had studied the effects of chemicals and pesticides on plants, animals, and water. She found that these chemicals disturbed the natural balance of the ecosystem, poisoning birds and fish, and endangering the humans who eat them. "The most alarming of all man's assault's upon the environment is the contamination of air, earth, rivers, and sea with dangerous and even lethal materials." Carson wrote, "This pollution is for the most part irrecoverable; the chain of evil it initiates not only in the world that must support life but in living tissues is for the most part irreversible. In this now universal contamination of the environment, chemicals are the sinister and little recognized partners of radiation in changing the very nature of the world—the very nature of its life" (p. 6).

Silent Spring sent a shock wave throughout the nation. Many people had assumed that the government protected them from harmful substances such as DDT. They were outraged to learn that industry might be poisoning them. The outcry was tremendous, the environmentalist movement grew, and Congress was forced to act.

Legislation and Other Government Initiatives

In 1969 Congress passed the National Environment Policy Act. This Act established a general policy for protecting the environment; it required that all government agencies give proper consideration to the environment before initiating or approving projects. In 1970 Congress passed the Clean Air Act and the OCCUPATIONAL SAFETY AND HEALTH ACT. The Clean Air Act regulates air emissions from area, stationary, and mobile sources. The Occupational Safety and Health Act provides for worker safety, protecting workers from toxic chemicals, excessive noise, mechanical dangers, poor climate conditions, and unsanitary settings. The Occupational Safety and Health Administration was created to enforce these standards nationwide.

In 1970, under President Richard Nixon, the ENVIRONMENTAL PROTECTION AGENCY (EPA) was formed. The EPA was established to enforce environmental standards, conduct research, help other organizations in reducing pollution through grants and technical assistance, and make recommendations to the president and the Council of Environmental Quality on ways to protect the environment. William D. Ruckelshaus was appointed the EPA's first administrator; he promised that the agency would "be as forceful as the laws that Congress has provided." Since its formation, the EPA has taken an active role in reducing hazardous emissions, restricting toxic wastes, and cleaning up oil spills and other environmental disasters.

In 1972, Congress passed the Federal Water Pollution Control Act Amendments, which would come to be known as the Clean Water Act (CWA). This Act established standards for regulating water pollution and gave the EPA the power to develop pollution control programs. The CWA also set water quality standards and limited contaminants in surface water. Industries were required to obtain a permit to discharge pollutants into water and were fined if they were found to be dumping waste into bodies of water.

The Act proved to be very effective. According to the EPA, in 1972 only a third of the nation's waters were safe for fishing and swimming; that had increased to two-thirds by the early twenty-first century. Wetland losses were estimated to be about 460,000 acres a year, whereas today they are estimated to be between 70,000 and 90,000 acres a year. Agricultural runoff in 1972 was estimated to cause 2.25 billion tons of soil to erode and phosphorus and nitrogen to be deposited in many waters; runoff has been cut by about one billion tons annually, and phosphorus and nitrogen deposits have decreased.

Congress also passed the Federal Insecticide, Fungicide, and Rodenticide Act in 1972. This Act authorized the EPA to study the effects of pesticides and to regulate their distribution. Users, from the small-time farmer to large utility companies, were required to register with the EPA if purchasing pesticides. Later amendments to the Act forced pesticide users to take certification exams. In addition, all pesticides used must be registered with the EPA.

The Endangered Species Act of 1973 was the first law passed specifically to protect plants, animals, and their habitats. The Act created two lists: one for endangered species and one for threatened species; anyone can petition for a plant or animal to appear on the list. Currently, 632 species are listed as "endangered"; 190 are listed as "threatened." Killing, trading, or transporting any of these species is expressly prohibited. The Act also allows the EPA to issue emergency suspensions of certain pesticides that may adversely affect endangered species.

The Safe Drinking Water Act of 1974 authorized the EPA to establish standards for owners or operators of public water systems. In 1976, Congress passed the TOXIC SUBSTANCES CONTROL ACT, which gave the EPA the power to track the 75,000 industrial chemicals being produced by or imported into the United States. This Act was accompanied by the Resource Conservation and Recovery Act, which granted the EPA the authority to regulate hazardous waste from "cradle to grave." Later amendments provided for the regulation of underground tanks storing hazardous materials such as petroleum and for the phasing out of waste disposal on land.

The 1980 Comprehensive Environmental Response, Compensation, and Liability Act provided a "SUPERFUND" for the EPA. The Act allows the EPA to respond quickly to oil spills and other disasters when those responsible cannot be found, or when the situation has become uncontrollable. The EPA can later recover costs from parties deemed responsible. This Act was strengthened by the Oil Pollution Act of 1990—a response to the *Exxon Valdez* disaster off of Prince William Sound in Alaska.

Conservation has also been advanced through management techniques. The Pollution Prevention Act of 1990 incorporated the efforts of government and industry to find cost-effective ways to reduce pollution. The Act made it easier for industries to comply with government regulations by opening the door for innovative operating strategies.

International Efforts

The Kyoto Protocol, which opened for signature before the United Nations in 1998, called for thirty-eight industrial countries to reduce their greenhouse gas emissions (which are thought to destroy earth's ozone layer, thus leading to global warming) by an average of 5.2 percent below 1990 levels by 2008–2012, including a 7 percent reduction by the United States. President George W. Bush has refused to sign the treaty. In May 2001, seventeen national science academies urged acceptance of Kyoto, declaring that "it is now evident that human activities are already contributing adversely to global climate change. Business as usual is no longer a viable option." In an address to the National Oceanic and Atmospheric Administration in February 2002, Bush called for voluntary action to slow the rising use of greenhouse gases.

Initially, the Bush administration had also expressed doubts as to how much of global warming was actually caused by humans. But in a dramatic turnaround in May 2002, the administration blamed human action for global warming for the very first time. Although Bush still declined to sign the treaty, a report was sent to the United Nations outlining the effects that global warming may have on the American environment.

Terrorism has brought a grim new face to conservation and preservation of resources. Fears have been expressed by both the government and the public that terrorists may, for example, try to contaminate drinking water. In June 2002, EPA administrator Christie Todd Whitman announced the first round of water security grants, part of a $53-million package designed to help water utilities across the nation address susceptibilities. Whitman noted that there are "168,000 public drinking water facilities," alerting the nation to possible widescale contamination. The grants will be divided among approximately 400 different areas. "These grants," Whitman declared, "will help ensure that the water people rely on is safe and secure."

BIBLIOGRAPHY

Brands, H. W. *TR: The Last Romantic*. New York: Basic Books, 1997.

Budiansky, Stephen. *Nature's Keepers: The New Science of Nature Management*. New York: Free Press, 1995.

Carson, Rachel. *Silent Spring*. Boston: Houghton Mifflin, 1962.

Findley, Roger W., and Farber, Daniel A. *Environmental Law in a Nutshell*. St. Paul, Minn.: West Publishing, 1983.

Gore, Albert. *Earth in the Balance: Ecology and the Human Spirit*. Boston: Houghton Mifflin, 1992.

Richardson, Joy. *The Water Cycle*. New York: Franklin Watts, 1992.

Snow, Donald, ed. *Voices from the Environmental Movement: Perspectives for a New Era*. Washington, D.C.: Island Press, 1992.

Stanley, Phyllis M. *Collective Biographies: American Environmental Heroes*. Springfield, N.J.: Enslow, 1996.

Weber, Michael L., and Judith A. Gradwohl. *The Wealth of Oceans*. New York: Norton, 1995.

David Burner
Ross Rosenfeld

See also **Clean Air Act; Clean Water Act; Endangered Species; Forest Service; Water Pollution; Yellowstone National Park; Yosemite National Park.**

WATERGATE. The largest scandal of Richard M. Nixon's presidency unfolded with the burglary on 17 June 1972 of the National Democratic Committee headquarters in the Watergate apartment-office complex in Washington, D.C. The burglars were employees of the Committee for the Re-election of the President (CRP, called "CREEP" by Nixon's opponents) and were supervised by members of the White House staff. Watergate came to symbolize the efforts of the Nixon administration to subvert the democratic order through criminal acts; the suppression of civil liberties; the levying of domestic warfare against political opponents through espionage and sabotage, discriminatory income tax audits, and other punitive executive sanctions; and attempted intimidation of the news media. President Nixon's direct role in White House efforts to cover up involvement in the Watergate break-in was revealed in a tape of a 23 June 1972 conversation with White House chief of staff H. R. Haldeman, in which Nixon discussed a plan to have the CIA pressure the FBI to cease investigation of the Watergate case by claiming that national security secrets would be threatened if the Bureau widened its investigations. It was after this so-called "smoking gun" tape was made public on 6 August 1974 that President Nixon resigned from office on 9 August 1974.

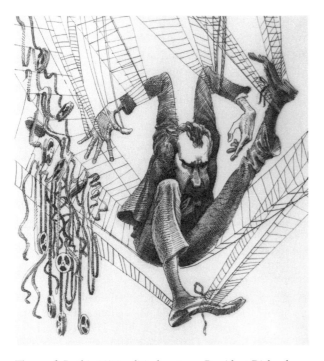

Trapped. In this 1974 political cartoon, President Richard Nixon is caught in a spider's web; tape recordings dangle at his side. LIBRARY OF CONGRESS

Beginnings

Watergate's roots can be traced to White House disappointment with the 1970 congressional elections. Fears that they foretold Nixon's possible defeat in 1972 were aggravated by massive antiwar demonstrations in Washington in 1971. These demonstrations were similar, the Nixon White House believed, to those that had brought down Lyndon B. Johnson's presidency. In an atmosphere of a state of siege, White House special counsel Charles W. Colson developed a list of enemies, including several hundred persons from various walks of life. To cope with the menaces it perceived, the administration recruited undercover agents and made plans for domestic surveillance.

After leaks to the press had led to news accounts, in May 1969, of secret American air bombing raids in neutral Cambodia, the telephones of reporters and of the staff aides of Henry A. Kissinger, then national security assistant to the president, were wiretapped. The White House was further jarred by the publication in June 1971 in the *New York Times* and other newspapers of the "Pentagon Papers," a confidential Defense Department study of decision making in the Vietnam War. In response, the White House increased the number of operatives trained in security and intelligence and established a "plumbers" unit to prevent "leaks." The Plumbers included E. Howard Hunt Jr., a former CIA agent, and G. Gordon Liddy, a former assistant district attorney in Dutchess County, New York. To secure information to prosecute or discredit Daniel Ellsberg, who had released the "Pentagon Papers," Hunt and other operatives in September 1971 broke into the office of Lewis Fielding, Ellsberg's psychiatrist, where they photographed records and papers.

In the first quarter of 1972, CRP raised unprecedented sums, from which various White House individuals, including Liddy, could draw directly. During the early presidential primaries the Plumbers and their hirelings engaged in espionage and sabotage against the candidacy of Senator Edmund S. Muskie, then considered the strongest potential Democratic presidential nominee. After Muskie's campaign foundered, similar activities were perpetrated against the two remaining leading candidates, Senator George McGovern, the eventual nominee, and Senator Hubert H. Humphrey. Liddy and others devised plans to disrupt the national Democratic convention and, through various contrived acts, to identify McGovern's candidacy with hippies, homosexuals, and draft evaders.

In January 1972 Attorney General John N. Mitchell, White House counsel John W. Dean III, and Jeb Stuart Magruder, an aide to White House Chief of Staff H. R. Haldeman and, in actuality, the chief administrator of CRP, attended a meeting held at the Justice Department. At that meeting Liddy presented a $1 million budgeted plan for electronic surveillance, photography of documents, and other activities for the approaching campaign. The plan was rejected as too expensive. At a second meeting in February, Liddy presented a revised plan and reduced budget. The approved plan centered on bugging

Watergate Committee. Chief counsel Samuel Dash (*second from right*) sits with (*left to right*) Senators Edward Gurney, Howard Baker, Sam Ervin, and Herman Talmadge. © CORBIS

Democratic National Committee headquarters at the Miami convention as well as the headquarters of the eventual Democratic presidential nominee. But the top priority target was the Democratic National Committee's headquarters at the Watergate complex in Washington and especially the office of the chairman, Lawrence R. O'Brien, whom the White House regarded as the Democrats' most professional political operative and a formidable competitor.

On the night of 27 May 1972 Liddy, Hunt, and James W. McCord Jr., another former CIA operative who had joined the Plumbers, along with a six-man group—chiefly Cuban exiles from Miami led by a former Hunt associate, Bernard L. Barker—taped doors leading to the Democratic headquarters, wiretapped the telephones in the offices, stole some documents, and photographed others. They subsequently monitored the bugs while making futile attempts to break into McGovern's Washington headquarters. Since one tap had been placed improperly in the initial break-in, a Plumbers team returned to the Watergate Democratic headquarters on 17 June. Frank Wills, a security guard at the complex, noticed that some doors had been taped open and removed the tape. When he later returned and found doors retaped, he summoned

the Washington police, and the five burglars, including McCord, were arrested and booked. E. Howard Hunt's White House telephone number was found on the person of two of the burglars, the first indication of White House involvement in the burglary.

The Cover-Up

A cover-up began (and never ended) in order to destroy incriminating evidence, obstruct investigations and, above all, halt any spread of scandal that might lead to the president. In his first public statement concerning Watergate on 29 August, Nixon declared that White House counsel John W. Dean III had "conducted a complete investigation of all leads" and had concluded that "no one in the White House staff" was "involved." Dean in fact coordinated the cover-up.

Hunt and four of the burglars pleaded guilty to all charges; McCord and Liddy stood trial and were convicted (30 January 1973) in the U.S. District Court of Judge John J. Sirica. Throughout the trial Sirica indicated that he believed that more than the seven men were involved. On 23 March, Sirica released a letter to him from McCord, in which McCord stated that higher-ups in CRP and the White House were involved, that the de-

John Dean. The fired White House counsel (*background*) is sworn in by Senator Sam Ervin, the colorful Senate Watergate committee chairman, on 25 June 1973, before the start of five days of testimony that proved devastating to the president. © CORBIS

fendants had been pressured to plead guilty, and that perjury had been committed at the trial. The president repeatedly professed ignorance of CRP and White House involvement in Watergate. However, his claims were eventually challenged when specific aspects of his own conduct were revealed in criminal trials of his associates, in investigations by the Senate Watergate committee (chaired by Senator Sam Ervin), in staff studies by the House Judiciary Committee, and in tapes of White House conversations.

In statements before the Senate Watergate committee, Dean revealed that the president had promised clemency to Hunt and had said that it would be "no problem" to raise the "million dollars or more" necessary to keep Hunt and other defendants silent. In an address on 30 April 1973 the president accepted "responsibility" for the Watergate events but denied any advance knowledge of them or involvement in their cover-up. A steady procession of White House aides and Justice Department officials resigned and were indicted, convicted (including Mitchell, Dean, Haldeman, and John D. Ehrlichman), and imprisoned. Nixon himself was named an unindicted coconspirator by the federal grand jury in the Watergate investigation, and the U.S. Supreme Court allowed that finding to stand. Relentless probing by Special Watergate Prosecutor Archibald Cox led Nixon to order his firing. Both Attorney General Elliot Richardson and Deputy Attorney General William Ruckelshaus resigned, refusing

to carry out Nixon's order. Robert H. Bork, the new Acting Attorney General, fired Cox. Leon Jaworski, Cox's successor, and the House Judiciary Committee, which considered impeachment of the president, were repeatedly rebuffed in requests for tapes and other evidence.

The impeachment charges that were ultimately brought against the president asserted that he had engaged in a "course of conduct" designed to obstruct justice in the Watergate case, and that in establishing the Plumbers and through other actions and inaction, he had failed to uphold the law. On 9 August 1974, faced with imminent impeachment, Nixon resigned as president. On 8 September 1974 his successor, Gerald R. Ford, pardoned Nixon for all federal crimes he "committed or may have committed or taken part in" while in office.

From the time of his resignation to his death in April 1994 Richard Nixon devoted much of his energy to rescuing his reputation from the long shadow of Watergate. For many Americans, acceptance of Ford's pardon by Nixon brought the presumption of felony guilt. Nixon fought attempts to make public his papers as well as the Watergate tapes. In public forums after his resignation Nixon minimized the ethical and legal misconduct of his staff and himself, focusing attention instead on the political context that led to his resignation. In 1990 Nixon's benefactors opened the Richard Nixon Library and Birthplace in Yorba Linda, California, without the benefit of the president's official papers, which are held, by act of Congress, in the Maryland facilities of the National Archives and Records Administration. After Nixon's death the tapes were made public and revealed an extensive pattern of Nixon's personal involvement and criminal action in Watergate.

BIBLIOGRAPHY

Bernstein, Carl, and Bob Woodward. *All the President's Men.* New York: Simon and Schuster, 1974.

Kutler, Stanley I. *The Wars of Watergate: The Last Crisis of Richard Nixon.* New York: Knopf, 1990.

Lukas, J. Anthony. *Nightmare: The Underside of the Nixon Years.* New York: Viking, 1976.

Rather, Dan, and Gary Paul Gates. *The Palace Guard.* New York: Harper and Row, 1974.

White, Theodore H. *Breach of Faith: The Fall of Richard Nixon.* New York: Atheneum, 1975.

Richard M. Flanagan
Louis W. Koenig

See also **Impeachment; Nixon Tapes; Nixon, Resignation of;** *and vol. 9:* **Nixon's Watergate Investigation Address.**

WATERPOWER is the product of falling water acting by impact, weight, or reaction on a wheel. For many centuries the simpler forms of waterwheels were made of wood and varied in diameter and breadth of rim, with flat or concave paddles or hollow troughs, known as buckets, attached around the circumference. Power came directly from water flow past a streamside (or boat-affixed) paddlewheel with paddles that dipped into the stream current. The noria, probably the most ancient of waterwheels and still widely used throughout the world, was of this type; it raised water from the powering stream by means of small vessels attached around the circumference.

A far more common and useful method of generating waterpower was to locate the wheel near an abrupt descent in the streambed (that is, a waterfall). By raising a simple dam of earth, rocks, or timber across the stream above the waterfall, the amount of descent was increased. The water was diverted into a ditch called a race and conveyed to the waterwheel, located beside or beneath the mill at a convenient site downstream. With a descent of several feet, a modest wheel in a small brook might deliver as much as two to three horsepower, sufficient to drive a small gristmill, sawmill, or fulling mill.

The watermills that served the frontier settlers of eighteenth- and nineteenth-century America greatly eased the more arduous tasks. The most common watermill on the American frontier was the gristmill, by which grain was reduced between millstones to the meal that was the basis of the settlers' diet. Later, the sawmill made it possible to replace log cabins with wood-frame dwellings.

Before the development of steam-driven machinery early in the nineteenth century, the alternative to the water-powered mill was the windmill. But the numerous and extensive river systems of the United States, particularly along the Atlantic coast, provided a wealth of waterpower. Waterpower fueled the early industrialization of the eastern seaboard. By 1840 there were well over fifty thousand gristmills and sawmills in use, half of them in the Middle Atlantic states and New England.

Waterpower complexes, of which the largest were found on the Merrimack and Connecticut Rivers in New England, provided the power base of some of the country's largest industrial centers, with the mills at Lowell, Massachusetts, driven by the powerful Pawtucket Falls, as the prototype and exemplar. These great waterpower complexes, dating from the 1820s, used great wooden wheels fifteen or more feet in diameter and of equal or greater width. These so-called breast-wheels were quite similar to the paddlewheels of river steamboats, except for the wooden troughs that replaced the flat paddles. The invention of the turbine marked an advance in efficiency, economy, and rotating speeds. Developed in Europe, particularly by the French engineer Benoit Fourneyron (1827), the turbine was improved in the United States, notably at Lowell, where Uriah A. Boyden, in 1844, and James B. Francis, in 1851, developed the most common type of modern water turbine. The other significant type of water turbine, the "impulse" turbine, for use in small streams that fall very steeply, was also developed in the United States.

After 1860 the rapid extension of the railway network doomed the widely distributed industries located along streams in small towns. As the advantages of large urban centers became apparent—increased labor supply; financial, commercial, and supply services; and transportation facilities—the centralization of manufacturing industries in large cities gathered momentum. Since few large cities possessed appreciable waterpower, their growth depended on steam power and access to coal, which was widely available through rail and water transport. Marked advances in the efficiency of steam engines and boilers in the late nineteenth century negated the cost advantage long enjoyed by waterpower. By 1870 steam power passed waterpower capacity in manufacturing nationwide, and in succeeding decades it left waterpower far behind.

The success of the Niagara hydroelectric power project of the early 1890s signaled the beginning of a new age in the history of waterpower. Based on the electrical transmission of energy, hydroelectric power bore little significant relation to the traditional, direct-drive waterpower in which each establishment, small or large, had its own power plant, with most establishments leasing the use of the water by which its wheels were driven. After 1900 hydroelectric power was produced in plants of enormous capacity and distributed over long distances by high-tension power lines.

BIBLIOGRAPHY

Hunter, Louis C. *A History of Industrial Power in the United States, 1780–1930.* Charlottesville: University Press of Virginia, 1979.

McKelvey, Blake. *Rochester, the Water-Power City, 1812–1854.* Cambridge, Mass.: Harvard University Press, 1945.

Pisani, Donald J. *To Reclaim a Divided West: Water, Law, and Public Policy, 1848–1902.* Albuquerque: University of New Mexico Press, 1992.

Pugh, Brinley. *The Hydraulic Age: Public Power Supplies Before Electricity.* London: Mechanical Engineering Publications, 1980.

*Louis C. Hunter/*A. R.

See also **Flour Milling; Industrial Revolution; Sawmills; Textiles;** *and vol. 9:* **Power.**

WATERWAYS, INLAND. The United States has an outstanding system of inland waterways, consisting of more than twenty-five thousand miles of navigable rivers and canals, of which twelve thousand miles are commercial waterways. The system, which by definition does not include the Great Lakes or coastal shipping lanes, carries more than 600 million tons of domestic freight each year. This amounts to approximately 16 percent of the total intercity freight movements in the country.

In the colonial period, water transportation was vital. The first settlements were along waterways, and countless vessels sailed the coastal and tidewater streams, serving the trade, travel, and communication needs of the colonies. The waterways also provided the initial travel routes that pioneers used to move west. Virginians and Marylanders traveled along the James and Potomac Rivers; Pennsylvanians advanced via the Susquehanna River and its tributaries; and New Englanders and New Yorkers followed the Connecticut and the Hudson–Mohawk river valleys into the interior.

After the Revolution, with the Appalachian Mountain barrier already breached by roads, the westward movement resumed. Travel by road, however, was expensive, slow, and very uncomfortable. Again the rivers supplied not only the bulk of the transportation needs but also determined the migration patterns of the trans-Appalachian settlers. The frontier population concentrated along the Ohio, the Mississippi, and other western rivers, which were soon teeming with the rude watercraft of the day.

Conflicting visions about the strategic importance of western rivers to the development of the young nation led to the first major sectional conflict among the states. In the 1783 Treaty of Paris, which had ended the Revolutionary War, Britain recognized the right of the United States to travel down the Mississippi River. Spain, however, was not a signator to the Treaty and in 1784 refused to allow American access to New Orleans. Western and southern settlers believed that use of the Mississippi was of crucial importance to the new nation. Some easterners, however, believed that westerners would have little reason to remain in the Union if they had free navigation of the river. After a year of fruitless negotiations with Spain, Congress abandoned its instructions to John Jay to insist on American navigation rights. Jay returned with a treaty that opened up Spanish markets to eastern merchants but relinquished export rights on the lower Mississippi for twenty years. The Jay-Gardoqui Treaty infuriated westerners and southerners. Congress rejected it in 1786. The question of American navigation of the Mississippi was finally settled by Pinckney's Treaty (1795), which gave Americans free access to the river. The United States acquired the whole Mississippi River Valley in 1803 with the LOUISIANA PURCHASE.

Two major developments of the early nineteenth century—steamboats and canals—enhanced the economic importance of inland waterways. The boats of the eighteenth century were propelled by wind power, water currents, and human energy. But wind power was generally unavailable on the inland waterways, and water currents went in one direction—downstream. On upstream trips, boats traveled very slowly and usually without passengers or freight. The harnessing of steam power allowed boats to carry goods and passengers in both directions on rivers and significantly reduced travel time. Following Robert Fulton's introduction of the steamboat in 1807, steamboating spread rapidly throughout the nation. It developed most fully on the western rivers, particularly after 1815, and by midcentury hundreds of steamboats regularly plied the unexcelled waterway network of the trans-Appalachian West.

Similarly, a mania for building canals swept the country in the early nineteenth century. The War of 1812 vividly demonstrated the need for improved transportation. But it was the completion of the phenomenally successful Erie Canal in New York in 1825 that touched off the rage for canals. When the canal era ended approximately twenty-five years later, there were nearly 4,000 miles of canals in the United States. Although most canal companies failed as their lines were superseded by the railroad, their contemporary economic impact in augmenting the natural waterways of the country was significant, and a few of them survived into the twentieth century, to be incorporated into the modern waterway network.

The railroad, introduced to America in 1830, came of age in the 1850s, giving increasingly effective competition to waterway transportation. In the battle for traffic after the Civil War, the railroads were the easy victors. They had the advantages of speed, directness, and continuity of service. The river shipping lines could not deter the railroad encroachments of the 1870s and 1880s. The nadir of the waterways came at the turn of the century, when the railroads were the undisputed masters of the transportation field. But before this decline, steamboating on the upper Missouri, the Red, the Arkansas, and several

Pacific Coast rivers had played a major role in the development of the West.

Just when the victory of the railroads seemed complete, however, a reemergence of the waterways occurred. This rebirth resulted from at least four factors: (1) government development of various waterways for multipurpose use, including flood control, irrigation, power production, recreation, and navigation; (2) national security considerations, reflecting the need for alternative transportation facilities, particularly following the development of submarines and their threat to oceanborne commerce; (3) a vastly improved maritime technology; and (4) the inherent economy of water transportation. The federal effort to restore the economic competitiveness of the inland waterways began in 1876 when President Grant signed the Rivers and Harbors Appropriations Act. In 1879, Congress created the Mississippi River Commission to unify development of Mississippi River navigation. Further appropriations for rivers and harbors followed.

By the turn-of-the-century, conservationists regarded waterway development as an integral component of conservation policy. But development of the waterways proceeded slowly until 1907, when President Roosevelt appointed a commission to prepare a comprehensive plan for improvement of the nation's waterways. The 1908 preliminary report of the Inland Waterways Commission and the alarming congestion of traffic on the railroads prior to World War I revealed the need for reviving the moribund waterways. As a result, the federal government not only began extensive canal and river canalization projects but also chartered the Inland Waterways Corporation in 1924 to operate a barge line on the Mississippi. Coupled with remarkable advances in marine technology—including the modern, diesel-powered tugboat; huge, special-purpose barges and tankers; and improved all-weather, day-and-night navigational systems—these developments have led to a significant return of traffic to the waterways.

As both cause and consequence of the increase in waterway traffic, the federal government, in the first three-quarters of the twentieth century, devoted increasingly greater sums to the development of navigational river and canal channels and harbors. Important twentieth-century projects included completion of the Atlantic Intracoastal and Gulf Intracoastal waterways—protected ship or barge channels stretching, in the one case, all the way from New England to the Florida Keys, excepting only a route across New Jersey, and in the other case, from Brownsville, Texas, as far as St. Marks, Florida. Other notable projects include the recanalization of the Ohio River, with new locks of 110 by 1,200 feet; the development of both the Columbia River and the St. Lawrence Seaway, the latter opened in 1959; and the opening of new channels in the South and Southwest, partly the result of the multifaceted Tennessee Valley Authority project initiated in the 1930s. Upon completion of the Tennessee–Tombigbee project in 1985, many resources were shifted to maintenance of existing waterworks. All of these programs, carried out by the U.S. Army Corps of Engineers, and not always without controversy, have been in accordance with the national transportation policy of fostering both cooperation and competition between the nation's railroads, waterways, highways, pipelines, and airlines.

BIBLIOGRAPHY

Alperin, Lynn M. *History of the Gulf Intracoastal Waterway.* Fort Belvoir, Va.: U.S. Army Institute for Water Resources, 1983.

Bourne, Russell. *Americans on the Move: A History of Waterways, Railways, and Highways.* Golden, Colo.: Fulcrum, 1995.

Hull, William J., and Robert W. Hull. *The Origin and Development of the Waterways Policy of the United States.* Washington, D.C.: National Waterways Conference, 1967.

Hunchey, James R., et. al. *United States Inland Waterways and Ports.* Fort Belvoir, Va.: U.S. Army Engineers Institute for Water Resources, 1985.

Hunter, Louis C. *Steamboats on the Western Rivers: An Economic and Technological History.* 1949. Reprint, New York: Dover, 1993.

Shaw, Ronald E. *Canals for a Nation: The Canal Era in the United States, 1790–1860.* Lexington: University Press of Kentucky, 1990.

Stine, Jeffrey K. *Mixing the Waters: Environment, Politics, and the Building of the Tennessee–Tombigbee Waterway.* Akron, Ohio: University of Akron Press, 1993.

Ralph D. Gray
Cynthia R. Poe

See also **Canals; Conservation; Inland Waterways Commission; Mississippi River; National Waterways Commission; River and Harbor Improvements; River Navigation; Rivers; Steamboats.**

WATTS RIOTS. During the summer of 1965, rioting broke out in Watts, an African American section of Los Angeles. By 1965 the successes of nonviolent protests seemed irrelevant to many African Americans segregated and mired in poverty and despair in urban ghettoes. Militancy increased, especially in Watts in south central Los Angeles, home to more than 250,000 African Americans. A not-so-routine traffic stop signaled the demise of the era of nonviolence.

On 11 August 1965 spectators accustomed to seeing black drivers pulled over by white police officers charged the officers with racism and brutality. Some simply yelled. Others hurled rocks, bricks, whatever they could find at the outnumbered police. Angry mobs assaulted white motorists, shattered store windows, and looted shops throughout the night. When dawn brought tranquility, police mistakenly declared that order had been restored. But that night Watts was in flames. Rioters armed themselves and passionately shouted, "Burn baby burn" and "Long live Malcolm X." Fires raged for four more days. Signs reading "Negro Owned" or "Owned by a Brother" pro-

Watts Riots. The sign placed in the middle of the street reads, "Turn left or get shot." © UPI/CORBIS-BETTMANN

tected some black businesses. Looting, violence, and bloodshed intensified, as rioters attacked whites, fought police, and shot at firefighters. Mobs repeatedly attacked reporters, and snipers aimed their rifles at members of the largely white press. Facing fewer obstacles, black reporters covered the story for major media outlets.

Only after the National Guard sent 14,000 soldiers to assist the 1,500 police officers did peace return to Watts. The official death toll reached 34, and 1,000 people suffered injuries. Police counted nearly 4,000 arrests. Some 30,000 rioters supported by 60,000 approving spectators caused more than $35 million in property damage. News of Watts unleashed a series of riots and racial disturbances in other American cities.

BIBLIOGRAPHY

Horne, Gerald. *Fire This Time: The Watts Uprising and the 1960s.* Charlottesville: University Press of Virginia, 1995.

Sears, David O., and John B. McConahay. *The Politics of Violence: The New Urban Blacks and the Watts Riots.* Washington, D.C.: University Press of America, 1981.

Paul J. Wilson

See also **Civil Rights Movement; Los Angeles; Riots, Urban.**

WAX PORTRAITS. The first American wax modeler, Patience Lovell Wright, made portraits of George Washington and Benjamin Franklin. Later, just after the American Revolution, itinerant modelers traveled the northern Atlantic coast. Johan Christian Rauschner and George M. Miller made many miniatures in varicolored wax, often jeweled, portraying the more prominent local worthies and their wives. Daniel Bowen copied Wright's Washington moderately well. Robert Ball Hughes of Boston modeled delicately in white wax. Giuseppi Volaperta made reliefs of three presidents in red wax. Reuben Moulthorpe of Connecticut molded heads in the round and made waxworks.

BIBLIOGRAPHY

Bolton, Ethel Stanwood. *American Wax Portraits.* Boston: Houghton Mifflin, 1929.

——. *Wax Portraits and Silhouettes.* Boston: Massachusetts Society of the Colonial Dames of America, 1914.

Ethel Stanwood Bolton / A. R.

See also **Art: Sculpture; Art: Self-Taught Artists.**

WAYNE, FORT, located at the joining of the St. Marys and St. Joseph Rivers to form the Maumee River in northeastern Indiana, was an important trade center for the Miami Indians from the 1600s on; they called it Kekionga. The French developed this strategic site into a military post called Fort Miami as early as the late 1680s, and it was occupied briefly by the British in the 1760s. American forces under General Anthony Wayne established Fort Wayne under the command of Colonel John F. Hamtramck on 22 October 1794. The Fort Wayne Indian Factory, a public trading post established at the site in 1802, increased its importance as a center of commerce between Indian fur trappers and American traders. The Treaty of Fort Wayne, signed at the post on 30 September 1809 by the United States and several Indian tribes, ceded about 2.5 million acres of present-day southern Indiana and Illinois to the United States in exchange for goods and annuities. Combined British and Indian forces besieged Fort Wayne during the War of 1812, and fighting continued through late 1813; after the war, Fort Wayne was decommissioned on 19 April 1819. A trading post and grist mill were built later that year, and on 22 October 1823 the U.S. Land Office sold off the rest of the land around the fort.

BIBLIOGRAPHY

Cayton, Andrew R.L. *Frontier Indiana.* Bloomington: Indiana University Press, 1996.

Madison, James H. *The Indiana Way: A State History.* Bloomington: Indiana University Press, 1986.

Rafert, Stewart. *The Miami Indians of Indiana: A Persistent People, 1654–1994.* Indianapolis: Indiana Historical Society, 1996.

Timothy G. Borden

See also **Indian Trade and Traders; Indian Treaties; Indiana; Miami (Indians); War of 1812.**

WAYS AND MEANS, COMMITTEE ON.

One of the most powerful and prestigious committees in the House of Representatives, this committee has general jurisdiction over all revenue measures, which constitutionally must originate in the House, and is responsible for managing the public debt, the tariff and trade laws, and the Social Security and Medicare systems. Until 1865, when the separate Appropriations Committee was created, it also had jurisdiction over virtually all spending measures. Legislation originating in the Committee on Ways and Means is privileged business, meaning that it may receive floor consideration ahead of other bills. Often, matters originating in this committee have very restrictive or closed rules, reducing or eliminating floor amendments.

Established in 1795 and made a formal standing committee in 1802, the Committee on Ways and Means is the oldest congressional committee. Strong leaders, such as Thaddeus Stevens, Robert Doughton, Wilbur Mills, and Daniel Rostenkowski, have chaired it. Eight eventual presidents, eight future vice presidents, and over twenty Speakers of the House have served on the committee. As a result of its wide jurisdiction, the Committee on Ways and Means has been at the center of many of the major legislative struggles throughout history—financing wars; managing trade, tariffs, and the debt; creating the social safety net; and sharing revenue with the states.

BIBLIOGRAPHY

Deering, Christopher, and Steven Smith. *Committees in Congress.* Congressional Quarterly Press, 1997.

Kennon, Donald R., and Rebecca M. Rogers. *The Committee on Ways and Means, A Bicentennial History, 1789–1989.* Washington, D.C.: Government Printing Office, 1989.

Brian D. Posler

See also **Congress, United States.**

"WE HAVE MET THE ENEMY, AND THEY ARE OURS."

On 10 September 1813, after defeating the British fleet in the Battle of Lake Erie, Oliver Hazard Perry, commander of the American fleet, dispatched one of the most famous messages in military history to Maj. Gen. William Henry Harrison. It read: "Dear Gen'l: We have met the enemy, and they are ours, two ships, two brigs, one schooner and one sloop. Yours with great respect and esteem. H. Perry." In 1970 cartoonist Walt Kelly famously paraphrased the statement as "We have met the enemy, and he is us" in an Earth Day poster that featured characters from his long-running strip *Pogo* and mourned the sad state of the environment.

BIBLIOGRAPHY

Welsh, William Jeffrey, and David Curtis Skaggs, eds. *War on the Great Lakes: Essays Commemorating the 175th Anniversary of the Battle of Lake Erie.* Kent, Ohio: Kent State University Press, 1991.

*Irving Dilliard/*A. E.

See also **Great Lakes Naval Campaigns of 1812; Navy, United States; Perry-Elliott Controversy; War of 1812.**

WEATHER SATELLITES

are robotic spacecraft that observe changes in terrestrial weather patterns. Their forecasting sharply reduces deaths from hurricanes and other violent weather. The first weather satellite, *TIROS I,* was launched in 1960 and functioned only eighty-nine days. *TIROS* (an acronym for Television and Infrared Observation Satellite) recorded television images of cloud patterns below, enabling meteorologists to track the movement of weather patterns and fronts. Weather satellites have since grown much more durable and can register more data, including wind speeds, atmospheric and surface temperatures, water temperatures, wave heights, and height of the polar ice caps. The U.S. government operates separate weather satellite programs for civilians and the military.

Weather satellites fall into two types. A geostationary satellite remains parked over a given point of the earth's equator, keeping continuous watch over a large portion of the earth from an altitude of 22,000 miles. A polar-orbiting satellite flies at about 500 miles in an orbit that carries it nearly over the earth's north and south poles. This satellite views a much smaller portion of Earth than a geostationary satellite but can make more detailed observations. The U.S. government typically has maintained two geostationary satellites and two polar-orbiting satellites in orbit at all times, but satellite weather forecasting ran into a snag in 1989, when the *GOES-6* failed in orbit. A replacement, *GOES-8,* was to have been launched on a space shuttle mission, but the *Challenger* shuttle explosion interrupted all shuttle launches. The replacement was further delayed until 1994 by technical problems. To fill the gap a European weather satellite was repositioned over the Atlantic Ocean to provide coverage of the eastern United States.

BIBLIOGRAPHY

Burroughs, William J. *Watching the World's Weather.* New York: Cambridge University Press, 1991.

Hubert, Lester F. *Weather Satellites.* Waltham, Mass.: Blaisdell Pub. Co., 1967.

*Vincent Kiernan/*H. S.

See also **Hurricanes; Meteorology; Space Program.**

WEATHER SERVICE, NATIONAL.

The National Weather Service (NWS) provides weather forecasts, climate and hydrologic data, and storm warnings for the United States and its territories.

Congress approved the creation of a federal weather service on 9 February 1870. Originally part of the Army Signal Service, the service became known as the Weather Bureau when the Department of Agriculture took control in 1891. In 1940 the bureau was shifted to the Department of Commerce. In October 1970 the Weather Bureau became part of the newly created National Oceanic and Atmospheric Administration (NOAA), and was renamed the National Weather Service.

The original weather service made forecasts from Washington, D.C., and offered climatological aid to farmers and businesses. The first regular forecasts (then called "probabilities") were published in 1871. In 1873 flood warnings were issued, and by the 1890s fruit growers were receiving special warnings by telegraph.

General weather forecasts were decentralized into district centers in the 1890s. National forecasts were updated four times daily starting in 1939; the popular five-day forecast appeared in 1940 and the thirty-day outlook was inaugurated in 1948. The Air Commerce Act of 1926 provided for the first regular aviation weather service. As forecasts improved, so did the means of communicating them: teletype (developed in the late 1920s) was followed by wire photo weather maps (1934) and facsimile transmission of weather maps (1950s), while radio and then television passed reports to the public.

Other midcentury innovations included recording rain gauges, the ceilometer, the telepsychrometer, and the recording river-flood gauge. Upper-air readings, once taken by weather balloons and kites, now were made by airplanes. Radar, developed as a military tool during World War II, greatly enhanced the bureau's weather-tracking abilities. The postwar growth of computers gave meteorologists another powerful new tool, allowing detailed data analysis and the creation of predictive models.

The National Aeronautics and Space Administration (NASA), founded in 1958, also relied on weather forecasts to make critical spacecraft launch and landing decisions. In turn, the new rockets allowed the launch of the first weather satellites. The *TIROS-9* satellite, launched in January 1965, offered the first complete ongoing coverage of the daylight portions of the earth; it was followed by the Geostationary Operational Environmental Satellites (GOES), first launched in November 1965, and the first launch (July 1972) of the Landsat series. By the end of the twentieth century, weather satellites surrounded the globe and their photos had become a key element in forecasting.

In the 1990s the NWS underwent a $4.5 billion modernization program. Included was the nationwide installation of NEXRAD (Next Generation Warning Radar) with so-called Doppler radar, capable of tracking directional shifts in wind-carried rain and alerting meteorologists to developing tornadoes. The development of the Internet allowed the general public, for the first time, on-demand access to satellite photos and other detailed NWS data.

The modern National Weather Service is charged with tracking and predicting life-threatening phenomena like hurricanes, tornadoes, snowstorms, and heat waves, as well as weather conditions conducive to natural disasters like forest fires. The NWS also plays a critical role in commercial aviation, delivering national forecasts and developing sensitive technology for predicting wind shear, microbursts, and other dangerous conditions. In 2001 the weather service had roughly 4,800 employees and an annual operating budget of approximately $740 million.

BIBLIOGRAPHY

Berger, Melvin. *The National Weather Service.* New York: John Day, 1971.

Shea, Eileen. *A History off NOAA.* Rockville, Md.: National Oceanic and Atmospheric Administration, 1987.

Whitnah, Donald R. *A History of the United States Weather Bureau.* Urbana: University of Illinois Press, 1961.

Ryan F. Holznagel
Donald R. Whitnah

WEBSTER V. REPRODUCTIVE HEALTH SERVICES, 492 U.S. 490 (1989), upheld provisions of a Missouri statute that restricted access to abortions, but declined to rule on whether the statute's declaration that human life begins at conception was constitutional. *Webster* involved a direct challenge to *ROE V. WADE,* 410 U.S. 113 (1973), which held that women have a constitutionally protected right to terminate a pregnancy. *Roe* decreed a trimester approach: as a woman's pregnancy progresses, the woman's right to obtain an abortion decreases, and the state's right to regulate abortion to protect the mother's health and the unborn child's potential life increases.

Sixteen years after *Roe,* the Supreme Court in *Webster* considered the constitutionality of a Missouri statutory prohibition on the use of public facilities or employees to carry out or assist in abortions unless it was necessary to save the mother's life. The statute's preamble stated that "the life of each human being begins at conception" and "unborn children have protectable interests in life, health, and well-being"; and the statute required that doctors ascertain the viability of an unborn child before performing an abortion.

The closely divided Court, in an opinion written by Chief Justice Rehnquist, ruled that the prohibition on using public resources to carry out abortions and the requirement for a physician to determine viability were both constitutional. The Court declined, however, to rule on the central issue of whether the preamble's assertion that life begins at conception was constitutional on the grounds that Missouri's courts had not yet ruled on whether the preamble formed part of the regulations of the statute.

In sum, notwithstanding shifts in the personnel of the court since *Roe*, including the appointment of three justices by President Reagan (who opposed abortion), the Supreme Court in *Webster* did not overrule *Roe*. The sharply divided Court, however, left the future of *Roe* uncertain; Justice O'Connor—who granted the vital fifth vote upholding the constitutionality of the statutory restrictions—declined to rule on whether the *Roe* framework was still valid. Many states responded by passing restrictive antiabortion laws in an effort to test the extent that a woman's right to an abortion merited constitutional protection. The lack of clarity from the *Webster* ruling thus set the stage for *Planned Parenthood of Southeastern Pennsylvania v. Casey*, 505 U.S. 833 (1992). In that case a splintered Supreme Court implicitly restructured the *Roe* standard by applying a less strenuous test for determining the constitutionality of abortion legislation.

BIBLIOGRAPHY

Craig, Barbara Hinkson, and David M. O'Brien. *Abortion and American Politics.* Chatham, N.J.: Chatham House, 1993.

Drucker, Dan. *Abortion Decisions of the Supreme Court, 1973–1989: A Comprehensive Review with Historical Commentary.* Jefferson, N.C.: McFarland, 1990.

Goldstein, Leslie Friedman. *Contemporary Cases in Women's Rights.* Madison: University of Wisconsin Press, 1994.

Mersky, Roy M., and Gary R. Hartman. *A Documentary History of the Legal Aspects of Abortion in the United States: "Webster v. Reproductive Health Services."* Littleton, Colo.: Fred B. Rothman, 1990.

Vitiello, Michael. "How Imperial Is the Supreme Court? An Analysis of Supreme Court Abortion Doctrine and Popular Will." *University of San Francisco Law Review* 34 (fall 1999): 49.

Elizabeth Lee Thompson

See also **Abortion.**

WEBSTER'S BLUE-BACKED SPELLER

WEBSTER'S BLUE-BACKED SPELLER is the popular name, derived from the blue paper covers, of Noah Webster's *Elementary Spelling Book*, published continuously since 1783 under several titles. Nearly 100 million copies have been printed; perhaps only the Bible has been more widely circulated in the United States. Webster, a nationalist, intended this book, eventually in conjunction with his dictionary, to develop an American form of English, with its own standard of spelling and pronunciation. He was largely successful in this effort, and the United States owes much of its linguistic uniformity to Webster's spelling book and dictionary.

BIBLIOGRAPHY

Monaghan, E. Jennifer. *A Common Heritage: Noah Webster's Blue-Backed Speller.* Hamden, Conn.: Archon Books, 1983.

Snyder, K. Alan. *Defining Noah Webster: Mind and Morals in the Early Republic.* Lanham, Md.: University Press of America, 1990.

Harry R. Warfel / s. b.

See also **Curriculum; Dictionaries; Education; Literature: Children's; McGuffey's Readers.**

WEBSTER-ASHBURTON TREATY

WEBSTER-ASHBURTON TREATY. The Webster-Ashburton Treaty resolved many disputed issues in British-American relations during the mid-nineteenth century. Of these, boundary disputes were the most prominent. After the War of 1812, the United States complained that Britain still habitually violated American sovereignty. The dispute over the northeastern boundary, between Maine and New Brunswick, Canada, had brought nationals of the two countries to the verge of armed hostility. This was settled by the treaty through what then appeared to be a wise compromise of territorial claims, which provided the present-day boundary line. (It was a concession that knowledge of Benjamin Franklin's Red-Line Map, not made public until 1932, would have made unnecessary, because the boundary had already been drawn.) The treaty also rectified the U.S.-Canada boundary at the head of the Connecticut River, at the north end of Lake Champlain, in the Detroit River, and at the head of Lake Superior. A useful extradition article and another providing for the free navigation of the St. John River were included in the treaty. Exchanges of notes covering the slave trade ensured the United States protection against "officious interference with American vessels" and the protection of "regularly-documented ships" known by the flag they flew.

BIBLIOGRAPHY

Bourne, Kenneth. *Britain and the Balance of Power in North America, 1815–1908.* Berkeley: University of California Press, 1967.

Peterson, Norma L. *The Presidencies of William Henry Harrison and John Tyler.* Lawrence: University Press of Kansas, 1989.

Samuel Flagg Bemis / a. g.

See also **Aroostook War; Canada, Relations with; Canadian-American Waterways; *Caroline* Affair; Great Britain, Relations with; Treaties with Foreign Nations.**

WEBSTER-HAYNE DEBATE

WEBSTER-HAYNE DEBATE. In the first years of Andrew Jackson's presidency, Senators Robert Y. Hayne of South Carolina and Thomas Hart Benton of Missouri shaped a potentially powerful Southern and Western alliance. At the level of partisan politics, Hayne supported the inexpensive sale of public lands for the West, and Benton supported low tariffs for the South. When Senator Samuel A. Foote of Connecticut proposed limiting the sale of public lands, Benton rose to denounce an eastern interest intent upon retarding the settlement of the West.

Hayne spoke in support of Benton, adding that high prices for western lands threatened to create "a fund for corruption—fatal to the sovereignty and independence of the states." Webster then took the floor to deny Benton's claim and to criticize Hayne's states' rights views. Webster also pointed to slavery as the source of the South's woes.

Hayne took the floor again and offered an impassioned defense of slavery and a detailed explication of the theory—increasingly identified with Vice President John C. Calhoun—that states had the right to "interpose" themselves when the federal government threatened their rights. Webster's second reply to Hayne, in January 1830, became a famous defense of the federal union: "Liberty and Union, now and forever, one and inseparable."

Just beneath the surface of this debate lay the elements of the developing sectional crisis between North and South. In April, after Hayne defended states' rights in the principal speech at the annual Jefferson Day dinner in Washington, President Jackson offered the first "volunteer" toast and echoed Webster's nationalism: "Our Federal Union. It must be preserved." Vice President Calhoun offered the second toast and endorsed Hayne's defense of states' rights: "The Union—next to our liberty, the most dear." The alliance of the West and the South collapsed and Benton soon emerged as a leading opponent of Calhoun and Hayne and their doctrine of nullification.

BIBLIOGRAPHY

Van Deusen, Glyndon G. *The Jacksonian Era: 1828–1848.* New York: Harper and Row, 1959.

Watson, Harry L. *Liberty and Power: The Politics of Jacksonian America.* New York: Farrar, Hill and Wang, 1990.

Louis S. Gerteis

See also **Nationalism; Sectionalism; States' Rights.**

WEBSTER-PARKMAN MURDER CASE. John

White Webster, a professor at Harvard College and lecturer at the medical school, was convicted on 30 March 1850 of the murder of Dr. George Parkman, a wealthy benefactor of the school and a prominent citizen of Boston. Webster was hanged in August 1850. The chief witness against him was Ephraim Littlefield, a janitor who found parts of Parkman's dismembered body in a waste-disposal vault at the medical school. Webster had been in debt to Parkman and had dishonestly sold property pledged as security. In a confession, supposedly obtained after his conviction, Webster attributed the crime to anger brought on by Parkman's attempts to deal with the situation. This confession, suspicions about the janitor's behavior, and several aspects of the trial have remained subjects of controversy to this day.

BIBLIOGRAPHY

Schama, Simon. *Dead Certainties: Unwarranted Speculations.* New York: Knopf, 1991.

Sullivan, Robert. *The Disappearance of Dr. Parkman.* Boston: Little, Brown, 1971.

Thomson, Helen. *Murder at Harvard.* Boston: Houghton Mifflin, 1971.

Robert E. Moody/c. p.

See also **Crime.**

WEDDING TRADITIONS. Weddings are cere-

monies marking a rite of passage. In the past, they ritualized the union of two or more people for purposes of securing property, heirs, and citizens and for strengthening diplomatic ties. Weddings united households, clans, tribes, villages, and countries. Such rituals took place in what we now know as the United States long before the arrival of nonindigenous peoples.

For Native Americans, the marriage ceremony was a very public celebration marking the transition of one spouse to the family and household of the other. Most often it was the male partner moving into the female's family in the mostly matrilineal cultures of North America. In the eastern United States, when a young man decided on a partner, he might woo her, but none of this took place in public—except his final approach, which might include his painting his face to appear as attractive as possible when he sought the intended's consent and the permission of her parents. To get that permission, the man might send ambassadors from his family with his intentions to the family of the woman. Depending on the meaning of the marriage in family, village, clan, or tribal terms, the parents consulted people outside their immediate family, such as a sachem or close members of their clan.

A two-part ceremony often followed such negotiations. First was a private reciprocal exchange between the couples' families, to ensure that if either partner decided to leave the marriage, the woman would not be disadvantaged in terms of losing her means of support. Second, a public acknowledgment of the union often included a feast for the village or the united clans. Before the assembly took part in the feast, the bride's father announced the reason for the gathering. Then they ate, and finally, the newly married couple returned home or were escorted to the quarters in which they would dwell for some or all of the years of their marriage.

The earliest immigrants to North America brought their wedding practices with them from Western Europe. Those rituals included witnesses to stand up with the couple before a minister, which may reflect an ancient practice of "marriage by capture" in which the groom, in kidnapping his bride-to-be, took many strong men with him, whereas the bride surrounded herself with women to keep off the aggressors. Bride prices or dowries were a carry-over of the practice of repaying the bride's father for the loss of her contribution to the family. Modern weddings continue the practice of having other young men and women stand up with the bride and groom, while gifts are brought for the couple, rather than the parents of the bride. Honeymoons may reflect the escape of the kidnapper and his captive. In the nineteenth-century South, wedding trips sometimes included several members of the wedding party and/or the family members of the bride and groom.

Courtship and marriage patterns among slaves were conditioned by their peculiar circumstances. Most prospective partners preferred to choose their spouses from plantations other than their own rather than choose someone they might have witnessed being whipped, raped, or otherwise used by white slave owners or overseers. Plantation owners frowned on such choices, however, because slave children followed the condition of their mother, which meant that if a male slave married off his plantation, his owner would not benefit from any children of the union.

After consent of parents, in the cases of freewomen brides, or owners, in the cases of slaves, the owner conducted a traditional ceremony or gave that over to a preacher, to be performed, if possible, in a church. Weddings often included many people from the plantation and neighboring plantations. Owners would sometimes open their big houses up for the occasion and provide feasts for the guests. A playful practice to show who would be in charge in the new household involved jumping over a broomstick. Whoever was able to jump over the broom backward without touching it would "wear the pants" in the family. If both partners sailed over without touching the stick, their marriage was destined for congenial relations.

The Chinese who immigrated to the United States in the middle of the nineteenth century in search for gold or work on the railroad were mostly men. Some left wives behind and lived as bachelors or used prostitutes imported from China. Often, Chinese or Japanese families sold their daughters to merchants, expecting them to marry upon arrival in the United States. However, whereas some of the girls and young women were set up in arranged marriages, others were enslaved for prostitution.

Part of the Spanish empire in the Americas extended up into what is now known as the American Southwest. Spanish culture mixed with Pueblo Indian culture to form a new combination of rituals. As with Native Americans in other parts of North America, the Pueblo experimented with sex and consummated marriage relationships before any ceremony took place, which the Spaniard missionaries found repugnant. They insisted on the adoption of the Catholic wedding ritual. There were three phases to the wedding ceremony. First, the bride's friends and relations escorted her to the church, where the wedding was performed by a priest, who also blessed the wedding ring provided by the groom. When the ceremony finished, the crowd escorted the newlyweds to the groom's home, celebrating with a feast and warding off evil spirits with gunfire. After the feast, the guests and the bride and groom danced late into the night. The dancing was an important ritual of community coherence.

BIBLIOGRAPHY

Axtell, James, ed. *The Indian Peoples of Eastern America: A Documentary History of the Sexes.* New York: Oxford University Press, 1981.

Blassingame, John. *The Slave Community: Plantation Life in the Antebellum South.* Rev. and enl. ed. New York: Oxford University Press, 1979.

Gutiérrez, Ramón A. *When Jesus Came, the Corn Mothers Went Away: Marriage, Sexuality, and Power in New Mexico, 1500–1846.* Stanford, Calif.: Stanford University Press, 1991.

Joyner, Charles. *Down By the Riverside: A South Carolina Slave Community.* Urbana: University of Illinois Press, 1984.

Rosen, Ruth. *The Lost Sisterhood: Prostitution in America, 1900–1918.* Baltimore: Johns Hopkins University Press, 1982.

Seligson, Marcia. *The Eternal Bliss Machine: America's Way of Wedding.* New York: Morrow, 1973.

Betsy Glade

See also **Indian Social Life; Marriage; Slavery.**

WEEDS. Etymologically, "weed" derives from the Old English word for "grass" or "herb," but during the Middle Ages the meaning has changed to indicate an undesirable plant that grows where it is not wanted, especially among agricultural plots. This has historically been the primary meaning of the word, although in the nineteenth century, American writers grew increasingly aware that calling a plant a "weed" was an arbitrary human judgment, as there is no natural category of weeds. In the words of Ralph Waldo Emerson, a weed "is a plant whose virtues have not yet been discovered." Today, biologists tend to share that opinion, since many of the plants that are designated as weeds are, in fact, closely related to popular crops. Indeed, "weed" has fallen out of usage among biologists, although those who study agriculture still find the term useful in discussions of weed control and management.

American weed control only developed out of the manual methods of pulling and hoeing in the early twentieth century, when salts and other chemicals began to be used as herbicides. However, since the 1970s, as environmental and health concerns have been raised, less toxic methods of weed control have been explored, although it has been found that any interference can have unintended ecological effects. For example, the introduction of a natural predator of an unwanted species—termed "biological control"—can devastate other local species or even, by reducing competition, cause a different species to grow out of control.

Moreover, "weed" has recently developed a new meaning in North America as a term that is applied to so-called invasive species, or non-native plants. Throughout the history of the Americas, as people have immigrated they have tended to bring along the flora and fauna of their homeland, thus intentionally—and at times unintentionally—introducing new species to the continents. Some of these non-native species have multiplied to such an extent that they threaten, or have already destroyed, the biological balance of local environments. This problem has been especially pronounced in Hawaii, Florida, California, and New York State. However, the term "weed" is generally not applied to all introduced or non-native plants but rather to those that are doing the greatest harm to biodiversity and are least controllable through human interference.

Scientists have discovered certain common characteristics among many of the most successful invasive species. They tend to be able to flourish in a variety of climactic zones and to reproduce easily and quickly over long periods with small seeds that are less likely to be eaten. However, non-native plants may also have an advantage in that they can exploit unfilled niches in their new lands while perhaps avoiding traditional enemies. Modern mobility and faster forms of transportation are exacerbating the problem in America and around the world.

Some of the most notorious invasive weeds in America today include kudzu, tumbleweeds, and leafy spurge. Kudzu, from Japan and perhaps originally China, is a semi-woody vine that came to dominate much of the American Southeast in the later twentieth century. Its introduction was encouraged by the American government early in the century to help improve soil and stop erosion, and attempts have continued for decades to undo the ecological damage that its widespread planting and subsequent spread have caused.

Tumbleweeds are now considered to be emblematic of the American West, and some tumbleweed species are indeed native to North America, while others originated in Europe and Asia. They do well with little water and were once cultivated in the hopes of being a food source for livestock. Leafy spurge, which was introduced from Europe and Asia in the early nineteenth century, is believed to be harmful to cattle if eaten. As with kudzu, attempts are being made to control tumbleweeds, leafy spurge, and other invasive weeds through biological, chemical, and manual methods to prevent further environmental and economic damage.

The history of American weeds is not only the story of importations and largely unsuccessful attempts to control non-native species, for native American species have also traveled to new lands. Notoriously, native ragweed, whose pollen causes Americans with hay fever to suffer every fall, has made an appearance in Europe, where it is spreading despite attempts to control it.

BIBLIOGRAPHY

Van Driesche, Jason, and Roy van Driesche. *Nature Out of Place: Biological Invasions in the Global Age.* Washington, D.C.: Island Press, 2000.

Zimdahl, Robert L. *Fundamentals of Weed Science.* San Diego, Calif.: Academic Press, 1993.

Caroline R. Sherman

See also **Agriculture.**

WEEKS ACT. The Weeks Act was a bill sponsored by Representative John W. Weeks of Massachusetts and approved by President William Howard Taft in March 1911. It authorized (1) interstate compacts for the purpose of conserving forests and water supply; (2) federal grants to states to help prevent forest fires upon watersheds of navigable waters; (3) acquisition of land by the federal government for the protection of watersheds, to be held as national forest land; and (4) the grant to states of a percentage of proceeds derived from national forests located within their boundaries, to be used for schools and public roads.

BIBLIOGRAPHY

Nash, Roderick Frazier, ed. *American Environmentalism: Readings in Conservation History.* 3d ed. New York: McGraw-Hill, 1990.

P. Orman Ray / c. w.

See also **Conservation; Fire Fighting; Water Law; Water Supply and Conservation.**

WELFARE CAPITALISM. Welfare capitalism is a system of private, employer-based social welfare provisions that first gained prominence in the United States from the 1880s through the 1920s. Promoted by business leaders during a period marked by widespread economic insecurity, social reform activism, and labor unrest, it was based on the idea that Americans should look not to the government or to labor unions but to the workplace benefits provided by private-sector employers for protection against the fluctuations of the market economy. Welfare capitalism, according to its proponents, was a new, more enlightened kind of capitalism, based on the ideals of corporate social responsibility and business-labor cooperation rather than unfettered individualism and class conflict. It was also a way to resist government regulation of markets, independent labor union organizing, and the emergence of a welfare state. For all its promise of industrial harmony, welfare capitalism was a way to keep private employers firmly in control of labor relations.

U.S. businesses began to adopt a variety of what were initially known as "welfare work" practices in the 1880s. From the beginning, the benefits employers offered were inconsistent and varied widely from firm to firm. "Welfare work" encompassed minimal benefits such as cafeteria plans and company-sponsored sports teams as well as more extensive plans providing retirement benefits, health care, and employee profit-sharing. By far the most elaborate and ambitious of the early plans were the company towns, such as the one established by and named for railroad car manufacturer George Pullman in 1881, just outside of Chicago, Illinois. In Pullman, as in the company towns established by textile mill owners in the South, workers lived in company-built houses, shopped at company-established stores, played at company-provided recreational facilities, went to company-hired doctors, and were often expected to worship at company-sanctioned churches.

Portraying themselves as benevolent father figures, many employers sought to exert parental authority and control over their workers as well. Thus, workers drawn to car manufacturer Henry Ford's promise of high ($5.00 a day) wages were subject to home inspections and a strict moral code as conditions of employment. Other employers offered cooking, hygiene, and language classes in efforts to regulate and "Americanize" their immigrant workers. Welfare capitalists went to greatest lengths, however, in efforts to quash independent union organizing, strikes, and other expressions of labor collectivism—through a combination of violent suppression, worker sanctions, and, as welfare capitalism became more widespread, benefits in exchange for loyalty.

By the 1910s and 1920s, welfare capitalism had become an organized movement with a diversifying base of business, social, scientific, and political support. It had also become the leading edge of the quest for corporate competitiveness and efficiency: benefit packages, employers reasoned, would attract a higher skilled, more productive, and stable workforce. Even at its height, however, welfare capitalism left the vast majority of workers without adequate social welfare protection and actively discriminated against low-skilled, non-white, and female wage-earners. Since employer benefits remained unregulated, companies could—and did—abandon their obligations during hard times.

The GREAT DEPRESSION of the 1930s brought the inadequacies of welfare capitalism into sharp relief, as NEW DEAL policymakers joined labor leaders and reform activists to establish the basis of the modern U.S. welfare state. Far from retreating, welfare capitalists subsequently adapted to the era of public provision and stronger labor unions. Private employer benefits, subsidized by tax incentives, became an essential supplement to the basic government safety net and a key bargaining chip in negotiations with organized labor. There is considerable cause for concern, then, that recent decades have seen a dramatic decline in the percentage of the U.S. workforce covered by employer-provided health, pension, and other benefits—especially as these declines have been accompanied by significant reductions in the public provisions of the welfare state.

BIBLIOGRAPHY

Gordon, Colin. *New Deals: Business, Labor, and Politics in America, 1920–1935.* Cambridge, U.K.: Cambridge University Press, 1994.

Jacoby, Sanford M. *Modern Manors: Welfare Capitalism Since the New Deal.* Princeton, N.J.: Princeton University Press, 1997.

Tone, Andrea. *The Business of Benevolence: Industrial Paternalism in Progressive America.* Ithaca, N.Y.: Cornell University Press, 1997.

Alice O'Connor

WELFARE SYSTEM. In the American vocabulary, "welfare" has often had a limited meaning, most commonly associated in public discourse with public assistance to mothers with dependent children. Yet government welfare can also be given a broader definition, as a general social safety net designed to support citizens in need. Under this definition, "welfare" refers to government protections for workers' incomes, which are often threatened by structural economic change under the free market system. In an economy in which workers rely on wages to support themselves, threats to income arise due to unemployment, sickness, old age, and loss of the family breadwinner. In the United States, then, government welfare has been a collection of different programs that includes unemployment insurance, health insurance, old-age pensions, accident insurance, and support for families with dependent children.

In the twentieth century, many nations in Western Europe built what became known as the "welfare state," a comprehensive system designed to protect citizens from the hazards of an industrial, capitalist economy. Compared with the European welfare state, the American welfare system is late developing, less extensive, haphazardly constructed, and reliant upon dispersed authority. While European nations instituted programs for old-age pensions and accident insurance near the turn of the twentieth century, the United States did not develop significant welfare programs until the 1930s under Franklin D. Roosevelt's New Deal. Unlike the European welfare state, the American welfare system has never included universal health insurance or guaranteed family incomes. Significant groups of Americans in need have not been covered by government welfare programs. Moreover, the American old-age pension system is based on worker contributions, and thus does little to redistribute wealth.

While the European welfare state was consolidated in the coherent programs of social-democratic or labor parties, the American welfare system has lacked a comprehensive structure. It was initially built as a response to emergency, during the economic crisis of the Great Depression. The American welfare system is characterized by dispersed authority. Unlike the nationalized European systems, responsibility for welfare has been shared by federal, state, and local governments, which has often led to wide disparities in welfare eligibility and benefits in different regions of the country.

Throughout its history, the American distribution of government welfare has been closely connected to cultural attitudes toward the poor. Americans have commonly distinguished between the deserving poor, who become needy through no fault of their own and are entitled to public assistance, and the undeserving poor, who are responsible for their own plight and who could escape poverty by developing a strong work ethic. Separating the deserving poor from the undeserving has often proved difficult. Nevertheless, for much of American history, many needy people have been seen as undeserving of public assistance. Because of a deeply held cultural belief in the "American dream," which holds that anyone can achieve economic advancement through hard work, Americans have characteristically attributed poverty to the moral failings of individuals.

In the American welfare system, the distinction between the deserving and the undeserving poor has translated into a division between social insurance and public assistance programs. Social insurance, which includes old-age pensions and unemployment insurance, has been available on a universal basis to those who earn it through work. Public assistance, such as aid to dependent children and general assistance for the very needy, is targeted at the poor and requires financial and moral evaluations for applicants to prove their worthiness for aid. The benefits of public assistance are typically less generous than those of social insurance. Recipients of public assistance have often been seen as undeserving of aid because they are not seen as having earned it through work. Public assistance has thus carried a social stigma. There is also a gender and racial dimension to the devaluation of public assistance in comparison to social insurance, as recipients of the former are disproportionately female and minority.

Welfare from the Colonial Period to the Progressive Era

Treatment of the poor in colonial America was based on the principles set forth in the Elizabethan poor law of 1601. According to this English law, each town or parish was responsible for the care of its own needy. The law distinguished between three categories of the poor: those who were unable to work due to sickness or age, who were to be given material aid; the able-bodied who were unable to find jobs, who were to be provided with work; and the able-bodied but unwilling to work, who were to be instilled with the work ethic. The two important legacies of this law were its stipulation that poor relief is a local responsibility and the burden that it placed on the needy to prove their worthiness for relief.

Operating on the principles of the Elizabethan poor law, American colonial governments took responsibility for providing for the needy in their localities, through so-called "outdoor relief"—material assistance granted on a case-by-case basis. Localities also auctioned off destitute persons to the lowest bidder, who would receive funds in exchange for caring for them. However, because they were seen as drains on government funds, strangers in need were often warned away from towns, even if they were sick or disabled.

Beginning in the late eighteenth century, however, increasing urbanization, immigration, population growth, and unemployment led to a rising poor population and the need for a more systematic approach to welfare. Although outdoor relief continued to be practiced, states and municipalities supported "indoor relief" by building institutions to provide for the permanently poor and to instill the able-bodied with habits of work discipline.

In general, poorhouses were inadequately funded. Moreover, they were often poorly administered, and those who ran them were often corrupt. They lumped together different classes of poor in the same institution: the old, the sick, and the mentally ill were housed with the able-bodied unemployed. Under such circumstances, poorhouses were unable to provide adequate care for the needy or instill work habits in the able-bodied. In part, poorhouses were meant to be unpleasant institutions, as the threat of having to live in the poorhouse was intended to deter the poor from idleness. By the beginning of the twentieth century, most poorhouses were transformed into homes for the old-aged who had no one else to care for them.

By the end of the nineteenth century, many European nations were beginning to build a welfare state. A number of American reformers, believing that government welfare would have to be altered to reflect the new hazards of an industrial economy, sought to emulate the European example. While these reformers failed in their efforts to develop European-style provisions for old-age pensions and unemployment insurance, the Progressive Era (1900–1921) did see the early growth of the American welfare system. For example, from 1911 to 1921, forty-two states introduced workmen's compensation legislation, which provided accident insurance to protect workers against job-related injuries.

In the Progressive Era, a powerful network of progressive middle-class women lobbied for mothers' pensions, and thirty-nine states developed mothers' aid programs from 1911 to 1921. Under these programs, states gave money to single mothers to help them defray the costs of raising their children in their own homes. The aid was meant to deter the use of child labor to help raise money for the family and to prevent the institutionalization of poor and fatherless children in orphanages, a common practice in the nineteenth century. However, in order to receive this aid, women had to prove that they were fit mothers with suitable homes. Often, the benefits given were inadequate, and the programs only reached a small portion of those in need—in 1931, only 93,620 of 1.5 million female-headed families received mothers' aid.

Progressives had the most success in instituting programs whose goal was protecting children. In 1912, the federal government established the U.S. Children's Bureau to gather information on the treatment of the nation's children. In 1921, Congress passed the Sheppard-Towner Act, giving matching funds to states to build maternal and child health facilities to fight infant mortality. Despite their accomplishments, Progressives failed to develop an extensive American welfare system—that task was not accomplished until the New Deal.

The New Deal and the Establishment of the American Welfare System

The severity of the Great Depression created new demands for government relief. After the stock market crash of 24 October 1929, millions of Americans lost their jobs and found themselves without adequate means of financial support. Between 1929 and the summer of 1932, the unemployment rate skyrocketed from 3.2 percent to 24.9 percent. In the face of this economic crisis, President Herbert Hoover stressed that relief for the needy should be the responsibility of private, local, and state relief agencies. Yet the need for assistance was staggering and could not be met by the institutions Americans had traditionally relied upon to provide public aid. In 1932, Congress established the Reconstruction Finance Corporation, which was authorized to lend $300 million in relief funds directly to the states. However, the true expansion of the American welfare system came during the presidency of Franklin Roosevelt, who took office in 1933. For the first time, the federal government committed itself to providing economic security for its citizens. By the end of the 1930s, the United States had become a world leader in social spending.

The first measures that Roosevelt took were temporary ones to relieve the immediate problems caused by the depression, though in doing so he became the first president to assert that the federal government should be responsible for the welfare of its citizens. In 1933, he appointed a dynamic administrator, Harry Hopkins, to lead government relief efforts and established the Federal Emergency Relief Administration (FERA). FERA provided funds to the states for the needy, both in the form of direct cash grants and on a matching basis. For the most part, the funds were distributed by the states with federal supervision. Work projects to provide jobs to the unemployed were administered by FERA, as well as the Civil Works Administration (CWA) and the Civilian Conservation Corps (CCC)—both created in 1933. By February of 1934, FERA, the CWA, and the CCC combined reached 28 million people, 20 percent of the American population.

The economic crisis provided an opportunity for liberals to pass European-style social welfare legislation that they had unsuccessfully advocated for years. In 1935, Congress passed Roosevelt's Social Security Act. This bill was designed to establish a more permanent system for government welfare. Roosevelt hoped that an expansive program of government security would protect Americans "against the hazards and vicissitudes of life."

In the short term, the law provided old-age assistance in the form of immediate payments for the destitute elderly. For the long term, however, the legislation established Old Age Insurance (OAI), a pension fund for American workers aged sixty-five and over. Social security, as OAI came to be called, was a fully federal program that granted standard benefits throughout the country. While there was a popular movement in favor of noncontributory old-age pensions paid for directly out of general government funds, OAI worked on a contributory basis, with workers and employers paying equal shares into the system. While workers had to contribute in order to receive social security, benefits did not correspond to the contributions that workers made in social security taxes. The New Dealers decided to make social security a contributory program in order to appease the demands of employers and because they believed that if it were a separate program with its own tax funds, it would be protected from political attack in the future.

The Social Security Act established unemployment insurance, also on a contributory basis, by providing for a cooperative federal-state program to provide payments for a set number of weeks to workers who had lost their jobs. The act also established a system of federal matching funds for the states for needy children, ADC (Aid to Dependent Children). Since each of these programs was administered by the states, payment amounts and eligibility requirements varied widely throughout the nation.

Eventually synonymous with the word "welfare," ADC was relatively uncontroversial at the time it was established. It was a less generous program and preserved its recipients' dignity less than OAI or unemployment insurance, however. At first, ADC only extended benefits to children, not to caregivers—when this was changed later, the program became AFDC (Aid to Families with Dependent Children). While social security was universally available to eligible workers, ADC recipients were means-tested. Since the aid was not distributed on a universal basis, ADC recipients were often stigmatized. In order to receive assistance, state officials had to certify need and worthiness of aid. Mothers had to prove that they provided a fit home for their children and that they adhered to an acceptable code of sexual conduct in order to be eligible for ADC. Until 1961, fathers of children aided under ADC had to be completely absent in order for the mothers to receive aid. The procedures that state agencies adopted to determine need often involved substantial invasions of privacy. Social workers intensely scrutinized the budgets of mothers, and some agencies conducted "midnight raids" of the women receiving aid to check for overnight male visitors—if they found one, assistance was withdrawn.

The welfare legislation of the New Deal was based on a distinction between "unemployables" and "employables." Unemployables such as the elderly, the disabled, and dependent children and their caregivers were to receive public aid without entering the labor market. Employables, however, were to be provided with jobs. In keeping with long-held American beliefs, the architects of the New Deal believed that it was morally damaging to substitute dependence on public aid for work. Therefore, the New Deal contained massive public works programs designed to provide work relief to the unemployed.

In 1935, Congress created the Works Progress Administration (WPA). Under Harry Hopkins, the WPA administered public works projects throughout the nation and employed workers of all skill levels at prevailing local wages. From 1935 to its elimination in 1943, the WPA employed between 1.5 and 3 million Americans at any one time, making it the largest civilian employer in the nation. During that period, it constructed or repaired 600,000 miles of road, built or rebuilt 116,000 bridges, and repaired 110,000 buildings. The CCC and the Public Works Administration (PWA) also provided jobs for public works during this period.

New Deal public works programs, however, were faced with the difficult problem of trying to reconcile the need to create jobs with the need to perform useful work in an efficient manner. Moreover, they were hampered by inadequate funding from Congress and could not rely on a fully developed federal bureaucracy to administer them. The WPA was unable to provide jobs for all of those who needed them and its wages were often insufficient. The WPA provision that it could only employ one family member indicated the prevailing gender expectation that men were to be the family breadwinners. Less than 20 percent of WPA workers were female.

While many New Dealers planned to make public employment a long-term federal commitment that could expand and contract with economic need, the public works programs were eliminated in 1943, as economic growth returned and the Roosevelt administration focused its attention on the war. In addition, New Dealers failed in their attempts to establish a system of national health insurance. Thus, while the New Deal did create a national welfare system, its programs were less ambitious than what many of its planners had anticipated.

In part, the inability of the New Dealers to develop a more extensive welfare system was due to resistance among conservative Democratic congressmen from the segregated South. Many in the South who would have benefited from such programs were unable to vote. Not only were virtually all African Americans disenfranchised, many poor whites were effectively prevented from voting by high poll taxes. Southern congressmen were instrumental in attaching limits to the programs that did pass, ensuring that federal welfare would not provide an economic alternative to work for the southern black labor force. For instance, southern congressmen saw to it that OAI excluded agricultural and domestic workers—60 percent of the nation's African Americans were in either of these categories.

Despite the broader ambitions of New Dealers themselves, the legacy of the New Deal was the two-tiered system established by the Social Security Act: a social insurance program that included old-age pensions and unemployment insurance, with benefits for workers of all social classes; and a public assistance program, ADC, targeted at the poor, that was less generous in its benefits and attached a humiliating stigma to its recipients. While the New Deal failed to establish a complete welfare state, the expansion of the American welfare system in this period was nevertheless dramatic. The amount of money the federal government spent on public aid increased from $208 million in 1932 to $4.9 billion in 1939.

From the War on Poverty to Welfare Reform

In the 1940s and 1950s, federal and state governments continued to assume the major financial and program role in providing welfare. The welfare system did not undergo significant expansion, however, until the 1960s. In 1964, Lyndon B. Johnson, acting on the plans of his predecessor, John F. Kennedy, launched the "War on Poverty." This public campaign had the ambitious goal of defeating poverty in the United States. However, its planners believed that economic growth would solve much of the problem, and so they avoided implementing expensive and controversial measures to fight poverty such as direct income maintenance and New Deal–style public works programs. Instead, the War on Poverty focused its energies on job training and education, launching programs such as Head Start, the Job Corps, and Upward Bound.

While the programs of the War on Poverty failed to match the extravagant rhetoric of the program, the American welfare system did expand. In 1965, Congress established the Medicare and Medicaid programs to provide medical assistance for the aged and for welfare recipients, respectively. Through these programs, a quarter of Americans received some form of government-sponsored medical insurance. Food stamps became more widely available and free to the poor: while, in 1965, the food stamp program provided only $36 million in aid to 633,000 people, by 1975 it granted $4.6 billion in aid to 17.1 million recipients. President Richard Nixon was unable to get Congress to pass the Family Assistance Plan in 1972, which would have provided a guaranteed minimum income to all families. However, Congress did pass Supplemental Social Security (SSI), which established an income floor on benefits paid to the aged, blind, and disabled.

Existing programs such as social security and Aid to Families with Dependent Children experienced tremendous growth during this period. Social security payments increased in amount and reached more people, as a greater percentage of the population became elderly and lived longer. The expansion of the welfare system substantially reduced poverty during this period, particularly among the elderly. From 1959 to 1980, the percentage of the elderly below the poverty line dropped from 35 percent to 16 percent.

In 1960, the AFDC program cost less than $1 billion and reached 745,000 families. By 1971, it cost $6 billion and reached over 3 million families. The expansion of AFDC was due in part to the concentration of poverty among certain demographic groups, such as African Americans and women. Due to the mechanization of southern agriculture, many African Americans moved northward into urban areas where the unemployment rate was high because of a decrease in factory jobs. The "feminization of poverty" left many women in economic need due to an increasing divorce rate, increasing out-of-wedlock births, and increasing rates of child desertion by fathers.

The expansion of AFDC was also due to a growing "welfare rights" consciousness that encouraged those eligible to receive aid and sought to remove the social stigma associated with it. This consciousness was promoted by groups such as the National Welfare Rights Organization (NWRO) and the Office of Economic Opportunity (OEO), a War on Poverty agency charged with seeking the "maximum feasible participation of the poor" in its programs. From 1968 to 1971, the Supreme Court decided a number of cases that expanded welfare rights. It struck down state residency requirements for AFDC eligibility, eliminated the rule that the father had to be entirely absent for aid to be given, and granted legal due process to those requesting welfare.

Although social security remained a much larger program than AFDC, AFDC became more controversial. Beginning in the mid-1970s, the expansion of the AFDC program fueled fears of a growing "welfare crisis." As inner cities suffered the effects of deindustrialization and high unemployment, poverty increasingly came to be associated with African Americans living in urban centers, who were often referred to in public discourse as an "underclass" living in a debilitating "culture of poverty." The public image of the AFDC recipient increasingly became that of the "welfare mom"—presumed to be an unwed African American. Here, the stigma of being poor and the stigma of single motherhood were combined to create a potent racial stereotype.

A new conservative critique of welfare gained increasing prominence by the 1980s. For leading conservatives such as Charles Murray and George Gilder, liberal social policy was itself responsible for keeping people in poverty. According to this critique, welfare programs kept recipients dependent on the state for support. Conservatives advocated reducing or abolishing AFDC payments, in order to provide poor people with the necessary incentive to become self-sufficient through work.

The conservative critique of the welfare system gained strength from an increasing distrust of the federal government. Changing gender expectations also help explain the new call for AFDC recipients to earn their living through work. The demand that the needy advance through work was a familiar one, but it had generally been applied only to men. Whereas in the New Deal single mothers were considered unemployable and kept out of the labor market, by the end of the century women were assumed to be a natural part of the labor force.

President Ronald Reagan acted on the growing conservative critique by slashing government welfare programs during the 1980s. Between 1982 and 1985 total funds spent on unemployment insurance went down 6.9 percent, food stamps went down 12.6 percent, child nutrition programs were cut 27.7 percent, housing assistance 4.4 percent, and low-income energy assistance 8.3 percent. While the Reagan administration decreased the money it spent on public assistance to the poor, it increased the budget of social security. Thus, while conservatives had success in reducing public assistance programs, existing social insurance programs that reached the middle class continued to enjoy substantial political support.

In 1992, Bill Clinton was elected president with a campaign pledge to "end welfare as we know it." However, he spent much of his energy in his first years in office in an unsuccessful attempt to extend the welfare system by providing all Americans with health insurance. After the 1994 election, a group of conservative Republicans took control of Congress and advocated the passage of welfare reform legislation. They were led by House Speaker Newt Gingrich, who pledged in his "Contract with America" to "replace the welfare state with the opportunity society."

In 1996, Congress passed the Personal Responsibility and Work Opportunity Reconciliation Act, designed to reduce the number of people receiving public assistance. This act repealed AFDC and replaced it with Temporary Assistance for Needy Families (TANF). Whereas AFDC had an open-ended federal commitment to provide matching funds to the states, TANF stipulated a set amount of money earmarked for parents with dependent children to be given to states by the federal government, shifting much of the responsibility for care of the needy back to the states. The act encouraged states to use a significant proportion of their funds not for cash payments but for job training, job placement, and education. The law stipulated that no family has a right to government assistance: states have no obligation to provide relief to needy families. States were given a number of incentives to cut their welfare caseloads. Under the new legislation, TANF caregivers were eligible for only five years of benefits over the course of their lives.

Those cut from the welfare rolls were expected to get a job in the private sector and support themselves with wages. However, states were under no obligation to address obstacles that many welfare recipients faced to working, such as low skills, lack of transportation, and the need for child care, though many states did choose to implement programs to address these obstacles. The jobs that were typically available for former AFDC recipients were low-wage service industry jobs that still left them below the poverty line. In 1997, median wages for workers who had left welfare were reported to be 20 percent of hourly wages for all workers.

The legislation succeeded in reducing the amount of people receiving aid for dependent children from 4.4 million at the time the law passed to 2.4 million in December

1999, though some of these reductions should be ascribed to the booming economy of the late 1990s. However, it was unclear how the system would work in more difficult economic times—for even if the need for assistance escalated, the federal government would not increase the amount of funds it granted to the states.

BIBLIOGRAPHY

Amenta, Edwin. *Bold Relief: Institutional Politics and the Origins of Modern American Social Policy.* Princeton, N.J.: Princeton University Press, 1998.

American Social History Project. *Who Built America?: Working People and the Nation's Economy, Politics, Culture, and Society.* 2d ed. 2 vols. New York: Worth, 2000.

Gordon, Linda, ed. *Women, the State, and Welfare.* Madison: University of Wisconsin Press, 1990.

Gordon, Linda. *Pitied but Not Entitled: Single Mothers and the History of Welfare, 1890–1935.* New York: Free Press, 1994.

Katz, Michael B. *The Undeserving Poor: From the War on Poverty to the War on Welfare.* New York: Pantheon, 1989.

———. *In the Shadow of the Poorhouse: A Social History of Welfare in America.* Rev. ed. New York: Basic Books, 1996.

Levine, Daniel. *Poverty and Society: The Growth of the American Welfare State in International Comparison.* New Brunswick, N.J.: Rutgers University Press, 1988.

Patterson, James T. *America's Struggle against Poverty in the Twentieth Century.* Cambridge, Mass.: Harvard University Press, 2000.

Piven, Francis Fox, and Richard A. Cloward. *Regulating the Poor: The Function of Public Welfare.* Updated ed. New York: Vintage, 1993.

Rodgers, Daniel T. *Atlantic Crossings: Social Politics in a Progressive Age.* Cambridge, Mass.: Harvard University Press, 1998.

Skocpol, Theda. *Protecting Soldiers and Mothers: The Political Origins of Social Policy in the United States.* Cambridge, Mass.: Harvard University Press, 1992.

Trattner, William I. *From Poor Law to Welfare State: A History of Social Welfare in America.* New York: Free Press, 1999.

Daniel Geary

See also **Children's Bureau; Civilian Conservation Corps; Head Start; Job Corps; Medicare and Medicaid; New Deal; Progressive Movement; Sheppard-Towner Maternity and Infancy Protection Act; Social Security; War on Poverty; Workers' Compensation; Works Progress Administration.**

WELLS, FARGO AND COMPANY.

The founders of the American Express Company, Henry Wells, William G. Fargo, and associates, organized Wells, Fargo and Company in 1852 to function as a western ally of American Express. The two companies divided the continent approximately at the Mississippi and Missouri rivers. Wells, Fargo and Company installed ocean service between New York and San Francisco via Panama, erected a fine office building in San Francisco, and began to operate not only in the gold region of California but over the entire Pacific coast. In less than ten years, it had eliminated or acquired nearly all competitors and dominated the Far West. In remote mining camps where the mails had not yet penetrated, it was the chief letter carrier; even after the mails came, many preferred it as more dependable. The company spread rapidly through the entire Rocky Mountain region and carried far greater amounts of gold, silver, and bullion than any other agency. In 1861, after the famous Pony Express failed, Wells, Fargo acquired it and extended its operations to western Canada, Alaska, Mexico, the West Indies, Central America, and Hawaii, and for a short time even carried letters to China and Japan. Later, it pushed its service eastward to the Atlantic coast. Along with all the other expresses, Wells, Fargo and Company merged with the American Railway Express Company in 1918, but continued to function for more than thirty years as a separate corporation on fourteen thousand miles of railway in Mexico and Cuba. As a subsidiary of American Express, Wells, Fargo became an armored-car service.

BIBLIOGRAPHY

Beebe, Lucius, and Charles Clegg. *U.S. West: The Saga of Wells Fargo.* New York: E. P. Dutton, 1949.

Hungerford, Edward. *Wells Fargo: Advancing the American Frontier.* New York: Random House, 1949.

Alvin F. Harlow / c. w.

See also **Gold Rush, California; Mail, Overland, and Stagecoaches; Pack Trains; Panama Canal; Pony Express.**

WEST, AMERICAN.

In the minds of people all over the world, the American West and the frontier often conjure up images of the blue-coated army, cowboys and Indians, buffalo, and stand-tall men like Davy Crockett, George Custer, Buffalo Bill Cody, and John Wayne. While these images are the stuff of great entertainment, they also make for bad history. The West and the frontier—the two are not the same—have been romanticized and blurred from the time of Buffalo Bill's "Wild West and Rough Riders" shows early in the twentieth century to the later radio, film, and television exploits of Tom Mix, the Lone Ranger, John Wayne, Clint Eastwood, Matt Dillon, and many others, both fictional and real.

A history of the American West must first distinguish the "West" from the "frontier," as the concept of the frontier does not exhaust the history of the West. As a target for settlement, the American West moved across the map for over three centuries, from just outside the stockades of colonial villages to the flatboats and steamboats of the Ohio and Mississippi valleys to the great cities of the Pacific Coast. Each of those regions indeed became, for a time, the frontier. For the period before 1920, then, it might make sense to identify the West with the frontier. But it has been nearly a century since homesteading ended, since city-dwellers outnumbered farm-dwellers in the United States, and since "the West" became, simply, the western half of the country. The post-1920 West has been neither the fabled West of cowboys and Indians, soldiers and gunfighters, nor the real—but historically past—land of millions of homesteaders.

The Spanish and French West

Just as the West cannot be identified wholly with the frontier, the frontier itself was not just a move westward, from Atlantic to Pacific. The first European settlers came north from Mexico into the present-day United States. In 1598, Juan de Oñate, "the last conquistador," led a mixed-race group of several hundred men, women, and children north across the Rio Grande River, at El Paso del Norte, into the pueblo country of present-day New Mexico; Spain's provincial capital was established at SANTA FE a few years later. For the next two-and-a-half centuries, Spanish soldiers, missionaries, and most importantly, settlers, pushed northward from Mexico into New Mexico, southern Arizona (from the 1690s), southeastern Texas (from 1716), and finally California (beginning with San Diego in 1769). When Mexico became independent in 1821, these areas became northern Mexico. By 1848, the United States had conquered and annexed this region, first through a migration to Texas so large that it overwhelmed the Spanish-speaking population, and then by force in the MEXICAN-AMERICAN WAR.

As the Spanish moved northward from Mexico, French settlers and fur traders moved southwestward from Canada's St. Lawrence Valley. French settlement began at Quebec in 1608 and by 1718 stretched thinly along the GREAT LAKES and the Mississippi all the way to New Orleans, long before any English or American colonial appearances west of the Appalachians. France lost these areas to Britain in 1763, not because of military incompetence, but simply on account of the difference in population: 65,000 French settled along the St. Lawrence, compared with nearly two million English colonists along the eastern seaboard.

The British and U.S. West

The English colonies began slowly, weakly, and very unpromisingly, starting with Jamestown, Virginia, in 1607. In 1700 the English colonial population was still only about 250,000, and births had just begun outnumbering deaths sufficiently to allow the colonies to survive without constant infusions of new migrants. In the decades that followed, however, the population boomed. By the 1740s English-speakers from Maine to Georgia reached a million, and by 1776, 2.5 million. They continued to settle the thirteen states, and some began crossing the Appalachians into Kentucky, Tennessee, and the upper Ohio Valley.

After about 1710, Americans doubled their numbers every twenty-two years or so, and they continued to do so well into the nineteenth century. High fertility was sustained by practically limitless new territory in which to expand. The peace treaty of 1783 that ended the Revolutionary War generously extended the new United States to the Mississippi River, and the LOUISIANA PURCHASE of 1803 doubled that area. By 1848 the United States had annexed Texas, the Southwest, and present-day Oregon, effectively reaching its continental limits after sixty-five years of unparalleled territorial expansion. By then, Russian outposts along the northern California coast had come and gone. Indians had been "removed" from their homelands in Tennessee, Indiana, and other eastern states, and resettled in and near the Indian Territory, present-day Oklahoma. Men and women were heading to Oregon and California along the OVERLAND TRAIL and the Latter-day Saints, to Utah by the MORMON TRAIL. A series of wars on the Great Plains and farther west, between the United States Army and Native Americans, sporadically erupted until 1890, "freeing" the Great Plains for settlement by Americans as well as hundreds of thousands of Irish, Germans, Scandinavians, Ukrainians, and many other Europeans.

The Federal Role

Between independence and the end of homesteading in the 1920s, the federal government encouraged westward migration. It enacted progressively more generous land laws. It encouraged European immigrants to come and settle. It protected settlers (and miners and cattlemen) by sending the military to subdue, round up, and if necessary annihilate Native Americans. It financed explorations beginning with Lewis and Clark's. It subsidized with huge LAND GRANTS the construction of railways that took settlers west and their farm products back east to markets. These policies resulted in an exceptionally fast-growing western population, acquiring and occupying more new territory than any in modern history. Homesteading—the creation of family farms on land previously considered "empty wilderness" (though Indians had been living on it for centuries)—became the reality for millions of men and women from the Midwest all the way to the Pacific, wherever there was enough water to permit it. High birth rates, large families, cheap and accessible land: these became the formula for a repeating process of westward expansion that continued until about 1920, when little land was left that could be homesteaded. Western farm settlement had reached its historic and practical limits on the high plains just east of the Rocky Mountains.

In the post-homestead decades after 1920, federal agencies continued to play a large role in the development of the West by building dams, selling mineral rights dirt-cheap (in the 1872 mining law, which was still in force in the early twenty-first century), subsidizing farmers large and small, creating highway systems (the U.S.-numbered roads that began in the 1920s and the interstates in the 1950s), managing national forests and parks, establishing military bases, and in many other ways.

The Urban West

Less heralded, but ultimately involving many more people, was the evolution of the urban West. SAN FRANCISCO began to boom with the Forty-Niner GOLD RUSH and reached a population of 100,000 in 1870, the first western city to do so. Los Angeles, a village of about 10,000 at that point, exploded after railroads arrived in the 1880s; it had passed San Francisco by 1920, soared beyond a million in 1930, and became the nation's second-largest city and metropolitan area in the early 1960s. Since then Los Angeles has become the most racially and ethnically diverse city, and California the first mainland state without a white majority, in the nation's history. Several hundred thousand African Americans, the majority women, arrived during World War II. For Asians, arriving in the American West meant an eastward, not westward, movement, starting with the Chinese who began coming after 1849 to the gold rush, followed by Japanese after 1890, Filipinos in the early twentieth century, and later South Asians, Vietnamese, and others. The American West assuredly included many Anglo-American homesteaders, but the full story must notice those who came from other directions—north from Mexico, south from Canada, and east from Asia; and also those who went not to farms but to cities and suburbs.

The West has always represented opportunity for Americans, from Puritan and Quaker colonists to mid-nineteenth-century Irish and German farmers and workers to the Asians and Latin Americans who have arrived in large numbers since the late 1960s. From the early 1700s to 1920, opportunity usually meant available farmland, but increasingly, through the nineteenth and twentieth centuries, cities provided opportunities as well—Chicago after its disastrous Great Fire of 1871, rebounding to over a million people by 1890; Los Angeles from the late 1880s on; Houston, Texas, and Silicon Valley in the 1990s. Opportunity did not always result in success. Many homesteading attempts failed, and many migrants to western cities did not achieve success. Yet the West remains America's fastest-growing region, as were the country's successive Wests for over three centuries.

BIBLIOGRAPHY

Hine, Robert V., and John Mack Faragher. *The American West: A New Interpretive History.* New Haven, Conn.: Yale University Press, 2000.

Limerick, Patricia Nelson. *The Legacy of Conquest: The Unbroken Past of the American West.* New York: Norton, 1987.

Milner, Clyde A., II, Carol A. O'Connor; and Martha A. Sandweiss. *The Oxford History of the American West.* New York: Oxford University Press, 1994.

Nugent, Walter. *Into the West: The Story of Its People.* New York: Knopf, 1999.

Rohrbough, Malcolm J. *The Trans-Appalachian Frontier: People, Societies, and Institutions, 1775–1850.* New York: Oxford University Press, 1978.

West, Elliott. *The Contested Plains: Indians, Goldseekers, and the Rush to Colorado.* Lawrence: University Press of Kansas, 1998.

Walter Nugent

See also **Explorations and Expeditions: U.S.; Frontier; Frontier Thesis, Turner's; Homestead Movement; Lewis and Clark Expedition; Oñate Explorations and Settlements; Western Exploration; Westerns; Westward Migration; Wild West Show.**

WEST COAST HOTEL COMPANY V. PARRISH,

300 U.S. 379 (1937), was a decision by the Supreme Court involving the constitutional validity of a Washington State statute creating a commission with power to fix minimum wages for women in the state. The Court thought that the close division by which the case of *Adkins v. Children's Hospital* (holding a similar act unconstitutional in 1923) had been decided—and changed economic conditions since that case—called for reconsideration of the constitutional issue in question: Does minimum-wage legislation constitute an undue infringement of the freedom of contract guaranteed by the due-process clause of the Fourteenth Amendment?

Chief Justice Charles Evans Hughes, speaking for the Court, reaffirmed the state's authority to interfere in labor contracts where it appeared that the parties were not equal in bargaining power or where the failure to intervene would endanger public health. The Court argued that to deny women a living wage imperiled their health and cast a burden on the community to support them. The enactment of a minimum-wage law for women, said the Court, was not a taking of "liberty" without "due process of law," and the Adkins case, being wrongly decided, should be overruled. Four justices, reiterating the arguments of the Adkins case, dissented. Dramatically ending a series of decisions overturning New Deal legislation, the *West Coast Hotel* opinion helped establish the legitimacy of federal economic controls and social welfare policies.

BIBLIOGRAPHY

Chambers, John W. "The Big Switch: Justice Roberts and the Minimum Wage Cases." *Labor History* 10 (1969): 49–52.

Leonard, Charles A. *A Search for a Judicial Philosophy.* Port Washington, N.Y.: Kennikat Press, 1971.

George W. Goble/A. R.

See also **Adkins v. Children's Hospital; Due Process of Law; Lochner v. New York; Minimum-Wage Legislation; Wages and Hours of Labor, Regulation of; Women in Public Life, Business, and Professions.**

WEST INDIES, BRITISH AND FRENCH. The terms British West Indies and French West Indies refer to those islands in the Caribbean formerly or presently under the British or French flags These terms lost any specific political meaning in the twentieth century. Britain continues to administer five possessions in the Caribbean as overseas territories: the Cayman Islands, the British Virgin Islands, the Turks and Caicos Islands, Anguilla, and Montserrat. These five territories are each governed

French West Indies. A depiction of slave quarters at a plantation on Saint Domingue, which became the Republic of Haiti in 1804 after a long slave uprising. THE GRANGER COLLECTION, LTD.

separately. The other islands comprising the former British West Indies achieved independence over a period beginning in the early 1960s and continuing into the 1980s.

French territories in the Caribbean are organized into two overseas departments and are treated as integral parts of France. One department consists of the island of Martinique; the other includes the island of Guadeloupe, part of the island of St. Martin, and several smaller island groups. Historically, France's largest and most important possession in the West Indies was Saint Domingue, which proclaimed its independence on 1 January 1804 as the Republic of Haiti. Independence came after years of protracted warfare with France, beginning with a slave uprising in 1791. Haiti is thus the first black republic, and the second-oldest independent country in the Western Hemisphere. (Only the United States achieved independence before Haiti.)

Relations between the United States and the islands prior to independence were largely determined by the state of relations between the United States and Britain and France. In the wake of the American Revolution, for example, many Americans who had remained loyal to the Crown fled to the British West Indies. Today, the majority of the white population of the Bahamas traces its descent to loyalists from South Carolina and Georgia who found refuge in those islands. During the Civil War, the South shipped cotton to England and purchased great quantities of weapons, ammunition, food, and other supplies from Britain. The Bahamas served as a major site for both British and Confederate ships running the Union blockade of Southern ports. Some blockade running also took place between Jamaica and ports on the Gulf Coast.

Since Haiti achieved independence long before any other state in the British and French West Indies, its relations with the United States are of particular interest. Because Haitian independence came as the result of a slave uprising, the southern slaveholding states viewed Haiti with fear and revulsion. Attempts to establish diplomatic relations between the United States and Haiti were repeatedly blocked by southern leaders. It was not until 1862, after the South had seceded, that Haiti and the United States finally established formal diplomatic relations. Haiti's history has been marked by frequent periods of authoritarian rule, instability, and widespread poverty. In July 1915, the United States landed marines there, following a protracted period of unrest that culminated in the killing of the country's president by an enraged mob. American intervention was motivated by fear of increased German influence in Haiti and a desire to protect foreign investments. The fact that U.S. marines did not leave Haiti until 1934 caused much resentment. From September 1957 until February 1986, Haiti was ruled by the Duvalier family. Dr. Francois "Papa Doc" Duvalier, who ultimately had himself declared president for life, governed the nation despotically until his death in April 1971, when he was succeeded by his 19-year-old son, Jean-Claude ("Baby Doc"). American relations with Haiti during the Duvalier era, which ended with the overthrow of Jean-Claude on 7 February 1986, were often strained. The United States has played a major role in trying to improve the political and economic climate in Haiti since then. During the late twentieth century and the early years of the twenty-first century, important issues in U.S.-Haiti relations included control of illegal im-

446

migration, and the fact that Haiti had become a major transshipment point for cocaine and other South American narcotics into the United States.

The United States has generally enjoyed friendly relations with the English-speaking Caribbean states since they received independence from Britain. In October 1983, however, U.S. forces, along with those of some Caribbean states, landed on Grenada to restore order in the wake of the murder of that nation's Marxist prime minister, Maurice Bishop, by rival elements in his government. In the last decades of the twentieth century, many states of the British West Indies served as transshipment points for South American narcotics destined for the United States. The Bahamas and the Cayman Islands, among other states and territories in the British West Indies, became major centers for offshore banking and other financial operations. Controlling narcotics and illegal financial transactions were significant issues in U.S. relations with the area in the opening years of the twenty-first century.

BIBLIOGRAPHY

Abbott, Elizabeth. *Haiti: The Duvaliers and Their Legacy.* New York: McGraw-Hill, 1988.

Braveboy-Wagner, Jacqueline Anne. *The Caribbean in World Affairs: The Foreign Policies of the English-Speaking States.* Boulder. Colo.: Westview Press, 1989.

Krehm, William. *Democracies and Tyrannies of the Caribbean.* New York: Lawrence Hill., 1985.

Williams, Eric Eustace. *From Columbus to Castro: the History of the Caribbean, 1492–1969.* New York: HarperCollins, 1971.

Jeffrey Kaplan

WEST POINT, in southeast New York State, is the site of the U.S. Military Academy (founded 1802). It is also the site of remains of two military posts, Forts Clinton and Putnam, built by the Continental army during the Revolution.

The swift collapse of the Hudson River defenses in October 1777, when in a fortnight Gen. Henry Clinton brought under British control the entire area from Manhattan Island north to Kingston, impressed on the Continentals the need for a proper defense. Moved to action by the urgent pleas of Gen. George Washington, the provincial congress of New York initiated a new survey of the Highlands of the Hudson, with the result that West Point was chosen as the site of the citadel for a strong system of defenses. The location was ideal. A plateau of about forty acres, lying more than 100 feet above the river level, formed a peninsula that dominated the water of a double right-angled bend of the river, as well as the river approaches, north and south, within cannon range. Moreover, the crests of two ridges west of the plateau could be fortified to meet a land attack.

Washington, who referred to West Point as the "key to America," made his headquarters there for the four

months following 28 July 1779. He was impelled to take charge by the urgencies of Baron Friedrich Wilhelm von Steuben who, writing of British plans of campaign, declared: "Whatever means they employ, I am positive their operations are directed exclusively to getting charge of this post and of the river as far as Albany. . . . On their success depends the fate of America." The seizure of West Point was always present in the British plans of campaign after 1777. Except for the British capture of Stony Point (May and July 1779) and Benedict Arnold's failed effort to turn the fort over to the British Army (1780), it was never threatened.

A corps of invalids (veterans) created by act of Congress, 20 June 1777, was transferred four years later to West Point, with the intention of using them as a cadre for the instruction of candidates for commissions. The germ of the idea that ultimately produced the U.S. Military Academy existed in that plan. In June 1784 Congress declared that "Standing armies in time of peace are . . . dangerous to the liberties of a free people," and accordingly reduced the army to eighty men, of which fifty-five were detailed to guard stores at West Point.

When domestic violence and foreign embroilments later forced Congress to increase the army, West Point became the garrison station of a corps of artillerists and engineers. Finally in 1802 Congress took the step that legally established the U.S. Military Academy at West Point. It is the oldest U.S. military post over which the country's flag has continuously flown.

BIBLIOGRAPHY

Ambrose, Stephen E. *Duty, Honor, Country: A History of West Point.* Baltimore: Johns Hopkins Press, 1966.

Atkinson, Rick. *The Long Gray Line.* Boston: Houghton Mifflin, 1989.

Palmer, Dave Richard. *The River and the Rock: The History of Fortress West Point, 1775–1783.* New York: Hippocrene Books, 1991.

Herman Beukema/A. G.

See also **Air Force Academy; Army, United States; Arnold's Treason; Military Academy; Naval Academy; Revolution, American: Military History; Volunteer Army.**

WEST VIRGINIA. The British landed on the Virginia coast in 1606 but exploration into the interior was slow. Besides curiosity, the main motivation for westward expansion was the fur trade, which played a large role in the commercial success of the colony. Sir William Berkeley, William Byrd, and Abraham Wood organized and financed a number of western expeditions. In 1671 Thomas Batts and Robert Fallam led the first expedition, organized by Abraham Wood, to travel far enough west to reach what would become the Virginia-West Virginia border. The rugged and mountainous physical characteristics of the territory earned the state the title of "the Switzerland of America." A relatively small population of Native Americans inhabited the area, the largest group of whom were the Iroquois. By 1669, the Iroquois and other groups like the Cherokees, Delawares, and Mingos used the land mostly for hunting and as a source of salt.

The first settler of record is Morgan Morgan who made his home in Berkley County at Bunker Hill in 1726. By the late 1700s, settlers, mostly Scotch-Irish and German, had penetrated the wilderness of the Allegheny Plateau. On the far western border, settlers arrived in Wirt County in 1796, and Wood County was organized in 1798. The first census reported 55,873 persons living within the borders of what would become West Virginia. By 1800 the number increased to 78,592. A number of towns incorporated during the 1780s: Lewisburg (1782), Clarksburg (1785), Morgantown (1785), Charles Town (1786), Frankfort (1787), and Middleton and West Liberty (1787). These first settlers were true pioneers entirely dependent on themselves and their environment for survival.

By the start of the nineteenth century, small industries such as saw mills, gristmills, salt manufacturing, and boatyards had started in the west. Transportation also improved and opened western Virginia for commercial pursuits. The opening of the Mississippi River meant businesses had a route around the region's mountains. Roads also developed. The 1818 Cumberland Road, from Cumberland to Wheeling, particularly benefited the west. However, it was the railroad that created the most change. As railroads penetrated through the trans-Allegheny region, populations in already settled areas doubled and even tripled, new places were settled, coal mines were opened, and other natural resources were harvested. As the region settled and became prosperous the west Virginians became more dissatisfied with the state's eastern government.

West Virginia remained part of the larger colony and then state of Virginia until the Civil War. Tension between the two regions of eastern and western Virginia was evident in the early nineteenth century. The Virginia constitution, adopted in 1776, provided the east with a number of advantages. For example, the document granted voting rights to white men owning twenty-five acres of worked land or fifty acres of unworked land, which favored the plantation culture of the east, not the small farmers of the west. The constitution also provided that slaves be taxed less than any other kind of property, which again benefited the east. To complicate matters the slave population was counted in determining representation in the state legislature. As a result of the east's dominance there was a corresponding distribution of funds. The majority of money for public works and government buildings went to the east.

In 1798 John G. Jackson, Harrison County delegate, presented the state government with a petition calling for amendments to the 1776 constitution. Although the petition was rejected, Jackson continued by writing for the *Richmond Examiner* with the pseudonym "A Mountaineer." His arguments became the foundation for reform. The legislature still refused to call a constitutional convention but made attempts to appease the westerners. The West, however, continued to voice their discontent and in 1828 the legislature finally agreed to a constitutional convention.

The western delegates had a number of goals including the extension of voting rights to all white men; representation based on white population; and election of county officials instead of appointment. The convention in Richmond on 5 October 1829 included past and future presidents, jurists, and an array of other statesmen. Unfortunately for the West, the convention's officers were elected using the traditional method, which meant the east had a distinct and profound advantage. Voters defeated every western goal. In response, every western delegate (except one too sick to attend) voted against the new constitution. Angered, some westerners called for immediate secession. In response the east granted some concessions over the next twenty years. However, the concessions still did not resolve the need to revise the 1776 constitution. A second convention called the Reform Convention convened in 1850. Despite the uneasy relationship between eastern and western delegates, they reached agreements on the remaining 1829 issues. The convention gave white males age twenty-one and older the right to vote; it made numerous offices elective; and it reformed the jury system.

During the 1850s the sectional troubles of the nation overshadowed Virginia's newfound harmony. Joseph Johnson, governor from 1852 to 1856, was the first popularly elected governor and also the first governor from the west. Johnson provided the western region with a real and psychological boost. Railroads continued to grow, as did commercial success. The region's population expanded and new counties formed. By the late 1850s, however, national tension over slavery began to disrupt Virginia. The two regions responded very differently to the growing sectional crisis. Westerners tended to remain moderate while the easterners were adamantly against abolition. Even after John Brown's 1859 raid on Harpers Ferry in western Virginia, the westerners remained moderate and calm, much to the chagrin of easterners who were outraged by Brown's actions.

Virginia as a whole was against secession. Even after the election of Abraham Lincoln and the secession of seven southern states in 1860 and early 1861, Virginia was still undecided. The course changed with Lincoln's call for volunteers after the 12 April 1861 firing on Fort Sumter, South Carolina. Virginia passed a secession ordinance on 17 April by a vote of eighty-five to fifty-five. Of forty-seven western delegates, thirty-two voted against secession, eleven favored secession, and four did not vote. The western delegates hurried back to their home counties and began to organize themselves for resistance.

A number of mass town meetings were held all over the west. The most significant of these was at Clarksburg organized by John S. Carlile. The meeting called for each West Virginia county to send five of its wisest men to Wheeling. During the first Wheeling Convention, 13–15 May 1861, Carlile's group wanted to separate from Virginia immediately. A more conservative group, led by Waitman T. Willey, wanted to wait until the people had a chance to vote on the secession ordinance. After three days of growing tension Carlile agreed to wait until the referendum.

The ordinance passed 23 May 1861. The second Wheeling Convention convened 11–25 June 1861, and nullified the secession ordinance and formed the "Restored" government of Virginia. On 24 October 1861, west Virginians voted 18,408 to 781 in favor of creating a new state. The constitutional convention met from 26 November 1861 until 18 February 1862. It outlined a new government and the physical boundaries of the state. According to the U.S. Constitution, any new state must have the permission of its parent state before it can achieve statehood. West Virginia asked the Restored government at Wheeling for permission to form a new state. On 13 May 1862, the Restored governor Francis Pierpont approved the formation of a new state. The West Virginia state bill went to Congress on 29 May 1862. After debate on the slavery issue the bill passed with one amendment. The Willey Amendment was a compromise; it provided for emancipation of slaves over twenty-one and the emancipation of younger slaves when they reached twenty-one. The bill passed and President Abraham Lincoln signed it on 31 December 1862. The people of the fifty western Virginian counties voted in favor of the statehood bill on 26 March 1863, and on 20 June 1863, West Virginia officially became the thirty-fifth state. Among other names considered for it were Kanawha, Western Virginia, Allegheny, and Augusta; of the forty-four votes the name "West Virginia" received thirty.

After the Civil War, Virginia and West Virginia struggled over an issue of compensation. After a number of legal battles, the U.S. Supreme Court ruled that West Virginia owed Virginia $12,393,930. The debt was paid off over time with the last installment made in 1939.

Throughout the Civil War the Union held the advantage in West Virginia. Supporters for both the Union and the Confederacy lived in West Virginia, and the war literally split families as some members fought for the North and others for the South. West Virginians also served in militias and irregular units sympathetic to the Confederacy. The fighting in the western theater was guerrilla in nature consisting of raids, arson, robbery, and intimidation.

Reconstruction was difficult for West Virginia, despite its Union loyalty. Hostility between former Confederate and Union soldiers was a serious problem. Some Confederate sympathizers continued violence causing Arthur Boreman, West Virginia's first governor, to recommend citizens organize themselves for protection. The majority of Confederate veterans, however, were not violent and in some cases federal troops were called to protect former Confederates from Unionist violence.

Another concern was that former Confederates, most of whom held Democratic views, would threaten the existence of the new state. Lincoln's reelection in 1864 lessened those fears, but his assassination in 1865 aroused them again. Governor Boreman traveled to meet with now President Andrew Johnson, who promised West Virginia his support. Boreman's administration also restricted former Confederates from holding public office and curtailed their voting rights. The laws did not relax until a new governor, William E. Stevenson, took office. By 1871, former Confederates were allowed to vote and hold office.

With restrictions removed, the Democrats slowly came to power in West Virginia, controlling the state from 1871 until 1897. The state held a constitutional convention in 1872 where sixty-six of seventy-eight members were Democrats. The new constitution omitted the word "white" from voter qualifications, placed executive power with the governor, and made changes in the judicial and legislative branches. The Democratic Party consisted of a diverse group of former Confederates, Unionists, former Whigs, and Bourbon Democrats. Republicans resumed control in 1897 and stayed in power until 1933 when Democrats regained their influence.

Sectional difference also affected the location of the state's capital. The capital was in Wheeling from 1863 until 1870. Associating the city with radical Republicanism, the Democratic legislature moved the capital to Charleston where it stayed until 1875. Charleston, however, was much smaller than Wheeling, and it was harder to reach since it did not have a railroad or an established structure for shipping. Legislators moved the capital back to Wheeling. Finally, in 1877 the legislature agreed to hold a referendum to establish a permanent capital. The voters chose among Charleston, Clarksburg, and Martinsburg; Charleston won and officially became the permanent capital of West Virginia on 1 May 1885.

In 1863 over 80 percent of West Virginians were involved in agriculture. The most important crop was corn, but wheat, oats, hay, and potatoes were also important. By the late nineteenth century, extractive industries such as coal mining, lumbering, and oil and gas production had overshadowed agriculture, taking wealth from the land without returning profit to the state.

The bituminous coal industry soared after the Civil War and climbed until the Great Depression. In 1914 coal production was 69,783,088 tons and by 1929 the production was 139,297,146 tons. The importance and place of coal in West Virginia created a new socioeconomic structure. As big business moved into the region the agrarian society became a mass of landless wage earners. Mining towns created a system of worker dependence on the company. A variety of people sought employment in West Virginia's mines, including newly freed slaves and new immigrants. As smaller coal companies consolidated into large powerful corporations they gained more and more influence over local and state governments. The vast wealth that coal mining generated went to absentee landowners who cared little about the land, environment, or people.

The United Mine Workers of America (UMWA), organized in 1890, attempted to unionize West Virginia's coal miners. The powerful companies used special police, blacklisting, and court injunctions to block the UMWA from even meeting. Miners often tried striking in hopes of securing better working conditions, which resulted in their eviction from the company-owned housing. Often tensions between miners and company guards led to violence. One of the most violent episodes, the Paint Creek Strike of 1912–1913, resulted in martial law. The other extractive industries, oil, gas, and timber, developed along similar lines. The cycle of feudalistic absenteeism and the extractive nature of West Virginia's industries ravaged the environment and left the people in poverty.

During World War I, UMWA membership increased from 7,000 members in 1913 to 50,000 members by the end of the war. World War I also brought interest in chemical and steel industries. Labor made some advances, such as a workers' compensation law, but the wartime demand and necessity of industrial goods outweighed other needs. The Great Depression hit the entire Appalachian region especially hard. A 40 percent reduction in coal production meant a rise in unemployment in an already economically depressed area. For people whose whole lives depended on the company town, the Red Cross and religious organizations were often the only places left to turn. Falling in line with the rest of the country, West Virginia began to vote out Republicans in favor of Democrats. Although at the close of World War II West Virginia shared the nation's prosperity, the state experienced a drop in population largely due to an increased use of technology. Mechanization reduced the need for employees, so people went elsewhere for work.

West Virginia had few public schools before the Civil War, but advances came quickly between 1872 and World War I. West Virginia University opened 2 September 1868, in Morgantown. Still, financing schools was hard for the poor region. West Virginia did, however, establish a minimum wage for teachers: about $22 a month. Between 1910 and 1925 the state saw a surge in the growth of high schools, but the depression meant education took a backseat to survival. The 1940s and 1950s brought a wave of reforms to the educational system, including better benefits for teachers, new textbooks, merging elementary and secondary schools, and programs like Head Start and Upward Bound. Education, however, remained a problem well into the 1980s, due to financial problems in the state. In 1984 the average public teacher's salary was more than $4,000 less than the national average. Despite efforts to enact legislation to improve salaries and redesign state education financing, West Virginia's schools continued to suffer. At the beginning of the twenty-first century, the state's high school and college graduation rates were the nation's lowest.

The governors during the 1960s began to initiate programs to help clean up the state's environment. William Wallace Barron created the Air Pollution Control Commission and a volunteer statewide clean-up program, and Hulett Carlson Smith's administration brought legislation to control air and stream pollution and strip mining. During the environmental movement of the 1970s, attention was finally given to the drastic impact extractive industries made on the region's land and people. Clear cutting and strip mining created pollution that ruined streams and landscapes. Government programs such as the Appalachian Regional Commission and private organizations strove to help rebuild the regions and increase money coming into the Appalachian regions with tourism. During the 1980s, West Virginia suffered severely from the recession and energy crisis. By 1984 the state had the nation's highest unemployment rate. Renewed attention helped to draw some people to the region. In 1970 the population was 1,744,237 and by 2000 the number had increased somewhat to 1,808,344 but both were still lower than the 1950 count of 2,005,552. In the year 2000 West Virginia's poverty rates remained the highest in the nation.

The population drop also cost West Virginia a congressional seat. Arch Alfred Moore Jr., governor from 1985 to 1989, developed a recovery program and tax cuts designed to attract new industries and revitalize the coal industry. While West Virginia failed to attract GM's Saturn automobile plant in 1985 (the plant went to Springhill, Tennessee), by 1990 over two hundred corporations were receiving tax credits and bolstering the state's economy. Jobs in the coal industry, however, continued to decline. The program of tax cuts also led to widespread corruption so severe that Moore was convicted of extortion in 1990. The next governor, William Gaston Caperton III (1989–1997), inherited the state's financial woes. To battle the long-term financial problems, he raised taxes and adopted a state lottery to no avail.

A great deal of financial help stemmed from the efforts of Senator Robert C. Byrd. In 1986 Byrd became chairman of the Senate Appropriations Committee and promised to bring more than $1 billion of federal projects to West Virginia by 1995; by 1992 he had exceeded that goal. Besides various highway and water projects, West Virginia also received a new federal prison and the FBI relocated its fingerprint center from Washington, D.C. to Clarksburg. The state also benefited from a new appreciation of Appalachian culture and art. Artists and novelists helped awaken the nation to West Virginia's beauty and plight while historians, sociologists, and anthropologists began to create a new body of scholarly interest and work about the region.

BIBLIOGRAPHY

Ambler, Charles Henry. *West Virginia*. New York: Prentice-Hall, 1940.

Rasmussen, Barbara. *Absentee Landowning and Exploitation in West Virginia, 1760–1920*. Lexington: University Press of Kentucky, 1994.

Rice, Otis. *The Allegheny Frontier: West Virginia Beginnings, 1730–1830*. Lexington: University Press of Kentucky, 1970.

——— and Stephen W. Brown. *West Virginia: A History*. Lexington: University Press of Kentucky, 1993.

West Virginia Division of Culture and History. Available from http://www.wvculture.org/.

Lisa A. Ennis

See also **Civil War; Virginia;** *Virginia v. West Virginia.*

WESTERN EXPLORATION.

Beginning with the first voyage of Columbus in 1492, the exploration of North America was a central component of the larger global contest between Europe's great imperial powers. Each sought to "discover" and thus claim the exclusive right to colonize vast geographic areas, using the wealth gained from the New World to enhance their economies in Europe and to monopolize global trade networks. Because the western half of North America was a vast borderland between several imperial concerns, the region that became the American West was an arena of particular contestation. Commencing with the arrival of Spanish conquistadores in the 1540s and continuing through nearly three centuries of French, British, and even Russian efforts to gain exclusive access to the peoples and resources of the region, western exploration reflected the shifting diplomatic and commercial concerns of these imperial rivals. They in turn shaped the nineteenth-century exploratory efforts of the United States, which sought to expand the territorial reach of the American government and assess the commercial potential of the region.

Spanish Exploration in the Southwest

Spanish interest in the lands north of Mexico followed the rapid conquests of the Aztec, Incan, and Mayan empires. Hoping to find equally wealthy civilizations, Francisco Vásquez de Coronado set out in 1540 to conquer the fabled Seven Cities of Cíbola. After crossing present-day Arizona, he traveled toward northwestern New Mexico, where he invaded the Zuni pueblos, which he believed were the Seven Cities. He soon left, disappointed by the lack of gold or silver among these people. Some of Coronado's lieutenants explored westward to the Colorado River, which they viewed from the rim of the Grand Canyon, and then moved eastward to the pueblos of the Upper Rio Grande. The following summer, hoping still to find cities of gold, Coronado headed northeast toward the central Great Plains, where he expected to find a wealthy city called Quivira. After reaching the villages of

the Wichita Indians in central Kansas, he ended his quest and returned to Mexico.

Coronado's search for Quivira was intended to bring him to the mythic Straits of Anián, the supposed Northwest Passage across the continent connecting the Pacific and Atlantic Oceans, a goal that also inspired the voyage of Juan Rodríguez Cabrillo along the California coast in 1542. While Cabrillo's expedition failed to find the straits, it did establish the northern boundary of the Spanish empire in the Americas at the present-day California-Oregon border. Cabrillo's rudimentary charts also identified areas along the coast that subsequently were used by the famed Manila Galleons from 1565 to 1815.

Except for a few expeditions in the service of colonization efforts in the Rio Grande valley or mapping potential landfalls for the Manila Galleons, the Spanish largely ceased both overland and maritime explorations of their northern frontiers until the eighteenth century. Notable exceptions included Sebastián Vizcaíno's exploration of the Pacific Coast in 1602, again in search of the fabled Straits of Anián, and Don Juan de Oñate's exploration of the central Great Plains in 1601 and the lower Colorado River in 1604–1605. Spanish administrators did not express a renewed interest in northern exploration until the 1760s and 1770s, and then only to stave off threats from Russian, French, and English designs in western North America. Beginning with a joint land and sea expedition led by Father Junípero Serra and Gaspar de Portolá in 1769, which led to the discovery of San Francisco Bay that year, Spain rapidly established important military and religious settlements along the California coast at San Diego (1769), Monterey (1770), and San Francisco (1776). The explorations of Juan Bautista de Anza and Father Francisco Garcés in the same era established land routes between these settlements and older colonies in present-day Arizona and New Mexico.

The French on the Great Plains

In an effort to expand France's vast fur-trading empire, a number of French traders pushed westward onto the Great Plains in the first half of the eighteenth century. Unlike the Spanish, these explorers did not attempt to establish permanent communities but instead focused on mapping navigable waterways, identifying potential Native trading partners, and searching for a route to the Pacific Ocean. From 1714 to 1718, Etienne de Véniard de Bourgmont traveled up the Missouri River as far as the Cheyenne River in present-day South Dakota, producing detailed information on the geography of the region and its inhabitants and securing a small fortune in peltry. These efforts were matched from 1739 to 1741, when the brothers Pierre and Paul Mallet traveled up the southern branch of the Platte River then down to Santa Fe. The Mallets were quickly forced to leave this Spanish outpost, and they returned to New Orleans by way of the Canadian and Arkansas Rivers. Between 1738 and 1743, Pierre de la Vérendrye and his two sons made repeated explo-

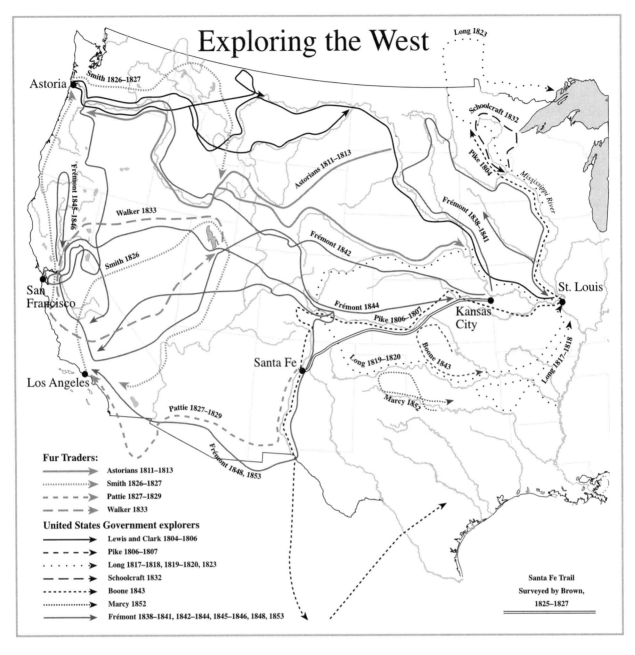

Exploring the West

Long 1823

Smith 1826–1827

Astoria

Schoolcraft 1832

Pike 1804

Mississippi River

Astorians 1811–1813

Frémont 1838–1841

Frémont 1845–1846

Walker 1833

Frémont 1842

Smith 1826

St. Louis

Frémont 1844

Pike 1806–1807

Kansas City

Boone 1843

Long 1817–1818

San Francisco

Santa Fe

Long 1819–1820

Los Angeles

Marcy 1852

Pattie 1827–1829

Frémont 1848, 1853

Fur Traders:

Astorians 1811–1813
Smith 1826–1827
Pattie 1827–1829
Walker 1833

United States Government explorers

Lewis and Clark 1804–1806
Pike 1806–1807
Long 1817–1818, 1819–1820, 1823
Schoolcraft 1832
Boone 1843
Marcy 1852
Frémont 1838–1841, 1842–1844, 1845–1846, 1848, 1853

Santa Fe Trail
Surveyed by Brown,
1825–1827

rations westward from Lake Superior to the upper Missouri River in present-day North Dakota and even as far as the Black Hills. While none of these explorers managed to find a route across the continent or to establish a serious challenge to Spanish trade in the Southwest, their travels did cement France's claims to the vast territory of Louisiana. Likewise, information they gathered provided the basis for various editions of Claude Delisle and Guillame Delisle's *Carte de la Louisiane et du cours du Mississippi* (1718), the most important map of central North America until the end of the century.

The English in the Pacific Northwest

Following the end of the Seven Years' War (known as the French and Indian War among the colonists) in 1763,

Great Britain assumed control of New France and the North American fur trade. English exploration of the continent's interior mirrored French objectives but mostly took place in the Canadian West. Some expeditions took in areas below the forty-ninth parallel, however, including David Thompson's remarkable efforts on behalf of the North West Company. In 1797–1798, Thompson completed a circuit that took him from western Lake Superior along the border established between the United States and British Canada in 1792 and down to the Mandan villages on the Missouri River. For the next several years, Thompson intermittently explored and established posts on the plains and mountains of present-day Alberta, then in 1807 he crossed the Rocky Mountains and discovered the source of the Columbia River. Over the next two years, he traveled south into present-day Idaho, Montana, and Washington, where he established trading posts and carefully mapped river courses, Native villages, and mountain ranges. He returned to the region in 1811 and explored down the Columbia River from Kettle Falls in northeastern Washington to the Pacific Ocean. Two years later, Thompson began work on his cartographic masterpiece, the massive *Map of the North-West Territory of the Province of Canada from Actual Survey during the Years 1792–1812.*

Thompson's efforts were augmented in subsequent years by traders who worked for the North West Company and its rival the Hudson's Bay Company, which eventually merged with the former in 1821. Most notable were the explorations of Donald McKenzie and Peter Skene Ogden, who together mapped vast portions of the interior Northwest from the Columbia River to the Gulf of California. From 1818 to 1821, McKenzie trapped and explored along the Snake River for the North West Company from the river's confluence with the Columbia to its headwaters in the Rocky Mountains. These efforts initiated the fur-trapping expeditions known as the Snake River brigades and described a significant portion of what became the Oregon Trail. Ogden made six separate expeditions between 1824 and 1830 on behalf of the Hudson's Bay Company, in part to stave off American commercial interests in the Pacific Northwest as well as to extend British interests farther south. Toward these two ends, from 1824 to 1830, Ogden explored nearly the entire region drained by the Snake River, most of the current state of Oregon south to Klamath Lake, a large portion of the Great Basin from the Great Salt Lake to the western reaches of the Humboldt River, and south from the Great Salt Lake to the Gulf of California then back north through California's Central Valley to the Columbia River.

Before embarking on these explorations of the interior West, the British used their maritime strength to survey the coast and assess Spanish and Russian colonization efforts. Sir Francis Drake sailed up the California coast in 1578 during his two-year circumnavigation of the globe. But the English did not return in earnest until Captain James Cook cruised the coast from present-day Oregon to southeastern Alaska in 1778 in another fruitless effort to discover a Northwest Passage. After Cook's death in Hawaii that winter, his ship, the *Endeavour,* returned to the area to engage Russian fur traders along the Aleutian Islands and the Bering Strait. George Vancouver sailed to the Northwest Coast in 1792 to search for the now doubted Northwest Passage but more importantly to assess the lucrative trade in sea otter pelts then carried on by the Russians and Spanish. His voyage brought him along the coastlines of present-day Oregon and Washington, one hundred miles up the Columbia River, through Puget Sound, and up the Inland Passage to southeast Alaska. Vancouver was a remarkable cartographer who, along with the later efforts of men like Thompson,

McKenzie, and Ogden, established the British in the Northwest and filled in one of the last unmapped portions of North America.

The Spanish, French, and Russians on the Northwest Coast

The English were not alone in their explorations of the Northwest. In the last quarter of the eighteenth century, the Spanish accelerated maritime exploration, including the voyages of Juan Francisco de la Bodega y Quadra (1779), Estéban Martinez (1788), Alejandro Malaspina (1791), and Juan Martinez (1793). While most of these concentrated on assessing the sea otter trade around Vancouver Island and the Gulf of Alaska and finding the still hoped for Northwest Passage, Juan Martinez gave careful attention to the coast between San Francisco and the Columbia River. The French navigator Jean-François de Galaup, comte de la Pérouse, also briefly covered much of this area in the summer of 1786, but the region was best known to Russian explorers. Beginning with the voyages of Vitus Bering and Aleksey Chirikov in 1741, the Russians made more than one hundred commercial voyages along the Gulf of Alaska over the next six decades. By 1812, under the auspices of the Russian-American Company, Russian traders and explorers had pushed as far south as Fort Ross on the California coast near Bodega Bay, which they occupied until 1841.

The United States and Nation Building

Even before he organized the Lewis and Clark Expedition of 1804–1806, Thomas Jefferson had long expressed an interest in westward exploration in the competitive terms defined by European imperial interests. The "purposes of commerce," as he instructed Meriwether Lewis, dictated the establishment of a strong American presence in the fur trade, the search for a water route across the continent, the assessment of imperial rivals in the Far West, and reports on the agricultural potential of Indian lands. Jefferson had privately sponsored two failed efforts to explore the West before the 1803 Louisiana Purchase allowed him to organize the first official U.S. exploration party under the command of Lewis and William Clark. Extending up the entire length of the Missouri River, across the Rocky Mountains, and eventually to the mouth of the Columbia River, the expedition proved that no easy water route existed across North America but otherwise achieved all of Jefferson's goals. The expedition also established American claims to the Columbia River, which had first been discovered by the Boston fur trader Robert Gray in May 1792, some five months before one of Vancouver's ships sailed up the river. Jefferson also organized two other exploring parties. The expedition under Zebulon Pike crossed the central Plains to the Colorado Rockies in 1806–1807 and took in the southern reaches of the Louisiana Purchase, and the expedition of Thomas Freeman and Peter Custis up the Red River in 1806 was short-lived.

In the ensuing decades, American exploration of the West was largely undertaken by fur trade expeditions. These included Jedediah Smith's journey from Salt Lake to southern California and back in 1826–1827, Joseph Walker's 1833 trek across the Sierra Nevadas, and the various adventures of Jim Bridger and Benjamin L. E. de Bonneville in the central and northern Rockies. The United States did mount an official scientific expedition of significance during the fur trade era, namely Stephen Long's exploration of the central Plains and the front range of the Rocky Mountains in 1820.

In 1838, the U.S. Army established a separate Corps of Topographical Engineers, which moved U.S. exploration away from older concerns with imperial rivals in the fur trade into the realm of conquest and nation building. Corps engineers explored much of the Southwest before and during the Mexican War, and John C. Frémont's reports found a wide audience among Americans eager to acquire new lands on the West Coast. The close of the Mexican War also led to an extensive boundary survey from the mouth of the Rio Grande to San Diego, California, in 1848–1855. In the mid-1850s, the most significant exploration of the American West involved the transcontinental railroad surveys (1853–1854), which reconnoitered four potential routes across the United States, roughly along the forty-fifth, thirty-eighth, thirty-fifth, and thirty-second parallels of latitude.

Immediately following the Civil War, most military explorations were conducted in the context of the Plains Indian wars, such as George Custer's expedition to the Black Hills in 1874. Farther west, Ferdinand V. Hayden, Clarence King, and John Wesley Powell conducted extensive scientific surveys of the western mountains and deserts. Focused on locating water and mineral sources on public lands, their work soon led to the creation of the U.S. Geological Survey (USGS) in 1879. Combining the offices of several government survey operations, the USGS completed the task of mapping the West by the end of the nineteenth century.

BIBLIOGRAPHY

Allen, John Logan, ed. *North American Exploration*. 3 vols. Lincoln: University of Nebraska Press, 1997.

Brebner, John Bartlet. *The Explorers of North America, 1492–1806*. London: A. C. Black, 1933.

Goetzmann, William H. *Exploration and Empire: The Explorer and the Scientist in the Winning of the American West*. New York: Knopf, 1966.

Meinig, D. W. *The Shaping of America*. Vol. 1. *Atlantic America, 1492–1800*. New Haven, Conn.: Yale University Press, 1986.

———. *The Shaping of America*. Vol. 2. *Continental America, 1800–1867*. New Haven, Conn.: Yale University Press, 1993.

Weber, David J. *The Spanish Frontier in North America*. New Haven, Conn.: Yale University Press, 1992.

Mark David Spence

See also **Cabeza de Vaca Expeditions; Colorado River Explorations; Conquistadores; Cook, James, Explorations of; Coronado Expeditions; Exploration of America, Early; Explorations and Expeditions: British, French, Russian, Spanish, U.S.; Frémont Explorations; Geological Survey, U.S.; Geophysical Explorations; Great Plains; Lewis and Clark Expedition; Northwest Passage; Oñate Explorations and Settlements; Pike, Zebulon, Expeditions of; Vancouver Explorations;** *and vol. 9:* **An Expedition to the Valley of the Great Salt Lake of Utah; Message on the Lewis and Clark Expedition; The Journals of the Lewis and Clark Expedition.**

WESTERN FEDERATION OF MINERS, a radical labor union founded among miners and smelters in the Rocky Mountains in 1893. At first affiliated with the American Federation of Labor (AFL), it broke away because of the AFL's conservative policies. The Western Federation called the strikes at Cripple Creek, Colo., in 1894, Leadville, Colo., in 1896, and the Coeur d'Alene district, in Idaho, in 1896 and 1897. Much bloodshed and violence marked these strikes, as militant union members clashed with company guards and strikebreakers, and with state and federal troops. Allied with the Industrial Workers of the World from 1905 to 1907, the Western Federation rejoined the AFL in 1911. In 1916 the union changed its name to the International Union of Mine, Mill, and Smelter Workers.

BIBLIOGRAPHY

Mellinger, Philip J. *Race and Labor in Western Copper: The Fight for Equality, 1896–1918*. Tucson: University of Arizona Press, 1995.

Stanley, Kathleen. "The Politics of the Western Federation of Miners and the United Mine Workers of America." In *Bringing Class Back in Contemporary and Historical Perspectives*. Edited by Scott G. McNall et al. Boulder, Colo.: Westview Press, 1991.

Suggs, George G. *Colorado's War on Militant Unionism: James H. Peabody and the Western Federation of Miners*. Norman: University of Okahoma Press, 1991.

Alvin F. Harlow/D. B.

See also **Coeur D'Alene Riots; Helena Mining Camp; International Union of Mine, Mill, and Smelter Workers; Leadville Mining District.**

WESTERN LANDS. When the thirteen colonies declared their independence from Great Britain, seven had overlapping and conflicting claims to western lands. These claims, which extended to the MISSISSIPPI RIVER, had been cut off by the PROCLAMATION OF 1763 and the Quebec Act of 1774. But, with independence, the states revived them, and Virginia undertook a campaign to recover its territory, which included the present states of Kentucky and West Virginia, and the territory north of the Ohio and east of the Mississippi rivers. The claims of Massachusetts, Connecticut, and New York cut across this northwest territory of Virginia. The claims of North and South Carolina and Georgia were south of Virginia, including the land between their present boundaries and the Mississippi.

The ownership of such vast areas by a few states aroused jealousy and ill-feeling among small states lacking western lands. They feared the western lands would give large states too much power, and Maryland refused to ratify the ARTICLES OF CONFEDERATION until landowning states surrendered their claims to the new government. The CONTINENTAL CONGRESS urged the states to cede their land claims to the central government, promising to erect new states there. Thus assured, New York and Virginia ceded their claims, but with unacceptable qualifications. New York's claims rested on Indian treaties of doubtful legality, but its cession greatly aided the movement. By 1781 Maryland was sufficiently convinced other states would follow and ratified the Articles of Confederation.

On 20 October 1783 Virginia again offered to cede its lands north of the Ohio, provided that it be allowed to reserve for itself a military district in the present state of Ohio to satisfy military grants made during the revolution. This offer was accepted on 1 March 1784. Virginia also retained its land south of the Ohio, which entered the Union in 1791 as the state of Kentucky. In 1785 Massachusetts ceded its claim to land in the present states of Michigan and Wisconsin, and in 1786 Connecticut ceded its western lands. Connecticut reserved a tract of 3.8 million acres in northeastern Ohio—called the Western Reserve—a part of which it set aside for the relief of those whose property had been destroyed by the British during the revolution. South Carolina ceded its land in 1787, as did North Carolina in 1790. After long delay, Georgia ceded its lands in 1802, but only after it sold vast tracts in the Yazoo Valley to land speculating companies under conditions of notorious fraud, roiling the political waters for a generation.

These cessions gave the Confederation a vast public domain of 221.99 million acres. But within the present states of Kentucky and Tennessee, the soil had already been granted to revolutionary war veterans, settlers, and land companies by Virginia and North Carolina, leaving the Confederation with only political jurisdiction. In 1785 the Confederation adopted a land ordinance to provide a method of disposing of the vast territory. In 1787 the Confederation adopted the Northwest Ordinance to provide a form of government for what came to be known as the OLD NORTHWEST. The land and government systems were not extended to the territory of the Southwest until later.

BIBLIOGRAPHY

Etcheson, Nicole. *The Emerging Midwest: Upland Southerners and the Political Culture of the Old Northwest, 1787–1861.* Bloomington: Indiana University Press, 1996.

Hibbard, Benjamin H. *A History of the Public Land Policies.* Madison: University of Wisconsin Press, 1965.

Hurt, R. Douglas. *The Ohio Frontier: Crucible of the Old Northwest, 1720–1830.* Bloomington: Indiana University Press, 1996.

Paul W. Gates / c. w.

See also **Colonial Charters; Land Bounties; Land Claims; Northwest Territory; Ordinances of 1784, 1785, and 1787; Western Reserve; Yazoo Fraud.**

WESTERN RESERVE. The Western Reserve, a part of northeastern Ohio lying along the south shore of Lake Erie and once belonging to Connecticut, is an irregular quadrilateral—with Conneaut, Youngstown, Willard, and Port Clinton at the corners. The charter that the Connecticut river towns obtained from Charles II in 1662 fixed the colony's boundaries north and south by parallels extending westward to the "South Sea" (Pacific Ocean). With royal disdain for the inconveniences of geography, King Charles granted parts of the same region to the Duke of York and to Admiral William Penn, while King James had already given Virginia a basis for a claim to all the territory included in Connecticut's boundaries beyond Pennsylvania.

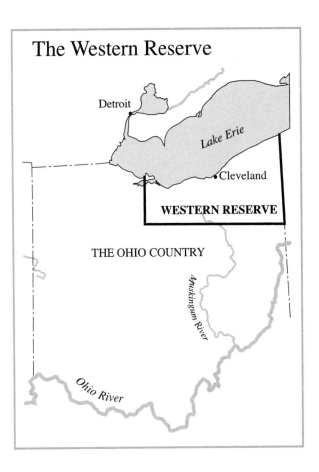

The Western Reserve

455

Following the American Revolution, these overlapping claims left the thirteen states to face serious territorial disputes. Small states without western lands, particularly MARYLAND, were loath to enter a union with great inequalities in public lands. Congress proposed that states cede their western lands, all or in part, to the Confederation, promising to admit the territories as new states on equal terms with the original thirteen. The states accepted the plan, launching the Confederation.

In 1786 Connecticut ceded its lands west of Pennsylvania except for a portion, the Western Reserve, that it attempted to keep as recompense for its relatively small size. It proceeded at once to plan for an advantageous disposal of its western estate. In 1792 it assigned 500,000 acres from the western end to the inhabitants of the Connecticut towns along the Long Island Sound as compensation for losses inflicted by British raids during the revolution. The "Firelands," as they called this western region, drew a steady stream of immigrants from Connecticut. In 1795 the Connecticut Land Company purchased the remaining portion of the Western Reserve, estimated at the time at more than 3 million acres.

Moses Cleaveland, one of the purchasers and general agent of the company, went west in 1796 to supervise a survey and other preparations for sale and settlement, finding a heavily forested area along the south shore of Lake Erie that was long unfavorable for extensive sale. The absence of any form of local government also for many years created a barrier to settlement. In 1800 Connecticut and the United States arranged by a joint agreement that the Western Reserve should be attached as a county to the newly formed Ohio Territory. Governor Arthur St. Clair gave it the name Trumbull County and proceeded to organize local government. Later, particularly after the completion of the ERIE CANAL in 1825, the population grew, resulting in Trumbull County's division and redivision into multiple counties.

The term "Western Reserve" ceased to have any territorial meaning and later lingered in the names of various commercial and banking enterprises, or in such instances as the Western Reserve Historical Society and the Western Reserve University. But Connecticut's Western Reserve developed as an extension of New England into the West. Names of families, towns, architecture, and social customs carried evidence of this transfer of population from the East and marked Western Reserve apart from other parts of the country until later industrialization and immigration blurred its origins.

BIBLIOGRAPHY

Campbell, Thomas F., and Edward M. Miggins, eds. *The Birth of Modern Cleveland, 1865–1930.* Cleveland, Ohio: Western Reserve Historical Society, 1988.

Lupold, Harry F., and Gladys Haddad, eds. *Ohio's Western Reserve: A Regional Reader.* Kent, Ohio: Kent State University Press, 1988.

Van Tassel, David D., ed. *The Encyclopedia of Cleveland History.* 2d. ed. Bloomington: Indiana University Press, 1996.

Elbert J. Benton / c. w.

See also **Cleveland; Colonial Charters; Connecticut; Pennsylvania; Western Lands; Duke of York's Proprietary.**

WESTERN UNION TELEGRAPH COMPANY.

The Western Union Telegraph Company resulted from the 1856 merger of Hiram Sibley's New York and Mississippi Valley Printing Telegraph Company and lines controlled by New York businessman Ezra Cornell. At Cornell's insistence, the newly formed venture was named Western Union to represent the consolidation of western telegraph lines.

During its first years, Western Union expanded rapidly by systematically acquiring its competitors. By 1861 it had completed the first transcontinental telegraph line, uniting the Union and providing rapid communication during the Civil War. The system proved so efficient that it prompted the U.S. government to discontinue the historic PONY EXPRESS. The company soon began experimenting with new technologies. In 1866 it introduced the first stock ticker, developed by then-employee Thomas Edison, and in 1871 it introduced money transfer as a complement to its existing telegraph business.

Having first declined to purchase the patent for Alexander Graham Bell's telephone, Western Union subsequently purchased the patents of Bell's competitor Elisha Gray. Western Union's foray into the telephone business proved unsuccessful, however. By 1879, faced with stiff competition from Bell, Western Union agreed to exit the industry. In return it received the promise that Bell would no longer operate a telegraph business.

By the early 1900s, the telephone industry had grown dramatically and the telegraph giant found itself a subsidiary of the American Telephone and Telegraph Company, which purchased Western Union in 1909. The U.S. government, however, fearing a monopoly, forced the sale of Western Union just four years later.

For many years the company continued to be an innovator in the communications industry. In 1914 it introduced the first consumer charge card; in 1924, it was one of several companies to develop a high-speed facsimile system. Ironically, facsimile services would eventually become a contributing factor in the decline of the telegraph industry.

Over the next several decades Western Union revenues began to fall. Fierce competition and the development of more efficient technologies for message delivery led to the decline of the telegram. Determined to remain a player in the telecommunications industry, Western Union diversified into Telex in 1958 and launched the country's first domestic communications satellite, *Westar I,* in 1974.

Yoggy, Gary A. *Riding the Video Range: The Rise and Fall of the Western on Television*. Jefferson, N.C.: McFarland, 1995.

Kristen L. Rouse

See also **Film; *Leatherstocking Tales;* Television: Programming and Influence**.

WESTWARD MIGRATION. The westward migration that resulted in the rapid settlement of the continental United States is perhaps the most compelling and important theme in American history. In no other place or time has such an immense region been settled so quickly by individuals and small groups of settlers who operated independent of, and at times in direct violation of, governmental policy. Of seminal importance in outlining westward migration in American history is the relationship of the frontier to the process of westward movement. Usually considered the area where the settled portions of civilization meet the untamed wilderness, the frontier moved west over time with the migrations of American settlers. The relocation and redefinition of the frontier thus in many ways came to define the process of westward migration, both as a delineating marker between settlement and wilderness and as a gateway to the "West."

Colonial Migrations

American westward migration actually began when the first English colonists came to the New World seeking land and socioreligious liberation. More generally, however, historians view the process of westward movement as having its genesis in the spread of settlement away from the Atlantic coast, a process that removed the frontier at places up to two hundred miles inland by the mid-eighteenth century. Despite significant variances in economics and political orientation within the American colonies, the first phase of westward migration exhibited the same trait that permeates American continental expansion as a whole—the individualistic pursuit of inexpensive, arable land.

In Virginia and Maryland, colonists initiated westward migration by moving into the interior in pursuit of new land for tobacco cultivation. Beginning in 1618, the headright system offered fifty acres of land to new migrants who promised to raise tobacco or to wealthy sponsors who paid for the passage of an emigrant, and fueled a westward flow of land hunters and tobacco farmers. The vast majority of desirable land in the tidewater region soon fell into the hands of an elite class of planter aristocrats, forcing lesser farmers and aspiring landowners to migrate farther west to obtain land. Conflicts with Indian inhabitants sporadically interrupted their migrations, but by 1750, Pennsylvanians, Virginians, and Marylanders had successfully established settlements along the entire length of the Potomac River, entered the Shenandoah Valley, and were poised to cross the Appalachian Mountains into the vast interior of the continent.

Westward migration from the New England colonies occurred in a similar fashion, although other factors besides securing land for export crops were at work. The strict religious orthodoxy imposed by the Puritan-led Congregational Church alienated many New England colonists, and spurred them to move west in pursuit of religious moderation. Environmental conditions were also an important consideration, as the rocky soil of tidewater New England was poorly suited for farming. Agricultural practices in New England centered upon the cultivation of subsistence food items, such as wheat and corn, rather than a marketable cash crop like tobacco, but the desire to open new lands to cultivation was no less influential than in Virginia. Beginning in 1636 with the Reverend Thomas Hooker and his followers, New Englanders moved into the lush Connecticut River Valley and spread out into other fertile regions of New England. Indian resistance to colonial encroachment in New England was fierce, but two significant conflicts—the PEQUOT WAR (1636–1637) and KING PHILIP'S WAR (1675–1676)—eliminated most native resistance and opened the interior of New England to migrant farmers. By 1750 New Englanders had reached west to New Hampshire and Vermont and stretched north as far as Maine.

Settlement and migration patterns differed in the middle colonies of New York and Pennsylvania. While the desire for land was no less fierce, powerful Indian groups managed to blunt much of the early westward flow of American colonists. The powerful Iroquois nations, who inhabited the rich lands from the Mohawk River in northeastern New York to the upper Allegheny watershed in northwestern Pennsylvania, checked colonial expansion into their territory by maintaining a system of satellite tribes, included the Lenapes (or Delawares), Shawnees, and Susquehannocks, who occupied the border region between the Iroquois and the colonials. All land sales or political treaties between these dependent peoples and the Americans required Iroquois acquiescence, a consequence of the subservient status forced on these peoples after the Iroquois conquest of many northeastern woodland Indians during the Beaver Wars (c. 1640–1680). This system worked remarkably well until the mid-eighteenth century, when increasing pressure for land in south-central Pennsylvania forced many Lenapes and Shawnees to migrate across the Appalachian Mountains into eastern Ohio. A flood of colonial migrants, led by fur traders and land speculators, followed on the heels of these retreating Native peoples.

Westward migration in the lower south, especially the Carolinas, developed slowly until 1718, when a long series of violent Indian wars finally ended. Most migration after that point was driven by the restricted access to western lands in Pennsylvania and New York. During the 1740s and 1750s, migrants from the middle colonies traveled down the Shenandoah Valley and settled in the western portions of present North Carolina. These settlers, many of whom were Scotch-Irish and Germans only re-

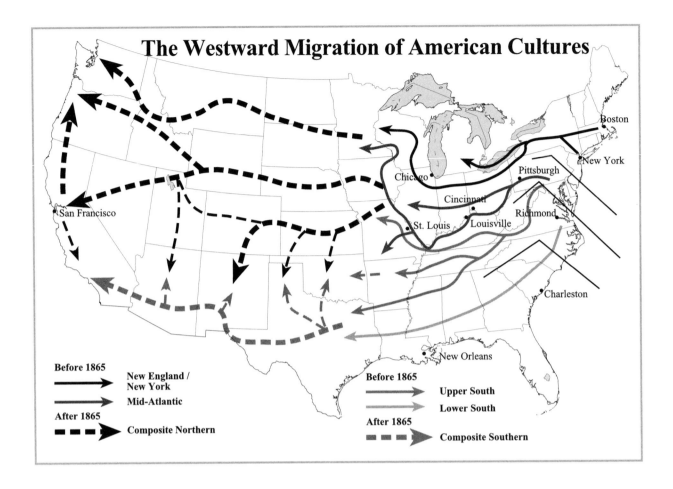

The Westward Migration of American Cultures

Before 1865

→ New England / New York

→ Mid-Atlantic

After 1865

⇢ Composite Northern

Before 1865

→ Upper South

→ Lower South

After 1865

⇢ Composite Southern

cently arrived in America, quickly filled the upland back-country on the eastern slopes of the Appalachians and began looking for routes of access to the lands beyond the mountains.

The Appalachian Frontier

The Appalachian Mountains, an older and smaller range than the Rockies that stretch nearly 1,500 miles from northeastern Alabama to northern Vermont and through which there are few natural passes, considerably hindered early migration into the interior of North America. By 1750, however, colonial fur traders, explorers, and land speculators had begun to cross over the Appalachians and return to eastern communities with tales of vast and rich lands to the west.

The first migrants to cross the Appalachians soon discovered that the mountains were not the only obstacles to westward settlement. The migrations of British colonists beyond the mountains was a principal cause of the North American phase of the Seven Years' War, also known as the FRENCH AND INDIAN WAR (1754–1761). In the early 1740s, migrants from Pennsylvania and Virginia aggressively advanced claims to the Ohio River valley, a territory the French in Canada considered their own. In 1753 the French launched an initiative to block further American expansion by erecting a line of forts along the

upper Ohio River corridor. American colonial efforts to stop the French from building Fort Duquesne at the forks of the Ohio River (present Pittsburgh, Pennsylvania) pre-cipitated the final contest between France and Great Britain for control of North America. The war's effect on the westward movement of American colonists was profound, as nearly all westward migration during the conflict came to abrupt halt when the Indian peoples living in the vicinity of present-day Ohio allied with the French and attacked the western fringes of colonial settlement in Pennsylvania, Virginia, and Maryland. In some places the frontier of settlement was driven eastward for several hundred miles as Indian warriors chased settlers towards the Atlantic. Only the capture of Fort Duquesne in 1758 and the subsequent defeat of a pan-Indian coalition in 1763–1764 reopened the trans-Appalachian region to American settlement.

After the war, migrants crossed the mountains in increasing numbers despite the British government's 1763 proclamation prohibiting settlement beyond the Appalachians. The British knew if the colonials continued their unrestrained encroachment upon Indian territory another Indian war would ensue, a situation they hoped to avoid. However, neither government prohibitions nor army blockades could stop the deluge of settlers that poured west after 1765. Separated by mountain ranges and hundreds of miles from the center of political authority in the East, migrants followed their own designs and ignored government policies that they deemed to be inconsistent with their interests. Their migrations were greatly assisted by two military roads left over from the war: the Braddock Road, which carried migrants from the headwaters of the Potomac River in western Maryland to Pittsburgh; and the Forbes Road, which ran from eastern Pennsylvania to also arrive at Pittsburgh. Not surprisingly, Pittsburgh became the launching point from which thousands of settlers migrated farther west down the Ohio River to settle portions of what are now West Virginia and eastern Ohio. Other routes through the Appalachians were also discovered during this time, including the Cumberland Gap, which afforded migrants access to eastern Kentucky and Tennessee.

By 1775 the frontier had been pushed beyond the Appalachian Mountains, but renewed war with Indian tribes living in the Old Northwest and the western Carolinas, this time as part of the American Revolutionary War, slowed the westward push. However, the war did not completely curb westward migration. Migrants continued to come west during the war—some to escape the ravages of war along the east coast, but most still seeking land and opportunity—and settled in the western Carolinas and Kentucky. At wars end in 1783, these migrants became the forerunners of American expansion into the Old Northwest.

Managed Expansion in the Midwest

In 1790 the population of the trans-Appalachian region was estimated at more than 120,000. The large number of Americans living west of the Appalachians made the management of westward migration a top priority for the new federal government, which hoped to peaceably maintain political authority over its western citizens and allow the settlers to extend the political boundaries of the young nation with their movements. The Northwest Ordinance of 1787 offered a solution by creating a model for managed expansion. The legislation provided for the organization of the NORTHWEST TERRITORY into new states by creating a defined set of conditions that assured the creation of civilian government in the newly settled regions and prepared the new territories for statehood. The system successfully managed the steady migration of settlers into the Old Northwest Territory, which eventually became the states of Ohio, Illinois, Indiana, Michigan, and Wisconsin.

While migrants settled the Old Northwest, President Thomas Jefferson purchased the Louisiana Territory from France in 1803. The immense new territory, a portion of which was explored and mapped by the famous Lewis and Clark expedition of 1804–1806, encompassed much of the interior land between the Mississippi River and the Pacific Northwest. Part of his planned program of expansion, Jefferson believed the Louisiana Territory provided the key to the future prosperity of the then-agrarian nation by

Adaptable Migrants. If a lack of wood on the Great Plains means that farmhouses had to be made largely of sod, like this one in Coburg, Neb., c. 1887, it should not be surprising if a cow found itself on the roof. LIBRARY OF CONGRESS

bringing a seemingly endless supply of potential farmland within American territorial borders.

It is highly unlikely that Jefferson realized just how quickly his vision would be put to the test. During the War of 1812 Indian resistance slowed migration into the fertile region lying between the Appalachian Mountains and the Mississippi River; yet, after the war thousands of Americans penetrated into the Old Southwest. The system of managed expansion that had proved so successful in the Old Northwest Territory was replicated in the South, and by 1836, several new states, including Tennessee, Alabama, Mississippi, and Arkansas, entered the union.

Technological advances in transportation made a more organized, manageable westward advance possible, and contributed to the rapid settlement of the Midwest. The completion of the Erie Canal in 1825 provided convenient access for thousands of New England migrants who eventually settled in Michigan, northern Illinois, and Wisconsin. In the south, steamboats assisted countless migrants moving up the Mississippi and Missouri Rivers into Arkansas and Missouri, where a staging ground for future migration into the trans-Mississippi West was established at Independence, Missouri, in 1827.

The Westward Expansion of Slavery

Westward migration also brought intense conflict over the place of slavery in the new territories. Western migrants brought with them two opposing socioeconomic systems: the free labor system that prevailed in the northern states and the South's slave-based plantation economy. Slavery had been abolished in most northern states during the early years of the republic and the 1787 Northwest Ordinance forbid the extension of slavery into any state created from the territory. However, the creation of the cotton gin, which invigorated cotton production by greatly simplifying the refinement process, and the profitability of sugar ensured that migrants from the South would seek to spread the institution of slavery into the West in an effort to replicate the plantation system of the Old South.

Initially the battle over the westward expansion of slavery centered upon the maintenance of political equality among the new states carved out of western territories. In 1820, the MISSOURI COMPROMISE temporarily stabilized the issue by creating a system by which one free and one slave state would be created from the western territories in order to maintain a balance of voting power in the Senate. This system functioned with a reasonable measure of success until the MEXICAN-AMERICAN WAR (1846–1848), the conclusion of which brought the southwestern portion of the United States under American control. Migration into the arid region was slow, with the notable exception of California, which attracted thousands of American migrants. In 1850, California's application for admission as a free state refueled the controversy over the expansion of slavery, triggering a decade of compromise and contention that saw widespread violence between migrants on either side of the debate, especially in Kansas. The violence escalated into the Civil War, a conflict that would settle the vexed slavery question for good.

The Trans-Mississippi West

During the Civil War, the frontier of American settlement generally followed the western limits of the states bordering the Mississippi River, along with a slight western tilt that included the eastern halves of Kansas and Nebraska. Beyond the edge of settlement lay expansive prairies that eventually gave way to the massive Rocky Mountains. Migrations into the trans-Mississippi West before the Civil War bypassed this vast interior—often referred to as the "Great American Desert" because of its comparative lack of water—and settled along the Pacific Coast, or in the case of the Mormons, in the mountain basin of present Utah. Even after the conclusion of the famous gold rush era, when hundreds of thousands of fortune seekers came west, most American migrants still followed the overland trails to their terminus along the Pacific Coast. California and Oregon had climates and environments more conducive to farming than the Great Plains and were rapidly populated, while the vast interior lay mostly vacant of American settlements.

In the 1860s, however, an increasing number of migrants turned their attention to the trans-Mississippi interior, where they came into conflict with the Indian tribes of the Great Plains and the Southwest. Most of these tribes, including the Sioux, Cheyenne, Comanche,

Conestoga Wagon. Large and heavy, it hauled trade goods as well as some families, though the lighter prairie schooner was more popular among westward migrants. LIBRARY OF CONGRESS

and Apache, allowed migrants to cross their territory but would not tolerate permanent settlements. When migrants began to push into the Dakotas, Colorado, and New Mexico in violation of native sovereignty, the Indians waged a determined resistance. Gradually, however, the United States Army subdued the Plains Indians and the Great Plains lay open to settlement.

Westward migration in the trans-Mississippi West took three forms, often classified as "frontiers." The first, the mining frontier, opened with the great rush of migrants to the mountainous regions following the discovery of gold in California. From 1848 to 1853, more than 250,000 prospectors flooded California, Nevada, Utah, and Colorado. The rush diminished significantly after the most workable deposits were exhausted and many mining communities disappeared. Yet the mining frontier helped lay the foundation for such major communities as Denver and San Francisco, communities that would become important political and social centers for continued migrations into the west.

The ranching, or cattle frontier, supplanted the miners after the Civil War. At first, cattle-ranchers settled in Texas to pursue range ranching, an activity requiring ranchers to drive huge herds of cattle hundreds of miles over open grasslands to designated slaughter depots. As railroads and refrigeration opened more eastern markets to beef, more sedentary forms of ranching took hold throughout the trans-Mississippi West, until cattle herds dominated the landscapes of Texas, Wyoming, Kansas, Nebraska, and the Dakota Territory. Some western migrants, no longer able to make a living as ranchers, returned to the Midwest and found employment in support industries in cities like Chicago, which became the leading center for meat processing and packaging in the United States.

On the heels of the ranchers came the farmer's frontier. Hundreds of thousands of migrants pushed into the trans-Mississippi West after the passage of the 1862 Homestead Act awarded free grants of 160 acres to anyone who would improve the land. By 1900 more than 80 million acres of homestead land had been handed out to nearly 600,000 applicants. During the 1880s and 1890s, these migrants-turned-farmers clashed with ranchers over land usage and water rights until a new invention—barbed wire—helped farmers oust ranchers from the open range and claim preemptive rights to the land. A significant percentage of these migrants were newly arrived foreign immigrants, who preferred to take their chances with western farming rather than endure life in the rapidly industrializing eastern cities, or former slaves who sought refuge from the racially exclusive environment of the American South. Yet, ethnic minorities seldom found increased opportunity or equality along the route west. African American migrants were often excluded from prime agricultural lands, leading many to settle in the growing cities where they formed ethnic neighborhoods along with similarly marginalized Mexican or Chinese immigrants.

Makeshift Covered Wagon. Any sort of covering, for protection from the elements, could turn an ordinary wagon into a covered wagon, like this one in Loup Valley, Neb., 1886.

Westward Migration as History: From Turner to the New Western School

The symbolic closing of the frontier, noted in historical terms by the pronouncement of the 1890 census that the continental United States had been completely settled and the frontier had become a thing of the past, marked the end of the most dynamic phase of westward migration in the nation's history. Yet, many Americans still migrate to the western portions of the country in pursuit of opportunity and advancement, a trend that has led generations of historians to ask "What makes the West so special?" Frederick Jackson Turner, a Wisconsin history professor, was the first to offer an answer. Turner's "Significance of the Frontier in American History," delivered in Chicago at the 1893 World's Columbian Exposition, argued that the experience of westward migration was directly responsible for creating the independence and resourcefulness that lay at the heart of American character. Turner believed that the "westering" experience was the root of American exceptionalism and that the process of frontier settlement had imbued Americans with a greater resourcefulness and fiercer love of democracy than any other people in the world. The Turner Thesis, as his theory became known, dominated the historical study of westward migration for nearly a century.

However, recent generations of scholars, collectively known as "New West Historians," have sharply criticized Turner's grand synthesis for its racial exclusiveness and triumphant paradigm. Among the New West School, the work of historians Richard White and Patricia Nelson Limerick has proven particularly influential. Their work has demonstrated that westward migration was much more complex than the inevitable Anglo-American conquest of the wilderness implied by Turner. In their estimation, all the peoples of the frontier, including American Indians, African Americans, Mexicans, Asians, and women, played important roles in westward migration, and that the active interaction of ethnic minorities in the migration process

463

helped define the parameters that guided westward movement. In the process, they have brought the topic of race relations from the periphery to the center in modern studies of westward migration. Moreover, these historians have classified the study of westward migration as "a legacy of conquest," a label that asserts the settlement process was a bitter struggle which ended in heartbreak and despair at least as often as success, a sobering realization that is noticeably absent from the Turnerian interpretation.

BIBLIOGRAPHY

Billington, Ray Allen. *Westward Expansion: A History of the American Frontier.* 5th Ed. New York: Macmillan, 1982.

Cayton, Andrew R. L., and Peter S. Onuf. *The Midwest and the Nation: Rethinking the History of an American Region.* Bloomington: Indiana University Press, 1990.

Cayton, Andrew R. L., and Fredrika J. Teute, eds. *Contact Points: American Frontiers from the Mohawk Valley to the Mississippi, 1750–1830.* Chapel Hill: University of North Carolina Press, 1998.

Limerick, Patricia Nelson. *The Legacy of Conquest: The Unbroken Past of the American West.* New York: Norton, 1987.

Mitchell, Robert D., ed. *Appalachian Frontiers: Settlement, Society, and Development in the Preindustrial Era.* Lexington: University Press of Kentucky, 1991.

Morrison, Michael A. *Slavery and the American West: The Eclipse of Manifest Destiny and the Coming of the Civil War.* Chapel Hill: University of North Carolina Press, 1997.

Nobles, Gregory H. *American Frontiers: Cultural Encounters and Continental Conquest.* New York: Hill and Wang, 1997.

Rohrbough, Malcolm J. *The Trans-Appalachian Frontier: People, Societies, and Institutions, 1775–1850.* New York: Oxford University Press, 1978.

White, Richard. *"It's Your Misfortune and None of My Own:" A History of the American West.* Norman: University of Oklahoma Press, 1991.

White, Richard, and Findlay, John M., eds. *Power and Place in the North American West.* Seattle: University of Washington Press, 1999.

Daniel P. Barr

See also **Duquesne, Fort; Frontier; Frontier Thesis, Turner's; Fur Trade and Trapping; Land Grants; Land Speculation; Migration, Internal; Ordinances of 1784, 1785, and 1787; Trans-Appalachian West;** *and vol. 9:* **Americans in Their Moral, Social, and Political Relations; Across the Plains to California in 1852; The Oregon Trail; A Pioneer Woman's Letter Home, c. 1856.**

WETLANDS are any of an array of habitats—including marshes, bogs, swamps, estuaries, and prairie potholes—in which land is saturated or flooded for some part of the growing season. According to the U.S. Fish and Wildlife Service, wetlands contain water-loving plants (hydrophytes) and hydric soils. They serve many ecological and practical purposes. Wetlands provide habitat and breeding sites for fish, shellfish, birds, and other wildlife; help maintain biological diversity (biodiversity); reduce the effect of floods by diverting and storing floodwaters;

Wetlands. Buena Vista Lagoon, in southern California near San Diego, is a tiny (200-acre) freshwater oasis for wildlife amid urban sprawl. NATIONAL ARCHIVES AND RECORDS ADMINISTRATION

provide protection from storm waves and erosion; recharge ground waters; and improve water quality by filtering out sediments, excess nutrients, and many chemical contaminants. Wetlands provide recreational, research, and aesthetic opportunities such as fishing, boating, hunting, and observing and studying wildlife.

Since 1780 human activity has destroyed more than half the wetlands of the United States, which now make up only 5 percent of the land surface of the contiguous forty-eight states, or 104 million acres. Nevertheless, they are extremely productive, exceeding even the best agricultural lands and rivaling rain forests in quantity and diversity of plant and animal life. More than half of the saltwater fish and shellfish harvested in the United States—and most of the freshwater sport fish—require wetlands for food, reproduction, or both. At least half of the waterfowl that nest in the contiguous states use the midwestern prairie potholes as breeding grounds. Wetland-dependent animals include bald eagles, ospreys, beaver, otter, moose, and the Florida panther.

Few people recognized the value of wetlands until the 1970s. Before then, most people considered wetlands to be wastelands. In an effort to make them more productive—primarily through agriculture or development—people destroyed them by draining, ditching, diking, or filling. Early legislation, such as the Swamp Lands acts of 1849, 1850, and 1860, allowed fifteen states on the MISSISSIPPI RIVER to "reclaim" wetlands for cultivation. By the mid-twentieth century, accumulating evidence, including U.S. Fish and Wildlife wetlands inventories in 1954 and 1973, made clear that destruction of wetlands was causing declines in fish and waterfowl. Federal, state, and local laws—notably the federal Clean Water Act of 1972 and amendments in 1977—attempted to regulate destruction.

Development, agriculture, and increasing pollution still threaten U.S. wetlands. One-third of wetland losses

Whaling. This engraving by Théodore de Bry, c. 1590, shows Indians pulling harpooned whales ashore. The Granger Collection Ltd.

have occurred in midwestern farmbelt states. All but three states (Alaska, Hawaii, and New Hampshire) have lost more than 20 percent of their wetlands. Biologists and economists agree that preserving wetlands is less expensive than attempting to restore those that have been damaged, and experts still argue whether it is even possible to restore wetlands and how scientists might measure restoration. The economic and biological feasibility of restoration is debated each time a developer seeks permission to build on a wetland, thus destroying it, and offers (or is required) to attempt to rehabilitate a second site in return. Many biologists feel that because damaged sites cannot be returned to their previous states, it may not be acceptable to allow this tradeoff.

BIBLIOGRAPHY

Council of Environmental Quality. *Environmental Trends*. Washington, D.C.: Executive Office of the President, 1989.

National Research Council. *Restoration of Aquatic Ecosystems: Science, Technology, and Public Policy*. Washington, D.C.: National Academy Press, 1992.

Susan J. Cooper / c. w.

See also **Conservation; Floods and Flood Control; Reclamation; Water Pollution; Wildlife Preservation.**

WHALING. Whaling, or the commercial hunting of whales, results in oil, ambergris, whalebone, meat, and other various by-products. Whale oil is used as a lubricant and as an additive in soapmaking, while ambergris is valued as a fixative in perfumes.

Native Americans had long hunted the great beasts by the time European settlers began to colonize the New World in the early seventeenth century. For the most part, indigenous people processed whale carcasses that washed up on beaches; however, some used canoes to pursue whales that swam into coastal waters.

By 1640, white settlers, who had brought with them knowledge of European whaling techniques, had established their own organized whaling efforts in Long Island and in parts of New England. The colonial whalemen towed harpooned whales to shore from small boats. They then removed blubber and bone, extracting the oil by boiling the blubber in large cast iron kettles called trypots.

Eventually, whale numbers near shore declined, and the colonists began hunting whales in single-masted sloops. As demand increased, whalemen undertook longer voyages of up to several years to find their quarry. The year 1774 saw the peak of colonial whaling when at least 350 vessels sailed from ports in Connecticut, Massachusetts, Rhode Island, and New York. Nantucket Island and New Bedford in Massachusetts eventually became important whaling centers. Other significant whaling ports included Provincetown, Massachusetts; New London, Connecticut; San Francisco; and Sag Harbor, New York.

Just two years later, the industry was collapsing because of the British blockade of colonial ports during the Revolutionary War; in addition, the Embargo of 1807 and the War of 1812 forced whaleships to lie idle. Several resourceful shipowners, the Rotches of New Bedford for example, went to France and conducted whaling from foreign shores.

Whaling burgeoned during the peaceful years that followed, and by the mid-1800s, the industry counted 736 vessels and seventy thousand people. Sperm whale oil peaked in 1843 with a production of 5.26 million gallons. Whale oil production reached 11.59 million gallons in 1845, and more than 5.65 million pounds of whalebone was retrieved in 1853.

The discovery of petroleum, a product superior to whale oil for lighting, in 1859 signaled the beginning of the end for the lucrative whaling industry. Other factors contributing to the decline of whaling included the loss of thirty-seven New Bedford vessels that were sunk during the Civil War followed by the Arctic disasters of 1871 and 1876, in which forty-five more New Bedford ships were lost to ice. The development of spring steel, which replaced the market for whalebone, coupled with diminishing whale populations, also contributed to the industry's downfall. The last American whaling vessel made final port in San Francisco on 28 October 1928, although several whaling voyages under the American flag were made from foreign ports until around 1938.

International Whaling Commission

After World War II, a convention held in Washington, D.C., resulted in the creation of the International Whaling Commission (IWC), an organization of twenty-four countries that participated in whaling. Regulating most of the world's whaling activities, the commission set specific limits on the numbers and species of whales that could be hunted. Today, the IWC lists forty-eight members worldwide, from Antigua to the United States. Besides setting catch limits and creating sanctuaries, the commission funds whale research.

The attempt to place limits on whaling has become a volatile issue. Many nations do not recognize IWC authority and have continued to hunt whales. In response, environmental and wildlife groups, among them Greenpeace, an environmental activist group, have made attempts to stop all whaling. The Japan Whaling Association contends that whaling is an integral part of Japan's history and culture and defends the country's continued whaling. Norway, the only country that objected to the IWC's 1982 moratorium on whaling, continues its whale hunts; in 2000, Norway took 487 small whales that yielded 713 tons of meat (valued at roughly $2.5 million) and ninety-six tons of blubber.

BIBLIOGRAPHY

Busch, Briton Cooper. *Whaling Will Never Do for Me: The American Whaleman in the Nineteenth Century.* Lexington: University Press of Kentucky, 1994.

Ellis, Richard. *Men and Whales.* New York: Knopf, 1991.

International Whaling Commission. Home page at http://www.iwcoffice.org.

Ronnberg, Eric A. R. *To Build a Whaleboat: Historical Notes and a Model Makers Guide.* Bogota, N.J.: Model Shipways Co., 1985.

Webb, Robert Lloyd. *On the Northwest: Commercial Whaling in the Pacific Northwest, 1790–1967.* Vancouver: University of British Columbia Press, 1988.

Works Progress Administration. *Whaling Masters.* New Bedford, Mass.: Old Dartmouth Historical Society, 1938.

Kym O'Connell-Todd

WHEAT. Throughout American history wheat has been the principal bread cereal. It was introduced by the first English colonists and early became the major cash crop of farmers on the westward-moving frontier. In colonial times its culture became concentrated in the middle colonies, which became known as the bread colonies. In the mid-eighteenth century, wheat culture spread to the TIDEWATER region of Maryland and Virginia, where George Washington became a prominent grower.

As the frontier crossed the Appalachian Mountains, so did wheat raising. The census of 1840 revealed Ohio as the premier wheat-producing state, but twenty years later Illinois took the lead; it retained its leading position for three decades, until Minnesota overtook it in 1889. Leadership moved with the farming frontier onto the GREAT PLAINS in the first years of the twentieth century. Census takers in 1909 found North Dakota to be the nation's top producer, followed by Kansas. Between 1919 and 1975 the order was reversed, except in 1934 and 1954, when Oklahoma and then Montana moved into second place. In the meantime, the soils of the COLUMBIA RIVER Valley became productive, with the state of Washington ranking fourth in wheat production in 1959.

The majority of the farmers east of the Mississippi River preferred soft winter wheat varieties, such as the Mediterranean (introduced in 1819), but those who settled the Great Plains found those varieties ill-adapted to the region's climates. Hard red spring wheats, such as Red Fife and Bluestem, proved more suited to the northern plains, while Turkey, a hard red winter wheat introduced into central Kansas by German MENNONITES who had immigrated from Russia, became popular on the southern plains. The introduction of these hard wheats prompted a major change in the technology of grinding of wheat into flour: a shift from millstones to rollers.

Wheat growers soon developed more varieties better adapted to different regions. Early maturing Marquis was introduced from Canada in 1912, and by 1929 it made up 87 percent of the hard spring wheat acreage in the United States. It proved susceptible to black stem rust, however, and after 1934 it lost favor to Thatcher and, in the late 1960s, to Chris and Fortuna varieties. On the southern plains, Tenmarq, released by the Kansas Agricultural Experiment Station in 1932, superseded Turkey and was in turn replaced first by Pawnee and later by Triumph and Scout. In the 1960s the wheat growers of the Columbia Valley began to favor a new short-stemmed soft white winter wheat, known as Gaines, which doubled yields in that area within a four-year period.

Whatever the variety, in the colonial and early national period farmers sowed wheat by broadcasting (scattering seed by hand over a wide area), reaped mature wheat using sickles, and threshed the harvested grain with flails. In rapid succession in the nineteenth century, sowing with drills replaced broadcasting, cradles took the place of sickles, and reapers and binders in turn replaced cradles. Steam-powered threshing machines superseded flails. In the 1930s the small combine joined reaping and threshing into a single operation. Such technological advances greatly increased the nation's wheat production while cutting the labor requirements per bushel.

The handling and marketing of wheat went through parallel changes. Initially, laborers sacked, shipped, and unloaded the harvest into storage warehouses by hand, but after the Civil War railroads began to construct large grain elevators at country railroad stations and even larger elevators in terminal markets. Grain exchanges there sold the wheat to flour millers and exporters, and a futures market developed for speculators. However, farmers soon accused elevator operators of undergrading, shortweighting, and excessive dockage and began to seek active control over marketing through the organization of cooperatives.

Since colonial times, American wheat growers have produced a surplus for export. Exports of wheat and flour varied from 868,500 bushels in 1814 to 223.8 million bushels in 1898, providing foreign exchange that helped to finance the nation's industrialization. However, expansion of acreage during World War I and contraction of overseas demand after the armistice created an accumulation of surpluses that could not be marketed. The resulting low prices prompted growers to seek government price supports, first through the McNary-Haugen Bill, which failed to become law, and later through the Agricultural Adjustment Act of 1933 and its many revisions. Increasing production, which reached one billion bushels in 1944, permitted an expansion of wheat and flour exports as part of the nation's foreign assistance programs. In fiscal year 1966 these exports amounted to 858.7 million bushels, of which some 571 million were disposed of as food aid. A disastrous drought in the Soviet Union in 1972 led to the sale of 388.5 million bushels to that country in one year and the conclusion in 1975 of an agreement to supply the Soviets with breadstuffs over a five-year period.

BIBLIOGRAPHY

Brumfield, Kirby. *This Was Wheat Farming: A Pictorial History of the Farms and Farmers of the Northwest Who Grow the Nation's Bread.* Seattle, Wash.: Superior Publishing, 1968.

Hadwiger, Don F. *Federal Wheat Commodity Programs.* Ames: Iowa State University Press, 1970.

Malin, James C. *Winter Wheat in the Golden Belt of Kansas.* Lawrence: University of Kansas Press, 1944.

Quisenberry, K. S., and L. P. Reitz. "Turkey Wheat: The Cornerstone of an Empire." *Agricultural History* 48 (1974): 98–110.

Robert G. Dunbar / c. w.

See also **Agriculture; Cereal Grains; Dry Farming; Elevators, Grain; Gristmills; Insecticides and Herbicides.**

WHIG PARTY represented the main national opposition to the Democratic Party from the mid-1830s until the early 1850s. Ostensibly, the party came together and took its name in hostility to the aggrandizement of executive power by President Andrew Jackson during his assault on the Bank of the United States in 1833–1834. In the 1836 presidential election, the northern and southern wings stood apart, offering different sectional candidates, but by 1839 they had come together behind a single candidate and a common set of policies. They elected two presidents, William Henry Harrison in 1840 and Zachary Taylor in 1848, both of whom soon died in office. Each won popular majorities in both the North and the South, while Whig congressmen throughout showed a high level of voting cohesion on most national issues, thus demonstrating that the party represented a nationwide coalition based on agreement on a nonsectional program.

In the North, especially in New England-settled areas, the party attracted Jackson's old antagonists, the National Republicans and the Antimasons. The former were somewhat conservative socially but liberal in religious matters, while the latter expressed the moral-reformist sentiments stemming from the evangelical revival, an influence that became more important as ethnocultural issues intensified in the 1840s. In the South, where the Jacksonians had been predominant, a new opposition appeared in the mid-1830s that drew its earliest support from those who objected to Jackson's assertive response to the nullification crisis and then exploited fears of northern abolitionist interference to arouse popular support. But at least as important for the southern party as for the northern party were widespread objections in more commercialized areas to the Jacksonians' assaults on the banking system and their resistance to state improvement programs. The panic of 1837 and the Democrats' refusal to countenance government help in the subsequent depression gave a common bond to Whigs all over the country, who thereafter acted together to promote positive government policies for economic advancement.

Those policies were not implemented after the 1840 victory, because John Tyler, the states' rights vice president who succeeded Harrison in 1841, obstructed passage of the party program. The Whigs never again enjoyed command of all branches of the federal government. However, they recovered control of the House of Representatives after 1846, when they had to take responsibility for financing a war against Mexico they had voted against. Thereafter, the Whigs were irredeemably divided by the problem of slavery expansion. Believing in positive national government, they needed a solution, whereas the localistic Democrats could evade the central issue. Moreover, some northern Whigs who represented strong antislavery strongholds made speeches in opposition to the Compromise of 1850 that undermined the efforts of southern Whigs to reassure their constituents that the party could still be trusted on slavery. Consequently, Whig support in the South fell decisively by 1852. Meanwhile, the northern Whigs faced large-scale Catholic immigration into seaboard cities, and their leaders' attempts to win immigrant votes condemned the party in some states to collapse amid the mass nativist movements of 1854. By 1856, many northern Whigs had stopped voting or turned to the Democrats as the party of national unity, but many more subsequently turned to the new Republican Party as the expression of northern views on the sectional issues of the day.

BIBLIOGRAPHY

Cooper, William J., Jr. *The South and the Politics of Slavery, 1828–1856*. Baton Rouge: Louisiana State University Press, 1978.

Holt, Michael F. *The Rise and Fall of the American Whig Party*. New York: Oxford University Press, 1999.

Howe, Daniel Walker. *The Political Culture of the American Whigs*. Chicago: University of Chicago Press, 1979.

Sellers, Charles. "Who Were the Southern Whigs?" *American Historical Review* 59 (1954): 335–346.

Donald J. Ratcliffe

See also **Bank of the United States; Compromise of 1850; Jacksonian Democracy; National Republican Party; Sectionalism.**

WHIP, PARTY. The term "party whip" refers to a high-ranking member of the U.S. congressional leadership for both the majority and minority parties. In American politics of the early twenty-first century, the party whip was an increasingly active and influential party leader in both the Senate and the House of Representatives.

In the House the party whip ranks immediately below the Speaker, who is the majority leader (if in the minority party, the whip is second behind the minority leader); in the Senate the whip is second in the party hierarchy behind the majority (or minority) leader. The whip's duties are to make sure that members are in Washington, D.C., and in the chamber during crucial votes; to forecast how members will vote; to persuade members to support the party leadership; to alert party leaders to shifting congressional opinions; and, occasionally, to distribute information on pending amendments or bills. Party whips usually attend important leadership meetings, including conferences with the president.

Party whips have been used in the British House of Commons since 1688 but were not employed in the U.S. Congress until 1899. Since the early 1960s the job of whip, although a party office, has become formalized, with offices, automobiles, staff, and office supplies, all paid for with public funds. Democratic and Republican parties in the House and Senate use differing methods of choosing whips and their assistants, but geography and party loyalty are important considerations. The post of party whip sometimes becomes a stepping-stone to a higher congressional party office.

In 2002, party whips were Tom DeLay (Republican majority) of Texas and Nancy Pelosi (Democrat minority) of California in the House and Harry Reid (Democrat majority) of Nevada and Don Nickles (Republican minority) of Oklahoma in the Senate. Pelosi was the first female party whip in congressional history.

BIBLIOGRAPHY

Polsby, Nelson W., ed. *Congressional Behavior*. New York: Random House, 1971.

Ripley, Randall B. *Majority Party Leadership in Congress*. Boston: Little, Brown, 1969.

Wise, Charles R. *The Dynamics of Legislation: Leadership and Policy Change in the Congressional Process*. San Francisco, Calif.: Jossey-Bass, 1991.

D. B. Hardeman / A. G.

See also **Blocs; Caucuses, Congressional; Congressional Record; Delegation of Powers; Implied Powers; Majority Rule; Rules of the House.**

WHISKEY. Many early colonial settlers were from Ireland and Scotland and were acquainted with the art of distilling whiskey, principally from malt. Many of the Irish and Scottish immigrants settled in western PENNSYLVANIA, which in the late seventeenth and early eighteenth centuries became a center of rye-whiskey making. In KENTUCKY, settlers discovered that whiskey could be produced from corn, which eventually became America's leading spirit. In 1792 there were 2,579 small distilleries throughout the United States. The drink emerged as a patriotic alternative to rum, which relied on imported molasses.

Whiskey became such a vital part of the economy that in 1794 western settlers organized in protest against a federal excise tax in the Whiskey Rebellion. Enormous distilling plants flourished in Kentucky, manufacturing sour mash, sweet mash, bourbon whiskey, and a small percentage of rye. Prohibition changed the business dramatically, destroying many long-established companies. In 1935 Kentucky produced 197 million gallons of whiskey. Producing a relatively low 104 million gallons in 1955, whiskey distillers in the United States put out 160 million gallons in 1970. By 1972 production had fallen to 126 million gallons.

Whiskey Rebellion. In this 1794 engraving, a mob forces a government tax collector—already tarred and feathered—to ride on a rail during the uprising in Pennsylvania. LIBRARY OF CONGRESS

BIBLIOGRAPHY

Crowgey, Henry G. *Kentucky Bourbon: The Early Years of Whiskey Making.* Lexington: University Press of Kentucky, 1971.

Rorabaugh, W. J. *The Alcoholic Republic: An American Tradition.* New York: Oxford University Press, 1979.

Alvin F. Harlow / H. S.

See also **Alcohol, Regulation of; Distilling; Prohibition; Rum Trade; Whiskey Rebellion.**

WHISKEY REBELLION (1794). Residents of the American backcountry in the 1790s were intensely democratic and resented the fiscal policies of the secretary of the treasury, Alexander Hamilton, which concentrated power in the hands of the upper classes. Their many grievances included the failure to open the MISSISSIPPI RIVER to navigation, the dilatory conduct of the Indian wars, the speculative prices of land, arduous and ill-paid militia duty, scarcity of specie, and the creation of a salaried official class. The excise law of 1791, which taxed whiskey—the chief transportable and barterable western product—furnished a convenient peg on which to hang these grievances, and for three years the opposition to this measure escalated.

Tensions erupted during the summer of 1794 in western Pennsylvania. Distillers caught violating the law were forced to travel to York or Philadelphia for trial, an onerous journey that would cost the value of the average western farm. Congress in May and June 1794 acknowledged the inequity and passed a measure making offenses against the excise law cognizable in state courts. While the bill was in Congress, the U.S. District Court of Pennsylvania issued a series of processes returnable to Philadelphia. However, these processes were not served until July, six weeks after the easing measure was passed. While serving a process, a federal marshal was attacked by angered residents in Allegheny County, and on 17 July several hundred men, led by members of a local "Democratic

society," besieged and burned the home of General John Neville, the regional inspector of the excise.

The attackers would probably have stopped there, but certain leaders robbed the mail and found in the stolen letters expressions that they used to incite an attack on PITTSBURGH. The southwestern militia was mustered at Braddock's Field on 1 August. The citizens of Pittsburgh were so alarmed that they exiled the odious townsmen, including Neville. The militia marched without violence on Pittsburgh on 2 August. Nevertheless, on 7 August President George Washington issued a proclamation ordering the disaffected westerners to their homes and called up the militia from Maryland, Virginia, Pennsylvania, and New Jersey.

On 14–15 August delegates from the Monongahela Valley met at Parkinson's Ferry, but were prevented from drastic measures by the parliamentary tactics of the moderates. A committee appointed by Washington met with a western committee and arranged to poll the people of the western counties on their willingness to submit. The vote was unsatisfactory, and Washington set in motion the militia army that had meanwhile been gathering in the East. The western counties were occupied during November, and more than a score of prisoners were sent to Philadelphia. All of them were acquitted or pardoned, or the cases were dismissed for lack of evidence.

The federal government had passed the first serious test of its enforcement powers. The rebellion strengthened the political power of Hamilton and the FEDERALIST PARTY. Circumstantial evidence seems to indicate that Hamilton promoted the original misunderstanding and sent the army west solely for that purpose. It is likely also that the defeat of the frontiermen encouraged investors to accelerate the economic development of the region that they had already begun.

BIBLIOGRAPHY

Baldwin, Leland D. *Whiskey Rebels: The Story of a Frontier Uprising.* Pittsburgh, Pa.: University of Pittsburgh Press, 1968.

469

Miller, John C. *The Federalist Era, 1789–1801*. New York: Harper and Brothers, 1960.

Slaughter, Thomas P. *The Whiskey Rebellion: Frontier Epilogue to the American Revolution*. New York: Oxford University Press, 1986.

Leland D. Baldwin / A. R.

See also **Amnesty; Distilling; Hamilton's Economic Policies; Insurrections, Domestic; Moonshine; Pennsylvania; Taxation.**

WHISKEY RING. During the Grant administration, a group of western distillers and Internal Revenue Service officials formed a conspiracy to evade the whiskey tax. After a lengthy investigation into the ring, Benjamin H. Bristow, the secretary of the treasury, procured the indictment of more than 230 persons, including the president's personal secretary, and the conviction of 110, including four government officials. The investigation turned up allegations that funds generated by the illegal abatements of taxes went to the REPUBLICAN PARTY to achieve a second term for Grant. The private secretary was acquitted, however, and no evidence implicated Grant himself.

BIBLIOGRAPHY

McDonald, John. *Secrets of the Great Whiskey Ring*. St. Louis, Mo.: W. S. Bryan, 1880.

McFeely, William S. *Grant: A Biography*. New York: W. W. Norton, 1981.

Simpson, Brooks D. *The Reconstruction Presidents*. Lawrence: University Press of Kansas, 1998.

John Francis Jr. / A. G.

See also **Belknap Scandal; Corruption, Political; Crédit Mobilier of America.**

WHITE CAPS were vigilante organizations arising in MISSISSIPPI, LOUISIANA, and NEW MEXICO in the late nineteenth century. Using the night-riding, terrorist tactics of the KU KLUX KLAN of the RECONSTRUCTION era, white farmers in southwestern Mississippi and the Florida parishes of Louisiana tried to drive black tenant farmers and lumber mill laborers from the area. Intervention from Governor Stone and some lengthy prison sentences crushed the movement in Mississippi in the mid-1890s, but Louisiana whitecapping turned into a feud that lasted well into the twentieth century. In New Mexico, Mexican American ranchers organized themselves as *Las Gorras Blancas* in 1888 to intimidate Anglo ranchers and business owners who fenced in what had been common grazing land.

BIBLIOGRAPHY

Bond, Bradley G. *Political Culture in the Nineteenth-Century South. Mississippi, 1830–1900*. Baton Rouge: Louisiana State University Press, 1995.

Hyde, Samuel C., Jr. *Pistols and Politics: The Dilemma of Democracy in Louisiana's Florida Parishes, 1810–1899*. Baton Rouge: Louisiana State University, 1996.

White, Richard. *"It's Your Misfortune and None of My Own": A New History of the American West*. Norman: University of Oklahoma Press, 1991.

Cynthia R. Poe
Mack Swearingen

See also **Fencing and Fencing Laws; Mississippi; Poor Whites; Populism; Vigilantes.**

WHITE CITIZENS COUNCILS. Southern opponents of racial integration organized white citizens councils to obstruct the implementation of the 1954 decision by the U.S. SUPREME COURT to end school desegregation, *Brown v. Board of Education of Topeka*. Originating in MISSISSIPPI, the councils advocated white supremacy and resorted to various forms of economic pressure against local advocates of desegregation. They attempted to win support for their views by describing the horrors that integrated education would supposedly bring. By the 1960s, as the pace of desegregation in southern schools accelerated, the councils grew steadily weaker. By the 1970s they were only of marginal importance.

BIBLIOGRAPHY

Patterson, James T. *Brown v. Board of Education: A Civil Rights Milestone and Its Troubled Legacy*. Oxford: Oxford University Press, 2001.

Jacob E. Cooke / A. E.

See also *Brown v. Board of Education of Topeka;* **Civil Rights Movement; Desegregation; Integration; Race Relations;** *and vol. 9:* **An Interview with Fannie Lou Hamer.**

WHITE HOUSE, the residence of every president of the United States since John and Abigail Adams became its first occupants on 1 November 1800. The selection of a site for the president's house in the new federal city of the District of Columbia was made by President George Washington and Major Peter ("Pierre") C. L'Enfant, the French-born planner of the city of Washington. The land they chose was on a ridge north of Tiber Creek (now enclosed in an underground conduit), with a majestic view down the Potomac River. In 1792, the commissioners of the federal city drew up a competition for the design of a house for the president. Among those entering the competition was an anonymous citizen who signed his entry "A.Z." and who was later revealed to be Secretary of State Thomas Jefferson. The winning design was the work of James Hoban, an Irish-born architect who modeled his entry after Leinster House in Dublin, Ireland. Hoban's design was built on eighteen acres on the south side of Pennsylvania Avenue, Northwest. The city's commissioners tried unsuccessfully to recruit European craftsmen and laborers to build the White House. Therefore, the

White House, like the early Capitol and other federal buildings, was largely built by slaves and free African Americans who worked alongside white workers. It was begun in 1792 and completed in 1800 at a cost of $232,372.

In 1807, during Thomas Jefferson's administration, the East and West Terraces were added to the mansion. In 1824, the South Portico was completed, and, in 1829, the North Portico. The terraces were the work of architect Benjamin Latrobe, and the two porticoes incorporated the designs of both Latrobe and Hoban. In 1948, a balcony was added to the South Portico at the request of President Harry S. Truman. The West Wing of the White House, which contains the offices of the president and his staff, was built in 1902 as a temporary office building. It was expanded over the years until its original size was doubled. The East Wing was completed in 1942, during World War II, to provide more office space; it houses the office of the first lady and her staff. Both wings were constructed at lower elevations than the residence. The West Terrace's swimming pool, built in 1933 for Franklin D. Roosevelt, was covered over in the late 1960s, during Richard Nixon's administration, so that it could serve as a press center.

Until Herbert Hoover's term (1929–1933), visitors were granted easy access to the White House. Americans then insisted on face-to-face contact with their leader and personal attention to their needs. That tradition originated with George Washington, who had begun a popular weekly presidential open house in New York City, the first seat of the federal government. There anyone was free to enter and shake the president's hand. Soon after, an hour was set aside twice weekly for similar receptions. John Adams, the first occupant of the White House, continued the tradition of opening the "people's house" to the public. During his term men seeking political favors could

White House. This photograph by Jack Delano shows the North Portico of the presidential residence in 1941, just before the completion of the East Wing and several years before the start of major renovations. LIBRARY OF CONGRESS

simply walk in the front doors, go upstairs, and enter the president's second-floor study. Over time, access varied with presidential style. The informal Andrew Jackson held receptions open to all, regardless of protocol. Martin Van Buren insisted on formal protocol, and was the first president to have police screen his well-wishers. The unpretentious Abraham Lincoln, whose study and living quarters were on the second floor of the White House, often woke to find audacious job-seekers loitering in the hall. By the time Herbert Hoover came to the White House in 1929, the tradition had evolved into an hour-long open house six days a week, when anyone could come and shake the president's hand or leave a gift. Meeting the president was as much a part of the tourists' Washington experience as a visit to the Capitol, and Hoover received 1,000 to 1,200 well-wishers daily. On New Year's Day 1930, 9,000 citizens lined up on the mansion's driveways to greet the president. Shortly after, he abolished the daily reception. Visitors still came to the White House, but were limited to the public rooms, which became more museum-like over the years. In times of national emergencies, the public rooms are closed to visitors.

Throughout its history, the White House has undergone extensive interior change and renovation. Only the exterior walls remained standing after the British set fire to the president's house on 24 August 1814, and James Monroe did not move into the White House until December 1817. In 1902, President Theodore Roosevelt commissioned a major refurbishing of the interior, and, between 1948 and 1952, during the Truman administration, the residence was completely gutted and renovated to make it structurally sound and to add two basement-level floors.

The precedent for housing the president at government expense was set in 1789, when Congress appropriated funds to rent and furnish a home for President Wash-

White House Grounds. This nineteenth-century illustration shows the public strolling around the grounds, with the South Portico behind them. The balcony, East Wing, and West Wing were not added until the twentieth century. © CORBIS

ington in New York City. Until 1905, presidents often sold aging White House furnishings in order to supplement the government furnishing allowance. Early sitting presidents also used their own funds to buy furnishings, and eventually presidents began raising private funds to refurbish or enhance the collections. In 1961, First Lady Jacqueline Kennedy began an extensive program to acquire American antique furnishings and paintings for the White House. Subsequent first ladies continued the practice, giving the White House an outstanding collection of American furniture from the late eighteenth and early nineteenth centuries as well as American paintings and decorative arts from the late eighteenth century to the early twentieth century. In 1979, First Lady Rosalynn Carter supported the establishment of the private, nonprofit White House Preservation Fund to help with new acquisitions and the refurbishment of state rooms. In addition, each new occupant of the White House had the opportunity to furnish the private living quarters and the working offices with pieces from a collection of items used by previous first families. Into the twenty-first century, the White House retained the classical elegance of an early nineteenth-century house and continued to serve as the home and office of the president of the United States and as a symbol of the government of the United States.

White House of the Confederacy. The wartime residence of Jefferson Davis in Richmond, Va. LIBRARY OF CONGRESS

BIBLIOGRAPHY

Bowling, Kenneth R. *The Creation of Washington, D.C.: The Idea and Location of the American Capital.* Fairfax, Va.: George Mason University Press, 1991.

Kapsch, Robert J. "Building Liberty's Capital: Black Labor and the New Federal City." *American Visions* 10, no. 1 (February/March 1995): 8–10.

Monkman, Betty C. *The White House: Its Historic Furnishings and First Families.* Washington, D.C.: White House Historical Association; New York: Abbeville Press, 2000.

Seale, William. *The President's House: A History.* Washington, D.C.: National Geographic Society, White House Historical Association, 1986.

White House Historical Association. Home page at www.white househistory.org.

Jane Freundel Levey

WHITE HOUSE OF THE CONFEDERACY

is a stately Greek revival mansion in Richmond, VIRGINIA, on the brow of steep Shockoe Hill across the wide ravine from old Church Hill. Designed by Robert Mills and built in 1818, it was bought by the City of Richmond on 11 June 1861; it was furnished and presented to the president of the Confederacy, Jefferson Davis. When he refused the gift, the Confederate government rented it. As the executive mansion, it was occupied by Davis as his official and private residence until he was forced to leave it by the approaching Union army on 2 April 1865. On 3 April the Union commander Godfrey Weitzel made the mansion his headquarters and entertained a visit from President

Abraham Lincoln the following day. After the federal government returned it to the city in 1870, the mansion was used as a public school.

Despite looting and fires throughout Richmond, the house was left largely intact. In her book *Jefferson Davis, A Memoir* (1890), Varina Davis, Jefferson Davis's wife, recalls the garden terraced down the steep hillside, the Carrara marble mantelpieces, the great high-ceilinged rooms, and the well staircases. On 12 June 1894 the city deeded the mansion to the Confederate Memorial Literary Society as a memorial to Jefferson Davis. It is now the home of the Museum of the Confederacy.

BIBLIOGRAPHY

Collier, Malinda W., ed. *White House of the Confederacy: An Illustrated History.* Richmond, Va.: Cadmus, 1993.

Collins, Bruce. *White Society in the Antebellum South.* London and New York: Longman, 1985.

McCardell, John. *The Idea of a Southern Nation.* New York: Norton, 1979.

Kathleen Bruce/A. R.

See also **Civil War; Confederate States of America; Richmond; Richmond Campaigns; Secession; Slavery; South, the: The Antebellum South.**

WHITE LEAGUE.

The White League, organized in Louisiana in 1874, was a broad-based paramilitary movement consisting of autonomous local "clubs" committed to WHITE SUPREMACY. It first appeared at Opelousas in April and then spread rapidly throughout the state. White

Leagues held large rallies, disrupted court sessions, and threatened to assassinate Republican officeholders in order to coerce them to resign from office and to drive both black laborers and Republicans from their homes. On 30 August leaguers were involved with the murder of six Republican officials from Red River Parish, and on 14 September the Crescent City White League successfully battled the Metropolitan Police and occupied the city hall, statehouse, and arsenal in New Orleans. They withdrew the next day, when federal troops arrived in the city. The league disappeared after having attained its objective with the election of a Democrat as governor in 1876.

BIBLIOGRAPHY

Foner, Eric. *Reconstruction: America's Unfinished Revolution, 1863–1877*. New York: Harper and Row, 1988.

Rable, George C. *But There Was No Peace: The Role of Violence in the Politics of Reconstruction*. Athens: University of Georgia Press, 1984.

Taylor, Joe Gray. *Louisiana: A History*. New York: W. W. Norton, 1976.

John S. Kendall / c. p.

See also **Louisiana; New Orleans Riots; Reconstruction; Vigilantes.**

WHITE PLAINS, BATTLE OF.

The first military movement after the Battle of Harlem (16 September 1776) came when the British general William Howe moved his army up the East River to cut off General George Washington's communication with New England. His slow advance gave Washington time to move north and take up a strong position on the high north of White Plains, New York. On 28 October Howe sent a detachment to gain Chatterton Hill, but the American general Alexander McDougall gained the hill first and held it until British reinforcements forced a retreat to the village. The British suffered about three hundred casualties, the Americans more than two hundred. On the night of 31 October, Washington withdrew into the hills five miles to the northwest.

BIBLIOGRAPHY

Kim, Sung Bok. "The Limits of Politicization in the American Revolution: The Experience of Westchester County, New York." *The Journal of American History* 80 (1993): 868–889.

Shy, John. *A People Numerous and Armed: Reflections on the Military Struggle for American Independence*. New York: Oxford University Press, 1976.

A. C. Flick / a. r.

See also **Harlem, Battle of; Loyalists; New York City; New York State; Revolution, American: Military History.**

"WHITE SQUADRON"

was the first group of modern American steel vessels (USS *Atlanta, Boston, Chicago,* and *Dolphin*) to be completed (1887–1888) after the naval decay following the Civil War. Congress had adopted a policy to modernize the navy in 1882 and required the use of steel in domestic manufacture. The White Squadron, named for the group's white-painted hulls, was the core of the "new Navy" of the 1890s, one capable of vying with major European powers for supremacy in the Pacific. The *Boston* participated in the Battle of Manila Bay (1 May 1898), which ended the Spanish-American War.

BIBLIOGRAPHY

Wimmel, Kenneth. *Theodore Roosevelt and the Great White Fleet: American Seapower Comes of Age*. Washington, D.C.: Brassey's, 1998.

Dudley W. Knox / a. r.

See also **Battle Fleet Cruise Around the World; Manila Bay, Battle of; Navy, United States; Spanish-American War; Warships.**

WHITE SUPREMACY

is the belief that members of the Caucasian race are superior in all ways to other groups or races in the world. In the history of the United States, white supremacy has existed as a means of justifying and preserving the nation as a white Christian country. The history of white supremacy is closely tied to the presence of slavery and the emergence, in the eighteenth and nineteenth centuries, of the theories and categorizations of groups and nations into races. In the United States the presence of slavery and its continuance and growth in the South served as a strong foundation for white supremacy. Also important was immigration, first of the Irish and later of eastern and Mediterranean Europeans, which heightened the belief in the superiority of whiteness, defined as White Anglo-Saxon Protestant.

The key group representing white supremacy was the Ku Klux Klan. Founded in Pulaski, Tennessee, in 1866 by Confederate colonel Nathan Bedford Forrest, its aim was to preserve the traditions of the Old South, which for the Klan focused primarily around the suppression of African Americans and the protection of white women. In its evolution during the early twentieth century, the Klan came to stand for "100 percent pure Americanism," a fervent belief in Protestant Christianity, and a staunch opposition to immigration. But still there remained a rock solid belief in the moral, intellectual, and physical superiority of white people. Through the years the Klan fragmented, reemerging at various periods; the largest regrouping occurred after World War I. The Klan arose again in the 1960s and 1970s as the civil rights movement was successfully attaining the desegregation of public accommodations and voting rights for black Americans. In the 1980s and 1990s the Klan once again appeared, but other groups formed in that period which also espoused white supremacy or white power.

A full generation after the successes of the civil rights movement, many white Americans exhibit an increased

Gertrude Vanderbilt Whitney. A portrait of the sculptor, art patron, and founder of the Whitney Museum of American Art in New York, the home of her own large collection and many works acquired since then. THE WHITNEY MUSEUM OF AMERICAN ART

tolerance of African Americans and a growing acceptance of racial equality. Nonetheless, the ethic of white supremacy is still very strong among some white Americans, namely those belonging or sympathetic to groups formed in the late twentieth century such as Posse Comitatus, the National Association for the Advancement of White People, the American Nazi Party, Aryan Nations, and World Church of the Creator. These groups have tried to recruit young people and have numerous sites on the Internet. They can be violent physically, with most of their attacks directed toward blacks, Jews, and immigrants. Their main goal is to return the nation to white people, root out what they see as a conspiracy between blacks and Jews to eliminate the white race, and regain pride and power for whites.

BIBLIOGRAPHY

Hamm, Mark S. *American Skinheads: The Criminology and Control of Hate Crime.* Westport, Conn.: Praeger, 1993.

Ridgeway, James. *Blood in the Face: The Ku Klux Klan, Aryan Nations, Nazi Skinheads, and the Rise of a New White Culture.* New York: Thunder Mouth's Press, 1990.

Charles Pete Banner-Haley

See also **Ku Klux Klan.**

WHITEWATER SCANDAL. *See* **Clinton Scandals.**

WHITNEY MUSEUM. Dedicated to the presentation and promotion of American art, especially modern and contemporary works, the museum was founded by Gertrude Vanderbilt Whitney (1875–1942) in 1930. Whitney, who was a sculptor acclaimed for her more traditional, figurative pieces, was interested in the avant-garde artistic movements centered around Greenwich Village in the early part of the twentieth century. In 1912, she leased a townhouse near her studio and founded the Whitney Studio at 8 West Eighth Street. In 1918, she created the Whitney Studio Club, which provided meeting and exhibition space for unrecognized artists; Edward Hopper had his first exhibition there. These were replaced in 1928 by the Whitney Studio Galleries. After the Metropolitan Museum of Art rejected her collection in 1929, she founded the Whitney Museum at 8–14 West Eighth Street. The museum opened on 18 November 1931 with 700 works of art, the vast majority from Whitney's private collection. It was run by Juliana Force (1876–1948), who had also run the Whitney Studio, and was originally supported by the Whitney family. The museum moved once before, finding its present home in 1966 in a building designed by Marcel Breuer and Hamilton Smith. It has a collection of some 12,000 objects, including every important American artist of the twentieth century. Its collection of Edward Hopper paintings is the largest in the world; numerous works by Alexander Calder and Georgia O'Keeffe are central to the collection on display. The museum also prides itself on its holdings of Stuart Davis and Reginald Marsh from the first half of the century and on its acquisition of works by Alex Katz, Agnes Martin, Louise Nevelson, Claes Oldenburg, Ad Reinhardt, and many others representing American art in the second half of the century. The museum, which is now public, is supported in part by members and visitors; it also relies upon its governing non-profit organization to secure city, state, and national grants, and to recruit corporate donors. The Whitney runs programs for teachers and students and provides on-line resources. The museum maintains its focus on living artists in accordance with its earliest constitution, which stated that the function of the Whitney was "to preserve, protect, and put on public view, paintings, drawings, and sculpture by American artists . . . and to contribute to the encouragement and development of art and artists, generally, in America, and to the education of the public."

BIBLIOGRAPHY

Berman, Avis. *Rebels on Eighth Street: Juliana Force and the Whitney Museum of American Art.* New York: Atheneum, 1990.

Haskell, Barbara. *The American Century: Art and Culture 1900–1950.* New York: Whitney Museum of American Art, 1999.

Phillips, Lisa. *The American Century: Art and Culture, 1950–2000.* New York: Whitney Museum of American Art, 1999.

Ruth Kaplan

See also **Art: Painting; Art: Sculpture.**

WICKERSHAM COMMISSION.

The Wickersham Commission was officially known as the National Commission on Law Observance and Enforcement. President Herbert Hoover appointed the commission in May 1929 with George W. Wickersham, an attorney and former cabinet member, as its chairman. Made up mostly of judges, lawyers, and educators, the panel represented all sections of the country. Divided into eleven subcommittees, it published its findings in fourteen lengthy reports in 1931. The first and most widely discussed was that on Prohibition. Others covered methods of dealing with juvenile delinquency, the cost of law enforcement, interrogation of criminal suspects, lawless practices in law enforcement, and the belief that criminals were mostly foreign born.

BIBLIOGRAPHY

Kim, Deok-Ho. *"A House Divided": The Wickersham Commission and National Prohibition.* Ph.D. thesis, State University of New York at Stony Brook, 1992.

Alvin F. Harlow / c. w.

See also **Investigating Committees; Nativism; Prohibition.**

WIGWAM, also known as a "wickiup," was a New England Algonquian word meaning "dwelling." The dome-shaped or oblong structures were made of bent poles covered with bark—especially birch bark. In some cases the winter covering was of mats or thatch. Because the structures were very simple, they could be easily disassembled and moved.

The English applied the term to all Iroquois and Algonquian dwellings from the Atlantic Ocean to the Mississippi River, and north of Carolina and Tennessee into Canada. Later, the term was applied to structures more correctly designated tepees.

BIBLIOGRAPHY

Yue, Charlotte. *The Wigwam and the Longhouse.* Boston: Houghton Mifflin, 2000.

Clark Wissler / j. h.

See also **Archaeology and Prehistory of North America; Architecture; Housing; Indian Technology.**

WILD WEST SHOW. The Wild West show was a popular, uniquely American form of entertainment that

Annie Oakley. In this illustration, the legendary sharpshooter, a star of Buffalo Bill's Wild West show for nearly twenty years, fires while standing on the back of a horse. © BETTMANN/CORBIS

Buffalo Bill. An 1896 photograph of William F. Cody, the former buffalo hunter and then operator of the famous Buffalo Bill's Wild West show, which toured the United States and Europe for more than thirty years. LIBRARY OF CONGRESS

promoted the image of a romantic and dangerous western frontier from its beginning in 1883 until the 1930s.

William "Buffalo Bill" Cody staged the first Wild West show in 1883. Cody's experiences as a performer as well as a Pony Express rider, army scout, buffalo hunter, and participant in Indian wars preceded his first show. In 1872, while serving as a hunting guide for the Grand Duke Alexis of Russia, Cody recruited the Brulé Sioux Spotted Tail and members of his tribe to entertain the duke with war dances and participate in a buffalo hunt. Dime novelist Ned Buntline wrote four novels and a magazine serial featuring "Buffalo Bill," a hero based on Cody. Cody played himself in Buntline's play *The Scouts of the Prairie* (1872) and continued to appear in plays until he began his Wild West shows.

In 1882, Cody held the "Old Glory Blow Out," a Fourth of July celebration and predecessor of the Wild West show in North Platte, Nebraska, featuring riding and roping competitions. The first show billed as "Wild West" was Cody's "Wild West, Mountain, and Prairie Exhibition" on the Omaha, Nebraska, fairgrounds opening 19 May 1883. It included a demonstration of Pony Express riding, an Indian attack on a Deadwood stagecoach, a glass ball shooting competition, and buffalo roping. Sharpshooter Annie Oakley joined Cody's "Wild West" in 1884, and the Sioux chief Sitting Bull joined the following year. Cody hired hundreds of "Show Indians" to

perform in his exhibitions, despite charges by social reformers and Bureau of Indian Affairs officials that the show exploited the Indians and emphasized savagery.

Wild West shows remained popular through the 1890s. Two other popular shows were "Pawnee Bill's Historic Wild West," which opened in 1888, and the "101 Ranch Real Wild West," beginning in 1907. Cody's "Wild West" toured Europe in 1887, 1889, and 1902, and performed for Queen Victoria's Golden Jubilee in 1887. In 1891, Cody's show became "Buffalo Bill's Wild West and Congress of Rough Riders of the World," expanding to include Russian, Mexican, Argentine, and Arab horsemen as well as American cowboys and Indians. The show reached the height of its popularity in 1893 with performances in conjunction with the World's Columbian Exposition in Chicago. To the exposition performances, Cody added a reenactment of "Custer's Last Charge," which became a standard feature of the Wild West show.

As life on the frontier became more settled, Cody and other Wild West showmen began to dramatize contemporary events, including the Spanish-American War and the Boxer Rebellion in China. The shows declined in popularity during World War I. The "101 Ranch" made a comeback in 1925, and Wild West performances continued into the 1930s as circus acts. The last major show was "Colonel Tim McCoy's Real Wild West and Rough

Riders of the World," which ran for only one month in 1938.

Wild West shows sustained the romantic image of frontier life in well into the twentieth century. Although few Wild West shows survived World War I and the Great Depression, their influence continues in rodeos and television and film westerns.

BIBLIOGRAPHY

Moses, L. G. *Wild West Shows and the Images of American Indians, 1883–1933.* Albuquerque: University of New Mexico Press, 1996.

Reddin, Paul. *Wild West Shows.* Urbana: University of Illinois Press, 1999.

Russell, Don. *The Wild West: A History of Wild West Shows.* Fort Worth, Tex.: Amon Carter Museum of Western Art, 1970.

Christine Whittington

WILDCAT MONEY

was currency issued by wildcat banks during the nineteenth century, particularly during the period 1830–1860. Wildcat banks earned their name by locating their main offices in remote places where it would be difficult for noteholders to present notes for payment. Bankers would often start wildcat banks with specie borrowed just long enough to show the banking commissioners, leaving the banks themselves with insufficient hard money to do legitimate business. These banks created a confusion in the currency and led the secretary of the treasury, Salmon P. Chase, to demand a national bank currency.

BIBLIOGRAPHY

Bray, Hammond. *Banks and Politics in America, from the Revolution to the Civil War.* Princeton, N.J.: Princeton University Press, 1957.

James D. Magee / S. B.

See also **Banking: Bank Failures; Financial Panics; Money; Specie Circular.**

WILDCAT OIL DRILLING.

Wildcatters are independent oil hunters willing to take chances with regard to where they drill. Wildcat drillers accounted for many of the early oil finds, thus helping create the commercial petroleum industry in the United States around 1860. Many productive oil fields were discovered by wildcatters.

Wildcat drilling success comes from low operating costs and the ability to mobilize quickly. By the 1930s these ventures had become less common due to rising costs as shallow fields were tapped out, forcing oil hunters to drill deeper. Drilling expenses on deep holes that produced nothing ruined many independent operators.

BIBLIOGRAPHY

Miles, Ray. *King of the Wildcatters: The Life and Times of Tom Slick, 1883–1930.* College Station: Texas A&M University Press, 1996.

Tait, Samuel W., Jr. *The Wildcatters: An Informal History of Oil Hunting in America.* Princeton, N.J.: Princeton University Press, 1946.

T. L. Livermore
Terri Livermore

WILDERNESS, BATTLES OF THE.

On 4 May 1864 Gen. Ulysses S. Grant's army prepared to cross the Rapidan River in Virginia to attack General Robert E. Lee's forces. But the move had been anticipated. Instead of attacking the Union troops in the act of crossing, as might have been expected, Lee withdrew to the Wilderness, a heavily wooded and tangled region, where the Union's two-to-one superiority in numbers and artillery would be somewhat neutralized. Grant directed his main movement at Lee's right, hoping to move clear of the Wilderness before effective resistance could be offered. Lee, however, countered rapidly. Road divergence separated his two wings; Confederate General James Longstreet, expected to support either wing, was late in arriving. On 5 May Grant attacked. Confederate generals Richard S. Ewell on the left and Ambrose P. Hill both held firm until night ended the fighting.

The next day Grant resumed his attack, and Hill's troops were driven in confusion. Lee personally rode among the fleeing men to rally and lead them back into battle. As the cry "Lee to the rear" rose on every side, Longstreet's tardy command arrived and struck with suddenness and fury, driving Grant's men back. Ewell, on Lee's left, repulsed all attacks. In the midst of success, Longstreet was wounded by his own men, just as General Thomas J. ("Stonewall") Jackson had been at Chancellorsville a year earlier (2 May 1863). Soon afterward fighting ceased for the day.

It is doubtful whether Longstreet's wounding had any important effect on the outcome of the day's fighting. The troops on both sides were very disorganized, the hour was late, and little more could have been accomplished. On 7 May the two armies faced each other from behind their hasty breastworks. The two days had seen bitter fighting in difficult terrain for battle. Thousands of acres of tangled forest, interlaced undergrowth, and scrub trees impeded movement, and the narrow roads were little more than paths. Cavalry and artillery were useless. Vision was limited to short distances, and, once the fighting began, control passed to local commanders. The brush caught fire and many wounded were burned to death.

Perceiving the uselessness of again assaulting Lee's lines, Grant decided to move by the flank toward Richmond, thus forcing Lee to come and meet him. As Grant's advance troops reached their objective of Spotsylvania Courthouse, Lee's men were in position to meet the threat. The first act was completed of a bitterly fought campaign replete with brilliant strategical and tactical movements.

BIBLIOGRAPHY

Gallagher, Gary W., ed. *The Wilderness Campaign.* Chapel Hill: University of North Carolina Press, 1997.

Priest, John M. *Victory Without Triumph: The Wilderness, May 6th and 7th, 1864.* Shippensburg, Pa.: White Mane, 1996.

Rhea, Gordon C. *The Battle of the Wilderness, May 5–6, 1864.* Baton Rouge: Louisiana State University Press, 1994.

Scott, Robert G. *Into the Wilderness with the Army of the Potomac.* Bloomington: Indiana University Press, 1985.

Steere, Edward. *The Wilderness Campaign: The Meeting of Grant and Lee.* Harrisburg, Pa.: Stackpole Books, 1960.

Thomas Robson Hay / A. R.

See also **Civil War; Cold Harbor, Battle of; Richmond Campaigns; Spotsylvania Courthouse, Battle of; Virginia.**

WILDERNESS ROAD ran from eastern Virginia through the mountain pass known as the Cumberland Gap, to the interior of Kentucky and through to the Ohio country. This road, first used by wandering herds of buffalo and, later, Indian hunters, was later utilized by Daniel Boone for the Transylvania Company. Boone's company traveled from the treaty ground at Fort Watauga, by way of the Cumberland Gap, through the mountains and canelands of Kentucky to the Kentucky River, where they chose to settle the fortified town of Booneboro. At first, the road was little more than a footpath or packhorse trail. Spasmodic but insufficient measures were taken by the Virginia government to enlarge and improve the crowded thoroughfare. After Kentucky became a separate state, renewed efforts to grade, widen, and reinforce the road began. Sections of the road were leased to contractors who, in consideration of materials and labor furnished to maintain the road, were authorized to erect gates or turnpikes across it and collect tolls from travelers. For more than half a century after Boone's party traveled the road, the Wilderness Road was a principal avenue for the movement of eastern immigrants and others to and from the early West. Only the Ohio River offered an alternative route to the West. Thousands of settlers moved west through these converging highways. The Wilderness Road is still an important interstate roadway and constitutes a part of U.S. Route 25, known as the Dixie Highway.

BIBLIOGRAPHY

Chinn, George Morgan. *Kentucky Settlement and Statehood, 1750–1800.* Frankfort: Kentucky Historical Society, 1975.

Faragher, John Mack. *Daniel Boone: The Life and Legend of an American Pioneer.* New York: Holt, 1992.

Krakow, Jere. *Location of the Wilderness Road at the Cumberland Gap.* Washington, D.C.: National Park Service, 1987.

Speed, Thomas. *The Wilderness Road: A Description of the Routes of Travel by which the Pioneers and Early Settlers First Came to Kentucky.* Louisville, Ky.: J. P. Morton., 1886.

Samuel M. Wilson / H. S.

See also **Cumberland Gap.**

WILDFIRES have always shaped the landscape. Many are not caused by humans, but by lightning, which is a major cause of wildfires, particularly in the West. In the twentieth century, governments at all levels tried to suppress wildfires. In the second half of the century, the environmental movement introduced the notion that wildfires were ecologically beneficial, and in 1972 the National Park Service adopted, experimentally, a policy of letting some wildfires burn; in 1976 the policy was adopted generally and became known as the "let-burn" policy. In 1978 the U.S. Forest Service adopted the same policy. Most such fires, designated "prescribed fires," burned less than 100 acres. In years of drought, however, there were major problems. In 1977, 175,000 acres of California wilderness burned in the Marble Cone fire. In 1979 wildfires in California, Oregon, Idaho, Montana, and Wyoming burned more than 600,000 acres. In 1981 a swamp fire in Florida consumed 300,000 acres. Three years later 250,000 acres of Montana forest and range burned, and in 1987, 200,000–300,000 acres in Oregon burned.

The worst wildfire season since World War II came in 1988; more than 6 million acres burned, 2.2 million of them in Alaska. Fires around Yellowstone National Park were shown on television and had a major public effect. As drought in the West persisted, wildfires continued to pose major risks. Yosemite National Park closed temporarily in 1990 because of a nearby wildfire. In 1991 a wildfire raced through a residential section of Oakland, Calif., killing at least twenty-four people. In 1993 a spectacular wildfire in the brushland north and south of Los Angeles burned the houses of many celebrities and caused nearly $1 billion in damage. In 1994 more than fourteen firefighters were killed fighting wildfires in Colorado and elsewhere in the West; acreage burned again exceeded one million acres. The extension of suburban development into wilderness areas in the 1990s made the fire risk to property and human life even more acute, ensuring that debates over fire management would continue to preoccupy both homeowners and policy leaders into the next century.

BIBLIOGRAPHY

Pyne, Stephen J. *Fire in America: A Cultural History of Wildland and Rural Fire.* Princeton, N.J.: Princeton University Press, 1982.

Nancy M. Gordon / L. T.; A. R.

See also **Conservation; Disasters; Fire Fighting; Forest Service, United States; Interior, Department of the; Western Lands.**

WILDLIFE PRESERVATION. In the colonial and early national period, a distinctively American conception of nature combined spiritual and aesthetic appreciation with antipathy and exploitation. Despite public outcries and literary appeals for the preservation of American forests and wildlife, economic considerations often took precedence over social concerns. By the twentieth century, this struggle between ideals had evolved into a central debate in the American conservation movement between utilitarian conservationists intent on scientific control and idealistic preservationists committed to wilderness protection from, rather than for, humans. This conflict can also be seen as a direct result of the relationship between human and nature that emerged from the scientific revolution. The confident push to gain control over natural processes reached its height during the seventeenth and eighteenth centuries, when it was believed that through human ingenuity and the application of reason one could gain mastery over and understanding of nature. The widespread belief in the Baconian creed that scientific knowledge meant technological power was still tempered, nevertheless, by the ideal of stewardship.

Scientists and artists alike challenged the exploitative nature of American forestry and hunting practices on religious and spiritual grounds. While Baconians justified the power of science as the culmination of a fallen but redeemed humanity, English Romantics brought a revival of interest in the physical and spiritual links that had once existed between nature and society. The Romantic writers, combining a heightened sense of self with a heightened sympathy for the otherness of the natural world, celebrated the individuality of living things. This interest in nature was shown in Victorian times in plant and animal collections and conservatories.

Following the tradition of his transcendentalist mentor Ralph Waldo Emerson (1803–1882) and a generation of English Romantics, Henry David Thoreau (1817–1862) went beyond his predecessors' discussion of the wilderness and embarked on a journey to uncover the universal spiritual truths to be found in natural objects. Thoreau argued that by uncovering all the laws of nature, the harmony and the interrelationships that had been lost to the misuse of the powers of civilization could be rediscovered. By affirming the call to rebel against the commercial and industrial interests in society and promoting the simplification of life through the contemplation and appreciation of the wild, Thoreau came to embody the pastoral tradition. Thoreau has been subsequently hailed as the originator of the deep ecology and biocentric philosophy that finds in nature moral instruction.

In creating a national identity associated with nature, earlier Americans had underlined the incomparable size of its wilderness and added to it European deistic ideas and Romantic assumptions about the value of wild country and species. This made American wilderness not only a cultural and moral resource but also a basis for national pride. The appreciation of nature's beauty, however, was insidiously combined with the widespread image of nature as an abundant and inexhaustible storehouse of resources. Her inexpressible beauty was only overshadowed by her fecundity.

This faith in ever-renewing nature concealed the problem of slaughtering wildlife. Consequently, wildlife preservation efforts in the colonial and early national period reflected the limits of legislative reform and the primacy of commercial prerogatives. As overharvesting represented the biggest threat to wildlife, restrictions on hunting were justified on protective grounds. Deer, buffalo, or water fowl were preserved and the financial future of the hunter secured. Colonial wildlife legislation, such as the first game law passed by the town of Newport for the protection of deer in 1639, regulated the killing of wildlife but was confined to the protection of traditional game species. Ordinances provided for a closed hunting season, but lack of enforcement made these laws ultimately ineffective.

By the early nineteenth century, reformers had advocated the need to encourage not only aesthetic appreciation of nature but also responsible governance. In his best-selling series *Leatherstocking Tales*, James Fenimore Cooper expertly combined a Romantic vision of the wilderness as a valuable moral influence, a source of beauty, and a place of exciting adventure with an emphasis on the uniqueness of the American environment. Cooper employed the idea that man should govern resources by certain principles in order to conserve them.

In 1842, the Supreme Court upheld the doctrine of state ownership of wildlife in cases like *Martin v. Waddell*. In the decision, Chief Justice Roger Taney argued that the state of New Jersey had jurisdiction over oysters in a mudflat claimed as property by the landowner because the interest of the public trust prevailed over that of the individual. The few additional Supreme Court cases to follow that considered the validity of state authority unanimously supported the decision. In 1896, state jurisdiction was expanded in *Geer v. Connecticut*, which upheld a conviction under state law for possessing game birds with the intent to ship them out of Connecticut. The Court's opinion provided a historical treatise on governmental control while sparking a long and continuing debate about the respective powers of the state and federal governments over wildlife.

Lacey Act

The decision set the stage for the Lacey Act (1900), the first step in the field of federal wildlife regulation. By the end of the nineteenth century, the federal government had finally responded to the mobilization of preservationist interest groups and the public outcry against overexploitation. In the 1870s, sportsmen groups, although engaged in hunting and fishing, had both realized the need for conservation and had tripled in number to more than three hundred. Sportsmen clubs created a powerful lobby that pushed for game laws, facilitated the development of

479

YELLOWSTONE NATIONAL PARK and similar game preserves, and played a crucial role in the expansion of the outdoor recreation industry. Prominent members of the Boone and Crockett Club, established in 1887, included President Theodore Roosevelt, Chief Forester Gifford Pinchot, and Representative John F. Lacey, sponsor of the Lacey Act that ended massive market hunting. The Lacey Act made it illegal to transport birds across state boundaries if they had been taken in violation of any other law in the nation. While it faced stiff opposition from states rightists, the Act passed behind the growing support of established groups like the League of American Sportsmen and northeastern chapters of the AUDUBON SOCIETY. Although limited to the regulation of interstate commerce in wildlife and initially criticized as a toothless legislative measure, subsequent amendments strengthened enforcement and extended provisions to all wild animals and some wild plants. Most important, the Lacey Act served as the cornerstone of federal efforts to conserve wildlife. The Act not only gave the federal government broader enforcement powers in the area of interstate commerce, it also gave the secretary of agriculture the power to influence foreign commerce by prohibiting the importation of animals deemed a threat to agriculture or horticulture.

As a number of economically and aesthetically important species received increasingly widespread public attention in the second half of the nineteenth century, the federal government was compelled to expand its role. Beaver had become virtually extinct east of the Mississippi River and scarce nationwide by the mid-1800s. The decline of salmonids in the Pacific Northwest prompted the U.S. Fish Commission to send an ichthyologist to the Columbia River in the 1890s. The precipitous decline of bird species was reflected with the heath hen, a heavily hunted subspecies of prairie chicken, which disappeared around the turn of the century, in the death of the last clearly identified passenger pigeon in the wild in 1900, and in the warnings of famed ornithologist James G. Cooper that the California condor was on the verge of extinction. In response to the depletion of several bird species, the Lacey Act authorized the secretary of agriculture to adopt all measures necessary for the "preservation, introduction, and restoration of game birds and other wild birds" while remaining subject to various state laws. Although this was a cautious move toward wildlife management by the federal government, it was an unequivocal statement of public over private authority.

The widely publicized plight of the buffalo also signaled the ineffectiveness of state jurisdiction over wildlife, the results of commercial overexploitation, and the potential value of federal intervention. Heavily hunted for the hide market and slaughtered in the campaign against Native Americans, the buffalo, which had been so plentiful within living memory, was nearing extinction; the fight to save this symbol of America brought wildlife preservation dramatically to the attention of the public.

National Parks and Scientific Management

Following the Homestead Act of 1862, an immense public campaign to make citizens landowners, American land use philosophy shifted toward preservation. The first federal attempt to protect wildlife on a designated area appears to be the 1864 transfer of Yosemite Valley from the public domain to the state of California. The creation of Yellowstone National Park in 1872 followed, but the endangered buffalo were not adequately protected until the passage of the Yellowstone Park Protection Act of 1894. Preservation efforts were also strengthened by the Forest Reservation Creation Act of 1881, which allowed the president to set aside areas for national forests. President Benjamin Harrison quickly created the Afognak Island Forest and Fish Culture Reserve in Alaska by executive order, making wildlife concerns a central element in the proposal. These types of preservation efforts became an international phenomenon in the opening decades of the twentieth century, with national parks established in Sweden, nature preserves set aside in the Netherlands, and the National Trust set up in Great Britain. The second American response to the sudden realization that resources were limited was to develop techniques for the scientific management of wilderness areas in order to maximize yields and eliminate waste. These methods included the utilitarian ethic embodied by forestry guru Gifford Pinchot (1865–1946), who endorsed as the main principle of economic development the preservation of the greatest good for the greatest number.

President Theodore Roosevelt embodied the ideal of progressive reform and signaled a dramatic change in federal policy and environmental ethics. Roosevelt declared that conservation of natural resources was central to American life and put the issue of CONSERVATION at the top of the country's agenda. Supporting an environmental ethic based on stewardship, utility, and scientific management, Roosevelt revolutionized American conservation efforts by taking more action than any prior president to preserve wildlife habitat. By the time he left office, he had created the first official wildlife refuge at Pelican Island, Florida, expanded the national wildlife refuge system to fifty-one protected sites, increased the size of national forests from 42 million acres to 172 million acres, and preserved eighteen areas as national monuments, including the Grand Canyon and the Petrified Forest.

Expanding Federal Authority

In response to the public mood recognized by Roosevelt, Congress continued to expand federal holdings by establishing the Wichita Mountains Forest and Game Preserve in 1905, the National Bison Range in 1908, and the National Elk Refuge in 1912 (the first unit officially referred to as a "refuge"). Then in 1913, an expansive 2.7 million acres were set aside by President William Howard Taft when the vast Aleutian Island chain was added to the system. In the wake of the Lacey Act, the Supreme Court secured the constitutional authority of federal wildlife regulation with a series of judgments cementing the government's role in preservation. The constitutionality of the landmark Migratory Bird Treaty Act of 1918 was first upheld in *Missouri v. Holland* (1920). The case established the supremacy of federal treaty-making power by upholding the protective duty of the federal government over state claims of ownership of wildlife. Justice Oliver Wendell Holmes disposed of the ownership argument in two ways. First, he explained that wild birds were not the possession of anyone. Second, he insisted that the Constitution compelled the federal government to protect the food supply, forests, and crops of the nation. The federal government assumed unprecedented responsibility for wildlife jurisdiction due to the migratory nature of the protected species and employed the first federal wildlife enforcement officers through the Biological Survey. In 1934, the passage of the Migratory Bird Hunting and Conservation Stamp Act (known as the Duck Stamp Act) created a major stimulus for funding the refuge system. What remained unclear was the extent of federal obligation and affiliated power.

The government had prohibited all hunting in Yellowstone National Park since 1894 without officially sanctioned jurisdiction, but a more concrete answer to the issue of property rights and responsibilities was provided by *Hunt v. United States* (1928). The case involved the secretary of agriculture's directive to remove excess deer from the Kaibab National Forest. While the secretary insisted that the deer threatened harm to the forest from overbrowsing, state officials arrested people for carrying out the orders. The Supreme Court decision was explicit. The power of the federal government to protect its lands and property superseded any other statute of the state. The relationship between federal and state authority, nevertheless, remained a hotly contested issue to be revisited by the Court for decades.

Kleppe v. New Mexico (1978) provided a firm foundation for the basis of federal authority in property disputes. The Wild Free-Roaming Horses and Burros Act of 1971, designed to protect all unbranded and unclaimed horses and burros on public lands as living symbols of the historic West, was upheld with the argument that the federal government had the power to regulate and protect its wildlife regardless of state interests. *Palil v. Hawaii Department of Land and Natural Resources* (1981) carried Kleppe's suggestion of federal ownership a step further. Upholding the Endangered Species Act of 1973, the judgment found that preserving a natural resource may be of such importance as to constitute a federal property interest.

These decisions illustrate changes in the focus of wildlife preservation policy from preventing overharvesting to addressing the larger problem of habitat destruction. While the first acknowledgment of the federal responsibility to protect habitats on a national scale can be traced to late-nineteenth and early-twentieth century presidential and congressional efforts, a series of legislative landmarks in the following decades extended the scope of federal preservation efforts. The Migratory Bird Conser-

vation Act of 1929 established a special commission for the review lands to be purchased by the Department of the Interior to protect areas crucial to waterfowl reproduction and remains a major source of authority for refuge acquisition. The Fish and Wildlife Coordination Act of 1934 also set an important precedent by requiring water development agencies to consider wildlife preservation in the planning process. The Federal Aid in Wildlife Restoration Act of 1937 provided the necessary fiscal foundation for wildlife administration by setting aside funds from taxes on ammunition for state agencies.

Legislation and the Professionalization of Ecology

The profession of wildlife management also evolved in the 1930s as Aldo Leopold (1887–1948) taught the first courses in wildlife management at the University of Wisconsin and his *Game Management* (1933) became the first textbook. In 1934, President Franklin Roosevelt appointed Leopold, Jay Norwood "Ding" Darling, and Thomas Beck to a special committee to study and advise him on the waterfowl problem in 1934. The committee undertook a campaign to alert the nation to the crisis facing waterfowl due to drought, overharvest, and habitat destruction. Darling was subsequently appointed head of the Bureau of Biological Survey in 1935. J. Clark Salyer was brought in to mange the fledgling refuge program, and for the next thirty-one years had a profound influence on the development of the refuge system. The Biological Survey subsequently established ten land grant universities equipped with research and training programs. Leopold was one of the first to recognize the shift from overharvest to habitat degradation as the primary threat to wildlife, his recommendations as chairman of the American Game Policy Committee established a new land ethic and fostered the blossoming of a new expertise in ecology. Along with the professionalization trend, new scientific organizations proliferated, among them the American Institute for Biological Sciences, the Conservation Foundation, and the International Union for Conservation of Nature and Natural Resources. With the merging of the Biological Survey and the Bureau of Fisheries in 1940, to form the Fish and Wildlife Service, which presided over an expanding system of wildlife refuges and sanctuaries, the stage was arguably set for a broader view of wildlife preservation.

The professionalization of ecology, the exposure of widespread environmental degradation in Rachel Carson's *Silent Spring* (1962), and the subsequent dawning of the American environmental movement collectively pushed the legislative evolution of wildlife preservation forward at an increased pace in the 1960s. The Fish and Wildlife Act of 1956 had established a comprehensive national fish and wildlife policy, making increased acquisition and development of refuges possible. The National Wildlife Refuge System Administration Act of 1966 provided further guidelines and directives for administration and management of the refuge system. In 1966, Congress passed the Endangered Species Preservation Act in an attempt to protect habitat for endangered vertebrate species by

481

creating new wildlife refuges. The 1969 Endangered Species Conservation Act extended the policy to invertebrates and directed the secretary of interior to facilitate an international convention of species preservation. The Convention on International Trade in Endangered Species of Wild Fauna and Flora (CITES), which convened in Washington, D.C., in the spring of 1973, set the stage for the most far-reaching wildlife statute in U.S. history.

In an attempt to bridge the gaps between competing interests, the Endangered Species Act (ESA) of 1973 intended to recognize the aesthetic, ecological, educational, historical, recreational, and scientific value of wildlife and plants. The ESA went beyond many earlier preservation efforts by mandating the conservation of entire ecosystems and requiring all federal departments and agencies to utilize their authority to further the purposes of the Act. Although it passed amidst a wave of environmental lawmaking in the early 1970s, the near unanimous support of Congress, and the endorsement of President Richard Nixon, debates continued in the wake of ESA. The longstanding issue of federal and state regulatory authority remained but was overshadowed by competing private interests. Conservationist organizations like the World Wildlife Fund and Nature Conservancy, along with activist organizations like the SIERRA CLUB and National Wildlife Federation, utilized the ESA as an effective tool to protect threatened and endangered species like the highly publicized northern spotted owl. Meanwhile, the loose-knit but widespread Wise Use movement led efforts to stop ESA's intrusion into the lives of private landowners. As special interest groups have consistently shaped wildlife preservation efforts since the nineteenth century, confronting the relationship between social and economic prerogatives, the formation of powerful lobbying groups on each side of the debate in recent years has ensured that wildlife preservation will remain a pivotal political issue for decades to come.

BIBLIOGRAPHY

Bean, Michael J., and Melanie J. Rowland, eds. *The Evolution of National Wildlife Law*. Westport, Conn.: Praeger, 1997.

Czech, Brian, and Paul R. Krausman. *The Endangered Species Act: History, Conservation, Biology, and Public Policy*. 3d ed. Baltimore: Johns Hopkins University Press, 2001.

Matthiessen, Peter. *Wildlife in America*. 3d ed. New York: Viking, 1987.

Reiger, John F. *American Sportsmen and the Origins of Conservation*. Corvallis: Oregon State University Press, 2001.

Tober, James A. *Who Owns the Wildlife? The Political Economy of Conservation in Nineteenth Century America*. Westport, Conn.: Greenwood Press, 1981.

Eric William Boyle

See also **Endangered Species.**

WILKES EXPEDITION.

The Wilkes Exploring Expedition began life as the U.S. Exploring Expedition of 1836, authorized by Congress to chart the southern Pacific beyond Hawaii. After delays, Commander Charles Wilkes led six ships into the area in 1838. He was accompanied by several scientists, including a geographer, a geologist, and a naturalist. It was an amazingly comprehensive voyage, touching Antarctica and Australia in the south, and then ranging northward to the Oregon coast. In between, he completed his charge by not only enumerating and describing the Marianas and Fijis, but other islands as well. The scientific data and samples of that expedition were important enough to later studies that the artifacts he collected ultimately wound up in the permanent collections of several national museums, including the Smithsonian and the U.S. Botanical Garden.

His charts have proven invaluable as well, even during World War II. By planting the American flag on several previously unknown islands, Wilkes provided the basis for later nineteenth-century American possession of several of them, including Wake Island of World War II fame. His explorations and charting of the northern Pacific and his landfall at the tip of Puget Sound at Fort Nisqually immediately bolstered American claims to what later became the Oregon Territory. The Expedition thus played a part directly in all American involvement in the Pacific for the century following his return to the United States in 1842.

A competent scientist in his own right as well as a naval officer, his wide-ranging Pacific explorations between 1838 and 1842 also helped to bolster later American claims in Antarctica, including Wilkes Island.

BIBLIOGRAPHY

Dupree, A. Hunter. *Science in the Federal Government: A History of Policies and Activities*. Baltimore: Johns Hopkins University Press, 1986.

Merk, Frederick. *Manifest Destiny and Mission in American History: A Reinterpretation*. Cambridge, Mass.: Harvard University Press, 1995.

Carl E. Prince

WILLIAM AND MARY, COLLEGE OF.

The College of William and Mary is a state university located in Williamsburg, Virginia. The college has a long and distinguished history. Chartered by William III and Mary II on 8 February 1693, the college drew its support from the English crown, the Established Church, and the colonial government of Virginia. It was the successor to a proposed university at Henrico, Va., which had been destroyed during a 1622 Indian uprising before its completion. William and Mary's first president, the Rev. James Blair, was also rector of Bruton Parish Church in Williamsburg and commissary in Virginia of the bishop of London. The College of Arms in London granted a coat of arms to the college on 14 May 1694. The first college building was erected in 1695; it was rebuilt and enlarged after a fire in 1705.

Redesigned after fires in 1859 and 1862, it was restored to its eighteenth-century appearance in 1928–1930 with funds donated by John D. Rockefeller, Jr., and renamed the Sir Christopher Wren Building. Still in use today, the Wren Building is the oldest academic building in continuous use in North America. The building is named after its architect, who also designed St. Paul's Cathedral in London. Two other early college buildings were also restored beginning in 1928: the Brafferton, constructed in 1723 with funds from the estate of the physicist Robert Boyle as a school for Indians; and the President's House, built in 1732, which beginning with Blair has served as the official residence.

Many of the students of the early college were leaders in the American Revolution, including Thomas Jefferson, James Monroe, Richard Bland, Peyton Randolph, Edmund Randolph, and Benjamin Harrison; John Marshall and John Tyler also attended the college. In 1776 the Phi Beta Kappa Society was organized by a group of students, and that same year the college adopted the honor code system of conduct, the first American college to do so. Schools of medicine, law, and modern languages were established in 1779. The college was also the first American institution of higher learning to adopt a system of course electives for its undergraduates.

After the Declaration of Independence, the college formally broke ties with Great Britain. During the Revolutionary War the college was closed briefly in 1781, when it was occupied by British Gen. Charles Cornwallis. It closed again during the Civil War; and again from 1881 until 1888 for lack of funds. In 1888 a state grant enabled the college to reopen to educate male teachers, and in 1906 the property of the college was deeded to the Commonwealth of Virginia. The college became coeducational in 1918. Branches that opened during the 1920s in Richmond and Norfolk became, in 1962, Virginia's state-supported urban universities, Virginia Commonwealth University and Old Dominion University, respectively.

In 1967, William and Mary was redesignated a university without changing its traditional name. It is today the second-oldest college in the United States, behind Harvard College. It boasts an enrollment of 7,500 students, including 5,500 undergraduates, and draws students from all 50 states and over 75 countries.

BIBLIOGRAPHY

Morpugo, J. E. *Their Majesties' Royall Colledge: William and Mary in the Seventeenth and Eighteenth Centuries.* Williamsburg, Va.: College of William and Mary, 1976.

Ross Weeks Jr. / A. G.

See also **Harvard University; South, the: The Antebellum South; Tidewater; Universities, State; Yale University.**

WILLIAMS V. MISSISSIPPI, 170 U.S. 213 (1898), a test by Henry Williams, an African American, of Mis-

sissippi's constitution of 1890 and code of 1892, which required passage of a LITERACY TEST as a prerequisite to voting. Williams claimed that the franchise provisions denied blacks equal protection of the law guaranteed by the Fourteenth Amendment. The SUPREME COURT decided on 25 April 1898 that mere possibility of discrimination was not grounds for invalidating the provisions. Mississippi's ingenious exclusion device thus was upheld and blacks continued to be disfranchised under it.

BIBLIOGRAPHY

Ayers, Edward L. *The Promise of the New South: Life After Reconstruction.* New York: Oxford University Press, 1992.

Curtis, Michael K. *No State Shall Abridge: The Fourteenth Amendment and the Bill of Rights.* Durham, N.C.: Duke University Press, 1986.

Mack Swearingen / A. R.

See also **African Americans; Civil Rights and Liberties; Disfranchisement; Equal Protection of the Law; Jim Crow Laws; Mississippi Plan.**

WILLIAMSBURG, COLONIAL. Originally known as the Middle Plantation, the city of Williamsburg was a planned community from its origin. In October 1693, the Virginia General Assembly designated the Middle Plantation as the site for the "free school and college" of William and Mary, and after the state house in Jamestown burned to the ground in October 1698, the Middle Plantation became the seat of government. Named Williamsburg, in honor of King William III, the city included many new innovations. A 1699 act of the Virginia General Assembly divided the city into half-acre lots, with a directive that no house could be built within six feet of the main street, known as Duke of Gloucester Street. This act called for the creation of a brick capitol building, the first in the American colonies, so that the governor and General Assembly could be housed in Williamsburg, as well as the construction of a brick prison. The city progressed quickly in the early years of the governorship of Alexander Spotswood, and in May 1722, the city of Williamsburg incorporated. As a result, the mayor, recorder, and aldermen were designated as justices of peace within the city limits and were empowered to hold a monthly hustings court. In addition, one delegate could be sent to the HOUSE OF BURGESSES, provided his estate was worth two hundred pounds sterling if he were a Williamsburg resident, or five hundred pounds sterling if he were not. The original Williamsburg charter vested power in the hands of each corporation, such as the mayor or aldermen, yet the charter called for a division of powers between each group.

During the eighteenth century, Williamsburg became a major capital city, and played a role in the events leading to the American Revolution. On 30 May 1765, Patrick Henry spoke his famous words, "if this be treason, make the most of it" in denouncing the Stamp Act. Although the British Parliament repealed the Stamp Act in 1766, Virginia led the way in uniting the colonies in resisting British encroachments on the rights of person and property. Williamsburg also was at the forefront of industrialization, creating a factory for making woolen and linen cloth, as well as a tannery, carriage factory, wig factory, and snuff mill. In addition to the College of William and Mary, various schools, including schools exclusively for young women and African Americans, were established, and these continued in some form even during the Revolutionary War. In 1780, the state capital moved to Richmond, and Williamsburg once again became a rural county seat; the population dropped by about one-third to about 1,300.

Restoration in the Twentieth Century

The idea of re-creating the town of Williamsburg originated with W. A. R. Goodwin, a local minister, who requested assistance from Henry Ford, boldly asking Ford to underwrite the cost of restoring the town where George Washington, Thomas Jefferson, and Patrick Henry had lived and worked. When Ford did not respond, Goodwin approached John D. Rockefeller, who authorized Goodwin to purchase property in the town anonymously. Using 1790 as a cut-off date, Rockefeller had 720 buildings constructed after 1790 demolished and had eighty-two eighteenth-century buildings restored. The Rockefeller crew also rebuilt 341 buildings whose foundations remained. Completed in the mid-1930s, the Williamsburg reconstruction cost approximately $79 million.

Ignoring and Restoring History

The town only restored the society of the planter elite—no reference was made to the black half of the city's eighteenth-century population, the half that had been slaves. Rockefeller appeared to have chosen to ignore that portion of American colonial history.

In 1939, Rockefeller became the chairman of the board of Colonial Williamsburg and called for an aggressive public relations campaign. He brought troops to Williamsburg during World War II as inspiration to the city's residents. In the 1950s, Williamsburg expanded its public relations campaign in an attempt to attract visitors; the city brought foreign students and held workshops on democracy. During the presidency of Dwight Eisenhower (1953–1961) in particular, Williamsburg became the customary arrival point for heads of state on their way to Washington, D.C. However, a tour through Colonial Williamsburg remained a tour through the history of white America, and the sight of a "slave" was rare. During the 1950s, the Colonial Williamsburg Foundation restricted the jobs available to African Americans and allowed blacks to visit as paying customers on only one day a week. Three decades later, Colonial Williamsburg was ridiculed for having ignored history while concentrating on the resort quality of the town. In 1982, the city responded to criticism of its focus on elites and the "stopped-in-time" quality of the town by adding slavery to the

portrayal of colonial life. Colonial Williamsburg stopped short, however, of tackling the relationship between blacks and whites. Very little attention was paid to the institution of slavery until, on 10 October 1994, a slave auction was re-enacted as a part of the celebrations of the accession of George III to the throne. The 1994 summer programs had also included slave marriage re-enactments. The 1994 "slave auction" drew an initial crowd of two thousand to Duke of Gloucester Street for the re-enactment of the sale of four slaves during an estate auction. The NAACP and the Southern Christian Leadership Conference protested this auction and attempted to cancel the re-enactment. However, once the controversy had somewhat died down, it became clear that programming like this was needed. In March 1999, programming entitled "Enslaving Virginia" began, with African Americans making up nearly 10 percent of the almost six hundred living history re-enactors in Colonial Williamsburg.

By the turn of the twenty-first century, the city of Williamsburg covered nine square miles, and was a thriving business and cultural center. With both the College of William and Mary and Colonial Williamsburg, the city attracts over one million visitors each year.

BIBLIOGRAPHY

Cutler, William W. "Cultural Literacy, Historic Preservation, and Commemoration: Some Thoughts for Educational Historians." *History of Education Quarterly* 4 (2000): 477–482.

Hood, Graham. *The Governor's Palace in Williamsburg: A Cultural Study.* Williamsburg, Va.: The Colonial Williamsburg Foundation, 1991.

Tyler, Lyon Gardiner. *Williamsburg: The Old Colonial Capital.* Richmond, Va.: Whittet and Shepperson, 1907.

Wallace, Mike. *Mickey Mouse History and Other Essays on American Memory.* Philadephia: Temple University Press, 1996.

Jennifer Harrison

See also **Slave Trade; Slavery; William and Mary, College of.**

WILLIAMSON V. LEE OPTICAL (*Williamson v. Lee Optical Company*, 348 U.S. 483, 1955). From a seemingly mundane Oklahoma statute arose *Williamson v. Lee Optical Company*, one of the most significant post–New Deal decisions of the Supreme Court. The statute made it unlawful for any person not a licensed optometrist or ophthalmologist to fit or duplicate lenses for eyeglasses without a prescription. Because the statute in effect made it almost impossible for opticians to do business, a U.S. district court held the statute violated the due process and equal protection clauses. A unanimous Supreme Court, in an opinion by Justice William O. Douglas, reversed.

Williamson completed the Court's repudiation of its practice during the so-called *Lochner* era, following *Lochner v. People of the State of New York*, 198 U.S. 45 (1905), of invalidating economic regulations as violations of substantive due process. In *Williamson* the Court applied only the most deferential level of "rationality" review to the statute. The Court hypothesized a variety of possible reasons for the legislation, none of which was apparent from the face of the statute, and went as far as to acknowledge that the statute might "exact a needless, wasteful requirement." As long as some conceivable rational basis for the regulation at issue existed, courts would not disturb the legislative judgment, even if "unwise" or "improvident."

The Court also applied a deferential rational-basis review of the equal protection challenge. The problem of legislative categorization is "perennial," and even if the basis for classification is not obvious, the legislature can address the problem "one step at a time" or even select one aspect of a problem and "apply a remedy there, neglecting the others." *Williamson* rendered it almost impossible to use equal protection to challenge economic regulation unless the classification at issue depends on suspect classifications, such as race or sex.

BIBLIOGRAPHY

Rotunda, Ronald D., and John E. Nowak. *Treatise on Constitutional Law: Substance and Procedure.* 3d ed. Volume 2. St. Paul, Minn.: West, 1999. Good overview of trends in substantive due process jurisprudence after the New Deal.

Kent Greenfield

See also **Due Process of Law; Equal Protection of the Law.**

WILMINGTON RIOT. On 9 November 1898 a mass meeting of whites was held at Wilmington, NORTH CAROLINA, to protest black rule; most of the city offices were held by blacks, who outnumbered the whites seventeen thousand to eight thousand. The group demanded that the editor of the African American newspaper remove himself and his press by the next morning. When this demand was not met, six hundred armed whites destroyed the printing material and burned the building. In the ensuing riot some ten blacks were killed and three whites wounded. All of the city officials resigned and were succeeded by white Democrats.

BIBLIOGRAPHY

Cecelski, David S., and Timothy B. Tyson, eds. *Democracy Betrayed: The Wilmington Race Riot of 1898 and Its Legacy.* Chapel Hill: University of North Carolina Press, 1998.

Prather, H. Leon. *We Have Taken a City: Wilmington Racial Massacre and Coup of 1898.* Rutherford, N.J.: Fairleigh Dickenson University Press, 1984.

Hugh T. Lefler / A. R.

See also **African Americans; Civil Rights and Liberties; Disfranchisement; Magazines and Newspapers, African American; Riots.**

WILMOT PROVISO. Immediately after the beginning of the Mexican-American War (1846–1848), President James Polk asked Congress for $2 million, which he intended to use to buy a peace treaty with Mexico. A rider was attached to the bill on 8 August 1846, by David Wilmot, a little-known Democratic representative from Pennsylvania. The Wilmot Proviso, as it became known, would forbid the extension of slavery to any territory acquired from Mexico. The proviso caused a split among the Democrats as northerners supported it and southerners opposed it. Polk eventually got his appropriation, but Congress rejected the Wilmot Proviso after a bitter debate. The provision was reintroduced several times afterward, but never approved.

The implications of the Wilmot Proviso were far-reaching. Wilmot's action was on behalf of a group of northern Democrats who were angry over Polk's political appointments, his apparent proslavery actions in Texas, his compromise with Great Britain over the Oregon issue, and Polk's veto of a rivers and harbors bill supported by midwestern Democrats. Many northern Democrats were also resentful of the domination of the party by southerners, feeling they had made too many concessions to the southern wing in the past, and that the war with Mexico was an act of aggression designed to expand slavery. As a result, the Wilmot Proviso sparked what would become a rancorous national debate on the question of expanding slavery into the territories.

All but one northern state legislature endorsed the Wilmot Proviso, while southern legislatures expressed their determination to resist it. Southern slaveholders resented the proviso as it seemed to stigmatize them, suggesting that they were not the equals of northerners. More importantly, southerners feared that if slavery could not expand, the slave system would slowly be strangled once it was surrounded by free territories. Prominent senator John C. Calhoun of South Carolina argued that the territories were the common property of all the states, and Congress lacked the power to prevent persons from taking their property into a territory; therefore slavery was legal in all the territories. Failure to uphold this principle, Calhoun declared, would destroy the balance between the free and slave states. At the end of 1847, Michigan's Democratic senator Lewis Cass argued for what would become known as "popular sovereignty" by proposing that the territories decide the slavery question themselves. This idea attracted support from both northern and southern Democrats, each of whom interpreted the concept to fit their own views about the expansion of slavery.

Polk seems not to have understood the nature of the debate, holding that the slavery issue was a domestic problem and not a question of foreign policy. The president failed to recognize the question was, indeed, a major foreign policy issue. Expansion had been a significant aspect of American foreign policy since colonial days. The end of the Mexican-American War would leave either slave owners or anti-slave forces in control of an enormous amount of new territory; in time, the winner could control the government. Polk thought that Congress was raising the issue in order to embarrass him; he felt slavery could not exist in the poor soil conditions of northern Mexico.

The proviso served to heighten sectional animosity, and later efforts to pass the measure only provoked further debate. The modern Republican Party would be founded on the principle of halting slavery's expansion, and Abraham Lincoln would be elected to the presidency on a platform that promised to carry out the principles of the Wilmot Proviso.

BIBLIOGRAPHY

Foner, Eric. "The Wilmot Proviso Revisited." *Journal of American History* 56 (1969): 262–279.

Morrison, Chaplain W. *Democratic Politics and Sectionalism: The Wilmot Proviso Controversy.* Chapel Hill: University of North Carolina Press, 1967.

Gregory Moore

WINDMILLS. In the seventeenth century windmills stood in what are now New York and northern New Jersey, but they did not become a feature of American life until after the Civil War, and then generally in the western United States. The occupation of lands beyond the belt of regular rain, springs, streams, and shallow underground water tapped by hand-dug wells made windmills a necessity. Well-drilling machinery and practical mills made their use possible. Popularized in the 1870s, windmills came to dot the PRAIRIE states and the rough, arid, or semiarid lands beyond. They provided a way, before the invention of the gasoline engine, to supply water for personal and agricultural use.

The windmill became common only after barbed wire had made the control of waterings by private owners possible. It turned tens of millions of acres of waterless land into farms. It made garden patches and shade and fruit trees possible, even during the most parching droughts. It also brought running water into homes.

Nonetheless, the use of windmills to provide water in dry western states has not been an unmitigated good. For instance, since the 1940s, farmers from northern TEXAS to southern SOUTH DAKOTA have depended on water pumped from the Ogallala Aquifer to irrigate their crops. Although this massive subterranean aquifer is the largest in the world, those who rely on it are consuming its water at a faster rate than the aquifer can recharge it. Therefore, this practice is not sustainable. Calling the transformation of arid territory into farms "land reclamation" falsely implies that the so-called Great American Desert served no purpose before irrigation. The fact that an area does not easily support humans and their preferred crops does not render it worthless. A more sustainable use for windmills is in the production of electricity from wind power, an area in which Denmark excelled during the early 2000s.

BIBLIOGRAPHY

Hills, Richard Leslie. *Power from Wind: A History of Windmill Technology.* New York: Cambridge University Press, 1994.

MacDonnell, Lawrence J. *From Reclamation to Sustainability: Water, Agriculture, and the Environment in the American West.* Niwot: University Press of Colorado, 1999.

Opie, John. *Ogallala: Water for a Dry Land.* 2d ed. Lincoln: University of Nebraska Press, 2000.

Rowley, William D. *Reclaiming the Arid West: The Career of Francis G. Newlands.* Bloomington: Indiana University Press, 1996.

J. Frank Dobie/A. E.

See also **Agriculture; Dry Farming; Energy, Renewable; Frontier; Irrigation; Reclamation.**

Windmill. This early-twentieth-century photograph by Theodor Horydczak was taken on V Street, on the outskirts of Washington, D.C. LIBRARY OF CONGRESS

WINE INDUSTRY. In the early nineteenth century Nicholas Longworth, an optimistic and eccentric settler of Cincinnati, raised eyebrows when he planted grapes on his farmlands in southwestern Ohio. On occasion, easterners had tried making wine but had disliked the taste; Longworth's wine, however, seemed palatable. Like many wine makers in the nineteenth century, including Thomas Jefferson, Longworth championed wine as a beverage of temperance, arguing that it was more civilized than distilled spirits. But the wine industry faced formidable challenges. For most of the nineteenth century, wine making was a small-scale, agrarian undertaking concentrated in eastern states. Demand was largely local and most Americans preferred spirits or beer, which were much cheaper, to wine. Until the late twentieth century, wine consumption was very low in the United States. The industry has always been composed of growers and vintners, although many industry members have engaged in both supplying and processing. The production of wine has proved land and labor intensive and therefore unattractive to farmers seeking easier profits. Wine making in the 1800s, furthermore, was hampered by crop diseases and insects. By the end of the century, however, the development of fungicides and other scientific advances fostered an increase in grape growing and wine making.

California Wine

Another important development was the rise of the wine industry in California, particularly northern California, in the late 1800s, when it became the country's leading wine-producing state. As did many other industries, the wine industry experienced consolidation during this period. The California Wine Association (CWA), founded in 1894, organized the industry in that state, and in what is sometimes referred to as the "wine war," aggressively cut prices to put its competitors out of business. The leaders of the wine industry became financiers instead of farmers and wine merchants. During this period, demand for wine moved from the country to the city, and because of the CWA's push for a standardized product, the public favored sweet, fortified wines at cheap prices. By the advent of PROHIBITION in 1919, most Americans viewed wine just as they did distilled spirits: as a mass-produced, intemperate beverage. Moreover, they regarded American wine as inferior to European wine. Wine, earlier respected as a beverage of moderation, now became an easy target for the TEMPERANCE MOVEMENT.

Prohibition and Afterward

Prohibition had a devastating impact on the wine industry. Growers converted vineyards to other crops and most wineries were abandoned. Over 1,000 commercial wineries existed before Prohibition, but at Repeal in 1933, only 150 remained. The industry had a much more difficult time recovering from Prohibition than did the BREWING and distilling industries. In the several decades after Prohibition, American wine still had the reputation of being a cheap drink that "belonged in paper bags on skid row" (Lukacs, *American Vintage*, p. 94). The association between wine and spirits was strengthened during World War II when several large distillers aggressively entered the wine business. The distillers exited by the end of the 1940s, but the connection was cemented in the minds of many.

As did most other agriculturally based enterprises, wine making became a big business during the postwar years. The industry once again experienced consolidation,

going from around 1,300 commercial wineries in 1936 to only 271 in 1960. In the East, the largest wineries could be found in the Finger Lakes region of New York. In California two companies, E. and J. Gallo and United Vinters, dominated the industry and in 1967 Gallo claimed its place, which it still holds, as the world's largest winery.

The Turn toward Wine

The ascendance of the wine industry began in the 1960s when prosperous and well-traveled Americans developed a taste for table wines, which transported wine consumption from the gutter into sophisticated and affluent homes. The Gallos participated in this shift when they began to plant premium grapes and strove for excellence in their wine making. Also influential was Robert Mondavi, another California wine producer, who designed his wines to taste like those of France. Mondavi and others were able to manipulate grapes and wines to achieve desired tastes. Unlike the European wine industry, which was built on craft and tradition, the post-Repeal wine industry in America was based on technology and science after Prohibition severed American wine makers' association with the past. In the 1960s and after, the industry relied on research and experimentation and was closely associated with agricultural researchers at several land-grant universities. Also, big corporations such as Coca-Cola, Nestlé, and Schlitz Brewing entered the industry in hopes of earning large profits from a rising enterprise. Nestle succeeded in turning Beringer into an industry leader, but others, such as Coca-Cola, failed and deserted their effort. Although the wine industry established strong footholds in Oregon and Washington, the state of California, with over nine-hundred wineries, remained the leading wine-producing state in the nation, accounting for 90 percent (444 million gallons) of all U.S. wine production at the end of the twentieth century. The industry in California organized itself into the Wine Institute, while wineries across the nation are represented by another trade association, the Association of American Vintners.

The trend toward superior table wines meant that during the 1980s and 1990s America saw a rise in small premium wineries that produced wines scoring higher than French wines in international competitions. American wine makers, moreover, no longer copied European wines; instead, they developed exceptional qualities of their own. Despite the blossoming of the American wine industry during the last quarter of the twentieth century, wine consumption failed to soar. This was partly attributable to the new temperance movement of the 1980s, which focused on drunk driving, alcohol-related birth defects, and alcohol advertising abuses. But another reason for sagging consumption rates was that Americans ceased drinking generous amounts of cheap wines and were drinking less, but more expensive, premium wines. Some wine producers, however, did experience a boom in another wine product during the 1980s when the wine cooler enjoyed a brief vogue. In the 1990s, scientific reports linking moderate wine consumption to good health bolstered a rising popularity for wine in America.

BIBLIOGRAPHY

Barr, Andrew. *Drink: A Social History of America.* New York: Carroll and Graf, 1999.

Lukacs, Paul. *American Vintage: The Rise of American Wine.* Boston: Houghton Mifflin, 2000.

Pinney, Thomas. *A History of Wine in America from the Beginnings to Prohibition.* Berkeley: University of California Press, 1989.

Wine Institute: The Voice for California Wine. Available at http://www.wineinstitute.org.

Pamela E. Pennock

See also **Spirits Industry.**

WINNEBAGO/HO-CHUNK.

The American Indian tribe Winnebago called themselves Ho-chunk-gra (Ho-Chunk), "People with the Big Voice." In prehistoric times, they were the only Siouan-speaking tribe in the Great Lakes area, and their name Winnebago, "People of the Filthy Water," is Algonquian, given to them by nearby tribes, the Sac and Fox.

Previous to contact with Europeans, the Winnebago lived in present-day Wisconsin in villages of bark lodges. They farmed, growing corn, beans, squash, and tobacco; they also hunted small game in forests and along streams, living in lean-tos and tents on hunting trips.

Their social and governmental organization was rigid, with two groups, Sky and Earth, divided into clans. Each clan had specific responsibilities. The Sky group was divided into four clans: Thunder Clan—civic leaders; Hawk Clan—soldiers and life-or-death judges of captives; Eagle and Pigeon Clans—hunters and soldiers. The Earth group was divided into eight clans: Bear Clan—police; Wolf Clan—in charge of health and safety; Water-Spirit Clan—water supply; Deer Clan—counsel on environment and weather; Elk Clan—distribute fire; Buffalo Clan—messengers; Fish Clan—soldiers and village protection; and Snake Clan—listen for intruders and monitor sanitation.

The tribe's population was near 25,000 when French explorer Jean Nicolet met Winnebago warriors in the Green Bay area in 1634; three smallpox epidemics and war with the nearby Algonquin tribes decimated the Winnebago within six years; only a few hundred survived. Their social and government organization suffered.

The Winnebago were fierce, never shirking combat. With renewed numbers, they fought alongside the French in a war against the Iroquois League (1690–1697). In 1702, they changed sides and joined the Fox Alliance in fur trade disputes with the French. This shift in allegiance caused a split in the tribe. During the FRENCH AND INDIAN WAR (1755–1763) both factions sided against the British, but shifted sides to fight with the British against the colonials in the American Revolution (1776–1783). This al-

Winnebago (Ho-Chunk) Chief. A portrait of Four Legs, also called Thunder Speaker (his Indian names are rendered in various ways, including O'-Check-Ka here), painted in 1827 by James Otto Lewis and reproduced as a lithograph in an 1830s collection of Lewis's art. LIBRARY OF CONGRESS

liance held through the War of 1812, but the U.S. victory over the British forced the Winnebago to sign their first peace treaty with Washington. One faction signed the treaty, and the other did not, creating more internal strife.

Violent squabbles with whites about the mining of lead caused the Winnebago to lose land in treaty settlements. When the Winnebago lost the BLACK HAWK WAR of 1832, they lost additional land. By 1840, the Winnebago tribe had been removed from Wisconsin to "Neutral Ground" in Iowa; in 1846 the tribe was moved to Minnesota, first to the Long Prairie Reservation and then, in 1855, to the Blue Earth Reservation. In 1863 they were moved to Crow Creek, South Dakota Reservation. The following year they ceded Crow Creek and bought part of the Omaha tribe's reservation in present-day Nebraska. Following each move, some Winnebagos returned to Wisconsin, only to be forcefully removed again.

During the allotment era (1887–1934) the Winnebago lost 75 percent of their Nebraska reservation and experienced dissention within the tribe; a final split resulted in half the tribe returning to Wisconsin. The Winnebago Tribe of Nebraska incorporated in 1936; the Wisconsin branch, officially called the Ho-Chuck Nation, was not recognized until 1963. The reservation in Wisconsin covers parts of ten counties with tribal headquarters in Wisconsin Dells.

Both branches suffered under the reservation system until the 1990s. Under the AMERICAN INDIAN GAMING REGULATORY ACT of 1988, tribes were allowed to erect gambling halls offering bingo and incorporating casinos. Profits from gaming in both states have been invested in income-producing entities: hotels, shopping centers, technology businesses, and gas stations. As a result, the tribes' standard of living has been raised significantly.

BIBLIOGRAPHY

Prucha, Francis Paul. *American Indian Treaties: The History of a Political Anomaly.* Berkeley: University of California Press, 1994.

Radin, Paul. *The Winnebago Tribe.* 1923. Reprint, Lincoln: University of Nebraska Press, 1990.

Smith, David Lee. *Folklore of the Winnebago Tribe.* Norman: University of Oklahoma Press, 1997.

Wyman, Mark. *The Wisconsin Frontier.* Bloomington: Indiana University Press, 1998.

Veda Boyd Jones

WINTERTHUR. Opened to the public in 1951 just outside of Wilmington, Delaware, Winterthur Museum, Garden, and Library is a 966-acre country estate that principally includes a museum of the American decorative arts, a naturalistic garden, and a research library and academic center. Winterthur was the home of Henry F. du Pont, who assembled the core of the decorative-arts collection, arranged it in period rooms now numbering 175, created the garden in conjunction with the designer Marian Coffin, and began the library and graduate programs. Du Pont remained an active presence at Winterthur until his death in 1969. A nonprofit board of trustees and a professional staff now provide oversight and direction.

Du Pont graduated from Harvard University in 1903 and returned to Winterthur to manage the house and eventually the estate for his father, Henry Algernon du Pont. The land, which had been in the du Pont family since 1867, was settled in 1837 by Jacques Antoine Biderman, a business partner of the du Ponts, who named the estate Winterthur after the Swiss city that had been his ancestral home.

Henry F. du Pont, who would inherit Winterthur in 1926, created a great American country estate, modeled in part on European examples. He redesigned and expanded the gardens. He reorganized the farm and established one of the finest dairy herds in the United States. In the 1920s, he began to collect American antiques and interior architectural elements, which would lead to a dramatic expansion of his home.

Since 1951, Winterthur has been a distinguished museum of art and history, a showcase for a preeminent collection of American decorative arts. Ongoing garden restoration has helped to reclaim du Pont's original vision. The research library has evolved into a leading center for the study of material culture and the American arts with an active fellowship program. Winterthur also supports a nationally recognized publications program, conservation labs, and two leading graduate programs. The Winterthur Program in Early American Culture, founded in 1952, and the Winterthur–University of Delaware Program in Art Conservation, founded in 1974, are joint masters programs with the University of Delaware that have now graduated over 500 curators, conservators, and others who have helped to reshape the study and practice of material culture and the decorative arts.

BIBLIOGRAPHY

Cantor, Jay E. *Winterthur: The Foremost Museum of American Furniture and Decorative Arts.* 2d ed. New York: Harry N. Abrams, 1997.

Eversmann, Pauline K., and Kathryn H. Head. *Discover the Winterthur Estate.* Winterthur, Del.: Winterthur Publications, 1998.

Gary Kulik

See also **Art: Decorative Arts.**

WISCONSIN. Wisconsin's people have been molded by their diverse immigrant heritage, honest government born of midwestern progressivism, and glacial gifts of rich soils, scenic rivers, and about 9,000 freshwater lakes. Cradled between Lake Michigan, Lake Superior, and the Mississippi River, Wisconsin's population in 2000 was 5,363,675.

Exploration and Fur Trade

Prior to the arrival of Europeans, the Winnebago, Menominee, Chippewa, Potawatomi, Fox, and Sauk peoples lived in harmony with the rolling hills, grassland prairies, pine forests, and scattered marshlands that became the state of Wisconsin. Deer, wolves, bald eagles, trumpeter swans, sandhill cranes, geese, and other wildlife populated the land. Native Americans grew corn and potatoes, harvested wild rice, speared fish, and built over 90 percent of North America's effigy mounds.

Jean Nicolet in 1634 and subsequent French explorers recognized that the cold climate of the Lake Superior basin produced the richest fur-bearing animals in French North America. In 1673, the Jesuit Jacques Marquette and Louis Jolliet discovered the Fox River–Wisconsin River all-water route from Green Bay, via a one-mile land portage, to the Mississippi River. The Fox-Wisconsin river route connecting Forts Howard (Green Bay), Winnebago (Portage), and Crawford (Prairie du Chien) became the key to the Wisconsin fur trade for 150 years. Marquette named the area Wisconsin, which he spelled *Meskousing*, roughly translated as "a gathering of waters." French *voyageurs* (licensed traders) and *coureurs de bois* (woods rangers) lived among and intermarried with Native Americans. Wisconsin beaver pelts and other furs were shipped to France via Fort Mackinac and Montreal. The 1763 British victory in the French and Indian War resulted in Scottish fur merchants replacing the French in Montreal. British Canadians traded in Wisconsin even after the American Revolution, until the American John Jacob Astor gained control in the early 1800s.

Wisconsin Territory and Early Settlement

In 1832, the Sauk chief Black Hawk returned from Iowa with 1,000 Native American men, women, and children to farm the southwestern Wisconsin homelands from which they had recently been expelled by settlers. Unplanned conflict erupted between the U.S. Army and the Sauk, who retreated up the Rock River and westward to the Wisconsin River. Following a rejected surrender attempt at Wisconsin Heights, Black Hawk withdrew down the Wisconsin River toward Iowa. He was trapped near the Mississippi–Wisconsin River confluence in a massacre at Bad Axe that left 150 survivors. The Black Hawk War resulted in Native American cession of most Wisconsin land to the United States in 1832–1848, opening the way for rapid population growth, from 3,245 in 1830 to 305,391 in 1850.

The lead mine region of southwestern Wisconsin experienced an influx of migrants from the southern frontier of Kentucky, Tennessee, and Missouri in the 1830s. They worked the mines, and gave the "Badgers" nickname to Wisconsin, because they burrowed into the earth like badgers. Family wheat farmers and shopkeepers from Yankee New England and upstate New York migrated to southeastern Wisconsin via the Erie Canal and Great Lakes in even larger numbers. As the majority, their territorial representatives passed an 1839 law prohibiting "business or work, dancing . . . entertainment . . . or sport" on Sunday. European immigrants would later ignore those restrictions.

Previously a part of Michigan Territory, Wisconsin Territory was established in 1836. It encompassed present-day Wisconsin, Iowa, Minnesota, and the eastern Dakotas. The territorial legislature selected the pristine and unpopulated Four Lakes wilderness (which would become Madison) to be the permanent state capital location over numerous other contenders, because it was both scenic and centrally located between the two population centers of the wheat-farming southeast and lead-mining southwest. Additionally, the Whig politician and land speculator James Doty owned much Four Lakes property, some of which he generously shared with legislators.

Statehood and Civil War

Wisconsin became the thirtieth state in 1848, establishing a 15–15 balance between free and slave states. The Wisconsin constitution and ensuing laws implemented the frontier concepts of elected judges, voting rights for immigrant noncitizens, and property ownership rights for married women. Transplanted New Englanders, descended from the Puritans and carrying the religious conviction that slavery was a moral evil, meant that Wisconsin would become a flash point of abolitionism in the 1850s.

Underground railroad activity flourished in Wisconsin following the passage of the federal Fugitive Slave Act of 1850. Wisconsin church colleges (Beloit and Milton) established by New Englanders regularly helped runaway slaves. When the abolitionist newsman Sherman Booth was arrested for inciting a Milwaukee mob that freed the runaway Joshua Glover from jail, the Wisconsin Supreme Court nullified the Fugitive Slave Act. A group met in Ripon, Wisconsin, in response to the Booth arrest and the Kansas-Nebraska Act, and established the Republican Party. Despite competing claims, the Republican National Committee has historically recognized Ripon as the GOP birthplace.

About 75,000 Wisconsinites (10 percent of the 1860 population) served in uniform during the Civil War. Most of them trained at Madison's Camp Randall, where the University of Wisconsin football stadium of the same name now stands. The war stimulated prosperity for wheat farmers and lead miners. Wisconsin women who were active in the Sanitary Commission provided medical and food supplies to soldiers. They were instrumental in building convalescent hospitals for Union soldiers and Confederate prisoners in Wisconsin. Although most residents supported the war effort, antidraft sentiments were strong in some immigrant communities.

European Immigrants Populate Wisconsin

Wisconsin's population grew from 305,391 in 1850 to 1,315,497 in 1880, of which 72 percent were foreign born or of foreign parentage. Additional European immigrants helped double the population to 2,632,067 by 1920. More than one hundred foreign-language newspapers were printed in Wisconsin in 1900. Most European immigrants were poor farm laborers who were drawn to America's farm frontier, which included Wisconsin. Not only could they find familiar work, but over time could own farms that dwarfed the largest old-country estates.

Due to their diverse backgrounds, Wisconsin's immigrants usually settled in communities and neighborhoods with their own countrymen. Consequently, for example, Koshkonong developed a Norwegian identity, Berlin a German identity, Monroe a Swiss identity, and Milwaukee neighborhoods were clearly Polish or Irish or German. The Fourth of July was celebrated exuberantly in immigrant communities as a statement of loyalty to the United States.

Wisconsin was populated most heavily by immigrants from Norway and the Germanies, but large numbers of Irish, Poles, English, Danes, Swedes, Swiss, Dutch, Belgians, and others also came. Most Hispanics, Greeks, Italians, southeast Asians, and African Americans from the South arrived later. Norwegian farmers formed the power base of twentieth-century La Follette progressivism. Germans from Mecklenburg, Pomerania, and elsewhere organized the *turnverein* (gymnastics) and *liederkranz* (singing) societies. Many Finnish dockworkers in Ashland and Superior embraced International Workers of the World union radicalism. Racine's J. I. Case and Mitchell Wagon Works had "Danes only" employment policies for decades. Wisconsin's rich and varied immigrant heritage is still celebrated in annual community events such as Stoughton's Syttende Mai (17 May, Norwegian Independence Day), New Glarus' Heidi Festival and William Tell Pageant, Jefferson's *Gemuetlichkeit* Days, and Milwaukee's International Folk Fair.

Pine Lumbering: Paul Bunyan's Footprints

Pine lumbering dominated northern Wisconsin from 1865 to 1920. Lumber barons such as Governor Cadwallader Washburn and Senator Philetus Sawyer controlled state politics. Lumber operations determined rail routes in the region, and the depots became the hubs around which Wisconsin small towns developed. With the exception of iron mining communities (Hurley) and shipping centers, most northern Wisconsin communities began as lumber or sawmill towns.

Lumberjacks cut trees from dawn to dusk during harsh Wisconsin winters. They lived in barracks, and their enormous appetites became legendary. As melting ice cleared, lumberjacks conducted huge river drives and faced the constant dangers of logjams up to fifteen miles long. After logs were processed by downstream sawmills, Wisconsin lumber was used by Milwaukee, Chicago, Great Lakes ships, and Mississippi River steamboats for construction and fuel. Iron and copper mines in northern Wisconsin and upper Michigan consumed lumber for mine shafts and smelting. When the process to manufacture paper from wood pulp was developed, the once separate paper and lumber industries were linked. Dairy farms used lumber for barns, fences, and fuel.

Northern Wisconsin's economy rose and fell with lumbering. When only the pine barrens remained, land values and population of northern Wisconsin counties declined from 1920 to 1970. Tax-delinquent land and abandoned farms were all too common until after World War II. Remaining woodlands were located primarily in national and state forests and on reservations.

Red Barn Country: America's Dairyland

A sign over the barn door of the dairy farmer W. D. Hoard (who served as governor from 1889 to 1891) carried the reverent reminder that "This is the Home of Mothers. Treat each cow as a Mother should be treated." Dairying became Wisconsin's agricultural giant as the wheat belt shifted to Kansas in the post–Civil War decades. Norwegian, Dutch, and German immigrants were familiar with dairying. Hoard founded *Hoard's Dairyman* magazine (1885) and the Wisconsin Dairyman's Association, and successfully promoted mandatory annual tuberculin testing for cows. Refrigeration added extensive milk and butter sales to an already profitable international cheese market. The University of Wisconsin College of Agriculture provided inventions (cream separator and butterfat tester) and improved breeding, feeding, and sanitary techniques to all Wisconsin farmers. By 1930, there were 2 million cows and 2,939,006 people in Wisconsin, and in rural counties the cows were in the majority. After the 1930s, Rural Electrification Administration power lines allowed farmers to milk by machine instead of by hand.

Although Wisconsin became "America's Dairyland," some farmers concentrated on hogs, corn, vegetables, hay, and other grains. The Door County peninsula became a leading cherry producer. Potato and soybean expansion came later. Almost all farmers raised chickens and joined their area farm cooperative.

Wisconsin family farms became a basic social unit as well as an efficient food producer. Neighbors collectively "exchanged works" during planting and harvesting seasons, and helped "raise" each other's barns. Their children attended one-room country schools from first through eighth grade. Farm social life centered around barn square dances, church socials, the county fair, and the country school. Until the advent of the automobile and tractor, workhorses pulled the plough, and livery stables and hitching posts dotted village business streets.

Industry and Transportation

Wisconsin's early industry was related to agriculture. Farm implement manufacturing (J. I. Case and Allis-Chalmers), meatpacking (Oscar Mayer and Patrick Cudahy), and leather tanning created jobs. Flour milling was the leading industry in 1880, and was surpassed only by lumber products (Kimberly-Clark paper) in 1900. The dairy industry was number one by the 1920s. Wisconsin's numerous breweries (Miller, Pabst, Schlitz, and Huber among them) were established by German immigrants. Ice harvesting provided refrigeration for the early dairy, meat, and brewery industries.

In the twentieth century, automobile (General Motors and Nash) and motorcycle (Harley-Davidson) manufacturing grew along with small-engine (Evinrude and Briggs Stratton) production. Oshkosh-b-Gosh jeans, Kohler plumbing ware, Ray-o-Vac batteries, and Johnson's Wax became familiar names worldwide. Machine tools and missile-control systems were less familiar but equally important components of Wisconsin's economy.

Wisconsin transportation evolved with the state's industrial growth. Inefficient plank roads and the old Military Road gave way to Milwaukee-based railroads that linked the rest of the state to Great Lakes shipping. Madison and Milwaukee city streetcars, mule driven and then electric powered, were replaced by buses. Paved-road construction steadily accelerated in the twentieth century, spurred initially by pressure from bicyclists. By the late twentieth century, Wisconsin's Midwest Express had become a major airline.

Progressivism and Politics

Wisconsin became a twentieth-century laboratory for progressive reform under the leadership of Robert La Follette (governor, 1901–1906; U.S. senator, 1906–1925) and his successors. Progressives democratized state politics by establishing the open primary election system, and democratized economic opportunity by creating state regulatory commissions. Wisconsin passed the first workers' compensation (1911) and unemployment compensation (1932) laws in the nation. Legislation required the creation of adult technical schools statewide. Public utilities were regulated. La Follette's sons "Young Bob" (U.S. senator, 1925–1947) and Philip (governor, 1931–1933, 1935–1939) continued the progressive tradition. Progressivism in Milwaukee translated into Socialist Party control of city government from the 1890s to 1960. The Socialists stayed in power by being good-government moderates who created neighborhood parks, improved city services, and won votes from the German ethnic population.

Conservation of natural resources has been a hallmark of twentieth-century Wisconsin progressivism. The Forest Crop Law (1927) encourages reforestation. The U.S. Forest Products Laboratory in Madison conducts wood, pulp, and paper research with a goal of more efficient usage. The state buyout and restoration of the Horicon Marsh began in 1940. Governors Gaylord Nelson (1959–1963) and Warren Knowles (1965–1971) signed Outdoor Recreation Act programs that became international conservation models. U.S. Senator Nelson (1963–1981) sponsored the Wild and Scenic Rivers Act and founded Earth Day.

Wisconsin had been a one-party Republican state since the Civil War. In 1934, the La Follette brothers left the Republican Party and formed the Wisconsin Progressive Party. Following a decade of Progressive versus Republican rivalry, the Progressives disintegrated. Youth-

ful ex-Progressives joined the moribund Democratic Party and built it into a political equal of the Republicans by the 1960s.

Wisconsin during Two World Wars

During World War I, tensions ran high in Wisconsin. Many first-generation German Americans bought German war bonds prior to the U.S. entry into the war and were sympathetic to the old country throughout. Most Wisconsin families contributed their sons or home-front efforts to the war, even though the neutralist senator Robert La Follette and nine of the state's eleven congressional representatives voted against the declaration of war.

A generation later, Wisconsin was loyally in the World War II home-front lines with the rest of the nation. About 330,000 Wisconsin citizens served in uniform during the war, and more than 8,000 of them were killed in action. State industry rapidly converted to World War II production. The Badger Ordnance Works sprouted from farm fields near Baraboo to produce ammunition. General Motors and Nash Rambler plants assembled military vehicles. Ray-o-Vac developed leakproof batteries and manufactured shell casings and field radios. Allis-Chalmers made bomber electrical systems. Oscar Mayer packaged K rations. Manitowoc's Lake Michigan shipyard built 28 submarines, which would sink 130 Japanese and German warships. The University of Wisconsin developed the U.S. Armed Forces Institute to provide correspondence courses for soldiers recuperating in military and veterans' hospitals, many of whom enrolled at the University of Wisconsin on the GI Bill after the war.

Wisconsin Life in the Twenty-first Century

Cultural, educational, and recreational opportunities provide a high quality of life in modern Wisconsin. Free public education, the State Historical Society (1846), the Wisconsin School for the Visually Handicapped (1849), and America's first kindergarten (1856) established a state educational tradition. The University of Wisconsin (Madison) opened its classrooms in 1848 and was recognized worldwide as a leading research and teaching institution by 1900. The university's WHA Radio is America's oldest operating station. Alumni Research Foundation support has led to breakthroughs in cancer treatment. The Madison and Milwaukee Symphony Orchestras are nationally acclaimed. Two medical schools, at the University of Wisconsin (Madison) and the Medical College of Wisconsin (Milwaukee), result in high-quality health care throughout the state.

Wisconsin Badger football transcends the events on the field. Friday fish fries, Lutheran church lutefisk suppers, and Door County fish boils became beloved institutions. The Green Bay Packers, community-owned since the Great Depression, are so-named because the team founder, Curly Lambeau, a meatpacking-house worker, convinced his employer to buy the first uniforms. The annual Circus Train from Baraboo's Circus World Museum culminates in the Milwaukee Circus Parade. Northern Wisconsin holds the cross-country Birkebeiner ski race. Prior to the Milwaukee Brewers, baseball's Braves counted more than 300 booster clubs statewide during their Milwaukee years (1953–1965). Oshkosh hosts the annual Experimental Aircraft Association Fly-in. Wisconsin Dells' amphibious "ducks" (converted World War II landing craft) show river-and-woods scenery to tourists. Wisconsin's natural outdoor beauty invites people to fish, camp, hike, hunt, and boat.

BIBLIOGRAPHY

Gard, Robert E. *The Romance of Wisconsin Place Names.* Minocqua, Wis.: Heartland Press, 1988.

Leopold, Aldo. *A Sand County Almanac.* New York: Ballantine, 1970.

Logan, Ben. *The Land Remembers: The Story of a Farm and Its People.* Minnetonka, Minn.: Northword Press, 1999.

Thompson, William Fletcher, ed. *The History of Wisconsin.* 6 vols. Madison: State Historical Society of Wisconsin Press, 1973–1998.

Wisconsin Blue Book. Madison: Wisconsin Legislative Reference Library, 1931–. Various publishers before 1931. Biennial since 1879.

Wisconsin Cartographers' Guild. *Wisconsin's Past and Present: A Historical Atlas.* Madison: University of Wisconsin Press, 1998.

Wisconsin Magazine of History. Madison: State Historical Society of Wisconsin Press, 1917–.

Richard Carlton Haney

See also **Black Hawk War; Dairy Industry; French Frontier Forts; Fur Trade and Trapping; Lumber Industry; Milwaukee; Progressive Party, 1924; Sauk; University of Wisconsin; Wisconsin Idea.**

WISCONSIN IDEA.

The Wisconsin Idea was the cooperation between experts at the University of Wisconsin and state administrators under the Progressive Party in the early twentieth century. Under the leadership of Robert M. La Follette, Sr., Wisconsin Progressives established investigative commissions in such areas as taxation, railways (and later, public utilities), insurance, civil service, industry, conservation, and highways. The commissions often drew upon the expertise of university specialists, as when the economist Delos O. Kinsman helped to draft the 1911 state income tax law. Some university professors, such as Thomas Adams and Balthasar Meyer, even served as members of the various commissions.

BIBLIOGRAPHY

Doan, Edward Newell. *The La Follettes and the Wisconsin Idea.* New York: Rinehart, 1947.

Thelan, David P. *Robert M. La Follette and the Insurgent Spirit.* Boston: Little, Brown, 1976.

Louise Phelps Kellogg / A. G.

See also **Progressive Movement; Progressive Party, Wisconsin; Taxation; University of Wisconsin; Wisconsin.**

WISCONSIN RAILROAD COMMISSION V. CHICAGO, BURLINGTON AND QUINCY RAILROAD COMPANY,

257 U.S. 563 (1922). Congress, by the provisions of the TRANSPORTATION ACT OF 1920—which returned the railroads to private ownership—undertook to guarantee the railways "a fair return upon a fair valuation." Previously, the Wisconsin Railroad Commission had entered into an agreement with the defendant railroad, by which intrastate transportation of persons was to be provided at the rate of 2 cents a mile. After the passage of the federal act, the state commission sought to continue the agreement. The railway contended that, at such a rate, it could not earn the fair return contemplated in the law. The SUPREME COURT accepted this view and emphasized the fact that the INTERSTATE COMMERCE COMMISSION, under the Transportation Act of 1920, had valid power and the duty to raise the level of intrastate rates when such rates were so low as to discriminate against interstate commerce and unduly to burden it. This decision—together with the similar and companion case of *New York v. New York Central Railroad Company*—was the last step in a process by which the decisions in the earliest railroad rate cases were completely reversed.

BIBLIOGRAPHY

Hoogenboom, Ari, and Olive Hoogenboom. *A History of the ICC: From Panacea to Palliative.* New York: Norton, 1976.

W. Brooke Graves / A. R.

See also **Plumb Plan; Railroad Administration, U.S.; Railroad Rate Law; Railroads; World War I, Economic Mobilization for.**

WISE MEN

(1968). The term, whose authorship is obscure, refers to President Lyndon B. Johnson's select gathering in March 1968 of certain experienced officials (including several from earlier Democratic administrations) to advise him on VIETNAM WAR policy following the enemy's TET OFFENSIVE. A majority favored de-escalation. The term was later generalized to describe participants in President Jimmy Carter's similarly soul-searching Camp David conference in July 1979 and retrospectively by historians of other like groups, as in Walter Isaacson and Evan Thomas's *The Wise Men* (1986) and Robert D. Schulzinger's *The Wise Men of Foreign Affairs* (1984).

BIBLIOGRAPHY

Herring, George C. *America's Longest War: The United States and Vietnam, 1950–1975.* 2d ed. New York: McGraw-Hill, 1986.

Fraser Harbutt

WITCHCRAFT. No general agreement seems to have been reached in the United States on what witchcraft is, or was, or might be.

When the Puritans arrived in New England in the early seventeenth century, they soon saw evidence of witchcraft. Massachusetts Governor John Winthrop discerned it in the behavior of Anne Hutchinson in the 1630s. Hutchinson was deeply spiritual, highly intellectual, and openly critical of some clergymen's interpretations of religious doctrine. Her outspokenness and her charismatic appeal to other early New England settlers so disconcerted Winthrop and some of the colony's most influential ministers that they tried her as a heretic and banished her from the colony. At the time neither Winthrop nor his clerical allies explicitly said that her crime was witchcraft, though they called one of her female followers, Jane Hawkins, a witch and insinuated that Hutchinson and another of her allies, Mary Dyer, gave birth to demons. Only later, when he wrote his history of New England in the 1640s, did Winthrop speak openly about Hutchinson's witchcraft. Some people thought her a witch, he said, because she was so successful in drawing support from her neighbors for her heretical religious beliefs.

When Winthrop talked further about Hawkins, he linked her heresies to her medical knowledge and also denounced Margaret Jones for her medical practice and divination skills. Not all healers or prescient women or challengers of official theology were labeled witches, nor were these the only recurrent themes in the suspicions voiced. Still, when we consider the hundreds of accusations lodged over the course of the seventeenth century, especially in light of ministerial writings on the topic, the meanings of witchcraft for New England's early colonists begin to emerge.

New Englanders defined witchcraft as the use of supernatural power, usually but not always to harm. They believed that some human beings possessed extraordinary abilities that were darkly unnatural. Ann Hibbens drew suspicion in 1656 because she possessed knowledge that ordinary people lacked, in her case an awareness that two neighbors some distance away were speaking of her. George Burroughs, one of the few men and the only minister to be executed as a witch in New England, was accused of unusual strength—he could carry a full barrel of molasses with just two fingers of one hand. More commonly, accused witches were said to abuse their power, to kill rather than heal an ailing child, to obstruct ordinary domestic processes such as the making of butter or beer, or to invisibly attack the cattle or crops upon which their neighbors' prosperity rested. Katherine Harrison was known to spin more yarn than any other woman, and that was used against her in court in the 1660s, but a man's tale of how she hindered him from completing a garment he was weaving probably carried more weight with the jury that declared her a witch. Indeed, the motive that underlay the supposed act of witchcraft was part of how the crime was defined. If the deployment of superhuman

Witchcraft. Yvonne Frost, cofounder of the Church and School of Wicca in 1968, performs a ritual. BRAD AND SHERRY STEIGER

power itself was understood as witchcraft, more often accusers emphasized its angry, malicious, and vengeful use. Thus Eunice Cole stood accused of many acts, from unseemly speeches to consulting evil spirits, but the records that survive of her court appearances from 1656 to 1680 stress the viciousness of her character, motives, and personal attacks.

If witchcraft gained its everyday meanings through accusations and trials in local contexts, Puritans also understood witchcraft as a relationship between a human being and the devil. Because they insisted on finding clear evidence of a witch's alliance with Satan, ministers fleshed out this meaning in discussions of the nature, physical evidence, and purported benefits of the pact between the two, the danger of such a relationship to New England's spiritual mission, and the effects on those who resisted Satan's insatiable desire for more witches to serve him. Many young women lent invaluable support to Puritan definitions of witchcraft when they acknowledged the excruciating pain they felt (which the ministers told them they would feel) when they held out against Satan's attempts to lure them into witches' ranks.

To these two definitions of witchcraft must be added a third, New Englanders' implicit understanding of what kinds of people were likely to align themselves with Satan and do their neighbors harm. If historians of witchcraft at the turn of the twenty-first century generally accept that popular and elite conceptions of witchcraft coexisted in the seventeenth century and frequently overlapped, consensus falls apart over the more subtle meanings conveyed in the patterns visible in the lives of accusers and accused. For some, accused witches were the angry, malicious, and vengeful people their neighbors said they were, and they attempted to harm their neighbors through image magic, curses, and spells. For these scholars, witchcraft was a social reality, a set of practices that identified genuine witches. For other historians, the lack of evidence for such practices in most witchcraft records and widespread economic, religious, and social patterns linking accusers and the accused suggest that New England witchcraft is best understood as an expression of social and cultural anxieties among accusers rather than the malice of the accused. From this perspective, religion, psychology, and gender provide better analytical tools for deciphering the meanings of witchcraft than the biases of accusers.

However varied their interpretations, for the most part historians reject definitions of witchcraft as superstition, mental illness, and lies. At the turn of the twentieth century, the Salem outbreak of 1692 is recognized as merely one—if by far the most deadly—witchcraft event in the American colonies. Studies of New England are heavily influenced by recent attempts to understand Western witchcraft traditions in the contexts of early modern belief systems and world religions more generally. As scholars turn to anthropology, women's studies, and most recently, literary and visual culture studies for analytical tools and interdisciplinary frameworks, witchcraft history looks less like a narrative of the exceptional and more like a window into comparative social and cultural transformation.

American witchcraft history has also begun to incorporate the past three centuries. Although the trials came to an end in New England soon after the Salem outbreak and witchcraft was declared a superstition, belief persisted through the eighteenth century and, for a few, even longer. Mainstream Protestant ministers debated the existence of witches and witchcraft among themselves long after such discussion was no longer acceptable in public discourse; Christian fundamentalist churches continue to keep the fear of witchcraft alive in sermons and boycotts. Artists, poets, and writers of fiction picked up the threads where ministers and magistrates left off, creating children's stories and entertainment for adults that kept as much as it changed the image of the witch. Advertisers, too, found her useful in selling their wares, from lingerie to liqueurs to Halloween costumes. Witches drew followers as well as exploiters in the nineteenth century and, by the late twentieth century, in particular with the emergence of feminist neo-pagan movements, witches and witchcraft had been reclaimed as multifaceted symbols of resistance, emancipation, and social and spiritual rebirth.

BIBLIOGRAPHY

Butler, Jon. "Magic, Astrology and the Early American Religious Heritage." *American Historical Review* 84 (1979): 317–346.

Demos, John Putnam. *Entertaining Satan: Witchcraft and the Culture of Early New England.* New York: Oxford University Press, 1982.

Karlsen, Carol F. *The Devil in the Shape of a Woman: Witchcraft in Colonial New England.* New York: Norton, 1987.

Norton, Mary Beth. *In the Devil's Snare: The Salem Witchcraft Crisis of 1692.* New York: Knopf, 2002.

Salomonsen, Jone. *Enchanted Feminism: Ritual, Gender and Divinity among the Reclaiming Witches of San Francisco.* London and New York: Routledge, 2002.

Carol F. Karlsen

See also **Puritans and Puritanism; Salem Witch Trials;** *and* vol. 9: **Evidence Used Against Witches.**

WOBBLIES. *See* **Industrial Workers of the World.**

WOLFF PACKING COMPANY V. COURT OF INDUSTRIAL RELATIONS,

262 U.S. 522 (1923). Following a series of labor actions in 1920, the Kansas legislature passed an act declaring a compelling public interest in the manufacture of food and clothing, mining, public utilities, and transportation. A three-judge industrial court was given sweeping authority to fix wages and labor conditions. In 1923 a unanimous decision of the U.S. SUPREME COURT ended the industrial court by declaring the fixing of wages in a packing plant a deprivation of property and a denial of the freedom of contract guaranteed by the Fourteenth Amendment.

BIBLIOGRAPHY

Mason, Alpheus T. *William Howard Taft: Chief Justice.* New York: Simon and Schuster, 1964.

Tribe, Laurence H. *American Constitutional Law,* 3d ed. New York: Foundation Press, 2000.

Allen E. Ragan / A. R.

See also **Constitution of the United States; Contract Clause; Labor; Labor Legislation and Administration; Wages and Hours of Labor, Regulation of.**

WOLVES. Wolves once roamed most of the Northern Hemisphere, including much of the United States, Europe, and the Middle East. Like humans, wolves crossed the Bering land bridge during the Ice Age to range throughout North America, from the Arctic to central Mexico. Both wolf species, the gray *(Canis lupus)* and the red *(Canis rufus)*, were found in the United States, though the latter lived only in the Southeast. Most literature, popular knowledge, and economic concerns about the wolf involve the gray wolf, also known as the timber wolf. The appearance of the gray wolf varies from pure white in the Arctic to black, gray, and tan in the lower forests and grasslands. A pack animal with well-ordered social systems, the wolf's success depended on its ability to den, hunt, and defend its territory in groups of two to twenty. Adaptability to different climates and habitats, perhaps only excelled by humans, meant the size and number of prey determined the wolf's travels. Until the huge bison herds of the Great Plains were destroyed in the mid-nineteenth century, wolves were most abundant in North America's central prairies.

Most Native Americans revered the wolf, emulating its hunting tactics and incorporating the animal into their creation stories. The wolf was central to the Anishinabe (Ojibwa) culture of northern Michigan and was an important clan or totem animal for others. Europeans arrived from densely populated, agrarian countries with much darker attitudes. Though no human deaths from wolves have been reported in the United States, the wolf did compete for the same wild prey as settlers and killed domestic livestock when it could. Intense efforts quickly developed to eradicate the wolf in farming and ranching regions. In the 1840s prairie settlers poisoned wolves with strychnine, chased them with dogs, and shot them in circle hunts. Throughout the late nineteenth century local bounty programs paid for wolf scalps and pelts. Congress authorized funds in 1915 to trap and kill wolves on all public lands. By 1950 the wolf was nearly extinct in the United States. Only scattered packs remained in northern Minnesota and Michigan and remote regions of the Rocky Mountains.

Growing environmental concerns in the 1960s prompted the federal government to declare the wolf an ENDANGERED SPECIES in 1973. Governmental protections resulted in slow growth of wolf numbers, and in 1986 the first western-state wolf den in fifty years was found in Montana's Glacier National Park. Successful efforts to reintroduce the wolf to its former habitat in the 1990s, however, met resistance. To compensate, these programs allowed for payment for livestock killed and removal of the individual wolves responsible. American attitudes toward the wolf continued to be conflicted and passionate to the end of the twentieth century.

BIBLIOGRAPHY

Dinsmore, James J. *A Country So Full of Game.* Iowa City: University of Iowa, 1994. Focuses on Iowa and the Midwest and makes extensive use of settlers' letters, diaries, and other historic sources.

Mallard, Ann, ed. *Creatures of the Wild: Wolf.* London: PRC, 1998. Contains excellent color photographs by Alan Carey and Sandy Carey.

Webb, Walter Prescott. *The Great Plains.* Boston: Ginn, 1931.

Jan Olive Nash

Frances Willard. The president of the Woman's Christian Temperance Union from 1879 to 1898 (and its world organization from 1891 to 1898); she expanded the WCTU's campaigns from attacks on alcohol to the reform of prostitutes and prisons, as well as woman's suffrage. GETTY IMAGES

WOMAN'S CHRISTIAN TEMPERANCE UNION (WCTU) was dedicated to eliminating the consumption of alcohol. Founded in 1874, the WCTU was the largest women's reform organization of the nineteenth century. It had its origin in the 1873 Woman's Temperance Crusade, in which women across the country engaged in spontaneous protest, marching to saloons, singing hymns, praying, dumping liquor barrels, destroying property, and forcing liquor sellers to close their businesses. When closed saloons reopened several months later, temperance women decided to organize formally, calling for a national convention to be held in Cleveland 18–20 November 1874. Delegates from seventeen states attended, and the National Woman's Christian Temperance Union was founded with Annie Wittenmyer as president (1873–1878). Its membership, composed mainly of evangelical Protestants and limited to women, grew rapidly, and soon every state had a WCTU organization.

During its first five years, the organization focused on abstinence through moral suasion and education, but its activities broadened to include many women's rights reforms when Frances Willard became president in 1879. Willard was the organization's most famous and innovative leader (1879–1898). Guided by Willard's "Do Everything" motto, the organization embraced the moral reform of prostitutes, prison reform, and woman suffrage. Willard's "Home Protection" campaign argued that with the vote women could enact prohibition, and this became a major focus of the organization's efforts, particularly under its third president (1898–1914), Lillian M. Stevens, a Willard protege. The WTCU developed sophisticated political organizing and lobbying techniques at local, state, and national levels and also ran a large publishing company. In the 1880s it became an international organization working for prohibition and women's rights around the world. The WCTU was also the first large national organization to unite Northern and Southern women after the Civil War, and it included black women, although local chapters in both the North and South were usually segregated.

A powerful and influential reform group, the WCTU secured a number of political victories. It campaigned, for example, for state legislation requiring scientific temperance instruction in the public schools, which was accomplished by 1902. Its most well known accomplishment, however, was the passage of the Eighteenth (Prohibition) Amendment in 1919. After 1919, guided by its fourth president (1914–1925), Anna Gordon, the organization turned its attention to child welfare, social purity, and the "Americanization" of immigrants. Throughout the late 1920s and early 1930s, it also fought the repeal of Prohibition, a battle which it lost in 1933 and which left the WCTU considerably weakened.

In the early twenty-first century, the WCTU was still headquartered in Evanston, Ill., as it had been since Willard headed the organization. The emblem of the WCTU is a white ribbon bow with the motto "For God and Home and Everyland." In 1975 it had organizations in more than seventy nations and approximately 250,000 members in the United States.

BIBLIOGRAPHY

Bordin, Ruth. *Woman and Temperance: The Quest for Power and Liberty, 1873–1900.* Philadelphia: Temple University Press, 1981.

———. *Frances Willard: A Biography.* Chapel Hill: University of North Carolina Press, 1986.

Hays, Agnes Dubbs. *Heritage of Dedication: One Hundred Years of the National Woman's Christian Temperance Union, 1874–1974.* Evanston, Ill.: Signal Press, 1973.

Tyrrell, Ian R. *Woman's World/Woman's Empire: The Woman's Christian Temperance Union in International Perspective, 1800–1930.* Chapel Hill: University of North Carolina Press, 1991.

Willard, Frances E. *Glimpses of Fifty Years: The Autobiography of an American Woman.* Chicago: Woman's Temperance Publication Association, 1889.

*Edith Kirkendall Stanley/*L. T.

See also **Settlement House Movement; Suffrage: Woman's Suffrage; Temperance Movement; Women's Rights Movement.**

WOMAN'S EXCHANGE MOVEMENT. Started in 1832, the Woman's Exchange movement is one of the country's oldest continuously operating charitable movements. Numbering nearly one hundred across the United States in the nineteenth century, Exchanges were fashionable shops where women who had fallen on hard times could sell their home-produced merchandise on consignment. Exchanges combined elements of charity, cooperation, and retailing, and serve as early examples of utilizing the voluntary sector for quasi-commercial activity.

In the antebellum years, only two Exchanges are known to have existed. The first, the Philadelphia Ladies' Depository, was established by many of the city's elite women to provide a discreet and anonymous employment alternative to harsh conditions "fallen gentlewomen" faced in the industrial workplace. After the Civil War, the movement quickly accelerated across the nation. Fueled by notions of self-help and economic independence, the Exchanges became available to women of all classes to sell their home-produced merchandise. By 1891 more than 16,000 consignors nationwide sold merchandise at Exchanges.

The Exchanges offered both the consignors and the "lady managers" the opportunity to exert their entrepreneurial flair. The working-class consignors often exceeded the industrial wage and could create a market niche by selling specialized items such as needlework or edibles. The middle- and upper-class managers benefited as well by becoming retailing executives, a position formerly off-limits to women of their social status.

The movement provides an early example of women's efforts to legally incorporate their voluntary organizations and to collectively purchase commercial real estate. In addition to retail consignment shops, many Exchanges offered boarding rooms, vocational training, workspace for self-employed women, and tearooms, which often became well known.

In 2001 twenty-eight Exchanges are in business, primarily on the East Coast. Of this number, eight are the original nineteenth-century Exchanges. The others were formed in the twentieth century. Most Exchanges today are affiliated with the Federation of Woman's Exchanges, an umbrella organization started in 1934 to provide cohesion to the movement.

BIBLIOGRAPHY

Sander, Kathleen Waters. *The Business of Charity: The Woman's Exchange Movement, 1832–1900.* Urbana: University of Illinois Press, 1998.

Kathleen Waters Sander

WOMAN'S SUFFRAGE. *See* **Suffrage.**

WOMEN, CITIZENSHIP OF MARRIED. Although original U.S. nationality legislation did not limit eligibility by sex, by 1804 the law began to make distinctions for married women. By the mid-1800s a woman's citizenship became, in the event of marriage, subsumed under her husband's status. In a law passed 10 February 1855, American nationality was conferred upon an alien woman who married an American citizen. And married immigrant women, who generally could not petition for citizenship independently, acquired U.S. citizenship only when their alien husbands were naturalized. Any American woman who married an alien could lose her U.S. citizenship (acquiring that of her husband), particularly if she chose to reside abroad. Long-standing debate over whether and how to enforce this latter practice was settled by a 1907 law, which dictated that all women acquired their husband's nationality upon marriage. Thus an American woman was stripped of her citizenship upon marriage to an alien, regardless of her residence. A woman might regain her U.S. citizenship if her husband naturalized (she would acquire his new status) or if the marriage terminated (she could petition to regain her American nationality).

The passage of the Married Women's Act, also known as The Cable Act (22 September 1922), reversed this trend by making some women's citizenship independent of their marital status. Demanded by women's rights activists, this law allowed an American woman to retain her nationality after marrying an alien. She was, however, reclassified as a naturalized citizen, losing her native citizen status. And if an American woman married an alien ineligible for citizenship (mainly Asians), she was still reclassified as alien. Immigrant women, moreover, continued to acquire American nationality upon marriage to a U.S. citizen. And there existed no provisions for married immigrant women to apply for citizenship as individuals. Revisions to this Act in the 1930s and subsequent legislation have addressed these issues, making the citizenship of wives absolutely independent of their husbands and ending any disability by reason of marriage.

Since 1934, children of a marriage between a woman having U.S. citizenship and an alien can acquire American citizenship by descent (derivative citizenship) on two conditions: (1) the woman must have lived in the United States before the birth of the child for a minimum of ten years, five of which must have been after she had reached the age of fourteen; (2) the child must establish this claim by residing in the United States for a minimum of two years between the ages of fourteen and twenty-eight, unless the alien parent was naturalized in the United States before the child reached eighteen and the child had established a permanent residence in the United States before that age.

An alien woman married to a U.S. citizen and lawfully admitted to permanent residence in the United States may be naturalized after three years residence, provided she resided in the country for half that time. The requirements of prior residence and physical presence can be waived when an alien woman is married to an American citizen who is engaged in missionary work abroad or who is stationed abroad by the U.S. government, an international organization with U.S. membership, an American research institution, or an American business. All the provisions of the Immigration and Nationality Act of 1952 apply equally to men and women. U.S. citizenship may be acquired by birth in the country, by descent from an American citizen, or by naturalization.

BIBLIOGRAPHY

Bredbenner, Candice Lewis. *A Nationality of Her Own.* Berkeley: University of California Press, 1998.

Cott, Nancy. "Marriage and Women's Citizenship in the United States, 1830–1934." *American Historical Review* 103 (December 1998).

Alona E. Evans
Lisa Tetrault

See also **Citizenship; Immigration Restriction; Indian Citizenship;** *Minor v. Happersett;* **Naturalization.**

WOMEN, PRESIDENT'S COMMISSION ON THE STATUS OF,

was established by executive order of President Kennedy on 14 December 1961 after intense lobbying by the Women's Bureau director Esther Peterson and Dollie Lowther Robinson, an African American union worker. Eleanor Roosevelt chaired the twenty-six member commission that included Peterson, officers from the National Councils of Jewish, Catholic, and Negro Women, two labor leaders, two college presidents, the historian Caroline Ware, the attorney general, the secretaries of the departments of commerce, agriculture, labor, and health, education and welfare, and two Republican and two Democratic members of Congress.

President Kennedy charged the commission to review women's progress and make recommendations for further equality in six areas: federal civil service employment policies and practices; employment policies and practices of federal contractors; labor legislation; social insurance and tax laws; political, civil, and property rights; and new and expanded services women needed as wives, mothers, and workers. The commission report was due 1 October 1961. The commission members were reluctant to abandon the idea that women's family role meant different life patterns for women and men, so it compromised between complete equality and recognition of gender difference. It endorsed the principle of employment equality, but allowed for possible justifiable gender discrimination. For example, in order to protect women's "maternal functions" it did not seek to outlaw protective hours legislation for women. It called for equal access to education, but wanted girls also to be educated in caring for homes and families. Assuming male responsibility to support the family, it recommended no changes in the social security system. It did recommend abolishing existing state laws entitling the person who worked for pay to all family assets.

Betty Friedan, author of *The Feminist Mystique*, contended that even the tepid recommendations of the com-

Eleanor Roosevelt. Widow of President Franklin D. Roosevelt and lifelong social activist, toward the end of her life Eleanor Roosevelt contributed to the renewal and progress of the women's rights movement of the 1960s by chairing the President's Commission on the Status of Women. LIBRARY OF CONGRESS

mission were buried in the bureaucracy. But the commission drew national attention to the status of women, gathered an enormous amount of data, and became, in the words of the African American activist Pauli Murray, the "first high-level consciousness group" (Hartman, p. 53) of a renewed women's movement.

BIBLIOGRAPHY

Harrison, Cynthia. *On Account of Sex: The Politics of Women's Issues, 1945–1968.* Berkeley and Los Angeles: University of California Press, 1988.

Hartmann, Susan M. *From Margin to Mainstream: American Women and Politics since 1960.* New York: Knopf, 1989.

Maureen A. Flanagan

See also **Equal Rights Amendment; National Organization for Women.**

WOMEN AND THE PEACE MOVEMENT.

The Women's International League for Peace and Free-dom (WILPF) was created in 1915 and was active throughout the twentieth century. The WILPF was born out of a conference in The Hague that was attended by women from many countries, including those involved in World War I. Jane Addams, founder of Hull House, was a leader in organizing the WILPF as a transnational attempt by women to stop the war. Prior to the WILPF, the Women's Peace Party, a faction of the suffragist movement, had been committedly antiwar and was strongly involved in the groups emerging to prevent the entry of the United States into that conflict.

Before the birth of the modern peace movement, individual women had played a key role in social reform, and elements of the women's rights and abolitionist movements identified with peace causes. At the beginning of the twentieth century the peace movement was predominantly male in leadership and membership. Women, Emma Goldman among them, who had been active in socialist movements began to promote a specific transnational role for women. In Congress, Representative Jeanette Rankin voted against U.S. entry into both world wars.

Feminists such as Crystal Eastman and Emily Green Balch initiated a critical dialogue about patriarchy, domination, and war; like Goldmann, Addams, and others they stressed internationalism. As Rosika Schwimmer put it, "I have no country but the world." During the 1920s and 1930s, Dorothy Day, an absolute pacifist and Roman Catholic activist (she founded the *Catholic Worker*) kept the concept of world peace alive in the public arena. After World War II, Eleanor Roosevelt worked closely with Ralph Bunche to advance UN policies.

In 1960 Women Strike for Peace formed around the issues of nuclear testing; the organization stressed the responsibility of women to stop nuclear testing and protect future generations. The magazine *Liberation* was one of the earliest to engage in a dialogue about militarism and gender, in particular promoting the writings of nonviolent theorist and activist Barbara Deming. Deming critiqued the too-easy adoption of violent methods and support for wars of national liberation. The antiwar movement also received support from artists—singer Joan Baez gave concerts in support of the movement, raised funds, and became involved in nonviolence as a trainer and activist.

In the 1970s, women became a major, perhaps *the* major, constituency of the peace movement; many feminists, including Carol Cohn, addressed the issue of antimilitarism, critiquing the male language of strategy. The UN "Decade of the Woman" (1975–1985) led to increased global awareness of and involvement in the peace movement by women in the United States. Major women's demonstrations took place at the Pentagon in 1980 and 1981; Helen Caldecott, an Australian doctor, along with Randall Forsberg became the most prominent spokesperson for nuclear freeze in the United States.

Heartened by the success in 1981–1982 of the Greenham Common women's peace camp at a cruise missile base in the United Kingdom, American women gathered at the Seneca army depot in New York to establish a camp and blockade the base nonviolently. In Nevada, women engaged in major civil disobedience on Mother's Day 1987 against nuclear tests in that state.

During the twentieth century, the peace movement has been changed in terms of membership, leaders, and agenda. More women are now active in the peace movement than men, and leadership is divided equally between women and men.

BIBLIOGRAPHY

Alonso, Harriet. *Peace as a Women's Issue: A History of the U.S. Movement for World Peace.* Syracuse, N.Y.: Syracuse University Press, 1993.

Carter, April. *Peace Movements: International Protest and World Politics since 1945.* New York: Longman, 1992.

Cooney, Robert, and Helen Michalowksi. *The Power of the People: Active Nonviolence in America.* Culver City, Calif.: Peace Press, 1977.

Early, Frances. *A World Without War: How U.S. Feminists and Pacifists Resisted World War I.* Syracuse, N.Y.: Syracuse University Press, 1987.

Nigel J. Young

See also **Peace Movements.**

WOMEN IN CHURCHES. Religion was integral to the history of European settlement of North America, and in large measure the experiences and work of women shaped the history of church life in the United States. Within the first generation of the Puritan experiment in New England, three important forms of women's religious experience were apparent. First, women would play critical roles as pious participants in the religious institutions that were being built in the new society. Second, women's roles would link family with faith. And third, women were not always content to live according to existing expectations.

Supporting the Churches

The critical role of women in American churches persisted even as they were often restricted to public listening and private prayer. Female Puritans, no less than their husbands, were responsible for living a virtuous life, testifying to their personal faith before being granted admission to church membership. By the end of the seventeenth century, women were already outnumbering men in the churches, a reality that has never abated. During the Awakenings of the eighteenth and nineteenth centuries, women enthusiastically embraced the new democratic "religion of the heart" that was preached on the frontiers and in the cities. After the revival preachers moved on to the next location, community women often preceded their husbands and children into church membership.

In the early nineteenth century, Protestant women were instrumental in forming and supporting mission and moral reform societies. They collected money, established the networks of correspondence, and, by late in the century, had helped to make overseas missions one of America's largest corporate enterprises. Meanwhile, Catholic sisters were the vanguard of the educational and medical institutions that were formed to support Catholic life in the United States. Jewish sisterhoods quickly took their place as the organizational backbone of synagogue life. Even in late-twentieth-century society, many women's religious organizations remained among the most vital centers of church life, and women's voluntary labor sustained both local congregations and religious service agencies. With few other opportunities for leadership within the church, women consistently transformed their religious groups into powerful arenas of religious, social, and political action.

Church and Family

The spheres in which women were expected to expend their energy included religion and family, and the two were often linked. Early Puritan women maintained fierce loyalty to their churches, in part to make sure their children could be baptized and obtain salvation. Victorian homes may have been "ruled" by fathers, but it was mothers whose work created the everyday world in which children were nurtured in the faith. In turn, it was argued, it was motherly nurturing that would produce the morally responsible citizens on which a democracy depends. And when children and husbands were threatened by economic woes and moral ills, it was women who mobilized to defend the sanctity of their homes, even if it meant marching in protest or singing hymns at the door of the

Barbara Harris. Social activist, publisher, and editor, in 1989 she became the first female bishop consecrated in the U.S. Episcopal Church (Diocese of Massachusetts)—in fact, the first in the entire worldwide Anglican communion. AP/WIDE WORLD PHOTOS

Oveta Culp Hobby. The director of the Women's Army Corps during World War II is shown here with Dwight D. Eisenhower *(center)*, who appointed her the first secretary of health, education, and welfare in April 1953. WOMEN IN MILITARY SERVICE FOR AMERICA MEMORIAL FOUNDATION, INC.

Airforce Service Pilots (WASP), a quasi-military organization affiliated with the Army Air Forces, was organized, and in November, the Coast Guard formed the Women's Coast Guard Reserve (SPAR). The Marine Corps was the last to admit women, establishing the Marine Corps Women's Reserve (MCWR) in February 1943. On 1 July, President Franklin D. Roosevelt signed new legislation, and the WAAC dropped its auxiliary status, becoming the Women's Army Corps (WAC). Almost 400,000 women served in uniform during the war. This included more than 150,550 WACs, 100,000 WAVEs, 76,000 army nurses, 23,000 female marines, 13,000 SPARs, and nearly 1,100 WASPs. Some 7,000 African American WACs and nurses also served, but in segregated units. Restricted from going overseas, they faced daily discrimination. African Americans were not accepted into the navy or Coast Guard until November 1944. Two hundred Puerto Rican women also served as WACs during the war. At their peak strength, some 271,000 women were in uniform, including 100,000 WACs.

Although the combat exclusion law was in effect, women were shot at, killed, wounded, and taken prisoner; 432 American military women were killed during World War II, including 201 army nurses, 16 as a result of enemy action. Another 88 were taken prisoner of war, all but one in the Pacific theater. More than 1,600 nurses were decorated for bravery under fire and meritorious service. Thirty-eight WASPs were killed while towing targets or ferrying or testing planes. The women who

served were motivated by patriotism, religion, and a chance for adventure.

Despite their large numbers and immense contributions, only a handful of women were allowed to remain in the military after World War II, although with the Army-Navy-Nurse Act of 1947 and the Women's Armed Services Integration Act of 1948, the women's services became a permanent, integral part of the U.S. military. The Women's Armed Services Integration Act, however, restricted the number of women to 2 percent of the total force and barred them from serving aboard navy combat vessels and from duty in combat aircraft. It also capped their rank at colonel with only one per service. Because the Coast Guard was not included in the bill, a few SPARs remained in the Women's Coast Guard Reserve. In 1949, the air force organized the Air Force Nurse Corps and Air Force Women's Medical Specialist Corps.

The Korean and Vietnam Wars
Women continued to make major strides in the military between World War II and the Korean War. In 1950, President Harry Truman appointed Anna Rosenberg the assistant secretary of defense for manpower and personnel in 1950. She served in that position until 1953. The beginning of the Korean War in June 1950 saw a small initial surge in the number of women in the military. By June 1951, there were 28,000 women serving in the military. The services, however, did not attempt to recruit women because there was a large pool of draft-eligible males. So,

Drill. A photograph of military women undergoing exercise. © Hulton-Deutsch Collection/corbis

the increase in numbers was neither significant nor long term. In 1951, Secretary of Defense George C. Marshall appointed the Defense Advisory Committee on Women in the Services (DACOWITS), consisting of fifty prominent women educators, civic leaders, and business and professional women, to assist the defense establishment in recruiting women for the armed services. When the cease-fire was signed on 27 July 1953, the Pentagon began a phaseout, reducing the number of Americans in uniform, including women. In all, 120,000 women served during the Korean War.

Women volunteered in large numbers during the Vietnam War, and as the war progressed, they were assigned to wartime operational commands, serving in nontraditional fields such as intelligence, communications, and transportation. About 7,000 served and 7 were killed. In 1967, Congress removed the 2 percent ceiling on number and grade limitations and women became eligible for appointment to flag and general officer rank. In 1971, Colonel Jean Holm was selected as the first air force woman general, and the air force became the first service to allow pregnant women to remain in the service. It also changed recruiting rules to allow the enlistment of women with children. The other services soon followed suit. In 1973, the first women naval aviators received their wings, and three years later the first women army aviators received theirs. In 1976, the service academies began admitting women. The following year the first women air force pilots received their wings. In 1978, the Coast Guard removed all assignment restrictions based on gender.

From Grenada to the Persian Gulf and Beyond

The participation of women in military operations continued to grow during the military actions that followed Vietnam, and by the 1980s there were enough air force women flying to allow the formation of all-female crews. Some 170 women took part in Operation Urgent Fury in Grenada in 1983, including air force women in air transport crews. Later that year, 7 women were among the crews of the KC-135 tankers that refueled the F-111s that raided Libya. About 770 took part in Operation Just Cause in Panama in 1989. Women manned air force transport and refueling aircraft, a woman MP (Military Police) commanded troops in a firefight with Panamanian troops, and women army aviators came under fire for the first time. Three were awarded the Air Medal. Almost 41,000 women deployed to the Persian Gulf as part of Operations Desert Storm and Desert Shield in 1990–1991. Thirteen were killed, including 5 army women, and 21 were wounded as the result of SCUD missile attacks, helicopter crashes, or mines. Two were taken prisoner. Women in the Persian Gulf War endured the same hardships as men, served for the same principles, and played a key role in the war's successful outcome.

In 1991, Congress repealed the combat exclusion law, leaving policies pertaining to women to the secretary of defense. In 1993, Secretary of Defense Les Aspin moved to eliminate many of the remaining restrictions on military women. He ordered all the services to open combat aviation to women, directed the navy to draft legislation to repeal the combat ship exclusion, and directed the army and Marine Corps to study opening new assignments to women. That same year, Sheila E. Widnall became the first woman secretary of the air force. In 1994, more than 1,000 women took part in military operations in Somalia. Four years later more than 1,200 women were deployed to Haiti for peacekeeping duties and the first Marine Corps women aviators received their wings. From 1995 to 2002, more than 5,000 women had served in peacekeeping operations in Bosnia.

A significant proportion of all U.S. military women are African American. Indeed, African Americans account for a considerably higher percentage of military women than of military men (30 percent versus 17 percent). In 2002, the army had the highest proportion of African American women (36 percent of female personnel) and the air force had the lowest (almost 25 percent). Hispanic women accounted for a lower population of the armed forces (10 percent) than of the general population (11 percent). The marines had the highest representation of Hispanic women (15 percent of its women), while the air force had the lowest (7 percent). Finally, almost 15 percent of military women were officers, the same ratio of officers to enlisted personnel among military men.

BIBLIOGRAPHY

Feller, Lt. Col. Carolyn M., and Maj. Debra R. Cox. *Highlights in the History of the Army Nurse Corps*. Washington, D.C.: U.S. Army Center of Military History, 2000.

Friedl, Vicki L. *Women in the United States Military, 1901–1995: A Research Guide and Annotated Bibliography*. Westport, Conn.: Greenwood, 1996.

Holm, Jeanne. *Women in the Military: An Unfinished Revolution*. Novato, Calif.: Presidio Press, 1995.

Morden, Bettie J. *The Women's Army Corps, 1945–1978*. Washington, D.C.: Government Printing Office, 1990.

Poulos, Paula Nassen, ed. *A Woman's War Too: U.S. Women in the Military in World War II*. Washington D.C.: National Archives and Records Administration, 1996.

Putney, Martha S., *When the Nation Was in Need: Blacks in the Women's Army Corps during World War II*. Metuchen, N.J.: Scarecrow Press, 1992.

Seeley, Charlotte Palmer, Virginia C. Purdy, and Robert Gruber. *American Women and the U.S. Armed Forces: A Guide to the Records of Military Agencies in the National Archives Relating to American Women*. Washington, D.C: National Archives and Records Administration, 2000.

Treadwell, Mattie E. *United States Army in World War II: The Women's Army Corps*. Washington, D.C.: U.S. Army Center of Military History, 1991.

Women's Research and Education Institute. *Women in the Military: Where They Stand*. Washington, D.C.: Women's Research and Education Institute, January 1998.

Gilberto Villahermosa

See also **Discrimination: Sex; Gender and Gender Roles;** *and* vol. 9: **Hobby's Army.**

WOMEN IN PUBLIC LIFE, BUSINESS, AND PROFESSIONS. Women have played a crucial part in the economic development of the United States since the time of the first colonial settlers. Women (endentured, slave, and free) worked long hours beside men cultivating the land. The jobs of child care, housework, spinning, weaving, and sewing were always exclusively theirs, and farm wives and daughters often brought in cash by selling butter or eggs. Although there were no opportunities for professional training for women in the colonial era, they served as nurses, midwives, elementary school teachers, shopkeepers, and innkeepers. And colonial women (particularly single and widowed, who could own property) sometimes managed or owned farms and businesses. Other women achieved public prominence through their writings, stage careers, or public service. Mercy Otis Warren, for example, was a well-known poet and political author, and Mary McCauley ("Molly Pitcher") was made famous for her service in the American Revolutionary War.

In the early nineteenth century, a new gender ideology arose in which women were ostensibly restricted to the home, or "private sphere," while men's domain was defined as the "public sphere." While it did restrict women's activites and opportunities, the distinction was largely ideological, and women nevertheless occupied public space and carried on public activites. The first factory workers in the United States were, in fact, women. The new textile mills of the 1820s drew their labor pool from young, unmarried New England farm girls. Over the years conditions deterioriated and in the 1840s, Sarah Bagley, a millworker in Lowell, Mass., helped launch some of the first formal industrial labor protests in the country. Organized on a large scale, the female millworkers created a permanent labor organization in 1844, the Lowell Female Labor Reform Association, which was at the forefront of the labor movement in New England. And in 1846 they lent their support to the New England Labor Reform League, an umbrella organization headed by five men and three women. Bagley and other female millworkers were pioneers in the long and still ongoing battle to achieve benefits and equal opportunity for women workers.

By midcentury, many of the new industries employed women, especially since both the migration westward and the Civil War produced manpower shortages. Often, women did spinning and weaving tasks as well as piece work (such as collars for shirts) in their homes for outside employers. Soon they constituted almost a quarter of the industrial workforce, although on the lowest level of pay and status.

Along with the labor movement, the abolitionist movement afforded women the opportunity to become leading public figures. Women comprised a large portion of the membership in antislavery societies, and they played critical, public roles within the organizations from raising funds to organizing petition drives. Other women broke with convention, which did not allow women to speak in public before mixed sex (or so-called "promiscuous") audiences. Nevertheless, many bravely did, speaking out against slavery and for women's rights: most notably, Maria Stewart, a northern black woman, and Sarah and Angelina Grimke, two white sisters from a slave-holding family in South Carolina. The Grimkes were threatened both with physical assault and admonitions from authorities as they began to travel about addressing large, mixed sex audiences. Stewart, the Grimkes, novelist Harriet Beecher Stowe (*Uncle Tom's Cabin*, 1852), ex-slave Sojourner Truth (*Narrative of Sojourner Truth*, 1850), and others also wrote political tracts, novels, and memoirs against slavery which earned them substantial public notoriety. Countless women, like Harriet Tubman, took an active part in running the underground railroad by harboring and transporting runaway slaves. All served to inspire a new view of a woman's proper role. The women's rights movement grew out of these struggles. In 1848 several hundred women and sympathetic men met at Seneca Falls, N.Y., for a convention called by two abolitionists, Elizabeth Cady Stanton and Lucretia Mott. This gathering produced the SENECA FALLS DECLARATION OF RIGHTS AND SENTIMENTS, which set forth a clear picture of women's unequal civil status and demanded women's full citizenship and equal economic opportunity. The inclusion of a call for women's voting rights, however, was highly controversial and was nearly voted down. Modeled after the DECLARATION OF INDEPENDENCE, it has inspired many women in the struggle for justice. Beginning in 1850, women's rights conventions were held annually, until the outbreak of sectional conflict in 1861. During the Civil War, some women's rights activists campaigned for the abolition of slavery by Constitutional Amendment through organizations like the National Woman's Loyal League. After the war, many were bitterly disappointed when black men were enfranchised but women were not. In response, women organized the first national organizations devoted exclusively to women's rights: the National Woman Suffrage Association (NWSA), founded in May 1869 by Stanton and Susan B. Anthony; and the American Woman Suffrage Association (AWSA), founded in November 1869 by Lucy Stone. Both organizations devoted their energies to the question of the franchise. These women and others traveled the country speaking to crowds and organizing women, despite frequent opposition. Suffragists finally secured passage of the Nineteenth Amendment, which enfranchised women, in 1920, but many black women could not vote until the Voting Rights Act of 1965.

The Civil War and Reconstruction, women's activism, as well as an evolving economy forced changes in the roles of women. Although women could not vote for most of the nineteenth century, they were often eligible to hold public office. A number of women ran as candidates after the Civil War, sometimes winning local offices. Others were appointed to public offices, such as postmaster. In 1872, the controversial women's rights and free love advocate Victoria Woodhull became the first woman to run for President. In 1884 and again in 1888, suffragist and lawyer Belva Lockwood also ran for President as the candidate of the Equal Rights Party. Record numbers of women also entered waged work outside the home. In both the North and South, industry and agriculture functioned because of female labor, and for the first time women entered government office jobs in large numbers. Women also became a majority in the teaching and nursing professions. Both professions provided literate blacks with a route out of domestic service, as emancipation created a large demand for education and aid among the freed slaves. Universities began to open their doors to women after the Civil War. And more and more professions began to admit women, including the ministry and medicine, two of the most prestigious professions of the nineteenth century. In 1853, Antionette Brown Blackwell had been the first woman ordained in a mainstream denomination, and after the war, many other women ministers followed. After the pioneering efforts of Elizabeth Blackwell (Antionette's sister-in-law), who became the nation's first woman doctor in 1847, several female medical colleges were established, including E. Blackwell's own Women's Medical College of the New York Infirmary (1868). Women also fought for and won the right to practice law. In 1910, when records of women entering various professions were first kept, there were almost 7.5 million women in the job market: 19 percent of college professors, presidents, and instructors were women; 6 percent of doctors; 3.1 percent of dentists; 1 percent of lawyers; and 79 percent of librarians.

In the decades that followed the gains made by women in the professions slowed, although an increase in the number of women in the workforce continued, particularly during World War II, when large numbers of women entered manufacturing jobs (earning them the nickname "Rosie the Riviter"). In 1950, 34 percent of women worked for pay; by 1970 that figure had grown to 43 percent. But, in that same year, only 7 percent of the nation's doctors were women, as were only 2 percent of its dentists, 3.5 percent of its lawyers, and 19 percent of its college presidents, instructors, and professors. On the other hand, women moved into new professions in the previous decades, notably as natural scientists (11 percent) and as real estate salesmen and brokers (40 percent). In journalism, radio, and television broadcasting, women made relatively few inroads beyond the traditionally feminine spheres of the women's pages, entertainment, and hostessing of shows. A few notable women journalists, including Dorothy Thompson and Mary McGrory, earned national recognition, but opportunities for women in straight reportage and news analysis were limited by conventions and long-standing prejudice. In the field of publishing, despite the remarkable success of Katharine Graham, publisher of the *Washington Post*, women were still relegated to the largely supportive roles of subeditors and agents. As for the corporate economy, women top executives were few and far between; a survey by the *Harvard Business Review* in the late 1960s found so few women in management positions that there was nothing to study.

In 1975, fifty-five years after the Nineteenth Amendment, there were only 17 women among the 435 representatives in the House of Representatives and no women among the 100 senators. The percentage of representation for women in the state legislatures across the country was not significantly higher, and in city and county governments only slightly so. As of 1975 only three women had held cabinet rank in the history of the country—Frances Perkins as secretary of labor under Franklin D. Roosevelt, Oveta Culp Hobby as secretary of health, education, and welfare under Dwight D. Eisenhower, and Carla Hill as secretary of housing under Gerald R. Ford—and no woman had been asked to serve on the Supreme Court. In the federal government as a whole, only 147 women held the top positions (that is, grades GS 16 through 18) among the 849,421 in the civil service in 1968.

The 1970s witnessed the most energetic feminist activism since the suffrage campaign, and women's rights advocates challenged these minimal gains for women in public life, business, and professions. The percentage of women earning college degrees had increased from 22.7 in 1910 to 42.3 in 1970; and this advance, coupled with the great increase in the women's workforce, led to expectations of equivalent advances for women in status, pay, and advanced occupations. In 1966 the National Organization for Women (NOW) was formed, headed by author Betty Friedan. A number of other feminist groups followed, and "Women's Liberation" became a catch-all phrase for a new social movement demanding equal pay and equal opportunities for women in all spheres of life. Their efforts led to significant gains for women in some professions and to the institution of affirmative action programs in colleges and government. Both major parties radically increased the number of women representatives to the presidential conventions of 1972 and adopted strong women's rights planks. The elections of that year also increased the number of women in the House of Representatives to fifteen, although the lone woman senator, Margaret Chase Smith of Massachusetts, was defeated. An equal rights amendment was finally passed in the Senate by an overwhelming vote and at the end of 1975 had been ratified by thirty-four states. Women's organizations and sympathetic groups, particularly the Women's National Political Caucus (WNPC), formed in 1971, continued their lobbying efforts to secure passage of the amendment.

The women's movement was committed to a redefinition of social roles for both men and women. A new feminist credo urged that women play a larger public role and men take on more private responsibility for family care. By 1990, 57.5 percent of all women worked outside the home. Employment of married women with children younger than six rose sharply from 14 percent in 1951 to 30.3 percent in 1970 to 59 percent in 1990. Two-thirds of them were working full time. The sharp rise in women working outside the home, however, had more to do with economic pressure than with feminist politics. Understanding this reality, feminists demanded safe, affordable child care and equal wages for equal work. On average, working women earned only three-fourths of what a man earned for the same job. Until 1991 African American women consistently worked at rates higher than white women. In that year the median earnings for all women who worked full time and year round increased to 70 percent of those for men, up from 60 percent in 1971. Black women's median earnings rose in that period from 52 percent to 62 percent of those for men.

Working women in 1990 continued to concentrate in clerical, service, and sales work, as well as the historically female professions of teaching, nursing, library service, and social work, but feminist activism for enforcement of laws protecting job rights and enactment of legislation prohibiting sex discrimination in education permitted women to pursue more occupations. Between 1975 and 1990 women doubled their ranks in executive and managerial jobs (from 5.2 to 11.1 percent) and more entered the historically male professions and occupations. Between 1970 and 1991 the proportion rose from 4.7 to 19 percent of lawyers; 12.1 to 18.1 percent of physicians; and 2.7 to 14 percent of police officers. Although engineering remained virtually unbreached (women made up 8.2 percent of engineers in 1991), women advanced in most of the sciences, from less than 10 percent in 1973 to more than 25 percent by 1991. In 1988, 47 percent of Fortune 1000 companies reported women on boards of directors, up from 13 percent in 1976. In 1982 women owned 25 percent of U.S. firms (mostly sole proprietorships), and in 1987 receipts from women-owned firms accounted for 14 percent of the U.S. total.

As women claimed a full public role, they sought political positions at every level, drawing support from new national and local feminist political organizations. In 1971 women occupied 4.5 percent of the seats in state legislatures; by 1993 the proportion had grown to 20.4 percent. Seven women held mayoralties in 1971; twenty years later there were 151. From fifteen women in the 92nd Congress (1971–1973) numbers climbed slowly to thirty-two (three senators and twenty-nine representatives) on the eve of the 1992 election. With that election Congress expanded to fifty-four women members, forty-eight in the House and six in the Senate. The latter included the first African American woman senator, Carol Moseley Braun of Illinois; in the House there were nine African American women, one Asian/Pacific American woman (Patsy Mink of Hawaii), and three Latinas. Women also obtained a fairer share of places in the judiciary. By 1970 only six women had ever been named to the federal district and circuit courts; by 1992 they composed 13.4 percent of federal judicial officers and by 1993 two of the nine Supreme Court justices (Sandra Day O'Connor and Ruth Bader Ginsburg). During the course of the 1990s, conservatives also forwarded female candidates, and increasingly women in elected and appointed offices represent a broad political spectrum. By the 1990s the legitimacy of women in politics and the workforce was beyond question. But women were still underrepresented in many prestigious fields, and they continue to receive less pay for equal work. The assumption by men of a larger responsibility for family life has also been slow to emerge, and women continue to face the burden of managing the frequently conflicting demands of their private and public roles.

BIBLIOGRAPHY

Amundsen, Kirsten. *A New Look at the Silenced Majority: Women and American Democracy*. Englewood Cliffs, N.J.: Prentice-Hall, 1977.

Costello, Cynthia B., Shari E. Miles, and Anne J. Stone, eds. *The American Woman, 1900–2000: A Century of Change—What's Next?*. New York: Norton, 1998.

Epstein, Cynthia Fuchs. *Woman's Place: Options and Limits in Professional Careers*. Berkeley: University of California Press, 1970.

Flexner, Eleanor. *Century of Struggle: The Woman's Rights Movement in the United States*. Cambridge, Mass.: Belknap Press of Harvard University Press, 1959.

Giddings, Paula. *When and Where I Enter: The Impact of Black Women on Race and Sex in America*. New York: Bantam Books, 1984.

White, Deborah G. *Too Heavy a Load: Black Women in Defense of Themselves, 1894–1994*. New York: W. W. Norton, 1999.

Kristen Amundsen
Cynthia Harrison / L. T.

See also **Discrimination: Sex; Emily's List; Indentured Servants; Legal Profession; Medical Profession; Sexual Harassment; Slavery; Suffrage: Woman's Suffrage; Women's Rights Movement;** *and vol. 9:* **Letter to President Franklin D. Roosevelt on Job Discrimination; NOW Statement of Purpose; Women in Industry (Brandeis Brief); Women Working in World War II.**

WOMEN'S BUREAU was officially organized within the Department of Labor in 1920 to investigate and report on the conditions of working women. Its direct antecedent was the Women-in-Industry Service that had been established in 1918 to advise the Department on wartime labor standards for working women. As a bureau inside the federal government, the Women's Bureau does not initiate legislation nor does it have any oversight or enforcement capabilities. Its charge is to formulate standards and policies to promote the welfare of wage-earning women, improve their working conditions, increase their efficiency, and advance their opportunities for profitable employment. Mary Anderson, a shoeworker and organizer for the Women's Trade Union League in Chicago, was the first head of the Bureau, a position she held until 1944.

As a government office, the Women's Bureau became the official clearinghouse for collecting statistics on working women. In this capacity it performed the work done previously by voluntary, non-government groups such as the National Consumers' League (NCL). From its inception, the Bureau worked closely with the National Women's Trade Union League (NWTUL) to promote equal pay, minimum wage, and maximum-hours legislation; and worked toward eliminating night work and employment in dangerous industries. For decades, the Bureau also led an informal women's coalition that included the NCL, NWTUL, YWCA, the National Councils of Jewish, Catholic, and Negro Women, the League of Women Voters, the American Association of University Women, and women's affiliates in the AFL and CIO. Working together as a coalition, these women's organizations made considerable progress during the New Deal era in bettering conditions and industrial protections for working women. The Bureau played a key role in passage of the Fair Labor Standards Act of 1938.

Since Anderson's tenure, fourteen women have headed the Bureau. These directors have included African American, Hispanic, and Asian American women. They have been union organizers and business and professional women. Under their leadership, the Women's Bureau has continued to pursue the charge it was given in 1920. In the early 1960s, President John F. Kennedy elevated the status of the director of the Women's Bureau to Assistant Secretary of Labor.

The Bureau has participated in the International Labor Organization. It led the successful drive to have President Kennedy establish his Commission on the Status of Women in 1961. Since the 1960s, the Women's Bureau has lobbied for the Equal Pay Act of 1963, created employment initiatives for young and low-income women, and directed attention to the special needs of minority women. In 1982, the bureau initiated a drive to encourage employer-sponsored day care facilities, and in the 1990s worked for passage of the Family and Medical Leave Act of 1993. In 1999, the Bureau established a National Resource and Information Center to make information on issues concerning women more accessible to working women, as well as to their families and employers.

BIBLIOGRAPHY

Harrison, Cynthia. *On Account of Sex: The Politics of Women's Issues, 1945–1968*. Berkeley: University of California Press, 1988.

Storrs, Landon R.Y. *Civilizing Capitalism: The National Consumers' League, Women's Activism, and Labor Standards in the New Deal Era*. Chapel Hill: University of North Carolina Press, 2000.

The Women's Bureau website is: www.dol.gov/dol/wb.

Maureen A. Flanagan

See also **New Deal; Women's Trade Union League.**

WOMEN'S CLUBS are voluntary organizations that were originally formed by women who had been denied access to the major institutions of America's democratic

Falls, New York, where they ratified the DECLARATION OF SENTIMENTS. Based on the Declaration of Independence, the document proclaimed that men and women were "created equal," and that women should therefore have legal and social parity with men, including the right to vote. The declaration was greeted with a storm of criticism in newspapers and from religious leaders. By 1850, however, activists had organized similar gatherings in Ohio and Massachusetts and established an annual Woman's Rights Convention.

The campaign for dress reform became closely associated with the women's rights movement, as advocates such as Amelia Bloomer argued that the tight clothing women wore—especially whalebone corsets—was unhealthy and restrictive (see BLOOMERS). Many early women's rights advocates also became involved in SPIRITUALISM, a belief system based on direct communication with God and the dead, which offered women a greater voice in their religious life than did the male hierarchies of the Christian churches.

The events of the Civil War and Reconstruction dramatically affected the women's rights movement. As tensions between North and South intensified in the late 1850s, many women activists decided to devote themselves purely to abolition, until slavery had ended in the United States. After the Civil War, many women returned to the fight for women's rights, but new tensions soon split the movement. Radical Republicans lobbying for black male suffrage attacked women's rights advocates, believing that to demand the vote for women hurt their cause. Some women's rights activists, including Elizabeth Cady Stanton and Susan B. Anthony, turned to the Democratic Party, portions of which supported white woman suffrage in order to stop black men from securing the vote. In 1869 Stanton and Anthony formed the National Woman Suffrage Association, which focused on enfranchising white women; they insisted on female control of the organization and focused their energies on action at the federal level. Soon thereafter, the American Woman Suffrage Association formed as a rival group, turning to

Women's Rights. Women march in New York in 1912 for the right to vote; it was granted in that state in 1917 and nationwide three years later. LIBRARY OF CONGRESS

Republican and abolitionist men for leadership and agreeing to place black male suffrage ahead of votes for women, white or black, and to work at the state level. Both groups chose suffrage as their main issue, stepping back from an earlier, broader based agenda.

The women's rights movement continued to transform itself and to weather divisive tensions. In 1890 the two rival suffrage associations merged, forming the National American Woman Suffrage Association (NAWSA). Both constituent groups, despite their differences, had originally based their case for woman suffrage on the argument that men and women were naturally equal. Even as the two groups consolidated their strength, this view lost political ground, and older advocates found themselves replaced by younger, more conservative suffragists. The WOMAN'S CHRISTIAN TEMPERANCE UNION, the YOUNG WOMEN'S CHRISTIAN ASSOCIATION, and hundreds of other women's clubs began to focus on winning the vote, as they came to believe they could not accomplish their goals without official political power. The NATIONAL ASSOCIATION OF COLORED WOMEN, formed in part due to the exclusion of black WOMEN'S CLUBS from the GENERAL FEDERATION OF WOMEN'S CLUBS (formed in 1890), became a central player in fostering the black woman suffrage movement. While these clubs had different agendas, many of their members believed that the vote would allow women to bring their moralizing influence to bear on the problems of society; in other words, women should have the right to vote not because they were the same as men, but because they were different.

Despite the new interest from clubwomen, the last decade of the nineteenth century and the first decade of the twentieth proved disappointing for advocates of woman's suffrage. Although there were some victories early in this period—by 1896, women in Colorado, Idaho, Wyoming, and Utah could vote and a few Midwestern states had enfranchised women in school and municipal elections—the suffrage movement would not enjoy another major victory until 1910. Racial and ethnic prejudice continued to haunt and divide the movement. As Southern women became more involved in the suffrage issue, many white suffragists began to court Southern politicians by portraying woman's suffrage as a method to secure white supremacy. African American women, in response, formed their own suffrage organizations. Some advocates also argued that female enfranchisement would allow educated native-born women—and their middle-class concerns—to overrule the growing immigrant vote.

As suffragists fought amongst themselves, they also fought an active anti-suffrage campaign. Because many feminists were also socialists, and because women workers often earned minimal wages, business interests solidly opposed the women's movement. The liquor industry, alarmed by the coalition between temperance advocates and the suffrage movement, campaigned particularly vigorously against the vote for women. Many females joined the anti-suffrage forces as well, arguing that women did not desire the vote.

In early decades of the twentieth century several suffragists introduced new approaches that both reinvigorated and once again divided the movement. Elizabeth Cady Stanton's daughter, Harriot Stanton Blatch, founded the Equality League of Self-Supporting Women in 1907, bringing females from all classes and backgrounds together to work for suffrage. The League organized large, lavish suffrage parades that brought publicity and respect to the cause. Carrie Chapman Catt, who served as the president of NAWSA between 1900 and 1904, recruited both college-educated professionals and socially prominent women to the campaign. In 1912, Alice Paul and Lucy Burns took over NAWSA's Congressional Committee. The movement had employed a state-by-state strategy since the 1890s, hoping eventually to secure woman suffrage nationwide, but Paul and Burns believed only a push for a federal constitutional amendment would bring about victory. The two women also believed in more aggressive tactics than those employed by their parent organization, including picketing the White House and hunger strikes. Eventually Paul and Burns broke with the NAWSA, forming the Congressional Union (later the NATIONAL WOMAN'S PARTY) in 1914.

Despite the split, the woman's suffrage movement had become a vital force. When Catt returned to the NAWSA presidency in 1915, she emphasized the importance of both state and national activity. Women in Arizona, California, Kansas, Oregon, and Washington had secured the vote by 1912; by 1913, Illinois women could vote in presidential elections. In January 1918 the House of Representatives passed the Nineteenth Amendment, sometimes known as the Anthony Amendment; a year and a half later, the Senate passed it as well. Suffragists worked tirelessly for the next year to obtain ratification by the required 36 states. On 26 August 1920 American women finally had the right to vote.

While the women's rights movement focused its energies mainly on suffrage after 1869, it both fostered and was fed by other changes in women's lives. Women's access to higher education expanded, as both single-sex and coeducational institutions opened their doors (see EDUCATION, HIGHER: WOMEN'S COLLEGES). As a result, females could begin to enter, at least in small numbers, traditionally male professions, becoming authors, doctors, lawyers, and ministers. Women also became involved in other political causes, especially labor issues, and opened settlement houses to aid the poor. Although American women had not achieved equality, by 1920 they had traveled far.

BIBLIOGRAPHY

Braude, Anne. *Radical Spirits: Spiritualism and Women's Rights in Nineteenth-Century America.* 2d ed. Bloomington: Indiana University Press, 1989.

Buechler, Steven. *The Transformation of the Woman Suffrage Movement: The Case of Illinois, 1850–1920.* New Brunswick, N.J.: Rutgers University Press, 1986.

Clinton, Catherine, and Christine Lunardini, eds. *The Columbia Guide to American Women in the Nineteenth Century.* New York: Columbia University Press, 2000.

Cott, Nancy F. *The Bonds of Womanhood: "Woman's Sphere" in New England, 1780–1835.* 2d ed. New Haven, Conn.: Yale University Press, 1997.

DuBois, Ellen Carol. *Feminism and Suffrage: The Emergence of an Independent Women's Movement in America, 1848–1869.* Ithaca, N.Y.: Cornell University Press, 1999.

———. *Harriot Stanton Blatch and the Winning of Woman Suffrage.* New Haven, Conn.: Yale University Press, 1997.

Flexnor, Eleanor. *Century of Struggle: The Woman's Rights Movement in the United States.* Cambridge, Mass.: Belknap Press of Harvard University Press, 1996.

Ginzberg, Lori D. *Women and the Work of Benevolence: Morality, Politics, and Class in the Nineteenth-Century United States.* New Haven: Yale University Press, 1990.

Hewitt, Nancy A. *Women's Activism and Social Change: Rochester, New York, 1822–1872.* Ithaca, N.Y.: Cornell University Press, 1984.

Kerber, Linda K. *Women of the Republic: Intellect and Ideology in Revolutionary America.* Chapel Hill: Published for the Institute of Early American History by the University of North Carolina Press, 1980.

Kraditor, Aileen S. *The Ideas of the Woman Suffrage Movement, 1890–1920.* New York: Norton, 1981.

Lerner, Gerda, ed. *Black Women in White America: A Documentary History.* New York: Vintage Books, 1992.

Marilley, Suzanne M. *Woman Suffrage and the Origins of Liberal Feminism in the United States, 1820–1920.* Cambridge, Mass.: Harvard University Press, 1996.

Marshall, Susan E. *Splintered Sisterhood: Gender and Class in the Campaign Against Woman Suffrage.* Madison: University of Wisconsin Press, 1997.

Painter, Nell Irvin. *Sojourner Truth: A Life, a Symbol.* New York: Norton, 1996.

Ryan, Mary P. *Women in Public: Between Banners and Ballots, 1825–1880.* Baltimore: John Hopkins University Press, 1990.

Scott, Anne Firor. *Natural Allies: Women's Associations in American History.* Urbana: University of Illinois Press, 1991.

Wheeler, Marjorie Spurill. *Votes for Women!: The Woman Suffrage Movement in Tennessee, the South, and the Nation.* Knoxville: University of Tennessee Press, 1995.

Carol Andreas
Katherine Culkin

See also **Antislavery; Discrimination: Sex; Gender and Gender Roles; Suffrage: Woman's Suffrage; Women in Churches; Women in Public Life, Business, and Professions; Women, Citizenship of Married;** *and vol. 9:* **Human Rights Not Founded on Sex, October 2, 1837; The Seneca Falls Declaration; What If I Am a Woman?; When Woman Gets Her Rights Man Will Be Right.**

THE TWENTIETH CENTURY

The reemergence of the women's movement in the United States in the late 1960s is commonly referred to as the modern women's rights movement, the feminist movement, or the women's liberation movement. It is also known as second wave feminism, which serves to distinguish it from the period a century earlier when women in the United States first organized around demands for full citizenship. That earlier campaign, known as first wave, culminated with the passage of the Nineteenth Amendment in 1920, which legally (if not actually) barred discrimination in voting on the basis of sex. Feminists in the 1960s, like their predecessors, sought to alter their unequal political, social, and economic status. Although still vital in a variety of forms, the modern women's movement reached a high point in the late 1960s and early 1970s.

Simply put, feminism is the belief in the full economic, political, and social equality of males and females. But because women are often distinctly different from one another—divided by issues of class, race, and sexual orientation—how feminists defined women's problems and women's equality varied considerably. Consequently, the modern wave of feminism had many facets, and it changed during its initial decades as women confronted and acknowledged not only larger patterns of sexism in society, but also their differences from one another. There were underlying themes common to all those who sought to improve women's status, however. One was an opposition to sexism—the notion that there are political and social institutions as well as deep-seated cultural attitudes that discriminate against women, denying them the opportunity to reach their fullest potential. A second theme was the goal of individual self-determination—the claim that women should be free to choose their own paths in life, perhaps helped by but not constrained by men or other women. Finally, feminists insisted that the "personal is political." This conviction asserted that women's individual problems were legitimate, important political issues and that the only way to change the problems of battering, rape, low-paying jobs, unfair divorce laws, discriminatory education, or degrading notions of femininity was through political organizing and political struggle. Feminist critiques constituted not only a direct challenge to the gender system, but also to racism and capitalism.

The roots of the second wave lay, in part, in large-scale structural changes that occurred in the United States during the middle part of the twentieth century. Demographic change, including a rapidly falling birth rate, increased longevity, a rising divorce rate, and an increase in the age at which people married, radicalized the expectations of girls and women. They flooded into the full-time labor force, stayed in school longer, secured college and postgraduate degrees in increasing numbers, and linked their newfound sexual freedom with the desire to control their own reproduction. Other important origins included a variety of political protest movements, including the labor movement, the Civil Rights Movement,

New Left politics, and the counterculture of the 1960s. Women joined these movements in large numbers and often encountered deep and pervasive sexism within these radical movements. When Stokely Charmichael, a leader of the Student Non-Violent Coordinating Committee, for example, was publically asked in 1964 what was the position of women in the organization, he replied famously: "The only position for women in SNCC is prone." The growing dissatisfaction of women within these groups led many to insist that the organizations devote attention to women's issues, while others exited New Left movements, joining with one another to ignite the modern women's liberation movement.

The early 1960s saw two important events that perhaps signalled the beginning of the second wave. In December 1961, President John F. Kennedy established the President's Commission on the Status of Women. Chaired by Eleanor Roosevelt and comprised of female political, business, and education leaders, the commission was asked to report on the progress women had made in six areas, including federal civil service employment and labor legislation. Its final report, although certainly not viewed as radical by modern feminists, did call for greater equality in the workplace while at the same time trying to protect women's "maternal functions."

Writer and feminist Betty Friedan recognized that the commission was bogged down in bureacracy and that it would not bring about any real changes, so she decided to take matters into her own hands, leading to the second important event. In 1963, Friedan's book *The Feminine Mystique* was published and immediately caused an uproar. Called a "wake-up call to women," the book outlined Friedan's belief that women were tired of being trapped in the home as housewives and that the entire nation would benefit if women could escape that outdated role and assume a more productive place in the national workforce. With such controversial tactics as comparing being stuck in the role of housewife to spending time in a Nazi prison camp, *The Feminine Mystique* touched a nerve in women across the country and caused a social revolution, after which little was ever the same in the women's movement.

Spurred on by those early 1960s events, organizations and small groups appeared in the late 1960s and the 1970s as feminists grappled with the difficult question of how to act on these themes and insights. The largest and most structured of the new feminist organizations was the National Organization for Women (NOW), founded in 1966. It sought solutions at the policy level, fighting legal and legislative battles. One of their most famous campaigns centered around an unsuccessful attempt to secure passage of a Constitutional amendment known as the Equal Rights Amendment (ERA), which bared discrimination on the basis of sex. Its backers believed the amendment could be used to eliminate discrimination against women in education and the labor force as well as to safeguard women's reproductive freedom. Other groups work-

ing on the policy level included the Women's Equity Action League (1968) and the National Women's Political Caucus (1971). These groups, along with NOW, demanded equal employment opportunity, equal pay for equal work, an end to sexual harassment in the workforce and educational institutions, more equitable divorce and child-custody laws, and greater concern with violence against women. Most also supported pay equity or comparable worth, reproductive rights (including abortion), and greater domestic autonomy. They believed that many of these reforms would likely occur when the numbers of women at all levels of government increased. Toward this end, they also launched initiatives to increase the number of women in public office.

Other tactics for change included the development of consciousness-raising groups. Small discussion groups, these intimate forums sprung up in large numbers around the country and sought to raise women's consciousness about sexism and feminism. Women explored their struggles to become more assertive and to resist a socialization process that had taught them to be passive and self-denigrating. This technique was so successful that it has filtered into the general culture being deployed by a wide variety of groups today. Activists in many camps believed that street protests were the most effective way to communicate feminism's message to large numbers of people. Direct-action tactics included protests at the Miss America pageant in 1968; the hexing of the New York Stock Exchange by women dressed as witches from WITCH (Women's International Terrorist Conspiracy from Hell); the Women's Strike for Equality on 26 August 1970, involving more than 100,000 women throughout the country; and, later, huge demonstrations to assert women's right to abortion. Other activists worked for a feminist vision of change by organizing alternative institutions. Some formed separatist female communities. Some established rape hotlines and battered women's shelters; women's health clinics, food stores, publishers, a symphony orchestra, art galleries, bookstores, banks, and bars provided outlets for creative energies and entrepreneurial skills. Although there was much disagreement within the movement about which of these disparate tactics was most effective, their combined effect was staggering. They touched the lives of millions of Americans and began to transform the ways people thought about and acted toward women.

No sooner, however, had men and women begun to shift their behavior and attitudes than the male-dominated media began to ridicule and trivialize women's liberation and to publicize distorted accounts of women's activities. Most famously, the media branded the protesters at the Miss America Pageant in August 1968 as "bra burners." This event was never part of the protest, however. The press photograph of the purported incident was staged. Nevertheless, this image of the bra-burning, man-hating feminist registered powerfully and has persisted in the public mind. This backlash against women has taken a

Rallying for the Equal Rights Amendment, Houston, Tx., 1977. *From left:* Betty Friedan, Liz Carpenter, Rosalynn Carter, Betty Ford, Elly Peterson, Jill Ruckelshaus, and Bella Abzug. Note the presence of two first ladies, a congresswoman (Abzug), and a figure from the Johnson administration (former press secretary Carpenter). © BETTMAN/CORBIS

wide variety of forms and has been a powerful force, particularly throughout the 1980s, in halting and reversing many gains for women's equal human rights.

Some policy successes of the modern women's rights movement have included the 1963 Equal Pay Act, the 1964 CIVIL RIGHTS ACT, laws prohibiting discrimination in educational and credit opportunities, and Supreme Court decisions expanding the civil liberties of women. In 1972 Congress sent the Equal Rights Amendment to the states for ratification; despite approval from more than half the states it failed to obtain the necessary two-thirds needed by 1982. In 1973, the Supreme Court affirmed a women's right to privacy in *Roe v. Wade*, which legalized abortion. Subsequent gains included the Civil Rights Restoration Act of 1987, the Civil Rights Act of 1991, the Family and Medical Leave Act of 1993, and the Violence Against Women Act of 1994. Victories in state legislatures included laws establishing greater protection for battered women and victims of violent crime, reform of rape statutes, and laws providing for more equitable distribution of marital property following divorce, made necessary by the negative impact of no-fault divorce laws on women. At the same time, many states placed restrictions on women's constitutional right to obtain abortions and often interpreted no-fault divorce laws in ways that harmed women's economic status.

The women's movement remained a salient force for social justice and equity in the 1990s but faced new challenges and problems. Despite substantial gains in many

areas over thirty years, sexist attitudes and behavior endured. The gap between women's and men's incomes narrowed but persisted, with women earning approximately 25 percent less than men regardless of education. Abortion rights, while guaranteed, came under renewed attack and in many states were severely eroded. Sexual harassment was a recognized crime but nevertheless continued to compromise women's full equality. More women were running for and winning elective office than ever before but in 1994 women constituted only 10 percent of Congress. Women continue to be underrepresented in positions of leadership in corporations and universities. Many women earning their own incomes had to work a "second shift" because they remained responsible for most or all of their families' care, even in dual income households. And families headed by single women were among the poorest in the nation. These and other concerns shaped the ideological debates within feminism at the end of the twentieth century. The women's movement continued to contain within itself a plethora of differing analyses and opinions concerning women and social change.

One such debate focused on the issue of sexual violence. Feminists were divided about the role of pornography in engendering and encouraging the sexual violence rampant in the United States. Many who believed that pornography was a major cause of woman-centered violence called for strict regulation or outlawing of pornography as a violation of women's civil rights. Other feminists were concerned about the difficulty of defining

517

pornography, claiming that the real causes of violence against women are complex and rooted deep within our culture and social institutions. They argued that pornography is a form of free speech—however abhorrent—that must be tolerated in a democratic society. Disagreements were apparent as well on the question of how to define and punish such problems as sexual harassment, date rape, and marital rape. Some questioned the legitimacy of a "battered woman defense," giving women victims of systematic violence the right to strike back against their abusers. While all feminists agreed that gender-based crimes against women, including violent acts against lesbian women, were a virulent form of sexism that must be eradicated, they differed in their analyses of and remedies for these problems.

Another debate divided "difference" feminists from "equality" feminists. Difference feminists stressed that women resemble one another and differ from men in fundamental ways. They focused on the value of presumed feminine characteristics, claiming women's greater empathy, cooperation, intuition, and care and posited these as superior to those thought to characterize men. Although they frequently pointed to socialization rather than biology as the source of sex differences, these feminists believed women's characteristics are shared by all women and difficult if not impossible to alter. Equality feminism, in contrast, rejected the view that there are basic social and psychological differences between women and men. It focused on eliminating barriers to fulfilling individual potential. Equality feminism defined social justice in a gender-neutral fashion, anticipating a future that would provide women and men with opportunities to exercise individual choice on a wide range of issues, including reproduction, education, employment, legal rights, sexual orientation, and personal relationships. It rejected the traditional idea that women's differences from men are inherent or can ever be legitimately used to justify either sex's exclusion from any aspect of society or social life. The political ramifications of difference and equality feminism were many. They divided feminists who advocated special provisions for women in the labor force and the law from those who wanted equal treatment for women and men. One practical aspect of this debate concerned the appropriate remedy for the persistent disadvantages of women in the labor force. When compared to men, women earned less, were promoted less frequently, and continued to be segregated in "female" occupations. Most harmful of all was the pattern of interrupted work histories that characterized large numbers of women as they continued to drop out of the labor force in order to almost single-handedly rear children and care for their homes.

Insisting on preserving women's special relationship to home and children, difference feminists addressed women's disadvantaged position in the workforce with such solutions as the "mommy track." This special arrangement of part-time work enables female lawyers, for example, to spend more time at home without forgoing their law practices. Women retain their relationships with firms even though the ability to qualify as partners is delayed and salaries are considerably lower than are those of full-time lawyers. Equality feminists, however, rejected such special protections. Their search for remedies focused rather on finding ways to equalize men's and women's responsibilities for home and child care. Many equality feminists believed that parental leaves of absence from work when children are young or ill, expanded availability of low-cost and high-quality day care, and greater participation of men in fairly dividing responsibilities for housework and child rearing were the only real solutions to women's dual-workload problem. By the middle of the 1990s, however, neither difference nor equality feminists had been able to exercise the political power necessary to resolve women's continuing disadvantages in the labor force.

The ideologies of difference and equality separated feminists with respect to strategies for building the movement itself. Difference feminists tended to be wary of co-

Pro-Choice. Women attend a rally to support abortion rights, the most divisive and bitterly fought issue related to women's rights since the legalization of abortion in 1973. © UPI/CORBIS-BETTMANN

alitions, especially those with men. They were generally pessimistic about the possibility of changing what they saw as men's essentially intractable sexist attitudes and behavior and frequently claimed that only women can understand and fight women's oppression. As a result, feminists influenced by a difference model tended to be separatist, inward looking, and focused on what they saw as women's inevitable victimization. Their activism often took the form of trying to shield women from sexism, especially by separating them from its sources. Thus, one of their primary goals was the creation of all-women environments that were considered safe spaces, such as those at women's music festivals or retreats.

The ideology of equality feminism, in contrast, concentrated on eradicating sexism by removing its causes. For many equality feminists this included working in coalition with men to change their attitudes and behavior toward women. They focused on issues that could unite women and men of different social classes and races, such as the disproportionate poverty of U.S. women and their children, federal funding for abortions, and the need for day care. Their goal was to change those aspects of the society that engender sexism. They fought for fair laws and nonsexist legislation and staged large demonstrations and protests to create a broad-based, diverse, and effective movement for ending sexism.

The difference and equality debate raged within academic institutions. The establishment of women's studies courses and programs in almost every institution of higher education in the country was unquestionably one of the women's movement's most significant achievements. These programs and the women's centers with which they were often associated on college campuses altered the way scholars and students thought about issues of gender. Reversing a situation in which women and their contributions to history, science, and society were almost entirely ignored, women's studies courses educated millions of young people about the importance of both women and men to our cultural heritage and contemporary world. Despite their success, women's studies programs faced an identity crisis in the 1990s. On one side, equality feminists argued that the subjects of women and gender should be integrated into the curriculum and not require separate courses or programs. To them the primary goal of women's studies programs was to facilitate that integration. In contrast, difference feminists claimed that only an independent women's studies curriculum could fulfill the continuing need for courses dedicated to women's unique place in and approach to the world. Thus, feminists celebrated the many accomplishments of women's studies programs even as they disagreed about the strategy that should be adopted by such programs.

The women's movement remained a forum for debate, with issues, strategies, and tactics subject to controversy. While such diversity may have confused a public looking for simple definitions or perplexed those who wanted to know, finally, "What do women want?" its multi-

faceted nature was the movement's strength. The women's movement had room for everyone who agreed that sexism has no place in a society dedicated to social justice. The most important contribution of the women's movement of the late twentieth century was to improve women's lives by reducing obstacles to the full expression of their desires and choices. Feminists contributed to the wider society as well, because their activism was an important element in the continuing struggle for a more equitable and just society for all.

BIBLIOGRAPHY

Baxandall, Rosalyn F., and Linda Gordon, eds. *Dear Sisters: Dispatches from the Women's Liberation Movement.* New York: Basic Books, 2000.

Deslippe, Dennis A. *Rights, Not Roses: Unions and the Rise of Working-Class Feminism, 1945–1980.* Urbana: University of Illinois Press, 2000.

Echols, Alice. *Daring To Be Bad: Radical Feminism in America, 1967–1975.* Minneapolis: University of Minnesota Press, 1989.

Evans, Sara M. *Personal Politics: The Roots of Women's Liberation in the Civil Rights Movement and the New Left.* New York: Vintage Books, 1980.

Faludi, Susan. *Backlash: The Undeclared War Against American Women.* New York: Anchor Books, 1991.

Freedman, Estelle B. *No Turning Back: The History of Feminism and the Future of Women.* New York: Ballantine Books, 2002.

Rosen, Ruth. *The World Split Open: How the Modern Women's Movement Changed America.* New York: Viking, 2000.

White, Deborah G. *Too Heavy a Load: Black Women in Defense of Themselves, 1894–1994.* New York: W.W. Norton, 1999.

Joan D. Mandle/l. t.

See also **Birth Control Movement; Discrimination: Sex; Emily's List; *Feminine Mystique, The*; National Organization for Women; National Women's Political Caucus; Pro-Choice Movement; Rape Crisis Centers; Sexual Harrasment; Sexual Orientation; Sexuality; Suffrage: Woman's Suffrage; Women, President's Commission on the Status of; Women in Public Life, Business, and Professions; Women's Equity Action League; Women's Health; Women's Rights Movement; Women's Studies;** *and vol. 9:* **NOW Statement of Purpose.**

WOMEN'S STUDIES is an interdisciplinary university curriculum originating in the United States in the late 1960s. Almost simultaneously in 1969–1970, the first women's studies courses appeared in a handful of American universities, including Cornell University and San Diego State College (now University). By 1980 there were over 300 women's studies programs and departments in United States universities. That number had more than doubled again by 2000, and included nine Ph.D. programs (with at least one more in development). In addition, there were women's studies programs and departments at universities around the world, including many sites in Canada, Europe, South Africa, the United Kingdom, and Australia, as well as Japan, Korea, Lebanon, Mexico, Ireland, Sudan, Turkey, and Uganda.

In the late 1960s, as the proportion of women enrolled in colleges and universities increased, feminists identifying with a new women's liberation movement criticized American higher education for failing to address women's concerns on at least three levels: the lack of equal professional opportunities for women scholars and graduates (the "glass ceiling"); the absence of curricular content reflecting women's lives and contributions in the liberal arts, sciences, and technical fields; and the skewed, diminished, and often insulting experiences of women undergraduates and graduate students in and outside the classroom.

Unsurprisingly, as Marilyn Boxer has pointed out, many of the pioneers in developing women's studies courses were political activists, using the free university and civil rights movements as models for developing feminist perspectives in various disciplines and expanding women's access to male-dominated classrooms, programs, positions, and bodies of knowledge. Jean Fox O'Barr, for example, was five years beyond a political science dissertation that deflected questions about women when she began reading recent women's studies literature by Kate Millett, Robin Morgan, and others. As a result, O'Barr began questioning fundamental assumptions in her own discipline and eventually became a leader of the women's studies movement.

Women's studies scholars came from existing disciplines that, with the exception of home economics, were male-dominated. Women literary scholars and historians weighed in first, asking questions that repositioned women in their research and thus changed previous bodies of "knowledge." In literature, feminist scholars began to ask about the exclusion of women writers from the canon of "great" (and thus always studied) writers. In history, Marilyn Boxer cites Joan Kelly as recalling, "All I had done was to say, with Leonardo, suppose we look at the dark, dense immobile earth from the vantage point of the moon? . . . Suppose we look at the Renaissance from the vantage point of women?" (Boxer, p. 129). Kelly articulated the core perspective of women's studies. The add-women-and-stir approach, pasting women into existing pictures of historical process or social dynamics, did not generate transformative insights. Nor did it help to recognize individual women who did things that men usually do. Instead, significant changes in scholarship stemmed from shifted "vantage points." This shift usually involved identifying systems of values and priorities practiced by women, systems that might either supplement or challenge prevailing value systems that are enforced socially or politically. An example from historical scholarship is Nancy Cott's seminal articulation in 1977 of a "woman's sphere" of interpersonal relations in colonial and early national New England. In women's studies, perhaps even more than in other areas of study, we can often identify "clusters" of significant works elaborating new insights. In this area of colonial and nineteenth-century European American women's culture, Cott's book had been preceded by Barbara Welter's work and enriched by complementary theses offered by Linda Kerber, Mary Beth Norton, Kathryn Kish Sklar, Carroll Smith Rosenberg, and others.

The floodgates of revisionist scholarship opened in the 1970s and 1980s, not just in history, but also in anthropology, sociology, literature, communication, and psychology. Simultaneously, women scholars began feminist activism within their disciplinary organizations, creating women's caucuses and women's networking mechanisms, agitating for greater representation of women scholars on conference panels and in governing offices and committees, and identifying ways of mentoring women graduate students. The National Women's Studies Association was founded in 1977. Several notable journals of women's studies were established, including *Feminist Studies* in 1972 and *Signs* in 1975. *Sage*, founded in 1982, has become a widely respected journal in black women's studies.

The proliferation of courses, programs, and then departments of women's studies from 1970 through 2000 testifies to the development of an audience, a teaching faculty, and curriculum. Early women's studies advocates faced key questions about the content of the courses, the viability and structure of women's studies as a discipline, and the political mission of the enterprise. From the beginning, women's studies theorists have considered pedagogy an integral part of creating their discipline. Instructors have widely agreed that the dynamics of the classroom must somehow reflect and embody the theoretical struggles of the discipline. Would it be enough for a women's studies course to include content on women's lives, or must the course be taught from a feminist point of view? What was feminist pedagogy and what would a feminist classroom look like? Did traditional dynamics between instructor and students—grades, modes of address, even the arrangement of desks and chairs—echo prevailing power structures in a stultifying or an exemplary way? How would men experience a women's studies classroom, and how would a women's studies class experience men? Could men teach women's studies? Was there or should there be a difference between a women's studies course per se and courses in other home disciplines that reflected revised content on women?

The first courses constructed their content around women's experiences, which reflected the grassroots nature of liberationist politics as well as a democratic and particularist epistemology. Women's studies teachers found that the opening of the universities in the 1960s and 1970s brought in "nontraditional" students, often older women returning to school after raising children or after a divorce, to pursue education and credentials for new careers. This population has enriched women's studies classes by bringing perspectives and debates into the classroom that are relevant to postgraduate and non-college women. Most women's studies curricula are grounded by a specific introduction to women's studies course. Besides the introductory course, core curricula then may include courses on feminist theory and epistemology; political and legal issues; feminist perspectives on social structure and social power, race, class, sex and sexuality; and individual and family development issues.

Women's studies students generally take additional university courses allied with, or double-listed by, women's studies. These often include courses in sociology, history, anthropology, art and aesthetics, and literature. One of the thorniest sets of issues, and one that often lay beyond the control of the organizers of women's studies programs, concerned the structure of the women's studies program and the interaction between its administrative and curricular organization. Would it be more important to integrate women's content into a traditionally organized curriculum, or to create a beachhead of feminist scholarship and pedagogy? Would organization in a department isolate and "ghettoize" the women's studies endeavor? Would departmental status tempt faculty to abandon their mission to transform the entire university curriculum? Many early advocates of integration became converts to the departmental model because of the advantages of regular funding and tenure lines, which improved stability and seemed to bestow the stamp of legitimacy. Programs still far outnumbered departments as of 2001, but the number of women's studies departments continues its proportional increase. In institutions where the program model prevails, women's studies faculties usually have two homes, one in women's studies and one in another department.

Another set of issues that enriched and sometimes threatened to fragment the women's studies enterprise revolved around women's differences, particularly those of race, class, and sexuality. In 1969 Frances Beale updated the concept of "double jeopardy," the oppression of black women on the two counts of sex and race. African American women scholars, artists, and activists, as well as those of Asian, Native American, Hawaiian, Latina, and other racial and ethnic backgrounds, protested any assumption that women experienced a common set of life conditions, simply on the basis of sex. (The coining of the term "women of color" presented some of the same pitfalls of unintentional homogenization.) Powerful writings and performances helped create a new mosaic of images and understandings of the multiplicity of women's lives as lived in the United States and in other parts of the world. Often painfully, women's studies absorbed the idea that privilege was not just a category that separated women from men, but also women from each other.

Though there were many lesbian and bisexual scholars involved in the creation of women's studies on campuses across the United States, the women's studies movement resembled the women's movement in general in its initial ambivalence toward full and integrated recognition of non-heterosexual women. Interestingly, the evolution of gay and lesbian studies courses and programs in the last fifteen years has both reinforced the legitimacy of inclusion and, in some ways, diluted the impact of lesbian content in women's studies programs. The flip side of this dilemma, and one that echoes the uncomfortable position of black women in African American studies, is that lesbians often find themselves and their concerns underrepresented in queer studies programs that, of course, include gay men.

In the last decade of the twentieth century, women's studies scholarship grappled with the same theoretical dilemmas that troubled and enlivened other humanities and social science disciplines. Some scholars believed that postmodernist interpretations threatened to eviscerate feminism, while others saw postmodernist discourse as a metalanguage that would salvage the intellectual integrity of the women's studies project. As the ranks of women's studies professors increasingly include scholars exposed to women's studies as undergraduates, the professional as well as intellectual dynamics of the field will continue to evolve.

BIBLIOGRAPHY

Boxer, Marilyn Jacoby. *When Women Ask the Questions: Creating Women's Studies in America.* Baltimore: Johns Hopkins University Press, 1998.

O'Barr, Jean Fox. *Feminism in Action: Building Institutions and Community Through Women's Studies.* Chapel Hill, N.C.: University of North Carolina Press, 1994.

Winkler, Barbara Scott, and Carolyn DiPalma, eds. *Teaching Introduction to Women's Studies: Expectations and Strategies.* Westport, Conn.: Bergin and Garvey, 1999.

Mina Carson

See also **Education, Higher: Women's Colleges.**

WOMEN'S TRADE UNION LEAGUE, an organization of working-class and middle-class women (1903–1950) dedicated to improving the lives of America's working women. The Women's Trade Union League (WTUL) was founded in Boston in 1903 at a meeting of the American Federation of Labor, when it became clear that American labor had no intention of organizing America's women into trade unions. A British version of the organization had been in existence since 1873. The American group was the brainchild of labor organizer Mary Kenny O'Sullivan. It combined middle-class reformers and social workers such as Lillian Wald and Jane Addams, called "allies," and working-class activists such as Leonora O'Reilly. While national, it was active in key urban areas such as New York, Boston, and Chicago.

The organization's twin focus was on (1) aiding trade unions and striking women workers and (2) lobbying for "protective labor legislation." It was at its height from 1907 to 1922 under the direction of Margaret Dreier Robins. During the bitter New York garment worker strikes of

1909 through 1913, the WTUL proved to be a major source of support for the strikers. WTUL members walked picket lines, organized support rallies, provided much-needed public relations, raised strike funds and bail, and helped shape public opinion in the strikers' favor. In 1911, after the terrible TRIANGLE SHIRTWAIST FIRE killed 146 garment workers, the WTUL was at the forefront of reformers demanding stepped-up governmental responsibility over the workplace. When New York State created the Factory Investigating Committee in 1912, WTUL representative Mary Dreier was one of the commissioners.

After 1912, the WTUL branched out to Iowa, New Jersey, and Ohio to aid women strikers and investigate working conditions. The thrust of their attention after the garment strikes, however, was on legislation: an eight-hour workday, workplace safety, and minimum wages for women workers. Their success in fourteen states won them many supporters among women workers and reform circles but caused concern for the American Federation of Labor (AFL). Samuel Gompers, the AFL president, saw legislation as a threat to the core of labor: collective bargaining. Gompers saw politics as a blind alley for labor. This conflict can be seen in the uneasy relationship between trade union women and the WTUL. Labor leaders such as Rose Schneiderman and Pauline Newman spent years with the WTUL, the former as N.Y. President, but they never felt completely at home among the reformers.

Just prior to World War I, the WTUL began to actively campaign for woman's suffrage in the belief that if working women had the vote they could demand laws to protect them. During World War I the WTUL worked with the Department of Labor as more and more women joined the workforce. After the war, as returning soldiers replaced the women workers and the AFL returned to its "family wage" philosophy (husbands need to earn enough to keep their wives at home), the relationship between the WTUL and the AFL was strained.

Starting in the 1920s, the WTUL began an educational effort that had profound effects. Starting with the summer school for women workers at Bryn Mawr (and spreading to other women's colleges), the WTUL educated and trained a whole generation of women union activists.

During the New Deal years, with WTUL member Eleanor Roosevelt, the league focused its attention on retaining the gains they had made and aiding women during the depression. They slowly became less involved with organizing and more focused on legislation. They were active in the passage of the Fair Labor Standards Act and Social Security. But they were never able to repair their relationship with organized labor. They remained neutral during the bitter labor rivalry between the AFL and the newly formed industrial unions of the Congress of Industrial Organizations (CIO). After World War II they drifted and, lacking resources and active members, closed their doors in 1950.

BIBLIOGRAPHY

Davis, Allen. "The Women's Trade Union League: Origins and Organization." *Labor History* 5, no. 1 (Winter 1964).

Dye, Nancy Schrom. *As Equals and as Sisters.* Columbia: University of Missouri Press, 1980.

Harris, Alice Kessler. *Out to Work.* New York: Oxford University Press, 1982.

Orleck, Annalese. *Common Sense and a Little Fire.* Chapel Hill: University of North Carolina Press, 1995.

Richard A Greenwald

See also **Labor; Suffrage: Woman's Suffrage; Trade Unions.**

WOOD ENGRAVING. The earliest images produced in British North America were relief cuts engraved on wood blocks or type metal by printers such as John Foster (1648–1681), and others who worked anonymously. During the colonial period and later, these cuts appeared in publications such as almanacs, primers, newspapers, and periodicals and on broadsides, government proclamations, currency, and advertising materials. Artisans and skilled engravers used knives to incise type metal or planks of wood cut with the grain for illustrations and decorative ornaments during the colonial and the Revolutionary War periods. These images were inexpensive to produce and decorative. The skill and the training of the engravers varied from almost none to expert. Even well known silversmiths such as Paul Revere (1735–1818) and James Turner (1722–1759) made cuts for newspapers and broadsides, in addition to engravings on copper for an elite audience.

In England during the last quarter of the eighteenth century, Thomas Bewick and others made relief cuts using the burin of an engraver on the end grain of dense wood, particularly boxwood. In New York, Alexander Anderson (1775–1870), a self-taught engraver, followed their lead, producing thousands of cuts over his seventy-five-year career. Changing technology led to the use of wood engravings as the basis for stereotyped plates that could be produced to order for printers and publishers across the nation. Anderson's cuts appeared in tract society publications and children's books issued by publishers in New York and other cities in the Northeast.

During the 1840s, the training and skill of wood engravers improved; their engravings after drawings by artists such as Felix Octavius Carr Darley (1822–1888) and John Gadsby Chapman (1808–1889) graced the pages of novels, drawing manuals, Bibles, and other publications. The widespread popularity of the pictorial press, beginning with *Ballou's Pictorial* in Boston and *Frank Leslie's Illustrated Newspaper* in New York in the 1850s, led to the proliferation of images. The circulation of the copiously illustrated *Harper's Weekly* reached over 100,000 in the 1860s, bringing reproductions of designs by Winslow Homer (1836–1910) and other artists to a sizeable portion of the literate public. Depictions of camp scenes of the Civil

War made details of that conflict vivid to Americans everywhere. In the 1870s, reproductive wood engraving reached its height in *The Aldine,* a fine-art journal with full-page reproductions of paintings by European and American artists. The wood engraver and historian William J. Linton (1812–1897) considered the engravings that he did for that journal to be the best of his career.

In the 1870s, artists' drawings were transferred to wood blocks photographically, changing the role of the engraver from interpreter of an artist's drawing to copyist. The so-called New School of Engraving was characterized by prints that reproduced drawings exactly using short white lines and cross-hatching as well as dots to simulate stippling. Linton and his followers preferred the old methodology, but they were challenged by others who preferred exact facsimiles. The advent of photoengraving a few years later rendered the controversy moot.

During the twentieth century, artists turned to woodcuts and wood engraving as an artistic medium. Artists such as Arthur Wesley Dow (1857–1922), Rockwell Kent (1882–1971), Clare Leighton (1901–1988), Thomas Nason (1889–1971), Rudolph Ruzicka (1883–1978), Blanche Lazell (1878–1956), Louis Schanker (1903–1981), and Leonard Baskin (1922–2000) have created relief prints of great interest and originality.

BIBLIOGRAPHY

Acton, David. *A Spectrum of Innovation: Color in American Printmaking, 1890–1960.* New York: Norton, 1990.

Linton, William J. *American Wood Engraving: A Victorian History.* Watkins Glen, N.Y.: American Life Foundation and Study Institute, 1976.

Reilly, Elizabeth Carroll. *A Dictionary of Colonial American Printers' Ornaments and Illustrations.* Worcester, Mass.: American Antiquarian Society, 1975.

Wakeman, Geoffrey. *Victorian Book Illustration: The Technical Revolution.* Newton Abbot, U.K.: David & Charles, 1973.

Georgia Brady Barnhill

See also **Printmaking.**

WOODSTOCK. The Woodstock Music and Art Fair took place in Bethel in upstate New York from 15 to 17 August 1969. Attended by 450,000 people, it is remembered as the high point of the "peace and love" ethos of the period, largely because the disaster that the overcrowding, bad weather, food shortages, supposed "bad acid" (LSD), and poor facilities presaged was somehow avoided. Woodstock was originally conceived as a money-making venture by producers John Roberts, Joel Rosen-

Woodstock. One small corner of Max Yasgur's field in Bethel, N.Y., the setting for the three-day 1969 festival, on the third day.
© CORBIS

man, Artie Kornfield, and Michael Lang. However, poor planning and happenstance forced them to admit most attendees for free. They were left with a debt of $1.3 million and a site that cost $100,000 to restore. Credit for the festival's success should go to the endurance of the attendees and to the likes of Wavy Gravy and the Hog Farmers, the West Coast "hippies" who organized food and medical support for the crowd.

Many rock and folk luminaries—including Joan Baez, the Grateful Dead, Ten Years After, Joe Cocker, The Band, Sly and the Family Stone, Janis Joplin, The Who, Jefferson Airplane, and Crosby, Stills, and Nash—graced the hastily constructed stage. Cameras and recording equipment captured most performances, the best of which were subsequently released on a number of successful Woodstock albums and featured in an Academy Award–winning three-hour movie, *Woodstock—Three Days of Peace and Music* (1970).

To avert the feared crowd difficulties, the music continued virtually around the clock, stopping only for the recurrent rainfall. Jimi Hendrix, Sunday's headliner, eventually played at 8.30 A.M. on Monday to a thinning audience. Musicologists subsequently described his blistering rendition of "The Star Spangled Banner" as a defining moment in rock history. Less often stated is the fact that the high fees that many of the artists demanded and the star treatment that they received significantly altered the ethos and the economics of the rock music industry. Attempting to cash in on Woodstock nostalgia, the producers subsequently staged two more "Woodstock" festivals. The 1994 twenty-fifth anniversary concert in Saugerties, New York, attracted a crowd of more than 300,000 and featured some of the original acts, along with more contemporary artists. Sponsored by the likes of Pepsi and MCI and with tickets costing $135 apiece, the event is remembered mostly for its obviously commercial intentions. Woodstock 1999, featuring six-dollar bottles of water, three days of ninety-degree heat, and artists such as Kid Rock, Insane Clown Posse, and Limp Bizkit, ended in violence, rioting, and arson, with numerous reports of sexual assaults.

BIBLIOGRAPHY

Curry, Jack. *Woodstock: The Summer of Our Lives.* New York: Weidenfeld and Nicolson, 1989.

Makower, Joel. *Woodstock: The Oral History.* New York: Doubleday, 1989.

Spitz, John. *Barefoot in Babylon: The Creation of the Woodstock Music Festival, 1969.* New York: Viking, 1989.

Rick Dodgson

See also **Counterculture; Music Festivals; Music Industry; Rock and Roll.**

WOOL GROWING AND MANUFACTURE.

English, Dutch, and Swedish settlers introduced sheep raising into the Atlantic colonies early in the seventeenth century, and the practice became a familiar part of their economy, particularly in the North. Household manufacture of wool was widespread; cards, spinning wheels, and looms were standard equipment in many homes. Sheep were unimproved, the wool coarse, and the homespun rude but serviceable. Fulling mills, auxiliaries of the home industry, appeared early. Itinerant weavers were numerous, and weaving shops existed in most towns, although colonials who could afford them still imported woolen goods from England. English policy discouraged the growth of large-scale wool manufacture in the colonies. The American Revolution spurred efforts to expand both wool growing and manufacture.

Sheep Raising and Wool Production

Between the Revolution and the Civil War, the character of the wool industry changed substantially. The introduction of many Spanish merino sheep in the early nineteenth century enabled growers to provide a fine wool suitable to the needs of an expanding manufacture. By the mid-nineteenth century, modifications in the breed had produced a larger and less delicate American merino that had a heavier fleece. Wool production moved westward, and by 1860 Ohio, Michigan, and California (where the Spanish had introduced sheep in 1769) were among the five leading wool-producing states. Although the manufacture of wool was widely diffused, the great bulk of it was still located in southern New England and in the Middle Atlantic states.

Wool growing has long been of diminishing importance in the U.S. economy. Stock sheep numbered 51 million in 1884 and only 15 million in 1973, and since 1961 the number has declined annually. In the Wool Act of 1954 Congress sought by means of price support to encourage the annual production of about 300 million pounds of shorn wool, but the industry never met the goal. Imports of raw wool regularly exceeded the domestic clip. For most of the twentieth century the sale of sheep was the chief source of income from sheep raising; in 1969 only one-quarter of the farm income derived from sheep came from wool. Breeding has reflected the changing emphasis. Although sheep are raised in all the states, about three-quarters of the stock sheep in the mid-1970s were in South Dakota, Texas, and the states of the Far West, where operations were on a larger scale than elsewhere. The development of man-made fibers substantially reduced the mill consumption of scoured wool per capita, and by 1971 it was only nine-tenths of a pound. The downward trend in wool production indicated the greater profitability of other economic activities, a predictable development in a populous, urbanized, and industrial country.

Wool Manufacturing

Despite the increase in American flocks, raw or manufactured foreign wool still accounted for most of that fiber consumed in the United States during the mid-1800s. Household manufacture steadily declined during the Industrial Revolution as hundreds of mills powered by water or steam sprang up and as transportation improved. By 1860 the manufacture of woolens represented the largest capital investment (in 1,260 establishments) within the industry, carpet manufacture was well established, and the worsted industry was a lusty infant. Imports were large, while the market for the domestic product was confined to the United States.

The CIVIL WAR brought to both growers and manufacturers an unprecedented demand and prosperity. With cotton in short supply in the North, civilian demand for woolens increased as military needs skyrocketed. Wool production soared, and a new merino craze developed, profitable to eastern breeders. Entrepreneurs built new mills, enlarged old ones, and turned cotton machinery to wool manufacture. The war's end found farms and factories with enlarged productive capacities and the government with a huge surplus of clothing.

After 1865 U.S. wool manufacture faced numerous challenges such as population growth, improved transportation, business cycles, changing demands and fashions, public trade policy, wars, foreign and domestic competition, and the development of increasing numbers of man-made fibers. An outstanding development during the fifty years after 1865 was the rise of the worsted industry to a position of dominance over the carded wool industry. The growth of the ready-to-wear clothing industry changed marketing methods. The average size of wool manufacturing plants increased, whereas the number declined sharply. Most of the small, scattered local mills ceased production. By 1914 the American Woolen Company (organized in 1899) controlled thirty-six manufacturing plants and produced more than half of menswear worsteds and woolens. That company and many others gave way in turn to new corporate structures.

After World War II the southern Atlantic states became major producers, and by the 1960s and 1970s their mills consumed more wool than those of New England. Imports were of major concern to the industry, and Japan became the leading exporter of woven wool fabrics to the United States during the 1960s and 1970s. American exports, although not negligible, represented a small part of U.S. mill output. The greatest threat to American wool manufacture in the twentieth century was competition from man-made fibers, the production of which became significant in the 1920s and increased enormously during the 1960s, leaving no branch of wool manufacture unaffected. By the 1970s the relative position of wool in the American world of carpets, yarns, knit goods, and woven fabrics was weaker than ever.

The Wool Industry and Trade Policy

Wool growers and manufacturers have been deeply involved in the perennial debate over the formulation of public trade policy. Protection from foreign competition has been the goal of both groups. Before the 1860s, growers and manufacturers did not cooperate because most

Wool. This 1941 photograph by Irving Rusinow shows a man using his own equipment to go from one small farm to another in Shelby County, Iowa, shearing the farmers' sheep. NATIONAL ARCHIVES AND RECORDS ADMINISTRATION

manufacturers opposed the imposition of wool duties. In 1864 the National Association of Wool Manufacturers was formed, and in 1865 the National Woolgrowers' Association was established. Because it represented both agricultural and manufacturing interests and because its political influence was widely distributed, the alliance successfully secured high duties on imports of both wool and woolens and, to a considerable extent, made the tariff schedule concerned with these duties "the keystone of the arch of protection." During the making of the Payne-Aldrich tariff (1909) and the years of debate that followed, Schedule K became the most publicized tariff schedule in U.S. history. In 1971, President Richard M. Nixon, under great pressure, negotiated agreements with Japan, Taiwan, South Korea, and Hong Kong limiting their exports of the manufactures of wool and man-made fibers to the United States. Although protection has played a significant role in the history of wool growing and manufacture, it has been only one of several major influences.

BIBLIOGRAPHY

Cole, Arthur Harrison. *The American Wool Manufacture.* Cambridge, Mass.: Harvard University Press, 1926.

Crockett, Norman L. *The Woolen Industry of the Midwest.* Lexington: University Press of Kentucky, 1970.

Molloy, Peter M., ed. *Homespun to Factory Made: Woolen Textiles in America, 1776–1876.* North Andover, Mass.: Merrimack Valley Textile Museum, 1977.

Wentworth, Edward Norris. *America's Sheep Trails: History, Personalities.* Ames: Iowa State College Press, 1948.

Harry James Brown / c. w.

See also **Carpet Manufacture; Industrial Revolution; Manufacturing, Household; Tariff; Textiles.**

WORK. Humans have always worked. Work was key to our biological development, shaping our bodies and sharpening our minds. One million years ago we first worked stones into tools and half a million years ago first worked with fire. For the last ten thousand years we have worked the land and for five thousand years have worked metals. Although we have always worked, we have not always held the same opinions about work. A brief survey of those cultures that have most influenced American opinions about work will make this clear and at the same time provide the perspective necessary for understanding the significance of work in American culture.

Ancients

Work was held in low esteem among those ancient cultures that have most influenced American culture. The ancient Jews, Greeks, and Romans all held work to be inferior to leisure. According to all three traditions, our original condition was leisurely. According to Genesis, Adam originally resided in Eden before sinning and being cast out by God "to till the ground whence he was taken." And according to the pagan poets, a leisurely age once existed but was also somehow lost. The ancients held their condition, a condition in which labor was the norm, to be inferior to the original condition of leisure. Further, conceptions of labor as divine punishment existed among the ancients. For example, according to the ancient Jewish tradition, we must all bear the burden of the punishment handed down for Adam's sin by God. And, according to the ancient Greek tradition, Sisyphus had to labor perpetually, pushing a boulder up an incline again and again, for his own transgression against Zeus. Further still, in addition to these religious reflections of the low esteem in which the ancients held work, there existed etymological reflections. For example, the ancient Greeks used one word (πόνος) to signify both "labor" and "pain." And they used one word (βάναυσος) to signify both "mechanic" and "vulgar." Finally, there existed political reflections of the low esteem in which the ancients held work. All were dependent upon work in ancient times. But not all worked. Most did but some were at leisure. Those who worked were held to be inferior to those who did not. The latter ruled the former.

Medievals

Amidst the ruins of the Roman Empire, smaller and more introspective communities arose. Those who worked the land were not slaves but serfs. Pagan religions gave way to Christianity. And the church gained substantial worldly power. This last development led to a pervasive duality. On the one hand, as in ancient times, there were nobles that owned land and ruled. On the other hand, in contrast to ancient times, there was an autonomous church that also owned land and ruled. And so a political duality ex-

isted. For example, a serf might owe allegiance to a noble for land and protection in this world. Yet he might also owe allegiance to the church for the promise of transcendence of death and avoidance of Hell in the next. In addition to this political duality, a cultural duality existed. On the one hand, as in ancient times, work (that is, manual labor, skilled labor) was held to be inferior to the activities of noble leisure (war, politics, culture). On the other hand, in contrast to ancient times, work was also held to be inferior to sacred activities (prayer). For example, a young nobleman might seek worldly power and honor while a young peasant might be drawn to monastic seclusion and discipline (silence, poverty, chastity).

Moderns

Work came to be held in unprecedented esteem during the modern times, as it was elevated by both Protestant theologians and philosophers. Martin Luther (German theologian and reformer, 1483–1546) attacked the medieval ranking of work as inferior to monasticism, asserting that devotion to God did not require seclusion from secular activities. John Calvin (French theologian and reformer, 1509–1564) also attacked the medieval ranking of work, asserting that work glorified God by improving the world and the individual. Francis Bacon (British philosopher and statesman, 1561–1626) attacked medieval education, criticizing it for encouraging a love of sloth and privacy in his *Advancement of Learning* (1605). In *Leviathan* (1651), Thomas Hobbes (British philosopher, 1588–1679) attacked the medieval status of leisure as the original human condition, reasoning that humans originally led not Edenic lives of leisure but lives that were poor, nasty, brutish, and short. And John Locke (British philosopher, 1632–1704) attacked the medieval political order, positing that the world belonged not to leisured nobles or praying monks but to the industrious in his *Two Treatises on Government* (1690). Such opinions and the habits they engendered came to be known collectively as the Protestant work ethic centuries later, after the publication of *The Protestant Ethic and the Spirit of Capitalism* (1920) by Max Weber (German economist and social historian, 1864–1920). The Protestant work ethic was the antecedent of the American work ethic as America, in its youth, was predominantly Protestant and British.

American Work Ethic

Had the native American population been assimilated rather than eliminated by germs and steel, the American work ethic might have emerged as more of a hybrid between European and Native American opinions about work. Or had the Spanish Armada not been rebuffed in 1588 or had the French not been defeated on the Plains of Abraham in 1759, the American work ethic might have reflected Catholic opinions about work more and Protestant opinions about work less. But the Native American population was decimated and Catholic Spain and France eventually surrendered, ceded, or sold most of their territorial claims in North America. And so Protestant Britain became the dominant power in America. Many of those who came to America during colonial times were Calvinist (English Puritans, Scot-Irish Presbyterians, French Huguenots), and the American work ethic was at birth if not Calvinist simply then at least Calvinistic. In contrast to ancients who tended to hold work to be inferior to leisure, and in contrast to the medievals who tended to hold work to be inferior to monasticism, Calvin held work to be sacred. Like the ancients and medievals, Calvin too held work to simply be a means. But he held work to be the highest sort of means. He held work to be a means by which to improve the world to the glory of God and a means by which to improve oneself so as to prove oneself worthy of being saved by God. Even as opinions of work became less otherworldly—in other words, as the improvement of the world and of oneself became ends in themselves—the American work ethic remained at least Calvinistic insofar as it remained progressive, individualistic, and egalitarian. Progress depends on work, and so one should work for progress—an implication of this being that one should work as long as there is work to be done and not simply as long as necessity requires. Individually we are saved and only individually, for one cannot be saved by priestly forgiveness, and so one should primarily be concerned with oneself. And all should work. There should be no leisured class, whether a class of nobles or a class of monks. Leisure, once held to be the precondition for the highest things, should be recognized as the precondition for the lowest and thus should be discouraged. And all kinds of work contributing to the progress of the world should be esteemed. Moneymaking, which for millennia was viewed with suspicion, should be appreciated for its potential contributions to world progress. And manual labor, which for millennia was viewed as slavish, should be appreciated for its utility as discipline against sin and thus contribution to individual progress.

The opinions from which the American work ethic was derived were born in the shadows of the Roman ruins and the Christian castles of Europe, but they took root and flourished fully in America, in the absence of a landed nobility and the medieval church. There was infinite progress to be made in America, where work was more highly esteemed in part because there was a surplus not of workers but of work. Although those things that were honored in Europe were honored still, in America they were honored less. Land ownership was less of a point of distinction, for land was cheap and nearly all owned land. The finest tailors were thousands of miles away. Even then, there were not royal courts in which to make grand appearances. It could take months for news to reach Europe and more months still for monarchical praise and blame to be heard. In many ways America was neither a monarchy, aristocracy, or democracy but a work-tocracy. Whereas audiences once concerned themselves with leisured nobles (Achilles, Odysseus, Lancelot), Americans have concerned themselves with workers (Tom Joad, Willy Loman, Travis Bickle). And whereas leisured nobles once ruled almost exclusively (Alexander the Great, Julius Caesar, Henry V), America has been ruled by a canal boat pilot, storekeeper, and school principal (James A. Garfield, Harry S. Truman, Lyndon B. Johnson). No ancient emperor or medieval king ever made the assertion that President Theodore Roosevelt did, that "far and away the best prize that life offers is the chance to work hard at work worth doing" (Labor Day speech, 1903).

At no time have Americans been unified in their estimation of work, however. Even in the beginning, the American work ethic varied from occupation to occupation (farmer-craftsman), region to region (North-South), age to age (industrial-postindustrial), culture to culture (German Protestant–Irish Catholic), and individual to individual. Some have been openly critical of the American work ethic (Henry David Thoreau). Innumerable variations on the work ethic have existed, but there are perhaps six that best manifest what the American work ethic was, is, and will be. Three were prominent by the time the Declaration of Independence was signed in 1776 (Agrarian, Craft, Southern). A fourth emerged soon thereafter at the beginning of the nineteenth century (Entrepreneurial). And a fifth came of age at the end of the nineteenth century and dominated the twentieth (Industrial).

Agrarian Ethic

As in ancient and medieval times, most worked the land in 1776. Yet most of those who worked the land were neither slaves nor serfs. Most were free and independent, working land that they themselves owned. Free and independent farmers were widespread and highly esteemed. Farming in America offered a life of relative self-sufficiency. If one was willing to depend on nature and one's own labor, one could reduce one's odious dependence on other human beings. Most believed farming to instill virtue. The rigors of rural life were thought to have a chastening effect. Thomas Jefferson (author of the Declaration of Independence, president of the United States, and scientist), who was not a yeoman farmer himself, declared that if God had a chosen people it was those who labor in the earth, that genuine virtue was to be found in their breasts, and that their way of life was the way of life antithetical to corruption. He hoped that yeomen farmers would be the ruling class far into the future. Such opinions contrasted sharply with those of a more ancient scientist, Aristotle, who considered farmers to be incapable of genuine virtue and political rule because they lacked sufficient leisure. And such opinions contrasted sharply with those of the medieval church, for the church then taught those that worked the land to be obedient, not independent, and that priestly forgiveness, not toil, led to salvation. Even as America became less rural and more urban, the Agrarian Ethic remained a powerful cultural force.

Craft Ethic

As in ancient and medieval times, some were also craftsman in 1776. Although craftsmen were perhaps not as independent or as highly esteemed as farmers, they enjoyed a relatively high status in America. American craftsman tended to be more independent, less subject to poverty, and more admired than their European counterparts. Paul Revere was a silversmith. Benjamin Franklin (signer of the Declaration of Independence, author, and scientist) was himself a printer and included in his *Autobiography* a list of thirteen virtues indicative of those characteristics held in esteem by colonial craftsmen (temperance, silence, order, resolution, frugality, industry, sincerity, justice, moderation, cleanliness, tranquility, chastity, humility). This list differed markedly from the moral virtues discussed by Aristotle in his *Nicomachean Ethics* (courage, temperance, liberality, magnificence, magnanimity, ambitiousness, patience, friendliness, truthfulness, wittiness, justice). And it differed markedly from the teaching of the medieval church insofar as, among others, faith and charity and hope were absent. Franklin published numerous aphorisms that reinforced his thirteen virtues in *Poor Richard's Almanack* (1732–1757). Industry, for example, was reinforced with aphorisms such as "Early to bed and early to rise makes a man healthy, wealthy, and wise," "Never leave that till to-morrow which you can do to-day," and "Little strokes fell great oaks."

Such aphorisms were one means by which the American work ethic was sustained. Such means were necessary because virtue tended toward vice. Ancient virtue, for example, bred courage. Courage bred a capacity for conquest. A capacity for conquest bred pursuit of empire. And pursuit of empire eventually led to destructive failure or corruptive success. Similarly, the Protestant work ethic engendered industriousness. Industriousness engendered a capacity for wealth. A capacity for wealth engendered pursuit of wealth. And pursuit of wealth tended to lead eventually to a forgetting of the two Calvinistic purposes of work: work as discipline against sin and work as glorification of God through improvement of the world. In other words, work tended to wealth, which tended to idleness and idolatry. Hence aphorisms aimed at these particular tendencies entered the common language. For example, "Idle hands do the devil's work" and "God helps those who help themselves." John Wesley (founder of Methodism and Anglican missionary in America) recognized these tendencies and warned against them. "What way can we take that our money-making may not sink us to the nethermost hell? There is one way, and there is no other under heaven. If those who gain all they can and save all they can will also give all they can, then, the more they gain the more they will grow in grace and the more treasure they will lay up in heaven." But at no time did American farmers or craftsmen, for whom frugality was a cardinal virtue, keep themselves poor by giving away excess wealth. And, ever so slowly, the American work ethic became less suspicious of idleness and more idolatrous, less devout and more religiously devoted to material success as an end in itself. Although some do continue to maintain a decidedly Calvinistic disposition toward pleasure, living a joyless quest for joy by accumulating wealth but not using it. For example, retirees dying on mattresses filled with millions and CEOs with no time or energy for the pleasures their money might buy.

Southern Ethic

The Pilgrims who crossed the Atlantic Ocean aboard the *Mayflower* in 1620 were not the first to found a lasting settlement in the British colonies. A less Calvinistic group of colonists had founded Jamestown in 1607. The differences between these two colonies, Plymouth Colony located north of the Hudson River and Jamestown located south of the Hudson River, foreshadowed the most historically significant geographic variation on the American work ethic. In both the North and the South, most work was performed by yeomen farmers, craftsman, indentured whites, and black slaves. And although most white farmers in the South owned no slaves, there was a much greater reliance on black slavery in the South. In the southern variation on the American work ethic, work was, to a degree, considered not sacred but slavish. And there was a greater appreciation of leisure. Although no landed, hereditary, leisured class ever took root in America, southern opinions about work within the uppermost class were in many ways closer to those of the ancients and medievals than the moderns insofar as they held work more as something to be endured and leisure as something to be appreciated. Yet a fully leisured class never developed. Had the southern climate been milder, had primogeniture been established, had the Civil War not broken out (1861), or had the degree of destruction been less, the Southern Ethic might have developed more fully and balanced the Calvinistic elements of the American work ethic to a greater degree. But the South lost the Civil War and consequentially much of its influence. From colonial times until the Civil War, the South was in many ways an equal to the North. A majority of the leading generals during the American Revolution and a majority of the early presidents were from the South (George Washington, Thomas Jefferson, James Madison). But the victory of the North was so devastating that it took nearly a century for the region to recover. And the southern elite, those who held the least Calvinistic opinions about work, never did recover. And so the American work ethic came to reflect the Calvinistic opinions of New England more and the southern opinions about work less. Remnants of the Southern Ethic remain, of course. For example, the pace is still somewhat slower in the South. Yet the differences are not as substantial as they once were. Those in the South do basically the same kinds of work and hold basically the same opinions about work as people in every other part of the country.

Entrepreneurial Ethic

After the Revolutionary War, there was a push westward. Most were still farmers and some were still craftsman but nearly all were becoming more commercial. Enterprises were being undertaken. Roads and canals were being built.

Crops from west of the Alleghenies were feeding the growing urban populations in the East or being shipped to the markets of Europe. Visiting America in the first half of the nineteenth century, Alexis de Tocqueville (French political writer, 1805–1859), perhaps the keenest observer of American society, suggested that Americans approached life as a game of chance or a battle. This gambling spirit, prevalent on the frontier, was not as evident among the earliest farmers and craftsman of New England who tended to be more cautious, to view gain without pain suspiciously, and to prefer frugality to spending money to make money. And gambles often depended on or resulted in debt and dependency. Yet these traits were also accompanied by a certain strength of soul, as families frequently rebounded after losing all.

The miraculous element of the Entrepreneurial Ethic was widely celebrated, the making of something out of nothing. One such rags-to-riches story was that of Andrew Carnegie (industrialist and philanthropist) who emigrated at age thirteen from Scotland, began as a bobbin boy in a cotton mill, and ended as one of the richest men in America. As waves of immigrants came to America in the nineteenth century, many poor and without any particular skills, rags to riches became the ideal. Immigrants during the nineteenth century were less likely to speak English and more likely to settle in cities with those of similar backgrounds. Agrarian independence was less attainable for later immigrants as good land became scarcer and commercial farming required more capital. Those without land settling in cities became almost entirely dependent on wages and thus on the health of the American economy. And as many immigrants arrived without particular skills, the independence of the craftsman also became less attainable. Although most prefer to work for others, some do still work for themselves. Such small business owners perhaps best typify the Entrepreneurial Ethic today.

Industrial Ethic

In the beginning of the twentieth century, a majority worked either directly or indirectly in industry. Those on factory floors and those supporting the manufacturing process from offices performed increasingly specialized work. The independent farmer was a manager, a laborer, a mechanic, a buyer, and a seller whose work varied from season to season and was not timed. The independent craftsman and the entrepreneur performed a similar variety of tasks. This lack of specialization cultivated the intelligence. But work in industry, whether work performed by a laborer on the floor of a factory or work performed in the offices of a factory, was specialized. Efficiency was pursued by managers such as Frederick W. Taylor (industrial engineer, 1856–1915) who developed time and motion studies in order to increase efficiency. Reliability, consistency, and an ability to focus on repetitive tasks for long periods of time were the sorts of virtues that became part of the Industrial Ethic.

American Work Ethic in the Twenty-First Century

A variety of developments will likely shape the American work ethic in the coming century. Cultural diversity is higher than it has ever been. Political rights of racial minorities and women are now recognized. Economically America is less industrial and more service oriented. And perhaps of the greatest significance for the future, Americans now have a decidedly non-Calvinistic view of leisure and pleasure. Like the ancients, Americans now appreciate leisure, although in a way very different from the ancients and the medievals. Americans work hard and play hard. And unlike the Calvinists, Americans are more favorably disposed to pleasures of all kinds, performing work with the intention and expectation of enjoying the fruits of their labor.

BIBLIOGRAPHY

American Social History Project. *Who Built America? Working People and the Nation's Economy, Politics, Culture, and Society.* Volume 1: *From Conquest and Colonization to 1877.* Volume 2: *From the Gilded Age to the Present.* Edited by Bruce C. Levine et al. New York: Pantheon Books, 2001.

Applebaum, Herbert. *The American Work Ethic and the Changing Work Force.* Westport, Conn.: Greenwood Press, 1998.

Bernstein, Paul. *American Work Values: Their Origin and Development.* Albany: State University of New York Press, 1997.

Gutman, Herbert G. *Work, Culture and Society in Industrializing America: Essays in American Working-Class and Social History.* New York: Knopf, 1975.

Innes, Stephen, ed. *Work and Labor in Early America.* Chapel Hill: University of North Carolina Press, 1988.

———. *Creating the Commonwealth: The Economic Culture of Puritan New England.* New York: Norton, 1995.

Kolchin, Peter. *American Slavery, 1619–1877.* New York: Hill and Wang, 1993.

Maccoby, Michael, and Terzi, Katherine A. "What Happened to the Work Ethic?" In *The Work Ethic in Business.* Edited by W. Michael Hoffman and Thomas J. Wyly. Cambridge, Mass.: Oelgeschlager, Gunn, and Hain, 1981.

Matthaei, Julie A. *An Economic History of Women in America: Women's Work, the Sexual Division of Labor, and the Development of Capitalism.* New York: Schocken, 1982.

Rodgers, Daniel T. *The Work Ethic in Industrial America, 1950–1920.* Chicago: University of Chicago Press, 1978.

Travis Haglock

See also **Calvinism;** *Democracy in America;* **Labor; Protestantism.**

WORKERS' COMPENSATION is a system that requires employers to provide workers who suffer job-related injuries (and fatalities) with medical treatment and monetary compensation to replace lost income. Compensation laws were first adopted in western Europe in the late 1800s. The first workers' compensation laws to pass legal muster in the United States were enacted in 1911, and by 1920 all but five states had adopted them. The system arose due to the breakdown of its predecessor, the negligence system of liability, under which employers were required to exercise "due care" in protecting workers from danger, but could escape liability for an accident by persuading the courts that the employee had assumed the ordinary risks associated with the job, that a coworker had caused the accident, or that the worker himself had not exercised due care. In practice, the negligence system of liability meant that payment levels were low and uncertain—in the early twentieth century, roughly 40 percent of families received nothing after fatal accidents, and few families received benefits exceeding the deceased worker's annual earnings. In addition, rapid industrialization made the American workplace about the most dangerous in the world. Many states' courts became unwilling to accept the employers' standard defenses, and during the twentieth century's first decade, many states passed legislation barring the use of these defenses. This caused a crisis as employers' accident insurance premiums soared yet many workers still received minimal payments.

With the adoption of workers' compensation laws most of this uncertainty disappeared. Employers (or their insurers) were required to pay standard benefits spelled out by law. Payments generally replaced about one-half to two-thirds of injured workers' lost wages and employers wound up paying about 75 to 200 percent more to families of accident victims. Because each employer's insurance premiums became linked to its accident costs, employers gained a powerful incentive to improve workplace safety and accident rates fell—except in industries like coal mining, where workers could not be closely supervised and where the new, higher accident benefits meant that workers bore less of an injury's cost. However, employers also benefited from workers' compensation, despite their substantially increased insurance premiums. Employers' uncertainties fell, and their new costs were generally shifted to employees in the form of lower wages—except among unionized workers. In essence, workers were forced to buy insurance through their employers.

By 1940, about three-quarters of workers were covered by workers' compensation, a figure that exceeded 90 percent by the 1990s. For decades, workers' compensation costs were about 1 percent of covered payroll. Then, beginning in the early 1970s, costs began to increase, exceeding 2 percent in the early 1990s. The increase was driven by rising medical costs and the expansion of disability compensation to cover a wider range of workplace injuries and occupational diseases (such as back pains and carpal tunnel syndrome), despite falling rates of injury, illness, and fatalities. After peaking in the early 1990s, costs (as a percent of payroll) fell about 40 percent due to declining accident rates, active management of medical costs, more efficient return-to-work programs, and tightening eligibility standards.

BIBLIOGRAPHY

Fishback, Price V., and Shawn Everett Kantor. *A Prelude to the Welfare State: The Origins of Workers' Compensation.* Chicago: University of Chicago Press, 2000.

Robert Whaples

See also **Employers' Liability Laws; Insurance.**

WORKINGMEN'S PARTY. The Workingmen's Party was established in 1829 in NEW YORK CITY. It advocated the abolition of debtors' prison, lien laws for construction laborers, a ten-hour working day, and universal education. Under the leadership of the American reformer Fanny Wright and her young protégé, Robert Dale Owen, the movement spread rapidly. The agnostic teachings of Owen and Wright antagonized many people, however. The abandonment of the Tammany opposition to the mechanic's lien law and to the repeal of imprisonment for debt, together with the formation of the Whig Workingmen's Party in New York City, hastened the end of the Workingmen's Party.

BIBLIOGRAPHY

Foner, Philip S. *History of the Labor Movement in the United States.* New York: International Publishers, 1975.

Wilentz, Sean. *Chants Democratic: New York City and the Rise of the American Working Class, 1788–1850.* New York: Oxford University Press, 1984.

A. C. Flick / A. G.

See also **Debt, Imprisonment for; Jacksonian Democracy; Labor Parties; Tammany Hall.**

WORKS PROGRESS ADMINISTRATION. When he assumed the presidency, Franklin Roosevelt defied the insistence by his predecessor, Herbert Hoover, on maintaining the traditional taboo against the "dole." Instead, he created the Federal Emergency Relief Agency (FERA) with authority to make direct cash payments to those with no other means of support. However, both Roosevelt and Harry Hopkins, the former social worker he chose to head FERA, preferred work relief that would provide recipients the self-esteem of earning their keep and taxpayers the satisfaction of knowing they were getting something for their money. In that spirit the Civil Works Administration (CWA) replaced FERA in the winter of 1933 and soon employed over 2 million persons on roads, buildings, and parks. Despite the program's success, Roosevelt worried that the CWA's policy of paying wages equivalent to those in the private sector would make it too expensive to rescue many of the millions of unemployed. He turned then to Congress for something that would offer subsistence wages and thus a motivation to find permanent employment.

On 8 April 1935, the Emergency Relief Appropriations Act granted the president's request for $4.8 billion to fund the Works Progress Administration (WPA), the largest relief program in American history. Projects were supposed to have a nonpolitical social value and not compete with private enterprise. However, politics was a factor because state and local jurisdictions controlled the choice of almost all projects except those for the arts. Subsequent legislation heightened concerns by requiring Senate approval for any WPA official earning more than $5,000 a year. Yet, even with the patronage appointments this system facilitated and some misuse of funds, the WPA managed to do useful work with low overhead.

The main thrust of the WPA projects had to be directed toward semiskilled and unskilled citizens, whom the Great Depression had hit the hardest. There followed a major effort in the construction of public facilities that left a permanent WPA stamp on the landscape. By 1941, the agency had invested $11.3 billion in 8 million relief workers who built such diverse projects as 1,634 schools, 105 airports, 3,000 tennis courts, 3,300 storage dams, 103 golf courses, and 5,800 mobile libraries.

Unlike the traditional relief program focus on manual labor, the WPA sought to fit tasks to recipients' job experience on a broadly inclusive scale. A Women's Division offered suitable tasks and equal pay and, when it combined with the Professional Division, gave women influence beyond their 12 to 19 percent enrollment. The WPA also inspired the black Urban League to declare that discrimination had been kept to a minimum. The 350,000 blacks employed annually constituted 15 percent of all persons in the program, a percentage half again as great as the number of blacks in society, though less than their proportion of the unemployed. The WPA Education Program raised many thousands of black recipients to literacy and trained thousands more to be skilled craftsmen and teachers.

Following Hopkins's dictum that artists have to eat like everyone else, the WPA offered a place where artists could make use of their gifts. The Federal Theatre Project, headed by an adventuresome Vassar professor named Hallie Flanagan, entertained 30 million people with performances ranging from traditional classics to "Living Newspaper" depictions of current issues and vaudeville shows traveling in caravans to the hinterland. Painters decorated public buildings with murals; and the Federal Writers Project informed Americans about their country by producing city, state, and regional guides. The arts projects also pioneered integration. WPA orchestras performed works by black composers; the Theatre Project mounted operas and plays with all-black casts, and the Writers Project gave aspiring black writers like Richard Wright and Sterling Brown the chance to develop.

The WPA generated opposition as well. Cynics derided the program as a boondoggle for loafers. Other critics feared that the huge WPA workforce would become a pressure group able to control policies and elections. Their fears were inflamed when Hopkins insisted that the WPA should be enlarged and made permanent, given that the program never enrolled more than 3.2 million of the 8 to 15 million unemployed.

World War II ended the argument over the WPA. On 30 June 1943, with wartime production absorbing most of the unemployed, Roosevelt gave WPA its "honorable discharge," and three months later the agency mailed its last checks. Never since has there been a significant federal job creation program. Instead, the government has sought to resolve unemployment through fostering opportunity in the private sector for specific hard-core groups. The passage of the Employment Act of 1946, which had been proposed as a way of ensuring a decent living for all, emerged with power only to encourage that goal. Policymakers have further hedged their commitment by accepting the view that an unemployment rate of 4 to 6 percent is a hedge against the inflation that would result if labor were a scarce, expensive commodity.

BIBLIOGRAPHY

Brock, William R. *Welfare, Democracy, and the New Deal.* New York: Cambridge University Press, 1988.

Harris, Jonathan. *Federal Art and National Culture: The Politics of Identity in New Deal America.* New York: Cambridge University Press, 1995.

Hopkins, June. *Harry Hopkins: Sudden Hero, Brash Reformer.* New York: St. Martin's Press, 1999.

Alan Lawson

See also **New Deal.**

WORLD BANK, formally known as the International Bank for Reconstruction and Development, was primarily the brainchild of Henry Dexter White, the assistant secretary of the Treasury during Franklin Roosevelt's third administration. Wary of the lessons of the 1930s, White was convinced that private investors would be unable to provide adequately for postwar European reconstruction. Accordingly, White envisioned the bank as an institution to guarantee foreign securities and, if necessary, loan money directly to governments.

Plans for creating the bank existed as early as 1942. Alongside the INTERNATIONAL MONETARY FUND (IMF), the bank came into being during the BRETTON WOODS CONFERENCE in July 1944. Forty-four nations (twenty-seven of which were considered as "developing" countries) attended the conference, but the United States, Britain, France, and Canada primarily directed it. While the IMF was the outcome of intense negotiations between the United States and Britain, the bank's creation was largely controlled by America. Once established, the bank started with a $7.6 billion treasury, nearly all of which was fronted by the United States, to help rebuild war-torn Europe as well as aid in the development of Africa, Latin America, and Asia.

When it became clear that the needs of postwar reconstruction would far exceed the resources of the bank, and as the MARSHALL PLAN took over the job, the focus of the bank shifted to Third World development. The shift in lending to developing countries was far from smooth, however, as many countries could not afford the bank's interest rates, its financial resources were too small, and its charter forbade making direct loans to private enterprises. To offset these problems the International Finance Corporation (1956) and the International Development Association (1960) were created as affiliates of the bank, and it began to take its present-day shape.

The bank obtains its resources in three ways: money invested by member countries, issuing bonds, and net earnings on the bank's assets. In 2002 there were 138 members of the World Bank Group, each of which must also be a member of the IMF. Each member acts as a shareholder but, due to their size and resources, the United States, Japan, Germany, France, and the United Kingdom dominate policymaking. Headquartered in Washington, D.C., the bank concentrates on issuing loans for economic development in Africa, Asia, the Middle East, and Latin America. It invests money in projects designed to create stable, sustainable, equitable growth in developing countries. Project lending makes money available for tasks such as natural resource development. Loans can also be made to an entire sector of a country's economy—agriculture, for example—or can be designed to aid in reorganizing a country's institutions to orient their policies toward free trade. Finally, loans are made to temporarily relieve debt crisis.

Until the presidency of Robert McNamara (1968–1981) the bank showed little concern with poverty itself, but McNamara redefined the idea of "development" to include the relief of poverty. While critics charge that the bank has actually done little to alleviate long-term poverty, and while the bank itself recognizes that the tasks it sets for itself are daunting, its motto is "Our Dream is a World Free of Poverty."

BIBLIOGRAPHY

Brown, Bartram, S. *The United States and the Politicization of the World Bank: Issues of International Law and Policy.* London: Kegan Paul, 1991; New York: Routledge, 1992.

George, Susan, and Fabrizio Sabelli. *Faith and Credit: The World Bank's Secular Empire.* Boulder, Colo.: Westview Press, 1994.

Gwin, Catherine. *U.S. Relations with the World Bank, 1945–1992.* Washington, D.C.: Brookings Institution, 1994.

Kapur, Devesh, John Lewis, and Richard Webb. *The World Bank: Its First Half Century.* Washington, D.C.: Brookings Institution, 1997.

Erin Black

See also **International Monetary Fund.**

WORLD COURT. *See* **International Court of Justice.**

WORLD ECONOMIC CONFERENCE. In June 1933 representatives of the leading industrial nations met in London to discuss a collective international response to the Great Depression. The European nations, especially France, proposed immediate agreement on currency stabilization under a gold standard to prevent rampant inflation. Although he had long supported Wilsonian internationalism, President Franklin Roosevelt feared making any diplomatic agreement that might limit his future policy options in the event of a worsening depression. The administration therefore refused to agree to currency stabilization, pushing instead for tariff reduction. Unable to reach a compromise settlement, the conference adjourned without having reached any major agreements.

BIBLIOGRAPHY

Dallek, Robert. *Franklin D. Roosevelt and American Foreign Policy, 1932–1945.* New York: Oxford University Press, 1979.

Leuchtenburg, William E. *Franklin D. Roosevelt and the New Deal, 1932–1940.* New York: Harper and Row, 1963.

Jeannette P. Nichols / A. G.

See also **France, Relations with; Great Depression; New Deal; Tariff.**

WORLD TRADE CENTER, a seven-building complex that was located on a sixteen-acre site in lower Manhattan in New York City. The Port Authority of New York and New Jersey financed the $958 million cost of construction. The architect Minoru Yamasaki designed the two 110-story towers (numbers 1 and 2 World Trade) in the International Style; the Twin Towers, as they were called, were to be the tallest buildings in the world, a record they held in 1973. To achieve that height, the engineering firm of Worthington-Skilling recommended a tube structure in which columns on the exterior walls, and the inner core of the skyscrapers, bore the gravity load. A grill of lightweight steel trusses connecting the perimeter and core supported the floors. Given the proximity of the Twin Towers to two major airports, each tower was built to withstand the impact of a Boeing 707 aircraft.

Relying on the perimeter and core columns to provide vertical support created 10 million square feet of open commercial space, which was leased to import and export businesses, government agencies, financial firms, and restaurants. Groundbreaking occurred in 1966; tenants moved into the World Trade Center in December 1970. The last building in the complex, 7 World Trade, a forty-seven story building, was completed in 1985.

On 23 February 1993, a truck bomb tore through an underground parking garage beneath the Vista Hotel (3 World Trade), killing six people. The explosion produced a crater six stories deep and destroyed lateral supports throughout the damaged area. As a result of the bombing, building modifications were introduced to improve evacuation, with tenants receiving evacuation training, and ad-

World Trade Center. This 1973 photograph by Wil Blanche views the newly completed Twin Towers—for a year, the tallest buildings in the world—from the south, along West Street.
<small>NATIONAL ARCHIVES AND RECORDS ADMINISTRATION</small>

ditional fire command centers were established in the lobbies of the Twin Towers. On 11 September 2001, two hijacked Boeing 767 commercial airliners were flown into the Twin Towers, causing the collapse of both skyscrapers; 2,830 people, including 403 emergency personnel, died.

The Federal Emergency Management Agency (FEMA) led the effort in trying to determine the progression of the collapse, a task complicated by the removal of the beams to recycling centers and scrapyards during the recovery effort. The prevailing hypothesis is that the impact of the airliners sheared off the fireproofing on the trusses, which softened in the subsequent blaze; jet fuel pouring into the elevator shafts spread the fires to lower decks. With the integrity of the sagging floors compromised, it is believed that an unsupportable gravity load was redistributed to the core columns, leading to total structural failure. The damage of the initial impact was also being assessed.

Eight surrounding buildings either partially or totally collapsed that day, crushed by falling debris (3 World Trade) or gutted by fire (7 World Trade). Discussions about the future use of the site, referred to as "Ground Zero"—whether it should be dedicated solely as a memorial or reopened for mixed-use purposes—were ongoing at the end of 2002.

BIBLIOGRAPHY

Federal Emergency Management Agency. *World Trade Center Building Performance Study: Data Collection, Preliminary Observations, and Recommendations.* New York: Greenhorne and O'Mara, 2002.

Gillespie, Angus Kress. *Twin Towers: The Life of New York City's World Trade Center.* New Brunswick, N.J.: Rutgers University Press, 1999.

Seabrook, John. "The Tower Builder." *New Yorker* (19 Nov. 2001): 64–73.

Tristan Hope Kirvin

See also **New York City; 9/11 Attack.**

WORLD TRADE CENTER BOMBING, 1993.

On 26 February 1993, a powerful truck bomb was detonated in the underground parking garage of the World Trade Center in New York City. The blast blew a large hole through several floors. Six people were killed and scores wounded.

Searching through the rubble, federal investigators were able to locate a small piece of the rental truck that was used to transport the bomb. This critical clue led investigators to Mohammed Salameh and the discovery of a terrorist network operating in New York City. The investigation uncovered a vast conspiracy to target various New York City landmarks, including the United Nations, federal installations, and parts of the city infrastructure. Investigators also discovered a plan to bomb U.S. aircraft flying between Asia and the United States. Numerous suspects were arrested and charged with participating in the bombing and broader conspiracy. Ramzi Yousef was captured in Pakistan and extradited to the United States on the charge of masterminding the bombing. Omar Abdel Rahman, a fundamentalist Islamic cleric living in New York City, was also charged as a prominent co-conspirator.

The suspects were brought to trial in the federal district court for the Southern District of New York. Their efforts to challenge the indictments were denied by the court. In May 1994, four suspects were convicted for their role in the bombing and sentenced to 240 years in prison. In January 1996, ten other suspects, including Abdel Rahman, received heavy jail terms for their roles in the conspiracy. Two other suspects, including Yousef, were convicted and sentenced in 1998 to 240 years in prison for their role in the bombing. Yousef was also sentenced for his role in the 1994 bombing of a Philippines Airlines plane, which killed one passenger and crippled the aircraft. He was fined $4.5 million and ordered to pay $250 million in restitution to the victims.

BIBLIOGRAPHY

Mylroie, Laurie. "The World Trade Center Bomb—Who is Ramzi Yousef?" *National Interest* 42 (Winter 1995–1996): 3.

Reeve, Simon. *The New Jackals: Ramzi Yousef, Osama bin Laden, and the Future of Terrorism.* Boston: Northeastern University Press, 1999.

William J. Aceves

See also **New York City; Terrorism.**

WORLD WAR I. The United States did not enter World War I until April 1917, although the conflict had begun in August 1914. After an intense period of military buildup and imperial competition, war broke out in Europe between Germany and Austria-Hungary (the Central Powers) and Britain, France, and Russia (the Allies). Turkey quickly joined the Central Powers and Italy joined the Allies in 1915.

Prelude to Involvement

Immediately, President Woodrow Wilson issued a declaration of neutrality. He was committed to maintaining open use of the Atlantic for trade with all the European belligerents. However, British naval supremacy almost eliminated American trade with Germany while shipments to the Allies soared. To counter this trend, German U-boats (submarines) torpedoed U.S. merchant vessels bound for Allied ports. In May 1915, Germans sunk the British passenger ship *Lusitania*, killing 128 Americans. Strong protest from Wilson subdued the submarine campaign, but it would emerge again as the war ground on and became more desperate. In late January 1917, Germany announced it would destroy all ships heading to Britain. Although Wilson broke off diplomatic ties with Germany, he still hoped to avert war by arming merchant vessels as a deterrent. Nevertheless, Germany began sinking American ships immediately.

In February 1917, British intelligence gave the United States government a decoded telegram from Germany's foreign minister, Arthur Zimmerman, that had been intercepted en route to his ambassador to Mexico. The

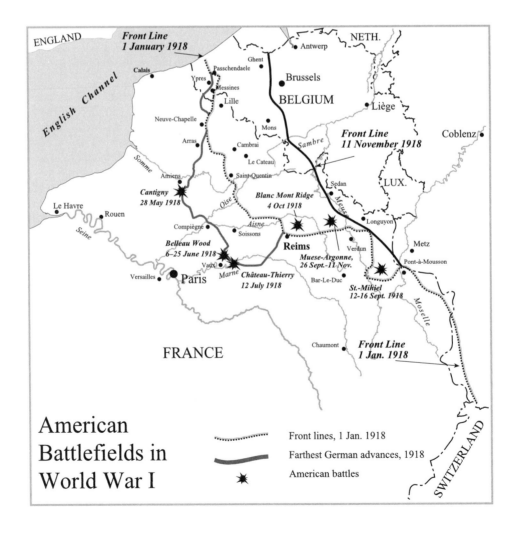

American Battlefields in World War I

········· Front lines, 1 Jan. 1918

━━━ Farthest German advances, 1918

✸ American battles

Gas Attack. American soldiers advance across a field in France in 1918. © CORBIS

Zimmerman Telegram authorized the ambassador to offer Mexico the portions of the Southwest it had lost to the United States in the 1840s if it joined the Central Powers. But because Wilson had run for reelection in 1916 on a very popular promise to keep the United States out of the European war, he had to handle the telegram very carefully. Wilson did not publicize it at first, only releasing the message to the press in March after weeks of German attacks on American ships had turned public sentiment toward joining the Allies.

Gearing Up for War: Raising Troops and Rallying Public Opinion

On 2 April 1917, Wilson asked Congress for a declaration of war and four days later all but six senators and fifty representatives voted for a war resolution. The Selective Service Act that was passed the following month, along with an extraordinary number of volunteers, built up the army from less than 250,000 to four million over the course of the conflict. General John Pershing was appointed head of the American Expeditionary Force (AEF) and led the first troops to France during the summer. Initially, the nation was woefully unprepared to fight so large a war so far from American soil. The task of reorganizing government and industry to coordinate a war and then of recruiting, training, equipping, and shipping out massive numbers of soldiers was daunting and would proceed slowly. The first serious U.S. military action would not come until April 1918, one year after declaration of war. It would take a gargantuan national effort,

one that would forever change the government and its relationship to the citizenry, to get those troops into combat.

Although there is strong evidence that the war was broadly supported—and certainly Americans volunteered and bought Liberty Bonds in droves—the epic scale of the undertaking and the pressure of time led the government, in an unprecedented campaign, to sell the war effort through a massive propaganda blitz. Wilson picked George Creel, a western newspaper editor, to form the COMMITTEE ON PUBLIC INFORMATION (CPI). This organization was charged with providing the press with carefully selected information on the progress of the war. It also worked with the advertising industry to produce eye-catching and emotional propaganda for various agencies involved in the war effort in order to win maximum cooperative enthusiasm form the public. Its largest enterprise was the Four Minute Men program, which sent more than 75,000 speakers to over 750,000 public events to rouse the patriotism of as many as 314 million spectators over the course of the war. The CPI recruited mainly prominent white businessmen and community leaders; however, it did set up a Women's Division and also courted locally prominent African Americans to speak at black gatherings.

Gearing Up for War: The Economy and Labor

The government needed patriotic cooperation, for it was completely unequipped to enforce many of the new regulations it adopted. It also had to maximize the productive resources of the nation to launch the U.S. war effort and prop up flagging allies. The WAR INDUSTRIES BOARD was charged with gearing up the economy to war production, but it lacked coercive authority. Even the Overman Act of May 1918, which gave the president broad powers to commandeer industries if necessary, failed to convince capitalists to retool completely toward the war effort. The government only took control of one industry, the railroads, in December 1917, and made it quite clear that the measure was only a temporary necessity. In all other industries, it was federal investment—not control—that achieved results. The EMERGENCY FLEET CORPORATION pumped over $3 billion into the nation's dormant shipbuilding industry during the war era. Overall, the effort to raise production was too little and too late for maximizing the nation's military clout. American production was just hitting stride as the war ended, but the threat that it represented did help convince an exhausted Germany to surrender.

The government also sought the cooperation of the American Federation of Labor (AFL) and involved its top officials in the war production effort, but very low unemployment emboldened union workers and it became difficult for the leadership to control the rank and file. Many workers connected Wilson's war goals—democracy and self-determination for nations—to struggles for a voice in their workplaces through union representation. However, the number of striking workers was lower in 1917 and 1918 than in 1916. The government hastily created labor arbitration boards and eventually formed a NATIONAL WAR LABOR BOARD (NWLB) in April 1918. The government had considerable success in resolving disputes and convincing employers to at least temporarily give some ground to the unions. When this novel arbitration framework disappeared along with government contracts in 1919, workers participated in the largest strike wave in the nation's history—over four million participated in walkouts during that year.

Women and African Americans in the War

For women workers the war also raised hopes, but as with labor as a whole, they were dashed after the conflict. The number of women working as domestic servants and in

The United States in World War I

African American Troops. Members of the all-black Fifteenth New York Infantry Regiment (commanded by white officers) stand at attention in France in 1918. Redesignated the 369th Infantry, the regiment served in combat with the French army. © CORBIS

laundering or garment making declined sharply during the war, while opportunities grew just as dramatically in office, industrial, commercial, and transportation work. The very limited place of women in the economy had opened up and government propaganda begged women to take jobs. However, few of these new opportunities, and even then only the least attractive of them, went to nonwhite women. Mainly confined to low-skilled work, many women were let go when the postwar economy dipped or were replaced by returning soldiers. Although women did gain, and hold on to, a more prominent place in the AFL, they were still only 10 percent of the membership in 1920. The government made some attempts through the NWLB to protect the rights of working women, although it backed off after the war. But women fought on their own behalf on the suffrage front and finally achieved the right to vote in 1920.

African Americans also made some gains but suffered a terrible backlash for them. There were ninety-six LYNCH-INGS of blacks during 1917 and 1918 and seventy in 1919 alone. Blacks were moving out of the South in massive numbers during the war years, confronting many white communities in the North with a substantial nonwhite presence for the first time. Northward migration by blacks averaged only 67,000 per decade from 1870 through 1910 and then exploded to 478,000 during the 1910s. This GREAT MIGRATION gave blacks access to wartime fac-

tory jobs that paid far better than agricultural work in the South, but like white women, they primarily did low-skilled work and were generally rejected by the union movement. The hatred that many of these migrants faced in the North forced them into appalling ghettos and sometimes led to bloodshed. In July 1917, a race riot in East St. Louis, Illinois, left thirty-nine African Americans dead. The recently formed NAACP championed justice and democratic rights for African Americans at a time when black soldiers were helping to guarantee them for the peoples of Europe. Although job opportunities would recede after the war, the new racial diversity outside the South would not—and neither would the fight for equal rights.

Repression and the War

The fragility of a war effort that relied on a workforce of unprecedented diversity and on cooperation from emboldened unions led the federal government to develop for the first time a substantial intelligence-gathering capability for the purpose of suppressing elements it thought might destabilize the system. The primary targets were anti-capitalist radicals and enemy aliens (German and Austro-Hungarian immigrants). The former group was targeted through the ESPIONAGE ACT of June 1917, which was amended by the Sedition Act in May 1918 after the Bolshevik Revolution in Russia convinced the government to seek even wider powers to control public speech. The Department of Justice, through its U.S. attorneys and Bureau of Investigation field agents, cooperated with local and state authorities to suppress radical organizers. Many government agencies developed at least some intelligence capacity and the private, but government-sanctioned, American Protective League recruited perhaps 300,000 citizen-spies to keep tabs on their fellow Americans. In this climate of suspicion, German-speaking aliens had the most cause to be afraid. War propaganda dehumanized Germans and blasted their culture and language. Well over a half-million enemy aliens were screened by the Department of Justice and were restricted in their mobility and access to military and war production sites. Several thousand enemy aliens deemed disloyal were interned until the conflict was over.

American Soldiers in Battle

The end of the war was nowhere in sight when U.S. troops first saw significant fighting in the spring of 1918, after the new Bolshevik government in Russia pulled out of the war in March and Germany switched its efforts to the western front. Under British and French pressure, General Pershing allowed his troops to be blended with those of the Allies—ending his dream of the AEF as an independent fighting force. Now under foreign command, American troops helped stop the renewed German offensive in May and June. The First U.S. Army was given its own mission in August: to push the Germans back to the southeast and northwest of Verdun and then seize the important railroad facilities at Sedan. The campaign got under way in September and American troops succeeded in removing the Germans from the southeast of Verdun, although the latter were already evacuating that area. The MEUSE-ARGONNE OFFENSIVE to the northwest of Verdun was launched in late September and proved to be much more bloody. Although the German position was heavily fortified, well over a million American soldiers simply overwhelmed all resistance. This massive and relentless operation convinced the German command that its opportunity to defeat the Allies before American troops and industry were fully ready to enter the fray had been lost. As exhausted as the United States was fresh, the Central Powers surrendered on 11 November 1918.

In the end, two million American troops went to France and three-quarters of them saw combat. Some 60,000 died in battle and over 200,000 were wounded. An additional 60,000 died of disease, many from the influenza pandemic that killed over twenty million across the globe

Trench Warfare. U.S. Marines fire from their trenches during the Meuse-Argonne offensive in the fall of 1918, which resulted in the signing of the armistice on 11 November.

in 1918 and 1919. Many surviving combatants suffered psychological damage, known as shell shock, from the horrors of trench warfare. The casualties would have been far greater had America entered the war earlier or been prepared to deploy a large army more quickly.

Wilson hoped that after the war the United States would become part of the League of Nations that was forming in Europe to ensure that collective responsibility replaced competitive alliances. But America was retreating inward, away from the postwar ruin and revolutionary chaos of Europe. The government was suppressing radicals at home with unprecedented furor in 1919 and 1920 in what is known as the Red Scare. Progressive wartime initiatives that further involved the government in the lives of its citizens withered against this reactionary onslaught. But the notion of government coordination of a national effort to overcome crisis had been born, and the Great Depression and World War II would see this new commitment reemerge, strengthened.

BIBLIOGRAPHY

Farwell, Byron. *Over There: The United States in the Great War, 1917–1918.* New York: Norton, 1999. Focuses on military action.

Greenwald, Maurine Weiner. *Women, War, and Work: The Impact of World War I on Women Workers in the United States.* Westport, Conn.: Greenwood, 1980.

Kennedy, Kathleen. *Disloyal Mothers and Scurrilous Citizens: Women and Subversion during World War I.* Bloomington: Indiana University Press, 1999.

Luebke, Frederick. *Bonds of Loyalty: German-Americans and World War I.* DeKalb: Northern Illinois University Press, 1974.

McCartin, Joseph. *Labor's Great War: The Struggle for Industrial Democracy and the Origins of Modern American Labor Relations, 1912–1921.* Chapel Hill: University of North Carolina Press, 1997. Focuses on workers and war production.

Preston, William, Jr. *Aliens and Dissenters: Federal Suppression of Radicals, 1903–1933.* Cambridge, Mass.: Harvard University Press, 1963. Focuses on home front repression.

Venzon, Anne Cipriano, ed. *The United States in the First World War: An Encyclopedia.* New York: Garland, 1995. Good general work.

Zieger, Robert. *America's Great War: World War I and the American Experience.* Lanham, Md.: Rowman and Littlefield, 2000. Stresses the home front.

Zeiger, Susan. *In Uncle Sam's Service: Women Workers with the American Expeditionary Force, 1917–1919.* Ithaca, N.Y.: Cornell University Press, 1999.

Adam Hodges

See also **Internment, Wartime; Palmer Raids; Riots; Sedition Acts; Women in Public Life, Business, and Professions;** *and vol. 9:* **America's War Aims: The Fourteen Points; Dedicating the Tomb of the Unknown Soldier; Peace and Bread in Time of War; The War in Its Effect upon Women; Letters from the Front, World War I, 1918; Lyrics of "Over There," 1917.**

WORLD WAR I, ECONOMIC MOBILIZATION FOR.

European demands for war supplies mobilized some sectors of the American economy before the United States entered World War I. Exports increased from $2.1 billion to $2.6 billion annually between 1911 and 1914 and jumped to $5.7 billion in 1916. Changes in the public sector were less dramatic. The government established the National Advisory Committee for Aeronautics, the U.S. Shipping Board, and the Council of National Defense, with an advisory commission, before 1917. But President Woodrow Wilson's policy of neutrality and the powerful peace sentiment in Congress and the rest of the country precluded systematic planning for a war economy.

The private nature of economic mobilization in the United States did not disappear after U.S. entry into the war on 6 April 1917. Throughout the spring and summer, volunteer committees of corporation executives tried to design production, transportation, and price schedules for army and navy supplies. Congress and the president, in the meantime, clashed over the nature of the government's economic policies and administrative controls, and the military services scrambled for supplies in an essentially free market. But much of the output of vital materials, such as steel and coal, had already been committed for months in advance to private and Allied purchasers.

In July 1917 the president increased the scope and power of the U.S. Shipping Board and established the War Industries Board (WIB) to regularize business-government relations. On 10 August Congress empowered the president to control food and fuel supplies and to fix a minimum price for wheat. Congress continued to yield to presidential initiatives in subsequent months, albeit reluctantly, and the War Trade Board, the Alien Property Custodian, and the Aircraft Board appeared in October. By that time, the administration had also taken the first tentative steps toward fixing prices on industrial raw materials.

Urgent Allied demands for ships and munitions, as well as transportation breakdowns in the desperate winter months of 1917–1918, touched off a much more rigorous extension of public economic controls in 1918. The president enlarged and redefined the functions of the WIB early in March and set up the National War Labor Board and the War Finance Corporation in April. The WIB's Price Fixing Committee negotiated a series of maximum prices with raw-material producers, and its Priorities Board broadened the range of restrictions on nonwar production. The military services launched a variety of internal reforms that made it easier for the board to coordinate its economic policies.

Wilson inaugurated a series of weekly meetings with his top war administrators in the spring of 1918, but the administration never fully centralized the responsibility for economic mobilization. The WIB offered the greatest potential for such a development, but the ARMISTICE OF NOVEMBER 1918 came before all aspects of economic mobilization were fully integrated. Achievements varied, therefore, from one sector of the economy to another. By the time of the armistice, for instance, there were surpluses in some agricultural products and industrial raw materials, while production lagged in ships and aircraft.

BIBLIOGRAPHY

Beaver, Daniel R. *Newton D. Baker and the American War Effort, 1917–1919.* Lincoln: University of Nebraska Press, 1966.

Cuff, Robert D. *The War Industries Board: Business-Government Relations During World War I.* Baltimore: Johns Hopkins University Press, 1973.

Urofsky, Melvin I. *Big Steel and the Wilson Administration: A Study in Business-Government Relations.* Columbus: Ohio State University Press, 1969.

Robert D. Cuff/c. w.

See also **Council of National Defense; Distribution of Goods and Services; National War Labor Board, World War I; Price and Wage Controls; Shipping Board, U.S.; War Finance Corporation; War Industries Board; War Trade Board.**

WORLD WAR I, NAVY IN.

The United States entered World War I on the side of the Allies in response to Germany's use of submarines against U.S. merchant ships. Under the assumption that the United States had insufficient antisubmarine warfare (ASW) capability to affect such a campaign, Germany had waged unrestricted submarine warfare. As its first task, the United States responded by temporarily setting aside a 1916 building program that was to give the nation the world's best navy in ten years and concentrating instead on building destroyers. The Navy dispatched Admiral William S. Sims, commander of the U.S. naval forces in Europe, to England on 9 April 1917. By July the Navy had dispatched thirty-five destroyers, and it sent additional ASW forces into the war zone as soon as bases to support them were provided. These ships were desperately needed: four-fifths of Britain's food, half its iron ore, and all other raw materials had to be imported. Allied shipping losses to German submarines were drastically high, exceeding 881,000 tons or more than 150 ships in April 1917 alone. To reduce these losses, the British began organizing merchant ships into convoys instead of patrolling fixed sea areas so that submarines had to avoid the convoy's ASW escort to make an attack.

The second critical task of the U.S. Navy was to transport the AMERICAN EXPEDITIONARY FORCES (AEF) to France before German armies on the eastern front, freed by the collapse of the Russian army after the 1917 revolution, could be employed on the western front. The initial American troop convoy, with the U.S. First Division, arrived at Saint Nazaire, France, on 24 June 1917. Over 300,000 American troops were in France when the Germans made their unsuccessful lunge at the Allied lines in the spring of 1918.

American flag shipping available for transport service included four hundred ships operating primarily in the coastal trade and another four hundred in production, but these could not carry the entire AEF. The Navy turned to the 104 German ships interned in U.S. ports, using the then-new technique of welding to quickly repair twenty ships damaged by their German crews. Mostly passenger ships, including the world's largest, *Vaterland* (renamed *Leviathan*), they formed a considerable segment of the Naval Transport Force commanded by Admiral Albert Gleaves. This force carried 911,047 soldiers to France, about half of them in former German ships. Another million U.S. troops were transported in British vessels.

The third major undertaking of the U.S. Navy in World War I was the North Sea mine barrage: the laying of 56,600 anchored mines between the Orkney Islands and the coast of Norway. This barrage was not completed by the war's end and had no impact on its outcome.

Other U.S. naval activities in World War I included using aviation, chiefly along the west coast of France; launching submarine chaser operations in the Mediterranean and Adriatic seas; providing a division of battleships with the British Grand Fleet and another at Bantry Bay, Ireland, to cover the English Channel ports; stationing a naval railroad battery of fourteen-inch guns on the western front; and operating in Russian waters, both in the White Sea and the Far East.

BIBLIOGRAPHY

Baer, George W. *One Hundred Years of Sea Power: The U.S. Navy, 1890–1990.* Stanford, Calif.: Stanford University Press, 1994.

Feuer, A. B. *The U.S. Navy in World War I.* Westport, Conn: Praeger, 1999.

Love, Robert W. *History of the U.S. Navy.* Harrisburg, Pa.: Stackpole Books, 1992.

McBride, William M. *Technological Change and the United States Navy, 1865–1945.* Baltimore: Johns Hopkins University Press, 2000.

Taussig, Joseph K. *The Queenstown Patrol, 1917: The Diary of Commander Joseph Knefler Taussig, U.S. Navy.* Newport, R.I.: Naval War College Press, 1996.

John D. Hayes/D. B.

See also **Aircraft Carriers and Naval Aircraft; Defense, National; Navy, United States; Submarines; Warships; Women in Military Service.**

WORLD WAR I TRAINING CAMPS.

To build the camps and cantonments required to train U.S. National Guard and National Army divisions during WORLD WAR I, the federal government created the construction division of the army in May 1917. Secretary of War Newton D. Baker ordered the building of sixteen wood-frame cantonments and sixteen NATIONAL GUARD camps, where troops would be quartered in hastily erected tents with

Black Soldiers. Although African Americans were segregated—under white officers—and generally given noncombat roles in the war, the U.S. Army's Ninety-second and Ninety-third divisions, some other units, and the pilots known as the Tuskegee Airmen all saw action. NATIONAL ARCHIVES AND RECORDS ADMINISTRATION

1937, and thereafter, as Germany's ally, planning further conquests.

The United States opposed this Japanese expansion diplomatically by every means short of war, and military staff planning began as early as 1938 for the possibility of a two-ocean war. American policymakers determined that the nation's security depended on the survival of the British Commonwealth in Europe and the establishment in the Pacific of a U.S. Navy defense line that must run from Alaska through Hawaii to Panama.

On 7 December 1941, a sneak attack by Japanese carrier-based planes surprised and severely crippled the U.S. fleet at Pearl Harbor, Hawaii, dooming American forces in the PHILIPPINES. Japan was now free to expand into Southeast Asia and the East Indies, toward Australia. On 8 December, Congress declared war on Japan, and on 11 December it responded to war declarations from Italy and Germany—allied to Japan by treaties—by similar declarations put through in a single day of legislative action in committees and on the floor of both houses of Congress.

Before the month of December was out, Churchill was again in Washington, bringing with him military and naval experts for what has been called the Arcadia conference. Within weeks Washington had created the Combined

Chiefs of Staff, an international military, naval, and air body that was used throughout the war to settle strategy, establish unified command in the separate theaters of war, and issue strategic instructions to theater commanders.

Organization, Preparation, and Strategy

Almost immediately after the declaration of war, under the first WAR POWERS ACT, the United States began a reorganization and expansion of the army and the navy, including the National Guard already in federal service. Increasing numbers of reservists were called to active duty, not as units but as individuals, to fill gaps in existing units, to staff the training centers, and to serve as officers in new units being formed. Additional divisions were created and put into training, bearing the numbers of World War I divisions in most cases, but with scarcely any relation to them in locality or in personnel of previously existing reserve divisions. New activities were created for psychological warfare and for civil affairs and military government in territories to be liberated or captured. The air force also underwent a great expansion, in personnel, in units, and in planes. Notable was the creation and shipment to England of high-level, precision daylight bombing units, which worked with the British to rain tons of bombs on enemy centers. Later they assisted the invasions and major attacks. Disrupting German factories and rail

Prisoners of War. A large group of captured American soldiers is guarded by Japanese troops in the Philippines, 1942. © CORBIS/BETTMANN

lines and weakening the entire German economy, the bombing campaign was extremely important in Hitler's downfall. The armed forces of the United States, in general, expanded their strength and put to use a host of details in tactics and in equipment that had been merely experimental in the preceding years. From new planes to new rifles, from motorization to emergency rations, from field radio telephones to long-range radar, progress was widespread.

In addition to new concepts of operation and new and improved mechanized matériel, there was an all-out popular war effort, a greater national unity, a greater systematization of production, and, especially, a more intense emphasis on technology, far surpassing the efforts of World War I. The U.S. effort would truly be, as Churchill predicted after the fall of France in 1940, "the new world with all its power and might" stepping forth to "the rescue and liberation of the old."

In an unprecedented burst of wartime legislative activity, Congress passed the Emergency Price Control Act and established the War Production Board, the NATIONAL WAR LABOR BOARD, the Office of War Information, and the Office of Economic Stabilization. Critical items such as food, coffee, sugar, meat, butter, and canned goods were rationed for civilians, as were heating fuels and gasoline. Rent control was established. Two-thirds of the planes of civilian airlines were taken over by the air force. Travel was subject to priorities for war purposes. There was also voluntary censorship of newspapers, under general guidance from Washington.

There was special development and production of escort vessels for the navy and of landing craft—small and large—for beach invasions. There was a program of plane construction for the air force on a huge scale and programs for the development of high-octane gasoline and synthetic rubber. Local draft boards had been given great leeway in drawing up their own standards of exemption and deferment from service and at first had favored agriculture over industry; soon controls were established according to national needs. By 1945 the United States had engaged more than sixteen million men under arms and improved its economy.

The grand strategy, from the beginning, was to defeat Germany while containing Japan, a strategy maintained and followed by the Combined Chiefs of Staff. The strategy was closely coordinated by Roosevelt and Churchill—except on one occasion when, in the early summer of 1942, Admiral Ernest J. King (chief of naval operations) and General George C. Marshall (army chief of staff) responded to the news that there would be no attempt to create a beachhead in Europe that year by suggesting a shift of U.S. power to the Pacific. Roosevelt promptly overruled them.

Campaign in the Pacific

Almost immediately after the strike at Pearl Harbor, the Japanese invaded the Philippines and overran American garrisons on Guam and Wake Island in late December. They soon captured Manila and then conquered the U.S. forces on the Bataan peninsula by April 1942, along with

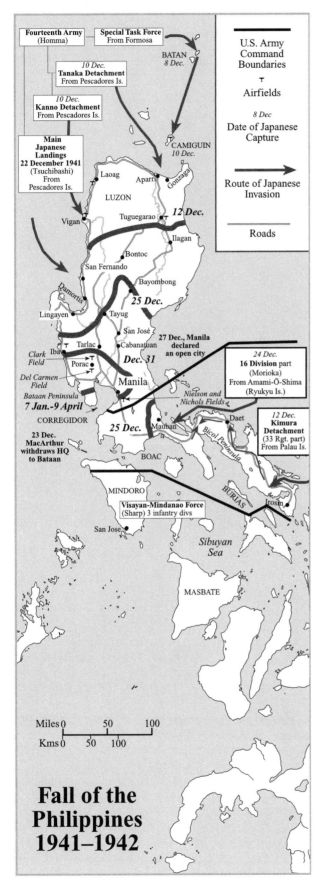

Fall of the Philippines 1941–1942

the last U.S. stronghold on Corregidor on 6 May. Japan then feinted into the North Pacific, easily seizing Attu and Kiska in the Aleutian Islands, which it held until March 1943.

Gen. Douglas MacArthur had been pulled out of the Philippines before the fall of Corregidor and sent to Australia to assume responsibility for protecting that continent against Japanese invasion, increasingly imminent since Singapore and Java had been taken. With great skill, MacArthur used American and Australian forces to check Japanese inroads in New Guinea at Port Moresby. He also used land and sea forces to push back the Japanese and take the villages of Buna and Sanananda, although not until January 1943. To block a hostile thrust against MacArthur's communications through New Zealand, marine and infantry divisions landed in the Solomon Islands, where they took Guadalcanal by February 1943 after bitter, touch-and-go land, sea, and air fighting.

Almost concurrently, the navy, with marine and army troops, was attacking selected Japanese bases in the Pacific, moving steadily westward and successfully hitting the Marshall Islands at Eniwetok and Kwajalein, the Gilberts at Makin and Tarawa, and—turning north—the Marianas at Guam and Saipan in June and July 1944. To assist the army's move on the Philippines, the navy and the marines also struck westward at the Palau Islands in September 1944 and had them in hand within a month. American control of the approaches to the Philippines was now assured. Two years earlier, in the Coral Sea and also in the open spaces near Midway, in May and June 1942, respectively, the U.S. Navy had severely crippled the Japanese fleet. MacArthur's forces returned in October 1944 to the Philippines on the island of Leyte. Their initial success was endangered by a final, major Japanese naval effort near Leyte, which was countered by a U.S. naval thrust that wiped much of the Japanese fleet. U.S. forces seized Manila and Corregidor in February 1945, thus bringing to a successful conclusion the BATAAN-CORREGIDOR CAMPAIGN.

American land and sea forces were now in position to drive north directly toward Japan itself. Marines had landed on Iwo Jima on 19 February and invaded Okinawa on 1 April, both within good flying distance of the main enemy islands. The Japanese navy and air force were so depleted that in July 1945 the U.S. fleet was steaming off the coast of Japan and bombarding almost with impunity. Between 10 July and 15 August 1945, forces under Adm. William F. Halsey destroyed or damaged 2,084 enemy planes, sank or damaged 148 Japanese combat ships, and sank or damaged 1,598 merchant vessels, in addition to administering heavy blows at industrial targets and war industries.

Until the island hopping brought swift successes in 1944, it had been expected that the United States would need the China mainland as a base for an attack on Japan. The sea and land successes in the central and western Pacific, however, allowed the United States, by the spring of 1945, to prepare for an attack on Japan without using

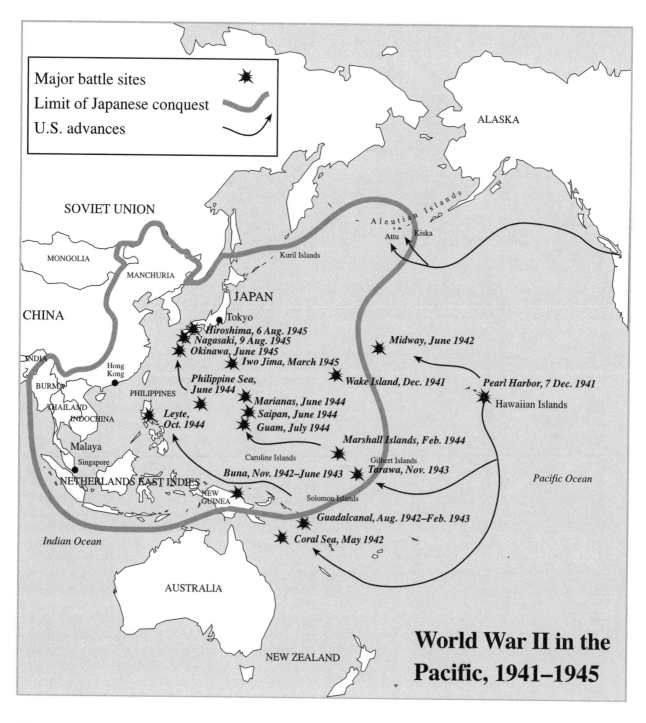

Major battle sites
Limit of Japanese conquest
U.S. advances

ALASKA

SOVIET UNION

MONGOLIA

MANCHURIA

CHINA

Aleutian Islands
Attu   Kiska

Kuril Islands

JAPAN
Tokyo

INDIA

Hong Kong

BURMA

PHILIPPINES

THAILAND

INDOCHINA

Malaya

Singapore

NETHERLANDS EAST INDIES

Hiroshima, 6 Aug. 1945
Nagasaki, 9 Aug. 1945
Okinawa, June 1945
Iwo Jima, March 1945
Philippine Sea,
June 1944
Midway, June 1942
Wake Island, Dec. 1941
Pearl Harbor, 7 Dec. 1941
Hawaiian Islands

Marianas, June 1944
Saipan, June 1944
Guam, July 1944
Marshall Islands, Feb. 1944

Leyte,
Oct. 1944

Caroline Islands

Gilbert Islands
Tarawa, Nov. 1943

Pacific Ocean

Buna, Nov. 1942–June 1943

NEW GUINEA

Solomon Islands

Guadalcanal, Aug. 1942–Feb. 1943

Indian Ocean

Coral Sea, May 1942

AUSTRALIA

NEW ZEALAND

World War II in the Pacific, 1941–1945

China as a base. This situation was the result of three major factors: (1) the new naval technique of employing the fleet as a set of floating air bases, as well as for holding the sea lanes open; (2) the augmentation and improvement of U.S. submarine service to a point where they were fatal to Japanese shipping, sinking more than two hundred enemy combat vessels and more than eleven hundred merchant ships, thus seriously disrupting the desperately needed supply of Japanese troops on the many islands; and (3) MacArthur's leapfrogging tactics, letting many advanced Japanese bases simply die on the vine. Not

to be overlooked was MacArthur's personal energy and persuasive skill.

Campaigns in Africa and Italy

Pressures, notably from Russian leaders, began building early in the war for an invasion of the European mainland on a second front. Because of insufficient buildup in England for a major attack across the English Channel in 1942—even for a small preliminary beachhead—U.S. troops were moved, some from Britain with the British and some directly from the United States, to invade northwest Africa from Casablanca to Oran and Algiers in November 1942. After the long coastal strip had been seized and the temporarily resisting French brought to the side of the Allies, British and American forces under the command of Gen. Dwight D. Eisenhower pushed east. The Germans were reinforced and concentrated. Sharp and costly fighting by air, army, and armor attacks and counterattacks, notably in February 1943 at the Kasserine Pass, ended with the Allied conquest of Tunisia and a great German surrender at Tunis, Bizerte, and Cape Bon. Meanwhile, at the CASABLANCA CONFERENCE in late January, Roosevelt and Churchill called for the "unconditional surrender" of the Axis powers. It would be a war to the finish, not a negotiated, temporary peace.

The next step was an invasion of Sicily, using large-scale parachute drops and perfected beach-landing skills, as a step toward eliminating Italy from the war. In September, Italy proper was invaded, the British crossing the Strait of Messina and the Americans landing at Salerno near Naples. Five days later, Italy surrendered, but the Germans occupied Rome and took control of the Italian government. After a long check midway up the "boot" of Italy on a line through Cassino, a dangerous landing was made at Anzio. Fierce German counterattacks there were stopped, and a following breakthrough carried U.S. forces past Rome, which fell on 4 June 1944. In July the Allied forces pushed through to the line of Florence and the

Liberated Rome. The U.S. Army's Eighty-fifth Division marches through an ancient Roman triumphal arch at the Porta Maggiore in June 1944. © CORBIS-BETTMANN

Arno River, the British on the east and the Americans on the west. Thereafter, although some British and American advances were made and a final offensive in April 1945 sent American troops to the Po Valley, Italy ceased to be the scene of major strategic efforts; the theater was drained to support the Normandy invasion, in southern France.

Invasion at Normandy and the Liberation of France

For the principal invasion of France, an inter-Allied planning staff had been created in March 1943 in London. In May the first tentative attack date was set, for early May of the following year, in what was called Operation Overlord. The buildup of units and supplies proceeded steadily for nearly a year, aided by improved successes against German submarines targeting seagoing convoys. Finally, after several weeks of delays, on 6 June 1944—popularly known as D DAY—the greatest amphibious invasion in history was launched across the English Channel, involving more than 5,300 ships and landing craft. It was a huge, carefully and intricately coordinated land, sea, and air action, with a precisely scheduled flow of reinforcements and supplies. The Germans anticipated that the Allies would land at Calais, so the landings along the Normandy coast caught the Germans completely by surprise.

The battle on the Normandy beaches on 6 June was vicious, particularly at Omaha Beach, where U.S. troops encountered stubborn German resistance. By nightfall the Allies had established a beachhead on the French coast, and within weeks they drove from the Normandy coast deep into the French countryside. Thick hedgerows provided the Germans with excellent defensive terrain, but relentless Allied aerial bombardment and a flank attack by U.S. infantry and tanks, under the command of Gen. George Patton, split the German lines.

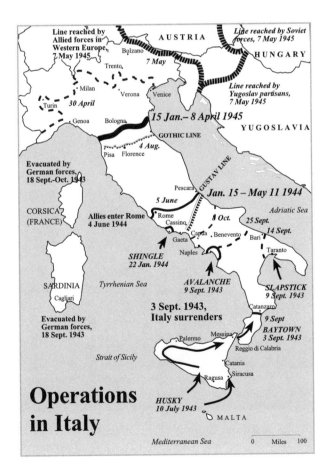

Operations in Italy

549

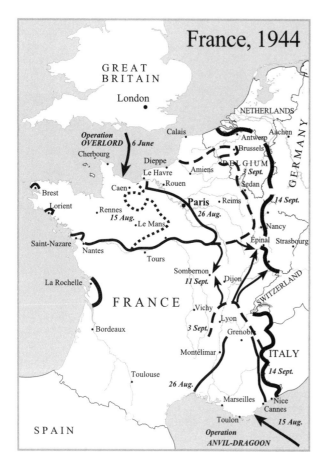

The Germans reacted to this penetration by finally drawing their reserve Fifteenth Army out of the Calais area, where it had been held by an Allied ruse and the threat of a second beach landing there. They struck directly west across the American front to try to cut off the leading U.S. troops who had already begun entering Brittany. This German effort was blocked by General Omar Bradley's forces. Relentless Allied attacks shattered German resistance in northern France and on 25 August Paris fell to American divisions with scarcely a battle.

The Germans retreated rapidly and skillfully for the distant frontier and their defense lines, except where they at points resisted the British in order to try and hold the seaports along the northern coast. While these events were taking place, a landing had been made in southern France on 15 August 1944, by a Franco-American force under U.S. command. It swept from the Riviera up the Rhone Valley and joined U.S. forces that had come east across northern France from Normandy. By September Brest fell into U.S. hands, and a German army in southwest France had surrendered, completely cut off. France was almost completely liberated from German occupation.

Battle of the Bulge and German Surrender

In the fall of 1944, Allied forces began the invasion of Germany, which many observers believed tottered on the brink of collapse. On 16 December, however, the Germans launched a sweeping counterattack that caught American and British forces completely by surprise. In several days of intense fighting, the outcome of the Battle of the Bulge hung in the balance. On Christmas Eve, however, an American counterattack sent German forces reeling. American air bombardments turned the German retreat into a crushing rout. The Battle of the Bulge was the Germans' final major effort of the war. They had used up their last major resources and had failed.

Through large-scale production and mass transportation, the U.S. air forces in Europe had been built to high strength so that they could take severe losses and still defeat the enemy. From bases in Britain and from bases successively in North Africa and Italy, American bombers had struck at the heart of the German economy. Through large-scale air raids, like those on Ploesti, Romania, a decisive proportion of German oil refinery production was disabled. German planes and tanks faced severe fuel shortages. German fighter planes, beaten back by the British in 1940, were later cut down by the Americans' heavily armed bombers and their long-range fighter escorts. Except for a short, sharp, and costly new campaign in the final month of 1944, German planes had ceased to be a serious threat. At the same time, to aid the ground troops, the U.S. fighter-bombers were taking to the air under perilous conditions over the Ardennes. German flying bombs (V-1s) and rocket bombs (V-2s) had continued to blast Britain until their installations were overrun in late March 1945, but they had no effect on ground operations or on air superiority as a whole.

George S. Patton. The colorful and controversial fighting general, photographed in Tunisia in 1943. LIBRARY OF CONGRESS

In February 1945 the American armies struck out into the Palatinate and swept the German forces across the Rhine. The enemy forces destroyed bridges as they crossed—all but one. On 7 March an advanced armored unit of the U.S. First Army approached the great railway bridge at Remagen, downstream from Koblenz, found it intact, dashed over it, tore the fuses from demolition charges, and drove local Germans back. Troops were hustled over the bridge for several days before it collapsed from damage, but by then pontoon bridges were in place.

Avoiding the heavily wooded Ruhr region in the center, the previously planned northern crossing of the Rhine was effected with navy, air, and parachute help on 2 March 1945; all arms drove directly eastward into Germany while the First and Third Armies drove eastward below the Ruhr, the First Army soon swinging north through Giessen and Marburg to make contact at Paderborn and Lippstadt with the northern force. More than 300,000 Germans were thus enclosed in the Ruhr pocket.

Germany's military strength had now all but collapsed. The British on the American left raced toward Hamburg and the Baltic. The U.S. First Army pressed through to Leipzig and met the Russians on 25 April 1945 at Torgau on the Elbe River, which had been established at the YALTA CONFERENCE as part of the posthostilities boundary with Russia. The U.S. Third Army dashed to-

Casualties of War. In this photograph by Billy Newhouse, taken in Belgium on 26 February 1945, American soldiers are placed in a truck to be taken for burial at a military cemetery. © CORBIS

ward Bavaria to prevent possible German retreat to a last stand in the south. The southernmost flank of the American forces swung southward toward Austria at Linz and toward Italy at the Brenner Pass. The U.S. Seventh Army, on 4 May, met the Fifth Army at Brenner Pass, coming from Italy, where German resistance had likewise collapsed. Germany asked for peace and signed its unconditional surrender at Allied headquarters at Reims on 7 May 1945.

Bombing of Hiroshima and Nagasaki; Japanese Surrender

Progress in the Pacific theater by this time had been substantial. U.S. ships and planes dominated sea and air close to Japan. Troops were soon to be redeployed from the European theater. Protracted cleanup operations against now-isolated Japanese island garrisons were coming to a close. American planes were bombing Tokyo regularly. A single raid on that city on 9 March 1945 had devastated sixteen square miles, killed eighty thousand persons, and left 1.5 million people homeless, but the Japanese were still unwilling to surrender. Approved by Roosevelt, scientists working under military direction had devised a devastating bomb based on atomic fission. A demand was made on Japan on 26 July for surrender, threatening the consecutive destruction of eleven Japanese cities if it did not. The Japanese rulers scorned the threats. President Harry S. Truman gave his consent for the use of the atomic bomb, which was dropped on Hiroshima on 6 August, killing 75,000. There were more warnings, but still no surrender. On 9 August, Nagasaki was bombed. Two square miles were devastated, and 39,000 people were killed. Five days later, on 14 August, the Japanese agreed to surrender. The official instrument of surrender was

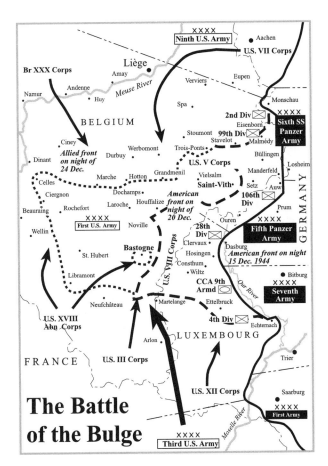

The Battle of the Bulge

signed on 2 September 1945, on board the battleship *Missouri* in Tokyo Bay.

The defeat of the Axis powers did not resolve all of the geopolitical issues arising from World War II. The spirit of amity among the Allied powers collapsed shortly after the war, as the United States and the Soviet Union rapidly assumed a position of mutual hostility and distrust. Germany was divided in half by the Allied victors, with West Germany aligned with the United States and East Germany with the Soviet Union. The United States also established security pacts with Japan and Italy, bringing them within the American defense shield against the Soviets. Ironically, therefore, during the Cold War the United States found itself allied with the former Axis nations and found itself at odds with its former ally, the USSR. Not until 1990, when the COLD WAR finally came to an end with the collapse of the Soviet Union, was Germany reunited as one nation.

BIBLIOGRAPHY

Blum, John Morton. *V Was for Victory: Politics and American Culture during World War II.* New York: Harcourt Brace Jovanovich, 1976.

Dallek, Robert. *Franklin D. Roosevelt and American Foreign Policy, 1932–1945.* New York: Oxford University Press, 1979.

Feis, Herbert. *The Road to Pearl Harbor: The Coming of the War between the United States and Japan.* Princeton, N.J.: Princeton University Press, 1950.

Linderman, Gerald F. *The World Within War: America's Combat Experience in World War II.* New York: Free Press, 1997.

Overy, Richard. *Why the Allies Won.* London: Jonathan Cape, 1995.

Rhodes, Richard. *The Making of the Atomic Bomb.* New York: Simon and Schuster, 1986.

Spector, Ronald H. *Eagle Against the Sun: The American War with Japan.* New York: Free Press, 1985.

Weinberg, Gerhard L. *A World at Arms: A Global History of World War II.* New York: Cambridge University Press, 1994.

Wyman, David S. *The Abandonment of the Jews: America and the Holocaust, 1941–1945.* New York: Pantheon Books, 1984.

*Elbridge Colby/*A. G.

See also **Air Power, Strategic; Aircraft Carriers and Naval Aircraft; Army of Occupation; Army, United States; Blockade; Cold War; Lafayette Escadrille; Mobilization; Naval Operations, Chief of; Navy, Department of the; Pearl Harbor; Unconditional Surrender; War Crimes Trials; War Department; World War II, Navy in;** *and* **vol. 9: America First; Franklin D. Roosevelt's Message on War Against Japan; Hobby's Army; The Japanese Internment Camps, 1942; Total Victory Speech; War and the Family; Women Working in World War II.**

WORLD WAR II, AIR WAR AGAINST GERMANY. On the eve of WORLD WAR II the German Air Force (GAF) was the most powerful in the world. How-

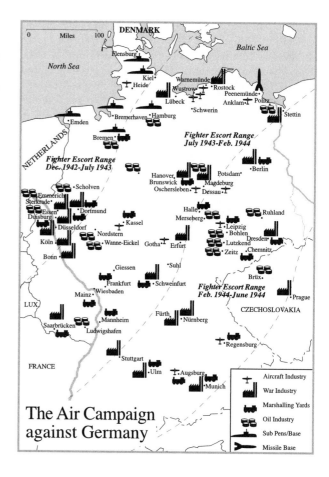

The Air Campaign against Germany

ever, it was designed primarily for the direct support of ground armies, a circumstance that would cripple it in its coming battle with the British Royal Air Force (RAF) and U.S. Army Air Forces (USAAF).

Overall Allied strategy for the war in western Europe called for an assault in force launched from Britain as a base and aimed at the heart of Germany. At the CASABLANCA CONFERENCE in January 1943, the RAF and USAAF made Allied air superiority a top priority. To cripple Adolf Hitler's plane production, the USAAF focused its initial bombing efforts on German aircraft and ball-bearing plants. Its effort during 1943 was disappointing, however, owing primarily to the severe losses suffered by bomber forces operating over Germany beyond the reach of escort fighters. Between February and May 1944, long-range escort fighters began to accompany the U.S. bombers all the way to their targets and back. Although German aircraft production continued to increase until September 1944, the GAF could not make effective use of the growing number of aircrafts because of (1) the loss of experienced GAF pilots brought on by the attempt to halt the bombing offensive, and (2) a critical gasoline shortage beginning in May 1944, which also made it difficult to train new GAF pilots.

In late 1944, the USAAF bomber forces concentrated on Germany's synthetic oil plants and transportation net-

Dresden. This 1946 photograph by Fred Ramage shows postwar commuters boarding a tram in the historic German city, which British and U.S. planes—and a firestorm caused by the intensive bombing—devastated in February 1945. HULTON/GETTY IMAGES

work. The GAF, already so weakened by June 1944 that it could not oppose the landings at Normandy, fell into disarray. Hopelessly outnumbered by the combined forces of the USAAF and RAF, and undergoing unceasing attack by day and night, the GAF had lost the battle. Not even the introduction of the new high-speed jet fighter (Messerschmitt 262) could stem the tide.

The inability of the German high command, including Adolf Hitler, to see the GAF as anything more than a supporting arm of the army contributed measurably to the Allied victory in the air. Despite the threat posed by Allied bombing from 1940 onward, it was late 1942 before any serious effort was made to increase the size and capabilities of the GAF. Then, when massive energies were applied to the task, the USAAF and RAF buildup already out-paced that of Germany, while the Allied bombing of the aircraft factories and fuel sources further hampered German efforts. With the destruction of surface transportation between and within its bases and factories during the winter of 1944–45, the GAF could offer but token resistance.

BIBLIOGRAPHY

Crane, Conrad C. *Bombs, Cities, and Civilians: American Airpower Strategy in World War II.* Lawrence: University Press of Kansas, 1993.

Craven, Wesley F., and James L. Cate, eds. *The Army Air Forces in World War II.* Washington, D.C.: Office of Air Force History, 1983.

Hooten, E. R. *Eagle in Flames: The Fall of the Luftwaffe.* London: Arms and Armour, 1997.

Schaffer, Ronald. *Wings of Judgment: American Bombing in World War II.* New York: Oxford University Press, 1985.

Sherry, Michael S. *The Rise of American Air Power: The Creation of Armageddon.* New Haven, Conn.: Yale University Press, 1987.

*David MacIsaac/*A. R.

See also **Air Force, United States; Air Power, Strategic; Aircraft Armament; Aircraft, Bomber; Aircraft, Fighter; Bombing; Normandy Invasion; Ploesti Oil Fields, Air Raids on; World War II, Air War Against Japan.**

WORLD WAR II, AIR WAR AGAINST JAPAN.

The first attack on Japan by American airmen in World War II was on 18 April 1942. In an extraordinary feat, they flew sixteen twin-engine B-25s off the carrier *Hornet* about 688 miles west of Japan and hit Tokyo and other nearby targets before heading for landing in China. This isolated raid, led by Lieutenant Colonel James H. Doolittle, came less than five months after Japan's attack on Pearl Harbor. By late 1943, anxious to begin a sustained air campaign against Japan, President Franklin D. Roosevelt arranged with British and Chinese authorities to build bases in India and western China for the B-29, a four-engine strategic bomber the prototype of which had gone into development in 1939. By the spring of 1944, 130 were available for deployment to India and China.

On 14 June 1944, B-29 crews struck Japan from China for the first time. Sixty-three planes bombed a steel plant on Kyūshū but caused only minor damage. Seven planes and fifty-five crewmen were lost on the raid. As mainland Japan lay beyond the B-29's 1,500-mile maximum combat radius, the U.S. airmen flew only five other missions against Japan from China. Mostly, they bombed closer enemy targets in Manchuria, China, Formosa, and Southeast Asia. By 29 March 1945, when the last raid was flown from the China-India theater, they had undertaken 3,058 individual sorties and dropped 11,691 tons of bombs on military and industrial targets.

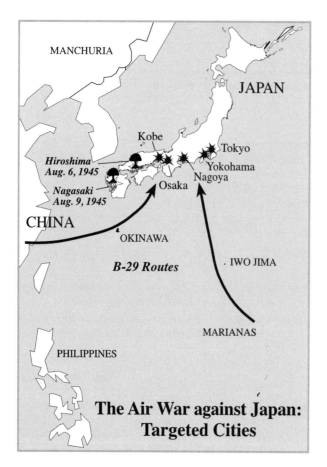

The Air War against Japan: Targeted Cities

The long-awaited sustained air war against Japan did not begin until U.S. forces had seized the Mariana Islands, beginning their assault on 15 June 1944. From Saipan, Tinian, and Guam, the B-29s could reach Japan's major industrial cities. Construction of runways on Saipan began even before the fighting there ended on 9 July 1944. The first bomber reached Saipan on 12 October. On 24 November, Major General Haywood S. Hansell launched the first air raid against Tokyo since Doolittle's raid. Nearly 90 B-29s struck at the enemy capital from an altitude of more than 25,000 feet, beyond the effective range of most Japanese aircraft and antiaircraft artillery. Their target—an aircraft plant—was almost completely obscured by clouds and was hit by only 24 planes. Sixty-four others bombed the general urban area. Although bomb damage was minimal, the Japanese soon began dispersing their industries, causing more disruption to their war production than did the initial B-29 attacks. Hansell staged six more raids in 1944.

These high-altitude bombing raids proved ineffective. In January 1945 Roosevelt's top airman, General Henry H. Arnold, replaced Hansell with Major General Curtis E. LeMay, who had commanded B-17s over Europe and the B-29s in the China-India theater. Other important changes followed. Washington directed that the B-29s carry more incendiaries on future raids, to take advantage of the known flammability of Japanese buildings. On 4 February a heavy incendiary strike against Kōbe destroyed 2.5 million square feet of the city's urban area. It was a precursor of the great fire raids.

The Japanese, meanwhile, had launched preemptive air strikes against the Saipan bases from Iwo Jima, a fortress island some 725 miles north of the Marianas. Between 26 November and 31 December 1944, some 80 Japanese planes had attacked and destroyed 11 B-29s on Saipan and damaged 43. American strategists determined to seize Iwo Jima; D day was set for 19 February 1945. Three days before, to support the invasion, a U.S. Navy fast-carrier force sailed into Tokyo harbor and launched more than 1,200 aircraft against Honshū targets, destroying some 500 Japanese planes. Navy carrier pilots returned to Japan on eighteen more occasions, bombing and strafing enemy facilities.

The B-29s, however, wreaked the greatest damage on Japan, LeMay having ordered his airmen to attack with incendiaries at altitudes of less than 8,000 feet, and individually rather than in formation. These new tactics were employed for the first time on the night of 9–10 March, when 285 bombers dropped two thousand tons of incendiaries on Tokyo. High winds fanned the flames into a huge firestorm that gutted 16 square miles in the city's center, killing 83,783, injuring 40,918, and leaving 1 million homeless. Similar fire raids were subsequently flown against Nagoya, Osaka, Kōbe, and fifty smaller Japanese cities. By midsummer, 180 square miles of Japan's urban area had been destroyed. To add to Japan's troubles, B-

Air War. U.S. Navy fighter planes, like these photographed during the June 1942 Battle of Midway, took part in significant raids on Japan in 1945. LIBRARY OF CONGRESS

29s dropped 12,953 mines in enemy waters, effectively blocking many Japanese ports and the Shimonoseki Strait.

The final blows came in August 1945. On 6 August a B-29 dropped the first atomic bomb on Hiroshima, killing 78,000 people and injuring 51,000. When Japanese officials did not immediately respond to Washington's call for surrender, a second atomic bomb was dropped 9 August on Nagasaki, killing 35,000 people and injuring 60,000. On 15 August, beset on all sides, Japan capitulated.

BIBLIOGRAPHY

Crane, Conrad C. *Bombs, Cities, and Civilians: American Air Power Strategy in World War II.* Lawrence: University Press of Kansas, 1993.

Dower, John W. *War without Mercy: Race and Power in the Pacific War.* 2d ed. New York: Pantheon, 1993.

Iriye, Akira. *Power and Culture: The Japanese-American War, 1941–1945.* Cambridge, Mass.: Harvard University Press, 1981.

Schaffer, Ronald. *Wings of Judgment: American Bombing in World War II.* New York: Oxford University Press, 1985.

Sherry, Michael S. *The Rise of American Air Power: The Creation of Armageddon.* New Haven, Conn.: Yale University Press, 1987.

Sherwin, Martin. *A World Destroyed: The Atomic Bomb and the Grand Alliance.* New York: Knopf, 1975; New York: Vintage Books, 1977.

Spector, Ronald H. *Eagle against the Sun: The American War with Japan.* New York: Free Press, 1985.

Carl Berger / A. R.

See also **Air Power, Strategic; Aircraft Armament; Aircraft, Bomber; Aircraft, Fighter; Bombing; Flying Tigers; Iwo Jima; World War II, Air War against Germany.**

WORLD WAR II, NAVY IN. President Woodrow Wilson, after World War I, was determined that the United States would be the foremost naval power both for the country's good and that of the rest of the world, and plans were made to modernize and expand the 1916 building program. But postwar isolation and disarmament sentiment was strong. The defeat of Wilson's Democratic party in 1920 led to a proposal for a naval disarmament conference in Washington, D.C. The four other major powers: Great Britain, Japan, France, and Italy, accepted, Japan reluctantly. Its outcome was a seeming agreement on battleship limitation: United States and Great Britain, 525,000 tons; Japan, 315,000 tons; France and Italy, 175,000 tons. To obtain Japan's consent, a clause was added forbidding new fortifications on any island possessions in the Far East. This clause in effect underwrote Japanese naval supremacy there. Another naval conference, held in London in 1930, limited cruiser tonnage, but the international climate worsened after the rise of Adolf Hitler and Japan's 1931 invasion of Manchuria, and all naval treaty limitations expired on 31 December 1936.

The United States did not even attempt to build up to its allowed treaty limitations until 1933 and thereby fell behind in naval strength, especially in the cruiser category. Construction was stepped up with the inauguration of President Franklin D. Roosevelt, who was fully aware that successful diplomacy depended on naval strength. His strong ally in Congress was Chairman Carl Vinson of the House Naval Affairs Committee. The National Industrial Recovery Act of 1933 was used to increase naval construction to reach full treaty strength, and the Vinson-Trammel Act of 1934 authorized 120 combat ships to be laid down in the next ten years. The Merchant Marine Act of 1936 provided for a revival of that deteriorated arm of national security.

Two qualitative revolutions took place in the navy during the post–World War I years. One was in naval aviation, led by Rear Adm. William A. Moffett, first chief of the Bureau of Aeronautics, 1921–1933, and Rear Adm. Joseph M. Reeves, who created the carrier task force between 1927 and 1931. The second was in engineering: ships adopted high-pressure steam, alternating electric current, high-speed diesel engines, and double-reduction gears, all initiated by Rear Adm. Samuel M. Robinson, chief of the Bureau of Engineering from 1931 to 1935.

Attack

World War II for the navy began in 1940 with Roosevelt's "short of war" policy. That year Congress authorized $4 billion for a two-ocean navy, and fifty destroyers were transferred to Great Britain in exchange for Atlantic bases. In 1941 U.S. destroyers began convoying in the western Atlantic. In the Pacific, Japanese forces moved toward Southeast Asia and in December attacked Pearl Harbor, Hawaii. The attack was made by a force of six carriers with 423 aircraft aboard. They struck the U.S. naval base at Pearl Harbor and the air stations nearby in several waves beginning at 7:55 A.M. on Sunday, 7 December 1941. One battleship was destroyed, another capsized, and four more sunk at their mooring. Several other types of ships were lost or damaged, 149 aircraft were destroyed, and 2,334 American servicemen were killed and 1,141 wounded. But no carriers were harmed; one was on the West Coast being repaired and two were at sea on missions delivering marine aircraft to Wake and Midway islands.

For Americans, Pearl Harbor was a disgraceful tragedy. For Japan it turned out to be a brilliant tactical victory but a lost opportunity when a second strike was not made on the Pearl Harbor base facilities, particularly the exposed oil tanks containing 4.5 million gallons of precious fuel. Destruction of the tanks would have forced the Pacific fleet back to the West Coast and broken the line of sea communications to Australia. Instead, a prostrate U.S. Navy was allowed several months to recover. Loss of the battleships but not the carriers resolved the long-standing controversy among U.S. naval officers as to which comprised modern capital ships.

Pearl Harbor gave Japan a temporary strategic success. Within hours after the attack there, Japanese military forces struck at the Philippines and Malaya. Declarations of war followed and a new maritime phase of World War II began. Then came several months of almost worldwide disaster at sea for Great Britain and the United States. Two British battleships were sunk off Malaya by Japanese aircraft. The remainder of American, Dutch, and British naval forces in the Far East and Indian Ocean were destroyed or scattered. The British naval base at Trincomalee, Ceylon, was bombed by the same carrier force that hit Pearl Harbor. But the Allies were not forced into a negotiated peace, as the Japanese had expected.

German Submarine Warfare

German submarines during the first six months of 1942 sank helpless merchant ships along the U.S. coast in the Atlantic, in the Gulf of Mexico, and in the Caribbean Sea. Allied losses in shipping amounted to 800,000 tons in June 1942, comparable to the losses of April 1917 in World War I, whereas German submarine sinkings by British and U.S. naval forces in the first six months of 1942 amounted to only the tonnage equivalent of one month of Germany's submarine production.

Karl Doenitz, the German admiral in charge of submarines, was perhaps the Allies' toughest naval opponent. He believed Germany could win the war by sinking an average of 750,000 tons of shipping per month. In March 1943 it looked as if he might do it. But in the next two months, the situation changed dramatically. In May 1943, U-boats were sunk in large numbers, thirty-one in the first twenty-two days. The Battle of the Atlantic was just about over.

Victory against the German submarines was primarily the result of British efforts; the United States' contribution was mostly in mass production of ships and weapons.

The Germans were defeated by the Royal Navy's battle-scarred escorts, by the Royal Air Force Coastal Command under navy control, and by British scientists with their microwave radar and operational analysis. Americans provided the small escort carrier used to cover the mid-Atlantic, which shore-based aircraft could not reach.

Pacific

The war in the Pacific was essentially a struggle for command of the sea. The combined efforts of all U.S. armed services were needed, but the first year of fighting was almost entirely a naval war. During December 1941 the Japanese effectively, if temporarily, neutralized American naval and air power in the Pacific. Through superior preparation, Japan's armed forces quickly achieved their original objectives, subjugating Malaya, Indonesia, and Burma. By the spring of 1942 they were confronted with the problem of what to do next to maintain the initiative; the choice was an advance toward Australia. The Japanese army, eagerly watching the weakened Soviet Union, would not release enough troops to invade Australia itself, so plans were made to occupy New Guinea, New Caledonia, and the Fiji Islands.

The Japanese offensive ground to a halt by June 1942 as they discovered that U.S. power in the Pacific had not been eliminated. The first carrier battle, in the Coral Sea (7–8 May 1942), checked the advance southward, and a decisive setback came shortly thereafter (4–6 June) at Midway Island in the Central Pacific. The real turning point in the war came in the last months of 1942 at Guadalcanal, where the navy afloat and the U.S. Marines ashore fought a bloody struggle against a desperate foe. When the United States gained complete control of the island early in 1943 the Japanese braced themselves for the American offensive they knew was coming. The offensive began in late 1943 with two major advances. One was the navy's drive directly through the Central Pacific, starting from the base in Hawaii. The Gilbert Islands were captured in 1943 and the Marshalls and Marianas in the spring and summer of 1944. The second advance, stemming from the initial campaigns in the South Pacific, was from Australia along the New Guinea coast toward the Philippines. The two drives joined at the Philippines in November 1944. The movement toward Japan then began with bloody assaults on Iwo Jima and Okinawa early in 1945.

American Submarine Warfare

Early 1944 saw the beginning of the American submarine campaign, which reduced the Japanese merchant marine to such a degree that the economy of that maritime nation was on the brink of collapse before the first atomic bomb was dropped. At the war's beginning, Japan had 6.9 million tons of shipping. It was not materially reduced until December 1943, when the faulty exploding mechanism in U.S. torpedoes was finally corrected. Within a year Japanese merchant tonnage was cut to 1.8 million, most of it confined to the Sea of Japan and the Inland Sea, both closed by mines to U.S. submarines.

Japanese antisubmarine operations were inept. Convoys remained small, so U.S. submarine attack groups—"wolf packs"—did not need to exceed four ships. American crew morale was high. Submarine duty was hazardous, but bold tactics paid off. Attacks by strategically located U.S. submarines against combat ships contributed largely to winning the Battle of the Philippine Sea (19–20 June 1944) and the Battle of Leyte Gulf (23–25 October 1944). Vice Adm. Charles A. Lockwood was the able commander of submarines, Pacific fleet.

Surface Warfare

Naval surface warfare developments during World War II may be divided into four categories: (1) carrier, (2) amphibious, (3) antisubmarine, and (4) mobile or afloat logistics. Except for antisubmarine operations all were products of the U.S. Navy's task force system of organization. Ships must be operationally prepared for modern, fast-moving naval warfare, while at the same time their maintenance, support, and constant replenishment are provided for. A ship functions only at sea but returns to port periodically to be reconditioned for sea duty. Combat operations therefore are separated in time from logistic support. The captain of a naval ship is responsible to two seniors; one is charged with a task within the navy's mission while a second oversees the ship's upkeep, supply, replenishment, and training.

This concept was most dramatically represented in the operations of the carrier task forces, which were normally composed of four aircraft carriers with protecting battleships, cruisers, and destroyers. In April 1944 task fleets were formed, the Third and Fifth fleets under Adm. William F. Halsey, Jr., and Adm. Raymond A. Spruance, respectively. The intent was to enable one campaign to follow quickly upon the last. The so-called "fleets" were actually only top commanders and staffs of task fleets and major task forces. One group would conduct an operation while the other planned the next. The ships were the same in both fleets, a fact the Japanese never learned.

The task fleets were composed primarily of carrier, amphibious, and mobile support task forces. Carriers, as the capital ships, operated within circular formations with their protecting ships around them. Manned aircraft offensive strikes were made chiefly by Grumman TBF bombers for level bombing and torpedo attacks and Douglas SBD planes for searches and dive-bombing. Grumman F6F fighters defended ships and aircraft. Radar and the proximity fuse were other developments that contributed to American naval success.

Amphibious assault operations included naval gunfire support, air support, ship-to-shore and shore-to-shore movements, and capturing of beachheads. American success in this new type of warfare was achieved chiefly with skillfully designed landing craft in adequate numbers. One type, the LST (landing ship tank), proved the most useful logistic craft of the war. Its ample tank deck made it suitable for hospital, repair, and many other support functions.

Mobile logistics enabled naval forces to remain indefinitely in the forward areas, close to the enemy, cruising at sea in virtually constant readiness. Combat ships were able to receive fuel and other supplies from service vessels either while under way or at anchorages near operating areas such as the Ulithi Atoll. Advance base facilities were maintained afloat at all times and techniques were contrived for transferring fuel, ammunition, stores, and personnel at sea.

Neglect of the peacetime American merchant marine required an enormous wartime shipbuilding program to move men and materials across two oceans. More than 3,500 ships were built, mostly 10-knot Liberty ships and 15-knot Victories. These were operated by the War Shipping Administration to provide for the ocean transport needs of the war economy and the armed forces.

The foremost naval figure of World War II was Adm. Ernest J. King, chief of naval operations and navy member of the Joint Chiefs of Staff. A forceful man, King insisted on the prosecution of the war in the Pacific although by agreement between Roosevelt and Prime Minister Winston Churchill of Great Britain, the European theater had priority.

Rich resources, an intelligent labor force, and freedom from bombing gave the United States an almost unlimited economic potential for war. A heartland facing two oceans, the United States could be allied in a continental war in Europe and fight a maritime war in the Pacific.

The extraordinary significance of naval operations on World War II's outcome made a deep impression on American policymakers. Indeed, six future U.S. presidents served in the Navy during World War II: John Kennedy, Lyndon Johnson, Richard Nixon, Gerald Ford, Jimmy Carter, and George H. W. Bush. Perhaps not surprisingly, therefore, since 1945 the United States has maintained the largest and most technologically sophisticated navy in the world.

BIBLIOGRAPHY

Blair, Clay. *Silent Victory: The U.S. Submarine War Against Japan.* Philadelphia: Lippincott, 1975.

Buell, Thomas E. *The Quiet Warrior: A Biography of Admiral Raymond Spruance.* Boston: Little, Brown, 1974.

Falk, Stanley. *Decision at Leyte.* New York: W.W. Norton, 1966.

Lewin, Ronald. *The American Magic: Codes, Ciphers, and the Defeat of Japan.* New York: Farrar Straus Giroux, 1982.

Potter, E. B. *Nimitz.* Annapolis, Md.: Naval Institute Press, 1976.

Prange, Gordon W. *At Dawn We Slept.* New York: Viking, 1991.

John D. Hayes/A. G.

See also **Aircraft Carriers and Naval Aircraft; Blockade; Coast Guard, U.S.; Convoys; Minesweeping; Naval Operations, Chief of; Navy, Department of the; Pearl Harbor;**

Spanish-American War, Navy in; Task Force 58; Underwater Demolition Teams; World War II.

WORLD WIDE WEB. *See* Internet.

WORLD'S FAIRS, sometimes called international expositions, originated with the 1851 London Crystal Palace Exhibition. The success of that venture in trumpeting the causes of industrialism, nationalism, and imperialism to an audience in excess of six million inspired the builders of nation-states in Europe and the United States to follow suit. The first wave of Victorian-era world's fairs concluded with World War I, but the collapse of capitalist economies in the 1920s precipitated a second wave of fairs held during the Great Depression. Following World War II, world's fairs, confronted with growing competition from electronic media and Disney-inspired theme parks, began to recede in number and importance. Projecting the failures of recent expositions back on the past would be anachronistic, however. From their inception in 1851 through the middle of the twentieth century, world's fairs played a primary role in giving form and substance to the modernizing world.

The success of London's Crystal Palace Exhibition, and especially the success of American exhibitors Cyrus McCormick and Samuel Colt in gaining rave reviews from the British press for their displays of reapers and revolvers, inspired a group of New York business leaders, including newspaper editor Horace Greeley and showman P. T. Barnum, to organize their own Crystal Palace Exhibition in New York City in 1853. The New York spectacle ran afoul of mounting sectional tensions in the United States and failed to win much support from the federal government. Before another world's fair would be held on American shores, the United States would undergo a civil war and an industrial depression, and find itself in the throes of growing class conflict between the rich and poor.

Inspired by the urgency of reconstructing the American nation after the Civil War, and by the ongoing parade of world's fairs in England, France, and Austria, Philadelphia civic authorities decided to hold a world's fair to celebrate the centenary of American independence from England. Fueled by concerns that the panic of 1873 would heighten conflict between social classes, the federal government determined to make the Philadelphia fair an instrument for winning over the hearts and minds of Americans to the newly reconstructed American nation-state. When President Ulysses S. Grant opened the fair in May 1876 in Fairmount Park, the fair boasted some of the largest buildings ever constructed, including Machinery Hall, which featured the 700-ton Corliss engine and Alexander Graham Bell's telephone. This fair, like most world's fairs, ran for only six months and, again like most others, lost money. There were, however, other ways of measuring success. For example, by the time it closed its gates, nearly ten million people had seen its exhibits and many local businesses had made money from the influx of exposition goers.

As the U.S. national economy continued to ricochet between boom and bust, and as Europeans, especially the French, continued to mount spectacular expositions, capped off by the 1889 Paris Universal Exposition with the Eiffel Tower as its centerpiece, numerous American cities considered hosting world's fairs. Some actually materialized. Louisville inaugurated the Southern Exposition in 1883, which ran annually until 1887, while New Orleans hosted the World's Industrial and Cotton Centennial Exposition in 1884–1885. It was, however, the competition between a dozen cities to hold a world's fair commemorating the 400th anniversary of Columbus's 1492 expedition that most clearly announced the medium's arrival as a mainstay of American cultural life.

In 1890, when Chicago business and financial elites persuaded Congress to award them the prize of organizing the World's Columbian Exposition, they set themselves the task of creating a world's fair that would surpass the one held in Paris the previous year. They targeted 1892 as the opening date, but poor weather conditions and labor strikes forced exposition authorities to postpone the formal opening until 1893. Despite the fact that the exposition buildings were still under construction, world's fair officials arranged for dedication ceremonies to take place in October 1892. For that occasion, they organized a nationwide celebration that featured schoolchildren across the country reciting, for the first time, the Pledge of Allegiance, which had been written by Francis J. Bellamy specifically to bring national attention to the fair and the first national Columbus Day holiday.

When the World's Columbian Exposition opened, it featured an inner core of palatial exhibition buildings intended to represent the claim that America represented the apex of the world's civilization. Designed by some of America's leading architectural firms, including Burnham and Root and McKim, Mead, and White, these buildings were dubbed the White City because they were all painted white. For some Americans, however, there was more to the name than the color of the buildings. Led by former abolitionist and African American political leader Frederick Douglass and by antilynching crusader Ida B. Wells, African Americans protested the racist policies of the fair that excluded all but a handful of African American exhibits. White, middle-class women also fought for inclusion in the fair and, unlike African Americans, were allowed to create their own building, used by some to advance the cause of women's suffrage. In addition to the White City, the fair also featured the Midway Plaisance, a mile-long entertainment strip that included ethnological villages intended, in part, to apply the lessons of social Darwinism to the struggle for survival between "races" of humanity. Dominated by its towering Ferris Wheel, the Chicago fair's answer to the Eiffel Tower, the World's Columbian Exposition became the defining event for America's fin-de-siècle generation. In a sense, it also became a defining event for America's young historical profession, for it was at a meeting of the American Historical Association organized in conjunction with this fair, that historian Frederick Jackson Turner read his paper on "The Significance of the Frontier in American History."

The Chicago fair ignited a world's fair-building craze in the United States. Atlanta (1895), Nashville (1897), Omaha (1898), Buffalo (1901), St. Louis (1904), Portland (1905), Jamestown (1907), Seattle (1909), San Diego (1915–1916), and San Francisco (1915–1916) all held world's fairs that hammered home to tens of millions of Americans the fundamental lesson that America's national reconstruction was on course and that the United States was well on the way toward becoming a global power. President William McKinley, who was assassinated at the 1901 Buffalo Pan-American Exposition, summed up the central theme of these fairs when he termed them "timekeepers of progress."

World War I, which erupted while world's fairs were in full swing in San Diego and San Francisco, called into doubt the meanings of both progress and civilization. At the conclusion of the war, however, Europeans quickly returned to the world's fair medium to rebuild their devastated economies and to shore up sagging faith in their imperial enterprises. The French had already led the way with an international colonial exposition in Marseilles in 1916, and were followed, in due course, by the British, who held a massive colonial exposition on the outskirts of London in 1924–1925. Not wanting to be left behind, a group of corporate capitalists and civic authorities in Philadelphia determined that the United States should hold a world's fair as well. Perhaps because America's economic prosperity left no need for reassurance and uplift, the 1926 Philadelphia Sesquicentennial Exposition was a total flop. Its financial losses and poor attendance led many observers to proclaim the end of the world's fair era.

They were wrong. Even before the 1929 stock market crash, several of Chicago's leading corporate capitalists were launching plans for a world's fair to commemorate the anniversary of the founding of Chicago and the fortieth anniversary of the 1893 fair. When the depression hit, they redoubled their efforts and, in 1933–1934, held the Century of Progress Exposition. Chief among its modernistic buildings was the Hall of Science, which distilled the exposition's central theme: "Science Finds; Industry Applies; Man Conforms." At least one performer at the fair refused to conform, however. Sally Rand amazed countless numbers of fairgoers with her notorious fan dance and gave the fair abundant publicity with her multiple arrests. Indeed, so successful was the 1933 fair in rekindling popular faith in the American economic and political systems that President Franklin Roosevelt personally urged exposition authorities to reopen it in 1934. By the time it closed, the Century of Progress Exposi-

Depression-Era World's Fair. This poster, dated 19 August 1940, promotes an exhibition of art from seventy-nine countries at the Utah Art Center, Salt Lake City. LIBRARY OF CONGRESS

tion had jump-started the stalled American world's fair movement.

In the wake of the Chicago fair, San Diego (1935–1936), Dallas (1936), Cleveland (1936–1937), San Francisco (1939–1940), and New York (1939–1940) held world's fairs that, in total, attracted some 100 million visitors. The fairs put thousands of people to work and held out the promise that America's best years lay in the future. Nowhere was this theme more in evidence than at the 1939 New York fair, which took as its theme "The World of Tomorrow." With exhibits created by some of the world's leading industrial designers, including Norman Bel Geddes (who designed the General Motors' Futurama show) and Henry Dreyfus (who designed Democracity), this fair gave visible form to the meaning of modernity and held out the promise that America, in the very near future, would escape from the ravages of the depression and become a consumerist paradise. This fair, like its immediate predecessors, also advocated the use of eugenics to solve America's social problems.

The fairs of the 1930s do not deserve credit for saving the United States from the depression. But, like the generation of Victorian-era fairs that mushroomed across the country between 1876 and 1916 in the midst of increasing class violence and mounting economic anxiety, the fairs of the Great Depression certainly helped restore middle-class confidence in U.S. political and economic institutions.

In the decade and a half following World War II, with the economy seemingly living up to the predictions of previous world's fair promoters, no world's fair was held in the United States. That situation changed when, in response to the Soviet Union's 1957 launch of the man-made satellite *Sputnik*, the federal government supported a bid by Seattle to host a world's fair dedicated to allaying national concerns about the United States lagging behind the Soviet Union in the race for control of outer space. With its "space gothic" architecture that featured the Space Needle, the Century 21 Exposition announced the preparedness of the United States to take on the Soviets in space. The next U.S. fair, the 1964–1965 New York World's Fair, with its Hall of Free Enterprise, announced the readiness of the United States to take up the Soviet challenge on this planet. Smaller fairs ensued, including the 1968 San Antonio HemisFair and Expo '74 held in Spokane. The Spokane fair, following the lead of Expo '67 in Montreal, put a new emphasis on environmentalism and helped prepare the way for the 1982 Knoxville International Energy Exposition and the 1984 New Orleans World Exposition. Both of the last-named fairs had severe financial problems and these contributed to the decision by Chicago civic authorities not to host a world's fair in 1992 to commemorate the quincentennial of Columbus's arrival in the New World.

World's fairs have been among the most formative influences in shaping the tone and texture of modern times. They have filled museums, including the Smithsonian Institution, with their exhibits and they have left vast urban parks, among them Chicago's Jackson Park, in their wake. They have introduced millions of Americans to technologies that range from the telephone and television to the airplane and computer. Because of their overt racism, they have met with resistance, especially from African Americans who successfully converted many fairs into laboratories of civil rights protest and litigation. At the beginning of the twenty-first century, especially in the wake of the billion-dollar loss sustained by the 2000 Hannover Exposition, many critics have suggested that, since world's fairs can no longer compete in a world dominated by television, theme parks, and the Internet, the end of the era of world's fairs is once again in sight. If, however, the primary function of world's fairs has been to provide cultural safety nets during times of economic and political crises brought on by the globalization of capitalism, it is doubtful that so powerful a medium will simply fade away.

BIBLIOGRAPHY

Findling, John E., and Kimberly D. Pelle. *Historical Dictionary of World's Fairs and Expositions, 1851–1988.* New York: Greenwood Press, 1990. Standard reference source.

Greenhalgh, Paul. *Ephemeral Vistas: The Expositions Universelles, Great Exhibitions, and World's Fairs, 1851–1939.* Manchester, U.K.: Manchester University Press, 1988.

Rydell, Robert W. *All the World's a Fair: Visions of Empire at American International Expositions, 1876–1916.* Chicago: University of Chicago Press, 1984.

———. *World of Fairs: The Century-of-Progress Expositions.* Chicago: University of Chicago Press, 1993.

Rydell, Robert W., John E. Findling, and Kimberly D. Pelle. *Fair America: World's Fairs in the United States.* Washington, D.C.: Smithsonian Institution Press, 2000.

Youngs, J. William T. *The Fair and the Falls: Spokane's Expo '74: Transforming an American Environment.* Cheney: Eastern Washington University Press, 1996.

Robert W. Rydell

See also **Centennial Exhibition; Ferris Wheel.**

WORMLEY CONFERENCE. The Wormley Conference was the name given to the series of conferences by which the controversy over the disputed election of 1876 was settled. The name grew out of the fact that the final conference was held at Wormley's Hotel in Washington, D.C., on 26 February 1877. Under the terms of the agreement, the Democrats permitted the counting of the electoral votes that would make Rutherford B. Hayes president of the United States; in return, the Republicans withdrew federal troops from the southern states, thus consenting to the overthrow of the Reconstruction governments in those states.

BIBLIOGRAPHY

Foner, Eric. *Reconstruction: America's Unfinished Revolution, 1863–1877.* New York: Harper and Row, 1988.

Woodward, C. Vann. *Reunion and Reaction: The Compromise of 1877 and the End of Reconstruction.* Boston: Little, Brown, 1966.

Hallie Farmer / A. G.

See also **Civil War; Democratic Party; Elections; Home Rule; Reconstruction; Republican Party.**

WOUNDED KNEE (1973). American Indian activism in the 1960s and 1970s culminated with the occupation of Wounded Knee on the Pine Ridge reservation in South Dakota by American Indian Movement (AIM) members. In early 1973 AIM leaders responded to requests from members of the Lakota community to enter Wounded Knee and establish an alternative political community within the Lakota Nation. Residents opposed the tribal government of Chairman Richard "Dick" Wilson, charging that Wilson abused and overextended his power by placing the tribal police force under his direct command and using violence and terror on community members who opposed his goals.

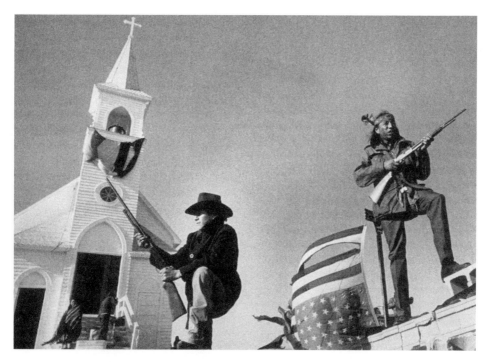

Wounded Knee, 1973. Indian activists stand outside Sacred Heart Catholic Church in Wounded Knee, S.D., during their months-long occupation of the town. © CORBIS

AIM had gained notoriety for its pan-Indian vision of community activism, self-awareness, and empowerment—bringing attention to the enduring economic and political struggles of Indian peoples. AIM members had occupied several reservation border towns, such as Gordon, Nebraska, to protest white racism and discrimination against Indians, and when invited to Pine Ridge, hundreds of Indian activists mobilized for an armed struggle. Under the leadership of Russell Means and Dennis Banks, AIM members declared themselves representatives of the legitimate leaders of the Oglala Nation, issued a series of demands, including the recognition of outstanding Lakota treaty rights, and seized the town of Wounded Knee in February 1973.

Because of Wounded Knee's infamous history as the site of the 1890 massacre and the attention it garnered in the best-selling book by Dee Brown, *Bury My Heart at Wounded Knee*, AIM's occupation attracted immediate press coverage and evoked deep sentiments throughout the United States. The image of armed Indian militants occupying historic monuments in protest of racism, injustice, and continued economic and political oppression resonated with many minority and activist communities, and AIM found sympathizers and supporters throughout the country.

As the standoff intensified, Wilson called in the National Guard. Heavily armed national guardsmen with advanced weaponry and assault vehicles laid siege to the AIM encampment. During the ensuing seventy-day siege, tens of thousands of rounds of ammunition were fired.

Two AIM members were killed, and one federal marshal was seriously injured. Facing daily terror and supply shortages, AIM members surrendered on 8 May 1973 and were quickly arrested. The ensuing trials, particularly those of Banks and Means, attracted national attention.

Violence continued to plague Pine Ridge, and in 1975 a shootout involving AIM leaders left two Federal Bureau of Investigation (FBI) agents and one Native American man dead. The FBI charged Leonard Peltier, a member of AIM, with killing the agents. Following his extradition from Canada, Peltier was tried and sentenced to life imprisonment. His controversial trial and sentence attracted condemnation from international legal observers, and many people consider Peltier the leading political prisoner of the United States.

BIBLIOGRAPHY

Brown, Dee. *Bury My Heart at Wounded Knee: An Indian History of the American West.* New York: Holt, Rinehart and Winston, 1971.

Matthiessen, Peter. *In the Spirit of Crazy Horse.* New York: Viking Press, 1983.

Smith, Paul Chaat, and Robert Allen Warrior. *Like a Hurricane: The Indian Movement from Alcatraz to Wounded Knee.* New York: New Press, 1996.

Ned Blackhawk

See also **Alcatraz; American Indian Movement; Bureau of Indian Affairs.**

WOUNDED KNEE MASSACRE marked the climax of United States efforts to subjugate Lakota-speaking Sioux Indians at the end of the nineteenth century. During 1890 a new religious movement called the Ghost Dance captured the loyalty of many western Indians. On the Sioux reservations, this movement attracted men and women who resented the government's heavy-handed tactics and were drawn to new rituals that promised an era of peace and future union with dead relatives. Unfortunately, just as tensions began to rise over the Ghost Dance, an inexperienced political appointee, Daniel Royer, took control of the agency at Pine Ridge, South Dakota. On 15 November, fearing that the ghost dancers might become violent, Royer called for military assistance. Tensions rose again on 15 December, when the Indians at Pine Ridge learned that Sitting Bull had been killed while being arrested on a nearby Standing Rock reservation. The agent there had believed arresting the old warrior would quell the Ghost Dance at his agency. Fearing similar action at the neighboring Cheyenne River reservation, the Miniconjou leader Big Foot gathered his followers and departed overland to join allies at Pine Ridge. Big Foot and his band were apprehended by elements of the Seventh Cavalry near Wounded Knee Creek on the Pine Ridge reservation on the evening of 28 December.

On the morning of 29 December, with troops deployed in a hollow square around the Indians, regimental commander Colonel George A. Forsyth ordered everyone in Big Foot's band to surrender their weapons. One warrior fired a concealed gun while being disarmed; the surrounding troops responded by opening fire. Hotchkiss guns on a nearby hillside fired indiscriminately into the Indian encampment gunning down those fleeing to safety. When the shooting stopped Big Foot, along with 145 others, including 45 women and 18 children, lay dead. The official death toll rose to 153 when seven of the fifty-one band members known to be wounded that day later died. In addition, an unknown number either were killed and carried from the scene by relatives or escaped and later died from their wounds. The army reported twenty-five soldiers dead and thirty-nine wounded; Forsyth's superiors asserted that some of the army casualties were victims of crossfire from their own comrades. His commander relieved him of his command and charged him with incompetence, but he was exonerated. Later, twenty

Wounded Knee. A view of the site shortly after the massacre on 29 December 1890, which left at least 150 Indians—and possibly far more—and 25 soldiers dead; many of the latter were killed inadvertently by other soldiers. © Bettmann/corbis

soldiers were awarded the Medal of Honor for their service in the massacre. Sioux leaders continue to protest these awards and to advocate the creation of a memorial park at the site.

BIBLIOGRAPHY
Utley, Robert. *The Last Days of the Sioux Nation.* New Haven, Conn.: Yale University Press, 1964.

Frederick E. Hoxie

WRITS OF ASSISTANCE were general search warrants issued to the customs officers by the colonial superior courts. They were first issued in Massachusetts in 1751 and remained fairly uncontroversial until 1761, when the old writs expired and customs officers had to apply for new ones to replace them. James Otis, an attorney who represented merchants who opposed the new writs, argued that they were unconstitutional, but he lost his case. Eventually, the courts issued new writs after the British government supported their legality. That closed the issue in Massachusetts.

The controversy resurfaced in 1767 when the Townshend Revenue Act authorized writs of assistance. Under the act, customs officers prepared the writs themselves and requested the attorney general in each colony to secure these writs from the superior court. This action made writs of assistance an issue in the superior court of every American province. Many judges objected to the form of the writs and questioned their constitutionality. In most courts, the issue dragged through 1772. This delay resulted in a direct refusal by most colonial courts, although many judges offered to issue writs of assistance in particular cases "as directed by law." Finally, in 1772, the customs officers reported that they had secured writs in East Florida, West Florida, South Carolina, Bahama, Bermuda, New Hampshire, Nova Scotia, and Quebec. Because the controversy over the writs of assistance surfaced in the superior court of every Anglo-American colony, it became a common grievance that merited attention in the DECLARATION OF INDEPENDENCE.

BIBLIOGRAPHY
Bailyn, Bernard. *The Ideological Origins of the American Revolution.* Cambridge, Mass.: Belknap Press of Harvard University Press, 1967.
Cook, Don. *The Long Fuse: How England Lost the American Colonies, 1760–1785.* New York: Atlantic Monthly Press, 1995.

O. M. Dickerson / S. B.

See also **Search and Seizure, Unreasonable; Townshend Acts;** *and vol. 9:* **The Writ of Assistance, 1762.**

WYANDOTTE CONSTITUTION. The Wyandotte Constitution, the charter under which Kansas became a state, was drafted at Wyandotte (now Kansas City,

Kansas) by the first territorial convention in which Republicans and Democrats participated (5–29 July 1859). It was adopted by popular vote on 4 October. It followed the constitution of Ohio as a model, prohibited slavery, and reduced Kansas to its present boundaries.

BIBLIOGRAPHY
Heller, Francis H. *The Kansas State Constitution: A Reference Guide.* Westport, Conn.: Greenwood Press, 1992.

Samuel A. Johnson / A. R.

See also **Border War; Kansas; Popular Sovereignty; State Constitutions.**

WYOMING. Called the last bastion of the "Old West," Wyoming retains some vestiges of its frontier past, and not just through the popular summer rodeos and as a backdrop for motion picture Westerns. Rainfall is scant, elevations are high, distances between populated places are long.

Admitted to the union as the forty-fourth state on 10 July 1890, Wyoming is the least populated of the United States, with fewer than 500,000 people occupying a land area of 97,818 square miles. Rectangular and without natural borders, Wyoming is bounded on the north by Montana, on the west by Idaho and Utah, on the south by Utah and Colorado, and on the east by Nebraska and South Dakota.

Early Wyoming
The earliest residents in Wyoming were prehistoric people dating from more than 11,000 years ago. Several Native American tribes occupied various parts of what is now Wyoming, including the Shoshone, Sioux, Cheyenne, Crow, Blackfeet, and Arapaho. The state has just one Indian reservation shared between the Shoshone and Northern Arapaho.

Wyoming always has been, as a popular saying goes, a "trail to somewhere else." The first Europeans in Wyoming were French Canadian fur trappers in the middle 1700s, interested in its fur resources but not planning to stay. By the 1820s, several hundred fur trappers sought furs and trade with native people. The fur trade rendezvous, conceived by William Ashley, was first held in Wyoming. Fur traders built what became Wyoming's first permanent settlement—Fort Laramie—in 1834. Sold to the U.S. Army in 1849, the fort became an important stopover for westward travelers and for the quartering of soldiers sent West to guard trails from Indians.

Wyoming remained a trail as a result of migration to Oregon and the later gold rush to California. Some 350,000 travelers used the Oregon-California-Mormon trail across the central part of Wyoming between 1841 and 1860. During the 1860s a series of skirmishes between native people and the army caused significant dislocations.

Despite its Old West image, Wyoming is a product of the transcontinental railroad. Prior to its construction in the late 1860s, there were few people in Wyoming beyond the military posts, stage stations, and ferry crossings. The railroad began construction across southern Wyoming in 1867. Railway depot towns were established, including Cheyenne, Laramie, Rawlins, Green River, and Evanston. Dozens of other "hell-on-wheels" towns did not survive.

At the time, the area was a part of Dakota Territory, governed from Yankton. Local residents wanted their own territory. The members of the Dakota legislature were anxious to cleave off the Wyoming part of their territory because it had little in common with the Eastern Dakotas, so they petitioned Congress to establish a separate territory. The name "Wyoming" is not indigenous, but was applied to the new territory by U.S. Representative James M. Ashley of Ohio, chairman of the House Committee on Territories, who suggested the name in honor of his boyhood home in the Wyoming Valley of Pennsylvania.

Women's Rights, Transportation, and Mineral Resources

Congress authorized the territory in 1868, but because of the pending impeachment trial of President Andrew Johnson, territorial officials were not appointed until after Johnson's successor, Ulysses S. Grant, was inaugurated. John A. Campbell of Ohio was the first territorial governor and Edward M. Lee of Connecticut the first territorial secretary. Neither had visited Wyoming prior to their appointments. The two men, with the help of the South Pass City saloonkeeper and legislator William Bright, convinced the first territorial legislature to give women equal rights, including the right to vote. Wyoming was the first government to do so, thus gaining the state's nickname, "The Equality State." Governor Campbell signed the suffrage bill on 10 December 1869, the date designated since 1935 as "Wyoming Day."

When Wyoming gained statehood in 1890, the state constitution guaranteed equal rights for women, thus making Wyoming the first state with such a constitutional provision, thirty years before all American women obtained the franchise. The other unique constitutional article stipulated state ownership of all waters within the state and specified the prior appropriation doctrine as a means of allocating water to users.

In 1924 Wyoming again gained national attention when Nellie Tayloe Ross became the first woman elected governor of any state. Estelle Reel, elected Wyoming's state superintendent of public instruction in 1894, had been the first woman in America to win statewide office.

The railroad engineer General Grenville Dodge determined much of the rail route across Wyoming and established the site of Cheyenne as a major railroad division point 8 July 1867. When Campbell first came to the territory, he designated Cheyenne his territorial capital. An article in the state constitution required an election to determine the location of the permanent capital. Since an election in 1904 failed to decide the issue, Cheyenne has remained the capital, albeit technically the temporary one.

Once the tracks for the transcontinental railroad had been laid across Wyoming, coal mines opened to supply the locomotives with fuel. Many of the earliest mines were owned by the Union Pacific Railroad or its subsidiary company. Because of the vast land grants deeded to the railroad as alternate sections twenty miles in both directions from the tracks, the railroad became (and remains) the largest private landowner in Wyoming, with an initial holding estimated at approximately 4.1 million acres. Because of its landholdings and its historic control over coal mining, the railroad was a significant force in Wyoming politics well into the twentieth century.

In the early 1900s, Wyoming again became a "trail to somewhere else" with the establishment of the Lincoln Highway, the nation's first transcontinental auto route. In the early 1920s, transcontinental airmail was flown across the state and airfields were established along the route, roughly paralleling the original transcontinental railroad line. Although air transport firms like United Airlines were once headquartered in Wyoming, the state now is home to no major airline. The busiest airport is in Jackson Hole, a destination for skiers, tourists, and many part-time residents.

Mineral development, starting with coal in the 1860s, remains a significant part of Wyoming's economy. The state has led the nation in coal production every year since 1988, with most of the coal coming from surface strip mines in the Powder River Basin in northeastern Wyoming.

Oil has been important in Wyoming history. In the early 1900s, the Salt Creek oil field in north-central Wyoming was one of the nation's largest oil producers. Casper, known as the Oil Capital of the Rockies, once was home to the world's largest gasoline refinery, the Standard Oil refinery, which was established in 1922. The nearby Teapot Dome Naval Petroleum Reserve lent its name to a national scandal in the 1920s, although no Wyomingite was directly involved in it. New oil discoveries were made in the 1970s in the "overthrust belt" of southwestern Wyoming, but oil production in the late twentieth century was in steady decline.

Trona, used in the production of glass and soap, was discovered in Wyoming in the mid-twentieth century. Nearly the entire national supply comes from the Green River Basin in southwestern Wyoming. Uranium, first discovered in great quantities in the 1950s, was produced in abundance in central Wyoming until demand began declining in 1980.

A Boom and Bust Economy

Because of the state's strong reliance on natural resources, it has been subject to extreme booms and busts. The fur trade was Wyoming's first boom and bust, followed several decades later by a bust in cattle ranching. The demise of coal-powered locomotives closed the coal mines in the 1950s, but coal production overtook all earlier records by the 1970s when the state's abundant coal, lying relatively close to the surface in deep seams, became an important fuel for power generation. Although low in BTUs, the low sulfur content met standards of the Clean Air Act and gave Wyoming coal competitive advantages in the last quarter of the twentieth century. From 1985 to the late 1990s, Wyoming suffered another economic bust, recovering only with the resurgence of natural gas prices and increased interest in coal bed methane production.

Agriculture was important in the development of Wyoming, particularly cattle raising. In the 1870s and 1880s, cattle companies formed in Europe and the East ran thousands of cattle on the open ranges of Wyoming. Competition and poor weather, culminating in the blizzard of 1886–1887, put many large companies out of business. This led to the Johnson County War of 1892, a conflict in which big operators sent a private army into Johnson County in north-central Wyoming to root out smaller ranchers who defied the rules set by the Wyoming Stock Growers Association. Two men, Nate Champion and Nick Ray, were killed by the cattle companies' men, who escaped conviction and punishment.

Crop agriculture has been limited as a consequence of aridity as well as the high average elevation and relatively short growing season. Nonetheless, some of the nation's first reclamation projects were built in Wyoming, and the dams allowed crop agriculture to proceed. Sugar beets, dry beans, and alfalfa are now important crops. Initially created to provide irrigation water to farmers, the dams also generate electricity for urban residents and give opportunities for recreational sports on the reservoirs.

Despite these water projects, experts promoted dry farming in eastern Wyoming in the early 1900s. The crops paid off until after World War I, when prices declined and the state was hit by a prolonged drought. By 1924, the state was in economic depression. In that one year alone, twenty-five banks failed. Many residents left the state, abandoning homesteads and closing businesses. New Deal programs, implemented almost a decade later, helped the economy but it was World War II that pulled the state out of its economic woes. In 1935, the state legislature debated new forms of taxation, rejecting a state income tax (promoted at the time by a bipartisan group of farmers and ranchers) and implementing instead a state sales tax. Wyoming remains one of only a handful of states without a state income tax. Sales taxes are augmented by mineral severance taxes, allowing for real property tax rates to remain among the lowest in the nation.

Following the Arab oil embargo of 1973, the state's economy entered another boom cycle. Cities such as Gillette and Rock Springs attracted national attention for runaway growth and problems of "impact." One of the main problems was the inability of the cities to house the huge influx of new residents. Also, the heavy strains of new, unexpected residents put pressure on water and sewer systems, streets, and law enforcement. Schools also recorded huge enrollments. Were it not for financial assistance from the state during the period, many of the cities would not have been able to handle the crunch. Legislative passage of a severance tax on minerals in 1969 guaranteed a source of funds to help mitigate the problems, even though mineral companies resisted the tax. Much of the severance tax revenues have gone into a Permanent Mineral Trust Fund, which had an estimated value of almost $3 billion in 2001. During the boom years of the early 1980s, as much as 40 percent of the state's budget was financed from severance tax revenues and state services were sustained during the bust years from 1985 to 1999.

Tourism, popularized by railroads in the nineteenth century, is also an important industry. Yellowstone National Park in Wyoming's northwest corner was established as America's first national park in 1872. Nearby Grand Teton National Park features spectacular mountain scenery as well as world-class ski areas nearby. Devils Tower National Monument, established as the first national monument in the United States in 1906, is located in northeastern Wyoming. The highly regarded Buffalo Bill Historical Center in Cody and celebrations such as Cheyenne Frontier Days attract tourists with the mystique of the Old West.

Tourism, the Environment, Manufacturing, and Education

Almost half of the state's land area is controlled by the federal government. Most of the federal land is held by the Bureau of Land Management, although the U.S. Forest Service manages vast tracts. Wyomingites remain split on environmental questions. In the 1990s, owners of ranches near Yellowstone unsuccessfully contested a plan of the federal government to reintroduce wolves into the park. Environmental organizations such as the regional-based Powder River Basin Resource Council have a substantial voice in Wyoming. In 2001, environmental groups pointed out the potential long-term damage caused by water discharges from coal bed methane wells in the Powder River Basin of northeastern Wyoming.

Manufacturing has never been significant to the state's economy. Since territorial days, Wyoming politicians have sought economic diversification, but with negligible results. Neither are defense expenditures a significant factor in Wyoming's economy. The only defense installation is Warren Air Force Base, the headquarters for the MX missile system. Silos that once housed Atlas and Minuteman missiles still dot the landscape of the southeastern part of the state. An airbase was located near Casper during World War II and a relocation center to hold Japanese and Japanese Americans operated between Cody and Powell during the World War II years.

The University of Wyoming, founded in 1886, is the only four-year university in the state. Seven community colleges provide two years of higher education. School district consolidation and equalization of school funding have been major political issues at the turn of the twenty-first century. In a series of decisions during the 1990s, the Wyoming Supreme Court ruled that educational spending must be as nearly equitable as possible.

Most Wyomingites live in small towns. The largest city, Cheyenne, has a population of just over fifty thousand people. Vast distances commonly separate towns. There are twenty-three counties. The legislature is bicameral, with a thirty-member Senate and sixty-member House elected from single-member districts.

Minority Groups and Racism

The population, very diverse when the railroad and coal mines hired workers of many nationalities, has become less so. The largest minority ethnic group is Mexican Americans. More than eleven thousand Native Americans live in Wyoming, most on the Wind River Reservation. The African American population is small and mainly concentrated in southern Wyoming.

Since the days of the frontier army forays against native people, racism has been present in Wyoming. More than two dozen Chinese miners were killed in the so-called Rock Springs massacre of September 1885, although most historians consider it a labor incident with racism in an incidental role. In 1969, the state and the University of Wyoming were rocked by the so-called Black 14 incident, which occurred when the university football coach kicked fourteen African American players off the team after they sought to wear black armbands in a game. The state and university gained national notoriety once again with the murder of gay university student Matthew Shepard in October 1998.

State Politics and Prominent Wyomingites

Until the late twentieth century, Wyoming had a competitive two-party system with national leaders coming from both political parties. U.S. Senator Francis E. Warren, the leader of the Republican Party in the state during the first decades of statehood, represented the state in the U.S. Senate for a record thirty-seven years until his death in 1929. John B. Kendrick, a popular Democrat, served as governor and then as U.S. senator until his death in 1933. Joseph M. Carey, first elected to the U.S. Senate in 1890, served as a Republican in the Senate but was elected governor as a Democrat in 1910. Other prominent political figures have included U.S. senators Joseph C. O'Mahoney (D), Gale McGee (D), and Alan K. Simpson (R). Vice President Richard Cheney represented Wyoming in the U.S. House of Representatives from 1979 until his appointment as secretary of defense in 1989. Except for the Progressive (Bull Moose) party in 1912 and Ross Perot's campaign in 1992, third parties have not had significant influence in the state.

Prominent Wyomingites have included the showman William F. "Buffalo Bill" Cody, the sports announcer Curt Gowdy, the attorney and television personality Gerry Spence, Esther Hobart Morris (the first woman in America to serve as a judge), the efficiency expert W. Edwards Deming, the country singer Chris LeDoux, the rocket pioneer G. Edward Pendray, the water engineer Dr. Elwood Mead, and Interior Secretary James Watt. Other famous Wyomingites include the Olympic wrestler Rulon Gardner, Chief Washakie, Crazy Horse, the artist Jackson Pollock, the former cabinet officer James Baker, the World Bank president James Wolfensohn, author Annie Proulx, the retailer J. C. Penney (the first Penney store, in Kemmerer, Wyoming, opened in 1902), and the mountain climber Paul Petzoldt.

BIBLIOGRAPHY

Annals of Wyoming: The Wyoming History Journal. Laramie: Wyoming State Historical Society, 1923–. Published quarterly.

Gould, Lewis Gould. *Wyoming from Territory to Statehood.* Worland, N.Y.: High Plains, 1989.

Hendrickson, Gordon, ed. *Peopling the High Plains: Wyoming's European Heritage.* Cheyenne: Wyoming State Archives and Historical Department, 1977.

Larson, T. A. *History of Wyoming.* 2d ed. Lincoln: University of Nebraska Press, 1978.

———. *Wyoming's War Years.* 1954. Reprint, Cheyenne: Wyoming Historical Foundation, 1994.

Roberts, Philip J., David L. Roberts, and Steven L. Roberts. *Wyoming Almanac.* 5th ed. Laramie, Wyo.: Skyline West Press, 2001.

Urbanek, Mae. *Wyoming Place Names.* Boulder, Colo.: Johnson, 1967.

Philip J. Roberts

See also **Cattle; Coal Mining and Organized Labor; Dry Farming; Fur Trade and Trapping; National Park System; Oil Fields; Reclamation; Suffrage: Woman's Suffrage; Teapot Dome Oil Scandal; Territorial Governments; Tourism; Westward Migration; Yellowstone National Park.**

WYOMING MASSACRE. On 2 July 1778 Patriot forces under the command of Zebulon Butler tried to launch a surprise attack against approximately 1,100 British soldiers and their Seneca allies who had moved down the Susquehanna River valley to prevent the expulsion of loyalists from the area near modern Wilkes-Barre, Pennsylvania. Unfortunately, Seneca scouts detected the advance, and the patriots were scattered. Only 60 of the more than 350 patriot troops managed to return to their base; Zebulon Butler and a small group fled the area entirely. Patriot leaders insisted afterward that British brutality and the savagery of their Indian allies had played a crucial role in the defeat. It was one of many confrontations where loyalist and patriot sentiment was mixed with concerns for secure land title and racial hatred.

BIBLIOGRAPHY

Calloway, Colin G. *The American Revolution in Indian Country: Crisis in Diversity in Native American Communities.* New York: Cambridge University Press, 1995.

Mancall, Peter. *Valley of Opportunity: Economic Culture Along the Upper Susquehannah, 1700–1800.* Ithaca, N.Y.: Cornell University Press, 1991.

Frederick E. Hoxie

WYOMING VALLEY, SETTLEMENT OF.

Until Europeans intruded just before the Revolution, the Wyoming Valley in Pennsylvania was largely the preserve of the Munsee Indians, a member of the Delaware Nation who dominated the region. Beginning about 1750, the arrival of white Europeans pressed the Indians gradually westward into the Ohio Valley.

The Wyoming Valley also became a Revolutionary-era bone of contention between Pennsylvania and Connecticut. Beginning in 1769 the valley was settled by Connecticut colonists, whose claim rested on grants issued by the Connecticut-incorporated Susquehanna Company (1754). By 1774, Pennsylvania settlers, with some success, made no less than five efforts to expel the Yankees; seventeen Connecticut settlements survived when, on 3 July 1778, the Wyoming massacre occurred. In a bloody raid carried out by 1,000 Loyalist Pennsylvanians and their Iroquois allies under the leadership of John Butler, the Whig stronghold Forty Fort was successfully assaulted and the rest of the New Englanders evicted from Pennsylvania. Butler's Rangers (who blamed the Indians although both were responsible) killed 360 pro-independence New Englanders, including women and children.

The massacre was a classic case of using the cover of the American Revolution to settle local scores. Persistent Connecticut settlers came back to the valley near the end of the war, only to have the Continental Congress court of arbitration decide land ownership in favor of the now-sovereign state of Pennsylvania. The Yankees could either leave or accept Pennsylvania rule. Not until the 1799 Compromise Act did Connecticut finally relinquish all claims to jurisdiction over the Wyoming Valley.

But if political jurisdiction favored the Pennsylvanians, the New England colonizers still determinedly held that part of the land resting on the old Susquehanna Company patents. These English ethnics confronted largely German settlers, as well as some "Yorkers" from New York State. The Wyoming Valley was thus the site of conflict as ethnic and state loyalties were tested in a lush, fertile agricultural area. As typical for nineteenth-century America, assimilation worked over the generations to diffuse, without however wholly eliminating, ethnic hostilities and exclusivity.

In the 1880s, rich anthracite coal deposits drew many new immigrants into the valley: Irish, Welsh, Poles, and other Slavs were prominent among the new wave. This influx was also ultimately absorbed into the already richly varied population. Although by the end of the century two generations of settlers from many lands called the valley their home the region's towns like Williamsport, Westmoreland, Towanda, and Wellsboro retained their Yankee influence, as seen in its architecture and in the New England village atmosphere that survived the earlier expulsion or assimilation of the settlers from Connecticut. The area's story profoundly challenges the perception that immigrant influx in the northeastern United States was only an urban phenomenon.

Wilkes-Barre and environs became the center of the anthracite coal industry by the beginning of the twentieth century. Mining (and its attendant poverty) in turn brought manufacturing plants attracted by the proximity to their chief energy source. Unusually bitter labor strife, common to areas combining mining and manufacturing, ensued. The United Mine Workers Union, very active in the valley, was largely responsible for the confrontational and class-oriented labor battles in urban and rural areas alike.

After World War I, anthracite production plummeted, an economic disaster rendered final by the Great Depression. Not even the economic prosperity that accompanied World War II could halt the economic demise of large portions of the Wyoming Valley. In the large cities of the region, Wilkes-Barre and Scranton, union affiliation remained strong even after World War II, when most of the anthracite mines had been inactive for a generation or more. Agriculture survives in the rural area of the valley, as does tourist-driven hunting and fishing, and some industrial diversification came out of the war. But postwar prosperity has been elusive in a region, which, until very recently, was locked into a permanent state of recession.

From a historical perspective, what happened more broadly in the United States in terms of ethnicity, immigration and labor also occurred in the Wyoming Valley. Beginning with the valley's earliest settlement by Europeans, tensions between Native Americans and white Europeans over land claims, between different ethnic and political groups deriving in part to land-company patent rights, and between classes as a result of heavy mining and manufacturing operations in large measure mirrored those taking place through significant parts of America.

BIBLIOGRAPHY

Bodnar, John E. *Anthracite People: Families, Unions and Work, 1900–1914.* Harrisburg, 1983.

Smith, Ernest Gray. *The Sesqui-Centennial of the Battle of Wyoming, July 2, 3, 4, 1778–1928.* Wilkes-Barre.

Works Projects Administraion Guide to Pennsylvania. New York, 1940.

Carl E. Prince

XYZ

"X" ARTICLE. This influential essay in the July 1947 issue of *Foreign Affairs*, "The Sources of Soviet Conduct," was written by State Department official George F. Kennan, using the pseudonym "Mr. X." Kennan, an experienced diplomat and senior advisor to U.S. ambassadors in Moscow, sent the State Department an 8,000 word report in February 1946 known as the "long telegram," urging the United States to view the Soviet leadership as an implacable, expansionist foe. In the "X" article, Kennan amplified his call for a strategy of "patient but firm and vigilant containment of Russian expansive tendencies" through the "adroit application of counterforce at a series of constantly shifting geographical and political points."

The article was widely circulated among the foreign policy bureaucracy, and won Kennan a position as head of the State Department Policy Planning Staff from 1947 to 1950 as well as the reputation of the father of containment. Soon, however, Kennan began to criticize containment policies, insisting that his vigorous language had been misunderstood. American foreign policy should not rely so heavily on military confrontation but on "counterforce," applying economic and political pressure while awaiting the Soviet Union's inevitable demise.

BIBLIOGRAPHY

Hixson, Walter L. *George F. Kennan: Cold War Iconoclast.* New York: Columbia University Press, 1989.

Miscamble, Wilson D. *George F. Kennan and the Making of American Foreign Policy, 1947–1950.* Princeton, N.J.: Princeton University Press, 1992.

Stephanson, Anders. *Kennan and the Art of Foreign Policy.* Cambridge, Mass.: Harvard University Press, 1989.

Max Paul Friedman

See also **Cold War; Foreign Policy; Russia, Relations with;** *and vol. 9:* **American Diplomacy.**

X-1 PLANE. The Bell X-1 plane was the first aircraft in the world to break the speed of sound on 14 October 1947. However, the work to accomplish this feat had begun over a decade earlier, as aerodynamicists such as Adolf Busemann began defining and studying the turbulences that appeared as a propeller aircraft approached the speed of sound, Mach 1. Machines experienced compressibility,

Chuck Yeager. The first pilot to break the sound barrier, standing next to his Bell X-1 plane, *Glamorous Glennis.* © UPI/ CORBIS-BETTMANN

an instability that shakes the machine and renders it uncontrollable. The Army–Air Force Scientific Board, together with the National Advisory Committee on Aeronautics (NACA, predecessor of the NATIONAL AERONAUTICS AND SPACE ADMINISTRATION), noted how measurements of airplane models in wind tunnels failed between the speed of Mach 0.8 and Mach 1.2, which meant that a specially built transonic machine was necessary. After considerable debate, in 1944 the NACA agreed to allow the U.S. Army Air Forces to procure a rocket-powered plane, deemed simpler than a jet-powered one for experimental purposes. The Bell Aircraft Corporation was awarded the project and constructed three prototypes, which were ferried from Niagara Falls, the company's factory site, to Muroc Army Air Field (now Edwards Air Force Base) in the California desert, where a series of ground and flight tests were conducted.

For the flight tests, the X-1 was partially sealed into the belly of a modified B-29 bomber and, once in the air, dropped to save on the amount of rocket propellant required for takeoff. Among the team of pilots testing the machine, Chuck Yeager was chosen to attempt the flight intended to break the speed of sound. He christened his machine *Glamorous Glennis* in honor of his wife. The B-29 with the X-1 inside took off and achieved 25,000 feet.

Yeager entered the X-1 (sitting in the machine from take-off was considered too dangerous), sealed the hatch, and dropped off. His rocket engines functioned perfectly, and after breaking the speed record (registering 700 mph, Mach 1.06) at an altitude of 43,000 feet, he glided to a dry lake landing. News of the successful flight test, however, was kept a secret for two months.

The Bell X-1 was used for further tests and became the first of a series of experimental aircraft that have allowed to push the boundaries of flight. The machine that first broke the speed of sound is now on display at the Smithsonian's National Air and Space Museum.

BIBLIOGRAPHY

Blackburn, Al. *Aces Wild: The Race for Mach 1*. Wilmington, Del.: Scholarly Resources, 1999.

Rotundo, Louis. *Into the Unknown: The X-1 Story*. Washington, D.C.: Smithsonian Institution Press, 1994.

Guillaume de Syon

See also **Rockets.**

XYZ AFFAIR of 1797–1798 led to an undeclared naval war between France and the United States. This diplomatic crisis had its beginnings in 1778, when the United States entered into a military alliance with the French; however, when the French were unable to completely fulfill the terms of the alliance, anti-French sentiments erupted in the United States. The 1794 JAY's TREATY, concluded between the United States and Britain, angered the French, who retaliated by seizing American ships at sea. In 1796, President George Washington attempted to replace the American minister to France, James Monroe, who had been friendly to the causes of the French Revolution, with Charles Pinckney, whom the French refused to accept. As a result, in 1797 Pinckney returned to France accompanied by John Marshall and Elbridge Gerry, to try to repair relations and to negotiate a new treaty. Bolstered by military victories, the French government asked for a $250,000 loan from the United States before agreeing to meet with the American representatives. Conveyed through three negotiators, a Swiss banker, Jean Hottinguer, known as "Mr. X" in correspondence from John Adams; an American banker in Hamburg, Germany, Mr. Bellamy, "Mr. Y"; and Lucien Hauteval, also Swiss, "Mr. Z," these requests met with outrage in the United States. Consequently, the mission failed, and the undeclared naval war ensued until the Convention of 1800 improved commercial relations between France and the United States.

BIBLIOGRAPHY

Smith, Mark A. "Crisis, Unity, and Partisanship: The Road to the Sedition Act." Ph.D diss., University of Virginia, 1998.

Stinchcombe, William. *The XYZ Affair*. Westport, Conn.: Greenwood Press, 1980.

Jennifer Harrison

YADDO, an artists' retreat in Saratoga Springs, New York, was founded in 1900 by Katrina "Kate" Nichols Trask (1853–1922) and the New York financier Spencer Trask (1844–1909), and was opened to artists in 1926. Its mansion, guesthouses, and studios are situated among more than four hundred acres of woodland, lake, and gardens. Yaddo is the largest artist-residency program in the United States, entertaining as many as two hundred guests annually (up to thirty-five at a time in the summer and twelve to fifteen in the winter). Guests typically remain for two to eight weeks. Advisory committees of artists review 1,100 applications annually. There are only two rules: studios may not be visited without an invitation, and visitors are admitted to the grounds only between 4 and 10 P.M.

Yaddo, heralded by the *New York Times* in 1926 as a "new and unique experiment [with] no exact parallel in the world of the fine arts," has been successful not only because of its physical facilities but because its sense has centered on the creative life. Its founders' reverence for art and artists has been transmitted in the stories told by the very artists it supports. The estate was named by four-year-old Christina Trask "because it makes poetry . . . . [Yaddo] sounds like shadow, but it's not going to be." It became the Trasks' means of revival after their four young children died and the original house called "Yaddo" burned to the ground in 1891. Their attitude is expressed in the motto in the phoenix mosaic (Tiffany) on the fireplace of the mansion: "Yaddo Resurgo ad Pacem." Katherine Anne Porter explained: "The Trasks were both quite complicated people, working within a perfectly conventional moral and religious and social code . . . both apparently had more than a streak of real mysticism, and both were as wildly romantic as any two Babes in the Woods."

The Philanthropist George Foster Peabody (1852–1938), who oversaw the financial affairs of the Trask fortune after Spencer Trask's death, and who became Katrina Trask's husband in the last year of her life, formally established Yaddo as a nonprofit corporation in 1923. Elizabeth Ames (1885–1977), appointed executive director of Yaddo in 1923, made the Trasks' dream a reality by inventing, in the words of John Cheever, "an administration so intelligent and comprehensive that at times when one found seven writers of vastly different temperaments working happily under the same roof it seemed magical" (Bird, "Elizabeth Ames," 1977). Ames served in this position until 1963, vindicated of Robert Lowell's charge (1949) that she headed a dangerous communist conspiracy. In the 1930s and 1940s Yaddo served as a haven from Nazi persecution for Jewish and left-leaning artists.

Notable guests have included Hannah Arendt, Milton Avery, James Baldwin, Leonard Bernstein, John Cheever, Aaron Copland, Philip Guston, Patricia Highsmith, Langston Hughes, Ted Hughes, Jacob Lawrence, Carson McCullers, Sylvia Plath, Katherine Anne Porter, Philip Roth, Meyer Schapiro, Clifford Still, Virgil Thomson, and William Carlos Williams. Yaddo is supported by grants from the New York State Council on the Arts, the National Endowment for the Arts, and private and corporate funding. Artists themselves act as patrons and board members.

BIBLIOGRAPHY

Bird, David. "Elizabeth Ames, Creator of Yaddo, Upstate Cultural Haven, Dies at 92." *New York Times*, 30 March 1977.

Cheever, Susan. "Yaddo Artists' Colony." *Architectural Digest*, August 1996, 34–38.

Ciccarelli, Barbara L. "Kate Nichols Trask." In *Dictionary of American Biography*. Edited by John A. Garraty, and Mark C. Carnes. Volume 21. *American National Biography*. New York: Oxford University Press, 1999.

Waite, Marjorie Peabody. *Yaddo, Yesterday and Today*. Saratoga Springs, N.Y.: Argus Press, 1933.

Patricia Trutty-Coohill

See also **Art: Painting; Artists' Colonies; National Endowment for the Arts.**

YAKAMA. Calling themselves Mamachatpam, the Native inhabitants of south central Washington State occupied the drainage of the Yakima River, a major tributary of the Columbia River. These five bands spoke Sahaptian languages and engaged in plant harvesting, hunting, and fishing, particularly salmon fishing. In the late twentieth century, nuclear waste, dams, and water diverted to irrigation destroyed many traditional foods. Although they suffered various epidemics, there were roughly 10,000 Yakamas at the end of the twentieth century, or double their estimated precontact population. The arrival of horses in the 1730s expanded their mobility and allowed the Yakamas to hunt bison on the northern Plains under the leadership of Weowich. The increased need for horse pastures led the Yakamas to explore the coastal meadows and villages east of the Cascade Mountains; this spread their language and led them to intermarry with other tribes in the region. By the mid-1800s, the Yakamas were led by three brothers, Kamiakin, Skloom, Shawaway, and their uncles, Teias and Owhi, who served as leaders of the native resistance during the 1855 Treaty War, which was fought in the aftermath of their forced land surrender. Despite strong pressures, such as withholding food and supplies, from the Methodist James Wilbur and both Oblate and Jesuit missionaries, Yakama beliefs and spiritual blessings continued to thrive at seasonal thanksgivings, or root feasts, held in mat lodges. In the late twentieth century, their prophet Smohalla preached for a return to Native American ways. His influence was enormous, and the community of his followers continued to shun all modern conveniences. With an industrial park and forestry reserves, Yakama Industries provided steady employment, as well as seasonal stoop labor in fields and orchards, while the Yakama nation pursued a major water rights case.

BIBLIOGRAPHY

Schuster, Helen. "Yakama." In *Handbook of North American Indians*. Vol. 13: *Plateau*. Edited by William C. Sturtevant. Washington, D.C.: Smithsonian Institution, 1998.

Jay Miller

See also **Tribes: Northwestern.**

YAKIMA INDIAN WARS. Following the American conquest of northern Mexico in the Mexican War (1846–1848), hundreds of thousands of white settlers and migrants traveled west along the Overland and Oregon Trails. Heading to the fertile river valleys of the Oregon and Washington Territories, white migrants brought devastating changes to the Northwest Coast and the Columbia River plateau. European diseases killed thousands of the region's Indians, settlers' herds and horses consumed precious grasses and water, and whites occupied and settled strategic valleys and passes. Throughout the Columbia River plateau, bands of Yakimas, Umatillas, Klikitats, Nez Perces, and Cayuses joined in extended trading and political alliances to head off the encroachment of white settlers.

Beginning in 1855, state authorities in Washington, led by Governor Isaac Stevens, negotiated a series of treaties and land cessions that recognized the power of interior tribes. The Yakima Treaty, signed on 9 July 1855, ceded more than 10 million acres to the U.S. government in exchange for over 1 million acres of reservation lands in which no white settlers could travel or settle without Yakima approval. Following the discovery of gold in the eastern Cascades that same summer, white prospectors and settlers crossed into Yakima territory without Indian agreement, and tensions escalated throughout the region. Prospectors consumed Indian resources and often indiscriminately attacked Indian parties.

Facing the loss of their traditional homelands and the destruction of many of their forests and game reserves, the Yakimas no longer trusted the promises of Stevens and other white authorities. When the region's Indian agents went to confer with Yakima leaders, including Chief Kamaiakin, they were killed. War, not hollow words, the Yakimas decided, would determine the future survival of their peoples. As the state militias in Oregon and Washington mobilized and attempted to prosecute those responsible for killing the agents, Yakima emissaries visited Indian communities throughout the region. Umatillas, Nez Perces, Spokanes, Klikitats, and other Indian groups began preparing for war.

The Yakima Wars involved not only affiliated bands of Yakimas but many of the region's other Indian groups, and military conflicts engulfed Indian communities. As allied Indian groups drove settlers from their farms and communities, threatening to push many whites further west to the Pacific, the U.S. Army mobilized and drove Indian groups further east of the Cascades and across the

Snake River. Long winter campaigns taxed resources and health on all sides. Following a series of losses in central and eastern Washington, the Yakimas and Spokanes sued for peace and settled onto reservations, where the story of the bravery and suffering of their people during these difficult years was often told.

BIBLIOGRAPHY

Pace, Robert E. *Yakima Indian Nation Bibliography.* Topenish, Wash.: Yakima Indian Nation Media Services, 1978.

Trafzer, Clifford E. *Yakima, Palouse, Cayuse, Umatilla, Walla Walla, and Wanapum Indians: An Historical Bibliography.* Metuchen, N.J.: Scarecrow Press, 1992.

Ned Blackhawk

See also **Indian Treaties; Tribes: Northwestern; Wars with Indian Nations: Later Nineteenth Century (1840–1900).**

YALE UNIVERSITY, an educational institution founded in 1701 as the result of a conservative reaction by Congregationalist leaders weary of what they identified as the increasing departure of Harvard College from its Calvinist heritage. Today, Yale consists of twelve graduate schools and Yale College, approximately 5,300 students who makeup the undergraduate arts and sciences division of the university. Approximately 975 full-time faculty instruct students in bachelor's, master's, and doctoral programs.

Like much of its earliest history, the date of Yale's founding is open to debate. Given the extant records, some place the date as 15 or 16 October 1701, when the Connecticut General Assembly approved a petition drafted by area clerics entitled "An Act for the Liberty to Erect a Collegiate School." This would-be charter of the "Collegiate School" presented the ministers with the charge of educating men "fitted for Publick employment both in Church and Civil State." With the petition approved, several ministers, among them James Pierpont of New Haven, Thomas Buckingham of Saybrook, Israel Chancy of Stratford, and Joseph Webb of Fairfield, met in Saybrook, Connecticut, on 11 November 1701, the other date offered as the founding, to plan a school for these stated purposes. With the exception of Gurdon Saltonstall, an advisor to Fitz-John Winthrop, soon-to-be governor of Connecticut, and the only founder not to be ordained, none of the careers of the men gathered at this event were, as the historian Brooks Mather Kelley remarked, "especially striking." There were other similarities as well. All but one were residents of Connecticut or Massachusetts and graduates of Harvard College. During this time the school remained little more than a proposal among a handful of clerics.

The following year, however, these designs turned into reality. Fifty-six year old Abraham Pierson, a minister in Killingworth, Connecticut, was appointed the first rec-

tor of the college. His first student was Jacob Heminway of East Haven, Connecticut, who began attending class in March 1702. Classes were held in the rectory of Pierson's church, with the first commencement taking place on 16 September 1702. With little fanfare the ceremony was held in the home of the Reverend Thomas Buckingham of Saybrook. Nathaniel Chauncey was the school's first graduate, receiving his master's degree. Chauncey was joined by four graduates of Harvard who were also conferred with M.A. degrees at this time. The following year, John Hart of Farmington, Connecticut, became the first candidate to officially receive a bachelor's degree from the school.

During its first several decades of service, the institution faced constant uncertainty. Despite the support of area residents and the Connecticut legislature, the school struggled financially. Student enrollment, a primary source of income, fluctuated from year to year, with as many as nine members in the class of 1714, followed by only three students in the class of 1715. Student discipline was also an early concern and was likely due, in part, to the age of incoming freshmen, who typically entered school at sixteen. Another obstacle in these initial educational efforts was the institution's library, which consisted of considerably dated works. These problems were further compounded by the debate among trustees concerning the location of the school. From 1701 to 1717, the college held its classes in numerous parsonages throughout Connecticut, including Hartford, Milford, New Haven, and Saybrook. It was not until 8 October 1717 that the college constructed its first building in New Haven. This ultimately settled a long-standing dispute among trustees as to where to permanently locate the school. Other developments at this time forever changed the institution's history.

In seeking greater financial stability for the college, Cotton Mather, alienated by the direction of Harvard's educational efforts, was asked to work on behalf of the Connecticut school. Mather wrote Elihu Yale, an employee of the East India Company who was appointed governor of Madras in 1687, asking for a charitable donation to the school. Yale eventually succumbed to Mather's requests, donating both money and personal effects to the college. In honor of this gift, the school named its first and only building after Yale. This situation, however, led to some confusion concerning the relationship between the name of the school and its lone building. Between 1718 and 1719 the names "Collegiate School" and "Yale College" were used interchangeably. By the spring of 1720, however, trustees referred to the school as Yale College in their letterhead, and the name appears to have quickly replaced the initial designation.

Enthusiasm for the GREAT AWAKENING of the mid-eighteenth century swept across the Yale campus leaving an indelible mark on the school. New Light preaching, calling people to repent while emphasizing a conversion experience as a sign of faith, flew in the face of Yale's new rector Thomas Clap, a conservative Congregationalist. The administration and student body clashed over theology on several fronts, with some students denied their degrees for propagating revivalism. In 1742 the situation became acute. Students refused discipline and religious instruction from those faculty they perceived to be unconverted. As a result, Clap closed the college, sending students home until the following academic term.

The late-eighteenth and nineteenth centuries witnessed Yale's growth from a fledgling, largely sectarian, school to a prominent university. During Ezra Stiles's presidency (1777–1793) changes were made to broaden the curriculum by introducing English, literature, and theater as subjects of study. Enrollments increased during these years averaging approximately 140 students at the college each year. Under the leadership of Timothy Dwight (1795–1817), Jeremiah Day (1817–1846), and Theodore Dwight Woolsey (1846–1871), the student population continued to grow as the foundation was laid to build the college into a premiere national educational institution. Two developments, the scientific method and the appointment of faculty to shaping the curriculum of their particular field, played a major role in Yale's pedagogical maturation. The first of what would become professional schools at Yale was also established at this time with the founding of the Medical Institution at Yale in 1810 and the Divinity School in 1832. In 1847, the department of philosophy and arts was established from which would emerge the Graduate School of Arts and Sciences. The nation's first art museum associated with an institution of higher education was also founded at this time.

In 1886 the Yale Corporation approved president Timothy Dwight's plan to change the name of the institution from Yale College to Yale University. In May 1887, this change was made legal, and Yale College became an undergraduate liberal arts department of Yale University. This name change more accurately reflected the academic life of the institution and mirrored the changes in higher education taking place in the late-nineteenth century. It was during the first half of the twentieth century that the institution began to truly reflect its university status. By 1920 its physical plant numbered over forty buildings and its endowment had grown to $25.5 million. Moreover, monetary power was taken away from its old constituent parts and concentrated in the university. With these changes Yale was able to attract and retain leading scholars, making it a world-renowned institution. Despite two wars and financial setbacks at times, Yale University continued to expand and diversify under the leadership of A. Whitney Griswold (1950–1963). Under Griswold, women were first admitted to Yale College in 1969, making the university truly modern.

BIBLIOGRAPHY

Kelley, Brooks Mather. *Yale: A History*. New Haven, Conn.: Yale University Press, 1974.

Pierson, George Wilson. *The Founding of Yale: The Legend of the Forty Folios*. New Haven, Conn.: Yale University Press, 1988.

Stevenson, Louise L. *Scholarly Means to Evangelical Ends: The New Haven Scholars and the Transformation of Higher Learning in America, 1830–1890*. Baltimore, Md.: Johns Hopkins University Press, 1986.

Warch, Richard. *School of the Prophets: Yale College, 1701–1740*. New Haven, Conn.: Yale University Press, 1973.

Kent A. McConnell

See also **Education, Higher: Colleges and Universities; Ivy League; New Lights.**

YALTA CONFERENCE. In early February 1945, U.S. President Franklin D. Roosevelt, British Prime Minister Winston Churchill, and Soviet Marshal Joseph Stalin met in the Black Sea port city of Yalta to discuss the postwar administration of Europe. At the time of the conference, Allied forces had pushed Nazi Germany to the brink of collapse, and all sides recognized that the end of World War II was imminent. Roosevelt hoped to use the conference not only as a planning meeting for the postwar period but also as a forum to establish a warmer personal relationship with Stalin. Although weakened by a deteriorating heart condition that took his life two months later, Roosevelt believed he could use his charm and skills of persuasion to win Stalin's confidence in American goodwill, thereby ensuring a peaceful postwar world order.

Despite Roosevelt's efforts, however, Stalin drove a hard bargain at Yalta. Roosevelt's physical weakness as a dying man and Churchill's political weakness as head of a dying empire left Stalin in the strongest bargaining position of the three. The fact that Soviet forces had numerical superiority over their American and British allies on the continent of Europe further strengthened Stalin's hand. After a week of negotiations, the three leaders announced agreement on (1) the occupation of Germany by the United States, Great Britain, the Soviet Union, and France in four separate zones; (2) a conference of the signatories of the United Nations Declaration to open at San Francisco on 25 April 1945, for the purpose of establishing a world peace organization; (3) a (then-secret) large-power voting formula in the new organization; (4) an eastern boundary of Poland mainly following the Curzon Line (which gave the Soviet Union about one-third of prewar Poland), for which Poland was to be compensated by unspecified German territory in the north and west, and a new, freely elected, democratic Polish government; and (5) freely elected democratic governments for other liberated European nations. A supplementary secret agreement provided for Soviet entry into the war with Japan in two or three months after Germany surrendered, and, in return, British and American acceptance of (1) the status quo of Outer Mongolia; (2) restoration to the Soviet Union of its position in Manchuria before the Russo-Japanese War (1904–1905), with safeguarding of Soviet

The Big Three. Meeting at Yalta are *(left to right)* Winston Churchill, an ailing Franklin D. Roosevelt, and Joseph Stalin. Library of Congress

interests in Dairen, Port Arthur, and the Manchurian railways; and (3) the cession to the Soviet Union of the Kurile Islands and the southern half of Sakhalin Island.

Contrary to Roosevelt's hopes, the conference failed to establish a spirit of trust between the United States and the Soviet Union. In the months and years following Germany's capitulation in May 1945, relations between Moscow and Washington steadily deteriorated, and a Cold War developed between the two rival superpowers. The Yalta conference became a major point of friction, as Americans charged the Soviets with systematically violating the Yalta agreements. Although at Yalta Stalin had agreed to support freely elected democratic governments in the liberated territories, he broke his pledges and brutally suppressed incipient democratic movements across Eastern Europe. The establishment of pro-Soviet puppet regimes in Eastern Europe led Churchill in a 1946 speech to accuse Moscow of having divided the continent with an Iron Curtain. In the United States, Republican critics accused the Roosevelt administration of having cravenly capitulated to Stalin's demands at Yalta. The controversy over Roosevelt's diplomacy at Yalta later became a major part of Senator Joe McCarthy's crusade of ANTICOMMUNISM in the early 1950s. The Republicans' accusation that Democratic administrations were "soft" on communism remained a significant feature of American presidential campaigns until the end of the Cold War.

BIBLIOGRAPHY

Clemens, Diane Shaver. *Yalta.* New York: Oxford University Press, 1970.

Divine, Robert A. *Roosevelt and World War II.* New York: Atheneum, 1967.

Gaddis, John Lewis. *The United States and the Origins of the Cold War, 1941–1947.* New York: Columbia University Press, 1972.

Charles S. Campbell/ T. G.

See also **Cold War; Germany, Relations with; Great Britain, Relations with; Iron Curtain; McCarthyism; Russia, Relations with; World War II.**

YANKEE. The *Yankee* was a famous privateer brig from Bristol, Rhode Island, with eighteen guns and 120 officers and men. During the War of 1812, it cruised off Halifax, Nova Scotia, and in the South Atlantic and took eighteen prizes worth nearly $1 million. In two later voyages, under Elisha Snow, the *Yankee* cruised off Ireland and in the Atlantic with success, one prize (the *San Jose Indiano*) netting $500,000. In six voyages it captured British ships worth $5 million, $1 million of which actually reached Bristol.

BIBLIOGRAPHY

Jones, Noah. *Journals of Two Cruises Aboard the American Privateer "Yankee."* New York: Macmillan, 1967.

Maclay, Edgar S. *A History of American Privateers.* New York: D. Appleton, 1899. Reprint, New York: B. Franklin, 1968.

Walter B. Norris / A. R.

See also **International Law; Privateers and Privateering; War of 1812.**

YANKEE, derived from the disparaging Dutch name Jan Kees (John Cheese) for New England Puritans in the 1660s, became a colloquial name for all New Englanders. Popularized by the British army march, "Yankee Doodle" (1750), it was adopted proudly by the Connecticut militia, and appeared in Royal Tyler's play *The Contrast* (1787), Seba Smith's *Major Jack Dowling* satires (1829), and James Russell Lowell's *Biglow Papers* (1848).

Southerners referred to Union soldiers as Yankees during the Civil War, but in World War I all American soldiers were dubbed Yankees. As an ethnic group, the Yankee descends from the Congregational British settlers of colonial New England, noted for their ingenuity and flinty character.

BIBLIOGRAPHY

Haywood, Charles Fry. *Yankee Dictionary: A Compendium of Useful and Entertaining Expressions Indigenous to New England.* Lynn, Mass.: Jackson and Phillips, 1963.

Peter C. Holloran

See also **New England Colonies; Puritans and Puritanism; Theocracy in New England.**

"YANKEE DOODLE" was a popular march in its day—easy to remember, adaptable to fife and drum, and appealing to the sense of humor. The origin of the tune, like that of the words, is uncertain; it probably was derived from an old English or Dutch folk song and was likely introduced to the American colonies by an English fife major of the Grenadier Guards about 1750. It was played in a Philadelphia ballad opera in 1767 and by English bands in America as early as 1768. It appeared in print first in Glasgow, Scotland, in 1782 and was published in the United States in 1794. The words assumed their present form about 1775. From the sarcastic tone, the author was surely a Tory or a Briton:

> Yankee Doodle came to town,
> Riding on a pony,
> Stuck a feather in his cap
> And called him [or "it"] Macaroni.

Early versions of the song included numerous verses. The origin of these may have been a satirical ballad, "The Yankee's Return From Camp," printed between 1810 and 1813. The verses were obviously written by Americans.

In the twentieth century, "Yankee Doodle" became something of a patriotic cliché. Variations of its melody and lyrics could be heard in numerous popular tunes, musical theatre scores, and movie sound tracks.

BIBLIOGRAPHY

Fedor, Ferenz. *The Birth of Yankee Doodle.* New York: Vantage Press, 1976.

Wilbur C. Abbott / A. R.

See also **Campaign Songs; Literature, Children's; Music: Early American; Tall Stories.**

YAP MANDATE. Under the terms of the Treaty of Versailles (1919) ending World War I, Japan received a mandate over the former German possessions in the Pacific Ocean lying north of the equator. They included the Marshall, Mariana (Ladrone), and Caroline Islands.

Although agreeing to a Japanese mandate over these Pacific islands, President Woodrow Wilson objected to the inclusion of Yap, a strategically significant cable relay island in the Carolines. The controversy was settled during the Washington Conference on the Limitation of Armaments, when the United States agreed to Japan's mandate over the island of Yap and in return obtained from Japan complete equality with respect to the cables.

BIBLIOGRAPHY

Buckley, Thomas H. *The United States and the Washington Conference, 1921–1922.* Knoxville: University of Tennessee, 1970.

Dingman, Roger. *Power in the Pacific: The Origins of Naval Arms Limitation, 1914–1922.* Chicago: University of Chicago Press, 1976.

Clarence A. Berdahl / T. G.

See also **Japan, Relations with; League of Nations; Versailles, Treaty of; Washington Naval Conference; World War I.**

YAZOO FRAUD. The Yazoo Fraud was one of the most spectacular and significant acts of land speculation in American history. In 1795 the Georgia legislature sold 35 million acres of its western lands, comprising the present states of Alabama and Mississippi, to four land companies for $500,000, or 1.5 cents an acre. The sale soon became a public scandal because nearly all the Georgia legislators who voted for the law had been bribed by agents of the land companies. In 1796 the newly elected Georgia legislature revoked the sale.

Georgia's repeal of the corrupt sale became a national political and legal issue for nearly twenty years. The land companies had quickly unloaded their dubious titles to speculators throughout the East. Many of these speculators, including leading politicians from both the Democratic-Republican and Federalist parties, organized themselves into the New England Mississippi Land Company and applied great pressure on the U.S. Congress and federal courts to award compensation for the land they claimed to have bought in good faith. In 1802 Georgia agreed to transfer its western lands to the United States for $1.25 million. But the Yazooists, as they were called, continued to push their campaign through a contrived legal case, *Fletcher v. Peck* (1810). This case eventually reached the U.S. Supreme Court, which ruled that the Georgia 1796 repeal act violated the contract clause of the Constitution of the United States. The legal doctrine of this decision helped to protect business interests from state regulatory actions until well into the twentieth century. Four years after the *Fletcher* decision, Congress enacted legislation providing $4.2 million to compensate the claimants, and the Yazoo land issue finally disappeared from the national scene.

BIBLIOGRAPHY

Coulter, E. Merton. *Georgia: A Short History.* Chapel Hill: University of North Carolina Press, 1947.

Elsmere, Jane. "The Notorious Yazoo Land Fraud Case." *Georgia Historical Quarterly* 51 (1967): 425–442.

Magrath, C. Peter. *Yazoo: Law and Politics in the New Republic.* Providence, R.I.: Brown University Press, 1966.

C. Peter Magrath / c. r. p.

See also **Fletcher v. Peck; Georgia; Land Speculation.**

Walter Reed. The U.S. Army surgeon whose commission learned how to defeat yellow fever. AP/Wide World Photos

YELLOW FEVER. The first reference to yellow fever in America is found in that indispensable sourcebook *The History of New England* (1647) by John Winthrop, governor of Massachusetts. The effort of the colonial court to exclude from Massachusetts the crew and the cargo of the ship that had brought the fever ("Barbados distemper") from the West Indies to America was the colonies' initial enforcement of quarantine. Later, in 1694, British ships that had sailed from Boston in an unsuccessful effort to capture Martinique brought back an epidemic of yellow fever, and subsequently, despite its endemic focus on the African coast, yellow fever emerged as a peculiarly American disease ("the American plague"). It spread through America as the African slave trade increased. With the single exception of smallpox, the most dreaded verdict on the lips of a colonial physician was "yellow fever."

The worst American epidemic of yellow fever occurred in 1793 and doomed the supremacy of Philadelphia among U.S. cities. Approximately 10 percent of the city's population died from the disease. Forty years later, the combined effects of yellow fever and cholera killed about 20 percent of the population of New Orleans. The last epidemic of yellow fever in the United States occurred in New Orleans in 1905.

Recurring epidemics of yellow fever and cholera led to the formation of municipal health boards in most major U.S. cities by mid-nineteenth century. But for much of that century, these agencies had few powers. Their lack of authority was, in part, due to distrust of the medical profession—a distrust fed by the inability of physicians to satisfactorily explain epidemic diseases. One camp of physicians argued that yellow fever was transmitted by touch and called for strict quarantines. Other physicians supported the "miasm" theory and argued that yellow fever was carried through the air by poisonous gases (miasm) emitted by rotting vegetation or dead animals. They called for swamp drainage and thorough cleaning of streets and abandoned buildings.

In 1900 the U.S. Army Yellow Fever Commission, with Walter Reed, James Carroll, Jesse W. Lazear, and Aristides Agramonte, was sent to track the pestilence in Cuba. The group, working with the aid of Carlos J. Finlay, demonstrated Finlay's theory that the infection is not a contagion but is transmitted by the bite of the female *Aëdes aegypti* mosquito. William Crawford Gorgas, chief sanitary officer of the Panama Canal Commission from 1904 until 1913, eliminated the mosquito in the region of the canal and made possible the building of the Panama Canal. Vaccines against the disease were developed in the early 1940s and today are required of anyone traveling to a hazardous area.

BIBLIOGRAPHY

Carrigan, Jo Ann. *The Saffron Scourge: A History of Yellow Fever in Louisiana, 1796–1905.* Lafayette: University of Southwestern Louisiana, Center for Louisiana Studies, 1994.

Ellis, John H. *Yellow Fever and Public Health in the New South.* Lexington: University Press of Kentucky, 1992.

Foster, Kenneth R., Mary F. Jenkins, and Anna Coxe Toogood. "The Philadelphia Yellow Fever Epidemic of 1792." *Scientific American* 279, no. 2 (August 1998): 88.

Humphreys, Margaret. *Yellow Fever and the South.* New Brunswick, N.J.: Rutgers University Press, 1992.

Victor Robinson / c. p.

See also **Epidemics and Public Health; Medicine, Military.**

YELLOW JOURNALISM. James Gordon Bennett, who founded the *New York Morning Herald* in 1835, was the first American publisher to introduce sensationalism in news stories, but not until the 1890s was the term "yellow journalism" applied to this kind of news presentation. In 1895 William Randolph Hearst, publisher of the *San Francisco Examiner,* purchased the *New York Morning Journal* and began a subscription war with Joseph Pulitzer's newspaper, the *New York World.* Pulitzer responded in 1896 by creating a color supplement for which staff cartoonist, Richard Outcault, produced a comic strip known

William Randolph Hearst. The newspaper publisher (and model for the tycoon in the film *Citizen Kane*) whose circulation wars with Joseph Pulitzer in the 1890s—including their battle for the comic strip "Yellow Kid"—gave rise to the phrase "yellow journalism" to describe their sensationalistic form of news coverage. LIBRARY OF CONGRESS

as the "Yellow Kid," named after the main character who wore a yellow nightshirt. The great popularity of this comic strip led Hearst to drop the price of his paper, to begin his own color supplement, and to hire Outcault away from the *World.* The role of Outcault's Yellow Kid character in these events lent the name "yellow journalism" to the circulation wars between the two papers and to the sensationalistic journalistic practices that this competition spawned.

Both New York City papers exploited the Cuban crisis of the 1890s, and the reporting surrounding these events was perhaps yellow journalism's most famous episode. Headlines screamed the latest developments and feature stories detailed Spanish atrocities. When a young Cuban woman was jailed for resisting rape, Hearst orchestrated her rescue by one of his reporters and publicized her travails widely. This lurid sensationalism fueled the anger of the American public and made it difficult for President McKinley to effect a peaceful resolution, particularly after Hearst published on 8 February 1898 a private letter by Spain's minister to the United States, which insulted McKinley. When the U.S. battleship *Maine* exploded in Havana harbor, Hearst had a field day. Although investigation ruled the explosion an accident, Hearst used his paper, including the comic strip character "the Yellow Kid," to denounce Spain and whip the American public into a frenzy for war. While some of their practices were outrageous, the tactics pioneered by Pulitzer's *World* and Hearst's *Journal* influenced the style and content of newspapers in most major American cities, and many of yellow journalism's innovations, such as banner headlines, sensational stories, copious illustrations, and color supplements have become a permanent feature of newspapers today.

BIBLIOGRAPHY
Bleyer, Willard G. *Main Currents in the History of American Journalism.* Boston: Houghton Mifflin, 1927.

Campbell, W. Joseph. *Yellow Journalism.* Westport, Conn.: Praeger, 2001.

Cohen, Daniel. *Yellow Journalism.* Brookfield, Conn.: Twenty-First Century Books, 2000.

Theodore G. Gronert
Lisa M. Tetrault

See also **Cuba, Relations with; Newspapers; Spain, Relations with; Spanish-American War.**

"YELLOW PERIL" was a racial epithet directed against persons of Asian descent that was fashionable in Europe and America in the late nineteenth and twentieth centuries. Its historical roots can be traced to the persistent theme in Western culture that the barbarian hordes of Asia, a yellow race, were always on the point of invading and destroying Christendom, Europe, and Western civilization itself. This interpretation of history contributed to racism in the United States.

"Yellow Peril." This political cartoon shows men of varied backgrounds joining together to lynch a Chinese immigrant, near a sign that reads "No Chinese need apply," c. 1880. Congress passed the Chinese Exclusion Act in 1882—one of a long series of harshly restrictive legislative measures aimed at Asians seeking to come to, or stay in, America. © CORBIS-BETTMANN

The spirit of this racial slur pervaded major aspects of American diplomacy, congressional legislation, federal-state relations, economic development, transportation, agriculture, public opinion, trade unionism, and education for more than eight decades. The Burlingame Treaty with China in 1868 encouraged the Chinese coolie (a source of cheap labor) to enter the United States to help build the Pacific railroads; however, these immigrants were denied U.S. citizenship under the Naturalization Act of 1790, which limited naturalized citizenship to white persons. Fifty-six years later, with the Immigration Act of 1924, Congress excluded nearly all Asians from the United States. Those restrictions were not eased until 1952 when Congress created quotas for Asian immigration and made people of all races eligible for naturalization.

In the interim, murder, personal and social humiliation, and physical brutality became the lot of the Asian residents, particularly Chinese workers in California and the mining camps of the mountain states. In the late nineteenth century, Chinese residents were targets of sporadic labor violence, which included boycotts and the destruction of Chinese businesses. In 1906, the San Francisco School Board ordered the segregation of all Japanese, Chinese, and Korean children in a separate Oriental school, an order that was rescinded a few months later. And state legislatures and Congress passed laws and en-

tered diplomatic treaties and agreements dealing with China and Japan that were designed to halt the yellow peril. These acts focused on immigration restriction and exclusion, naturalization prohibition, limitations on citizenship, prevention of free transit, and denial of rights to land ownership. The specifics of the yellow peril mania are evident in the CHINESE EXCLUSION ACTS, passed between 1880 and 1904, and in treaties and enactments with Japan, especially the treaties of 1894, 1911, and 1913 and provisions of the Immigration Act of 1907. The yellow peril fear peaked with the Immigration Act of 1924.

Thereafter, in its most gross form the yellow peril declined, although it emerged during the early days of World War II, after the bombing of Pearl Harbor and the confinement of Japanese Americans in camps. Nevertheless, with changes and modifications evident in new legislation, such as the McCarren-Walter Act of 1952, and administrative actions based on the exigencies of cold war foreign policies, the yellow peril was absorbed by other social forces and concerns of racism in the United States.

BIBLIOGRAPHY

Daniels, Roger. *Asian America: Chinese and Japanese in the United States Since 1850*. Seattle: University of Washington Press, 1988.

Higham, John. *Strangers in the Land: Patterns of American Nativism 1860–1925*. 2d ed. New York: Atheneum, 1978 (orig. pub. 1963).

Hing, Bill Ong. *Making and Remaking Asian America Through Immigration Policy, 1850–1990*. Stanford, Calif.: Stanford University Press, 1993.

Salyer, Lucy E. *Laws Harsh as Tigers: Chinese Immigrants and the Shaping of Modern Immigration Law*. Chapel Hill: University of North Carolina Press, 1995.

Takaki, Ronald T. *Strangers from a Different Shore: A History of Asian Americans*. New York: Penguin Books, 1990.

Charles Vevier / C. P.

See also **Asian Americans; Chinese Americans; Chinese Exclusion Act; Japanese Americans; Japan, Relations with; Race Relations.**

"YELLOW-DOG" CONTRACT, an agreement signed by a worker promising not to join a union while working for a company. Beginning during the period of LABOR unrest in the 1870s, companies used these agreements to prevent unions from securing a base in their firms. By the 1890s, labor advocates had secured laws prohibiting "yellow-dog" contracts in fifteen states, and, in 1898, Congress passed the Erdman Act, which outlawed "yellow-dog" contracts in the railroad industry.

As unions attempted to expand in the twentieth century, use of "yellow-dog" contracts increased, especially after the SUPREME COURT overturned the Erdman Act in 1908 (*Adair v. United States*) and a similar state law in 1915 (*COPPAGE v. KANSAS*). In 1917, the Supreme Court further ruled (*Hitchman Coal and Coke Company v. Mitchell*) that injunctions could be issued against unions trying to organize workers who had signed "yellow-dog" contracts. The use of these agreements, which spread rapidly after the *Hitchman* decision, hampered the growth of unions in such industries as coal, shoe, glass, full-fashioned hosiery, clothing, metal trades, and commercial printing trades.

With the 1932 NORRIS–LA GUARDIA ANTI-INJUNCTION LAW, Congress declared that "yellow-dog" contracts conflicted with public policy and that the courts could not enforce them. After the passage of the Wagner Act in 1935, the National Labor Relations Board ruled that employers were engaging in an unfair labor practice to demand that workers sign such an agreement. As a result of these two actions, the "yellow-dog" contract disappeared from the labor scene.

BIBLIOGRAPHY

Seidman, Joel I. *The Yellow Dog Contract.* Baltimore: Johns Hopkins University Press, 1932.

Steinfeld, Robert J. *The Invention of Free Labor: The Employment Relation in English and American Law and Culture, 1350–1870.* Chapel Hill: University of North Carolina Press, 1991.

Albert A. Blum / c. w.

See also **Closed Shop; National Labor Relations Act.**

YELLOWSTONE NATIONAL PARK.

Yellowstone National Park encompasses 3,468 square miles (2,219,823 acres) of Rocky Mountain terrain in Wyoming, Idaho, and Montana. Its enabling act, signed 1 March 1872 by President Ulysses S. Grant, withdrew lands from the public domain for use as a "public park or pleasuring ground" for the "preservation, from injury or spoliation, of all timber, mineral deposits, natural curiosities, or wonders . . . and their retention in their natural condition." The Yellowstone National Park Act established a significant conservationist precedent, leading to the formation of more than twelve hundred parks and preserves in more than one hundred countries. The national park idea represents one of the major, original contributions of the United States to world thought.

Native Americans utilized Yellowstone for hunting and fishing hundreds of years before whites frequented the region. In 1807 the trapper John Colter became the first Euro-American to visit Yellowstone. Information regarding Yellowstone's natural features remained scarce until the late 1860s, when several exploring parties surveyed the area. Cornelius Hedges, a Massachusetts-born Montana judge and member of the Washburn-Langford-Doane expedition in 1870, has often been credited with proposing Yellowstone as a national park, although historians have since questioned the validity of his claim. The Yellowstone National Park Act was drawn up by William H. Clagett, a Montana territorial delegate in Congress; Nathaniel Langford, territorial revenue collector and later first park superintendent; and Ferdinand V. Hayden, a member of the U.S. Geological Survey, whose 1871 expedition showered Congress with illustrations and photographs of Yellowstone's fantastical landscape. Yel-

Yellowstone National Park. The devastating wildfire of 1988 is battled from the air. © CORBIS

lowstone was under military stewardship from 1886 until 1918, when the newly created National Park Service (1916) took responsibility for its operation. California lawyer Horace M. Albright became Yellowstone's first civilian superintendent.

Yellowstone remains the largest national park in the contiguous United States. Its three thousand hot springs and two hundred geysers, including Old Faithful, signify the world's largest concentration of geothermal features. Yellowstone Lake represents the largest high-mountain lake in North America, covering 137 square miles at an elevation of 7,730 feet. There the Yellowstone River starts its 671-mile journey to the Missouri River, bequeathing the park its famous 1,200-foot deep Grand Canyon of the Yellowstone River and its Upper Falls and Lower Falls; the latter, almost twice as high as Niagara Falls, drops 308 feet. The park supports an array of wildlife, including grizzly and black bears, elk, bighorn sheep, moose, antelope, coyotes and more than two hundred varieties of bird. Yellowstone's protected wildlands provide vital habitat for threatened species, notably the once endangered trumpeter swan and the country's only continuously wild herd of bison.

Shifting biological theories, increased visitation, and external threats present decisive challenges for Yellowstone's managers. In the summer of 1988, 45 percent of the park was razed by fire, fueling criticism of official natural regulation policy. Affected areas have since recovered. In January 1995, following two decades of protracted debate and capacious biological studies, federal agencies reintroduced wolves to Yellowstone under the terms of the Endangered Species Act (1973). Wolves had been absent from the park since the 1920s, when they were eradicated as part of an official campaign to remove predatory animals. Yellowstone National Park, which observed its 125th anniversary in 1997, attracts more than 3 million visitors a year.

BIBLIOGRAPHY

Bartlett, Richard A. *Yellowstone: A Wilderness Besieged.* Tucson: University of Arizona Press, 1985.

Chase, Alston. *Playing God in Yellowstone: The Destruction of America's First National Park.* San Diego, Calif.: Harcourt Brace, 1987.

Haines, Aubrey L. *The Yellowstone Story: A History of Our First National Park.* Rev. ed. Niwot: University Press of Colorado, 1996.

Pritchard, James A. *Preserving Yellowstone's Natural Conditions: Science and the Perception of Nature.* Lincoln: University of Nebraska Press, 1999.

Karen Jones
John Vosburgh

See also **National Park System; Wildlife Preservation.**

YELLOWSTONE RIVER EXPEDITIONS (1819–1825) were planned by John C. Calhoun, secretary of War under President Jame Monroe, to intimidate British fur traders and the American Indians of the upper Missouri. Calhoun's decision to initiate these expeditions emerged from his expansionist political philosophy. Having supported the recent war against Britain (1812–1814), he was suspicious of decades-old alliances between the British and many American Indian tribes, and he devised strategies to secure United States control of the North American continent. The Yellowstone Expeditions were part of a larger military policy that included the reorganization of the war department, the maintenance of a standing army, and the development of infrastructure— particularly roads—that the army could use for defense.

The Yellowstone expeditions to navigate and survey the region produced mixed successes. General Henry Atkinson commanded the initial expedition of five steamboats, which were supposed to carry 1,100 men up the Missouri River in 1819. The river, however, proved unnavigable by steamboat. Two turned back at the start, and only one reached Council Bluffs (in present-day Iowa), halfway to the Yellowstone. Continued Indian attacks on American fur traders resulted in a second expedition in 1825 with 476 men under Atkinson. The party traveled in eight keelboats, arrived at the Yellowstone in August, and returned the same season. Ultimately, the Yellowstone River Expeditions furthered many of Calhoun's strategic goals for the Northwest. The parties surveyed and mappped out the Missouri River and its tributaries, built roads and forts to secure the region, and concluded treaties—which confirmed United States control of the territory—with fifteen Indian tribes.

BIBLIOGRAPHY

Bartlett, Irving H. *John C. Calhoun: A Biography.* New York: Norton, 1993.

Mancall, Peter C. *American Eras: Westward Expansion, 1800–1860.* Detroit, Mich.: Gale, 1999.

Tate, Michael. *The Frontier Army in the Settlement of the West.* Norman: University of Oklahoma Press, 1999.

Bliss Isely / S. B.

See also **Exploration of America, Early; Fur Trade and Trapping; Indian Land Cessions; Indian Treaties; Leavenworth Expedition; Long, Stephen H., Explorations of; Missouri River Fur Trade; Western Exploration.**

YORKTOWN CAMPAIGN (August–October 1781). On 19 October 1781, American and French troops forced the surrender of a sizeable British army at Yorktown, a decisive victory that reversed the war's momentum, and proved to be the last major engagement of the Revolutionary War.

By late 1780, the patriot cause arguably reached its low point: British victories at Charleston and Camden virtually destroyed the southern wing of the Continental Army; the American military supply system collapsed and

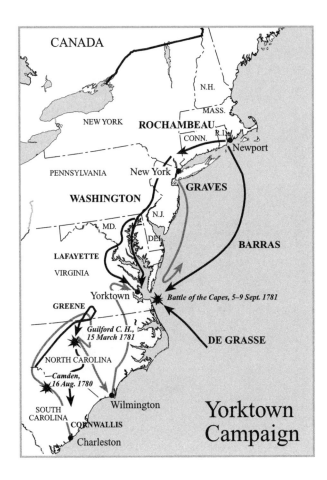

CANADA

N.H.

MASS.

NEW YORK

ROCHAMBEAU

CONN. R.I.

Newport

PENNSYLVANIA

New York

GRAVES

WASHINGTON

N.J.

MD.

DEL.

BARRAS

LAFAYETTE

VIRGINIA

Yorktown

Battle of the Capes, 5–9 Sept. 1781

GREENE

Guilford C. H., 15 March 1781

DE GRASSE

NORTH CAROLINA

Camden, 16 Aug. 1780

SOUTH CAROLINA

Wilmington

CORNWALLIS

Charleston

Yorktown Campaign

rampant inflation eroded the army's purchasing power; a weak Continental Congress provided ineffective political leadership; scarce resources led General George Washington to cancel military operations against New York City; and the alliance with France had yet to produce significant results. By contrast, British optimism remained high. Their "southern strategy"—securing one by one the southern colonies from Georgia northward—seemed to bear fruit.

By early 1781, the tide was turning. Lord Charles Cornwallis, who commanded British troops in the South, failed to eliminate resistance by pesky Continentals and militia under Major General Nathanael Greene. Unable to pacify South Carolina, Cornwallis moved his army into North Carolina. Failing to secure North Carolina, he proceeded into Virginia contrary to official orders. The British ministry was not displeased, however, for they hoped to secure this tobacco-rich region, prevent French incursions into the Chesapeake, and draw support from its supposedly large loyalist population. Moreover, Cornwallis's superior, Sir Henry Clinton, recognized that British occupation of Virginia could disrupt the flow of patriot supplies from the north to forces in the Carolinas if the British could obtain adequate naval support. But when Clinton learned that Admiral de Grasse's squadron

had left France for North America, he developed reservations about a Virginia campaign. Initially, the British commander instructed Cornwallis to abandon operations and reinforce New York; however, when the French fleet appeared to sail for the Chesapeake, Clinton directed Cornwallis to assume a defensive position there. The offensive-minded Cornwallis reluctantly followed orders to establish a fortified harbor along Virginia's coast. He selected Yorktown, a prosperous tobacco port of approximately 2,000 residents. His troops occupied the town on 1 August 1781.

The arrival of de Grasse's French squadron in the Chesapeake on 29 August proved key to the unfolding campaign. Washington had planned to besiege the main British army in New York, and had hoped that joint operations with the Comte de Rochambeau's French army and de Grasse's squadron would make that possible. But when he learned that the French fleet would make a brief foray into the Chesapeake, Washington shifted his attention southward. There, the Marquis de Lafayette, whose small American force opposed Cornwallis, informed Washington that the British position was vulnerable. Washington recognized the opportunity, and implementing diversionary measures to keep an unsuspecting Clinton in New York, he and Rochambeau secretly marched their armies to Virginia in mid-August.

By late August, Cornwallis detected de Grasse's arrival. On 5 September 1781, French and British naval forces collided in the Battle of the Capes, with de Grasse's larger squadron battering the ships of Admiral Thomas Graves. De Grasse extended his blockade of the lower Chesapeake Bay and the York River, while Graves's damaged ships returned to New York. Britain's military fortunes had rested upon naval superiority, and now France controlled Yorktown's waters. The allied armies' arrival in mid-September meant that Cornwallis's 8,300 men were completely surrounded by more than twice that number. At that point, he was faced with two choices: he could either attempt to break through allied lines into the hostile Virginia interior, or he could await a relief expedition. He chose the latter.

Washington and Rochambeau began their siege of Cornwallis's army, while Clinton prepared for its rescue. By 9 October, allied forces completed their first line of trenches, hauled up heavy artillery, and unleashed a devastating cannonade upon British defenses and nearby warships. Two days later, they began a second line only 300 yards from the enemy. When two British redoubts, numbers 9 and 10, blocked allied progress, Lafayette and the Baron de Vioménil each directed 400 American and French forces against the fortifications. On the night of the 14th, Colonel Alexander Hamilton's assault on number 10 and Vioménil's on number 9 quickly overcame resistance and captured the redoubts. With his defenses pummeled by enemy artillery, a desperate Cornwallis attempted a breakout. Late on the 16th, he began ferrying troops north across the York River to Gloucester, where

Surrender of General Cornwallis. John Trumbull's painting is ironic: Lord Charles Cornwallis did not show up; his subordinates tried to surrender to the French *(left)* and then were forced by General George Washington *(right, on a brown horse)* to surrender to his own deputy, General Benjamin Lincoln *(on the white horse).* NATIONAL ARCHIVES AND RECORDS ADMINISTRATION

they planned to surprise allied forces and escape the Yorktown trap. Luck was not with the British. A violent storm scattered the boats, and forced the redcoats' return. Cornwallis saw little choice but to negotiate his surrender, and on 19 October 1781, approximately 7,000 of the King's troops laid down their arms—the very same day that Clinton's expedition sailed to relieve Yorktown.

The battle's outcome was significant. For the United States and France, it reflected extraordinary coordination and cooperation in an age of poor communication. For Britain, it undermined Parliament's resolve to continue the war. Thereafter, both sides sought acceptable terms to conclude the fighting.

BIBLIOGRAPHY

Fleming, Thomas J. *Beat the Last Drum: The Siege of Yorktown, 1781.* New York: St. Martin's Press, 1963.

Pancake, John S. *This Destructive War: The British Campaign in the Carolinas, 1780–1782.* University: University of Alabama Press, 1985.

Sands, John O. *Yorktown's Captive Fleet.* Charlottesville: Published for the Mariners' Museum, Newport News, Va., by the University Press of Virginia, 1983.

Wickwire, Franklin and Mary. *Cornwallis: The American Adventure.* Boston: Houghton Mifflin, 1970.

Mark Thompson

See also **Revolution, American: Political History; Revolution, American: Military History;** *and vol. 9:* **Correspondence Leading to Surrender.**

YOSEMITE NATIONAL PARK, called "the greatest marvel of the continent" by journalist Horace Greeley, was also described by the naturalist John Muir as having "the noblest forests . . . the deepest ice-sculptured canyons." Located in the California High Sierra and consisting of 1,189 square miles (760,917 acres), Yosemite boasts one of the three largest exposed granite monoliths in the world, the El Capitan rock face, rising 3,600 feet from the valley floor. The 1,430-foot Upper Yosemite Falls is one of the world's five highest waterfalls. Only four trees, also California giant sequoias, surpass Yosemite's 2,700-year-old Grizzly Giant in size.

Native Americans occupied Yosemite 8,000 years ago. During the mid-1800s, the region belonged to the Southern Miwok nation. Captain Joseph Walker's trappers explored much of the surrounding area in 1833, but there is no known record of a white man entering Yosemite Valley until William Penn Abrams, a millwright, did so in 1849 while tracking a grizzly bear. State volunteers from the Mariposa Battalion under Major James D. Savage ventured into the hidden valley on 27 March 1851 seeking Indians. They named the area Yosemite after hearing one of the Miwoks exclaim *Yo-che-ma-te* or "some among them are killers."

James Hutchings guided the first tourists into Yosemite in 1855. The region swiftly gained fame for its unparalleled scenery, popularized through stunning panoramas created by the artist Albert Bierstadt and the photographer Carleton Watkins. Concern over the commercialization of the valley prompted calls for its protection. In 1864, President Abraham Lincoln signed an act of Congress granting Yosemite Valley and the Mariposa Grove of giant sequoia trees to California on condition that the areas would "be held for public use, resort, and recreation . . . inalienable for all time." The grant stimulated the creation of parks in other states.

Inspired by fears of private exploitation—notably expressed by the Scottish-American John Muir, who had been enraptured with Yosemite since visiting the area in 1868—Congress on 1 October 1890 authorized Yosemite National Park, which was created from about two million acres surrounding Yosemite Valley State Park. Following a series of boundary changes, California ceded Yosemite Valley to federal control in 1906.

From 1901 until 1913, Yosemite was at the center of a bitter controversy over San Francisco's attempts to get federal approval to build a dam in the park across the Tuolumne River. The dam, completed in 1923, destroyed the park's Hetch Hetchy Valley, similar in grandeur to Yosemite Valley, and described by its foremost defender Muir as "a mountain temple." Beginning in the 1960s, problems of traffic congestion and development in Yosemite Valley drew attention from resource managers and environmentalists. In the year 2000, annual visitation was 3.4 million.

BIBLIOGRAPHY

Huth, Hans. "Yosemite: The Story of an Ideal." *Sierra Club Bulletin* 33 (March 1948): 47–78.

Runte, Alfred. *Yosemite: The Embattled Wilderness.* Lincoln: University of Nebraska Press, 1990.

Russell, Carl P. *One Hundred Years in Yosemite: The Story of a Great Park and Its Friends.* Reprint. Yosemite, Calif.: Yosemite Natural History Association, 1992.

Karen Jones
John Vosburgh

See also **California; National Park System.**

"YOUNG AMERICA," a popular and widespread phrase culturally linked to the period 1840–1852, referred to anything that exhibited the youthful spirit of energy and enterprise characteristic of the times. Fundamentally an attempt to construct issues apart from sectional controversy, the phrase combined democratic universalism and aggressive nationalism with the notion of manifest destiny. Young Americanism was articulated by literary figures such as Ralph Waldo Emerson as an elevated nationalism and by political figures in the Democratic Party such as George Nicholas Sanders as uniting all sections on a platform of free trade, access to foreign markets, and annexation southward. After culminating in the amorphous Young America Democratic faction (1851–1856), the movement lost momentum and disappeared.

BIBLIOGRAPHY

Curti, Merle E. "Young America." *American Historical Review* 32 (1926): 34–55.

Gienapp, William E, ed. *Essays on American Antebellum Politics, 1840–1860.* College Station: Texas A&M University Press, 1982.

Grant, Susan-Mary. *North over South: Northern Nationalism and American Identity in the Antebellum Era.* Lawrence: University Press of Kansas, 2000.

S. F. Riepma / H. R. S.

See also **Democratic Party; Manifest Destiny; Nationalism; Sectionalism.**

YOUNG MEN'S AND YOUNG WOMEN'S HEBREW ASSOCIATION.

The first Young Men's Hebrew Association (YMHA) was organized in 1854 in Baltimore to develop Jewish community life. The facilities of early YMHAs consisted mainly of reading rooms, and the first paid worker was generally the librarian. The YMHAs differed from social clubs in that they were careful to ban card playing, gambling, and drinking. Immediately after the Civil War, YMHAs began to develop rapidly, especially in the South and Midwest. The sponsors of these associations were much impressed with the popularity of the Young Men's Christian Association (YMCA), and the YMHAs followed suit when the YMCAs introduced sports, health, and other physical education activities. From their early days, YMHAs included Jews of all shades of opinion and belief. Provision was also made for non-Jews as members. When Jewish immigrants from eastern Europe came to America in unprecedented numbers between 1881 and 1910, the YMHAs offered classes in citizenship and English, and at the same time expanded their Jewish educational and cultural activities. On 2 November 1913, the Council of Young Men's Hebrew and Kindred Associations (YMHKA) formed to coordinate the efforts of the YMHAs. During World War I, the group raised funds to secure rabbis for service at military posts. In 1917, the YMHKA created the Jewish Welfare Board (JWB) to develop an infrastructure to support Jewish military personnel.

While many of the YMHAs had auxiliaries to serve the needs of Jewish women, the first independent Young

Women's Hebrew Association (YWHA) began in New York City in 1902 under the leadership of Mrs. Israel Unterberg. Like Jewish settlement houses, the YWHA aimed to strengthen the Jewish community by focusing on the religious, mental, and physical lives of immigrant and working-class Jewish women. It offered courses in Hebrew, English, bookkeeping, dressmaking, gymnastics, basketball, tennis, and swimming. The physical education classes proved especially popular. Membership in the YWHA jumped from 30,000 in 1906 to 102,000 in 1913 and the all-female board of directors began opening new branches to meet the additional demand for facilities. By the 1920s, the YWHA had become heavily involved in promoting sporting activities for women. The New York branch hosted many national swimming competitions and, in 1924, the Women's Swimming Association meet became the first athletic event to be officiated entirely by women.

The JWB, which changed its name to Jewish Community Centers Association of North America in 1990, became the national governing body for the associations in 1921 and promoted the merger of YMHAs and YWHAs. After World War II, the YM/YWHAs broadened their character to become Jewish community centers—educational, cultural, and sports centers and places of assembly for the entire Jewish community—serving all ages. However, many retained the YM/YWHA name. By 2000, more than 275 YM/YWHAs, Jewish community centers, and their camps annually served over 1 million American Jews. The Jewish community centers had been so successful in responding to community needs that Jewish communities in Western Europe after World War II "imported" them as a means of rebuilding Jewish life.

BIBLIOGRAPHY

Borish, Linda J. "'An Interest in Physical Well-Being Among the Feminine Membership': Sporting Activities for Women at Young Men's and Young Women's Hebrew Associations." *American Jewish History* 87 (1999): 61–93.

Kraft, Louis. *A Century of the Jewish Community Center Movement, 1854–1954.* New York: Jewish Community Center Centennial Committee, 1953.

Rabinowitz, Benjamin. *The Young Men's Hebrew Associations: 1854–1913.* New York: National Jewish Welfare Board, 1948.

Lionel Koppman
Caryn E. Neumann

See also **Jews.**

YOUNG MEN'S CHRISTIAN ASSOCIATION

(YMCA). The first YMCA on North American soil was formed in Montreal on 25 November 1851, followed by one in Boston on 29 December 1851. Both were modeled on the YMCA founded by George Williams (1821–1905) in London on 6 June 1844. In 1855 the first YMCA World Conference reported fifty-five YMCAs in North America.

In 1853 the first African American YMCA was formed in Washington, D.C., by Anthony Bowen, a minister and former slave. For nearly a century YMCAs were segregated along racial lines, but in 1946 they began to desegregate, ahead of the nation.

In 1861 YMCAs split along North-South lines along with the rest of the nation, and membership declined as many young men joined the armies on both sides. Fifteen northern YMCAs formed the U.S. Christian Commission, offering its services to Union army soldiers and prisoners of war.

After the Civil War the YMCA regained organizational momentum and entered a phase of institutional expansion and proliferation of programs. The YMCA created new opportunities for Chinese immigrants in San Francisco (1875); for railroad workers in Cleveland (1872; YMCA Railroad Department, 1877); for Native Americans in Flandreau, South Dakota (1879); for industrial workers through the YMCA Industrial Department (1903); and for Japanese immigrants in San Francisco (1917). The organization named its first African American secretaries, William A. Hunton (1863–1916) and Jesse E. Moorland (1863–1940), in 1888 and 1898, respectively, and formed a Colored Work Department in 1923. In 1889 the YMCA began to send its secretaries abroad to spread the movement, focusing especially on China, Japan, and India.

In the United States the YMCA began to extend its concern with men's souls to include their bodies. This departure was captured by Luther Halsey Gulick (1865–1918) in his 1889 design of the YMCA's triangle logo inscribed with the words "spirit," "mind," "body." This approach, called "muscular Christianity," generated some of the YMCA's lasting contributions to U.S. culture. For example, in 1891 James Naismith invented basketball at the YMCA's Springfield, Massachusetts, Training School, and in 1895 the YMCA instructor William Morgan invented volleyball.

During both world wars the YMCA, under the leadership of John R. Mott (1865–1955), supported the U.S. war effort, offering religious, recreational, and relief work to soldiers, prisoners of war, and refugees. In World War I women's involvement in YMCAs grew as 5,145 women assisted as volunteer workers at home and abroad. In World War II the YMCA established outreach work in the ten internment camps in which the government detained Japanese Americans. During the war YMCAs administered relief work to 6 million prisoners of war in thirty-six countries. In recognition of the YMCA's effort with war refugees, Mott was awarded the Nobel Prize for peace in 1946.

After 1945 the YMCA continued to expand as an institution, but even high-ranking YMCA officials noticed that the movement's ideas and approaches were in need of revision. After 1975 the organization regained momentum. As Americans became more health conscious, the association's physical program took center stage. By the 1980s and 1990s the YMCA had rediscovered its earlier focus on character building, seeking to encourage positive values and behavior among American youths.

Following World War II the YMCA became a community service organization, integrated along race and gender lines. At the beginning of the twenty-first century 2,393 YMCAs served roughly 10,000 communities. Females constituted about half of the organization's 17 million members and about half of its staff.

BIBLIOGRAPHY

Davidann, Jon Thares. *A World of Crisis and Progress: The American YMCA in Japan, 1890–1930.* Bethlehem, Pa.: Lehigh University Press, 1998.

Elfenbein, Jessica I. *The Making of a Modern City: Philanthropy, Civic Culture, and the Baltimore YMCA.* Gainesville, Fla.: University Press of Florida, 2001.

Gustav-Wrathall, John Donald. *Take the Young Stranger by the Hand: Same-Sex Relations and the YMCA.* Chicago: University of Chicago Press, 1998.

Hopkins, Charles Howard. *History of the Y.M.C.A. in North America.* New York: Association Press, 1951.

Mjagkij, Nina. *Light in the Darkness: African Americans and the YMCA, 1852–1946.* Lexington: University Press of Kentucky, 1994.

Winter, Thomas. *Making Men, Making Class: The YMCA and Workingmen, 1877–1920.* Chicago: University of Chicago Press, 2002.

Xing, Jun. *Baptized in the Fire of Revolution: The American Social Gospel and the YMCA in China, 1919–1937.* Bethlehem, Pa.: Lehigh University Press, 1996.

Thomas Winter

See also **Evangelicalism and Revivalism; Philanthropy; Volunteerism.**

YOUNG PLAN. Named for its chief architect and promoter, American business executive Owen D. Young, the Young Plan attempted to depoliticize and establish the final terms of Germany's World War I reparations to the Allied Powers, namely France, Great Britain, Italy, and Belgium. Implemented in September 1930, the complex international agreement reduced the amount of Germany's annual payments and set the total indemnity near $25 billion (approximately $267 billion in 2001 dollars). Interest was to accrue annually at 5.5 percent with installments payable through 1988. The Young Plan ended France's occupation of the Rhineland, terminated Allied economic control over Germany, and created the BANK FOR INTERNATIONAL SETTLEMENTS (BIS). The onset of the Great Depression and a banking crisis in Central Europe made implementation of the Young Plan impractical. The Allies and Germany abandoned the agreement in June 1932.

BIBLIOGRAPHY

Leffler, Melvyn P. *The Elusive Quest: America's Pursuit of European Stability and French Security, 1919–1933.* Chapel Hill: University of North Carolina, 1979.

Jeffrey J. Matthews

See also **World War I, U.S. Relief in; World War I War Debts.**

YOUNG WOMEN'S CHRISTIAN ASSOCIATION. First established in Great Britain in 1855, the Young Women's Christian Association (YWCA) reached the United States in 1858. By 2002 the YWCA of the U.S.A. included 326 community associations, including campus and registered YWCAs and membership in the United States had reached two million. The YWCA's chief objective is to develop the full potential of the women it serves, most of them between the ages of twelve and thirty-five. The YWCA seeks to include women and girls of different racial, ethnic, socioeconomic, occupational, religious, and cultural backgrounds. Men and boys participate as associates in the YWCA. By the early twenty-first century the YWCA focused on eight key issues: childcare and youth development; economic empowerment; global awareness; health and fitness; housing and shelter; leadership development; racial justice and human rights; and violence prevention.

The National Board of the YWCA of the U.S.A. was formed in 1906. Its headquarters are in New York City. Active in both World War I and World War II, in 1941 the YWCA became one of six national organizations that contributed to the United Service Organizations. Delegates from YWCAs throughout the nation attend national conventions every three years and vote on policies, goals, and direction for the organization. The priority adopted at the convention in 1970, and reaffirmed in 1973, was to join with like-minded groups to use the YWCA's collective power to achieve a just and equal society, including the elimination of institutional racism. Related to that objective, the YWCA focused on the elimination of poverty, ending war and building world peace, increasing women's self-perception and changing society's expectations of them, and involving youth in leadership and decision making within the organization.

Members of the YWCA of the U.S.A. maintain that they are nonpolitical, but they encourage girls and young women to be politically active. In the late twentieth century the YWCA began campaigns to increase awareness about violence against women, including the support of legislation that would protect women and girls from violence. YWCA conventions also issued statements on difficult topics such as abortion, rape, HIV and AIDS education, and drugs and alcohol. The YWCAs provide residential halls, classes, athletic programs, recreational facilities, and lectures and forums on subjects of interest to women for its members. The YWCA also provides education on breast cancer prevention and care as well as sex education, and the organization continues programs in employment education and placement.

In 2002 YWCA work was being done in more than 326 associations in the United States and in 101 countries around the world. The YWCA of the U.S.A., an affiliate of the World YWCA, which has its headquarters in Geneva, Switzerland, participates in the World YWCA mutual service and development program. Each year it aids an average of thirty other national YWCAs through advisory staff, program grants, building loans, bringing trainees to the United States for observation and study, or a combination of some or all four methods.

BIBLIOGRAPHY

Mjagkij, Nina, and Margaret Spratt, eds. *Men and Women Adrift: The YMCA and the YWCA in the City.* New York: New York University Press, 1997.

Sarah E. Heath

See also **Young Men's and Young Women's Hebrew Association; Young Men's Christian Association.**

YOUTH ADMINISTRATION, NATIONAL

(NYA) was established by executive order on 26 June 1935 as a division of the WORKS PROGRESS ADMINISTRATION (WPA). It remained under WPA jurisdiction until 1939, then the Federal Security Agency became its home until September 1943, when it dissolved. The depression of the 1930s brought special hardship to American youth, preventing large numbers from entering the labor market and denying them the opportunity to attain or upgrade skills. President Franklin D. Roosevelt, influenced by his wife, Eleanor, and by WPA Director Harry L. Hopkins, established the NYA to devise useful work for some of the estimated 2.8 million young people who were on relief in 1935. NYA activities took two major directions: the student work program for youths in school (elementary to graduate), and out-of-school employment for the needy unemployed between the ages of sixteen and twenty-four.

The student work program eventually helped 2.1 million students find jobs in school laboratories, libraries, and playgrounds, at wages ranging from a maximum of $6 per month for secondary pupils to $30 per month for graduate students. Because most projects were inadequately supervised and tended to be irregular and of short duration, those who insisted on tangible evidence of achievement from relief activities criticized the in-school program as a waste of taxpayer dollars. The out-of-school program ultimately aided 2.6 million people. Those participating in the program received on-the-job training in the construction trades, metal and woodworking, office work, recreation, health care, and other occupations. NYA workers also performed useful tasks in parks, national forests, and other outdoor recreational areas along lines similar to the CIVILIAN CONSERVATION CORPS. In the cities, enrollees resided at home, but the NYA established resident centers for group projects in rural areas. Because out-of-school NYA programs focused on skills development and visibly productive work, they were less criticized.

The NYA brought desperately needed relief to a vital sector of the American population at minimal expense. The average annual cost to the federal government of the student program was about $75 per enrollee, and the out-of-school worker cost the government about $225 annually. In an average year (such as 1938), the NYA employed about 500,000 youths—150,000 in school and the rest in the community—at a total cost of about $58 million. It was a minimal investment in the skills and self-respect of young people, but the program was nonetheless unpopular with congressional conservatives, in part because of the strong liberalism of NYA Director Aubrey Williams. Despite partisan criticism, the NYA was remarkable for its absence of political overtones. Unlike much of the NEW DEAL, the agency was almost completely decentralized, with many of the projects being administered by states and communities.

BIBLIOGRAPHY

Rawick, George. "The New Deal and Youth." Madison, Wisc.: Unpublished Ph.D. dissertation, University of Wisconsin (1957).

Reiman, Richard A. *Planning the National Youth Administration.* Athens: University of Georgia Press, 1992.

Otis L. Graham Jr. / c. w.

See also **Great Depression.**

YOUTH MOVEMENTS,

as the organized expression of viewpoints held autonomously by a large number of young people, have been rare in the United States. Not until the 1960s did an autonomous youth movement in the sense familiar to people in many other nations achieve a full growth in America. Yet, throughout much of the twentieth century and into the twenty-first, young people on college campuses have taken conspicuous part in social causes of various kinds.

The largest manifestations of student activism in the period before World War I involved settlement-house work and Christian missionary endeavors. From the 1910s through the 1930s, some college students in the Young Women's Christian Organization forged ties with working-class women to try to improve their working conditions, rather than to proselytize. The Intercollegiate Socialist Society (ISS), founded in 1905 and later renamed the League for Industrial Democracy, had about 1,300 undergraduate members in seventy campus chapters at its peak before World War I. During the 1920s, an independent student voice on public issues began to be heard. The National Student Forum (1921–1929), a clearly liberal organization, was important chiefly because of its weekly newspaper, the *New Student*, which combined intercollegiate news with liberal commentary.

Campuses first became prominent centers of radical activity in the 1930s, with the main focus on foreign policy. Communist Party members and sympathizers played an important role, especially through the American Student Union (1935–1940), a merger of the Communist-led National Student League (1932–1936) and the student affiliate of the social-democratic League for Industrial Democracy. Antiwar sentiment spread far and wide, as an estimated 500,000 students took part in demonstrations or rallies against war in 1936, the third year of such demonstrations. An undetermined but large number of students took the Oxford Pledge, promising refusal to fight in a war if the United States became involved. For the most part the 1930s student movement focused on off-campus issues, except threats to campus freedom of expression.

The 1930s student movement was overshadowed by World War II, and a national climate of intense anticommunism stifled a brief radical political revival in the late 1940s. The federal government and some everyday Americans treated dissenting political ideas as suspect, and left-leaning teachers and students were subjected to various forms of harassment, including loss of jobs. In this atmosphere the only visible "student" group in the 1950s was the National Student Association (NSA) established in 1946, which soon came to depend on covert funding from the Central Intelligence Agency for its survival; the subsidies were given in the belief that the NSA, which took fairly liberal stands on many issues, could be a credible front for the U.S. government in dealing with foreign student groups.

It was the civil rights movement that broke this long period of quietude. Beginning in 1960, students at black colleges in the South held sit-ins at whites-only lunch counters demanding the right to equal service, and student protest groups across the South founded the STUDENT NONVIOLENT COORDINATING COMMITTEE (SNCC). Sympathetic students on predominantly white northern campuses joined SNCC's efforts, and SNCC became an organization of full-time field-workers risking their lives by challenging racial discrimination in some of the most firmly segregationist areas of the Deep South. Student participation in civil rights activity continued, most notably in the Mississippi Summer Project of 1964, in which northern volunteers shared the work and dangers of the civil rights organizers.

The 1960s saw numerous other campus movements. During the early 1960s, an antinuclear movement arose. The Student Peace Union (founded 1959) reached its peak of activity in 1961–1962, with about 2,000 members. In the free speech movement at the University of California, Berkeley, in the fall of 1964, participants criticized the modern state university as being factorylike in its operation and purposes.

By the mid-1960s, the campus-based movement known as the New Left had emerged. Growing out of the civil rights movement and the free speech movement (along with smaller but similar protest movements at a number of schools), it was greatly stimulated by the escalation of the Vietnam War in 1965. The New Left, whose main organizational vehicle was the STUDENTS FOR A DEMOCRATIC SOCIETY (SDS)—although it was much broader than SDS—was the only American radical movement that centered on young people rather than being an adult movement with a following among youth. SDS broke off its nominal affiliation with the social-democratic League for Industrial Democracy in 1965 and did not affiliate with any other political group. The New Left focused on racial oppression at home and American imperialism abroad, rather than on class issues. Offering a rebellious youth culture and cogent criticism of the way of life that America offered to its young people, the movement brought in hundreds of thousands of sympathizers. Even though SDS disintegrated in 1969, spontaneous campus protest remained strong through the 1969–1970 school year. The American invasion of Cambodia in 1970, coupled with the killing of four KENT STATE University students by the Ohio National Guard, touched off the greatest wave of campus protests in American history, and hundreds of colleges were closed by protesting students or worried administrators. This was the last major thrust of the student revolt of the 1960s, however. Campuses became quieter over the next several years, partly from cynicism over the benefits of protest and partly from the withdrawal of U.S. troops from Vietnam in 1973.

In the 1980s, despite increasing conservativism overall, student activism revived around the issue of racial apartheid in South Africa. Students at campuses across the nation pitched tents in campus "shantytowns" and conducted other protest activities to draw attention to the sordid conditions under which most black South Africans were forced to live. The antiapartheid movement pressured college and university administrations to divest of their holdings in companies that did business in or with South Africa.

In the 1990s and the early twenty-first century, students at a number of major universities launched protests against the use of sweatshops by the manufacturers of college-logo clothing. At the same time, a new, more liberal leadership in the AFL-CIO, the nation's major labor organization, showed increasing interest in organizing previously unorganized groups (such as low-wage chicken processing jobs). The organization began holding "Union Summers," programs in which college students spent a summer learning how to do labor organizing. On many campuses, students and hourly workers joined in "Living Wage" campaigns, seeking to raise wages above the federally mandated minimum. As the twenty-first century opened, political youth movements appeared to be growing again and forging ties beyond campus.

BIBLIOGRAPHY

Bloom, Alexander, ed. *Long Time Gone: Sixties America Then and Now.* New York: Oxford University Press, 2001.

Brax, Ralph S. *The First Student Movement: Student Activism in the United States during the 1930s.* Port Washington, N.Y.: Kennikat Press, 1981.

James P. O'Brien / D. B.

See also **Antiwar Movements; Civil Rights Movement; Coeducation Movement.**

YUGOSLAVIA, RELATIONS WITH. The lack of any significant and tangible U.S. interests in the Balkans through most of American history has meant that the United States often has dealt with Yugoslavia in the context of larger international struggles and interests, particularly World War II and then the Cold War. American policy primarily has been dictated by greater concerns, not by any intrinsic value the United States places on Yugoslavia.

American relations with Yugoslavia date back to the creation of that multiethnic state in December 1918, a result of the collapse of the Austro-Hungarian empire at the end of World War I. Although Yugoslavia was ostensibly a reflection of Woodrow Wilson's principle of national self-determination, the twentieth-century Yugoslav state brought together under one government several peoples, including the Serbs, the Croats, and the Bosnian Muslims.

In the period between the world wars, U.S. policy toward the new nation was practically nonexistent. There were no significant American economic interests in Yugoslavia. There was little American capital invested there, and the volume of trade was minimal. During World War II, Yugoslavia became a matter of concern to the United States once it too became a victim of Nazi aggression in March 1941. U.S. policy was to support resistance forces in Yugoslavia fighting against the German and Italian armies. Even so, the United States tended to let the British, who had more experience in the region, take the lead. Following Winston Churchill, the United States gave aid first to Chetnik forces loyal to the prewar royal government, and then shifted its aid to Josip Broz Tito's partisans toward the end of the war, when it became apparent that they were the more effective fighting force. The only hard and fast rule Franklin Roosevelt's administration had regarding the region was its steadfast resistance to the idea of introducing American combat troops anywhere in the Balkans. The American military refused to entertain the idea at any point in the war. With that one restriction, the single American concern was to damage the Axis powers.

After the war, American policy toward Yugoslavia became a function of the Cold War. From 1945 to 1948, while Tito (who prevailed in the internal power struggle) was Joseph Stalin's loyal communist ally, the United States was implacably hostile to the Yugoslav regime. After Moscow's heavy-handed attempts to dominate Yugoslavia led Tito to split with Stalin in June 1948, the United States slowly inched closer to Tito, supporting his regime rhetorically, economically, and finally militarily, all in the name of keeping Yugoslavia out of the Soviet orbit. The United States and Yugoslavia signed a bilateral military agreement in November 1951 that had the practical effect of incorporating the communist state into NATO's defensive plans for Europe. Tito came to rely on a steady stream of U.S. economic aid to prop up his economy, and the United States grudgingly tolerated his attempts to organize Third World nations into a neutralist bloc, as long as he remained independent of Moscow and thus a useful example for the United States of a communist leader who was not under the thumb of the Kremlin.

This remained American policy throughout the Cold War. It was not based on any fondness for Tito, his ideology, or his government, but on a desire to place a thorn in the side of the Soviet Union. When the Cold War came to an abrupt end, the United States was left with no policy for Yugoslavia. Having viewed the country through the prism of World War II and then the Cold War for nearly fifty years, Yugoslavia had no clear meaning for the United States in the absence of a common enemy.

Upon Tito's death in 1980, no single leader emerged to replace him. Instead, the Yugoslav government was run by the leaders of the republics, who shared a revolving presidency. The state limped along through the 1980s, but the collapse of the Soviet empire in eastern Europe in 1989 removed the last force holding the republics together. Slovenia, Croatia, Bosnia, and Macedonia all declared their independence of Yugoslavia and set up separate states. The wars that followed the breakup of Yugoslavia presented a new challenge to American policy. Throughout the 1990s, America's struggle to define a coherent and effective policy vacillated between a desire to act to end the bloodshed and a fear of becoming trapped in a foreign policy quagmire.

President George H. W. Bush avoided any direct American role in Yugoslavia, and his successor, Bill Clinton, initially followed suit. Eventually the fear of a wider war that might destabilize Europe and international outrage over atrocities committed (particularly by Serb forces in Bosnia) forced the Clinton administration to act, both diplomatically and militarily. The United States brokered the Dayton agreement in 1995 that ended the fighting in Bosnia, and American-led NATO air strikes in 1999 forced the Yugoslav government of Slobodan Milosevic to allow NATO occupation of Kosovo. At the start of the twenty-first century, American military forces were part of NATO peacekeeping forces in both Bosnia and Kosovo, but the often stated preference of George W. Bush to withdraw American forces from peacekeeping missions seemed to signal a return to a more hands-off American policy in the region.

BIBLIOGRAPHY

Beloff, Nora. *Tito's Flawed Legacy: Yugoslavia and the West, 1939–1984.* Boulder, Colo.: Westview Press, 1985.

Brands, H. W. *The Specter of Neutralism: The United States and the Emergence of the Third World, 1947–1960.* New York: Columbia University Press, 1989.

Heuser, Beatrice. *Western Containment Policies in the Cold War: The Yugoslav Case 1948–53.* London and New York: Routledge, 1989.

Lees, Lorraine M. *Keeping Tito Afloat: The United States, Yugoslavia, and the Cold War.* University Park: Pennsylvania State University Press, 1997.

Mark S. Byrnes

See also **Kosovo Bombing.**

YUKON REGION, an area associated with the Yukon River and the Yukon Territory in northwest North America. The Yukon River, formed by the confluence of the Lewes and Pelly Rivers, flows northwest through the Yukon Territory into Alaska and then southwest from the junction with the Porcupine River to empty across an immense delta (eighty to ninety miles wide) into the Bering Sea. At 1,979 miles in length, the Yukon River is the third longest river in North America. Due to its extreme northern location, much of the river is frozen from October through June.

The Yukon Territory takes its name from the Yukon River, which drains more than two-thirds of the Yukon's 205,345 square miles. Yukon probably derives from the Gwich'in Indian word "Youcon" meaning "great river." The Yukon's human history is thought to have begun in prehistoric times with the crossing of humans from Eurasia. By the time of the first known European explorer, Martin Frobisher (1576), the region was home to many Native American peoples such as the Dene, the Inland Tlingit, the Gwitch'in, the Han, the Kaska, the Tagish, and Tutchone. These groups led a mostly nomadic life, migrating with their primary food source, caribou. Frobisher was in search of the Northwest Passage while subsequent explorers were seeking new sources for fur trade and new knowledge of the region.

The Canadian government acquired the Yukon from the Hudson Bay Company in 1870 and administered it as part of the Northwest Territories. The famous gold rush in the Klondike River region in the 1890s brought thousands of people to the Yukon. This great influx prompted the Canadian government to pass in 1898 the Yukon Act, which created a separate Yukon Territory with its capital at Dawson. In 1952, the capital was moved to Whitehorse.

In 1999 the population of the Yukon Territory was 31,070 with the majority of the people living in the capital city. The region is dominated by the great mountains that form the western margin of North America. The Saint Elias range in southwestern Yukon Territory contains Mount Logan (19,850 feet), the highest mountain in Canada. The location of the mountains influences the climate, which is primarily continental subarctic, with long, cold, dry winters and short, dry, warm summers. The moun-

On the Yukon Trail. Thousands took the route through the Yukon, in Alaska and northwestern Canada, during the Klondike gold rush, especially in 1897–98. © UPI/CORBIS-BETTMANN

tains block the mild Pacific air from reaching most of the region. Much of the Yukon has continuous permafrost, which limits road and building construction. In the early 2000s the Yukon's economy was dependent on mining (zinc, silver, gold, and copper), forestry, and tourism. Nearly a quarter of a million people annually visit the largely pristine wilderness and the historic sites of the Klondike Gold Rush.

BIBLIOGRAPHY

Coates, Kenneth S., and William R. Morrison. *Land of the Midnight Sun: A History of the Yukon.* Edmonton, Alberta, Canada: Hurtig, 1988.

Janet S. Smith

See also **Klondike Rush.**

ZENGER TRIAL. Although appointed governor of the New York and New Jersey colonies in 1731, Colonel William Cosby did not arrive until 1732. In the interim, New York politician Rip Van Dam served as acting governor of New York and Lewis Morris did the same for

Zenger Trial. Soldiers burn copies of John Peter Zenger's newspaper during the 1735 case that set an important legal precedent for America's future, concerning both libel and freedom of the press. Library of Congress

the New Jersey colony. Both collected the governor's salary. Shortly after Cosby arrived, he sought to recover half the governor's salary from each of his predecessors. His suit in 1733 against Van Dam ended abruptly when New York's chief justice, Lewis Morris, ruled that New York's supreme court justice could not act as an equity court to hear Cosby's case. Cosby summarily removed Morris, replacing him with James De Lancey, a young politician allied with Cosby.

In November 1733, Morris and his allies James Alexander and William Smith hired John Peter Zenger to publish an anti-Cosby newspaper—the *New York Weekly Journal*, which was the first opposition paper in America. The paper attacked Cosby with satire, humor, and irony, as well as serious essays on politics and government. Through innuendo, but not by name, the paper compared Cosby to a monkey and suggested he was tyrant. In January 1734, New York Chief Justice De Lancey urged a grand jury to indict Zenger for libel, but that body refused. In November 1734, a sheriff arrested Zenger, but again the grand jury refused to indict him. Nevertheless,

in January 1735, the prosecutor charged Zenger with the misdemeanor of libel. Zenger's attorneys, James Alexander and William Smith, challenged the legality of De Lancey's appointment as chief justice, and De Lancey responded by disbarring both lawyers.

De Lancey appointed a pro-Cosby lawyer to represent Zenger, but when the trial began in July 1735, Andrew Hamilton of Philadelphia, the most famous attorney in the colonies, represented Zenger. The traditional defense in a libel case was to argue that the defendant did not actually publish the material. To the shock of everyone present, Hamilton, using a brief largely written by Alexander, admitted that Zenger had published the allegedly libelous newspapers, but then argued that Zenger should be permitted to prove the truth of his publications. This claim ran counter to English law, which held that a defamatory publication was libelous, whether true or not, and that, in fact, "the greater the truth [of the libel], the greater the scandal." Speaking directly to the jury, Hamilton attacked this theory, noting that it came out of the repressive star chamber during the reign of England's King James I. Hamilton argued that the significant political differences between England and America called for a different law of libel, and thus he urged the jury to give a general verdict of not guilty. De Lancey instructed the jury to follow the traditional English practice in libel cases, and hold Zenger guilty of publication, leaving it to the Court to determine if the publication was libelous. The jury ignored De Lancey and acquitted Zenger.

The jury's verdict did not change the law of libel in America or Britain, but it became a political force, putting colonial governors on notice that American juries would be supportive of those printers who attacked the largely unpopular royal officials. In the 1790s, both Britain and America adopted the twin principles of James Alexander's brief: that truth should be a defense to a libel and that juries should decide both the law and the facts of a case.

BIBLIOGRAPHY

Finkelman, Paul, ed. *A Brief Narrative of the Case and Tryal of John Peter Zenger: Printer of the New York Weekly Journal.* St. James, N.Y.: Brandywine Press, 1987.

Paul Finkelman

See also **Civil Rights and Liberties; Libel.**

ZIMMERMAN TELEGRAM. Tensions arising from German submarine action during World War I provoked the United States to sever diplomatic relations with Germany on 3 February 1917. On 24 February, the British delivered to the U.S. ambassador in London an intercepted German telegram dated 19 January declaring that unrestricted submarine warfare would begin on 1 February. The note, sent by German Foreign Secretary Arthur Zimmerman to the German minister in Mexico, expressed the fear that the United States would abandon neutrality and directed the minister to arrange an alliance between Mexico and Germany and to urge Japan to switch to the German side. Mexico was to attack the United States on its southwestern border and recover Texas, New Mexico, and Arizona. The publication of the note on 1 March caused popular indignation against Germany and played a significant role in Congress's affirmative response to President Woodrow Wilson's request, on 2 April, for a declaration of war against Germany.

BIBLIOGRAPHY

Tuchman, Barbara W. *The Zimmermann Telegram.* New York: Macmillan, 1966.

Richard E. Yates / c. w.

See also **Germany, Relations with; Mexico, Relations with; Submarines; World War I, Navy in.**

ZINC INDUSTRY. Zinc was first introduced commercially in the United States during the 1850s, with small-scale smelting plants in New Jersey, Pennsylvania, Illinois, Missouri, and Arkansas, near sources of ore and fuel. The principal early use of zinc was in the production of brass, a zinc-copper alloy. The first known domestic zinc production was at the Washington, D.C., arsenal in 1835, by Belgian workers. A furnace was built primarily to produce zinc for making brass to be used in standard weights and measures.

Early zinc production used oxidized forms of the ore, reduced by externally heating closed clay vessels containing a mixture of ore and coal. The vaporized zinc was condensed and cast into slabs. As ore deposits were worked to greater depths during the 1880s, larger quantities of sulfides and smaller quantities of oxides occurred. This required new technology for preroasting the sulfides to form crude oxides. As a result of this technology, sulfuric acid became a by-product of the zinc industry. Development of zinc-lead ore fields in Missouri, Kansas, and Oklahoma in 1895 gave a great impetus to the building of gas-fired zinc smelters in the region. The discovery of natural gas in and west of this area fueled developments, and the tri-state region became known as the Gas Belt. Westward migration created a great need for galvanized, zinc-coated steel for fencing, corrugated sheet metal, and brass hardware. In 1852, Samuel Wetherill invented a grate furnace to produce zinc oxide from oxidized ores, a so-called American process that was perfected in the last half of the nineteenth century.

During the first quarter of the twentieth century, as new mining districts were opened up in the Rocky Mountain area, in Tennessee, and in Virginia, the froth flotation technique for separating sulfide minerals from associated rock became the major mode of production. Demand for zinc during WORLD WAR I led to great expansion of the U.S. zinc mining and smelting industry. It also spurred introduction of the electrolytic process in 1916, which used electrical energy as a substitute for coal and gas in freeing zinc from its mineral compounds. In the course of improving the process, it became possible to produce high-purity zinc. The uses for this zinc were vast, enabling mass production of intricate, precision shapes. When alloyed with aluminum, zinc products were instrumental in the burgeoning automobile and appliance industries beginning in the 1930s. New smelting techniques recovered cadmium as a by-product, which is valuable for its attractive and durable finish when plated onto other metals.

The U.S. zinc industry built up during World War I was the largest in the world and remained so through the end of WORLD WAR II. The smelting segment of the U.S. industry ranked first in tonnage of zinc produced until 1971, when a combination of economic factors, environmental pressures, and shifting patterns of foreign-resource allocation resulted in nearly one-half of the domestic smelters ceasing operation in a two-year period. Of the 1.4 million tons of zinc used annually in the United States as of the early 1970s, only about 40 percent was mined domestically. By 2002, the United States was the fifth-leading producer of zinc worldwide, with production expected to rise to just over 400,000 metric tons by the year 2004. Between 2000 and 2004, U.S. zinc consumption was expected to rise 1.5 percent to more than 1.45 million metric tons annually. In everyday life, zinc is largely unrecognized, although it has many uses, including as a protectant against rust on galvanized steel containers and highway guardrails, as an alloy component in die-cast cases for transistor radios or automobile carburetors, in brass alloy water faucets, as zinc oxide in white house paint or rubber tires, as a chemical compound additive for animal nutrition, and as a self-contained source of electrical energy in flashlight batteries.

BIBLIOGRAPHY

Faloon, Dalton B. *Zinc Oxide: History, Manufacture, and Properties as a Pigment.* New York: Van Nostrand, 1925.

Gent, Ernest V. *The Zinc Industry: A Mine to Market Outline.* New York: The American Zinc Institute, 1940.

Gibson, Arrell M. *Wilderness Bonanza: The Tri-State District of Missouri, Kansas, and Oklahoma.* Norman: University of Oklahoma Press, 1972.

Smith, Duane A. *Mining America: The Industry and the Environment, 1800–1980.* Lawrence: University Press of Kansas, 1987.

Carl H. Cotterbill / h. s.

See also **Industrial Revolution.**

ZIONISM. The emergence of modern political Zionism in the late nineteenth century did not inspire great enthusiasm on American shores. German American Jews, who numbered about 200,000 at the time Theodore Herzl convened the First Zionist Congress in 1897, rejected calls for creation of a Jewish state. Reared in the classical Reform movement, they considered the United States

The American Zionist movement enjoyed its most rapid growth under the leadership of the famed attorney and eventual Supreme Court justice Louis Brandeis. According to Brandeis, American Jews could support the Zionist cause without sacrificing their status as loyal American citizens. His "Brandeisian synthesis" described the United States in pluralist terms, encouraging ethnic difference and drawing strong parallels between the aspirations of Americans and Zionists. With Brandeis's support, President Woodrow Wilson backed Great Britain's November 1917 Balfour Declaration, which promised a Jewish homeland in Palestine.

For the next twenty-five years the Zionist movement suffered from political infighting, financial difficulties, and an American political culture unsympathetic to its long-term goal. During the 1920s conflicting leadership styles ruined any hope of consensus, while the Great Depression diverted needed dollars from organizational coffers. American isolationism and the rise of domestic anti-Semitism in the 1930s discouraged Jewish leaders from adopting an aggressive Zionist stance.

U.S. entry into World War II and word of Adolf Hitler's "final solution" mobilized American Jews behind the Zionist cause. By 1948 membership in Zionist organizations swelled to 1 million as American Jews from across the denominational spectrum rallied for Jewish statehood. Even the once anti-Zionist Reform movement abandoned its opposition to Zionism during its 1937 rabbinic convention in Columbus, Ohio. A small group of Reform rabbis formed the anti-Zionist American Council for Judaism, but it faded quickly with news of Nazi atrocities.

President Harry S. Truman recognized the state of Israel a mere eleven minutes after the new Jewish state declared its independence in May 1948. While a few American Jews immigrated to Israel in the 1950s and early 1960s, most advanced the Zionist cause with financial contributions to Israel and resisted the call for a physical return to Zion. Philanthropic Zionism dominated the movement for the first twenty years of the postwar period.

At the time of the 1967 Six Day War, American Zionism underwent a fundamental transformation, as many young Jews rejected the humanitarian-based Zionist views of their parents and embraced a form of Jewish nationalism that encouraged aliyah (immigration, literally to rise up). Jewish high school students looked forward to spending a summer in Israel, while undergraduates took advantage of overseas study programs to matriculate at the Hebrew University of Jerusalem. In the 1990s several Jewish philanthropists endowed the birthright program, promising every North American Jew a free trip to Israel.

In the late twentieth century American Jews took a more active role in domestic Israeli politics, especially around issues of religious pluralism. Both the Conservative and Reform movements established Jerusalem campuses for their respective seminaries and lobbied Israeli government officials for greater recognition of nontra-

Rabbi Arthur J. Lelyveld. The Reform Jewish leader of many organizations was also active in the civil rights movement. As executive director of the Committee on Unity for Palestine in the Zionist Organization of America, he and two other Zionists met with President Harry S. Truman in 1946 and were instrumental in convincing him to back the creation of Israel. Fairmount Temple

their "New Zion" and feared that Jewish nationalism might compromise their standing as loyal American citizens. At its 1885 Pittsburgh meeting, the Reform movement's Central Conference of American Rabbis declared, "We consider ourselves no longer a nation but a religious community and therefore expect neither a return to Palestine . . . nor the restoration of any of the laws concerning the Jewish state."

The arrival of over 2 million eastern European Jews between 1880 and 1920 altered the demographic profile of American Jewry and opened new doors for the Zionist movement. Reared in traditional Judaism or in the socialist movements of the Old World, the new arrivals proved more sympathetic to the idea of a Jewish homeland. In 1884 a small group of Jews in New York City formed the nation's first Zionist organization, Hoveve Zion (literally the lovers of Zion). By 1898 a number of American Zionist groups merged into the Federation of American Zionists, counting some ten thousand members across the country.

ditional forms of Jewish expression. They demanded recognition of their clergy's right to perform weddings and conversions, staged protests at Jerusalem's Western Wall, and sought inclusion on local religious councils.

American immigration to Israel also reflected a fundamental political shift. Between 1967 and 1973 almost sixty thousand American Jews packed their belongings and moved to the Jewish state. Most hailed from nontraditional religious backgrounds and viewed their aliyah as an opportunity to help create an idealistic Jewish homeland. By the 1990s though the number of American immigrants plummeted to fewer than three thousand a year.

Despite their strong support for the state of Israel, American Jews have never considered mass immigration to the Jewish state a viable option. Zionism has remained a minority movement in the United States.

BIBLIOGRAPHY
Cohen, Naomi W. *American Jews and the Zionist Idea.* New York: Ktav, 1975.
Halperin, Samuel. *The Political World of American Zionism.* Detroit: Wayne State University Press, 1961.
Urofsky, Melvin I. *American Zionism from Herzl to the Holocaust.* Garden City, N.Y.: Doubleday, 1975.

Marc Dollinger

See also **Israel, Relations with; Jews.**

ZONING ORDINANCES are local measures regulating the use of land and the physical characteristics of structures in specified zones. As early as 1908 the Los Angeles City Council created three residence and seven industrial districts, with no manufacturing establishments permitted in the residence areas. During the following decade developers of high-quality housing subdivisions joined with upscale retailers along such posh thoroughfares as New York City's Fifth Avenue in a campaign for zoning ordinances to protect existing property values. In 1913 Minnesota and Wisconsin empowered cities to create residence zones similar to those in Los Angeles. Three years later New York City adopted the first comprehensive zoning ordinance. It divided the city into residence, commercial, and unrestricted zones and regulated the height and area of structures.

New York City's example inspired cities throughout the nation to embrace zoning, and at the end of 1923, 218 municipalities with more than 22 million inhabitants had zoning ordinances. In 1924 the federal Department of Commerce issued a model state zoning enabling act intended to spur the adoption of additional zoning measures and to guide states in the drafting of statutes. State courts repeatedly upheld the constitutionality of zoning ordinances, and in 1926 the U.S. Supreme Court added its imprimatur in *Euclid v. Ambler Realty Company.* The Court held that local zoning measures were a legitimate exercise of the states' police power.

Criticism of zoning persisted, however. Most municipalities adopted zoning ordinances without drafting comprehensive city plans, thus the zoning provisions did not reflect carefully considered planning goals. Zoning ordinances were drafted primarily to protect or to enhance property values; they were not necessarily designed to achieve well-planned urban development. During the second half of the twentieth century, concern about the adverse effects of exclusionary zoning grew. Suburban municipalities adopted ordinances prohibiting multifamily housing and mandating large lots and a high minimum floor area for single-family residences. Such zoning provisions ensured that only the affluent would be able to live in the municipality; the poor were effectively excluded. In 1975, in *Southern Burlington County NAACP v. Township of Mt. Laurel,* the New Jersey Supreme Court held that exclusionary zoning violated the state's constitution. Some other state courts and legislatures also took action against such zoning, though at the close of the twentieth century zoning ordinances remained significant weapons for defending economic and social privilege.

BIBLIOGRAPHY
Scott, Mel. *American City Planning since 1890.* Berkeley: University of California Press, 1971.
Toll, Seymour I. *Zoned American.* New York: Grossman, 1969.

Jon C. Teaford

See also **City Planning.**

ZOOLOGICAL PARKS. Although royal animal collections and popular traveling menageries had existed for centuries, true zoological gardens—organized, permanent exhibitions of animals intended for public education and enjoyment—emerged only in the wake of the Enlightenment, that eighteenth-century intellectual movement celebrating science, reason, and order. The first public animal collections opened in major European cities such as Vienna, Paris, Amsterdam, London, and Berlin during the late-eighteenth and early-nineteenth centuries. In most cases these gardens were established by private zoological societies that believed that their collections would provide scientific interest, natural history instruction, and cultural improvement for their cities' growing bourgeoisie. American zoological gardens took somewhat longer to develop—in part because most antebellum cities lacked the requisite cultural capital to establish major civic institutions, in part because American audiences already enjoyed a number of other sites for live-animal amusement, from itinerant circuses and country fairs to the eclectic museums of Charles Willson Peale and P. T. Barnum. (BARNUM'S AMERICAN MUSEUM in New York also boasted the nation's first public aquarium, opened in 1856.) By the 1860s, though, the attraction of more substantial, permanent, respectable animal gardens had become too compelling for civic-minded American elites to ignore.

Entrance to Zoo. Large animal cut-outs greet visitors as they walk through the gate of the Memphis Zoo in Memphis, Tenn. According to Morey and Associates in a study of sixty-three zoos throughout the United States, total paid attendance per zoo increased in 2001, with an average of more than 710,000 people visiting each zoo. © MEMPHIS CONVENTION & VISITORS BUREAU

The First American Animal Gardens: 1860s–1900s

A few leading zoo boosters explicitly followed the lead of their European predecessors. The Zoological Society of Philadelphia, modeled largely on its London counterpart, was chartered in 1859, though the Civil War postponed the opening of the Society's garden until 1874. The Cincinnati Zoological Garden debuted one year later, drawing its inspiration from the festive animal parks of Germany. Both institutions embraced the twin goals of "instruction and recreation" and proclaimed themselves to be civic institutions of the highest order, allied with the libraries, concert halls, museums, and other cultural attractions of the Gilded Age metropolis. In most American cities, though, zoos developed not as philanthropic endeavors but rather as adjuncts to municipal parks departments. New York's CENTRAL PARK Menagerie appeared in the early 1860s, partly as a result of unsolicited public donations of animals to the city. Chicago's Lincoln Park boasted its own zoo by 1868, with the first inhabitants—a pair of swans—coming from the Central Park Menagerie. By the end of the nineteenth century, over twenty American cities from Baltimore to Boise had opened their own municipal zoos, with most open to the public free of charge. Not surprisingly, these public facilities tended to be more modest affairs than the society-run gardens, but what they lacked in funding they more than made up in popularity, with weekend attendance running into the tens of thousands.

Whether privately or publicly administered, American zoos generally adhered to a common design tradition. Animals were typically housed in barred cages or fenced corrals, often organized taxonomically (all birds together, all cats together) rather than geographically or ecologically. Most exhibition buildings were simple utilitarian shelters, but some parks constructed elaborate animal houses with ornamental features echoing the prevailing

architectural styles of the animals' native lands. The grounds of most American zoos covered no more than forty or fifty acres, and while winding paths and ample trees provided a pleasant pastoral atmosphere, little attempt was made at simulating the creatures' natural habitat.

Near the end of the nineteenth century, however, two new facilities pioneered a revolutionary new design model, that of the so-called "zoological park." The National Zoological Park, a branch of the SMITHSONIAN INSTITUTION, was established by Congress in 1889 as a "city of refuge" for endangered North American species, with only a fraction of its 160 acres to be dedicated to public exhibition. Ten years later the New York Zoological Society opened its park of approximately 261 acres in the Bronx, with similar plans for preserving native fauna. A driving spirit (and the first director) for both parks was William Temple Hornaday, a former chief taxidermist for the Smithsonian, whose outrage at the indiscriminate slaughter of American bison led to a long career promoting wildlife conservation and popular education in natural history. By the early 1900s both zoological parks saw their original conservationist missions fade, as funding difficulties and visitor demand led to the development of more "traditional" zoological collections, stocked not with bison and elk but with elephants and lions. (After 1902, the New York Zoological Society also operated a hugely popular aquarium, first at Castle Garden in Manhattan's Battery Park, later at Coney Island in Brooklyn.) Nevertheless, the more expansive vision of both landscape and mission seen in Washington and the Bronx profoundly influenced future generations of zoo designers and directors.

The Age of Spectacle and Showmanship: 1910s–1950s

A further shift toward naturalistic design came in the early-twentieth century, thanks to the influence of German animal dealer and zoo director Carl Hagenbeck. At his Tierpark near Hamburg, opened in 1907, Hagenbeck oversaw the construction of vast barless enclosures, outdoor panoramas that displayed a variety of species in a roughly "natural" landscape of artificial rock, with animals and visitors separated only by strategically hidden moats. While some American zoo directors refused to build such exhibits, citing concerns for the safety of both animals and visitors, several parks in the Midwest and West eagerly adopted the new designs during the interwar years, recognizing their potential for adding drama and spectacle to the zoogoing experience, as well as offering the appearance of freedom for the animals. In Denver, Detroit, St. Louis, San Diego, and the Chicago suburb of Brookfield, zoo visitors gaped at bears, big cats, and hoofed stock exhibited in the open air, with nary a bar or fence in sight.

These dramatic new designs were abetted by an emerging ideal of "showmanship." Needing to compete with a booming mass culture, zoo directors of the 1920s and 1930s developed a variety of new features that emphasized entertainment over education. From trained chimpanzee performances to elephant rides to concerts and restaurants, these added attractions encouraged visitors to see the zoo as a cultural resort. Such attractions were also promoted more professionally and aggressively by more publicity-minded directors like George Vierheller of St. Louis, whose unabashed endorsement of zoos' entertainment value represented a conspicuous change from the more scientific and educational aims of William Temple Hornaday. The popular success of "showmanship" helped zoos to survive the trials of the Great Depression and World War II. At a time when their funding might easily have disappeared, zoos actually managed to secure millions of dollars in government aid, particularly under the New Deal's Works Progress Administration (WPA), by presenting themselves as beloved, even essential, elements of their respective communities.

During the postwar years, American zoos continued to enjoy tremendous popularity. Riding the crest of the baby boom, zoos proudly promoted themselves as purveyors of wholesome "family entertainment" that parents and children could delight in together. Dozens of parks opened special "children's zoos" featuring tame, pettable creatures, often displayed in fanciful storybook settings. Lincoln Park's R. Marlin Perkins developed the first zoo-based television program, *Zoo Parade*, in 1949, showcasing his zoo's colorful animal personalities and soon inspiring several imitators. In both of these new arenas, zoo animals symbolically became family pets, neatly domesticated for children's enjoyment.

Reinventing the Zoo: 1960s–1990s

Yet beneath these family-friendly innovations lurked serious financial and philosophical problems, and by the 1960s and 1970s, many zoos had fallen on hard times. Declining urban tax bases forced many cities to decrease their support for municipal zoos, leading to a marked deterioration in the parks' physical plants. When zoos could afford to construct new buildings, they often favored starkly antiseptic enclosures of tiled walls and glass-fronted cages, designed to ensure the animals' health but destined to provoke criticism. Indeed, a growing movement for animal welfare and animal rights increasingly condemned zoos' "naked cages," contrasting them with the lushness and vitality of the animals' natural habitats (habitats familiar to many Americans through popular wildlife documentaries, such as Marlin Perkins's *Wild Kingdom*). (New commercial competitors provided even more challenges to zoos, as drive-through safari parks and sea-life theme parks provided visitors with more spectacular attractions and better customer service.) All of these developments reinforced a general trend of decreasing attendance at the nation's zoos, and the consequent loss of income and popularity further exacerbated the problems of financing and image. Underfunded and under attack, the American zoo itself appeared to be an endangered species.

Over the last quarter of the twentieth century, however, zoos rebounded by dramatically altering their identities—physically, philosophically, professionally, and politically. Innovative exhibit designers abandoned cages and moats in favor of "landscape immersion," an exhibition model that used ample vegetation and carefully controlled sightlines to create strikingly realistic replicas of the animals' native habitats. (Improved technology allowed for similarly elaborate, naturalistic exhibits at the score of new American aquariums that opened during the last three decades of the century.) Curators from across the country organized cooperative captive breeding programs, or Species Survival Plans (SSPs), highlighting the zoo's role as a "Noah's ark" for creatures facing extinction in the wild. The American Association of Zoological Parks and Aquariums (AAZPA)—later renamed the American Zoo and Aquarium Association (AZA)—became an independent entity in 1972, ending its decades-long association with a municipal-parks organization and gradually reinventing itself as both monitor and promoter of the nation's zoos. Finally, a wave of privatization swept the zoo world, as cash-strapped city governments turned their animal collections over to private zoological societies (which then had to recruit corporate donors and raise admission fees in order to pay the bills).

Yet, while these changes prompted many observers to declare a wholesale "zoo revolution" by the 1990s, the fundamental attraction of zoos remained much the same as it had been nearly a century-and-a-half before: the deep-seated human desire to see active, entertaining, charismatic animals up close and in the flesh. Indeed, at the dawn of the twenty-first century, American zoos were attracting over 130 million visitors a year—a figure greater than the annual attendance at all professional baseball, football, basketball, and hockey games combined. Such astonishing popularity suggests that zoological parks will continue to shape and reflect Americans' ideas of entertainment and education, of civilization and the wild, of people and animals, for many generations to come.

BIBLIOGRAPHY

Croke, Vicki. *The Modern Ark: The Story of Zoos, Past, Present, and Future.* New York: Scribners, 1997. Accessible popular survey.

Hanson, Elizabeth A. *Animal Attractions: Nature on Display in American Zoos.* Princeton, N.J.: Princeton University Press, 2002. Especially valuable on collecting and display of zoo animals.

Hoage, R. J., and William A. Deiss, eds. *New Worlds, New Animals: From Menagerie to Zoological Park in the Nineteenth Century.* Baltimore: Johns Hopkins University Press, 1996.

Horowitz, Helen Lefkowitz. "Seeing Ourselves through the Bars: A Historical Tour of American Zoos." *Landscape* 25, no. 2 (1981): 12–19.

Hyson, Jeffrey N. "Jungles of Eden: The Design of American Zoos." In *Environmentalism in Landscape Architecture.* Edited by Michel Conan. Washington: Dumbarton Oaks Research and Library Collection, 2000.

Kisling, Vernon N., Jr., ed. *Zoo and Aquarium History: Ancient Animal Collections to Zoological Gardens.* Boca Raton, Fla.: CRC Press, 2001.

Mullan, Bob, and Garry Marvin. *Zoo Culture.* 2d ed. Urbana: University of Illinois Press, 1999. Provocative study by sociologist and anthropologist.

Jeffrey Hyson

See also **Marine Biology; Ornithology.**

ZOOLOGY. Zoology is the area of systematic biology that studies the animal kingdom. Systematic biology (or just systematics) is "the scientific study of the kinds and diversity of organisms" (Simpson, p. 7). The animal kingdom is one of at least five kingdoms into which organisms are now divided; the others are plants, fungi, protoctists, and bacteria. The last two kingdoms comprise only unicellular organisms: protoctists include all unicellular organisms formerly considered animals, among them amoebas and paramecia, as well as several types of unicellular algae; bacteria are unicellular organisms lacking a differentiated cellular nucleus. Animals and plants are multicellular organisms, but plants have cell walls and animals do not. Fungi may be unicellular or multicellular, but do not develop through embryological stages, as do plants and animals. Therefore, animals may be loosely defined as multicellular organisms that lack cell walls, but develop through embryological stages.

Zoology is divided into different fields: MAMMALOGY (the study of mammals), ORNITHOLOGY (birds), HERPETOLOGY (reptiles and amphibians), ichthyology (fish), entomology (insects), malacology (mollusks, from snails with and without shells to squids and octopuses), and helmintology (worms, from earthworms to flatworms), among others. Zoologists usually specialize in the study of only one group or of closely related groups of animals. If a zoologist specializes in extinct animals, of which only fossil remains are known, he is called a paleozoologist (the term paleontologist includes the paleobotanists, who study plant fossils). Zoogeography is a special field of zoology that studies the geographical distribution of animals and is closely linked with research on the evolution of animal species.

Classification

One of zoology's main purposes is to identify all animals through classification. Classification is accomplished by comparing the characters, or features, of groups of animals. These characters may be of very different nature: morphological characters refer mainly to body structures, whereas histological and cytological characters are those of body tissues and cells, respectively. The number and forms of the chromosomes (karyology) are also considered a distinctive feature, but methods of DNA complementation ("molecular systematics") are being used increasingly. The presence, absence, or even the structure of certain biochemical compounds are used as characters.

Certain physiological functions (for example, temperature regulation) are also considered in classification.

The rules and procedures for classification constitute a division of zoology called animal taxonomy. Various opinions about whether characters should be differentially weighed (i.e., some characters should be considered more important than others), and on how they should be weighed have been voiced since the eighteenth century. Carolus Linnaeus (1707–1778), the founder of modern taxonomy, maintained that characters should be weighed according to their functional value, whereas Michel Adanson, a French naturalist, thought they should be arbitrarily selected.

Modern classification has relied mostly on weighed characters; however, in the twentieth century insect taxonomists began using quantitative (numerical and graphic) methods, bringing about new debate on this matter. The tendency now called phenetics, initiated by Russian taxonomist E. S. Smirnov in the 1920s, proposed methods for comparing unweighed characters to determine overall similarity, whereas another tendency, now known as cladism, developed by the German zoologist Willi Hennig in the 1950s, insisted on weighing characters according to their evolutionary importance. In the 1970s and 1980s, discussions took place in the United States between the supporters of both. As a result of this debate, numerical methods (which allow for the use of computers) were perfected; this brought about a certain degree of compromise between the differing quantitative approaches, but not between the underlying philosophies. The use of cladistic criteria, however, seems to have prevailed.

Characters and Conservation

Characters used for classification are generally determined in laboratories and natural history cabinets, but other features can only be studied in the field. Captive animals are not usually reliable when studies of behavior (ethology) or of relations between animal populations and their environment (ecology) are intended. Field studies are an important part of zoological research. Although they do contribute to classification, they also stand by themselves as a valuable source of information for species conservation. The only true way to preserve a species is within its own typical habitat (i.e., the natural conditions in which it lives).

By using an array of characters, many previously undescribed species are discovered every year. In their research, zoologists often go further than mere classification, contributing to a better understanding of biological processes and discovering previously unknown qualities of animals. For example, a collateral result of the study of insect pheromones (hormones that attract the opposite sex) was the use of some compounds in pest control that, unlike traditional insecticides, do not contaminate the environment. Research on sounds produced by certain dangerous or obnoxious animals have also served to devise methods to repel them without damaging the environment.

596